Introduction

This book has profiles of all-time greats of sport. The continuing problem in its preparation was the matter of just who to include. My first thoughts of identifying about 1000 people were either eased or aggravated, depending how one looks at it, when the publishers encouraged me to expand the numbers so that we could produce a really definitive volume.

With well over 2600 sports men and women included, not to mention the horses and greyhounds, I trust that readers will find all the biggest names. However, having agreed on a long list of obvious candidates, any experts would then produce substantially different lists, at least in the second half of such compilations. I started with about 1700 names and have added more, and deleted some, as the work progressed. However, the final selection was not just mine, because early on I invited Ian Buchanan and Bill Mallon to join me in this project. We divided the sports between us, and then exchanged our drafts. We each have a different perspective, with Bill of course providing an American viewpoint to the British ones of Ian and myself. Our interests are in any case sufficiently widespread that we can claim to take an international stance, and we now have great delight in presenting the fruits of our labours.

The biggest representations are obviously from the major sports, but we have spread the net wide to include the most notable practitioners from many less obviously popular ones as well. We have also tried to include the most famous sports men and women from each major sporting nation.

We have not stuck to rigid structures for the biographies, the length of which vary considerably. However, for several sports, such as baseball and cricket, career details are summarised in standard formats. Such statistics are usually up to the end of the last completed season, although the text may include more topical details.

This can be regarded as a complementary publication to my *Guinness Encyclopedia of Sports Records and Results*. Like that publication, which is published biennially, I hope that this book may appear in subsequent editions. Every year new stars emerge and their biographies can be added in future. We will, of course, also be happy to consider adding any names from the past that readers may feel should belong in such a work.

Many people have helped in providing me and co-authors with information. Our thanks to them all, but mine go above all to Ian and Bill for their enthusiasm and expertise and to my editor at Guinness Publishing, Charles Richards. He has suffered my delivery of copy to him for editing rather later than I would have liked, and has not only read our efforts most carefully but has also contributed many helpful comments, not least from his own encyclopaedic knowledge of football.

I have endeavoured to include as much information as possible up to the very last stage of the production process at the end of July 1993.

Peter Matthews

Acknowledgements

In the course of compiling this book over the past three years we have consulted many reference sources and many experts. We have also of course tapped into our accumulated data over lifetimes of sports 'nuttery', and many others have helped us with our various projects over the years. It is very difficult, therefore, for this list to be comprehensive, so if we have missed anybody from the following list then please accept our apologies and thanks.

We would, then, like to mention the following, some of whom have helped with just one or two queries and some whose assistance has been profound.

Reg Abbott, Australian rugby league
Howard Bass, winter sports
Naomi Beinart, South Africa
Anthony Bijerk, Netherlands
Dennis Bird, ice skating
Roberto Carmona, Italy
Pete Cava, baseball
Marion Collin, women's cricket
Gabor Kobzos, Hungary/Switzerland
Robert Gate, rugby league
Stan Greenberg, Olympics
David Guiney, Ireland
Matti Hannus, Finland
John Jenkins, Great Britain
Maurice Jones, speedway
Erich Kamper, Austria
Ove Karlsson, Sweden
Ken Knelly, US horse racing
Fred Lake, archery
Alan Little, tennis
Peter Lovesey, athletics
Wolf Lyberg, Sweden
Bob Mason, hockey
Giuseppe Odello, Italy
A.J.Oldham, croquet
Guy Oliver, football
Sue Peard, badminton
David Powell, skiing
Paul Ramlow, harness racing
John Randall, horse racing
Chris Rhys, rugby union
Runfried Rissmann, Germany (GDR)
Hugh Soar, archery
Bernt Solaas, Norway
Zoltán Subert, Hungary
Isao Sugawara, Japan
Priit Tänava, Estonia
Sergey Tikhonov, Russia
Luis Vinker, Argentina
David Wallechinsky, Olympics
Louis Weisscher, Netherlands
Rob Whittingham, bowling
Ture Widlund, Weightlifting
Tadeusz Wolejko, Poland
Mark Young, USA

THE GUINNESS INTERNATIONAL WHO'S WHO OF SPORT

Peter Matthews

Ian Buchanan Bill Mallon

GUINNESS PUBLISHING

PETER MATTHEWS is Editor of *The Guinness Book of Records*, having previously been sports editor for ten years. He commentates on his speciality, athletics, for ITV and Channel 4. Guinness published the third edition of his *Encyclopedia of International Sports Records and Results* in 1993. He is editor of the *International Athletics Annual* and his other works include *Who's Who in British Athletics* (1990).

IAN BUCHANAN is a leading athletics and Olympic historian whose previous books include *British Olympians*, published by Guinness in 1991, the *Encyclopedia of British Athletics Records*, and *The US National Championships in Track & Field* with Bill Mallon. He is a member of the British Society of Sports Historians, the Association of Track & Field Statisticians, and the British Olympic Association.

Dr BILL MALLON is the leading US Olympic historian. A graduate of Duke University where he was twice named among the Outstanding College Athletes of America, he was a professional golfer on the PGA Tour 1975-9. He co-authored *The Golden Book of the Olympics* with Erich Kamper in 1993 and *Quest for Gold: The Encyclopedia of American Olympians* with Ian Buchanan in 1984.

Published in Great Britain by Guinness Publishing Ltd, 33 London Road, Enfield, Middlesex

Cover design by Ad Vantage Studios, photographs courtesy of Allsport (London and Los Angeles)
Text design and layout by Amanda Ward
Typeset in Times and Gill Sans
Printed and bound in Great Britain by The Bath Press, Bath, Avon

A catalogue record for this book is available friom the British Library

ISBN 0-85112-980-3

Editor's Notes

Certain conventions have been used for displaying statistical material for various sports. Note that career figures are generally given to the end of the last completed season before press date, although references may be made in the biographies of current players to milestones achieved since.

Seasons that cross over years are shown in the format e.g. 1992/3. A span of successive years is shown in the format e.g. 1961-7, for each year from 1961 to 1967. Note that e.g. 1992-3 therefore indicates in the calendar years 1992 and 1993, rather than the 1992/3 season.

American football
Career statistics for the NFL may be listed for passing, rushing, receiving and touchdowns (TD).

Athletics
Event distances are shown in metres (m), yards (y), kilometres (km) or miles (M). Distances recorded for field events are generally shown in metres. Times are in seconds or minutes and seconds (e.g. 27:39.4 is 27 minutes, 39.4 seconds).

The letter w after a time indicates wind-assisted in excess of the limit permitted for record purposes of 2 metres per second. The letter i indicates an indoor performance. A personal best performance may be indicated by the letters pb.

Baseball
Career records are shown for the major leagues - NL (National League) and AL (American League).

For batting the format is: years of career, number of hits, and average (hits to at-bats), home runs (HR), runs batted in (RBI). Stolen bases (SB) may also be shown

For pitching the format is: earned run average (ERA), which is the average number of earned runs scored against a pitcher per nine innings, win-loss record (W-L), and number of strikeouts (SO).

Basketball
Career records are shown for NBA (National Basketball Association) players. These also include, where indicated, figures for play in the ABA (American Basketball Association), formed in 1967, which merged with the NBA in 1976.

Figures given may include: points, assists or rebounds, and averages (av.) per game played (also ppg for points per game).

Boxing
Career records list number of wins (W) followed by wins inside the full distance in parentheses, losses (L), and draws (D). Biographies may detail wins by knockout (KO) and technical knockout (TKO).

Canoeing

Races are designated with K for kayak and C for Canadian canoes, followed by the number of canoeists, e.g. C2 is Canadian pairs.

Cricket
Career figures are shown under three categories: a) Test matches, b) One-day internationals, c) First-class matches.

The number of Tests or one-day internationals is shown, with the span of Test and first-class careers. Then batting figures: number of runs, and average runs per completed innings, number of centuries (100s) and highest score (HS). Then bowling figures: wickets and average runs per wicket, best bowling in an innings (BB). Then total catches and stumpings.

Note * indicates an unfinished (not out) innings.

Cycling
Times are in seconds or minutes and seconds. e.g. 3:40.62 is 3 minutes, 40.62 seconds.

Harness racing
Times are recorded in fifths of a second, but for convenience are shown in this book in decimals. So 1:49.4 is 1 minute, 49 and two fifth-seconds.

Ice hockey
Career records are shown for NHL (National Hockey League) players. These also include, where indicated, figures for play in the WHA (World Hockey Association), which was contested as a rival to the NHL from 1972/3 to 1978/9.

Figures given may include: number of games played, goals and points (goals plus assists). For goalkeepers the average number of goals conceded per match (GAA) may be listed.

The summaries include annual NHL award winners:
Hart Memorial Trophy: the player adjudged to be the most valuable to his team.
Art Ross Trophy: the league's leading points scorer in regular season games.
Calder Memorial Trophy: the player who was selected as the most proficient in his first year in the NHL.
James Norris Memorial Trophy: the defense player who demonstrates the greatest all-round ability throughout the season.
Vezina Trophy: the best goalkeeper.
Lady Byng Memorial Trophy: the player adjudged to have exhibited the best type of sportsmanship and gentlemanly conduct combined with a high standard of playing ability.
Conn Smythe Trophy: the most valuable player for his team in the play-offs.
Lester B Pearson Award: the NHL's outstanding player as selected by the NHL Players' Association.

Speed skating
Times are in seconds or minutes and seconds (e.g. 3:40.62 is 3 minutes, 40.62 seconds).

Swimming
Times are in seconds or minutes and seconds (e.g. 3:40.62 is 3 minutes, 40.62 seconds). IM is individual medley.

Triathlon
Times are shown in hours: minutes: seconds for the total times for swimming, cycling and running.

Weightlifting
Weights lifted and weight-categories are shown in kilograms.

Abbreviations

av.	average
cc	cubic capacity
d	days
hr	hours
kg	kilograms
km	kilometres
km/h	kilometres per hour
m	metres
min	minutes
mph	miles per hour
m/s	metres per second
sec	seconds
y	yards
yr	years

In dates, months are usually abbreviated to their first three digits.

Countries

Note that in the headings countries are generally abbreviated only when the names are more than five characters in length

Alg	Algeria
Ant	Antigua
Arg	Argentina
Arm	Armenia
Aus	Australia
Aut	Austria
Bah	Bahamas
Bar	Barbados
Bel	Belgium
Ber	Bermuda
Bls	Belorus
Bra	Brazil
Bul	Bulgaria
Can	Canada
Chl	Chile
Chn	China (People's Republic)
Col	Colombia
Cs	Czechoslovakia
Cyp	Cyprus
Den	Denmark
Ecu	Ecuador
Egy	Egypt
Eng	England
Est	Estonia
Eth	Ethiopia
Fin	Finland
Fra	France
FRG	Federal Republic of Germany
GDR	German Democratic Republic
Geo	Georgia
Ger	Germany
Gha	Ghana
Gre	Greece
Guy	Guyana
Haw	Hawaii
Hol	Holland/Netherlands
Hun	Hungary
Ice	Iceland
Ina	Indonesia
Ind	India
Ire	Ireland
Ita	Italy
Jam	Jamaica
Jap	Japan
Ken	Kenya
Kgz	Kirghizstan
Kzk	Kazakhstan
Lat	Latvia
Lie	Liechtenstein
Lit	Lithuania
Lux	Luxembourg
Mal	Malaysia
Mex	Mexico
Mol	Moldova
Mor	Morocco
NI	Northern Ireland
Nig	Nigeria
NKo	North Korea (Korean DPR)
Nor	Norway
NZ	New Zealand
Pak	Pakistan
Pan	Panama
Par	Paraguay
Phi	Philippines
Pol	Poland
Por	Portugal
PR	Puerto Rico
Rho	Rhodesia
Rom	Romania
Rus	Russia
SAf	South Africa
Sco	Scotland
Sen	Sénegal
Sin	Singapore
SKo	Korea (South)
Som	Somalia
Spa	Spain
Sri	Sri Lanka
Swe	Sweden
Swi	Switzerland
Tai	Taiwan
Tan	Tanzania
Tha	Thailand
Tjk	Tadjikstan
Tri	Trinidad & Tobago
Tun	Tunisia
Tur	Turkey
Uga	Uganda
UK	United Kingdom of Great Britain & N.Ireland
Ukr	Ukraine
Uru	Uruguay
USA	United States
USSR	Soviet Union
Uzb	Uzbekistan
Ven	Venezuela
Wal	Wales
WI	West Indies
Yug	Yugoslavia
Zam	Zambia
Zim	Zimbabwe (formerly Rhodesia)

Governing Bodies, Sports Organisations, Awards etc

Specified here in English

AAA	Amateur Athletic Association (UK)
AAU	Amateur Athletic Union (USA)
AFC	American Football Conference
AFL	American Football League
AL	American League
ATP	Association of Tennis Professionals
FA	Football Association
FIBA	International Basketball Federation
FIDE	International Chess Federation
FIE	International Fencing Federation
FIFA	International Association Football Federation
FIG	International Gymnastic Federation
FIH	International Hockey Federation
FINA	International Amateur Swimming Federation
FIQ	International Bowling Federation
FIS	International Ski Federation
FITA	International Archery Federation
GP	Grand Prix
IAAF	International Amateur Athletic Federation
IBF	International Boxing Federation
ISU	International Skating Union
ITF	International Tennis Federation
LPGA	Ladies Professional Golfers Association
MCC	Marylebone Cricket Club
MVP	Most Valuable Player
NASCAR	National Association for Stock Car Auto Racing
NBA	National Basketball Association (USA)
NBL	National Basketball League (USA)
NCAA	National Collegiate Athletic Association (USA)
NFC	National Football Conference (USA)
NFL	National Football League (USA)
NHL	National Hockey League (USA)
NL	National League
PGA	Professional Golfers Association
PRCA	Professional Rodeo Cowboys Association
RAC	Royal Automobile Club
TT	Tourist Trophy
UCI	International Cycling Union
UEFA	Union of European Football Associations
UIPMB	International Union of Modern Pentathlon and Biathlon
UIT	International Shooting Union
WBA	World Boxing Association
WBC	World Boxing Council
WBO	World Boxing Organisation

See also Editor's Notes for specific abbreviations for particular sports.

Hank AARON (USA)

BASEBALL

Henry Louis Aaron. b. 5 Feb 1934 Mobile, Alabama.

One of the greatest ever right fielders and all-round hitters in baseball. In April 1973 he hit a home run in Atlanta off Al Downing, the 715th of his career, to break the legendary record of 714 career home runs by Babe Ruth. Aaron, who went on to a career record of 755, played most of his career with the Braves, starting in Milwaukee in 1954, and moving with the team to Atlanta in 1966. He was traded back to Milwaukee with the American League Brewers for the last two years of his career. One of the first great blacks in major league baseball, he found discrimination in the southern United States even after breaking Ruth's record. He later stated that he received a lot of hate mail from racists who were upset that he had upstaged Ruth. He is now an executive in the Atlanta Braves organisation.
Career 1954-76: 3771 hits Avg .305, HR 755. Best seasons: 1959 - .355, 39 HR, 123 RBI; 1963 - .319, 44 HR, 130 RBI.

Giuseppe ABBAGNALE (Ita)

Carmine ABBAGNALE (Ita)

ROWING

Giuseppe Abbagnale. b. 24 Jul 1959, Carmine Abbagnale b. 5 Jan 1962 both at Pompeii.

Brothers who won a record nine world titles at the coxed pairs, 1981-2, 1984-5, 1987-91, including the Olympics of 1984 and 1988. Giuseppe made his international début in 1976, when he was ninth at the coxed pairs at the World Juniors. He was eighth in the World Juniors at eights in 1977 and seventh at coxed pairs at the 1980 Olympics. Carmine made his international début at the 1981 European Cup and that same year the brothers won the first of their string of world titles. They were second at the Olympics in 1992 and at the Worlds in 1986 and third in 1983. Very fast rowers, but one-paced and they could not respond to the finish of the Searle brothers from Britain at the 1992 Olympics. **Giuseppe Di Capua** (b. 15 Mar 1958 Salerno) has been their cox for all their major championships.
Together the brothers lived near the ruins of the ancient city of Pompeii and trained on salt water in a Mediterranean Bay near Naples. Giuseppe is a bank employee and Carmine has stood unsuccessfully for parliament. A third brother, **Agostino**, was also a renowned rower who won a gold medal at the 1988 Olympics in the quadruple sculls.

Kareem ABDUL-JABBAR (USA)

BASKETBALL

né Ferdinand Lewis 'Lew' Alcindor. b. 16 Apr 1947 New York.

With Bill Russell and Wilt Chamberlain, one of the three greatest centers to play basketball. He began his career as Lew Alcindor at Power Memorial High School in New York city, where he was the subject of a great recruiting war. He went to UCLA whom he helped to three straight NCAA titles. Drafted by the Milwaukee Bucks, the giant (2.18 m *7'2"*) Alcindor led them to an NBA title in 1971, his second year in the league. By then he had embraced the Muslim faith and changed his name to Kareem Abdul-Jabbar. He played for 6 years with Milwaukee but was then traded to the Los Angeles Lakers where he played until 1989. With the Lakers he won five more NBA titles. He retired as the leading career scorer in NBA history, with 38,387 points in 1560 games 1970-89 av. 24.6. Play-offs: 5762 points in 237 games av. 24.3. He was also voted league MVP a record six times, 1971-2, 1974, 1976-7, 1980 and appeared in 18 All-Star games.
NBA career: also 17,440 rebounds, av. 11.2.

ABDUL QADIR (Pak)

CRICKET

Abdul Qadir Khan. b. 15 Sep 1955 Lahore.

The best leg-spin bowler of the 1980s, Abdul Qadir made his Test début on the Pakistan tour to England in 1977 and had his best series against England in 1987/8

when he took 30 wickets at 14.56 in 3 Tests, including 9-56 and 4-45 to help Pakistan to an innings victory in the First Test at Lahore. In 1982/3 he took 103 wickets, the first bowler ever to take more than 100 in a Pakistan season. He had some difficulties with the authorities in Pakistan, and seemed to end his Test career prematurely.
67 Tests 1977-90: 1029 runs at 15.59, HS 61; 236 wkts at 32.80, BB 9-56; 15 catches.
102 One-day Ints: 634 runs at 15.09, HS 41, 131 wickets at 25.68, BB 5-44; 21 catches.*
First-class 1975-91: 3636 runs at 18.74; 2 100s HS 112; 897 wickets at 23.43, BB 9-49; 76 catches.

Bobby ABEL (UK)

CRICKET
Robert Abel. b. 30 Nov 1857 Rotherhithe, Surrey, d. 10 Dec 1936 Stockwell, Surrey.

'The Guv'nor' was one of the smallest of top-class batsmen (1.62m *5'4"*) but was a masterly opener. He played for Surrey and was 31 when he made his Test début. He exceeded 2000 runs in eight successive seasons 1895-1902, including a record 12 centuries in 1900 and then a record 3309 runs (at 55.15) in a season in England in 1901. His best score of 357* came when he carried his bat through Surrey's 811 v Somerset at The Oval in 1899. He was also a right-arm slow round-arm bowler and a fine slip fielder.
13 Tests 1888-1902: 744 runs at 37.20, 2 100s HS 132; 13 catches.*
First-class 1881-1904: 33,124 runs at 35.46, 74 100s HS 357; 263 wickets at 24.00, BB 6-15; 586 catches.*

Sid ABEL (Can)

ICE HOCKEY
Sidney Gerald Abel. b. 22 Feb 1918 Melville, Saskatchewan.

He played most of his career with the Detroit Red Wings, centering for Gordie Howe and Ted Lindsay, except for his last season with the Chicago Black Hawks. He was a good scorer but was better known as a creative playmaker. After he finished playing, Abel became a coach and later a general manager for both the Red Wings and the St Louis Blues.
NHL career 1938-54 - 613 games, 189 goals, 472 points. Best year: 1949/50 - 34 goals, 69 points. Hart Trophy 1949.

Harold ABRAHAMS (UK)

ATHLETICS
Harold Maurice Abrahams. b. 15 Dec 1899 Bedford, d. 14 Jan 1978 Enfield, Middlesex.

The Olympic 100m champion of 1924, whose feat was later immortalised in the film *Chariots of Fire* (1981). He set British 100m records at 10.6 in heat, semi-final and final and also won a silver medal in the sprint relay. In his first Olympics in 1920 he was eliminated in the quarter-finals of the 100m and 200m and helped Britain to 6th in the 4x100m. He set four British records at the long jump from 7.19 in 1923 to 7.38 in 1924, and this remained the record for 30 years. He might have become the first English 25-footer (7.52m) but for breaking his leg in May 1925, an injury that terminated his career. He set a record with eight individual event wins for Cambridge University in the annual match against Oxford: 100y 1920-3, 440y 1923, and long jump 1920, 1922-3. AAA champion at 100y 1924 and long jump 1923-4, he was coached by Sam Mussabini.
Other bests: 100y 9.6w downhill and 9.9 (1924), 220y straight track 21.6 (1923), 200m 22.0 (1924).
Following his retirement he devoted a lifetime of service to the sport, as team manager, broadcaster, journalist, statistician and official, serving on the AAA's General Committee from 1926, becoming secretary in 1931 and president in 1976. He was Hon. Treasurer of the BAAB 1946-69 and its chairman 1969-75. Awarded the CBE in 1957 as secretary of the National Parks Commission, which he joined after 13 years as a barrister. Harold's elder brothers Adolph and Sidney were both knighted, the former for services to medicine and the latter for legal work. Sidney was also a fine long jumper, AAA

champion in 1913, competing in the 1906 and 1912 Olympics.

Rosemarie ACKERMANN (GDR)

ATHLETICS

née Rosemarie Witschas. b. 4 Apr 1952 Lohsa.

A great high jumper, who was the Olympic champion in 1976 and European champion in 1974. She had many classic competitions with Sara Simeoni, over whom she had in all an 8-5 advantage. She set seven world records from 1.94m in 1974, to equal the record that Yordanka Blagoyeva (Bul) had set in 1972, to the historic first two-metre clearance in West Berlin on 26 Aug 1977. She was the last world record-setter to use the straddle style.

At the Olympics she was also 7th in 1972 and 4th in 1980, and at the Europeans she was 2nd in 1978. She was European Indoor champion three times 1974-6, GDR champion six times 1973-4, 1976-7 and 1979-80 and was the winner at the European Cup Final three times and the World Cup once.

Janet ACKLAND (UK)

BOWLS

Janet Ackland. b. 19 Dec 1938 Somerset.

World singles champion and the leading Welsh lady bowler. After winning bronze medals in the pairs and fours at the 1977 World Championships she took the singles title 11 years later. Representing Wales, she was the second UK player to win the World singles, Norma Shaw (Eng) having won the title in 1981. She was Welsh champion in singles, triples and fours and won her first international cap in 1973. In 1980 she gave up her job as an art teacher to become a full-time bowler.

ADEMIR (Bra)

FOOTBALL

Ademir Marques de Meneses. b. 8 Nov 1922 Recife.

A dangerous striker who also performed well in the outside-left position. He was the leading scorer in the 1950 World Cup with four of his nine goals coming in the match against Sweden. In all he scored a total of 31 goals in 37 internationals. He first signed for Recife but later played for Vasco da Gama, for whom he scored 303 goals in 461 games, and Fluminense (1946-7) who between them won the Brazilian League six times when Ademir was in the team. A succession of injuries after the 1950 World Cup curtailed his playing career, finally ending in 1956, after which he went into broadcasting.

His father, **Domingos da Guia** starred for Brazil as a defender in the 1938 World Cup.

Jean AERTS (Bel)

CYCLING

Jean Aerts. b. 8 Sep 1907 Laken-Brussels, d. Jun 1992.

The first man to win both the world amateur (1927) and professional (1935) road race championships. In 1927 the professionals and amateurs rode concurrently at the Nurburgring in Germany and Aerts finished 5th overall, but was the highest ranked amateur. He was an excellent sprinter which helped in the world championships but he lacked the climbing ability to be a factor in the major tours. He used his sprinting ability to win 11 stages of the Tour de France, including six in 1933, but even then his climbing kept his finish down to only 9th place. He won the Paris-Brussels in 1931.

Andre AGASSI (USA)

TENNIS

Andre Agassi. b. 29 Apr 1970 Las Vegas, Nevada.

An exciting and charismatic player who won the Wimbledon singles title in 1992. Coached from the age of 13 by Nick Bolletieri, he turned professional at 16, and ranked third in the world at 18 in 1988, when he was a semi-finalist at the French and US Opens. The hard-hitting, agile right-hander did not quite live up to his early promise in the ensuing years, although he remained ranked in the

world's top ten at the end of each year. He lost in three Grand Slam finals, French 1990-1 and US 1990 before his Wimbledon triumph. He won the ATP World Championship in 1990. He made his Davis Cup début in 1988 and helped the US to win in 1990 and 1992; his career record (all singles) won 19 (including all 10 in 1991-2), lost 4. Career earnings $5,351,203.
His father Mike (né Emmanuel Agassian) was an Armenian, who had emigrated from Iran to the USA in 1952. He boxed at the Olympics, and had a brief career as a pro in the USA; he was also a tennis coach for a while.

Giacomo AGOSTINI (Ita)

MOTOR CYCLING
Giacomo Agostini. b. 16 Jun 1942 Lovere, near Brescia.

The most successful rider in the history of World Championship motorcycling. He won a record 15 world titles: seven at 350cc, 1968-74, and eight at 500cc 1966-72 and 1975, and he won a record 122 Grand Prix races (54 at 350cc and 68 at 500cc) in the championship series between 1965 and 1977, including a record 19 in 1970.
His interest in motorcycling started when his father bought him a Vespa scooter at the age of nine, and his first road race was in 1961. From then he rode for Morini, winning the 1964 Italian 250cc championship, until signed by MV in 1965, when he was second in the World Championship at 500cc to Mike Hailwood. He rode for MV Agusta until 1973, when he was beaten by team-mate Phil Read for the 500cc title, then for two years with Yamaha 1974-5, and on a variety of machines in 1976. On the Isle of Man he won ten TT races between 1966 and 1972. An idol in his native Italy he was also in demand, with his wholesome good looks, as a model and in films. After his racing career was over he managed the Yamaha team before Kenny Roberts took over, and in 1992 returned to head the Cagiva team. His younger brother **Felice** (b. 1955) was a useful moto-cross rider.

Tonny AHM (Den)

BADMINTON
Tonny Kristine Ahm. b. 21 Sep 1914 Gentofte, d. 2 Apr 1993. née Olsen.

In a long career she won more than 50 national titles at badminton, including eight senior titles each at ladies singles and doubles and three at mixed doubles 1936-52, and represented Denmark internationally for 23 years. At the All-England Championships she won 12 titles between 1939 and 1952; six at women's doubles with Ruth Dalsgard in 1939, Kirsten Thorndahl 1947-8 and 1950-1 and Aase Jacobsen 1952; four mixed doubles with Paul Holm, 1947 and 1950-2, and the singles in 1950 and 1952.

Georges AILLERES (Fra)

RUGBY LEAGUE
Georges Ailleres. b. 3 Dec 1934 Rieumes, Haute-Garonne.

Captain of Toulouse Olympique and France, he initially played in the second row before moving to prop. He made the first of his 34 international appearances in 1961/2 and after playing for the team that lost in the World Cup final of 1968 to Australia he captained the national team in 1969-70. He started his career with Lézignan, moving to Toulouse, who he captained until 1971.

John AKII-BUA (Uga)

ATHLETICS
John Akii-Bua. b. 3 Dec 1949 Kampala.

When he won the Olympic gold medal for 400m hurdles at Munich in 1972 he ran 47.82 to take a phenomenal 0.3 off the world record that David Hemery had set four years earlier at high altitude.
One of 43 children, Akii-Bua had taken up hurdling in 1967, reaching world class in 1970, when he was 4th at the Commonwealth Games. He was African champion in 1973, but hopes of additional Olympic glory were dashed with the African boycott of the 1976 Games.
He escaped from Idi Amin's Uganda and settled in Germany in 1979 before compet-

ing without success at the 1980 Olympics. In 1971 he had won the Ugandan decathlon title with 6933 points.

Pierre ALBALADEJO (Fra)

RUGBY UNION

Pierre Albaladejo. b. 13 Feb 1933 Dax.

A drop goal specialist who was, at one time, France's most capped fly-half. He set an international record by dropping three goals against Ireland in 1960. In an 11-year international career beginning in 1954 he won 30 caps at fly half or full back and scored 104 points from penalties, conversions and 12 dropped goals but surprisingly he never scored a try in an international match. After retirement, he concentrated on his restaurant business.

Florian ALBERT (Hun)

FOOTBALL

Florian Albert. b. 15 Sep 1941 Hercegszántó.

A complete centre-forward who possessed fine positional and tactical skills and could shoot with either foot. After signing for Ferencváros as a 17-year-old he made his international début against Sweden in June 1959, when still aged 17, and went on to score 31 goals in 75 internationals. He was European Footballer of the Year in 1967 and was in the Ferencváros team which won the Fairs Cup in 1965.

His talents were such that he only bothered to train spasmodically and this, coupled to the fact that he was able to exert excessive influence in important club matters, did not make him popular with his team-mates. He was undoubtedly a selfish and uncommitted player and even his most enthusiastic admirers had their reservations. On his retirement in 1974 he became a journalist.

Carlos ALBERTO (Bra)

FOOTBALL

Carlos Alberto Torrès. b. 17 Jul 1944 Rio de Janeiro.

The team's captain, he marshalled the defence of the Brazilian side that won the 1970 World Cup, when he scored the fourth and best goal in the final. An attacking full back, that was one of eight goals he scored in 58 international appearances 1963-77. He played for Santos.

Tenley ALBRIGHT (USA)

FIGURE SKATING

Tenley Emma Albright. b. 18 Jul 1935 Newton Center, Massachusetts. Later Gardiner.

The first American woman to win both an Olympic and a world figure skating title. After finishing second to Jeannette Altwegg at the 1952 Olympics she won her first US senior Championship later that year and retained the title for the next four years. In 1954 she won the world title and after successfully defending her crown in 1955 took the Olympic title the following year, when she finished first in both the compulsory and free figures to beat her team-mate Carol Heiss. Two weeks later she lost her world title to Heiss but soon re-established her supremacy when she took her fifth and final US title in March 1956. All these successes were achieved while she was a student at the exclusive Radcliffe College, but when she retired from skating in 1957 she entered Harvard Medical School and graduated four years later. She married lawyer Tudor Gardiner in 1962 and she is today a practising surgeon and a member of the Board of the US Olympic Committee.

Amy ALCOTT (USA)

GOLF

Amy Strum Alcott. b. 22 Feb 1956 Kansas City, Missouri.

Her five wins in the majors include a record three, 1983, 1988 and 1991, in the Dinah Shore Classic, with the 1979 Peter Jackson Classic and the 1980 US Open. She became the LPGA Tour's sixth millionaire in 1983 and the third to win over $2 million in 1988. She had won the US Girls' Junior Amateur title in 1973.

LPGA career earnings 1975-92: $2,850,188 with 29 victories.

Terry ALDERMAN (Aus)

CRICKET

Terence Michael Alderman. b. 12 Jun 1956 Subiaco, Perth, Western Australia.

Alderman, a right-arm medium-fast bowler, enjoyed his greatest success on English wickets, where he became the only player ever to twice exceed 40 wickets in a Test series, 42 at 21.26 in 1981 and 41 at 17.36 in 1989. He was markedly less successful elsewhere, although a most capable performer, as his next best, also against England, was 16 wickets in the 1990/1 series. In all against England he took 100 wickets in 17 Tests. He played for Western Australia and in England for Kent in 1984 and 1986 and Gloucestershire 1988. He lost some years in Test cricket through going on a 'rebel' tour to South Africa.

41 Tests 1981-91: 203 runs at 6.54, HS 26; 170 wickets at 27.15, BB 6-47; 27 catches.*

65 One-day Ints: 32 runs at 2.66, HS 9, 88 wickets at 23.36, BB 5-17; 29 catches.*

First-class 1974-93: 1307 runs at 8.32, HS 52; 956 wickets at 23.74, BB 8-46; 190 catches.*

Alexandre ALEKHINE (USSR/Fra)

CHESS

Alexandre Aleksandrovich Alekhine (né Alyokhin) b. 31 Oct 1892 Moscow, d. 24 Mar 1946 Estoril, Portugal.

World chess champion 1927-35 and 1937-46. Nordic champion 1912; German champion 1914; Russian champion 1909, 1914 (joint), 1920. Alekhine learnt chess from his mother and had his first major success at Stockholm in 1912, at which time he was studying law in Moscow. He had a difficult time following the Russian Revolution and emigrated to Switzerland in 1921, but then deserted his Swiss wife and became a French citizen in 1925. He beat Capablanca for the world title in 1927, but thereafter avoided his potentially greatest rival. He lost the world title to Euwe in 1935 but regained it from him two years later, holding it until his death. A hard drinker, he earned disrepute with anti-Semitic articles in World War II.

Vasiliy ALEKSEYEV (USSR/Rus)

WEIGHTLIFTING

Vasiliy Ivanovich Alekseyev b. 7 Jan 1942 Pokrovo-Shishkino, Ryazan Oblast.

Alekseyev has the greatest competitive record of any super-heavyweight lifter in history. As a 28 year-old miner in 1970 he made a late start to international sport, but his pioneering training methods brought him instant and continuing success. From 1970 until 1978 he was undefeated, winning two Olympic gold medals (1972, 1976), was world or Olympic champion for eight successive years (1970-77), and won eight European championships, not entering in 1976.

Alekseyev set a record number of world records for any sport, with 80 between 24 Jan 1970 and 1 Nov 1977; he received bonuses for each world record and craftily broke each record by the smallest of margins. For the press he set 17 from 210.5 kg to 236.5, his range for 4 at snatch was 177 to 187.5 and he made 32 improvements for the jerk from 221.5 to 256, with 9 for total. He ended his career sadly as he failed three times to lift a weight in the snatch at the 1980 Olympics in Moscow. He was married to a woman aptly named Olympiada and he became chief coach of the Soviet team.

Markku ALÉN (Finland)

RALLYING

Markku Alén. b. 15 Feb 1952 Helsinki.

A charismatic driver with a record equalling 19 wins in world championship rallying races to the end of the 1992 season. He has never won the World Championship, but was second in 1986 and 1988, and third in 1979, 1983-4 and 1987. He started racing in Volvos, but was with Fiat/Lancia 1974-89, before joining Subaru in 1990. His major wins have included the 1000 Lakes Rally 1976, 1978-80, 1987-8, and the RAC Rally 1988.

Pete ALEXANDER (USA)

BASEBALL

Grover Cleveland Alexander. b. 26 Feb

1887 Elba, Nebraska, d. 4 Nov 1950 St Paul, Nebraska.

Alexander set a National League pitching record with 373 games won in his career. Slightly more than a year's World War I service interrupted a streak in which he won 30 games in three consecutive seasons 1915-17 (31-10, 33-12, 30-13). In 1916 he also recorded an amazing 16 shutouts, still the major league record. He played for Philadelphia 1911-17 and 1930, Chicago 1918-26, St Louis 1926-9, leading the NL by earned run average for five years (equals record), in 1915-17, 1919-20; for strikeouts in six years, 1912, 1914-17 and 1920; and for percentage won in 1915. He played a notable part in the World Series victory by St Louis Cardinals in 1926, when he struck out Tony Lazzeri when called from the bullpen in the seventh inning of the seventh game and went hitless in the remaining two innings. He had only average speed, but had an excellent curveball and superb control, and achieved his magnificent record despite suffering from epilepsy and the alcoholism which plagued him late in his career.
Career pitching 1911-30: ERA 2.56; W-L 373-208, SO 2198.

Muhammad ALI (USA)

BOXING

Muhammad Ali (Haj). né Cassius Marcellus Clay. b. 17 Jan 1942 Louisville, Kentucky.

He called himself 'The Greatest' and few who saw him box in his prime will dispute it. His magical abilities were perhaps best described by Mark Kram of *Sports Illustrated*, writing before the first Ali-Frazier fight: "He will be the first in the ring, so look at him with honest eyes because you will probably never see such impeccable talent again.... He is a Balanchine, a Dali, the ultimate action poet who has lifted so primordial an act to eloquent, sometimes weird, beauty."
He first gained international prominence as Cassius Clay by winning the light-heavyweight gold medal at the 1960 Rome Olympics. In February 1964, he upset Sonny Liston to win his first heavyweight championship. Shortly afterwards he embraced the Muslim faith and took the name Muhammad Ali. No fighter defeated him for the rest of the 1960s.
Ali was however defeated by the US draft board when he refused induction to the service based on a conscientious objection. Eventually, Ali won his battle in the Supreme Court but his title was stripped and the best years of his career were lost, as he did not fight for over three years. He returned in 1970 and the next year lost a much ballyhooed title fight against Joe Frazier. In 1974, Ali regained the heavyweight championship against George Foreman and after losing to Leon Spinks in 1978, hebecame the only man to hold the title three times when he defeated Spinks in a rematch. Ali won 22 world title fights and lost 3.
Career record: W - 56 (37), L - 5, D -0.

Liz ALLAN-SHETTER (USA)

WATER SKIING

Elizabeth Allan-Shetter. b. 12 Jul 1947.

Generally acclaimed as the greatest women's water skier in history. From her début in 1962 to retirement in 1975 she never failed to win at least two events in the US national championships, with 42 titles in all. She was world overall champion in 1965, 1969, and 1973 and won eight individual event world championships; both are records. In 1969, she won a unique grand slam by sweeping all four titles. She won the Masters Cup for women on each of the nine times that she entered. She also won in 1972, when water skiing was held as a demonstration sport at the Olympics for the only time.

Tony ALLCOCK (UK)

BOWLS

Anthony Allcock. b. 11 Jun 1955 Thurmaston, Leicestershire.

A specialist at the indoor game who won two World Indoor singles titles, 1986-7, and six pairs titles, 1986-7 and 1989-92 partnering David Bryant. He also won the English Indoor singles twice.
Outdoors he became the youngest ever world champion when he joined with Jim

Hobday and David Bryant to win the triples in 1980 at the age of 24. He won further gold medals at fours in 1984 and team in 1980 and 1988. In August 1987 he gave up his job as principal of a day centre for mentally handicapped adults in Stroud to devote more time to the game. He did not win his first English Outdoor singles title until 1990 but he was again the champion in 1991. In 1992 he had a great year, winning the British Isles singles and then the World title. Awarded the MBE 1989.

Gubby ALLEN (UK)

CRICKET

(Sir) George Oswald Browning Allen. b. 31 Jul 1902 Sydney, Australia, d. 29 Nov 1989 London.

While he was a fine, hostile fast bowler and a more than useful attacking batsman, Allen's cricket was limited by his business career, and he made an even bigger impact as an administrator. He was treasurer of the MCC 1964-76 and its president 1963-4 and chairman of the Test selectors 1955-61. After Eton and Cambridge University he played infrequently for Middlesex, but had many successes in major games. He played in the 'Bodyline' series in 1932/3, although not bowling that style himself, and he did much to restore his nation's reputation in Australia when he led the England team to tour there in 1936/7. When not really fit enough, at the age of 45, he was persuaded to take the England team to the West Indies in 1947/8. Awarded the CBE, and then knighted in 1986 for services to cricket.

25 Tests 1930-48: 750 runs at 24.19, 1 100 HS 122; 81 wickets at 29.37, BB 7-80; 20 catches.

First-class 1921-50: 9232 runs at 28.67, 11 100s HS 180; 788 wickets at 22.23, BB 10-40; 131 catches.

Marcus ALLEN (USA)

AMERICAN FOOTBALL

Marcus LeMarr Allen. b. 26 Mar 1960 San Diego, California.

The Heisman Trophy winner for the University of Southern California in 1981 when he had 2342 yards gained rushing, for an NCAA season's record. Joining the Los Angeles Raiders as a running back he was Rookie of the Year in the AFC in 1982 and won the MVP award at the January 1984 Super Bowl. In 1985, when he led the AFC in rushing, he shared the NFL player of the year award with Walter Payton. To the end of the 1992 season he had 98 career touchdowns in the NFL, and in 1993 moved to the Kansas City Chiefs.

Mark ALLEN (USA)

TRIATHLON

Mark Allen. b. 12 Jan 1958 Glendale, California.

The most successful triathlete in the history of the sport. A San Diego county lifeguard, passionate about surfing, he was inspired to take up triathlon by watching the Hawaii Ironman on television in February 1982, when Julie Moss collapsed yards from the finish line. He entered his first triathlon in June 1982 and finished fourth behind the three top names in the sport, Dave Scott, Scott Molina and Scott Tinley; two races later he beat them all. He won the Hawaii event himself four times consecutively 1989-1992, with record times of 8 hr 9 min 16 sec in 1989, after years of frustration at that race, and again in 1992 with 8:09:08. He also married Moss in 1989. His greatest race has been the Nice event in which he has won all ten times he has entered (1982-6, 1989-93). He was also winner of the inaugural world triathlon championship in 1989 and in his career to June 1993 has won 67 of the 90 triathlons he has contested, including 20 in succession 1988-91. He began as a swimmer and was an All-American backstroker at the University of California at San Diego. Known as 'The Grip', he is a prolific and indeed obsessive trainer.

Phog ALLEN (USA)

BASKETBALL

Forrest Clare Allen. b. 15 Nov 1885 Jamesport, Missouri, d. 16 Sep 1974 Lawrence, Kansas.

The first great basketball coach. He played

for the game's founder, James Naismith, at the University of Kansas 1905-07, and then took over as head coach in 1908. He coached for 46 years, missing only a few years in the 1910s when he studied osteopathic medicine, and in this time won 771 games with a winning percentage of .771. Almost single-handedly he was responsible for basketball being added to the Olympic programme in 1936. In 1952 he was honoured when he was named to coach the US Olympic team which won a gold medal.

Richard ALLEN (India)

HOCKEY

Richard John Allen. b. 4 Jun 1902 Bengal.

India's greatest goalkeeper in the years when they dominated world hockey. After keeping a clean sheet in five matches at the 1928 Olympics, he was only a reserve at the 1932 Games but was recalled for the 1936 Olympics where he played in four of India's five matches. The only goal he conceded in nine Olympic matches was in the 1936 final when India beat Germany 8-1.

Bobby ALLISON (USA)

MOTOR RACING

Robert Arthur Allison. b. 3 Dec 1937 Miami.

Driver of the year in the USA in 1972. His interest in motor racing began at school, after which he opened a garage with his brother Donnie in 1956. Between 1962 and 1966 he won national titles in various divisons of modified and special cars, and then joined the Grand National circuit. In his career he has 84 victories in NASCAR stock car races, third equal on the all-time list, and earnings of $7,102,233. He peaked at ten wins in 1971 and 1972 and was Winston Cup champion in 1983. He retired in 1988 after sustaining serious injuries in a crash, but returned to competition in 1993.

His son **Davey** (b. 25 Feb 1961 Hollywood, Florida) was a leading NASCAR driver until he was killed after a helicopter that he was piloting crashed at Talladega Speedway, Alabama on 6 July 1993, at the age of 32. Davey had 19 victories in 191 starts, including the Daytona 500 in 1992, having been second to his father in 1988. He was 'Rookie of the Year' in 1987 and had earned $6.7 million in his career.

José ALTAFINI (Bra/Ita)

FOOTBALL

José Altafini. b. 24 Jul 1938 Piracicaba. Known as Mazzola at 1958 World Cup.

One of the few men to have played for two different countries in the World Cup. A centre-forward, who was especially strong in the air, he began his career with Palmeiras and, although he had already signed for AC Milan, he played for Brazil in the 1958 World Cup. Then known as Mazzola, he used Altafini when he wnent to Italy, to avoid confusion with their famous player of that name (qv). He spent seven seasons with Milan and played for Italy in the 1962 World Cup. While with Milan he scored 120 League goals and both Milan's goals when they beat Benfica 2-1 in the 1963 European Cup final.

In 1965 he moved to Napoli and then in 1972 to Juventus and, at the age of 35, was in their team in the 1973 European Cup final. He finished his playing days with the Swiss Second Division club Chiasso, who he joined in 1976.

Rudi ALTIG (FRG)

CYCLING

Rudi Altig. b. 18 Mar 1937 Mannheim.

An outstanding pursuit cyclist, winner of world titles as an amateur 1959 and professional 1960-1, who became a top road sprinter. His lack of ability as a climber limited him in the major tours, although he did win the 1962 Vuelta à España. He also won the Tour of Flanders 1964 and Milan-San Remo 1968. His 1966 professional world road championship came at home in Germany when he outsprinted Jacques Anquetil for the title. Altig was also the winner of 23 six-day races, won 13 German championships and set world records at 1000m and 5000m. Although he never won the Tour de France he wore the yellow jersey for a total of 18 days between 1962 and 1969 and was third in 1966. Altig supplemented his training with yoga, often standing on his head between heats of track races. He had trained as an automobile electrician and after his racing days became a coach to the German team. He set world indoor records for 5km with a standing start of 6:07.6 as a pro in 1962 and for 1km with a flying start of 1:09.6 as an amateur in 1959.

Jeannette ALTWEGG (UK)

FIGURE SKATING

Jeannette Eleanor Altwegg. b. 8 Sep 1930 India. Later Wirz.

The only British woman to win both a world and an Olympic figure skating title since Madge Syers in 1908. Altwegg made her début at the World Championships in 1947 when she placed fifth and later that year was runner-up in the junior Lawn Tennis Championships at Wimbledon. She then decided to concentrate on skating and showed consistent improvement each year. She finished fourth at the 1948 World Championships, third in 1949, second in 1950 and finally took the title in 1951. She won a bronze medal at the 1948 Olympics before winning a gold medal at the 1952 Games, after which she retired. She was also British champion four times, 1947-50, and twice European champion, 1951-2. She declined all offers to turn professional and took up a teaching post at a children's orphanage in Switzerland. Awarded the CBE in 1953, she married a Swiss, Marc Wirz, but they were divorced in 1973. One of their daughters, Cristina, won the World Curling Championship in 1983.

Lance ALWORTH (USA)

AMERICAN FOOTBALL

Lance D. Alworth. b. 3 Aug 1940 Houston, Texas.

Alworth led the NCAA in 1961 with 61 punt returns in his senior year at the University of Arkansas. But in the pros he made his reputation as one of the greatest wide receivers in history. Blessed with blazing speed he was known as 'Bambi' for his youthful features. He began his career in the AFL in 1962 with the San Diego Chargers before the merger of the two leagues and finished his career with the Dallas Cowboys from 1970-3. Alworth had a career total of 542 receptions for 10,266 total yards to rank fourth on the all-time receiving list at his retirement, and his average yards per reception of 18.9 is the best among the top twenty all-time pass receivers. He scored 85 touchdowns and was known as a 'big-play' receiver.

Curtley AMBROSE (Ant)

CRICKET

Curtley Elconn Lynwall Ambrose. b. 21 Sep 1963 Swetes Village.

For the Leeward Islands Ambrose took a record 35 wickets in the Red Stripe Cup competition in 1988 and his Test début followed immediately. He speedily established himself as the leading fast bowler in world cricket, reaching his peak for the West Indies against Australia in 1992/3 when he took 33 wickets in the five Tests at an average of 16.42. In England he has played for Northamptonshire from 1989.
42 Tests 1988-93: 582 runs at 11.41, HS 53; 190 wickets at 21.42, BB 8-45; 9 catches.
90 One-day Ints: 359 runs at 13.80, HS 26; 136 wickets at 20.80, BB 5-17; 22 catches.*
First-class 1986-92: 1603 runs at 15.56; HS 59; 420 wickets at 22.12, BB 8-45; 26 catches.

Leslie AMES (UK)

CRICKET

Leslie Ethlebert George Ames. b. 3 Dec 1905 Eltham, Kent, d. 26 Feb 1990 Canterbury.

A high class wicket-keeper/batsman, who three times achieved the wicket-keeper's double of 1000 runs and 100 dismissals. His 128 dismissals (79 ct, 49 st) in 1929 and 122 (70, 52) in 1928 remain unassailable as the two highest totals of dismissals in a first-class season. In 1932 he again achieved over 100 dismissals (104), and this total included 64 stumpings, again an

all-time record, as is his 418 career stumpings, many off the Kent leg-spinner 'Tich' Freeman. He scored over 1000 runs in a season 17 times, with a peak of 3058 at 58.80 in 1933. Back problems caused him to concentrate virtually exclusively on his batting from 1939.
A free-scoring batsman, easily good enough to play for England in that rôle alone, he was manager and secretary of Kent 1960-74, playing a major part in that county's outstanding success after his own playing days were over. In 1950 he was the first professional ever to be appointed an England selector, serving for eight seasons. He also played League football for Clapton Orient and Gillingham.
47 Tests 1929-39: 2434 runs at 40.56, 8 100s HS 149; 74 catches, 23 stumpings.
First-class 1926-51: 37,248 runs at 43.51, 102 100s HS 295; 24 wickets at 33.37, BB 3-23; 703 catches, 418 stumpings.

Dennis AMISS (UK)

CRICKET
Dennis Leslie Amiss. b. 7 Apr 1943 Harborne, Birmingham.

Athough he made his début in Test cricket in 1966, Amiss did not establish himself for several years until he became Warwickshire's opening batsman in 1972. From then he was England's most prolific scorer, until in common with many others he struggled against the pace of Lillee and Thomson in 1974/5. Against the West Indies in 1973/4 he made 663 runs at 82.87 in 5 Tests, with a great match-saving 262* at Kingston. His Test career ended in 1977 when he went to play in World Series Cricket in Australia, but he continued to score massively for his county. He exceeded 1000 runs for 23 successive seasons in England 1965-87, with bests of 2239 at 55.97 in 1984 and 2110 at 65.93 in 1976. Awarded the MBE.
50 Tests 1966-77: 3612 runs at 46.30, 11 100s HS 262; 24 catches.*
18 One-day Ints: 859 runs at 47.72, 4 100s HS 137; 2 catches.
First-class 1960-87: 43,423 runs at 42.86, 102 100s HS 262; 18 wickets at 39.88, BB 3-21; 418 catches.*

Manuel AMOROS (Fra)

FOOTBALL
Manuel Amoros. b. 1 Feb 1952 Nîmes.

A fine defender who won a French record 82 international caps (1 goal), many as captain. He played for France in the World Cups of 1982 and 1986 and the European Championships of 1984 and 1992. Formerly with AS Monaco, he helped Marseille to win four successive French League titles 1989-92.

Abdelfattah AMR BEY (Egy)

SQUASH
Abdelfattah (David) Amr Bey. b. 14 Feb 1910.

The first of only two men to have won the British Open and the British Amateur Championship in the same season. Initially an outstanding lawn tennis and polo player, he was introduced to squash when he arrived in England in 1928 as part of the Egyptian Davis Cup squad. After reaching the semi-finals of the British Amateur in 1930 he won the title the following year and apart from 1934, when he did not compete due to injury, he won every year 1931-7. It took him five games to beat the veteran Dugald Macpherson in 1931, but he did not lose a single game in the next five finals. In 1932 he successfully challenged Don Butcher for the Open Championship and defended once against Butcher and three times against Jim Dear before retiring unbeaten in 1938.
A career diplomat, he gave up competitive squash when he was appointed Egyptian Ambassador to the United Kingdom in 1938 at the early age of 28.
Different versions of his name appear in record books: 'Bey' is a title of rank and the letter 'D' was adopted to differentiate from an identically named nephew. This became David through common usage, but it was never an official given name.

Hjalmar ANDERSEN (Nor)

SPEED SKATING
Hjalmar Andersen. b. 12 Mar 1923 Rødøy.

The dominant speed skater of the early

1950s. He was all-round World, European and Nordic champion each year 1950-2. At the 1952 Olympics he won three gold medals, 1500m, 5000m and 10,000m. His 11 seconds margin of victory at 5000m was the largest ever at the event, and at 10,000m he also had a huge measure of superiority, 16:45.8 to 17:10.6. He then retired but returned in 1954 to win a fourth Nordic title and place 2nd at the European Championships. He set four world records at 5000m and 10,000m, and his famous 16:32.6 at the latter stood for eight years. *Other personal best times: 500m 43.7, 1500m 2:16.4, 5000m 8:06.5.*

Bob ANDERSON (UK)

DARTS

Robert Anderson. b. 7 Nov 1947.

A civil servant from Swindon, Anderson began playing darts at five but did not represent England until he was 33. He steadily reached the top, winning his first major title in 1986. That year he partnered John Lowe to win the first World Pairs title, and won the first of three successive World Masters titles. In 1987 he won the British Open and World Matchplay and in 1988 he became the World Professional champion. He was also British Matchplay champion in 1988-9.

Gary ANDERSON (USA)

SHOOTING

Gary Lee Anderson. b. 8 Oct 1939 Holdredge, Nebraska.

A self-taught, left-handed marksman, who dominated free rifle shooting during the 1960s. In addition to winning two Olympic gold medals (1964 and 1968), he won seven individual world titles, 11 US titles and 11 gold medals at the Pan-American Games. Additionally, he set seven world records. After graduating from Hastings College in Nebraska, he initially planned further studies in theology but later opted for a political career and rose to become a Nebraska state senator. He also served as executive director of the National Rifle Association for many years.

Paul ANDERSON (USA)

WEIGHTLIFTING

Paul Edward Anderson. b. 17 Oct 1932 Toccoa, Georgia.

A contender for the strongest man who has ever lived. He had a short but meteoric career in Olympic-style lifting, winning the US championship in the heavyweight class in 1955 and then, later in the year, taking the world title by a margin of 37.5kg, unheard of in world competition. He won a gold medal at Melbourne in 1956 in a surprisingly close competition with Humberto Selvetti of Argentina; they tied in weight lifted, but Anderson won because, at 310 lb, he was the lighter of the two. Anderson set three world records at press (to 185.5kg) and two at jerk (best 197kg) in 1955 and made three improvements to the total record 1955-6. He set hundreds of records since as a powerlifter. He has bench-pressed 625 lb, squatted with 1,200 lb, dead-lifted 820 lb, and done three repetitions in the squat with 900 lb. In addition he performed a back-lift off trestles, supporting 6270 lb - the greatest weight ever lifted by a human.

Sparky ANDERSON (USA)

BASEBALL

George Lee Anderson. b. 22 Feb 1934 Bridgewater, South Dakota.

Generally acknowledged as the top manager in major league baseball in the 1970s and 1980s. He played only one year of major league, as a second baseman with the Philadelphia Phillies in 1959. After retiring in 1963, he spent five years as a minor league manager and in 1970 was named manager of the Cincinnati Reds. For the next eight years he guided baseball's dominant team, 'The Big Red Machine', as they won five National League pennants and two World Series, 1975-6. Anderson was inexplicably released by Cincinnati in 1978, but quickly hired by the Detroit Tigers for whom he is still the manager (1993). In 1984 he led the Tigers to a World Series win and in that year he also became the first manager to win 100 games in a season in both the

American and National Leagues. In 1993 he became the sixth major league manager to win 2000 games.

Willie ANDERSON (USA)

GOLF

William Anderson. b. May 1880 North Berwick, Scotland. d. 1910 Philadelphia, Pennsylvania.

The only person to have won the US Open three consecutive times, 1903-5 after wining earlier in 1901, he still ties the record for most wins. He also won the Western Open in 1902, 1904, 1908-9. Anderson emigrated from Scotland in 1895 with his father and became the club professional at Onwentsia Club near Chicago, wintering in St Augustine, Florida. He had an unorthodox swing characterised by a flat plane with a bent left arm but a full hip turn. His early death is usually attributed to alcoholism.

Adolf ANDERSSEN (Ger)

CHESS

Karl Ernst Adolf Anderssen. b. 6 Jul 1818 Breslau, d. 18 Mar 1879 Breslau.

The winner of the first truly international chess tournament in London in 1851, which meant that he was regarded as the world's strongest player until his defeat by Paul Morphy in 1858. After Morphy's retirement he was again regarded as world chess 'champion' 1862-6.
A professor of mathematics in Breslau, he was an attacking player and had great positional understanding. He won many major tournaments although less impressive in match-play.

Arne ANDERSSON (Swe)

ATHLETICS

Arne Andersson. b. 27 Oct 1917 Trollhättan.

His middle distance rivalry with Gunder Hägg was a feature of the war years of the 1940s in neutral Sweden. He ran four world records, 3:45.0 for 1500m in 1943 and three at the 1 mile: 4:06.2 in 1942 , 4:02.6 in 1943, when he took two seconds off Hägg's 1943 mark, and 4:01.6 in 1944 when he beat Hägg's record of 4:02.0. That last record came in July after he had earlier run a three-quarter mile world best of 2:56.6 and his fastest ever 1500m of 3:44.0 behind Hägg's world record of 3:43.0. In 1945 Hägg improved the world mile record to 4:01.3 with Andersson second in 4:02.2.
Arne first came to prominence with a national record of 3:48.8 to win the 1500m in the annual match against Finland in 1939, and he was Swedish champion at 1500m 1943-4. With Hägg he was suspended from amateur competition in 1945 for allegedly taking money.
Other best times: 800m: 1:50.8 (1942), 1000m 2:21.9 (1944), 2000m 5:12.6 (1944), 3000m 8:11.4 (1942), 2 miles 8:51.4 (1942), 5000m 14:18.2 (1941).

José ANDRADE (Uru)

FOOTBALL

José Léandro Andrade. b. 20 Nov 1898 Bella Vista, Montevideo, d. 5 Oct 1957.

One of the legends of the early days of Uruguayan football. A brilliant right-half with Nacional, he was in the winning team at both the 1924 and 1928 Olympic Games and in the South American Championships of 1923, 1924 and 1926. Although troubled by injury, he was recalled to the national team for the first World Cup at Montevideo in 1930 which Uruguay won. He ended his playing career with Peñarol in 1933, but his nephew, **Victor Rodriguez**, carried on the family tradition and was the right-half for the winning team at the 1950 World Cup and played with distinction in 1954.

Georges ANDRÉ (Fra)

RUGBY UNION and ATHLETICS

Georges André. b. 13 Aug 1889 Paris, d. 4 May 1943 Tunisia.

A notable Olympic athlete from the Racing Club de France who played on the wing for France seven times in 1913 and 1914 but was on the losing side in every match. He competed in four Olympic Games from 1908 to 1924, winning a

silver medal in the 1908 high jump and in 1920 taking a bronze in the 4 x 400m relay as well as 4th place at 400m hurdles. In 1924 he took the Olympic oath on behalf of the competitors. He set nine French records in athletics (at 110m, 200m and 400m hurdles, and at high jump) and won 21 French championships.
Known as 'The Bison' he was a physical education teacher and was killed in action in North Africa at the age of 53. His son Jacques was French champion at 110m hurdles in 1938.

Mario ANDRETTI (USA)

MOTOR RACING

Mario Gabrielle Andretti. b. 28 Feb 1940 Montona, near Trieste, Italy.

After learning in dirt track and stock car racing with his twin brother Aldo, he achieved fame on his first drive at Indianapolis, when he achieved pole position and placed third in the race itself in 1965; he won the 500 in 1969. He won the USAC national title in 1965-6 and 1969 and was runner-up in 1967-8. He had his first Formula One drive in 1968 and his first Grand Prix win in South Africa in 1971. USAC commitments prevented him from concentrating on Formula One until 1975. With Lotus from 1976, he placed third in 1977 and won the world title in 1978, when he won six Grands Prix. His world championship career total was 12 wins in 128 Grand Prix races and 180 points. Returning to racing in the USA, he won the 1984 Indy Car World Series. In 1993, at the age of 53, he won his 52nd Indy Car races from 380 starts and took his career earnings past $10 million for fifth on the all-time money list at $9,775,939. He is second to A J Foyt on the all-time list for races won. He is seventh on the all-time money list for the Indianapolis 500 itself with $2,628,419 from 27 races.
Andrettti's family came from Italy to Nazareth, Pennsylvania in 1957.
His son **Michael** (b. 5 Oct 1962) is one place ahead of him on the Indy Car all-time money list at $10,197,503, with 27 career wins in 145 Indy Car series races to the end of 1992. In 1991 Michael was second in the Indianapolis 500 and was overall Indy Car champion. Mario, with Michael as one of his co-drivers, was third in the 1983 Le Mans 24-hour race.

Rob ANDREW (UK)

RUGBY UNION

Christopher Robert Andrew. b. 18 Feb 1963 Richmond, Yorkshire.

England's most capped fly-half, playing 51 times in that position and once at full back from 1985 to 1993, captaining England once and scoring 148 points with an English record of 14 dropped goals. He added a further two dropped goals in his five Tests for the British Isles, two in 1989 against Australia and three in 1993 against New Zealand. He played for Nottingham andWasps and for a brief spell with Toulouse in France in 1991-2.
A Cambridge blue 1982-4, he also captained the University at cricket, and became a chartered surveyor.

Nikolay ANDRIANOV (USSR/Rus)

GYMNASTICS

Nikolay Yefimovich Andrianov. b. 14 Oct 1952 Vladimir.

The winner of a men's record 15 Olympic medals at gymnastics, seven gold, five silver and three bronze from 1972 to 1980. He won six individual golds: one in 1972, four in 1976 and one in 1980, when he also took a team gold. At the World Championships he won the gold for rings in 1974, with four silvers including the combined exercises, going on to win that title in 1978, when he again won on his best discipline, the rings, and added two silvers; he also won with the Soviet team in 1979, also taking an individual silver. He had started his international career at the 1971 Europeans, where, a late substitute, he surprised with six medals including bronze overall. He improved to 2nd in 1973 and to win in 1975; in all he had 8 golds, 6 silvers and 2 bronze in individual European competition. He was also overall champion at the World Cup in 1975 and 1977, when he shared the title with Vladimir Markelov.

Howard ANGUS (UK)

RACKETS and REAL TENNIS

Howard Rea Angus. b. 25 Jun 1944 Watford, Hertfordshire.

Angus matched Peter Latham and Jim Dear's achievement of winning world titles at both rackets and real tennis, and was the first amateur to do so.
He excelled at all racket games at Winchester and Cambridge. At real tennis he was the British Amateur champion 16 times between 1966 and 1982 and he only failed to win the title in 1981. He also won the doubles eight times. After an unsuccessful challenge for the World title in 1974 he beat Gene Scott (USA) two years later and remained the champion until 1981.
His record as a rackets player was equally impressive, winning the British Amateur singles and doubles title four times each. Between 1972 and 1977 he played Willie Surtees (GB/USA) four times in challenge matches for the world title and was successful in his second challenge in 1973. He was particularly disappointed to lose the fourth challenge in 1977 as he was, at the time, the world real tennis champion and he had hoped to match Latham's record of holding both titles simultaneously.

Denise ANNETTS (Aus)

CRICKET

Denise Annetts. b. 30 Jan 1964.

Australia's top run-scorer in women's one-day internationals with an aggregate of 1047 runs at an average of 43.63 and a highest score of 100* from 104 balls against England at Christchurch on 25 Jan 1992. This was prior to the 1993 World Cup, in which she captained Australia.
She has a remarkable Test average of 81.90 for her 819 runs, which includes two centuries, one of them the Test record score of 193 for Australia v England at Collingham in on 23-24 Aug 1987. Annetts and Lindsay Reeler (110*) put on 309 runs for the 3rd wicket to set a Test record partnership for any wicket before Annetts was run out.

Jacques ANQUETIL (Fra)

CYCLING

Jacques Anquetil. b. 8 Jan 1934 Mont-Saint-Aignan, d. 17 Nov 1987 Boos, near Rouen.

One of the greatest cyclists ever and known as the man who could break nobody, but who could not be broken. His wins were never spectacular, but his major tour victories were always carefully planned and steadily ridden. Anquetil's only weakness was as a road sprinter. He was an excellent climber, but his forté was as a time trialist. He had five wins in the Tour de France (1957, 1961-4) and wore the *maillot jaune* for a total of 51 days, the third highest ever. He is also one of the few top professional cyclists to have won an Olympic medal, having helped France to a bronze in the 1952 team road race. The greatest disappointment of his career was that he never managed to win the world professional road race title, his lack of sprinting ability hampering that effort, and his best was second in 1966. In 1956 he was French champion and second in the Worlds at pursuit and set world records for the 1 hour with 46.159 km and for 20km with 25:57.40. In 1967 he achieved 47.493 km in 1 hour and his last major race win came in 1969. Decorated as Chevalier of the Légion d'honneur by General de Gaulle in 1966, he became president of the French professional cyclists union and director of the French world championships team.
Other major victories: Giro d'Italia 1960, 1964; Vuelta à España 1963; Ghent-Wevelgem 1964; Bordeaux-Paris 1965; Liège-Bastogne-Liège 1966; Paris-Nice 1957, 1961, 1963; Grand Prix de Nations 1953-8, 1961, 1965-6; Dauphiné-Libéré 1963-5.

Cap ANSON (USA)

BASEBALL

Adrian Constantine Anson. b. 11 Apr 1852 Marshalltown, Iowa, d. 14 Apr 1922 Chicago, Illinois.

The biggest star in baseball in the nineteenth century, and a great hitter. He was the first man to get 3,000 hits, and batted over .300 for 25 seasons. He was not a good fielder, however, recording 58 errors in 1884 at first base, still a major league record for that position. Anson was also a playing manager during much of his career and was known as a martinet who was known to enforce his rules with his fists. He was also well-known as a racist, and was probably responsible for setting the integration of baseball back many years. In the 1880s, several blacks played in the major leagues until Anson refused to allow his teams to take the field and play against them.

Career 1876-97: Avg. .329, HR 97. Best seasons: 1881 - .399; 1886 - .371, 147 RBI.

Earl ANTHONY (USA)

BOWLING

Earl Roderick Anthony. b. 27 Apr 1938 Tacoma, Washington.

The greatest champion in the history of the Professional Bowlers' Association (PBA) with a record 41 titles on the Tour. His first title came in 1970 at Seattle. He retired briefly in 1984 but came back in 1988 to bowl on the senior PBA Tour, retiring from that in 1991. Besides his PBA titles, Anthony also won the ABC Masters in 1977 and 1984. He was voted PBA Player of the Year six times (1974-6, 1981-3). The only gap in Anthony's great career was his failure ever to win the US Open. He was the first bowler to win over $100,000 in one season ($107,585 in 1975) and the first to win $1 million in career prize money when he won the PBA National Championship at Toledo, Ohio in 1982. His career total was $1,361,931. He was nicknamed 'The Doomsday Stroking Machine' for his smooth delivery and winning style. He was an excellent athlete who began his sporting career as a minor league pitcher with the Baltimore Orioles organisation (Vancouver Triple A team in 1958-9). At his retirement he announced plans to devote his time to golf, at which he was a scratch player.

Kalle ANTTILA (Finland)

WRESTLING

Kaarle Johan Jalmari Anttila. b. 30 Aug 1887, d. 1 Jan 1975.

Anttila is one of just three wrestlers to have won Olympic gold medals in both classes (Kristjan Palusalu and Ivar Johansson are the others). He won the lightweight freestyle in 1920 and the Greco-Roman featherweight in 1924. He was world Greco-Roman featherweight champion 1921-2.

Isao AOKI (Japan)

GOLF

Isao Aoki. b. 31 Aug 1942 Abiko, Chiba Prefecture.

The finest ever Japanese golfer. He has won the most money and the most victories of any player on their tour, leading the money list in 1976 and 1978-80, with 52 Japanese PGA victories. He has also had success worldwide, notably winning the World Matchplay in 1978. Though he has never won any major tournament in the USA or Britain he has contended in both Opens, finishing second in the US Open in 1980 at Baltusrol. His style is most unorthodox, as he uses a flat, hands-dominated swing. His putting, which is outstanding, is also unusual in that he addresses the ball with the toe of the putter high in the air.

Saïd AOUITA (Mor)

ATHLETICS

Saïd Aouita. b. 2 Nov 1959 Kenitra.

The world's best 5000 metres runner of the 1980s, when he was unbeaten at that distance for ten years. He won the Olympic title in 1984 and the World title in 1987. His other titles include the World Student Games 1500m 1981, African 1500m 1984 and World Indoor 3000m 1989, and he was the IAAF Grand Prix overall champion in 1986, 1988 and 1989.

His range of distance-running ability was unprecedented, for having run 27:26.11 for 10,000m he stepped down to the 800m to take the Olympic bronze in 1988 with a best of 1:43.86. Injury then prevented him from taking part in the 1500m after reaching the semi-finals, and further injury caused him to miss the 1992 Olympics. Thus his 1983 World bronze medal remained his best in a major 1500m final, although he won the African title in 1984, after second place in 1982 (and third at 800m). He was beaten by Steve Cram at Nice in 1985 when they became the first and second men to better 3:30 for 1500m, but a month later he took the world record with 3:29.46. In between he set a 5000m world record at 13:00.40 and he broke that with 12:58.39 in 1987. He added world records at 2000m 4:50.81 in 1987, and at 3000m with 7:29.45 in 1989; these records were characterised by following a pace exactly on schedule, with a finishing kick to break the previous mark by a small margin.

Luis APARICIO (Ven)

BASEBALL

Luis Ernesto Aparicio Montiel. b. 29 Apr 1934 Maracaibo.

Aparicio played shortstop his entire career, beginning in 1956 with the Chicago White Sox. He later played for the Baltimore Orioles and Boston Red Sox, and was briefly traded back to the White Sox. Aparicio returned speed to the game of baseball after an absence of decades. He led the American League in stolen bases in his first nine years (topping 50 three times, with a peak of 56 in 1959). He was also a superb fielder, leading AL shortstops in fielding average eight times and winning nine Gold Gloves. In 1984 he became the first Venezuelan to be elected to the Hall of Fame.

Career 1956-73: 2677 hits Avg. .262; SB 506.

Joseph APESTEGUY (Fra) see CHIQUITO de CAMBO

Mikael APPELGREN (Swe)

TABLE TENNIS

Mikael Appelgren. b. 15 Oct 1961 Stockholm

Nicknamed 'The Apple', he was the winner of the singles a record three times, 1982, 1988, 1990, at the biennial European Championships. He was also doubles champion in 1988, and in five winning Swedish teams between 1980 and 1992. With Ulf Carlsson he won the world doubles title in 1985 and was in the winning Swedish team in 1989, 1991 and 1993 after three successive second places. Competed in the Olympic Games of 1988 and 1992. He made his international début in 1977, and he won a European Junior doubles and team gold medals in 1979, the World Cup in 1983 and the European Top-12 title in 1982 and 1990.

Syl APPS (Can)

ICE HOCKEY

Charles Joseph Sylvanus Apps. b. 18 Jan 1915 Paris, Ontario.

The Bobby Orr of his era, Apps was a true 'All-Canadian' boy, proficient in several sports. As an undergraduate at McMaster University in Hamilton, Ontario, he won the pole vault at the 1934 British Empire Games. He returned home to lead McMaster to the Canadian intercollegiate football championship. After graduation, he remained an amateur and finished 6th in the pole vault at the 1936 Olympics with his best performance of 4.00m.

He then began his hockey career which was spent entirely as a center with the Toronto Maple Leafs. His all-round ability was supplemented by long hours of extra work and he was an immediate success as rookie-of-the-year in the NHL. He was an excellent skater and stickhandler, centering the DAD Line (Drillon-Apps-Davidson). During his playing career he began forays into the political arena as well.

After his retirement, he became a member of the Ontario Legislature and later was a member of the Canadian cabinet.

NHL career 1936-48 - 423 games, 201 goals, 432 points. Best years: 1936/7 - 29 assists, 45 points; 1937/8 - 29 assists, 50 points. Calder Trophy 1937, Lady Byng Trophy 1942.

Rodica ARBA (Rom)

ROWING

Rodica Arba. née Puscatu. b. 5 May 1962 Bucharest.

The most titled woman rower in Olympic history, with four medals. She shares this honour with her compatriot Olga Bularda-Homeghi, with whom she has won most of her titles. As Rodica Puscatu she won an Olympic bronze in 1980 at Moscow in the eights. She and Bularda-Homeghi added a gold medal in 1984 at Los Angeles in the coxless pairs. In between she had won three medals at the world championships - 3rd in the 1981 coxless pairs, 3rd 1982 coxed fours, and 2nd 1983 coxless pairs. Her 1984 gold started her on a winning pattern, as she and Bularda-Homeghi won the world coxless pairs title in 1985-7 and also at the 1988 Olympics. She added a silver in the eights at Seoul to give her her fourth Olympic medal.

Eddie ARCARO (USA)

HORSE RACING

George Edward Arcaro. b. 19 Feb 1916 Cincinnati, Ohio.

In his 31-year career, 1931-61, he rode 4779 winners (then the third highest ever total) from 24,092 mounts to set a record money figure of $30,039,543. He is the only jockey to ride two horses to the Triple Crown in the USA: *Whirlaway* in 1941 and *Citation* in 1948. He rode the winner of the Kentucky Derby five times, the winners of the Preakness Stakes and Belmont Stakes six times each, and the Jockey Club Gold Cup ten times.

Apprenticed in 1929, he was highly popular and an excellent judge of pace. Known as 'Banana Nose', he was an ardent campaigner for jockeys' rights.

Maurice ARCHAMBAUD (Fra)

CYCLING

Maurice Archambaud. b. 30 Aug 1906 Paris, d. 3 Dec 1955 Le Raincy.

A solid rider who became most famous as a time trialist. His 1932 victory in the Grand Prix de Nations occurred in the inaugural of the race now considered the time trialing championship of the world. His ability against the clock also helped him set his hour record of 45.84 km in Milan at the famed Vigorelli velodrome in 1937. He won the Paris-Nice race in 1936 and 1939.

Fred ARCHER (UK)

HORSE RACING

Frederick James Archer. b. 11 Jan 1857 Cheltenham, d. 8 Nov 1886 Newmarket.

The greatest jockey of the 19th century, Fred Archer was champion jockey in England for 13 successive years, 1874-86, up to his suicide at the age of 29. He had ridden 2748 winners from 8084 mounts from 1870. His annual tally of winners rose each year from 1870 to 1878: 2, 3, 27, 107, 147, 172, 207, 218, 229; the last four were new annual records. After again totalling over 200 in 1881-2, he set further new records from 1883 to 1885: 232, 241, 246. He rode five Derby winners, and in all won 21 classics, 12 of them for Lord Falmouth. At 5 ft 10 in (1.78m) tall Archer was forced to adopt savage dieting in order to ride at some three stone below his natural weight of 11 stone. This wasting drastically affected his health and while seriously ill with typhoid fever, and also affected by the death of his wife Nellie two years earlier, he shot himself.

The son of William Archer, who rode the winner of the 1858 Grand National, Fred was apprenticed to Mathew Dawson at the age of 11 and was stable jockey for that great trainer from 1874. Allied to his masterly natural horsemanship he possessed enormous drive and determination to succeed, making him very hard on his horses, but a great friend to backers of them.

Nate ARCHIBALD (USA)

BASKETBALL

Nathaniel Archibald. b. 2 Sep 1948 New York.

Archibald combined the ability to score and playmake as well as any guard that has ever played. In 1973 he led the NBA in scoring and assists, the only time this has ever been accomplished, averaging 34.0 points and 11.4 assists per game. For his first seven years in the league (with Cincinnati and Kansas City) he averaged 24.8 ppg. In 1977 he tore his Achilles tendon and, although he played for 6 more years after sitting out the 1977/8 season, he was never again the same player. In 1981, he helped the Boston Celtics to an NBA championship.

Ossie ARDILES (Arg)

FOOTBALL

Osvaldo César Ardiles b. 3 Aug 1952 Córdoba.

He started his career with Instituto Córdoba in 1969, turning professional in 1971, and moved to Huracán in 1975. During this time he studied to be a lawyer before winning 42 international caps for Argentina, for whom he played a leading part as the midfield playmaker in their World Cup victory in 1978. He was an intelligent, skilful player who became highly popular in England when he arrived with his compatriot Ricky Villa to join Tottenham Hotspur, for whom he played in 238 Football League games 1978-88 and won an FA Cup winners medal in 1981 and the UEFA Cup in 1984. He had a spell with Paris St Germain in the aftermath of the Falklands War in 1982/3. He played five games for Blackburn Rovers in 1987/8 and five with Queens Park Rangers 1988/9. Appointed manager of Swindon Town in 1989, he had spells with Newcastle United 1991-2 and West Bromwich Albion 1992-3 before returning to manage Spurs in June 1993.

Paul ARIZIN (USA)

BASKETBALL

Paul Joseph Arizin. b. 9 Apr 1928 Philadelphia, Pennsylvania.

A consensus All-American and College Player of the Year in his final year at Villanova. He then played with the Philadelphia Warriors for his entire professional career to 1962. Apart from 17 points per game as a rookie he averaged more than 20 points per game every year. He led the league in scoring in 1952 and 1957 and helped the Warriors to the NBA championship in 1956. He was named to the NBA Silver Anniversary Team in 1971.
NBA career: 16,266 points, av. 22.8.

Jimmy ARMFIELD (UK)

FOOTBALL

James Christopher Armfield. b. 21 Sep 1935 Denton, Manchester.

Winner of 43 caps for England at right-back 1958-66, including a run of 37 consecutive appearances and 15 as captain. Although he represented Lancashire Schools at rugby, he decided on a football career and signed for Blackpool as an amateur in 1951. He turned professional in September 1954 and made his League début three months later, going on to make 566 League appearances for Blackpool before he retired in 1971. He also played nine times for England in under-23 internationals and made 12 appearances for the Football League.
Two months after retiring in May 1971 he was appointed manager of Bolton Wanderers and after moving to Leeds United in 1974/5 he guided them to the European Cup final that season. On leaving Leeds in July 1978 he became a regular broadcaster on BBC radio.
The outstanding feature of his game was the strength of his tackle and he was at his peak in the 1962 World Cup.

Tommy ARMOUR (USA/UK)

GOLF

Thomas Dickson Armour. b. 24 Sep 1895 Edinburgh, Scotland. d. 13 Sep 1968 Larchmont, New York.

Armour was a machine gunner in the tank corps in World War I, when he was wounded and lost the sight of one eye. Legend has it that after taking eight pieces of shrapnel in his shoulder, he jumped from his tank and killed a German soldier with his bare hands. He also became a legendary figure in golf. After winning the 1920 French Amateur, he moved to America. He uniquely played for Britain against the Americas 1921 and for the

USA against Britain 1926. His major victories were the US Open 1927, US PGA 1930, British Open 1931, Canadian Open 1927, 1930, 1934.
At one time he became known as the greatest iron player in the world, the greatest raconteur, the greatest drinker, and the greatest and most expensive teacher in golf. Though his tournament record was outstanding, Armour's later fame rested primarily on his reputation as a teacher and he authored one of the great instructional books ever, *How to Play Your Best Golf All the Time*.

Henry ARMSTRONG (USA)

BOXING

Henry Armstrong. b. 12 Dec 1912 Columbus, Mississippi, d. 22 Oct 1988 Los Angeles, California. né Henry Jackson, Jr.

'Homicide Hank' was brought up in St Louis but at 19 he hitchhiked to Los Angeles to begin professional boxing, first known as 'Melody' Jackson. Thus started a career in which he become the first man to hold three different titles simultaneously. His first title was won at featherweight in 1937 when he knocked out Pete Sarron. In May 1938 he defeated Barney Ross to add the welterweight, and in August 1938 he claimed the lightweight with a decision over Lou Ambers. Armstrong held various crowns through 1940 when he lost his welterweight title to Fritzie Zivic. After losing a rematch, Armstrong briefly retired, having contested 26 world title fights, of which he won 22 and drew 1. He fought until 1945 before settling on a life as an ordained minister of the Baptist Church. He published an autobiography *Gloves, Glory and God*.
Career record: W - 152 (100), L - 21, D -8.

Warwick ARMSTRONG (Aus)

CRICKET

Warwick Windridge Armstrong. b. 22 May 1879 Kyneton, Victoria, d. 13 Jul 1947 Darling Point, Sydney.

A tall, slim figure when he first played for Australia, he was a huge man by the time of his retirement, as he weighed over 20 stone *127kg* when he captained the team to England in 1921. He was a very successful all-rounder, a hard-hitting right-handed batsman, and a bowler whose pace slowed as he got heavier from fast medium to legbreaks. He achieved the remarkable feat of the double of 1000 runs and 100 wickets on three of his four tours to England, in 1905, 1909 and 1921, with that 1905 tour his best at 1902 runs av. 50.05 and 122 wickets av. 18.20. He made his début for Victoria in 1898/9 and first came to England in 1902. He captained Australia in 10 Tests after World War I and had the unmatched record of 8 wins and 2 draws with no defeats. He was accused of arrogance but he had much to be arrogant about, and he became a very successful businessman.
50 Tests 1902-21: 3868 runs at 29.74, 6 100s HS 159; 87 wickets at 33.59, BB 6-35; 44 catches.*
First-class 1898-1922: 16,158 runs at 46.83, 45 100s HS 303; 832 wickets at 19.71, BB 8-47; 274 catches.*

Cathy ARNAUD (Fra)

JUDO

Catherine Arnaud. b. 5 Feb 1963 Bordeaux.

World judo champion at under 56kg in 1987 and 1989, and European champion each year 1987-90. French champion 1983, 1987-9. A most dynamic attacker, she was third at the 1988 Olympics when judo was a demonstration sport and also at the 1984 World Championships.

René ARNOUX (Fra)

MOTOR RACING

René Arnoux. b. 4 Jul 1948 Pontcharra, Grenoble.

Had a long Formula One career, with a best world championship placing of third in 1983. The first of his seven Grand Prix wins was in Brazil 1980. In all he totalled 181 points from 149 starts. Drove for Martini and Surtees 1978, Renault 1979-82, Ferrari 1983-5, Ligier 1986-9.
Trained as a mechanic, he was on the French national karting team, before win-

ning the Formula Renault title for the Martini team in 1973 and 1975. He was European Formula Two champion in 1977 after second place in 1976.

Inga ARTAMONOVA (USSR)

SPEED SKATING

Inga Artamonova. b. 29 Aug 1936 Moscow, d. 4 Jan 1966 Moscow. Later Voronina.

Winning four world overall speed skating titles, she established a record which has twice been equalled but never beaten. She won her first world overall title on her championship début in 1957 and was again champion in 1958, 1962 and 1965. She also placed second in 1963 and in her seven appearances won a total of twelve individual events.

Because of injury she missed the World Championships and the Olympic Games both in 1960 and 1964 but enjoyed an outstanding year in 1962, setting three world records in late January (500m 44.9, 1500m 2:19.0, 3000m 5:06.0), and winning three out of four individual events at the World Championships three weeks later. Her marriage to Sergey Voronin, the Soviet national coach, ended in tragedy when he stabbed her to death after a family quarrel. Voronin was later sentenced to seven years imprisonment.

Vladimir ARTEMOV (USSR)

GYMNASTICS

Vladimir Artemov. b. 7 Dec 1964 Moscow.

Artemov won four Olympic gold medals in 1988, taking those for parallel bars and horizontal bar as well as the combined exercises and team. He was also world champion at parallel bars in 1987 and 1989, when he shared the title with Li Jing. USSR champion 1986.

Before 1988 however, he had been known as a perennial runner-up, having placed second at the 1984 Friendship Games, the 1985 World Championships and the 1986 Goodwill Games as well as third overall at the 1987 Worlds.

Alberto ASCARI (Italy)

MOTOR RACING

Alberto Ascari. b. 13 Jul 1918 Milan, d. 26 May 1955 Monza.

World champion driver in 1952 and 1953 for Ferrari, when the competition was contested by Formula Two cars, winning 11 of the 14 races in those years. He started in motorcycle races in 1936 and progressed to cars in 1940, when he drove the first car produced by Enzo Ferrari in the Mille Miglia. After the war he raced for Maserati in 1947-8, before joining Ferrari, with his first major success in the 1949 Italian GP. Drove for Lancia in 1954, when he won the Mille Miglia, and in 1955, when he crashed into the harbour at Monaco and four days later was killed while testing a Ferrari sports car at Monza.

A gentle, even placid man, he was very self-disciplined and able to drive precisely, within his limits. His father **Antonio** (1888-1925) was also a great driver, driving an Alfa Romeo to victory in the 1924 Italian and 1925 Belgian Grands Prix before being killed in the French GP at Montlhéry at the age of 36, the same age at which his son died.

Richie ASHBURN (USA)

BASEBALL

Donald Richard Ashburn. b. 19 Mar 1927 Tilden, Nebraska.

'Whitey' Ashburn was a center fielder who played his entire career in the National League, mostly for the Philadelphia Phillies, but at the end of his career also with the Chicago Cubs and New York Mets. Unlike the glamour center fielders of his era - Mays, Mantle, Snider - he was not a power hitter, never recording 10 home runs in a single season. He was primarily a singles hitter who hit for average.

He was also one of the all-time great outfielders, possessing great range. He has since become a top broadcaster for the Phillies.

Career 1948-62: 2574 hits Avg. .308. Best seasons: 1958 - .350; 215 hits.

Arthur ASHE (USA)

TENNIS

Arthur Robert Ashe, Jr. b. 10 Jul 1943 Richmond, Virginia, d. 6 Feb 1993 New York.

The first black male to win a Grand Slam tournament. After some notable successes at scholastic and collegiate level, he won the 1968 US Open and National (amateur), the 1970 Australian Open and then Wimbledon in 1975. Between 1963 and 1978 he only lost 5 of his 32 Davis Cup singles in 18 ties and from 1981 to 1985 was non-playing captain of the US team. He turned professional in 1969 and retired in 1980 having suffered a heart attack the previous year. Ashe was ranked in the top three in the US for 11 years although two years service as an Army officer restricted his play from 1967 to 1969. His game owed much to his topspin ground strokes and a fast, flat first serve. He helped to found the Association of Tennis Professionals' Tour and was its president from its creation in 1974 to 1979.
From a blood transfusion while undergoing the second of two heart operations he contracted the HIV-virus, and died from pneumonia cauised by AIDS in 1993.
Ashe is now remembered as much for what he accomplished out of tennis as for his achievements on court. A proud black man, he became a quiet, dignified crusader for racial equality and civil rights in the United States, in South Africa, and the world. He set up research foundations to fight the deadly AIDS virus, and the world mourned at his untimely death.

Evelyn ASHFORD (USA)

ATHLETICS

Evelyn Ashford. b. 15 Apr 1957 Shreveport, Louisiana. Married to basketball player Ray Washington.

Ashford was in the forefront of women's sprinting for an unparalleled time, her span of Olympic competition running from 1976, when she was fifth in the 100m, to 1992 when she was a semi-finalist and won a third successive sprint relay gold medal. She won the individual 100m in 1984 and the silver medal in 1988. At 100m with auto timing she ran 33 sub-11 second times (including 10 wind assisted), with five US records and world records at 10.79 in 1983 and 10.76 in 1984.
She ran the 200m less often, but set four US records with a best of 21.83 in 1979, and had seven years in the world top ten, with 27 successive finals wins 1978-86.
She won the 100m and 200m double at the 1979 Pan-American Games and at the World Cups of 1979 and 1981. She was third at 100m in the World Championships of 1991, but had previously met with misfortune at this even, pulling up with a hamstring injury in the 1983 100m final and having to withdraw through injury in 1987 after qualifying at 200m. She studied at UCLA and was US champion at 100m 1977, 1979 and 1981-3; 200m 1977-9, 1981 and 1983.
World indoor bests: 50y: 5.77 and 5.74 (1983), 60y: 6.54 (1982). Other bests: 60m 7.15i (1990), 400m 51.08 (1984).

Eric ASHTON (UK)

RUGBY LEAGUE

Eric Ashton. b. 24 Jan 1935.

An outstanding leader who captained Wigan in six Challenge Cup finals, taking the trophy 1958-9 and 1965. He won 26 caps for Great Britain and led them to victory in the 1960 World Cup and the Ashes on the 1960 tour of Australia. After being turned down by St Helens, he was signed by Wigan who had noted his talents while he was playing rugby union as a national serviceman. Although he scored 231 tries and 448 goals his major contribution was as a playmaker for his winger, Billy Boston, and on the 1958 and 1962 Great Britain tours of Australia he scored a total of 51 tries but again created many openings for his wing men. He was player-coach at Wigan 1963-9 and after retirement remained as coach until 1973 when he moved to St Helens. A natural leader and master tactician who coached Great Britain and England. He was awarded the MBE in 1966 and was the first rugby league player to be honoured in this manner.

ASIF IQBAL (Pak)

CRICKET

Asif Iqbal Razvi. b. 6 Jun 1943 Hyderabad, India.

A delightful batsman, fast of foot with wristy drives and cuts. He was a highly regarded captain of Kent in 1977 and 1981-2, having played for them from 1968, and for Pakistan in 1979-80 at the end of his Test career when he had returned to Tests after playing in World Series cricket. Asif made his first-class début for Hyderabad in India before emigrating to Pakistan in 1961 and made his Test début as a medium-fast bowler. He took 18 wickets at 13.77 in three Tests in New Zealand in 1965. However, from 1967 when he scored his maiden Test century against England at The Oval, batting at No.9 and putting on a Test record 190 for the 9th wicket with Intikhab Alam in 170 minutes, he concentrated on batting. His uncle **Ghulam Ahmed** (b. 4 Jul 1922) played 22 Tests for India as an off-spinner 1948-59.

61 Tests 1964-80: 3575 runs at 38.85, 11 100s HS 175; 53 wickets at 28.33, BB 5-48; 36 catches.

10 One-day Ints: 330 runs at 55.00, HS 62, 16 wickets at 23.62, BB 4-56; 7 catches.

First-class 1959-82: 23,375 runs at 37.28, 45 100s HS 196; 291 wickets at 30.58, BB 8-45; 304 catches.

Bob ASKIN (USA)

RODEO

Robert Askin. b. 1908 Rochester, New York, d. 1985 Miles City Veterans Hospital.

The original 'Mr. Rodeo', he never won a world championship because he competed in an era before one was selected, but he was the champion by acclamation several times. In Toronto in 1926, Askin made rodeo history when he rode the legendary 'unrideable' bronc *Midnight*. In 1936, he repeated the performance in Omaha by riding another 'unrideable' bronc *Five Minutes to Midnight*. He rode horses competitively starting from 1923 until the early 1950s.

Cash ASMUSSEN (USA)

HORSE RACING

Brian Keith Asmussen. b. 15 Mar 1962 Agar, South Dakota. name legally changed to Cash.

He won the Eclipse Award in the USA in 1979 as the outstanding apprentice with 236 winners. In 1981 he won the Japan Cup on *Mairzy Doates* and a year later went to France to ride for Stavros Niarchos and trainer François Boutin. He now races mostly in Europe, and was champion jockey in France, 1985-6, 1988-90. In 1988 he was the first jockey to ride 200 winners in a season in France.

A fine horseman, his father Keith was a jockey as was his younger brother Steve for a while before becoming a trainer.

Nigel ASPINALL (UK)

CROQUET

George Nigel Aspinall. b. 29 July 1946 Reading, Berkshire.

Winner of the President's Cup a record 11 times between 1969 and 1985. He also won the Open Championship eight times and his total of ten wins (with three different partners) in the men's doubles equalled the record set by John Solomon and Edmund Cotter. Other successes included victories in the men's championship (1973, 1983) and the mixed doubles (1973, 1982, 1987). An accomplished all-round player from the Bristol club, he favoured a straightforward style of play, eschewing unnecessary embellishments and his particular strength was his shooting.

Recognised as the world's best player from 1969, when he won all his matches in the Test series against Australia. Graduate of Bristol University and a freelance computer programmer.

Polina ASTAKOVA (USSR/Ukr)

GYMNASTICS

Polina Grigoryevna Astakova. b. 30 Oct 1936 Donetsk, Ukraine.

To the three Olympic team gold medals that she won, in 1956, 1960 and 1964, this graceful gymnast added golds on the asymmetric bars and third overall in both 1960 and 1964, with two more silver and a bronze at other apparatus. She helped the USSR to win the World team title in 1958 and 1962.

Doug ATKINS (USA)

AMERICAN FOOTBALL

Douglas L Atkins. b. 8 May 1930 Humboldt, Tennessee.

A huge (2.03m *6'8"*, 123 kg *270 lbs*), talented athlete in high school, who attended the University of Tennessee on a basketball scholarship. Atkins also played football at Tennessee, making All-American as a tackle and becoming a first-round draft choice of the Cleveland Browns. He played two seasons with them and from 1955 to 1966 for the Chicago Bears. He was an intimidating defensive end, who was both agile and immensely strong. George Halas said that Atkins was the best defensive player he ever saw. He played in seven Pro Bowls and was elected All-Pro three times.

Geoffrey ATKINS (UK)

RACKETS

Geoffrey Willoughby Thomas Atkins. b. 20 Jan 1927.

By successfully challenging Jim Dear in 1954 he became only the third amateur to win the world rackets title since the championship was instituted in 1820. He successfully defended the title against challenges from James Leonard (1963 and 1968) and Charles Swallow (1964 and 1970). When he resigned the title in 1971, at the age of 44, he had been champion for 17 years which beat Peter Latham's record for the longest tenure.
Between 1952 and 1963 he won the British Amateur title five times and the doubles three times. After winning the world rackets title in 1954, he lived in Chicago for the next 20 years winning the US Open in 1958 and 1968 and the US Amateur eight times between 1954 and 1970. A classic stylist with effortless footwork, his outstanding career could hardly have been predicted as, while at Rugby School, he was only second string in the school pair for one year.

Aubert Puig (Fra) see PUIG

Red AUERBACH (USA)

BASKETBALL

Arnold Auerbach. b. 20 Sep 1917 Brooklyn, New York.

The most successful coach in professional basketball history, with 1037 wins to 548 losses in NBA regular season and play-off games.
Auerbach played basketball at George Washington University, briefly coached in high school, and then served in the US Navy during World War II. In 1946 he became head coach of the Washington Capitols in the fledgling NBA and in 1950 was named head coach of the Boston Celtics where he established his greatness. In 1957 he coached the Celtics to their first NBA championship. They lost in the NBA play-offs the next season, but Auerbach then led the Celtics to eight consecutive NBA titles. He then retired to become their general manager and later was named club president. He was known for his trademark 'victory cigar', which he would light on the team bench when he knew the game was in hand.

Mike AULBY (USA)

BOWLING

Michael Aulby. b. 25 Mar 1960.

Aulby reached the peak of his outstanding PBA career with two superb years in 1985 and 1989, in both of which he won over $200,000, with a record $298,237 in the latter. He was named the PBA Rookie of the Year in 1979, PBA Player of the Year in 1985, and the Bowling Writers Bowler of the Year in 1985 and 1989. In 1989 he won the US Open, the ABC Masters, and four PBA Titles. Only a third-place finish at the PBA National Championship preventing him from totally dominating the Tour that year.
To the end of 1992 he had 20 PBA titles and career earnings of $1,262,160.

Berit AUNLI (Nor)

NORDIC SKIING

Berit Kristine Aunli. née Kvello. b. 9 Jun 1956 Stjørdal.

Cross-country skier, who had a great year in 1982 when she won three gold medals at the World Championships, 5km and 10km and relay, with a silver at 20km. That year she also won the World Cup title. She competed at three Olympic Games. She was 5th in the 4 x 5km relay in 1976, and won a bronze medal on the Norwegian relay team in 1980. In 1984 she completed a complete set of Olympic medals with relay gold and a silver at 5km as well as placing 4th at 10km.

In 1985 she won a relay silver and had two individual fourth places at the World Championships. She won 15 Norwegian titles: 5km 1977-8 and 1980-2; 10km 1977, 1980-2; 20km 1978, 1980; relay 1977-8, 1980-1.

Her husband **Ove** (b. 12 Mar 1956) won Olympic silver (relay) and bronze (15km) in 1980. Her father **Kristen** (b. 19 Oct 1931) was the Norwegian champion at 50km in 1957.

Didier AURIOL (Fra)

RALLYING

Didier Auriol. b. 18 Aug 1958 Montpelier.

In 1992 he achieved a season's record six wins in world championship races to bring his career total to 12, but still was only third overall behind Sainz and Kankkunen. With his co-driver Bernard Occelli (b. 20 May 1961 Nice) he started the year by winning the Monte Carlo Rally (as he had in 1990), following with wins in Corsica, Acropolis, Argentina, 1000 Lakes, and Australia.

He started rallying in 1979 and with Occelli was French champion in 1986 in a Metro 6 R 4 and in 1987-8 in a Ford Sierra-Cosworth. From 1989 to 1991 he was successively 4th, 2nd and 3rd for the World Championship.

Auriol and Occelli switched from Lancia to Toyota for 1993 and won their first race for them, the Monte Carlo Rally.

Bunny AUSTIN (UK)

TENNIS

Henry Wilfred Austin. b. 26 Aug 1906 Croydon, Surrey.

Stalwart of the British team which held the Davis Cup from 1933 to 1936. After winning the Public Schools title while at Repton, he went on to captain Cambridge and the year after leaving University he made his Davis Cup début. Between 1929 and 1937 he played in 48 Davis Cup rubbers (all of them singles) and won 36. A singles semi-finalist at Wimbledon five times, he lost in the final to Vines in 1932 and Budge in 1938. He was also runner-up to Henner Henkel (Ger) at the 1937 French Championships. His only significant singles success outdoors was at the 1937 British Hard Court Championships but he won the British Indoor title in 1934 and 1937.

As a doubles player, he again narrowly missed top honours; in the mixed doubles he was the losing finalist at the US Championships (1929), the French Championships (1931) and Wimbledon (1934). At men's doubles he reached the semi-finals at Wimbledon (1926-7) and the French Championships (1931). He retired at the end of the 1937 season and devoted himself to the cause of Moral Rearmament.

'Bunny' Austin lacked the physique to play a power game but his superlative armoury of ground strokes made him one of the most respected players of his era.

Tracy AUSTIN (USA)

TENNIS

Tracy Ann Austin. b. 12 Dec 1962 Rolling Hills Estate, Los Angeles, California.

A child star whose meteoric rise to the top was ended by injury. A powerful range of shots on both the forehand and backhand took her to 27 US Junior titles in various age groups and she won a host of major titles while still a teenager. In 1979, at the age of 16 yr 271 days, she became the youngest player ever to win the US singles and after losing in the semi-finals in 1980 she regained the title in 1981. She also won the 1979 Italian and 1981 Canadian titles. With her brother, John, she won the Wimbledon mixed doubles in 1980, the only sister-brother pairing ever to do so. After some unexpected defeats, she missed part of the 1984 season with a fractured arm and never recovered her earlier form.

Earl AVERILL (USA)

BASEBALL

Howard Earl Averill. b. 21 May 1902 Snohomish, Washington, d. 16 Aug 1983 Everett, Washington.

'Rock' Averill's career was shortened by a back injury, so that he played only 12 years in the major leagues. Although he was was only 1.75m *5'9"*, 78 kg *172 lbs*, he possessed plenty of power. He homered in his first major league at-bat and averaged over 20 home runs and almost 100 RBIs during his career. He was the only outfielder selected to play in the first six All-Star Games. At that game in 1937 he achieved some measure of infamy when his line drive broke the toe of Dizzy Dean, and effectively ended Dean's career.
Career 1929-41: 2020 hits Avg. .318, HR 238; RBI 1164. Best season: 1935 - .378, 232 hits.

Nikolay AVILOV (USSR/Ukr)

ATHLETICS

Nikolay (Mykola) Viktorovich Avilov. b. 6 Aug 1948 Odessa.

The Olympic decathlon champion in 1972, when he set a world record of 8454 points (8466 on the current tables) and won by over 400 points. He was also fourth in the Olympics in 1968 and won the bronze medal in 1976, but surprisingly did not win a European medal, placing 4th in 1969. World Student Games champion 1970, and USSR champion 1972, 1975 and 1976. His best individual events were 110mh 14.20 and 14.0 hand-timed, high jump 2.14m and long jump 7.68m.
A popular, confident athlete, he was able to achieve an enviable blend of relaxation and concentration when attempting the multi-event competitions. He retired in 1980 and is now a lawyer.

AZAM KHAN (Pak)

SQUASH

Azam Khan.

The younger of two brothers who dominated British squash for more than a decade. Originally a tennis coach, he came to England in December 1952. In each British Open from 1953 to 1959 he lost to his legendary elder brother, Hashim Khan, three times in the semi-finals and three times in the final. Azam, near perfection technically, finally took the British Open title in 1958, beating his nephew Mohibullah Khan in the final, and after defending the title against Roshan Khan the following year he again beat Mohibullah in 1960 and 1961. After four successive victories he was forced to retire from tournament play in 1962 as a result of a severe injury to his Achilles tendon.

Mohammad AZHARUDDIN (India)

CRICKET

Mohammad Azharuddin. b. 8 Feb 1963 Hyderabad.

In each of his first three Test matches he made a hundred, a unique cricketing achievement. A brilliant, wristy stroke-player, his power has grown as he has put on a little weight from those early days. He took over the captaincy of India in 1990, but after averaging 75.75 and 85.20 in his first two Test series in charge, his batting and his team's results were very disappointing for a couple of years. In early 1993 there were suggestions that he would be dropped from the captaincy after a poor tour of South Africa, but then he returned to his best with a marvellous 182 in the First Test against England and he led his team to convincing wins in all three Tests. In 1989 he equalled the Test record with five catches in an innings.
55 Tests 1984-93: 3553 runs at 45.55, 12 100s HS 182; 46 catches.
154 One-day Ints: 3914 runs at 34.33, 3 100s HS 108; 12 wickets at 39.00, BB 3-19, 58 catches.*
First-class 1984-92: 9378 runs at 54.20, 31 100s HS 226; 7 wickets at 76.14, BB 2-33; 110 catches.

Shirley BABASHOFF (USA)

SWIMMING

Shirley Frances Babashoff. b. 31 Jan 1937 Whittier, California.

The winner of eight Olympic medals and setter of eleven world records at freestyle swimming. Babashoff started swimming at the age of nine and won the first of four successive AAU titles at 200m freestyle in 1972 with her first individual world record of 2:05.21. She added further AAU outdoor titles with 100m in 1973 and 1975, 400m 1974-5 and eight indoors, and in all set 17 US records at individual events.
At the 1972 Olympics she was silver medallist at 100m and 200m and won gold at 4x100m relay. At the 1973 Worlds she took four silver medals at 100m, 200m and both relays. In 1974 she set world records for 200m, twice recording 2:02.94, and at 400m, 4:15.77, and in 1975 she was the star of the World Championships when she beat Kornelia Ender to win the 200m and also won the 400m. She was second at 100m, third at 800m and fourth at 200m individual medley, and anchored both US relay squads to silver medals.
She set further world records with 400m 4:14.76 in 1975, 800m 8:39.63 in 1976 and five at 4 x 100m freestyle relay. Although she improved at 400m to 4:10.46 and at 800m to 8:37.59 at the 1976 Olympics, those were in second place to Petra Thümer (GDR), and she took two more silvers at 200m behind Ender and at 4 x 200m. She did, however, win gold at 4 x 100m. Trained by Mark Schubert at the Mission Viejo Club in California.
Other bests: freestyle 100m 56.95, 200m 2:00.69, 800m 8:34.04, all in 1976.
Her elder brother **Jack** (b. 13 Jul 1955) won silver medals for 100m freestyle at the 1976 Olympics and 1975 Pan-American Games.

Steve BACKLEY (UK)

ATHLETICS

Steven James Backley. b. 12 Feb 1969 Sidcup, Kent.

The world's top javelin thrower in his first two years as a senior in 1989, when he won the European and World Cup events and the World Student Games gold medal, and in 1990, when he won Commonwealth and European titles and became the first British male thrower ever to set a world record. After retaining his World Student title he was held back in 1991 by an abductor muscle injury, and met his first failure at a major event when he did not qualify for the final of the World Championships. He rebounded with a UK record three weeks later, and in New Zealand in January 1992 he achieved the first 90m throw (91.46) with the revised javelin specification, but with further injury problems was restricted to the bronze medal at the Olympics. A shoulder injury then kept him out of action until July 1993.
He had won the European Juniors in 1987 and in 1988 set a world junior record and placed second at the World Juniors. His first world records in 1990 were 89.58 in Stockholm with a Sandvik javelin, and 90.98 at Crystal Palace on just his second throw with a Németh model. When this was banned at the end of 1991 his 89.58 was reinstated as the record. UK champion 1988-92, AAA 1989 and 1992. He competes for Cambridge Harriers and postponed his sports science studies at Loughborough University.

Max BAER (USA)

BOXING

Maximillian Adalbert Baer. b. 11 Feb 1909 Omaha, Nebraska, d. 21 Nov 1959 Hollywood, California.

Nicknamed the 'Livermore Larruper', Baer was known as much for his hedonistic delights as for his powerful right-hand punch. He turned professional in 1929 and used that powerful right, one of the greatest punches ever, to defeat Primo Carnera in 1934 and win the heavyweight title, although he gave away over 23 kg *50 lb*. Baer lost his first title defence to James Braddock and never again fought for the title. He settled in Hollywood where his hail-fellow-well-met personality brought him great acclaim.
Career record: W - 70 (52), L - 13, D -0.

Edgar BAERLEIN (UK)

RACKETS and REAL TENNIS

Edgar Maximilian Baerlein. b. 13 Dec 1879 Manchester. d 3 Jun 1971 Midhurst, Sussex.

Winner of the British Amateur rackets singles a record 9 times and the British Amateur real tennis singles 13 times. The promise he had shown as a player of court games at Eton and Cambridge was quickly fulfilled in the senior ranks. His run of championship successes at rackets was only interrupted when he fractured his skull in a motorcycle accident. He also won the Amateur rackets doubles six times between 1902 and 1920.

Although Baerlein did not concentrate on real tennis until after World War I, he won the British Amateur singles 13 times between 1912 and 1930 and this remained the record until Howard Angus won for a 14th time in 1979. He also won the doubles 11 times between 1920 and 1937. In 1931 he won the first British Open Championship at the age of 51 and at the time of his final championship victory in the 1937 doubles he was, incredibly, aged 57. Despite this host of Championship successes, his finest victory came in the Bathurst Cup in 1923 when he became the only man to beat the great American, Jay Gould, at real tennis in a 20 year period extending from 1907 to 1926.

Braulio BAEZA (Pan/USA)

HORSE RACING

Braulio Baeza. b. 26 Mar 1940 Panama City, Panama.

A brilliant horseman, after riding a record 309 winners in Panama in 1959 he moved to the USA; there he topped the money list each year from 1965 to 1968 and again in 1975. He won the Eclipse award as outstanding jockey in 1972 and 1975, and retired having ridden 3140 winners in the USA. He took up training in 1978.

On a rare trip to Europe he rode *Roberto* at York in 1972 to hand *Brigadier Gerard* the only defeat of his career.

Federico BAHAMONTES (Spain)

CYCLING

Federico Martin Bahamontes. b. 9 Jul 1928 Val de Santo Domingo.

Bahamontes was a small man who was one of the greatest *grimpeurs* in cycling history. His record of six King of the Mountains titles (1954, 1958-9, 1962-4) in the Tour de France remains unbeaten, and he won the Tour in 1959. His nickname was the 'Eagle of Toledo' for his hometown of Toledo, Spain. The biggest disappointment of his career must be that he never won the Vuelta à España, although he was King of the Mountains in that race in 1957 and 1958.

Trevor BAILEY (UK)

CRICKET

Trevor Edward Bailey. b. 3 Dec 1923 Westcliff-on-Sea, Essex.

'Barnacle' Bailey's epic partnership with Willie Watson to save England from defeat by Australia at Lord's in 1953 made him a national hero. By then however he was mid-way through a Test career which lasted for just under ten years and which many experts felt ended prematurely. A most astute tactician, he could well have made a most successful captain at Test level, as he had been for Essex 1961-6. He won his blue at Cambridge University 1947-8 and played for Essex 1946-67. He was a true all-rounder as he proved his worth in Tests both as a fast-medium bowler and a generally obdurate batsman. He was also a very fine close-in fielder. He achieved the double of 1000 runs and 100 wickets in eight seasons, and in 1959 became the only player since 1937 to have scored 2000 runs and taken 100 wickets in a season. For many years he has provided expert analysis for the BBC Radio team on cricket. At soccer he won an FA Amateur Cup medal in 1952 with Walthamstow.

61 Tests 1949-59: 2290 runs at 29.74, 1 100 HS 134; 132 wickets at 29.21, BB 7-34; 32 catches.*

First-class 1945-67: 28,642 runs at 33.42, 28 100s HS 205; 2082 wickets at 23.13, BB 10-90; 428 catches.

Erin BAKER (NZ)

TRIATHLON

Erin Margaret Baker. b. 23 May 1961 Kaiapoi.

Baker won her first triathlon in Australia in 1984, and reached the top with wins at Nice in 1985 and 1988, and when she set a course record 9 hr 35 min 25 sec in winning the Hawaii Ironman in 1987. That record was improved by over 30 min in 1988 by Paula Newby-Fraser, with Baker second. In 1990 Baker won three Ironman races, including the prestigious Hawaii race in 9:13:42. She was triathlete of the year in 1988 and 1989, and was the first women's world champion in 1989. Her success is primarily because of her world-class abilities as a distance runner. In 1991 she announced plans to devote full time to running for the next year in an effort to make the 1992 New Zealand Olympic marathon team; although unsuccessful she recorded her best time of 2:35:49. She married triathlete Scott Molina in 1990. Awarded the MBE 1992.

Frank BAKER (USA)

BASEBALL

John Franklin Baker. b. 13 Mar 1886 Trappe, Maryland, d. 28 Jun 1963 Trappe.

'Home Run' Baker earned his nickname despite hitting less than 100 career home runs. The impetus for the nickname came from two home runs he hit in the 1911 World Series which won games off Christy Mathewson and Rube Marquard. Baker was actually a better hitter for average, and was also an excellent fielding third baseman. He played his early career with the Philadelphia Phillies as part of the $100,000 infield (1B - Stuffy McInnis, 2B - Eddie Collins, SS - Jack Barry), and helped them win four pennants in five years. In 1916 he was traded to the New York Yankees after sitting out 1915 in a salary dispute. He was the biggest drawing card for the Yankees until the arrival of Babe Ruth.

Career 1908-22: 1838 hits Avg. .307, HR 96; RBI 987. Best season: 1913 - .337, 12 HR, 117 RBI.

Percy BAKER (UK)

BOWLS

Edwin Percy Baker. b. 18 Jul 1895 Weston-Super-Mare, Somerset, d. 3 Jan 1990 Poole, Dorset.

Winning four singles titles over a 23-year period, 1932, 1946, 1952 and 1955; he was the most successful bowler at the English Championships until the arrival of David Bryant. He also won the pairs twice (1950 & 1962) and the triples in 1960, and won a silver in the singles at the 1958 Commonwealth Games. He settled in Dorset after serving in France and the Balkans in World War I and won 11 county singles titles over a 37-year period. He represented Dorset from 1927 to 1969 and first played for England in 1933 but was not a regular member of the team until 1949, becoming the team captain in 1950. His distinguished career ended in 1971 when, at the age of 76, he won the Bournemouth Open pairs. In his last years he was totally blind.

Reg BAKER (Aus)

BOXING

Reginald Leslie Baker. b. 8 Feb 1884 Sydney, New South Wales, Australia, d. 1 Dec 1953 Los Angeles.

'Snowy' Baker was one of the greatest all-round athletes in Australian sporting history. He was considered of national calibre in no less than 29 sports and represented Australia internationally in five - rugby union, diving, boxing, swimming and water polo. At the 1908 Olympics he competed in swimming, diving, and boxing, winning a silver medal in the latter at middleweight. His loss in the finals to Johnny Douglas, later England cricket captain, was the only time he was defeated as a boxer in his career. While at Sydney University he won blues in athletics, cricket, football and rowing.

Baker later became a well-known boxing referee. After World War I he moved to Hollywood where he became a famous equestrian and taught many movie stars to ride. In addition, he starred in five movies.

Enid BAKEWELL (UK)

CRICKET

Enid Bakewell. b. 18 Dec 1940.

England's finest all-round woman cricketer, a right-hand opening bat and left-arm orthodox spinner. She made a century, 113 v Australia, on her Test début in 1968, and was the first woman player to do a double of 1000 runs and 100 wickets on tour, with 1031 runs at 39.65 and 118 wickets at 9.77 in Australia and New Zealand in 1968/9. With 68 and 112 not out and match figures of 10-75 (3-14 and 7-61) for England v West Indies at Edgbaston in 1979 she achieved a match double never before achieved by a man or woman in an Test match for England. This was also one of three occasions in which she took five wickets in an innings and scored a century in the same Test. She holds the National Cricket Association advanced coaching award and still plays for her club and the East Midlands, as well as being an England selector.

12 Tests 1968-79: 1078 runs at 59.88, 4 100s HS 124; 50 wickets at 16.62.
23 One-day Ints: 500 runs at 35.71, 2 100s; 25 wickets at 21.12.

Iolanda BALAS (Rom)

ATHLETICS

Iolanda Balas. Later Söter. b. 12 Dec 1936 Timosoaru.

Balas, who was 1.85m tall, achieved the greatest domination of an event ever seen in the history of athletics. She set 14 world records for the women's high jump, from 1.75m in Bucharest on 14 Jul 1956 to 1.91m at Sofia on 16 Jul 1961, to set a record for any event (since surpassed by Sergey Bubka). By the end of 1963 she had jumped 1.80m or higher in 72 competitions, yet it was not until 27 Sep 1964 that another woman, Michele Brown (Aus), jumped as high. By the end of her career Balas had jumped 1.80m or higher in 94 competitions while the rest of the world had a count of five between them. From her fifth place at the Olympic Games on 1 Dec 1956 she won 150 consecutive competitions until she lost to Dagmar Melzer (GDR) on 11 Jun 1967. She was Olympic champion in 1960 and 1964, European champion in 1958 and 1962 (and silver medallist in 1954), won the first European Indoor Games title in 1966 and a record eight World Student titles between 1954 and 1961. She was Romania's first European and Olympic medallist in athletics, and won 16 successive national titles from 1951, at the age of 14, to 1966. At the end of 1967 she married her coach Ian Söter, who set the Romanian men's record at 2.05m in 1956. Her style was described as a cross between a scissors and the Eastern cut-off.

BALBIR SINGH (India)

HOCKEY

Dosanth Balbir Singh. b. 10 Oct 1924 Haripur, Jullundur.

Winner of three Olympic gold medals, 1948-56, he captained the Indian team at the 1956 Games. A forward, he also won a gold medal at the 1966 Asian Games (and silver in 1958). He managed the Indian team 1962-82 and became director of sports for the Punjab Government. He lit the flame at the opening ceremony for the 1982 Asian Games.

Nikolay BALBOSHIN (USSR/Rus)

WRESTLING

Nikolay Fyodorovich Balboshin. b. 8 Jun 1949 Potsdam, GDR.

In 1976 at Montreal, Balboshin put on one of the most dominating displays ever in Olympic wrestling. He had five matches, and won all of them by pins, needing only 16 minutes 48 seconds of action to complete all five matches. This was his only Olympic appearance but as a heavyweight he won Greco-Roman world championships in 1973-4 and 1977-9 and six European titles 1973, 1975-9. From 1973-9 he was Soviet champion as well. From 1973 to 1980 he lost only three major championships: second at the 1974 Europeans, and unplaced at the 1975 Worlds when he was injured and at the 1980 Olympics when he collapsed with a ruptured right Achilles tendon. In 1984 he tried a comeback and took the bronze medal at the Europeans. His speciality was the Cross-body-hold, which he applied with much skill and elegance.

András BALCZÓ (Hun)

MODERN PENTATHLON

András Balczó. b. 16 Aug 1938 Kondoros.

The most successful modern pentathlete at the World Championships with a record six individual and seven team titles between 1960 and 1970. After placing second in 1959 and third in 1961 he was individual champion in 1963, 1965-7 and 1969 as well as finally winning Olympic gold at the age of 34 in 1972. His team titles included the Olympic gold medals in 1960 and 1968. At the Olympics he was also 4th in 1960 and silver medallist in 1968, when he was beaten by Björn Ferm (Swe) by just 11 points, equivalent to four seconds in the cross-country running, which was one of Balczó's great strengths. He was a typewriter mechanic.

Ercole BALDINI (Italy)

CYCLING

Ercole Baldini. b. 26 Jan 1933 Villanova de Forli.

In 1956 Baldini had one of the greatest years in amateur cycling history. He won the world pursuit title, broke the world hour record twice at Milan (44.870km and 46.39361km) and ended the year with the Olympic gold in the individual road race. He turned professional later in 1956 and Italian cycling fans envisioned him as the next *campionissimo*. However, although he won the world professional road race title in 1958, he was never quite as successful as a professional rider. His other major wins were in the 1958 Giro d'Italia and the 1960 Grand Prix de Nations.

Alan BALL (UK)

FOOTBALL

Alan James Ball. b. 12 May 1945 Farnworth, Lancashire.

A resolute and constructive midfield player who was the youngest member of England's World Cup winning team in 1966. Encouraged by his father, a former professional and manager of Halifax Town and Preston North End, he signed amateur forms for Blackpool in 1961, turning professional the following year. He was transferred for British record fees to Everton in August 1966 for £110,000 and then in December 1971 when he went to Arsenal for £220,000. He moved in 1976 to Southampton before returning to Blackpool as player-manager in 1980; he then returned to Southampton in 1981 and he closed his playing career with Bristol Rovers in 1983. During this period he also played in the USA, Canada and Hong Kong. After only a few months at Bristol he moved to Portsmouth, serving first as youth coach and then as manager before reverting to a coaching position.

During his outstanding career he won a host of honours: 72 England caps; six appearances for the Football League and eight England Under-23 caps. He played in two FA Cup finals, for Everton 1968 and Arsenal 1972, and one League Cup final for Southampton 1979, but was on the losing side on each occasion. He was, however, a member of the Everton team which took the Football League title in 1970.

John BALL (UK)

GOLF

John Ball Jr. b. 24 Dec 1861 Hoylake, Cheshire, d. 2 Dec 1940 Halkyn, Flintshire.

The greatest amateur of his time. He won the British Amateur a record eight times, 1888, 1890, 1892, 1894, 1899, 1907, 1910 and 1912, the last at age 51, and he played in the tournament from the first time it was staged in 1885 until 1921. In 1890 he became the first amateur and the first Englishman to win The Open, and achieved another first by completing a double with the Amateur that year. All this despite not playing for three years at his peak when he served with the Cheshire Yeomanry in the Boer War from 1899. Ball revolutionised swing theories with his technique. He was the first to use an open stance and an upright swing, enabling him to hit highly-lofted shots landing near the target rather than always playing a run-up game. His father owned the Royal Hotel, which overlooked the links at Hoylake.

Ivar BALLANGRUD (Nor)

SPEED SKATING

Ivar Ballangrud. b. 7 Mar 1904 Lunner, Hadeland, d. 1 Jun 1969 Trondheim.

The most versatile of the early speed skaters who won international honours over a wide range of events during an usually lengthy career. He was a stylish skater with an economical stride. At the Olympics he won the 5000m and was second at 1500m in 1928, was second at 10,000m in 1932 and at his peak in 1936 won the 500m, 5000m and 10,000m and placed second in the 1500m. His tally of seven Olympic medals matched the total of Clas Thunberg in 1924-8, and this remains the record for the most speed skating medals. Ballangrud's record at the World Championships was even more impressive. Between his début in 1924, when he placed fifth overall, to his final appearance in 1939, when he was fourth, he won the overall title four times (1926, 1932, 1936 and 1938), the 1500m and 10,000m four times each, and won his best event, the 5000m, seven times. He was also European champion in 1929-30, 1933 and 1936. He set four world records at 5000m, with a best of 8:17.2 in 1936, and others at 3000m, 4:49.6 (1935) and 10,000m, 17:14.4 (1938). He also set Norwegian records at 1000m 1:29.3 (1937) and 1500m 2:19.0 (1936).

Severiano BALLESTEROS (Spain)

GOLF

Severiano Ballesteros. b. 9 Apr 1957 Pedraña, Spain.

The greatest golfer ever produced in Spain and probably continental Europe. He was also for many years in the 1980s a strong contender as the finest player in the world. He first achieved fame in 1976 when he finished 2nd in the British Open when only 19. In 1979 he won that championship, the first continental European to do so since Arnaud Massy (Fra) in 1907, and won again in 1984 and 1988. He won the World Matchplay in 1981-2, 1984-5 and 1991 and became the first European winner of the US Masters in 1980, winning again in 1983.

Ballesteros is the leading career money-winner on the European Tour with £3,153, 819 from 1974 to 1992. His 51 victories are far ahead of any rival, and he headed the money list in 1976-8, 1986, 1988 and 1991. He helped Spain to win the World Cup in 1976 and 1977 and has been an inspiration to the European team in the Ryder Cup, in which he has compiled the most successful record, winning 17, losing 8 and halving 5 of his 30 matches in six Cups 1979-91.

He is the nephew of former Spanish great, Ramon Sota.

Kork BALLINGTON (SAf)

MOTOR CYCLING

Hugh Neville Ballington. b. 10 Apr 1951 Salisbury, Southern Rhodesia.

World champion at both 250cc and 350cc in 1978 and 1979 for Kawasaki. He won 31 Grand Prix races 1976-80, 17 at 250cc and 14 at 350cc. Having started racing in 1967 in Pietermaritzburg, he won national titles at 50, 175 and 500cc classes before winning a 'Rider to Europe' scholarship. He eventually broke into the top class in 1976. He left Europe after the 1980 season, but in 1987 he won the Daytona 100 on a Honda.

Karin BALZER (GDR)

ATHLETICS

Karin Balzer. née Richert. b. 5 Jun 1938 Magdeburg.

Balzer had a most successful career as a high hurdler and made a record 55 international appearances for the GDR. She set her first world record at 80m hurdles with 10.5 in 1964, five months before becoming the first GDR athlete to win an Olympic title in a wind-aided 10.54, after running the fastest ever 80m on auto-timing of

10.65 in the semi-finals. Having taken the silver in 1962, she went on to three successive European hurdles titles, at 80m in 1966 and the new distance of 100m in 1969 and 1971, adding a relay silver in 1971 and 5th at the 100m in 1969.
She was also European indoor hurdles champion at 50m/60m for five successive years, 1967-71, and won the European Cup final races of 1967 and 1970. In the Olympics, however, she was less successful, with 5th place in 1968 and 3rd in 1972. GDR champion seven times at high hurdles between 1962 and 1971, and at pentathlon 1962-3, long jump 1963 and 200m 1968.
She set six world records at 100m hurdles, from 13.3 in 1969 to 12.6 in 1971, with an auto-timed best of 12.90 in 1962. Indoors her 16 world hurdles bests included peaks of 6.7 for 50m, 7.4 for 60y and 8.0 for 60m.
Other bests: 100m 11.3 (1969), 200m 23.4 (1964), pentathlon 4790 (1964).

Billy BANCROFT (UK)

RUGBY UNION

William John Bancroft. b. 2 Mar 1871 Swansea, d. 3 Mar 1959 Swansea.

An unorthodox full-back for Swansea, who played for Wales in 33 consecutive matches, 11 of them as captain. His international career lasted from 1890 to 1901 and he also played cricket for Glamorgan from 1897 to 1914. In 1893 he scored the decisive penalty from a drop kick which gave Wales their first home win over England. He is said to have invented the screw kick.
He was a cobbler by trade. His younger brother, **Jack** (1879-1942), won 18 caps as full back (1909-14) scoring 88 points which stood as a Welsh record for many years, including a record eight conversions against France in 1910.

Ernie BANKS (USA)

BASEBALL

Ernest Banks. b. 31 Jan 1931 Dallas, Texas.

Banks may be the most beloved Chicago Cub player of all time. His cheerful outlook made him popular, as did his love of the game, epitomised by his frequently used phrase, 'Let's play two!'. He was also a superb baseball player. He began his career as a shortstop, but played the second half of his career as a first base. Between 1957 and 1960 he recorded 40 home runs for four straight seasons, in 1958 he set a shortstop season's record of 47 home runs, and in 1958-9 became the first National Leaguer to win back-to-back MVP Awards. His greatest disappointment was that the Cubs, with whom he played his entire career, never won a pennant and he never played in a World Series.
Career 1953-71: 2583 hits Avg. .274, HR 512; RBI 1636. Best seasons: 1958 - .313, 47 HR, 129 RBI. 1959 - .304, 45 HR, 143 RBI.

Gordon BANKS (UK)

FOOTBALL

Gordon Banks. b. 30 Dec 1937 Sheffield, Yorkshire.

Universally recognised as the greatest goalkeeper in the world during his peak years. Discovered while playing for a Sheffield works club, he played only one season for Division III Chesterfield before moving to Leicester City in 1959 and to Stoke City in 1967. He set a (then) record for an England goalkeeper by winning 73 caps 1963-72. The highlight of his career was as a member of the England team which won the 1966 World Cup although many other honours came his way. He won Football League Cup winners medals for Leicester in 1964 and Stoke 1972 and his outstanding performance in the latter final did much to earn him the award as the Footballer of the Year. Perhaps the one outstanding save of his career was that against Pelé in the 1970 World Cup.
An eye injury sustained in a road accident in August 1972 virtually ended his career although he recovered sufficiently to play briefly in the USA. He later held coaching or managerial posts with Port Vale, Telford United and Stoke City. His game was built on brilliant positional play and superb anticipation and reflexes. He was awarded the MBE in 1970.

Willie BANKS (USA)

ATHLETICS

William Augustus Banks. b. 11 Mar 1956 Travis Air Force Base, California.

The ebullient Banks made the triple jump into a star event by the force of his own personality in the 1980s, encouraging crowds to clap him down the runway to an accelerating tempo. After four US records and two world low-altitude bests from 1981 to 1985, he set a world record with 17.97m at the 1985 TAC Championships in Indianapolis. At the same venue three years later he became the first man to triple jump over 18 metres, with wind-assisted jumps of 18.06 and 18.20 at the US Olympic Trials. He also set a world indoor best with 17.41 in 1982.
He won the World Cup triple jump in 1985 and the World Student Games title in 1979, but otherwise his best was silver at the 1983 World Championships and at the Pan-American Games of 1979 and 1989. At the Olympics he was sixth in both 1984 and 1988. He won the US Olympic Trials in 1988 and also in 1980, when the Carter boycott prevented him from competing in Moscow. TAC champion 1980-1, 1983, 1985. Best long jump 8.11 (1981).
A graduate of UCLA, he became a sports consultant and has been coaching at Chukyo University, Nagoya, Japan. Married Louise Romo (pbs 800m 1:59.63 '85, 1500m 4:09.29 '84) in 1986.

Johnny BANNERMAN (UK)

RUGBY UNION

(Lord) John Macdonald Bannerman. b. 1 Sep 1901 Glasgow, d. 10 Apr 1969 Tidworth, Hampshire.

Educated at Shawlands Academy, Glasgow High School and Glasgow University, he had already won 28 caps in the Scottish pack when he went up to Balliol College, Oxford to take a course in agricultural economics. He won his Blue in 1927 and 1928 and went on to win a total of 37 international caps 1921-9; this remained a Scottish record until 1962.
He was Factor to the Montrose Estates from 1930 to 1952 and held many civic and political posts. Notably, he served as President of the Scottish RFU in 1954-5, as the Lord Rector of Aberdeen University and as Chairman and President of the Scottish Liberal Party. He was created a Life Peer in 1967.

Roger BANNISTER (UK)

ATHLETICS

(Sir) Roger Gilbert Bannister. b. 23 Mar 1929 Harrow, London.

On 6 May 1954 he achieved one of the most celebrated deeds in the history of sport, with the first sub four-minute mile, running 3:59.4 at Iffley Road, Oxford. Six weeks later John Landy (Aus) improved the mile record to 3:57.9, but Bannister in this, his last season before concentrating on his medical career, beat Landy in a race dubbed 'The Mile of the Century' to win the Empire Games title at 1 mile in Vancouver. Bannister ran 3:58.8 and Landy 3:59.6, the first time two men had beaten four minutes in one race. Bannister then added the European title at 1500m. He set four British records at 1500m to 3:42.2 in 1954 and four at 1 mile, his first being 4:03.6 in 1953. He had been third in the European 800m in 1950 and a disappointed 4th at 1500m in the 1952 Olympics.
He was awarded the CBE in 1955 and became a distinguished neurologist. He was knighted in 1975 for his services to medicine, was Chairman of the Sports Council 1971-4, and has been Master of Pembroke College, Oxford since 1985.
Best time for 880y 1:50.7 (1953).

Warren BARDSLEY (Aus)

CRICKET

Warren Bardsley. b. 7 Dec 1882 Nevertire, Warren, New South Wales, d. 20 Jan 1954 Collaroy, New South Wales.

Bardsley scored over 2000 runs on the first three of his four tours to England, in 1909, 1912 and 1921, and at that time was compared with Clem Hill as Australia's greatest ever left-handed batsman. In 1909 at The Oval he became the first batsman to score a century in each innings of a Test

match. He played for New South Wales and was also a splendid outfielder.
41 Tests 1909-26: 2469 runs at 40.47, 6 100s HS 139; 12 catches.*
First-class 1903-28: 17,025 runs at 49.92, 53 100s HS 264; 112 catches.

Franco BARESI (Ita)

FOOTBALL
Franco Baresi. b. 8 May 1960 Travagliato.

An elegant player who is widely regarded as the best sweeper in world football. He won his first cap against Romania in 1982, three years after his elder brother **Giuseppe** won the first of his 18 caps. He threatened retirement from international football in 1992, but was persuaded to return after poor performances by the national side and by May 1993 had made 69 appearances for Italy (with 1 goal). He helped AC Milan to win the European Cup in 1989 and 1990 and Italian league titles in 1979, 1988, 1992 and 1993.

Charles BARKLEY (USA)

BASKETBALL
Charles Wade Barkley. b. 20 Feb 1963 Leeds, Alabama.

One of the most unusual players in basketball history. At 'only' 1.96 metres *6'5"* he is almost too small to play forward in the NBA, but at 115 kg *253 lbs*, he is so strong that he plays power forward with the very best and was voted the MVP in 1992/3. His size prompted a tremendous nickname, 'The Round Mound of Rebound' and in 1987 he led the league in rebounding. He played collegiately at Auburn and his entire professional career with the Philadelphia 76ers until he was traded to the Phoenix Suns for 1992/3. For them he had a great first season, being elected the league MVP, although he was just a little overshadowed by Michael Jordan, when Phoenix were beaten 4-2 by the Chicago Bulls in the playoffs finals. Barkley has been All-NBA first-team since 1988. He starred on the US Olympic gold-medal winning 'Dream Team' in 1992.
NBA career: 16,128 points, av. 23.5. 8007 rebounds, av. 11.7.

Viktor BARNA (Hun)

TABLE TENNIS
né Gyözö Viktor Braun. b. 24 Aug 1911 Budapest, d. 28 Feb 1972 Lima, Peru.

Winner of 15 world and 20 English Open individual titles; both totals being records. Within 12 months of taking up the game as a 15 year-old at Budapest Commercial High School he won the junior championship of Hungary and the following year, 1929, he won the world men's doubles. This marked the beginning of a phenomenal record at the World Championships. He won the singles five times, 1930, 1932-5, and was only prevented from claiming a record six consecutive victories when he lost to Miklós Szabados in the 1931 final. He also won the men's doubles eight times, 1929-35 and 1939, and the mixed doubles twice, 1932, 1935. His final world title came in the men's doubles in 1939 when he made a comeback after breaking his playing arm in a motor accident in 1935. He was also a member of seven winning Swaythling Cup teams. At the English Open he claimed a record 20 victories between 1931 and 1953 (5 singles, 7 men's doubles and 8 mixed doubles). His successes were built on a complete all-round game and a particularly strong back-hand attack.
He emigrated to France in 1932 and later settled in England, who he represented internationally after adopting citizenship. After retirement he wrote extensively on the game and represented the sports goods manufacturers, Dunlop. He died of a heart attack while on a South American promotional tour . At the time of his death he was the only man to have attended every World Championships either as a player or as a journalist.

Sidney BARNES (UK)

CRICKET
Sidney Francis Barnes. b 19 Apr 1873 Smethwick, Staffordshire, d. 26 Dec 1967 Chadsmoor, Staffordshire.

Regarded by many as the greatest of bowlers. He operated at varying paces from fast to slow-medium, employing a beautifully balanced action to impart both swing and spin, with immense accuracy. He played only a limited amount of county cricket for Warwickshire 1894-6 and Lancashire 1899-1903, as for the rest of his career he played for minor counties and in the leagues. That, and perhaps his aloof attitude, meant that he played in only ten Tests in England. Yet his Test record is magnificent. In just four matches for England in South Africa 1913/4 he set an unchallenged record for a Test series with 49 wickets at an average of 10.93. That included a match analysis of 17-159 (8-56 and 9-103), a Test record until surpassed by Jim Laker in 1956. His 189 Test wickets remained the record until passed by Clarrie Grimmett in 1936. In all matches in his career he took 6229 wickets at an average of 8.33, including 1432 wickets at 8.15 for Staffordshire in the Minor Counties Championship and 4069 wickets over 38 years in league and club cricket at the staggering average of just 6.03.

27 Tests 1901-14: 242 runs at 8.06, HS 38; 189 wickets at 16.43, BB 9-103; 12 catches.*

First-class 1895-1930: 1573 runs at 12.78, HS 93; 719 wickets at 17.09, BB 9-103; 72 catches.

Jonah BARRINGTON (UK)

SQUASH

Jonah Paul Barrington. b. 29 Apr 1941, Stratton, Cornwall.

The greatest British squash player. He won many major tournaments, including the British Open every year from 1967 to 1973 except for 1969 when he lost to Cam Nancarrow (Aus) in the semi-finals, and the British Amateur three times, 1967-9. His greatest year was 1968 when he also won the Egyptian Open, the Australian Amateur and the South African Amateur. His greatest rival was the Australian, Geoff Hunt, and although Barrington won many of their matches Hunt beat him in the final of the 1967 World Amateur and frustrated Barrington's plans to turn professional as the reigning world champion. He finally turned professional in February 1969 and through his match winnings, endorsements, coaching clinics and exhibitions he became the first man to be handsomely remunerated by the game. A left-hander, his game was built on supreme physical fitness, tenacity and endurance. He was educated at Cheltenham College and Trinity College, Dublin and in July 1973 he married Madeline Ibbotson (née Wooller), an international middle-distance runner and the former wife of Derek Ibbotson, who set a world record for 1 mile in 1957.

Ken BARRINGTON (UK)

CRICKET

Kenneth Frank Barrington. b. 24 Nov 1930 Reading, Berkshire, d. 14 Mar 1981 Needham's Point, Bridgetown, Barbados.

The news of Barrington's death from a heart attack during the Third Test of the England tour of the West Indies in 1981 deeply saddened cricket lovers all over the world. This much loved and respected man was assistant manager for the England team on what was a most troubled tour. His playing career had been cut short by a mild heart attack at the age of 38. Initially joining Surrey as a bowler, his promise as a batsman was soon evident, although his leg-breaks later seemed under-utilised. He made his Test début at the age of 24 with two matches in 1955, but had to wait four years for another chance. By then he had tightened up his defence and became a highly productive and sound batsman, ever determined to sell his wicket dearly. This led at times to accusations of slow play, and he was omitted from the Test team for a match against New Zealand in 1967 after taking over seven hours to make 137, but otherwise England were very glad of his determination and consistency virtually throughout the 1960s. He averaged 101.60 for 508 runs in 1964/5 against South Africa, but his most vital contribution was probably his 582 runs at 72.75 against Australia in 1962/3, far ahead of the rest of the team (and 1763 at 80.13 in all first-class games). He scored over 2000 runs in a season three times: 2499 at 54.32 in 1959, 2070 at 59.14 in 1961 and 2059 at 68.63 in 1967.

82 Tests 1955-68: 6806 runs at 58.67, 20 100s HS 256; 29 wickets at 44.82, BB 3-4; 58 catches.
First-class 1953-68: 31,714 runs at 45.63, 76 100s HS 256; 273 wickets at 32.62, BB 7-40; 513 catches.

Mike BARROWMAN (USA)

SWIMMING
Michael Ray Barrowman. b. 4 Dec 1968 Asunción, Paraguay.

Olympic champion at 200m breaststroke in 1992, when he set his sixth world record for the event, recording 2:10.16. His first record had been 2:12.90 in the US Championships in 1989, and he also set world records when winning at the 1989 Pan-Pacific Championships, 1990 Goodwill Games and 1991 World Championships. He also set a US 220y record to win the 1990 NCAA title for the University of Michigan. Other bests: 100m breaststroke 1:02.02 (1991), 200m IM 2:01.79 (1992), 400m IM 4:19.75 (1991).

Ernest BARRY (UK)

ROWING
Ernest Barry. b. 12 Feb 1882 London, d. 21 Jul 1968 Twickenham, Middlesex.

Barry had a very long career as an oarsman, winning his first major title in 1900 with the Putney Coat and Badge, and he added Doggett's Coat and Badge in 1903. He lost to Frank Arnst (Aus) when he first challenged for the world professional title in 1910, but reversed that setback to claim the title in 1912, and defended it three times before World War I interrupted sporting matters. In 1919 Alf Felton (Aus) defeated him over the Putney to Mortlake course, but Barry reclaimed the title by defeating Felton a year later and retired shortly thereafter.

Rick BARRY (USA)

BASKETBALL
Richard Francis Dennis Barry III. b. 28 Mar 1944 Elizabeth, New Jersey.

One of the greatest forwards ever to play professional basketball. He attended the University of Miami and then began his NBA career in 1965 with the San Francisco Warriors. He sat out the 1967/8 season in a contract dispute and played in the ABA for four years. He was an outstanding scorer, but was also considered the best passing forward ever, pre-Larry Bird. He is also the all-time leader in free throw shooting, with a career average a shade under .900, but which rounds out to that august figure. Since his retirement he has become an announcer for televised basketball broadcasts.
Career: NBA and ABA 25,279 points, av. 24.8; NBA 18,395 points, av. 23.2.

Ron BARRY (Ire)

HORSE RACING
Ron Barry b. 28 Feb 1943 Limerick.

Champion National Hunt jockey in 1972/3 with 125 winners, including the Cheltenham Gold Cup on *The Dikler*. His total broke the 20-year-old record for a season, and he was champion again the following year. He was apprenticed to T Shaw in Ireland for five years, and came to Britain in 1964, riding his first winner that year at Ayr. At his retirement in 1983 he had ridden 823 winners under NH rules.

Gino BARTALI (Italy)

CYCLING
Gino Bartali. b. 18 Jul 1914 Ponte a Ema.

A world class professional cyclist for 26 years, the longest career of any top rider. He was best known as a climber, and on both occasions that he won the Tour de France (1938 and 1948) he also won the King of the Mountains title. In the Giro d'Italia, which he won in 1936-7 and 1946, he was King of the Mountains seven times, 1935-7, 1939-40 and 1946-7. He was also a good enough sprinter to record several victories in the one-day classics. Other major victories: Tour de Suisse 1946-7, Milan-San Remo 1939-40, 1947, 1950; Zürich Championship 1946, 1948; Tour of Lombardy 1936, 1939-40.
He had a great rivalry with Fausto Coppi, who succeeded Bartali as the *campionis-*

simo among Italian cycling fans. Owner of Bartali International Corporation, bicycle manufacturers.

Greg BARTON (USA)

CANOEING

Gregory Mark Barton. b. 2 Feb 1959 Jackson, Michigan.

Double gold medallist at the 1988 Olympic Games at kayak canoeing over 1000m, in the K1 and the K2 with Norman Bellingham. These were the first gold medals for the USA at canoeing for 36 years. Barton also won bronze medals at K1 1000m in 1984 and 1992, and had also made the 1980 US Olympic team. He was World Champion at K1 1000m in 1987 and at K1 10,000m in 1985 and 1987.
He overcame the disability of being born with club feet and no calf muscles to become the finest ever US canoe racer. Employed as an engineer with Ocean Kayak Ltd.

Carmen BASILIO (USA)

BOXING

Carmen Basilio. b. 2 Apr 1927 Canastota, New York.

Basilio is remembered as one of the toughest fighters of all time and he was a world champion four separate times. In 1953 he won his first championship, defeating Billy Graham for the New York state welterweight title, but lost to Kid Gavilan in a bid for the world title. He finally claimed the world welterweight crown in 1955 when he defeated Tony de Marco. He lost and regained the welterweight title in 1956 before turning to the middleweights, at which in 1957 he won the title by defeating 'Sugar Ray' Robinson. Robinson however won the 1958 rematch. The former Syracuse onion-picker had three more unsuccessful title fights to bring his record to 5 wins and 6 losses in world title fights before retiring in 1961. He was known as a colourful fighter who never gave an inch in any battle.
Career record: W - 56 (27), L - 16, D -7.

Billy BASSETT (UK)

FOOTBALL

William Isiah Bassett. b. 27 Jan 1869 West Bromwich, d. 8 Apr 1937.

The greatest right-winger of the 19th century, winning 16 England caps at a time when opportunities for international selection were restricted to matches between the Home Countries. He played for West Bromwich Albion throughout his senior career, winning FA Cup medals in 1888 and 1892 and playing in his third FA Cup final in 1895 when WBA lost to Aston Villa. Small and speedy, his accurate centres were a feature of his game during an era when wingers never strayed far from the touchline.
He was appointed a West Bromwich Albion director in 1905 and served as Chairman of the club from 1908 until his death. From 1930 to 1937 he was a member of the FA Council and the Football League Management Committee.

Cliff BASTIN (UK)

FOOTBALL

Clifford Sydney Bastin. b. 14 Mar 1912 Exeter, Devon, d. 3 Dec 1991 Exeter.

A brilliant outside-left who, by the age of 19, had won the highest honours. He played in the League for Exeter City when aged only 15 and moved to Arsenal in 1929 soon after turning professional. He was a major contributor to the successes of their great team which won the League five times (1931, 1933-35, 1938) and the FA Cup twice (1930, 1936). He also played in the 1932 Cup Final, when Arsenal lost to Newcastle United. In 1930 he set a record, which was to last for 34 years, of being the youngest-ever Wembley Cup finalist. In the 1932/3 season he scored 33 League goals which was a record for a First Division winger. He won 21 England caps 1932-8, and made his last League appearance in 1946. With his devastating shot and ice-cool temperament, Bastin was the most accomplished winger of his generation although he also played at inside-left and occasionally at wing-half with notable success.

Throughout his career he was troubled by deafness and the problem became more acute in his later years when he was a publican in Devon.

Waldemar BASZANOWSKI (Pol)

WEIGHTLIFTING

Waldemar Baszanowski. b. 15 Aug 1935 Grudziadz.

One of the greatest lifters ever pound-for-pound and the first man to clean & jerk 2.5 times his bodyweight. He won gold medals in both 1964 and 1968 at the Olympics in the lightweight (67.5kg) class and was World Champion in 1961 and 1965, with second places at 67.5kg in 1962-3 and at 75kg 1966, and European champion at 67.5kg in 1961, 1965 and 1968. From 1961 to 1971 he set 24 world records, including his greatest day, 26 Jun 1964, when he broke the world overall record three times in the same competition. A great technician who did very well in the quick lifts of snatch and clean & jerk, he took the world records for those disciplines to 137.5kg and 173kg respectively. Now trains in Asia.

William BATTEN (UK)

RUGBY LEAGUE

William Batten. b. 26 May 1889 Kinsley, nr. Fitzwilliam, Yorkshire, d. 27 Jan 1959 Wakefield, Yorkshire.

One of the great pioneers of the game. He began as a winger with Hunslet but soon moved to centre and played in all three Tests in the first ever series against Australia in 1908/09, scoring two tries in the first Test. As an incisive runner in the centre and a devastating tackler he was a great favourite with the crowd who particularly appreciated his ability to jump over would-be tacklers. When he moved to Hull in 1913 his transfer fee of £600 doubled the previous record and in 1920 he received the first benefit to exceed £1000. He won nine Great Britain caps with Hunslet from 1908 and his tenth and final cap in 1921 with Hull. After 11 years with Hull he played briefly for Wakefield Trinity and Castleford.

Cliff BATTLES (USA)

AMERICAN FOOTBALL

Clifford Franklin Battles. b. 1 May 1910 Akron, Ohio, d. 28 Apr 1981.

At West Virginia Wesleyan, Battles proved his all-round athletic ability by captaining the football, baseball, basketball and track teams. He also earned a Phi Beta Kappa key and was a Rhodes candidate. In 1932 he joined the Boston Braves of the NFL. The Braves became the Redskins in 1933 and in 1937 moved to Washington. He became a great running back, leading the NFL in rushing in 1932 (as a rookie) and 1937. After a contract dispute in the spring of 1938, Battles refused to give in to Redskins owner George Marshall and retired at the age of 28. He later became a college and professional (Brooklyn Dodgers of the AAFC) football coach.

Grant BATTY (NZ)

RUGBY UNION

Grant Bernard Batty. b. 31 Aug 1951 Greytown.

An outstanding winger from Wellington who won 15 caps for New Zealand 1972-7. He made his international début on the 1972/3 tour of Britain when he played in all five Tests. He was probably at his best on the 1976 tour of South Africa when, although troubled by a knee injury, he played in all four Tests. His final international appearance was in the opening Test against the visiting British Lions in 1977. After being selected for the second Test he was obliged to withdraw due to the recurrence of problems with his knee and he announced his retirement.
Although small, his approach to the game was excessively physical and his robust style of play was poorly received everywhere - except in his native New Zealand.

Sammy BAUGH (USA)

AMERICAN FOOTBALL

Samuel Adrian Baugh. b. 17 Mar 1914 Temple, Texas.

The first great professional passer and quarterback. He played collegiately at

Texas Christian University and his entire pro career, 1936-52, with the Washington Redskins. He led the NFL in passing in 1937, 1940, 1943, 1945, 1947, and 1949, and had a career record of 21,886 yards from 1693 pass completions. He was also a superb punter, leading the NFL in that category each year 1940-3. A true all-round player in the days of one-platoon football, Baugh led the league in interceptions in 1943. In 1969, for the 100th anniversary of college football, he was chosen the all-century quarterback. Most of his passing records have been surpassed as the game has changed into a wider open one, but at his retirement, Baugh led all NFL quarterbacks in virtually all categories. After his retirement he coached at Hardin-Simmons and coached the New York Titans of the AFL in 1960-1 and the Houston Oilers in 1964.

Alex BAUMANN (Can)

SWIMMING

Alexander Sasa Baumann. b. 21 Apr 1964 Prague, Czechoslovakia.

A medley swimmer who excelled at all four strokes. He set four world records at the 200m IM, from 2:02.78 in 1981 to 2:01.42 in 1986 and two at 400m IM, 4:17.55 and 4:17.41 in 1984; his last world records at each event came when winning gold medals at the Los Angeles Olympics, Canada's first swimming golds since 1912. Commonwealth gold medallist at both 200 and 400 IM in 1982 and 1986, with a fifth gold at the medley relay in 1986 and at 4 x 100m freestyle, bronze in 1982 and silver in 1986. World Student Games champion at both medley events in 1983. At the World Championships in 1986 he was beaten into second place at 200m IM and third at 400m IM by his successor as the world's top medley swimmer, Tamás Dárnyi. Coached by Jeno Tihanyi, Baumann was a member of the Canadian Olympic team that did not compete in 1980. His family went to New Zealand in 1967 and as his parents did not want to return to Czechoslovakia after the Soviet invasion they went to Canada two years later, settling in Sudbury, Ontario. There Alex's father became sociology professor at Laurentian University, where Alex later studied political science.

Daniel BAUTISTA (Mex)

WALKING

Daniel Bautista Rocha. b. 4 Aug 1952.

The leader of a generation of top-class walkers, he became the first Mexican Olympic gold medallist at athletics when he won the 20km walk title in 1976. At this distance he also won the 1975 Pan-American title in 1975 and the World Cup race in 1977 and 1979, and set world records on the track twice: 1:23:31.9 in 1977 and 1:20:06.8 in 1979. In 1980 he was disqualified when leading at the Olympics. He set track walking bests three times each at 10,000m 15,000m and at 1 hour to bests of 39:31.5 (1979), 59:33.0 (1980) and 15,121m (1980) respectively, and a world road best of 2:03:06 for 30km in 1980. 50km best 3:51:11 in 1979.

Jim BAXTER (UK)

FOOTBALL

James Curran Baxter. b. 29 Sep 1939 Hill of Beath, Fife.

One of the finest attacking midfield players in the world in the 1960s. He began his career with Raith Rovers in 1957 and won a Scottish Under-23 cap in 1959, but his superlative talents were not fully appreciated until he moved to Rangers later that year. While he was at Ibrox he won the majority of his 34 Scottish caps (1961-8) and Rangers won the Scottish League and Scottish Cup three times each and the Scottish League Cup four times. They were also finalists in the European Cup Winners' Cup in 1961. He also played for the Rest of the World against England in 1963. A broken leg in December 1964 seemed to have ended his career but he still commanded a substantial fee when he was transferred to Sunderland 1965 and then Nottingham Forest 1967. After two undistinguished years at Nottingham he was given a free transfer in 1969 when he returned briefly to Rangers before becoming a publican in Glasgow.

With his superb distribution of the ball from the left-half position and his seemingly effortless control of his territory, he is remembered with respect by all who saw him play when he was at his best. Unfortunately, this memory is rather flawed by the lethargy and aloofness which marked his final seasons.

Filbert BAYI (Tan)

ATHLETICS

Filbert Bayi. b. 23 Jun 1953 Karutu, near Arushu.

An exciting front-runner, he made his international début at the 1972 Olympics, when he ran in the heats of the 1500m and 3000m steeplechase. A year later he burst into world-class, winning the African Games 1500m, and later running the year's fastest 1500m of 3:34.6 as well as 3:52.86 for a mile, behind Ben Jipcho's 3:52.17. On 2 Feb 1974 at Christchurch, New Zealand at the Commonwealth Games he ran one of the greatest of world records as he stormed away from the field in the 1500m, through 400m in 54.4 and 800m in 1:51.8 and yet held on to clock 3:32.16 to win from John Walker 3:32.52 and Jipcho 3:33.16. Bayi was also 4th at 800m at those Games. On 17 May 1975 in Kingston, Jamaica, Bayi again blazed away to lead all the way as he improved the 1 mile world record to 3:51.0. Later that year Walker improved the record with the first sub-3:50 mile, but politics prevented the keenly-awaited clash between Walker and Bayi at the 1976 Olympics, which Tanzania boycotted. In 1977 Bayi again won the African 1500m, and in 1978 he was 2nd to Dave Moorcroft in the Commonwealth 1500m. In 1980 Bayi returned to the steeplechase and built up a huge lead at the Olympics, only to be caught by Bronislaw Malinowski, so having to settle for the silver medal.

Bayi later took a degree in physical education and sports administration at the University of Texas in El Paso, while competing on the US road running circuit. He is now the head coach of the Tanzanian army team.

Other best times: 800m 1:45.32 (1974), 2000m 4:59.21 (1978), 3000m 7:39.27 (1980), 2M 8:19.45 (1980), 5000m 13:18.2 (1980), Marathon 2:16:16 (1986), 3000m steeplechase 8:12.48 (1980).

Elgin BAYLOR (USA)

BASKETBALL

Elgin Baylor. b. 16 Sep 1934 Washington, DC.

The first great player to play the game above the basket. As a 1.96m *6'5"* forward he possessed great driving and leaping ability. He began his college career at Idaho, where he played one year before Idaho de-emphasised sports, and then transferred to Seattle where he led the nation in scoring in 1957. In 1958, as a senior, Baylor was the nation's second leading scorer (31.5 ppg) and third leading rebounder (19.3 per game). He was drafted by the Minneapolis Lakers in 1958 and quickly became the league's most prolific scorer prior to the arrival of Wilt Chamberlain.

Baylor played his entire career with the Lakers, although they moved to Los Angeles in 1960. He was voted Rookie of the Year in 1959 and was named to the league All-Star first team for 10 of his first 11 years in the NBA. His two greatest years were 1960/1 when he averaged 34.8 ppg for a full season and 1961/2 with 38.3 ppg for 48 games. In that year he sustained a severe knee injury and he was never quite the same again, although he did average 34 ppg in 1962/3. At his retirement in 1971, Baylor was the second leading scorer in NBA history, after Chamberlain. He played little in his last two years because of injuries. The one missing achievement from his record was an NBA Championship. In 1971/2, the Lakers finally won the NBA title, but Baylor had retired shortly after the season began.

NBA career: 23,149 points, av. 27.4.

Bob BEAMON (USA)

ATHLETICS

Robert Beamon. b. 29 Aug 1946 Jamaica, New York.

His long jump of 8.90m to win the

Olympic long jumpwas long regarded as a contender for a perpetual world record. At 2 $^1/_2$ inches over 29 feet, it was not only the first 29 ft jump, but also the first over 28 ft. Beamon, who was the favourite for the title but known as an inconsistent jumper, took full advantage of the maximum permitted wind aid and the 2247m high altitude of Mexico City to add an amazing 55cm to the world record and nearly two feet to his own best of 8.33m (27ft 4 in). No other athlete bettered even 28 feet (8.53m) until 1980, and the record was eventually bettered when Mike Powell jumped 8.95m at Tokyo in 1991.
Beamon himself, having achieved everything in just a few seconds activity, never again jumped over even 27ft, falling an inch short in 1969, in which year he suffered a serious hamstring injury.
He was second in the 1967 Pan-American Games and was AAU champion outdoors in 1968 and 1969 and indoors in 1967 and 1968. While at North Carolina A&T he was NCAA champion indoors at long and triple jumps in 1968, and he graduated from the University of Texas at El Paso in 1970. He became a social worker.
Other bests: 100y 9.5 (1966), triple jump 16.02i (1968).

Mrs R C J BEATON (UK) see GOWER

Bill BEAUMONT (UK)

RUGBY UNION

William Blackledge Beaumont. b. 9 Mar 1952 Preston, Lancs.

Although both totals have now been bettered, Beaumont formerly held the record as England's most capped prop (34) and for captaining England a record number of times (21). He was an inspirational captain and in 1980 led England to their first Grand Slam in 23 years. Later in the year he captained the British Lions in South Africa before his distinguished career was ended by injury in 1982. That year he was awarded the OBE.
After leaving Ellesmere College, he joined Fylde and represented England Under-23s, Lancashire, North Western Counties and the North of England who he led to a memorable victory over the 1979 All Blacks. He developed a successful career as a TV commentator and personality.

Franz BECKENBAUER (Ger)

FOOTBALL

Franz Beckenbauer. b. 11 Sep 1945 Munich.

The only man to both captain and manage a winning World Cup team. After playing for SC München 1954-8, he joined Bayern Munich in 1958, and won a German record 103 caps between 1965 and 1977. He played in the World Cup final 1966 and semi-final 1970 before leading West Germany to victory in 1974. Twice European Footballer of the Year (1972, 1976) he led Germany to the 1972 European Championship and captained Bayern Munich to a hat-trick of victories in the European Cup 1974-6. In 1977 he moved to New York Cosmos and, apart from a spell with Hamburg 1980-2, he stayed with the American club until his retirement in 1984 when he was appointed manager of West Germany.
In 1986 he took his team to the World Cup final and in 1990 they again met Argentina in the final where they avenged their defeat of four years earlier. Later in 1990 Beckenbauer signed as technical director for Marseille but the appointment was not an unqualified success. At the end of 1992 he signed a four-year contract worth an estimated £2 million as adviser to the Japanese League team Mitsubishi Urawa.
A superb tactician with fine individual skills, he was at his best in switching from defence to attack. He is credited with inventing the rôle of the attacking sweeper and he had an immense influence on the development of the game. Voted as the best European player of all-time in 1990.

Boris BECKER (Ger)

TENNIS

Boris Becker. b. 22 Nov 1967 Leimen.

The first German, the first unseeded player and the youngest-ever winner of the Wimbledon singles at 17 yrs 227 days in 1985. After this sensational début he retained the title the following year when he was still younger than any other winner. He was not at his best in 1987 because of injury and coaching problems but he came back in 1988 to win the Masters and lead Germany to victory in the Davis Cup. In 1989 he won the US Open for the first time, took his third Wimbledon title and again captained his country in the Davis Cup when Germany beat Sweden in the final for the second successive year. In 1991 he reached his fourth successive Wimbledon final, where he lost to fellow-German Michael Stich after having gone down to Stefan Edberg in the 1988 and 1990 finals. In 1991 he won the Australian Open and in 1992 the ATP Tour World Championship at singles and the men's doubles with Stich at the 1992 Olympic Games. In 1993 after indifferent form in other tournaments, he reached his seventh Winbledon semi-final, losing there to Pete Sampras. He has a superb record in the Davis Cup as he has lost only one of 34 singles matches 1985-92, and that to Sergio Casal (Spa) in a 'dead' rubber in 1987; he also has 11 wins in 17 doubles. A superb volleyer with excellent court coverage, by the end of 1992 he was fourth on the all-time money list with $11,670,442. West German Sportsman of the Year 1985-6 and 1989.

David BEDFORD (UK)

ATHLETICS

David Colin Bedford. b. 30 Dec 1949 London.

A hugely popular and flamboyant distance runner, Bedford played a major part in re-establishing the popularity of athletics in Britain in the early 1970s. His extrovert appearance, sometimes including red socks, delighted the crowds. An early example of his uninhibited approach was when he won the Southern junior and senior cross-country titles within an hour. He won the International cross-country titles as a junior in 1969 and senior in 1971, but disappointed in major track races, where his lack of a finishing kick let him down, so that he was 6th in the 1971 European 10,000m, 12th at 5000m and 6th at 10,000m in the 1972 Olympics, and 11th at 5000m and 4th at 10,000m at the 1974 Commonwealth Games.

He was National cross-country champion in 1971 and 1973, and won five successive AAA titles at 10,000m from 1970 to 1974, including the world record of 27:30.8 in 1973, adding the 5000m title in 1972. In addition to four at 10,000m from 28:24.4 at the age of 19, his British records included the following bests: 2000m 5:03.16 (1972), 3000m 7:46.4 (1972), 5000m 13:17.21 (1972), 3000m steeple-chase 8:28.6 (1971).

Persistent leg injuries brought his running career to a premature close, but he remained very actively involved with his club, Shaftesbury Barnet Harriers, and with the International Athletes Club in the promotion of athletics. He is now secretary of the AAA of England.

Bishen BEDI (India)

CRICKET

Bishen Singh Giansingh Bedi. b. 25 Sep 1946 Amritsar.

Probably the finest slow left-arm bowler of his era, his beautiful rhythmic action and mastery of his craft brought him great success from his first-class début at the age of 15 for Northern Punjab. He moved to play for Delhi in 1968 and captained them for more than a decade in the Ranji Trophy. He also played for Northamptonshire 1972-7.

He led the outstanding Indian spin attack of the 1960s and 1970s, becoming his country's leading wicket-taker in Tests, and to first to reach 200. He captained the team very positively in 22 Tests, which included his most successful series against Australia in 1977/8 when he took 31 wickets at 23.87, although losing the series 2-3.

67 Tests 1966-79: 656 runs at 8.98, HS 50; 266 wickets at 28.71, BB 7-98; 26 catches.*

10 One-day Ints: 31 runs at 6.20, HS 13; 7 wickets at 48.57, BB 2-44; 4 catches.

First-class 1961-82: 3584 runs at 11.37, HS 61; 1560 wickets at 21.69, BB 7-5; 172 catches.

Chuck BEDNARIK (USA)

AMERICAN FOOTBALL

Charles Philip Bednarik. b. 1 May 1925 Bethlehem, Pennsylvania.

As the son of Czech immigrants who worked in steel factories, Bednarik used that background to become one of the toughest football players ever. He is remembered now as the last of the two-way players, playing center on offense and linebacker on defense. He played his entire career in Pennsylvania - high school at Liberty High in Bethlehem, college at the University of Pennsylvania, and professionally with the Philadelphia Eagles from 1949-62. Famed coach George Allen once linked Bednarik with Dick Butkus as the 'two hardest-hitting tacklers ever'. Bednarik's best remembered tackle is one which stopped New York Giants running back Frank Gifford in the 1960 NFL Championship. Seen on national television, it gave Gifford a concussion, hospitalised him, and he later retired for one year as a result.

Alec BEDSER (UK)

CRICKET

Alec Victor Bedser. b. 4 Jul 1918 Reading, Berkshire.

World War II held back Alec Bedser's introduction to Test cricket, but he was an immediate success against India in 1946, when he took 24 wickets at 12.41 in three matches, including 7-49 and 4-96 on his début. For the next eight years his accurate in-swing bowling, with a most effective leg-cutter, was the mainstay of the England attack, and at times he seemed to carry the attack almost single-handed.

He took 30 wickets at 16.06 against Australia in 1950/1 and reached his peak effectiveness against Australia in the Ashes winning series of 1953, when he started with 7-55 and 7-44 at Trent Bridge and took 39 wickets at 17.48 in the five Tests, passing Grimmett's record number of wickets in a Test career. Amazingly within two years that was over, as the new young fast bowlers Frank Tyson, Brian Statham and Fred Trueman took charge.

Alec's twin brother **Eric** was an off-spinning all-rounder (14,716 runs at 24.10, 833 wickets at 24.95), but did not progress beyond a Test trial. Both gave stalwart service to Surrey, playing major rôles as that county won seven consecutive championships 1952-8.

Alec was an England Test selector from 1961 and chairman for a record 13 seasons 1969-81; he also manged several England touring teams. He was awarded the OBE in 1964 and the CBE in 1982.

51 Tests 1946-55: 714 runs at 12.75, HS 79; 236 wickets at 24.89, BB 7-44; 26 catches.

First-class 1939-60: 5735 runs at 14.52, 1 100 HS 126; 2082 wickets at 23.13, BB 10-90; 428 catches.

Jutta BEHRENDT (GDR)

ROWING

Jutta Behrendt. née Hampe. b. 15 Nov 1960 Berlin.

A top woman sculler of the 1980s, when she won the Olympic single sculls in 1988 and world titles at singles in 1983 and 1986 and at quad sculls in 1985 and 1987. She won World silver medals at double sculls in 1981 and quad sculls in 1982. Her first GDR Championship medal was bronze at coxed fours in 1977, but thereafter all her successes were at sculling, with two singles and four quad sculls titles in this most competitive environment.

Igor BELANOV (USSR)

FOOTBALL

Igor Belanov. b. 25 Sep 1960 Odessa.

Belanov was the outstanding player for the USSR in the World Cup of 1986, in which year he was voted European Footballer of the Year, and when they were runners-up in the 1988 European Championships. After an outstanding first division début season for Chernomorets Odessa he played for Dynamo Kiev, who won the European Cup-Winners' Cup in 1986. He scored eight goals in 33 internationals for the USSR.

Jean BELIVEAU (Can)

ICE HOCKEY

Jean Arthur Beliveau. b. 31 Aug 1931 Trois Rivières, Québec.

'Le Gros Bill' Beliveau spent his entire pro career as a center for the Montreal Canadiens when they were the dominant team in ice hockey, following the great Maurice Richard as their leader, and they-may never have had a more beloved hockey player. Beliveau was a first-team all-star seven times, and second-team four times. Known for his quiet dignity and unselfishness, he played despite numerous injuries which would have hampered lesser players. His jersey number, 4 was retired by the Canadiens, for whom he became a public relations specialist.

NHL career 1950-71 - 1125 games, 507 goals, 1219 points. Playoffs: 162 games, 79 goals, 126 points. Best years: 1955/6: 47 goals, 88 points; 1958/9: 45 goals, 91 points; 1960/1: 58 assists, 90 points. Hart Trophy 1956, 1964; Ross Trophy 1956, Smythe Trophy 1965.

Bobby BELL (USA)

AMERICAN FOOTBALL

Robert Lee Bell. b. 17 Jun 1940 Shelby, North Carolina.

The first outside linebacker inducted into the Pro Football Hall of Fame, Bell played collegiately at quarterback, linebacker, and defensive and offensive line for the University of Minnesota. A truly versatile athlete, he played in the pros with the Kansas City Chiefs from 1963-75. Chiefs' coach Hank Stram considered him the greatest athlete he had ever seen in pro football. He played him at linebacker and occasionally at center, but considered using him as a safety and tight end. He played in six AFL All-Star Games and three Pro Bowl contests after the merger of the leagues.

DAVID BELL (AUS)

HOCKEY

David Bell. b. 11 Mar 1955.

A teacher from Perth, he represented the Old Aquinians club and Western Australia. Making his international début in 1975, he took over the captaincy of the Australian team in 1984 and retired two years later, having won 186 caps in the midfield. In the World Cup he won gold in 1986 and bronze in 1978 and 1982; and he was also a silver medallist at the 1976 Olympic Games.

James BELL (USA)

BASEBALL

James Thomas Bell. b. 17 May 1903 Starkville, Mississippi, d. 8 Mar 1991 St Louis, Missouri.

'Cool Papa' Bell never played in the major leagues, the victim of his skin colour and the discrimination of his era, but in 1974 he was finally allowed to join the men he should have competed against for years when he was elected to the Hall of Fame. He played in the Negro Leagues between 1922 and 1946 with several teams. Bell is considered by many the fastest baseball player ever. Satchel Paige said that Bell was so fast that he could switch off the light in a room, and jump into bed before the room got dark. In an exhibition against the Cardinals in 1935, he scored from second on a sacrifice fly. And in 1948, in an exhibition against the Indians, he scored from first on a sacrifice, although he was by then 45 years old. He was tenth on the all-time list of batting average in the Negro Leagues, although records are far from complete.

Career batting: Avg. est .340-350.

Walt BELLAMY (USA)

BASKETBALL

Walter Jones Bellamy Jr. b. 24 Jul 1939 New Bern, North Carolina.

Bellamy was the starting center on the 1960 Olympic gold medallists. He played for Indiana University and made most all-America teams in 1960 and 1961 before being drafted by the Chicago Packers. He starred in the NBA from the start - he was Rookie of the Year in 1962, leading the league in field-goal percentage (with a new record of .519) and averaging 31.6 points

and 19 rebounds a game. During a 14-year career which saw him play for five teams, he was one of the top centers in the league. Because of a trade from New York to Detroit in 1968, Bellamy played 88 games that year, still an NBA record.
NBA career 20.941 points av. 20.1; 14,241 rebounds av. 13.7.

Peter BELLISS (NZ)

BOWLS
Peter James Belliss. b. 12 Nov 1951.

The first New Zealander to win the world singles title and also the first from his country to win the world pairs. After winning the singles at Aberdeen in 1984 he failed to retain the title on his home ground at Auckland in 1988 but made up for his disappointment by skipping Rowan Brassey to the pairs gold. Like Brassey, he turned to bowls when his career as a first-class rugby player ended. He first played bowls for New Zealand in 1978 and became a regular member of the team in 1981. He won the Commonwealth singles bronze medal in 1982, but was not selected for the 1990 Commonwealth Games team as he had previously played in South Africa.

Sergey BELOGLAZOV (USSR/Ukr)

WRESTLING
Sergey Alekseyevich Beloglazov. b. 16 Sep 1956 Kaliningrad, Russia. né Serhiy Alekseyevitch Bilohlazov (Ukrainian).

Beloglazov had one of the longest careers of any wrestler at international level. He joined the USSR national team in 1977 and won the bantamweight (57kg) freestyle gold medal at both the 1980 and 1988 Olympics. He would almost certainly have won a third but for the 1984 Soviet Olympic boycott. He won the European title in 1979, 1982, 1984 and 1987-8, and was World champion in 1981, 1983 and 1985-7 at 57kg and in 1982 at 62kg. He was also the World Cup winner in 1979-81, 1983, and 1986. His twin brother, **Anatoliy**, won the Olympic freestyle wrestling gold medal at flyweight (52kg) in 1980 and was world junior champion at 48kg in 1975 and world champion at 48kg in 1977, 52kg in 1978 and 57kg in 1982. In 1990 Sergey was the first former Soviet hired as a US college wrestling coach, by Lehigh University.

Ludmila BELOUSOVA (USSR)

FIGURE SKATING
Ludmila Belousova. b. 22 Nov 1935 Ulyanovsk. Later Protopopov.

With her husband, Oleg Protopopov, she was twice an Olympic gold medallist and a four-time World and European champion in pairs figure skating. Following her marriage in 1957, she retained her maiden name of Belousova for sporting purposes and with her husband formed a classic partnership. Their balletic movements, overhead lifts and a one-handed death spiral during which Ludmila's blonde hair swept the ice were movements which countless other skaters have sought to emulate. After placing ninth at the 1960 Olympics, they won the title in 1964 and 1968. Finishing as runners-up in the World and European Championships in 1962, 1963 and 1964, they won both titles in 1965 and were again successful for the next three years. By 1969 Ludmila was aged 33 and her husband Oleg 36, and after defeats by fellow-Russians, Aleksey Ulanov and Irina Rodnina, at both the World and European Championships they decided to turn professional. As the first Russians to become international champions in any branch of figure skating their influence on the sport in the Soviet Union had been immense and they were both accorded the supreme accolade of Honoured Masters of Soviet Sport. To the chagrin of the Soviet authorities this brilliant pair of figure skaters later defected to Switzerland.

Sergey BELOV (USSR)

BASKETBALL
Sergey Aleksandrovich Belov. b. 23 Jan 1944 Nashchekova, Tomsk Oblast.

Sergey Belov played guard for the Soviet national team from 1967 until 1979. He won three Olympic medals, bronzes in

1968 and 1976 and a gold medal in 1972. In addition, Belov played on teams which won the world championships in 1967 and 1974 and European championships in 1967, 1969, 1971, and 1979. He helped CSKA Moscow win the European Champions' Cup in 1969 and 1971.

Richie BENAUD (Aus)

CRICKET

Richard Benaud. b. 6 Oct 1930 Penrith, New South Wales.

Benaud was the first Australian to reach 2000 runs and 200 wickets in Test cricket. He was the best leg-break and googly bowler of his generation and went on to be the game's foremost communicator as a journalist and brilliant TV commentator for BBC and Channel Nine. He was a PR consultant for World Series Cricket.

He was a forcing middle-order batsman who on his first tour to England in 1953 hit 11 sixes in an innings at Scarborough of 135, and against the West Indies in 1955 scored 121, reaching his 100 in 78 minutes. He was also one of the greatest ever fielders in the gully.

With his high, fluent action, his bowling developed steadily, hitting its peak at the end of the 1950s. In South Africa in 1957/8 he set a season's first-class record with 106 wickets at 19.39, and he took 30 wickets in the Tests. He followed that with 31 against England in 1958/9, followed by 18 in three Tests against Pakistan and 29 against India in 1959/60.

He played for New South Wales throughout his career, captaining them from 1955 to 1964. He was one of the greatest ever Australian captains; of his 28 Tests iin charge 1958-64, he won 12 and lost 4 as well as the tied Test against the West Indies in 1961. Awarded the OBE in 1961. His brother **John** (b. 11 May 1944) captained New South Wales and played three Tests for Australia 1972-3.

63 Tests 1952-64: 2201 runs at 24.45, 3 100s HS 122; 248 wickets at 27.04, BB 7-72; 65 catches.

First-class 1948-68: 11,719 runs at 36.50, 23 100s HS 187; 945 wickets at 24.73, BB 7-18; 254 catches.

Gilbert BENAUSSE (Fra)

RUGBY LEAGUE

Gilbert Benausse. b. 21 Jan 1932 Carcassonne, Aude

With two tries and four goals he inspired France to their first-ever win in England at Wigan in February 1962. He joined Carcassonne at the age of 17 and went on to win a French record 48 international caps between 1951 and 1964, mostly at stand-off but occasionally at centre or on the wing, ending his career in 1968 with Lézignan. He was a master of the drop goal and his side-step and dummy were features of his creative game. His brother **René** won two international caps in 1960 as a three-quarter.

Johnny BENCH (USA)

BASEBALL

Johnny Lee Bench. b. 7 Dec 1947 Oklahoma City, Oklahoma.

Bench played his entire career with Cincinnati and was a stalwart of the Big Red Machine teams of the mid-1970s which won several World Series. For most of that time he was the top catcher in major league baseball, although he ended his last few years playing primarily first and third base. A top slugger, he set a record at 325 home runs for a catcher (since broken). He also won the MVP Award in 1970 and 1972. He was also known for his superb defensive abilities behind the plate, and after his first few years, baserunners rarely challenged his arm.

Career 1967-83: 2048 hits Avg. .267, HR 389; RBI 1376. Best seasons: 1970 - 45 HR, 148 RBI; 1972 - 40 HR, 129 RBI.

Chief BENDER (USA)

BASEBALL

Charles Albert Bender. b. 5 May 1884 Crow Wing County, Minnesota, d. 22 May 1954 Philadelphia, Pennsylvania.

A half-Chippewa Indian who attended the Carlisle Indian School. He spent most of his career with the Philadelphia Athletics 1903-14. His best pitch was the 'talcum

ball' in the days when it was legal to doctor the ball. Connie Mack, the manager of the A's, said Bender was the one pitcher he would want for a must-win game. Although he won 20 games only twice (1910, 1913), he had three seasons in which his ERA was below 2.00.
Career pitching: 1903-25 ERA 2.46; W-L 212-128, SO 1711; Best season: 1910 - 23-5, 1.58 ERA.

Stellan BENGTSSON (Swe)

TABLE TENNIS

Stellan Bengtsson. b. 26 Jul 1952 Falkenberg.

After 10 successive wins by Asian players he brought the world singles title back to Europe in 1971. He also won the world men's doubles with countryman Kjell Johansson in 1973 and both Bengtsson and Johansson were members of the Swedish team which won the Swaythling Cup for the first time that year. He also enjoyed a brilliant season in 1972 when he won the English, French, Yugoslav and European singles. At the biennial European Championships he won the doubles in 1976 and was a member of five winning Swedish European teams.
A child prodigy, he abandoned his studies in 1969 to concentrate full-time on the game. Always superbly fit, his left-handed backhand attack was exceptional.

Wilfred BENITEZ (USA)

BOXING

né Wilfredo Benitez. b. 12 Sep 1958 New York.

In March 1976 Wilfred Benitez outpointed Antonio Cervantes to win the WBA light-welterweight championship; at 17 years 173 days he became the youngest professional world champion ever. He later abandoned that title and won the welterweight championship in January 1979. He lost this title in 1980 to 'Sugar Ray' Leonard, but in May 1981 claimed the WBC light-middleweight crown by knocking out Maurice Hope. He lost that title in 1982 to Thomas Hearns. Benitez was a lightning fast boxer known for his skill more than for his knockout punch. He won eight and lost two world title fights.
Career record: W - 51 (30), L - 6, D -1.

Phil BENNETT (UK)

RUGBY UNION

Philip Bennett. b. 24 Oct 1948 Felinfoel.

After progressing through the Welsh Secondary Schools and Youth teams he went on to play for Llanelli, the Barbarians, Wales and the British Lions. His greatest asset was his ability to beat opponents with a jink, dummy or side-step and these talents led to 29 caps (8 as captain) for Wales and 8 Test appearances for the Lions. Bennett usually played at fly half and in 25 of his matches for Wales and in all four Tests for the 1974 Lions he partnered scrum half Gareth Edwards. During his international career 1969-78 he set numerous scoring records including a then world record 210 points in international matches and a record equalling 38 points in the 1976 Championship season. After touring with the Lions to South Africa in 1974 he captained the team in New Zealand in 1977 and is only the second Welsh player to have captained the Lions. He played in every Test on each tour.
Awarded the OBE in 1978 after retiring from international rugby, he continued to play for Llanelli for a number of seasons. He is still involved in the game as a TV commentator.

Joan BENOIT (USA), see SAMUELSON

Doug BENTLEY (Can)

ICE HOCKEY

Douglas Wagner Bentley. b. 3 Sep 1916 Delisle, Saskatchewan, d. 24 Nov 1972 Saskatoon, Saskatchewan.

A left wing, he was not an immediate star as he failed to make NHL teams three times before being picked up by the Chicago Black Hawks, finishing with two years for the New York Rangers. He played on the same line as his brother Max, 1940-3 and with New York in 1953-4. Bentley retired after the 1951 season to

become a coach with Saskatoon of the Western Hockey League, but was coaxed out of retirement by his brother and then joined the Rangers. In his first game after two years of retirement he scored a goal and had three assists. He then went back to coaching although he made a brief comeback in 1962 with the Los Angeles Blades of the WHL.
NHL career 1939-54 - 566 games; 219 goals, 543 points. Best years: 1943/4: 38 goals, 77 points; 1948/9: 43 assists, 66 points. Ross Trophy 1943.

Max BENTLEY (Can)

ICE HOCKEY

Maxwell Herbert Lloyd Bentley. b. 1 Mar 1920 Delisle, Saskatchewan, d. 19 Jan 1984 Saskatoon, Saskatchewan.

Known as the 'Dipsy Doodle Dandy from Delisle', Max Bentley is considered one of the most exciting centers ever to play hockey. He starred with his older brother Doug and Bill Mosienko on the Chicago Black Hawks Pony Line from 1940-7. All three were diminutive by hockey standards, but they were unparalleled stickhandlers and playmakers who were stopped only by rough play. After seven years, Max was traded to the Toronto Maple Leafs, whom he helped turn into the power of the NHL, as they became the first team to win three straight Stanley Cups, 1947-9, adding a fourth in 1951. In his last year in the NHL, 1953/4, the Bentley brothers were reunited for a last hurrah.
NHL career 1940-54 - 646 games, 244 goals, 300 points. Best years: 1945/6: 30 goals, 61 points; 1946/7: 29 goals, 72 points. Hart Trophy 1946, Ross Trophy 1946-7; Lady Byng Trophy 1943.

Nino BENVENUTI (Italy)

BOXING

Giovanni Benvenuti. b. 26 Apr 1938 Isola d'Istria.

A handsome and stylish boxer, he became a national hero in 1960 when he won the Olympic welterweight title at Rome. He turned professional early the next year and won the light-middleweight world championship in 1965. In April 1967 he defeated Emile Griffith to win the middleweight championship. Griffith won a return bout, but Benvenuti took the rubber match. Benvenuti held the world title until 1970 when he lost to Carlos Monzon, who again defeated Benvenuti in May 1971, at which time the great Italian champion retired with a record of eight wins in 12 world title bouts.
Career record: W - 82 (35), L - 7, D -1.

Pierre BERBIZIER (Fra)

RUGBY UNION

Pierre Berbizier. b. 17 Jun 1958 Lannemazan.

A scrum-half who made his international début against Scotland in 1981 and helped France win the Grand Slam in his first international season. Although with 56 caps he is France's most capped scrum-half, he was never an automatic choice for the team. During the years he played at international level (1981-91) France called on three other scrum-halves and he also lost his place for 'political' reasons after a well publicised dispute with coach Jacques Fouroux. Berbizier later took over the duties of national coach himself. A physical education teacher, he played for Lourdes before moving to Agen.

Jack BERESFORD (UK)

ROWING

Jack Beresford Jr. b. 1 Jan 1899 Chiswick, Middlesex, d. 3 Dec 1977 Shiplake-on-Thames, Oxfordshire.

Beresford was one of the most titled rowers ever and also had an amazingly long career, rowing both sculls and sweep oars. He won five Olympics medals: at single sculls silver 1920 and gold 1924, eights silver 1928, coxless fours gold 1932, and double sculls gold 1936. He was preparing to compete in 1940 when the war intervened. At Henley, he won the Diamond Sculls four times, 1920 and 1924-6; the Nickalls Challenge Cup at coxless pairs with Gordon Killick 1928-9, and the Double Sculls Challenge Cup with Dick Southwood 1939. Beresford also won

the Wingfield Sculls for seven consecutive years from 1920. He rowed for the Thames, Leander, and Kingston clubs, coached and managed the British Olympic rowing team in 1952. He was honoured with a CBE in 1960.
His father **Julius** (b. 29 Jun 1868, d. 29 Sep 1959) was also a notable oarsman, winning the Silver Goblets in 1911.

Patty BERG (USA)

GOLF
Patricia Jane Berg. b. 13 Feb 1918 Minneapolis, Minnesota.

The first great woman professional golfer; she helped start the LPGA in the late 1940s and was elected its first president. She led the LPGA tour in victories won in 1953, 1955 and 1957, with a career total of 57 tournament wins (including 13 pre-LPGA), and was money leader in 1954, 1956-7. She was also one of the first four inductees into the LPGA Hall of Fame.
Berg had been a child prodigy who took up golf at the age of 12. She was runner-up in the US Women's Amateur at 17 and at 19, and won the title at 20 in 1938. She played on the US Curtis Cup team in 1936 and 1938, and after winning 29 amateur championships turned pro in 1940, the first woman to do so, even though at first she played exhibitions for Wilson Sporting Goods as there were no tournaments for her to play. She won the first US Women's Open in 1946 and her hole-in-one at the 1959 US Open was the first by a woman in a US Golf Association competition. Her seven wins in the Titleholders Championship, 1937-9, 1948, 1953, 1955 and 1957, and in the Western Open, 1941, 1943, 1948, 1951, 1955, 1957-8, at that time major championships, were both records. She continues to play into her 70s though she has recently undergone a total hip replacement.
She served as a lieutenant in the Marine Corps in 1942-5. Her numerous honours include being named the Associated Press woman athlete of the year in 1938, 1943 and 1955. In 1976 she became the first woman to receive the Humanitarian Sports Award in recognition of her work against cerebral palsy. In 1978 the LPGA established the Patty Berg Award for outstanding contributions to women's golf.

Gerhard BERGER (Aut)

MOTOR RACING
Gerhard Berger. b. 27 Aug 1959 Wörgl.

A consistent Formula One racer, with a best world championship placing of third in 1988. The first of his eight Grand Prix wins was in Mexico 1986. From 1984 to the end of July 1993 he totalled 259 points from 141 starts. He drove for ATS 1984, Arrows 1985, Benetton 1986, Ferrari 1987-9 and 1993, McLaren 1990-2. He won the German Alfasud Trophy in 1981 and was third in the European F3 championship in 1984.

Ingrid BERGHMANS (Bel)

JUDO
Ingrid Berghmans. b. 24 Aug 1961. Later Vallot

The most successful woman judo player in the history of the sport, with a record six world titles. She won at Open class in 1980, 1982, 1984 and 1986 and at under 72kg in 1984 and 1989, and has also won four silver medals and a bronze. She also won the 1988 Olympic 72kg title in 1988 when judo was a demonstration sport and was European champion at 72kg in 1985, 1988-9 and Open 1983, 1987-8.
She married Belgian judo player Marc Vallot in 1990.

Richard BERGMANN (Aut/Pol/UK)

TABLE TENNIS
Richard Bergmann. b. 1919 Vienna, d. 5 Apr 1970.

Winner of four men's singles world titles between 1937 and 1950, Bergmann would almost certainly have exceeded Viktor Barna's record of five victories had his career not been interrupted by World War II. Born in Austria of a Polish father and Italian mother, he first took part in the World Championships as a 16-year-old in 1936 when he helped Austria to their first

Swaythling Cup victory and reached the semi-finals of the singles. The following year he became the youngest man ever to win the world singles and after being a losing finalist in 1938 he again won the title in 1939, when he also won the men's doubles with Barna.
When the Germans annexed Austria in 1938, Bergmann fled to England and after serving in the RAF took British nationality. He was again world singles champion in 1948 and 1950 and was a member of the British team which won the Swaythling Cup in 1953. At the English Open he won the singles a record six times between 1939 and 1954. Rated as the greatest defensive player in table tennis history, he eventually left England and settled in America.

Yogi BERRA (USA)

BASEBALL

Lawrence Peter Berra. b. 12 May 1925 St Louis, Missouri.

One of the greatest catchers the game has ever seen but he has almost become better known for the many malapropisms he uttered.
For the New York Yankees he played in a record 14 World Series, and was a champion in 10 of them, setting the World Series career record with 71 base hits in 259 at bats in his 71 games. His total of 39 runs batted in is second only to Mickey Mantle's 40 in World Series games.
The ultimate winner, one opposing manager said that Berra was not a great hitter but he was the game's best from the 7th inning on. He was also known as a great bad-ball hitter. As a catcher he had almost no weaknesses. He had a good throwing arm and was an excellent backstop and fielder, but his handling of his pitchers was his strength. In 1955, Berra became the first man to win three MVP awards, 1951, 1954-5 (AL). He became a coach and manager; as a manager he won pennants with the 1964 Yankees and the 1973 Mets. His son Dale played for Pittsburgh in the National League.
Career 1946-65: 2150 hits Avg. .285, HR 358.

Livio BERRUTI (Italy)

ATHLETICS

Livio Berruti. b. 19 May 1939 Turin.

The Olympic champion at 200 metres in Rome in 1960, when he became the first non-North American to win this title. He caught the public's imagination by wearing dark glasses and equalled the world record with 20.5 in both semi-final and final (20.65 and 20.63 on auto timing). He was then a chemistry student at the University of Padua and these Olympics proved to be his career highlight as he went on to place 5th in the 1964 Olympics and 7th in the 1966 Europeans at 200m as well as winning the 100m silver medal at the 1963 World Student Games.
Italian champion at 100m and 200m each year 1957-62, he had set the first of three Italian records at 100m with 10.4 in 1957, improving to 10.2 in 1960, and nine Italian records at 200m from 21.1 in 1959. Now an advertising and PR manager.

Ray BERRY (USA)

AMERICAN FOOTBALL

Raymond Emmett Berry. b. 27 Feb 1933 Corpus Christi, Texas.

A great wide receiver, considered to have achieved his fame with as little natural talent as any receiver ever. He was neither fast nor big, but he had spider-web hands, and a work ethic which saw him run the best routes of any receiver in football history. He played his entire career 1955-67 with the Baltimore Colts where, with quarterback Johnny Unitas, he formed one-of the greatest quarterback/receiver duos in pro football history. Berry later became a professional coach, most recently with the New England Patriots.
NFL career: 9275 yards receiving av. 14.7, 68 touchdowns.

Roland BERTRANNE (Fra)

RUGBY UNION

Roland Gaston Bertranne. b. 6 Dec 1949 Ibos, Haute-Pyrénées.

With 39 international appearances in the centre and 13 on the wing, his total of 69 caps 1971-81 was a French record until beaten by Serge Blanco. A brilliant attacking player he was also thoroughly dependable and this quality, often lacking in French backs, helped him keep his place throughout a period of unsettled selections. He still holds the French record for playing in 46 consecutive internationals. A draughtsman by profession he played for Bagnères.

Jay BERWANGER (USA)

AMERICAN FOOTBALL
John Jacob Berwanger. b. 19 Mar 1914 Dubuque, Iowa.

The first winner of the Heisman Memorial Trophy in 1935, playing for the University of Chicago. He played both ways, as did all players in that era, but his fame rested on his ability as a running back. He also was an excellent track athlete, competing as a sprinter and decathlete. He never played professionally, preferring to enter the business world. He remained in football as a collegiate referee for several years.

George BEST (UK)

FOOTBALL
George Best. b. 22 May 1946 Belfast.

One of the most talented players in the history of the game. Sadly, his unacceptable off-field behaviour hastened his retirement and tarnished his image. Before being beset by alcohol-related problems his skills as a striker or winger were universally admired. He made his Football League début for Manchester United and won the first of his 31 international caps for Northern Ireland before he had reached his 18th birthday. He was English and European Footballer of the Year in 1968 and played a vital part in Manchester United's defeat of Benfica in the European Cup that year. Between 1963 and 1973 he made 349 League appearances for Manchester United, scoring 134 goals but towards the end of this period signs of his excesses were already apparent. He began to miss club and international training sessions with worrying regularity and he was dropped from the Manchester United and Ireland teams. After a while, the managers were prepared to overlook his lapses and he regained his place in both sides. The recovery was short-lived, the physical and mental decline continued and although he made a brief comeback with Los Angeles Aztecs and Fulham (and won his final cap in 1977) his brilliant but tragic career in football was all but over, although he played briefly for league teams in the USA, Scotland and England, ending with five games for Bournemouth in 1983.

Natalya BESTEMYANOVA (USSR)

FIGURE SKATING
Natalya Bestemyanova. b. 6 Jan 1960 Moscow.

Bestemyanova and **Andrey Bukin** (b. 10 Jun 1957 Moscow) were the successors as ice dance world champions to Jayne Torvill and Christopher Dean. They were World champions 1985-8 and won Olympic gold in 1988. After 8th at the 1980 Olympics and 3rd in the 1981 Worlds, they were runners-up to Torvill and Dean at the 1982 and 1983 World Championships and 1984 Olympics. Their first important titles were those of the USSR 1982-3 and the Europeans 1983. Bestemyanova provided the explosive personality, while Bukin was quiet and strong.

Pauline BETZ (USA)

TENNIS
Pauline May Betz. b. 6 Aug 1919 Dayton, Ohio. Later Addie.

One of the greatest of the American women players who dominated the game immediately after World War II. She won three US singles titles (1942-4) during the war years and soon showed her worth when she first encountered top-class international competition. In 1946 she took her fourth US title, won at Wimbledon and narrowly lost in the final of the French Championships after holding two match points. But she won the mixed doubles in Paris with Budge Patty that year and also played in the Wightman Cup. She was precluded from defending her Wimbledon

title in 1947 when earlier in the year she was suspended for merely *discussing* a possible professional contract.
Although not a classic stroke player, she possessed an excellent all-round game and was expected to win further honours in the amateur ranks.

Brian BEVAN (Aus)

RUGBY LEAGUE
Brian Bevan. b. 24 Jun 1924 Sydney, d. 3 Jun 1991 Blackpool, Lancashire.

A former stoker in the Australian Navy who had played rugby union for Randwick High School as a winger, he first played for Warrington in November 1945 and became the greatest try scorer in the history of the game, with a career record of 796 tries in English rugby league. In 1954, in only his eighth season with Warrington, he scored his 462nd try, bettering Alf Ellerby's 15-year-old record which had been set over 14 seasons and two Australasian tours. Bevan twice scored seven tries in a match and claimed a hat-trick no less than 69 times, his most prolific season being 1952/3 when, with 72 tries, he fell eight short of Albert Rosenfield's record set in 1913/14. After 16 seasons with Warrington, he spent two years with Blackpool Borough before retiring in 1964. Although unathletic in appearance, frail, spindly-legged and balding, he was a winger of exceptional speed and his side-step, swerve and change of pace invariably upset the best laid defensive plans.
His father Rick had played for Eastern Suburbs in the 1920s and his brother Owen also played league football in England with Leigh and Warrington.

Udo BEYER (GDR)

ATHLETICS
Udo Beyer. b. 9 Aug 1955 Eisenhüttenstadt.

The outstanding shot putter of the late 1970s and early 1980s. He was ranked first in the world each year from 1977 to 1984, except 1983, when, as in 1976, he was second. At four Olympic Games he won in 1976, was third in 1980, when he suffered a pulled back muscle, was fourth in 1988, but did not qualify for the final in 1992.
He emerged with five European junior records in 1973-4 and won the European Junior title in 1973. He went on to win the Europeans in 1978 and 1982, World Student Games 1979, eleven successive GDR titles 1977-87, and both European and World Cup Finals in 1977, 1979 and 1981. He set world records at 22.15m in 1978, 22.22 in 1983 and 22.64 in 1986. He continued through to 1992 but with gradually reducing success, placing third in 1986 and fifth in 1990 at the Europeans, and taking sixth place at the World Championships of 1983 and 1987.
His sister **Gisela** (b. 16 Jul 1960) was 4th in the discus at the 1980 Olympics and 1982 Europeans and 5th at the 1983 Worlds and his brother **Hans-Georg** (b. 3 Sep 1956) won an Olympic handball gold medal in 1980.

Miki BIASION (Italy)

RALLYING
Massimo Biasion. b. 7 Jan 1958 Bassano del Grappa.

World rallying champion 1988-9, winning the Safari Rally in each of those years. His 16 world championship wins include the Monte Carlo Rally in 1987 and 1989, and the San Remo Rally 1987-9. He started rallying in Opels, always with co-driver Tiziano Siviero. Moved to Lancia in 1983 with immediate success, winning the European title, and on to Ford in 1992.

Nino BIBBIA (Italy)

TOBOGGANING
Nino Bibbia. b. 15 Mar 1922 Bianzine, Sondrio.

The greatest of all Cresta Run riders and an Olympic gold medallist in 1948 in the skeleton event which is only included in the Olympic programme when the Winter Games are held at St Moritz. Between 1950 and 1973 he won the Grand National and the Curzon Cup a record eight times each, winning both events in 1960, 1962 and 1964. In 1965 he broke both the main

Cresta speed records setting new times from the Top and Junction. His success was based on a fast start and a superb steering technique. Although Italian-born he settled in St Moritz when he took up tobogganing seriously and virtually all his racing was on the Cresta.

Terry BIDDLECOMBE (UK)

HORSE RACING

Terence Walter Biddlecombe. b. 2 Feb 1941 Hartbury Court, Gloucestershire.

Champion National Hunt jockey three times in the 1960s. He started his career in 1957/8, had his first winner at Wincanton in 1958 and turned professional in 1960. His first championship in 1964/5 was with 114 winners, when he was first jockey to Fred Rimell, and he then placed successively 1, 2, 3, 1=, 3 in the NH jockeys championship, with one more century, 102 in 1965/6. In all he rode 909 winners under NH rules 1958-74. Won the Cheltenham Gold Cup on *Woodland Venture* in 1967. The extrovert son of a Gloucestershire farmer, he was very tall for a jockey; a strong rider with fast reactions, renowned for his courage and horsemanship.

Abebe BIKILA (Eth)

ATHLETICS

Abebe Bikila. b. 7 Aug 1932 Mout (later given as 1933 Jatto, Debre Birham). d. 25 Oct 1973.

Bikila surprised the world when he won the 1960 Olympic marathon as a complete outsider in a world best ever time of 2:15:16.2, running barefoot. That was his third race at the distance and his first outside his hometown of Addis Ababa. He was a member of the Imperial Bodyguard, having joined the Army at the age of 19, and trained under the guidance of the Swede Onni Niskanen.

In 1964 he became the first man ever to retain an Olympic marathon title when he won in Tokyo, this time wearing shoes, in another world best time of 2:12:11.2. He had had an operation for appendicitis only six weeks earlier, and yet finished looking exceedingly fresh! He said that he could have run for another ten kilometres.

In his career he won 12 of his 15 marathons, his last being when a recurrence of an injury caused him to drop out of the 1968 Olympic marathon. Track bests: 10,000m 29:00.8 (1966), 1 hour 19,946m (1962).

He suffered severe injuries, including a broken neck, in a car accident in 1969. Paralysed, he died four years later.

Rolf BILAND (Swi)

MOTOR CYCLING

Rolf Bilan. b. 1 Apr 1951 Birmenstorf.

Five times world sidecar champion, 1978-9, 1981, 1983 and 1992, riding for Yamaha on the first four occasions and LCR Krauser in 1992. He started his Grand Prix career in 1974 and between 1975 and June 1993 had 62 Grand Prix victories at sidecar racing, easily the most ever for this category. He was also second overall in 1977, 1980, 1982, 1988 and 1991, and third in 1975, 1985 and 1987. An all-out racer, after previously riding Yamaha he rode Krauser bikes in 1986-90 and LCR 1991.

Abdi BILE (Somalia)

ATHLETICS

Abdi BileAbdi b. 28 Dec 1962 Las Anod.

In 1987 Bile became the first Somali world champion at any sport, when he won the 1500m in Rome. He had competed at the 1984 Olympics, reaching the 1500m semi-finals, and came to top class while he studied marketing at George Mason University, USA. For them he won the NCAA title in 1985 and 1987. He missed the 1988 Olympics due to a stress fracture in his left foot, but in 1989 he won the Oslo Dream Mile and World Cup 1500m, with national records at 800m, 1000m, 1500m and 3000m. He also won the Grand Prix 1500m title in 1987 and 1989. After missing a year through injury he returned to form in 1993.

Best times: 800m 1:43.60 (1989), 1000m 2:14.50 (1989), 1500m 3:30.55 (1989), 1 mile 3:49.40 (1988), 2000m 4:59.77 (1987), 3000m 7:52.23 (1989).

Fred BILETNIKOFF (USA)

AMERICAN FOOTBALL
Frederick Biletnikoff. b. 23 Feb 1943 Erie, Pennsylvania.

One of the greatest pass receivers in football history. He played collegiately at Florida State University and for his entire American professional career, 1965-78, with the Oakland Raiders. He was not blazingly fast, but was blessed with great hands and ran very precise pass routes. For ten straight seasons he caught over 40 passes in a season. In 1980 he made a brief comeback in Canada with the Montreal Alouettes and caught 38 passes for that club. He was MVP when Oakland won the Super Bowl in 1977.
NFL career: 8974 yards received av. 15.2, 76 touchdowns.

Dmitriy BILOZERCHEV (USSR)

GYMNASTICS
Dmitriy Bilozerchev. b. 22 Dec 1966 Moscow.

In 1983 at the age of 16 years 315 days he became the youngest ever world champion, adding three individual titles to the all-around. He had to miss the 1984 Olympics through the Soviet boycott, but won the Friendship Games title. However, after winning the European title in both 1983 (when he won golds on three individual apparatus) and 1985 (with golds at five of the six apparatus), he had a very serious car accident in which his left leg was shattered into more than 40 pieces; amputation was even considered. He made an enormously courageous return to fitness, even having to suffer a further operation on his right ankle in December 1986, but he came back to regain the 1987 world title and to take his total of world gold medals to a record seven. He was thus favourite for the 1988 Olympic title, but after a bad mistake on his favourite apparatus, the horizontal bar, had to settle for bronze in the all-around event. He did however win gold medals at the pommel horse and rings. European Cup winner 1983 and 1985, World Cup 1983 and 1987 and USSR all-around champion 1983, 1985 and 1987.

Alfredo BINDA (Italy)

CYCLING
Alfredo Binda. b. 11 Aug 1902 Cittiglio, d. 19 Jul 1986.

Binda succeeded Constante Girardengo as the *campionissimo* among Italian cycling fans. His greatest successes came within Italy, with the Giro d'Italia in 1925, 1927-9 and 1933 (when he was also King of the Mountains), but he was also superb in the world road championship. His record of three wins in that race (1927, 1930, 1932) is still unbeaten, and he was also third in 1929. Binda was so dominant in his day that in 1930, the organisers of the Giro d'Italia paid him the equivalent of the winner's prize not to start, because it ruined the suspense of the race. He also won the Tour of Lombardy 1925-7 and 1931.

David BING (USA)

BASKETBALL
David Bing. b. 24 Nov 1943 Washington, DC.

Bing, who played guard and was known more as a scorer than a playmaker, starred collegiately at Syracuse University, graduating in 1966. He was drafted by the Detroit Pistons and in 1967 was named NBA Rookie of the Year. He was first-team All-NBA in 1968 and 1971 and he led the league in scoring in 1968 (1242 points av. 27.1). In 1989 he was elected to the Naismith Memorial Basketball Hall of Fame. Since retirement, Bing has settled in Detroit where he has been a great success as a businessman in several different companies.
NBA career: 901 points, av. 20.3.

Blanche BINGLEY (UK)

TENNIS
Blanche Bingley. b. 3 Nov 1863 Greenford, Middlesex, d. 6 Aug 1946 Pulborough, Sussex. Later Hillyard.

A player whose career was noted not only for its many successes but also for its longevity. She first played at Wimbledon in 1884 and, at the age of 49, made her

27th and final appearance in 1913. During the intervening years she won the singles six times (1886, 1889, 1894, 1897, 1899-1900) with a 14-year interval between her first and last title. She was unfortunate to be a contemporary of the incomparable Lottie Dod who beat her four times in the Challenge Round and once in the All-Comers' Final. She was also the singles champion of Germany (1897, 1900), Ireland (1888, 1894, 1897) and Wales (1888) and won the All England doubles in 1897, 1901 and 1906 before the event was given full Championship status.
The majority of her titles were won after her marriage in July 1887 to Commander George Hillyard RN, secretary of the All England Club from 1907 to 1924.

Matt BIONDI (USA)

SWIMMING

Matthew Nicholas Biondi. b. 8 Oct 1965 Moraga, California.

Biondi won eleven Olympic swimming medals, one in 1984 (gold at 4x100m freestyle relay), seven in 1988 (gold at 50m and 100m freestyle and all three relays, silver at 100m butterfly, bronze at 200 free); and three in 1992 when he was second at 50m and fifth at 100m free, swam on the winning US 4 x 100m freestyle team and gained a final gold (his eighth at the Olympics) for 4 x 100m medley, although he swam only in the heat and not the final.
He won gold medals at 100m free and both 100m relays at the World Championships in both 1986 and 1991. In 1986 he added a silver and three bronze for a record seven medals at one Championships, and in 1991 silver at 50m free.
He set his first world record with 49.24 for 100m freestyle in the heats of the US Championships in 1985, improving to 48.95 in the final. He added further records at 48.74 in 1986 and 48.42 in 1988. He also set three world records at 50m freestyle: 22.33 in 1986 and 1987 and 22.14 in 1988, and has set world records at all three relays, including three at 4 x 100m free. Very tall at 2.01m and 95kg with an 8 ft armspan. He studied at the University of California, Berkeley and was co-founder of the Delphys Foundation for Marine Study with David Berkoff (b. 30 Nov 1966), who set three world records for 100m backstroke in 1988.
Other best times: freestyle 50m 21.85 behind Tom Jager's world record 21.81 in 1990, 200m 1:47.72 (1988), 100m butterfly 53.01 (1988).

Larry BIRD (USA)

BASKETBALL

Larry Joe Bird. b. 7 Dec 1956 French Lick, Indiana.

One of the greatest basketball forwards, despite not possessing the talents of many other great players. He began college at Indiana University but soon transferred to Indiana State, which he led to be NCAA runner-up in 1979 before being drafted by the Boston Celtics, for whom he played his entire pro career. He was relatively slow and not a great jumper, but his outside shooting was superb, his passing was unrivalled among any big men, and the court presence and ability that made his team-mates better made him a superstar. He helped the Celtics win NBA titles in 1981, 1984 and 1986 and he was voted NBA MVP each year from 1984 to 1986. Late in the 1980s he was hampered by injuries to his heels and back and was slightly less dominant. Though past his prime he was held in such regard that he was named to the 1992 US Olympic basketball team, the first ever to feature NBA players and was elected captain of the 'Dream Team', helping them to win the tournament. After the Olympics, he retired because of his chronic back problems.
NBA career: 1980-92 21,791 points, av. 24.3.

Molla BJURSTEDT (Nor/USA)

TENNIS

Anna Margrethe Bjurstedt. b. 6 Mar 1884 Oslo, d. 22 Nov 1959 Stockholm, Sweden. Later Mallory.

A trained masseuse who emigrated to America in December 1914 after winning the Norwegian Championship ten times between 1904 and 1914 and a bronze medal at the 1912 Olympic Games. In her first US Championships in 1915 she defeated the favourite, Hazel Wightman, in the All Comers final and then won the Challenge round by default. She retained the title the following year and won again in 1918, 1920-2 and 1926. She also won the US women's doubles twice (1916-17) and the mixed doubles three times (1917, 1922-3).

She married New York stockbroker Franklin Mallory in 1919. Winning a total of 12 US outdoor titles she is rated as the greatest American player until the emergence of Helen Wills Moody but she failed to produce her best form when playing overseas. Her best performance at Wimbledon was to reach the 1922 final but she was eliminated in the quarter-finals in 1921 and 1923 and the semi-finals in 1920 and 1926. Her place in sporting history is assured, as the only player to beat Suzanne Lenglen in singles after World War I. This was at the 1921 US Championships when Lenglen, having lost the first set, defaulted during the first game of the second set. Molla Mallory played in five Wightman Cup teams between 1923 and 1928 and retired from tournament play in 1929 as a result of a knee injury. A fluent linguist, she worked for the US Office of Censorship during World War II.

Ian BLACK (UK)

SWIMMING

Ian Macintosh Black. b. 27 Jun 1941 Aberdeen.

Britain's Sportsman of the Year in 1958 after winning three gold medals at the European Championships: 400m and 1500m freestyle and 200m butterfly; along with the 220y butterfly gold and silvers at 440y freestyle and 4 x 220y relay at the British Empire Games.

His one world record was the inaugural mark, 5:08.8 at the 440y individual medley. He ended his brief career with fourth places and European records at the Olympic Games, at 400m in 4:21.8 and on Britain's 4 x 200m relay team. He actually dead-heated with John Konrads for the bronze at 400m, but was relegated to fourth on a technicality. He also set European records for 200m butterfly, 2:18.7 in 1960, and 400m IM, 5:08.8 in 1959.

ASA champion at each of 110y, 220y and 440y freestyle and 220y butterfly in 1958 and 1959. In 1958/9 he set British records at all freestyle distances from 100y to 1 mile as well as three of the four at butterfly and at 400m/440y IM.

Jack BLACKHAM (Aus)

CRICKET

John McCarthy Blackham. b. 11 May 1854 North Fitzroy, Melbourne, d. 28 Dec 1932 Melbourne.

The first great Australian wicket-keeper, he came to England on the first eight Australian tours from 1878 to 1893, captaining the last team. He usually stood up to the stumps, where his concentration and dexterity earned him the title of the 'prince of wicket-keepers'. He was also a useful, unorthodox, late order batsman.

35 Tests 1876-95: 800 runs at 15.68, HS 74; 36 catches, 24 stumpings.

First-class 1874-94: 6395 runs at 16.78, 1 100 HS 109; 2 wickets; 273 catches, 180 stumpings.

Blagoi BLAGOEV (Bul)

WEIGHTLIFTING

Blagoi Blagoev. b. 4 Dec 1956 Preslav.

Blagoev began lifting in 1972 and made a major breakthrough in 1976 when he finished 2nd at the European Championships. At the Montreal Olympics he finished second in the 82.5 kg class but was disqualified when the drug test revealed he had taken anabolic steroids. His first international championship came in 1979 when he won the Europeans, but he was forced to compete early in his career against Yurik Vardanyan, who usually had the better of their match-ups, taking gold to Blagoev's silver at the 1980 Olympics. In 1981, having moved up to the 90 kg class, Blagoev won the first of three consecutive world championships, but the boycott of the 1984 Olympics denied him a final chance at Olympic gold. World Cup winner in 1982 and 1983. He became an Australian citizen in 1993.

Bonnie BLAIR (USA)

SPEED SKATING
Bonnie Kathleen Blair. b. 18 Mar 1964 Cornwall, New York.

An outstanding woman speed skating sprinter who first made the US Olympic team in 1984, at the age of 19. After winning the world short track 500m title in 1986 she set a world 500m record of 39.43 in 1987 on a standard track. She improved that year to 39.28 and in 1988 when she took the Olympic title in 39.10, a record which still stands (1993). She also placed third in the 1000m at the 1988 Olympics. She confirmed her position as the world's fastest woman sprinter when she won the 1989 World Sprint Championship with a record points score. At her third Olympics in 1992 she successfully defended her 500m title and won her third Olympic gold in the 1000m.

Hector BLAKE (Can)

ICE HOCKEY
Hector 'Toe' Blake. b. 21 Aug 1912 Victoria Mines, Ontario.

A tough left winger who played for fourteen years in the NHL, all for Montreal teams; one year with the Maroons, and his last thirteen years with the Canadiens. Blake skated on the Punch Line with Maurice Richard and Elmer Lach.
He is best remembered, however, as the greatest coach in the history of the NHL. He coached the Montreal Canadiens from 1955 to 1968 and in that time led them to eight Stanley Cups, including five in a row, 1956-60.
Career 1932-48 - 578 games, 235 goals, 527 points. Hart Trophy and Ross Trophy 1939 (24 goals and 37 assists), Lady Byng Trophy 1946.

Doc BLANCHARD (USA)

AMERICAN FOOTBALL
Felix Anthony Blanchard Jr. b. 11 Dec 1924 McColl, South Carolina.

'Mr Inside' to Glenn Davis's 'Mr Outside' at the US Military Academy. These two led West Point to three straight unbeaten seasons and the teams were named AP national champions in 1944 and 1945. In those two years, Blanchard at full back averaged 5.9 yards per carry and in 1945 he won the Heisman Memorial Trophy. He also starred as a sprinter and shot putter at which in 1945 he was IC4A indoor champion. He never played professionally, as he fulfilled his military commitment after college by serving as a jet fighter pilot. He retired from the service in 1971 as a colonel.

Danny BLANCHFLOWER (UK)

FOOTBALL
Robert Dennis Blanchflower. b. 10 Feb 1926 Belfast.

One of the most thoughtful players of the post-war era, whose skills at right-half provided countless opportunities for his forwards. After joining Barnsley from Glentoran of the Irish League in 1948, he moved to Aston Villa in 1951, but only after joining Tottenham in December 1954 were his talents fully appreciated. He captained Spurs to the Cup and League double 1961, the FA Cup 1962 and the European Cup Winners' Cup 1963.
He was voted Footballer of the Year in 1958 and 1961. After winning a record 56 caps for Northern Ireland, a leg injury caused his retirement at the end of the 1963/4 season. Apart from a brief spell as manager of Chelsea, he concentrated on journalism, writing mainly for the *Sunday Express*. Unusually, for a top-name sportsman, he wrote his own copy but his career as a television commentator never flourished. He undoubtedly had all the necessary qualities but he refused to compromise his views in order to conform with the authorities. In more recent years he faced hard times.
His younger brother **Jackie** (b. 7 Mar 1933), who played for Manchester United and Northern Ireland, was injured in the Munich air crash of 1958.

Serge BLANCO (Fra)

RUGBY UNION

Serge Blanco. b. 31 Aug 1958 Caracas, Venezuela.

Playing 93 times for France since his début in 1980 he has the distinction of being the world's most capped player. He won 81 caps as a full back and 12 as a winger and his total of 38 international tries is a French record.

Brilliant in attack, he scored some of the greatest individual tries ever seen. Like many great attacking full backs he was sometimes inconsistent in defence, a quality which also marked his goal kicking. In the 1987 World Cup he scored the try which gave France victory over Australia in the semi-final and in 1990 he captained France on their tour of Australia when his try from 90 metres out in the second Test was rated as one of the greatest ever.

Born in Venezuela, he moved to France as a child and played for Biarritz throughout his career.

George BLANDA (USA)

AMERICAN FOOTBALL

George Frederick Blanda. b. 17 Sep 1927 Youngwood, Pennsylvania.

Blanda became more and more of a football legend as he became 'too old' to continue playing. Having played college football at Kentucky, he was drafted in the 12th round of the 1949 NFL draft, but rarely started at quarterback in the NFL with Chicago. In 1960 he joined the Houston Oilers of the nascent AFL and became a starter, leading the Oilers to three straight championship games, winning the AFL title in 1960 and 1961 and playing quarterback for them until 1967 when he was traded to the Oakland Raiders. With the Raiders his main duty initially was to kick field goals, but he often came on in relief for starter Daryle Lamonica and won several games in the last minutes when he was over 40 years old. Blanda became pro football's leading all-time scorer in 1971 and at his retirement in 1975 at age 48 had taken his points to 2002, still the all-time record, as is his total of 340 games played.

NFL career 1949-74: 26,920 yards from 1911 pass completions, 47.7%, 236TD.

Fanny BLANKERS-KOEN (Hol)

ATHLETICS

née Francina Elsje Koen. b. 26 Apr 1918 Amsterdam. Married her coach, the Dutch triple jumper Jan Blankers.

The heroine of the 1948 Olympics when she won four gold medals in London, at 100m, 200m, 80m hurdles and sprint relay. At the European Championships she won the same individual events in 1950, but took silver in the relay; having won gold at hurdles and relay in 1946 and bronze at 100m and 200m in 1938.

Her exceptional versatility is shown by the fact that she set 16 world records at eight different events, including two at 100y to 10.8 in 1944, three times at 11.5 for 100m 1943-50, 24.0 for 200m in 1950, three at 80m hurdles to 11.0 in 1948, three high jump marks at 1.67, 1.69 and 1.71 in one competition in 1943, long jump of 6.25 in 1943 and pentathlon of 4692 points in 1951 as well as two at 4x110y relay. She won 58 Dutch titles between 1936 and 1955 at individual events: 13 at 100m, 12 at 200m, 11 at 80m hurdles, 10 high jump, 9 long jump, two shot and one pentathlon. Her first Dutch record had been 2:29.0 for 800m in 1935 and she also competed at the Olympics in 1936 when she was fifth at high jump and sprint relay, and in 1952 when she failed to finish in the 80m hurdles through injury. Her children were born in 1942 and 1945. A statue was erected in her honour in Amsterdam.

Carol BLAZEJOWSKI (USA)

BASKETBALL

Carol Ann Blazejowski. b. 29 Sep 1956 Elizabeth, New Jersey.

'The Blaze' was one of the early American women's collegiate stars. She played at Montclair State (New Jersey) from 1974-8 and was renowned for her jump shot. She averaged 30.1 points per game for her career, finishing with averages of 33.5 and 38.6 in her final two seasons. She was an alternate to the 1976 Olympic team but in 1980 was named to the ill-fated US Olympic team which did not compete. She then signed a three-year contract with the New Jersey Gems of the Women's Basketball League. She averaged 30 ppg in her first season but the league subsequently folded. In 1979 she was the leader of the first US team to win a world championship.

Stefan BLÖCHER (Ger)

HOCKEY

Stefan Blöcher. b. 25 Feb 1960 Wiesbaden.

A forward with successively Limburger HC, Rot-Weiss Köln and SC Frankfurt 1880, he won 210 outdoor and 46 indoor caps. In 1988 he was appointed captain of the German team. He won Olympic silver medals in 1984 and 1988, a silver in 1982 and bronze 1986 in the World Cup and in the European Cup he won gold in 1978 and bronze in 1983 and 1987. He also won three gold medals in the Champions Trophy 1986-8.

Oleg BLOKHIN (USSR/Ukr)

FOOTBALL

Oleg Blokhin. b. 5 Nov 1952 Kiev.

From his début in 1972, he made a record 109 international appearances for the USSR, scoring 39 goals, also a national record. With them he won Olympic bronze 1972 (tied) and 1976, and played in the World Cup finals in 1982 and 1986. He was European Footballer of the Year in 1975.

He played for seven Dynamo Kiev USSR championship winning teams, scoring a goal for them in their 3-0 wins over Ferencváros in 1975 and over Atletico Madrid in 1986 in the finals of the European Cup-Winners' Cup, and all three goals in their two-leg win in the European Super Cup in 1975. He had been a student at the Kiev state institute of physical culture and ended his major career with Styen in Austria.

Stig BLOMQVIST (Swe)

RALLYING

Stig Blomqvist. b. 29 Jul 1946 Örebro.

World champion in 1984 and the winner of 14 races in the Championship series from 1970. A spectacular and versatile driver, he has a record seven wins in the Swedish Rally, 1971-3 , 1977 and 1979 in Saabs, 1982 and 1984 in Audi Quattros. He won the RAC Rally in 1971 in a two-stroke Saab with Arne Hertz as his co-driver and again with Björn Cederberg in an Audi Quattro in 1983.

Steve BLOOMER (UK)

FOOTBALL

Stephen Bloomer. b. 20 Jan 1874 Cradley Heath, Worcs, d. 16 Apr 1938 Derby.

A prolific scorer from the inside-right position whose 28 goals for England in 23 appearances (1895-1907) remained a record for 50 years. After playing in local minor leagues he joined Derby County in 1892 and twice was in their losing FA Cup Final team (1898-9) but because of injury he missed the 1903 Final when Derby again lost. Shortly after he left for Middlesbrough in 1906, Derby County were relegated but after four years with Middlesbrough he returned to Derby for a final three seasons and led them to the Second Division Championship in 1912 at the age of 38.

Despite his frail physique, he possessed an incredibly powerful shot and in 674 League and Cup games he scored a total of 394 goals. The main criticism of his game was that he was more concerned with adding to his personal goal tally than with providing scoring chances for his teammates. After playing his last game for Derby in 1914, he went to Berlin as a coach and was interned in Germany during World War I. After the war, he served Derby in various capacities until the time of his death although his duties at the Baseball Ground were interrupted at various times by coaching appointments in Canada, Spain and Holland. His daughter married Alfred Quantrill, another England international from Derby County.

Heather BLUNDELL (Aus) see McKAY

Colin BLYTHE (UK)

CRICKET

Colin Blythe. b. 30 May 1879 Deptford, Kent, d. 8 Nov 1917 Passchendaele, Belgium.

A classical slow left-arm bowler, who was killed in the Great War. He took 100 wickets or more in 14 of his 16 seasons with Kent, with a peak of 215 at 14.54 in 1909, despite suffering from epilepsy. He was a master of flight, and really formidable on 'sticky' wickets. In 1907 he had his most successful Test series, with 26 wickets at 10.38 against South Africa, and for Kent v Northants he took 17 wickets in a day (10-30 and 7-18).

19 Tests 1901-10: 183 runs at 9.63, HS 27; 100 wickets at 18.63, BB 8-59; 6 catches. First-class 1899-1914: 4443 runs at 9.87, HS 82; 2506 wickets at 16.81, BB 10-30; 206 catches.*

Chris BOARDMAN (UK)

CYCLING

Christopher Boardman. b. 26 Aug 1968 Clatterbridge, Wirral.

When Chris Boardman won the Olympic pursuit title in 1992, much attention was focused on his revolutionary Lotus bicycle. That perhaps distracted attention from some of the greatest riding ever seen at an Olympics. From a pre-Games best of 4:31.4, he set Olympic records in the preliminary rounds with times of 4:27.357 and 4:24.496, and the latter was later recognised as the world record for the distance, when the lists were rationalised in 1993. Boardman went even faster in the Olympic final and completed 4000m in about 4:22, but by then he had eased up and the race was over, because he achieved the unprecedented feat of catching his opponent, Jens Lehmann (Ger), who started half a lap ahead, at 4:11 to end the race.

Boardman won a Commonwealth bronze medal at team pursuit in 1986 and competed at the 1988 Olympics; he also won a series of national titles. In 1993 he prepared to attack the classic world record for the 1 mile. Six days before his attempt the Scot Graeme Obree smashed the record set by Francesco Moser at 51.151km in 1984, with 51.596km. Boardman was undaunted, however, and powered to a distance of 52.270km at Bordeaux on 23 Jul 1993. That day he was invited to join Miguel Induráin on the rostrum of the Tour de France which swept into the French city that day, and immediately began to receive offers to join the professional road racers.

Louis BOBET (Fra)

CYCLING

Louison Bobet. b. 13 Mar 1925 St Méen-le-Grand, d. 13 Mar 1983 Biarritz.

Bobet was a self-made rider, relying on tenacity rather than any natural abilities. He was a superb climber but at first was a poor time trialist until he willed himself to improve in that discipline and eventually became the first man to win three consecutive times in the Tour de France, 1953-5, having first worn the yellow jersey in 1948. In the peloton, he was the most highly respected rider, as much for his class and determination as for his skill. Once, while well behind in Liège-Bastogne-Liège during terrible weather (it was actually snowing), he rode on rather than quit. At the race banquet that night, he entered to a standing ovation from his fellow riders, one of whom announced, 'A great champion is here.'

He was world road race champion in 1954, and was also second in 1957 and 1958. His retirement was typical of his style. In the 1959 Tour, sick for many days, he forced himself to ride to the highest pass in the race, then got off his bike and bid the peloton farewell. It was said of him that there have been greater all-rounders, but no greater champions.

Other major victories: Milan-San Remo and Tour of Lombardy 1951; Paris-Nice and Grand Prix de Nations 1952; Milan-San Remo and Dauphiné-Libéré 1955; Paris-Roubaix 1956; Bordeaux-Paris 1959; King of the Mountains - Tour de France 1950, Giro d'Italia 1951.

Vsevolod BOBROV (USSR)

FOOTBALL

Vsevolod Bobrov. b. 1 Dec 1922 Mershansk, Tambov Oblast, d. 1 Jul 1979 Moscow.

A high-scoring centre-forward who captained the 1952 Olympic soccer team and also won an Olympic gold medal for ice hockey in 1956. He initially played for Dynamo Leningrad and after guesting for the Moscow Dynamo team which toured Britain in 1945 he joined the Red Army team which dominated Russian soccer in the post-war years. He later played for Spartak. Although the USSR team were eliminated by Yugoslavia in the first round of the 1952 Olympic soccer tournament, Bobrov's hat-trick forced a 5-5 draw and he scored the opening goal in the replay before Yugoslavia went on to win 3-1.

Anatoliy BOGDANOV (USSR)

SHOOTING

Anatoliy Bogdanov. b. 1 Jan 1931 Leningrad.

The first Soviet Olympic champion and the winner of 25 gold medals at the Olympic Games, World and European Championships. Only two years after taking up the sport he won the free rifle at the 1952 Olympics and four years later won his second Olympic gold in the small bore rifle, three positions. Between these two victories he performed brilliantly at the 1954 World Championships, winning six events and setting the first of his three world records in the free rifle.

Phil BOGGS (USA)

DIVING

Philip George Boggs. b. 29 Dec 1949 Akron, Ohio, d. 4 Jul 1990 Miami, Florida.

He won the first three world titles at springboard diving in 1973, 1975 and 1978, as well as the Olympic gold in 1976. While at Florida State University he was the NCAA highboard champion for 1971 and he won AAU springboard titles outdoors in 1975 and indoors 1972-5.
He was a captain in the US Air Force when he won his Olympic title. He left the service to go to the University of Michigan Law school, and has worked as a TV commentator on diving.

Wade BOGGS (USA)

BASEBALL

Wade Anthony Boggs. b. 15 Jun 1958 Omaha, Nebraska.

In the modern age when merely hitting .300 is considered superb batting, Boggs sported a lifetime average of .356 in seven years up to 1988. That has been surpassed by only three people in baseball history - Ty Cobb, Rogers Hornsby and Joe Jackson. Having started his third-base career in 1982 with the Boston Red Sox, when he batted .349, he did not fall below .300 until the 1992 season when he dropped to .259, his worst ever. He was afterwards traded to the New York Yankees. His peak average was .368 in 1985 and he set a major league record by getting 200 hits in seven consecutive seasons 1983-9. His career was interrupted when it was revealed that he had had a long-standing extra-marital affair with Margo Adams, who sued him for palimony support, and since that relevation in 1989, Boggs' batting ability has declined somewhat, although he made the All-Star team in 1993.
Career 1976-92: 2098 hits Avg. .338, HR 85, 687 RBI.

Svetlana BOGINSKAYA (USSR)

GYMNASTICS

Svetlana Boginskaya. b. 9 Feb 1973 Minsk, Belarus.

Reached the top in women's gymnastics with World and European all-round titles in 1989. In 1990 she retained her European title and became only the third woman at those championships to win gold medals at each of the four disciplines. She had made her international début in 1987, and at the 1988 Olympics was the individual bronze medallist at all-around, won gold medals at the horse vault and with the Soviet team, and silver for floor exercises. She competed for the Trudovye Rezervy sports society in Minsk, having taken up gymnastics at the age of six.

Brian BOITANO (USA)

FIGURE SKATING

Brian Anthony Boitano. b. 22 Oct 1963 Mountain View, Calfornia.

An adventurous skater who made history at the 1983 World Championships when he became the first person ever to land all six triple jumps (Salchow, Lutz, Axel, toe loop, loop and flip) in competition; he placed 7th . He won the first of his three US titles in 1985 and in 1986 he dethroned the Russian, Aleksandr Fadeyev, at the World Championships. A fall while attempting a quadruple loop ruined his chances of defending his world crown in 1987 but he recaptured the title in 1988 after earlier winning the Olympic gold medal. Like most modern Olympic ice skating champions he soon turned professional but is remembered not only as possibly the best technical skater of all-time but also for his outstanding artistry and athleticism. With other professionals he returned to competition under new rules in 1993.

Jean BOITEAUX (Fra)

SWIMMING

Jean Boiteaux. b. 20 Jun 1933 Marseille.

The first French Olympic gold medallist at swimming, when he was a surprise winner of the 400m freestyle title in 1952 in an Olympic record time of 4:30.7. His father leapt into the water to congratulate his son before some swimmers had even finished. Jean's mother (Bibienne Pellegry) had swum on the French 4x100m teams that placed fifth at both the 1924 and 1928 Olympics.

In 1950 he took silver medals at both 400m and 1500m in the European Championships. In 1951 he set European records at 400m, 500m, 800m and 1500m, with a world record at 4 x 200m relay. At individual and relay events he won a total of 44 French championships, retiring after his Olympic 6th place at 1500m in 1956.

Michael BONALLACK (UK)

GOLF

Michael Francis Bonallack. b. 31 Dec 1934 Chigwell, Essex.

A master of the short game, Bonallack was the greatest British amateur player of the modern era. He is the only man to have won the British Amateur three consecutive times, 1968-70, following his earlier victories in 1961 and 1965. He set a record by winning the English Amateur title five times, 1962-3, 1965, and 1967-8, and in the final in 1968 went round Ganton in 61 strokes. He was also four times English Amateur Stroke Play champion, 1964, 1968-9 and 1971. He played on eight consecutive Walker Cup teams, 1959-73, with his record: won 8, lost 14, halved 3; he was also a member of the 1957 team but did not play. He played seven times in the World Amateur Team Championship, 1960-72, winning with the GB & Ireland team in 1964. He succeeded Keith McKenzie as chairman of the Royal & Ancient in 1983. Awarded the OBE 1971. His sister **Sally** played for Britain in the Curtis Cup and was English Women's champion in 1968. His wife **Angela** (née Ward) was twice English Ladies' Champion, 1958 and 1963.

Olga BONDARENKO (USSR/Rus)

ATHLETICS

née Olga Krentser. b. 2 Jun 1960 Slavgorod, Altayskiy Kray.

Petite (1.54m, 41kg) distance runner with a formidable finishing kick, who won the European 3000m in 1986 and the Olympic 10,000m in 1988. She also won silver medals at the 1985 European Indoor 3000m, 1986 European 10,000m and the 1987 World Indoor 3000m. In 1985 she had won the European Cup 10,000m but misjudged the finish of the World Cup, kicking in with a lap to go and having to struggle on to third place. USSR champion 3000m 1985, 1987; 5000m 1985; 10,000m 1984-5, 1987.

Before her major championship success she ran world records for 10,000m in 1981 and 1984 as well as a world indoor best for

3000m of 8:42.3 in 1986. After three years out she returned to competition, and after second place in the CIS 10,000m she competed at the 1992 Olympics. A teacher, she competed for Volgograd SA.
Best times: 1500m 4:05.99 (1986), 3000m 8:33.99 (1986), 5000m 14:55.76 (1985), 10,000m 30:57.21 (1986).

Barry BONDS (USA)

BASEBALL

Barry Lamar Bonds. b. 24 Jul 1964 Riverside, California.

The son of Bobby Bonds (qv) he joined Pittsburgh Pirates in 1986 after the conclusion of his college career at Arizona State. After 7 years with the Pirates, he was signed by the San Francisco Giants, where his father was coach, for 1993, by when he was being freely discussed as the greatest player in the game. He led the National League in slugging percentage in 1990 (.565) and 1992 (.624) and was elected MVP each of those seasons. He is an outstanding outfielder, winner of Gold Gloves awards each year 1990-2.
Career 1986-92: 984 hits Avg. .275, HR 176, 556 RBI.

Bobby BONDS (USA)

BASEBALL

Bobby Lee Bonds. b. 15 Mar 1946 Riverside, California.

One of those players whose greatness never seemed to approach that predicted of him. Although he had an excellent career, it never seemed to be enough for his critics and did not match his extraordinary potential. Still, Bonds became the greatest combination of power and speed ever seen when he combined for 30 home runs and 30 stolen bases in five seasons (1969, 1973, 1975, 1977-8), the first player to do so more than once. His biggest weakness was his tendency to strikeout; he did that 187 times in 1969 for a major league record, and broke it with 189 in 1970. His other 'curse' was that he broke in as an outfielder with the San Francisco Giants and he was expected to be the next Willie Mays; great as he was, he could not quite satisfy the Giants' fans in that way. In his later years, Bonds was much travelled, playing in New York, California, Chicago (White Sox and Cubs), Texas, Cleveland, and St Louis.
Career 1968-81: 1886 hits Avg. .268, HR 332; SB 461.

André BONIFACE (Fra)

RUGBY UNION

André Boniface. b. 14 Aug 1934 Monfort-en-Chalosse, Londes.

Playing as a wing or centre he scored 11 tries in his 48 international appearances. His international career, which lasted 13 seasons 1954-66, was then the longest of any Frenchman although Francis Haget subsequently played for 14 seasons 1974-87. André Boniface was a sports shop owner. In 18 of his international matches his brother, **Guy** (b. 6 Mar 1937, d. 31 Oct 1967 in a car accident), was also playing in the French back division. Guy, who played with André for Mont-de-Marsan where he was a café proprietor, made a total of 35 international appearances.

Giampiero BONIPERTI (Ita)

FOOTBALL

Giampiero Boniperti. b. 4 Jul 1928 Barengo, Novara.

A versatile forward from Juventus who won 38 international caps 1946-60, and played in the 1950 and 1954 World Cup. On his international début in the 1946/7 season, Italy lost 5-1 to Austria and two years passed before he won his second cap. With Juventus he scored 177 goals in 444 games from 1947 to 1961 and won five League Championship medals and two Cup finals, captaining the team during the latter part of his career. At club and international level he played at centre-forward, inside-right and outside-right but never really specialised in any of these positions. He played at centre-forward in the 1950 World Cup and was inside-right, and captain, four years later. In the FA Anniversary match at Wembley in 1953 he scored twice for the Rest of the World against England.

He later became a highly successful businessman and president of Juventus.

David BOON (Aus)

CRICKET

David Clarence Boon. b. 29 Feb 1960 Launceston.

By the time that the Australian team came to England in 1993 David Boon was being recognised by his captain, Allan Border, as his team's premier batsman. He confirmed that on the tour, with three centuries in the first four Tests, his third being his 50th in first-class cricket. He may not have the style of some of his team-mates but his dependability either as an opener or as a number three has become more and more established. He is certainly Tasmania's most successful Test cricketer.
He exceeded 500 runs in a Test series for the first time against England in 1990/1, and did so again against India in 1991/2.
74 Tests 1984-93: 5314 runs at 43.91, 14 100s, HS 200; 73 catches.
142 One-day Ints: 4524 runs at 35.34, 5 100s HS 122; 36 catches.
First-class 1978-93: 14,503 runs at 45.75, 42 100s HS 227; 6 wickets; 176 catches.

Willie BOONE (UK)

RACKETS

William Robin Boone. b. 12 July 1950 Norwich, Norfolk.

After winning the 1968 Public Schools Championship for Eton he developed into the most consistent of current players. He was World champion from 1984 to 1986, British Open champion in 1984 and 1986 and winner of the British Amateur title eight times between 1976 and 1990. Remarkably, he was a finalist every year during this 15-year period. He also won the doubles nine times between 1975 and 1986.
A hard-hitting left-hander with a devastating service, he first challenged for the world title in 1979 when he failed to take a game off William Surtees. In 1984 he beat John Prenn (UK) in Montreal and then at Queen's to take the World Championship but two years later the title again passed to Prenn. He remains a top-class player and in 1991 won the US amateur title for both singles and doubles.

Allan BORDER (Aus)

CRICKET

Allan Robert Border. b. 27 Jul 1955 Cremorne, Sydney.

Border has displayed an astonishing level of consistency and fitness over his 16 years as an international cricketer, holding records for the most Test matches and one-day international matches played and the most runs and catches in Test cricket. Averaging 50 virtually throughout his Test career, he passed 10,000 runs and then Sunil Gavaskar's record number of runs in early 1993. He made his Test début against England in 1978. After three matches he was dropped for the 6th Test of that series, but thereafter has not missed a single one, playing in 142 consecutive Tests for Australia to July 1993.
From when he took over in 1984 to the fourth Test of the 1993 series against England, when his team ensured the retention of the Ashes, he captained Australia in 82 Tests (a world record), winning 27 of them. Border scored his 26th century and 2nd double century in Tests in the 4th Test against England in 1993.
He also captained Australia to win the World Cup in 1987. As a middle order left-handed batsman, he has frequently made runs when most needed and his resilience has been vital for his country, during a period in which there were several weak sides. His slow left-arm bowling has met with some success, notably his 7-46 and 4-50, remarkably the best ever figures in Tests by an Australian captain, against the West Indies at Sydney in 1989. He played in England for Essex in 1986 and 1988.
141 Tests 1978-93: 10,262 runs at 51.05, 25 100s, HS 205; 38 wickets at 38.84, BB 7-46; 140 catches.
255 One-day Ints: 6172 runs at 30.55, 3 100s HS 127; 65 wickets at 29.21, BB 3-20; 117 catches.*
First-class 1976-93: 23,947 runs at 51.72, 65 100s HS 205; 96 wickets at 38.11, BB 7-46; 320 catches.

Arne BORG (Swe)

SWIMMING

Arne Borg. b. 18 Aug 1901 Stockholm, d. 6 Nov 1987.

Borg set 32 world records between 1921 and 1929 at freestyle distances from 300y to 1 mile. His 400m best of 4:50.3 in 1925 was not bettered until 1931 and his 1500m best of 19:07.2 lasted for 11 years. That time came at the second European Championships, held in 1927, when he won all three freestyle events contested - 100m, 400m and 1500m, having won the latter two at the first European meeting in 1926.
At the Olympic Games in 1924 Borg was second at 400m and 1500m (with his twin brother Åke fourth and sixth respectively), and fourth at 100m with a bronze medal in the 4x200m relay. In 1928 he won the 1500m and was third at 400m.
A debonair and highly popular man, he loved his pleasures and did not like anything to get in their way. Thus he fell foul of the authorities when he avoided his military call-up to take a holiday in Spain. He was imprisoned on his return, but received such quantities of food and drink as presents that he gained 8 kilograms during his sentence.

Björn BORG (Swe)

TENNIS

Björn Rune Borg. b. 6 Jun 1956 Södertälje.

A superlative match player who completely dominated the game during his peak years. On grass, having been junior champion in 1972, he won Wimbledon for five successive years, 1976-80, and on clay courts he won the French Open a record six times, 1974-5, 1978-81, and was twice the winner of the Italian Open, 1974 and 1978. On clay he was a three-time winner of the US Pro title, 1974-6, and the only surfaces he never truly mastered were the American hard courts with their exceptionally high bounce. He reached the final of the US Open on four occasions but lost each time.
He was also the Masters champion in 1979 and 1980. He won his first Wimbledon title without losing a set in the tournament.
His contribution to Swedish tennis was immense and he led his country to their first ever Davis Cup triumph in 1975.
From 1972 to 1980 he won 37 of his 40 singles in Davis Cup competition and 7 of 15 doubles. He had 109 weeks ranked as the world's number one in 1977-81. At the end of 1981 he retired from serious tournament play and restricted himself to exhibitions and special matches. A succession of business failures led to a number of attempts at a comeback but each was unsuccessful and short-lived.
Borg had a powerful serve and his counter attacking topspin shots both on the forehand and on his double-handed backhand were as good as any in the history of the game.

Julius BOROS (USA)

GOLF

Julius Nicholas Boros. b. 3 Mar 1920 Fairfield, Connecticut.

Boros did not turn professional until he was 29, but had an excellent career, with 18 US PGA tour victories and wins in the US Open in 1952 and 1963 and the PGA in 1968, when at 48 he became the oldest ever winner. He led the PGA tour in money earnings in 1952 and 1955. From 1950 to 1970, Boros finished in the top ten nine times in the US Open, a record matched only by the likes of Hogan, Nicklaus, and Palmer.
He won 9, lost 3 and halved 4 of his 16 Ryder Cup matches , playing four times between 1959 and 1967. He was noted for his fluid, almost nonchalant, swing.

Jean BOROTRA (Fra)

TENNIS

Jean Robert Borotra. b. 13 Aug 1898 Arbonne, Basses-Pyrenées.

Universally known as the 'Bounding Basque' he was one of the 'Four Musketeers' who won the Davis Cup for France for six successive years 1927-32. Between 1922 and 1947 he won 36 (19 singles, 17 doubles) of his 54 Davis Cup rubbers. He won 13 doubles titles at the

major championships and also had a fine record in the singles, winning Wimbledon in 1924 and 1926, the Australian Championships in 1928 and the French title in 1931. His most impressive record was in Covered Court events where he won the French singles 12 times, the British title 11 times and was twice US champion.
He was a remarkably durable player: he played his final Davis Cup tie when he was approaching his 49th birthday and continued to play competitively until he was well into his eighties. He tied Wentworth Gore's record of playing at 35 Wimbledon Championships to his last appearance as the oldest ever competitor at 64 years 320 days in 1964, subsequently adding many more in the veteran's event. Borotra served as Minister of Sport 1940-2 before being imprisoned by the Germans and he was later awarded the Chevalier de la Legion d'Honneur.

Valeriy BORZOV (USSR/Ukraine)

ATHLETICS

Valeriy Filipovich Borzov. b. 20 Oct 1949 Sambor, near Lvov.

Olympic champion at both 100m and 200m in 1972, when he ran European records of 10.07 (in a quarter-final) and 20.00 respectively. He added an Olympic silver medal at the sprint relay in 1972 and two bronze medals, at 100m and relay, in 1976. He won three European 100m titles, 1969, 1971 and 1974, and the 200m in 1971, the sprint treble at the 1968 European Juniors, and 13 USSR titles, seven at 100m, six at 200m. Indoors he won seven European titles at 50m/60m, 1970-2 and 1974-7, showing amazing consistency by winning each of the last four in 6.58 or 6.59 secs. He also tied the world hand-timed best with 6.4 in 1968 and 1974.
He was the complete sprinter, strong in all aspects of the event; a fine starter, good pick-up, a smooth and relaxed style, and above all he had a supreme temperament. He studied biomechanics at the Kiev Institute of Physical Culture and married the great gymnast Lyudmila Turishcheva.

Mike BOSSY (Can)

ICE HOCKEY

Michael Bossy. b. 22 Jan 1957 Montreal, Québec.

'The Goal Machine', whose greatest claim to fame came in 1981 when he equalled the record of the great Maurice Richard with 50 goals in 50 games. Bossy broke in with the New York Islanders in 1977 and immediately his genius was evident. From 1980-3 he was the leader of the Islanders team which won four consecutive Stanley Cup titles. He retired after the 1986/7 season when a chronic back injury prevented him from playing anymore.
NHL career 1977-87: 752 games, 573 goals, 1,126 points. Playoffs: 129 games, 85 goals, 160 points. Best years: 1978/9: 69 goals; 1980/1: 68 goals. Lady Byng Trophy 1983-4, 1987; Smythe Trophy 1982.

Billy BOSTON (UK)

RUGBY LEAGUE

William John Boston. b. 6 Aug 1934 Cardiff, Wales.

A high-scoring winger who attracted the attention of League scouts while playing the Union code as a national serviceman. He signed for Wigan in 1953 and the following year became the first coloured British player to tour Australia. He won the first of his 31 Great Britain caps in the second Test against Australia and his four tries in the second Test against New Zealand equalled the individual try scoring record for a Test match. His total of 36 tries was also a new record for a tour of Australia.
Boston again toured Australia in 1962 when he scored a further 22 tries and he played in the World Cup tournaments in 1957 and 1960. He scored a career total of 560 tries, of which 482 were for Wigan. His speed and powerful hand-off made him one of the most spectacular players of his era. He played for Wigan in six Challenge Cup finals and later played occasionally for Blackpool Borough before becoming the landlord of a hotel next to Wigan's Central Park ground.

Ralph BOSTON (USA)

ATHLETICS

Ralph Harold Boston. b. 9 May 1939 Laurel, Mississippi.

Boston won a complete set of Olympic medals at the long jump: gold in 1960, silver in 1964 and bronze in 1968. He also won the Pan-American title in 1963 and 1967 and AAU titles outdoors six times from 1961 to 1966 as well as indoors in 1961.

He was the first long jumper to surpass Jesse Owens, when he jumped 8.21m at Walnut on 12 Aug 1960 and in all set six world records. With his second, 8.24 at Modesto on 27 May 1961, he became the first man to surpass 27 feet and finally set the mark at its pre-Beamon 8.35, which he achieved at Modesto on 29 May 1965. He recorded an even better jump of 8.49 at the US Olympic Trials in Los Angeles on 12 Sep 1964, but this had wind assistance over the permissible limit, at 2.6 m/s. While at Tennessee State University he won the NCAA long jump title in 1960.

Other bests: high jump 2.05m, triple jump 15.89m, 100y 9.6, 120y hurdles 13.7.

Naas BOTHA (SAf)

RUGBY UNION

Hendrik Egnatius Botha. b. 27 Feb 1958 Breyten, Transvaal.

Although his international career was curtailed by South Africa's exclusion from world rugby, he won 23 caps (1980-89) and on his country's return to the international game in 1992 he led the Springboks against New Zealand and Australia and later in the year captained the touring side to France and England, before announcing his retirement. He is South Africa's highest scorer in international matches and most capped fly-half, with 311 points in 28 games and a record 18 dropped goals, including three against South America in 1980 and against Ireland in 1981, both in Durban.

His superb kicking abilities attracted the attention of American Football managers and in 1983 he had a trial with the Dallas Cowboys with a view to turning professional. Nothing came of the idea and on his return he was reinstated by the South African Rugby Board.

His wife **Karen** (b. 17 Jan 1967, née Kruger) set the South African women's long jump record at 6.85m in 1990 and competed at the 1992 Olympics.

Ian BOTHAM (UK)

CRICKET

Ian Terence Botham. b. 24 Nov 1955 Heswall, Cheshire.

The charismatic all-rounder became a folk hero in England after his exploits in the 1981 Test series against Australia. He had quickly made his mark in Test cricket from his début in 1977, taking his 100th wicket just 2 years and 9 days later with hostile swing bowling. He achieved the double of 1000 runs and 100 wickets in a record 21 Tests, and went on to further records, with 2000 runs and 200 wickets in 42 Tests and 3000 runs and 300 wickets in 71. He reached a record number of wickets in Tests with his 326th in 1985, and although he added to that figure in seven years afterwards, at a much slower pace, he has been overtaken by others. For England against Pakistan at Lord's in 1978 he became the only player to score a century (108) and take eight wickets in an innings (8-34) in the same Test, and against India in 1980 achieved a unique century (114) and 13 wickets (6-58 and 7-48) in a Test match. In his later years his experience has been of value to England in one-day cricket, and on his day his majestic batting can turn any game. In 1985 he hit a record 80 sixes during a first-class season.

He captained England for 12 Tests 1980-1, but that included two tough series against West Indies, and he was unsuccessful. His form was affected and he stood down after two matches against Australia in 1981. He bounced back, however, with his greatest triumphs in the next four Tests. In the 3rd Test at Headingley came a match-winning 149 not out, scoring a hundred off only 87 balls; in the 4th a spell of five wickets for 1 run in 28 balls, in the 5th an even better hundred, his century coming off 86 balls; and in the 6th ten wickets in the match. In

1982 against India at Lord's he made 208, his 200 coming off 219 balls, the fastest Test double century ever.

He played for Somerset 1974-86 (captain 1984-5), leaving acrimoniously after the county had dispensed with the services of Vivian Richards and Joel Garner; Worcestershire 1987-91 and Durham 1992-3, announcing his retirement from first class-cricket in July 1993. He also played League football for Scunthorpe United as a striker. Awarded the OBE 1992.

102 Tests 1977-92: 5200 runs at 33.54, 14 100s HS 208; 383 wickets, at 28.40, BB 8-34; 120 catches.

116 One-day Ints: 2113 runs at 23.21, HS 79; 145 wickets at 28.54, BB 4-31; 36 catches.

First-class 1974-93: 19,399 runs at 33.97, 38 100s HS 228; 1172 wickets at 27.22, BB 8-34; 354 catches.

Jim BOTTOMLEY (USA)

BASEBALL

James Leroy Bottomley, b. 23 Apr 1900 Oglesby, Illinois, d. 11 Dec 1959 St Louis, Missouri.

'Sunny Jim' Bottomley was a first baseman with the St Louis Cardinals, except for three years with Cincinnati. He averaged .300 for eight years, and batted in 100 runs for six consecutive years 1924-9. He is perhaps best known for holding the major league record for most RBIs in a game - 12 in 1924. His biggest weakness was his fielding, and he led the National League in errors four times.

Career 1922-37: 2313 hits Avg. .310, HR 219; RBI 1422. Best season: 1925 - .367, 225 hits.

Mikhail BOTVINNIK (USSR)

CHESS

Mikhail Moiseyevich Botvinnik. b.17 Aug 1911 Kuokkala, Finland.

World chess champion from 1948, when uniquely the title went to the winner of a tournament, to 1957 when he lost to Vasiliy Smyslov. He regained the title from Smyslov in 1958, but lost to Mikhail Tal in 1960, and became the first to win for a third time by beating Tal in 1961. He lost to Tigran Petrosyan in 1963.

An electrical engineer and graduate of the Leningrad Polytechnic Institute, he was USSR champion in 1931, 1933, 1939, 1941, 1944-5 and 1952. He achieved chess master status in 1927, grandmaster in 1935 and international grandmaster in 1950. After achieving his doctorate in technical sciences in 1952, from 1955 he was a senior scientist at the USSR Research Institute for Electroenergetics and he received the Order of Lenin in 1957. The title of his 1981 autobiography was *Achieving the Aim*, a reflection of the dedication and very thorough preparation that he brought to his play.

Frank BOUCHER (Can)

ICE HOCKEY

Frank Boucher. b. 7 Oct 1901 Ottawa, Ontario, d. 12 Dec 1977 Kemptville, Ontario.

Considered by hockey experts to epitomise clean, textbook hockey, Boucher literally retired the Lady Byng trophy, as after winning it seven times in eight years 1928-31 and 1933-5, it was decided that the trophy should be given to him permanently. A replacement was struck, and although Boucher played for five more years, he never won it again. He was a center who played most of his career with the New York Rangers and became most famous centering the fabled line with Bill Cook at right wing and Bunny Cook at left wing. Before breaking into pro hockey, Boucher spent some time as a Mounty with the Royal Canadian Mounted Police. After his retirement, he coached the Rangers from 1938-48, and then served as their general manager for the next seven years.

NHL career 1921-38, 1943-4 - 557 games, 161 goals, 423 points. Best year: 1929/30: 36 assists, 62 points.

Lou BOUDREAU (USA)

BASEBALL

Louis Boudreau. b. 17 Jul 1917 Harvey, Illinois.

Boudreau played most of his career with

the Cleveland Indians, although he ended up by playing for two years with the Boston Red Sox. He was a playing manager for his last nine years with the Indians and later managed the Red Sox, the Athletics, and the Chicago Cubs. A superb fielding shortstop, he led the AL shortstops in fielding average eight times, in double plays five times, and in putouts four times. He was also an excellent hitter, batting over .300 four times.
Career 1938-52: 1779 hits Avg. .295, HR 68; RBI 789. Best seasons: 1944 - .327, 45 doubles; 1948 - .355.

Johnny BOWER (Can)

ICE HOCKEY

John William Bower. b. 8 Nov 1924 Prince Albert, Saskatchewan.

After playing goalie for many years in the American Hockey League with the Cleveland Barons, Bower played for 18 years in the NHL, retiring at 46, ancient for a hockey player. He broke in with the New York Rangers but was quickly sent back to the minors and then was traded to Toronto in 1958 and made his fame with the Maple Leafs. One of the toughest goalies of all time, playing despite multiple injuries; his face alone received over 200 stitches during his career.
NHL career 1953-70 - 549 games, 2.52 GAA, 37 shutouts. Vezina Trophy 1961, 1965.

Everett BOWMAN (USA)

RODEO

Everett Bowman. b. 12 Jul 1899 Hope, New Mexico, d. 25 Oct 1971 Arizona.

One of the pioneers of rodeo competition and a charter member of the Rodeo Association of America (in 1929), the forerunner of today's Professional Rodeo Cowboys Association. Had there been official competition in the 1920s, Bowman would have been world champion many times. From 1929 however he won the all-around world championship in 1935 and 1937, calf roping in 1929, 1935, and 1937, steer wrestling 1930, 1933, 1935 and 1938, and steer roping in 1937. He was the first president of the Cowboys Turtle Association, the first organisation of rodeo cowboys.

Geoffrey BOYCOTT (UK)

CRICKET

Geoffrey Boycott. b. 21 Oct 1940 Fitzwilliam, Yorkshire.

The most dedicated of batsmen, he achieved a record number of runs for England, and in his penultimate Test at Delhi on 23 Dec 1981 passed the world record total of Gary Sobers. He made his Yorkshire début in 1962 and two years later first played for England. He was an obvious first-choice opener for the next two decades, except for the period 1974-7 when he made himself unavailable for Test cricket. That was in the middle of a generally unsuccessful eight years as captain of Yorkshire. He returned to Tests against Australia in 1977, and on his home ground at Headingley became the first player to score his 100th first-class hundred in a Test match. He captained England four times as deputy for Mike Brearley in 1977-8.
He averaged over 50 in 19 seasons in England, including a record 11 consecutive years 1970-80, and is the only batsman to average more than 100 in two English seasons: with his best aggregate of 2503 runs at 100.12 in 1971 and again with 1538 runs at 102.53 in 1979. Awarded the OBE 1980.
Seen by many an an obsessively selfish player, and a man who was the the midst of many turmoils at Yorkshire County Cricket Club both as a player and as a committee member, his great batting was backed by profound knowledge of the game and he has become a most authoritative TV commentator.
108 Tests 1964-82: 8114 runs at 47.72, 33 100s HS 246; 7 wickets, BB 3-47; 33 catches.*
36 One-day Ints: 1082 runs at 36.06, 1 100 HS 105; 5 wickets at 21.00, BB 2-14; 5 catches.
First-class 1960-87: 43,423 runs at 42.86, 102 100s HS 262; 45 wickets at 32.02, BB 4-14; 264 catches.*

Cecil BOYD-ROCHFORT (UK)

HORSE RACING

(Sir) Cecil Boyd-Rochfort. b. 16 Apr 1887 Middleton Park, Co. Meath, Ireland, d. 17 Mar 1983 Kelnahard Castle, Co. Cavan.

The first British trainer to win over £1 million in career prize money, he was leading trainer in 1937-8, 1954-5 and 1958. He joined Atty Persse in 1906 and became assistant trainer to Captain R H Dewhurst in 1908. In 1912 he was appointed racing manager to Sir Ernest Cassel. He started training at Newmarket in 1921, based at Freemason Lodge from 1923, and in his 47 years as a trainer, 25 of them for the Royal Family, he won 13 classics. He won the St Leger six times and was especially noted for his stayers. His greatest horses included *Alcide* and *Meld*, and he had just one Derby winner, *Parthia* in 1959.
A tall and elegant Old Etonian, he was awarded the Croix de Guerre in World War I while serving in the Scots Guards with his elder brother Arthur, who won the VC and was later to breed many famous horses at the Tally-Ho Stud in Ireland. Boyd-Rochfort was created KCVO in the 1968 New Year Honours List. On his retirement at the end of that year he handed over to his stepson Henry Cecil.

Raelene BOYLE (Aus)

ATHLETICS

Raelene Ann Boyle. b. 24 Jun 1951 Victoria.

The Olympic silver medallist at 200m in both 1968 and 1972, she was one of the favourites in 1976, but was disqualified for two false starts in her semi-final. At 100m she was 4th in 1968 and 1976 and took the silver in 1972. At the Commonwealth Games she won a record nine medals, the sprint treble in 1970 and 1974, and after a silver at 200m in 1978 returned to win the 400m and take a silver at 4x400m in 1982. World relay records at 4x200m 1976 and 4x220y 1969. Australian champion at 100m and 200m 1970-3 and 1976-7, and at 400m 1980 and 1982.
Best times: 100m 11.20 (1968), 200m 22.45 (1972), 400m 51.08 (1982).

József BOZSIK (Hun)

FOOTBALL

József Bozsik. b. 28 Nov 1925 Budapest, d. 31 May 1978 Budapest

The greatest of all Hungarian half-backs and the general of the 'Magic Magyars' of the 1950s. He made his international début against Bulgaria in 1947 and played his 100th and final game for his country against Uruguay in 1962. He also played internationally as a centre-forward or inside-forward.
Beginning his career with Honvéd before the war, he won five post-war Championship medals with them. After winning an Olympic gold medal in 1952, he played in the World Cup in 1954 and 1958, but after helping Hungary qualify in 1962 he did not play in the finals that year. Possibly his greatest game was at Wembley in 1953 when he masterminded Hungary's 6-3 defeat of England to become the first Continental team ever to defeat England at home.
He was elected to the National Assembly in the early 1950s and unlike some of the touring Honvéd team he chose to return home after the 1956 uprising. After retirement, he opened a small shop in Budapest before taking up an appointment as Honvéd's coach in 1966. He was a demanding task master and soon resigned when it became apparent that his advice was being ignored. He subsequently declined many lucrative offers to coach abroad.

Jack BRABHAM (Aus)

MOTOR RACING

John Arthur Brabham. b. 2 Apr 1926 Hurstville, NSW.

In 1966 he became the first man to win the world drivers' championship in a car of his own design, having previously won for Cooper-Climax in 1959 and 1960. In his world championship career from 1955 to 1970 he won 14 Grand Prix races from 126 starts, totalling 261 points.
Having studied engineering, he began racing in midget speedway cars in Australia, winning national titles 1948-51.

He came to England in 1955, working with Charles and John Cooper, and with their support built himself a Cooper-Bristol, with which he made his World Championship début in the 1955 British Grand Prix. His first championship wins were the Monaco and British GP in 1959, when he won a closely contested world title. In 1960 he dominated the Formula One scene, winning five consecutive races. With his designer Ron Tauranac he introduced the Brabham car to Formula One in 1962. He was awarded the OBE in 1966 and knighted in 1979.
A tough, reclusive man 'Black Jack' was fiercely competitive throughout his career. His sons, Gary, David and Geoff are all racing drivers. At Le Mans in 1993 **Geoff** (b. 20 Mar 1952) drove the winning car, while David won the GT class.

James BRADDOCK (USA)

BOXING

James Joseph Braddock. b. 7 Jun 1906 New York, d. 29 Nov 1974 North Bergen, New Jersey.

The 'Cinderella Man' was one of the most unlikely of heavyweight champions. He began fighting professionally in 1926 as a welterweight and gradually added weight until he fought as a heavyweight in 1930. He retired in 1933 and worked as a docker in Hoboken. After a year out, however, the depression caused his return. He won three fights to become a contender, and in 1935 overcame quoted odds of 10-1 to defeat Max Baer and win the world heavyweight title. Braddock never successfully defended his title, losing in 1937 to Joe Louis. He fought once more and then retired.
Career record: W - 46 (27), L - 23, D -4.

Bill BRADLEY (USA)

BASKETBALL

William Warren Bradley. b. 28 Jul 1943 St Louis, Missouri.

A renaissance man if ever there was one, Bill Bradley was the greatest college basketball player of the mid-1960s, averaging 30.1 points per game in his three years at Princeton and wining an Olympic gold medal in 1964. In 1965 he became the first basketball player to win the Sullivan Award. Eschewing the normal route of immediate pro stardom, he instead accepted a Rhodes Scholarship to study at Oxford. There he played occasionally in European leagues and found that he missed the competition of top-flight basketball. He joined the New York Knicks in the middle of the 1967/8 season amidst much media hype. He was basically a disappointment that first season and it was attributed to the fact that, at 6' 5" and of only average speed, he didn't fit in at either guard or forward. Eventually, however, he became a consummate team player and helped the New York Knicks to win two NBA championships in his 11-year pro career to 1977. He was elected to the US Senate from New Jersey in 1978.

Pat BRADLEY (USA)

GOLF

Patricia Bradley. b. 24 Mar 1951 Westford, Massachussets.

In 1986 Pat Bradley broke the women's earnings record for professional golf, and has been the first to pass successive career milestones of $2 million, $3 million and $4 million. Until her great year of 1986 when she won three majors, the LPGA, Dinah Shore and her second successive du Maurier Classic, she had been a highly consistent performer on the tour but without achieving eminence. She was, however, in the top ten money winners each year from 1976 to 1987 and headed the list in 1983 and 1986-7. After suffering from hyperthyroidism in 1988 she returned to top the list again in 1989 and 1991. She had won the Peter Jackson Classic in 1980 and the US Open in 1981.
Her first important title was the New Hampshire Amateur in 1967 when she showed much promise at several sports. Concentrating on golf she was named an All-American in 1970 while at Florida International University, from which she graduated in physical education.
LPGA career earnings 1974-92: $4,347,706 with 31 victories.

Don BRADMAN (Aus)

CRICKET

(Sir) Donald George Bradman. b. 27 Aug 1908 Cootamundra, New South Wales

His prodigious scoring achievements can leave no doubt about his status as the greatest batsman who ever lived. He averaged very nearly 100 throughout his career, failing to achieve that in Tests only when he was bowled by Eric Hollies for 0 on his emotional farewell at The Oval in 1948. The keen eye and exceptional technique and concentration of the Little Masters (he was 1.70m *5' 7"*) brought him all imaginable batting records in his first-class career which started with a century on his début for New South Wales in 1927. He made his Test début against the visiting England team a year later, making 18 and 1 in the First Test. He was omitted for one match, but returned with 79 and 112, and was thereafter a fixture in the Australian side until his retirement. He moved to South Australia, whom he captained from 1935 to 1948.

His century in every 2.9 innings played is a far higher rate than any other great batsman, and his 100s include a record 37 over 200 and 6 over 300 with the then highest ever score of 452* (in 6 hrs 55 mins) for New South Wales v Queensland at Sydney on 4 and 6 Jan 1930. Later that year he made the first of his four hugely successful tours of England, when he started with 236 at Worcester, and after a century in the 1st Test and a double hundred in the 2nd he scored 334 in 383 mins in the 3rd at 21 years 318 days. His aggregate of 974 runs at 139.14 in the five matches remains the all-time Test record. On that tour he scored 2960 runs at 98.66 in first-class matches and scored over 2000 runs on his three other tours to England. He captained Australia in 24 Tests 1936-48, winning 15 and losing 3.

He scored over 1000 runs 12 times in the limited Australian first-class seasons, with a record aggregate in just his second season, and in 1938/9 he tied the record with six successive centuries in first-class cricket. In his Sheffield Shield career he scored 8926 runs at 110.19. He was knighted in 1949 for his services to cricket and made a Companion of the Order of Australia in 1979. He has been a successful stockbroker and businessman and a quiet but most significant influence on cricket. He has written several books and served two three-year terms as chairman of the Australian Cricket Board.

52 Tests 1928-48: 6996 runs at 99.94, 29 100s HS 334; 2 wickets; 32 catches.
First-class 1927-49: 28,067 runs at 95.14, 117 100s HS 452; 36 wickets at 37.97, BB 3-35; 131 catches, 1 stumping.*

Don Bradman - first-class career

Year	*Country*	*Runs*	*Average*	*100s*
1927/8	Aus	416	46.22	2
1928/9	Aus	1690	93.88	7
1929/30	Aus	1586	113.28	5
1930	Eng	2960	98.66	10
1930/1	Aus	1422	79.00	5
1931/2	Aus	1403	116.91	7
1932/3	Aus	1171	61.63	3
1933/4	Aus	1192	132.44	5
1934	Eng	2020	84.16	7
1935/6	Aus	1173	130.33	4
1936/7	Aus	1522	86.22	6
1937/8	Aus	1437	89.81	7
1938	Eng	2429	115.66	13
1938/9	Aus	919	153.16	6
1939/40	Aus	1475	122.91	5
1940/1	Aus	18	4.50	-
1945/6	Aus	232	116.00	1
1946/7	Aus	1032	79.38	4
1947/8	Aus	1296	129.60	8
1948	Eng	2428	89.92	11
1948/9	Aus	216	54.00	1

Terry BRADSHAW (USA)

AMERICAN FOOTBALL

Terry Paxton Bradshaw. b. 2 Sep 1948 Shreveport, Louisiana.

The quarterback of one of the greatest football teams ever, the Pittsburgh Steelers of the 1970s. Bradshaw played high school football in Louisiana where he also set a national high school record in the javelin (74.66m 1966), and collegiately at Louisiana Tech. He was the first player chosen in the 1970 NFL draft, but was not an immediate success as a quarterback. However, the Steelers, who had been a poor team for many years, were building a dynasty and Bradshaw, who possessed a

rifle arm and great athletic abilities, proved to be the perfect man for the team. Under his leadership the Steelers won eight division titles and four Super Bowls, 1974-5, and 1978-9, at the time a record. He retired in 1984 because of elbow injuries.
Bradshaw's first marriage was to Melissa Babish, a former Miss Teen-Age America, while his second was to well-known Olympic figure skater, JoJo Starbuck. Both ended in divorce and he has subsequently remarried. He is now a popular football announcer on television.
NFL career 1949-74: 27,989 yards from 2105 pass completions, 54.0%, 212 TD.

Liam BRADY (Ire)

FOOTBALL
William Brady. b. 13 Feb 1956 Dublin.

One of the most gifted footballers ever to play for Ireland, for whom he made a record 72 international appearances between 1974 and 1990. Sadly he never had the opportunity to play in a World Cup competition or indeed the finals of any international competition. He came to England to make his Football League début at the age of 17 with Arsenal, for whom he played in midfield in three successive FA Cup finals 1978-80, but was only on the winning team in 1979. He was also a member of the team which lost the 1980 European Cup Winners' Cup to Valencia on penalties.
In 1980 he went to Italy, where he played for seven years, successively with Juventus (guiding them to two League championships), Sampdoria, Internazionale and Ascoli, before returning to England to play for West Ham. He was elected Football Writers' Player of the Year in Britain in 1979. A highly skilful playmaker, particularly strong with his left foot.

Lyudmila BRAGINA (USSR)

ATHLETICS
Lyudmila Ivanovna Bragina. b. 24 Jul 1943 Sverdlovsk.

Bragina ushered in a new era in women's distance running when she set world records at 1500m in the heat, semi-final and final of the 1972 Olympic Games in Munich with times of 4:06.47, 4:05.07 and 4:01.38. Before the Games she had set her first world record, 4:06.9 in Moscow. At 3000m she was the first woman to break 9 minutes, with 8:53.0 in 1972 and ran the first record recognised by the IAAF at this distance, 8:52.74 in 1974. She took an astonishing 18.28 secs off Grete Waitz's record, when she ran 8:27.12 to win for USSR v USA in 1976.
At 1500m she was 4th in 1969 and 6th in 1971 at European Championships, third in the European Cup in 1970 and 1973, USSR champion in 1968-70 and 1972-4, and returned to the Olympics for fifth place in 1976. At 3000m she won the 1974 European silver medal, and in 1977 won the European Cup and was second in the World Cup.

Alberto BRAGLIA (Italy)

GYMNASTICS
Alberto Braglia. b. 23 Mar 1883 Campogallano, Modena, d. 5 Feb 1954.

Braglia was the Olympic champion at combined exercises in 1908 and 1912, when he also won a team silver. In 1906 he had also won a silver and a bronze medal at the all-round contests. He joined a circus as an acrobat in 1912 and was chief coach to the 1932 Italian Olympic team, which was the most successful of all Italian teams.

James BRAID (UK)

GOLF
James Braid. b. 6 Feb 1870 Earlsferry, Fifeshire, d. 27 Nov 1950 London.

The first man to win the British Open five times: 1903, 1905-06, 1908 and 1910; he was also second thrice. He was a tall, quiet man who drove the ball great distances. At the turn of the century he was one of the 'Great Triumvirate' with J H Taylor and Harry Vardon. Braid was a founding member of the British PGA, whose match-play championship he won four times, 1903, 1905, 1907 and 1911. He was a joiner by trade before going to London as a club-maker in 1893 and turning professional in 1896. He served as the professional at Walton Heath for 45 years, helping make it one of England's finest courses, and was famed as a golf course architect.

Gerhardt BRAND (SAf)

RUGBY UNION

Gerhardt Hamilton Brand. b. 8 Oct 1906 Cape Town.

In 46 internationals for the Springboks from 1928 to 1938 he amassed a record 293 points, all but six from the boot. Having played his early rugby as a half back or three-quarter, he took up the full back position when he started playing for Western Province. He became not only a great kicker but a fine defensive player. On the 1931/2 Springbok tour of Britain he dropped a goal against England that was measured at 85 yards from kick to landing.

Mike BREARLEY (UK)

CRICKET

John Michael Brearley. b. 28 Apr 1942 Harrow, Middlesex.

Although he was a good-class county batsman, Brearley did not fulfil his early batting promise in Tests. He gained his place for his batting, but once he had taken over the England captaincy from Tony Greig in 1977, he played simply because he was a genius as a captain; an inspiration to his team and a great communicator. He won 18 and lost 4 of his 31 matches as captain. He may have been fortunate that many of those wins were against Australian teams weakened by defections to World Series cricket, but his return in 1981 to take over from Ian Botham was the stuff of legend as he helped to revitalise Botham and the team, winning three of the four Tests. He scored a record 4310 runs in his four years at Cambridge where he also kept wicket and took a 1st in Classics. In 1964 he scored 2178 runs at 44.44 and was voted Best Young Cricketer of the Year. He captained the England under-23 team to Pakistan in 1966/7, where he made his highest ever score of 312*. Remarkably that tour was in the middle of a period when he did not play first-class cricket but trained as a psychologist and taught philosophy at the University of California and Newcastle University. He returned to full-time cricket when asked to take on the Middlesex captaincy in 1971, and had considerable success in his 12 years in charge, during which time the county won 3 Championships and shared another, and 2 Gillette Cups. Awarded the OBE in 1978.

39 Tests 1976-81: 1442 runs at 22.88, HS 91; 52 catches.
25 One-day Ints: 510 runs at 24.28, HS 78; 12 catches.
First-class 1961-82: 25,185 runs at 37.81, 45 100s HS 312; 3 wickets; 418 catches, 12 stumpings.*

Scobie BREASLEY (Aus)

HORSE RACING

Arthur Edward Breasley. b. 7 May 1914 Wagga Wagga.

After riding more than 1000 winners in Australia, where he was champion jockey thrice, Breasley went to England in 1950. There, as first jockey for Noel Cannon, he rode 139 winners in his first two years, including the 1951 2000 Guineas winner *Ki Ming*, but returned to Australia in 1952. However, he was back in 1953 and remained to be champion jockey four times, 1957, 1961-3, exceeding 100 winners in a year each year from 1955 to 1965 and in 1967, and reaching a peak of 179 in 1962. He was first jockey for Sir Gordon Richards from 1956. A master of the art of waiting, he retired in 1968 with a total of 2161 winners from 9716 starts in Britain, including two Epsom Derbys: *Santa Claus* 1964, *Charlottown* 1966 (when at 25 he was the oldest ever winning jockey).
He trained at Epsom for six years, and then in France and the USA, but settled in the West Indies in 1980. In Australia he was apprenticed to Pat Quinlan in 1928, rode his first winner that year, and his first big race win was in the 1930 Sydney Metropolitan at the age of 16. He rode five winners of the Caulfield Cup, 1942-5 and 1952.

Harry BREECHEN (USA)

BASEBALL

Harry David Breechen. b. 14 Oct 1914 Broken Bow, Oklahoma.

Harry 'The Cat' Breechen played his entire career in St Louis, with the Cardinals 1940-52 and with the Browns in 1953. His finest moments came in the biggest games of all, as he won four games and lost one in three World Series with an ERA of 0.83, the second-best ever. His peak fame came in 1946 when he pitched the Cardinals to three victories.
Career pitching: ERA 2.92; W-L 133-92. Best season: 1948 - 20-7, 2.24.

Andreas BREHME (FRG)

FOOTBALL

Andreas Brehme. b. 9 Nov 1960 Hamburg.

A defender who scored from a penalty to enable West Germany to beat Argentina 1-0 in the 1990 World Cup Final. He also played in the team that were runners-up in 1986. From Barmbeck-Uhlenhorst, he moved to Saarbrücken FC 1980, FC Kaiserslautern 1981-6 and to Bayern Munich in 1986, helping them to win the League title that year. He made his international début in 1984 and in that year also played at the Olympic Games. By 1992 he had played in 74 international matches (with 8 goals) for Germany. In 1988 he went to Italy to play for Inter Milan, helping them to win the Italian League in 1989 and the UEFA Cup 1991.

Paul BREITNER (FRG)

FOOTBALL

Paul Breitner. b. 5 Sep 1951 Kolbermoor.

An attacking left-back for West Germany's World Cup winning team in 1974, scoring goals against Chile and Yugoslavia and from a penalty against Holland in the final. Earlier he had played a vital rôle in West Germany's victory in the 1972 European Championship and was a member of the Bayern Munich team which won the 1974 European Cup. At the end of the 1974 season he moved to Real Madrid but returned to Germany with Eintracht Brunswick in 1977 as a midfield player. He later played again for Bayern.
A maverick on and off the field, he had said that he would not play again for Germany after 1974, but did and scored Germany's only goal in their 3-1 defeat by Italy in the 1982 World Cup final. He played in 48 internationals for Germany.

Hallgeir BRENDEN (Nor)

NORDIC SKIING

Hallgeir Brenden. b. 10 Feb 1929 Tyrsil.

Cross-country skier, who won the Olympic gold at 18km in 1952 and 15km in 1956, with silver medals on the Norwegian relay team in 1952 and 1960. He won 12 Norwegian titles between 1951 and 1961, 6 at 15 or 18km, 3 at 30km and 3 relay. A farmer and lumberjack, he was also an international athlete, who won Norwegian 3000m steeplechase titles in 1953 and 1954, with a best of 8:54.6 in 1954.

Roger BRESNAHAN (USA)

BASEBALL

Roger Philip Bresnahan. b. 11 Jun 1879 Toledo, Ohio, d. 4 Dec 1944 Toledo.

One of the first great catchers in major league baseball. He is credited with introducing the use of shinguards for catchers, although that is disputed by some. He played for six different teams in his career, but most of his best years came with the New York Giants1902-08 when he caught Christy Mathewson and Joe McGinnity, and helped the Giants win pennants in 1904 and 1905. In 1945, Bresnahan became the first catcher elected to the Hall of Fame. He claimed (incorrectly) that he was born in Tralee, Ireland, and was thus nicknamed 'The Duke of Tralee'.
Career 1897-1915: 1251 hits Avg. .279.

George BRETT (USA)

BASEBALL

George Howard Brett. b. 15 May 1953 Glendale, West Virginia.

During his long career with the Kansas

City Royals, Brett has established himself as the greatest hitting third baseman in baseball history, although in recent years he has played more often at first. He batted over .300 eleven times between 1975 and 1990. His greatest year was 1980, when he became the first player since Ted Williams to seriously flirt with batting .400, finishing the season at .390 and with 118 RBI; he was an obvious choice for AL MVP that year. Three times, Brett has led the AL in hitting, his most recent being in 1990, when, supposedly in the twilight of his career, he batted .329. Late in the 1992 season he became the 18th major leaguer to record 3000 hits, with season's bests of 215 in 1976 and 212 in 1979, and in May 1993 he took his career home runs past 300.

Career 1971-92: 3005 hits Avg. .307, HR 298; RBI 1520.

Siegfried BRIETZKE (GDR)

ROWING

Siegfried Brietzke. b. 12 Jun 1952 Rostock.

Brietzke earned the first of three Olympic gold medals in 1972 in the coxless pairs with Wolfgang Mager and then won twice at coxless fours. In 1976 he was joined by Mager, Andreas Decker and Stefan Semmlerand, and in 1980 it was the same team with Jürgen Thiele replacing Mager. Brietzke also won world coxless fours titles in 1977 and 1979, and the coxless pairs with Mager in 1975, before becoming a coach.

Barry BRIGGS (NZ)

SPEEDWAY

Barry Briggs. b. 30 Dec 1934 Christchurch.

World speedway champion in 1957, 1958, 1964 and 1966 and runner-up in 1962, 1968 and 1969, he made a record 17 consecutive appearances in the World Championship finals 1954-70, and also rode in 1972, setting a competition record of 201 points in 87 races. The only person to take a point off Briggs in his four winning years was Jack Geran who beat him in a heat in 1957. Other successes included two wins in the World Team championship for Great Britain, 1968 and 1971, and for New Zealand in 1979; six consecutive victories in the British League Riders' Championship 1965-70; and seven wins in the British League Team Championship: five with Wimbledon and one each with Southampton and Swindon.

He came to England from his native New Zealand in 1952 and rode for Wimbledon, New Cross, Southampton, Swindon, and then Wimbledon again before finally joining Hull. He retired from British League racing at the end of the 1972 season but returned in 1974 to spend two seasons with Wimbledon. After riding for Hull in 1976 he finally ended his career. He was awarded the MBE for his services to the sport in 1973, the first speedway rider to be so honoured.

Karen BRIGGS (UK)

JUDO

Karen Briggs. b. 11 Apr 1963 Hull, Yorkshire.

Britain's most successful judo player at World championships with four titles: under 48kg in 1982, 1984, 1986 and 1989. She was also European champion in 1982-4 and 1986-7 and won the Japanese Open title 1983-6 and 1988.

Debbie BRILL (Canada)

ATHLETICS

Deborah Brill. b. 10 Mar 1953 Mission, British Columbia.

The first woman to use the 'flop' style effectively at the high jump as she pioneered the 'Brill bend' in 1967. She became the youngest ever Commonwealth champion in 1970 at 17 years 137 days, took the silver medal in 1978 and won again in 1982. Despite 'dropping out' as a hippy for a while, between 1970 and 1984 she set 17 Commonwealth high jump records, as well as eight indoor marks equalling or bettering the record, the most for any athlete at any event. After the birth of her son Neil in 1981 she set a world indoor best at 1.99m in 1982 and had an outdoor peak of 1.98 in 1984. She made four Canadian Olympic teams, although she was unable to compete in 1980 due to the boycott, but her best placing was only 5th in 1984. Pan-American champion in 1971, World Cup winner in 1979 and 11 times Canadian champion outdoors.

Frankie BRIMSEK (Can)

ICE HOCKEY

Francis Charles Brimsek. b. 26 Sep 1915 Eveleth, Minnesota.

Brimsek replaced Tiny Thompson, a well-respected netminder for the Boston Bruins in 1938, and the fans resented the newcomer. But Brimsek silenced them quickly with six shutouts in seven games during his first 12 games in the NHL. Thus he became 'Mister Zero'. During that stretch he recorded 231 consecutive minutes of scoreless goaltending. He was known for his lightning reflexes with his glove hand, although his footwork was only ordinary. He was also the first truly outstanding American to make it in the Canadian-dominated NHL.

NHL career 1938-50 - 514 games, 2.70 GAA, 40 shutouts. Vezina Trophy 1939, 1942; Calder Trophy 1939.

Valerie BRISCO (USA)

ATHLETICS

Valerie Brisco. b. 6 Jul 1960 Greenwood, Mississippi.

As Valerie Brisco-Hooks (she was formerly married to sprinter Alvin Hooks) she won three Olympic gold medals in 1984, a feat previously achieved by only three other women. Her victory celebration with coach Bob Kersee was especially ecstatic. She ran her best ever times to take the Olympic titles at 200m 21.81 and 400m 48.83 and her third gold was at the 4 x 400m relay.

Her first international success was a sprint relay gold and fourth place at 200m in the 1979 Pan-American Games, but her bests that year of 23.16 (and 22.53w) for 200m and 52.08 for 400m were not improved until her sensational breakthrough in 1984. She had given birth to a son in 1982. She continued competing until 1989, but although regularly highly ranked in the world did not quite recapture the brilliance of 1984. On the US 4 x 400m relay team she won Pan-American gold and World bronze in 1987, and an Olympic silver in 1988 after placing fourth in the individual 400m. She was TAC 400m champion in 1984 and at 200m indoors in 1984-5. Her best time for 100m was 10.99 (1986).

Eric BRISTOW (UK)

DARTS

Eric John Bristow. b. 25 Apr 1957 Stoke Newington, London.

'The Crafty Cockney' became the leading player when darts reached its peak popularity as a television sport in the early 1980s. He was a precocious talent, making his England début at 18 and taking over from John Lowe as World No. 1 in January 1980. In that year a film of his lifestyle *Arrows* was released.

Bristow has most wins in the World Masters (1977, 1979, 1981, 1983-4), the World Professional Championships (1980-1, 1984-6), World Matchplay (1985 and 1988), British Open (1978, 1981, 1983, 1985-6) and the World Cup singles (1983, 1985, 1987, 1989) and has played on seven winning England teams in the latter tournament. He also won the *News of the World* Championship in 1983-4, the British Matchplay in 1982-3 and 1986, and with Peter Locke the World Pairs in 1987. In addition to his five wins he has also been beaten in five World Championship finals. He was awarded the MBE in 1989.

Janette BRITTIN (UK)

CRICKET

Janette Ann Brittin. b. 4 Jul 1959.

England's most-capped woman cricketer, playing in 19 Tests and 37 one-day internationals. A fluent opening bat, she scored her first Test century, 144*, in the 1st Test against New Zealand at Headingley in 1984. In the subsequent two Tests of that series her scores were 96, 63 and 35, for an overall average of 112.67, the highest for a woman in a three-match Test series. She also proved to be a useful occasional spin-

ner and took 3-27 in the 2nd Test against Australia in 1984/5. Her 138* against the International XI at Hamilton in January 1982 is the highest ever in the World Cup by an England player. She is now the second highest run-scorer in women's Test cricket and the highest ever in one-day internationals. She has also played hockey for England, and is a sales administrator for British Airways.
19 Tests 1979-92: 1193 runs at 45.88, 3 100s; 9 wickets at 46.11.
37 One-day Ints: 1186 runs at 35.93, 2 100s; 8 wickets at 14.2.

Punch BROADBENT (Can)

ICE HOCKEY
Harry Broadbent. b. 13 Jul 1892 Ottawa, Ontario, d. 6 Mar 1971 Ottawa.

Broadbent earned his nickname of Punch because of the power he packed in his fists. But he was also well known as a prolific goal scorer and in 1922, set a record which lasted until Gretzky when he scored goals in 16 consecutive games. He played right wing for four Stanley Cup winners, three with the Ottawa Senators and one with the Montreal Maroons. He also played for the New York Americans.
NHL career 302 games, 124 goals, 168 points. Ross Trophy 1922 (32 goals, 46 points).

Lou BROCK (USA)

BASEBALL
Louis Clark Brock. b. 18 Jun 1939 El Dorado, Arkansas.

The greatest base-stealer ever before the Ricky Henderson era. Brock began his career in 1961 with the Chicago Cubs, but in 1964 he was traded to the St Louis Cardinals for Ernie Broglio, in what was considered one of the most lopsided trades in baseball history, and stayed there for the rest of his career. During that time, he recorded over 3,000 hits. As a lead-off batter, he batted almost .300 lifetime, and in 1974, as well as batting .306, he broke Maury Wills' record for stolen bases in a season when he pilfered 118. At his retirement, Brock held the major league record for stolen bases in a career with 1730. Henderson eventually broke both records.
Career 1961-79: 3023 hits Avg. .293, HR 149; SB 1730.

Walter BRODA (Can)

ICE HOCKEY
Walter Broda. b. 15 May 1914 Brandon, Manitoba, d. 17 Oct 1972 Toronto, Ontario.

Except for two years off to serve in World War II, Turk Broda served as the goalkeeper for the Toronto Maple Leafs for 16 years, helping them to win six Stanley Cups. Large, chubby, and rather slow, he did not look like a professional goalie, but he was one of the greatest ever and was renowned for playing his best in the biggest games and at the most critical moments of those games. After his playing days, he coached minor league hockey until his death.
Career 1936-52 - 629 games, 2.53 GAA, 62 shutouts. Vezina Trophy 1941, 1948

John BROMWICH (Aus)

TENNIS
John Edward Bromwich. b. 14 Nov 1918 Sydney, New South Wales.

One of the great doubles players who was denied further honours by World War II. His only major singles victories were at the Australian Championships (1939, 1946) but with countryman Adrian Quist he formed an outstanding doubles partnership. They won the Australian title on eight successive occasions, 1938-40 and 1946-50, with the War causing the cancelling of the Championships in 1941-5. They were also US champions in 1939, won Wimbledon in 1950 and only lost once in 21 Davis Cup rubbers. Bromwich also won 19 of 31 Davis Cup singles. He had some notable doubles successes with other partners, winning the 1948 Wimbledon and 1950 US titles with Frank Sedgeman and the 1949 US title with Bill Sidwell. His hopes of the doubles Grand Slam in 1950 were spoiled when he and Quist went out in the semi-finals at the French Championships. He also had a fine

record in the mixed doubles. After winning the Australian title with J Wilson in 1938, he partnered Louise Brough after the war and together they won the 1947 US, and 1947 and 1948 Wimbledon titles.
With his softly strung racket and two-handed forehand, Bromwich was a distinctly unorthodox player but, whatever his methods, he built one of the finest records of any doubles player.

Norman BROOKES (Aus)

TENNIS

(Sir) Norman Everard Brookes. b. 14 Nov 1877 St Kilda, Melbourne, Victoria, d. 28 Sep 1968 South Yarra, Melbourne.

The first great Australian player and the first great left hander; and the first overseas or left-handed player to win a Wimbledon championship. On his début there in 1905 he won the All Comers' singles but lost to Laurie Doherty in the Challenge Round. He also reached the All Comers' final of the men's doubles with Alf Dunlop (NZ/Aus). Brookes again played at Wimbledon in 1907 and 1914, winning the singles and men's doubles, with Anthony Wilding, in both years. He made his fourth and final visit to Wimbledon in 1924 and, at the age of 46, reached the fourth round of the singles. He also won the Australian singles in 1911, the US doubles in 1919 and the Australian doubles in 1924.
Brookes played a major part in Australasia's early Davis Cup successes. Between 1905 and 1920 he was a member of six winning teams and in 1912 and 1920 the team that lost in the Challenge Round; his overall Davis Cup record was to win 18 of 25 singles and 10 of 14 doubles. A prominent businessman, he became the first president of the LTA of Australia in 1926 and held office for 28 years. In 1939 he was knighted in recognition of his services to tennis.

David BROOME (UK)

EQUESTRIAN

David McPherson Broome. b. 1 Mar 1940 Cardiff.

Has a record six wins in the King George V Gold Cup, on six different horses, between 1960 on *Sunsalve* and 1991 on *Lannegan*. Three times European champion - on *Sunsalve* in 1961, and then riding *Mister Softee*, his greatest horse in 1967 and 1968. He was world champion on *Beethoven* in 1970 and helped Britain win the team championship in 1978.
He won two individual show jumping bronze medals at the Olympics in 1960 and 1968, but having turned professional in 1973 he could not compete at the Games, until the rules changed and he was selected again in 1992. He would have achieved a record for any sport by a British competitor with a 32-year-span, but a last-minute injury meant that he was unable to compete.
A farmer, he was awarded the OBE in 1970.

Louise BROUGH (USA)

TENNIS

Althea Louise Brough. b. 11 Mar 1923 Oklahoma City, Oklahoma. Later Clapp.

Possibly the finest of an outstanding group of US women players in the post-World War II era. In the singles she won at Wimbledon in 1948-50 and 1955, was US champion in 1947 and Australian champion in 1950, but it was her doubles partnership with Margaret Osborne/du Pont that made her one of the legends of the game. Between 1942 and 1957 they won the US title 12 times (1942-50, 1955-7), were five times Wimbledon champions (1946, 1948-50, 1954) and won the French title three times (1946-7, 1949). During this 15 year period they only lost eight matches and have been rated as the best doubles pairing - men or women - in history. Both were fine exponents of the serve and volley game. Brough won her 21st major women's doubles at the 1950 Australian Championships with Doris Hart. She was also a four-time winner of the mixed doubles both at Wimbledon (1946-8, 1950) and the US Championships (1942, 1947-9). At Wimbledon, she won all three titles in 1948 and 1950. To this impressive roll of championship honours she could add an impeccable Wightman

Cup record, winning all 22 of the rubbers she played between 1946 and 1957. After marrying Alan Townsend Clapp in 1958 she began a brief career as a professional in 1961.

Al BROWN (Panama)

BOXING

Alphonse Theodore Brown. b. 5 Jul 1902 Panama City, d. 11 Apr 1951 New York.

'Panama Al' Brown, who was fluent in seven languages, was one of the tallest bantamweights ever at 180 cm *5' 11"*. His tremendous reach gave him a great advantage over others of this weight. He won his first title in 1929 by defeating Vidal Gregorio and in 1931 he gained universal recognition as bantamweight champion. He held the title until 1935, winning 11 world title fights, and fought as a professional until 1944.

Career record: W - 120 (58), L -19, D -11.

David BROWN (Aus)

RUGBY LEAGUE

David Michael Brown. b. 4 Apr 1913 Hurstville, Sydney, d. 23 Feb 1974 Sydney.

A fast, long-striding centre with exceptional ball handling skills and a remarkable talent for long-range goal kicking. He was first selected for New South Wales at 18, and as a 20-year-old he scored a record total of 285 points (19 tries, 114 goals) in 32 matches on Australia's 1933/4 tour of Great Britain.

He was also a prolific scorer for Eastern Suburbs and in 1935 scored 385 points which smashed Dally Messenger's 270 points in 1911, and which remained a scoring record for an Australian season until bettered by Mick Cronin in 1978. He scored a one game record 45 points (5 tries and 15 goals) against Canterbury. At the end of that season, in which his 38 tries in 15 games was also a record, Brown led the Australian tour of New Zealand, scoring 74 points (10 tries, 22 goals) in four games. The following year he became, at 23, the youngest player ever to captain Australia against England, who were touring. One of his opponents in 1936 was the Warrington forward Jack Arkwright, who recommended Brown to his club and at the end of the tour the Australian joined the Lancashire club. He returned home on the outbreak of war and led Easts as player-coach in 1940. After retirement the following year, he held a variety of jobs, including managing the family surf-sheds, and in 1962 he spent three months in South Africa attempting to promote the League code. In 1964 he coached the South Africans against the visiting Australians but the tour was not a success and the idea of introducing rugby league into South Africa was eventually abandoned.

9 Tests 1933-6: 7 tries, 26 goals, 73 points.

Doris BROWN (USA)

ATHLETICS

Doris Elaine Brown. née Severtsen. b. 17 Sep 1942 Gig Harbor, Washington. Later Heritage.

Winner of the International cross-country title on the first five occasions that the race was run, 1967-71. That alone settled her claim to be the first great woman distance runner from the USA, but she also won five AAU track titles outdoors: 800m 1969, 1500m/1M 1966, 1969, 1974; 2M 1971, and four indoor mile titles 1967-8 and 1971-2, as well as five at cross-country 1966, 1968-71.

Greater international championship success was thwarted by the fact that when she was at her best the longest event was the 800m, and at that distance she was 2nd in the 1967 and 1971 Pan-Americans and 5th at the 1968 Olympics. She qualified for the US team at the new event of 1500m at the 1972 Olympics but did not compete through injury.

Prior to IAAF recognition of the event she set a world record for 3000m in 1971 at 9:26.9 en route to 2 miles in 10:07.0. She also set three US records at 1500m and four at 1 mile. She was assistant women's coach on US teams in the 1980s and coached at Seattle Pacific University.

Other bests: 800m 2:01.9 (1968), 1500m 4:14.6 (1971), mile 4:39.6 (1971), marathon 2:47:35 (1977).

Jim BROWN (USA)

AMERICAN FOOTBALL

James Nathaniel Brown. b. 17 Feb 1936 St Simons Island, Georgia.

Most of his records have been broken, but there has never been a greater running back than Jimmy Brown. His all-around ability as an American athlete is possibly surpassed only by Jim Thorpe, although throughout his life, Brown has remained a very controversial figure.
Brown played high school sports at Manhasset High, excelling in football and also setting the Long Island basketball scoring record, which survived until future Duke superstar Art Heyman broke it. Brown attended Syracuse University where he was a football All-American in his junior and senior years and was also a starting forward on the basketball team. His best collegiate sport may however have been lacrosse, at which some experts consider him the greatest player ever. In 1954 he was tenth in the AAU decathlon, in his only try at that difficult endeavour. He was drafted first by the Cleveland Browns in 1957 and quickly became the greatest running back in football history. He played for nine years and led the NFL in rushing every year except 1962. He rebounded from that in 1963 by gaining 1863 yards, a record which stood until O J Simpson's 2003 yards in 1973. Brown ended his career at the top, retiring while still the best running back in the game. His lifetime yardage total was later broken by Walter Payton, but nobody has ever approached the career carry average of 5.2. He was 1.88m *6'2"* and 106 kg *233 lb* at his peak, and also possessed great speed for his era. He never missed a game and was knocked out of a game only once. Basketball coach Bobby Knight, in discussing Brown, paid him what he considered the ultimate compliment, 'He never, ever, ran out of bounds.'
After retiring from football he began a movie career. He was an outspoken black man, and was often criticised and ostracised for some of the stands he took. This hampered his acting efforts and some critics' memory of his abilities.
NFL career 1957-65 Rushing: 12,312 yards av. 5.2, 106 touchdowns. Receiving: 2499 yards av. 9.5. 20 touchdowns.

Joe BROWN (USA)

BOXING

Joe Brown b. 18 May 1926 New Orleans, Louisiana.

An all-services lightweight champion before he turned professional in 1946. He did not get a title bout until 1956, when he defeated 'Bud' Smith for the lightweight title. He successfully defended the championship twelve times in the next six years before losing to Carlos Ortiz in 1962. He retired from boxing in 1970.
Career record: W - 104 (48), L - 42, D -12.

Larry BROWN (USA)

BASKETBALL

Lawrence Harvey Brown. b. 14 Sep 1940 Brooklyn, New York.

At a shade under 178 cm *5' 10"*, Larry Brown shares with Sam Balter the distinction of being the shortest US Olympic basketball player. Brown played his college ball at North Carolina and then two years of AAU play with the Akron Goodyears. At his height, and with his deadly outside shot, he was far better suited for the ABA with its 3-point goals, and from 1967-72 he played there as a steady performer. In 1969 he played with the champion Oakland Oaks and led the league in assists.
Since retiring as a player he has been one of the game's best, and most travelled, coaches. He started with the Carolina Cougars of the ABA and moved in 1974 to the Denver Nuggets. He stayed with the Nuggets when they joined the NBA in 1976 but in 1979 left to take over at UCLA. He returned to the NBA after two seasons, but moved on after another two seasons to accept the head coaching job at the University of Kansas.

Mordecai BROWN (USA)

BASEBALL

Mordecai Peter Centennial Brown. b. 19 Oct 1876 Nyesville, Indiana, d. 14 Feb

1948 Terre Haute, Indiana.

'Three Fingered' Brown lost the end of his right index finger and had his small finger paralysed by an accident in a corn shredder when he was only seven years old. He was still able to pitch and used his unusual hand to perfect a great knuckleball. Between 1904 and 1910 he posted an ERA of under 2.00 every year, with a low of 1.04 in 1906, which is still a National League Record. He also won 20 or more games for six straight seasons from 1906. He helped the Chicago Cubs win National League pennants in 1906-08 and 1910, and helped the Chicago Feds to the Federal League title in 1915.
Career pitching: 1903-16: ERA 2.06; W-L 239-130, SO 1375; Best seasons: 1909: 27-9, 1.31 ERA; 1906: 26-6, 1.04 ERA.

Mary BROWNE (USA)

TENNIS
Mary Kendall Browne. Later Smith. b. 3 Jun 1891 Santa Monica, California, d. 19 Aug 1971 Laguna Hills, California.

Winner of nine US Championships before World War I, she won three further titles in post-war years when tennis often took second place to her golfing ambitions. Before the war she won all three titles at the US Championships for three consecutive years (1912-14), winning three finals on the same day in 1912. After her 1914 victories she disappeared from national tennis until 1921 when she won the US women's and mixed doubles. She then dropped out of tennis again until 1924 and won her final US title in the women's doubles in 1925. The following year she won her only Wimbledon title in the women's doubles. At the end of the 1926 season she contracted to play a series of professional matches against Suzanne Lenglen, but in almost 40 matches, she failed to win once and only managed to win two sets. In view of the obvious mismatch, the arrangement was terminated and Browne opened a sports store in Cleveland. As a golfer, she won many State Championships and the first year she entered for the US Amateur golf championship (1924) she lost in the final having beaten the redoubtable Glenna Collett in the first round. After her marriage to Dr Kenneth Smith ended in divorce she continued her career as a successful portrait painter.

Jacques BRUGNON (Fra)

TENNIS
Jacques 'Toto' Brugnon. b. 11 May 1895 Paris, d. 20 Mar 1978 Paris.

The doubles specialist of the 'Four Musketeers'. Initially he partnered Henri Cochet but also had an equally successful partnership with Jean Borotra. With Cochet he won the Wimbledon doubles in 1926 and 1928 and the French doubles in 1927, 1930 and 1932. Partnering Borotra, he won Wimbledon in 1932 and 1933, the Australian title in 1928 and the French Championships in 1928 and 1934. As late as 1948 Brugnon and Borotra reached the fourth round at Wimbledon when their combined ages exceeded 100 years. Other successes included victories in the French mixed doubles with Suzanne Lenglen in 1925 and 1926. Between 1923 and 1934 he won 22 of his 30 Davis Cup doubles and all three of his singles.

Valeriy BRUMEL (USSR/Russia)

ATHLETICS
Valeriy Nikolayevich Brumel. b. 14 Apr 1942 Tolbuzino, Siberia.

A great high jumper, who started his international career at the age of 18 in 1960, when he won the Olympic silver medal at 2.16m, the same height as the winner, Robert Shavlakadze. From then he was supreme in world high jumping, winning the European title in 1962 and the Olympics in 1964, although on the latter occasion he only won on the count-back from John Thomas, who cleared the same height of 2.18. Brumel was Soviet champion four times, 1960-3.
He set six world records, taking it up a centimetre at a time from 2.23 to 2.28 in the three years 1961 to 1963. His great rival, the American John Thomas, had set the previous record at 2.22 in 1960. Brumel first exceeded this indoors with 2.25 at Leningrad on 29 Jan 1961, before

embarking on his record-breaking outdoors. No other jumper exceeded his 2.28 until 1970, but Brumel's career was cut short by a serious motor-cycle accident on 7 Oct 1965, when he suffered multiple fractures in his right leg. He made a very brave recovery and showed his tenacity by high jumping 2.06m in 1969.
Not especially tall for a high jumper at 1.85m, he was a fine all-rounder with bests for 100m of 10.5 and long jump 7.65m.

Avery BRUNDAGE (USA)

ATHLETICS/IOC

Avery Brundage. b. 28 Sep 1887 Detroit, Michigan, d. 5 May 1975 Garmisch-Partenkirchen, Germany.

A superb athlete who became one of the best known, and perhaps least liked, administrators in the history of international sports. He attended the University of Illinois, graduating in civil engineering in 1909. He started his own construction company but continued to compete as an athlete, winning the US all-around track & field championship in 1914, 1916, and 1918, and placing 6th in the pentathlon and failing to finish the decathlon at the 1912 Olympics in Stockholm.
Brundage was AAU president 1928-35 and president of the US Olympic Committee 1928-52. In 1935-6 he staunchly defended Nazi Germany's right to host the Olympics and was elected to the International Olympic Committee in 1936 as a reward for his efforts to stave off an American boycott. He served as IOC vice-president 1946-52 and president 1952-72.
His tenure as IOC president was marked by his autocratic behaviour and anachronistic strict insistence on pure amateurism in the Olympics. He stepped down after the Munich Olympics of 1972 after the greatest tragedy in Olympic history when 11 Israelis were savagely murdered by Arab terrorists at the Olympic Village. At the memorial ceremony for them, Brundage rather rudely compared the murders to an attempted Olympic boycott of African nations, but declared that the 'Games must go on.'

Pierre BRUNET (Fra)

ICE SKATING

Pierre Brunet. b. 28 Jun 1902 Paris, d. 27 Jul 1991 Boyne City, Michigan.

At the Olympic Games Pierre Brunet was eighth in the individual ice skating in 1924 and ninth in 1928, but it was with **Andrée Joly** (b. 16 Sep 1901 Paris, d. 30 Mar 1993 Boyne City) in the pairs that he achieved his greatest successes.
After taking Olympic bronze in 1924, the French couple were gold medallists in 1928 and 1932 and won the world title four times, 1926, 1928, 1930 and 1932. They were also European champions in 1932. Pierre was French individual champion seven times between 1924 and 1931 and Andrée won ten successive individual women's titles 1921-30; together they won 11 French pairs titles between 1924 and 1935. After they married, they turned professional in 1936 and settled in America, where they founded a prestigious skating school. Pierre coached such stars as Carol Heiss and Donald Jackson, and their son, Jean-Pierre, was one of only two men to defeat Richard Button.

Bear BRYANT (USA)

AMERICAN FOOTBALL

Paul William Bryant. b. 11 Sep 1913 Moro Bottoms, Arkansas, d. 26 Jan 1983 Tuscaloosa, Alabama.

Bryant was given the nickname 'Bear' because, as a boy, he wrestled a bear in Fordyce, Arkansas for money. He played football at the University of Alabama 1932-6 and then became a football coach. In 1945 he was named head coach at Maryland and also coached at Kentucky and Texas A&M before he was appointed head coach in 1958 at his alma mater, where he became a legend. In his 25 years there he led Alabama to the national championship six times (1961, 1964-5, 1973, 1978-9), more than any college football coach in history, and had a record of 232-46-9. His career record was 323-85-17, the 323 wins a college football record (since surpassed). Bryant was named National Coach of the Year three times. He took

Alabama to 24 consecutive bowl games and his overall bowl record was 15-12-2.

David BRYANT (UK)

BOWLS

David John Bryant. b. 27 Oct 1931 Clevedon, Yorkshire.

The most successful bowler in the history of the game with the greatest number of wins at all the major championships. He has a total of six victories at the World Outdoor Championships, winning the singles in 1966, 1980 and 1988, the triples 1980 and the Leonard Trophy (team) 1984 and 1988. At the World Indoors he won the singles the first three years the Championships were held, 1979-81, and the pairs, with Tony Allcock, six times, 1986-7, 1989-92. His record at the English Outdoor Championships is no less remarkable, winning (or sharing) 16 titles between 1957 and 1985. He won the singles six times, 1960, 1966, 1971-3, 1975; the pairs three times, 1965, 1969, 1974; the triples three times, 1966, 1977, 1985; and the fours with the Clevedon team four times, 1957, 1968-9, 1971. He also won the English Indoor singles a record nine times between 1964 and 1983. Other notable successes include seven British Isles titles (four singles, one pairs, one triples and one fours) from 1957 to 1987 and five gold medals at the Commonwealth Games (four singles between 1962 and 1978 and the fours 1962).
With his skill, showmanship and impeccable manners, he has done more than any man to promote and popularise the game and he was awarded the MBE in 1969 and CBE 1980 for his services to the sport.

Olga BRYZGINA (USSR/Ukr)

ATHLETICS

Olga Bryzgina. née Vladykina. b. 30 Jun 1963 Krasnokamsk, Perm.

Married to sprinter Viktor Bryzgin. Both won Olympic gold medals in 1988, Viktor in the 4 x 100m relay, Olga in the 400m and 4 x 400m relay, on which she contributed a 47.7 leg to the USSR's world record. She ran her fastest ever time for an individual 400m with 48.27, her fourth Soviet record, behind Marita Koch's world record in the 1985 World Cup and she was also second to Koch in the 1986 Europeans. After Koch's retirement she took the 1987 World gold medal with silver in the relay.
Her daughter Lisa was born in November 1989 and she returned to competition in 1991, ducking under 50 secs for the first time since 1988 when she was fourth in the World final. She improved further to 49.05 for the 1992 Olympic silver, adding another gold medal at the relay. USSR 400m champion in 1984, 1985 and 1991. An economics student, she competed for Lugansk Dynamo.

Sergey BUBKA (USSR/Ukr)

ATHLETICS

Sergey Nazarovich Bubka. b. 4 Dec 1963 Voroshilovgrad (now Lugansk).

The surprise world champion in 1983, he went on to dominate the world of pole vaulting, and was not beaten in a championship from then until his sixth place in the Europeans after injury earlier in 1990. He has set 16 world pole vault records, the most at any event, from 5.85m in 1984 to 6.13m in 1992, including the world's first six-metre jump at Paris in 1985. He has also set 18 world indoor records from 5.81 in 1984 to 6.15 in 1993. On 15 Mar 1991 he became the first vaulter to clear 20 feet when he set his 13th world indoor record at 6.10m.
His championship gold medals include: Olympics 1988; Worlds 1983, 1987 and 1991; World Indoors 1985, 1987, 1991; Europeans 1990; European Indoors 1985; World and European Cup 1985. The only other blot on his immaculate record was his failure to clear a height at the 1992 Olympics.
A master of his craft, he combines great speed and strength with brilliant gymnastic ability and has been one of the few athletes in the history of sport to compete regularly over many years at a different level from all rivals. Bubka now represents OSC Berlin and commutes from meetings

around the world, living in Paris and his home in Donetsk.

His elder brother **Vasiliy** (b. 26 Nov 1960) has a pole vault best of 5.86m (1988), was European silver medallist in 1986 and World Indoor bronze in 1985.

Bubka's world records

Outdoors

5.85	Bratislava	26 May 1984
5.88	Paris	2 Jun 1984
5.90	London	13 Jul 1984
5.94	Rome	31 Aug 1984
6.00	Paris	13 Jul 1985
6.01	Moscow	8 Jul 1986
6.03	Prague	23 Jun 1987
6.05	Bratislava	9 Jun 1988
6.06	Nice	10 Jul 1988
6.07	Shizuoka	6 May 1991
6.08	Moscow	9 Jun 1991
6.09	Formia	8 Jul 1991
6.10	Malmö	9 Aug 1991
6.11	Dijon	13 Jun 1992
6.12	Padua	30 Aug 1992
6.13	Tokyo	19 Sep 1992

Indoors

5.81	Vilnius	15 Jan 1984
5.82	Milan	1 Feb 1984
5.83	Inglewood	10 Feb 1984
5.87	Osaka	15 Jan 1986
5.92	Moscow	8 Feb 1986
5.94	Inglewood	21 Feb 1986
5.95	New York	28 Feb 1986
5.96	Osaka	15 Jan 1987
5.97	Turin	17 Mar 1987
6.03	Osaka	11 Feb 1989
6.05	Donyetsk	17 Mar 1990
6.08	Volgograd	10 Feb 1991
6.10	San Sebastian	15 Mar 1991
6.11	Donetsk	19 Mar 1991
6.12	Grenoble	23 Mar 1991
6.13	Berlin	21 Feb 1992
6.14	Liévin	13 Feb 1993
6.15	Donetsk	21 Feb 1993

Charles BUCHAN (UK)

FOOTBALL

Charles Murray Buchan. b. 22 Sep 1891 Plumstead, London, d. 25 Jun 1960 Monte Carlo.

A brilliant attacking player in any of the three inside-forward positions, although his subtleties frequently confused his colleagues and limited his international appearances for England to only six matches, 1913-24.

After signing for Southern League club Leyton in 1910 he moved to Sunderland one year later. In the 1912/3 season he helped them to the First Division Championship and the FA Cup final where they lost to Aston Villa. His career was interrupted by the War in which he won a Military Medal serving with the Grenadier Guards and was later commissioned in the Sherwood Foresters. He won the last of his six international caps in 1924 and moved to Arsenal the following year.

At the age of 33, he was one of the first signings of the legendary Herbert Chapman who had recently taken over as manager at Highbury. Arsenal paid Sunderland a basic £2,000 plus a further £100 for each goal Buchan scored in his first season. He scored 21 and Arsenal's original down-payment was more than doubled. His most important contribution at Highbury was the development of the 'third-back' game which he devised with Chapman to counter the new offside rule. He captained Arsenal to their first FA Cup final in 1927 and, as with Sunderland 15 years earlier, he was on the losing side.

On his retirement in 1928, he became a journalist and was the football and golf correspondent for the *Daily News* and the *News Chronicle* following the amalgamation of the two papers. He was also a commentator for BBC Radio and in 1951 founded the popular magazine, *Football Monthly*. He died while on holiday with his wife in the South of France.

Buck BUCHANAN (USA)

AMERICAN FOOTBALL

Junious Buchanan. d. 10 Sep 1940 Gainesville, Alabama, d. 16 Jul 1992 Kansas City, Missouri

The top defensive lineman of the old AFL. He played collegiately at Grambling under legendary coach Eddie Robinson. Drafted in 1963 by the Dallas Texans (later the Kansas City Chiefs) in the first round, he played with them through the 1975 season. He started in six AFL All-Star Games and the first two Pro Bowls after the merger of the leagues. He combined great size with tremendous speed and agility for a defensive tackle. He may have been the greatest pass rusher in football history. After his retirement he directed the Kansas City Special Olympics and spent some time as an assistant coach in the NFL.

Willie BUCHANON (USA)

AMERICAN FOOTBALL

Willie James Buchanon. b. 4 Nov 1950 Oceanside, California.

Buchanon played defensive back at San Diego State and with the Green Bay Packers for most of his NFL career. He is considered one of the greatest ever cornerbacks. He was drafted in the 1st round in 1972 and starred with the Packers until 1978 at which time he was traded to the San Diego Chargers. He was NFL Rookie of the Year in 1972 and made the 1974 and 1978 Pro Bowls. He later became a high school teacher.

Georges BUCHARD (Fra)

FENCING

Georges Buchard. b. 21 Dec 1893 Harfleur. d. 22 Jan 1977.

His record of winning three individual world épée titles (1927, 1931, 1933) was equalled by Aleksey Nikanchikov (USSR) in 1970 but has not been bettered. He was unable to repeat his World Championship successes at the Olympic Games but placed second in the individual event in 1928 and 1932, and took four épée team medals, golds in 1924 and 1932, silver in 1928 and bronze in 1936. He competed in 120 internationals for France and was European épée champion in 1925, 1931 and 1933.

Frank BUCKLE (UK)

HORSE RACING

Francis Buckle. b. 1766 Newmarket, d. 5 Feb 1832 Peterborough.

From his success on *John Bull* in the 1792 Derby to 1827 he rode 27 English classic winners: nine Oaks, six 1000 Guineas, five each 2000 Guineas and Derby, two St Leger. This record was eventually passed by Lester Piggott in 1984. He started riding in 1783 at a weight of just 3st 13lb *25kg* and rode until the age of 65 in 1831. He was for many years first jockey to Robert Robson.

Renowned for his integrity, as well as being a great jockey, specialising in well-timed finishes, he was also a successful farmer near Peterborough.

Zola BUDD (SAf/UK)

ATHLETICS

Zola Budd. b. 26 May 1966 Bloemfontein. Now Pieterse.

A teenage prodigy, she set an unofficial world record for 5000m at 15:01.83 in South Africa in January 1984 shortly before emigrating to Britain to take advantage of her ability to become a British citizen due to her grandfather's British nationality - as long as she did this before her 18th birthday. With the help of the *Daily Mail* the nationality papers were put through in extraordinary time, and Budd's career as a British athlete began, as it continued, in a blaze of publicity.

She went to the Los Angeles Olympics but there in the 3000m final Mary Slaney fell over Budd's legs and Budd herself faded from the lead to 7th. She set a total of 14 world junior bests 1983-5, and achieved her greatest success with world cross-country titles in 1985 and 1986, and on the track in 1985 when she won the European Cup 3000m and set a world record for 5000m with 14:48.07 in London. In 1986 she set a world indoor record for 3000m and was 4th at 3000m and 7th at 1500m in the Europeans, but was not permitted to run in the Commonwealth Games. With injuries and unhappiness in her adopted country she eventually returned for good to South Africa in 1988. She married Mike Pieterse on 15 Apr 1989 and gradually returned to competition. She ran at the 1992 Olympics and showed a return to form with 4th in the 1993 World cross-country.

National titles: SA 1500m 1982-3, 1991;

3000m 1982-3, 1990-1; UK 1500m 1984, WAAA 3000m 1985, 1500m 1986. Other best times: 800m 2:00.9 (1984), 1500m 3:59.96 (1985), 1M 4:17.57 (1985), 2000m 5:30.19 (1986), 3000m 8:28.83 (1985)

Don BUDGE (USA)

TENNIS

John Donald Budge. b. 13 Jun 1915 Oakland, California.

The first man to win the Grand Slam and rated by many experts as the greatest player of all-time. He made his Davis Cup début in 1935 when he lost to both Perry and Austin of Great Britain, but these were to be his only defeats in 21 Davis Cup singles; he also won 6 of 8 doubles.

He was a semi-finalist at Wimbledon in 1935 and 1936 and a finalist at the 1936 US Championships where he won his first major title in the men's doubles (with Gene Mako). For the next two years he was unbeatable. In 1937 he won all three titles at Wimbledon (doubles with Mako and mixed with Alice Marble), and the singles and mixed doubles (with Marble) at the US Championships. He went even better in 1938 when he was uniquely a triple Wimbledon champion for the second successive year (and won the singles without losing a set), took all three titles at Forest Hills, and achieved wins in the French and Australian singles which gave him the distinction of being the first-ever player to win the Grand Slam.

In November 1938 he turned professional and sensationally beat Fred Perry and Ellsworth Vines on his pro début. Budge continued to enjoy considerable success as a professional until service as a US Army Air Corps officer interrupted his career. A shoulder injury inhibited his play after the war but he continued to compete at the top-level until 1955.

His return of service was as good as any player in history but his rolled backhand was his main strength. As the first player to turn the backhand from a defensive into an attacking stroke he changed the shape of the game.

Maria BUENO (Bra)

TENNIS

Maria Esther Andion Bueno. b. 11 Oct 1939 São Paulo.

A graceful, artistic player whose encounters with the more robust Margaret Court were one of the highlights of the tennis scene for almost a decade. Equally talented as a singles or doubles player, the majority of Bueno's successes came at Wimbledon, where she won the singles three times (1959-60, 1964) and five women's doubles titles (1958, 1960, 1963, 1965-6), and in the US at Forest Hills, where she won four singles (1959, 1963-4, 1966) and four women's doubles (1960, 1962, 1966, 1968). In 1960 she completed the Grand Slam of women's doubles titles winning the Australian with Christine Truman and the French, Wimbledon and US titles with Darlene Hard. At the French Championships that year she won her only major mixed doubles title. Other successes included victories in the Italian singles in 1958, 1962, 1965 and the women's doubles in 1962. Her career was hampered, and finally ended, by injury and although her win-loss record against Margaret Court was not in her favour she will be remembered as the last woman champion who did not rely on the power game.

Gianni BUGNO (Italy)

CYCLING

Gianni Bugno. b. 14 Feb 1964 Brugg, Switzerland

After third place in 1990 Bugno became the fourth man to win the World road race championship in successive years, 1991-2. By then, in a professional career that started in 1985, he had achieved 48 victories in major races. His best year was1990 when he won the overall World Cup title, the Giro d'Italia, Milan-San Remo and Wincanton Classic. In the Tour de France he has had four stage wins from his first in 1988, but has yet to win the race, placing 7th in 1990, 2nd in 1991 and 3rd in 1992.

Andrey BUKIN (USSR) see Natalya BESTEMYANOVA.

Olga BULARDA (Rom)

ROWING

Olga Bularda. née Olga Homeghi. b. 1 May 1958.

Her four Olympic rowing medals is the most by any woman, an honour she shares with fellow Romanian Rodica Arba-Puscatu, with whom at coxless pairs she won the Olympic title in 1984 and 1988, and the World in 1985-7. As Homeghi she had won a bronze medal in the 1980 double sculls with Valeria Racila-Rosca and as Bularda rowed with the Romanian coxless fours that won in 1984 and the eight which took the silver medals in 1988.

Jim BUNNING (USA)

BASEBALL

James Paul David Bunning. b. 23 Oct 1931 Southgate, Kentucky.

A power pitcher who won over 100 games in both the American and National League and also pitched a no-hitter in both leagues. He began his career in 1955 with the Detroit Tigers (AL) and stayed with that team until 1964 when he was traded to the Philadelphia Phillies (NL). He played for the Pittsburgh Pirates in 1968-9 and was briefly an LA Dodger in 1969, before finishing his last two years 1970-1 with the Phillies. At his retirement, Bunning had 2855 strikeouts, then second only to Walter Johnson. Bunning later entered politics and earned a seat in the U.S. House of Representatives from Kentucky. He also lost a gubernatorial bid in that state.
Career pitching: ERA 3.27; W-L 224-184, SO 2855; Best season: 1958: 20-8, 2.70 ERA.

Haydn BUNTON (Aus)

AUSTRALIAN RULES FOOTBALL

Haydn William Bunton. b. 5 Jul 1911 Albury, New South Wales, d. 5 Sep 1955 Adelaide.

Regarded by many as the greatest of all Australian rules players, with his speed and stamina making him the ideal rover. He was spotted by a VFL talent scout and signed for Fitzroy (for both football and cricket) in 1930. He became the first man to win three Brownlow medals (1931-2 and 1935), awarded annually to the fairest and best VFL player. He was also second in 1934. In 1938 he moved to Subicao where he won the Sandover Medal, the Brownlow equivalent in the Western Australia League, three times, 1938-9 and 1941. Near the end of his career he moved to play for Port Adelaide in South Australia in 1945, before becoming a coach and then an umpire. He played a total of 213 games in the three States, kicking 438 goals, and he represented Victoria 15 times.
His son **Haydn Bunton, Jr** won the Sandover Medal when playing for Swan Districts in 1962, for a unique father and son achievement. He captained the Western Australia side which, in 1961, won its first Australian championship carnival in 40 years and had earlier played for and coached Norwood in South Australia.

Frank BURGE (Aus)

RUGBY LEAGUE

Frank Burge. b. 14 Aug 1894 Darlington, New South Wales, d. 5 Jul 1958 Sydney.

'Chunky' Burge was one of the greatest try-scoring forwards in the history of the game. During the 1921/2 Australian tour of England he scored 33 tries in only 23 matches, the most ever scored by a forward on tour. At the age of 14 he was the youngest player ever in first grade, for South Sydney, and first played for New South Wales at 16. He played for Glebe 1911-23, and after playing and coaching in country areas he returned to Glebe in 1926, although he broke a leg after three matches. He then captained and coached St George 1927-30 and later coached North Sydney.
His elder brothers **Peter** (b. 14 Feb 1884, d. Jul 1956) and **Albert** 'Son' (b. 3 Jun 1887, d. 1943) both played for Australia at rugby union and Peter also played at rugby league . A fourth brother, Laidley, also played for New South Wales.
13 Tests 1914-22: 7 tries, 7 goals, 35 points.

David BURGHLEY (UK)

ATHLETICS

David George Brownlow Cecil (Lord Burghley). b. 9 Feb 1905 Stamford, Lincolnshire, d. 22 Oct 1981 Stamford. Later Marquess of Exeter KCMG.

The Olympic champion at 400m hurdles in 1928, he had also competed at 110m hurdles in 1924 and went on to win a relay silver medal and place 4th at 400m hurdles in 1932 (in his best ever time of 52.01). At the first Empire Games, in 1930, he won gold medals at both 440y hurdles and 4 x 440y relay, and he won five AAA titles at 440y hurdles, 1926-8, 1930 and 1932 and three at 120y hurdles, 1929-31. He held British records at all hurdles events, with bests of 14.5 for 120y and 24.3 for 220y. Just a year after his last Olympic appearance he became a member of the International Olympic Committee (at the age of 28) and in 1936 he was elected President of the Amateur Athletic Association and Chairman of the British Olympic Association. In 1946 he became President of the International Amateur Athletic Association and was Chairman of the Organising Committee of the 1948 Olympic Games.
A graduate of Cambridge University, he was MP for Peterborough from 1931 to 1943, when he was appointed the Governor of Bermuda. He succeeded his father to become the 6th Marquess of Exeter in 1956.

Beryl BURTON (UK)

CYCLING

Beryl Burton. née Charnock. b. 12 May 1937 Leeds. Married Charles Burton in 1955.

The greatest distaff rider ever produced in Britain, she was chiefly renowned as a time trialist, though in the early 1960s few women could beat her at any discipline. In 1967 she covered 446.19 km in a 12-hour time trial, which was then 9.25 km beyond the British men's record, and in 1968 she rode 100 miles in 3hrs 55:05, only 12 years after the first British man had broken four hours for that distance. At the world championships her medal collection was as follows: individual pursuit - 5 gold (1959-60, 1962-3, 1966), 3 silver, 3 bronze; road race - 2 gold (1960, 1967), 1 silver. She was the first woman to be allowed to compete at the highest level against men when she rode in the Grand Prix de Nations. World outdoor records ratified: 3km 4:16.6 and 4:14.9 in 1964, 20km 28:58.4 in 1960. She collected an unprecedented number of British titles, 25 times all-round time trial champion 1959-83 and winner of 72 individual road TT titles, 14 track pursuit titles and 12 road race titles to 1986. Awarded the MBE 1964 and the OBE 1968.
Her daughter Denise (b. Jan 1956) competed with her at the 1972 World Championships.

Mike BURTON (USA)

SWIMMING

Michael Jay Burton. b. 3 Jun 1947 Des Moines, Iowa.

The Olympic champion at 1500m freestyle in both 1968 and 1972 and at 400m in 1968, 'Mr Machine' Burton made huge improvements on the world records for long distance freestyle swimming during his career. At 800m he set records at 8:43.3 in 1968 and 8:28.8 in 1969, and at 1500m set five records from 16:41.6 in 1966 to 15:52.58 at the Olympics in 1972, when he set a US record 8:25.86 for 800m en route. In all he set 16 US records, with 400m in 4:06.6 (1968), and won nine AAU titles at 1500m/1650y outdoors 1966-9, 1971 and indoors 1966-9 as well as the indoor 500y in 1967. His huge training mileage set new standards.
When Burton was ten months old his family moved from Iowa to Sacramento in California, where he was coached by Sherman Chavoor at the Arden Hills club. He was severely injured when hit by a truck while cycling at the age of 12, but overcame this, although his knee tendon surgery was repeated in 1970 between his Olympic successes.
His other successes included the World Student Games and Pan-American 1500m titles in 1967 and NCAA outdoor titles at 500y 1970 and 1650y 1967-8 and 1970

while at UCLA. After retirement from competition he continued as a coach and in the late 1970s became technical director for the world governing body, FINA.

Matt BUSBY (UK)

FOOTBALL

(Sir) Matthew Busby. b. 26 May 1909 Orbiston, Lanarkshire.

One Scottish international cap in 1933 and an FA Cup winners medal for Manchester City the following season were the highlights of a rather modest playing career (Manchester City 1929-36, Liverpool 1936-9) but as a manager he has few peers. He served as manager of Manchester United from 1945-1969 and guided them to unprecedented heights. They won the European Cup (1968); the FA Cup twice (1948, 1963) and the Football League Championship five times (1952, 1956-7, 1965, 1967). Many of these successes were achieved after eight team-members had tragically lost their lives in the Munich air disaster in 1958.
Busby himself was close to death after the air crash but he survived to rebuild his team and he continued to serve the game for many years. Appointed to the Manchester United board in 1971 he became club President in 1982 and held high office in the Football League Management Committee. He was awarded the CBE in 1958 and knighted in 1968.

Sabine BUSCH (GDR)

ATHLETICS

Sabine Busch. b. 21 Nov 1962 Erfurt.

Turned from 400m flat running to hurdling with immediate success in 1985, as she ran a GDR 400mh record 53.83 on her début, followed by a world record of 53.55. In 1987 she won the world title with a second gold at the 4 x 400m relay, and improved the GDR record to 53.24, although by then the world record had been improved to 52.94 by Marina Stepanova. She had also won gold medals on the GDR 4 x 400m relay team at the 1982 Europeans (when she was 4th at 400m), 1983 Worlds and 1986 Europeans (2nd at 400m hurdles). In the 1988 Olympics she was 4th at hurdles and won a bronze medal in the relay, and she achieved wins at 400m hurdles in the 1985 and 1987 European Cups and 1985 World Cup. She became a lecturer for the Turingian Sports and Social Ministry.

Dick BUTKUS (USA)

AMERICAN FOOTBALL

Richard Marvin Butkus. b. 9 Dec 1942 Chicago, Illinois.

Butkus is considered the hardest-hitting defender in football history. He played linebacker and center in college at the University of Illinois, was an All-American in 1963 and in 1964, when he finished third in the Heisman Memorial Trophy balloting, as close as any defensive player has ever come to winning that award. He won the Knute Rockne Award in 1963-4 as the nation's top collegiate defensive player. Butkus played with the Chicago Bears 1965-73 as a middle linebacker and made nine Pro Bowl teams, and was All-Pro six times (1965, 1967-70, 1972). He was voted the greatest middle linebacker of the 1960-84 era by the Pro Football Hall of Fame. Knee injuries eventually forced his retirement.

Emilio BUTRAGUEÑO (Spa)

FOOTBALL

Emilio Butragueño Sánchez. b. 22 Jul 1963 Madrid.

Despite being rejected by both Real and Atletico Madrid as a boy he has spent a decade as a highly successful striker for Real, whom he joined from their second division nursery team Castilla in 1982. He scored two goals on his senior début in 1984 and has been a prolific scorer ever since, helping his team to the League title 1986-9 and the UEFA Cup 1985 and 1986. Has scored a Spanish record 26 goals in 69 internationals 1984-93, including four against Denmark in the 1986 World Cup and against Albania in a European Championship qualifying match in 1990. Came third in European Footballer of the Year polls in both 1986 and 1987. Nicknamed 'El Buitre' (the Vulture).

Jeff BUTTERFIELD (UK)

RUGBY UNION
Jeffrey Butterfield. b. 9 Aug 1929 Heckmondwike, Yorkshire.

Winning 28 caps in consecutive matches between 1953 and 1959 he was England's most capped centre until David Duckham surpassed his record. After leaving Cleckheaton GS he played for the local club, the Army and Loughborough Colleges before becoming a regular in the Northampton and Yorkshire teams.
Although Butterfield only played alongside Phil Davies in the centre nine times for England, they formed an outstanding partnership on the Lions tour of South Africa in 1955 and were rated as one of the greatest pair of centres in history. He went on a second Lions tour to Australia and New Zealand in 1959 but a thigh injury, which ended his representative career, kept him out of the Test team. As the proprietor of The Rugby Club in London he maintains close contact with the sport and has served as an England selector.

Frank BUTTERS (UK)

HORSE RACING
Joseph Arthur Frank Butters. b. 1878 near Vienna, Austria, d. 1 Jan 1958 Northampton.

From 1926 to 1949 he trained 1019 winners in Britain and was leading trainer eight times, 1927-8, 1932, 1934-5, 1944, 1946 and 1949. His 15 classic winners included *Bahram*, winner of the Triple Crown in 1935, and *Mahmoud*, the 1936 Derby winner.
His father Joseph went to Austria in 1873 to ride for Emperor Franz Josef. He later trained in Austria and in Newmarket from 1903 to 1926. Frank also trained in Austria prior to internment in World War I. He then ran a stable in Italy before coming to Britain in 1926 to train for Lord Derby at Stanley House, Newmarket. His contract with Lord Derby expired in 1930, when he took a lease on the Fitzroy House stables. He was forced to retire in 1949, suffering brain damage when he was knocked off his bicycle by a lorry.

Dick BUTTON (USA)

FIGURE SKATING
Richard Totten Button. b. 18 Jul 1929 Englewood, New Jersey.

With his athletic style he set a new trend in figure skating and in his amateur career, which lasted from 1943 to 1952, he was only defeated twice. In 1944 he was the first skater to achieve the double lutz in competition and in 1952 the first to do a triple loop. He was world champion for five consecutive years 1948-52, twice Olympic champion, 1948 & 1952, three times North American champion, seven times US champion 1946-52, and once European champion. He uniquely held all these five major titles simultaneously in 1948 which was the last year the European Championship was open to non-Europeans. The following year he became the first ice skater to win the James E Sullivan Memorial Trophy as the best US amateur athlete.
After the 1948 Olympics, Button enrolled at Harvard University and pioneered a new programme of multi-rotation jumps which took him to an unprecedented number of major titles. Having obtained his law degree he practised at the Washington DC bar and became a distinguished TV commentator, wrote two books on skating and in 1980 created and promoted the highly lucrative World Professional Figure Skating Championship. In 1981 he won an Emmy Award for his outstanding television work which embraced a number of sports and was not restricted to figure skating.

Tamara BYKOVA (USSR/Rus)

ATHLETICS
Tamara Bykova. b. 21 Dec 1958 Azov, near Rostov-on-Don

A most consistent high jumper, she set three world records, 2.03 and 2.04m 1983, 2.05m 1984. The first came in the European Cup, when she was beaten on count-back by Ulrike Meyfarth, and this was one of seven second places she achieved (with no wins) in European and World Cup events between 1981 and 1989.

She also won the European Championship silver in 1982 and World Indoor silver medals in 1989 and 1991. She had however won the European Indoors and World title outdoors in 1983, and went on to take European Indoor and World outdoor silvers in 1987, with 7th place in the Worlds in 1991. At the Olympics she was 9th in 1980, missed out in 1984 through her nation's boycott and took a bronze in 1988.
A student of education, who competed for Moskva SA, she received a three-month ban for a positive test for ephedrine at the 1990 Goodwill Games. USSR champion 1980, 1982-3, 1985, 1989 and World Student Games winner 1983. In all she set eight USSR records from 1.97m in 1980 and three world indoor bests, 2.00, 2.02 and 2.03 in 1983.

Galina BYSTROVA (USSR)

ATHLETICS

Galina Petrovna Bystrova. née Dolzhenkova. b. 8 Feb 1934 Nachichevan, Azerbaidzhansk SSR.

European champion in 1958 and 1962 at the pentathlon, at which event she set two world records with 4846 in 1957 and 4872 points in 1958. She also ran a world record for 80mh with 10.6 in 1958. At the Olympic Games she was 4th in 1956 and 5th in 1960 at 80m hurdles and won a bronze medal at pentathlon in 1964.

Lee CALHOUN (USA)

ATHLETICS

Lee Quency Calhoun. b. 23 Feb 1933 Laurel, Mississippi, d. 22 Jun 1989 Erie, Pennsylvania.

The Olympic champion at 110 metres hurdles in 1956 and 1960. He emerged very fast in 1956 while at North Carolina College; indoors he tied the world record at 6.0 for 50y hurdles and won the first of two successive AAU 60y hurdles titles, and outdoors he won the NCAA/AAU double and tied with Jack Davis at the US Olympic Trials. Then he just beat Davis to take the Olympic title, as both men ran 13.5 (13.70 to 13.73 on auto timing), into the wind on a slow track, in what was acclaimed at the time as one of the greatest races ever. In 1957 he repeated his AAU/NCAA double.
In August 1957 he was married on the 'Bride and Groom' television show and his wife won $2500 worth of goods and a $6000 swimming pool, although the Calhouns later gave the pool to a boys' club. This was seen by the AAU as an infringement of the amateur regulations and Calhoun was suspended so that he missed the 1958 season. He returned to competition in 1959, when he took the Pan-American silver and won his third AAU title. In 1960 he equalled the world record for 110mh with 13.2 in Berne, and then won his second Olympic title. His victory margin was even closer than it had been in 1956: 13.98 to 13.99 for Willie May. He was an assistamt coach to the 1976 US Olympic team

Didier CAMBÉRABÉRO (Fra)

RUGBY UNION

Didier Cambérabéro. b. 9 Jan 1961 La Voulte.

Holder of the world record for scoring most points in an international match, with 30 against Zimbabwe in the 1987 World Cup. He also tied the record with three dropped goals against Australia at Sydney in 1990. He scored a French record 354 points, winning 36 caps at fly-half, 1985-93, and following his father, B (b. 27 May 1936 La Voulte), who was capped 14 times (1961-8) in that position. His uncle, **Lilian** (b. 15 Jul 1937 La Voulte), also won 13 caps as a scrum-half 1964-8.

Enrico CAMICI (Italy)

HORSE RACING

Enrico Camici. b. 1912 Barbaricina. d. 17 Mar 1991.

First jockey to the Tesio stable, in all he rode 4801 winners. He rode five winners of the Italian Derby between 1943 and 1957, including on *Tenerani* 1947 and *Botticelli* 1954, and the Prix de l'Arc de Triomphe on *Ribot* 1955 and 1956, and *Molvedo* 1961.

Roy CAMPANELLA (USA)

BASEBALL

Roy Campanella. b. 19 Nov 1921 Philadelphia, Pennsylvania, d. 26 Jun 1993 Woodland Hills, California.

'Campy' Campanella played his best years in the Negro Leagues, catching for the Baltimore Elite Giants from 1937 until 1945. In 1946 he was signed by the Brooklyn Dodgers and spent two years in their farm system before graduating to the majors in 1948. For the next ten years he was the top catcher in the National League, helping the Dodgers to pennants in 1949, 1952-3, and 1955-6. He was the first man to win three MVP awards, 1951, 1953 and 1955, in the National League. In early 1958 his career was ended by an automobile accident, in which he sustained injuries which left him partially paralysed from the waist down and he spent the rest of his life needing a wheelchair. At the time, his home run total of 242 was the most ever by a catcher.
Career 1948-57: 1161 hits Avg. .276, HR 242. Best season 1953 - .312, 142 RBI.

Donald CAMPBELL (UK)

MOTOR RACING

Donald Campbell. b. 23 Mar 1921 Horley, Surrey, d. 4 Jan 1967 Coniston Water.

An engineer by training, and also with quite a reputation as a playboy, he emulated his father Malcolm (qv) by breaking both land and water speed records; they were two of only three men to hold both records simultaneously. Donald set the land speed record with 403.14 mph *648.77 km/h* on Lake Eyre salt flats, Australia in 1964, and broke the water speed record seven times from 202.32 mph *325.60 km/h* on Ullswater Lake in a jet-propelled hydoplane on 23 Jul 1955 to 276.279 mph *444.615 km/h* on Lake Dumbleyung, Australia on 31 Dec 1964.
In his last, and fatal water speed record attempt in his turbo-jet engined Bluebird he achieved an unofficial speed of 328 mph 528 km/h. on Coniston Water in England before his boat was wrecked and he was killed. Awarded the CBE.

Earl CAMPBELL (USA)

AMERICAN FOOTBALL

Earl Christian Campbell. b. 29 Mar 1955 Tyler, Texas.

Campbell played high school football in Tyler and was one of the most highly sought after football players ever in that football-mad state. He went to the University of Texas where he won the Heisman Memorial Trophy in 1977 in his senior year. He was chosen by the Houston Oilers as the 1st pick of the 1978 NFL draft and led the NFL in rushing as a rookie, the first time that had been accomplished since Jimmy Brown in 1957, ensuring his selection as Rookie of the Year. He was also voted NFL MVP in his first three years in the league, 1978-80. Shortly thereafter, his ability declined slightly due to injuries and less protection from his linemates. He was traded in 1984 to the New Orleans Saints, for whom he played for two years. He was a bull-like runner who punished defenders at 1.80m *5'11"* and 102 kg *225 lb.*
NFL career 1979-85 Rushing: 9407 yards av. 4.3, 74 touchdowns. Receiving: 806 yards av. 6.7.

John CAMPBELL (Can)

HARNESS RACING

John D Campbell. b. 8 Apr 1955 London, Ontario.

Campbell's harness racing feats are such that he was inducted into its Living Hall of Fame in 1990 at the age of 35, the youngest ever to be so honoured. He has dominated the lists of leading money winners for more than a decade, leading the year list nine times, 1979-80, 1983, 1986-90 and 1992, so that at the end of 1992 he headed the career earnings list at $109,024,606 (from 1972), more than $30 million ahead of the runner-up Hervé Filion. He has driven many world champions, but pride of place goes to the colt *Mack Lobell*, the first of his three Hambletonian winners, and the filly *Peace Corps*, arguably the best trotters of all-time for their sex, and trotters of the year in respectively 1987-8 and 1989.

Campbell made his reputation at Detroit and Windsor area tracks, before moving his base to Meadowlands, New Jersey when that track opened in the mid 1970s. His father Jim was a respected horseman in western Ontario.

Malcolm CAMPBELL (UK)

MOTOR RACING

(Sir) Malcolm Campbell. b. 11 Mar 1885 Chislehurst, Kent. d. 31 Dec 1948 Reigate, Surrey.

A pilot in World War I, he had started flying in 1909, and he raced motor cycles from 1906 and started motor racing in 1910. He called his cars *Bluebird* after a play by Maeterlinck he had seen in 1912. Following a successful racing career he turned to pursuing the world land speed record which he improved nine times, taking it from 146.16 mph *235.21 km/h* in 1924 to 301.13 mph *484.6 km/h* in 1935. He was the first man to exceed 300 mph on land. He was knighted in 1931.
In 1937 he wrested the world water speed record from the American Gar Wood with a speed of 208.4 km/h *129.5 mph* on Lake Maggiore, Italy. The following year he inproved this record to 210.67 km/h *130.91 mph* on Lake Hallwil, Switzerland, and in 1939 made a third improvement to the record with a speed of 228.10 km/h *141.74 mph*. His son Donald (qv) also set both land and water speed records; they were two of only three men to hold both records simultaneously.

Milt CAMPBELL (USA)

ATHLETICS

Milton Gray Campbell. b. 9 Dec 1933 Plainfield, New Jersey.

While an 18 year-old high school student Campbell won the Olympic silver medal in the decathlon. Four years later he won the gold medal with his best ever score of 7937 points (7565 on the current tables). He was especially talented at the hurdles and in 1957 he improved the world indoor record for 60y hurdles to 7.0 (twice) and outdoors tied the world record for 120 yards at 13.4. He won the AAU decathlon in 1953 and both AAU and NCAA titles at 120y hurdles in 1955 while at the University of Indiana.
He also excelled at football, playing for the Cleveland Browns in the NFL and Montreal Alouettes in the CFL, as well as swimming and karate.

Ollie CAMPBELL (UK)

RUGBY UNION

Seamus Oliver Campbell. b. 3 Mar 1954 Dublin.

Scoring 217 points in 22 matches (1976-84) he was Ireland's leading points scorer in international rugby until Michael Kiernan surpassed his total in 1988. With one dropped goal and six penalties against Scotland in 1982 he scored 21 points to set an Irish record for the most points in an international match. Although this record has since been beaten, his 52 points in a championship season (1983) remains an Irish record.
Campbell won international honours as a fly half and as centre and after touring Australia with Ireland in 1979, he went with the British Lions to South Africa in 1980 and New Zealand in 1983. He was the top scorer for the Lions on both tours. Educated at Belvedere College, he played for Old Belvedere and Leinster, and today holds a senior appointment in the textile industry.

David CAMPESE (Aus)

RUGBY UNION

David Ian Campese. b. 21 Oct 1962 Queanbeyan, ACT.

One of the most exciting running backs of modern times. First capped in 1982 at the age of 19, by July 1993 he had played for Australia a record 74 times and his total of 54 international tries is by far the world record. His unorthodox play often caused problems, never more so than against the 1989 Lions when he was caught in possession trying to run the ball out of defence and the resulting try gave the Test series to the visitors. He was also suspect in more orthodox defensive situations but his scoring record amply compensated for these

deficiencies. Fast, elusive and using a unique 'goose step' when a tackle seemed imminent, he was one of the most entertaining players of his era.
Played for Queanbeyan, ACT when he won his first international cap, and then for Randwick in New South Wales, and, having turned down many offers to play rugby league, for Mediolanum, Milan in Italy during the Australian close season.

Billy CANNON (USA)

AMERICAN FOOTBALL

William Anthony Cannon. b. 8 Feb 1937 Philadelphia, Pennsylvania.

Billy Cannon knew the best and worst that life can bring a man. He played college football at Louisiana State University (LSU) where he was the idol of a state. He was voted All-American in both 1958 and 1959 and won the Heisman Memorial Trophy in 1959. A running back and defensive back, Cannon was also an excellent sprinter and shot putter. As a college football player his greatest moment came for LSU against Mississippi in 1959, when, late in the game with LSU behind, he fielded a punt on the 11-yard line and returned it 89 yards for a touchdown to give his team a 7-3 win. He signed with the AFL's Houston Oilers and led the AFL in rushing in 1961. He was traded to the Oakland Raiders in 1964 and became one of the league's best tight ends. While playing pro football, Cannon studied dentistry, which he practised after retiring in 1971. In 1983, he was put on trial for his part in a massive counterfeiting scheme, was found guilty, and eventually imprisoned.
NFL career 1960-70: Rushing: 2455 yards av. 4.1, 17 touchdowns. Receiving: 3656 yards av. 15.5, 47 touchdowns.

Morny CANNON (UK)

HORSE RACING

Herbert Mornington Cannon. b. 21 May 1873 Stockbridge, Hampshire, d. 1 Jun 1962 Hove, Sussex.

Champion jockey in England 1891-2, 1894-7, with a peak of 182 winners in 1892. He won 6 classics, including the Triple Crown on *Flying Fox* in 1899. He was a natural horseman and a great judge of pace; but he refused to adopt the crouching style when that was introduced at the turn of the century. His first winner came the day before his 14th birthday in 1887, and he was champion while still a teenager. He gave up riding in 1907.
His father **Tom Cannon** (b. 23 Apr 1846 Eton, d. 1917) rode 1544 winners in his career, including 13 classics between 1866 and 1889; and he trained *Busybody* to win the 1000 Guineas and Oaks in 1884. Thomas was champion jockey in 1872 with 87 winners. Joseph Cannon (1849-1933), younger brother of Thomas, rode three classic winners, as did his son Noel (1897-1959) and Mornington's brother Kempton (1879-1951). Lester Piggott was a great-grandson of Thomas Cannon, whose daughter Margaret married Ernest Piggott.

Ernesto CANTO (Mex)

WALKING

Ernesto Canto. b. 18 Oct 1959.

The best 20km walker of the mid-1980s, when he won the World title in 1983 and Olympic in 1984. He was also Central American champion in 1982, 1986 and 1990, and at the World Cup won in 1981 and was second in 1983 and 1991. He was also second in the 1983 Pan-American Games. At subsequent Olympics he was disqualified in 1988 and was only 29th in 1992. He set world walking records at 20km, 1:18:40.0 and 1 hour, 15,253m in 1984.
Other best times: Track 3000m 11:50.0 (1983), 5000m 18:38.71i (1987), 10,000m 39:29.2 (1984). Road 30km 2:08:49 (1990), 50km 3:51:10 (1982).

Tony CANZONERI (USA)

BOXING

Tony Canzoneri. b. 6 Nov 1908 Slidell, Louisiana, d. 9 Dec 1959 New York.

After winning the New York state amateur bantamweight championship in 1924, Canzoneri, a former shoeshine boy, turned professional in 1925. He fought for world

crowns at four weight classes, and won titles in the featherweight (1927), lightweight (1930), and junior-lightweight (1931) classes. Canzoneri was always popular because of his rough, aggressive style. His first title came in 1927 when he outpointed Johnny Dundee at featherweight. From then he was always a champion at some weight or another until 1937 when Lou Ambers defeated him for the lightweight crown. Canzoneri retired at the end of 1939. In all he had 22 world title fights, of which he won 12 and drew one.
Career record: W - 141 (44), L - 24; D - 10.

José CAPABLANCA (Cuba)

CHESS

José Raul Capablanca y Graupera. b. 19 Nov 1888 Havana, d .8 Mar 1942 Manhattan Chess Club, New York, USA.

Perhaps the greatest ever natural chess player, he was world champion 1921-7 and lost only 34 games in his adult career, 1909-39, the least by any world champion. He learnt to play at age 4 by watching his father. He attended Columbia University in New York 1906-7 and after his first major success at San Sebastián in 1911 became a commercial attaché with the Cuban Foreign Office, a career which allowed him plenty of time for travel and chess. His influence on the game was enormous, especially on opening play, and he was a fine writer on the game. After surprisingly losing the world title to Alekhine in 1927 he was not permitted a re-match.

Joaquin CAPILLA (Mex)

DIVING

Pérez Joaquin Capilla. b. 23 Dec 1928 Mexico City.

Mexico's only Olympic diving champion, Capilla worked his way steadily to the gold that he gained at highboard in 1956, having taken the bronze in 1948 and the silver in 1952. He also won the springboard bronze in 1956. Pan-American champion at both events in 1951 and 1955. AAU champion at highboard 1953 and both events 1954. His brother Alberto also competed as a diver at the 1952 and 1956 Olympic Games.

Rudolf CARACCIOLA(Ger)

MOTOR RACING

Rudolf Caracciola. b. 30 Jan 1901, d. 28 Sep 1959 Kassel.

The greatest German driver of the inter-war years. After spending the war years in Switzerland, he became a naturalised Swiss citizen. Nicknamed 'Caratsch'.
He started racing motorcycles and in hill climbs in 1922, and joined Mercedes in 1923, for whom he drove for the rest of his career, except for a spell with Alfa Romeo in 1932. He won the German Grand Prix at Avus in 1926 and five times at the Nürburgring, 1928, 1931-2, 1937 and 1939, as well as 23 other top international races up to 1939. He also set 17 world speed records. In 1933 he smashed his thigh in practice at Monaco, and this injury troubled him for the rest of his life, although he continued to race for a further 20 years. He was especially skilful in wet conditions.

Antonio CARBAJAL (Mex)

FOOTBALL

Antonio Carbajal. b. 7 Jun 1929 Guanajuato

The only player to have appeared in five World Cup finals tournaments. He kept goal for Mexico in 1950, 1954, 1958, 1962 and 1966 playing 11 games in all, although he let in four on his début against Brazil in 1950. As an amateur with España he played in the 1948 Olympic Games after which he signed as a professional with León and remained with them until his retirement after the 1966 World Cup. Three years later he became León's coach.

Vicki CARDWELL (Aus)

SQUASH

Vicki Cardwell. b. 1955 Adelaide. née Hoffman.

A former South Australian junior tennis champion who became the world's leading

squash player. Her first major success in her new sport came in 1978 when she won the Australian Amateur title and reached the final of the British Open. She won the Australian Open in 1979-80 and 1982-4, and the British Open for four successive years 1980-3. During this period she surprisingly lost in the 1981 World final to her fellow Australian Rhonda Thorne, but at the next World Championships in 1983 reversed the result. Having won all the honours available to her she retired after giving brth to her son Joshua in 1985.
A small, hard-hitting, attacking player, she did not win as many major Championships as some of her predecessors, but she played in an era when the standards of play were far higher than they had ever previously been.

Rod CAREW (Pan)

BASEBALL

Rodney Cline Carew. b. 1 Oct 1945 Gatun, Canal Zone.

Carew played 19 years in the major leagues, starting in 1967 with the Minnesota Twins as a second baseman. He later shifted to first base and in 1979 was traded to the California Angels, where he remained until his retirement after the 1985 season. He was known primarily as the best hitter in baseball for much of his career and led the American League in hitting seven times, 1969, 1972-5, and 1977-8. He finished with a career average of .328, the highest in the major leagues since the retirements of Ted Williams (1961, .344) and Stan Musial (1963, .331). In 1977, Carew's .388 (239 hits) was the highest since Williams' identical mark in 1957, and for much of the season, Carew flirted with the magical .400 mark. He also reached 200 hits in 1973, 203 at .364, 1974, 203 at .364 and 1976, 200 at .331.
Career batting: 3053 hits Avg. .328, HR 92; SB 353.

Johnny CAREY (UK/Ire)

FOOTBALL

John Joseph Carey. b. 23 Feb 1919 Dublin, Ireland.

A player of remarkable versatility who won international honours in six different positions. Joining Manchester United as a 17-year-old in 1936 he remained at Old Trafford until 1953 and scored 17 goals in 306 appearances. He was a member of the team which defeated Blackpool 4-2 to win the FA Cup in 1948 and were League Champions in 1951/2.
As an international, he played 29 times for Ireland and 9 times for Northern Ireland (including 2 Victory Internationals). He captained the Rest of Europe against Great Britain at Hampden Park in 1947 and was Footballer of the Year in 1949. Initially an inside-forward, he later moved to wing-half and then to full-back before becoming a wing-half again: he occasionally played in other positions and was a competent substitute goalkeeper. Although lacking pace his intelligent distribution of the ball made him one of the outstanding full-backs of his generation.
When he retired in 1953, he became manager of Blackburn Rovers and took them back into the First Division in 1958. He moved on to Everton, Leyton Orient and Nottingham Forest before returning to Blackburn in 1969. After Rovers dropped to Division III for the first time in their history in 1971, he was replaced.

Max CAREY (USA)

BASEBALL

Max George Carey. né Maximilian Carnarius. b. 11 Jan 1890 Terre Haute, Indiana.

Played for 17 years (1910-26) with the Pittsburgh Pirates in the National League and finished his career (1926-9) with the Brooklyn Dodgers. Carey was renowned for his fielding and his range in patrolling center at Forbes Field in Pittsburgh.
He was an average hitter for the era, but he was a great baserunner, leading the National League ten times in stolen bases. His 1922 record of 51 stolen bases in 53 attempts is the best ever percentage per attempt for a season.
Career batting: 2665 hits Avg. .285; SB 738.

Rick CAREY (USA)

SWIMMING

Richard John Carey. b. 13 Mar 1963 Mount Kisco, New York.

The top backstroke swimmer of the 1980s, he won the Olympic 100m and 200m double in 1984, adding a third gold in the medley relay. At the 1982 World Championships he had won gold medals at 200m and medley relay, with a silver at 100m.

Carey first came to national prominence with a win at 200m in the 1977 US junior Olympics. He qualified for the US Olympic team in 1980, but lost his chance to compete through the boycott and his first US national title and record came indoors in 1981. That year he went to the University of Texas at Austin, where he studied aerospace engineering and was coached by Eddie Reese; he won the NCAA title at 100m 1983-4 and 200m 1982-4. Carey broke John Naber's seven year-old world backstroke records with times of 55.44 and 55.38 at 100m and 1:58.93 at 200m at the 1983 US Championships. Two weeks later at the Pan-American Games he lowered the record for 100m to 55.19 and also won gold medals at 200m and medley relay. He improved his US record for 200m to 1:58.86 when winning the US Olympic Trials in 1984. After the Olympics Carey won five further US titles in 1985-6.

Will CARLING (UK)

RUGBY UNION

William David Charles Carling. b. 12 Dec 1965 Bradford-on-Avon, Wiltshire.

First appointed captain of England in 1988 at the age of 22 he quickly established himself as England's most successful leader. A strong running centre, he played a major role in the successive Grand Slam victories in 1991-2. He is easily England's most successful captain, with 26 wins in 35 games to March 1993 and he also holds the record as England's most capped centre (42). He was spoken of as a possible captain of the 1989 Lions tour to Australia but was unable to tour due to a leg injury and, although he was selected for the tour to New Zealand in 1993, Gavin Hastings was preferred as captain. Carling played in just the first of the three Tests on that tour. After attending Sedbergh and Durham University Carling played for the Harlequins and joined the Army but resigned his commission to devote more time to rugby. Awarded the OBE in 1991.

Erik CARLSSON (Swe)

RALLYING

Erik Carlsson. b. 5 Mar 1929 Trollhättan.

The top rally driver of the early 1960s, he bridged the gap between the amateur drivers and the professionals of the modern era. After motorcyling and car racing, his first major rally drive was in 1953, and he joined Saab as a works driver in 1957, when he achieved his first big wins, including the 1000 Lakes Rally, in a small but distinctive Saab 96 powered by a two-stroke 850cc engine.

He did not immediately test his skills outside Scandinavia but in 1960 scored the first of his three successive wins in the RAC. After winning the Acropolis Rally in 1961, victories in the Monte Carlo Rally followed in 1962 and 1963 and his tiny Saab is the smallest car ever to have won this race. He retired from international competition at the end of the 1964 season. That year he married Pat Moss, sister of Stirling Moss, and herself a most consistent rally driver.

Steve CARLTON (USA)

BASEBALL

Steven Norman Carlton. b. 22 Dec 1944 Miami, Florida.

One of the great left-handed pitchers of all time and also one of the worst interviews, as for much of his career he refused to speak to the press. He was renowned as a power pitcher and strikeout artist. His greatest year was 1972 when he won the Cy Young Award with the last-place Philadelphia Phillies, posting a record of 27-10, winning an amazing 46% of all the Phillies victories that season, when he was a triple crown winner, leading the National

League in wins, ERA (1.98), and strike-outs (310). Carlton finished his career with 329 wins, second only to Warren Spahn among left-handers, and with 4131 strike-outs, second only to Nolan Ryan among all pitchers. He won further NL Cy Young Awards in 1980 (24-9, 286 SO, 2.34 ERA) and 1982 (23-11, 286 SO, 3.10 ERA).
Career pitching 1965-88: ERA 3.22; W-L 329-244, SO 4136.

JoAnne CARNER (USA)

GOLF

JoAnne Carner. née Gunderson. b. 4 Mar 1939 Kirkland, Washington.

'The Great Gundy' may be the greatest American distaff amateur of all time. She was a member of four Curtis Cup teams and had five US Amateur wins, 1957, 1960, 1962, 1966 and 1968, and may have equalled Glenna Collett Vare's six had she not elected to turn professional in 1970. That decision came late in her career, and may have been sparked by her victory in the 1969 LPGA Burdine's Invitational. Carner, a very long hitter known to all as 'Big Mama' for her size and friendly personality, was an immediate gallery favourite on the LPGA Tour, where she was one of the two or three best players but never quite established dominance. She won the US Women's Open in 1971 and 1976 and the Peter Jackson Classic in 1975 and 1978. She led the LPGA money list in 1974 and 1982-3.
LPGA career earnings 1970-92: $2,649,642 with 42 victories.

Primo CARNERA (Italy)

BOXING

Primo Carnera. b. 26 Oct 1906 Sequals, Venice, Italy, d. 29 Jun 1967 Sequals.

The largest heavyweight champion ever, with a peak weight of 122kg *270 lb*. He had an expanded chest measurement of 137cm *57in* and the longest reach (finger-tip to fingertip) of 217cm *85.5in*. Before beginning professional boxing, he worked as a wrestler and strongman in a circus. He was managed by Léon See, a Frenchman who oversaw his career in London and Paris, and arranged for him to travel to the United States. There, several carefully selected opponents allowed the giant with minimum boxing skills to advance to a title bout. In 1933, Carnera, at a weight of 118kg *260 lb*, defeated Jack Sharkey for the heavyweight championship. He lost the title in 1935 to Max Baer and then retired in 1936. 'The Ambling Alp' was swindled for much of his career and lost all his boxing earnings, but had better fortune later as a professional wrestler.
Career record: W - 88 (69), L - 14, D -0.

Kiki CARON (Fra)

SWIMMING

Christine Caron. b. 10 Jul 1948 Paris.

The best known French woman swimmer, she set six European records for 100m backstroke in 1963-4, with her 1:08.6 in 1964 also a world record, although she improved to 1:07.9 when she took the Olympic silver later that year behind Cathy Ferguson's world record 1:07.7. Kiki also set five European records at 200m backstroke from 1963 to 2:27.9 in 1966. At 100m backstroke she was European champion in 1966 and US champion in 1965.
She was coached by Suzanne Berlioux, and in her career, which lasted until 1971, won 29 French titles including 11 at 100m backstroke, 7 at 200m backstroke and one each at 100m and 200m butterfly and 400m IM. Her sister Annie was a French champion and record setter at breaststroke and butterfly.
She started a singing career in 1970.

Connie CARPENTER (USA)

CYCLING

Helen Constance Carpenter. b. 26 Feb 1957 Madison, Wisconsin. Later Carpenter-Phinney.

One the greatest athletes in American sporting history. She won 12 US cycling championships, more than any man or woman in history. She also won four medals at the world championships in both the pursuit and road race, including the pursuit title in 1983. Her finest moment came in the 1984 Olympic road race, the first ever for women, when she outlasted America's Rebecca Twigg to narrowly win the gold medal. At the finish she 'threw' her bike, using a move taught to her by her husband, Davis Phinney, who was a bronze medallist at the 1984 Olympics in the team time trial, and later rode professionally for the 7-Eleven team. Carpenter-Phinney also competed in the 1972 Olympics as a speed skater, though she was only 15 at the time. In addition she rowed for the University of California in the national collegiate championships.

Georges CARPENTIER (Fra)

BOXING

Georges Carpentier. b. 12 Jan 1894 Liévin-les-Lens, Pas-de-Calais, d. 28 Oct 1975 Paris.

The handsome, debonair Frenchman, known as 'The Orchid Man', was the idol of many a Parisian female in the 1920s, and is still the most beloved French boxer ever.

He fought mostly as a light-heavyweight, holding the world crown in that class from 1920-22. Briefly, while Jack Johnson was world heavyweight champion, Carpentier fought at that weight and was acclaimed the white heavyweight champion of the world. Shortly after that escapade, he became a hero in the French air force in World War I, winning a *Croix de Guerre* for bravery. After the war, he returned to win his world title and reign supreme among French athletes. In 1921 he lost a much heralded heavyweight title bout to Jack Dempsey. Carpentier retired in 1927 and remained a revered figure in Paris, where he owned a top-class restaurant, until his death.

Career record: W - 93 (56), L - 15, D -6.

Henry CARR (USA)

ATHLETICS

Henry William Carr. b. 27 Nov 1942 Montgomery, Alabama.

Olympic champion at 200m and 4 x 400m relay in 1964. He set three world records at 220 yards, 20.4 and 20.3 in 1963, improving to 20.2 in 1964, when his time to win the Olympic title was 20.36, a record on automatic timing.

He showed that he could have been one of the greatest 400m athletes of all-time, running the anchor leg of the US team's world record of 3:00.5 in Tokyo 1964 in 44.5, and the previous year he had helped the Arizona State University team set a world record at 4 x 440 yards. However, he ran the individual event only rarely, with a best time of 45.4 in 1963. He didn't need to stretch himself to run the longer distance as he was supreme at half a lap, at which he was AAU champion in 1963 (when he tied with Paul Drayton) and 1964, and NCAA champion in 1963.

He played American football with limited success 1965-7 with the New York Giants and Detroit Lions.

Other bests: 100y 9.3 (1963), 100m 10.2 (1964).

Tom CARROLL (Aus)

SURFING

Thomas Carroll. b. 26 Nov 1961 Sydney.

After winning the Pepsi-Pro junior title in 1977, Carroll joined the World pro surfing tour in 1980, won the World Cup in 1982 and became world champion in 1984 and 1985. Short at 1.68m *5' 6"* but with powerful legs, he signed surfing's first $1 million contract in 1988.

Jimmy CARRUTHERS (Aus)

BOXING

James Carruthers. b. 5 Jul 1929 Paddington, NSW, d. 16 Aug 1990 Sydney.

After winning the Australian amateur bantamweight title Carruthers first boxed internationally at the 1948 Olympics, where he had to withdraw from the quarter-finals due to an eye injury. He turned professional in 1950, won the Australian championship in his ninth pro fight, and the world bantamweight championship in 1952 by defeating South Africa's Vic Toweel. This made him the first Australian world champion since Young Griffo was a disputed champion in 1890. Carruthers relinquished the crown after three successful defences when he retired in 1954, having won all 19 of his professional fights. He ran a pub and refereed fights, then in 1961 made a brief, unsuccessful, return to the ring, losing four of six fights. *Career record: W - 21 (13), L - 4, D -0.*

Willie CARSON (UK)

HORSE RACING

William Hunter Fisher Carson. b. 16 Nov 1942 Stirling, Scotland.

On 22 May 1990 he became the fourth jockey to ride 3000 winners in Britain. He was the first Scot to be champion jockey, winning five times, in 1972-3, 1978, 1980 and 1983.

He started his career as an apprentice with Gerald Armstrong in Yorkshire in 1957, moving to Gerald's son Sam at Newmarket at the end of the 1962 season, soon after his first winning ride, at Catterick on 19 Jul 1962. It was not until 1972 that he rode his first classic winner, *High Top* in the 2000 Guineas, but by 1991 he had won each of the five classics, 16 wins in all. He had a career total of 3434 winners in Britain to the end of 1992, with more than 100 winners each year from 1971 to 1992, except for 1984, with successive peaks of 145 in 1971, 163 in 1973, 182 in 1978 and 187 in 1990. In 1990 he set a prize money record in Britain of £2,903,976. He met with particular success from 1977 when he became first jockey to Major Dick Hern, and for him rode the Derby winners *Troy* in 1979 and *Henbit* in 1980. He considers *Nashwan*, his third Derby winner (1989), to have been the best horse that he has ever ridden.

A most determined rider, his cheerful personality, and infectiously cackling laugh, was brought to the widest audience when he regularly took part on the BBC's *Question of Sport*. Awarded OBE 1983.

Don CARTER (USA)

BOWLING

Donald James Carter. b. 29 Jul 1926 St Louis, Missouri.

Carter dominated the world of bowling from 1950 until 1964 and in 1970 was voted by bowling writers as the greatest of all-time. He was almost unbeatable in the early and mid-1950s and continued to be one of the top bowlers after the formation in 1958 of the PBA, of which he was a charter member. He eventually won seven PBA titles, and was the first bowler to win the 'Grand Slam' of PBA Nationals, the BPAA US Open title four times (1953-4, 1957-8), the World Invitational five times (1957, 1959-62), and the ABC Masters Championship in 1961. He was voted Bowler of the Year six times, 1953-4, 1957-8, 1960, and 1962. He had a unique bent-elbow style.

Raich CARTER (UK)

FOOTBALL

Horatio Stratton Carter. b. 21 Dec 1913 Hendon, Sunderland.

Capped six times before World War II and seven times afterwards, his 14 year international career (1934-47) was the longest of any England inside-right. After winning schoolboy international honours he signed as a professional for Sunderland in 1931 and was a member of the team which won the Football League in 1936 and the FA Cup in 1937. After appearing as a guest player for Derby County during World War II he signed for them in December 1945 and won a second FA Cup winners medal in 1946. In March 1948 he moved to Hull City, where he also had some managerial responsibilities, and took them to the Third Division (North) title in 1949. During a brief spell with Cork Athletic he won an FA of Ireland Cup winners' medal in 1953 at the age of 40 and later managed Leeds, Mansfield and Middlesbrough.

He was probably at his best during the war years when he played between Stanley Matthews (right-wing) and Tommy Lawton (centre-forward) in the unofficial internationals. Undoubtedly, his finest peacetime performance came in the 1946 FA Cup Final when his brilliant understanding with Peter Doherty at inside-left led to a 4-1 victory for Derby. A powerful marksman with superb ball control and distribution, he ranks as one of the greatest inside-forwards. He was also an accomplished cricketer and played three first-class matches for Derbyshire in 1946.

Rosemary CASALS (USA)

TENNIS

Rosemary Casals. b. 16 Sep 1948 San Francisco, California.

One of the great doubles players of her era. Partnering Billie Jean King she won the doubles at Wimbledon five times (1967-8, 1970-1, 1973), the US title twice (1967, 1974) and the Italian title once (1970). Casals was also a women's doubles winner at Forest Hills with Judy Dalton in 1971 and with Wendy Turnbull in 1982, and in Rome in 1967 with Leslie Turner. In the mixed doubles she won at Wimbledon in 1970 and 1972 with Ilie Nastase and at the US Championships in 1975 with Richard Stockton. She was a member of the US Wightman Cup and Federation Cup teams in 1967 and 1976-81.
The daughter of El Salvadoran immigrants, she was brought up by relatives and learned the game on public courts in San Francisco. In 1970, following the dispute over prize money for women, she was one of the nine players who led a breakaway and played in the first Virginia Slims tournament.

Pat CASH (Aus)

TENNIS

Patrick Cash. b. 27 May 1965 Melbourne, Victoria.

After winning the 1982 Junior singles at Wimbledon and the US Open he led Australia to victory in the Davis Cup the following year. At 19 he reached the singles semi-finals at Wimledon and the US in 1984, but was beset by injuries over the next few years and did not win a Grand Slam title until Wimbledon in 1987. That year he also reached the Australian singles final and he was only beaten in that event 8-6 in the final set by Mats Wilander in 1988. Since then this talented serve and volleyer has never been completely free of injury and has failed to recapture his earlier form. He was the ITF junior world champion in 1981.

Vera CÁSLAVSKÁ (Cs)

GYMNASTICS

Vera Cáslavská. b. 3 May 1942 Prague.

The graceful, vivacious blonde-haired Cáslavská delighted spectators and TV viewers worldwide with her beautiful gymnastics at the Olympic Games of 1964, when she won three gold medals and a silver, and in 1968 when she took four golds (one shared) and two silvers. She had also won a team silver in 1960 to take her overall Olympic medal haul to 11.
She made her international début in 1958 when she won a European team silver, and she won her first European title on the beam in 1959. She was World overall champion in 1966, with gold medals at the vault in 1962 and 1966, and overall European champion in 1965, when she equalled Latynina's feat of winning all five individual titles, and in 1967.
In 1968 Soviet tanks rolled into her hometown of Prague, and Cáslavská, a keen supporter of the new Czech régime, had to go into hiding for a while. Two months later she was a heroine of the 1968 Olympics in Mexico City. She performed her floor exercises fittingly to 'The Mexican Hat Dance' and the day after collecting her final gold medal, she married **Josef Odlozil** (b. 11 Nov 1938), who had won a silver medal for 1500m at the 1964 Olympics. Returning home she presented her four gold medals to the ousted Czech leaders.
In 1989 she was appointed president of Czechoslovakia's national Olympic committee.

Billy CASPER (USA)

GOLF

William Earl Casper Jr. b. 24 Jun 1931 San Diego, California.

Although one of the great players of the era from 1955-1975, Casper was forced to yield the limelight to Arnold Palmer and Jack Nicklaus and was rarely given the credit he deserved. Only five players have ever won more PGA tournaments than Casper's 51 (1956-75) and he was nine times chosen to the Ryder Cup team, playing in a record 37 matches for the USA, winning 20, losing 10 and halving 7 in the eight times that he played. He was US Open champion in 1959 and 1966 and won the 1970 Masters. He also won the Vardon Trophy five times (1960, 1963, 1965-6, 1968), a record matched only by Lee Trevino, and led the money list on the PGA Tour in 1966 and 1968. Casper was primarily known as the greatest putter on the PGA Tour, but he played a solid, all-round game, not hitting the ball long but controlling it well, usually with a slight fade. He continues to play on the PGA Senior Tour.

Hopalong CASSADY (USA)

AMERICAN FOOTBALL

Howard Cassady. b. 2 Mar 1934 Columbus, Ohio.

Cassady achieved most of his football fame as a running back for Ohio State in the mid-1950s. He was a unanimous All-American selection in 1954 and 1955 and in his senior year won the Heisman, Maxwell, and Walter Camp Trophies as college football's top player. His college coach, Woody Hayes, once stated that 'The greatest player I ever had playing for me was Hop Cassady.' Cassady played in the NFL for seven years, 1956-62, but he was small for the professional game and never dominated it as he had in college.

Cassius CLAY, see Muhammad ALI

Ken CATCHPOLE (Aus)

RUGBY UNION

Kenneth William Catchpole. b. 21 Jun 1939.

A brilliant scrum half, renowned for the speed of his passing, who captained Australia in 13 of his 27 international appearances 1961-8. Educated at The Scots College and Sydney University, his partnership with his New South Wales and Randwick colleague Phil Hawthorne (who later captained Australia at rugby league) was one of the features of world rugby in the 1960s. After retiring from international rugby he pursued his career as a chemical engineer and became a commentator for the Australian Broadcasting Commission.

Tracy CAULKINS (USA)

SWIMMING

Tracy Anne Caulkins. b. 11 Jan 1963 Winoma, Minnesota.

The winner of a record 48 US national titles in her career 1977-84, achieving a first by also setting records at all strokes. Caulkins began swimming in Tennessee at the age of eight and made her international début in 1976. In 1977 she set AAU Championship records at 100y and 200y breaststroke short-course and 200m and 400m individual medley long-course. She had a sensational year in 1978, when she broke or tied 27 world and American records and won a record five gold medals at the World Championships: both individual medleys, 200m butterfly and two relays, as well as silver at 100m breaststroke. She set world records at 200m butterfly 2:09.87, 200m IM 2:15.09 and 2:14.07, and 400m IM 4:40.83, and at the age of 15 became the youngest ever winner of the Sullivan Award.

In 1980 she improved her 200m IM world record to 2:13.69 but was denied her chance of Olympic glory by the US boycott. A student of communications at the University of Florida, for whom she won 12 individual NCAA titles, she won both medley events at the 1983 Pan-Ams and eventually got her Olympic chance in 1984. In Los Angeles she ended her career fittingly with three gold medals, at both medley events and the relay, improving her US records to 2:12.64 for 200m and 4:39.24 at 400m. At breaststroke she set six US records at both 100m and 200m to 1:09.53 and 2:32.43 in 1981.

Other bests: freestyle 100m 56.57 (1978), 200m 2:01.04 (1981); backstroke 100m 63.97 (1984), 200m 2:15.15 (1982); 100m butterfly 59.98 (1980).

Steve CAUTHEN (USA)

HORSE RACING

Stephen Mark Cauthen. b. 1 May 1960 Walton, Kentucky.

The only jockey to have won both the Kentucky and Epsom Derbys. He achieved prodigious riding success in the USA as a teenager, before coming to Britain. There he rode 1704 winners (including 10 classics) from his first ride on 7 Apr 1979 to the start of 1993 when he retired after the ending of his very successful contract to ride for Sheikh Mohammed. He now lives in Kentucky, works on the family farm and commentates on racing for TV.
He rode his first winner *Red Pipe*, trained by his uncle, at Riverdown, Kentucky on 17 May 1976, just five days after his first race, and the following year he was the top jockey in the USA, with 487 winners and $6,151,750, a prize money record, and the Eclipse Award. The following year he won the Triple Crown on *Affirmed*., but, moving to California, he hit a run of 110 consecutive losers in Jan-Feb 1979.
He was brought over to Britain by Barry Hills and Robert Sangster and in his first year achieved a classic success in the 2000 Guineas on *Tap On Wood* and rode 52 winners. His total increased each year to 61, 87 and 107, his first century, in 1982. He then rode over 100 winners each year to 1992, with successive peaks of 130 in 1984, 195 in 1985 and 197 in 1987; on each occasion being champion jockey. He succeeded Lester Piggott as first jockey for Henry Cecil, and for him rode four classic winners in 1985, the fillies' triple crown on *Oh So Sharp* and his first Derby winner *Slip Anchor*. Two years later he won the Derby on *Reference Point*. A superb and sympathetic horseman, with great race judgement and a charming personality.

Evonne CAWLEY (Aus) see GOOLAGONG

Henry CECIL (UK)

HORSE RACING

Henry Richard Amherst Cecil. b. 11 Jan 1943 near Aberdeen.

The leading trainer in Britain nine times between 1976 and 1990; in 1985 he was the first to achieve season's winnings of over £1 million and in 1988 broke a record which had stood for 120 years with a total of 180 winners (from 446 starts). He had over 100 winners 11 times between 1978 and 1990, with previous best totals of 109 in 1978, 128 in 1979 and 132 in 1985.
After attending agricultural college and working in Europe and the USA he was assistant trainer to his step-father Sir Cecil Boyd-Rochfort (qv) 1964-8, before starting training at Freemason Lodge, Newmarket in 1969. In 1976 he moved to Warren Place, previously used by his father-in-law Noel Murless (qv). His first Classics winner was *Bolkonski* in the 1975 2000 Guineas and his first Derby winner *Slip Anchor* in 1985, in which year he won four of the five Classics, as *Oh So Sharp* took the fillies' triple crown.

Johnny CECOTTO (Ven)

MOTOR CYCLING

Alberto Cecotto. b. 25 Jan 1956 Caracas.

Riding for Yamaha, he made a sensational start to his Grand Prix career in 1975 when he won the French 250cc and 350cc races at the age of 19 and went on to win the 350cc title, the youngest ever world champion, and to place fourth at 250cc.
Born of Italian parents, his father owned a garage and bought him a 750cc Honda, on which he had his first races, but it was on a Yamaha that he won the Venezuelan 1000cc titles in 1973 and 1974 before coming to race in Europe. In his career between 1975 and 1980 this exciting rider won 14 Grand Prix races, nine at 350cc, three 500 cc and two 250cc, and was champion at 750cc in 1978.
In 1983-4 he contested 18 world championship motor races, but his best placing was sixth in the 1983 US GP West. He won the Daytona 200 race in the USA in 1976.

Michel CELAYA (Fra)

RUGBY UNION

Michel Celaya. b. 27 Jul 1930 Biarritz.

With 50 international appearances (1953-61) at lock or No.8, he was France's most capped player until Roland Bertranne bettered his record. Appointed captain for the 1958 tour of South Africa he was injured in the first match and Lucien Mias led the team in the Test series when France scored a memorable victory. Celaya made three further tours of South Africa, as assistant manager in 1971 and 1975 and as coach in 1980. He played for Biarritz, then Montluçon and Stade Bordelais before returning to Biarritz.

Orlando CEPADA (USA/PR)

BASEBALL

Orlando Manuel Cepada Penne, b. 17 Sep 1937 Ponce, Puerto Rico.

Cepeda began his career with the San Francisco Giants in 1958 and stayed with them until 1966 when he was traded to the St Louis Cardinals. A first baseman, he was the first great Latin player in the major leagues, and some consider him still the greatest ever. He was very popular in San Francisco until knee injuries limited his effectiveness. Still, in 1966 with the Cardinals he earned the Comeback Player of the Year Award and in 1967 helped them win the World Series. His knee injuries then severely hampered his play and he was traded several times before his 1974 retirement. Cepada was considered a certainty for the Hall of Fame at his retirement. However, he was later convicted of marijuana possession and spent ten months in prison and this has weighed against him in the minds of the Cooperstown selectors.
Career 1958-74: 2351 hits Avg. .297, HR 379. Best season: 1961 - .311, 46 HR, 142 RBI.

Miroslav CERAR (Yug)

GYMNASTICS

Miroslav Cerar. b. 28 Oct 1939 Ljubljana.

An expert on the pommel horse at which he took the Olympic gold medal in 1964 and 1968, and won three successive World titles, 1962, 1966 and 1970. His final triumph to seal 12 years at the top in gymnastics came in his home town of Ljubljana. He was all-around European champion in 1961 and 1963, won a World gold medal at parallel bars in 1962, and an Olympic bronze at horizontal bar in 1964 and was Yugoslav champion for 13 successive years.
A lawyer, he added a new dimension to pommel horse skills, increasing the length of the exercise, and he was the first to show real aptitude in shears and extension in the double leg circle.

Marcel CERDAN (Fra)

BOXING

Marcellin Cerdan. b. 22 Jul 1916 Sidi-bel-Abbès, Algeria, d. 27 Oct 1949 Azores.

The son of a butcher, Cerdan turned professional at 17 and won the French middlewight title in 1938. In 1942 he won the European title and in 1948, at 32, he won the world middleweight title by knocking out Tony Zale. He held the title only briefly, losing it in 1949 to Jake LaMotta. Preparing for a return bout against LaMotta, Cerdan was killed when his plane crashed in the Azores.
Cerdan was the most beloved boxer in France after Georges Carpentier. His idolatry was helped by a well-publicised love affair with French chanteuse Edith Piaf. His son **Marcel Cerdan Jr** (b. 4 Dec 1943) had a successful professional boxing career.
Career record: W - 119 (74), L - 4, D -0.

Raymond CEULEMANS (Bel)

BILLIARDS

Raymond Ceulemans. b. 12 Jul 1935.

Winner of a record 20 world titles at three-cushion billiards. He was the champion in 1963-73, 1975-80, 1983, 1985 and 1990.

Wilt CHAMBERLAIN (USA)

BASKETBALL

Wilton Norman Chamberlain. b. 21 Aug 1936 Philadelphia, Pennsylvania.

Considered by some as the greatest basketball player ever. At 2.18m *7' 2"* and close to 135kg *300lb*, Chamberlain was enormous for his era of the late 1950s and 1960s. He re-wrote the record book as the most prolific scorer and rebounder the game has ever seen. His greatest scoring feat was surely his season average of 50.5

points per game (4029 points in 80 games) in 1961/2. On 2 Mar 1962 he set an NBA record likely to stand forever when he scored 100 points in a single game against the New York Knicks. He led the NBA in scoring each year 1960-6 and in rebounding eleven times, with the record of 55 rebounds in a single game. He is the only player to have led the league in all three major statistical categories, having led the league in assists in 1968.

The only criticism about Chamberlain was that he did not win enough. He was twice All-American at the University of Kansas but in the NCAA Championship game of 1958, his Kansas team lost in triple overtime to the University of North Carolina. That pattern persisted in the NBA, wherehe started with the Philadelphia Warriors in 1960, after first playing briefly with the Harlem Globetrotters. He played for the Warriors when they moved to San Francisco in 1963 before returning to Philadelphia with the 76ers. He spent the last four years of his career with the Los Angeles Lakers, retiring in 1973.

For most of his career his teams played second fiddle to the great Boston Celtic dynasty, led by their dominant center, Bill Russell. He did, however, play on two Championship teams, the 1967 Philadelphia 76ers and the 1972 Los Angeles Lakers, and both warrant strong consideration as the greatest professional teams ever. After his playing career ended, Chamberlain stayed in the limelight by making movies and sponsoring both track athletes and volleyball teams.

NBA career: 31,419 points in 1045 games, av. 30.1, an average exceeded only by Michael Jordan; a record 23,924 rebounds, av. 22.9. Playoffs: 3607 points in 160 games, av. 22.5.

John CHAMBERS (UK)

ADMINISTRATION

John Graham Chambers. b. 12 Feb 1841 Llanelli, d. 4 Mar 1883 Earl's Court, London.

After rowing for Cambridge in the Boat race 1862-3, Chambers won the 7 mile walk at the AAC Championships in 1866, but his influence as an administrator far exceeded any mark he made as a competitor. Educated in France before Eton and Cambridge, there was scarcely any sport in Britain which did not benefit from his influence.

He founded the Inter-Varsity Sports, staged the FA Cup final in 1873, and instituted amateur championships in billiards, boxing, cycling and wrestling. He devised the Queensberry rules for boxing and rewrote the rules for billiards, yet still found time to edit a national newspaper, coach the Cambridge crew to four successive Boat Race wins, and row beside Captain Webb when he swam the Channel. He also managed the Lillie Bridge sports ground. This almost unbelievable frenzy of activity came partly as a result of having to earn his living after his father, a wealthy Welsh landowner, made some unwise investments. Whatever the motive, the contribution of Chambers to British sport was immense. Sadly the prodigious workload took its toll and he died at the early age of 40.

Mrs R.L.CHAMBERS (UK) see DOUGLASS

Frank CHANCE (USA)

BASEBALL

Frank Leroy Chance. b. 9 Sep 1877 Fresno, California, d. 15 Sep 1924 Los Angeles.

The first baseman in the famous poem about the double play combination 'Tinkers-to-Evers-to-Chance'. He played first base most of his career, which was spent with the Chicago Cubs 1898-1912 and the New York Giants 1913-14; from 1905 he was a superb playing manager with those teams. He led the Cubs to four pennants in five years 1906-10. In 1906 the Cubs won 116 games, which still stands as a major league record.

He was a good first baseman but far from one of the greatest ever. His fame rests primarily on the poem and his managing career.

Career batting: Avg. .296. Best season: 1906 - .319, 103 Runs.

Bhagwant CHANDRASEKHAR (Ind)

CRICKET

Bhagwant Subramanya Chandrasekhar. b. 17 May 1945 Mysore.

Bowling medium-paced leg breaks and googlies he was a vital member of the great Indian spinning combinations of the 1960s and 1970s. His finest performances came against Engand in the early 1970s. At The Oval in 1971 he took 6-38 in an inspired spell in the second innings to destroy England's batting and pave the way for India's first ever victory against England, and in the 1972/3 series in India he took 35 wickets at 18.91 including his best Test analysis of 8-79 at Delhi. His right arm was withered due to polio as a child, but that did not seem to inhibit his bowling with it, and he used a very fast arm-action. He played for Mysore throughout his career, and was a negligible batsman, one of the few great Test players who took more wickets than he scored runs, and with a record number of 23 ducks (in his 41 completed Test innings).
58 Tests 1963-79: 167 runs at 4.02, HS 22; 242 wickets at 29.74, BB 8-79; 25 catches. First-class 1963-80: 600 runs at 4.61, HS 25; 1063 wickets at 24.03, BB 9-72; 107 catches.

Herbert CHAPMAN (UK)

FOOTBALL

Herbert Chapman. b. Jan 1875 Kiveton Park, Sheffield, d. 6 Jan 1934 Hendon, London.

A man who raised the profession of football manager to new heights. He created teams at both Huddersfield Town and Arsenal that won three consecutive English League titles.
Having trained as a mining engineer, he signed as a professional footballer for Northampton in 1901, moving to Notts County in 1903 and Tottenham Hotspur 1905, before returning to Northampton as player-manager in 1907. He took over as secretary-manager of Leeds City in 1912. His glory days started when he took over at Huddersfield in 1921, leading them to win the FA Cup in 1922 and to start their run of League titles 1924 to 1926. In 1925 he moved to Arsenal, and under his managership, until his death in office in 1934, they were the leading team in the country. An authoritative figure, but one who was a great innovator, tactically and technically.

Frank CHAPOT (USA)

EQUESTRIAN

Frank Davis Chapot. b. 24 Feb 1932 Camden, New Jersey.

Chapot competed in Olympic show jumping six times, winning two silver medals in the team event, and having a highest individual placing of fourth in 1968. At the Pan-American Games he won two gold medals and one silver in show jumping and, in 1966, he placed second in the European Championship to become the first American medallist in this event.

Greg CHAPPELL (Aus)

CRICKET

Gregory Stephen Chappell. b. 7 Aug 1948 Unley, South Australia.

A beautifully correct right-handed batsman, who surpassed Don Bradman's record number of runs for Australia. His Test career average of well over 50 showed that he was a batsman of the very highest class. A brilliant slip fielder, he also set a Test record for most catches, including a record seven in a match against England at Perth in December 1974, and was a useful medium-paced swing bowler. He succeeded his brother Ian as captain of Australia, and although he was a much less flamboyant character, led his team to victory in 21 of the 48 matches in which he was in charge from 1975 to 1983. Against New Zealand at Wellington in March 1974 Greg set a record for the most runs in a Test (since passed by Graham Gooch), with the rare feat of a 200 and a 100, 247* and 133; the achievement was made unique by the fact that Ian also scored two centuries, 145 and 121, in this match. Greg's peak series aggregate was 702 at 117.00 in 6 Tests against West Indies in 1975/6. He played for South Australia 1966-73, Queensland as captain 1973-84,

and in England gained much experience playing for Somerset in 1968-9. Awarded the MBE. His younger brother **Trevor** (b. 21 Oct 1952) played three Tests for Australia in 1981.
87 Tests 1970-84: 7110 runs at 53.86, 24 100s HS 247; 47 wickets at 40.70, BB 5-61; 122 catches.*
74 One-day Ints: 2331 runs at 40.18, 3 100s HS 138; 72 wickets at 29.11, BB 5-15; 23 catches.*
First-class 1966-84: 24,535 runs at 52.20, 74 100s HS 247; 291 wickets at 29.95, BB 7-40; 376 catches, 1 stumping.*

Ian CHAPPELL (Aus)

CRICKET
Ian Michael Chappell. b. 26 Sep 1943 Unley, South Australia.

An abrasive character, a hard-playing and successful right-handed batsman, who led Australia to victory in 15 of the 30 Tests in which he was captain. His encouragement of the practice of 'sledging', verbal abuse of his opponents on the cricket field, brought him much criticism and the game into disrepute, but his results and tactical appreciation were undeniable. He played for South Australia, whom he captained from 1970 to 1976, and was also a useful leg-break bowler and an outstanding slip fielder.
His grandfather **Victor Richardson** (1894-1969) played 19 Tests for Australia 1924-36, and captained them five times, and his brother **Greg** (qv) succeeded him as Australia's leader. Ian continued to play for Australia under Greg both before and after both the Chappells, with most of their team, defected to play for Kerry Packer's World Series Cricket. He became a commentator and presenter with Packer's Channel 9 TV.
75 Tests 1964-80: 5345 runs at 42.42, 14 100s HS 196; 20 wickets at 65.80, BB 2-11; 105 catches.
16 One-day Ints: 673 runs at 48.07, HS 86; 2 wickets at 11.50, BB 2-14; 5 catches.
First-class 1961-80: 19,680 runs at 48.35, 59 100s HS 209; 176 wickets at 37.57, BB 5-29; 312 catches, 1 stumping.

Bob CHARLES (NZ)

GOLF
Robert James Charles. b. 14 Mar 1936 Carterton.

Charles won national championships in four decades, with the New Zealand Open in 1954, 1966, 1970, 1973 and 1980. He is universally acclaimed as the greatest left-handed golfer of all-time. In addition, in his prime some people considered him the finest putter in the world. His career peaked in 1963 when he defeated Phil Rodgers in a play-off to win the British Open. He also won the World Match-play title in 1969 and had five victories on the US PGA tour. From 1986 he has been highly successful on the PGA Seniors tour, lying second on the all-time money list with $3,642,545 and 18 tournament victories. He won the British Senior Open in 1993. Awarded the OBE and then the CBE in 1991.

Ezzard CHARLES (USA)

BOXING
Ezzard Mack Charles. b. 7 Jul 1921 Lawrenceville, Georgia, d. 27 May 1970 Chicago, Illinois.

In 1939 Charles won the golden gloves middleweight title and he turned professional the next year. After Joe Louis retired the National Boxing Association nominated Charles to fight Joe Walcott for the vacant heavyweight title in 1949. Charles won on points and defended the title eight times, including a victory over a comebacking Joe Louis in 1950. In July 1951 he lost the title to Walcott. Charles attempted to regain the heavyweight championship against Walcott in 1952 and twice against Rocky Marciano in 1954 but failed each time. After his retirement he was wheelchair bound for his last years and died aged only 48.
Career record: W - 96 (58), L - 25, D -1.

John CHARLES (UK)

FOOTBALL
William John Charles. b. 27 Dec 1931 Cwmdu, nr. Swansea.

Winning the first of his 38 caps in 1950

shortly after his 18th birthday he was then the youngest-ever Welsh international. During his years in Italy he was not always available for international selection, otherwise he would have been capped far more often. Signed as an amateur by Leeds United when only 15, he initially played at centre-half but soon made a successful switch to centre-forward. His goalscoring abilities were a major factor in Leeds' promotion to the First Division in 1956 and the following season, after he had topped the First Division scorers with 38 goals, he was transferred to Juventus for a British record transfer fee of £65,000. He helped Juventus win the Italian Cup twice and the League three times. In August 1962 Charles returned to Leeds, but after playing in 11 matches he joined Roma. His return to Italy was equally brief as after only 10 games he signed for Cardiff City and then after a further 8 games he retired from first-class football and became player-manager of Hereford United and later Merthyr Tydfil.
Blessed with a magnificent physique he scored many goals with his head but he also had a fierce shot and was an excellent distributor of the ball. During his five years in Italian football he never lost his reputation for fine sportsmanship and was known to the fans as the 'Gentle Giant'.
His brother **Mel** (b. 14 May 1935 Swansea) played 31 internationals for Wales 1955-63.

Rik CHARLESWORTH (Aus)

HOCKEY

Dr Richard Ian Charlesworth. b. 6 Feb 1952 Subiaco, Perth, Western Australia.

A four-time Olympian and one of Australia's greatest players. After making his Olympic debut in 1972, he won a silver medal in 1976 but because of the 1980 boycott his third Olympic appearance was delayed until 1984. In 1988 he played in his fourth Olympic tournament. He represented Australia 234 times and since 1983 has been the member of the House of Representatives for Perth.
He was also a useful cricketer, a left-handed batsman who played in 47 matches for Western Australia in the 1970s, scoring 2327 runs (av. 30.22) in first-class cricket with a top score of 101 not out.

Bobby CHARLTON (UK)

FOOTBALL

Robert Charlton. b. 11 Oct 1937 Ashington, Northumberland.

After signing for Manchester United as an amateur in 1953 he turned professional the following year and remained with the club for virtually his entire playing career. The 8-year contract he signed with United in 1968 is the longest in League history.
His total of 106 caps (1958-70) stood as an England record until beaten by Bobby Moore in 1973. He played in every forward position except outside-right, and his total of 49 goals remains an England record. A survivor of the Munich air disaster he played with his elder brother, Jackie, in England's 1966 winning World Cup team and was voted Footballer of the Year for both Europe and England that year. He was awarded the OBE in 1969 and the CBE in 1974.
At club level he scored 198 goals in 606 League appearances for Manchester United and helped them win the European Cup 1968, the FA Cup 1963 and the Football League 1957, 1965 and 1967.
After retiring in 1973 he became manager of Preston North End and played for them in 1974/5. He later served briefly as a director of Wigan Athletic and in 1984 was appointed a director of Manchester United. He now runs a football coaching school.
His powerful, accurate shooting, particularly from long range, was the hallmark of his game but his fine all-round skills made him one of the most admired players of his generation.

Eddie CHARLTON (Aus)

SNOOKER

Edward Charlton. b. 31 Oct 1929 Merewether, New South Wales.

Charlton was the winner of a record 14 Australian snooker titles between 1964 and 1984, but World Championship success just eluded him. He was beaten by John

Pulman in a World championship challenge in 1968 and, a semi-finalist eight times between 1971 and 1982, lost to Ray Reardon in the 1973 and 1975 finals, the latter by 30-31. He also unsuccessfully challenged Rex Williams for the World Professional title at Billiards in 1975.
A fine all-round sportsman, 'Fast Eddie' was in the surf boat crew that won the 1950 Australian championship, had a successful career as an amateur middleweight boxer and played first-grade soccer and rugby league. He started playing billiards at nine, and became a professional snooker player in 1963. He won the BBC Pot Black series in 1972-3 and 1980.

Jack CHARLTON (UK)

FOOTBALL

John Charlton. b. 8 May 1935 Ashington, Northumberland.

Although he signed professional forms for Leeds United in 1952, he did not win his first England cap until 1965 when he was almost 30. He remained with Leeds throughout his career scoring 70 goals in 629 League appearances. He won the last of his 35 England caps in 1970 and retired three years later. At centre-half he was a stalwart of England's World Cup winning side in 1966 and helped Leeds to a host of honours: League Division II 1964, League Cup 1968, League Division I 1969, FA Cup 1972 and the Inter-Cities Fairs Cup 1968 and 1971. In 1967 he was voted Footballer of the Year.
Between 1973 and 1985 he served as manager of Middlesbrough (twice), Sheffield Wednesday, and Newcastle United. In February 1986 he took over as manager of Ireland, steering them to their best ever success in international competition. He has also hosted a popular TV programme on angling. Awarded the OBE 1974.

Chris CHATAWAY (UK)

ATHLETICS

(Rt. Hon.) Christopher John Chataway. b. 31 Jan 1931 Chelsea, London.

The 'Red Fox' was a charismatic athlete who went on to distinguished careers in several fields. He was a friend and Oxford colleague of Roger Bannister, whom he helped to the first sub-four minute mile in 1954. Two months later he was second in the AAA 3 miles, sharing the world record with winner Fred Green, before going on to beat Green to win the Empire Games 3 miles. He took the silver medal behind Vladimir Kuts in the European 5000m, running 14:08.8 to the world record of 13:56.6 by Kuts. In an epic race under the floodlights of the White City in October 1954, both men smashed that record as Chataway gained his revenge and just won 13:51.6 to 13:51.7. Fittingly he ended that year by being voted the first BBC Sports Personality of the Year.
In Olympic 5000m finals Chataway led for much of the last lap in 1952 but fell after being passed by Emil Zátopek and staggered home in 5th place; he was 11th in 1956. He was AAA 3 miles champion in 1952 and 1955, when he ran a world record 13:23.2. He set British records also at 2000m 5:09.4 (1955), 3000m 8:06.2 (1954) and 2 miles 8:41.0 (1954) and had other best times: 1500m 3:43.6 (1955), 1 mile 3:59.8 (1955).
On 25 Sep 1955 he became the first newscaster on Independent Television and he was a Conservative MP 1959-66 and 1969-74, with ministerial positions from 1970-4 before retiring from politics to a business career. He is now chairman of the Civil Aviation Authority.

Julio César CHÁVEZ (Mex)

BOXING

Julio César Chávez. b. 12 Jul 1962 Ciudad Obregón.

The top boxer in the world, pound-for-pound, in the 1990s. He turned professional in 1980 after just 13 amateur fights and won the WBC super-featherweight title in 1984, holding it until he relinquished it in 1987 to contest the WBA lightweight title against Edwin Rosario, whom he stopped easily. Chavez later unified that title and has since added the world junior-welterweight (super light) championship, WBC 1989 and IBF 1990. He remains undefeated at all weight

classes, the longest run by any world champion, including 24 successful world title fights to May 1993. His 23rd win, over Greg Haugen, was in front of a world record 130,000 crowd at the Aztec Stadium in Mexico City in March 1993. A relentless attacker, described by Angelo Dundee as the toughest boxer ever.
Career record: W - 87 (75), L - 0, D -0 to May 1993.

Jack CHESBRO (USA)

BASEBALL

John Dwight Chesbro. b. 5 Jun 1874 North Adams, Massachusetts, d. 6 Nov 1931 Conway, Massachusetts.

'Happy Jack' Chesbro started with the Pittsburgh Pirates, spent seven years 1903-09 with the New York Highlanders (later Yankees), and finished with the Boston Red Sox. In 1904 he enjoyed one of the finest seasons in baseball history. He started 51 games, completed 48, pitched 455 innings, had an ERA of 1.82 and won 41 games (a 20th century record) while losing only 12, with 239 strikeouts. He later built a chicken farm in Conway, coached baseball at Amherst College and played semi-pro baseball.
Career pitching 1899-1909: ERA 2.68; W-L 198-132, SO 1265.

CHI Cheng (Taiwan)

ATHLETICS

Chi Cheng. b. 15 Mar 1944 Hsinchu. Later Reel.

A stylish and graceful all-rounder who set ten world records. Three of these were set in 1969, 26.2 for 200m hurdles and two times of 10.3 for 100y. The rest came during her extraordinary 1970 campaign, when she won all 83 competitions at distances from 50y to 440y, 80m to 200m hurdles, long jump and relays. She had won 70 of 71 in 1969 too! After equalling the world record for 100y at 10.3, she ran the first ever 'even time' by a woman, 10.0 at Portland on 13 Jun 1970, recorded on automatic timing as 10.10. She also ran records for 200m 22.4 (22.62 auto) and 100m hurdles 12.8 (12.93) in Munich on 12 July, for 100m 11.0 (11.22), and 220y 22.7 and 22.6. In 1969 she ran a world record for 200m hurdles with 26.2 in her first race at the event. Sadly a 'snapping hip' injury cut short her career thereafter despite very brave attempts and several operations to try to overcome the problem. What feats she might have achieved at the 1972 Olympics will remain a matter for speculation.
From an 11.1 for 100y in 1964 Chi set a record 44 Asian records, moving to the USA to study physical education at California Polytechnic College, where she was coached by Vince Reel, whom she later married and subsequently divorced. At the 1968 Olympics she was 3rd at 80m hurdles and 7th at 100m. She was elected to the Taiwan senate in 1981 and heads the national athletics federation.
Other bests: 440y 52.5 (1970), long jump 6.42i (1970), pentathlon 4844 (1968).

Claudio CHIAPUCCI (Ita)

CYCLING

Claudio Chiapucci. b. 28 Feb 1963.

An outstanding climber, King of the Mountains in the Tour de France in 1991 and 1992, but not so strong at time trials. This has meant that he has yet to be able to overcome Miguel Indurían to win the overall race, although after 81st place in his first Tour in 1989, he wore the Maillot Jaune for eight days in 1990 and has been 2nd, 3rd, 2nd and 6th in successive years. It has been a similar story in the Giro d'Italia, in which he was 2nd in 1991 and 1992 and 3rd in 1993.
He turned professional in 1985, with his first major wins coming in 1989. He won the Milan - San Remo classic in 1991

Sam CHIFNEY (UK)

HORSE RACING

Samuel Chifney. b. 1753 Norfolk, d. 8 Jan 1807 Fleet Prison, London, to which he had been committed for debt.

He brought new skills and tactics to jockeyship, often saving his horses for a late swoop,. Apprenticed in 1770 to Foxe's stable in Newmarket, he was the first jockey to win the Derby and Oaks double in the same year, 1789, and rode three more Oaks winners. After being employed to ride the Prince of Wales's horses he was involved in scandal in 1791 when Escape finished last in a race at Newmarket at 2/1 on. The Prince retired from the Turf and Chifney was strongly suspected of pulling the horse. A dandy, his lack of modesty was shown by his biography entitled Genius Genuine. One son Samuel (1786-1854) was also a talented jockey, and rode the winners of nine classics between 1807 and 1843, and another **William** (1784-1862) trained five classic winners.

CHIQUITO de CAMBO (Fra)

PELOTA

né Joseph Apesteguy. b. 10 May 1881 Cambo, Basses-Pyrénées. d. 1955.

The greatest player in history who was the world's No.1 from the turn of the century until his defeat by Jean Urruty in 1938. He was a major influence in the development of the game, and instrumental in promoting the building of most of the major frontons. Although he enjoyed substantial earnings during his lengthy career, he died a poor man. His talents are commemorated by a memorial in his home town, where the fronton named after him is one of the most famous pelota courts in the world.

Louis CHIRON (Monaco)

MOTOR RACING

Louis Alexandre Chiron. b. 3 Aug 1899 Monaco, d. 22 Jun 1979.

After a very long career he holds the record for the oldest driver ever to contest a world championship race, sixth at Monaco in 1955 at 55 years 292 days. He won the 1954 Monte Carlo Rally in a Lancia. A charismatic figure, he was in charge of the Monaco Grand Prix after his retirement from racing in 1956.

In the 1920s he began his racing career in Bugattis, and also raced for Alfa and briefly Mercedes. His most successful year was 1928 when he won six Grand Prix races, and he won the French Grand Prix four times, 1931, 1934, 1937, 1947.

Galina CHISTYAKOVA (USSR/Rus)

ATHLETICS

Regina Galina Chistyakova. b. 26 Jul 1962 Izmail, Ukraine.

A top-class long jumper, setting the world record at 7.52m in 1988 (her fourth USSR record), she has become one of the major pioneers of the women's triple jump, setting a world best of 14.52m in 1989, with five world indoor bests at this event as well as one at long jump.

Major long jump titles won: World Indoors 1989, European Indoors 1985, 1989-90; European Cup 1985 and 1989; World Cup 1989. European silver medallist 1986, Olympic bronze 1988.

Married to Aleksandr Beskrovniy (European Junior triple jump champion 1979, with best of 17.53m in 1984), she gave birth to a daughter in 1983.

Nadezhda CHIZHOVA (USSR/Rus)

ATHLETICS

Nadezhda Chizhova. b. 29 Sep 1945 Usolye-Sibirskoye, Siberia. Later Baryshnikova.

At the shot she achieved the unprecedented feat of four successive European titles between 1966 and 1974 and won a set of Olympic medals: gold 1972, silver 1976, bronze 1968. She also won five European indoor titles, and the European Junior shot/discus double in 1964, with six Soviet titles, 1967-70, 1972 and 1974. She also had three European Cup victories.

Her championship success was augmented by ten world records from 18.67m in 1968 to 21.45m in 1973; all but the last were ratified by the IAAF.

Eddy CHOONG (Mal)

BADMINTON

Ewe-beng Choong. b. 1930.

Despite being only 1.58m *5' 2"* tall, the 'pocket prodigy from Penang' was a dynamic badminton player and the champion player during the 1950s. He came to England to study law and brought immense vitality to the game in Britain. At the All-England Championships he was singles champion in 1953-4 and 1956-7 and won the men's doubles with his elder brother Choong Ewe-Leong (**David** b. 5 Apr 1929) each year 1951-3, adding the mixed doubles with June White in 1953. He helped Malaya to win the Thomas Cup in 1955 and was All-Malayan singles champion in 1957. After retiring as a player he coached Tan Aik Huang to win the All-England title in 1966 and raced motor cars.

CHUANG TSE-TUNG (China)

TABLE TENNIS

Chuang Tse-tung. b. 1942.

The son of a Peking doctor, he joined the Chinese team in 1959 after some outstanding performances as a schoolboy. At the three successive World Championships, held biennially 1961-5, Chuang was a member of the winning Swaythling Cup team and beat Li Fu-jung in the singles final on each occasion. It was later revealed that the results in these finals had been pre-arranged by the Chinese team management In 1964 he was appointed a member of the National People's Congress but with the coming of the Cultural Revolution he fell foul of the new authorities. Reports that he had been killed by the Red Guards proved to be ill-founded and he won a fourth Swaythling Cup gold medal in 1971 when China returned to international competition after their self-imposed absence in 1965.

He was an exciting attacking player who had an all-round mastery of the penholder grip and was particularly strong on the half-volley. As a student at a physical culture college he brought an exceptional degree of fitness to his game.

Aleksandra CHUDINA (USSR)

ATHLETICS

Aleksandra Georgiyevna Chudina. b. 6 Nov 1923, d. 28 Oct 1990 Moscow.

One of the most remarkable all-rounders in the history of sport, she set world records at three different events in athletics, played for the USSR's world championship winning volleyball team, and excelled also at ice hockey, basketball, cycling and tennis. Physically, at 1.88m tall and weighing 73kg, she stood out amongst her fellow competitors.

She set five world records for the pentathlon, although the first three, 1947-50, were not recognised. Her ratified marks were 4704 points in 1953 and 4750 in 1955. She ran on the USSR's world record setting 4 x 200m team in 1950 and high jumped 1.73m in 1955.

Her opportunities for winning major championship medals were restricted by the fact that the USSR did not compete at the 1948 Olympics and also that the pentathlon was not included until 1964, but her amazing versatility was shown in Helsinki in 1952, when she won the silver medal at the javelin and bronze at both high jump and long jump. She won the European pentathlon in 1954, and had been high jump silver medallist in 1946.

She won ten World Student Games titles at five events and between 1945 and 1956 won 31 Soviet outdoor titles at individual events, nearly twice as many as the next best ever: nine at pentathlon, seven each at high jump and long jump, four javelin, three at 80m hurdles and one at 400m.

She led the world year lists with personal bests at 400m, 58.6 in 1946; long jump, 6.24 in 1953; and javelin, 52.75 in 1953. She also ranked in the world's all-time top ten at 80m hurdles when she ran 11.3 in 1950. Her shot best was 14.33 in 1955.

Viktor CHUKARIN (USSR/Ukr)

GYMNASTICS

Viktor Ivanovich Chukarin. b. 9 Nov 1921 Mariupol (now Zdhanov), d. 26 Aug 1984 Lvov.

In 1952 when the USSR entered the Olympic family, Chukarin, at the age of 30 and a World War II prisoner-of-war, won the all-around gymnastic title, adding a team gold and two gold and two silver medals at individual apparatus. A teacher, he successfully defended his overall title in 1956 and took his Olympic medal collection to 11, with two more gold, a silver and a bronze. In between these triumphs he was the overall World champion in 1954, with individual success on parallel bars. His first national title came at horizontal bars in 1948 and he was USSR all-round champion in 1949-51 and 1955. He became head of gymnastics at the Lvov Institute of Physical Culture.

Héctor CHUMPITAZ (Peru)

FOOTBALL

Héctor Chumpitaz. b. 12 Apr 1944 Lima.

Often quoted as the most capped player from any country, but although between 1963 and 1982 he appeared in each of the 150 matches played by the Peruvian team, these included 49 games against club sides. This still leaves him, however, as the most capped Peruvian of all-time. He began his career with Municipal before moving onto the more prestigious Lima clubs of Universitario and Sporting Cristal. A centre-back he led Peru into the 1970 World Cup.

Clive CHURCHILL (Aus)

RUGBY LEAGUE

Clive Bernard Churchill. b. 21 Jan 1927 Merewether, nr. Newcastle, New South Wales, d. 9 Aug 1985 Sydney.

Although standing only 5ft 7in *1.70m* he was a devastating tackler and a fast elusive runner; an excellent touch finder and an accurate left-footed goal kicker; the outstanding full back of the immediate post-war era. Many rated 'The Little Master' as Australia's greatest ever rugby league player.

Having joined South Sydney from Central Newcastle he played 155 first grade games for them 1948-58, playing in five premiership winning teams. He then coached Northern Suburbs to the Brisbane premiership in 1959 and coached with much success in New South Wales and Queensland until his retirement in 1975. He made his Test début for Australia in 1948 and made 34 international appearances, 32 in consecutive matches before a broken arm forced him to miss the three Tests against New Zealand in 1956. He also set a record by captaining Australia in 24 consecutive matches, his first appearance as captain being before he had led any representative side and when he was still only vice-captain of his club. He made seven overseas tours including trips to Britain and France in 1948/9, 1952/3 and 1956/7, with a fourth visit as coach in 1959/60. He rated as his career highlight the match on 22 Jul 1950 when he captained Australia to beat England 5-2 at Sydney to regain the Ashes for the first time for 30 years. After his first tour of Britain, Workington offered £10,000 for his services but the transfer ban which operated between England and Australia prevented him joining the Lancashire club. His memory is perpetuated by the Clive Churchill Medal, awarded annually to the best player in the Sydney Premiership Grand Final.

Waldemar CIERPINSKI (GDR)

ATHLETICS

Waldemar Cierpinski. b. 3 Aug 1950 Neugattersleben.

Cierpinski emulated the feat of Abebe Bikila by winning two Olympic marathon gold medals. He was a surprise winner at Montreal in 1976 in an Olympic and GDR record of 2:09:55, but maintained top-class form in ensuing years as he was fourth in the 1978 Europeans, won his second Olympic gold in Moscow, was second in the European Cup in 1981 and won that event in 1983, when he also took the World bronze. In all he won 11 of his 28 marathons 1974-85. He had started his international career at the steeplechase, at which he was GDR champion in 1972, before making his marathon début in 1974. *Track bests: 1500m 3:42.2 (1974), 5000m 13:36.6 (1975), 10,000m 28:28.2 (1975), 3000m steeplechase 8:32.4 (1974).*

Johan CLAASSEN (SAf)

RUGBY UNION

Johannes Theodorus Claassen. b. 23 Sep 1930 Prince Albert.

In addition to making 105 appearances for Western Transvaal as a speedy lock he played 28 times for his country which was then a record. He had mixed fortunes when

captaining South Africa; in two matches against France in 1958 he led the Springboks in the only home Test series they had lost since 1896, but on the other seven occasions 1961-2 when he was captain, South Africa won every match. Together with 'Salty' Du Rand he formed an outstanding second row and they played together in 10 internationals.
Educated at Potchefstroom University, Claassen became a schoolmaster and was coach on the South African tour of France in 1968 and 1974 and of Australia in 1971. In 1981 he was manager of the tour to New Zealand.

King CLANCY (Can)

ICE HOCKEY

Francis Michael Clancy. b. 25 Feb 1903 Ottawa, Ontario.

King Clancy excelled at every level of ice hockey. As a player he was a defenseman for the Ottawa Senators and Toronto Maple Leafs, but in one memorable Stanley Cup game he played all six positions on the ice, including goalie. When he went to Toronto in 1930, it was then the biggest trade in hockey history. He became a referee, serving the NHL in that capacity from 1937 to 1949. From 1953 to 1956 he was the coach of the Toronto Maple Leafs and then moved into administration; he was an assistant to the Maple Leafs' general manager and club president.
NHL career 1921-37 - 593 games, 137 goals, 280 points. Best year: 1929/30: 17 goals, 40 points.

Dit CLAPPER (Can)

ICE HOCKEY

Aubrey Victor Clapper. b. 9 Feb 1907 Newmarket, Ontario, d. 20 Jan 1978 Peterborough, Ontario.

An unusual hockey star in that he played both forward (right wing) and defense during his career with the Boston Bruins, whom he helped win six regular season championships and three Stanley Cups. He started out as a right winger, and switched to defense in 1939. For his last three years, Clapper was a player-coach. His most memorable seasons came when he, Cooney Weiland and Dutch Gainor combined to form the Dynamite Line.
NHL career 1927-47 - 833 games, 228 goals, 474 points. Best year: 1929/30: 41 goals, 61 points.

Douglas CLARK (UK)

RUGBY LEAGUE

Douglas Clark. b. 2 May 1891 Ellenborough, Cumberland, d. 1 Feb 1951 Birkby, Huddersfield, Yorkshire.

A loose forward of immense strength who was also well-known as a wrestler. He first played for the amateur club Brookland Rovers before signing for Huddersfield in 1909.
During the 1914 tour of Australia he was one of the heroes of the famous 'Rorke's Drift Test' when Great Britain, although reduced to only ten men, held on to win 14-6 and clinch the series. For most of the match Clark played with a broken thumb and collar bone. Severely gassed during the war, he was discharged with a 95% disability but made a second tour of Australasia in 1920. Nine of his eleven Great Britain caps came during the 1914 and 1920 tours of Australia and New Zealand. He played in three winning Challenge Cup and five Championship final teams.

Dutch CLARK (USA)

AMERICAN FOOTBALL

Earl Harry Clark. b. 11 Oct 1906 Fowler, Colorado, d. 5 Aug 1978 Canon City, Colorado.

Clark played college ball at Northwestern and then Colorado College and was named All-American as a running back in both his junior and senior years. In 1931 he was signed by the Portsmouth Spartans of the NFL and he led the NFL in scoring in 1932. He then quit pro football for a year, serving as a coach at the Colorado School of Mines. He returned in 1934 with the same team, which was by now the Detroit Lions, and played with them until 1938, again leading the league in scoring in 1935 and 1936. In his last two years he served as a player-coach, and after his retirement coached in the NFL through 1941. He was subsequently elected to both the College and Pro Football Halls of Fame.

Jim CLARK (UK)

MOTOR RACING

James Clark. b. 14 Mar 1936 Kilmany, Fife, d. 7 Apr 1968 Hockenheim.

World drivers' champion in 1963 and 1965, he beat Fangio's record with 25 Grand Prix wins in his career, including a record seven wins in a year in 1963. He totalled 274 points from his 72 races 1960-8.
The son of a Scottish sheep farmer, he began racing in 1956, when he had several class wins in a Sunbeam. He progressed rapidly, with 12 wins in 20 starts in a D-type Jaguar in 1958 and great success in Lotus Elite and Jaguar cars in 1959, before making his move into single-seater racing. He made his World Championship début in 1960 for Lotus, for whom he drove for the rest of his career. His first win was at Pau in 1961 and in addition to his two world titles, he was second in 1962 and third in 1964 and 1967. He competed in many types of racing, winning the Indianapolis 500 in 1965, having shaken the Americans by taking second place in a rear-engined Lotus-Ford there in 1963. Killed at Hockenheim when his Formula Two Lotus left the track and hit a tree in the opening round of the European F2 Championship. A great, natural driver, he was highly consistent, always seeming in total control of his car, bringing an unprecedented level of technical perfection to driving.

Bobby CLARKE (Can)

ICE HOCKEY

Robert Earle Clarke. b. 13 Aug 1949 Flin Flon, Manitoba.

Clarke played his entire 15-year career with the Philadelphia Flyers, helping them to win the Stanley Cup in 1974 and 1975. Dave Schultz, the Flyers' enforcer, said of Clarke, 'He was the heart and soul of our club.' He persevered to become a great hockey star despite being a diabetic who took insulin shots daily throughout his professional career. He was a tough, all-round player, with guts in abundance. He used that to make himself the most valuable player on the top team of the mid-70s.
NHL career 1969-84: 1144 games, 358 goals, 1210 points. Playoffs: 135 games, 42 goals, 119 pts. Best years: 1974/5: 89 assists, 116 points; 1975/6: 89 assists, 119 points. Hart Trophy 1973, 1975-6; Masterton Trophy 1972, Lester Pearson Award 1974, Selke Trophy 1983.

Don CLARKE (NZ)

RUGBY UNION

Donald Barry Clarke. b. 10 Nov 1933 Pilhama.

New Zealand's most capped full back whose all-round talents were often overshadowed by his phenomenal kicking abilities. A big man, he made his All Black début in the third Test against the 1956 Springboks when his brother Ian was also in the side. After scoring 8 points in New Zealand's 17-10 victory Don established himself as his country's first choice full back for the remainder of his career. He played in 31 internationals, missing only the second Test against the Wallabies in 1964 due to a knee injury which forced his retirement at the end of the season.
His 207 points was a record for international rugby until beaten by Andy Irvine (Scotland) but stood as a New Zealand record until bettered by Grant Fox in 1988. On the 1957 All Black tour of Australia Clarke scored a record 163 points and he set what was then a world record when he kicked six penalties in the first Test against the 1959 Lions.
His brother **Ian** (b. 5 Mar 1931 Kaponga) played in 24 Tests.

Ron CLARKE (Aus)

ATHLETICS

Ronald William Clarke. b. 21 Feb 1937 Melbourne.

The hero of a generation of distance runners, he didn't just break records but took them into entirely new territory. For instance when he won the 1965 AAA 3 miles he took his own record from 13:00.4

to 12:52.4 and in Oslo four days later he smashed his month-old time for 10,000m of 28:14.0 with 27:39.4. Sadly however he didn't win a major championship gold medal, though he does own one, as, in one of the most heart-warming stories in the world of sport, the great Emil Zátopek gave him one of his.
Clarke set a world junior record for the 1 mile with 4:06.8 in 1956 andat the end of that year carried the Olympic torch into the stadium in Melbourne, but he slipped into obscurity before returning in 1961. He was Australian champion at 3 miles/5000m 1965-9, 6 miles 1966, and 10,000m 1969-70.
In part Clarke's finishing kick let him down, but he was also cruelly deprived at his peak of Olympic glory due to the 1968 Games being held at the high altitude of Mexico City. It seems inconceivable that he would not have run away from his rivals at sea-level, but he ran himself into collapse with 6th at 10,000m and 5th at 5000m. He had won the Olympic bronze at 10km in 1964, when he was also 9th at 5000m and marathon, and won Commonwealth silvers at 3 miles in 1962, both 3 and 6 miles 1966, and 10,000m 1970. He later had serious heart surgery, which he always felt was attributable to excess strain at high altitude.
His bests at his world record distances: 2 miles 8:19.6 (1968), 3 miles 12:50.4 (1966), 5000m 13:16.6 (1966), 6 miles 26:47.0 (1965), 10,000m 27:39.4 (1965), 10 miles 47:12.8 (1965), 20km 59:22.8 (1965), 1 hour 20,232m (1965).

His elder brother **Jack Clarke** (b.1933) had also been a highly promising runner, as well as excelling at cricket, but he decided to follow in the footsteps of their father Tom and to play Australian Rules football for Essendon, whom he captained 1959-64. In 1953, at 19, he was chosen for the All-Australian side and he represented Victoria 29 times, captaining them from 1959. He played for Essendon in five Grand Finals from 1951; they won the last two, in 1962 and 1965.

Leslie CLAUDIUS (India)

HOCKEY
Leslie Walter Claudius. b. 25 Mar 1927.

Of the seven Indians who have won three Olympic gold medals for hockey, only Leslie Claudius and Udam Singh have also won a silver medal. Claudius, who played at right-half, won gold in 1948, 1952 and 1956 and silver in 1960 when he captained the team.

Roger CLEMENS (USA)

BASEBALL
William Roger Clemens. b. 4 Aug 1962 Dayton, Ohio.

The Boston Red Sox pitcher has been the American League winner of the Cy Young Award three times, 1986-7 and 1991. He was also the League MVP in 1986, after a great first full season in which he had an ERA of 2.48 and 238 strikeouts. On 29 Apr 1986 he set the major league single game record of 20 strikeouts in a nine-inning game. After success at high school he went to San Jacinto JC and then to the University of Texas. Tall, 1.93m *6'4"*, and powerful, he has been a dominant figure in the AL for several years and shares the AL record for seven consecutive seasons with 200 or more strikeouts, 1986-92.
Pitching career 1984-92: ERA 2.80, W-L 152-72, SO 1873.

Roberto CLEMENTE (USA/PR)

BASEBALL
Roberto Clemente Walker. b. 18 Aug 1934 Carolina, Puerto Rico, d. 31 Dec 1972 San Juan, Puerto Rico.

The first Latin player to be elected to the Hall of Fame. He played his entire career with the Pittsburgh Pirates and recorded an even 3000 hits. As a rightfielder he had no equal during his playing days, possessing a rifle arm with which he led the National League five times in outfield assists. He won 12 straight Gold Gloves for his defensive prowess. He averaged better than .350 in three seasons, with a peak of .357 in 1967, and was probably deserving of more acclaim. He spoke out against what he

considered prejudice because of his Latin background but he was also hampered by not playing in New York or Los Angeles, nearer the nation's media centres.
Clemente died in a plane crash when he was helping carry emergency supplies to earthquake victims in Nicaragua. The usual five-year waiting period was waived and he was elected to the Hall of Fame in 1973.
Career 1955-72: 3000 hits Avg. .317, HR 240.

Brian CLOSE (UK)

CRICKET

Dennis Brian Close. b. 24 Feb 1931 Rawdon, Leeds, Yorkshire.

Against New Zealand in 1949 Close became the youngest ever England Test cricketer at 18 years 149 days. He never quite fulfilled his youthful promise as an off-spin bowler and hard hitting left-handed batsman, but was turned to on many occasions by England, especially when someone with his great fortitude was needed to stand up to fast bowlers. He was also an outstandingly brave close-to-the-wicket fielder. His Test career was full of gaps, but he was a popular hero when he came into a demoralised team to lead them to victory in the final Test against West Indies in 1966. That was the first of six wins in his seven matches as captain, as he continued most successfully against India and Pakistan in 1967. He was then dropped after using time-wasting tactics in a county match for Yorkshire, whom he led very successfully from 1963-70 in which time they won four Championships. After falling out with his native county, he went to Somerset, whom he captained 1972-7. In 1976 he was recalled, at the age of 45, to the England team to take on the West Indies pace bowlers and he battled on to score 166 runs av. 33.20 in three matches. The title of his autobiography *I Don't Bruise Easily* admirably summed up his qualities. He played League football for Leeds United, Arsenal and Bradford City. Awarded the CBE.
22 Tests 1949-76: 887 runs at 25.34, HS 70; 18 wickets at 29.55, BB 4-35; 24 catches.
3 One-day Ints: 49 runs at 16.33, HS 43; 1 catch.
First-class 1949-86: 34,994 runs at 33.26, 52 100s HS 198; 1171 wickets at 26.42, BB 8-41; 813 catches, 1 stumping.

Brian CLOUGH (UK)

FOOTBALL

Brian Howard Clough. b. 21 Mar 1935 Middlesbrough.

Clough only played twice for England (in 1959), but before his playing career was ended by serious injury at the age of 29 he had established the highest ever goals per game average in the Football League. He totalled 251 goals in 274 games as a centre-forward; 197 for Middlesbrough (1955-61) and 54 for Sunderland (1961-4); all but the last three of these games were in the second division.
He became an inspirational and highly successful manager in his own unique style, initially in partnership with Peter Taylor, with whom he had played at Middlesbrough. Starting with Hartlepool United (1965-7) they moved to Derby County (1967-73), steering them to the second division title in 1969 and to become League champions in 1972. After brief spells with Brighton (1973-4) and 44 days with Leeds United (without Taylor) in 1974, he was manager of Nottingham Forest from 1975 to his retirement in 1993 (with Taylor 1976-82). Under Clough Forest were League champions and League Cup winners in 1978, European Cup and League Cup winners in 1979, European Super Cup and European Cup winners in 1980 and League Cup winners in 1989 and 1990. Awarded the OBE 1991.
His son **Nigel** (b. 19 Mar 1966) played for him at Nottingham Forest and played 11 times for England 1989-93, before being transferred to Liverpool in June 1993.

John COBB (UK)

MOTOR RACING

John Rhodes Cobb. b. 2 Dec 1899 Esher, Surrey, d. 29 Sep 1952 Loch Ness.

Cobb broke the world land speed record three times in his Railton Mobil Special,

with speeds of 350.20 mph *563.58 km/h* in 1938, 369.74/ *595.02* in 1939 and 394.19/ *634.37* in 1947. He was the first man to exceed 400 mph on land, reaching 403.1 mph *648.7 km/h* on a one-way run in 1947. Awarded the Segrave Trophy 1947.
A big man who with his careful, methodical approach, was a perfect test driver, he preferred to race big cars. His first race win was in 1925, and he set many records at Brooklands, including the outer circuit lap record at 215.43 km/h. At one time he held every world record from 1 hour to 24 hours.He was a fur broker by profession. He was killed when attempting the world water speed record on Loch Ness in his jet-engined *Crusader*, after becoming the first man to exceed 200 mph on water. His first run averaged 206.89 mph *332.95 km/h* for a mile with a peak speed of about 240 mph *385 km/h.*

Ty COBB (USA)

BASEBALL

Tyrus Raymond Cobb. b. 18 Dec 1886 Narrows, Georgia, d. 17 Jul 1961 Atlanta, Georgia.

'The Georgia Peach' was the first player elected to baseball's Hall of Fame and is considered by some experts as the greatest player of all time. His greatest ability lay in being able to get hits, reach first base, steal a base and then score. With a career total of 4190 hits he is second all-time to Pete Rose. He led the American League in batting eleven times, in steals six times and in runs scored five times. He also batted over .400 in three different seasons (248 hits at .420 in 1911, 227 at .410 in 1912 and 211 at .401 in 1922). He was a ruthless player with a vindictive personality, who was highly unpopular among his peers in the league. Still, that personality probably made him the great player that he was. He played the outfield for the Detroit Tigers from 1905-26 and spent his last two seasons with the Philadelphia Athletics. After his retirement, Cobb became quite wealthy through some investments in the Coca-Cola company in his native Atlanta.
Career 1905-28: Avg. .366; hits: 4190, HR 118; SB 892.

Henri COCHET (Fra)

TENNIS

Henri Jean Cochet. b. 14 Dec 1901 Villeurbanne, nr Lyons, d. 1 Apr 1987 Paris.

One of the 'Four Musketeers' who was a member of the winning Davis Cup team six times between 1922 and 1933. One of the greatest volleyers the game has ever seen he won seven Grand Slam singles titles: Wimbledon 1927, 1929; US 1928; and the French 1926, 1928, 1930 and 1932, having earlier won the French title in 1922 before overseas players were permitted entry.
His Wimbledon success in 1927 was extraordinary. In the final he lost the first two sets to Jean Borotra, and was 2-5 down in the final set, saving six match points. He had similarly lost the first two sets in the quarter-final against Frank Hunter (USA) and against Bill Tilden in the semi-final, and then he was 1-5 down in the third set! In the doubles, he formed a successful partnership with Jacques Brugnon: together they won Wimbledon 1926 and 1928, and the French 1927, 1930 and 1932, and they won 7 of the 11 Davis Cup rubbers they played together. Between 1922 and 1933, Cochet won 44 (34 singles, 10 doubles) of his 58 Davis Cup rubbers.
Cochet turned professional in 1933 but was reinstated as an amateur after the war and reached the final of the 1949 British Hard Court championships at the age of 49.

Mickey COCHRANE (USA)

BASEBALL

Gordon Stanley Cochrane. b. 6 Apr 1903 Bridgewater, Massachusetts, d. 28 Jun 1962 Lake Forest, Illinois.

Considered to be one of the three or four greatest catchers ever; his lifetime average of .320 is the highest ever for a catcher in major league history. He first demonstrated his leadership qualities as a football quarterback, punter and running back at Boston College. He played his first nine years with the Philadelphia Athletics, leading them to

the championship for three consecutive years 1929-31. He played out his career for four years with the Detroit Tigers, helping them win two pennants and a World Series in 1935, but his career ended in May 1937 when he sustained a fractured skull on a pitch thrown by Yankee Bump Hadley. He later coached and served in multiple scouting and administrative positions for the Yankees and Tigers. Major league great Mickey Mantle was named after Mickey Cochrane.
Career 1925-35: 1652 hits Avg. .320, HR 119; RBI 832. Best season: 1932: 23 HR, 11 RBI, .293 BA.

Sebastian COE (UK)

ATHLETICS

Sebastian Newbold Coe. b. 29 Sep 1956 Chiswick, London.

The complete middle distance runner, Coe is Britain's most prolific world record setter, with nine outdoors and three indoors. His bests at 800m (1:41.73) and 1000m (2:12.18) remain unsurpassed more than a decade later. After taking the silver medal for 800m behind his great rival Steve Ovett he won the Olympic 1500m title in 1980. Four years later he repeated the silver at 800m and then retained his 1500m title, having made a wonderful recovery from serious illness in 1983.
After placing third in the European Junior 1500m in 1975, his first major title was the European Indoor 800m in 1977, and his first world record was 800m in 1:42.40 at Oslo on 5 Jul 1979. Twelve days later at the same venue he set the 1 mile record with 3:48.95, improving his personal best by a remarkable 8.72 secs. He set further records of 3:48.53 and 3:47.33 in 1981. At 1500m he ran a world record 3:32.03 at Zürich in 1979, before losing the record to Ovett.
A title that gave him as much pleasure as his Olympic successes was the European gold at 800m in 1986, for at that, perhaps his best distance, he had been favourite in both 1978 and 1982 , and yet had to settle for bronze and silver respectively. He had had to withdraw from the 1986 Commonwealth Games through viral illness, so his return to fitness was all the more welcome and he went on to add the European silver behind Steve Cram at 1500m, and to miss the 1500m world record narrowly at Rieti, when he ran his best ever time of 3:29.77.
He raced the longer distance less often but was undefeated in a 1500m or 1 mile final from 14 Sep 1976 to 24 Jun 1983.
Controversially omitted from the 1988 Olympic team after failing in the trials through illness, he was second to Abdi Bile in the 1989 World Cup 1500m, but ended his career with a disappointing sixth place in the 1990 Commonwealth Games.
An economics graduate of Loughborough University, he served as vice-chairman of the Sports Council 1986-9 and was elected as Conservative MP for Falmouth and Camborne in 1992. Awarded MBE in 1982, OBE 1990.
Other best: 400m 46.87 (1979).

Paul COFFEY (Can)

ICE HOCKEY

Paul Douglas Coffey. b. 1 Jun 1961 Weston, Ontario.

Began his hockey career in the NHL with the Edmonton Oilers, and, skating alongside Wayne Gretzky, he won three Stanley Cups and two Norris Trophys, 1985-6, in his first seven years in the league. One of the top defensemen in the league, he then played for the Pittsburgh Penguins, where he continued to shine in a different rôle, leading a second-division club 1987-92, Los Angeles 1992 and Detroit 1992-3.
Coffey will forever be remembered for one play. In the 1984 Canada Cup, in the decisive fifth game, the USSR and Canada tied at 2-2 and entered sudden death. Twelve minutes into overtime, two Soviet forwards were away on a break, with only Coffey between them and the goal. Coffey not only broke up the breakaway, he stole a pass and streaked towards the Soviet goal, passing to Mike Bossy who scored the winning goal.
NHL career 1980-93. 953 games, 871 assists, 1201 points. Playoffs: 123 games, 92 assists, 136 points. Best year: 1985/6: 90 assists, 138 points.

Rocky COLAVITO (USA)

BASEBALL

Rocco Domenico Colavito. b. 10 Aug 1933 New York.

Colavito captured the imagination of the fans of the Cleveland Indians, for whom he played the outfield for his first five years in the majors. He was primarily a power home-run hitter and reached 300 home runs faster than all but four players in major league history. He hit over 20 home runs for 11 straight seasons 1956-66. In 1960, Cleveland's fans lost their hero when he was traded straight up to Detroit for singles hitter and batting champion Harvey Kuehn. With Detroit he had his greatest year in 1961, hitting 45 homers and knocking in 140 runs. He later played with Kansas City, Chicago, the New York Yankees, the Los Angeles Dodgers, and again for the Indians from 1965-7. In his last year, with the Yankees, Colavito, who had been brought up as a pitcher-outfielder, pitched in and won one game. He is the last position player to have recorded a pitching win in the major leagues. He had also pitched one game in 1958 with the Indians and retired with a 0.00 ERA. *Career 1955-68: 1730 hits Avg. .266, HR 374; RBI 1159.*

John COLEMAN (Aus)

AUSTRALIAN RULES FOOTBALL

John Coleman. b. 1929, d. 1973.

A hugely popular and brilliantly successful goal kicker in his short career in the VFL, with 537 goals in 99 matches. After kicking 137 goals in 1947 and 160 in 1948 for the provincial team, Hastings, he was signed by Essendon and was an immediate success. He kicked 12 goals in his first match, against Hawthorn in 1949, and kicked 100 goals that year, when he gained selection to the Victoria team. He increased his tally to 120 in 1950 and also led the league with 103 in 1952 and 97 in 1953. However, in 1954 he was forced to retire due to a serious knee injury. He coached Essendon to win the VFL premierships in 1962 and 1965, but died at 44 following a heart attack in 1973.

Cecilia COLLEDGE (UK)

FIGURE SKATING

Magdalena Cecilia Colledge. b. 28 Nov 1920 Hampstead, London.

World figure skating champion, six times British champion and the youngest ever British Olympic competitor. The daughter of a Wimpole Street specialist, she was inspired to take up skating after watching Sonja Henie win her second world title at the Ice Club, Westminster in 1928. Her parents arranged lessons with the renowned Jacques Gerschwiler and in January 1932 she placed second to Megan Taylor at the British Championships. The following month she went to Lake Placid, USA for the Winter Olympics and at the age of 11 yrs 76 days set a record, which still stands, of being the youngest female Olympic competitor from any country in any sport. She was second in the European Championships that year and went on to win six British Championships 1935-8 (two in 1937) and 1946. After finishing second to Sonja Henie at both the 1935 Worlds and the 1936 Olympics, she won the World title in 1937 and the European each year 1937-9. In 1938 she lost her World title to Megan Taylor, her teammate at the 1932 and 1936 Olympics. After serving with the forces as a driver with the Mechanised Transport Corps during the war, she turned professional in July 1946 and in 1951 emigrated to America where, for more than 25 years, she was attached to the prestigious Skating Club of Boston.

Glenna COLLETT VARE (USA)

GOLF

Glenna Collett. b. 20 Jun 1903 New Haven, Connecticut, d. 10 Feb 1989 Gulfstream, Florida. Married Edwin H Vare in 1931.

Collett Vare won a record six US Women's Amateur titles, 1922, 1925, 1928-30 and 1935. She won an estimated 50 major amateur championships, including seven Eastern Amateurs and six North & South Amateurs and the French Amateur in 1925. She also played on the Curtis Cup team from 1932 until 1948. The only omission from Vare's record was her failure to win the British title. In 1925 she lost an early round match to Joyce Wethered, her only rival as the greatest female player of the era. In 1929, Vare and Wethered matched up in the British final, waging a classic battle, with Wethered prevailing 2 & 1.

The Vare Trophy, for the lowest stroke average on the LPGA tour is named in her honour.

Eddie COLLINS (USA)

BASEBALL

Edward Trowbridge Collins Sr. b. 2 May 1887 Millerton, New York, d. 25 Mar 1951 Boston, Massachusetts.

Collins played major league ball for parts of 25 seasons, playing in over 100 games in 19 years as a second baseman with the Philadelphia Athletics and the Chicago White Sox in the American League. His baseball career began at Columbia University, where he used the pseudonym Eddie Sullivan to sneak into a few games with the Athletics. He led the American League in fielding average nine times and was the key member of Connie Mack's '\$100,000 Infield' which led the Athletics to pennants in 1909-11 and 1913-14. During his career, Collins batted over .300 for 18 seasons. He ranks 5th in career stolen bases with 743. He became a general manager and part-owner of the Boston Red Sox.

Career 1906-30: 3311 hits Avg. .333; RBI 1299; SB 743. Best seasons: 1920: 222 hits, .372; 1911: .365; 1923: .360; 1912: .348, 137 Runs.

Peter COLLINS (UK)

SPEEDWAY

Spencer Peter Collins. b. 24 Mar 1954 Urmston, Manchester.

In a remarkable 1973 season he established himself as one of the world's leading riders at an unusually early age. Beginning his career as a 17-year-old with Rochdale in 1971, he moved to Belle Vue the following year, and in 1973, when still only 19, he scored maximum points for Britain when they won the World Team Championship. In 1976 he won the World Individual Championship, the first British winner since Peter Craven 14 years earlier. A member of the winning British team five times, 1973-5, 1977 and 1980. He is also the most successful British rider in the World Pairs, winning four times with different partners, Malcolm Simmons in 1977, David Jessup in 1980, Kenny Carter in 1983 and Chris Morton in 1984.

Mário COLUÑA (Por)

FOOTBALL

Mário Coluña. b. 6 Apr 1935 Magude, Mozambique.

One of the first great players to come out of Africa. Signed by Benfica in 1954 from a local club in the Portuguese colony of Mozambique, he was an immediate success on his arrival in Lisbon. He won the first of his 73 caps (57 on a stricter definition) for Portugal as a centre-forward but soon specialised in the inside-left position and later as a left-half. Coluña captained Portugal in the 1966 World Cup and played for Benfica in five European Cup finals being on the winning team in 1961 and 1962. After recurring injury problems ended his career with Benfica he moved to France and finished his playing days with Lyon.

His main attribute was a ferocious left-footed shot but he was also noted for his athleticism and he held the Mozambique long jump record for many years.

Nadia COMANECI (Rom)

GYMNASTICS

Nadia Comaneci. b. 12 Nov 1961 Onesti, Moldavia.

In 1976 she was the first gymnast in Olympic history to be awarded a perfect score (10.0) and she was awarded seven in all. Her first two came on the asymmetric bars and beam in the team competition at which Romania were silver medallists, and she added gold medals and five more tens at both those individual exercises.

Trained as a gymnast from the age of six,

she made her junior international début in 1971 and became a narrow favourite for Montreal after winning four gold medals at the 1975 European Championships.

Her bravery and agility took women's gymnastics to new levels. She went on to retain her European overall title in 1977 and 1979, with three more gold medals at individual events, but was beaten into 4th place overall at the 1978 Worlds, where she won gold on the beam. By the 1980 Olympics she had grown considerably; nonetheless she was second overall and won gold medals at beam and floor exercises. In all she won nine Olympic medals, five gold, three silver and one bronze. Her last competition was a win at the 1981 World Student Games.

In November 1989 she defected from Romania, and settled in North America.

Earle COMBS (USA)

BASEBALL

Earle Bryan Combs. b. 14 May 1899 Pebworth, Kentucky, d. 21 Jul 1976 Richmond, Kentucky.

The lead-off hitter on the greatest team ever, the 1927 New York Yankees. He played next to Babe Ruth, covering the massive centerfield of Yankee Stadium. Combs played his entire 12-year career with the Yankees 1924-35. His speciality was the 3-base hit, as he led the league three times, with 23 in 1927, 21 in 1926, and 22 in 1930. Although big at 1.83m *6ft* and 84 kg *185 lb*, he was the fastest player on the Yankees, but their power made it unnecessary for him to steal many bases. Combs batted below .300 only twice, with .299 in 1926, and .282 in his last year. He later coached with the St Louis Browns, Boston Red Sox, and Philadelphia Phillies.

Career 1924-35: 1866 hits Avg. .325. Best season: 1927: Avg. .356, hits: 231.

Denis COMPTON (GB)

CRICKET and FOOTBALL

Denis Charles Scott Compton. b. 23 May 1918 Hendon, Middlesex.

Brilliant right-handed batsman and unorthodox slow left-arm bowler. He received his county cap for Middlesex in 1936, when at 18 he was the youngest ever to score 1000 runs in his début season. He was England vice-captain on the tour to Australia in 1950/1 and Middlesex joint captain with Bill Edrich in 1951-2. His 300 v North-Eastern Transvaal at Benoni 3-4 Dec 1948, made in 181 minutes, is the fastest ever triple century.

In 1947 he set English season's record figures unlikely ever to be broken, of 3816 runs (av. 90.85) and 18 centuries, four of them in the Test series with South Africa. He charmed and thrilled large crowds with his dashing strokeplay. A year later a knee injury incurred at football flared up and his mobility throughout the rest of his career was often severely impaired. At soccer he played outside-left for Arsenal, gaining an FA Cup winners medal in 1950 after the League title in 1947/8, and he won 14 wartime England international caps.

A batting genius, he brought sparkle to the cricket and soccer fields of post-war England, and was undoubtedly the most popular sportsman of the era. *Daily Express* Sportsman of the Year 1947 and 1948. Astutely managed by Bagenal Harvey, he was one of the first professional sportsmen to build on their appeal, most notably through his Brylcreem advertisements. Awarded the CBE for services to cricket 1958, he has written several books, worked as a journalist, PR consultant and advertising agency director.

His elder brother **Leslie** (1912-84) kept wicket for Middlesex 1938-56 and, also an Arsenal footballer, played twice for England at soccer, winning his first cap at the age of 38 in 1950.

78 Tests 1937-57: 5807 runs at 50.06; 17 100s HS 278; 25 wickets at 56.40, BB 5-70; 49 catches.

First-class 1936-64: 38942 runs at 51.85, 123 100s HS 300; 622 wickets at 32.27, BB 7-36; 415 catches.

Charles CONACHER (Can)

ICE HOCKEY

Charles William Conacher. b. 20 Dec 1910 Toronto, Ontario., d. 30 Dec 1967 Toronto.

Charles Conacher played 12 years in the NHL, mostly for the Toronto Maple Leafs. He eventually became an even better hockey player than his more heralded older brother, Lionel, though he never quite matched his versatility. He achieved most of his fame during a seven-year tenure on the Leafs with Busher Jackson and Joe Primeau - the Kid Line. A right wing, he was NHL scoring champion in 1934 and 1935, with the latter his best year at 36 goals and 57 points. He was 1st-team All-Star 1934-6, and 2nd-team All-Star in 1932 and 1933. After his retirement, he briefly coached the Chicago Black Hawks.
NHL career 1929-41 - 460 games, 225 goals, 398 points.

Lionel CONACHER (Can)

ICE HOCKEY

Lionel Pretoria Conacher. b. 24 May 1901 Toronto, Ontario, d. 26 May 1954 Ottawa, Ontario.

There have been few athletes from any country who excelled in as many sports as Canada's great all-rounder, Lionel 'Big Train' Conacher, who was voted the greatest Canadian athlete of the first half of the 20th century. His best sport may have been ice hockey, at which he played defense for 12 years in the NHL, twice playing on Stanley Cup champions. At 18 he played for the Ontario rugby league champions. At 19 he won the Canadian light-heavyweight boxing championship, and he later fought an exhibition with Jack Dempsey. He played professional baseball in the minor leagues with the Triple A Toronto Maple Leafs. In 1921, Conacher played for the Toronto Argonaut football team which won the Grey Cup as the champions of the Canadian football league; and he considered football his favourite sport. In 1922 Conacher played for the Toronto Maitlands, winners of the Ontario Amateur Lacrosse League. After this incredible athlete retired from the playing fields, he entered politics, serving several terms in the Ontario parliament.
NHL career 1925-37: 498 games, 80 goals, 185 points.

Jean CONDOM (Fra)

RUGBY UNION

Jean Condom. b. 15 Apr 1960 St Andre de Seigneux.

As a hard working lock he was virtually a fixture in the French team in the 1980s. Between 1982 and 1990 he won 61 caps - a record for a French lock - and had eleven different partners in the second row. First capped when playing for Boucau, he moved to Biarritz in 1986.

Mike CONLEY USA)

ATHLETICS

Michael Alexander Conley. b. 5 Oct 1962 Chicago.

The greatest ever combined exponent of long jump and triple jump. He has consistently shown a remarkable ability to produce his best with his final jump and has won many championships in this fashion, most notably in his Olympic triumph in 1992. He was already assured of the gold medal but was desperately unlucky as he triple jumped 18.17m, 20 cm better than the world record, but it was the only wind assisted jump of the competition, at 2.1 m/s, a mere 0.1 over the limit.
At World Championships he was third at long jump and fourth at the triple in 1983, following with 2nd and 8th in 1987, and 3rd at the triple in 1991. He won the World Cup long jump in 1985, but thereafter met with greatest success at the triple jump, his championships including the World Indoors 1987 and 1989, World Cup 1989. Goodwill Games 1986, Pan-American 1987, and US 1984, 1987-9 and 1993.
He won the NCAA double indoors and out for the University of Arkansas in 1984 and 1985. Fourth at the US Trials, he missed the 1988 Olympics, but won the Grand Prix triple jump and was second overall.
He had been an outstanding high school basketball player, and has combined his athletics with coaching and dog training.
Best performances: long jump 8.43 (1985), 8.63w (1986); triple jump 17.87 (1987), 18.17w (1992); 200 metres 20.21/20.12w (1985), 20.0 hand timed (1984). World indoor triple jump best of 17.76 in 1987.

Billy CONN (USA)

BOXING

William David Conn Jr. b. 8 Oct 1917 Pittsburgh, Pennsylvania, d. 29 May 1993 Pittsburgh.

The Irish-American was world light-heavyweight champion from 1939-41. As evidenced by his few knockouts, he was known as a very skilled boxer, but not a great puncher. In 1941 he challenged Joe Louis for the heavyweight championship and almost won, as after 12 rounds, Conn was ahead of the Brown Bomber by a wide margin. In the 13th round, however, he got overconfident and started slugging with Louis, who promptly scored a TKO. After World War II, Conn fought Louis again in 1946 but lost more easily by a KO in the 8th. He soon retired and became well known as an artist.
Career record: W - 63 (14), L - 12, D -1.

Dennis CONNER (USA)

YACHTING

Dennis Walter Conner. b. 16 Sep 1942 San Diego, California.

The helmsman of the winning yacht three times in the America's Cup, on *Freedom* (1980) and *Stars and Stripes* (1987 and 1988). Although he joined Charles Barr and Harold Vanderbilt as the only three-time winners of the Cup, he was also the only American skipper who failed to retain the Cup in the 132-year history of the event when he lost to the Australian challenger in 1983. He was also starting helmsman in 1974 with Ted Hood as skipper.
His father was a tuna fisherman in San Diego, where Conner learnt his yachting. Educated at San Diego State University, he has been a full-time professional yachtsman for many years. He has won 26 world championships in various classes from the Star in 1971, and won an Olympic bronze medal in 1976 in the Tempest class.
A big man, he gained notoriety in his younger days with his fiery temper and erratic behaviour, but has always been fiercely competitive.

Hal CONNOLLY (USA)

ATHLETICS

Harold Vincent Connolly. b. 1 Aug 1931 Somerville, Maine.

Setter of seven world records at the hammer. His first record was an unratified 66.71m at Boston on 3 Oct 1956, and he followed with six official records from 68.54m in 1958 to 71.26m in 1965. He competed at four Olympics, winning at his first attempt in 1956, which he followed by marriage to the women's discus champion **Olga Fikotova** (Cs) (b. 13 Nov 1932) . Both competed for the USA at the next three Olympic Games and Olga competed for a fifth time in 1972. Their son James won the NCAA decathlon and was second in the World Student Games in 1987. Hal later married Pat Winslow (at pentathlon, 7th 1964 and 6th 1968 at the Olympics). Hal was AAU champion nine times at the hammer, 1955-61, 1964-5 and three times at the 35lb weight indoors, 1960, 1965-6. He originally took up hammer throwing to strengthen his left arm, which had been slightly withered at birth.

Maureen CONNOLLY (USA)

TENNIS

Maureen Catherine Connolly. b. 17 Sep 1934 San Diego, California, d. 21 Jun 1969 Dallas, Texas. Later Brinker.

Although her career was ended by injury at the age of 19, 'Little Mo' was the first woman to win the Grand Slam and one of the great players of all-time. In the space of four years she won nine Grand Slam singles titles (six of them in successive tournaments): Wimbledon (1952-4), US (1951-3), French (1953-4) and Australian (1953). Her three major doubles titles came in 1954 when she won the Australian women's and the French women's and mixed. After winning her first US title when only 16, she lost only four matches throughout the remainder of her career. She was never beaten in the singles in her three appearances at Wimbledon from age 17. She also won all nine rubbers she played in the Wightman Cup 1952-4.
In 1954 she looked a certainty to take her

fourth successive US singles but shortly before the Championships a crushed leg in a riding accident ended her career at a tragically early age. In 1955 she married Norman Brinker, a member of the US equestrian team, and she died of cancer aged only 34.
A determined baseline player with a powerful drive on both wings, she would surely have set unparalleled records had her career run its full span.

George CONNOR (USA)

AMERICAN FOOTBALL

George Connor. b. 21 Jan 1925 Chicago, Illinois.

Connor played football at Holy Cross in 1942 and earned All-American honours as a freshman. He then joined the US Navy during World War II. After the war, he entered Notre Dame and in 1946 and 1947 was again named to the All-American team as a tackle. In 1946 he won the first ever Outland Trophy, for the nation's top collegiate lineman. In 1950 he was named to the all-time half-century All-American team. As a professional Connor played for the Chicago Bears 1948-55 as an offensive tackle and defensive linebacker. He was later elected to the Pro Football and College Football Halls of Fame.

Jimmy CONNORS (USA)

TENNIS

James Scott Connors. b. 2 Sep 1952 East St Louis, Illinois.

After winning the 1971 NCAA singles while at UCLA, Connors matured quickly and as early as 1974 he enjoyed the best season of his career winning Wimbledon, the US Open and Australian titles. He was denied the opportunity of winning the Grand Slam when he was refused entry to the French Open as he had not joined the ATP. Connors won the US Open again in 1976, 1978 and 1982-3 and was the Masters champion in 1977, but he never managed a second singles victory at either Wimbledon or the Australian Open. In the doubles he won Wimbledon in 1973 and the US Open in 1975. He also had a host of other singles victories in such events as the WCT Finals, the US Indoor and the US Clay Courts but failed to win a Grand Slam title after 1983. He did, however, continue to play with distinction at the highest level until his retirement in 1992 after which he developed his career as a TV commentator. His final glory came in 1991 when he reached the semi-finals at the US Open.
A left hander with a double-fisted backhand, powerful ground strokes and a superb return of service, he re-established the effectiveness of baseline play after a period of domination by serve-volley specialists. He set a men's record for the professional era with 109 singles titles 1972-89, with career earnings of $8,471,435, and ranking as the world number one for 268 weeks 1974-83.

Adolfo CONSOLINI (Italy)

ATHLETICS

Adolfo Consolini. b. 5 Jan 1917 Costermano, d. 20 Dec 1969.

A great discus thrower for more than two decades. He won three European titles (1946, 1950 and 1954) in five championships. At the Olympics his record was: 1st 1948, 2nd 1952, 6th 1956, 17th 1960 in Rome, when he took the oath on behalf of the competitors. He won 15 Italian titles between 1939 and 1960 and also set three world records, all in Milan from 53.34m in 1941 to 55.33m in 1948. His best mark was his sixth European record 56.98m in 1955.

Learie CONSTANTINE (Tri)

CRICKET

(Sir, later Baron) Learie Nicholas Constantine. b. 21 Sep 1902 Petit Valley, Diego Martin, d. 1 Jul 1971 Hampstead, London, England.

A marvellous exciting cricketer, whose figures do not begin to do justice to his abilities. He was one of the hardest hitters of a cricket ball, with spectacular innings at all levels of cricket so that crowds flocked to see him, not least in the Lancashire Leagues, where he achieved an unmatchable reputation and helped Nelson to eight league titles in his ten years with them. He was an astute bowler, sometimes bowling medium-fast but capable of extreme pace, and also a brilliant fielder, one of the greatest ever seen. He toured England four times between 1923 and 1939. The respect of his fellow players was shown by his election as captain of the Dominions team against England in 1945. His years of studying law were rewarded when he was called to the Bar of the Middle Temple in 1954, and he achieved notable success in politics and race relations. He was High Commissioner in Britain for Trinidad and Tobago in 1962-4, was knighted in 1962 and created a Life Peer in 1969.

His father **Lebrun** (1874-1942) was a leading West Indies batsman in the days before they came into Test cricket, and father and son played together for Trinidad in 1923.

18 Tests 1928-39: 635 runs at 19.24, HS 90; 58 wickets at 30.10, BB 5-75; 28 catches.

First-class 1921-45: 4475 runs at 24.05, 5 100s HS 133; 439 wickets at 20.48, BB 8-38; 133 catches.

Bill COOK (Can)

ICE HOCKEY

William Osser Cook. b. 9 Oct 1896 Brantford, Ontario.

Cook did not break into the NHL until he was 30 years old. He had an invitation to try out for pro hockey when he was 20, but he was called to serve in World War I. When he came home, he was given a piece of land as reward for his service and he began farming. In 1922 he resumed his hockey, however, with the Saskatoon Sheiks of the Western Hockey League, and led the WHL in scoring three consecutive years.

A right wing, Cook played for the New York Rangers his entire NHL career. He was part of a great line with Frank Boucher and his brother, Bun Cook.

NHL career 1926-37 - 452 games, 223 goals, 355 points. Ross Trophy 1927 (33 goals, 37 points), 1933 (28 goals, 50 points).

Ashley COOPER (Aus)

TENNIS

Ashley John Cooper. b. 15 Sep 1936 Melbourne, Victoria.

After winning the Australian singles in 1957 Cooper enjoyed a great season in 1958, winning Wimbledon, the US and Australian Championships but spoiling his Grand Slam prospects by losing to Sven Davidson (Swe) in the French semi-finals. He also won the US and French men's doubles in 1957 and the Australian and French doubles in 1958. He only played in two Davis Cup ties, 1957-8; on both occasions Australia successfully defended the trophy. He turned professional at the end of the 1958 season but his solid, reliable style was not well suited to the pro game.

Charlotte COOPER (UK)

TENNIS

Charlotte Reinagle Cooper. b. 22 Sep 1870 Ealing, Middlesex, d. 10 Oct 1966 Helensburgh, Scotland. Later Sterry.

After winning three Wimbledon singles, 1895-6 and 1898, as Miss Cooper, she won two further titles, 1901 and 1908, following her marriage to Alfred Sterry in January 1901. At the time of her fifth victory in 1908 she was aged 37 yrs 282 days and is the oldest winner of the women's singles. She also won the All England mixed doubles with Laurie Doherty in 1901 and 1902 before the event was given full championship status. Away from Wimbledon, she won two singles (1895, 1898) and four mixed doubles titles at the Irish Championships and also won both the Welsh (1888) and Scottish (1899) singles. She also won two gold medals (singles, mixed doubles) at the 1900 Olympic Games to become the first woman from any country to win an Olympic title. Her daughter, Gwen, was a Wightman Cup player in 1927 and her son, Rex, served for many years as vice-chairman of the All England Club. One of the longest-lived of all champions, she attended the Wimbledon 75th anniversary celebrations in 1961 when in her 91st year and she died aged 96.

Henry COOPER (UK)

BOXING

Henry William Cooper. b. 3 May 1934 Bellingham, Kent.

Cooper held the British and Commonwealth professional heavyweight championships from 1959-70 and was also thrice European champion at that weight. He was a skilful boxer with a powerful left hook, but his biggest fault was that he cut easily, leading to his nickname, 'Bleeding 'Enry'.

Perhaps Cooper's greatest hour came in a losing cause. In 1963 he floored Muhammad Ali in the fourth round of a non-title fight, only the bell saving Ali. However in round five, Cooper was cut and the fight had to be stopped. Cooper, who was awarded the OBE in 1969, retired in 1971 after losing his British title to Joe Bugner.

He was hugely popular in Britain and has retained that celebrity status to this day. He was twice voted by the BBC as Sports Personality of the year (1967 and 1970).

Career record: W - 40 (27), L - 14, D -1.

Lionel COOPER (Aus)

RUGBY LEAGUE

Lionel Cooper. b. 18 Feb 1923 West Wynlong, New South Wales, d. June 1987 Sydney.

A strong-running winger from Eastern Suburbs and New South Wales who played for Australia in three Tests in 1946 before joining Huddersfield early in 1947. He had switched from playing Australian Rules to rugby league only in 1945.

While with Huddersfield he was their leading try scorer for seven seasons and in 1951/2 scored 71 tries; only nine short of the world record set almost 40 years earlier by his club-mate and fellow Australian, Albert Rosenfeld. His 10 tries against Keighley in 1951 remains a club record. He headed the League try-scoring list three times and his career total of 432 tries was also a Huddersfield record. He played 10 times for 'Other Nationalities' in the international championship before returning to Australia in 1955.

Malcolm COOPER (UK)

SHOOTING

Malcolm Douglas Cooper, b. 20 Dec 1947 Camberley, Surrey.

The winner of two Olympic gold medals, six World Championships and four Commonwealth Games titles. He first took up shooting as a schoolboy in New Zealand where his father was stationed as a lieutenant in the Royal Navy. Following his return to England he developed into one of the world's finest marksmen. After a relatively undistinguished performance at the 1972 and 1976 Olympics he missed the 1980 Games because of the boycott, but in both 1984 and 1988 he was Olympic champion in the sma%%ll bore rifle, three positions.

His host of other outstanding performances include gold medals at each of the five World Championships held between 1978 and 1990. Particularly notable were the 1985 Europeans where he won all five individual events and the 1986 Worlds where he set five world records. His wife **Sarah** (b. 23 Mar 1949) was a member of the Olympic shooting team in 1988 and together they won the small bore rifle, pairs, at the 1986 Commonwealth Games.

Roy COOPER (USA)

RODEO

Roy Cooper. b. 13 Nov 1955 Hobbs, New Mexico.

The all-time money leader on the pro rodeo (PRCA) circuit with $1,374,953 from 1975 to 1992, having become the second million dollar earner in 1987. Cooper was world champion at calf roping 1976 and 1980-4, and completed triple victory in 1983 with not only steer roping, but also the all-around title, when he improved the yearly money record to $153,391.

Fausto COPPI (Italy)

CYCLING

Fausto Angelo Coppi. b. 15 Sep 1919 Castellania, d. 2 Jan 1960 from a tropical illness contracted in Upper Volta.

Probably the greatest Italian sporting hero

ever, Coppi was 'the' *campionissimo* - the champion of champions. He first raced in 1937 and turned professional in 1940, but because of World War II his career did not begin seriously until he was 26 years old. Had he not missed the war years, his record might rival even that of Eddy Merckx. Coppi's only weakness as a rider was as a sprinter, but he was so strong that he rarely needed that talent. In 1949, Coppi effectively ended the rivalry of Gino Bartali with the greatest stage ride ever seen at the Giro. On a mountain stage crossing the Alpine passes of Maddalena, Vars, Izoard, Montgenevre and Sestrières, Coppi dropped Bartali shortly before the Izoard climb and won the stage by more than 20 minutes. Other monumental victories which testify to his strength were his 6 minute victory margin in the 1950 Flèche-Wallonne and his 14-minute margin in the 1946 Milan-San Remo.

By the end of his career he had won 118 road races. The world 1 hour record that he set with 45.848km in 1942 lasted until 1956.

World titles: Pro road race 1953, Pro Pursuit 1947, 1949 (2nd 1948). Major victories: Tour de France 1949, 1952; Giro d'Italia 1940, 1947, 1949, 1952-3; Milan-San Remo 1946, 1948-9; Paris-Roubaix and Flèche-Wallonne 1950, Grand Prix de Nations 1946-7; Tour of Lombardy 1946-9, 1954. King of the Mountains - Tour de France 1949, 1952; Giro d'Italia 1948-9, 1954.

Cyril CORBALLY (Ire)

CROQUET

Cyril Corbally. b. c.1880 Ireland. d. 1946 Ireland.

The most successful croquet player of all-time until the arrival of Humphrey Hicks. He won the Open Championship at his first attempt in 1902 and was only defeated twice in the six other Opens in which he played until 1913. He also won the mixed doubles in 1903 and 1911 and with his brother Herbert the men's doubles in 1913. One of the greatest of an early school of Irish players who introduced the centre-stance to England, which quickly and virtually permanently replaced the side-stance favoured by the Victorian English players. Corbally only came to England twice after the War, winning the men's championship in 1926, but on his second visit in 1934 he only played in provincial tournaments. For someone who suffered from ill health as a young man and had been advised to take up croquet as a form of 'gentle exercise' he showed a remarkable aptitude for the game and his record of five Open championship wins (1902-03, 1906, 1908, 1913) was not beaten until Hicks scored his sixth victory in 1950.

Jim CORBETT (USA)

BOXING

James John Corbett. b. 1 Sep 1866 San Francisco, California, d. 18 Feb 1933 Bayside, New York.

Nicknamed 'Gentleman Jim' for his polished manners and elegant speech, Corbett was the first man to bring science into boxing. He studied his opponents, facing them from an orthodox stance, and using a straight left and a powerful right.

He turned professional in 1884 after an outstanding amateur career. In 1892 he knocked out John L. Sullivan in the 21st round, becoming the first man to win the heavyweight championship under the Marquess of Queensberry rules. Corbett had one successful defence, but lost the title to Bob Fitzsimmons in 1897. He made two attempted comebacks against Jim Jeffries but lost by late round knockouts in both 1900 and 1903.

Career record: W - 11 (7), L - 4; D -2.

Angel CORDERO (USA)

HORSE RACING

Angel Tomás Cordero Jr. b. 8 Nov 1942 Santurce, Puerto Rico.

After a serious accident on 12 Jan 1992 he retired from riding having won 7057 races, the third highest total of all-time, and second to Laffit Pincay in money earnings with a career total of $164,526,217. He headed the jockey's money winning table in the USA in 1976, 1982 and 1983 and won the Eclipse Award for outstanding

jockey in the latter two years.
From a racing family, many of whom rode professionally, Angel had his first winner in 1960 at the local El Commandante track and was leading jockey there with 124 winners in 1961. Going to the USA in 1962, he was at first unsuccessful, but after returning in 1965 he became leading jockey in New York in 1967 and in 1968 rode 345 winners. He rode the winner of the 100th Kentucky Derby in 1974, *Cannonade*, and followed with further wins in 1976 and 1985, along with two wins in the Preakness Stakes and one in the Belmont.
A sometimes controversial rider, he was regularly suspended for his forceful riding tactics.

Kresimir COSIC (Yug)

BASKETBALL
Kresimir Cosic. b. 26 Nov 1948.

The first great Yugoslav basketball player and the first to train overseas. He attended Brigham Young University, where he played basketball for three years. At 2.06m *6'9"*, he played power forward or center and won three Olympic medals - gold in 1980 and silver in 1968 and 1976. He also helped Yugoslavia win two world championships (1970, 1974) and three European championships (1973, 1975, 1977). With Cibona Zagreb he won the European Cup-winners Cup in 1982.

Paul COSTELLO (USA)

ROWING
Paul Vincent Costello. b. 27 Dec 1894 Philadelphia, Pennsylvania, d. 17 Apr 1986.

The first Olympic rower to win three consecutive gold medals in the same event (1920-24-28 at double sculls), a feat later matched by Vyacheslov Ivanov and Pertti Karpinnen in the single sculls. Costello won two US titles in the single sculls, 1919 and 1922, but he was best known as a double sculler. In that boat, partnered mostly by his cousin John Kelly and later by Charles McIlvaine, he won innumerable national titles, both in the US and Canada.

Edmond COTTER (UK)

CROQUET
Edmond Patrick Charles Cotter. b. 1904.

Although he had played croquet as a boy, he did not take up the game seriously until 1947 when he was aged 43. In 1949 he won the President's Cup at his first attempt and repeated his victory five times in the next 11 years. He also won the Open Championship in 1955, 1958 and 1962, the men's championship four times, 1952, 1954, 1963 and 1969; the mixed in 1951 and, with John Solomon, he won the Open doubles ten times.
His game, which was based on an attacking approach, was a welcome development after the defensive attitude which had become prevalent in the game since the war. Cotter was also a scratch golfer but in addition to his sporting talents he brought a fine brain to the game. He was a classics master at St.Paul's School, an international bridge player and the compiler of the crossword puzzle in the *Financial Times*.

Fran COTTON (UK)

RUGBY UNION
Francis Edward Cotton. b. 3 Jan 1947 Wigan, Lancashire.

Making his England début in 1971, he went on to become England's most capped prop before poor health ended his career in 1981 with 31 caps to his credit. He toured with the British Lions to South Africa in 1974 and New Zealand in 1977 and only missed one of the eight Tests over the two tours. On his third Lions tour to South Africa in 1980 he was afflicted with severe chest pains and it was thought his life was in danger. He recovered sufficiently to regain his place in the England team against Wales in 1981 but recurrent leg infections soon brought about his final retirement. A forceful personality and inspiring leader with Loughborough Colleges and Coventry, he led the North-West Counties to victory over the All Blacks in 1972. He also captained England and the Lions in some of their Provincial matches. His father was a rugby league international.

Henry COTTON (UK)

GOLF

Thomas Henry Cotton. b. 26 Jan 1907 Holmes Chapel, Cheshire, d. 22 Dec 1987 London.

After the Americans became dominant in golf in the early part of the 20th century, only Henry Cotton really challenged this until the 1980s. He won the British Open three times, 1934, 1937 and 1948, in 1937 defeating a field that contained the whole US Ryder Cup team. He played on three Ryder Cup squads, captained the team in 1947 (as well as the team that did not play in 1939) and was non-playing captain in 1953. He was PGA Match Play champion in 1932, 1940 and 1946. With Walter Hagen and Bobby Locke, he was one of the first three professionals to be accorded honorary membership by the Royal & Ancient Golf Club. Cotton will always be remembered for the round of 65 which he shot in winning the 1934 Open at Sandwich which inspired the popular golf ball, the 'Dunlop 65'. He made only sporadic trips to the United States, winning only one tournament on their PGA Tour. After leaving school he had three assistantships before becoming a full professional in 1926. At the end of his playing career Cotton became a well-known golf pundit, journalist and course architect and settled in Portugal. He was awarded the MBE in 1946, and shortly before his death heard that he was to be knighted in the 1988 New Year's Honours List.

Pierre de COUBERTIN (Fra)

OLYMPICS

Baron Pierre de Fredi. b. 1 Jan 1863 Paris, d. 2 Sep 1937 Geneva, Switzerland.

Coubertin believed in the Greek athletic ideal of perfection of mind and body, and for many years directed his energies to achieving his dream of reintroducing the Olympic Games, part of his campaign for broadening and restructuring education. In 1889 he was commissioned by the French government to form a universal sports association and he visited other European nations to gather information. He made public his views on 25 Nov 1892 at the Sorbonne in Paris. These led to the formation of the International Olympic Committee in 1894 and thence to the staging of the Olympic Games, which were opened in Athens on Easter Monday 1896. He was president of the IOC from 1896 to 1925, and on his retirement, by when the Games had become firmly established, he was given the title of Honorary President.

Fred COUPLES (USA)

GOLF

Frederick Stephen Couples. b. 3 Oct 1959 Seattle, Washington.

For long promising greatness, Couples had his finest year in 1992 when he pushed Nick Faldo off the World no.1 spot for a week in March, won the Masters, led the PGA money-list for the year with $1,344,188, and won the World Cup for the USA with Davis Love III. Previously his most important wins had come in the 1984 Tournament Players Championship and the 1991 Johnny Walker World Championship. He won the Vardon Trophy in both 1991 and 1992. He played in the Ryder Cup in 1989, losing both matches, but won 4 of 5 in 1991. A graduate of the University of Houston.

PGA career earnings 1981-92: $5,466,915 with 9 victories.

Jim COURIER (USA)

TENNIS

James Spencer Courier. b. 17 Aug 1970 Sanford, Florida.

A very strong, aggressive and athletic player Courier has achieved his greatest success so far on clay courts, winning the French title in 1991 and 1992, and runner-up in 1993. He also won the Australian title in 1992 and 1993. After a previous best of quarter-finals in 1991, he showed that he had the game to succeed on grass as well, by reaching the Wimbledon final in 1993, where he lost to Pete Sampras.
A prominent junior from the Nick Bollettieri school, he leapt into top world class in 1991 when, in addition to his French win, he reached the final of the US

Open, losing there to Stefan Edberg. Courier ranked number two in the world at the end of that year and reached top ranking for the first time in February 1992. At the end of 1992 he had career tour earnings of $4,846,459. In the Davis Cup his record 1991-2 is won 3 lost 5, as he helped the US to win in 1992.

Yvan COURNOYER (Can)

ICE HOCKEY

Yvan Serge Cournoyer. b. 22 Nov 1943 Drummondville, Ontario.

'The Roadrunner' was the fastest skater in the NHL in the 1960s and early 70s. He played his entire NHL career as a right wing with the Montreal Canadiens and played for eight Stanley Cup champions. At 170 cm *5' 7"* and 80 kg *175 lb*, he was small, but his speed made him a top goal scorer. He also had a brilliant shot, both off the slapper and with his wrist shot.
NHL career 1963-79 - 968 games, 428 goals, 863 points. Playoffs: 147 games, 64 goals, 127 points. Best years: 1968/9: 43 goals, 87 points; 1971/2: 47 goals, 83 points. Smythe Trophy 1973.

Margaret COURT (Aus) see SMITH

Robin COUSINS (UK)

FIGURE SKATING

Robin John Cousins. b. 17 Aug 1957 Bristol, Gloucestershire.

Having placed 10th behind John Curry in 1976, Cousins became only the second British male to win an Olympic figure skating gold medal in 1980. A superb display of free skating gave him a narrow victory over Jan Hoffman (GDR), but Hoffman got his revenge at the World Championships and a World title was the one honour which eluded Cousins, as he had won a bronze medal in 1978 and silver in 1979. The son of a former Millwall goalkeeper, he combined his skating activities with his studies at Bristol but after his Olympic victory he turned professional and in 1989 was appointed head of coaching at a new advanced training centre in Southern California.

Bob COUSY (USA)

BASKETBALL

Robert Joseph Cousy. b. 9 Aug 1928 New York.

The first famous playmaking guard produced in the NBA. He graduated from Holy Cross as an All-American in 1950 and was drafted by the Chicago Stags. That team disbanded before he played for them, so he became a solid scorer as well as a playmaker for the Boston Celtics while they won six NBA Championships. He was named to the first-team All-Star side for 10 straight years, 1952-61 and led the NBA in assists for eight consecutive years, 1953-60. Cousy was known for several razzle-dazzle type moves which were pioneering for his era - no-look passes and behind-the-back dribbles and passes. After his retirement in 1963 he coached at Boston College until 1969, and then in the NBA for 5 years with the Cincinnati Royals and Kansas City Kings. In 1969-70, he played in 7 games for the Royals as a player-coach.
NBA career 6955 assists, av. 7.5.

Alberto COVA (Italy)

ATHLETICS

Alberto Cova. b. 1 Dec 1958 Inverigo, Como.

Cova completed a major championship treble at 10,000 metres with the 1984 Olympic title, having earlier won the 1982 European and 1983 World titles. In all these races he displayed a devastating finishing kick off a much faster second half. After a third and a second in 1983, he scored a double win at 5000m and 10,000m in the 1985 European Cup Final, but his run of success ended with second in the 1986 European 10,000m.
Best times: 1500m 3:40.6 (1985), 3000m 7:46.40 (1983), 5000m: 13:13.71 (1982), 10,000m: 27:37.59 (1983).

Gordon COVENTRY (Aus)

AUSTRALIAN RULES FOOTBALL

Gordon Coventry. b. 1901, d. 1968.

Between 1920 and 1937 he played 306

games for Collingwood, which was then a record for a Victoria League player. In this period he scored a record 1299 goals, an average of 4.24 per game, heading the VFL goal kicking lists in six seasons, and four times exceeding 100 with a peak of 124 in 1929. In that year he twice set a record for a single match, with 16 goals against Hawthorn and 17 against Fitzroy. His nine goals against Richmond in 1928 remains the record for a Grand Final. He also kicked 100 goals for Victoria in 25 inter-state matches.
His brother **Sidney** (1899-1976) played 227 games for Collingwood, captaining the club to four consecutive VFL premierships 1927-30, and winning the Brownlow medal in 1927. He was known as the best ruckman in the VFL.

Ronnie COVE-SMITH (UK)

RUGBY UNION

(Dr) Ronald Cove-Smith. b. 26 Nov 1899 Edmonton, Middx, d. 9 Mar 1988 Brighton, Sussex.

A lock-forward with Old Merchant Taylors he was capped 29 times by England and was on the losing side in only five of those matches. He captained the British Lions in South Africa in 1924 and led England to a Grand Slam win in 1928. After holding a commission in the Grenadier Guards during the war he went up to Cambridge and won his blue in 1919-21; in his third year he captained Cambridge in the first University Match to be played at Twickenham. He also represented Cambridge at swimming and water polo. After University he enjoyed a distinguished career in medicine.

Colin COWDREY (UK)

CRICKET

(Sir) Michael Colin Cowdrey. b. 24 Dec 1932 Pulumala, Ooatacamund, India.

Undoubtedly a great batsman, elegant with all the strokes and so determined that he was flown out to Australia after three years out of Test cricket at the age of 42 to face Lillee and Thomson at their fiercest when the England batting was falling away before them. And yet he did not quite satisfy his admirers when sometimes his batting became over-introspective, as if he could not quite come to terms with his own genius. That genius was obvious from his earliest days when he went straight into the Tonbridge team at the age of 13 and was the youngest schoolboy ever to play in a Lord's match. He lost his youthful ability as a leg-break bowler, but immediately after leaving Oxford University he made his Test début against Australia in 1954/5 to rave reviews, with a hundred in his third Test. Over the next 20 years he passed the records of Wally Hammond for most runs for England and catches in Test cricket. He captained England in 27 Tests between 1959 and 1969, but never in Australia despite making six tours there. He was one of the longest serving of county captains, leading Kent from 1957 to 1971. He made 1000 runs in a season 27 times, in South Africa, West Indies and Australia as well as 21 times in England, with a peak of 2039 at 63.42 in 1965. Awarded the CBE 1972, he was president of the MCC in 1986/7 and chairman of the ICC for several years. He was knighted for his services to cricket in 1992. His son **Christopher** (b. 20 Oct 1957) played in six Tests for England 1984-8, the last as captain and another son **Graham** also plays for Kent.
114 Tests 1954-75: 7624 runs at 44.06, 22 100s HS 182; 120 catches.
1 One-day Int: 1 run.
First-class 1950-76: 42,719 runs at 42.89, 107 100s HS 307; 65 wickets at 51.21, BB 4-22; 638 catches.

David COWENS (USA)

BASKETBALL

David William Cowens. b. 25 Oct 1948 Covington, Kentucky.

A fiery redhead who played the game with an intensity that matched his hair colour. He played collegiately at Florida State and for most of his professional career with the Boston Celtics. Though much shorter than the average NBA center at 2.06m *6'9"*, his intensity and desire allowed him to master the position. He was NBA co-Rookie of the Year (with Geoff Petrie) in 1971 and NBA Most Valuable Player in 1973. Led by Cowens, the Celtics won NBA championships in 1974 and 1976. He was something of a free spirit who, though a rich man because of his NBA salary, decided he wanted to be a cab driver one summer and drove a taxi in Boston for the experience. He retired in 1980, although still a potent force, because he had lost the desire that so epitomised his game. He made a one season return to the court in 1982 with the Milwaukee Bucks but then retired for good. In 1978-9 he was a player-coach for the Celtics.

Buster CRABBE (USA)

SWIMMING

Clarence Linden Crabbe. b. 7 Feb 1910 Oakland, California, d. 23 Apr 1983 Scottsdale, Arizona.

An American hero when he won the 400m freestyle gold at the 1932 Olympics, he forsook intentions to practise law to become a film star with Paramount Studios. Known as the 'King of the Serials' he made in all some 192 movies, playing such characters as Buck Rogers and Tarzan, but he became best known for the 40 episodes of Flash Gordon.

His family moved to Hawaii when he was two years old, but he returned to study at the University of Southern California. At the 1928 Olympics he took the bronze at 1500m and was fourth at 400m freestyle. In all he won eleven AAU titles outdoors, including the 1 mile each year 1927-31, and he set a world record for 880y with 10:20.4 in 1930.

He was selected for the 1936 Olympics at water polo, but was not allowed to compete as he had appeared in advertisements.

Steve CRAM (UK)

ATHLETICS

Stephen Cram. b. 14 Oct 1960 Gateshead.

Achieved a unique treble at 1500m with Commonwealth (1982), European (1982) and World (1983) titles, before returning from injury to take the 1984 Olympic silver medal.

He had run on the UK team that had set a world record at 4 x 800m relay in 1982, but first entered the world record lists as an individual in 1985, when he ran three world records in 19 days: at 1500m 3:29.67, 1 mile 3:46.32 and 2000 metres 4:51.39, times which remained his best (and the mile time still a world record) eight years later.

He set a world age-17 mile best with 3:57.43 in 1978 and in that year made his championships début at the Commonwealth Games. The next year he won the European Junior title at 3000m and in 1980 was 8th in the Olympic 1500m. In 1986 Cram became the third man to win the Commonwealth 800m/1500m double and then won gold (1500m) and bronze (800m) at the Europeans. Since then he has increasingly suffered from calf and other leg injuries. At his third Europeans he was 5th at 1500m in 1990, and he has won seven national senior titles: AAA 1500m 1981-3, 800m 1984, 1986, 1988; UK 5000m 1989.

Other bests: 800m 1:42.88 (1985), 1000m 2:12.88 (1985), 3000m 7:43.1 (1983), 2 miles 8:14.93 (1983), 5000m 13:28.58 (1989).

Christl CRANZ (Ger)

ALPINE SKIING

Christl Cranz. b. 1 Jul 1914. Later Borchers.

The winner of a record number of world titles at Alpine skiing, with seven individual, slalom 1934 and 1937-9, and downhill 1935, 1937 and 1939; and five combined, 1934-5, 1937-9. She also won the Olympic gold medal for the Alpine Combination in 1936, when although only sixth in the downhill her two slalom times were far superior to the rest of the field. Her brother Heinz-Rudolf (1918-41) was 6th in the Olympic Alpine combination in 1936.

Lorraine CRAPP (Aus)

SWIMMING

Lorraine Joyce Crapp. b. 17 Oct 1938 Sydney, New South Wales. Later Thurlow.

The first woman to break five minutes for

the 400m freestyle, when she smashed through that barrier with 4:50.8 at Townsville on 25 Aug 1956. In that same race she set world records also at 200m, 220y and 400y with 2:19.3, 2:20.5 and 4:52.4 respectively. On 20 October in Sydney she improved those records to 2:18.5, 2:19.1, 4:47.2 and 4:48.6 in one 440y race and set the 100m at 63.2, a time she improved five days later to 62.4. Back in January 1956 she had set her first world record with 10:30.9 for 800m and 10:34.6 for 880y. She thus went into the Melbourne Olympics in December as the clear favourite for the freestyle titles. Although she was beaten into second place at 100m by her team-mate Dawn Fraser, she easily beat Fraser to take the gold medal at 400m in 4:54.6 and won a second gold at 4 x 100m.

At the Commonwealth Games she won both 110y and 440y titles with bronze at medley relay in 1954, and in 1958 took gold at 4x110y, silver at 110y and bronze at 440y. Her career ended with a silver in the freestyle relay at the 1960 Olympics, but she swam a mediocre leg, having been disciplined by Australian team officials for leaving the Olympic village to spend the night with her husband Bill Thurlow, whom she had married just before the Games. In all she set 16 individual and seven relay world records, 17 of these 23 coming in 1956.

Australian freestyle champion 110 and 220y 1954, 440y 1954-6.

Michel CRAUSTE (Fra)

RUGBY UNION

Michel Crauste. b. 6 Jul 1934 St-Laurent de Gasse, Landes.

A flanker and No.8 with Racing Club de France and Lourdes, he won a then record 63 caps for France between 1957 and 1966. An aggressive and sometimes abrasive forward, he captained his country in South Africa in 1964 when France won the only Test 8-6. Known as 'Le Mongol', because of his black moustache. He won French Championships with Racing Club de France in 1959 and Lourdes in 1960 and 1968.

Danie CRAVEN (SAf)

RUGBY UNION

Daniel Hartman Craven. b. 11 Oct 1910 Lindley, Orange Free State, d. 4 Jan 1993 Stellenbosch.

Although winning 16 international caps he eventually became better known as an administrator and one of the most influential figures in world rugby.

He was first capped in 1931 while a theological student at Stellenbosch University even though he had not yet represented his Province. He won international honours as fly-half, scrum-half, centre and No.8 and played in four different positions in consecutive Tests against Australia in 1933. Craven captained South Africa four times and later served as coach, manager and selector of the national team, and as President of the South African Rugby Board from 1956, he exerted considerable influence as a member of the International Rugby Board. He became joint-president of the racially integrated South African Rugby Football Union on its creation in February 1992. With degrees in anthropology, psychology and physical education from the University of Stellenbosch, he became head of the PE department there in 1947 and subsequently director of sport and recreation until his retirement in 1975.

Peter CRAVEN (UK)

SPEEDWAY

Peter Theodore Craven. b. 21 Jun 1934 Liverpool, d. 1963 Edinburgh.

World champion in 1955 and 1962, and the only English rider to win two world titles - although Welshman Freddie Williams had been a double winner in 1950 and 1953. In ten consecutive championships 1954-63 Craven scored 96 points in all. His career was cut short at the age of 29 when he died from injuries sustained during a crash in Edinburgh. He started in the minor leagues with Liverpool and Fleetwood before beginning a 10-year association with First Division Belle Vue. He was one of the most spectacular and popular of the post-war riders and was still in the top flight when he met his premature death.

Jack CRAWFORD (Aus)

TENNIS

John Herbert Crawford. b. 22 Mar 1908 Albury, New South Wales, d. 10 Sep 1991 Cessnock, NSW.

A classic stylist who wore long sleeved shirts and played with an old fashioned square-topped racquet. In the changing game of the 1930s his appearance and manner recalled the pre-war era and he was the last of the great champions to rely almost entirely on ground strokes.
He never played in the US Championships but won titles at all the other majors. At Wimbledon he won the singles 1933, doubles 1935 and mixed 1930; at the Australian Championships he won the singles 1931-3 and 1935; doubles 1929-30, 1932, 1935; and the mixed 1931-3; and at the French he won the singles and men's doubles 1935 and the mixed 1933. The 1933 Wimbledon final when Crawford repelled the hard-hitting Ellsworth Vines with his classic ground strokes is rated as one of the greatest ever. Between 1928 and 1937 he won 36 out of 58 Davis Cup rubbers.

Sam CRAWFORD (USA)

BASEBALL

Samuel Earl Crawford. b. 18 Apr 1880 Wahoo, Nebraska, d. 15 Jun 1968 Hollywood, California.

'Wahoo Sam' Crawford is the all-time major league leader with 309 triples and led the league six times in that category, once (1902) in the National League with the Cincinnati Reds, and five times with the Detroit Tigers of the American League. He is also the only player in major league history to have led both leagues in home runs - the National League in 1901 with 16 for the Reds, and the American League in 1908 with 7 for the Tigers. In addition, Crawford led the league in RBI three times, 1910, 1914-15. He played outfield his entire career, but in later years also made appearances at first base.
Career 1899-1917: 2964 hits Avg. .309; SB 366. Best season 1911: Avg. .378, 115 RBI.

Ben CRENSHAW (USA)

GOLF

Ben Daniel Crenshaw. b. 11 Jan 1952 Austin, Texas.

Crenshaw had dominated the amateur ranks, winning three successive NCAA titles 1971-3 for Texas, and every title available except the US Amateur. He led the PGA qualifying school in 1973 by 17 shots and then won his first tournament on tour - the San Antonio Texas Open. He led the World Open tournament at Pinehurst the next week briefly, but he eventually faltered and finished only second. He never fulfilled the intense expectations placed on him and it took until 1984 for him to win a major - The Masters, having lost in a play-off for the PGA in 1979 and placed second twice in both the British Open and US Masters. Crenshaw, however, has been one of the great champions by his manner, if not for his victories. He is the ultimate gentleman, hailed by one and all as a friend. He is also known as a golf historian and collector. In early 1991, for his contributions and classy demeanour on course, he was awarded by the USGA the Bobby Jones Award for meritorious contributions to the game of golf.
PGA career earnings 1973-92: $5,129,902 with 16 victories.

Bob CROMPTON (UK)

FOOTBALL

Robert Crompton. b. 26 Sep 1879 Blackburn, Lancashire, d. 15 Mar 1941 Blackburn.

Unchallenged for the position of England's right-back from 1902 to 1914, he won a total of 41 caps which stood as an England record until beaten by Billy Wright in 1952. He joined Blackburn Rovers in 1896 and remained with the club until his retirement in 1920 which, at the time, was the record for the time spent by a player with one club. Crompton won two Football League championship medals (1912, 1914) and played 17 times for the League in representative matches.
One year after his retirement he was appointed a director of Blackburn and

served as team manager from 1926 to 1931. In 1935 he accepted the job as manager of Bournemouth & Boscombe Athletic but stayed less than one year and from 1938 until his death he was honorary manager of his old club. His physical strength enabled him to play a robust game to great effect and he was a master of the shoulder charge. Despite his style he was known as a scrupulously fair player. A plumber by trade.

Joe CRONIN (USA)

BASEBALL

Joseph Edward Cronin. b. 12 Oct 1906 San Francisco, d. 7 Sep 1984 Osterville, Massachusetts.

Cronin played shortstop for 20 years in the major leagues. He broke in with the Pittsburgh Pirates and later played for seven years with the Washington Senators, the last two as player-manager, but he is best remembered for the 11 years in which he was player-manager with the Boston Red Sox. He retired in 1945, and managed for two more years. He then spent 11 years in the front office of the Red Sox and in 1959 became the first former player elected a league president, serving in that capacity until the mid-1970s.
Career batting: 2285 hits Avg. .301, HR 170; RBI 1424. Best seasons 1930: .346, 203 hits.

Michael CRONIN (Aus)

RUGBY LEAGUE

Michael William Cronin. b. 28 Jun 1951 Kiama, New South Wales.

A strong-running centre, nicknamed 'The Crow', whose greatest asset was his prowess as a goal kicker. In 1978 he scored 405 points from 35 games to break Dave Brown's 1935 record of 385 points during an Australian season. With 77 points from 12 matches he was the highest scorer during Australia's 1973 tour of England and during the 1979 Great Britain tour of Australia he kicked a record 10 goals in the first Test and his total of 54 points (24 goals, 2 tries) remains a Test series scoring record. Between 1973 and 1982 he won 33 caps and his total of 309 international points (141 goals, 9 tries) is another Australian scoring record. He played for Gerringong 1969-76 and then for Parramatta 1977-86, as well as for New South Wales 1973-83. A publican at his family hotel in Geeringong.

Martin CROWE (NZ)

CRICKET

Martin David Crowe. b. 22 Sep 1962 Henderson, Auckland.

A right-handed batsman, whose exceptional class was apparent from his Test début at the age of 19. It was not until 1985 that he averaged 50 in a Test series, but he has done so on many occasions since. He took over the New Zealand captaincy in 1990 and has held on to the job despite some hostile criticism from his local media. In his first home Test as captain, against Sri Lanka at Wellington in 1991, he scored the highest score, 299, by a New Zealander in Test cricket, and with Andrew Jones put on 467 for the 3rd wicket, a world record Test partnership for any wicket. Awarded the MBE in 1992. His elder brother **Jeffrey** (b. 14 Sep 1958 Cornwall Park, Auckland) played in 39 Tests for New Zealand 1983-90 (captain in 6), scoring 1601 runs at 26.24 with 3 hundreds; and 74 one-day internationals in which he made 1520 runs at 25.76. Awarded the MBE 1992.
66 Tests 1982-93: 4777 runs at 46.83, 15 100s HS 299; 14 wickets at 48.42; 61 catches.
133 One-day Ints: 4412 runs at 38.70, 3 100s HS 105; 29 wickets at 32.89, BB 2-9; 64 catches.*
First-class 1979-93: 17,791 runs at 57.02; 63 100s HS 299; 117 wickets at 32.97, BB 5-218; 200 catches.

Johan CRUYFF (Hol)

FOOTBALL

Johan Cruyff. b. 25 Apr 1947 Amsterdam.

In 1971 he was the first Dutchman to be voted European Footballer of the Year, and with further awards, 1973-4, the first man to be honoured three times. Born near the

Ajax ground he played for them from 1964-73, making his international début in September 1966. In 1967 he helped Ajax to win the Dutch League and Cup double, as with 33 goals he was the top scorer in the League. In all he helped Ajax to six Dutch League championships and four Dutch Cups between 1966 and 1973, as well as the European Cup each year 1971-3. He then moved to Barcelona in the first million dollar deal. He captained Holland in the 1974 World Cup final and retired in 1978 having won 48 caps and scored 33 goals. His retirement was short-lived and he signed for Los Angeles Aztecs, then playing for the Washingon Diplomats 1979-80 and Levante in Spain 1981, before in 1982 he returned to play for Ajax and Feyenoord. He managed Ajax from 1985. Overall he scored 215 goals in Dutch League games, 47 League goals for Barcelona and 25 in the North American Soccer League. As player or manager he has won nine Dutch championships, adding those of 1982-4 to his earlier successes, and eight Dutch Cups, adding 1983-4 and 1986-7. He took Ajax to victory in the European Cup-Winners Cup in 1987. Repeating as a manager his move as a player to Barcelona, he took them to victory in the Cup-Winners' Cup in 1989 and European Cup in 1992, with the Spanish League title each year 1991-3 and the Spanish Super Cup 1992.
Slighty built, he was supremely gifted in virtually every department and was one of a group of talented players who raised Holland to a power in world soccer.

Joaquim CRUZ (Bra)

ATHLETICS
Joaquim Carvalho Cruz. b. 12 Mar 1963 Taguatinga, Brasilia.

Olympic champion at 800 metres in 1984, he has been the only man to threaten seriously the world record set by Seb Coe in 1981, as he missed that by just 0.04 when he ran 1:41.77 in 1984.
Cruz won the Pan-American junior titles at 800m and 1500m in 1980 and set a great world junior record at 1:44.3 at the age of 18 in 1981. In 1983 he took the World bronze medal at 800m. He missed the 1986 season due to Achilles tendinitis and had surgery; and he also had to miss the 1987 World Championships, but he won the Pan-American 1500m that year and returned for Olympic silver in 1988. Further Achilles problems prevented a resumption of his career. He was NCAA champion for the University of Oregon at 800m in 1983-4 and at 1500m 1984.
Other bests (all South American records): 1000m 2:14.09 (1984), 1500m 3:34.63 (1988), 1 mile 3:53.00 (1984).

Larry CSONKA (USA)

AMERICAN FOOTBALL
Lawrence Richard Csonka. b. 25 Dec 1946 Stow, Ohio.

Csonka followed Jimmy Brown, Ernie Davis, Jim Nance, and Floyd Little in the great Syracuse tradition of bruising full-backs. He made All-American teams as a junior and was a unanimous selection as a senior in 1967. He was selected as the outstanding player in the 1968 College All-Star Game and was drafted by the Miami Dolphins, with whom he played to 1974 and in 1979, in his last season before retirement. He played for Memphis Southmen of the World Football League 1974-5 and for the New York Giants 1976-8. He was a bruising, punishing runner who earned the tough yards for the Dolphins and was a member of the 1972/3 team which won all 17 games and the Super Bowl. Csonka was Super Bowl MVP when Miami won again in 1974.
NFL career 1968-79: Rushing: 8081 yards av. 4.3, 64 touchdowns. Receiving: 820 yards av. 7.7, 4 touchdowns.

Teofilo CUBILLAS (Peru)

FOOTBALL
Teofilo Cubillas. b. 8 Mar 1949 Lima.

Peru's greatest ever player, and the inspiration of their fine team in the 1970 World Cup in which they were unlucky to meet Brazil as early as the quarter-finals, losing 4-2. Cubillas played again in the World Cups of 1978 and 1982 and guided Peru to win the 1975 South American

Championship. He was a speedy attacker and a magnificent striker, scoring 25 goals in full international matches. South American Footballer of the Year in 1972, he moved from Alianza Lima to FC Basel, Switzerland for 6 months in 1973 and then to FC Porto in Portugal, where he delighted the fans as a midfielder for four years. He returned to Alianza in 1977, before playing for Fort Lauderdale in the USA from 1979.

Candy CUMMINGS (USA)

BASEBALL

William Arthur Cummings. b. 18 Oct 1848 Ware, Massachusetts. d.16 May 1924 Toledo, Ohio.

Cummings played in the major leagues from 1872 until 1877. It was only a six-year career, but he won 124 games in his first four years, an average of 31 a year. He also played for five teams in both the National Association and the National League. His fame is based on his being credited with the invention of the curve-ball, which he said that he developed as a 14-year-old throwing clamshells on the Cape Cod beaches where he grew up.

Glenn CUNNINGHAM (USA)

ATHLETICS

Glenn V Cunningham. b. 4 Aug 1909 Atlanta, Kansas, d. 10 Mar 1988 Menifee, Arkansas.

A great miler of the 1930s, who set world records outdoors at 880y, 1:50.9 in 1933 when he was runner-up but shared the same time as Charles Hornbostel at the NCAAs; 800m 1:49.7 in Stockholm in 1936; and mile 4:06.7 at the Princeton Invitational in 1934. Indoors he set world bests at 1000y, 2:10.1 in 1935; three times at 1500m to 3:48.4 in 1938; and three times at a mile as well as an over-sized track best of 4:04.4 in 1938. His 1500m best was 3:48.0 in 1940.

At the University of Kansas he was NCAA champion at 1500m/1 mile in 1932 and 1933, and at the end of his brilliant 1933 season, when he also won the AAU double of 800m and 1500m, he won the Sullivan Award. He was AAU champion outdoors at 1500m each year 1935-8, and indoors at 1500m in 1934-5 and 1938-9. Over 1500m at the Olympic Games he was 4th in 1932 and took the silver medal behind Jack Lovelock in 1936.

He triumphed despite a severe childhood accident when his legs were badly burned at the age of seven and it was originally thought he would never walk again. He earned a PhD in physical education from New York University in 1938, and taught in Iowa on his retirement in 1940. Later he bought a ranch in Kansas, where he cared for orphans and troubled youngsters.

John CURRY (UK)

FIGURE SKATING

John Anthony Curry. b. 9 Sep 1949 Birmingham, Warwickshire.

The first Englishman to win an Olympic figure skating title. After winning the British junior Championship in 1967 he won his first senior title in 1970. Steadily improving performances in the World and European Championships and 11th place at the 1972 Olympics led to invaluable sponsorship from the American millionaire, Ed Moseler. This enabled him to train under the renowned coach Carlo Fassi in ideal conditions in Colorado. The benefits were soon apparent and in 1975 he placed second in the European and third in the World Championships. He won the European title in 1976 and then gave a superb performance to take the Olympic gold medal. He quickly consolidated his position by winning the World title and then turned professional and was able to negotiate a highly lucrative contract.

He produced and starred in a successful Ice Show but he never forgot his early financial hardships and was a generous supporter of the National Skating Association. Awarded the OBE 1976.

Ann CURTIS (USA)

SWIMMING

Ann Elisabeth Curtis. b. 6 Mar 1926 Rio Vista, California. Maried Gordon Cuneo.

The top female swimmer at the 1948

Olympics, when she won gold medals at 400m and 4 x 100m freestyle and silver at 100m. That year she won the Sullivan Award.

She started swimming at the age of nine but her coach Charles Sava, at the Crystal Plunge Club of San Francisco, kept her out of competition until the age of 17. She then came to the fore immediately and won 18 US outdoor titles and 11 indoors 1943-8, with world records at 440y 5:07.9 in a 25y pool (1947) and 880y 11:08.6 (1944). A graduate of the University of California at Berkeley, she runs the Ann Curtis School of Swimming.

Betty CUTHBERT (Aus)

ATHLETICS

Elizabeth Cuthbert. b. 20 Apr 1938 Merrylands, Sydney.

At the age of 18 Cuthbert was the heroine of the Melbourne Olympics in 1956, when she won three sprints gold medals. After her individual victories at 100m and 200m she helped the Australian team to two world records in the relay. In all she was responsible for 18 world records, from her first, 23.2 for 200m in September 1956, to the 52.01 that she ran to win a fourth Olympic gold medal, at 400m in 1964.

In between her Olympic wins she had met with lesser success. At the Commonwealth Games she had been overshadowed by team-mate Marlene Matthews in 1958, when she was 4th at 100y and 2nd at 220y with silver also in the relay, and in 1962 although she took a relay gold, she was 5th at 220y and went out in the semis at 100y. She was injured at the 1960 Olympics. Australian champion 220y 1956 and 1960, 440y 1963. It was revealed in 1979 that she was fighting multiple sclerosis.

Other bests: 60m 7.2 (1960), 100y 10.4 (1958), 100m 11.4 and 11.2w (1956), 220y 23.2 (1960).

David CUTLER (UK)

BOWLS

David J Cutler. b. 1 Aug 1954 Redruth, Cornwall.

At the age of 18 in 1972 he became the youngest-ever winner of an English title, with the triples. Between 1974 and 1984 he won five major EBA titles, including the English singles in 1979. He made his debut for England in an outdoor international in 1975 and won numerous caps, both indoors and outdoors, up to 1988. He is the owner of a bowls equipment business and part-time civil servant in Plymouth.

Louis CYR (Can)

WEIGHTLIFTING

Louis Cyr. b. 11 Oct 1863 St Cyprien de Napierville, Québec, d. 10 Nov 1912 Montreal, Québec.

The French-Canadian was the first strongman to gain worldwide acclaim. Standing only 174 cm *5'8"* but weighing between 125-143 kg *275-315 lb* in his prime, Cyr was a colossus of all-round strength. He began work as a lumberjack which surely helped develop his strength, and his feats around Montreal reached Richard Fox, who edited *The Police Gazette* in New York and who became Cyr's patron and promoter. With Fox's help Cyr went on tour and competed against all the renowned strongmen of his era. On 27 May 1895, in a backlift, Cyr raised *c.*1820 kg (4300 lb) in what was for years the greatest weight ever raised by a human. His pre-eminence is exemplified by the fact that he never dodged a contest with any man and was never defeated in his prime (1881-1906). Like many large men, he developed kidney failure and died of that disease, aged only 49.

Bjørn DÆHLIE (Nor)

NORDIC SKIING

Bjørn Dæhlie. b. 19 Jun 1967 Råholt.

At the 1992 Winter Olympics the two Norwegians, Dæhlie and Vegard Ulvang, dominated the cross-country skiing. Together they took gold medals with the Norwegian relay team and Dæhlie added those for 25km combined and 50km classical, with silver at 30km and 4th at 10km. He was also world champion in 1991 at 15km freestyle, and in 1993 at 25km combined and 30km classical, with relay golds both years. He won the cross-country World Cup in 1992 and 1993 after placing 3rd in 1990 and 3rd equal in 1991.

Kenny DALGLISH (UK)

FOOTBALL

Kenneth Mathieson Dalglish. b. 4 Mar 1951 Dalmarnock, Glasgow.

A player of prodigious talent who was equally successful as a manager. Joining Celtic in 1970 he helped them to win nine major titles: the Scottish Cup (1972, 1974-5, 1977), Scottish League (1972-4, 1977) and Scottish League Cup (1975).

After 10 years he moved to Liverpool in 1977 for the then British record fee of £440,000. His successes in major competitions were continued at Anfield and he was a member of the team which won the European Cup (1978, 1981, 1984), the FA Cup 1986, the Football League six times (1979-80, 1982-4, 1986) and the League Cup for four consecutive years (1981-4).

He followed 112 League goals at Celtic with 118 for Liverpool and is the only man to have scored 100 goals in both the English and Scottish Leagues.

In June 1985 he was appointed as player-manager at Liverpool and in his first season led the club to the League and Cup double. He repeated the league championship success in 1988 and 1990. He made his last League appearance in May 1989 and in February 1991 he shocked the football world by suddenly resigning, but he came back into the game in October when he took over as manager of Blackburn Rovers, helping them win promotion from Division Two in 1991/2.

He won a record 102 Scottish caps 1971-86, and equalled Denis Law's scoring record of 30 goals for Scotland. He was awarded the MBE in 1985 and he was both Player of the Year (1979, 1983) and Manager of the Year (1986, 1988, 1990).

One of the greatest of all British forwards, he will be remembered for his determined and incisive finishing when in the opponents' goal area.

Andy DALTON (NZ)

RUGBY UNION

Andrew Grant Dalton. b. 16 Nov 1951 Dunedin.

Playing in 35 Tests between 1977 and 1985, he was New Zealand's most capped hooker and was only on the losing side in five international matches. Injury and business commitments prevented him winning further honours.

He was also held in high regard when he took over the captaincy of the All Blacks and the accuracy of his line-out throwing was a feature of his game.

His father, **Raymond** (b. 14 Jul 1919 Te Awamutu) was also capped twice in 1947 as a prop forward.

Maurizio DAMILANO (Italy)

WALKING

Maurizio Damilano. b. 6 Apr 1957 Scarnafigi.

Damilano won the 1980 Olympic title at 20 kilometres walk after two men ahead of him were disqualified close to the finish; his twin brother Giorgio came in 11th. Maurizio went on to take bronze medals in 1984 and 1988 and just missed another with fourth place in 1992. He became World champion in 1987 and retained that title in 1991 with his first sub 1 hr 20 min time (1:19:37), becoming the oldest world champion, although Yuriy Sedykh took that distinction later the same day.

In four European Championships he won just one medal, silver in 1986, while in the biennial World Cup he achieved a record seven placings in the top eight, with a best of 2nd in 1985. He showed his speed with a silver medal in the 1985 World Indoors at 5000m.

He started his walking career in 1972, and from his fourth place in the European Junior 10km in 1975 retained consistently top-class form, winning 19 Italian walks championships in all. He retired after setting world records in October 1992 at 30,000m (2:01:44.1) and 2 hours (29,572m).

Stanley DANCER (USA)

HARNESS RACING

Stanley F Dancer. b. 25 Jul 1927 New Egypt, New Jersey.

The first driver to win more than $1 million in a season, a feat he achieved in 1964. He was also the leading money-winning driver in 1961-2 and 1966. Beginning as a stable boy in Long Island, New York, from his first win in 1947, he steadily built up his stable and in all he had 3720 race wins and earned $26,684,756 in his career. He trained and drove seven Harness Horses of the Year, including *Nevele Pride* 1967-9 and *Albatross* 1971-2.

Ray DANDRIDGE (USA)

BASEBALL

Raymond Dandridge. b. 1913 Richmond, Virginia.

The greatest third baseman of the old Negro Leagues, where he played for Detroit Stars, Newark Dodgers, Newark Eagles, and New York Cubans. Only the prejudices of the time prevented him from being acclaimed one of the greatest ever in the major leagues. He got his chance at organised professional ball in 1949 when he signed with the Minneapolis Millers of the American Association, the New York Giants' farm club. He hit .311 and was AA Rookie of the Year but his age, and probably racial quotas, prevented him from being called up to the majors. He was a superb fielder and also excelled as a hitter.

Ludvik DANEK (Cs)

ATHLETICS

Ludvik Danek. b. 6 Jan 1937 Horice.

The winner of a complete set of Olympic medals at the discus, gold 1972, silver 1964 and bronze 1968, before placing ninth at his fourth Games in 1976. At European Championships he won in 1971 and was second in 1974 in five appearances. He won 13 Czechoslovak titles 1963-69 and 1971-6, and the 1965 AAU. He set nine CS discus records from 57.22 in 1963, with three world records in 1964-6, and a best of 67.18m in 1974.

Beth DANIEL (USA)

GOLF

Elizabeth Ann Daniel. b. 14 Oct 1956 Charleston, South Carolina.

The third highest career money winner on the US LPGA Tour. She was US Amateur champion in 1975 and 1977 and played in the Curtis Cup of 1976 and 1978, winning 7 of her 8 matches, before turning pro with immediate success. In her first year on the tour she won the Patty Berg Classic and then headed the yearly money list in 1980 (a record $863,578), 1981 and 1990. Surprisingly it was not until 1990 that she won a major, the LPGA Championship.
LPGA career earnings 1979-92: $3,692,665 with 27 victories.

Charles DANIELS (USA)

SWIMMING

Charles Meldrum Daniels. b. 24 Mar 1885 Dayton, Ohio, d. 9 Aug 1973 Carmel Valley, California.

The pioneer of the American crawl, having modified it from the previously known Australian crawl, he won five gold medals, one silver and two bronze at the Olympic Games. In 1904 he had won golds at 220y, 440y and 4 x 50y freestyle with silver at 100y and bronze at 50y; in 1906 he won the 100m and in 1908 he won the 100m and bronze at 4 x 200m.
He set seven world records between 1907 and 1911, with best times of 100y 54.8, 100m 68.2, 220y 2:25,4, 300m 3:57.6, 500m 7:03.4, as well as various bests at other distances. He won AAU titles outdoors from 100y to 1 mile: 100y 1905-8, 220y 1904-8, 440y 1904, 1906-10, 1 mile 1906, 1908-9 and the indoor 100y in 1906, 1909-11. Daniels was a fine all-round sportsman, also winning New York AC championships at bridge and squash, and he became a top amateur golfer.

Adrian DANTLEY (USA)

BASKETBALL

Adrian Delano Dantley. b. 28 Feb 1955 Washington, DC.

Dantley came from basketball powerhouse

DeMatha High School in suburban Washington and then attended Notre Dame. As a sophomore and junior he was a first-team all-American in college. After playing on the 1976 Olympic gold medal winning team, he claimed hardship and declared himself eligible for the NBA draft. He started out his NBA career with Buffalo, but has since played for Indiana, Los Angeles, and Utah. He was named Rookie of the Year in 1977 and his best year was 1981 when he was an NBA All-Star Second Team selection as well as leading the league in scoring (2452 points, av. 30.7).
NBA career 1977-91: 23,177 points, av. 24.3.

Fred DARLING (UK)

HORSE RACING

Frederick Darling. b. 15 May 1884 Beckhampton, Wiltshire, d. 9 June 1953 Beckhampton.

Leading trainer in Britain six times: 1926, 1933, 1940-2 and in his last season of 1947. He trained 19 classic winners, including seven of the Derby, tying the record.
He came from a notable racing family; his great-grandfather Sam had ridden the winner of the St Leger in 1833, his father Sam (1852-1921) was a successful trainer with seven classic winners, and his elder brother Sam (1881-1967) also trained at Newmarket.
Fred was an apprentice jockey to his father before taking out a trainer's licence in 1907. After training in Germany he took over his father's stables at Beckhampton in 1913 and produced his first classic winner when *Hurry On* won the 1916 St Leger. His best horses included the 1942 Triple Crown winner *Sun Chariot* and *Tudor Minstrel*. He was a fierce disciplinarian, totally dedicated to his profession.

Tamás DARNYI (Hun)

SWIMMING

Tamás Darnyi. b. 3 Jun 1967 Budapest.

Gold medallist at both 200m and 400m individual medley events at the 1985, 1987 and 1989 European Championships, 1986 and 1991 World Championships, and at the Olympic Games in both 1988 and 1992.
He showed unprecedented ability to peak for the big occasion in setting world records at both events at the 1987 Europeans, 2:00.56 and 4:15.42 respectively, again at the 1988 Olympics in 2:00.17 and 4:14.75, and at the 1991 Worlds, 1:59.36 and 4:12.36. In 1989 he won a third European gold medal, at 200m butterfly, and at this event he was the World bronze medallist in 1991.
He had started swimming at the age of six, but had to overcome problems with his sight. His left eye was hurt in a snowball fight at the age of 12, and it was discovered two years later that he had a detached retina. Already European Junior champion in 1982, he had four operations in 1982-3, spending four months in hospital. His comeback was complete as he took three Hungarian titles in 1984 before embarking on his marvellous career which has brought him gold medals at every major event that he has contested. His first European record was at 200m IM in 1986. By 1991 he had taken his number of Hungarian titles to 46. He has been studying hotel and catering management in Budapest. Swam for Ujpesti Dózsa SC and later Budapesti Rendészeti SE, and coached since 1979 by Tamás Széchy.
Other bests: 200m backstroke 2:01.97 (1986), 200m butterfly 1:58.25 (1991).

André DARRIGADE (Fra)

CYCLING

André Darrigade. b. 24 Apr 1929 Narrosse, Landes.

Darrigade, nicknamed 'Dédé' was a great road sprinter who was able to win many smaller races in Europe, but his lack of ability as a climber cost him dearly in the major tours. However, he did manage to win the first stage of the Tour de France five times, relying on his great sprint, and in all he had 22 stage wins in the Tour. He was French road champion in 1955 and won the Tour of Lombardy in 1956. His greatest year was 1959 when he won the world championship and the points jersey in the Tour de France (which he also won in 1961). Tragedy had befallen him at the end of the 1958 Tour when he lost control on the tour of the velodrome at the end of the final stage, killing an official and sustaining a serious head injury himself. In the world championships he was also 2nd in 1960, 3rd in 1957 and 1958 and 4th in 1963.

Benoit DAUGA (Fra)

RUGBY UNION

Benoit Dauga. b. 8 May 1942 Montgaillard, Landes.

A lineout specialist who won 63 caps (1964-72) and who still shares with Michel Crauste the distinction of being the most capped French forward. He toured South Africa in 1967 and as captain in 1971. His career ended with a serious injury while playing for his club Mont-de-Marsan in 1975. Paralysed in the arms and legs, he finally recovered after many months in hospital.

Willie DAVENPORT (USA)

ATHLETICS

Willie D Davenport. b. 8 Jun 1943 Troy, Alabama.

Olympic champion in Mexico City in 1968, when he ran the fastest ever automatically timed 110m hurdles in 13.33. The following year in Zürich he equalled the official (hand timed) world record at 13.2.
In all he competed at four Olympic Games at athletics, failing to qualify in 1964 after being a surprise winner of the US Trials, and placing fourth in 1972 and third in 1976. He then went on to compete at the Winter Olympics in 1980 on the US 4-man bobsled team. AAU champion at 120y hurdles in 1965-7, he tied for the title in 1969 with Leon Coleman. Indoors he was AAU champion at 60y hurdles in 1966-7 and 1969-71, and set world hurdles records with 5.9 and 5.8 for 50y (1968-9), 6.6 for 50m (1965) and thrice 6.8 at 60y (1969-70).
Flat best times: 100y 9.5 (1968), 100m 10.3 (1969).

Alan DAVIDSON (Aus)

CRICKET

Alan Keith Davidson. b. 14 Jun 1929 Lisarow, Gosford, New South Wales.

An outstanding left-arm fast bowler, who was also a powerful batsman and a brilliant fielder either close to the wicket or in the deep. He made his début for New South Wales in 1949/50 and for Australia on the tour to England in 1953. He met with little success in Tests until the 1957/8 tour to South Africa when he captured 25 wickets average 17.00, and from then took 23 or more wickets in each of his five Test series until his last against England in 1962/3, except for 13 in 3 matches against Pakistan in 1959/60. Against West Indies in 1960/1 he took 33 wickets at 18.54. Awarded the OBE.
44 Tests 1953-63: 1328 runs at 24.59, HS 80; 186 wickets at 20.58, BB 7-93; 42 catches.
First-class 1949-63: 6804 runs at 32.86, 9 100s HS 129; 672 wickets at 20.90, BB 7-31; 168 catches.

Bruce DAVIDSON (USA)

EQUESTRIAN

Bruce Oram Davidson. b. 31 Dec 1949 Newburgh, New York.

The only rider to have won two individual World three-day event titles, on *Irish Cap* in 1974 and *Might Tango* in 1978. He also won a world team gold in 1974. He made his Olympic début in 1972, when he won a team silver, followed by team gold in 1976 and 1984. He competed in a fourth Olympic Games in 1988. He attended Iowa State, and at the Pan-American Games took a team gold and individual silver in 1975.

Bob DAVIES (USA)

BASKETBALL

Robert Edris Davies. b. 15 Jan 1920 Harrisburg, Pennsylvania.

Davies attended Seton Hall University on a baseball scholarship arranged by the Boston Red Sox. In college he turned his attention to basketball. Graduating in

1942, he joined the US Navy during the war, playing for the Great Lakes Naval Training Station team which won the All-Service title in 1943. He then played pro basketball for ten seasons, making All-NBA (and all-NBL, the NBA's forerunner) seven times. In 1970 he was named to the NBA's 25th Anniversary All-Star team, and was voted the sixth greatest player of the first half-century. After retirement, he briefly coached several sports at Gettysburg College and then became an executive with the Converse Rubber Company.

Gerald DAVIES (UK)

RUGBY UNION

Thomas Gerald Reames Davies. b. 7 Feb 1945 Llansaint.

A fast, elusive runner, Gerald Davies was one of the most exciting backs of any era. Winning 11 caps at centre and 35 on the wing, he shares with Gareth Edwards the Welsh record for the most international tries (20, with a further three for the British Lions).

From Queen Elizabeth GS, Carmarthen he went to Loughborough College and then to Cambridge University where he won his blue 1968-70. In 1970 he withdrew from international rugby to concentrate on his finals at Cambridge but on his return the following year he helped Wales to the Grand Slam. After University, Gerald Davies played for Cardiff, London Welsh and the Barbarians.

On the 1968 Lions tour of South Africa injury restricted his Test appearances to one match, but he was at his best on the 1971 tour of Australia and New Zealand when he played in all four Tests. He declined invitations to tour South Africa in 1974 and New Zealand in 1977. He is now the rugby correspondent of *The Times*.

Lynn DAVIES (UK)

ATHLETICS

Lynn Davies. b. 20 May 1942 Nantymoel, Glamorgan.

Gold medallist at the long jump at the 1964 Olympics, 1966 Europeans and 1966 and 1970 Commonwealth Games. His confidence destroyed by Bob Beamon's epic jump, he was only ninth in the 1968 Olympics, but he came back to win the 1969 European silver and to take part again in the Olympics in 1972, when he did not qualify for the final.

Also in the Europeans he was fourth in 1971 and twelfth in 1962 outdoors, and was first in 1967 and second in 1969 indoors. He was AAA champion five times outdoors and three times indoors. His eight UK records were headed by his best jump of 8.23m *27ft* at Berne on 30 Jun 1968. He made 43 international appearances for the UK from 1962, when he made his début at the European Championships (11th at long jump). That year he was also 4th in the Commonwealth long jump.

Coached and inspired by Ron Pickering, he was a most tenacious competitor and a great ambassador for sport. Davies later became technical director of Canadian athletics (1973-6) and British team manager before taking up a broadcasting career with BBC Wales.

Other bests: 100y 9.5 (1964), 100m 10.4 (1967), triple jump 15.43m (1962).

Wayne DAVIES (Aus)

REAL TENNIS

Wayne Foster Davies. b. 1955 Geelong, Victoria.

A professional initially attached to the Melbourne Tennis Club and later the New York Racquet Club. After unsuccessfully challenging Chris Ronaldson for the world real tennis title in 1985, he took the title two years later. He is still reigning champion and is the first Australian to hold the World title.

In doubles he formed a particularly effective partnership with fellow Australian Lachlan Deuchar, and together they won the World Invitation Doubles in 1988 and 1990 and were the British Open doubles champions1984-9. Davies defended his world titlein 1993 against Deuchar and won narrowly, 7-6. Although not as physically robust as many of his rivals, Davies has few equals in the execution of the volley and the forcing forehand.

W J A DAVIES (UK)

RUGBY UNION

William John Abbott Davies. b. 21 Jun 1890 Pembroke, d. 26 Apr 1967 Teddington, Middlesex.

For US Portsmouth, Royal Navy and England, 'Dave' Davies and Cyril Kershaw had few rivals as a half-back pairing. They were partners in the England team a record 14 times and in their four seasons together, England won the International Championship twice and shared it once. Davies captained England in 11 of his 22 internationals (1913-23) and held the record as England's most capped fly-half until 1989 when the record passed to Rob Andrew. The only time he was on the losing side in an international was on his début against South Africa in 1913. He was noted for his left-footed drop kicks and elusive running.
A regular naval officer, he was awarded the OBE in 1919 for his work with the naval constructor corps.

Ernie DAVIS (USA)

AMERICAN FOOTBALL

Ernest Davis. b. 14 Dec 1939 New Salem, Pennsylvania, d. 18 May 1963 Cleveland, Ohio.

In 1961 Davis became the first black man to win the Heisman Memorial Trophy, while at Syracuse University, following in the footsteps of his idol, Jimmy Brown. He was selected for All-American teams for three straight years, and was a unanimous selection as a senior. He also broke Brown's Syracuse records for total yards gained, touchdowns, and points scored.
He was selected by the Buffalo Bills of the AFL and was the first pick of the 1961 NFL draft by the Washington Redskins. Before signing with the Redskins, however, he was traded to the Cleveland Browns. Shortly before his rookie season, Davis became ill and was diagnosed as having leukemia. He never was able to play a down of professional football and the highly popular running back died less than one year later.

Fred DAVIS (UK)

SNOOKER

Fred Davis. b. 14 Feb 1913 Whittingham Moor, near Chesterfield.

He played billiards and snooker at the highest level for more than 60 years, from winning the national under-16 billiards title in 1929 to ending his professional career in 1990. He succeeded his elder brother Joe as world snooker champion in 1948, and the following year became the first professional to defeat Joe on level terms. He was also world snooker champion in 1949 and from 1951-6, having been beaten in the final in 1940 and 1947. He won the Professional Match-play championship for the first five (1952-6) of its six years as the world's top tournament. When he emulated his brother by winning and later retaining the world professional billiards title in 1980 he became the oldest ever world champion at any sport.
His other major titles: UK pro billiards 1951, *News of the World* snooker 1958-9, Australian Open snooker 1960. Awarded the OBE.

Glenn DAVIS (USA)

AMERICAN FOOTBALL

Glenn Woodward Davis. b. 26 Dec 1924 Burbank, California.

'Mr Outside' teamed with 'Doc' Blanchard ('Mr Inside') to give Army the greatest one-two running punch of the 1940s. Together they led the US Military Academy to three consecutive undefeated seasons and two national championships, 1944-5. In his college career, Davis had an incredible average of 10.1 yards per carry and finished second in the Heisman Memorial Trophy voting in 1944 and 1945 (to Blanchard in 1945), finally winning in 1946.
He was possibly the greatest all-round athlete ever at West Point, where he also played baseball and basketball and ran track. He was very fast, with Army records of 9.7 for 100y and 20.9 for 220y, once being timed in 10.0 seconds for 100y in full football uniform while carrying a football. In the West Point physical fitness test,

Davis set the school record with 926.5 of a possible 1,000 points. The Brooklyn Dodgers offered Davis $75,000 to play pro baseball but he turned them down. After serving his mandatory military service commitment, he played two years of professional football (1950-1) with the Los Angeles Rams, but his career was hampered by an old knee injury which forced his premature retirement.

Glenn DAVIS (USA)

ATHLETICS

Glenn Ashby Davis. b. 12 Sep 1934 Wellsburg, West Virginia.

A marvellously talented all-round athlete, Davis won the 1956 Olympic title at 400m hurdles in his first year at the event, having earlier run the first ever sub-50 second time in only his ninth race. He improved the world record for 400m hurdles to 49.2 in 1958 (and also set a record at 440y hurdles at 49.9) and won further Olympic gold medals in 1960 at 400mh and the 4x400m relay. In his final year of 1960 he also set a world record at 200m hurdles of 22.5, a time which has never been bettered, although the event is no longer on the record schedule.

He won four AAU hurdles titles, 1956-8 and 1960. He was also a world class runner at the flat quarter-mile, at which he set two world records (45.8 and 45.7) and was NCAA champion for Ohio State University in 1958. He had a short pro football career, 1960-1, with the Detroit Lions and Los Angeles Rams.

Other bests: 100m 10.3 (1958), 200m 21.0 (1958).

Greg DAVIS (Aus)

RUGBY UNION

Gregory Victor Davis. b. 27 Jul 1939 Matamata, New Zealand, d. 24 Jul 1979 Rotorua, New Zealand.

On moving from his native New Zealand to play for Drummoyne in Sydney, Australia in 1963, he won the first of his 39 Australian caps that year. A powerful No.8, he captained Australia in 16 consecutive Tests and led them on the tours to France in 1971 and New Zealand in 1972. He worked in the wholesale meat and wool business and died from a brain tumour at the early age of 39.

Hal DAVIS (USA)

ATHLETICS

Harold L Davis. b. 5 Jan 1921 Salinas, California.

Davis would surely have been the favourite for Olympic sprint titles, but his chances were dashed by World War II. He set world records at 100y, 9.4 in 1942, and 100m, 10.2 in 1941, and was AAU champion at 100m in 1940, 1942-3 and at 200m each year 1940-3. For the University of California he won the NCAA sprint double at 100y and 220y in 1942-3.

Best at 220y (straight track): 20.4 (1942) and 20.2w (1941). He was a poor starter, but a brilliant finisher.

Joe DAVIS (UK)

BILLIARDS and SNOOKER

Joseph Davis. b. 15 Apr 1901 Whitwell, Derbyshire, d. 10 Jul 1978 Hampshire.

Supreme at snooker and second only to Walter Lindrum at billiards, he is the only man to have held the World title at both games simultaneously. He learned to play in his father's public house and first qualified for the World Championship in 1922 when he lost to Tom Newman in the final. He was again beaten by Newman in the final on his second and third appearances in 1926 and 1927, but finally became the world billiards champion the following year and retained the title until beaten by Walter Lindrum in 1933. His best championship break, without the aid of repetitive sequences, was 2,052 in 1930.

In 1926, two years before becoming the world billiards champion, he won the world snooker title and remained unbeaten at that game until 1955, and was so superior to the rest of the world that he retired from championship play after winning the title for the 15th time in 1946. In 1955 he became the first man to make a maximum break of 147 under championship conditions. Between 1928 and 1965 he compiled

687 century breaks.
More than any man, he was responsible for turning snooker into a world game and his personality and business acumen brought considerable financial benefit both to himself and to the game in general. Awarded the OBE in 1963.

John DAVIS (USA)

WEIGHTLIFTING

John Henry Davis. Jr. b. 12 Jan 1921 Smithtown, New York, d. 13 Jul 1984.

Davis was undefeated from 1938 to 1953 and in that period won two Olympic gold medals (1948, 1952), six World Championships (1938, 1946-7, 1949-51), 11 National Championships, and the 1951 Pan-American Games gold medal. He was the first lifter to clean and jerk over 400 lb, and the second man to total over 1,000 lb for three lifts. He set 18 world records in 1946-51: 3 press, 8 snatch, 4 jerk (to 182kg) and 3 total. His only defeat before his retirement came at the 1953 World Championships when, hampered by a thigh injury, he was second to Douglas Hepburn (Can).

Steve DAVIS (UK)

SNOOKER

Steve Davis. b. 22 Aug 1957 Plumstead, London.

The dominant snooker player of the 1980s, when with flawless technique he won 22 ranking tournaments compared to the next best of five (Ray Reardon) and was world champion in 1981, 1983-4 and 1987-9, runner-up twice and once a semi-finalist. His other major titles have included the British Open in 1981-2, 1984 and 1986; the UK Open 1980-1 and 1984-7; Benson & Hedges Masters 1982 and 1988. He also has a record four World Cup appearances on the winning team, for England 1981, 1983, 1988-9. Awarded the MBE in 1988. After winning the British junior title at billiards in 1976, he turned professional in 1978 and under the careful guidance of Barry Hearn soon made his mark. In 1980 he beat the defending champion Terry Griffiths in the second round of the World Championship, before winning his first title the following year.
In the 1990s he hit, by his standards, a poor patch, and he went 27 months without winning a ranking tournament until two in early 1992. He then had to wait another year until he beat Stephen Hendry in the final of the European Open in 1993. He followed that with his 7th win in the B&H Irish Masters, his 66th professional tournament victory.

Victor DAVIS (Can)

SWIMMING

Victor Davis. b. 10 Feb 1964 Waterloo, Ontario, d. 13 Nov 1989 Montreal, Québec.

A champion breaststroke swimmer and a great rival of Adrian Moorhouse, he won the Olympic 200m in 1984 in 2:13.34 by over two seconds. That was his third world record, his first being 2:14.77 when he won the 1982 World title. At 100m he took Olympic silver in 1984 (in his best time of 61.99) and was fourth in 1988, and also won silver medals at medley relay in 1984 and 1988. In both the World Championships and Commonwealth Games he had won the 200m and silver at 100m in 1982, and won the 100m with second at 200m in 1986.
His grandfather, Al, had been a boxing coach. Davis himself showed bad temper on a number of occasions, notably when kicking a chair across the pool and joining a walk-out of the Canadian team at the 1982 Commonwealth Games after they had been disqualified following a flying take-over between Davis and Dan Thompson in the medley relay, an event in which they had finished first very clearly. He died two days after being struck by a car following a brawl outside a bar.

John DAWES (UK)

RUGBY UNION

Sydney John Dawes. b. 29 Jun 1940 Chapel of Ease, Monmouth.

A shrewd tactical centre who won 22 caps for Wales 1964-71. In 1971 he led Wales to the Grand Slam and at the end of the season he was appointed captain of the Lions for the tour of New Zealand. He was the first Welshman to be honoured with the captaincy and under his leadership the Lions became the only British side to win a Test series in New Zealand. He retired from the international game at the end of the tour but returned to captain the Barbarians to a memorable victory against New Zealand in 1973. When he finally gave up playing he maintained his interest in the game notably as coach of the Welsh national team and the 1977 Lions. He was awarded the OBE for his services to the game.

While at Loughborough College, he won many University representative honours and most of his club rugby was with London Welsh who became one of the most exciting teams in the country under his leadership.

Pete DAWKINS (USA)

AMERICAN FOOTBALL

Peter Miller Dawkins. b. 8 Mar 1938 Royal Oak, Michigan.

A single wing tailback at college football with the US Military Academy at West Point, leading his team to an undefeated record in 1968, when he won the Heisman and Maxwell Trophies as the nation's top college football player. He began his mandatory military commitment, but was soon thereafter awarded a Rhodes Scholarship and studied for two years at Oxford, where he won a rugby football Blue.

Dawkins had an outstanding military career. He served two tours in Vietnam, won two Bronze Stars, an air medal, and the Joint Service Commendation Medal. He later studied at Princeton, earning a Master's Degree. In 1983 he became the Army's youngest full general and it was predicted that he would possibly go on to become Army Chief of Staff. Future political office was also expected for him. But Dawkins surprisingly retired from the Army and became an investment banker. He ran for the Senate in New Jersey after his retirement but was defeated.

Mat DAWSON (UK)

HORSE RACING

Mathew Dawson. b 9 Jan 1820 Gullane, Haddingtonshire. d. 18 Aug 1898 Newmarket.

A great Scottish trainer, who produced 28 classic winners: six each of the 1000 Guineas, Derby and St Leger and five each of the 2000 Guineas and Oaks. His greatest horse was, however, not a classic winner, *St Simon*. He was apprenticed to his father, George, at Stamford Hall, Haddingtonshire, and at 18, prior to training on his own account, became head lad for his brother **Thomas** (1809-80), who trained at Middleton from 1830 and had five classic winners. His younger brothers **John** and **Joseph** trained four and five classic winners respectively. In 1885 Mathew handed over his Heath House stable at Newmarket to his nephew **George** (c.1853-1913), who added ten classic wins to the family tally, but Mathew continued to train and won four classics for Lord Rosebery in 1884-5.

A bluff man, always immaculately dressed, he was widely respected, and had a contempt for heavy betting. He was one of the first trainers to run a private stable, at Newmarket, rather than train privately for a specific owner.

Ronnie DAWSON (Ire)

RUGBY UNION

Alfred Ronald Dawson. b. 5 Jun 1932 Dublin.

An outstanding leader who captained the 1959 British Lions in Australasia after winning only nine of his 27 Irish caps 1958-64. As hooker for Dublin Wanderers and Leinster he made his international début against Australia in 1958 when he scored a try in Ireland's first-ever win against a touring side.

After missing much of the 1960 season due to a broken leg, he captained the Barbarians to victory over the South Africans in 1961. On retirement, he became a successful coach and accompanied the 1968 Lions to South Africa as assistant manager. An architect by profession, he served as Barbarians committee member and was elected to the International Rugby Board in 1974.

Ned DAY (USA)

BOWLING

Edward Patrick Day. b. 11 Nov 1911 Los Angeles, California, d. 26 Nov 1971 Milwaukee, Wisconsin.

Day was considered the greatest bowler of the first half of the 20th century. His first major title was the Petersen Classic in 1943. He won the US Open (then the BPAA All-Star) in 1944 and was voted Bowler of the Year in both 1943 and 1944. In 1959 he won the first ever televised bowling event, the Championship Bowling Tournament in Toledo, Ohio. He was an excellent writer on the game as well, writing several popular instructional books. He was considered an articulate spokesman and promoter of the sport.

Pat DAY (USA)

HORSE RACING

Patrick Alan Day. b. 13 Oct 1953 Brush, Colorado.

Winner of three Eclipse Awards as outstanding jockey in the USA, 1984, 1986 and 1987. He rode the most winners in the USA each year 1982-4, with successive totals of 397, 455 and 400. At the end of 1992 he was fourth on the all-time money list at $126,017,280 and rode 5727 winners from 1972. At Arlington on 13 Aug 1989 he set a North American record by riding the winner of eight of the nine races.

Christopher DEAN (UK)

ICE DANCE

Christopher Colin Dean. b. 27 Jul 1958 Nottingham, Notts.

His partnership with Jayne Torvill produced some legendary performances in ice dancing. They joined forces in 1975 after both had achieved some success with previous partners and they won the first of a record six successive British titles three years later. After placing fifth at the 1980 Olympics they established themselves as performers of the highest class by winning the World and European Championships in 1981. After successfully defending both titles in 1982, they won their third successive World title in 1983 after missing the Europeans because of injury. Their performance at the 1984 Olympics in Sarajevo will go down in history as one of the greatest sporting exhibitions of all-time. Their brilliant interpretation of Ravel's *Bolero* drew a six (the maximum score) from each of the nine judges for artistic presentation and their total of twelve sixes for the entire competition broke all previous records. It seemed at the time that this performance was the ultimate but four weeks later the judges awarded a total of thirteen sixes to secure their fourth consecutive World title. Throughout their career they received a record total of 136 sixes. They then turned professional and were a huge success with their ice show.

In 1990 Dean became engaged and later married to the French-Canadian **Isabelle Duchesnay** (b. 18 Dec 1963) who with her brother **Paul** (b. 31 Jul 1961) won the 1991 world ice dance title and silver medals at the 1992 Olympics.

Dixie DEAN (UK)

FOOTBALL

William Ralph Dean. b. 21 Jan 1907 Birkenhead, Lancashire, d. 1 Mar 1980 Liverpool.

A robust, high-scoring centre-forward who was renowned for the power and direction of his heading. Joining Everton from Tranmere Rovers in 1925, he stayed at Goodison Park until 1938, scoring 379 goals in 437 League matches. His greatest season was 1927/8 when he scored 60 goals in 39 League matches to set a record which still stands. That year he also scored 22 goals in other competitions to bring his season's total to 82.

The previous season he had claimed 12 goals in his first international season, uniquely scoring in each of his first five matches for England. In total he scored 18 times in his 16 international matches 1927-33. While he was with Everton they won

the Football League in 1928 and 1932, and the FA Cup in 1933. In 1938 he moved to Notts County but played only nine games before transferring to Sligo Rovers where he helped the club to the final of the FA of Ireland Cup (1939).
Dean, who was nicknamed 'Dixie' because of his swarthy complexion, retired on the outbreak of war and was a licensee in Chester until overtaken by ill-health in 1964. He died at Goodison Park after an Everton v Liverpool match and the death of this football legend was mourned far beyond Merseyside.

Dizzy DEAN (USA)

BASEBALL

Jay Hanna Dean. b. 16 Jan 1911 Lucas, Arizona, d. 17 Jul 1974 Reno, Nevada.

Dean pitched for 12 years in the majors, mostly with the St Louis Cardinals and Chicago Cubs. But he had only six full seasons, during which he established his reputation as one of the toughest pitchers ever. As a rookie in 1932 he won 18 games and led the National League in shutouts, strikeouts, and innings pitched. During the next four seasons, he won 102 games, including 30-7 in 1934 and 28-12 in 1935. In 1937 he had 13 wins and appeared headed for another 20+ win season by the All-Star Game, but there he was struck in the foot by an Earl Averill line drive and sustained a broken toe. He attempted to come back before it was healed and developed shoulder problems which essentially ended his career. He pitched until 1941, and made a brief return in 1947, but he won only 16 more games in the major leagues. He later became a very popular broadcaster of baseball games, known for his lack of grammar and frequent malapropisms.
Career pitching 1930-47: ERA 3.04; W-L 150-83, % .644, SO 1155.

Jim DEAR (UK)

RACKET GAMES

James Patrick S. Dear. b. 1910 Fulham, London.

The only man to have been British Open champion at rackets and real tennis and squash, adding world titles at the first two. A pupil of the great Peter Latham, he started as a ball boy at Queen's Club in 1924 before becoming, at the age of 17, an apprentice professional at Prince's Club. Initially he excelled as a squash player, losing challenges for the British Open to Amr Bey (Egy) for three successive years, 1935-7, before taking the title in 1938. He lost it to Mahmoud Karim in the last Open held on a challenge basis in 1946. He became the outstanding rackets and real tennis player of his generation, taking the British Open title at real tennis in 1938 and 1954, and at rackets in 1946, 1951 and 1960.
In 1947 he beat Kenneth Chantler (Can) for the vacant world rackets title, retaining it until beaten by Geoffrey Atkins in 1954. He unsuccessfully challenged Pierre Etchebaster for the world real tennis crown in 1948 but when Etchebaster retired in 1955 Dear beat Albert 'Jack' Johnson (USA) for the vacant title. Johnson made a successful challenge in 1957 and Dear never regained the title. He was a notable coach at Eton, Queen's Club, Wellington College and the New York Racquet Club. Although not an exceptionally hard hitter he was a master of the angles and change of pace and he used the drop shot to great effect at all the sports. Awarded the MBE in 1960.

Dave DeBUSSCHERE (USA)

BASKETBALL

David Albert DeBusschere. b. 16 Oct 1940 Detroit, Michigan.

After graduation from the University of Detroit in 1962, DeBusschere was drafted by the Detroit Pistons of the NBA and the Chicago White Sox of the American League. He was a pitcher for the White Sox and played two seasons of major league baseball 1962-3, appearing in 36 games, winning 3, losing 4, and recording a lifetime ERA of 2.91. He retired from baseball in 1963 when he was named the player-coach of the Pistons, whom he coached in 1964-7. The muscular 1.98m *6'6"*, 107 kg *235 lb* DeBusschere, a strong rebounder and defensive player, was a forward with the Pistons until 1968 and then for the New York Knicks, whom he helped win an NBA championship in 1973. He has since been involved with several professional basketball teams in a management capacity.

Rob DE CASTELLA (Aus)

ATHLETICS

Francois Robert de Castella. b. 27 Feb 1957 Melbourne.

'Deke', a very strong runner who stayed clear of injuries for many years, won the first World marathon title in 1983 and was Commonwealth champion in both 1982 and 1986. He had set a world best time of 2:08:18 when he won at Fukuoka in 1981 and after the world best had been taken down to 2:07:13, he improved to 2:07:51 when he won at Boston in 1986. Always in contention, but never a medallist, he was successively 10th, 5th, 8th and 26th at Olympic Games from 1980 to 1992.

He won nine of his 24 marathons to 1993, eight times running sub 2:10 times. His other wins included the Rotterdam marathon of 1983 and 1991. On the track he set Commonwealth records at 20km (58:37.2) and 1 hour (20,516m) in 1982 and had bests of 5000m 13:34.28 (1981) and 10,000m 28:02.73 (1983). Awarded the MBE in 1982. A biophysicist, he is director of the Australian Institute of Sport in Canberra, and is married to cross-country international Gayelene Clews.

Guy de CLERCQ (Bel)

WATER SKIING

Guy de Clercq. b. 1923 Groot-Bygaarden.

Guy de Clercq tied for the overall title and won the jumps at the first World Championships at water skiing in 1949 at Juan-le-Pins, France. He again won the jumping in 1950 at Cypress Gardens. He was European champion in 1949 in jumping and overall, and also won the European jumping championship in 1951. His brother **Claude** was European overall champion in 1947, and from 1950 until 1952, with a further eight individual titles.

Max DECUGIS (Fra)

TENNIS

Maxime Omer Decugis. b. 24 Sep 1882 Paris, d. 6 Sep 1978 Biot.

The most successful of all Olympic players during an era when these tournaments attracted most of the world's leading players. He won a total of six Olympic medals (4 gold, 1 silver, 1 bronze) between 1900 and 1920 including victories in the mixed doubles in 1906 partnering his wife, Marie, and in 1920 with Suzanne Lenglen. As a boy he spent eight years at school in England and played much of his tennis at the Connaught Club, Woodford. He won a number of junior events in England, including the Renshaw Cup which was the forerunner of the British Junior Championships. He was one of the pioneers of the centre court attack and developed into the first great French player. Between 1902 and 1920 he won 33 titles (8 singles, 14 doubles, 11 mixed doubles) at the French (closed) Championships. Although he never progressed beyond the semi-finals of the Wimbledon singles (1911-12) he won the doubles with Andre Gobert in 1911. They were the first French players to win a Wimbledon title and their defeat of the holders Wilding and Ritchie (UK), who had never previously lost a championship match, was an impressive performance. Decugis played in the first six French Davis Cup ties, from 1904 to his last appearance against Belgium in 1919 when France won their first tie.

Ed DELAHANTY (USA)

BASEBALL

Edward James Delahanty. b. 30 Oct 1867 Cleveland, Ohio, d. 2 Jul 1903 Niagara Falls, New York.

'Big Ed' Delahanty was one of the first great baseball sluggers. He was by far the best known of five brothers to have played major league baseball. He played multiple positions, having broken in as an infielder, but he spent the bulk of his career in the outfield and at first base. In 1896 he became the second man to hit four home

runs in one game. He played most of his career with the Philadelphia Phillies, but in 1890 he jumped to the Players' League to join the Cleveland team for one year. In 1902 he was traded to the Washington Senators. In June 1903, he was suspended for breaking training rules. On the trip home he was ordered off the train by the conductor for his drunk and disorderly conduct. He staggered off, through an open drawbridge and was swept over Niagara Falls to his death.
Career 1888-1903: 2591 hits Avg. .346; RBI 1464. Best season: 1899: .410, 238 hits, 137 RBI.

Flemming DELFS (Den)

BADMINTON

Flemming Delfs. b. 7 Sep 1951 Gentofte.

In 1977 he won the singles title at the first World Championships as well as at the All-England Championships. He also matched the record by winning three European singles titles, successively from 1976 to 1980, having been the European Junior champion in 1969. He won the Nordic singles in 1976 and the Danish in 1977 and 1979. He was a formidable exponent of the backhand, but took training a shade too casually to sustain his position at the top of the sport.

Pedro DELGADO (Spain)

CYCLING

Pedro Delgado Rodrigo. b. 15 Apr 1960 Segovia.

'Perrico' Delgado has been one of the great riders in the major tours from the 1980s. But he has had to fight against Bernard Hinault and Greg LeMond and thus won less than perhaps was expected of him. His strength has been his ability as a climber. He is also a good time trialist but his inability to sprint well costs him dearly and has prevented him from winning any one-day classics. He turned professional in 1982 and after second place in 1987 won the Tour de France in 1988, a feat which had been expected of him for years. His victory was tarnished because he tested positive after one stage for the masking agent, probenecid. He was not disqualified because probenecid was not prohibited by the UCI, although it was by the IOC. Its presence in his urine raised the question of what other pharmacology it was masking, however. He was 3rd in the Tour in 1989 and 4th in 1990. He won the Vuelta à España in 1985 and 1989.

Luis DELIS (Cuba)

ATHLETICS

Luís Mariano Delis. b. 6 Dec 1957 Guantanamo.

Delis compiled an impressive record in major championships at the discus, always winning a medal until he was suspended for two years for a positive drugs test in 1990. At his only Olympics he was third in 1980, at the World Championships he was second in 1983 and third in 1987, and he was Pan-American champion in both 1983 and 1987, after taking bronze in 1979. He also won the Pan-American shot in 1983. At the four World Cups he contested, 1979 to 1989, he was successively 3rd, 2nd, 3rd, 2nd.
His six Cuban discus records from 1979 were topped with 71.06m in 1983 and he had a shot best of 19.89 in 1982.

Renato Della VALLE (Italy)

POWERBOATING

Renato Della Valle. b. 7 Nov 1942 Casalmaggiore.

The most successful offshore powerboat racer in history. He won the renowned Cowes-Torquay Offshore Race for four consecutive years, 1982-5, and in 1982 he also won the Offshore Class 1 World Championship.
In his home town of Casalmaggiore in the Cremona region, there is a great tradition of boat racing on the river Po.

Alex DELVECCHIO (Can)

ICE HOCKEY

Peter Alexander Delvecchio. b. 4 Dec 1931 Fort William, Ontario.

One of the most sportsmanlike of players -

he three times won the Lady Byng Trophy 1959, 1966 and 1969 - Delvecchio survived not on brawn, but on brain. Having played center for the Detroit Red Wings for 24 years, 'Fats' Delvecchio became their coach for two years and then moved up to become general manager of the only professional team for whom he had ever played.
NHL career 1950-1974 - 1,549 games, 456 goals, 1,281 points. Playoffs: 121 games, 69 assists, 104 points. Best years: 1965/6: 31 goals, 69 points; 1968/9: 25 goals, 83 points.

Jimmy DEMARET (USA)

GOLF

James Newton Demaret. b. 24 May 1910 Houston, Texas, d. 28 Dec 1983 Houston.

Demaret was one of the most popular golfers ever and a great one as well. He was known for his sartorial splendour but also as a superb iron player. Early in his career he played primarily in Texas, winning the Texas PGA Championship five times consecutively 1934-8. His greatest year was 1947 when he won the Vardon Trophy for low scoring average, won six PGA Tour events, and was the leading money winner. He won the Masters that year and in 1940 and 1950. In his career he had 31 US PGA Tour victories and played on the Ryder Cup teams of 1947, 1949 and 1951, wiining all six matches that he played.

Charles Pahud De MORTANGES (Hol)

EQUESTRIAN

Charles Ferdinand Pahud De Mortanges. b. 13 May 1896 The Hague, d. 8 Apr 1971.

The only rider to have successfully defended an Olympic individual championship in the three-day event, winning on *Marcroix* in 1928 and 1932. He added team golds in 1924 (when he was 4th individual) and 1928, and a team silver in 1932, but was unplaced in his fourth Games in 1936. Then a lieutenant in the Dutch Hussars he bought *Marcroix* specifically to ride in the 1928 Games at Amsterdam. He later became a General, and was an IOC member 1946-64 and an honorary member until his death. He was also Chief of the Military House and Grand Master of Ceremonies of HM the Queen of the Netherlands.

Jack DEMPSEY (USA)

BOXING

William Harrison Dempsey. b. 24 Jun 1895 Manassa, Colorado, d. 31 May 1983 New York.

Dempsey grew up fighting in the mining towns of the old west. When he turned professional in 1914, his older brother, Bernie, was also a professional, boxing as Jack Dempsey. William Dempsey thus started out as 'Kid Blackie' and then 'Young' Dempsey but later also took the name Jack as his professional name.
He won the heavyweight championship in 1919 by savagely defeating Jess Willard. His manager, Tex Rickard, used Dempsey's new-found popularity to make him one of the best known heavyweights ever. In 1920 he fought Georges Carpentier in front of the first million-dollar gate, a feat he repeated the next year against Luis Firpo. Dempsey finally lost his title to former light-heavyweight champion Gene Tunney in 1926, and in the rematch in 1927 he floored Tunney, who remained on his knees a total of 14 seconds as Dempsey did not quickly go to the neutral corner. Tunney later won that fight, known as 'The Long Count' for the controversial knockdown, by decision. After his retirement in 1931 Dempsey owned a popular restaurant in New York and was a very highly paid referee.
Career record: W - 60 (49), L -7, D -7.

Stewart DEMPSTER (NZ)

CRICKET

Charles Stewart Dempster. b. 15 Nov 1903 Wellington, d. 14 Feb 1974 Wellington.

A stylish opening batsman, whose Test average of 65 shows how much New Zealand missed him when he decided to concentrate on playing for Sir Julien Cahn's team and for Leicestershire 1935-9

(captain 1936-8). He first played for Wellington at 17 in 1921/2 and was very successful in 'unofficial Tests' against England before taking his place in New Zealand's first ever full Test in January 1930 against England. He also played in a few matches for Warwickshire in 1946.
10 Tests 1930-3: 723 runs at 65.72, 2 100s HS 136; 2 catches.
First-class 1921-48: 12,145 runs at 44.98, 35 100s HS 212; 8 wickets at 37.50, BB 2-4; 94 catches, 2 stumpings.

Willy den OUDEN (Hol)

SWIMMING
Willemijntje den Ouden. b. 1 Jan 1918 Rotterdam.

Her 13 individual world records included the first sub 1 minute time for the 100 yards freestyle, as she swam 59.8 in 1934. Her other records included four at 100m to 64.6 (1936), three at 200m to 2:25.3 (1935) and 400m in 5:16.0 (1934). Her final 100m mark stayed as a record for 19 years 359 days.
At the age of 13 she won a relay gold and was second at 100m in the 1931 European Championships. At this event in 1934 she won further gold medals at 100m and relay and was second at 400m, and in 1938 she won a relay silver. At the Olympic Games she took silver medals at 100m and relay in 1932, but disappointed in 1936 with fourth at 100m, although she took a relay gold.

João Carlos DE OLIVEIRA (Bra)

ATHLETICS
João Carlos de Oliveira. b. 28 May 1954 Pindamanhangaba, near São Paulo.

At the high altitude of Mexico City in 1975 de Oliveira won the Pan-American long jump and then the triple jump title with 17.89m. This added 45cm to the world record held by Viktor Saneyev and compared to his own previous best of 16.74. Hampered by sciatica the Brazilian was third at the 1976 Olympics (and fifth at long jump), but won at the World Cups of 1977, 1979 and 1981. In December 1981, however, he was involved in a traffic accident and after seven operations eventually had to have his right leg amputated below the knee.
In 1978 he tied Saneyev's world low-altitude best of 17.44 and in 1979 he retained both his Pan-American titles and set a long jump best of 8.36. He was third again at the 1980 Olympics, although most unfortunate to have a series of big jumps ruled as trailing leg fouls, inexplicably in the eyes of many observers.

Ralph De PALMA (USA)

MOTOR RACING
Ralph De Palma. b. 1883 Troia, Italy, emigrating to the USA when he was ten, d. 31 Mar 1956 South Pasadena, California.

The greatest driver of his era in the USA. He started racing in 1907 on dirt tracks in New York, with a career lasting until 1934. He won the US National Championship in 1912, 1914, and the Indianapolis 500 in 1915. In the war he worked as an aero engineer and was second in the 1921 French Grand Prix. In 1919 in a Packard at Daytona Beach he set the US and world land speed record of 241.19 km/h *149.875 mph*. Thereafter he concentrated on exhibition events, set stock car records for Chrysler, and worked as a consultant in the oil industry.

Pete DESJARDINS (USA)

DIVING
Ulise Joseph Desjardins. b. 10 Apr 1907 Manitoba, Canada. d. 6 May 1985.

Olympic champion at both springboard and highboard diving in 1928, having won the springboard silver and placed sixth at highboard in 1924. In the springboard event in 1928 he became the first diver at an Olympics to be given a perfect 10.0 score, gaining two such marks. AAU champion at both events each year 1925-7. Only 1.60m *5' 3"* tall he was known as 'The little bronze statue from Florida'. Moved with his family to Miami Beach, Florida as a child. An economics graduate from Stanford University, he turned professional and made many notable tours in the USA and Europe with Billy Rose's

Aquacades in the 1930s, still being featured up to the 1960s.

Kent DESORMEAUX (USA)

HORSE RACING

Kent Jason Desormeaux. b. 27 Feb 1970.

As a teenager in 1989 Desormeaux broke the record for the most wins by a jockey in a year in the USA. His total was 597 from 2312 rides, and won him the Eclipse Award as jockey of the year. He won another Eclipse in 1992 when he was the top money-winning jockey at $14,193,006. He had also won the Eclipse Award as apprentice of the year in 1987. He was then riding in Maryland, but he moved to Southern California in 1990. By May 1993 at the age of 23 he had already ridden 2478 winners

Hans DEUTGEN (Swe)

ARCHERY

Hans Deutgen. b. 28 Feb 1917, d. 3 Oct 1989.

Deutgen won more world individual archery championships than any other man, winning each year 1947-50, having been runner-up in 1946 to Ejnar Tang-Holbæk (Den). He also won a world team gold medal in 1948. Oddly, Deutgen fared less well in the Nordic Championships, never winning the title, but taking 2nd in 1949 and 3rd in 1951. He was Swedish champion each year from 1947 to 1950, and finished 2nd in 1953. He competed for the Stockholms Bågskjutningsklubb. He competed while archery was not an Olympic sport.

Donna de VARONA (USA)

SWIMMING

Donna Elizabeth de Varona. b. 26 Apr 1947 San Diego, California. Later Mrs Pinto.

At the age of 13 she was the youngest member of the US Olympic swimming team in 1960, when she swam in the relay heats. She had already set her first world record, with 5:36.5 for 400m individual medley, a few weeks earlier, but there was then no medley event on the Olympic programme. Four years later she won gold medals at the 400m individual medley and in the medley relay, and by then had become clearly established as the world's best.

From that first world record she added five more at 400m medley, taking the time down to 5:14.9 in 1964, and set one at 100m backstroke with 1:08.9 in 1963. She also swam on the Santa Clara Swimming Club team that set world records for 4 x 100m at both freestyle and medley events in 1964. She also set three US records at 200m IM to 2:29.9 (1964). AAU champion outdoors at 100m backstroke 1962, 400m IM 1960-1, 1963-4.

Her beauty as well as her swimming talent made her cover girl on such magazines as *Life*, *Time*, *Saturday Evening Post* and *Sports Illustrated*. After her retirement at the age of 17 she attended the University of Los Angeles and later became a television commentator and activist for women in sport. She served on several Presidential sports committees and as a special consultant to the US Senate. Her father Dave was a football star at the University of California.

Gail DEVERS (USA)

ATHLETICS

Gail Devers. b. 19 Nov 1966 Seattle. Married Ron Roberts in June 1988.

The fastest ever woman sprinter-hurdler. She won the 100m at the 1987 Pan-American Games, and in 1988 was the NCAA 100m champion and made the US Olympic team at 100m hurdles. Then, however, a serious thyroid disorder (Graves's Disease) caused her to miss competition in 1989-90. Her condition deteriorated so much that she was close to having to have a foot amputated, but then she made an astonishingly speedy return to the top in 1991. In that year she won the US 100m hurdles title (as she did again in 1992) and was second in the World Championships, adding a US record of 12.48. In 1992 she was a surprise winner of the Olympic 100m and added a second

gold in the sprint relay, but tripped over the last hurdle when well clear of the field in the 100m hurdles. In 1993 she won the World Indoor 60m title in a US record 6.95 and the US 100m title outdoors.
Other bests: 50m 6.10i (1993), 200m 22.71/22.55w (1987), 400m 52.66 (1987), 55mh 7.58i (1992), 60mh 7.93i (1992), long jump 6.77 (1988).

Roberto De VICENZO (Arg)

GOLF

Roberto De Vicenzo. b. 14 Apr 1923 Buenos Aires.

Known as one of the most gracious of all golf champions, he won over 100 major international championships among his 230 career victories, which is probably the largest number of golf championships recorded by any man. But he will forever be known for one tournament he did not win - the 1968 Masters. In that tournament, De Vicenzo shot a last round 66 to tie Bob Goalby for first place, seemingly forcing a play-off. But De Vicenzo signed an incorrect scorecard, signing for a four on the seventeenth hole, when he actually made a three. The score had to stand, giving him a 67 and victory to Goalby without a play-off. De Vicenzo commented, 'What a stupid I am'.
Major victories: British Open 1967 (2nd 1950, 3rd six times 1948-69); Individual World Cup 1969, 1972; Team World Cup 1953. 4 US PGA Tour victories.

Dawie DE VILLIERS (SAf)

RUGBY UNION

(Dr) Dawid Jacobus De Villiers. b. 10 July 1940 Burgersdorp.

Graduating through the Stellenbosch University, Western Province and Junior Springbok teams he became South Africa's most capped scrum-half. In 17 of his 25 international appearances he partnered Piet Visagie. De Villiers captained the Springboks a record 22 times including tours of Australia, France, New Zealand and the British Isles. He served as a Member of Parliament for seven years before being appointed South Africa's Ambassador in London in 1979. On his return home he became a cabinet minister and leader of the Cape National Party in 1989.

John DEVITT (Aus)

SWIMMING

John Devitt. b. 4 Feb 1937 Sydney, New South Wales.

Having been second at 100m to Jon Henricks at the 1956 Olympics, he succeeded his compatriot as the best sprint swimmer in the world. He took a gold medal and a world record at 4 x 200m in 1956 and won the Olympic title at 100m in 1960, with a bronze in the relay. He was, however, most fortunate to take that gold, on a casting vote from the judges, despite the fact that all three timekeepers had made Lance Larson of the USA the winner. Devitt set two world records at 100m (54.6) in 1957 and two at 110y (55.2 in 1957 and 55.1 in 1959), with a total of ten world records on Australian relay teams. He was Commonwealth gold medallist at 110y and 4 x 220y relay in 1958 and Australian champion at 110y 1957-8 and 1960.

Roger DE VLAEMINCK (Bel)

CYCLING

Roger de Vlaeminck. b. 24 Aug 1947 Eeklo.

One of the great riders in history, but one who had to battle Eddy Merckx for supremacy throughout his career. He is one of the few great professional cyclists also to have claimed cyclo-cross championships, winning the amateur world title in 1968 and professional in 1975. Such ability enabled him to win the bone-shattering Paris-Roubaix four times (1972, 1974-5, 1977) - still a record - and defeat Merckx several times in the process, including by the record winning margin in the race, 5 mins 21 secs in 1970. He was second in the 1975 world pro road race.
Other major victories: Tour de Suisse 1975; Milan-San Remo 1973, 1978-9; Tour of Flanders 1977; Het Volk 1969, 1979; Flèche-Wallonne 1971, Liège-

Bastogne-Liège 1970; Zürich Championship 1975; Paris-Brussels 1981; Tour of Lombardy 1974, 1976; Points Jersey Giro d'Italia 1972, 1974-5.
His elder brother **Eric** (b. 23 Aug 1945 Eeklo) won a record number of world cyclo-cross titles, with the Amateur and Open 1966 and Professional each year 1968-73.

Frank DEVLIN (Ire)

BADMINTON

Joseph Francis Devlin. b. 16 Jan 1900 Dublin, d. 27 Oct 1988 Clane, Co. Kildare.

The best badminton player of his era, he won successive All-England singles titles 1925-9, with a sixth win in 1931. He also won seven men's doubles, the first with George Sautter (Eng) in 1922 and the rest with his compatriot 'Curly' Mack; and five mixed doubles, the first two with the top tennis player Kitty McKane. In 1931 he became a teaching professional initially at Winnipeg in Canada, then after a tour of Australasia and Malaysia he settled in the USA, in New York and then Baltimore. His daughters Judith (see Hashman) and Susan were both outstanding players for the USA.
At the age of 12 he lost half a heel due to osteomyelitis, but while lying in bed spent hours hitting a shuttle against the wall; this developed his powerful and supple wrist.

Susan DEVOY (NZ)

SQUASH

Susan Devoy. b. 4 Jan 1964 Rotorua.

The first New Zealand woman to be world champion, she established a dominance over the women's game unparalleled since the retirement of Heather McKay, winning the World title with relentless power in 1985, 1987 and 1990-2. Her only setback came in the 1989 final when she surprisingly lost to Martine le Moignan (UK). After taking her fifth world title in October 1992 in impressive style, she announced that she would take a complete rest from the game at the end of the 1992 season, planning to start a family with her husband and coach John Oakley.
She also won the British Open for seven successive years, 1984-90, and took the title for an eighth time in 1992. She was awarded the MBE in 1988.

Ted DEXTER (UK)

CRICKET

Edward Ralph Dexter. b. 15 May 1935 Milan, Italy.

A splendid, authoritative batsman, whose powerful straight driving was a particular feature of his game. His great natural talent was also shown in his lively medium-fast bowling and fine fielding, and he was a top-class golfer. His authority and command made him an obvious choice as captain and he led Cambridge University 1958, Sussex 1960-5 and England 1961-4. Yet he was an unenterprising captain, whose interest in the game often seemed to dull. He is currently a controversial chairman of the England cricket committee. His majestic innings of 70 against the West Indies at Lord's in 1963 showed him at his best, but he also showed his character with match-saving innings against Australia of 180 in 1961 and 174 in 8 hours in 1964. In 1964 he stood unsuccessfully for Parliament against Jim Callaghan in Cardiff and retired from cricket the following year. He was persuaded to return three years later and made 203* for Sussex in his first innings. That earned him a Test recall for two matches against Australia.
62 Tests 1958-68: 4502 runs at 47.89, 9 100s HS 205; 66 wickets at 34.93, BB 4-10; 29 catches.
First-class 1956-68: 21,150 runs at 40.75, 51 100s HS 205; 419 wickets at 29.92, BB 7-24; 233 catches.

Brigitte DEYDIER (Fra)

JUDO

Brigitte Deydier. b. 12 Nov 1958 Meknês.

World judo champion at under 66kg at three successive championships, in 1982, 1984 and 1986, before placing third in 1987 and second at the 1988 Olympics when judo was a demonstration sport. She was also European champion at 61kg in 1979 and at 66kg 1984-6.

Kazimierz DEYNA (Pol)

FOOTBALL

Kazimierz Deyna. b. 23 Oct 1947 Stargard Szczecinski, d. 1 Sep 1989 San Diego, California.

The second most capped player and second highest scorer in international football for Poland, with 45 goals and 102 caps. He was an attacking midfield player with Wlokniarz Gdansk, LKS Lodz and then Legia Warsaw, with whom he won two championships and a cup winner's medal. He captained Poland during their most successful period, helping them to win the 1972 Olympic title, take third place in the 1974 World Cup and second in the 1976 Olympics. In his 100th international, during the 1978 World Cup, he missed a penalty. He also played for Manchester City and the San Diego Sockers, and while with them died in a road accident.

DHYAN CHAND (India)

HOCKEY

Dhyan Chand. b. 28 Aug 1905 Allahabad, d. 3 Dec 1979.

Winner of three Olympic gold medals as a centre-forward and the greatest of all hockey players. He learned the game from British officers while serving as a Sepoy in the Army and had his first experience of international competition in 1926 on a tour of Australia and New Zealand with the Indian Army team. Two years later he won his first Olympic gold medal and was again on the winning team in 1932 and 1936. In his last Olympic match he contributed six goals to India's 8-1 victory over Germany in the 1936 final. He was top-scorer when the Indian team toured East Africa in 1947-48 but declined selection for the 1948 Olympics when he would have been assured of a record fourth gold medal. He retired from the Army as a Major and became a coach at the National Sports Institute.

His ball control and dribbling skills have never been matched and although a prolific scorer himself his greatest asset was the creation of scoring chances for his teammates. His younger brother, Roop Singh, was also a member of the winning team at the 1932 and 1936 Olympics, and his son Ashok Kumar won an Olympic bronze medal in 1972.

Klaus DIBIASI (Italy)

DIVING

Klaus Dibiasi. b. 6 Oct 1947 Solbad Hall, Austria.

Dibiasi achieved the unique feat of winning three successive Olympic titles, at highboard diving in 1968, 1972 and 1976, with silver medals at highboard in 1964 and springboard in 1968, setting a record of five medals for diving. He also won the first two world titles at highboard diving in 1973 and 1975, and was second at springboard on both occasions. European champion at highboard 1966 and 1974 and springboard 1974, and second at both events 1970.

He was European Cup winner at springboard 1969, 1971 and 1973, highboard 1965, 1967, 1971 and 1975, and from 1963 to 1975 he won 18 Italian titles, 7 at springboard and 11 at highboard.

He was the first Italian to win an Olympic swimming or diving gold medal. Although he was born in Austria, his Italian parents returned to Bolzano in Northern Italy. Tall and fair-haired Klaus was coached by his father Carlo who was Italian springboard champion 1933-6 and 10th in the 1936 Olympics. Klaus succeeded his father as coach to the Italian team in 1977.

Eric DICKERSON (USA)

AMERICAN FOOTBALL

Eric Demetric Dickerson. b. 2 Sep 1960 Sealy, Texas.

One of the greatest running backs of the 1980s. A tremendous athlete who had played football and basketball in high school, and was Texas state high school 100 yards champion, he played college football at Southern Methodist (SMU) and broke all SMU and Southwest Conference records for yards gained and touchdowns. Selected by the Los Angeles Rams, he was the second choice in the 1983 NFL Draft.

His rookie year saw him gain an NFL-leading 1808 yards and in 1984 he broke O.J. Simpson's record for rushing yards gained in a season, with 2105 yards. Dickerson has since played for the Indianapolis Colts, then a year with the Los Angeles Raiders, before moving to the Atlanta Falcons in 1993. Although known as one of football's greatest runners, he has also earned a reputation for being difficult to coach, and has never played for a champion team. He is second on the all-time list with 13,168 yards gained rushing to 1992, reaching 10,000 in the fewest games ever (91).

Bill DICKEY (USA)

BASEBALL

William Malcolm Dickey. b. 6 Jun 1907 Bastrop, Louisiana.

Many experts consider Dickey the greatest catcher ever. He played his entire career with the New York Yankees, bridging their dynasties of the Ruth/Gehrig and DiMaggio eras. He was known as an expert handler of pitchers and caught over 100 games for 13 straight years, a major league record at the time. He never played another position in the major leagues. He was a player-manager for part of 1946 when he returned after the war and then coached the Yankees 1947-57.
Career 1928-46: 1969 hits Avg. .313, HR 202; RBI 1210. Best season: 1936: .356, 107 RBI.

Jimmy DICKINSON (UK)

FOOTBALL

James William Dickinson. b. 24 Apr 1925 Alton, Hampshire, d. 8 November 1982 Alton.

His 764 League appearances for one club stood as a record until 1980. He played his first game for Portsmouth as an amateur in 1943 and made his final appearance on his 40th birthday in 1965.
He was virtually an automatic choice for England from 1949 to 1957, winning 45 caps at left-half and 3 at right-half when he changed flanks to accommodate the youthful Duncan Edwards. He seemed assured of further international honours until he switched to centre-half for Portsmouth, although he knew he could not command a regular England place in that position. Towards the end of his career in club football he played at left-back. Dickinson played for Portsmouth in the First, Second and Third Divisions of the Football League and was a stalwart of the team which won the Division I title in 1949 and 1950.
Following his retirement in 1965 he continued to serve the club as public relations officer, scout, secretary and finally as manager from April 1977 to May 1979 when he retired on medical advice. Jimmy Dickinson was the epitome of an ideal club player and was never once cautioned by the referee throughout his lengthy career. In recognition of his fine example he was awarded the MBE in 1964.

Michael DICKINSON (UK)

HORSE RACING

Michael William Dickinson. b. 3 Feb 1950 Gisburn, Yorkshire.

In a meteoric career as a National Hunt trainer he was champion in three of his four years, setting a record of 120 winners (from 259 runners) in 1982/3, including the unique feat of saddling the first five horses in the Cheltenham Gold Cup on 17 Mar 1983.
Formerly a top jockey, he took over his father Tony's stables at Harewood, West Yorkshire in 1980. In 1984 he handed over to his mother, Monica, and became private trainer for Robert Sangster on the flat at Manton in Wiltshire. Despite producing the most modern training centre in Britain he achieved a mere four successes in his first year of 1986 and was sacked by Sangster in November that year. He then left to train in Maryland, USA.

DIDI (Bra)

FOOTBALL

Valmar Pereira. b. 8 Oct 1928 Campos.

A midfield star who was twice in a World Cup winning team (1958, 1962). He joined Fluminense in 1950 and won his first international cap two years later. In all he scored 20 goals in 68 international appearances. In 1956 he moved to Botafogo but in 1958 he was transferred to Real Madrid where his arrival was not welcomed by Alfredo Di Stéfano who was not prepared to consider any rivals for the title of the 'World's Greatest Player'. In an attempt to relieve the unsatisfactory situation, Didi was loaned to Valencia but eventually he asked for his contract to be rescinded and in 1960 he returned to Botafogo. After taking his old club to the League title in 1961 and 1962 he became manager of Sporting Cristal in Peru at the end of 1962. As a manager, he proved a great success and was asked to take charge of the Peruvian national team for the 1970 World Cup. Under his guidance, Peru's performance exceeded expectations and they reached the quarter-finals. In 1971 he moved to Argentina where he managed River Plate.

A serious knee injury as a child left him with a slight limp but he overcame the handicap by dedicated practice and spent many hours perfecting his famous 'dry leaf' kick. He was the pioneer of this curving dead-ball shot which is now part of every great player's armoury.

Mildred 'Babe' DIDRIKSON (USA)

ATHLETICS and GOLF

Mildred Ella Didrikson. Original family name Didriksen. b. 26 Jun 1911 Port Arthur, Texas, d. 27 Sep 1956 Galveston, Texas. Married professional wrestler George Zaharias.

Named as the female athlete of the half-century by Associated Press in 1950, she has an outstanding claim to be the most versatile sportswoman ever. She won two gold medals (80m hurdles and javelin) and a silver (high jump) at the 1932 Olympics and set world records at those three very different events 1930-2. She was an All-American basketball player each year 1930-2 and set the world record for throwing the baseball 90.22m *296 ft*.

Switching to golf she won the US Women's Amateur title in 1946 and the US Women's Open in 1948, 1950 and 1954. She also excelled at various other sports and was nicknamed 'Babe' after baseballer Babe Ruth for hitting 13 home runs in a game against boys.

Her world records set in 1932 lasted as US records for decades: 80m hurdles 11.7 not beaten until 1956; high jump 1.65m to 1948; javelin 40.80m to 1956. She also set a US long jump record of 5.69m in 1930 which lasted to 1953, and an unofficial world record for 100y of 11.0 in 1931. Her three year championship career in track and field included AAU titles at 80m hurdles 1931-2, javelin 1930-2, long jump 1931, high jump and shot 1932.

After her Olympic success she toured in vaudeville and with her own basketball team, before achieving golfing success starting with the Texas state championship in 1935. Having been earning up to $1000 a week on an exhibition tour with Gene Sarazen she was declared a professional, but regained her amateur status by staying out of competition for three years. She turned pro again in 1948. After contracting cancer in 1953 she made a courageous return to win the 1954 US Open by a record 12 strokes, but eventually lost her battle against the disease and died in 1956 a year after having to give up golf.

Wilfried DIETRICH (FRG)

WRESTLING

Wilfried Dietrich. b. 14 Oct 1933, d. 3 Jun 1992.

The winner of a record five Olympic medals in wrestling and accomplished at both Greco-Roman and freestyle. All of his Olympic medals were won in the unlimited class; his first was a silver at Greco-Roman in 1956, then in 1960 at Rome he medalled in both styles, a gold in freestyle and a silver in Greco-Roman; and he earned bronze medals at Greco in 1964 and freestyle in 1968. He also won five medals in the world championships between 1957 and 1969, three at freestyle and two at Greco-Roman, but his only win was in 1961 at the unlimited freestyle. In 1967 he also won that division in the European championships.

Sjoukje DIJKSTRA (Hol)

FIGURE SKATING
Sjoukje Rosalinde Dijkstra. b. 28 Jan 1942 Akkrum.

In 1964 she became the first woman since Sonja Henie in 1936 to win the World, Olympic and European figure skating titles in the same year. She began her international career as a 13-year-old in 1955 when she finished last at the World Championships, but showed steady improvement and in 1960 won her first European title and placed second to Carol Heiss at both the Olympics and the World Championships. For the rest of her career she was unbeaten, winning three World titles, 1962-4, four further European titles, 1961-4, and Olympic gold in 1964.

Harrison DILLARD (USA)

ATHLETICS
William Harrison Dillard. b. 8 Jul 1923 Cleveland.

Dillard was the hot favourite for the 1948 Olympic title at 110m hurdles, but sensationally failed to qualify for the US team when he hit three hurdles at the Olympic Trials. Nonetheless, such was his ability that he made the team at the flat 100m and won the Olympic title. Four years later he duly won the Olympic 110m hurdles, and at both Games he added gold medals at the sprint relay.
Dillard, who was short for a hurdler at 1.78m *5' 10"*, and nicknamed 'Bones' due to his scrawniness at school, first came to the fore in 1942 when he was fifth in the AAU 400m hurdles and 2nd and 3rd in the AAU Junior 110mh and 200mh. After war service in the army, he resumed his collegiate career at Baldwin-Wallace College, Ohio, where he studied commerce and won 201 of 207 sprint and hurdles finals. He compiled a win streak of 82 consecutive sprints and hurdles races, indoors and out, from 31 May 1947 to 26 Jun 1948. He was AAU hurdles champion at 110m 1946-7 and 1952 and at 200m 1946-7, and eight times indoors, 1947-53 and 1955; NCAA champion at both 120y and 220y hurdles in 1946 and 1947. He ran world records of 13.6 for 120 yards hurdles in 1948, and for 220 yards hurdles on a straight track of 22.5 in 1946 and 22.3 in 1947. Indoors he set five world hurdles bests at 50y to 6.0 in 1953; also ten at 60y, six at 7.2 (1947-8) and four at 7.1 (1948-56). Sullivan Award winner 1955.
Flat bests: 100y 9.4 (1949), 100m 10.3 (1947), 200m 20.8 (1948).

Dom DiMAGGIO (USA)

BASEBALL
Dominic Paul DiMaggio. b. 12 Feb 1917 San Francisco.

'The Little Professor' was the smallest of the DiMaggio brothers and was always overshadowed by Joe. But he played 11 major league seasons with the Boston Red Sox, missing from 1943-5 because of war service. Like his brother Joe, he began his professional career with his hometown San Francisco Seals in the Pacific Coast League. He was an outstanding fielder and was a perennial All-Star in centerfield.
Career 1940-53: 1680 hits Avg. .293.

Joe DiMAGGIO (USA)

BASEBALL
Joseph Paul DiMaggio. b. 25 Nov 1914 Martinez, California.

'Joltin Joe' or 'The Yankee Clipper' is remembered as one of the finest baseball players ever. He was the acknowledged leader of several of the greatest New York Yankee teams. In addition, he set numerous statistical standards to measure his greatness, notably his streak of hitting in 56 consecutive games in 1941, a mark which has still not been approached.
But DiMaggio was more than a leader and a statistical stalwart; he was the hero of a generation, known as much for the grace and élan with which he played the game, for which he was immortalised in both song and verse. In 1968, Paul Simon wrote the lyrics to the song 'Mrs. Robinson', which asked the plaintive question, "Where have you gone, Joe DiMaggio? A nation turns its lonely eyes to you." And in 1952, Santiago, the hero of Ernest Hemingway's *The Old Man and the Sea,*

asked himself, "My head is not that clear. But I think the great DiMaggio would be proud of me today."
DiMaggio retired in 1951. He was briefly married to Marilyn Monroe, Jan-Oct 1954, and in later years he owned a restaurant in San Francisco and became a popular commercial spokesman.
Career 1936-51: 2214 hits Avg. .325, HR 361; RBI 1537. Best seasons: 1939: .381, 126 RBI. 1940: .352, 133 RBI. 1937: .346, 46 HR.

Philippe DINTRANS (Fra)

RUGBY UNION

Philippe Dintrans. b. 29 Jan 1957 Tarbes.

Winning 50 caps between 1979 and 1990 he is France's most capped hooker. He toured to New Zealand in 1979, South Africa in 1980, and captained France in New Zealand in 1984 and on their 1985 tour of Argentina.

Piero D'INZEO (Italy)

EQUESTRIAN

Piero D'Inzeo. b. 4 Mar 1923 Rome.

The D'Inzeo brothers were guided in their riding careers by their father, Carlo Costante D'Inzeo, a Warrant Officer in the Cavalry of the Royal Army. Piero followed his father into the academy, and in 1946 joined the Cavalry jumping team. He first competed at the Olympics in 1948, when he was forced to ride his reserve horse and was eliminated at the first fence. He uniquely competed at show jumping at eight Olympics, each year to 1976, winning six medals. In 1960 at Rome, Piero was second to his brother Raimondo in the individual event, having also won a team silver in 1956, and he took four bronze medals - individual 1956 and team 1960, 1964, and 1972. In 1952 he was sixth in the three-day event.
Piero was European champion in 1959 and second in 1958, 1961 and 1962; Italian champion in 1973 and 1975; and won the King George V Gold Cup three times.

Raimondo D'INZEO (Italy)

EQUESTRIAN

Raimondo D'Inzeo. b. 2 Feb 1925 Poggio Mirteto, Rieti.

Raimondo D'Inzeo competed in a record equalling eight Olympic Games (3-day event 1948, and seven at show jumping 1952-76). He shares this record with Danish yachtsman Paul Elvström, Bahamian yachtsman Durward Knowles, and his brother, Piero. Raimondo won five Olympic medals including an individual show jumping gold in 1960 at Rome when Piero was second, with silvers in 1956 in both the individual and team event, and team bronzes in 1960, 1964, and 1972. He was also the world individual champion in both 1956 and 1960 and Italian champion 1968, 1970-1. The last Nations Cup team win for the brothers was in 1977.
Although originally interested in engineering, he followed his brother into the Army, and reached the rank of Colonel.

Marcel DIONNE (Can)

ICE HOCKEY

Marcel Elphege Dionne. b. 3 Aug 1951 Drummondville, Ontario.

The top center in the NHL in the late 1970s, until the advent of Wayne Gretzky. Dionne started out with the Detroit Red Wings but played for the Los Angeles Kings 1975-86 and then for the New York Rangers. By 1986 Dionne, a scoring machine, had moved into second place in the NHL all-time rankings of points scored, behind Gordie Howe. The only prize missing from Dionne's career was post-season success. He has had the misfortune to play for some very mediocre teams, and has never played for a Stanley Cup winner. His best scoring years were 1979/80 when he won the Ross Trophy with 53 goals and 137 points, and 1980/1 with 58 goals and 135 points.
NHL career 1971-89 - 1,348 games, 731 goals, 1,771 points. Lady Byng Trophy 1975, 1977; Lester Pearson Award 1979-80.

Alfredo Di STÉFANO (Arg, Col, Spa)

FOOTBALL

Alfredo Di Stéfano Lauthe. b. 4 Jul 1926 Buenos Aires.

A deep-lying centre-forward of such prodigious talent that even such clubs as Real Madrid fashioned their game plan around his skills. Starting in 1944 with Ríver Plate, he was already an established star when he joined the exodus to the high paying Colombian League in 1949 to play for Millonarios Bogotá. After four years the Colombian venture failed and he went to Real Madrid where he found a suitable stage for his skills. He was a member of the team which won the first five European Cup competitions 1956-60, the Spanish League eight times (1954-5, 1957-8, 1961-4) and the World Club Cup in 1960. He set scoring records wherever he played and topped the Spanish League scoring for five of the six seasons 1954-9, with a record 49 goals in 58 European Cup games.

In 1964 Di Stéfano moved to Español (Barcelona), but after two years took up a coaching appointment with Elche before returning home to Argentina in 1968 where, despite a hostile reception from the press, he revived the fortunes of Boca Júniors. In 1970 he returned to Spain to become manager of Valencia and took them to their first League title for 24 years. He later had two short spells as manager of Real Madrid. He represented three countries: 7 caps for Argentina, 3 for Colombia and 31 for Spain, for whom he scored 23 goals. Although idolised by the crowds, his unapproachable, dour and selfish manner did not endear him to his contemporaries or the media. Despite these off-field failings, his performances on the pitch were matchless and, with the possible exception of Pelé, he is recognised as the greatest forward of all-time.

Mike DITKA (USA)

AMERICAN FOOTBALL

Michael Keller Ditka. b. 18 Oct 1939 Carnegie, Pennsylvania.

Ditka played college football at Pittsburgh and then had a superb 12-year pro career with the Chicago Bears, Philadelphia Eagles, and Dallas Cowboys. He was termed the prototype of the modern tight end; known for his legendary toughness, often playing while injured. He caught 427 passes, then the NFL record for tight ends, for 5913 yards and 43 touchdowns. He became an even better known coach; an assistant at Dallas from 1973 until appointed head coach of the Chicago Bears on 20 Jan 1982. He made the Bears into an NFL powerhouse, winning the Super Bowl in 1986 with one of the great defensive teams of all time. He was sacked as head coach of the Bears on 6 Jan 1993 after 112 wins to 68 losses in his 11-year career, including a 15-1 record in 1985.

Aleksandr DITYATIN (USSR/Rus)

GYMNASTICS

Aleksandr Nikolayevich Dityatin. b. 7 Aug 1957 Leningrad.

At the 1980 Olympic Games in Moscow Dityatin achieved set a record for any sport at one Games by winning eight medals, uniquely at all eight categories for gymnastics. He won gold medals for overall individual and team and on the rings, with four silver and a bronze. He was awarded a ten for his horse vault, the first perfect score ever awarded to a male gymnast at the Olympics.

Tall for a gymnast at 1.78m, he won the combined exercises bronze at the 1975 Europeans and progressed steadily. In the 1976 Olympics he was 4th all-around and won two silvers, at rings and as a member of the USSR team. He was the World Cup overall champion in 1978 and 1979, and was World overall champion in 1979 with individual success at vault and rings. He added a World gold at the rings in 1981, and in all won 12 World Championship medals, 7 gold, 2 silver and 3 bronze.

George DIXON (Can)

BOXING

George Dixon. b. 29 Jul 1870 Halifax, Nova Scotia, d. 6 Jan 1909 New York

Nicknamed 'Little Chocolate' because of his size and his race, he was a very skilful

boxer, who after claiming the bantamweight title in 1890, won the world featherweight championship in 1892. He defended the title several times but lost to Solly Smith in 1897. However, in 1898 and 1899, Dixon defeated Dave Sullivan and Eddie Santry to regain all versions of the featherweight championship. He lost his title in 1900 to Terry McGovern and fought until retiring in 1906. In all he won 18 and drew 2 of 22 world title fights.
Career record: W - 51 (27), L - 28, D -46.

Aurelia DOBRE (Rom)

GYMNASTICS

Aurelia Dobre. b. 6 Nov 1972.

In 1987 she became the youngest ever world overall champion at gymnastics, winning the title at the age of 14 years 352 days. She added golds on the balance beam and with the Romanian team, and two bronze medals. A year later she was 6th overall at the Olympics. She had won a bronze medal at the 1986 European Juniors.

Larry DOBY (USA)

BASEBALL

Lawrence Eugene Doby. b. 13 Dec 1924 Camden, South Carolina.

Doby was the second black man, after Jackie Robinson, to play major league baseball in the 20th century. He was also the first to break the colour barrier in the American League, as he broke in with the Cleveland Indians and played most of his career with them. He was an outfielder for most of his career, although he played infield in his first year. He played in the All-Star Game each year 1949-54 and twice led the American League in home runs (32 in 1952 and 32 again in 1954). He also led in RBI in 1954 with 126. He later coached in the majors and became one of the first blacks to manage in the major leagues, with the Chicago White Sox for one year, 1978.
Career 1947-59: 1515 hits Avg. .283, HR 253; RBI 1011.

Lottie DOD (UK)

TENNIS

Charlotte Dod. b. 24 Sep 1871 Bebington, Cheshire, d. 27 Jun 1960 Sway, Hampshire.

An all-rounder of prodigious talent who was never beaten in five appearances at Wimbledon, winning the singles in 1887-8 and 1891-3. She was aged 15 yrs 285 days when she first won in 1887 and she remains, to this day, the youngest-ever Wimbledon champion. Throughout her career she only lost five open singles before retiring from competitive tennis, aged only 21, after the 1893 Wimbledon. She then turned to other sports and played hockey for England in 1899-1900 and won the British women's golf championship in 1904 after being a semi-finalist in 1898 and 1899. She was also won a silver medal for archery at the 1908 Olympic Games.

Bobby DOERR (USA)

BASEBALL

Robert Pershing Doerr. b. 7 Apr 1918 Los Angeles.

From 1937 until 1951 Doerr played second base for the Boston Red Sox. He never played another position in the majors, nor he did ever play for another team. He also appeared in over 125 games every year except his first and last. He was a reliable, steady performer, whose value to the team was never measured in the box score. He played in eight All-Star Games and was generally considered the top second baseman of his era. He also had excellent power, hitting 223 career home runs, but he never batted below .270, with a high of .325 in 1944. He later coached for almost 30 years in the majors.
Career 1937-51: 2042 hits Avg. .288, HR 223; RBI 1247.

Laurie DOHERTY (UK)

TENNIS

Hugh Laurence Doherty. b. 8 Oct 1875 Wimbledon, Surrey, d. 21 Aug 1919 Broadstairs, Kent.

The younger of two brothers who dominated world tennis at the turn of the

century. On leaving Westminster School, he attended Trinity College, Cambridge, winning his blue from 1896-8. The Doherty brothers were one of the most formidable doubles teams in history. They won the Wimbledon doubles for eight consecutive years (1897-1905) with the first two victories coming while Laurie was still at Cambridge. They also won the US title in 1902 and 1903, the Olympic title in 1900, and were unbeaten in the five Davis Cup doubles they played together. Laurie also won all seven singles that he played in the Davis Cup between 1902 and 1906.
He won the All-Comers' singles at Wimbledon in 1898 but lost to Reggie in the Challenge Round. He later won the title for five straight years 1902-06. He was Olympic champion in 1900 and in 1903 became the first overseas player to win the US Championships.
He was renowned for his speed around the court and with his smash and volley he was an unusually aggressive player for his era. After poor health forced him to give up the game in 1906 he concentrated on golf and played several times in the Amateur Championships. War service in the RNVR further damaged his health and he died one year after the war ended.

Reggie DOHERTY (UK)

TENNIS

Reginald Frank Doherty. b. 14 Oct 1872 Wimbledon, Surrey, d. 29 Dec 1910, Kensington London.

After winning the Wimbledon singles from 1897 to 1900, he lost to Wentworth Gore in the 1901 Challenge Round after his doctor had forbidden him to play. His younger brother, Laurie, then won the title from 1902 to 1906 and, apart from this lapse in 1901, the brothers dominated the Wimbledon singles for a full decade. Like his brother he was educated at Westminster and Trinity College, Cambridge and they won many major doubles titles together (see Laurie Doherty). His ground strokes, particularly on the backhand, provided a perfect complement to his brother's more aggressive style. In eight Davis Cup rubbers (3 singles, 5 doubles) the only match he lost was his singles against William Larned in 1903. Despite warnings about his health, he continued to play in selected tournaments after his last appearance at Wimbledon in 1906. After winning both the singles and the doubles (with George Hillyard) at the 1909 South African Championships he died the following year. Gates at the south-east entrance to Wimbledon were named after the brothers.

Basil D'OLIVEIRA (UK)

CRICKET

Basil Lewis D'Oliveira. b. 4 Oct 1931 Signal Hill, Cape Town, South Africa.

A prodigious player in Cape Coloured cricket in South Africa, he was prevented by Apartheid from making his mark at first-class level. He was, however, encouraged by John Arlott to come to England, where he started by playing for Middleton in the Central Lancashire League. He showed that he could make the transition to the highest grade on two Commonwealth tours and, despite being well into his 30s, was persuaded by Tom Graveney to join Worcestershire in 1964. Thus began a happy career with the county, playing until the age of 48 in 1980, and coaching thereafter. He graced the English game with his calm authority and was an outstanding success as a Test cricketer from making his début at 34, a hard-hitting middle order batsman who exerted great power from a very short backlift, and an accurate medium-paced seamer.
His original omission from the England team selected to tour South Africa in 1968 was itself a disgrace, but when he was eventually added to replace the injured Tom Cartwright, a selection surely essential after he had scored 158 in the final Test against Australia that summer, he was not allowed to come by the South Africans and the tour was cancelled. Amid all the controversy his quiet dignity was greatly admired. Awarded the OBE in 1969.
His son Damian played for Worcestershire from 1982.
44 Tests 1966-72: 2484 runs at 40.06, 5 100s HS 158; 47 wickets at 39.55, BB 3-

46; 29 catches.
4 One-day Ints: 30 runs at 10.00, HS 17; 3 wickets at 46.66; 1 catch.
First-class 1961-80: 18,919 runs at 39.57, 43 100s HS 227; 548 wickets at 27.41, BB 6-29; 211 catches.

Amédée DOMENECH (Fra)

RUGBY UNION
Amédée Domenech. b. 3 May 1933 Narbonne.

Capped both at prop and at No.8, he represented France 52 times. A hotelier, he played for Narbonne, Vichy and Brive. First capped in 1954, he held his place in the French team for four years until his unorthodox, roving style lost favour with the selectors. After adopting a more traditional style of prop-forward play, he was recalled to the national team after an absence of two years and played in all four Tests on the 1961 tour of Australasia. He went on to win a total of 52 caps before his international career ended in 1963. Nicknamed 'The Duke'.

Walter DONALDSON (UK)

SNOOKER
Walter Weir Wilson Donaldson. b. 2 Feb 1907 Coatbridge, Scotland, d. 24 May 1973 Newport Pagnell, Buckinghamshire.

The first man to succeed Joe Davis as world snooker champion, beating Fred Davis to take the title in 1947. After losing the rematch in 1948 he regained the title in 1950. He was beaten by Fred Davis in the final of the Professional Match-play championship in its first three years, 1952-4, and then retired from competitive play, having been a professional from the age of 16. He had been the first British Boys champion at billiards in 1922 and won his first Scottish title in 1928.

Yordanka DONKOVA (Bul)

ATHLETICS
Yordanka Lyubchova Donkova. b. 28 Sep 1961 Yana, Sofia.

Donkova displayed the finest ever sprint hurdling by a woman in 1986-8, with very sharp speed and technique, running 26 sub-12.50 times. She set five world records: four in 1986, and a best of 12.21 in 1988. She was European champion in 1986 (and won a silver in the 4 x 100m relay) and Olympic champion in 1988, but only 4th at the 1987 Worlds.
She was a semi-finalist in the 1980 Olympics and took the 1982 European silver medal. At the 60m hurdles indoors she set a word record of 7.74 in 1986 and after three medals in earlier years won the European Indoor title in 1989. She gave birth to a son in February 1991 and returned to competition in 1992, when she won the Olympic bronze medal. Competes for Levski Spartak, Sofia.
A talented all-rounder, she had a heptathlon best of 6187 points in 1987 when she was seventh in the European Cup. She lost three fingers on her right hand in an accident on her fifth birthday.

Martin DONNELLY (NZ)

CRICKET and RUGBY
Martin Paterson Donnelly. b. 17 Oct 1917 Ngaruawahia.

One of the greatest of all left-handed batsmen and a fine cover point, Donnelly had but a short cricket career, and only played in two Test series, both in England; as a 19 year-old in 1937 and again in 1949, when he made 462 runs at 77.00 in the four Tests, including a majestic 206 at Lord's. He scored another Lord's hundred for the Dominions against England in 1945.
He played for Wellington and Canterbury in New Zealand before the War, and afterwards came to England where he obtained his blue at Oxford University 1946-7 and played one match for Middlesex in 1946 and 20 for Warwickshire 1948-50. He also played one match for England as a centre at rugby in 1947.
7 Tests 1937-49: 582 runs at 52.90, 1 100 HS 206; 7 catches.
First-class 1937-61: 9250 runs at 47.44, 23 100s HS 208; 43 wickets at 39.13, BB 4-32; 74 catches.*

Steve DONOGHUE (UK)

HORSE RACING

Steven Donoghue. b. 8 Nov 1884 Warrington, d. 23 Mar 1945 London.

The idol of the racing public in England in the 1920s, he was champion jockey for ten successive years, 1914-23, riding over 100 winners in a season five times, with a peak of 143 in 1920. He rode 14 classic winners between 1915 and 1937, including six Derby winners, with a record three in succession 1921-3.
He struggled to gain a foothold in racing, and after an apprenticeship with John Porter he went to France, where he rode his first winner in 1905. After success in Ireland, where he was champion in 1908, he returned to England in 1911 as first jockey to Atty Persse, for whom he rode his first great horse *The Tetrarch* in 1913. Later in his career he rode *Brown Jack* to win the Queen Alexandra Stakes at Ascot each year from 1929 to 1934. After his 1000 Guineas and Oaks double on *Exhibitionnist* in 1937 he retired, having ridden 1845 winners. He trained for a while, but did not meet with much success. A charming man, he had great courage and showed his horsemanship with his balance and superb hands.

Christian d'ORIOLA (Fra)

FENCING

Christian d'Oriola. b. 3 Oct 1928 Perpignan, East Pyrenees.

Winner of four world titles (1947, 1949, 1953-4) and two Olympic gold medals (1952, 1956) in the individual foil, he dominated the event in the years immediately following World War II. He was also a member of four winning teams at the World Championships, 1947, 1951, 1953, 1958. In all he won a total of six Olympic medals (4 gold, 2 silver) with the individual silver in 1948, team gold in 1948 and 1952 and team silver in 1956. He was also French champion ten times.
An agile left-hander, with a natural sense of time and distance, he had exceptionally fast reflexes and developed into a fine technician under the guidance of the publican in his local village of Perpignan. He retired after the 1956 Olympics but returned to competition in 1958 and placed seventh at the 1960 Olympics. He was awarded the Legion d'Honneur in 1971, when he was non-playing captain of the French team.
A cousin of the great horseman Pierre Jonquères d'Oriola, he was an insurance broker, and his son Fred became an international fencer.

Pierre Jonquères D'ORIOLA (Fra)

EQUESTRIAN

Pierre Jonquères d'Oriola. b. 1 Feb 1920 Corneilla-del-Vercol, Pyrénées-Orientales.

The Olympic individual show jumping champion in 1952 at Helsinki on *Ali Baba* and twelve years later in 1964 at Tokyo on *Lutteur B.*, when at 44 years 266 days he became the oldest show jumping gold medallist. He also won team silver medals in 1964 and 1968 and placed 6th in 1956, 18th in 1960 and 17th in 1968. In World Championships he was 3rd in the inaugural event in 1953, 2nd in 1954 and 4th in 1955 before becoming the oldest champion at 46 in 1966, so that he ties with Hans Günter Winkler as the only man to have won three individual World or Olympic show jumping titles. He was second in the 1959 Europeans. A wine grower by profession, he was taught to ride by his father, also a distinguished horseman, and made his international début in 1947, in which year he won the King George V Gold Cup, and in all to 1971 he won over 300 international events.

Tatyana DOROVSKIKH (USSR/Ukr)

ATHLETICS

Tatyana Dorovskikh. b. 12 Aug 1961 Sekretarka, Orenburg. née Khamitova, then Samolenko.

A silky smooth runner with a deceptively fast finish, she achieved the World Championships double at 1500m and 3000m in 1987. She had not needed to run very fast times until she took 9.47 sec off her best to win the Olympic 3000m title in 8:26.53 in 1988, adding a bronze medal at

the 1500m. Her son Nikolay was born in January 1990 and she returned to competition in 1991, winning gold at 3000m and silver at 1500m in the World Championships. In 1992, with little racing behind her although she had taken a silver in the European Indoor 3000m, she again excelled at the Olympics, taking silver at 3000m and fourth in a fast 1500m, when she ran her fastest ever time of 3:57.92.
An engineering graduate, competing for Zaporozhye Spartak. She married walking coach Viktor Dorovskikh in 1988 (he had placed fifth in the 1978 European 50 km walk).
Doubling up at 1500m and 3000m she had also been 2nd and 5th in the 1986 Europeans, 2nd and 1st at the 1987 World Indoors, and, varying her distances, won the 800m and was second at 1500m in the 1987 European Cup.
Best 800m 1:58.56 (1985).

Tony DORSETT (USA)

AMERICAN FOOTBALL

Anthony Drew Dorsett. b. 7 Apr 1954 Rochester, Pennsylvania.

Dorsett (pronounced Door-SET) is one of the great running backs in football history. After high school football in Aliquippa, Pennsylvania he was highly recruited, finally enrolling near his home at the University of Pittsburgh. Though small at only 1.80m *5'11"* and 82 kg *180 lb*, in 1973 he became the first freshman to become first-team All-American in 29 years. He rushed for a record 6032 yards in college, including 2510 in his senior year, and won the 1976 Heisman Memorial Trophy. He was drafted by the Dallas Cowboys and played for them from 1977-87, finishing his career with the Denver Broncos. His career total yards gained is third on the all-time list. Dorsett was known for his speed, and his acceleration in the first few yards off the ball may be unsurpassed in football history.
NFL career 1977-88: Rushing: 12,739 yards av. 4.3, 77 touchdowns; Receiving: 3554 yards av. 8.9, 14 touchdowns.

Johnny DOUGLAS (UK)

CRICKET and BOXING

John William Henry Tyler Douglas. b. 3 Sep 1882 Clapton, Middlesex, d. 19 Dec 1930 off Læso, Denmark.

An obdurate right-handed batsman and skilful fast-medium bowler, with pronounced late swing. He completed the double five times in English seasons. He was a born leader and captained England in 18 of his 23 Tests, from his first when he deputised for Pelham Warner in 1911, and Essex from 1911 to 1928.
He won an England amateur cap for soccer, and in 1908 won the Olympic title for middleweight boxing. He was presented with his gold medal by his father, who was then president of the Amateur Boxing Association. Douglas lost his life with his father when the boat in which they were returning from Finland sank following a collision and both were drowned.
23 Tests 1911-25: 962 runs at 29.15, 1 100 HS 119; 45 wickets at 33.02, BB 5-46; 9 catches.
First-class 1901-30: 24,531 runs at 27.90, 26 100s HS 210; 1893 wickets at 23.32, BB 9-47; 364 catches.*

Dorothea DOUGLASS (UK)

TENNIS

Dorothea Katharine Douglass. b. 3 Sep 1878 Ealing, Middlesex, d. 7 Jan 1960 Kensington, London. Later Mrs Lambert Chambers.

The winner of seven Wimbledon singles championships between 1903 and 1914, she narrowly missed an eighth title when she held two match points against Suzanne Lenglen in the 1919 Challenge Round. The following year she again met Lenglen in the Challenge Round but at the age of 41 was overwhelmed by the 21-year-old.
The daughter of an Ealing vicar, Dorothea Douglass won the Wimbledon singles, 1903-04 and 1906, and following her marriage to Robert Lambert Chambers in April 1907 she won four more titles (1910-11, 1913-14) as a married woman. She was also a winner of the women's doubles (1903, 1907) and the mixed doubles (1906,

1908, 1910) at Wimbledon before they became full championship events.
She won her doubles in the 1925 Wightman Cup and played again in 1926 aged 47; two years later, as she approached her 49th birthday, she made her final challenge at Wimbledon in the women's doubles. In 1928 she became a professional coach. She was also a fine badminton player and won the All England women's doubles in 1903 and the mixed doubles the following year. Additionally, she played hockey for Middlesex.
The finest British player of the pre-World War I era, her strength was her forehand. Although a semi-permanent wrist injury restricted her power, she used an angled cross-court shot to great effect.

Heike DRECHSLER (GDR/Ger)

ATHLETICS

Heike Drechsler. née Daute. b. 16 Dec 1964 Gera.

The youngest gold medallist of the 1983 World Championships, she has long jumped consistently over 7 metres ever since and became Olympic champion in 1992. In 1981 she won the European Junior long jump and set world junior records of 6.91m in 1981 and 6.98 in 1982, in which year she was fourth at the European seniors. Evidence of her all-round ability was shown by a world junior record at the heptathlon in 1981. She set eight GDR long jump records from 7.14 in 1983 to 7.48 in 1988, with three world records, 7.44 1985, and 7.45 twice in 1986, and equalled with 7.48 for a unified German record in 1992.
She made a sensational breakthrough in 1986 into a great sprinter, starting with the GDR indoor 100 yards title in a world indoor record 10.24, and going on to equal Marita Koch's world record of 21.71 twice over 200m. In 1987 she ran a 400m relay leg in 50.0 in the European Cup, but a run of 27 successive long jump wins was ended through injury at the World Championships and she had to withdraw from the relay.
Major championships medals (LJ = long jump): Olympics 1988: 2nd LJ, 3rd 100m and 200m; Worlds: 1983: 1st LJ; 1987: 2nd 100m, 3rd LJ; 1991: 2nd LJ, 3rd 4x100m; Europeans: 1986: 1st LJ and 200m; 1990: 1st LJ, 2nd 200m. World Indoors 1987: 1st LJ and 200m. She also won the long jump at the European Indoors 1986-8, European Cup 1983, 1987 and 1991; World Cup 1985. She was GDR champion at LJ 1981, 1983-8, 1990; 200m 1986, 1988; and German champion LJ 1992, 100m 1992.
She was the overall Grand Prix champion in 1992, having been runner-up in 1990, winning the long jump title each year. Indoors she has set six world records at long jump, three at 100 yards and one at 200m. She has been coached by her father-in-law, Erich Drechsler, and competes for TuS Jena. Her son, Toni, was born on 1 Nov 1989. She was trained as an optical instrument maker.
Other bests: 100m 10.91 and 10.80w (1986), high jump 1.88i (1992), heptathlon 5812 points (1981).

Paddy DRISCOLL (USA)

AMERICAN FOOTBALL

John Leo Driscoll. b. 11 Jan 1895 Evanston, Illinois, d. 29 Jun 1968 Chicago, Illinois.

A running back and also a superb punter, Driscoll played college football at Northwestern in 1915-6, but in the summer of 1917 he played 13 games with the Chicago Cubs, thereby losing his collegiate eligibility. He enrolled in the Navy in 1917, and in 1919 played in the Rose Bowl for the Great Lakes Blue Jackets, leading them to a 17-0 victory over Mare Island. In 1920 he joined the Decatur Staleys of the fledgling NFL. He played in the NFL until 1929, from 1920-5 with the Chicago Cardinals and from 1926-9 with the Chicago Bears. He later was head coach at Marquette University and briefly coached the Bears in 1956.

Jaroslav DROBNY (Cs/Egy)

TENNIS

Jaroslav Drobny. b. 12 Oct 1921 Prague.

An immensely popular player who beat the

favourite, Jack Kramer, on his Wimbledon début in 1946 before going out in the semi-finals. He reached the singles final in 1949 and 1952 before finally winning the title at his ninth attempt in 1954.
Essentially a clay court player, Drobny won the French singles in 1951-2 and the Italian singles in 1950-1 and 1953. He also won the Italian doubles four times between 1951 and 1956, playing with a different partner each time. He won both doubles at the 1948 French Championships.
He was a member of the Czech Davis Cup team from 1946-9, winning 37 out of 43 rubbers, and he won a silver medal with their ice hockey team at the 1948 Olympics. He left Czechoslovakia as a political refugee in 1949 and took out Egyptian citizenship the following year. In 1960 he became a naturalised British subject but he was technically an Egyptian when he won at Wimbledon in 1954. Notwithstanding his big serve, he was also a fine touch player and the first left-handed Wimbledon singles champion since 1914.

Guy DRUT (Fra)

ATHLETICS

Guy Drut. b. 6 Dec 1950 Oignies, Pas-de-Calais.

Olympic champion at 110m hurdles in 1976 and second in 1972; European champion in 1974. He also won the European indoor 50m hurdles title in 1972. He ran three world records in 1975, headed by his hand-timed 13.0 at Berlin. His auto-timed best was 13.28, also in 1975. Indoors he set several European hurdles records, with bests of 6.0 for 50y, 6.51 for 50m, and 7.5 for 60m. A talented all-rounder, he had a pole vault best of 5.20m, with 7.56m for long jump and 7424 points for decathlon. Between 1970 and 1980 he was eight times French champion at 110m hurdles and also set eight French records 1969-75.

Ken DRYDEN (Can)

ICE HOCKEY

Kenneth Wayne Dryden. b. 8 Aug 1947 Hamilton, Ontario.

Tall and cerebral, Dryden may be the greatest goalie of the 'masked' era. He broke in late in the 1970/1 season, and immediately took over the nets in helping the Montreal Canadiens win the Stanley Cup. Unusually for a goalie, he was known, after a barrage had ended, for his pose of calmly leaning on the posts with his stick dug into the ice. After three excellent years in the nets, Dryden, who had graduated from McGill Law School, retired to take a job as a lawyer in Montreal. It was actually a salary protest as Dryden was upset with his pay but the Canadiens would not budge. However, after a poor year, they enticed him to return and from 1975 until his eventual retirement in 1979, Dryden was nonpareil, the outstanding goalie in the NHL. In only eight years he led the Canadiens to six Stanley Cups. After his retirement he took up law, but also works as a television commentator for ice hockey broadcasts.
NHL career 1970-79 - 397 games, 2.24 GAA, 46 shutouts. Vezina Trophy 1973, 1976-9; Calder Trophy 1972, Smythe Trophy 1971.

Don DRYSDALE (USA)

BASEBALL

Donald Scott Drysdale. b. 23 Jul 1936 Van Nuys, California, d. 3 Jul 1993 Montreal, Canada.

Drysdale was one of the most feared pitchers of the 1960s. This was part due to his blazing fastball and his size 1.95m *6'5'*, which brought his side-arming fastball down to the batter from on high. He was also famous for knocking down batters, holding the modern major league career record of 154 hit batters, and leading the NL in this category five times. His philosophy was oft-quoted, 'If one of our guys went down, I just doubled it. No confusion there. It didn't require a Rhodes Scholar.' He played for Brooklyn for two years and then for the Los Angeles Dodgers for the rest of his career. There he and Sandy Koufax were one of the greatest pitching duos in major league history. Drysdale's 58 consecutive scoreless innings in 1968 was a major league record until Orel Hershiser achieved 59 in 1988. He was

one of the greatest hitting pitchers ever, with 29 career home runs and twice had a slugging average of over .500. He played in five World Series, winning in 1959, 1963 and 1965, and was selected to ten All-Star games. He became a popular entertainer and broadcaster and later married Ann Meyers (qv), one of the greatest female basketball players ever.
Career pitching 1956-69: ERA 2.95; W-L 209-167, SO 2486; Best seasons: 1962: 25-9, .735, 2.84 ERA. 1965: 23-12, .657, 2.78 ERA.

David DUCKHAM (UK)

RUGBY UNION
David John Duckham. b. 28 Jun 1946 Coventry.

One of the most exciting runners seen in British rugby in recent years. A wonderful attacking player either in the centre or on the wing, he played for Coventry and England in both positions and on the wing for the British Lions in three Tests during their 1971 tour of New Zealand. One of his finest performances came on this tour when he scored five first-half tries and added a sixth in the second half in the provincial match against West Coast-Buller. Capped 36 times by England 1969-76, he was on the winning side in only 10 matches. He scored 10 international tries and in addition to his attacking flair he was superb in defence.

Arthur DUFFEY (USA)

ATHLETICS
Arthur Francis Duffey. b. 14 Jun 1879 Roxbury, Massachusetts, d. 25 Jan 1955 Arlington, Massachusetts.

Equalled the world record for 100 yards five times at 9.8, before becoming the first to run 9.6. He achieved this in the IC4A Championships at Travers Island, New York in 1902. The time was, however, rescinded as an AAU record as he was said to have violated amateur rules. He used specially made running shoes, rather than the standard equipment manufactured by the all-powerful AAU president James L Sullivan.

Slightly built at 1.70m and 62kg, he was an ultra-fast starter and won the AAU 100 yards in 1899 and the AAA title in England each year 1900-03 in 10.0. A student at Georgetown University, he was clear favourite for the Olympic 100m title in 1900, but pulled a muscle when in the lead at the halfway point of the final and failed to finish. In 1901 he was credited with an amazing 5.0 for 50y indoors as a professional.
He later became a columnist on the *Boston Post.*

Mary DUGGAN (UK)

CRICKET
Mary Beatrice Duggan. b. 1925, d. 1973.

The leading wicket-taker in women's Test cricket, with 77 wickets at 13.49 in her 17 Tests for England 1948-63. She was a left-arm medium-fast swing bowler in her early career and later a spin bowler, and captained England 1957-63. She achieved her best Test bowling performance at St Kilda's Cricket Ground, Melbourne in February 1958, when she took 7-6 in 14.5 overs, including 11 maidens, against Australia. This was one of five times that she took five or more wickets in a Test innings. She also scored 662 runs at 24.51, including two 100s, in Tests, and was the first woman to score a century and take five wickets in the same Test, 108 and 6-55 from 40 overs against New Zealand at Christchurch in 1957.
She was elected president of the Women's Cricket Association in 1972, and was vice-principal of Dartford College of PE.

Vic DUGGAN (Aus)

SPEEDWAY
Victor John Duggan. b. 10 Aug 1910 West Maitland, New South Wales.

In 1947 Duggan dominated British speedway, winning 297 of 348 races for Harringay, the Match Race Championship and the London Riders' Championship. His only failure was when he crashed when looking well set for the British Championship. He won that title, however, the following year. When the World

Championship was revived in 1949 he was a hot favourite but a broken collar-bone cost him his chance of competing. His brother Ray rode with him at Harringay, but was killed at the Sydney Sports Ground Speedway in January 1950, and Vic's interest declined thereafter. He had begun racing in the mid 1930s in Sydney and won a contract to race in England, where he qualified for the 1939 World Championships which were cancelled due to the outbreak of War. He was Australian champion in 1945 and 1947-8.

Jeff DUJON (Jam)

CRICKET

Peter Jeffrey Leroy Dujon. b. 28 May 1956 Kingston.

The leading wicket-keeper in one-day international cricket, and the world's best wicket-keeper batsman of the 1980s. In 1989 he passed Deryck Murray's record number of dismissals in Tests for West Indies. He was left out of the West Indies side from 1991, and dropped out of first-class cricket for a year, but returned with striking batting success for Jamaica in the 1993 Red Stripe Cup.

81 Tests 1981-91: 3322 runs at 31.94, 5 100s HS 139; 267 catches, 5 stumpings.
169 One-day Ints: 1945 runs at 23.15, HS 82; 183 catches, 21 stumpings.*
First-class 1975-93: 9732 runs at 39.24, 21 100s HS 163; 434+ catches, 19 stumpings.*

Geoff DUKE (UK)

MOTOR CYCLING

Geoffrey E. Duke. b. 29 Mar 1923 St Helens, Lancashire.

The motor cycling hero of the 1950s, he is considered to be the first of the modern-style racers. He won six world titles: riding for Norton at both 350cc and 500cc in 1951 and at 350cc in 1952, and for Gilera at 500cc in 1953-5. In all he won 22 500cc races and 11 350cc races, and was awarded the OBE after his feat of winning both titles in 1951. He helped to change the traditional racing attire as he got a tailor in his native St Helens to make one-piece leathers for him, giving reduced wind resistance. A supremely stylish and skilful rider with an especial 'feel' for his machines.

His interest in the sport was kindled by a visit to the Isle of Man in 1939, and during the War he instructed army motor cycle despatch riders. His competitive career began as a member of the BSA trials team and he made his road racing début at the age of 26 in 1948 on a 350cc Norton in the Manx Grand Prix. He won his first senior TT on the Isle of Man in 1950, won again in 1951 and 1955, and also won the junior race in 1951-2. He briefly, but unsuccessfully, switched to motor racing for Aston Martin in 1953. Gilera quit racing in 1957, and after declining success Duke retired in 1960.

Charles DUMAS (USA)

ATHLETICS

Charles Everett Dumas. b. 12 Feb 1937 Tulsa, Oklahoma.

The first ever 7ft high jumper officially, a feat he achieved when, at the age of 19, he cleared 7ft 0 5/8 in *2.15m* at the US Olympic Trials at Los Angeles in 1956. He went on to win the Olympic title that year in an Olympic record 2.12m. He was AAU champion for five successive years 1955-9 and won the Pan-American title in 1959, before finishing sixth at the 1960 Olympics when he suffered from a knee injury.

Nina DUMBADZE (USSR)

ATHLETICS

Nina Yavovlevna Dumbadze. b. 23 Jan 1919 Tbilisi, Georgia, d. 14 Apr 1983. Later Dyachkova.

She revolutionised women's discus throwing in the 1940s with seven improvements on the world record, although her first four improvements on the record, from 49.11m in 1939 to 50.50 in 1946, were not put forward for ratification because the USSR were not then members of the IAAF. With their return to international competition she won the European title in 1946 and 1950 and was third in her first Olympics, in 1952 at the age of 33. The IAAF recognised her records of 53.25 in 1948 and 53.37 in 1951. After Nina Romashkova had thrown 53.61 in 1952, Dumbadze achieved the greatest ever improvement by adding 3.43m to that with her final record of 57.04. This remained unsurpassed for eight years. Eight times Soviet champion, 1939, 1943-4, 1946-50, she was also placed 2nd or 3rd each year 1951-5.

Joey DUNLOP (UK)

MOTOR CYCLING

William Joseph Dunlop. b. 25 Feb 1952 Ballymoney, Northern Ireland.

He has become the most successful rider in Isle of Man TT races and has won a record five Formula One motor cycling world titles, 1982-6 (2nd 1987-8). In 1992 and 1993, when he won at 125cc, he first equalled Mike Hailwood's record of 14 Isle of Man TT wins and then passed it with a 15th win. He emulated the latter's record with three wins in a year, at Senior, Junior and Formula One in both 1985 and 1988. He was Formula One winner each year 1983-8 and his other TT wins were Jubilee 1977, Classic 1980 and 1987. He set the TT lap record of 190.66 km/h *118.48 mph* on a Honda in 1984. A pub landlord in Co. Antrim, who began racing in 1970, he was awarded the MBE in 1986. His brother Robert won the 125cc TT in 1989.

Richard DUNWOODY (UK)

HORSE RACING

Thomas Richard Dunwoody. b. 18 Jan 1964.

A fine horseman, who quickly established himself as a leading National Hunt jockey. He rode his first winner in 1983 and was third in the amateur championship in 1983/4. Turning professional he was runner-up to Peter Scudamore in the jockeys championship in 1989/90 with 102 winners, 1990/1 with 127 and in 1991/2 with 137. He succeeded the latter as chief jockey for Martin Pipe and as champion in 1992/3 with 173 winners and season's record prize money of £1,088,320. At the end of the season, by when his career total of winners had reached 910, he was awarded the MBE. He rode *Desert Orchid* to several of his major race victories, and also won the Grand National on *West Tip* in 1986, the Cheltenham Gold Cup on *Charter Party* in 1988 and the Champion Hurdle on *Kribensis* in 1990.

Margaret DU PONT (USA)

TENNIS

Margaret Evelyn Du Pont. née Osborne. b. 4 Mar 1918 Joseph, Oregon.

One of the great doubles players whose partnership with Louise Brough was a feature of the game in the immediate post-war years. After winning the US doubles with Sarah Cooke in 1941, she paired-up with Brough and together they won 18 major doubles titles: Wimbledon (1946, 1948-50, 1954), the US Championships (1942-50, 1955-7) and the French Championships (1946-7, 1949). As a singles player she won the Wimbledon (1947), US (1948-50) and French (1950) titles. She also won 10 major mixed doubles titles with various partners. She is the oldest ever US champion, the mixed doubles with Neale Fraser at 44 yrs 125 days in 1962, and the oldest at Wimbledon, 42 yrs 166 days for the mixed in 1960, 15 years after her singles victory. To this impressive list of championship successes she could add an impeccable Wightman Cup record winning all 18 rubbers she played (10 singles, 8 doubles).

Although not a spectacular player, her thoroughly efficient game was based on consistent serving and accomplished net play. In 1947 she married William du Pont, Jr who, back in 1941, had first suggested her partnership with Louise Brough.

Frik DU PREEZ (SAf)

RUGBY UNION

Frederick Christoffel Hendrik Du Preez. b. 28 Nov 1935 Rustenberg.

A lock and flanker with Northern Transvaal, he was capped a record 38 times (31 at lock, 7 as flanker) by South Africa between 1960 and 1971. His record was equalled by Jan Ellis in 1976 but has not yet been surpassed. He toured France and the British Isles with the Springboks in 1960/1 and made a second tour of Britain in 1969/70. His last tour was to Australia in 1971.

Jean DUPUY (Fra)

RUGBY UNION

Jean Dupuy. b. 25 May 1934 Vic-de-Bigorre, Haute-Pyrénées.

Making his international début in 1956 he won 40 caps, 38 on the wing, and on his retirement in 1964 he held the record as the most capped French winger. Dupuy, who scored 19 international tries, toured South Africa in 1956 and Australasia in 1961. He played for Tarbes where he worked as an insurance agent.

Roberto DURAN (Pan)

BOXING

Roberto Duran. b. 16 Jun 1951 Guarare.

A hard-hitting puncher Duran earned the nickname of having 'Hands of Stone' early in his career. In 1972 he defeated Scotland's Ken Buchanan to win the world lightweight championship. He never lost that title, but after 12 defences relinquished it in 1979 to challenge 'Sugar Ray' Leonard for the world welterweight title. Duran won that first fight with a brilliant display, but in the return match eight months later he was stopped in the eighth round, uttering the now famous comment, 'No más, no más!' (No more, no more). In 1983, Duran defeated Davey Moore to win the WBA light-middleweight championship, but the 1980s were marked by his gaining a great deal of weight and retiring and returning to fight multiple times. He won the WBC middleweight title from Iran Barkley in 1989, but lost later that year to Leonard in the last of his 21 world title fights, of which he had won 16. By then he was but a shadow of the great warrior he had been in the early 1970s but he continued to fight into 1993.
Career record: W - 89 (61), L - 9, D -0.

Bill DURNAN (Can)

ICE HOCKEY

William Durnan. b. 22 Jan 1916 Toronto, Ontario, d. 31 Oct 1972 Toronto.

Big Bill Durnan was considered the top goaltender in the NHL during his short career of seven seasons, in which he won the Vezina Trophy six times, 1944-7, 1949-50. He led the Montreal Canadiens to four regular season championships and two Stanley Cups. Huge for the era at 188 cm *6' 2"*, 91 kg *200 lbs* he also had lightning reflexes and was ambidextrous. He retired in the middle of the play-offs in 1950, feeling that his reflexes had slowed and his nerves were betraying him.
NHL career 1943-50 - 383 games, 2.36 GAA, 34 shutouts.

Sammy DUVALL (USA)

WATER SKIING

Samuel E. Duvall III. b. 9 Aug 1962 Greenville, South Carolina.

Duvall has a men's record four overall world championships (1981, 1983, 1985 and 1987). He excels as a jumper, at which he won the 1983 and 1987 world titles, and the Masters title in 1979, 1980, 1982, 1987-9. He was the first American to jump over 200 feet, and set a world record at 62.4m *205 ft*. Duvall has also won the US Masters tricks title in 1982 and 1985. To 1990 he won 13 US national titles.
His sister **Camille** won the world title at slalom in 1985.

Jack DYER (Aus)

AUSTRALIAN RULES FOOTBALL

Jack Dyer. b. 1913.

A legendary ruckman, whose fearsome play earned him the title 'Captain Blood'. During his 19-year career he played 310 games for Richmond, his club's record until passed by Kevin Bartlett in 1979, and kicked 443 goals. In that time Richmond, whom he captained and coached 1941-9, won the VLF premiership three times. He represented Victoria 16 times.
When he gave up playing he coached Richmond for three more seasons and later

became a popular radio and television commentator.

Eddie EAGAN (USA)

BOXING and BOBSLEIGH

Edward Patrick Francis Eagan. b. 26 Apr 1898 Denver, Colorado, d. 14 Jun 1967 New York.

The only man to have won a gold medal at both the Summer and Winter Olympic Games. After graduating from the University of Denver in 1917 he served as a lieutenant in the Artillery and in 1919 won the Allied Forces middleweight boxing title in Paris and the US amateur heavyweight title. He later attended both Yale and Harvard Law Schools and was still at Yale when he won his first Olympic title, the light-heavyweight title in 1920. In 1922 he went to Oxford as a Rhodes Scholar, and while there made his second Olympic team in 1924 when he lost in the semi-finals of the heavyweight division. In 1926-7 he toured the world with his fellow Oxford blue, the Marquis of Clydesdale (later the Duke of Hamilton) and they took on the amateur champions of all the countries they visited. Following his marriage to Margaret Colgate, the toothpaste heiress, in 1927 he gave up boxing and devoted more time to his legal practice and to bobsledding, at which he won a second Olympic gold medal in 1932 as a member of the four-man team.

Dale EARNHARDT (USA)

MOTOR RACING

Ralph Dale Earnhardt. b. 29 Apr 1952 Concord, North Carolina.

By the end of 1992 Earnhardt was by some $3.5 million the all-time money leader on the NASCAR list with $16,159,762. He set a season's record $3,083,956 in 1990 when he won nine races and had 18 top five finishes, and had been champion five times, 1980, 1986-7 and 1990-1, a total second only to Richard Petty. Known on the circuit as 'Ironhead', he began racing at the age of 19. His father, Ralph, was a stock car racing driver and when he died in 1973 he bequeathed Dale two racing cars. From dirt track racing he progressed to late model sports cars 1975-8. He was NASCAR Rookie of the Year in 1979, but went from one win that year to five in 1980, when he took his first title with the then season's record $588,926.

Dennis ECKERSLEY (USA)

BASEBALL

Dennis Lee Eckersley. b. 3 Oct 1954 Oakland, California.

Eckersley has had two distinct careers. He began as a fireballing right-handed starter with the Cleveland Indians and Boston Red Sox, winning 89 games in his first six seasons. He then began to have difficulties with alcohol abuse, but recovered to become a fitness fanatic. He was traded to Chicago and eventually the Oakland Athletics, where he was shifted to the bullpen. With Oakland he has become perhaps the greatest relief pitcher ever. He has had over 30 saves in five consecutive seasons 1988-92, with a peak of 51 in 1992 (the second highest ever figure), when he won the AL Cy Young Award and was elected MVP. He had remarkably few failed save opportunities in 1991-2. He still throws hard, but now mostly from a sidearm, underhand type delivery which has baffled batters since he has gone to the bullpen.

Career 1975-92: ERA 3.43; saves 239, W-L 181-145; Best seasons: 1978: 20-8, .714; 1992: 7-1, .875, 1.91 ERA, 51 saves.

Stefan EDBERG (Swe)

TENNIS

Stefan Bengt Edberg. b. 19 Jan 1966 Västervik.

A worthy successor to Björn Borg and Mats Wilander as Sweden's leading player. He won the junior singles title at all four Grand Slam tournaments in 1983 and soon became a major force. He met Boris Becker in the Wimbledon singles final for three successive years, taking the title in 1988 and 1990 but losing in straight sets in 1989. He did, however, beat Becker in the 1989 Masters final. Edberg reached his sixth Wimbledon semi-final in 1993, and was also Australian champion in 1985 and 1987 (and beaten in the final by Jim Courier in 1992 and 1993) and the US champion in 1991 and 1992. He has not won the French title but was a finalist in 1989. In 1991 his earnings of $2,363,575 were a record for one season, and by the end of 1992 he was second on the all-time money list with $13,339,075. World number one for 72 weeks in 1990-2. With his Davis Cup partner, Anders Jarryd, he won the US and Australian doubles in 1987 but in recent years he has concentrated on the singles in order to minimise the risk of aggravating his injury problems. He won bronze medals at singles and doubles at the 1988 Olympics. He made his Davis Cup début in 1984, and helped Sweden to win the Cup that year and again in 1985 and 1988; his win-loss record is 22-9 in singles, 11-8 in doubles.

Pat EDDERY (Ire)

HORSE RACING

Patrick James John Eddery. b. 18 Mar 1952 Newbridge, Galway.

In 1974 Eddery became the youngest champion jockey for 50 years, and won again in 1975-7, 1986 and 1988-90. In 1990, with 209, he became the first jockey to ride more than 200 winners in a season in Britain for 38 years, and in 1991 he became the fifth jockey to ride 3000 winners in a career in Britain.

Pat was apprenticed to Frenchie Nicholson at Cheltenham, and his first winner was in 1969, Alvaro at Salisbury. He became first jockey to Peter Walwyn in 1972 and first rode 100 winners in a year in 1973, when he was champion apprentice. The following year he rode Polygamy in the Oaks, the first of his nine English classic winners to 1993. Perhaps the greatest horse that he rode was Grundy, on whom he won English and Irish Derbys and the King George in 1975. He rode a total of 3251 winners in Britain to the end of 1992, with over 100 each year from 1973 to 1992, except in 1982.

His father Jimmy had been Irish champion jockey seven times and won the 1955 Irish Derby, and his brothers Paul (b. 14 Jul 1963) and David (b. 4 Apr 1966) are also riders. His wife Carolyn is the daughter of the great jockey Manny Mercer.

Jaap EDEN (Hol)

SPEED SKATING

Jaap J Eden. b. 19 Oct 1873 Haarlem, d. 3 Feb 1925 Haarlem.

The first speed skater to achieve prominence under organised championship conditions. At the first official World Championships at Amsterdam in January 1893 he won the 500m, 1500m and 5000m and although he fell in the 10,000m became the first overall champion. At the early championships a skater had to win three of the four races on the programme to be declared the overall champion. He achieved this again in 1895, when also second at 500m, and in 1896 when he won all four races, the first of only four men ever to achieve this feat. In 1894 he won the 10,000m and was second at 500m and 1500m. In 16 World Championship races, he won 11, placed second in three and fell in the other two; a phenomenal record which would have been even better had he not lost the lottery which decided first place in the 500m in 1894 after he had tied with Oscar Frederiksen (Nor).

He had competed with limited success at the first unofficial European Championships in 1891, and made his only appearance at the official Championships in 1894 in Norway where he did much of his training. He won the 5000m with a world record which remained unbeaten for 17 years; an exceptional period during an era of rapid development in the sport. His three other world records all came at the World Championships: 1500m (1893) and 10,000m (1894 and 1895). He was also the World sprint cycling champion in 1893 and was one of the first individuals to demonstrate the affinity between these sports.

Best times: 500m 48.2, 1000m 2:25.4 (1895), 5000m 8:37.6 (1894), 10,000m 17:56.0 (1895).

Trudy EDERLE (USA)

SWIMMING

Gertrude Caroline Ederle. b. 23 Oct 1906 New York.

On 6 Aug 1926 Ederle became the first woman to swim the English Channel, crossing from Cap Gris-Nez to Deal in 14 hr 39 min, at that time faster than any man had achieved. Two years earlier at the 1924 Olympics she won a gold medal in the 4 x 100m freestyle relay and bronze medals at 100m and 400m freestyle. She is also the youngest swimmer ever to have set a world record; at 12 years 298 days she swam 880 yards in 13 min 19.0 sec at Indianapolis on 17 Aug 1919. In all she set nine world records from 100m (72.8 in 1923) to that 880 yards distance. She turned professional in 1925. On her return to the US following her Channel record she received a huge ticker-tape reception in New York in her honour. She toured the US and Europe as a vaudeville act, but suffered a breakdown and became deaf due to damage to her eardrums. She recovered and taught swimming to deaf children.

Bill EDRICH (UK)

CRICKET

William John Edrich. b. 26 Mar 1916 Lingwood, Norfolk, d. 24 Apr 1986 Chesham, Buckinghamshire.

The golden summer of 1947 was lit by the genius of Denis Compton, but also by his Middlesex and English team-mate Bill Edrich, whose 3539 runs (av. 80.43) has been exceeded only by Compton's 3816. Edrich's rich promise was immediately evident and he made his England début in 1938 at the age of 22, having started the year with 1000 runs before the end of May. At first he met with little success at the highest level, only 67 runs in 6 innings in the summer series against Australia, but the selectors persevered with him and their trust was eventually rewarded with his breakthrough 219 in the 'Timeless Test' in Durban. His DFC, awarded for his war-time service as a squadron leader, mirrored his bravery and determination as a batsman, and he gave great service to England after the War, living life to the full. He was also for several years a tearaway fast bowler. Joint captain of Middlesex with Compton in 1951-2 and sole captain 1953-7, on leaving the first-class game in 1958 he returned to minor counties cricket with Norfolk, for whom he had played prior to joining Middlesex, leading them with much distinction and playing for them until he was 55. He also played League football for Norwich City and Tottenham Hotspur. His three brothers Eric, Geoffrey and Brian all played first-class cricket.

39 Tests 1938-55: 2440 runs at 40.00, 6 100s HS 219; 41 wickets at 41.29, BB 4-68; 39 catches.

First-class 1934-58: 36,965 runs at 42.39, 86 100s HS 267; 479 wickets at 33.31, BB 7-48; 526 catches,1 stumping.*

John EDRICH (UK)

CRICKET

John Hugh Edrich. b. 21 Jun 1937 Blofield, Norfolk.

Followed his older cousin Bill as a splendidly determined batsman and gully fielder for England. A left-handed opener who played for Surrey, captaining the county 1973-7 and also taking over the England captaincy as deputy in one Test for Mike Denness in 1975. His peak was reached in 1965 when he scored a majestic 310* against New Zealand at Headingley. Scoring over 1000 runs each year 1959-77, he had a peak of 2482 in 1962, one of six years over 2000. He played for Norfolk on either side of his first-class career. Awarded the MBE.

77 Tests 1963-76: 5138 runs at 43.54, 12 100s HS 310; 43 catches.*

7 One-day Ints: 223 runs at 37.16, HS 90.

First-class 1956-78: 39,790 runs at 45.47, 103 100s HS 310; 311 catches.*

Sigfrid EDSTRÖM (Swe)

OLYMPICS

Johannes Sigfrid Edström. b. 21 Nov 1870 Gothenburg, d. 18 Mar 1964.

The president of the International Olympic Committee from 1946 to 1952, having been president of the International

Amateur Athletic Federation from 1912, when he helped to organise the Stockholm Olympics, to 1946, and an IOC member from 1920. In addition to this 40-year service to international sport he was an outstanding administrator in Scandinavian sport. He had been a good sprinter with bests of 11.0 for 100m and a Swedish record 16.4 for 150m in 1891.

Duncan EDWARDS (UK)

FOOTBALL

Duncan Edwards. b. 1 Oct 1936 Dudley, Worcestershire, d. 21 Feb 1958 Munich, Germany.

A teenage prodigy whose brilliant career was ended when he died from injuries received in the Munich air disaster. He made his début for Manchester United as a 16-year-old amateur in April 1953 and two years later, almost to the day, he won the first of his 18 England caps: aged 18 years 183 days he is England's fourth youngest-ever international.

In 1956 and 1957 he helped Manchester United win the Football League. In 1957 they were also FA Cup finalists and reached the semi-finals of the European Cup in their first venture into Continental competition. In February 1958 Edwards played his last match for United in Belgrade and two weeks later he met his tragic death at the age of 21. He was rated as the complete player and during his relatively brief career he established himself as one of the greatest wing-halves.

Gareth EDWARDS (UK)

RUGBY UNION

Gareth Owen Edwards. b. 12 Jul 1947 Gwaun-cae-Gurwen.

After winning his first cap for Wales as a 19-year-old against France in 1967, the Cardiff scrum-half never missed a match for Wales throughout his career, playing 53 consecutive internationals until his last against France in 1978. In only his fifth international, against Scotland in 1968, he was appointed captain and at the age of 20 years, 7 months he is the youngest player ever to captain Wales.

He toured with the British Lions to South Africa in 1968, New Zealand in 1971 and South Africa again in 1974 playing in a total of 10 Tests on the three tours. His partnership with fly-half Barry John was the foundation of many successes for Cardiff, Wales and the Lions.

His 53 caps stood as a Welsh record until beaten by J.P.R.Williams in 1981 but remains the record for a scrum half. His record 20 tries for Wales has been equalled by Gerald Davies but has not yet been bettered. In 1975 he was awarded the MBE for his services to the game.

Shaun EDWARDS (UK)

RUGBY LEAGUE

Shaun Edwards. b. 17 Oct 1966 Wigan, Lancashire.

After captaining England schoolboys at both League and Union he signed as a professional on his 17th birthday and soon repaid the world record fee for a schoolboy of £35,000 which Wigan had paid for his services. In 1984, at 17yr 201 days, he became the youngest player ever to appear in a Challenge Cup final; the following season when he played against France at the age of 18yr 135 days he was, at the time, Britain's youngest-ever international. In 1988, when still only 21, he became the youngest-ever captain of a winning Challenge Cup team when Wigan beat Halifax at Wembley. By 1993 he had played in 31 consecutive winning Challenge Cup games for Wigan as the all-conquering team won the Cup for six successive years. Adding his first final in 1984, when Wigan lost, and a win in 1985, he has equalled the record of appearing in eight Challenge Cup finals.

His first international honours came as a full back and although he was usually selected as a stand-off he also played for Great Britain as a scrum half. He has won 18 international caps (plus 3 appearances as a substitute) although the total would undoubtedly have been greater had he not returned from the 1988 tour of Papua New Guinea and Australia after being injured in the first game.

Theresa EDWARDS (USA)

BASKETBALL

Theresa Edwards. b. 19 Jul 1964.

One of the greatest female guards ever to play basketball. She played collegiately at the University of Georgia, where she was a consensus All-American in 1984 and 1985. Her record is unmatched by women in international competition, with gold medals at the 1984 and 1988 Olympics, and a bronze medal in 1992. She was also the playmaking leader of winning teams at the 1986 and 1990 World Championships, the 1986 and 1990 Goodwill Games, and the 1987 Pan-American Games.

Joseph EGAN (UK)

RUGBY LEAGUE

Joseph Egan. b. 19 Mar 1919 Wigan, Lancs.

After signing for Wigan as a full-back in 1937, World War II deprived him of his best playing years but he developed into the outstanding hooker of the post-war era. He won 14 caps for Great Britain and toured Australia and New Zealand in 1946 and 1950. He led Wigan to victory in the 1948 Challenge Cup and after 13 years with the club moved to Leigh as player-coach in 1950. After he gave up playing in 1956, he returned to Wigan as coach and later moved to Widnes. In seven seasons as a coach he took his teams to the Challenge Cup final four times. Wigan won the trophy in 1958 and 1959 and were the losing finalists in 1961, and Widnes were the winners in 1964.

Krisztina EGERSZEGI (Hun)

SWIMMING

Krisztina Egerszegi. b. 16 Aug 1974 Budapest.

The most successful swimmer of the 1992 Olympic Games, as she won gold medals at both 100m and 200m backstroke and 400m individual medley. She was World champion at both backstroke events in 1991, and later that year broke long-standing world records with 1:00.31 for 100m and 2:06.63 for 200m.

In 1987 she was 5th at 200m backstroke at the Europeans and at the 1988 Olympics, after placing runner-up to Kristin Otto at 100m backstroke, she won the 200m in a new Olympic record, beating the much bigger and more powerful GDR swimmers into second and third places. At 14 years and 40 days she became the youngest swimmer ever to take Olympic gold. At European Championships she won three silver medals in 1989, and three golds (100m and 200m backstroke, and 400m medley relay) in 1991.

Even when she was just ten, Roland Matthes had commented on her perfect technique and had predicted that she would leave the rest of the world behind in the backstroke. Before her 18th birthday the schoolgirl had fulfilled his prophecy. Coached by Lászlo Kiss.

Other bests: 200m IM 2:16.03 (1989), 400m IM 4:36.54 (1992).

Oscar EGG (Swi)

CYCLING

Oscar Egg. b. 2 Mar 1890 Schlatt, d. 9 Feb 1961 Nizza.

An exceptional all-rounder who set the world hour record three times, recording 42.360 km in 1912, 43.775 km in 1913 and 44.247 km in 1914. He also campaigned vigorously on behalf of his records. When his 1912 record was beaten by Richard Weise in 1913 he demanded that the track on which he, Egg, had set the record be remeasured. It was found to be longer than expected and this enabled Egg to keep the record. In 1933 Jan van Hout broke Egg's record and Egg now demanded a measurement of the track on which van Hout rode. It was found to be short but the record was soon broken by Maurice Richard.

Egg was Swiss track sprint champion for 12 consecutive years, at one time set the world record for the six-day, and was also superb at motor-paced races and tandem track racing. He won the 1914 Paris-Tours race and eight six-day races, and made a fortune selling Oscgear, an early derailleur he helped invent. He later trained Switzerland's only two Tour de France winners, Ferdi Kubler (1950) and Hugo Koblet (1951).

Annelie EHRHARDT (GDR)

ATHLETICS

Annelie Ehrhardt. née Jahns. b. 18 Jun 1950 Ohrsleben.

The top woman high hurdler of the early 1970s, and an immaculate technician, she was Olympic champion in 1972 and European in 1974 after taking the European silver in 1971. Her 12.59 for 100m in winning the 1972 Olympics was the inaugural world record on automatic timing, and on hand timing she set new marks at 12.5 in 1972 and 12.3 in 1973. She came to the fore when winning the 1968 European Junior title at 100m hurdles, won the European Cup races of 1973 and 1975 and was GDR champion in 1970 and 1972-4. Indoors she was European champion at 60m hurdles in 1972 and 1973 with silver medals in 1971 and 1975, and set many world indoor records with bests of 6.6 and 6.74 for 50m and 7.90 for 60m hurdles.

Andrea EHRIG (GDR)

SPEED SKATING

Andrea Ehrig. b. 1 Dec 1960 Dresden. née Mitscherlich, then Schöne, later Ehrig.

The winner of seven Olympic speed skating medals. She started with the silver at 3000m in 1976, although she slipped to 6th at 1500m and 4th at 3000m in 1980. In 1984 she won the 3000m and took silver medals in the 1000m and 1500m. She set world records in 1984 for 1500m 2:03.34, 3000m 4:20.91, and 5000m 7:34.52, and improved the latter in 1985 and twice in 1986 to a best of 7:20.99. She improved her times at the 1988 Olympic Games, with personal bests when second to Yvonne Van Gennip in both the 3000m and 5000m and she also won a bronze medal in the 1500m. She was a nurse and medical student, and married first to Ingolf Schöne and then in 1985 to Andreas Ehrig (b. 20 Oct 1959), who competed at two Olympics as a speed skater with a best placing of 4th at 500m in 1984.

Best times, all in 1988: 500m 40.71, 1000m 1:19.32, 1500m 2:01.00, 3000m 4:12.09, 5000m 7:17.12.

Ilona ELEK (Hun)

FENCING

Ilona Elek. b. 17 May 1907 Budapest, d. 24 Jul 1988 Budapest. Later Schacherer 1936, then Hepp.

With three world and two Olympic titles, she has won more major individual championships than any other woman fencer. A determined left-handed competitor, rather than an outstanding stylist, her career spanned World War II: she was the world individual foil champion in 1934 and, at the age of 48, she won a team gold medal and placed fifth in the individual event in 1955. During this period she won individual Olympic gold medals in 1936 and 1948 and a silver in 1952. Her victory in 1948, at the age of 41yr 78d, gave her the record of being the oldest woman ever to win an Olympic gold medal for fencing, and in 1952 she added the record of being the oldest medallist when she took the silver aged 45yr 72d. Her outstanding Olympic record was, however, surpassed by her performances at the World Championships where she won 11 gold medals (individual 1934-5, 1951 and team 1933-5, 1937, 1952-5), 5 silver medals and 1 bronze.

Mark ELLA (Aus)

RUGBY UNION

Mark Gordon Ella. b. 5 Jun 1959 La Perouse, Sydney.

An outstanding schoolboy fly half who went on to win 25 international caps. A regular tourist, he first captained Australia on the 1982 tour of New Zealand when only 23, and when he led Australia to the UK in 1984 he set a record by scoring a try in each of the internationals against the four Home Countries. A fine all-round player with a brilliant eye for an opening, he retired at the early age of 25 mainly because of disagreements with coach Alan Jones. Contrary to expectations he declined many lucrative offers to join leading rugby league clubs. His twin, **Glen** (b. 5 Jun 1959) and his younger brother, **Gary** (b. 23 Jul 1960) were each capped four times by Australia.

Carl ELLER (USA)

AMERICAN FOOTBALL

Carl Lee Eller. b. 25 Jan 1942 Winston-Salem, North Carolina.

A defensive tackle who was a stalwart on the Minnesota Vikings' Purple People Eater defense, although he played the last two of his 15 pro seasons with the Seattle Seahawks. He was All-Pro five times and appeared in six Pro Bowl Games, helping the Vikings get to four Super Bowl Games, although never winning. He had played for the University of Minnesota in college. After his playing career, Eller began his own career and management counselling programme, helping many NFL players with drug rehabilitation.

Bill ELLIOTT (USA)

MOTOR RACING

William C Elliott. b. 8 Oct 1955 Dawsonville, Georgia.

Champion stock car racing driver who won the Winston Cup series in 1988 after two years as second, two thirds and a fourth. His career earnings reached $12,651,025 with 39 wins to the end of 1992.

The son of a car dealer, he started racing as a youngster and had his first NASCAR victory in 1983. In 1985 he set a seasonal record with earnings of $2,383,187 and won the Daytona 500, a victory he repeated in 1987.

Charlie ELLIOTT (UK)

HORSE RACING

Edward Charles Elliott. b. 3 Oct 1904 Newmarket, d. 6 Jan 1979 London.

A stylish jockey, he ended Steve Donoghue's run of ten years as champion jockey by tying with him in 1923 and then became champion himself in 1924 with 106 winners while still apprenticed to Jack Jarvis. Between 1923 and 1949 he rode the winners of 14 English classics, and also raced a lot in France where from 1929 he rode for Marcel Boussac, for whom he rode 4 winners of the French Derby and 3 of the Prix de l'Arc de Triomphe. Elliott also trained for Boussac from 1953 to 1958 before returning to train at Newmarket, where he had come from a local racing family, until his retirement in 1963.

Herb ELLIOTT (Aus)

ATHLETICS

Herbert James Elliott. b. 25 Feb 1938 Subiaco, Western Australia.

Elliott had just two years, 1958 and 1960, at the head of world middle distance running, yet in that short time he established such a reputation that he remains many experts' selection as the greatest ever. Undefeated at 1500m or 1 mile from 1954 he set world records for the former with 3:36.0 in 1958, 2.1 secs off the old mark, and 3:35.6 when he won the Olympic title in 1960 by a huge margin with Michel Jazy runner-up in 3:38.4. This was a classic performance from Elliott, who ran away from the field from 950m. At 1 mile he improved Derek Ibbotson's 1957 record of 3:57.2 to 3:54.5 in Dublin in 1958, shortly after winning the Commonwealth Games double at 880y and 1 mile. Coached by Percy Cerruty, Elliott had run world junior bests at distances from 1500m to 3 miles in 1957. Australian champion 880y and 1 mile 1957-8, 1960. He went to Cambridge University in 1961 but ended his running career at 23, still surely with years of potential achievement ahead. He is now managing director of the sportswear company Puma Australia.

Other bests: 880y 1:47.3 (1958), 1000m 2:19.1 (1960), 2 miles 8:37.6 (1958).

Jan ELLIS (SAf)

RUGBY UNION

Jacobus Hendrik Ellis. b. 5 Jan 1943 Brakpan.

A flanker from South West Africa (now Namibia) who shares with Frik Du Preez the record of being the most capped Springbok of all-time. He made his international début against New Zealand in 1965 and won his 38th cap in the first Test against New Zealand in 1976. He was dropped for the remainder of the series and thus lost the chance to better Du Preez's record.

Paul ELVSTRØM (Den)

YACHTING

Paul Bert Elvstrøm. b. 25 Feb 1928 Gentofte (Hellerup), Copenhagen.

Winner of the Firefly class in 1948 and the Finn class in 1952, 1956 and 1960, he was the first sportsman to win individual gold medals at four successive Olympic Games. He also competed at the Games of 1968, 1972, 1984 and 1988 to become one of only four men to have taken part in eight Olympics, and he is also one of the four Olympians whose career spanned 40 years. He was a reserve in 1964. His daughter, **Trine** (b. 6 Mar 1962), crewed for him in the Tornado class Danish yachting team in 1984 and 1988, the first time in Olympic history that a father and daughter had competed together. Together they won the European titles in the Tornado class in 1983-4. A second daughter, Ann Christine, was an Olympic reserve in 1988. He also won 13 world titles in seven different monotype classes. In 1954 he started a sail manufacturing company which became a worldwide operation and was so successful that Elvstrøm's status was scrutinised by the IOC Eligibility Commission in 1972.

Keith ELWELL (UK)

RUGBY LEAGUE

Keith Elwell. b. 12 Feb 1950 Widnes, Cheshire.

Played a record 239 consecutive games as hooker for Widnes between May 1977 and September 1982. His decision to withdraw from the England team against France in 1981 in order to maintain his unbroken sequence of club appearances affected his international prospects and he only played three times for Great Britain and twice for England. Between 1972 and 1985 he won 28 winners or runners-up medals in major competitions. He is one of only three men to have played in seven Challenge Cup finals and was on the winning side four times, 1975, 1979, 1981 and 1984.

Roy EMERSON (Aus)

TENNIS

Roy Stanley Emerson. b. 3 Nov 1936 Blackbutt, Queensland.

Emerging as Australia's leading player after being in the shadow of Hoad and Rosewall, he won all the major singles titles: Wimbledon (1964-5), US (1961, 1964), French (1963, 1967) and Australian (1961, 1963-7). His six Australian and 12 Grand Slam singles titles remain as records. In 1966 he was favourite to win his third successive Wimbledon but he fell and injured his shoulder in his quarter-final against Owen Davidson (Aus).

Emerson had an equally impressive record as a doubles player, winning the French title six times, the US four times and Wimbledon and the Australian three times each. In the Davis Cup, he was uniquely in the winning team on eight occasions, losing only in 1963 in the nine successive (1959-67) Challenge Rounds in which he played, and in which he won 15 of 18 rubbers. A notable sprinter as a schoolboy, his speed around the court was one of the features of his game.

Kornelia ENDER (GDR)

SWIMMING

Kornelia Ender. b. 25 Oct 1958 Plauen. Later Matthes, then Grummt.

Ender tied Dawn Fraser's women's record by winning eight Olympic swimming medals: gold at 100m and 200m freestyle, 100m butterfly and 400m medley relay in 1976; silver at 200m individual medley, 400m medley relay and 400m freestyle relay in 1972 and at the latter in 1976. At 1.78m in height and 72.5kg in weight she was far bigger and more powerful than most of her rivals.

Her first world record came at the age of 14 in 1973 when she took 0.25 off Shane Gould's best with 58.25 sec. for 100m freestyle, and from then until 1976 she set a total of 23 at individual events, more world records than anybody in the history of women's swimming at the currently ratified events. These comprised ten at 100m freestyle (to 55.65), four at 200m freestyle (to 1:59.26), six at 100m butterfly (to 1:00.13), two at 200m individual medley (to 2:17.14) and one at 100m backstroke (1:01.62). At each of the first two World Championships in 1973 and 1975 she won four golds (100m freestyle and butterfly, and both 4x100m relays) and added silvers at 200m IM in 1973 and 200m freestyle in 1975. She also took four golds at the 1974 Europeans (100m and 200m freestyle and both relays). GDR champion at freestyle 100m 1973-5, 200m 1975; 100m butterfly 1973-6, 200m IM 1971-3, 100m backstroke 1976.

She was married to Roland Matthes (qv) 1968-72 and then to **Steffen Grummt** (b. 15 Sep 1959), who was a top-class decathlete (best score 8261 points 1982, 4th Europeans 1982, 8th Olympics 1980) before turning to bobsledding at which he was world champion at 4-man and silver medallist at 2-man in 1985.

Klaus ENDERS (FRG)

MOTOR CYCLING

Klaus Enders. b. 2 May 1937 Giessen, near Frankfurt.

The most successful sidecar racing champion, with a record six world titles, 1967, 1969-70 and 1972-4, riding BMW machines. In all he had 27 Grand Prix wins, 23 with Rolf Engelhardt and 4 with Wolfgang Kalauch. Enders had started racing in 1960, both solo and sidecars. In 1971 he had a year driving BMW cars before returning to sidecar racing. He retired from racing in 1974 after disagreements with his sponsor Gerhard Heukerot and with Dieter Busch, who built his outfits and prepared his BMW engines.

Yukio ENDO (Japan)

GYMNASTICS

Yukio Endo. b. 18 Jan 1937 Akita.

The winner of five Olympic gold medals, with the Japanese team in 1960, 1964 and 1968, the individual all-around title and parallel bars in 1964 and silvers for floor exercises in 1964 and vault in 1968. A brilliant technician, he was also World champion at floor exercises in 1962, when he won a total of seven medals; he added three more in 1966, helping Japan to win the team title on both occasions. A professor from the Nippon University, he became coach and then team leader of the Japanese Olympic gymnastics team.

Ingrid ENGEL (GDR)

DIVING

Ingrid Engel. née Kramer. b. 29 Jul 1943 Dresden. Later Gulbin.

The Olympic champion at both highboard and springboard diving in 1960, she retained her springboard title in 1964 as Frau Engel, but was second at highboard. European champion at both events in 1962 by huge margins. After her second marriage, as Frau Gulbin she was fifth at springboard in 1968.

Her first major championships had been the 1958 Europeans at which she placed fourth at springboard, after leading going into the last dive, and eighth at highboard. European Cup winner at springboard 1963 and 1967, highboard 1963.

Jannie ENGELBRECHT (SAf)

RUGBY UNION

Jan Pieter Engelbrecht. b. 10 Nov 1938 Cape Town.

Winning 33 caps between 1960 and 1969 he is South Africa's most capped winger. In his final international match against Australia in 1969 he scored twice to equal John Gainsford's former Springbok record of eight tries. He also shared with Gainsford the record of being the most capped South African but both these records have since been beaten.

Exceptionally fast and with a devastating swerve, Engelbrecht had no serious rival for his place in the Springbok team and 32 of his 33 caps came in consecutive matches. He toured the British Isles and France in 1960, New Zealand in 1965 and France in 1968.

Educated at Stellenbosch University, he was a farmer and economist and played for Western Province.

Karin ENKE (GDR) see KANIA

Irene EPPLE (FRG)

ALPINE SKIING

Irene Epple. b. 18 Jun 1957 Seeg-Allgau.

At the giant slalom she won the World Cup in 1982 and the Olympic silver in 1980. At downhill she was second in the 1978 World Championships and built a great reputation yet did not win a Grand Prix race at the event until Val d'Isère 1984. A World Cup competitor from 1973, she won 11 races 1980-4, with best overall placings of second 1982 and third 1979. She also competed at the 1976 and 1984 Olympics and was German champion at downhill 1973, 1978 and 1981 and at giant slalom 1975-6 and 1978.

Her younger sister **Maria** (b.11 Mar 1959 Seeg) was world champion at giant slalom in 1978 and had five World Cup race wins 1981-5.

Julius ERVING (USA)

BASKETBALL

Julius Winfield Erving II. b. 22 Feb 1950 Hempstead, New York.

'Dr J' was the most spectacular player of the old ABA and when the ABA merged with the NBA in 1976 he joined the Philadelphia 76ers and assumed that role in the NBA as well. Erving is considered by many the flashiest, most flamboyant player ever and was known as an articulate spokesman for his sport. He had huge hands which enabled him to palm the ball easily and control it while in flight. That, combined with superb jumping ability and the ability to hang in the air, made him the star of many highlight films. He was, however, far more than a spectacular leaper and was one of only seven players to average over 20 points and 20 rebounds during a full college career. In the pros, he is the only man, other than Kareem Abdul-Jabbar, to have scored 30,000 points, taken down 10,000 rebounds, and passed for over 5,000 assists, combining his ABA and NBA marks. His career began at the University of Massachusetts, where he acquired the nickname, 'The Doctor'. Previously, as a New York schoolyard legend, he was known simply as 'Julius of New York'. He joined the Virginia Squires in the ABA in 1971, moving to the New York Nets two years later. He was ABA scoring leader three times, the league's MVP three times and led the Nets to championships in 1974 and 1976. Elected MVP in the NBA in 1981. Off the court, his refined manner, elegance and grace belied his spectacular actions on it.

NBA/ABA career 30,026 points, av. 24.2. NBA 18,364 at 22.0.

Phil ESPOSITO (Can)

ICE HOCKEY

Philip Anthony Esposito. b. 20 Feb 1942 Sault Ste. Marie, Ontario.

A big center who broke in with the Chicago Black Hawks in 1963 and who became the best center in the league after he was traded to the Boston Bruins in 1967. For them he led the league in goal scoring for six consecutive years 1970-5, scoring over 50 goals in the last five, and also leading the league in scoring in 1969, 1971-4. He set new records with 77 assists and 126 points in1968/9, 76 goals and 152 points 1970/1, and again had 77 assists in 1973/4. With Espo, the Bruins won two Stanley Cups. He was not a great skater, nor did he have a rocket shot like Hull, but he was an immovable force in front of the goal crease, and scored most of his goals because of his quick hands and accurate shot. Esposito played the last five years of his career with the New York Rangers. After his playing retirement, he briefly coached the Rangers, and he is now part owner of an NHL expansion franchise in Florida.

NHL career 1963-81 - 1282 games, 717 goals, 1590 points. Playoffs: 130 games, 61 goals, 137 pts. Hart Trophy 1969, 1974; Lester Pearson Award 1971, 1973.

Tony ESPOSITO (Can)

ICE HOCKEY

Anthony James Esposito. b. 23 Apr 1943 Sault Ste. Marie, Ontario.

Having begun his career with the Montreal Canadiens, Esposito was traded to the Chicago Black Hawks after only one year.

There he became one of the top goalies of his era. He never got to play with his brother Phil, who was traded to the Bruins by the Black Hawks in 1967, but Tony was so dominating in the nets that it was said only his brother, at the time the greatest center in the NHL, could beat him. Phil once said, "I know how to do it, but I'm not telling." Tony's goals against average of 1.77 in 1971/2 was the lowest in the NHL for 21 years.
NHL career 1968-84 - 886 games, 2.92 GAA, 76 shutouts. Vezina Trophy 1970, 1972, 1974.

Pierre ETCHEBASTER (Fra)

REAL TENNIS

Pierre Etchebaster. b. 3 May 1894 (or 8 Dec 1893) St Jean-de-Luz, d. 24 Mar 1980 St Jean-de-Luz.

World champion at real tennis for 27 years, a period only surpassed by Edmund Barre (Fra) who reigned for 33 years (1829-62). A Basque who learned his tennis in Bordeaux, Etchebaster was a pelota champion and outstanding handball player before being apprenticed to work in his uncle's store in Chile in 1909. His sporting career suffered a further set-back when he was called up for military service in 1914, but after being demobilised in 1919 he returned to France to work in the family bakery and soon became champion in all the Basque games. In 1922 he became a professional in Paris and was invited to learn to play real tennis. Within two years he was national champion and he first challenged for the world title in 1926 when he lost to Fred Covey. Two years later he took the title from Covey and made a record seventh and final defence of his title in 1952 in New York, where he had settled in 1930 on taking up an appointment as head professional at the Racquet and Tennis Club. He retired undefeated in 1955, a year after, at the age of 60, he had beaten his successor James Dear 7-4, the closest anyone had come to beating him. He was a swift, rhythmic player with a powerful serve, great footwork and endurance.

EUSÉBIO (Por)

FOOTBALL

Eusébio Ferreira da Silva. b. 25 Jan 1942 Lourenço Marques, Mozambique.

Often known as the 'European' Pelé, he was, in fact, African although he starred in European football for more than a decade. He signed for Benfica from SC Lourenço Marques in his native Portuguese East Africa (Mozambique) in 1961 and helped the Lisbon club to a host of honours. Between 1961 and 1973, Benfica won the Portuguese League ten times and Eusébio was the top scorer in the League in seven of these years; they also won the Portuguese Cup five times and retained the European Cup in 1962, with Eusébio scoring twice in the final against Real Madrid. He was also three times a losing finalist with Benfica in this competition. From 1968 Eusébio suffered from knee injuries, and after playing for Toronto Metros he returned to Benfica as coach in 1977. For Benfica he scored 316 goals in 294 league games.
An inside-forward, he was possessed of one of the strongest shots ever seen in football and, with nine goals, was the leading scorer in the 1966 World Cup, with a total of 41 goals in 64 internationals for Portugal.

Max EUWE (Hol)

CHESS

Dr Machgielis Euwe. b. 20 May 1901 Amsterdam, d. 26 Nov 1981 Amsterdam.

World amateur champion in 1928 and Netherlands champion 13 times between 1921 and 1955, Euwe became World chess champion 1935-7. He was, however, the only amateur world champion at chess since Paul Morphy, and after playing only sporadically for some years, withdrew from match play in 1948.
Euwe graduated from the University of Amsterdam, became a professor of mathematics and data processing, and was director of the Netherlands Research Centre for Information Sciences 1958-64. He was president of the International Federation of Chess (FIDE) 1970-8.

Chick EVANS (USA)

GOLF

Charles Evans Jr. b. 18 Jul 1890 Indianapolis, Indiana. d, 6 Nov 1979 Chicago, Illinois.

Though a great player before 1911, Chick Evans' career took off when James Braid convinced him in that year to change from the baseball grip to the Vardon grip. He went on to become the first player to win the US Open and Amateur in the same year (1916). He won the US Amateur again in 1920 and other major wins were the Western Open 1910, French Amateur 1911 and the Western Amateur 1909, 1912, 1914-15, 1920-3.

The strength of Evans' game was his iron play and he often drove with an iron. He had a very long career, playing in the US Open in 1953, aged 63, and the US Amateur in 1961, aged 71. He established the Evans Scholarship Foundation, which gives college scholarships to deserving caddies.

Eric EVANS (UK)

RUGBY UNION

Eric Evans. b. 1 Feb 1921 Droylsden, Manchester, d. 12 Jan 1991 Stockport.

After attending Loughborough College 1939-42 and serving as a Sergeant in the Border Regiment, Evans joined Sale immediately after the war. Although he made his England début against Australia in 1948 as a loose-head prop he soon established a reputation as an outstanding hooker, although not winning a regular place in the team until 1953. Evans went on to win 30 caps - just one short of Wavell Wakefield's England record - and made his final international appearance in 1958 at the age of 37. Having proved himself as an inspiring leader for Lancashire, for whom he made 105 appearances, he captained England 13 times beginning in 1956. In 1957 he led England to their first Grand Slam since 1928 and England were again unbeaten in 1958. Originally a school teacher he was later an industrial relations officer and was appointed an England selector in 1963.

Godfrey EVANS (UK)

CRICKET

Thomas Godfrey Evans. b. 18 Aug 1920 Finchley, Middlesex.

An automatic choice for England as wicket-keeper in the 12 years after World War II. A genial and extrovert character, he was always in the action, but his showmanship was matched by his brilliance. He made his Kent début in 1939, but then had to wait until 1946 for his first full season, taking over the England 'keeping in the final Test of that summer. He was a hard-hitting batsman, and it was totally out of character when he set the all-time record by remaining at the crease for 97 minutes without scoring against Australia in 1947. In contrast he scored 98 before lunch on the way to his second Test century against India in 1952. He passed Bert Oldfield's record number of dismissals (130) in Test cricket in 1954 and went on to be the first to 200 dismissals (and 2000 runs). At his retirement he had played in a record 91 Tests. Awarded the CBE in 1960.

91 Tests 1946-59: 2439 runs at 20.69, 2 100s HS 104; 173 catches, 46 stumpings. First-class 1939-69: 14,882 runs at 21.22, 7 100s HS 144; 2 wickets; 816 catches, 250 stumpings.

Janet EVANS (USA)

SWIMMING

Janet B Evans. b. 28 Aug 1971 Fullerton, California.

The supreme long distance freestyle woman swimmer of the late 1980s, she radically improved the world records from 400m to 1500m. Her first records came in 1987 with 4:05.45 for 400m, 8:22.44 at 800m and 16:00.73 for 1500m. In 1988 she improved the record for 800m to 8:17.12 and that for 1500m to 15:52.10 in March, and then set further world records when winning the Olympic titles for 400m in 4:03.85 and 800m in 8:20.20. She won a third gold medal with a US record 4:37.76 for 400m individual medley.

A further world record for 800m came in 1989, 8:16.22 at the Pan-Pacific Championships, where she also won the

400m free and IM. At the end of that year she was awarded the Sullivan Award. After winning the 400m, 800m and 1500m freestyle gold medals at the 1990 Goodwill Games, she won two golds (400m, 800m) and a silver (200m) at the World Championships and three golds and a silver at the Pan-Pacifics in 1991.
She spent two years at Stanford University, where she won five NCAA titles, but dropped out to concentrate on preparation for the 1992 Olympics. There, although no longer swimming as fast as she had as a teenager, she won the 800m and took silver at 400m, her first defeat at 400m since the 1986 Goodwill Games. By 1993 she had won a total of 33 US national titles.
Other best times: 200m free 2:00.27 (1990), 200m IM 2:15.15 (1989), 200m back 2:13.66 (1990).

Lee EVANS (USA)

ATHLETICS

Lee Evans. b. 25 Feb 1947 Madera, California.

Evans won the Olympic title for 400 metres in 1968 in 43.86 and anchored the US team to a relay gold in 2:56.16. Both times remained as world records until 1988, with the latter equalled by the US Olympic team in Seoul but remaining as a joint record until 1992. Evans had threatened to withdraw from the 400m final in protest against the expulsion from the US team and Olympic village of John Carlos and Tommie Smith following their 'Black Power' salutes on the victory rostrum; however, Smith and Carlos persuaded him to take part.
Evans had earlier improved the world best for 400m to 44.06, but this was disallowed as he wore illegal 'brush' spikes. He won the Pan-American title in 1967, the 1968 NCAA title, representing San Jose State, and five AAU titles, 1966-9 and 1972. He also ran a world best for 600m of 1:14.3 in 1968 and ran on the San Jose State team that set world records for 4x220y and 4x200m in 1967. He turned professional in 1972, after placing only fourth in the US Olympic Trials.

John EVERS (USA)

BASEBALL

John Joseph Evers. b. 22 Jul 1883 Troy, New York, d. 28 Mar 1947 Albany, New York.

'These are the saddest of possible words; Tinkers-to-Evers-to-Chance.' Thus began the poem by Franklin Adams that immortalised the Chicago Cub infield of 1906-08. Led by Johnny Evers, who played second base, shortstop Joe Tinker, and first baseman Frank Chance, the Cubs won pennants in all three years and the World Series in 1907-08. Evers was probably the top second baseman of the first two decades of the 20th century and his greatest feats were performed at the biggest moments as he starred several times in the World Series. He played for the Cubs 1902-13, before moving to Boston.
Career 1902-29: 1658 hits Avg. .270.

Chris EVERT (USA)

TENNIS

Christine Marie Evert. b. 21 Dec 1954 Fort Lauderdale, Florida. Later Lloyd, then Mill.

After some notable successes as a junior, she turned professional on her 18th birthday and went on to win 18 Grand Slam singles titles. She won the French title a record seven times, 1974-5, 1979-80, 1983 and 1985-6. She was a six-time winner at the US Open (1975-8, 1980, 1982) and won Wimbledon three times (1974, 1976, 1981) and the Australian twice (1982 and 1984). Between 1974 and 1986 she won at least one Grand Slam singles title every year and in her 18 appearances at Wimbledon she reached the semi-finals or better 17 times.
In 1974 she won the French doubles with Olga Morozova and retained the title in 1975 partnering Martina Navratilova with whom she also won Wimbledon in 1976. Between 1971 and 1985, she won all 26 of her singles matches in the Wightman Cup and 8 of her 12 doubles matches, and has an unsurpassed record in the Federation Cup, winning 40 of 42 singles, including her first 29, and 16 of 18 doubles from

1977 to 1989, helping the US to win seven times. She set a record, since surpassed by Martina Navratilova, of 157 singles titles, and had career earnings of $8,896,195. Her steady baseline play and two-fisted backhand were especially suited to clay courts. After her marriage to the English player John Lloyd ended in divorce she married the US Olympic skier Andy Mill in 1988.

Patrick EWING (USA)

BASKETBALL

Patrick Aloysius Ewing. b. 5 Aug 1962 Kingston, Jamaica.

A master shot blocker, an intimidating defender and considered to be the best jump-shooting big man ever, Ewing stands 2.13m *7ft* tall and weighs 109 kg *240 lbs*. In 1980 he was the first High School player invited to the US Olympic Trials and although he did not make the team then, he was a member of the gold medal winning team in 1984. By then he was in the middle of a dazzling collegiate career at Georgetown University, whom he steered to 3 NCAA finals in 4 years, winning in 1984. He was voted college player of the 1980s. The No.1 draft in 1985 he was signed by the New York Knicks, for whom he has starred ever since, averaging over 20 points per game every season. His current contract brings him in $33 million over 6 years.

NBA career 14,252 points, av. 23.7; 6121 rebounds.

Ray EWRY (USA)

ATHLETICS

Raymond Clarence Ewry. b. 14 Oct 1873 Lafayette, Indiana, d. 29 Sep 1937 New York.

A practitioner of the now arcane standing jumps, Ewry earned everlasting fame by winning a record ten Olympic gold medals, including those at the Intercalated Games of 1906: both high jump and long jump in 1900, 1904, 1906 and 1908; and the triple jump in 1900 and 1904.

His standing jump bests: HJ 1.65m 1900, LJ 3.47m 1904, TJ 10.85m 1901. AAU champion at both standing HJ and LJ 1898, 1906-7; LJ only 1909-10; and indoors at LJ 1898, 1906-7 and 1909-10. His exercising began after he was confined to a wheelchair having contracted polio as a child. He was at Purdue University from 1890 and 1897, graduating in mechanical engineering, and then moved to New York where he worked as a hydraulics engineer.

George EYSTON (UK)

MOTOR RACING

(Capt.) George Edward Thomas Eyston. b. 28 Jun 1897 Bampton, Oxfordshire, d. 11 Jun 1979 West Orange, New Jersey, USA.

Eyston set three world land speed records, 502.436 km/h in 1937, 556.002 and 575.330 in 1938, and many other speed records in cars of all sizes between 1926 and 1954. Awarded Segrave Trophy 1937. A skilled engineer, he raced motorcyles before and after his distinguished service in World War I, then took up car racing from 1923. Also a fine rower and yachtsman, he was awarded the OBE in 1948.

François FABER (Lux)

CYCLING

François Faber. b. 26 Jan 1887 Aulnay-sur-Iton, France, d. 9 May 1915 Garency, France.

Faber is, with Charley Gaul, one of the two greatest riders ever produced by Luxembourg. His career victories were compressed into five great years and his major wins were Tour of Lombardy 1908, Tour de France and Paris-Brussels 1909, Paris-Tours 1909-10, Bordeaux-Paris 1911, Paris-Roubaix 1913.

Red FABER (USA)

BASEBALL

Urban Charles Faber. b. 6 Sep 1888 Cascade, Iowa, d. 25 Sep 1976 Chicago.

Faber was one of the greatest spitball pitchers of all time. He played his entire 20-year major league career with the Chicago White Sox, a team whose habitual appearance in the second division certainly

prevented him from winning more games. He learned the spitball in 1911 after a sore arm ruined his early major league tryouts, although like most early spitballers he threw that pitch sparingly, using it for variety and surprise. He was a superb control pitcher, who rarely walked or hit batters. He allowed very few home runs.
Career pitching 1914-33: ERA 3.15; W-L 254-213, SO 1471; Best seasons: 1921: 25-15, .625, 2.47 ERA. 1915: 24-14, .632, 2.55 ERA.

Giacinto FACCHETTI (Ita)

FOOTBALL

Giacinto Facchetti. b. 18 Jul 1942 Treviglio.

A speedy, attacking left-back who scored more international goals for Italy and more league goals in Italy (59 in 476 games for Internazionale) than any other full-back. Initially a centre-forward with CS Trevigliese, he signed in 1960 for Inter, who converted him into a left-back despite the fact that he was naturally right-footed. He played in a record 94 matches for Italy 1962-77, surpassing the long-standing Italian record of Umberto Caligaris, also a left-back, when he played in his 60th international in September 1971. He took over as captain in his 25th match in 1966.
He was a stalwart of the Inter teams which won the European Cup and World Club Championship in 1964 and 1965, and the Italian league 1963, 1965-6, 1971. A member of the World Cup squad in 1966 and 1970, he was surprisingly dropped from the Italian team in 1972 but returned to play in the World Cup in 1974.

Roy FACE (USA)

BASEBALL

Elroy Leon Face. b. 20 Feb 1928 Stephentown, New York.

Probably the first great relief pitcher, Face pitched 15 of his 16 years in major leagues with the Pittsburgh Pirates. In 1959 his 18-1 record set a major league record for winning percentage for one season with .947; those wins included 17 won in relief, still a record. He holds the National League record for most games finished (574) and most games pitched for one club (802). He was also one of the first pitchers to utilise a forkball, now usually called a split-fingered fastball.
Career pitching: 1953-69 ERA 3.48; W-L 104-95, SO 877.

Arsen FADZEYEV (USSR/Rus)

WRESTLING

Arsen Fadzeyev. b. 5 Sep 1962.

Fadzeyev won world or Olympic freestyle wrestling lightweight (68kg) gold medals each year from 1983 to 1992, except for 1984, when the USSR boycotted the Olympic Games. So he had two Olympic and six world titles to tie the record for the second highest ever tally. He was world junior champion at 57kg in 1981 and in 1985-6 he was also the World Cup winner and European champion.

Leandro FAGGIN (Italy)

CYCLING

Leandro Faggin. b. 18 Jul 1933 Padova, d. 6 Dec 1970 Padova.

Faggin possesses one of the greatest records ever among pursuit cyclists. After placing successively 1st, 3rd and 2nd for the world amateur title in 1954-6, he was professional champion three times, 1963 and 1965-6, second in 1958, 1962 and 1964, and third in 1961 and 1967-8.
The individual pursuit did not become an Olympic event until 1964, but he took the Olympic gold medals of 1956 at the kilometre time trial and the team pursuit. He was 12 times Italian pursuit champion and three times set new records for the 5000m unpaced on the track, from 6:15.4 as an amateur in 1956 to 6:02.4 as a pro in 1961. He also set an amateur world record for 1 kilometre with 1:09.2 in 1956. Shortly after his retirement from cycling he died tragically young at the age of 37.

Luigi FAGIOLI (Italy)

MOTOR RACING

b.9 Jun 1898 Osimo, d. 20 Jun 1952 Monaco.

His racing success started in 1926, gaining

in prominence with Maserati from 1929 and he won the 1931 Monza Grand Prix. Moving to Enzo Ferrari's Alfa Romeo team he won the 1933 Italian GP, and for Mercedes the 1934 Italian and 1935 Monaco and Barcelona Grands Prix. After the war he returned to racing and joined the Alfa Corse team, placing third in the World Championship in 1950 and winning the 1951 French GP, when he shared the car with Fangio. He died after crashing in practice for a sports car race.

FALCÃO (Bra)

FOOTBALL

Paulo Roberto Falcão. b. 16 Oct 1953 Santa Catarina.

A superbly talented midfielder he played for Brazil in the World Cups of 1978 and 1982, and scored six goals in 32 international appearances. He moved from Porto Alegre to star for AS Roma, when they lost on penalties to Liverpool in the 1984 European Cup Final. Returning to Brazil, he played for São Paulo.

Nick FALDO (UK)

GOLF

Nicholas Alexander Faldo. b. 18 Jul 1957 Welwyn Garden City, Hertfordshire.

Nick Faldo established a position in the early 1990s as the finest golfer in the world, with a great record in the majors. Having been an England boys and youth international, he turned professional in 1976, coming 8th on the European money list in 1977 and 3rd in 1978 when he won his first major tournament, the PGA Championship. He won that title again in 1980-1 and in 1989. Faldo took time out to remodel his swing, but by the late 1980s his steady play had brought him to the top of the world's players. In 1990 he came very close to contending for the Grand Slam of golf. He won the US Masters for the second successive year and the British Open (as he had done in 1987) and between those two, he came within a lipped-out 15-foot putt of tying for the US Open championship at Medinah, having to settle for third equal.

A big man at 1.91m *6' 3"*, he won the World Matchplay in 1989 and 1992, and that same year with his third British Open and the Johnny Walker World Championship he had worldwide earnings of £1,558,978, a world record. In 1993 he played superbly at the British Open, equalling the tournament record with a 63 in the 2nd round, but had to settle for 2nd place, on his 36th birthday, as his aggregate of 269 left him two shots behind Greg Norman. From 1977 to 1991 Faldo played in eight Ryder Cups, tying Seve Ballesteros for a European record 17 wins, with 12 losses and 2 halves. The leading money-winner in 1983 and 1992, his career European tour earnings are £3,108,574 with 25 wins 1976-92. He has also added $1,732,676 from the US PGA tour. Awarded the MBE 1988.

Juan Manuel FANGIO (Arg)

MOTOR RACING

Juan Manuel Fangio. b. 24 Jun 1911 Balcarce.

World champion at Formula One in 1951 and each year from 1954 to 1957. He won 24 of his 51 Grand Prix races, an unsurpassed success rate, and scored 277.14 points.

His father, a house painter, was an Italian immigrant to Argentina, where Fangio worked as a garage mechanic before starting racing at the age of 17. At 21 he opened his own garage and built his own racing car, but his racing was confined to South America, mostly racing Chevrolet cars, until 1949. During the war he had been a taxi driver. In the previous year the Argentine Automobile Club had bought two Maseratis to oppose the top European drivers visiting Argentina, and Fangio had been selected to drive one. Learning much from this experience he went to Europe in 1949 and had a brilliant series of victories. He was then invited to join Alfa Romeo for the first World Championship season of 1950 when he narrowly lost the title to Giuseppe Farina, but won for them the following year. In 1952 he drove for Ferrari before his season was cut short by injury, but he returned in 1953 with Maserati for

second place in the World Championship. In his four successive years as champion he started with Maserati, switched to Mercedes halfway through 1954, moved to Ferrari for 1956 and returned to Maserati in 1957. He retired after a few races in 1958 and built up a large motor business in Argentina.
Fangio set the standard for all the great drivers that followed; he allied great stamina and concentration, with a fierce competitiveness, to his ability to nurse his cars with enormous care.

Nino FARINA (Italy)

MOTOR RACING

(Dr) Giuseppe Farina. b. 30 Oct 1908 Turin, d. 30 Jun 1966 Alguebelle, France.

A lawyer, Dr Farina was the first ever world champion at Formula One at the age of 44 in 1950. His family were famous coachbuilders, and his uncle Pinin Farina was the world famous designer. His first major race win was in a Maserati at Brno in 1934 and he was Italian champion for Ferrari's Alfa Romeo team in 1938 and 1939. After the war he had success in Maseratis and Ferraris, but in 1950 he became part of the Alfa Corse team, winning at Silverstone, Monza and Berne to take that world title. Although not champion again and somewhat temperamental, he raced consistently in the World Championship Grands Prix he contested, placing fourth with Alfa in 1951, and then 2nd, 3rd, 8th and 5th with Ferrari 1952-5. He retired from racing in 1957 and died in a road accident in France nine years later.

Gizi FARKAS (Hun)

TABLE TENNIS

Gizella Farkas. b. 16 Nov 1925 Miskolc. Later Gervai.

The first great woman player to emerge in the post-World War II era. After winning the first three post-war world women's singles titles 1947-9, she was a finalist at the next four championships, losing on each occasion to Angelica Rozeanu. Her appearance in seven consecutive singles finals matched the record of her compatriot Maria Mednyánszky. Between 1947 and 1954 she won a total of 10 world titles (3 singles, 3 doubles, 4 mixed doubles) and in 1947 and 1949 she won all three events.

Ken FARMER (Aus)

AUSTRALIAN RULES FOOTBALL

Kenneth William Farmer. b. 1910 Adelaide, d. 1982.

The greatest forward in the history of South Australian rules football. In his first season for North Adelaide he kicked 62 goals and he went on to amass the Australian record of 1419 goals from 224 matches in 13 league seasons. He added 81 goals in 17 representative matches. His feat of scoring more than 100 goals for eleven consecutive years, 1930-40, still stands as the record. His peak total of 134 in 1936 was a SA State record. After his playing career ended he stayed on as coach at North Adelaide and led them to the premiership in 1949 and 1951, having won as a player in 1930 and 1931.

Aubrey FAULKNER (SAf)

CRICKET

George Aubrey Faulkner. b. 17 Dec 1881 Port Elizabeth, d. 10 Sep 1930 Walham Green, London, England.

Faulkner was one of the trio of South African googly bowlers who made an enormous impression when they visited England in 1907. He bowled at slow-medium pace with a dangerous faster yorker. He was his country's greatest all-rounder, a very strong batsman, who met with his greatest successes against England in 1909/10 with 545 runs at 60.65 and 29 wickets at 21.89, and in Australia in 1910/11 when he scored 732 runs at 73.20 (and 1534 runs on the tour). In England in 1912 he made 1075 runs and took 163 wickets. Awarded the DSO in World War I, he afterwards set up the Faulkner School of Cricket in London, where he established a great reputation as a coach. He committed suicide in 1930.
25 Tests 1906-24: 1754 runs at 40.79, 4 100s HS 204; 82 wickets at 26.58, BB 7-84; 20 catches.

First-class 1902-24: 6366 runs at 36.58, 13 100s HS 204; 449 wickets at 17.42, BB 7-26; 94 catches.

FAZAL MAHMOUD (Pak)

CRICKET

Fazal Mahmoud. b. 18 Feb 1927 Lahore.

Fazal made his début in first-class cricket for Northern India and nearly made the Indian team to England in 1946. After partition he became Pakistan's leading bowler, operating at medium-fast pace with swing and leg-cutters, and being particularly effective on matting wickets, but had to wait until 1952 for his country's first Test match. He played the leading rôle in Pakistan's first Test victory when he took 12 wickets for 94 in the match against India in October 1952 and in their first victory over England with 6-52 and 6-46 at The Oval in 1954. He captained Pakistan in 10 Tests 1959-61 and became a senior Police Inspector.

34 Tests 1952-62: 620 runs at 14.09, HS 60; 139 wickets at 24.72, BB 7-42; 11 catches.

First-class 1943-64: 2602 runs at 23.02, 1 100 HS 100; 460 wickets at 19.11, BB 9-43; 38 catches.*

Tom FEARS (USA)

AMERICAN FOOTBALL

Thomas Jesse Fears. b. 3 Dec 1923 Los Angeles, California.

Fears played all his football in Los Angeles. He played in high school for Manuel Arts High School of LA, collegiately at UCLA, and professionally with the Los Angeles Rams. As a wide receiver he led the NFL in catches from 1948-50. In 1950 he set a still-standing record by catching 18 passes in a single game. He was not exceptionally fast but was big for an end (1.88m *6'2"*, 98 kg *216 lb*) and ran very precise patterns. He coached football after his playing retirement, and was head coach of the New Orleans Saints 1967-70.

NFL career 1948-56: 5397 yards gained receiving av. 13.5, 38 touchdowns.

Beattie FEATHERS (USA)

AMERICAN FOOTBALL

William Beattie Feathers. b. 4 Aug 1908 Bristol, Virginia, d. 11 Mar 1979 Winston-Salem, North Carolina.

Feathers played college football at the University of Tennessee and for seven years in the NFL, for the Chicago Bears 1934-7, Brooklyn Dodgers 1938-9, and Green Bay Packers 1940. He was very quick and in 1934 became the first NFL running back to gain over 1000 yards in a single season with 1004 (on 101 carries), a mark no other runner approached for 13 years. He later became a college coach, coaching both football and baseball, finishing as head baseball coach at Wake Forest 1972-6.

Lewis FEILD (USA)

RODEO

Lewis Feild. b. 28 Oct 1956 Salt Lake City, Utah.

The world all-around champion at pro rodeo each year 1985-7, the first rough-stock cowboy since Larry Mahan in 1973 to claim the title. He was also bareback bronc champion in 1985-6. He became a PRCA member in 1980 and by the end of 1992 he was third on the all-time list for career earnings with $1,163,340. Despite his championships and money winning titles, Feild actually competes less than some cowboys, preferring to stay at home in Utah with his wife and three children.

Petra FELKE (GDR/Ger), see MAIER.

Bob FELLER (USA)

BASEBALL

Robert William Andrew Feller. b. 3 Nov 1918 Van Meter, Iowa.

'Rapid Robert' Feller was one of the greatest pitchers and strikeout artists in history. In 1962 he was elected to the Hall of Fame in his first year of eligibility, the first pitcher to have received that honour since Walter Johnson, and in 1969 he was voted the greatest living right-handed pitcher in ceremonies celebrating baseball's centen-

nial. He was a true phenomenon, being signed as a 17 year-old in 1936. In his first major league start he struck out 15 St Louis Browns, and later that year struck out 17 players in one game. During his career, Feller pitched three no-hitters and a major league record 12 one-hitters. His 348 strikeouts in 1946 when he went 26-15 was a record (though since disputed, as Rube Waddell has been found to have struck out 349 in 1904), until Sandy Koufax broke it in 1965 with 382 in one season. Feller was the league leader in wins six times, strikeouts seven times, and innings pitched five times.
Career pitching 1936-56: ERA 3.25; W-L 266-162, SO 2581.

Ian FERGUSON (NZ)

CANOEING

Ian G Ferguson. b. 20 Jul 1952.

Winner of four Olympic gold medals at kayak caneoing. At the 1980 Olympics he was 7th at K1 500m and 8th at 1000m. He then retired and opened a video games business in Auckland. However, with increased help he returned to competition and won a silver medal at 500m at the 1983 World Championships. Then in 1984, at the age of 32, he won three gold medals at the Los Angeles Olympics, at K1 and K2 500m and K4 1000m. Paul McDonald joined him in the latter two canoes, and together they retained the K2 500m titles at the 1988 Olympics, with a silver at 1000m, and were 8th at K2 1000m in 1992. Ferguson is an accountant by profession.

Tom FERGUSON (USA)

RODEO

Thomas R Ferguson. b. 20 Dec 1950 Tahlequah, Oklahoma.

Ferguson won the title of world's all-around champion cowboy for an unmatched six consecutive years, 1974-9. In 1976 he also became the first cowboy to post earnings of $100,000 for a single year, and a decade later he became the first to record career earnings of $1 million, with a final figure of $1,145,880. He had great all-around ability, but was not a true specialist in a single event; he won only three world titles in single events - calf roping in 1974 and steer wrestling in 1977-78. At 5ft 11in and 175 lb he was smaller than many practitioners at those disciplines, but triumphed through skill and coolness. Ferguson attended California Polytechnic at San Luis Obispo before he led the school's 1973 rodeo team to the national collegiate title, and was an immediate success on turning pro.

Enzo FERRARI (Italy)

MOTOR RACING

Enzo Ferrari. b. 20 Feb 1898 Modena, d. 14 Aug 1988 Modena.

The cars bearing his name have been the most successful in the history of motor racing, with Ferrari winning the Constructors' Championship eight times between 1961 and 1983 and enjoying 93 race wins from 434 Grands Prix during his lifetime.
Enzo drove for Alfa Romeo in the 1920s before poor health terminated his racing career. He established the Scuderia Ferrari in 1929, racing Alfa Romeos throughout the 1930s. He first built and ran his own cars in 1940, initially under the cover company Auto Avio Costruzzioni, as he was not allowed under the terms of his severance from Alfa to use his own name until 1947. He went on to become the most influential figure in motor sport as well as establishing his company as a premier manufacturer of luxury sports cars. He sold 50% of the business to Fiat in 1969, but remained president until 1977.

Adhemar FERREIRA DA SILVA (Bra)

ATHLETICS

Adhemar Ferreira da Silva. b. 29 Sep 1927 São Paulo.

He dominated triple jumping in the early 1950s, winning 60 successive competitions 1950-6. When he equalled Naoto Tajima's 14-year-old triple jump mark with 16.00m at São Paulo on 3 Dec 1950 he became the first Brazilian world record holder at any event. He added a further four world

records, improving to 16.01 in 1951, 16.12 and 16.22 in the 1952 Olympic final, and finally to 16.56 to win his second Pan-American title at altitude in Mexico City in 1955.
He won a second Olympic title in 1956 and was Pan-American champion in 1951 and 1959, and South American in 1952, 1954 and 1958. He also competed at the Olympics in 1948 (11th) and 1960 (14th).

Vyacheslav FETISOV (USSR)

ICE HOCKEY
Vyacheslav Fetisov. b. 20 Apr 1958 Moscow.

The greatest defenseman ever produced by the Soviet Union, winning Olympic gold medals in 1984 and 1988 after silver in 1980, and world titles in 1978, 1981-3 and 1986. He started playing ice hockey at the Central Army sports school in 1968, joining the CASC team in 1976. He played for the USSR from 1977 to 1988, after winning European Junior gold medals in 1975 and 1976. No less an authority than Wayne Gretzky called him 'the best I've ever played against'. In 1983 he was drafted by the New Jersey Devils of the NHL but few thought he would ever play for them. However, after *glasnost* and *perestroika*, Fetisov was able to join the Devils in late 1988. He has been a solid player in the NHL, though perhaps not quite as good as expected. Some of that could be related to his age as he started his pro hockey career in his 30s.

Helena FIBINGEROVÁ (Cs)

ATHLETICS
Helena Fibingerová. b. 13 Jul 1949 Vicemerice. Later Smiderová.

She scored an emotional triumph in the women's shot in the World Championships at Helsinki in 1983, for it was her first win outdoors in a long major championships career. In 1986 she competed in a record sixth European Championships, at which she had won silver medals in 1978 and 1982 and bronze in 1974. Indoors she holds the record for the most European titles, with eight wins between 1973 and 1985. She was undefeated by a Czechoslovak shot putter for 18 years 1969-87. At the Olympic Games she was 7th in 1972 and 3rd in 1976.
She set world shot records with 21.99m in 1976 and 22.32m in 1977, the last of 25 national records (from 16.32 in 1970), and also recorded six world indoor bests from 20.36m in 1974 to 22.50m in 1977, a mark unsurpassed outdoors until 1984. She married shot-putter Jaroslav Smid in 1977.

Anja FICHTEL (Ger)

FENCING
Anja Fichtel. b. 17 Aug 1968 Tauberbischofsheim. Married name Mauritz.

The 1988 Olympic champion at women's foil in both individual and team events, and world champion individual in 1986, 1990 (2nd in 1989) and team in 1985, 1989 and 1993. She was also world junior champion in 1985, 1988 and World Cup winner 1990.
She won seven consecutive German titles, 1986-92, and in the latter year came back speedily after giving birth to a son to take part at her second Olympics, taking a team silver medal. Coached by the 1976 Olympic épée champion Alexander Pusch.

Jackie FIELDS (USA)

BOXING
né Jacob Finkelstein. b. 9 Feb 1908 Chicago, Illinois, d. 3 Jun 1897.

Jacob Finkelstein began boxing as a youth of 14 in Chicago. He was trained by a former fighter, Marty Fields, and he shortly adopted Fields' name as his own. As Jackie Fields, at 16 years 162 days, he became the youngest ever Olympic boxing champion, at featherweight. He turned professional later that year and worked for five years until he won the world welterweight title in 1929 by outpointing Jack Thompson. He lost the title in 1930 to Thompson, but regained it in 1932 before relinquishing it for good when he lost to Young Corbett in 1933. Fields retired the next year after one more fight.
Career record: W - 74 (30), L - 9, D -3.

James FIGG (UK)

BOXING

James Figg. b. c.1695 Thame, Oxfordshire, d. 8 Dec 1734 London.

Generally reckoned to be the first recognised world heavyweight champion at the old prize ring methods of fighting. He became widely known in 1719 as an all-round athlete in such sports as quarter-staff, cudgel fighting and small backsword, but he was best known as a fighter. Figg was considered the world bare-knuckle champion from 1719 until 1734 when George Taylor claimed the title. Figg was also well known as a teacher of boxing, setting up booths in many local fairs to ply his trade.

Michela FIGINI (Swi)

ALPINE SKIING

Michela Figini. b. 7 Apr 1966 Prato-Leventina.

The surprise Olympic downhill racing champion in 1984, when at 17 years 314 days she became the youngest ever skiing gold medallist. She had won her first World Cup race just two weeks earlier. In 1985 she won the world title at downhill. In the World Cup she won 26 races in all to 1990, including 17 downhill. She was the overall winner in 1985 and 1988, won the downhill series in 1985 and 1987-9, tied for the giant slalom title in 1985, and won the super G series in 1988.

Laurent FIGNON (Fra)

CYCLING

Laurent Fignon. b. 16 Aug 1960 Tournan-en-Brie.

Fignon has been called the Professor because of his background. Unlike many professional cyclists, he attended college (though only briefly) where he was studying to become a veterinarian. However, the lure of the peloton was too much and he became one of the great riders in the world. He came to glory at the 1983 Tour de France when he humbled four-time champion Bernard Hinault, and he won again in 1984. But Fignon's personality came out there also, as, after one stage in which he dropped the great champion, Fignon mocked him in the press. Fignon staged a classic battle with Greg LeMond in the 1989 Tour de France, leading going into the last leg but losing out by 8 seconds, the closest finish in Tour history, when LeMond made up 58 seconds on the last leg, a time trial. Other major victories: Criterium International 1982, 1990; Flèche-Wallonne 1986, Milan-San Remo 1988-9, Giro d'Italia and Grand Prix des Nations 1989. He was King of the Mountains in the 1984 Giro d'Italia.

Elias FIGUEROA (Chile)

FOOTBALL

Elias Figueroa. b. 25 Oct 1946 Quilpue.

South American Player of the Year for three successive years 1974-6. A commanding centre-half, he played first for Santiago Wanderers and then Unión Calera in Chile, but then spent most of his 20s with Peñarol in Uruguay and Porto Alegre in Brazil. With Peñarol he won three national championships and one Copa Libertadores He retired at the age of 38, having played out his career with Palestino, Fort Lauderdale Strikers (USA) and Colo Colo. He won 70 caps for Chile 1967-82, playing for them in the World Cup finals tournaments of 1966, 1974 and 1982.

Hervé FILION (Can)

HARNESS RACING

Hervé Filion. b. 1 Feb 1940 Angers, Québec.

He has achieved more wins than any driver in the history of North American harness racing, with 13,750 to January 1993, nearly double the total of the second most successful, with earnings of $77,773,049 to 1992. He won his first harness race at the age of 13 near his home in Québec and started his professional career in 1961. He was the first driver to achieve 400 winners in a season in 1968, the first to 500 in 1971 and 600 in 1972, and he set all-time records with 637 in 1974, 798 in 1988 and 814 in 1989. He has been the top driver in terms of number of wins 13 times from 1968, and by money earned seven times 1970-4, 1976-7. He has usually raced twice a day, commuting from his afternoon meeting to a night one by helicopter.

Rollie FINGERS (USA)

BASEBALL

Roland Glen Fingers. b. 25 Aug 1946 Steubenville, Ohio.

Distinctive for his pitching ability as well as his handlebar moustache, Rollie Fingers is usually considered the greatest relief pitcher in modern baseball history and was the first reliever to be elected to the Hall of Fame. He pitched for nine years with the Oakland Athletics, helping them win three consecutive World Series victories. He was the World Series MVP in 1974. From 1977-80 he was with the San Diego Padres in the National League and finished his career in the American League with the Milwaukee Brewers. In 1981 he was the AL Cy Young and MVP winner. During his career he pitched in 944 games, saving 341 of them, with a season's high of 37 in 67 games in 1978. His best pitches were a sinker and slider, but late in his career he added a forkball to his repertory.

Career pitching 1968-84: ERA 2.90; W-L 114-118; saves 341.

Tom FINNEY (UK)

FOOTBALL

Thomas Finney. b. 5 April 1922 Preston, Lancashire.

A high-scoring winger of exceptional ability who also won international honours as a centre-forward. After playing for Preston North End in the 1941 war-time Cup Final his career was interrupted by service in the Eighth Army in North Africa and it was not until 1946 that he played his first League game for Preston. One month later he made his international début at outside-left against Scotland and went on to win 76 caps for England, missing a further 11 caps through injury. At the time, only Billy Wright, who was in the same team as Finney in all but two of his internationals, had played more times for England. Finney won 40 caps at outside-right, 33 at outside-left and 3 as centre-forward, scoring on his début in each position. His total of 30 goals for England stood as a record for a number of years.

He remained with Preston throughout his career, scoring a record 187 goals in 433 League matches between 1946 and 1960, and he served as president of the club in 1975-6. Voted Footballer of the Year in 1954 and 1957, he was awarded the OBE in 1961 and the CBE in 1992. Finney owns an electrical and plumbing contracting firm in his home town.

Bobby FISCHER (USA)

CHESS

Robert James Fischer. b. 9 Mar 1943 Chicago.

He became world chess champion when he beat Boris Spassky in 1972 at the age of 29, then the youngest ever, and was then acclaimed by some, including past champion Mikhail Tal, as the greatest ever chess genius. A prodigy, he became the youngest ever US junior champion at the age of 13 in 1957, the youngest ever grandmaster in 1958 and turned professional at 16. He was US champion eight times from 1958 to 1966. However, he played no games in competition while world champion and was stripped of the title in 1975 for refusing to defend against Anatoliy Karpov. By then he had attained the highest ever Elo rating of 2785. He became a recluse, living in Southern California, and did not play major competitive chess again until a sudden re-emergence in 1992, when he played for a $5 million purse against his old rival Spassky (who had dropped to 99th in world rankings). Fischer immediately showed his old brilliance and won ten games to five, but offended against UN sanctions as games were staged in Serbia, and faced prosecution in the USA.

Carsten FISCHER (Germany)

HOCKEY

Carsten Fischer. b. 29 Aug 1961 Duisburg.

Winning silver in 1984 and 1988 and gold in 1992, he was a medallist at three successive Olympic Games. He also won gold medals in the 1991 European Cup and in the Champions Trophy 1986-8 and 1991-2. He plays in defence for HTC Uhlenhorst Mulheim, and to 1992 had won 212 outdoor and 13 indoor caps. He is a doctor of medicine.

Allison FISHER (UK)

SNOOKER

Allison Fisher. b. 24 Feb 1968 Peacehaven, Sussex.

The best ever woman snooker player, she has won a record six world titles, in 1985-6, 1988-9, 1991 and 1993. She won her first national title in 1983 and won the UK Women's Open title each year 1986-90. In 1992 she recorded the highest break by a woman, 133.

Carlton FISK (USA)

BASEBALL

Carlton Ernest Fisk. b. 26 Dec 1947 Bellows Falls, Vermont.

In his 24th season in the major leagues, 'Pudge' Fisk played his 2226th game as a catcher on 22 Jun 1993 to pass the previous all-time record. He played for the Boston Red Sox 1969-80, and from then for the Chicago White Sox until he was released by them a week after his record game. He also holds the major league record for most home runs by a catcher. He was 'Rookie of the Year' in 1972, but early in his career he had a penchant for being injured though he has since been remarkably durable, in part due to rigorous off-season training. In the 1975 World Series, Fisk hit what may be the most widely seen home run in baseball history. The series that year between the Red Sox and the Cincinnati Reds is considered the greatest ever by most experts and the highlight was Game Six. It was won in the 12th inning by a Fisk home run. The shot, easily long enough, was barely fair, and television cameras followed Fisk down the first base line as he waved and urged the ball to stay in. It did and he exulted around the basepaths in a moment that has been replayed multiple times in highlight films.

Career 1969-93: 2346 hits Avg. .269; HR 376; RBI 1330. Best seasons: 1975: .331, 1977: .315, 26 HR, 102 RBI, 1985: 37 HR, 107 RBI.

Billy FISKE (USA)

BOBSLEIGH

William Mead Lindsay Fiske III. b. 4 Jun 1911 New York, d. 17 Aug 1940 Chichester, Sussex, England.

The youngest ever bobsleigh gold medallist at the Winter Olympics. When only 16yr 260d he steered the winning 5-man bob at the 1928 Olympics and he won a second gold medal in 1932 as driver of the winning 4-man bob. He was a superb Cresta rider, winning the Grand National in 1936 and 1938 and the Curzon Cup in 1935 and 1937. Educated at Cambridge University, where he narrowly failed to get a golf blue, he married the Countess of Warwick and joined the RAF on the outbreak of war. He was the first American pilot to be killed in the Battle of Britain and there is a memorial to him in St.Paul's Cathedral. The AAU named the Billy Fiske Memorial Trophy for 4-man bobsled in his honour.

Emerson FITTIPALDI (Bra)

MOTOR RACING

Emerson Fittipaldi. b. 12 Dec 1946 São Paulo.

The youngest ever world champion at Formula One at the age of 25 in 1972, he was again champion in 1974. In his forties he became champion at Indy Car racing in the USA.

The son of a motor racer and journalist, Emerson's motoring success started in Brazil following his elder brother Wilson. He won his first motorcycle race at 15, and at 17 was racing go-karts and showing his entrepreneurial abilities by founding Fittipaldi Motoring Accessories in São Paulo. His thriving enterprises are now based in Miami. After winning the Brazilian Formula Vee title, he came to England in 1969 and shot to notice by winning the Lombard F3 title. From his Grand Prix début in 1970, in which year he won

the US Grand Prix at Watkins Glen, to 1975 he won 14 Grand Prix races, driving for Lotus 1970-3 and McLaren 1974-5. In 1976 he formed his own team racing under the banner of the Brazilian sugar company Copersucar, but he gave up Grand Prix racing in 1980, achieving a career total of 281 points from 144 races. A careful and consistent driver, he started Indy Car driving in 1984 with Pat Patrick's team and later joined Penske, for whom he won the series in 1989. By the end of 1992 he was sixth on the all-time Indy Car series money list at $9,093,158. In the Indianapolis 500 itself he won for Penske in 1989 and 1993, and this took him to second on the all-time money list with $3,744,604.
His nephew Christian (b. 18 Jan 1971) has been a Formula One driver from 1992, and his cousin Wilson Fittipaldi (b. 25 Dec 1943) drove in 35 Grands Prix 1972-5.

Billy FITZGERALD (Can)

LACROSSE

William James Fitzgerald. b. 1888 St Catherines, Ontario, d. 1926.

Considered the greatest lacrosse player ever in Canada, the home of the sport. He started his career with the St Catherines Athletics and helped them win the Globe Shield from 1905 to 1912 and led them to undefeated seasons in 1907-08. In 1909, Fitzgerald turned professional with the Toronto Lacrosse Club. He became a hero sought out by fans and promoters everywhere. Shortly before World War I, he was lured to Vancouver with the then unheard-of salary of $US 5,000 and led them to the Minto Cup, the professional world championship. He then alternated playing between Toronto and Vancouver until he retired in 1922. He later became a lacrosse referee and coached mostly in the United States, at Hobart College, Swarthmore College, and West Point.

Bob FITZSIMMONS (UK/USA)

BOXING

Robert Fitzsimmons. b. 26 May 1863 Helston, Cornwall, d. 22 Oct 1917 Chicago, Illinois.

The first man to win three world titles and the only English-born professional world heavyweight champion. He grew up in New Zealand where he was apprenticed as a blacksmith. He was spotted winning a local contest by the renowned visiting fighter Jem Mace, who encouraged him to begin a professional career. Fitzsimmons won his first world title as a middleweight in 1891 when he knocked out Jack 'The Nonpareil' Dempsey. He then set his sights on the heavyweight crown and annexed that title by knocking out Jim Corbett in 14 rounds in 1897. At 75kg *165lb* he remains the lightest ever champion. Fitzsimmons, by then a naturalised American, lost the title in his first defence in 1899 to Jim Jeffries. He also lost a re-match to Jeffries in 1902, but in 1903 added his third world title, claiming the recently created light-heavyweight crown by defeating George Gardner. He lost that title in 1905 but boxed until 1914, when he was 52 years old.
Career record: W - 40 (32), L - 9, D -0.

James FITZSIMMONS (USA)

HORSE RACING

James Edward Fitzsimmons. b. 23 Jul 1874 Brooklyn, New York, d. 11 Mar 1966 Miami, Florida.

The trainer of two Triple Crown winners, *Gallant Fox* in 1930 and *Omaha* in 1935, and of ten other horses that won Triple Crown races. He was leading trainer in the USA by money won in 1936, 1939 and 1955, when he trained the Horse of the Year *Bold Ruler*.
His nickname of 'Sunny Jim' was thoroughly deserved of this lovely man, respected by all.

John FLANAGAN (Ire/USA)

ATHLETICS

John Jesus Flanagan. b. 9 Jan 1873 Kilbreedy, Co. Limerick, d. 4 Jun 1938 Kilmallack, Co. Limerick

The father of modern hammer throwing, he won three Olympic gold medals, 1900, 1904 and 1908, and set 18 world records. His first world record was 44.46m at

Clonmel, Ireland on 9 Sep 1895, and his last 56.19m at New Haven, USA on 24 Jul 1909, when he was 41 years and 196 days. That remains the oldest at which a track and field world record has been set. He was the first man to surpass 45m (in 1897) and 50m (in 1899). He emigrated from his native Ireland to the USA in the autumn of 1896 and dominated the event for the next decade. He returned to Ireland in 1911 and in his final international appearance won the hammer for Ireland against Scotland. In the USA between 1897 and 1908 he was AAU champion seven times at hammer and six times at 56lb weight, and he won AAA hammer titles in 1896 and 1900. In the 1904 Olympics he also took a silver medal at the 56lb weight throw and was fourth in the discus.

A charming and gentle man, in his early days he was a fine all-round athlete, with second places at both high jump and long jump at the 1895 Irish Championships.

Nat FLATMAN (UK)

HORSE RACING

Elnathan Flatman. b. 1810 Holton St Mary, Suffolk, d. 20 Aug 1860 Newmarket.

Champion jockey in England for 13 successive seasons, 1840-52, he set six progressive records for most winners in a season from 50 in 1840 to 104 in 1848. An honest and dependable jockey, he rode 10 classic winners between 1835 and 1857. He was apprenticed to William Cooper at Newmarket in 1825. His career was ended by a heavy fall in 1859.

Peggy FLEMING (USA)

FIGURE SKATING

Peggy Gale Fleming. b. 27 Jul 1948 San Jose, California. Later Jenkins.

After winning her first US senior title as a 15-year-old, she went on to win three world titles and an Olympic gold medal during a relatively brief career. In 1963 she took her first title as a senior at the Pacific Coast Championship and the following year she won her first US title and placed sixth in the Olympic Games. She retained her US title for the next four years and was world champion each year 1966-8, having placed third in 1965. She added Olympic gold in 1968 and then turned professional, signing a long-term $500,000 contract. She took part in the professional skating championships and appeared on TV both as a commentator and in commercials. She was also a goodwill ambassador for UNICEF and is today married to Dr Gregory Jenkins.

Curt FLOOD (USA)

BASEBALL

Curtis Charles Flood. b. 18 Jan 1938 Houston, Texas.

An outstanding centerfielder who won Gold Gloves from 1963-9, and a solid hitter who batted over .300 seven times during his 15 major league years, mostly with the St Louis Cardinals. He will, however, be remembered for other reasons. In 1969, the Cardinals traded Flood to the Philadelphia Phillies, a trade that Flood refused and fought. He challenged baseball's time-honoured 'reserve clause' which bound a player inextricably to his team. The suit eventually went to the Supreme Court, where Flood lost. He came back in 1971 with the Senators but played only 13 games. Though he lost his battle, he started a war that the players eventually won, as the reserve clause was later overturned and baseball players now have virtually complete free agency. This resultant escalation of several magnitudes in player salaries is due in large part to the courage of Curt Flood, who likened 'being owned by a baseball team' to 'being a slave 100 years ago'.

Career 1956-71: 1861 hits Avg. .293.

Ray FLOYD (USA)

GOLF

Raymond Loren Floyd. b. 14 Sep 1942 Fort Bragg, North Carolina.

Floyd has had a long, steady career, marked by his victories in three of the four major championships, lacking only the British Open in which he finished 2nd in 1978 and 3rd in 1981. He won the PGA in 1969 and 1982, the Masters in 1976 and the US Open in 1986, at the time the oldest

ever to do so. He nearly became the oldest ever to win the Masters, as he was runner-up in both 1990, when he lost to Nick Faldo at the second hole of a play-off, and in 1992. Early in his career, Floyd had a reputation as a playboy which was thought to hamper his progress. But after a marriage in the early 1970s, he became a redoubtable force in the majors.
In 1992 he won $1,178,908, $741,918 on the PGA tour and a further $436,990 on the seniors tour. He has played in seven Ryder Cup ties from 1969, and after being non-playing captain in 1989 returned to play in 1991; his overall record stands at won 9, lost 15, halved 3.
PGA career earnings 1961-92: $4,907,480 with 22 victories.

Imre FÖLDI (Hun)

WEIGHTLIFTING
Imre Földi. b. 8 May 1938.

Hungary's greatest ever weightlifter. He was the Olympic bantamweight (56kg) champion in 1972, after being 6th in 1960 and second in both 1964 and 1968, and was 5th at his fifth Games in 1976.
He was European champion at 56kg in 1962, 1968 and 1970-1, and at 60kg in 1963, having initially placed with third at 56kg in 1959. He set 20 world records: nine at 56kg - three for the press from 115kg in 1961 to 125kg in 1969 and six for the three-lift total from 355kg in 1964 to 377.5kg in 1972; and 11 for the press at 60kg from 123.5 kg in 1962 to 137.5 kg in 1972.

Just FONTAINE (Fra)

FOOTBALL
Just Fontaine. b. 18 Aug 1933 Marrakech, Morocco.

In 1958 he scored a record 13 goals in a World Cup Finals tournament, including a hat-trick in France's opening game against Paraguay and four in their 6-3 win over West Germany to take third place. In all he scored 27 goals in 20 international appearances for France 1956-60, as he formed a great partnership with Raymond Kopa. A broken leg on 20 Mar 1960 followed by another on 1 Jan 1961 meant that Fontaine was forced to announce his premature retirement from the game in 1962.
A centre forward, he started his playing career in Morocco, before moving to Nice, helping them to win the French Cup in 1954. He won French league honours with Nice in 1956 and with Reims in 1958 (also winning the Cup that year) and 1960, in both seasons the league's leading goalscorer. He became a sports writer and the first president of the French Professional Footballers Union in 1963. In 1967 he was briefly director of the French national team.

Frank FORBERGER (GDR)

ROWING
Frank Forberger. b. 5 Mar 1943 Meissen.

Forberger was the stroke of the renowned Einheit Dresden four (with Frank Rühle, Dieter Grahn and Dieter Schubert), who competed for 11 years and were never beaten in international competition. They won the Olympic gold medal in the coxless fours in 1968 and 1972. At the world championships, they were victorious in 1966 and 1970 and they were European champions in 1967 and 1971.

Bernard FORD (UK)

ICE DANCE
Bernard Ford. b. 27 Sep 1947 London.

World, European and British Ice Dance champion for four consecutive years, 1966-9, his partnership with Diane Towler brought a new dimension to the sport. Coached by Gladys Hogg, the world's foremost instructor, their exciting and daring style to music, which was initially thought to be unsuitable for ice dancing, was in sharp contrast to the impeccable elegance and footwork which was the characteristic of previous British champions. Their innovative talents established them as the greatest of all ice dancers until the arrival of Torvill and Dean. They relinquished their amateur status in 1969 to coach at Streatham and were both awarded the MBE. Despite their coaching activities they maintained their competitive interest and won the World Professional Championship at Wembley in 1969.

Horace FORD (UK)

ARCHERY

Horace Alfred Ford. b. 1822 London, d. 24 Jun 1880 Bath.

The greatest British archer of the 19th century; he won 12 Grand National titles, eleven of them consecutively from 1849 to 1859, with a final championship in 1867. In 1857 he scored 1251 points for the Double York Round, which was a British record for that competition, shot in two directions at any open meeting, until 1960. This was done with traditional long-bow and wooden arrows. He was a Glamorgan colliery owner and was the author of *Archery: its theory and practice* which was first published in 1856 and which remains a classic.

Malcolm FORD (USA)

ATHLETICS

Malcolm Worthington Ford. b. 7 Feb 1862 Brooklyn, New York, d. 8 May 1902 New York.

From a well-known American literary family, Ford was a hugely talented all-round athlete, who won 14 AAU titles and set a world long jump record of 7.08m in 1886. His first titles came in 1883 when he won the US high jump and long jump and the Canadian high jump. Later that year he fell out with his family and was disowned by his father, who felt that it was beneath any Ford to take part in sports. He continued to compete, however, and in 1884 won the US 100y and long jump, going even better with the triple of 100y, 220y and long jump and also winning the all-around title in 1885 and 1886. In 1887 he was suspended for professionalism, but was later reinstated temporarily and in this time he won the AAU all-around in 1888 and long jump in 1889. In 1891 he toured Europe, performing athletic feats in a circus. On his return he took up writing and married a wealthy New York heiress; he was, however, left out of the will of his father, who died that year. A few years later Ford's wife divorced him and he was left penniless, forced to borrow from his wealthy brothers and sisters. They grew increasingly irritated with this, especially his best known brother, the novelist Paul Ford. Malcolm lost a bitter court struggle in which he sued his entire family for a share of their wealth. In late 1901 Paul Ford, an invalid, told Malcolm he would support him no longer. The story came to a tragic end when on 8 May 1902 in New York, Malcolm walked into Paul's office and shot him dead, then turning the gun on himself and committing suicide.

Whitey FORD (USA)

BASEBALL

Edward Charles Ford. b. 21 Oct 1928 New York.

The top pitcher on the top team in baseball, the New York Yankees, in the late 1950s and early 1960s. His lifetime .690 winning percentage ranks him first all-time among modern pitchers with 200 or more wins. He was not a power pitcher but relied on his control and craftiness to dominate the opposing teams. He helped the Yankees win 11 American League pennants. In the World Series he was particularly outstanding as he ranks first all-time in wins (10), losses (8), games and games started (22), innings pitched, hits, bases on balls, and strikeouts. In the three World Series 1960-2, Ford pitched 33 consecutive scoreless innings, breaking a record formerly held by Babe Ruth. In 1961 he was the Cy Young winner and the World Series MVP.
Career pitching: ERA 2.74; W-L 236-106, SO 1086; Best season: 1961: 25-4, 3.21 ERA.

George FORDHAM (UK)

HORSE RACING

George Fordham. b. 24 Sep 1837 Cambridge, d. 11 Oct 1887 Slough.

Easily the top jockey of his generation, he passed Nat Flatman's record with progressive totals for winners in a year of 108 in 1856, 118 in 1859, 146 in 1860 and 166 in 1862, as he was champion jockey 14

times, 1855-63, 1865, 1867-9, 1871, with a career total of 2587 winners, 1851-84. He retired in 1875, but due to failure of investments was forced to return to riding in 1878. From then until 1884 he rode a further 482 winners, and brought his total of classic winners to 16, including his first Derby in 1879.
Although he grew stronger, he weighed just 54lb when he started his successful riding career, apprenticed to Richard Drewitt. Known as 'The Demon' he rode with shorter leathers than contemporary jockeys and was renowned for keeping his mounts balanced and for his honesty.

George FOREMAN (USA)

BOXING

George Foreman. b. 22 Jan 1948 Marshall, Texas

One of the most powerful punchers ever, Foreman had little experience in 1968 when he won the AAU title, the Olympic trials and the Olympic Games. He became famous as, after winning the final bout, he took a small American flag and waved it to the four corners of the auditorium. It was especially significant given the tenor of the times and the protests of black athletes Tommie Smith and John Carlos on the Olympic victory platform in Mexico City. Foreman quickly turned professional and began knocking out fighters left and right. In 1973 he fought Joe Frazier for the heavyweight title and punished him - flooring him seven times in the second round before the fight was stopped. Foreman successfully defended the title twice but on 30 Oct 1974, in 'The Rumble in the Jungle, in Zaire, Muhammad Ali stopped him in eight rounds. Foreman was never a championship factor again, and after two lacklustre years, became a practising minister in Texas. However, in 1987, by then weighing close to 300 lb, he began a comeback and was unbeaten until in April 1991 he fought for the heavyweight title again and lost a decision to Evander Holyfield. He was considering retirement following his loss to Tommy Morrison for the WBO world title in June 1993.
Career record: W - 72 (67), L - 4, D - 0.

Karl-Heinz FÖRSTER (FRG)

FOOTBALL

Karl-Heinz Förster. b. 25 Jul 1958.

Once rated the best stopper in Europe, he was in the West German teams that won the 1980 European Championships and were runners-up in the 1982 and 1986 World Cup Finals, and in all played in 81 internationals 1978-86. With VfB Stuttgart he won the Bundesliga in 1984, and in 1986 he transferred to Olympique Marseille in France, helping them to French titles in 1989-92.

Dick FOSBURY (USA)

ATHLETICS

Richard Douglas Fosbury. b. 6 Mar 1947 Portland, Oregon.

The pioneer of the Flop style of high jumping which bears his name. His use of the backwards layout technique brought him instant fame when he won the 1968 Olympic gold medal with 2.24m. That was the climax of a year in which he had progressed from a best of 2.08m in 1967.
He had developed the style from 1963 when he had been using the 'scissors' technique and started leaning further and further back.
He won the NCAA high jump in 1968 and 1969 and indoors in 1968. A graduate of Oregon State, he is now a civil engineer.

Bob FOSTER (USA)

BOXING

Robert Wayne Foster. b. 15 Dec 1938 Albuquerque, New Mexico.

One of the greatest light-heavyweight champions ever. At 191cm *6' 3"* he was very tall for the weight and he tried several times to compete as a heavyweight but never fared well there. Foster first won the light-heavyweight championship in 1968 by knocking-out Dick Tiger, and successfully defended the title 14 times before retiring in 1974. He fought Joe Frazier for the heavyweight championship in 1970 but lost by a KO in the second. Foster is now a sheriff in Albuquerque.
Career record: W - 56 (46), L - 8, D -1.

Brendan FOSTER (UK)

ATHLETICS

Brendan Foster. b. 12 Jan 1948 Hebburn, Co. Durham.

In the 1970s Foster became Britain's most successful distance runner. At 1500m he won Commonwealth 1970 and European 1971 bronze medals and was 5th at the 1972 Olympics, before steadily moving up in distance. He set world records for 2 miles, 8:13.68 in 1972, and for 3000m, 7:35.2 at the opening of the Gateshead track in 1974. His greatest victory was in the 1974 European 5000m when he destroyed the field with a 60.2 eighth lap, running a championship best 13:17.21 despite hot and humid conditions. Earlier in the year he had just lost in an epic duel to Ben Jipcho in the Commonwealth 5000m, setting a British record of 13:14.6 (he was also 7th at 1500m). He won the European Cup 5000m in 1973 and 1975, and at the end of that year made the fastest ever début at 10,000m, 27:45.43, to win at the Coke meeting at Crystal Palace. The following year he was weakened by illness and had to settle for the Olympic bronze at this distance; following this with 5th at 5000m, after setting an Olympic record 13:20.34 in his heat.

He won AAA titles at 5000m in 1973-4 and 1976, and in 1978 added the 10,000m, when he ran a world record time of 27:30.3. He went on to win the Commonwealth title at 10,000m and the bronze at 5000m, but this took the edge off his running so that three weeks later he was 4th in the European 10km, although running 27:32.65, in the fastest ever mass finish. In 1979 he won his third European Cup title, at 10,000m, but was below his best in his final major race, 11th at the 1980 Olympics. He also set British records at 1500m 3:37.64 (1974) and 2000m 5:02.93 (1975) and had other bests of 1 mile 3:55.9 (1972), marathon 2:15:49 (1980).

Awarded the MBE 1976, he has become a successful athletics promoter, notably in the North-East of England, businessman, managing director of Nova International, and a TV commentator for the BBC.

Greg FOSTER (USA)

ATHLETICS

Gregory Foster. b. 4 Aug 1958 Maywood, Illinois.

Three times world champion outdoors, winning the 110m hurdles in 1983, 1987 and 1991, and once indoors, the 60m hurdles in 1991. He ranked for 15 years in the world top ten (a record for any running event) for 110mh, 1977-87 and 1989-92, including ten years in the top two. He was silver medallist at the 1984 Olympics, but did not make the teams for the next two Games. He was fourth at the US Trials in 1992 and in 1988 had competed at the Olympic Trials wearing a plaster cast for a compound fracture of his left forearm three weeks earlier. He broke his arm again in two places playing basketball in January 1989, and served a three month ban after a positive drugs test on 19 Jan 1990.

He set a US record for 110m hurdles with 13.22 in 1978, before being slightly overshadowed by Renaldo Nehemiah in the next three years, running his fastest ever time of 13.03 behind Nehemiah's world record in Zürich in 1981. Foster ran a record 56 (and 4 wind assisted) sub-13.30 times, including 20 sub-13.20. He set a world indoor record of 7.36 for 60m hurdles in January 1987, and bests for 50 yards hurdles, 5.88 in 1986, and 50 metres hurdles, 6.35 in 1985. A graduate of UCLA, his other major wins at 110m hurdles: World Cup 1991, TAC 1981, 1983, 1986-7 and 1991; NCAA 1978, 1981 (and 200m 1979); US Olympic Trials 1984. He was also AAU sprint hurdles champion indoors six times: 1983-5, 1987-8, 1991.

Other bests: 100m 10.28 (1979), 200m 20.20 (1979).

Dan FOUTS (USA)

AMERICAN FOOTBALL

Daniel Francis Fouts. b. 10 Jun 1951 San Francisco.

Fouts is second on the all-time list for yards gained passing, with 43,040 yards and 254 touchdowns as quarterback for the San Diego Chargers. He established NFL

records for the most 300-yard passing games (51) and most 3000-yard seasons (6), with three consecutive 4000-yard seasons, 1979-81. He played in six Pro Bowls, and had been at the University of Oregon.
NFL career: 3297 pass completions, 58.8%, 254 TD.

Grant FOX (NZ)

RUGBY UNION
Grant James Fox. b. 16 Jun 1962 New Plymouth.

After winning international honours at schoolboy, colts, university and junior levels he made his All Black début against Argentina in 1985. He failed to win a regular place in the New Zealand team until the 1987 World Cup when he played in every match and kicked 126 points, including an international record ten conversions against Fiji. Playing at fly half, he developed into a prodigious place kicker and he holds virtually every New Zealand record in that department. In all matches in All Black colours Fox passed 1000 points in the first Test against the Lions in June 1993 and only Michael Lynagh has bettered his total of 620 international points, which Fox achieved in 45 Tests to the end of July 1993. Playing for Auckland, his 746 points is a record in Ranfurly Shield matches and he has nearly 4000 points in all first-class matches. He is managing director of Harvard Sports Management.

Neil FOX (UK)

RUGBY LEAGUE
Neil Fox. b. 4 May 1939 Sharlston, Yorkshire.

With a total 6220 points in 828 matches he is the most prolific scorer of all-time. Although he scored 358 tries, his phenomenal scoring feats were based on his left-footed goal kicking abilities and during his career he kicked 2575 goals at club, county and international level.
He made his début for Wakefield Trinity as a 16-year-old in 1956 and won all his 29 Great Britain caps with the club. He also played briefly for Bradford Northern, Hull Kingston Rovers, York, Bramley and Huddersfield. As a member of Wakefield's winning Challenge Cup team in 1960 he set an individual scoring record for a Wembley final of 20 points (7 goals; 2 tries). Two years later he dropped three goals and scored one try in the Challenge Cup final against Huddersfield and was awarded the Lance Todd Trophy as Man of the Match.
He used his powerful physique to good effect in the centre but in the latter part of his career he played as a forward. After retirement he coached Underbank amateurs and was awarded the MBE in 1983 for his services to the sport.

Nellie FOX (USA)

BASEBALL
Jacob Nelson Fox. b. 25 Dec 1927 St Thomas, Pennsylvania, d. 1 Dec 1975 Baltimore, Maryland.

Fox played for 19 years in the major leagues, mostly with the Chicago White Sox, whom in 1959 he led to their first pennant in 40 years. For his leadership efforts, he was named the American League MVP that year. He played in 798 consecutive games 1956-60, a record for a second baseman. He also batted over .300 in six different seasons and led the league in hits four times, 1952, 1954, 1957-8.
Career 1947-65: 2663 hits Avg. .288.

Richard FOX (UK)

CANOEING
Richard Munro Fox. b. 5 Jun 1960 Winsford, Cheshire.

The winner of a record five world titles for canoe slalom in the K1 class, 1981, 1983, 1985, 1989 and 1993, also winning five team gold medals at the biennial championships, each year 1981-7 and in 1993. He was one of the favourites for gold when canoe slalom was reintroduced to the Olympic Games in 1992 after a 20-year absence, but had to settle for the bronze medal. He is a marketing consultant.
His wife **Myriam Jérusalmi** (Fra) (b. 24 Oct 1961) was the women's world champion at canoe slalom K1 in 1989 and 1993,

and runner-up in 1987. She also won team gold medals with the French team in 1983, 1985, 1989, 1991 and 1993. She was the World Cup winner each year 1989-91.

Jimmy FOXX (USA)

BASEBALL

James Emory Foxx. b. 22 Oct 1907 Sudlersville, Maryland, d. 21 Jul 1967 Miami, Florida.

'Double X' Foxx is one of the greatest power hitters in baseball history. He played mostly first base for the Philadelphia Athletics and Boston Red Sox in his 20-year career. His top year was 1933 when he won the Triple Crown (.356, 48 HR, 163 RBI), and he was named as American League MVP in 1932-3 and 1938. When Foxx retired in 1945 his 534 home runs was second only to Babe Ruth. He led the league in home runs four times, despite playing against Ruth, Lou Gehrig, Hank Greenberg and Joe DiMaggio during his career, and is one of only five players to have hit 50 home runs in two seasons (58 in 1932 and 50 in 1938). He also was a prodigious run producer, driving in over 100 runs for 13 consecutive seasons 1929-41. His post-baseball career saw him have many difficulties; he drank heavily and lost most of his money in failed investments. He did some coaching and radio announcing in his later years.
Career 1925-45: 2646 hits Avg. .325, HR 534; RBI 1452.

A J FOYT (USA)

MOTOR RACING

Anthony Joseph Foyt, Jr. b. 16 Jan 1935 Houston.

The first man to win the Indianapolis 500 four times, 1961, 1964, 1967 and 1977, he qualified for a record 35 successive Indy 500s 1958-92. In all he completed a record 4914 laps and 12,285 miles in the race. He also won a record seven USAC National Championships, 1960-1, 1963-4, 1967, 1975 and 1979, and at Indy car racing he had career earnings of $5,357,589, achieving an all-time record 67 wins. He displayed great racing versatility, as he was very successful in sports car racing, winning the Le Mans 24-hour race with Dan Gurney in 1967, and at stock car racing, completing a unique driving triple by winning the Daytona 500 in 1972. He was USAC dirt car champion in 1971 and USAC stock car champion in 1968, 1978 and 1979.
This exceptionally strong driver started racing in 1953, joined USAC in 1957 and drove his first Indy car in 1958. With his father A J Sr (Tony) he built cars with Ford engines bearing his own name.
A flamboyant character yet a model driver, cool and precise in all that he did, he now raises cattle and thoroughbred horses on his 1500-acre ranch.

John FRANCOME (UK)

HORSE RACING

John Francome. b. 13 Dec 1952 Swindon.

A marvellous horseman, he passed Stan Mellor's record total of winners under National Hunt rules, totalling 1138 winners from 5072 mounts over jumps from 1970 to 1985.
He first rode at the age of four, and achieved much success in gymkhanas, becoming a British show jumping international in 1969, in which year he joined the stable of Fred Winter, for whom he was first jockey 1975-85. He won on his first NH ride, a 3 miles hurdles race at Worcester on 2 Dec 1970. Champion jockey seven times, in 1975/6, 1978/9 and each year from 1980/1 to 1984/5, tying with Peter Scudamore in 1981/2; his most wins in a season was 131 in 1983/4. He rode *Midnight Court* to win the Cheltenham Gold Cup in 1978 and *Sea Pigeon* to win the Champion Hurdle in 1981. Awarded the MBE 1986. Now a writer and TV commentator.

Dawn FRASER (Aus)

SWIMMING

Dawn Lorraine Fraser. b. 4 Sep 1937 Balmain, Sydney.

The greatest woman swimmer of her era, the fiery and fun-loving Dawn Fraser had a long and brilliant career until given ten years suspension by Australian swimming officials for misbehaviour at the 1964 Olympics; a shocking and ridiculously heavy-handed decision, despite her long record of problems with the authorities. She had led a midnight raid to steal a souvenir flag from the Emperor's Palace in Tokyo and had been arrested, but the charges were dropped and the Emperor gave her a souvenir flag. Although the ban was later reduced to four years, her competitive career was over.

Fraser won the Olympic 100m freestyle title at three successive Games, a unique achievement for any swimming event. Her eight Olympic medals, since tied by Ender, is also a women's record. In 1956 she beat her team-mate Lorraine Crapp in 62.0, her third world record at the event, and also won gold at 4x100m freestyle and silver at 400m. In 1960 she added silver medals at 4 x 100m freestyle and medley relays, and she took another freestyle relay silver in 1964. At 400m she was fifth in 1960 and fourth in 1964.

The youngest of eight children, she set 27 individual world records, with 11 in all at 100m from 64.5 in the Australian Championships in 1956 to 58.9 in 1964, a time that was not bettered until eight years later. She broke the minute barrier for the first time in 1962. Her best time for 220y was 2:11.6 in 1960 (also her fourth world record for 200m) and her best for 100y was 56.9.

At the Commonwealth Games she won six gold medals: 110y and 4x110y freestyle 1958 and 1962; 440y and medley relay 1962; with two silvers, 440y and medley relay in 1958.

She won 23 Australian titles: freestyle 100m/110y 1956, 1958-62, 1964; 200m/220y 1955-6, 1958-62, 1964; 400m/440y 1958, 1960-2, 1964; 100m butterfly 1960 and 1962; 200m IM 1959.

Named Australian of the Year in 1964, awarded the MBE in 1967. A film of her life *Dawn!* was released in 1979. She became a publican in Balmain and represented that district in the New South Wales parliament 1988-91.

Neale FRASER (Aus)

TENNIS

Neale Andrew Fraser. b. 3 Oct 1933 St Kilda, Melbourne, Victoria.

A stalwart of Australian tennis who made a notable contribution to his country's Davis Cup successes both as a player and as captain. Between 1958 and 1963 he won 18 of his 21 rubbers and was a member of the winning team four times 1959-62. He was later non-playing captain of the team which won the Cup in 1973, 1978 and 1983.

In Championship singles, Fraser won Wimbledon in 1960 and the US title in 1959 and 1960, but achieved his greatest successes in the men's doubles, winning all the major titles. He won at Wimbledon twice (1959, 1961) and was a three-time winner at each of the other Grand Slam tournaments: US (1957, 1959-60), French (1958, 1960, 1962) and Australian (1957-8, 1962). He also won five Grand Slam mixed doubles titles.

A left-hander with a powerful but unspectacular serve-volley game, he was one of the most consistent players of his era. Awarded the MBE in 1974.

Joe FRAZIER (USA)

BOXING

Joseph Frazier. b. 12 Jan 1944 Beaufort, South Carolina

Frazier is one of the great heavyweight champions of all time. It is sad that he fought in the same era as Muhammad Ali because he did not get the acclaim that Ali did and that he deserved. He emerged internationally when he won a gold medal as a heavyweight at the 1964 Olympics. He managed that despite a broken thumb which he had sustained in the semi-finals. It was typical of this gutsy fighter. He first won the heavyweight world championship in 1970 by stopping Jimmy Ellis in five rounds. He defended the title four times before being knocked out by George Foreman in 1973. Frazier fought three tremendous battles with Ali. The first, in 1971, was the fight of the century, a battle of undefeated heavyweight champions,

and Frazier won by a decision in 15 rounds. Frazier was on the losing end in the next two fights, but all three were great spectacles. Ali later stated that fighting Joe Frazier was 'the closest thing to death I ever want to know'.
Frazier was very short for a heavyweight, and he made no pretence of back-pedalling. He always came at his opponent like a Sherman tank, willing to trade three punches to land one pulverising blow. After losing his heavyweight title, he continued to fight for a few years before retiring in the mid 1970s.
Career record: W - 32 (27), L - 4, D -1.

Walt FRAZIER (USA)

BASKETBALL
Walter 'Clyde' Frazier II. b. 29 Mar 1945 Atlanta, Georgia.

A lizard-quick guard with the New York Knicks for 10 years of his 13-year NBA career, known as the epitome of 'cool'. He helped the Knicks to win NBA Championships in both 1970 and 1973. Heralded for his defense, his quick hands terrorised opposing guards and earned him a nomination to the NBA All-Defensive First Team for seven consecutive years 1969-75. He could also score, as he averaged 18.9 points during his career, with a season best of 23.3 points per game in 1971/2. Off the court he was famous for his flashy and expensive clothes, which frequently included mink coats and wide-brimmed hats, and for driving a Rolls-Royce to the Knicks home games at Madison Square Garden. His last three years were with the Cleveland Cavaliers, and he became a broadcaster for the New York Knicks cable television network.

Sylvie FRÉCHETTE (Can)

SYNCHRONISED SWIMMING
Sylvie Frechette. b. 27 Jun 1967 Montréal.

The 1991 world champion at synchronised swimming, when she was awarded seven perfect scores of 10 in the solo event to establish a world record score of 201.013. She was undefeated from 1990 to 1992, when she was beaten into second place at the Olympic Games by Kristen Babb-Sprague (USA).
Having begun synchro swimming at the age of eight, she was Canadian junior champion in 1981-2, Commonwealth Games champion 1986 and 1990, World Cup winner in 1991 after being second in 1989, and Canadian senior champion 1989-92. She studied physical education at the University of Montréal.

Frank FREDERICKSON (Can)

ICE HOCKEY
Frank Frederickson. b. 11 Jun 1895 Winnipeg, Manitoba, d. 28 May 1979 Toronto, Ontario.

Frederickson, of Icelandic descent, was renowned in Canada as an amateur hockey player. In 1920 he led the Winnipeg Falcons (representing Canada) to the Olympic title. Frederickson scored both goals in a 2-0 victory over the USA in the final. He then played in the NHL for five years until a knee injury ended his career. He later became a college hockey coach and also wrote hockey instructional articles for newspapers for several years.
NHL career 1926-31 - 165 games, 39 goals, 73 points. Best year 1926/7: 18 goals, 31 points.

Gert FREDRIKSSON (Swe)

CANOEING
Gert Fridolf Fredriksson. b. 21 Nov 1919 Nyköping.

The most successful canoeist in Olympic history, with six gold medals, a silver and a bronze. He started in 1948 by winning both K1 titles, at 1000m and at 10,000m. He retained the 1000m title in both 1952 and 1956, while at 10,000m he was second in 1952 and won again in 1956. At his fourth Olympics in 1960 he teamed with Sven-Olov Sjödelius to win the K2 1000m and was 3rd at K1 1000m. He was just as successful at World Championships, winning the K1 500m in 1948 and 1954, K1 1000m in 1950 and 1954 and three titles at 4 x 500m relay. He started canoeing in 1937 and won a record total of 71 Swedish titles from his first in 1942.

David FREEMAN (USA)

BADMINTON

(Dr) David Guthrie Freeman. b. 6 Sep 1920 Pasadena, California.

In 1938 Freeman was US junior champion at both singles and doubles at lawn tennis, but then concentrated on badminton and swept all before him to gain a reputation as the game's greatest ever player until he retired in 1949. He sealed his career in 1949 with remarkably easy wins, dropping only 24 points in his last eight games, to gain the All-England men's singles title. He made a brief comeback in Toronto in 1953, when he lost just one game, only his third since 1939!
He was US singles champion each year 1939-42 and after the interruption of the War, when he was a surgeon in the US Army, again in 1947-8. He was also men's doubles winner at five successive championships 1940-8 and mixed doubles winner with Sally Williams each year 1940-2.
Not especially powerful, but he was patient and immensely precise, making his opponents make the errors, as he was nearly flawless.

Tich FREEMAN (UK)

CRICKET

Alfred Percy Freeman. b. 17 May 1888 Lewiston, Kent, d. 28 Jan 1965 Bearsted, Kent.

With his slow leg-spin bowling Freeman captured an enormous haul of wickets for Kent in the 1920s and 1930s. He made his début in 1914, missing four seasons due to the War. Every year from 1920 to 1934 he took over 100 wickets in a season, and after his all-time record of 304 at 18.05 in 1928, took over 200 every year to his penultimate year of 1935. He took all ten wickets in an innings three times and twice took 17 wickets in a match. Just 1.58m *5'2"* tall, he was most impressively accurate for a bowler of his type. He only played 12 times for England and only twice against Australia, so although his Test figures were nowhere near as impressive as his county ones, his worth at the highest level was not fully explored.

12 Tests 1924-9: 154 runs at 14.00, HS 50; 66 wickets at 25.86, BB 7-71; 4 catches.*
First-class 1914-36: 4961 runs at 9.50, HS 66; 3776 wickets at 18.42, BB 10-53; 238 catches, 1 stumping.

Urs FREULER (Swi)

CYCLING

Urs Freuler. b. 6 Nov 1958 Glarus.

The greatest rider in the points race on the track, winning the world professional title each year 1981-7 and 1989. He has also been superb in the keirin, world champion in 1983 and 1985, although he has not raced professionally in Japan, the home of that event. He has also ridden on many winning six-day event teams and was the points winner in the 1984 Giro d'Italia. At one kilometre he set two world records outdoors with a best of 1:06.091 (1983) and one indoors, 1:06.603 (1981). He also set the 500m flying start record indoors at 28.486 in 1981. Prior to turning professional, Freuler, a car mechanic, was Swiss sprint champion in 1978 and finished third in the world amateur points race in 1979.

Artur FRIEDENREICH (Bra)

FOOTBALL

Artur Freidenreich. b. 18 Jul 1892 São Paulo, d. 20 Nov 1969.

During a first-class career from 1909 to 1934 he scored an unprecedented total of 1329 goals. These included 9 in 17 internationals 1916-30 in the rare matches that Brazil played as a national team in those years. A centre-forward, his clubs included Germania, Ipiranga, Americano, Paulistano, São Paulo and Flamengo.

Heike FRIEDRICH (GDR)

SWIMMING

Heike Friedrich. b. 18 Apr 1970 Karl-Marx-Stadt.

A most successful freestyle swimmer in the 1980s. She was world champion at 200m and 400m and both freestyle relays in 1986 and Olympic champion at 200m

and silver medallist at 400m in 1988. She won a total of nine European gold medals: five in 1985, 100m and 200m freestyle and all three relays; four in 1987, 200m and 400m and both freestyle relays. The world record of 1:57.55 for 200m that she swam at the 1986 GDR championships still stood seven years later and she also set three European records for 400m to 4:05.94 in the 1988 Olympics.
She first emerged internationally when she was European Junior champion at 100m freestyle and three relays in 1984, and her first GDR senior titles were at 100m and 200m, 1985. Coached by Joachim Rother and Bernd Köhler at SC Karl-Marx-Stadt.
Other bests: 50m 26.10 (1985), 100m 55.71 (1985), 800m 8:28.91 (1988).

Frank FRISCH (USA)

BASEBALL

Frank Francis Frisch. b. 9 Sep 1898 Bronx, New York, d. 12 Mar 1973 Wilmington, Delaware.

'The Fordham Flash' played mostly at second base for the New York Giants 1919-26 and the St Louis Cardinals 1927-37. For his last five years he was a player-manager. He batted over .300 in thirteen different seasons. Despite that, he was mostly known for his expert fielding and his leadership ability. His nickname came from his years at Fordham University, where he played football, baseball, basketball and track, before graduating in 1919. After he finished playing, Frisch managed for ten more years in the major leagues.
Career 1919-37: 2880 hits Avg. .316; SB 419; RBI 1244. Best season: 1923: .348, 223 hits.

Morten FROST (Den)

BADMINTON

Morten Frost Hansen. b. 4 Apr 1958 Nykøbing Sjælland.

A dogged player who was the best European badminton exponent in the 1980s, winning the continental men's singles title in 1984 and 1986. He lost in the final of the World Championships in 1985 and 1987. After three successive years as runner-up he won the All-England singles in 1982, 1984 and 1986-7. He won three Danish junior titles, and eight Nordic titles from 1978.
He was also a useful high jumper before concentrating on badminton, where he used speedy footwork and lightning-fast reflexes.

C B FRY (UK)

CRICKET

Charles Burgess Fry. b. 25 Apr 1872 West Croydon, Surrey, d. 7 Sep 1956 Hampstead, Middlesex.

Renaissance man, his brilliance at all pursuits seemed to know no limits. England captain in six Test matches in 1912 (won 4, drawn 2), he would have led the team much more had he been available for tours. He set a world long jump record with 7.17m on 4 Mar 1893 and three times won that event for Oxford University v Cambridge. He also won his blue for soccer, at which he played for England in 1901 and for Southampton in the 1902 FA Cup final; and he would have won one for rugby as well but for injury. He played cricket for Sussex 1894-1908 (captain 1904-8), and occasionally for Hampshire 1909-21. His greatest season was 1901, when he scored 3147 runs (av. 78.67), including 13 hundreds of which six were in successive innings, still a record. He was a fast-medium bowler, but was called for throwing in 1898.
A first-class honours graduate in classics, he failed to be elected for parliament although he stood several times as a Liberal, but after World War I he was India's representative at the League of Nations. He also declined an offer to be King of Albania. An avid conversationalist, broadcaster and author, he edited boys' magazines and directed his naval training ship *Mercury* with his martinet wife from 1909.
26 Tests 1896-1912: 1223 runs at 32.18, 2 100s HS 144; 17 catches.
First-class 1892-1921: 30,886 runs at 50.22, 94 100s HS 258; 166 wickets at 29.34, BB 6-78; 240 catches.*

Shirley FRY (USA)

TENNIS

Shirley June Fry. b. 30 Jun 1927 Akron, Ohio. Later Irvin.

First ranked in the US top ten in 1944 and a Wimbledon quarter-finalist in 1948, she was generally overshadowed in her early years by her American contemporaries. Her first major singles title came with the 1951 French. In 1956 she won at Wimbledon and at Forest Hills and in 1957 she won the Australian title. At the time, Doris Hart and Maureen Connolly were the only other players to have won all four Grand Slam singles titles.
She also had a fine record as a doubles player partnering Doris Hart, and between 1950 and 1954 they won four times at the French and US Championships and three times at Wimbledon. Their most notable success came at Wimbledon in 1953 when they won both the semi-final and the final 6-0, 6-0 and lost only four games throughout the whole event. Fry also won the Australian doubles in 1957 and the mixed doubles at Wimbledon in 1956. She played in six Wightman Cup matches between 1949 and 1956 winning 10 of her 12 rubbers. She was ranked No.1 in the world in 1956. On her retirement in 1957 she married Karl Irvin and following his death in 1976 she devoted her time to coaching in Connecticut.

Ruth FUCHS (GDR)

ATHLETICS

Ruth Fuchs. née Gamm. b. 11 Dec 1946 Egeln.

Fuchs won 113 of 129 javelin competitions from 1970 to 1980, amazing consistency for such an unpredictable event over such a span of time. These included two Olympic (1972 and 1976) and two European (1974 and 1978) titles as well as four European Cup Final and two World Cup victories. She won eleven GDR titles from her first in 1967. Her first appearance at a major championships was when she took the bronze medal in the 1971 Europeans and her last was 8th place at the 1980 Olympics, when she was suffering from a back injury. The first of her ten GDR javelin records was at 60.60m in 1970, and she added 2.36m to the world record with 65.06m at Potsdam in 1972, improving five more times to 69.96m in 1980. She remained influential in GDR athletics and served on the IAAF Women's Committee.

Shojo FUJII (Japan)

JUDO

Shojo Fujii. b. 11 May 1950 Shozo, Kagawa Prefecture.

World champion at under 80kg in 1971, 1973 and 1975 and at under 78kg in 1979; tying the record for most judo titles. He did not, however, compete at the Olympics as he was defeated at the All-Japan championships in 1976 by Isamu Sonada, who went on to win the title. A graduate of Tenri University and now an assistant professor, Fujii has coached the Japanese Olympic teams.

Joe FULKS (USA)

BASKETBALL

Joseph Fulks. b. 26 Oct 1921 Birmingham, Kentucky, d. 21 Mar 1976 Eddyville, Kentucky.

The first prolific scorer of the NBA, leading the league in its first sesaon in 1946/7 with 1389 points, av. 23.2. In 1949 he scored 63 points in a game against the Indianapolis Jets, at the time a professional record. Having played college basketball at Murray State to 1943, he was drafted and played with the San Diego Marines. In 1947 he joined the Philadelphia Warriors of the Basketball Association of America, a forerunner of the NBA, and was first-team all-NBA 1946-9.

Bozo FULTON (Aus)

RUGBY LEAGUE

Bob Fulton. b. 1 Dec 1947 Warrington, Lancashire, England

A very strong and unorthodox centre or five-eighth, who was rated as one of the most damaging players ever in broken play. He emigrated with his family to Australia at the age of three and joined Manly at the age of 18. He was named their captain two years later and won three premierships with Manly, scoring two tries in their 10-7 win over Cronulla in what was rated as the most brutal Grand Final of all in 1973. Having scored 510 points in 213 matches from 129 tries, 57 goals and 5 field goals for Manly, he moved on to play for Eastern Suburbs from 1977 to his retirement as a player in 1979. Since then he has been a highly successful coach. He made 20 international appearances for Australia 1968-78, playing in three World Cup series and one world championship and captaining the team on their tour to Britain and France in 1978.

Ove FUNDIN (Swe)

SPEEDWAY

K Ove Fundin. b. 23 May 1933, Tranås.

His record of five individual world titles has only been surpassed by Ivan Mauger, and from 1956 to 1965 he never placed out of the first three in the championship, scoring 173 points from 15 finals 1954-65, 1967-9. His final international appearance was at Wembley in 1970 when he was a member of the winning Swedish team in the World Team Championship for the sixth time. He spent most of his career with Norwich but also rode briefly for Long Eaton and Belle Vue. Swedish champion 1956-7, 1960, 1962, 1964, 1966-7, 1969-70.

Danny GABLE (USA)

WRESTLING

Danny Mack Gable. b. 25 Oct 1948 Waterloo, Iowa.

America's best-known wrestler, and thought by some experts to have been the greatest yet produced in the United States. In his career at Iowa State University 1967-70 he won 118 bouts and lost just once, to Larry Owings in the 1970 NCAA final, which concluded a total run of 182 successive victories at high school and college. Gable was already known as a workaholic and the most dedicated wrestler in the sport, but the loss spurred him on to even greater efforts. As a lightweight he won the 1969 and 1970 AAU titles and the Pan-American and World titles of 1971.

He severely injured his knee shortly before the 1972 Olympics, but in 21 matches at the US Trials and the Olympics he gave up just one point - wrestling basically on one leg. At Munich he achieved the amazing feat of winning his gold medal in the lightweight class with no opponent scoring a point off him in six matches. Gable competed sporadically thereafter but has become America's top wrestling coach, leading University of Iowa teams to nine consecutive NCAA tournament victories, 1978-86, and eleven overall through 1992.

Rosemarie GABRIEL (GDR) - see KOTHER.

Jean GACHASSIN (Fra)

RUGBY UNION

Jean Gachassin. b. 23 Dec 1941 Bagnères-de-Bigorre, Haute-Pyrénées.

A highly versatile player who was capped in every position outside the pack except at scrum-half. Only 1.52m *5'4"* tall and weighing a modest 63kg *138lb* he is one of the smallest players to have won international honours but his brilliant running earned him 32 caps between 1961 and 1969. He played for Lourdes where he was a schoolmaster, until becoming trainer and player for Stade de Bagnères in 1969.

Rowdy GAINES (USA)

SWIMMING

Ambrose Gaines IV. b. 17 Feb 1959 Winter Haven, Florida.

The Olympic champion at 100m freestyle in 1984, when he set an Olympic record of 49.80, and to which he added further gold medals at both 4 x100m relays, freestyle and medley. He would have been heavy favourite to win four gold medals in 1980 but lost that chance due to the US boycott. That year he set a US record of 49.61 for 100m and a world record of 1:49.16 for 200m. He added world records for 100m

with 49.36 in 1981 and for 200m with 1:48.93 in 1982.
In the World Championships in 1978 he won two freestyle relay golds and 200m silver; and in 1982 he was second at both 100m and 200m with three relay golds. He also won seven Pan-American gold medals, 200m 1979, 100m 1983, both freestyle relays in 1979 and all three relays (as well as the 200m bronze) in 1983. First NCAA title for Auburn University 1979. Best 50m 22.78 (1982). Recently he has had health problems with a neuromuscular disorder.

John GAINSFORD (SAf)

RUGBY UNION

John Leslie Gainsford. b. 4 Aug 1938, Germiston.

At one time he held the Springbok record both for the most international appearances (33) and the most tries scored (8). Both records were later equalled by Jan Engelbrecht and subsequently beaten but Gainsford remains South Africa's most capped centre. His international career lasted from 1960 to 1967 and he toured the British Isles and France in his first international season. He played for Western Province and after working in insurance he moved to the wine trade.

Gary GAIT (Can)

LACROSSE

Gary Gait. b. 5 Apr 1967 Victoria, British Columbia.

Considered by some lacrosse experts to be the greatest player in the modern history of the game. A midfielder, he joined with his twin brother, Paul, to lead Syracuse University to two NCAA Championships and was first-team All-American as a sophomore, junior and senior as well as the leading scorer in Syracuse lacrosse history. He set NCAA tournament records for total goals, goals in a game, and goals in one tournament. He grew up playing box lacrosse. At Claremont High in British Columbia he was also All-Province in basketball and rugby and captained the basketball team.

Paul GAIT (Can)

LACROSSE

Paul Gait. b. 5 Apr 1967 Victoria, British Columbia.

Paul Gait grew up playing basketball, rugby, soccer and box lacrosse in his native British Columbia. He and his twin brother, Gary, earned scholarships to Syracuse University where they became the greatest brother tandem in the history of lacrosse. A midfielder, he helped lead Syracuse to two NCAA championships, was named the MVP of the NCAA finals in 1989, and was an All-American in both his junior and senior years.

Kaosai GALAXY (Tha)

BOXING

Kaosai Galaxy. b. 15 May 1959 Petchaboon.

Kaosai Galaxy won the WBA bantamweight title on 2 Nov 1984 and retained that title with 19 successful defences to December 1991 before retiring undefeated. On 9 May 1988 his twin **Kaokor** won the WBA bantamweight title, losing it, regaining and losing again, all in 1989, for a unique family world title feat.

Jean GALIA (Fra)

RUGBY LEAGUE

Jean Galia. b. 20 Mar 1905 Ille-sur-Tet, d. 18 Jan 1949 Toulouse.

As a lock forward he won 20 rugby union international caps between 1927 and 1931 before becoming the prime mover in the introduction of the League game into France in 1933. He made five international appearances at rugby league and was trainer, selector and captain of the first French team to visit England in March 1934. His name was given to the Galia Club de Perpignan.

Hughie GALLACHER (UK)

FOOTBALL

Hugh Kilpatrick Gallacher. b. 2 February 1903 Bellshill, Lanarkshire, d. 11 June 1957 Low Fell, Gateshead, Co. Durham.

The greatest centre-forward of his era and possibly the greatest Scottish player of all-time in that position. Starting his professional career with Airdrieonians in 1921, he moved to Newcastle in 1925 and then played for Chelsea (1930-4), Derby County (1934-6), Notts County (1936-8), Grimsby Town (1938) and Gateshead (1938-9). During his 21 seasons in League football he scored 387 goals in 543 matches for seven different clubs. For Scotland he scored 22 times in 20 matches, including a Scottish record of 5 goals against Northern Ireland in 1929. One of his finest international performances came at Wembley in 1928 when, although he failed to score, he was in the Scottish line-up whose 5-1 defeat of England earned them immortality as the 'Wembley Wizards'.
Although short in stature (1.65m *5'5"* tall) he scored many of his goals with his head. A mercurial player with superb ball control, he won a Scottish Cup winners medal with Airdrie in 1924 and he was with Newcastle when they won the Football League in 1927. From a humble background, he found it difficult to cope with the fame and money which his football talents brought him. His problems with alcohol increased over the years and the day before he was due to appear in court for ill-treating his daughter he threw himself in front of an express train.

Joe GANS (USA)

BOXING

né Joseph Gant. b. 25 Nov 1874 Baltimore, Maryland, d. 10 Aug 1910 Baltimore.

Gans was a black fighter who suffered because of the racial discrimination of the era. It prevented him from fighting in certain places, meeting certain opponents and often he was asked to fight 'to orders'. He first fought for the world lightweight title in 1900 against Frank Erne. For inexplicable reasons he asked the referee to stop the fight in the 12th. But in May 1902 he again challenged Erne for the title and knocked him out in 1:40 of the first. Gans held the lightweight title until 1908 when he was stopped by Battling Nelson in the 17th. In 1904 he made an abortive attempt to win the welterweight crown. He retired in 1909 and succumbed to tuberculosis one year later.
Career record: W - 120 (55), L - 8, D -10.

GAO MIN (China)

DIVING

Gao Min. b. 7 Sep 1970 Zihong, Sichuan Province.

Started diving training at the age of nine, changing from highboard diving to 3m springboard with coach Xu Yiming in 1985. From the 1986 World Championships she has been undefeated in major competition, winning world titles in 1986 and 1991 (at both 1m and 3m) and Olympics in 1988 and 1992. In 1988 she had become the first female diver to score over 600 points in a springboard competition, and took the Olympic title with 580.23 to the runner-up's 534.33. In 1992 she had an even more decisive victory with 572.400 to 514.140 for the silver medallist.

Nona GAPRINDASHVILI (USSR/Geo)

CHESS

Nona Terentyevna Gaprindashvili. b. 3 May 1941 Zugdidi, Georgia.

Women's world chess champion from 1962 until her defeat by Maya Chiburdanidze in 1978 after four successful defences. She was USSR women's champion 1964, 1973-4, 1981 (joint) and 1983. She reached international master status in 1962, women's grandmaster in 1976 and international grandmaster in 1980.

Anders GÄRDERUD (Swe)

ATHLETICS

Anders Gärderud. b. 28 Aug 1946 Stockholm.

Gärderud ran four world records at 3000m steeplechase, from 8:20.7 in 1972 to 8:08.02 to win the 1976 Olympic title. The latter was his first major title since he won the 1964 European Junior Games 1500m steeplechase. Despite immense talent, and fast flat times as well as steeplechase records, he had gone out in the heats of the Olympics in 1968 and 1972 and the Europeans in 1966. In European finals he was only tenth in 1971 but was second in 1974.

He was a coach to the Swedish team after his retirement and from 1993 took charge of the national women's team.

Best times: 800m 1:47.2 (1968), 1500m 3:37.73 (1974), 1M 3:54.45 (1975), 3000m 7:47.8 (1972), 5000m 13:17.59 (1976), 10,000m 28:59.2 (1973).

Wayne GARDNER (Aus)

MOTOR CYCLING

Wayne Gardner. b. 11 Oct 1959 Wollongong, New South Wales.

A brash, even daredevil rider, he became world 500cc champion in 1987, the first Australian to win this title. Riding for Honda, his brilliant, confident season that year thrust him into prominence. He was runner-up in 1986 and 1988. He achieved the first of four wins in the Suzuka 8 hours in 1982 and was British Formula I champion in 1983. From his Grand Prix début in 1983 and his first success in 1986 to his retirement at the end of the 1992 season, he won 17 races at 500cc.

Tamara GARKUSHINA (USSR)

CYCLING

Tamara Garkushina. b. 1 Feb 1946 Lipetsk region.

From 1970 to 1974 she was unchallenged at the women's pursuit, winning five consecutive world championships on the track, having also won in 1967. In 1969 she finished second in the world to her fellow countrywoman Obodovskaya, but did not compete in 1968. Though she occasionally rode on the roads she never placed in the world championships in that event. In 1964 she improved the world record for 3km standing start from 4:01.7 to 3:52.5 on the Olympic velodrome in Montreal.

Don GARLITS (USA)

MOTOR RACING

Donald Glenn Garlits. b. 14 Jan 1932 Florida.

'Big Daddy' set a series of barrier-breaking records for drag racing. He was the first US drag racer to exceed 170 and 180 mph and set top fuel records by passing 190 mph for the first time in 1963, 200 mph *321.8 km/h* in 1964, 240 mph in 1973, 250 mph in 1975 and 270 mph in 1986; all speeds for terminal velocity at the end of a quarter-mile *402.2m* strip. From 1975 to 1992 he won a record 35 Top Fuel races and was NHRA champion at Top Fuel in 1975 and 1985-6. Credited with developing the rear-engined dragster, he became president of the American Hot Rod Association.

Joel GARNER (Bar)

CRICKET

Joel Garner. b. 16 Dec 1952 Christchurch.

'Big Bird' was one of the greatest of bowlers, not the fastest of the powerful West Indian line-ups of his generation, but from his height of 2.03m *6'8"* able to generate steep bounce off the pitch. He made his début in Tests just a year after starting his first-class career for Barbados, and took 25 wickets in a series against Pakistan. His peak success came in 1984 when he took 31 wickets at 16.87 against Australia and 29 wickets at 18.62 against England, both in 5-Test series. He reaped great success in England for Somerset 1977-86, playing a major rôle in their one-day successes in the Gillette Cup 1979 and NatWest Trophy 1983, and his greatest one-day triumph was a spell of 5-4 in 11 balls to seal the West Indian victory in the 1979 World Cup final. Awarded the MBE.

58 Tests 1977-87: 672 runs at 12.44; HS 60; 259 wickets at 20.97; BB 6-56; 42 catches.

98 One-day Ints: 239 runs at 9.19, HS 37, 146 wickets at 18.84, BB 5-31; 30 catches.

First-class 1976-88: 2964 runs at 16.74; 1 100 HS 104; 881 wickets at 18.53; BB 8-31; 129 catches.

Dick GARRARD (Aus)

WRESTLING

Richard Edward Garrard. b. 21 Jan 1909.

Garrard had one of the longest careers of any wrestler ever and he had to overcome adversity to do so. He began wrestling quite late, in 1929 at age 20, and qualified for the 1936 Olympics where he lost two matches and was eliminated. On his way home he was nearly killed in an automobile accident in Colorado. A doctor at the Denver hospital where he was taken told him, "You'll never wrestle again," but only eight months later, Garrard was defending his Australian title.

From 1931 until his retirement in 1956 he never lost a match in Australia, posting a lifetime mark of 516 wins and 9 losses. At the Empire and Commonwealth Games he won the gold medal three times, 1934, 1938 and 1950, and lost only on a split points decision in 1954. He won a silver medal at welterweight in the 1948 Olympics, a gold at the 1939 Pan-Pacific Games and every Victoria State title from 1930 to 1956. Garrard competed in the 1954 World Championships and was selected for the Australian team for the 1956 Melbourne Olympics, but, at 47 years old, did not compete due to injury and retired. He was then president of the Australian Wrestling Union and had not been beaten in a match in Australia for 25 years. Awarded the OBE in 1977.

GARRINCHA (Bra)

FOOTBALL

Manoel Francisco dos Santos. b. 28 Oct 1936 Pau Grande, d. Jan 1983.

A brilliantly talented right-winger whose remarkable individual skills compensated for his rejection of a disciplined style of team play. Starting as an inside-right with his local club, Pau Grande, he was signed by Botafogo in 1953 and won the first of his 50 caps two years later. He made a great contribution to Brazil's victory in the 1958 World Cup and in 1962, although sent off in the semi-final, he was again in the winning World Cup team.

After a pay dispute with Botafogo he moved to Corinthians and played in the World Cup for a third time in 1966, but following a car accident in 1965 and an obvious lack of fitness he was a shadow of his former self. As his decline continued he ended his career with a succession of lesser clubs in France and Italy before finally returning to Olaria in Brazil. His form at the end of his career was an embarrassment to those who remembered him as one of the greatest right-wingers in football. He died of alcoholic poisoning at the age of fifty.

Edward GARRISON (USA)

HORSE RACING

Edward Henry 'Snapper' Garrison. b. 9 Feb 1868 New Haven, Connecticut, d. 28 Oct 1930 Brooklyn, New York.

The highest paid US jockey of the 1880s and 1890s. Having won over $2 million in nearly 700 races, he retired in 1897 to become a trainer and racing official. He had worked as a blacksmith and learnt his skills as a jockey at the stable of William C Daly. He considered *Tammany* to have been the greatest horse that he had ridden. His hallmark was his spectacular finishing burst, since known as a Garrison finish.

Steve GARVEY (USA)

BASEBALL

Steven Patrick Garvey. b. 22 Dec 1948 Tampa, Florida.

Garvey began his career as a third baseman with the Los Angeles Dodgers, but he moved to first base in 1973 after four unspectacular seasons and could not be ousted from that position. He was the top National League first baseman of the 1970s and started the All-Star game at that position for seven straight years. He eventually played in a National League record 1207 consecutive games. He was decidedly unspectacular, but he was known for his steadiness, his durability, and his squeaky clean image. He spent the last five years of his career with the San Diego Padres and retired with four Gold Gloves and a lifetime .996 fielding average. His Mr Clean image was tarnished late in his

career by revelations that he had fathered several children out of wedlock, shortly after the highly publicised break-up of his marriage.
Career 1969-87: Avg. .294, HR 272; RBI 1308. Best seasons: 1978: .316, 202 hits, 1979: .315, 204 hits.

Paul GASCOIGNE (UK)

FOOTBALL
Paul John Gascoigne. b. 27 May 1967 Dunston, Gateshead.

The most talked-about footballer at the start of the 1990s, as a midfield player he was the inspiration of the England team at the 1990 World Cup, at which he was voted Best Young Player in the Tournament. Later he was voted BBC Sports Personality of the Year.
He joined Newcastle United as an apprentice in 1982 and captained their team to victory in the FA Youth Cup in 1985, in which year he made his Football League début. He played for England Under-21s in 1987 and signed for Tottenham Hotspur for a British record fee of £2 million in July 1988, making his England début in September that year, when he was also voted PFA Young Footballer of the Year. The Italian league club Lazio offered £8 million for him, but that fee was eventually cut to £5.5 million when Gascoigne finally signed in June 1992. His career was severely threatened by his own horrendous tackle in the 1991 Cup Final as a result of which he was out of action for more than a year. Despite being yet to regain full fitness he made a triumphant return to the England side in the final months of 1992. By May 1993 he had scored 5 goals in 25 internationals for England. Headstrong and controversial, he undoubtedly has a brilliant talent with a great sense of balance and position, although 'Gazza' mania in the media threatened to get out of hand at one stage.

Reg GASNIER (Aus)

RUGBY LEAGUE
Reginald William Gasnier. b. 12 May 1939 Sydney.

After only a few weeks in first grade rugby in Sydney he made his Test début against New Zealand and before the season was over he was selected for the 1959 tour of Britain and France. As a 20-year-old he made a spectacular début against Great Britain, scoring three tries in the first Test, and he returned home having quickly established the reputation of being one of the great centres of all-time. He made two further tours to Europe, but on his third visit in 1967, when he captained the Australian team, a broken leg in the first Test and a further breakdown in France ended his playing career. He played in 36 Tests and two World Cup matches and also toured New Zealand twice. Gasnier excelled in many sports at school before opting for rugby league for St George, for whom he played 1958-67

Mike GATTING (UK)

CRICKET
Michael William Gatting. b. 6 Jun 1957 Kingsbury, London.

Gatting made his Test début at 20 in 1977, but took a long time to make his mark. Finally, after consistently averaging over 50 for year after year in county cricket with pugnacious and exciting batting, he broke through on the tour to India in 1984/5, making his maiden century in his 31st Test and 54th innings, and scoring 207 three Tests later. He went on to considerable batting success until 1987, although his form declined in Tests thereafter. He captained England 23 times including success in the Ashes series against Australia in 1986/7, but after losing the captaincy after a series of incidents, he led a 'rebel' tour to South Africa in 1989/90, which meant a three-year Test ban. He returned to Tests in 1992/3.
He has captained Middlesex for over ten years from 1983, playing a major rôle in their Championship successes of 1985 and 1990 and four one-day trophies. He has exceeded 1000 runs in 15 seasons, including once overseas, and over 2000 three times, with a peak of 2257 at 68.39 in 1984. His brother Steve played League football as a defender for Arsenal,

Brighton and Charlton Athletic from 1978.
72 Tests 1977-93: 4136 runs at 37.26, 9 100s HS 207; 4 wickets, at 79.25, BB 1-14; 54 catches.
92 One-day Ints: 2095 runs at 38.36, 8 100s HS 115; 10 wickets at 33.60, BB 3-32; 22 catches.*
First-class 1975-93: 28,935 runs at 50.06, 73 100s HS 258; 154 wickets at 29.12, BB 5-34; 379 catches.

Hartwig GAUDER (GDR/Ger)

WALKING

Hartwig Gauder. b. 10 Nov 1954 Vaihingen, Württemberg.

An outstanding walker for two decades, his feat of winning European junior (10km 1973), European (50km 1986), Olympic (50km 1980) and World (50km 1987) titles is matched only by Daley Thompson and Khristo Markov. At 50 kilometres walk he also won bronze medals at the 1988 Olympics (when he recorded his best ever time of 3 hrs 39 mins 45 secs), 1990 Europeans and 1991 Worlds, and was 4th in the 1982 Europeans and 6th at the 1992 Olympics. At the World Cup he won in 1985 and was second in 1981 and 1987. He has concentrated on the 50 kilometres, but at 20km he had a best time of 1:20:51 in 1987 and was 7th in the 1978 Europeans, and he set a world indoor 1 hour best with 14,906m in 1986. He won GDR titles at 20km 1975-6, 1985-6; 50km 1979, 1982, 1986; and the German 50km in 1993.
He trained as an architect and competed for TSV Erfurt; coached by **Siegfried Herrmann** (b. 7 Nov 1932), the stylish runner who set a world record for 3000m at 7:46.0 in 1965. Gauder's family moved from West Germany when he was five.

Lucien GAUDIN (Fra)

FENCING

Lucien Gaudin. b. 27 Sep 1886 Arras, Pas-de-Calais, d. 23 Sep 1934.

A double Olympic champion in 1928 and probably the greatest technical fencer of the 20th century. He won an Olympic individual gold medal in the épée and foil in 1928, at the age of 42, and in the team event with both weapons in 1924. He also won a silver medal in the foil team event in 1920 and 1928. Rather surprisingly, he was only once a world champion (in a non-Olympic year) when he took the épée title at the first Championships in 1921. European champion at the épée in 1922. From 1906 he won nine successive French titles at the foil.

Charly GAUL (Lux)

CYCLING

Charly Gaul. b. 18 Dec 1932 Ash.

The greatest cyclist ever produced by Luxembourg and one of the greatest climbers produced by any nation, He was also renowned for riding very well in bad weather conditions. Known as 'The Angel of the Mountains' for his skill as a *grimpeur*, he earned the nickname in the 1955 Tour de France when, in a mountain stage crossing the cols of Aravis, Telegraphe, and Galibier, he won by 14 minutes. He was King of the Mountains in that race in 1955 and 1956, and won the Tour in 1958. He was third in the 1954 world pro road race championship and won the Giro d'Italia in 1956 and 1959, with the Giro King of the Mountains title also in 1959.

Sunil GAVASKAR (India)

CRICKET

Sunil Manohar Gavaskar. b. 10 Jul 1949 Bombay.

A superstar of Indian sport, a great batsman who passed Geoffrey Boycott's record 8114 runs made in Test cricket in 1983, and took his total past 10,000 by his retirement. A very small man, he was possessed of an immaculate technique and was able to concentrate for long innings but also to adapt his style to the need to score fast when required.
He scored prodigiously in schools cricket before making his début for Bombay at the age of 17. He scored 774 runs (av. 154.80) in just four matches on his Test début against the West Indies in 1971, and continued to display his great talent

throughout his career, which ended fittingly with his first century at Lord's in the bicentenary Test in August 1987. He took over the Indian captaincy in 1978 and scored 732 runs at 91.50, including four centuries, in six Tests against the West Indies in his first series in charge. He was then replaced by Venkataraghavan on the tour to England in 1979, but continued to thrive, with his 221 at The Oval rated as one of the greatest of Test innings. He led India again from the following winter until 1983 and again in 1984-5, but tended to adopt an overly negative approach. He was also a fine slip fielder and an occasional medium pace bowler.
His uncle Madhav Mantri played four Tests for India 1951-5, and his brother-in-law was Gundappa Viswanath (qv).
125 Tests 1971-87: 10,122 runs at 51.12, 34 100s HS 236; 108 catches.*
108 One-day Ints: 3092 runs at 35.13, 1 100 HS 103; 1 wicket; 22 catches.*
First-class 1966-87: 25,834 runs at 51.46, 81 100s HS 340; 22 wickets at 56.36, BB 3-43; 293 catches.

Don GAY (USA)

RODEO

Don Gay. b. 18 Sep 1953 Dallas, Texas.

Now considered the greatest bull rider ever among rodeo cowboys. From 1974 to 1981 he was the leading money winner at this event on the PRCA circuit and he was world champion each year except in 1978 when he was upset by Butch Kirby. In 1974 he broke the money winning record for bulls which had been set by the legendary Jim Shoulders and had stood since 1954, but went on to further improve this record each year to 1981. Gay was considered very outspoken among cowboys and was popular with the fans and the media. He used that to his advantage and made many commercial appearances.

Kenneth GEE (UK)

RUGBY LEAGUE

Kenneth Gee. b. 23 Sep 1916 Wigan, Lancashire, d. 17 April 1989 Wigan.

An uncompromising prop forward of impressive physique. After signing for Wigan in 1933 he waited two seasons for a place in the first team but soon established himself as an indispensable member of the pack. He played 33 times for England, won 17 caps for Great Britain and toured Australasia in 1946 and 1950. In many of his international appearances he played alongside his club-mate Joe Egan, the Wigan hooker, and their combined strength and understanding of each other's play provided a formidable scrummage base. Unusually for a forward, Gee was also a talented goal kicker, his best season being in 1949/50 when he kicked 133 goals.

Anton GEESINK (Hol)

JUDO

Antonius J Geesink. b. 6 Apr 1934 Utrecht.

When judo was added to the Olympic programme in 1964 in Tokyo, the giant Dutchman, 1.98m and 121kg, provided a shocking upset for the Japanese by winning the Open title. He was, however, the favourite, for in 1961 he had become the first non-Japanese judo player to win a world title. He had been third in the first ever World Championships in 1956 and also won a record number of European titles, winning the open category in 1953-4, 1957-60, 1962-4 and 1967 and the over 93kg in 1962-4. In 1967 he retired to become a professional instructor.

Lou GEHRIG (USA)

BASEBALL

Henry Louis Gehrig. b. 19 Jun 1903 New York, d. 2 Jun 1941 Riverside, New York.

Universally acknowledged as the greatest first baseman ever and a legendary name in the pantheon of baseball heroes. The name conjures images of the stoic, durable 'Iron Horse', but it also evokes memories of a man whose steel-like body betrayed him, who died young from a disease now named after him.
There was only a brief 'Era of Gehrig' but he passed the torch from Babe Ruth to Joe DiMaggio as the leader of the Yankee dynasty. He played in 2130 consecutive

games, a major league record not approached until the recent feats of Cal Ripken, who still has a few years to go to equal that record. The streak began in 1925, when regular Yankee first baseman Wally Pipp sat out a game with a headache. It ended on 2 May 1939, when Gehrig took himself out of the line-up. In between, he won a Triple Crown (1934: .363, 49 HR, 165 RBI), led the American League in runs batted in five times, including a still-unequalled American League record of 184 in 1931; hit for the cycle twice, hit four home runs in one game, and had over 100 RBI and scored 100 runs all 13 full seasons of his career.

His withdrawal in 1939 was because of his failing strength and coordination. He never played again, although as captain he took out the line-up card every day. Later that season, he was diagnosed with a rare, progressive neuromuscular disease, amyotrophic lateral sclerosis, known forever after as Lou Gehrig's Disease. On 4 Jul 1939, the Yankees honoured him at Yankee Stadium. Gehrig's speech, again the stuff of legends, saw him proclaim 'Today I consider myself the luckiest man on the face of the earth.' The waiting period for the Hall of Fame was waived for him and he was admitted late in 1939. He died only two years later.

Career 1923-39: 2721 hits Avg. .340, HR 493; RBI 1990.

Charlie GEHRINGER (USA)

BASEBALL

Charles Leonard Gehringer. b. 11 May 1903 Fowlerville, Michigan, d. 21 January 1993 Detroit.

Gehringer was an outstanding fielder and excellent hitter for the Detroit Tigers, and had good power for a second baseman. He led the league in fielding percentage for his position nine times. He retired in 1942, became general manager of the Tigers in 1951 and was their vice-president 1953-9. In 1969, he was named the game's greatest living second baseman by a special committee of baseball writers.

Career 1924-42: 2839 hits Avg. .320, HR 184; RBI 1426. Best seasons: 1937: .371, 209 hits. 1929: .339, 215 hits. 1934: .356, 214 hits, 134 Runs.

Francisco GENTO (Spa)

FOOTBALL

Francisco Gento López. b. 21 Oct 1933 Guarnizo, Santander.

A speedy, vivacious and consistent outside-left. After playing for Rayo Cantabria and Real Santander, he signed for Real Madrid in 1953 and stayed with them for the remainder of his career, playing for them in six European Cup winning teams (1956-60, 1966) and twice on the losing side in the final (1962, 1964). When di Stéfano left the club in 1964, Gento took over as captain and he later captained Spain for whom he won 43 caps, including matches in the 1962 and 1966 World Cup. He finally retired in 1971, having played in 761 matches scoring 253 goals for Real Madrid, helping them to win 12 Spanish League titles, but he remained with the club as trainer of their junior teams.

Bernie GEOFFRION (Can)

ICE HOCKEY

Bernard Geoffrion. b. 16 Feb 1931 Montreal, Québec.

'Boom-Boom' Geoffrion was so nicknamed because of his renowned shot - the sound was that of the stick hitting the puck and the puck hitting the endboards. He played with the Montreal Canadiens in the 1950s when the team that many consider the greatest ever won six Stanley Cups, and finished his career with the New York Rangers from 1966. He was a top right-winger and productive scorer, but he was better known for his wild sense of humour. His best season was 1960/1 when, with 50 goals and 95 points, he became the second man - after Maurice Richard - to score 50 goals in one season. After his playing days ended, Geoffrion coached the Rangers and Atlanta Flames for several years.

NHL career 1950-68 - 883 games, 393 goals, 822 points. Playoffs: 132 games, 58 goals, 118 pts. Awards: Hart Trophy 1961, Ross Trophy 1955, 1961; Calder Trophy 1952.

Peter GEORGE (USA)

WEIGHTLIFTING

Peter Tony George. b. 29 Jun 1929 Akron, Ohio.

Between 1947 and 1956 George ran up an impressive record in major competition. At the Olympics he was middleweight (75kg) champion in 1952 and silver medallist in 1948 and 1956. He won five World titles (67.5kg 1947 and 1953, 75kg 1951, 1954-5) and was runner-up at 75kg in 1949 and 1950. He also won two Pan-American Games gold medals and was a five-time national champion. His three world records were all at 75kg jerk (to 164.5kg in 1950). He attended Kent State University and then went to dental school at Ohio State, before becoming an orthodontist in Hawaii; he is a past president of the Hawaiian Dental Association.

Walter GEORGE (UK)

ATHLETICS

Walter Goodall George. b. 9 Sep 1858 Calne, Wiltshire, d. 4 Jun 1943 Mitcham, Surrey.

As an amateur George set numerous world records at distances from 1000y, 2:18.0 (1881) to 18,555m in 1 hour (1884), with other bests including 3/4 mile 3:08 3/4 (1882); 1 mile 4:18.4; 2 miles 9:17.4; 3 miles 14:39; 6 miles 30:21.2; 10,000m 31:40 and 10 miles 51:20 (all in 1884). He uniquely won AAA titles at four events, 880y, 1M, 4M and 10M in both 1882 and 1884, the first three events on the same day, and he also won the 1 and 4 miles in 1880 and the National cross-country in 1882 and 1884.

George turned professional in 1885 for his great series of races against William Cummings, highlighted by his win at 1 mile in 1886 in 4:12.8, a time that was not bettered by an amateur until 1915, although George himself was reported to have run 4:10.2 in a time trial in 1885. He also ran several series of match races against Lawrence Myers.

His brother Alfred, ten years his junior, won one AAA and three AAU titles.

Aladár GEREVICH (Hun)

FENCING

Aladár Gerevich. b. 16 Mar 1910 Jászberény, d. 15 May 1991 Budapest.

Winner of ten Olympic medals (9 sabre, 1 foil) over a 28 year period. As a member of the winning sabre team at every Olympic Games from 1932 to 1960, he is the only man in history, at any sport, to win gold medals at six successive Games. Individually, he won a gold in 1948, when he did not lose a single bout, a silver in 1952 and a bronze in 1936. He was also a member of the foil team which placed third in 1952. He was aged 50yr 178d when he won his final sabre team title in 1960, the oldest fencing gold medallist in Olympic history. His record of winning three individual sabre titles at the World Championships (1935, 1951, 1955) has been equalled but not surpassed and he is rated as the greatest sabreur in history. He was fencing coach at the Vasa sports club in Budapest into his 70s.

Other members of his family also had distinguished records in Olympic fencing. His son **Pál** (b. 10 Aug 1948) won bronze medals in the sabre team event (1972, 1980) and was world champion in1977; his wife **Erna Bogen** (b. 31 Dec 1906) won a bronze in the foil in 1932 and his father-in-law **Albert Bogen** (1882-1961) won a silver medal in 1912 for Austria as a member of the sabre team. In all, this remarkable family won a total of 14 Olympic medals (7 gold, 2 silver, 5 bronze).

GERMANO (Por)

FOOTBALL

Germano de Figuereido. b. 18 Jan 1933 Lisbon.

After a late start, his international career was ended by injury but during the brief period he was at his peak there was no finer centre-half in Europe. In 1960, when he was aged 27, second division Atlético Club de Portugal accepted a token transfer fee from Benfica and Germano helped them to an unexpected victory over Barcelona in the 1961 European Cup final.

He was in the team which retained the trophy the following year but cartilage troubles caused him to miss the World Club Championships in 1961 and 1962 and the European Cup campaign in 1962/3. He played in his third European Cup final in 1965 when Benfica lost to Internazionale. During his injury-interrupted career he won 23 caps for Portugal.

Bernhard GERMESHAUSEN (GDR)

BOBSLEIGH

Bernhard Germeshausen. b. 28 Aug 1951 Heiligemstadt.

Winner of three Olympic gold medals at bobsleigh, a record shared with his partner, Meinhard Nehmer. Together they won the two-man bob in 1976 and were both members of the winning four-man crew in 1976 and 1980.

Germeshausen also won an Olympic silver in the 1980 two-man and was world champion at two-man in 1981 with Hans-Jürgen Gerhardt, and at four-man in 1977 and 1981. In European Championships at four-man he won two gold and a silver, and at two-man a gold and three silvers. Like many of the GDR bobsledders he was formerly an athlete, scoring 7534 points for the decathlon in 1972, and was ideally built at 1.90m tall and 96 kg in weight.

GÉRSON (Bra)

FOOTBALL

Gérson de Oliveira Nunes. b. 11 Jan 1941 Niterói.

A brilliant midfield tactician who masterminded Brazil's 1970 World Cup victory. While with Flamengo he was a member of Brazil's 1960 Olympic team but he moved to Botafogo in 1963 where he provided the inspiration which took them to the league title in 1967 and 1968. The following year, Botafogo, wrongly believing Gérson to be past his best, agreed to his transfer to São Paulo where he led an undistinguished team to second place in the Brazilian League in 1971. Early in 1972 a broken ankle in a charity match effectively ended his career during which he was capped 83 times by Brazil.

Ute GEWENIGER (GDR)

SWIMMING

Ute Geweniger. b. 24 Feb 1964 Karl-Marx-Stadt.

An outstanding breaststroke swimmer, who won the 1980 Olympic and 1982 World gold medals at 100m and medley relay, and who set six world records at 100m from 1:10.20 in 1980 to 1:08.51 in 1983. She also swam the 200m individual medley in 2:11.73 in 1981, and this lasted as the world record until 1992.

At the 1982 Worlds she also took silver medals at 200m breaststroke and individual medley. She won nine European golds: both breaststroke titles, the 200m medley and medley relay in both 1981 and 1983, with the 100m butterfly in 1981. She also won a silver at 400m medley in 1981, when her five medals were a Championship record.

Other best times: 200m breaststroke 2:29.52 (1984), 100m butterfly 60.40 (1981), 400m IM 4:45.43 (1981).

Nicknamed 'Bones' due to her tall, slim and loose-limbed build.

Lance GIBBS (Guy)

CRICKET

Lancelot Richard Gibbs. b. 29 Sep 1934 Georgetown, then British Guiana.

A cousin of Clive Lloyd, Gibbs was an outstanding off-break bowler who passed Fred Trueman's Test record number of wickets in his last Test match. He headed the Test averages in his first series, with 17 wickets at 23.05 against Pakistan in 1958, and his best hauls were 26 wickets against England in 1963 and Australia in 1973.

He played in England for Warwickshire 1967-73 and had his best year in 1971 with 131 wickets at 18.89. He was a great bowler on hard wickets, where his considerable powers of spin were needed. He was also a fine gully fielder, though no batsman.

79 Tests 1958-76: 488 runs at 6.97, HS 25; 309 wickets at 40.63, BB 8-38; 52 catches.

3 One-day Ints: 2 wickets at 29.50, BB 1-12.

First-class 1954-76: 1729 runs at 8.55, HS

43; 1024 wickets at 27.22, BB 8-37; 203 catches.

Althea GIBSON (USA)

TENNIS

Althea Gibson. b. 25 Aug 1927 Silver, South Carolina. Later Darben.

The first black player to achieve prominence in the game. As the daughter of a South Carolina sharecropper who moved his family to New York in 1930, her early career was inhibited by racial restrictions. It was not until 1950 that she became the first black competitor at the US National Championships, when she came close to beating the redoubtable Louise Brough. She was nearly 30 years old when she won her first Wimbledon singles in 1957 and she retained the title the following year. She also won the US singles in 1957-8 and the French title in 1956. In the doubles she won Wimbledon three times, 1956-8, the French title in 1956 and the Australian in 1957. Her only major success in the mixed doubles was at the 1957 US Championships.

She only played twice in the Wightman Cup, suffering a surprise loss to 17-year-old Christine Truman in the 1958 singles. At the end of that season she turned professional and enjoyed some modest success as a singer and actress, and as a golfer she won one LPGA tournament. In 1965 she married William Darben and from 1975 to 1977 served as athletic commissioner for the State of New Jersey.

Bob GIBSON (USA)

BASEBALL

Robert Gibson. b. 9 Nov 1935 Omaha, Nebraska.

Gibson was one of the great pitchers of the 1960s and 1970s, but should also be remembered as one of the great all-round athletes to have played major league baseball. He attended Creighton University on a basketball scholarship and briefly played with the Harlem Globetrotters. In the major leagues he played his entire 17 years with the St Louis Cardinals. He was an outstanding fielder (winning nine consecutive Gold Gloves) and batter, with 24 career home runs. In 1970 he posted a .303 batting average. But it was as a pitcher that he made his mark.

Big, powerful, fast, and unafraid to throw inside, he terrified opposing batters. His 1968 season, in which he posted a 1.12 ERA, is one of the greatest in modern history by a pitcher, and would have been greater had the Cardinals given him better run support (he won 22-9 and had 268 strikeouts). He bettered the latter total in 1970 with 274 and struck out 200 batters in a season nine times. He led the National League in shutouts four times. He was also at his best in the big games, winning the clinching victory in both the 1964 and 1967 World Series. In the 1968 World Series, he struck out 35 Detroit Tigers, albeit in a losing cause, and this included a record 17 in one game. From 1963 to 1972 he averaged almost 19 wins per season.

Career pitching 1959-75: ERA 2.91; W-L 251-174,, SO 3117; Best seasons: 1968: 22-9, 1.12 ERA, 268 SO. 1970: 23-7, 3.12 ERA, 274 SO.

Josh GIBSON (USA)

BASEBALL

Joshua Gibson. b. 21 Dec 1912 Buena Vista, Georgia, d. 20 Jan 1947 Pittsburgh, Pennsylvania.

The greatest player never to play in the major leagues and possibly the greatest catcher ever. He was a power hitter bar none and his lifetime average of .384 is the best ever for the Negro Leagues. He was known for his ability to hit a baseball prodigious distances. He blasted one in Monessen, Pennsylvania that was measured at 175m *575 feet*, and it has been claimed that he is the only man to hit a fair ball out of Yankee Stadium.

In his 13-year career, first with the Homestead Grays and then the Pittsburgh Crawfords, Gibson led the Negro League nine times in home runs and four years in batting average. He was a solid catcher, who improved during his career, but his hitting overshadowed his defensive abilities. He died from a stroke when aged only 35.

Mike GIBSON (UK)

RUGBY UNION

Cameron Michael Henderson Gibson. b. 3 Dec 1942 Belfast.

Universally recognised as one of the greatest centres of all-time. Beginning his career with Campbell College, he later played for Trinity College, Dublin, Cambridge University, North of Ireland FC and the Barbarians. He won 69 caps for Ireland (1964-79) establishing what was then the record as the world's most capped player. Although winning 25 caps as a fly-half and four on the wing he will remembered as the complete centre.
He and Willie John McBride are the only players to go on five British Lions tours. Gibson played in all four Tests for the Lions in New Zealand in 1966 and 1971 and South Africa in 1968, but did not play in the Tests against South Africa in 1974 or New Zealand in 1977. A Belfast solicitor by profession, he was awarded the MBE for his services to the game.

George GIFFEN (Aus)

CRICKET

George Giffen. b. 27 Mar 1859 Adelaide, d. 29 Nov 1927 Adelaide.

A great all-rounder, who was often referred to as the 'WG Grace of Australia'. His 475 runs and 34 wickets (av. 24.11) in the 5 Tests against England in 1884/5 remains an unmatched all-round performance in a Test series, and was the first time that any bowler had taken 30 or more wickets. He became the first player to achieve the double of 1000 runs and 100 wickets in Tests and the first Australian to exceed 10,000 runs and 1000 wickets in first-class cricket. On three of his five tours to England he did the double, with a best of 1424 runs and 154 wickets in 1886. Earlier that year he became the first Australian to take 17 wickets in a first-class match, and in 1891 had the unique achievement of a double century and 16 wickets in a match: 271, 9-96 and 7-70 for South Australia v Victoria at Adelaide. He was a determined and aggressive right-handed batsman and slow-medium bowler, but, particularly for the often weak South Australian teams for whom he played throughout his career, he was inclined to over-bowl himself. He captained Australia four times in 1894/5.
31 Tests 1881-96: 1238 runs at 23.35, 1 100 HS 161; 103 wickets at 27.09, BB 7-117; 24 catches.
First-class 1877-1904: 11,758 runs at 29.54, 18 100s HS 271; 1023 wickets at 21.29, BB 10-66; 195 catches.

Frank GIFFORD (USA)

AMERICAN FOOTBALL

Frank Newton Gifford. b. 16 Aug 1930 Santa Monica, California.

Gifford was one of football's 'Golden Boys'. He starred as a running back at Southern California, and in 1952 joined the New York Giants, with whom he played his entire NFL career. He played both offense and defense and in 1953 was named to the All-NFL Defensive Team. In 1954 Vince Lombardi became the Giants offensive coach and chose Gifford to be his halfback to run the power sweep. Over the next decade Gifford was one of the biggest stars in the NFL. In addition to being a top running back and pass receiver, he was good-looking, well-spoken, and earned numerous commercial endorsements. In the 1960 NFL Championship Game, he was blindsided by Philadelphia Eagles linebacker Chuck Bednarik, sustained a severe concussion and retired for a year, but returned in 1962-4. Gifford has become one of the very best television sportscasters, hosting both ABC's Monday Night Football and Wide World of Sports. In 1986, he married Kathie Lee Johnson (his third wife), a well-known television talk-show host and singer.
NFL career 1952-64: 5434 yards gained receiving av. 14.8, 43 touchdowns; 3609 yards gained rushing.

Josh GIFFORD (UK)

HORSE RACING

Joshua Thomas Gifford. b. 3 Aug 1941 Huntingdon.

Champion National Hunt jockey four

times: 1962/3, 1963/4, 1966/7 and 1967/8, with a top figure of 122 winners in 1966/7. Under NH rules between 1959 and 1970 he rode a total of 643 winners. He gained his trainer's licence in 1970 and trains at The Downs, Findon, Sussex, where he took over from Ryan Price, for whom he had been first jockey. He trained *Aldaniti* to win the 1981 Grand National.
He started riding on the flat from 1951, apprenticed to Sam Armstrong, and had his first winner 14 days before his 15th birthday. After 51 winners on the flat, increased weight pushed him to jumping from 1959. He married show-jumper Althea Roger-Smith. Awarded the MBE 1989. His younger brother Macer rode *Larbawn* to victory in the 1968 Whitbread Gold Cup.

Gillian GILKS (UK)

BADMINTON

Gillian M Gilks. née Perrin. b. 20 Jun 1950 Epsom, Surrey.

The most successful woman badminton player in Europe in the 1970s, she had special success at doubles with a record 10 European titles, four women's and six mixed at the biennial European Championships between 1972 and 1986. She was also European singles champion in 1974 and 1976, and took five European silver medals. At the All-England Championships she was singles champion in 1976 and 1978, took three women's doubles with different partners and five mixed doubles titles, three with Derek Talbot and two with Martin Dew. At the Commonwealth Games of 1974 she won the treble of women's singles and both doubles. Her most successful World Championships were the first, in 1977, when she won silver medals at singles, beaten by Lena Köppen, and at mixed doubles, partnering Derek Talbot; she added bronze medals in 1983 and 1987. She also won the mixed doubles with Talbot at the 1972 Olympics when badminton was a demonstration sport, and in all won 27 English national titles between 1968 and 1988, 9 singles, 7 women's doubles and 12 mixed doubles.
She had a long and distinguished career from winning the All-England under-15 singles at the age of 12 and her first senior international at 16, and made a record number of 111 international appearances for England, although that might have been even higher but for several brushes with the badminton authorities. Awarded the MBE in 1976 and elected Sportswoman of the Year by the British Sports Writers in 1974 and 1976.

GILMAR (Bra)

FOOTBALL

Gilmar Neves dos Santos. b. 22 Aug 1930.

Brazil's goalkeeper in their successful World Cup teams in 1958 and 1962. Starting his career as a boy with Jabaquara AC, he signed professional forms in 1950 but the following year moved to Corinthians where he stayed for 10 years before being transferred to Santos in 1961. By accepting a modest transfer fee, Corinthians indicated they thought his career was nearing its end but his years with Santos proved to be his best. He won six league medals (1962, 1964-5, 1967-9), South American Cup and World Club Championship medals in 1962 and 1963 and a second World Cup medal in 1962. After making his international début in the 1963 South American Championship he went on to win 100 caps (95 on a stricter definition), conceding 97 international goals and being on the losing side only 14 times.

Artis GILMORE (USA)

BASKETBALL

Artis Gilmore. b. 21 Sep 1949 Chipley, Florida.

Gilmore starred in college at Jacksonville University. In 1971 he opted for the ABA and played for five years with the Kentucky Colonels. In 1976 he moved to the NBA where he played for the Chicago Bulls and later the San Antonio Spurs. He was a huge 2.18m *7'2"*, 123 kg *270 lb* center who remains the NBA career leader in blocked shots and holds the NBA career average record for field goals at .599. With

1329 games played in his 18-year professional career, he ranks second behind only Kareem Abdul-Jabbar.
NBA/ABA career 24,941 points, av. 18.8; 16,330 rebounds, av. 12.3.

Felice GIMONDI (Italy)

CYCLING

Felice Gimondi. b. 29 Sep 1942 Sedrina.

At the time of his retirement, only Eddy Merckx and Fausto Coppi had won more international titles than Felice Gimondi did in his career. Gimondi won the Tour de l'Avenir in 1964 and then turned professional. In his first year he won the Tour de France, though he had been included in the race only as a last-minute substitute. Gimondi was a good climber, an excellent time trialist, and a proficient road sprinter. He was later overshadowed by Merckx, but in 1973 Gimondi defeated Merckx in the finishing sprint to win his only rainbow jersey as world professional road champion, having been 3rd in 1970 and 2nd in 1971. Retired in 1976 and is now an insurance agent and cycling manager.
Other major victories: Giro d'Italia 1967, 1969, 1976; Vuelta à España 1968, Tour of Lombardy 1966, 1968; Paris-Roubaix 1966, Paris-Brussels 1966, 1976; Grand Prix de Nations 1967-8, Milan-San Remo 1974.

Luciano GIOVANETTI (Italy)

SHOOTING

Luciano Giovanetti. b. 25 Sep 1945 Pistoia.

Olympic gold medallist in 1980 and 1984 and the only man to win two Olympic titles at trap shooting. His attempt to win three successive Olympic gold medals failed badly when he placed no higher than 18th at Seoul in 1988.

George GIPP (USA)

AMERICAN FOOTBALL

George Gipp. b. 18 Feb 1895 Laurium, Michigan, d. 14 Dec 1920 South Bend, Indiana.

Gipp is far more famous for his deathbed soliloquy than for his football career. But as a running back for the Notre Dame Fighting Irish from 1917-20, he set school records for yards gained rushing which lasted until the 1980s. He was also a superb baseball player, playing in the minor leagues in the summer between school seasons. Though a tremendous athlete, Gipp was famous for his gambling, pool playing and drinking habits. In his senior year he developed pneumonia and died in mid-season. His deathbed speech to coach Knute Rockne has become legendary. It is perhaps apocryphal, but Gipp supposedly told Rockne to exhort the Notre Dame team someday, 'when the odds are against them, when things look bleak, win one for the Gipper.' Rockne used the speech several times as a half-time motivational tool which never failed to bring a victory to the Irish. It was later immortalised in a movie in which future US President Ronald Reagan played Gipp.

Marc GIRARDELLI (Lux, ex-Aut)

ALPINE SKIING

Marc Girardelli. b. 18 Jul 1963 Lustenau, Austria.

He has been overall World Cup champion a record five times, 1985-6, 1989, 1991 and 1993; with second place in 1987 and third in 1984 and 1992. He made his World Cup début in 1979 and had 40 victories from 1983 to January 1993, including successes at each discipline. Despite several serious injuries he has been the finest and bravest ski racer of the past decade, with intense concentration. After a smashed left knee in 1983 he returned the following season to win five World Cup slaloms.
He was slalom world champion in 1991, also 2nd in 1985 and 1993, 3rd 1989, 4th 1987; and world champion at Alpine combination 1987 and 1989. After disputes with the Austrian federation he became a naturalised Luxembourg citizen, although he now lives in Switzerland. This citizenship change meant that he had to miss the 1984 Games and did not make his Olympic début until 1988. Then he was below par after smashing his elbow a

month earlier and was 9th in the downhill. Eventually he gained his first Olympic medals, silver at giant slalom and super G, in 1992.

Constante GIRARDENGO (Italy)

CYCLING

Constante Girardengo. b. 18 Mar 1893 Novi-Ligure, d. 9 Feb 1978.

The first *campionissimo* for Italian cycling aficionados. In addition to his major tour wins, the Giro d'Italia 1919 and 1923, and the Tour of Lombardy 1919, 1921-2, and one-day classics, he won the Milan-San Remo race seven times, 1918, 1921, 1923, 1925-6 and 1928, and was Italian road race champion from 1913-25. With a break for World War I, that was nine consecutive national championships, a record unmatched in any country for road riders. He competed almost exclusively in Italy but late in his career won several six-day races in Germany. He held the Italian 1 hour record from 1917 to 1926.

Alain GIRESSE (Fra)

FOOTBALL

Alain Giresse. b. 2 Aug 1952 Langoiran.

A gifted midfield player, who helped France to win the 1984 European Championships. He was part of the great French midfield of the 1980s, with Michel Platini, Jean Tigana and Bernard Genghini, and won 47 caps (with 6 goals) 1974-86. He played in 579 League games in France to 1985, the third highest ever total. With Girondins de Bordeaux he won French championships in 1984-5 and the cup in 1986. He ended his career with Marseille.

Silke GLADISCH (GDR/Ger), see MÖLLER.

Maxi GNAUCK (GDR)

GYMNASTICS

Maxi Gnauck. b. 10 Oct 1964 Berlin.

After placing second in the all-around at the 1979 Worlds and 1980 Olympics, Gnauck became European champion in 1981, when she won four of the five individual titles. That year she went on to World titles at three individual apparatus as well as team gold. In 1983 she repeated her World Championships success at her speciality, the asymmetric bars, on which she had won the Olympic gold in 1980, when she also won two bronze medals. She was 2nd overall in the 1985 Europeans.

Kitty GODFREE (UK)

TENNIS

Kathleen Godfree. née McKane. b. 7 May 1896 Bayswater, London, d. 19 Jun 1992 London.

One of the world's outstanding players of the early 1920s and a worthy successor to Dorothea Lambert Chambers as the British No.1. She first entered Wimbledon in 1919 and reached the final four years later where she lost to Suzanne Lenglen. She was singles champion in 1924 beating Helen Wills, who was making her Wimbledon début, in a classic final. This was the only defeat that Wills-Moody suffered in nine appearances at Wimbledon. In 1926 McKane married Leslie Godfree while on a tennis tour to South Africa and then, while Kitty won her second singles title after losing to Lenglen in the 1925 semifinals, they became the only married couple ever to win the Wimbledon mixed doubles. As Miss McKane she had earlier won the mixed doubles at Wimbledon in 1924 and the US Championships in 1925. In the women's doubles she was the US champion in 1923 and 1927, the World Hard Court champion in 1923 and an Olympic gold medallist in 1920. At the Olympic Games of 1920 and 1924 she won five medals (1 gold, 2 silver, 2 bronze) - a record for a woman tennis player. She played in the first Wightman Cup in 1923 and made her seventh and final appearance in 1934 when she also played at Wimbledon for the last time. At badminton she won four All-England singles titles 1920-2 and 1924, the women's doubles with her sister Margaret in 1921 and 1924, and the mixed with Frank Devlin in 1924-5. She was also a member of the English lacrosse team in 1918.

Marlies GÖHR (GDR)

ATHLETICS

Marlies Göhr. née Oelsner. b. 21 Mar 1958 Gera.

Her outstanding sprinting career includes a record number of European Cup victories, winning at both 100m and sprint relay at all six finals 1977-87, and five European outdoor gold medals, including a hat-trick of 100m titles, 1978, 1982 and 1986. She won five European Indoor titles at 60m (1977-9, 1982-3) and was also twice second and twice third in that event. The first woman to run a sub 11-second 100 metres, she ran a record 36 such times, including 3 with excess wind assistance, between 1977 and 1988. She set three world records at 100m, 10.88 in 1977 and 1982 and 10.81 in 1983, and for GDR relay teams nine at 4x100m and one at 4x200m. Indoors she set three world bests at 60 metres to 7.10 in 1980.
She started her sprinting career with 100m silver and relay gold at the 1975 European Juniors. In 1976 she was 8th at her first Olympics, and although she took relay gold in 1976 and 1980 she never won an Olympic 100m title as she was 2nd in 1980 and went out in the semi-finals in 1988. At 100m she was World Student champion in 1979 and had World Cup wins in 1977 and 1985.
She ran the 200m only rarely, but was second in the 1978 Europeans and had a best time of 21.74 in 1984, then just 0.03 off the world record. She was GDR champion ten times at 100m, 1977-85, 1988, and twice at 200m, 1978, 1984. A psychology student she ran for SC Motor Jena. Gave birth to daughter Nadja in 1989.

Sid GOING (NZ)

RUGBY UNION

Sidney Milton Going. b. 19 Aug 1943 Kawakawa.

New Zealand's most capped scrum-half. A tough, aggressive player whose attacking breaks around the scrum or from the line-outs were a feature of his game. After first representing the NZ Maoris in 1965, he played in the NZ Trials the following year and made his début for the All Blacks against Australia in 1967. He went on to win 29 caps prior to his retirement in 1977 and scored 10 tries in Test matches.
He was voted the outstanding Maori player every year from 1967 to 1972 and was awarded the MBE for his services to the game. His brother, Ken, was also an All Black and a third brother, Brian, won representative honours with the New Zealand Maoris.

Marielle GOITSCHEL (Fra)

ALPINE SKIING

Marielle Goitschel. b. 28 Sep 1945 Sainte-Maxime, Var.

At the 1964 Olympics the Goitschel sisters each won gold and silver medals. The older sister **Christine** (b. 9 Jun 1944) won the slalom, with Marielle second, and two days later Marielle won the giant slalom from Christine. Meanwhile their younger sister Patricia won the French junior title. In 1968 Marielle won the slalom but was only seventh at the giant slalom.
Marielle won three successive world titles at the Alpine Combination, 1962 (at the age of 16), 1964 and 1966, and took the giant slalom title in 1966. She was also second in 1966 at slalom and at the downhill, but years later was declared to have won the latter title as the original winner, Erika (Erik) Schinegger, was found to be a man!
After the 1968 Olympics and second place in the world championships at the Combined, Marielle announced her retirement. Her nephew **Philippe** was second at speed skiing when this was a demonstration sport at the 1992 Olympics, and set a world speed record at 233.615 km/h on 21 Apr 1993.

Vladimir GOLUBNICHIY (USSR/Ukr)

WALKING

Vladimir Stepanovich Golubnichiy. b. 2 Jun 1936 Sumy.

A outstanding walker, who competed in five Olympic 20km walks. After winning in 1960, he was 3rd in 1964 and became the first athlete to regain an Olympic title since Paavo Nurmi when he won a second gold in 1968. He then added a silver in 1972 to tie the record of four successive medals at any athletics event; finally he was 7th in 1976. He also won a complete set of European 20km medals: 1st 1974, 2nd 1966 and 3rd 1962, and was Lugano Trophy runner-up in 1967 and 1970. He set the first of three world track records at 20km with 1:30:35.2 at the age of 19 in 1955, and his best ever 20km time was 1:23:55 on a road course 21 years later. USSR champion at 20km walk 1960, 1964-5, 1968, 1972 and 1974 with 13 placings in the first three.

Lefty GOMEZ (USA)

BASEBALL

Vernon Louis Gomez. b. 26 Nov 1908 Rodeo, California, d. 17 Feb 1989 Larkspur, California.

A left-handed pitcher renowned as much for his zaniness as his pitching ability, although he was a top pitcher and the ace of the New York Yankee staff during much of their heyday in the 1930s. Early in his career Gomez was renowned for his blazing fastball but as injuries hounded him he became a finesse pitcher. He ended his career with one game for the Washington Senators in 1943. His 6-0 record is the most wins without a loss ever for a pitcher in the World Series.

Career pitching: ERA 3.34; W-L 189-102, SO 1468; Best seasons: 1934: 26-5, 2.33 ERA; 1937: 21-11, 2.33 ERA.

Wilfredo GOMEZ (PR)

BOXING

Wilfredo Gomez. b. 29 Oct 1956 Los Morjas

One of the greatest punchers ever seen in the lighter weight divisions. His 40 of 42 victories won inside the distance included an amazing stretch of 32 consecutive bouts. His first world title came in 1977 when he won the WBC super-bantamweight by knocking out Yum Dong-kyun in 12. He never lost that title but, after 17 successful defences, relinquished it in 1984 to challenge for the WBC featherweight title, which he won by outpointing Juan LaPorte. In 1985 he won the WBA junior-lightweight title by a decision over Rocky Lockridge, but he lost that crown in his first defence. He won 20 of 23 title fights at various weights, an outstanding record.

Career record: W - 42 (40), L - 3, D -1.

Pancho GONZALES (USA)

TENNIS

Richard Alonzo Gonzales. b. 9 May 1928 Los Angeles, California.

Often rated as the finest player of all-time, he turned professional in 1949 and ranks as one of the few great players never to have won the Wimbledon singles, as he was denied the opportunity of competing in the major tournaments until the arrival of Open tennis in 1968.

Before turning pro he won the US singles and the US Clay Court title in 1948 and 1949. In 1949 he made his only amateur appearance at Wimbledon and, although seeded No.2 in the singles, he lost in the fourth round to Geoff Brown (Aus). He did, however, win the doubles both at Wimbledon and in Paris with Frank Parker in 1949.

His record as a professional got off to a poor start when he was decisively beaten (96-27) in a series of matches against Jack Kramer but he was World Professional singles champion from 1954 to 1962. When Open tennis began in 1968 Gonzales was well past his best but he reached the semifinals of the French Open that year and in 1969 he won the longest-ever match at Wimbledon, defeating Charlie Pasarell (USA) in a 112-game, five hours 12 minutes singles match. This included the equal longest ever set at Wimbledon, the first, which Gonzales lost 22-24.

Gonzales never had a single tennis lesson but his phenomenal natural ability took him to the top and kept him there for an incredible 24 years. He was first ranked in the World top ten in 1948 and in 1972, at the age of 44, he was still ranked ninth. After retirement he became a teaching professional in Las Vegas.

Raúl GONZALES (Mex)

WALKING

Raúl Gonzáles. b. 29 Feb 1952.

Gonzáles had a fitting climax to a distinguished career when he won the gold medal for 50 kilometres walk and silver at 20 kilometres at his fourth Olympic Games in 1984. His earlier successes had included World Cup wins at 50km in 1977, 1981 and 1983, and the Pan-American titles of 1979 and 1983, to which he added silvers at 50km in 1987 and at 20km in 1983. He had set world track walking records at 30km (2:11:53.4 in 1979) and twice at 50km (3:52:23.5 in 1978, 3:41:38.4 in 1979), and world road bests at 30km (2:07:29 in 1979) and twice at 50km in 1978, with a best of 3:41:20.

Graham GOOCH (UK)

CRICKET

Graham Alan Gooch. b. 23 Jul 1953 Leytonstone, London.

A powerful batsman who reached his peak as England captain with scores of 333 and 123 (a Test record match aggregate) against India at Lord's in 1990. That year he also became the first player to score over 1000 Test runs in an English summer (306 v New Zealand, 752 at 125.33 v India) and his 2746 runs at 101.70 was the highest in a first-class season in England since 1961. He made his Test début in 1975, but had to wait until 1978 for a second chance, from when he established himself as an England regular, except for a three-year ban after he had captained an English 'rebel' tour to South Africa in 1982. After captaining England twice in 1988, he returned to the job in 1990 and led the team by the personal example of his magnificent batting, although often it seemed with no great tactical acumen. He resigned after losing the Ashes series in 1993 with a record of 10 wins in his 34 matches as captain.

He has played for Essex from 1973, captaining them in 1986-7 and from 1989. To the end of the 1992 season he holds the runs records for all three English one-day competitions: 7157 in the Sunday League, including the record score of 176 in 1983; 2261 in the Gillette/NatWest Cup; and 4402 in the Benson & Hedges Cup, including the record score of 198* in 1982. He is also a useful medium-pace swing bowler. Awarded the OBE in 1991.

101 Tests 1975-93: 7620 runs at 43.05, 17 100s HS 333; 22 wickets at 40.63, BB 3-39; 97 catches.

120 One-day Ints: 4206 runs at 37.89, 8 100s HS 142; 36 wickets at 39.88, BB 3-19; 44 catches.

First-class 1973-93: 36,404 runs at 48.08, 100 100s HS 333; 233 wickets at 34.48, BB 7-14; 482 catches.

Brian GOODELL (USA)

SWIMMING

Brian Stuart Goodell. b. 2 Apr 1959 Stockton, California.

Double Olympic freestyle champion in 1976. His times of 3:51.93 for 400m and 15:02.40 for 1500m improved the world records of 3:53.08 and 15:06.66 he had set a month earlier in winning the US trials. After graduating from Mission Viejo High School in 1977, Goodell went to UCLA and won nine NCAA titles 1978-81. He improved his 400m world record to 3:51.56 in 1977, won two gold medals at the 1979 Pan-American Games and nine AAU titles, but lost his Olympic chance in 1980 due to the boycott. In that year he set a US record for 800m with 7:59.66.

Gail GOODRICH (USA)

BASKETBALL

Gail Charles Goodrich, Jr. b. 23 Apr 1943 Los Angeles, California.

After helping UCLA to win NCAA Championships in both 1964 and 1965, he joined the Los Angeles Lakers in the NBA, moving on to the Phoenix Suns and New Orleans Jazz. He was a small, quick guard who averaged over 20 points in a season five times. He played in five all-star games and was named to the All-NBA First Team in 1974. In 1972 he was a vital cog in the Laker team considered by many to be the greatest NBA team ever; during that season they won 33 consecutive games.

NBA career: 19,181 points, av. 18.6.

Andy GOODWAY (UK)

RUGBY LEAGUE

Andrew Goodway. b. 6 Jun 1961 Castleford, Yorkshire.

After winning 11 Great Britain caps with Oldham he moved to Wigan in July 1985 for £65,000, then a record fee for a forward. He won a further 12 caps with his new club.
He made an impressive international début against France in 1983, scoring a try from the second row. His robust play frequently failed to meet with the approval of the referee.

Evonne GOOLAGONG (Aus)

TENNIS

Evonne Fay Goolagong. b. 31 Jul 1951 Barellan, New South Wales. Later Cawley.

Born in a remote part of Australia and of partly Aboriginal parentage, she had an unusual tennis background but after her natural talents had been refined by coach Vic Edwards she developed into a great and popular champion. Having been Australian junior champion in 1970, she first won the Wimbledon singles as a 19-year-old in 1971 and although she was again a finalist in 1972, 1975 and 1976, she did not win again until 1980. In 1975 she married Roger Cawley and their first child, Kelly, was born the following year. Evonne's 1980 Wimbledon victory was the first by a mother since Dorothea Lambert Chambers in 1914.
She was also the Australian Open champion four times, 1974-6, 1978, and won the French 1971, South African 1972 and Italian 1973 titles. She was a fine doubles player winning Wimbledon 1974, the Australian Open 1971, 1974-6, and the South African 1971-2. She represented Australia in the Federation Cup from 1971 to 1982, winning 33 out of 38 rubbers. Although possessing a fine range of strokes, her greatest strength was her instinctive volleying which served her particularly well on the hard surfaces of her native Australia. She was awarded the MBE in 1972.

Fortune GORDIEN (USA)

ATHLETICS

Fortune Everett Gordien. b. 9 Sep 1922 Spokane, Washington, d. 10 Apr 1990 Fontana, California.

Gordien was consistently at the forefront of world discus throwing for a decade from his first number one ranking in 1947. He threw world records with 56.46m and 56.97 in 1949 and with 58.10 and 59.28 in 1953. At the Olympics he never quite did himself justice, with the bronze in 1948, 4th place in 1952 and silver in 1956. While at the University of Minnesota he was NCAA champion each year 1946-8 and won the AAU discus 1947-50 and 1953-4. Pan-American champion 1955 (and second at shot). He had a shot best of 16.51 in 1947, when he was second in the AAU and third in the NCAA.
He became a cattle rancher in Oregon.

Wentworth GORE (UK)

TENNIS

Arthur William Charles Gore. b. 2 Jan 1868 Lyndhurst, Hampshire, d. 1 Dec 1928 Kensington, London.

A player of remarkable durability who competed at every Wimbledon over a span of 39 years and 35 Championships 1888-1927. He played a total of 182 matches at Wimbledon and won 121 of them. He won the singles three times, 1901, 1908 and 1909, and the men's doubles in 1909. He is the only player to have won a singles title over the age of 40, in 1908 and at 41 yr 182 days in 1909. In 1912 at 44, he added the distinction of being the oldest Wimbledon singles finalist when he lost to Tony Wilding in the Challenge Round. Wentworth Gore played in the first British Davis Cup team at Boston in 1900 and reached the semi-finals of the US championships that year. He played again in the Davis Cup in 1907 and 1912. Other successes included gold medals in the men's singles and men's doubles at the 1908 Olympics. An outstanding baseline player with a strong forehand, his speed around the court allowed him to protect his extremely vulnerable backhand.

Aleksandr GORSHKOV (USSR)

ICE DANCE
Aleksandr Georgiyevich Gorshkov. b. 8 Oct 1946 Moscow.

He partnered his wife, Lyudmila (née Pakhomova), as they won the first Olympic ice dance title in 1976 and together won a record six World Championships, 1970-4 and 1976.

Goose GOSLIN (USA)

BASEBALL
Leon Allen Goslin. b. 16 Oct 1900 Salem, New Jersey, d. 15 May 1971 Bridgeton, New Jersey.

Goose Goslin played outfield for 18 major league seasons, 12 of them spent with the Washington Senators. He was a superb hitter, for both average and power, although his defensive abilities in the outfield were almost non-existent. He led the league in batting in 1928 with an average of .379, and twice (1923, 1925) led the American League in triples. His best year for home runs was 1930 when he hit 37. In 1924 Goslin led the Senators to the only world championship they ever won. In that series he hit .344, with three home runs and seven RBI.
Career 1921-38: 2735 hits Avg. .316, HR 248; SB 175; RBI 1609.

Frank GOTCH (USA)

WRESTLING
Frank Alvin Gotch. b. 27 Apr 1878 Humboldt, Iowa, d. 16 Dec 1917 Humboldt.

Possibly America's greatest professional wrestler ever, holding that title when professional wrestling was not for showmen but was truly a sport. He won the championship in 1904 when he defeated Tom Jenkins. He then challenged George Hackenschmidt for the world title. In the match at Chicago in April 1908 Gotch won in a 2 hr 3 min match and in September 1911 he repeated the victory, defeating Hackenschmidt in straight falls. Gotch became an American hero and toured the country and the world. He boxed briefly and considered challenging Jack Johnson for the world championship, but demurred. Gotch won almost 400 matches during his career and was undefeated again from 1908.

Arthur GOULD (UK)

RUGBY UNION
Arthur Joseph Gould. b. 10 Oct 1864 Newport, d. 2 Jan 1919 Newport.

An outstanding leader who captained Wales a record 18 times in 27 international appearances between 1885 and 1897. He led Wales to their first Triple Crown in 1893 and at the time of his retirement he was Wales' most capped player. His retirement was marked by the Welsh RU with the gift of a house which resulted in Ireland and Scotland refusing to play Wales in 1897 as they considered this an act of professionalism. Gould was appointed to the committee of the Welsh RU in 1897 and became a selector the following year.
He was one of six brothers who all played for Newport and three of whom were capped by Wales. He was twice placed in the AAA 120 yards hurdles and used his speed to great effect as a full back or in the centre.

Jay GOULD (USA)

REAL TENNIS
Jay Gould, Jr. b. 1888, d. 26 Jan 1935 Margaretville, New York.

The greatest ever American player. The son of the railroad multi-millionaire, he was able to play from an early age on a private court on the family's New Jersey estate where he retained a personal professional. Later, when he entered the family business he had his private court built at their New York offices.
He held the US Amateur title from 1906-26 without the loss of a single set. Between 1909 and 1932 he also won the US Amateur doubles 19 times - 8 with Tevis Huhn, 6 with Joseph Wear and 5 with William Wright. In 1907 he became the first American to win the British Amateur title and after retaining the title

the following year he won a gold medal on the only occasion real tennis was included in the Olympics. The highlight of his career came in 1914 when he successfully challenged Fred Covey (UK) for the world title in Philadelphia and became the first amateur ever to be world champion. On the outbreak of war in Europe he resigned the title and did not make a further challenge in the post-war years.

From 1907 until his retirement in 1926 the only singles match he lost was to Edgar Baerlein in the Bathurst Cup in Paris in 1923 and his only doubles defeat came in the 1925 US Amateur when, partnered by Joseph Wear, they lost to the brothers, Suydam and Fulton Cutting.

Shane GOULD (Aus)

SWIMMING

Shane Elizabeth Gould. b. 23 Nov 1956 Brisbane.

Between July 1971 and January 1972 she set world records at all five freestyle distances from 100m to 1500m. At the 1972 Olympics she swam 12 races in eight days, starting with the gold medal at 200m individual medley in a world record 2:23.07, but then losing at 100m for the first time for two years as she took the bronze medal. She came back to set world records in winning gold medals at 400m (4:19.44) and 200m (2:03.56), and then took silver at 800m in 8:56.39 behind the world record set by Keena Rothhammer. A year later, at the age of 16 years 9 months, disenchanted with the incessant demands of training, she announced her retirement. Other best times: 110y/100m 58.5 (1972) and her final world record 1650y (and 1500m) 16:56.9 in February 1973.

She was coached by Forbes Carlisle from the age of 13, and was Australian champion at freestyle 100m and 400m 1971-3; 200m 1971 and 1973; 800m 1972; 200m individual medley 1971 and 1973.

David GOWER (UK)

CRICKET

David Ivon Gower. b. 1 Apr 1957 Tunbridge Wells, Kent.

A sublime left-handed batsman. He never scored the mass of runs in first-class cricket of many other great batsmen, but significantly his average is much higher in Tests than in other matches. For many years he has charmed cricket watchers with his batting, but he was churlishly dropped by the England selectors after playing with considerable success in 1990-1. An incident in which he borrowed an airplane and 'buzzed' his colleagues seemed more important to them than his batting. Recalled, however, in 1992 he averaged 50 in three Tests against Pakistan and passed Geoffrey Boycott as England's leading run-scorer in Test cricket. There was then a national outcry over his non-selection for the winter tour to India.

Gower made his first-class début for Leicestershire in 1975, playing for them until 1989, captain 1984-6. He then switched to play for Hampshire. He started a law degree course, but gave that up to concentrate on cricket. His class was swiftly recognised and he made his Test début at the age of 21. Between 1982 and 1989 he captained England 32 times but was not a great success, apart from a 2-1 win over India in 1984/5 followed by a 3-1 win in 1985 against Australia, in which Gower himself had his most successful series with 732 runs at 81.33, including his Test highest of 215 at Edgbaston. Awarded the OBE 1992.

117 Tests 1975-92: 8231 runs at 44.25, 18 100s HS 215; 74 catches.

114 One-day Ints: 3170 runs at 30.77, 7 100s HS 158; 44 catches.

First-class 1973-93: 25,203 runs at 40.00, 49 100s HS 228; 269 catches, 1 stumping.

Lily GOWER (UK)

CROQUET

Lilias Mary Gower. b. 1877, d. 29 Jul 1959, West Kensington, London. Later Beaton.

The first great woman croquet player and the first lady to win the Open Championship. She learned her tactics entirely from an instructional book and her tournament début at Budleigh Salterton in 1898, when she beat the defending champion, was the first time she had ever played

on a full-sized court and the first time she had even seen a first-class game. After this astonishing start, she won the first of her three successive victories in the women's championship the following year. A fourth victory came many years later when, as Mrs Beaton, she took the title in 1928.
She was the equal of most of her male contemporaries and in 1905 she became the first woman to win the Open title, beating R C J Beaton, whom she married later in the year, in the final.

W G GRACE (UK)

CRICKET

Dr William Gilbert Grace. b. 18 Jul 1848 Downend, Bristol, d. 23 Oct 1915 Mottingham, Kent.

'The Champion' bestrode cricket for 40 years, taking it from a rural pursuit into a national sport, as he himself became the best known figure in the land; a figure that changed over the years from the athletic young man who made an immediate impact as a teenager to the portly giant who played his last Test at the age of 50 and made his last first-class appearance in 1908. His run-scoring dwarfed his contemporaries. In 1871 when he became the first player to exceed 2000 runs in a season and made a record ten centuries, his total of 2739 runs was at an average of 78.25, while the next best averaged 37.66. He again exceeded 2000 in 1876, 1887 and, just when some thought his powers were declining, again in 1895 and 1896. He made the first ever first-class triple century, 344 for MCC v Kent in 1876, and followed that a few days later with 316 for Gloucs v Yorkshire. In his early days he was also by far the best all-rounder in the country, bowling slow round-arm deliveries, with a best season of 191 wickets (av. 12.94) in 1875. He did the double of 1000 runs and 100 wickets eight times, and in 1873 and 1876 became the first to achieve 2000 runs and 100 wickets. He was also a magnificent catcher, whose career total has been surpassed only by Frank Woolley.
WG was often seen at his best in the Gentlemen v Players matches, transforming the fortunes of the Gentlemen, for whom he scored 6008 runs including 15 100s, and took 271 wickets. He played for Gloucestershire 1868-99 (captain 1870-98) and then ran the London County team 1900-04.
He qualified as a doctor, but left his practice to locums whenever there was cricket to be played. In his youth he was also a fine athlete. In August 1866 WG achieved a unique double when he scored 224*, then the highest ever first-class score, for England v Surrey at the Oval, but missed the second day of the match to run at the first National Olympic Association meeting at Crystal Palace, where he won the 440 yards hurdles. At a slower pace, in 1903 he was elected the first president of the English Bowling Association.
His brother **Edward** Mills (1841-1911) preceded him as the leading batsman in England and both Edward and George **Fred**erick (1850-80) each played with WG in the first Test match ever played in England, against Australia at The Oval in 1880. In that match WG scored 152, the first century by an England batsman in Tests. He captained England in his last 13 Tests from the age of 40.
22 Tests 1880-99: 1098 runs at 32.29, 2 100s HS 170; 9 wickets at 26.22, BB 2-12; 39 catches.
First-class 1865-1908: 54,896 runs at 39.55, 126 100s HS 344; 2876 wickets at 17.92, BB 10-49; 887 catches, 5 stumpings.

Steffi GRAF (Ger)

TENNIS

Stefanie Maria Graf. b. 14 Jun 1969 Brühl.

A phenomenal junior who first achieved a WTA ranking at the age of 13 in 1982 and who won her first Grand Slam title in 1987 when still eight days short of her 18th birthday. She was, at the time, the youngest-ever winner of the women's singles at the French Open. She won in Paris for a second time in 1988, went on to complete the Grand Slam and concluded an outstanding year by winning the Olympic singles in Seoul. In 1989 she successfully defended her Wimbledon, US and Australian titles but defeat by Arantxa

Sánchez (Spa) in the French final cost her a second consecutive Grand Slam. By her own high standards, 1990 was a disappointing year: although she won the Australian title for the third successive year, she lost to Monica Seles in the final at the French Open, to Gabriela Sabatini (Arg) in the US Open final and went out to Zina Garrison (USA) in the Wimbledon semi-finals. Troubled by injury, illness and family problems, her period of near invincibility seemed to be drawing to a close but she came back to win Wimbledon each year 1991-3, although after a record 186 weeks ranked as the world's number one 1987-91 she had to settle for number two status to Monica Seles, regaining the top ranking in June 1993 after Seles had been forced out of action. At the end of 1992 Graf was second on the all-time money list with $10,332,673 and in 1993 passed the 71 career tournaments won by Billie-Jean King to move to the fourth highest in the professional era, as she won her seventh German and third French singles titles. By then she had been continually in the world top two for six years.
Her only Grand Slam doubles title came in 1988 when she won at Wimbledon with Gabriela Sabatini. A superb athlete, she epitomises the modern serve-volley power game, with the most powerful single-handed forehand in the women's game.

Gillis GRAFSTRÖM (Swe)

FIGURE SKATING

Gillis Emanuel Grafström. b. 7 Jun 1893 Stockholm, d. 14 Apr 1938 Potsdam, Germany.

A three-time winner of both the Olympic and world figure skating titles who was noted for originating various spins and turns. His first Olympic victory was in 1920 and after defending his title at the next two Games he was probably only deprived of a fourth gold medal in 1932 by a knee injury while training at Lake Placid, finishing in second place. A noted amateur poet and painter, he was a highly individual character and was more interested in skating as an aesthetic pastime than for its competitive opportunities. Despite his lengthy career he only competed in four World Championships, winning in 1922, 1924 and 1929 after 7th in 1914, and he never even entered for the European Championships. Although Swedish, he spent much of his life in practice as an architect in Germany and London. It was while he was in Germany that he married Celia, the great-grand-daughter of the composer Felix Mendelssohn-Bartholdy.

Otto GRAHAM (USA)

AMERICAN FOOTBALL

Otto Everett Graham, Jr. b. 6 Dec 1921 Waukegan, Illinois.

Graham enrolled at Northwestern University on a basketball scholarship in 1939. He also played football and baseball for the Wildcats, and eventually played professional basketball as a guard in 1945-6 with the Rochester Royals of the old National Basketball League, a forerunner of the NBA. In 1944 he became the only college athlete to be named All-American in both football and basketball. In 1946 he joined the Cleveland Browns of the All-American Football Conference (AAFC) and played with them as the dominant quarterback of his era until his retirement in 1955. Each year 1947-9 he was the MVP of the AAFC, leading the Browns to four straight championships in the fledgling pro football league. In 1950 the Browns joined the NFL and continued their dominance, with conference titles for six consecutive seasons 1950-5, and the Championship in 1950, 1954, and 1955. He later became a college and pro football coach.
AAFC/NFL career 1946-55: 23,584 yards from 1464 pass completions, 55.8%, 174 TD.

Dieter GRAHN (GDR)

ROWING

Dieter Grahn. b. 20 Mar 1944 Zobten.

A member of the renowned Einheit Dresden four, who competed for 11 years and were never beaten in international competition.
See Frank FORBERGER for details.

Red GRANGE (USA)

AMERICAN FOOTBALL

Harold Edward Grange. b. 13 Jun 1903 Forksville, Pennsylvania, d. 28 Jan 1991 Lake Wales, Florida.

'The Galloping Ghost' is one the greatest legends in football history, one of its greatest running backs ever, and is probably responsible for professional football becoming a popular sport prior to World War II. He first played for the University of Illinois, wearing Number 77, which he also made famous. He was the best college running back from 1923-5, but it was a game against Michigan in his junior year that stands out as his finest. Then he scored four touchdowns in the first 12 minutes on runs of 95, 67, 56, and 44 yards. He added a fifth touchdown later in the game, and also threw one touchdown pass. In 41 minutes he carried the ball 15 times for 402 yards, and completed six passes. In 1925 he was signed to play pro football with the Chicago Bears. Prior to then pro football had laboured in anonymity, as American football fans preferred the college sport, but Grange was so popular that he helped establish the NFL as a professional league. He played until 1934, when a knee injury forced his retirement.

Tom GRAVENEY (UK)

CRICKET

Thomas William Graveney. b. 16 Jun 1927 Riding Mill, Northumberland.

A majestically elegant batsman, who was also a safe close fielder. Although his class was apparent from when he made his Test début in 1951, for some years he did not prove as successful in Tests as perhaps he should have, although that may have been due to some distrust of his abilities when more work-a-day qualities were appreciated. He did not play in Tests between 1959 and 1962. Then he averaged 100.25 in a 4-Test series against Pakistan, but after faring less well against Australia in 1962/3 he was again dropped and did not reappear until 1966. He had played for Gloucestershire 1948-60, but left the county after losing the captaincy (1959-60). He moved to Worcestershire, and there found the best form of his career. He helped them to their first ever championship in 1964, and captained them in 1968-70. Somewhat belatedly the England selectors recognised his marvellous consistency and recalled him to the Test side at the age of 39 in 1966, when he averaged 76.50 in four matches against the West Indies. For the next three years he excelled for England, until he lost his place due to a petty squabble over activity on the rest day of a Test match. He captained England once against Australia in 1968.

He scored over 1000 runs in a season 22 times, including twice overseas, and over 2000 seven times, with a peak of 2397 in 1956. Awarded the OBE. His brother Ken captained Gloucestershire in 1963-4 and Ken's son David has since captained Gloucestershire and Durham.

79 Tests 1951-69: 4882 runs at 44.38, 11 100s HS 258; 1 wicket; 80 catches.
First-class 1948-72: 47,793 runs at 44.92, 122 100s HS 258; 80 wickets at 37.96, BB 5-28; 550 catches, 1 stumping.

Ken GRAY (NZ)

RUGBY UNION

Kenneth Francis Gray. b. 24 Jun 1938 Porirua.

Initially a lock, he moved to prop in 1961 and became one of the lynch-pins of the great All Black pack of the mid-1960s. Apart from missing two matches through injury, he played in every Test match between 1963 and 1969. He toured Britain in 1963/4 and 1967 and Australia in 1968, and he played in the home series against Australia in 1964, South Africa in 1965, the British Lions in 1966, France in 1968 and Wales in 1969. In all he played in 24 Tests and, showing unusual mobility for a prop, he scored nine international tries.

Rocky GRAZIANO (USA)

BOXING

né Thomas Rocca Barbella. b. 1 Jan 1921 New York (although he gave his birthdate as 7 Jun 1922 when he deserted from the army in 1942), d. 22 May 1990 New York.

World middleweight champion 1947-8. A tough fighter who emerged from a life of crime on New York's Lower East Side to take up pro boxing in 1942 and have three savage world title fights against Tony Zale. He lost the first in 1946 when the fight was stopped in the sixth round, but in the second in July 1947 he knocked out Zale in the sixth to become champion. Just under a year later Zale regained the title with a third round KO. Graziano lost his boxing licence for a year but returned to carry on boxing until 1953. An all-out attacking fighter with little defensive subtlety but great courage, he was elected to the Boxing Hall of Fame in 1971.

His autobiography *Somebody Up There Like Me* was made into a film, with Paul Newman playing the boxer, in 1956, and he had a successful and lucrative career as an actor as well as popularising the name Rocky for boxers and being a model for the Rocky films of Sylvester Stallone.

Career record: W - 67, L - 10, D -6

Jimmy GREAVES (UK)

FOOTBALL

James Peter Greaves. b. 20 Feb 1940 Poplar, London.

A mercurial inside-forward with an extraordinary flair for goalscoring. He played for Chelsea 1957-61, AC Milan 1961, Tottenham Hotspur 1961-70 and West Ham United 1970-1, and scored on his début for each club. He also scored in his first game for England and for the England Under-23 team.

He scored a record 357 goals in 517 matches in the First Division and was the leading scorer in the Division for six seasons. A further 55 goals in FA Cup ties, 44 for England, and many more in representative matches, made him one of the most exciting and entertaining players of his era. His finest years came while he was with Tottenham who he joined after a brief, unhappy spell in Italy with AC Milan. He played a vital rôle in the team which won the FA Cup in 1962 and 1967, and the European Cup-Winners' Cup in 1963.

He played 57 times for England 1959-67, 42 while with Spurs, but his greatest disappointment was that he was left out of the team for the closing stages of the 1966 World Cup. Only Bobby Charlton and Gary Lineker, who played in many more matches, have scored more goals for England.

Following his retirement in May 1971, he had little involvement in football, preferring to concentrate on his varied business interests but he later made occasional appearances for Chelmsford and Barnet. Having overcome alcoholism, he has now found his metier as a TV personality.

Harry GREB (USA)

BOXING

Edward Henry Greb (né Berg). b. 6 Jun 1894 Pittsburgh, Pennsylvania, d. 22 Oct 1926 Atlantic City, New Jersey.

Nicknamed 'The Human Windmill' because of his all-action style, he also fought almost continuously, taking part in 299 bouts in his career with 44 in 1919 alone. He rarely trained, keeping in condition by continuously fighting. He was unbeaten in a sequence of 178 bouts between 1916 and 1923, but these included 117 'no decisions' of which five were unofficial losses.

Greb is best known as the only fighter ever to have defeated Gene Tunney, beating him in 1922 for the US light-heavyweight title. The punishment was so severe that Tunney spent the following week in bed. Greb won the world middleweight crown in 1923 by decisioning Johnny Wilson. After six successful defences he lost it in 1926 to Tiger Flowers and also lost a rematch. He died later that year from complications from surgery.

Career record: W - 264 (49), L - 23, D -12.

Lucinda GREEN (UK)

EQUESTRIAN

Lucinda Jane Green. b. 7 Nov 1953 London. née Prior-Palmer.

An outstanding three-day eventer who achieved a record six Badminton victories. Her first was in 1973 on *Be Fair*, whom her parents had bought her as a 15th birthday present, and the others were: *Wide*

Awake 1976, *George* 1977, *Killaire* 1979, *Regal Realm* 1983 and *Beagle Bay* 1984. She was European Champion on *Be Fair* in 1975 and on *George* in 1977, and World champion on *Regal Realm* in 1982, when she also won a team gold. She also won at Burghley in 1977 and 1981. She competed at two Olympics; in 1976 when *Be Fair* broke down in his last competition, and in 1984 when she was sixth individually and took a team silver. With the British team she boycotted the 1980 Games. Awarded the MBE in 1978, she married the Australian rider David Green (b. 28 Feb 1960) in 1981. David competed for Australia at the 1988 Olympics.
Her first international appearance was in 1971 when she was a member of the winning British team at the European Junior Championships. A natural cross-country rider, she worked hard at becoming equally proficient at show jumping and dressage.

Hank GREENBERG (USA)

BASEBALL

Henry Benjamin Greenberg. b. 1 Jan 1911 New York, d. 4 Sep 1986 Beverly Hills, California.

One of the greatest of sluggers, although injuries, military service and an early retirement kept his career numbers below many of his peers. He played one game in the majors in 1930, but started his career in earnest in 1933 with the Detroit Tigers with whom he remained until 1946 when he joined the Pittsburgh Pirates for one last year. During that time he led the American League in home runs four times, his greatest effort being his 58 home runs in 1938, a mark surpassed only by Babe Ruth and Roger Maris. His 183 RBI in 1937 (when he batted .337) are also second in American League history only to Lou Gehrig. Greenberg played mostly first base and a little outfield. He missed most of the 1936 season due to a fractured wrist, and did not play in 1942-4 because of injuries and the war. He later became a baseball executive, retiring in 1963 to become a successful investment banker.
Career batting: 1638 hits Avg. .313, HR 331; RBI 1276.

Joe GREENE (USA)

AMERICAN FOOTBALL

Charles Edward Greene. b. 24 Sep 1946 Temple, Texas.

A quiet, well-spoken man who was anything but mean, 'Mean Joe' Greene earned his nickname in college at North Texas State for the way he dominated offenses from his defensive tackle position. In 1969 he was drafted by the Pittsburgh Steelers, whom he helped to become the dominant football team of the 1970s. Greene was named All-NFL as a defensive lineman from 1970-5. He helped the Steelers win four Super Bowls, 1975-6, 1979-80, and helped established the 'Steel Curtain' as the dominant defense in pro football. He was a unanimous selection to the NFL's All-Decade team for the 1970s. He retired in 1981 and has since been an assistant coach with the Steelers. In 1980, he earned a Clio Award for a famous television commercial he made for Coca-Cola in which he gave his jersey to a small boy.

Nancy GREENE (Can)

ALPINE SKIING

Nancy Catherine Greene. b. 11 May 1943 Ottawa, Ontario.

An attacking skier, in 1968 she won the Olympic gold at giant slalom and silver at slalom and was World champion at Alpine Combination. She also won the first two overall and giant slalom World Cup titles, 1967-8, winning 14 races over those two years. US downhill champion in 1960, 1965 and 1967; in 1965 she won all four titles, adding the slalom, giant slalom and Alpine Combination.

Gordon GREENIDGE (Bar)

CRICKET

Cuthbert Gordon Greenidge. né Lavine. b. 1 May 1951 Black Bess, St Peter.

An exciting opening batsman. For much of his career he established outstanding partnerships, with Barry Richards for Hampshire and with Roy Fredericks and then, most notably, Desmond Haynes (qv) for the West Indies. With his family he

came to live in Reading, England from the age of 14, but, although he played for England Schoolboys at 16, chose to return to play in his native Barbados for a couple of winters and to play his Test cricket for the West Indies (captaining them once in 1988). He hit the ball very hard indeed, with his straight driving a special feature, and achieved many devastating innings; his match-winning 214* from 241 balls at Lord's in 1984 was one of four Test double centuries. At some time he held records for the highest scores in each of the English one-day competitions.
108 Tests 1974-91: 7558 runs at 44.72, 19 100s HS 226; 96 catches.
128 One-day Ints: 5134 runs at 45.03, 11 100s HS 133; 1 wicket; 45 catches.*
First-class 1970-92: 37,354 runs at 45.88, 92 100s HS 273; 18 wickets at 26.61, BB 5-49; 516 catches.*

Hal GREER (USA)

BASKETBALL

Harold Everett Greer. b. 26 Jun 1936 Huntington, West Virginia.

Greer played for 15 years in the NBA, first with the Syracuse Nationals and later with the Philadelphia 76ers. Collegiately he played at Marshall College in his hometown in West Virginia. He was 2nd-team all-NBA for seven consecutive years 1963-9 and in 1967 he was the sparkplug of the 76ers team which won the NBA Championship and is still considered one of the greatest professional teams of all-time. He averaged 19.2 points from 21,586 career points and averaged over 20 points for eight seasons. He is remembered for one quirk rarely seen: he always shot a jump shot at the free throw line. He played in 10 NBA All-Star Games. When he retired in 1973, Greer held the record for most games played in the NBA (1122) and still stands 5th on the all-time list through 1993.

Forrest GREGG (USA)

AMERICAN FOOTBALL

Alvis Forrest Gregg. b. 18 Oct 1933 Birthright, Texas.

Perhaps the finest epitaph on Forrest Gregg's career was given him by his pro coach, Vince Lombardi, who said that Gregg was the finest football player he ever coached. An offensive tackle, he played for Southern Methodist (SMU) in college and with the Green Bay Packers from 1956-70 in the pros. He spent the 1957 season in military service, and finished his career with one final season in 1971 with the Dallas Cowboys. Gregg was named All-Pro eight times in 15 years, and played in nine Pro Bowls. He helped the Packers win five NFL Championships and the first two Super Bowl titles in 1966-7, adding a third Super Bowl ring with the Cowboys in 1971. He later became a successful coach with the Packers, the Cleveland Browns, and Cincinnati Bengals in the NFL, the Toronto Argonauts of the Canadian Football League, and ended his career at his alma mater, SMU.

Andy GREGORY (UK)

RUGBY LEAGUE

Andrew Gregory. b. 10 Aug 1961 Wigan, Lancashire.

A tough, aggressive scrum-half who joined Widnes in 1979 and later moved to Wigan. The only player to appear in eight Challenge Cup finals, he was on the winning side a record seven times; with Widnes in 1981 and 1984 and with Wigan in 1988-92. His only disappointment was with Widnes in 1982, when they lost to Hull after a replay. He played in four series against Australia but was on the losing side each time.
He made his international début against France in 1981 and went on to win 24 caps (plus one appearance as a substitute).

Jack GREGORY (Aus)

CRICKET

Jack Morrison Gregory. b. 14 Aug 1895 North Sydney, d. 7 Aug 1973 Bega, New South Wales.

A tall, powerful man, with Ted McDonald he formed one of the great fast bowling attacks, and one that was far too good for England and South Africa in the first three

Test series after World War I. He was also a fine aggressive left-handed batsman, although he was a right-arm bowler. He came to the fore with the Australian Imperial Forces team in England in 1919 and for Australia against England in 1920/1 he scored 442 runs at 73.66 and took 23 wickets at 24.17 as well as a record 15 catches in the five Tests. In 1921, when he did the double of 1000 runs and 100 wickets on a tour of England, he took 19 wickets in the Tests and in 1921/2 in South Africa he took 15 wickets at 18.93 and averaged 51.25 with the bat in the three Tests. At Johannesburg in that series he made the fastest ever Test century in terms of time; going on to 119 he reached his 100 in just 70 minutes off 67 balls. Thereafter, although a useful all-rounder, his powers declined somewhat. His father Charles had played, as he did, for New South Wales and his cousin Syd (qv) preceded him as a Test cricketer.
24 Tests 1920-8: 1146 runs at 36.96, 2 100s HS 119; 85 wickets at 31.15, BB 7-69; 37 catches.
First-class 1919-29: 5661 runs at 36.52, 13 100s HS 152; 504 wickets at 20.99, BB 9-32; 195 catches.

Syd GREGORY (Aus)

CRICKET
Sydney Edward Gregory. b. 14 Apr 1870 Randwick, Sydney, d. 1 Aug 1929 Randwick.

Known as 'Little Tich' as he stood just 1.62m *5' 4"*, Syd Gregory had made a record number of 58 Test appearances by his retirement in 1912. His batting was technically correct and he was also a magnificent cover point. He captained New South Wales from 1894 to 1912 and Australia in six Tests at the Triangular Tournament in 1912, when several leading Australian players refused to play in a row over terms. The team was weak and Gregory, at 42, well past his best. He is the only Australian to have batted in every position in the batting order in Tests.
His father **Ned** (1839-99) and uncle **Dave** (1845-1919) (captain) played in the first ever Test match in 1877, and Jack Gregory (qv) was his cousin. His brother **Charles** (1878-1910) scored 383 for New South Wales v Queensland in 1906, then the highest first-class score by an Australian.
58 Tests 1890-1912: 2282 runs at 24.53, 4 100s HS 201; 25 catches.
First-class 1889-1912: 15,192 runs at 28.55, 25 100s HS 201; 2 wickets; 174 catches.

Tony GREIG (UK)

CRICKET
Anthony William Greig. b. 6 Oct 1946 Queenstown, South Africa.

Greig will be remembered as the leading henchman of Kerry Packer in recruiting players for World Series Cricket. He was at the time a highly successful captain of England, who inspired a series win in India in 1976/7. The revelation of his World Series preparations brought him much abuse, notably from those who had never been comfortable with the fact that a South African born man could become England captain, and he lost the captaincy although he played under Mike Brearley in 1977 before the Packer series began. He continued to be a leading figure in the Packer organisation and a TV commentator in Australia. Such notoriety distracts attention from the fact that he had a superb temperament for Test cricket, achieving notable success as a middle-order batsman and a medium pace or off-break bowler, and instilling great spirit into a flagging England side. Born of a Scottish father and South African mother, he qualified to play for Sussex at the age of 20, and captained them in 1973-7. He made his England début against the Rest of the World in 1970 and was the tallest player at 2.02m *6' 7 1/2"* to play for England.
His brother **Ian** (b. 8 Dec 1955) played in two Tests for England in 1982 and played for Cambridge University 1977-9, Sussex 1980-5 and Surrey as captain 1987-91.
58 Tests 1972-7: 3599 runs at 40.43, 8 100s HS 143; 141 wickets at 32.20, BB 8-86; 87 catches.
22 One-day Ints: 269 runs at 16.81, HS 48; 19 wickets at 32.57, BB 4-45; 7 catches.

First-class 1965-78: 16,660 runs at 31.19, 26 100s HS 226; 856 wickets at 28.85, BB 8-25; 345 catches.

Wayne GRETZKY (Can)

ICE HOCKEY

Wayne Gretzky. b. 26 Jan 1961 Brantford, Ontario.

'The Great One' was a scoring sensation by the age of ten and lived up to all expectations to become ice hockey's greatest ever goal scorer and Canadian hero. Playing as a centre, he has smashed all NHL scoring records, taking just over ten years to surpass the 1850 career points that Gordie Howe amassed over 26 seasons. Gretzky played for the Edmonton Oilers from 1979 until joining the Los Angeles Kings in a $15m deal in 1988. He has won the Hart Trophy as NHL MVP a record nine times, 1980-7 and 1989, the Ross Trophy for leading scorer a record eight times, 1980-7 and 1990, and the Leston Pearson Award for the outstanding player five times 1982-5, 1987. Gretzky has dominated the game with skill, stickhandling, and an unequalled vision. He does not have the strength of a Howe or Hull, nor the speed or an Orr or Cournoyer, but it is likely that no player has ever controlled the puck better, nor understood the nuances of the game better.

He learned to skate at the age of 6 and although he broke all scoring records with Sault Ste. Marie Greyhounds, some experts felt that his relatively small size would inhibit his progress. However, he joined Indianapolis Racers in the WHA for 1978/9 at the age of 17 and scored 110 points in 60 games. He was the youngest ever goal scoring leader in the NHL in his first season 1979/80, when he also won the Lady Byng Memorial Trophy for the most gentlemanly player, and set new season's records for goals, 1981/2; for assists, five times from 109 in 1980/1 to 163 in 1985/6; and for points, three times from 164 in 1980/1 to 215 in 1985/6.

He assisted the Oilers to four Stanley Cup victories, 1984-5 and 1987-8, and won the Smythe Trophy as the play-offs MVP in 1985 and 1988. To the end of the 1992 season he stretched his records for goals and assists in the Stanley Cup play-offs to 95 and 211 respectively. A chronic back injury in early 1992 threatened his career, but he returned to the NHL in January 1993. He again won the Lady Byng Trophy in 1991 and 1992. He is married to actress Janet Jones.

Career: 1124 games, 811 goals, 2438 points. NHL: 1044 games, 765 goals, 2328pts. Playoffs: 156+ games, 110 goals, 346 pts.

Gretzky's NHL record

Season	*goals*	*assists*	*points*
1979/80	51	86	137
1980/1	55	109	164
1981/2	92	120	212
1982/3	71	125	196
1983/4	87	118	205
1984/5	73	135	208
1985/6	52	163	215
1986/7	62	121	183
1987/8	40	109	149
1988/9	54	114	168
1989/90	40	102	142
1990/1	41	122	163
1991/2	31	90	121
1992/3	16	49	65

Rosey GRIER (USA)

AMERICAN FOOTBALL

Roosevelt Grier. b. 14 Jul 1932 Cuthbert, Georgia.

One of the greatest defensive tackles in football history. He played collegiately at Penn State and began his NFL career in 1955 with the New York Giants. Except for missing 1957 because of military service, he played for them until 1962 when he was traded to the Los Angeles Rams. Grier had been a dominant defensive lineman for the Giants but for the Rams, with Deacon Jones, Merlin Olsen, and Lamar Lundy, Grier became part of what some consider the greatest ever defensive line, the 'Fearsome Foursome'. Literally a giant of a man (1.96m *6'5"* and 136 kg *300 lb*), Grier became a well-known actor and television personality after his retirement as a player. He was also active in politics and supported the ill-fated campaign of Robert Kennedy for the 1968 presidential nomination. After Kennedy was shot and killed at the Ambassador Hotel in Los Angeles, Rosey Grier tackled and subdued the assassin Sirhan B. Sirhan, and supported Kennedy with Rafer Johnson, the 1960 Olympic decathlon gold medallist.

Bob GRIESE (USA)

AMERICAN FOOTBALL

Robert Allen Griese. b. 3 Feb 1945 Evansville, Indiana.

As a star quarterback at Purdue University 1964-6, he was runner-up in his senior season to Steve Spurrier in the Heisman Memorial Trophy balloting. Griese, however, had by far the better professional career, as a quarterback for the Miami Dolphins. He was All-Pro in 1971 and 1977, and played in the Pro Bowl six times. In 1972 and 1973 he led the Dolphins to Super Bowl titles, avenging a 1971 loss to the Dallas Cowboys. In 1973, the Dolphins had the single greatest season in pro football history, uniquely winning all 17 games they played that year. Since his retirement, Griese has become a popular television football analyst.
NFL career 1967-80: 25,092 yards from 1926 pass completions, 56.2%, 192 TD.

Archie GRIFFIN (USA)

AMERICAN FOOTBALL

Archie Mason Griffin. b. 21 Aug 1954 Columbus, Ohio.

Griffin played professional football for seven years with the Cincinnati Bengals, but he is far more famous for his college career at Ohio State. As a running back for the Buckeyes he was the only player to win the heralded Heisman Memorial Trophy twice, in 1974 and 1975. He was the first college running back to gain over 5000 yards running, carrying for 5177 yards at an average of 6.1 per carry, and he rushed for over 100 yards in 31 consecutive games. He became a sports administrator at Ohio State after his NFL retirement. He briefly played in the USFL in 1985 with the Jacksonville Bulls.

Emile GRIFFITH (USVI)

BOXING

Emile Alphonse Griffith. b. 3 Feb 1938 St Thomas, US Virgin Islands

Griffith won world professional titles five times in a career that spanned from 1958 until 1977. He won the world welterweight title three times (1961, 1962, and 1963) and the middleweight twice (1966 and 1967), and had several classic battles against Benny 'Kid' Paret, Luis Rodriguez and Nino Benvenuti. The nadir of his career came on 24 Mar 1962 when he regained the world welterweight title from Benny 'Kid' Paret (b. 3 Apr 1962). Griffith pummelled Paret in the 12th round and Paret died several days later from head injuries sustained during the fight.
Career record: W - 85 (23), L - 24, D -1.

Florence GRIFFITH-JOYNER (USA)

ATHLETICS

Delores Florence Griffith. b. 21 Dec 1959 Los Angeles.

'Flo-Jo' was the athlete of 1988 as she produced astonishing sprinting. She first captured the headlines with her amazing series of runs at the US Trials, especially her world record time of 10.49 in the quarter-final of the 100m, which was followed by a US record of 21.77 for 200m. She showed brilliant form at the Olympics, where she won the 100m in a wind-assisted 10.54, then set two world records at the 200m, 21.56 in the semi-final and 21.34 in the final, and completed triple gold at the sprint relay. She then earned a silver at 4 x 400m relay with a 48.07 leg. Her four medals equalled the women's Olympic record. Her attire in 1988 was equally impressive and she formerly had six-inch fingernails on her left hand!
While at UCLA she won NCAA titles at 200m in 1982 and at 400m in 1983. At 200m she had been a silver medallist at the 1984 Olympics and 1987 Worlds (where she won a gold at sprint relay). Best time for 400m was 50.89 in 1985. Sullivan Award winner 1988.
She married **Al Joyner** (b. 19 Jan 1960 East St Louis), the 1984 Olympic triple

jump champion, in October 1987, and their daughter Mary Ruth was born on 14 Nov 1990.

Terry GRIFFITHS (UK)

SNOOKER

Terry Griffiths. b. 16 Oct 1947 Llanelli.

Winner of the World Professional title at his first attempt in 1979, Griffiths has not won again but has remained one of the world's best with his steady, deliberate play. He was Welsh Amateur champion in 1975 and won the English Amateur in 1977 and 1978 before turning professional. He helped Wales win the World Cup in 1979 and 1980, and in 1980 won the Benson & Hedges Masters. In 1982 he won the Mercantile Credit Classic and the UK Open, and in 1988, when he was beaten by Steve Davis in the final.

Burleigh GRIMES (USA)

BASEBALL

Burleigh Arland Grimes. b. 9 Aug 1893 Emerald, Wisconsin, d. 6 Dec 1985 Clear Lake, Wisconsin.

Grimes was a right-handed pitcher whose primary claim to fame is that he was the last legal spitball pitcher in the major leagues. He was a fiery competitor who often threw inside to keep batters off the plate. After his playing career with seven different teams he managed the Los Angeles Dodgers for two years, and then for over 10 years in the minors.

Career pitching 1916-34: ERA 3.53; W-L 270-212, SO 1512. Best seasons: 1928: 25-14, 2.99 ERA; 1920: 23-11, 2.22 ERA.

Clarrie GRIMMETT (Aus)

CRICKET

Clarence Victor Grimmett. b. 25 Dec 1891 Caversham, Dunedin, New Zealand, d. 2 May 1980 Adelaide.

Unprepossessing in appearance - small, wizened of face and prematurely bald, with a somewhat round-arm action, Grimmett was a superb leg-break bowler with great control. He played for Wellington in his native New Zealand before the first World War, and played a few matches for Victoria after he had moved to Australia. It was not, however, until he started playing for South Australia in 1924/5 that he came to prominence and he made his Test début at the age of 33. It was a sensational start as he took 11-82 in the match against England at Melbourne in 1925. Despite his very late start he went on to take a Test record number of 216 wickets and many felt his Test career ended prematurely, particularly as he took 44 wickets at 14.59 in his last series, against South Africa in 1935/6, with 7-100 and 6-73 in his last match.

His 513 wickets in the Sheffield Shield competition is the all-time record.

37 Tests 1925-36: 557 runs at 13.92, HS 50; 216 wickets at 24.21, BB 7-40; 17 catches.

First-class 1911-41: 4720 runs at 17.67, HS 71; 1424 wickets at 22.28, BB 10-37; 139 catches.*

Judy GRINHAM (UK)

SWIMMING

Judith Brenda Grinham. b. 5 Mar 1939 Hampstead, London. Married journalist Peter Rowley, now Mrs Roe.

In 1956 when she won the Olympic 100m backstroke she became Britain's first swimming gold medallist for 36 years. In so doing she set an initial long course world record of 1:12.9, adding further records at 110y (and the shorter 100m) with 1:11.9 in 1958 when she won the Commonwealth Games title. There, in Cardiff, she also won a gold medal on England's world record-breaking medley relay team and took a bronze in the freestyle relay. She achieved a unique hat-trick by adding the European backstroke title that year, and also won a silver at freestyle relay and bronzes at 100m freestyle and medley relay. She was ASA champion at 110y backstroke in 1955-6, 1958, and at freestyle 220y 1957 and 110y 1958.

She swam for the Hampstead Ladies SC, where she was coached by Reg Laxton. After her retirement following the 1958 season she wrote for the *Daily Express*.

Later she coached swimming and became the national training officer for Dr Barnardo's.

Yevgeniy GRISCHIN (USSR)

SPEED SKATING

Yevgeniy Grischin. b. 23 Mar 1931 Tula.

The leading sprinter in world speed skating in the late 1950s and early 1960s and winner of four Olympic gold medals. A member of the USSR cycling team at the 1952 Olympics he was in the Russian speed skating team from 1952 to 1968. In the World Championships he was third overall in 1954 and 1956 but his record at 500m was unparalleled; in eight starts between 1954 and 1963 he won the event six times and he also won the Olympic title in 1956 and 1960. Additionally, he was the Olympic champion at 1500m in both years but never managed to win the world title at this distance although he placed second three times. He was European all-round champion in 1956.
At 500m he set four world bests and on 27 Jan 1963 he recorded 39.6, the first sub-40 sec time. He also set world records for 1000m (1:22.8) and 1500m (2:09.8) in 1955 and made a further improvement to the 1500m record to 2:08.6 the following year. On retirement he became a coach to the national team.

Dick GROAT (USA)

BASKETBALL and BASEBALL

Richard Morrow Groat. b. 4 Nov 1930 Swissvale, Pennsylvania.

One of the greatest two-sport athletes in history. A native of Pennsylvania, he starred collegiately at Duke University where he played both basketball and baseball. He was an All-American guard playing basketball for Duke in both 1951 and 1952. He also made All-American as a baseball shortstop in those two years, batting .370 and .386 in his junior and senior years. Groat briefly played pro basketball in 1952-3 with the Fort Wayne (later Detroit) Pistons. He spent 1953-4 in the military and then turned to pro baseball. He is best remembered as a top shortstop with the Pittsburgh Pirates, with whom he played through 1965. In 1960 he was named National League MVP as the Pirates won the World Series. Groat finished his career with the Philadelphia Phillies in 1966 and the San Francisco Giants in 1967, and a .286 batting average.

Michael GROSS (FRG)

SWIMMING

Michael Gross. b. 17 Jun 1964 Frankfurt.

Known as 'The Albatross' for his huge 2.25m arm span, the 2.02m tall German won a record 13 medals at three world championships 1982-90: five gold, five silver and three bronze. His individual event wins were at 200m freestyle and butterfly in both 1982 and 1986.
At the 1984 Olympic Games he set world records when he won the 200m freestyle in 1:47.44 and the 100m butterfly in 53.08, but was surprisingly only second to Jon Sieben at 200m butterfly and won another silver at 4x200m freestyle relay (with the fastest ever 200m split, 1:46.89). He won the 200m butterfly in 1988 in an Olympic record 1:56.94, and added a relay bronze. He set ten world records at individual events: three more at 200m freestyle in 1983-4, 3:47.80 at 400m freestyle in 1985, four at 200m butterfly to 1:56.24 in 1986. Other best: 100m freestyle 50.13 (1988). He also set world short course records: freestyle 200m 1:44.50 (1982), 400m 3:42.40 (1985), 800m 7:38.75 (1985); butterfly 100m 52.9 (1984), 200m 1:54.78 (1985). He set 67 German records in all.
With 13 gold medals, four silvers and a bronze he had a record 18 medals in four European Championships, winning three individual events, 200m freestyle, 100m and 200m butterfly, in both 1983 and 1985. In 1983 he won four golds and a silver, with three world records in five days, and in 1985 he also swam on three winning FRG relay teams, for a record six golds at one Championships. He also won 200m butterfly titles in 1981 and 1987 and the 4 x 200m in 1987. He had won his first national title in 1979, winning four events, but had to miss the 1980 Olympics due to the boycott.

Johan GRØTTUMSBRÅTEN (Nor)

NORDIC SKIING
Johan Grøttumsbråten. b. 12 Feb 1899 Sørkedalen, Oslo, d. 24 Jan 1983.

The winner of three Olympic gold medals, the Nordic Combined in 1928 and 1932 and the 18km cross-country in 1928. He had also won three medals in 1924, silver at 18km, and bronze at 50km and combined. At the World Championships he won the combined in 1926 and the 18km and combined titles in 1931.

Wally GROUT (Aus)

CRICKET
Arthur Theodore Wallace Grout. b. 30 Mar 1927 Mackay, Queensland, d. 9 Nov 1968 Brisbane.

Grout's eight catches in an innings for Queensland v Western Australia in 1960 remains the record for first-class cricket, although subsequently equalled twice. By then he was firmly established as Australia's wicket-keeper, and in January 1964 he passed Bert Oldfield's record number of dismissals for Australia in Tests. His 23 victims in 1960/1 against the West Indies tied the then Test series record. He was a good enough batsman to have opened occasionally for Queensland.
51 Tests 1957-66: 890 runs at 16.77, HS 74; 163 catches, 24 stumpings.
First-class 1946-66: 5168 runs at 22.56, 4 100s HS 119; 3 wickets; 473 catches, 114 stumpings.

Lefty GROVE (USA)

BASEBALL
Robert Moses Grove. b. 6 Mar 1900 Lonaconing, Ohio, d. 22 May 1975 Norwalk, Ohio.

Considered the greatest left-handed pitcher ever by some experts. When with the Philadelphia Athletics he led the American League in strikeouts for seven consecutive years 1925-31. He was also famous for his violent temper. A fireballer in his early days, he hurt his arm in mid-career, and with the Boston Red Sox, for whom he played from 1934, he was more of a crafty pitcher. In his later years he also mellowed and became quite genial. He holds the record for 593 strikeouts at bat by a pitcher in a career.
Career pitching: 1925-41 ERA 3.06; W-L 300-141, SO 2266. Best seasons: 1931: 31-4, 2.06 ERA; 1930: 28-5, 2.54; 1928: 24-8, 2.58; 1932: 25-10, 2.84; 1933: 24-8, 3.21.

Alex GROZA (USA)

BASKETBALL
Alexander John Groza. b. 7 Oct 1926 Martins Ferry, Ohio.

The biggest star of the Kentucky teams of the late 1940s. The 2.01m *6'7"* forward played for two seasons in the NBA with the Indianapolis Olympians, of which he was part-owner. He was an excellent player, making first-team all-league both years, and was twice runner-up for the scoring title to big George Mikan. He was also one of the league's top rebounders. He later returned to his home state of Kentucky and when the ABA was formed in 1967 he was instrumental in bringing a team to play in his home state, the Kentucky Colonels. In 1970, as general manager, he also took over the reins as an interim coach for two games, winning both. In 1974 the call of coaching lured him back and he coached half a season, but with little success, for the San Diego Conquistadors of the ABA, succeeding Wilt Chamberlain. His older brother, Lou, became quite well known as a place-kicker for the Cleveland Browns.

Gheorge GRUIA (Rom)

HANDBALL
Gheorge Gruia. b. 2 Oct 1940.

Widely considered to be the best handball player in the world when he was a member of the Romanian team which was victorious in the World Championships of 1964 and 1970.
He scored more than 600 goals in his 126 internationals for Romania and also won an Olympic bronze medal in 1972. He was a PE teacher and played for Steaua Bucharest.

Wille GRUT (Swe)

MODERN PENTATHLON

William Oscar Guernsey Grut. b. 17 Sep 1914 Stockholm.

In 1948, when he was a captain in the artillery, he won the Olympic modern pentathlon title by the most overwhelming margin ever. He finished first in three of the five disciplines, riding, fencing and swimming, and was fifth at shooting and eighth at running. That year he was also second in the demonstration pentathlon event at the Winter Olympics and was declared Sweden's sportsman of the year. He then succeeded Sven Thofelt as Sweden's team manager and became secretary-general of the sport's international governing body, the UIPMB in 1960.
At the age of 16 Grut was Swedish schoolboy champion and record holder at 100m freestyle swimming, and a year later, in 1932, was Swedish champion at 100m, 400m and 1500m. He beat Arne Borg's national record for 200m in 1932 (2:16.0). Wille had planned to study medicine but after his father had lost much of his money opted instead to become a soldier. In 1936 as a second lieutenant in the artillery he was a reserve on the Swedish Olympic swimming team in Berlin, and started his pentathlon training. In 1938 he won the first of five Swedish titles at the five-event discipline and had a brilliant victory against Germany.
His father, Torben Grut, was a finalist in the Swedish tennis championships and was also a distinguished architect who designed the Stockholm Stadium for the 1912 Olympics.

Ruud GULLIT (Hol)

FOOTBALL

Ruud Gullit. b. 1 Sep 1962 Amsterdam.

Initially a sweeper, he later became an outstanding midfield attacking player. Powerful at 1.93m tall, he won the first of his 65 caps (with 17 goals to May 1993) on his 19th birthday in 1981 while with Haarlem, before going to Feyenoord the following year. After a move to PSV Eindhoven (1985) he was transferred to AC Milan for a then world record fee of £5.5 million, and in his first year in Italy (1987) he was voted both European and World Footballer of the Year.
In 1988 he helped Milan to the Italian League Championship and led Holland to victory in the European Championship, but unfortunately he sustained a knee injury in a friendly game from which he never fully recovered. Despite recurring problems with his knee, he helped Milan to two victories in the European Cup (1989, when he scored twice in the final, and 1990) and two further league titles 1992-3 before joining Sampdoria in July 1993. His father played football for Surinam and his mother was Dutch.

Erik GUNDERSEN (Den)

SPEEDWAY

Erik Gundersen. b. 8 Oct 1959 Jerne, Esbjerg.

He made speedway history in 1985 when he became the first man to hold simultaneously the world title at individual, pairs, team and long track events. In all he won 17 world titles: three individual (1984-5, 1988), five pairs (1985-9), two long track (1984, 1986) and seven team (1981, 1983-8).

George GUNN (UK)

CRICKET

George Gunn. b. 13 Jun 1879 Hucknall Torkard, Nottinghamshire, d. 29 Jun 1958 Cuckfield, Sussex.

In his long career he scored over 35,000 runs, yet that figure could well have been higher but for his somewhat eccentric attitude. That may well also have cost him the chance of playing more Tests, for he played only once (in 1909) in England despite his fine record. On his Test début in 1907 he made 119 and 74 against Australia, and although he did not live up to that, the fact that he announced his intentions to do something special on his 50th birthday and then scored 164 for Notts v Worcester showed his genius. At that age he played four Tests for England in the West Indies in 1930, after a record

interval of 17 years and 316 days since his previous selection. His uncle **Billy** (1858-1921) played 11 Tests for England 1887-99 and his brother **John** (1876-1963) played 6 Tests for England 1901-05. In 1931 he and his son George V Gunn both scored centuries for Nottinghamshire v Warwickshire, a unique feat in the first-class game.
15 Tests 1907-30: 1120 runs at 40.00, 2 100s HS 122; 15 catches.*
First-class 1902-32: 35,208 runs at 35.96, 62 100s HS 220; 66 wickets at 35.68, BB 5-50; 473 catches

Dan GURNEY (USA)

MOTOR RACING
Daniel Sexton Gurney. b. 13 Apr 1931 Port Jefferson, Long Island, New York.

His win in the 1967 Belgian GP was the first Grand Prix win by an American driver in an American car since 1921. Very tall at 1.88m *6ft 2in* for a racing driver, he bought his first car in 1948 and began his serious racing career in sports cars in 1955 when he was working as an engineer in California. He made his European début in a Ferrari at Le Mans in 1958 and his first World Championship race was a sixth place at Reims in the 1959 French Grand Prix. He switched to BRM for 1960 but met with more success with Porsche in 1961, when he was equal third in the championship. He continued to be well placed each year, for Porsche 1962 and Brabham 1963-5, but then set up a manufacturing business with Carroll Shelby and raced his cars under the name Eagle. His cars proved unreliable in Formula One but he had that one success at Spa in 1967. He raced in a McLaren from 1968 until his retirement in 1970, his world championship career record being four wins and 133 points from 86 races. In the Indianapolis 500 he was second in 1968 and 1969, and third in 1970, and he won at Le Mans in 1967 with A J Foyt. Now president of All American Racers, his Eagle cars have been highly successful in the USA, wining the Indianapolis 500 in 1968, 1973 and 1975.

Koji GUSHIKEN (Japan)

GYMNASTICS
Koji Gushiken. b. 12 Nov 1956 Osaka.

The winner of the Olympic gold medal in 1984 after the closest all-around competition for 60 years, as he came from only 5th place after the preliminaries. At individual events he won a medal of each colour and gained a team bronze. At World Championships he was 3rd overall in 1981, with gold for parallel bars, and 2nd in 1983, with gold for rings. A PE teacher, he was coached by Eizo Kenmotsu.

Tomas GUSTAFSON (Swe)

SPEED SKATING
Sven Tomas Gustafson. b. 28 Dec 1959 Katrineholm.

The first Swede to win the Olympic 5000m speed skating title. He made his way steadily to the top, placing 19th and 9th in the World Championships of 1978 and 1979 before his undistinguished Olympic début in 1980 when he was 7th at 1500m and 12th at both 5000m and 10,000m. At the three World Championships from 1981 to 1983 he progressed to 6th, 5th and 2nd, before reaching the top at the 1984 Olympics when he won the 5000m and was second at 10,000m. In 1988 he not only successfully defended his 5000m title but also won the 10,000m in the world record time of 13:48.20. At his fourth Games in 1992 he was 13th at 5000m. World junior champion 1979-80 and Swedish all-round champion 1978, 1982-3, 1986, 1988-90.
Other bests: 500m 38.10, 1500m 1:53.22, 5000m 6:44.51.

Ray GUY (USA)

AMERICAN FOOTBALL
William Raymond Guy. b. 22 Dec 1949 Swainsboro, Georgia.

Considered the greatest punter in pro football history and the first ever selected in the first round of the NFL draft after his college career at Southern Mississippi. Guy led the NFL in punting four times and played in seven Pro Bowls. In his 14-year career, 1973-86, with the Oakland Raiders, he had only one punt blocked. Though his average distance did not approach any records, Guy was known for the incredible height of his punts, which gave them a very long hang-time and prevented returns. An excellent athlete, Guy was drafted as a baseball pitcher by the Cincinnati Reds (1969, 1973), Houston Astros (1971), and Atlanta Braves (1972).

Dezsö GYARMATI (Hun)

WATER POLO

Dezsö Gyarmati. b. 23 Oct 1927 Miskolc.

Gyarmati has been considered the greatest ever water polo player. He began his career in 1943 and won Olympic medals at each Games from 1948 to 1964 - gold in 1952, 1956 and 1964, silver in 1948 and bronze in 1960. He was also a member of the Hungarian European championship winning teams of 1954 and 1962. Highly versatile, as well as being ambidextrous, he could play at back or forward. From 1967 he coached the Hungarian team, taking them to Olympic gold in 1976. Later he was a member of the Hungarian Parliament.

His wife **Éva** (née **Székely**, b. 3 Apr 1927) was Olympic champion at 200m breaststroke in 1952 and silver medallist in 1956. She was second in the European 200m breaststroke in 1947 and set world records for 100m breaststroke (using the then permissible butterfly stroke) with 1:16.9 in 1951 and twice for 400m individual medley with 5:50.4 in 1953 and 5:40.8 in 1955. She won a total of 29 Hungarian titles.

Dezsö and Éva's daughter **Andrea** (b. 15 May 1954) won European swimming gold medals in 1970 at 200m backstroke and 100m butterfly, and also took silver at 100m backstroke and freestyle relay. She broke the world record for 100m butterfly with 63.80 in the heats of the 1972 Olympics, but although she improved to 63.73 in the final she just failed to emulate her parents as Olympic champion for she placed third as two others also beat the world record; she also won the silver medal at 100m backstroke in Munich, and in 1973 was third in the World 200m backstroke. In all she set 12 European records at backstroke events, with bests of 65.93 for 100m (1973) and 2:24.3 200m (1972). Keeping gold in the family, Andrea married the 1968 Olympic kayak canoeing champion Mihály Hesz.

Christl HAAS (Aut)

ALPINE SKIING

Christl Haas. b. 19 Sep 1943 Kitzbühel.

At downhill skiing she was the Olympic champion in 1964 and bronze medallist in 1968. In 1991 she placed her gold medal in the coffin of Germot Reinstadler, killed at Wengen at the age of 20. His mother Traudi Eder had skied with Haas on the Austrian team in the 1960s.

George HACKENSCHMIDT (Rus)

WRESTLING

George Hackenschmidt. b. 2 Aug 1878 Tartu, Estonia, d. 19 Feb 1968 London, England.

Of German, Swedish, and Russian descent, 'The Russian Lion' was considered the strongest man in the world at the turn of the century. He won the 1898 Greco-Roman amateur world wrestling championship and then turned professional in June 1900, by which time he was already known as a strongman who toured extensively throughout Europe. In April 1901 he became world professional Greco-Roman champion in Vienna and had two historic matches with Frank Gotch, although losing them both. Some older wrestling experts considered Hack to have been past his prime by then. He was a prisoner of war of the Germans in World War I, and became a British citizen in 1945. He used neither alcohol nor tobacco and in his later years was a strict vegetarian.

Andy HADEN (NZ)

RUGBY UNION

Andrew Maxwell Haden. b. 26 Sep 1950 Wanganui.

One of the dominant figures in world

rugby for more than a decade. At 1.99m 6'6 $^1/_2$" he is one of the tallest-ever All Blacks and after making his début against the Lions in 1977 he was an automatic choice as lock. He played for New Zealand a record 117 times, including 41 Tests. These impressive totals would undoubtedly have been greater but for his volatile and controversial character. After playing in 22 consecutive Tests he missed the first Test against Scotland in 1981 as he was under suspension for fighting in a club match. He was unavailable for the tour to Britain in 1983 as he was promoting his recently published book, and he missed the tour to Australia in 1984 when his amateur status was under investigation. He was the pioneer of off-season play in Europe and for a time played for Harlequins (England) on Saturdays and Algida (Italy) on Sundays.

His various off-field activities often strained relationships with officialdom but on the field few men have made a greater contribution to New Zealand rugby.

Richard HADLEE (NZ)

CRICKET

(Sir) Richard John Hadlee. b. 3 Jul 1951 Christchurch.

Steadily developed into the world's top fast-medium bowler, ending his career with a Test record number of wickets. He had equalled Ian Botham's record of 373 wickets in December 1987, but did not pass it until 12 Nov 1988, going on to take his 400th wicket in his 80th Test. His 36 Test innings taking five wickets or more is also well ahead of the next best of 27 by Botham. He also became a top-class all-rounder as his left-handed batting (he bowled right) improved steadily. In 1990 he became the first Test cricketer to take the field after being knighted (previously awarded MBE 1980). The impressive Test match feats of this most intelligent bowler played a major part in enabling New Zealand to achieve series successes for the first time over Australia home and away and over England away.

He played for Canterbury from 1971, and in 1978-87 for Nottinghamshire in England, where he set himself specific targets, achieving in 1984 the first double of 1000 runs and 100 wickets since 1967, made so much harder since the reduction in the first-class programme.

His father **Walter** (b. 4 Jun 1915) scored 543 runs at 30.16 in 11 Tests 1937-51 and captained New Zealand 1946-51, and Richard's elder brothers both played for New Zealand: **Dayle** (b. 6 Jan 1948), a fast-medium bowler, took 71 wickets at 33.64 in 26 Tests, and **Barry**, a batsman, played in 2 one-day internationals. Walter and Richard are the only fathers and sons to have hit Test centuries for New Zealand.

86 Tests 1973-90: 3124 runs at 27.16, 2 100s HS 151; 431 wickets, at 22.29, BB 9-52; 39 catches.*

115 One-day Ints: 1749 runs at 21.59, HS 79; 158 wickets at 21.56, BB 5-25; 27 catches.

First-class 1971-90: 12,052 runs at 31.71, 14 100s HS 210; 1490 wickets at 18.11, BB 9-52; 198 catches.*

Åge HADLER (Nor)

ORIENTEERING

Åge Hadler. b. 14 Aug 1944 Bergen.

Winner of the World Championship in 1966 and 1972, the first of the three men who have won the title twice. He also won the bronze medal in 1968, and in the relay took gold in 1968, silver 1974 and bronze 1966 and 1970. He was Norwegian champion in 1966-7, 1970-1 and 1973 as well as at long distance in 1968-9 and 1973, and Nordic champion in 1969 and 1971.

His wife **Ingrid** (b. 12 Feb 1946 Trondheim) (née Thoresen) was individual world champion in 1970, and took the silver medal in 1968, adding gold in 1968, silver in 1974 and bronze in 1966 and 1970 in the relay.

Cliff HAGAN (USA)

BASKETBALL

Clifford Oldham Hagan. b. 9 Dec 1931 Owensboro, Kentucky.

A forward known for having one of the great hook shots in basketball history. He played collegiately at Kentucky where he starred as a forward. Graduating in 1954, he was drafted by the Celtics, but never played in Boston as he was traded to the St Louis Hawks, where he played his entire NBA career 1956-66. Hagan was a member of an NCAA championship team (1951) and NBA championship team (1958), and the 1954 Kentucky team which he captained was undefeated (25-0) but could not play for the NCAA title because it was on probation. He ended his professional career with three seasons as player-coach with the Dallas Chaparrals of the ABA and later returned to his alma mater, where he served as athletic director from 1975 until 1989.

Walter HAGEN (USA)

GOLF

Walter Charles B Hagen. b. 21 Dec 1892 Rochester, New York, d. 5 Oct 1969 Traverse City, Michigan.

Hagen brought respectability to professional golf and his dashing style, loved by spectators, made him golf's most colourful personality and one of the best-loved golfers ever. In addition, he was a great champion. He protested against the second-class treatment of professionals, who often were not allowed to enter the clubhouse at major tournaments. After the 1923 British Open, in which he finished 2nd, he refused to attend the presentation ceremony because of that affront and instead invited spectators to the pub where he was staying. Hagen's four consecutive wins in the US PGA, 1924-7, following an earlier win in 1921, mark the only time any player has won the same major or indeed any US PGA tournament four times consecutively. He won the US Open in 1914 and 1919, the British Open 1922, 1924, 1928-9, Canadian Open 1931, Western Open 1916, 1921, 1926-7, 1932 and the French Open 1920. In five Ryder Cups 1927-35 he won 7, lost 1 and halved 1 of his 9 matches.

Hagen was known for all-night parties, a chauffeur-driven limousine, and his sartorial splendour. He played easily and loosely, but could concentrate intensely when necessary. His motto was, 'Never hurry and don't worry. You're here for just a short visit, so don't forget to stop and smell the flowers along the way.'

Gunder HÄGG (Swe)

ATHLETICS

Gunder Hägg. b. 31 Dec 1918 Hällersjö.

Hägg ran 16 world records at all events in the war years 1941-5: three each at 1500m (to 3:43.0 in 1944), 1 mile (best 4:01.4 in 1945) and 2 miles (8:42.8); two at 2000m (5:11.8) and 3 miles (13:32.4); and one each at 3000m (8:01.2), 5000m (13:58.2, the first sub-14 minute time) and 4 x 1500m relay. With his great rival Arne Andersson, he was suspended from amateur competition in November 1945, so did not contest the international meetings after the war. He was Swedish champion at 1500m in 1941 and at 5000m in 1944 and 1945, and was unbeaten on a tour in the USA in 1943.

A smooth and powerful front runner, Hägg, trained by Gösta Olander at Vålådalen, reached world class in 1940 and had his greatest year in 1942, when he set ten world records in 82 days from 1 July to 20 September.

Marvin HAGLER (USA)

BOXING

Marvelous Marvin Hagler. b. 23 May 1952 Newark, New Jersey

Hagler was such a great middleweight that he was nicknamed 'Marvelous Marvin'; he liked the tag so much that he eventually had his name legally changed. He was that rare boxer who possessed great technical skills and also had a knockout punch with either hand. He did not earn a title fight for seven years, as the champions avoided him because he was so good. In his first bout against Vito Antuofermo on 30 Nov 1979, Hagler earned only a draw in a hotly disputed decision. However, he won the middleweight title in 1980 by stopping Alan Minter in three rounds. After 12 successful title defences Hagler retired after losing a much-ballyhooed fight against Sugar Ray Leonard in 1987.

Career record: W - 62 (52), L - 3, D -2.

Christine HAHN (GDR)

ROWING

née Christine Scheiblich. b. 31 Dec 1954 Wilsdruff.

The greatest ever female sculler. She won the initial Olympic gold medal in women's sculling in 1976 at Montreal and won the first four world championships in single sculls, in 1974-5 and 1977-8. She then retired to train as a physiotherapist. Married to Ulrich Hahn, who was world champion at two-seater luge 1974-5.

Mike HAILWOOD (UK)

MOTOR CYCLING and MOTOR RACING

Stanley Michael Bailey Hailwood. b. 2 Apr 1940 Oxford, d. 23 Mar 1981 Birmingham.

The supreme motorcyclist of the early 1960s, one of the most exciting periods in the history of the sport, and many experts' choice as the greatest of all-time. He became the youngest ever world champion in 1961 at 250cc, and won further world titles at 500cc 1962-5 and at both 250cc and 350cc, 1966-7. After switching to motor racing, he returned to win the motorcycling Formula One world title in 1978.

'Mike the Bike' was started in his motorcycling career by his father Stan, a wealthy motorcycle dealer in Oxford, at the age of 17 in 1957 on a 125cc MV. Four years later he was world champion. He won a total of 76 Grand Prix races between 1961 and 1967, displaying consummate skill and natural ability by winning on different bikes: 2 at 125cc, 21 at 250cc, 16 at 350cc and 37 at 500cc, mostly for MV Augusta and Honda, including a record 19 in one year, 1966. He set a record which stood until 1993 with 14 wins in Isle of Man TT races between 1961 and 1979, winning three events in one year in both 1961 and 1967. Awarded the MBE in 1968.

On four wheels he met with less success as he did not win a Formula One Grand Prix, but he scored 29 world championship points 1971-4, with a best place of second in the 1971 Italian GP driving a Surtees-Ford. He won the European Formula Two title in 1972.

He died in a car accident in Birmingham.

George HAINSWORTH (Can)

ICE HOCKEY

George Hainsworth. b. 26 Jun 1895 Toronto, Ontario, d. 9 Oct 1950.

Although he did not begin his NHL career until he was 31 years old, the diminutive goalie (1.68m *5' 6"*, 68 kg *150 lb*) became one of the greatest ever.

Playing for the Montreal Canadiens from 1926-33 and the Toronto Maple Leafs for the remainder of his career, Hainsworth holds the record for lowest career goals against average, and his 94 total shutouts is second only to Terry Sawchuk, who recorded 103 but played more than twice as many games as Hainsworth. He also set an NHL record in 1929 when he recorded 22 shutouts for the season, a record which has never been approached.

NHL career 1926-37 - 465 games, 1.91 GAA, 94 shutouts. Vezina Trophy 1927-9.

Veikko HAKULINEN (Fin)

NORDIC SKIING

Veikko Johannes Hakulinen. b. 4 Jan 1925 Kurkijoki.

Hakulinen won seven Olympic medals for cross-country skiing: gold at 50km in 1952, gold at 30km with silver at 50km and relay in 1956 (4th at 15km), and a gold (relay), silver (50km) and bronze (15km) in 1960 (6th at 30km). In 1960, at 35 years 52 days, he was the oldest ever Olympic Nordic skiing gold medallist and he competed in a fourth Games in 1964 at biathlon. At that new sport he had won a world team silver in 1963.

He was also world cross-country skiing champion at 15km in 1954 and 1958, with golds at 4x10km in 1954 and 1960, to confirm his status as the outstanding skier of his era.

A forestry technician at Valkeakoski, he was small at 1.73m but quick and agile, and has continued competing happily at skiing, running, rowing, and ski orienteering well into his sixties.

It is planned that a lifesize statue of him will be unveiled at Valkeakoski for his 75th birthday in 1995.

George HALAS (USA)

AMERICAN FOOTBALL

George Stanley 'Papa Bear' Halas. b. 2 Feb 1895 Chicago, d. 31 Oct 1983 Chicago.

Considered by many as the 'Father of the NFL', for the influence he had upon the National Football League of which he was one of the founders. He played football, baseball and basketball at the University of Illinois, graduating in 1918, and then played for the Great Lakes football team at the US Naval training centre, being named MVP of the Rose Bowl in 1919. He briefly played professional baseball with the New York Yankees after his Naval discharge, before in 1922 helping to start the Chicago Bears in the fledgling NFL. His name is still synonymous with the team, for whom he played for a few years, co-owned, and coached until 1968. As a coach he was a pioneer, using daily practices, classroom instructions, game films, and assistant coaches for the first time. He was nick-named 'Papa Bear' although the combative, often crusty Halas was often at odds with fellow owners and players.

Olivér HALASSY (Hun)

WATER POLO

Olivér Halassy. né Haltmayer. b. 31 Jul 1909 Ujpest, d. 10 Sep 1946 Budapest.

Despite losing his left foot below the ankle as a child in a tram accident, Halassy was considered to be the greatest midfield player of the 1930s. A great personality and popular leader, after a silver medal in 1928 he won gold with the Hungarian team in the Olympic Games of 1932 and 1936 and at the European Championships of 1931, 1934 and 1938. He was almost as good a swimmer as a water polo player, winning the European 1500m title in 1931 and 25 Hungarian titles. An auditor by profession, he was shot dead while walk-ing down the street in Budapest.

Murray HALBERG (NZ)

ATHLETICS

Murray Gordon Halberg. b. 7 Jul 1933 Eketahuna.

Halberg overcame the handicap of a with-ered left arm, due to a rugby injury in 1950, to be Olympic 5000m champion in 1960 and win the Commonwealth 3 miles in 1958 and 1962. His international career had started with fifth place at 1 mile in the 1954 Commonwealth Games and he was 11th at 1500m at the 1956 Olympics. He set world records at 2 miles (8:30.0) and 3 miles (13:10.0) in 1961 and had a 5000m best of 13:35.2 in 1961. At 10,000m he was 5th in 1960 and 7th in 1964 at the Olympics. Coached by Arthur Lydiard from 1952, Halberg was NZ champion at 1 mile 1954-7 and 1960, 3 miles 1958-62 and cross-country 1953.

Other best times: 1500m 3:38.8 (1958), 1 mile 3:57.5 (1958), 6 miles 27:32.8 (1964), 10,000m 28:33.0 (1964).

Gary HALL (USA)

SWIMMING

Gary Wayne Hall. b. 7 Aug 1951 Fayetteville, North Carolina.

Hall set his first world record for 400m individual medley at 4:43.3 in 1968, but at the Olympics was narrowly defeated by team-mate Charles Hickcox. The follow-ing year he smashed the time that Hickcox had improved to 4:39.0, with first 4:38.7 and then an astonishing 4:33.9. He made two further improvements to 4:31.0 in 1970 and 4:30.81 in 1972, and also set world records at 200m backstroke, 2:06.6 in 1969; 200m butterfly, 2:05.0 in 1970; and three at 200m IM from 2:09.6 in 1969 to 2:09.3 in 1972. Other bests: freestyle 400m 4:08.5, 1500m 16:32.8. He was also the first man to better 4 minutes for 400 yards IM with 3:58.2 in 1971.

His final two world medley records were set in the US Championships in 1972, but he had lost his peak form by the time of the Olympics a month later, as he 'blew up' in both medley races to place 4th at 200m and 5th at 400m, but did get a silver at 200m butterfly.

Coached by Doc Councilman, Hall won seven individual NCAA titles and led Indiana University to four successive team titles. In all he won 23 AAU titles and set 23 US records in a long career which went on to the 1976 Olympics, where he won the bronze medal at 100m butterfly. Having graduated from Indiana in zoology, Hall went to the University of Cincinnati School of Medicine and has become a distinguished opthalmologist. His son Gary Hall Jr set US junior records for 50m (23.18) and 100m (50.91) freestyle in 1992.

Glenn HALL (Can)

ICE HOCKEY

Glenn Henry Hall. b. 3 Oct 1931 Humboldt, Saskatchewan.

Hockey historian Stan Fischler rates Hall as the greatest goalie ever to play the game. 'Mr Goalie' broke in with the Detroit Red Wings in 1952, but was traded in 1957 to the Chicago Black Hawks, for whom he played for 10 years before finishing his career with four seasons for the St Louis Blues. He pioneered the 'butterfly' method of goaltending, with the skates fanned out towards the posts and the knees pointed inward. He was very nervous, often vomiting before games, but his hair-trigger reflexes made him almost unstoppable in the goal.

NHL career 1952-71 - 906 games, 2.51 GAA, 84 shutouts. Vezina Trophy 1963, 1967, 1969; Calder Trophy 1956, Smythe Trophy 1968.

Lars HALL (Swe)

MODERN PENTATHLON

Lars Hall. b. 30 Apr 1927 Karlskrona, d. 26 Apr 1991 Täby.

The only man to win two individual Olympic gold medals at the modern pentathlon, in 1952 and 1956 . He also won a team silver in 1952. World individual champion in 1950 and 1951 and a member of the winning Swedish team each year 1949-51 and 1953. A carpentry instructor, he was the first non-military Olympic champion at his sport.

Wes HALL (Bar)

CRICKET

Wesley Winfield Hall. b. 12 Sep 1937 Christchurch.

Hall came with the West Indies to England on their tour in 1957 but made little impact and did not play in the Tests. However, he made a dramatic start in Test cricket with 30 wickets at 17.66 in his first series against India in 1958/9, and for the next few years he was the world's leading fast bowler, making a formidable partnership with Charlie Griffith for the West Indies. His pace and his success declined after 1965. Also a useful, hard-hitting batsman, he played his first-class cricket in the West Indies mostly for Barbados, but also for Trinidad 1966-70, and played in Australia for Queensland in 1961-2. He has become a leading politician and sports minister in Barbados.

48 Tests 1958-69: 818 runs at 15.73, HS 50; 192 wickets at 26.38, BB 7-69; 11 catches.*

First-class 1956-71: 2673 runs at 15.80, 1 100 HS 102; 546 wickets at 26.14, BB 7-51; 58 catches.*

Marja-Liisa HÄMÄLÄINEN (Fin)

NORDIC SKIING

Marja-Liisa Hämäläinen. b. 10 Sep 1955 Simpele, Karelia. Later Kirvesniemi.

Hämäläinen completed a unique triple with three cross-country skiing gold medals at the 1984 Olympics at 5km, 10km and 20km; she also won a bronze medal at the relay. She had previously competed at the 1976 and 1980 Games, although with a best individual placing of only 18th.
After her 1984 successes she married **Harri Kirvesniemi** (b. 10 May 1958), who won Olympic bronze medals at 4 x 10km relay in 1980 and 1984.
After gold on the Finnish relay team in 1978 and silver medals at 5km and 10km in 1985, Marja-Liisa finally became world champion at 15km (and relay) in 1989. She competed again at the Olympics in 1988, when she took a relay bronze and was fifth at 5km, and at a fifth Games in 1992, when she was ill and did not succeed. She won a further World silver medal at 5km in 1991.
A farmer's daughter from near the Russian border, she trained as a physiotherapist and her Olympic triumph came at the age of 28

after she had been written-off by Finnish journalists. Her first success was in the relay team at the 1971 European Juniors. She was the World Cup winner in 1983 and 1984.

Dorothy HAMILL (USA)

FIGURE SKATING

Dorothy Stuart Hamill. b. 26 Jul 1956 Chicago, Illinois. Later Martin, then Forsythe.

US figure skating champion each year 1974-6 and the 1976 Olympic and world champion. After taking up skating at the age of eight, she made steady progress through junior and regional competitions until shortly after she won her first US senior title in 1974 she placed second at the World Championships. She turned professional after her 1976 successes and signed a number of lucrative contracts for ice shows and with the media. She was married briefly to the son of the movie star Dean Martin, but in March 1987 she married Kenneth Forsythe, a doctor of sports medicine.

Scott HAMILTON (USA)

FIGURE SKATING

Scott Scovell Hamilton. b. 28 Aug 1958 Toledo, Ohio.

America's most successful figure skater since the days of Dick Button and the Jenkins brothers. As a healthy, normal child he suddenly stopped growing at the age of five when he contracted a rare disease and although he was eventually cured, he never grew beyond 5ft 3in (1.60m). After trying gymnastics, he did not take up skating until the age of ten and almost nine years passed before he made an impact on the national scene. In 1977, he placed ninth at the US Championships and improved to third the following year. He was at the Olympics in 1980 and won in 1984, and was world champion each year 1981-4. He then turned professional. With other professionals he returned to competition under new rules in 1993.

Walter HAMMOND (UK)

CRICKET

Walter Reginald Hammond. b. 19 Jun 1903 Dover, Kent, d. 1 Jul 1965 Durban, South Africa.

The greatest England batsman of his generation who set a record for most runs in Test cricket, passing Jack Hobbs' total of 5410 in 1937 and going on to be the first to score 6000 and 7000 runs. With 336 not out in 318 minutes against New Zealand in 1933 he set the then highest Test score, and his feat of leading the English first-class averages for eight successive seasons, 1933-9 and 1946, has never been matched. He was also a magnificent all-rounder, an incomparable slip fielder with a season's record 78 catches in 1928, and a fine medium-fast bowler. He made his Gloucestershire début in 1920 but was prevented from playing for them regularly in his early years due to being born in Kent, and he then missed the 1926 season through serious illness. Thereafter he swept all before him and broke into the England team, where he became the dominant force. In 1928/9 against Australia he set a series record of 905 runs at 113.12 in the five Tests. He changed status from professional to amateur and became England's captain in 1938. Twelve times he exceeded 2000 runs in a season, with three years over 3000 and a peak of 3323 at 67.81 in 1933. He scored his 100th first-class century at 31, the youngest ever to reach this milestone. His 36 career double centuries is exceeded only by Don Bradman. He settled in South Africa after his retirement.

85 Tests 1927-47: 7249 runs at 58.45, 22 100s HS 336; 83 wickets at 37.83, BB 5-36; 110 catches.*

First-class 1920-51: 50,551 runs at 56.10, 167 100s HS 336; 732 wickets at 30.58, BB 9-23; 819 catches, 3 stumpings.*

Andy HAMPSTEN (USA)

CYCLING

Andy Hampsten. b. 7 Apr 1962 Great Plains, North Dakota.

Hampsten is second only to Greg LeMond among American professional cyclists. He first became well known in 1984 when he made the Olympic team, although he did not compete there, his lack of a finishing sprint hampering him in a one-day race. It has remained his *bête noire* as a professional as well. Riding exclusively for 7-Eleven (now Motorola), Hampsten is best known for his toughness and his ability as a climber. His victory in the 1988 Giro d'Italia (when he also won the King of the Mountains title) came primarily because of a brutal ride over the Gavia Pass in a blinding snowstorm. Only he and Eric Breukink rode well and broke well clear of the field. It gave Hampsten the pink jersey which he maintained to the finish. In 1992, Hampsten achieved his greatest stage victory when he won the ride to L'Alpe d'Huez during the Tour de France. He won the Tour de Suisse in 1986-7.

Kurt HAMRIN (Swe)

FOOTBALL

Kurt Hamrin. b. 14 Nov 1934 Stockholm.

One of the most dangerous right wingers, he was a fine elusive dribbler, small but with great pace, who also had a fierce shot. He scored 54 goals in 62 first division games for Slona in Sweden, before being transferred to Juventus in Italy in 1956. There he had a slow start so he was loaned to Padova, with whom he regained his goalscoring form. He starred for Sweden when they were runners-up to Brazil in the 1958 World Cup, scoring a spectacular goal in the semis against West Germany. He was then signed by Fiorentina and reached his peak in his nine years with them, helping them to the European Cup-Winners' Cup in 1961 and to Italian Cups in 1961 and 1966. In 1967 he moved to AC Milan and with them won the Italian league title and the European Cup-Winners' Cup in 1968 and then the European Cup in 1969, before moving on to play for Napoli 1970-1.

He scored 190 goals in Italian football and but for his long sojourn there would have made many more than his 32 appearances for Sweden, in which he scored 16 goals.

HAN Aiping (China)

BADMINTON

Han Aiping. b. 22 Apr 1962.

With wins in 1985 and 1987 she was the first woman to win two singles titles at the World Badminton Championships. In 1985 she also won the women's doubles with Li Lingwei and achieved the same double at the All-England Championships. With Li Lingwei she was also World Cup doubles champion in 1986 and 1987.

Gerhard HANAPPI (Aut)

FOOTBALL

Gerhard Hanappi. b. 9 Jul 1929 Vienna, d. 23 Aug 1980 Vienna.

Winner of a record 93 caps for Austria, he was capped in every position except in goal and on the left-wing. After a 0-6 defeat by Czechoslovakia in 1962 he was dropped from the national team and although he was selected for the next game he declined the invitation and refused to play for Austria again.

Hanappi began his career with Wacker Wien and as a 17-year-old helped them to the League title in his first full season, 1947/8. He made his international début in 1948 before moving to SK Rapid Wien in 1950 where he remained until his retirement in 1965. Helped Austria to their best ever World Cup place, third in 1954. One of the most popular Austrian players of all time, he was voted Footballer of the Year eight times. After retirement he built up a thriving practice as an architect and designed the West-Stadion in Vienna.

Chip HANAUER (USA)

POWERBOATING

Lee Edward Hanauer. b. 1954 Seattle, Washington.

Hanauer trails only Bill Muncey in total number of powerboat races won, with 45 career victories from 1979-93. From 1982 to 1988 he won the APBA Gold Cup seven consecutive times, breaking the 66-year-old record of Gar Wood, who won six. Hanauer won again in 1992, and in 1993 he recorded a record ninth victory, break-

ing Muncey's previous record of eight. His first victory came only months after Muncey, whom he succeeded as driver of a new Atlas Van Lines hydroplane, was killed at Acapulco.
Hanauer graduated from Washington State University in 1976 and began his unlimited hydroplane career later that year. He has won six unlimited national championships and eight overall APBA national championships. He retired briefly in 1990-1, when he dabbled in auto racing, but signed again with Budweiser in 1992. He has a degree in education and teaches emotionally disturbed children in Seattle.

HANIF MOHAMMAD (Pak)

CRICKET
Hanif Mohammad. b. 21 Dec 1934 Junagadh, Gujerat, India.

The 'Little Master' played in all but 2 of Pakistan's first 57 official Tests. In the first against India in 1952, he was, at 17 years 300 days, the world's youngest Test wicket-keeper, although he soon dropped the 'keeping to concentrate on batting. He could play all the strokes, but will best be remembered for his immaculate defence. On 11 Jan 1959, batting on his home ground for Karachi v Bahawalpur, he was run out off the last ball of the day when he had scored 499 runs (in 10 hr 35 min), the highest ever score in first-class cricket. A year earlier he had played the longest innings ever in first-class cricket, when he scored 337 in 16 hr 10 min for Pakistan v West Indies at Bridgetown, Barbados. He captained Pakistan in 11 Tests 1964-7, but was criticised for his negative attitude. He was also an off-break bowler.
Three of his brothers also played Test cricket (see Mushtaq Mohammad), and his son **Shoaib Mohammad** (b. 8 Jan 1961) scored 2443 runs at 46.98 with 7 centuries in 39 Tests 1983-92, often matching his father's tenacity.
55 Tests 1952-69: 3915 runs at 43.98, 12 100s HS 337; 1 wicket; 40 catches.
First-class 1951-76: 17,059 runs at 52.32, 55 100s HS 499; 53 wickets at 28.50, BB 3-4; 178 catches, 12 stumpings.

Cornelia HANISCH (FRG)

FENCING
Cornelia Hanisch. b. 12 Jun 1952 Frankfurt.

One of four women to have won three individual world foil titles. She was champion in 1979, 1981 and 1985, and was also a member of the winning FRG team in 1985, after taking team silver medals in 1977, 1981 and 1983. She was unable to take part in the 1980 Olympics due to the boycott, when surely the best fencer in the world, but in 1984 she won a team gold medal and a silver in the individual event. She won her first FRG title in 1976, and won again in 1978-80 and 1982. She is a PE and history teacher.

Ned HANLAN (Can)

ROWING
Edward Hanlan. b. 12 Jul 1855 Toronto, Ontario, d. 4 Jan 1908 Toronto.

Hanlan was once dubbed 'the first world champion of anything'. He became the world professional sculling champion in May 1879 when he defeated William Elliott (UK) in England over the Tyne course. He remained world champion until 1884 when he lost to William Beach (Aus). In his prime, he was only 1.73m and about 70 kg (*5'8", 155 lb*), but he was immensely powerful, rowing very low cadences. Although he did not actually invent the sliding seat, he was the first to master it. He was nicknamed 'The Boy in Blue' for the characteristic sky blue outfit he wore in competition. In his career he lost only six of 350 races. A statue to his memory was erected in 1926 over the rowing grounds of the Canadian National Exhibition (near Toronto) and the end of the Toronto Island where he trained was then re-christened Hanlan's Point.

Ellery HANLEY (UK)

RUGBY LEAGUE
Ellery Hanley. b. 27 Mar 1961 Leeds, Yorkshire.

Gifted and versatile and equally talented as a forward or a back, he has won 34 caps

(plus 1 appearance as a substitute) in four different positions; stand-off, centre, wing and loose forward. He was signed by Bradford Northern from a Leeds amateur club in 1978 but did not play a full Division I match for three years. Once established as a first-team player, he set a variety of records. His 55 tries in the 1984/5 season was the highest-ever by anyone other than a winger, and after his transfer to Wigan for a record fee of £150,000 in 1985 his record breaking continued. In his first season with Wigan he scored 63 tries, again a record for a non-winger, and 30 of these came from the loose forward position which was yet another record.
On the 1984 tour of Australia he played as a winger, scoring 12 tries in 17 matches, and on the 1988 tour he became the first coloured player to captain Great Britain. The highlight of the tour was a victory in the Third Test which was Great Britain's first win over Australia for ten seasons. In September 1991 he moved to Leeds. His outstanding achievements were acknowledged when he was awarded the MBE in 1990.

John HANNAH (USA)

AMERICAN FOOTBALL

John Allen Hannah. b. 4 Apr 1951 Canton, Georgia.

An offensive guard considered by many experts as the greatest ever to play football. He played collegiately at Alabama, where was was also a conference champion as a wrestler, shot putter and discus thrower, and from 1973-85 in the NFL with the New England Patriots. Though the Patriots have historically been one of the weakest professional teams, Hannah had little to do with that. He played in nine Pro Bowls and was named All-Pro eight times. Since his retirement he has started a second career as a stock broker.

Alf and Frank HANSEN (Nor)

ROWING

Alf Hansen. b. 13 Jul 1948 Oslo.

Frank Hansen. b. 4 Aug 1945 Oslo.

At double sculls the brothers were Olympic champions in 1976 and world champions in 1975, 1978-9 (2nd in 1974). The elder brother Frank had won the Olympic silver medal with Svein Thögersen in 1972, when Alf competed in the coxed fours, before they joined forces. Alf had made his World Championships début at eights in 1969 and took a bronze medal at coxed fours in 1970. After Frank retired Alf was partnered by Rolf Thorsen, and at the World Championships they were successively 3rd, 1st and 2nd 1981-3, and both were in the Norwegian quadruple sculls team that took silver medals at the 1987 World Championships and 1988 Olympics, when Alf was 40. Alf won 57 Norwegian titles 1968-89 and Frank 43 1965-85.
Frank was an electrician, and became national coach 1987-92, and Alf an employee of the Norwegian telephone company.

Rudolf HARBIG (Ger)

ATHLETICS

Rudolf Harbig. b. 8 Nov 1913 Dresden, d. 8 Mar 1944 on the Eastern Front in World War II.

An immensely gifted runner but deprived of Olympic opportunity due to the War. Harbig took the bronze medal at 4 x 400m at the 1936 Olympics, after going out in a heat of the 800m. He won 55 consecutive races at various distances 1938-40, including the gold medal at 800m (and 4 x 400m relay) at the 1938 European Championships. He reached his pinnacle of form with 800m in 1:46.6 for Germany against Italy at Milan on 15 Jul 1939, and this remained a world record for 16 years. A month later Harbig added the world record for 400m with 46.0, again convincingly beating his arch-rival Mario Lanzi, and in 1941 he added further world records, 1000m in 2:21.5 and at 4 x 800m relay.
Coached by Waldemar Gerschler, Harbig was German champion at 400m 1942, 800m 1936-41.

Darlene HARD (USA)

TENNIS

Darlene Ruth Hard. b. 6 Jan 1936 Los Angeles, California.

A fine doubles player who won the women's event at Wimbledon four times (1957, 1959-60, 1963), the US Championship six times (1958-62, 1969) and the French championship three times (1955, 1957, 1960). She was also a three-time winner of the mixed doubles at Wimbledon (1957, 1959-60) and won it twice at the French Championships (1955, 1961). She lost in the Wimbledon singles final to Althea Gibson in 1957 and to Maria Bueno in 1960, but she won the French singles in 1960 and the US singles in 1960-1. She was a member of the US Wightman Cup team from 1957 to 1963, winning 10 of her 14 rubbers, and she played in the Federation Cup in 1963. Her powerful serve and baseline play were the outstanding features of her excellent all-round game.

Glenn HARDIN (USA)

ATHLETICS

Glenn Foster Hardin. b. 1 Jul 1910 Derma, Mississippi, d. 6 Mar 1975 Baton Rouge, Louisiana.

Olympic champion at 400m hurdles in 1936. He had won the silver medal behind Bob Tisdall in 1932, but was accorded the world record with a time of 52.0 (51.85 on automatic timing) because Tisdall had knocked over the final hurdle, and according to the rules then in force that meant that his time of 51.7 could not be ratified. Hardin went on to dominate the event, not losing another race in his career, improving the record to 51.8 when he won the 1934 AAU title, and smashing that a month later in Stockholm when he ran 50.6, a time that was not to be bettered until 1953. Hardin also set an unratified world record time of 22.7 (although only 23.14 on electronic timing) for 220 yards hurdles on a straight course to win the 1934 NCAA title. He won the NCAA double for Louisiana State University at 220y and 440y hurdles in 1933 and 1934 and was AAU 400m hurdles champion in 1933-4, 1936. His best 440y time was 46.8 (1934), then the second fastest ever run. Glenn's son Billy was the NCAA champion and competed at the Olympics at 400m hurdles in 1964.

Dusty HARE (UK)

RUGBY UNION

William Henry Hare. b. 29 Nov 1952 Newark, Notts.

Scorer of a world record 7337 points in first-class matches from 1971 to 1989, comprising 1800 for Nottingham, 4427 for Leicester, 240 for England, 88 for the British Lions and 782 in other representative matches. He set new records with 44 points in the 1984 season's International Championship and for the most points in a Championship match with 19 against France in 1983. Although these records have now been surpassed, Dusty Hare remains one of the most reliable full-backs ever to represent England. Capped 25 times between 1974 and 1984 he only failed to score in his first two international matches, and on his retirement he was England's most capped full-back. With 240 points he was also England's leading scorer. Despite these impressive performances and his general all-round reliability, he was never a fixture in the England XV and was dropped five times during his international career. He toured New Zealand with the 1983 British Lions but failed to win a Test place.

Despite the demands made on his time as a farmer, he found time to play cricket in the summer and made 10 first-class appearances for Nottingham 1971-7. Awarded MBE 1989.

Franco HARRIS (USA)

AMERICAN FOOTBALL

Franco Harris. b. 7 Mar 1950 Fort Dix, New Jersey.

At Penn State, he teamed up with Lydell Mitchell to form a redoubtable running backfield. Mitchell was thought to have more pro potential but Harris became by far the better of the two in the NFL, where he helped Pittsburgh Steelers to win four Super Bowls, being voted MVP in 1975. He holds the Super Bowl career record for the most yards rushing (354) and the most touchdowns (4). Harris played for 13 years in the NFL, finishing his career with one year at the Seattle Seahawks. He gained over 1000 yards eight times and is fifth on the all-time list for career rushing yards. *NFL career 1972-84: Rushing: 12,120 yards av. 4.1, 91 touchdowns; Receiving: 2287 yards av. 7.4, 9 touchdowns.*

Reg HARRIS (UK)

CYCLING

Reginald Hargreaves Harris. b. 31 Mar 1920 Bury, Lancashire, d. 22 Jun 1992 Macclesfield, Cheshire.

Britain's greatest ever track sprint cyclist. He began track racing in 1936 and in 1947 he was world amateur champion, but at the 1948 Olympics he was hampered by a recent recovery from a broken arm and won only silvers in the individual and tandem sprint races. Shortly thereafter he turned professional and became the first sprinter to win a world professional championship in his first attempt, going on to four sprint titles, 1949-51 and 1954, and to place 2nd in 1956 and 3rd in 1953. As a professional he set two world records for the unpaced kilometre from a standing start outdoors, with 1:09.8 in 1949 and 1:08.6 in 1952, which stood for over 21 years. He also set two indoor records at 1 kilometre with a best of 1:08.9 in 1955. Seventeen years after his retirement in 1957 he made an amazing return to racing in 1974, and won the British sprint championship.

Doris HART (USA)

TENNIS

Doris Jane Hart. b. 20 Jun 1925 St Louis, Missouri.

Although a childhood illness left her with restricted use of her right leg, she developed into a formidable competitor, winning 33 Grand Slam titles. In the singles she won Wimbledon (1951), US (1954-5), French (1950, 1952) and Australian (1949) titles and in the women's doubles she won Wimbledon (1947, 1951-3), US (1951-4), French (1948, 1950-3) and Australian (1950). She was even more successful as a mixed doubles player winning at Wimbledon and at the US Championships 1951-5, adding the French 1951-3, and Australian 1949-50 for a total of 15 Grand Slam victories. The first eight of these up to 1952 were with Frank Sedgman and the rest with Vic Seixas.

As a member of the Wightman Cup team from 1946 to 1955 she won 22 out of 24 rubbers, but possibly her greatest feat was to win all three titles at Wimbledon in 1951 with the loss of only one set (in the mixed doubles). In 1955 she became a coaching professional.

Leon HART (USA)

AMERICAN FOOTBALL

Leon Joseph Hart. b. 2 Nov 1928 Turtle Creek, Pennsylvania.

Hart played end at Notre Dame and in 1949 became the first lineman to win the Heisman Memorial Trophy as college football's outstanding player. That year he also won the Maxwell Award and Knute Rockne Trophy and served as senior class president. Hart played eight years of pro football with the Detroit Lions, was twice an All-Pro and played on three NFL championship teams.

Bill HARTACK (USA)

HORSE RACING

William John Hartack Jr. b. 9 Dec 1932 Edensburg, Pennsylvania.

He rode 417 winners in the USA in 1955, and was the leading jockey in both races and money won, setting new money records in 1956 of $2,343,955 (347 wins) and in 1957 of $3,060,051 (341 wins), the latter remaining a record until 1967. In 1957 he also won a record 43 stakes races. In his 22-year career he rode 4272 winners in the USA, from his first at the age of 19 at Waterford Park, West Virginia in 1952. He won five Kentucky Derbys, two of them in track record time, three Preakness and

one Belmont Stakes. From 1981 he was a racing official and TV commentator.
A fiery character, he often preferred to set the pace, urging his horses on energetically.

Gabby HARTNETT (USA)

BASEBALL

Charles Leo Hartnett. b. 20 Dec 1900 Woonsocket, Rhode Island, d. 20 Dec 1972 Park Ridge, Illinois.

One of the great catchers in major league history. He played 20 seasons in the majors, 19 with the Chicago Cubs, and he caught for all of those seasons. His best season ever was 1930 when he hit .339 with 37 homers and 122 RBI. He led the league in fielding average for catchers six times, four times in putouts, six times in assists, and seven in double plays. Joe McCarthy, the great manager, labelled Hartnett 'The Perfect Catcher'. After he retired as a player, he managed for five years in the minors and then opened a recreation centre and bowling alley.
Career 1922-41: 1912 hits Avg. .297, HR 236; RBI 1179.

Rudy HARTONO (Ina)

BADMINTON

Rudy Hartono Kurniawan. b. 18 Aug 1948. Formerly Rudy Niohapliane.

The top badminton player of the 1970s, Hartono won a record eight men's singles titles at the All-England Championships, 1968-74 and 1976, his run interrupted when Svend Pri (Den) beat him in 1975. Having retired in 1978, he returned to win the singles at the second World Championships in 1980. He first represented Indonesia in the Thomas Cup in 1967, and was a member of their winning team on three successive occasions, 1970, 1973 and 1976, displaying great skill at both singles and doubles. He won the singles when badminton was a demonstration sport at the 1972 Olympic Games, when his younger sister Utami Dewi was the beaten ladies' finalist.
He was an elegant player, very fast around the court, and with a devastatingly accurate smash.

Doug HARVEY (Can)

ICE HOCKEY

Douglas Norman Harvey. b. 19 Dec 1924 Montreal, Québec.

Despite a style so laconic it bordered on nonchalance, Harvey is considered by many as the greatest defenseman ever to play the game, although never the offensive threat that Bobby Orr would become. He won the Norris Trophy as the league's best defenseman seven times, 1955-8, 1960-2, a record since surpassed only by Orr. Harvey was a first-team all-star for ten of eleven years (1952-62, save 1959) and had no weaknesses. He was a member of the team considered the greatest ever - the Montreal Canadiens of the 1950s, which won six Stanley Cups. In 1961 he was traded to the New York Rangers, and retired three years later after injuries limited his playing time in 1964. He came out of retirement in 1966, playing only two games for the Detroit Red Wings, but he played a full season for the St Louis Blues in 1968/9 before retiring for good.
NHL career 1947-69 - 1113 games, 88 goals, 540 points. Best year: 1954/5: 43 assists, 49 points.

Neil HARVEY (Aus)

CRICKET

Robert Neil Harvey. b. 8 Oct 1928 Fitzroy, Melbourne.

A brilliant left-handed batsman and a great cover fielder. He was a small man at 1.67m *5'6"* who used sparkling footwork and an immaculate technique. He was Australia's most prolific run scorer in the 15 years after World War II, and at the time of his retirement only Don Bradman had scored more runs for Australia. In 1948 he made his Test début against India, scoring 153 in his second Test, and he followed that with 112 in his next Test, his first against England. Against South Africa in 1952/3 he scored 834 runs at 92.66, the fourth highest aggregate in a Test series, and on his previous series there in 1949/50 he averaged 132.00 for 660 runs. His most successful tour of England was 1953, with 2040 runs at 65.80. Awarded the MBE. His

brother **Mervyn** (b. 29 Apr 1918) played one Test for Australia in 1947 and another brother Ray also played for Victoria.
79 Tests 1948-63: 6149 runs at 48.41, 21 100s HS 205; 3 wickets at 40.00; 62 catches.
First-class 1946-64: 21,699 runs at 50.93, 67 100s HS 231; 30 wickets at 36.86, BB 4-8; 228 catches.*

Armin HARY (FRG)

ATHLETICS
Armin Hary. b. 22 Mar 1937 Quierschied, Saarland.

The Olympic 100m champion of 1960, Hary was renowned for his blitz starting. He set a Saarland decathlon record with 5376 points in 1956, but became a German citizen from 1957, and a year later came to the fore. After second place in the 1958 German 100m championships to Manfred Germar, when both men equalled the European record, Hary caused an upset when he beat Germar to win the European 100m title.
On 21 Jun 1960 in Zürich, Hary twice ran the 100m in 10.0; the first time was annulled as the starter confessed that he should have recalled the runners for a false start by Hart, but the second was ratified as the first 'even-time' world record for 100m. It was recorded as 10.25 on automatic timing, while the first race had been timed at 10.16; at the time, hand timings were officially recognised. At the Rome Olympics later in the year he displayed his brilliant starting and impressive early acceleration, holding off the challenge of Dave Sime (USA) to win in 10.2 (10.32 to 10.35 auto). Hary then ran the second leg for the German team that set world records of 39.5 in both the heats and final of the 4 x 100m relay. The USA finished ahead, but were disqualified, so the Germans took the gold medal.
Hary was German champion at 100m and 200m in 1960 and had a 200m best (around half a turn) of 20.5 that year. Indoors he set three European bests for 60y at 6.1 in 1958.
Hary was very much an individualist and he tried to cash in on his Olympic fame in films. That was unsuccessful, but a knee injury in a car crash determined his retirement. He became a businessman, but in 1980 he received a 2-year prison sentence, later commuted to a suspended sentence for fraud.

HASHIM KHAN (Pak)

SQUASH
Hashim Khan. b. c.1915 Nawakilla, Peshawar.

Although Geoff Hunt and Jahangir Khan ultimately won more major championships, Hashim is still regarded by many as the greatest squash player of all time. The son of the chief steward at the Peshawar Club, he was appointed professional at the nearby RAF base in 1942 and after winning the All-India Professional title in 1944 he dominated the game at home until he went to England in 1950. He won the British Open that year beating the four-time champion Mahmoud Karim. Although his exact birth-date is not recorded, he was approximately 35 years old at the time, a very advanced age for the sport. In all, he won the British Open seven times in eight years, losing only to his cousin Roshan in 1956. After losing to his younger brother Azam in the 1958 semi-finals, he went to live in America and became the professional at Uptown Athletic Club, Detroit in 1960. Between 1955 and 1963 he won the US Open three times and the US Professional title three times. He also won the British Professional Championship five times, the North American and Canadian titles three times each and was twice the Australian Open champion. Although resident in America he returned to England each year to play in the Vintage Open which he won for six successive years, 1978-83, being aged approximately 68 when he won his last title.

Judy HASHMAN (USA/UK)

BADMINTON
Judith Margaret Hashman. née Devlin. b. 22 Oct 1935 Winnipeg, Canada.

The daughter of Irishman Frank Devlin

(qv) and an English mother, she became the most successful woman badminton player in the history of the All-England Championships, with ten singles titles, 1954, 1957-8, 1960-4 and 1966-7. She also won seven women's doubles titles, once with Tonny Holst-Christensen and six with her elder sister **Susan** Devlin (later Peard). That is a record for one pair, and the sisters also won a record ten US women's doubles titles together.
A formidably determined match player, Judy won a record 12 US women's singles titles, 1954, 1956-63, 1965-7, 12 women's doubles and 8 mixed doubles. She helped the USA to three wins in five Uber Cup series, but having lived in England from 1960 she played for them in 1970-2. In 1978 she was appointed England team manager and coach, although that was short-lived as she came into dispute with the Badminton Association. A fine all-rounder, she represented the US at junior level at tennis and was a member of the US lacrosse team for five years.
Her sister Susan was a member of the US Uber Cup team 1957-62 and of the Irish team 1963-9. She directed badminton coaching for school children in Ireland 1960-84.

Lindsay HASSETT (Aus)

CRICKET
Arthur Lindsay Hassett. b. 28 Aug 1913 Geelong, Victoria, d. 16 Jun 1993 Bateman's Bay, New South Wales.

A great, little (1.67m *5'6"*) batsman, who succeeded Don Bradman as a very popular captain of Australia, leading them in 24 Tests 1949-53. He toured England in 1938, 1948 and 1953, with 1563 runs at 74.42 in 1948 his best return. He was also the captain of the Australian Services team in England in 1945. He played for Victoria, captaining them from 1946 to 1953. His superb technique meant that he had few superiors amongst Australians on wet wickets, although he curbed his attacking batting to a more defensive mode in his later years. A man of impish humour, he became a much respected commentator on the game after his retirement. Awarded the MBE in 1953. His brother Dick played as a batsman and leg-spinner for Victoria.
43 Tests 1938-53: 3073 runs at 46.56, 10 100s HS 198; 30 catches.*
First-class 1932-54: 16,890 runs at 58.24, 59 100s HS 232; 18 wickets at 39.05, BB 2-10; 170 catches.

Gavin HASTINGS (UK)

RUGBY UNION
Andrew Gavin Hastings. b. 3 Jan 1962 Edinburgh.

Hastings succeeded Andy Irvine as Scotland's record points scorer in international rugby. By April 1993 he had scored 424 points in 45 matches for Scotland, including 123 in World Cup matches. He has added a further 28 in three games for the British Lions against Australia in 1989 and 38 against New Zealand in 1993.
A Cambridge blue in 1984 and 1985, he made his début for Scotland as full back in 1986 with his brother **Scott** (b. 4 Dec 1964) in the centre. He scored 18 points in that match and set a record for the International Championship series with 52 points in the season. In 1987 he set a Scottish scoring record with 27 points in a match against Romania, 2 tries, 8 conversions and one penalty goal.
A charismatic figure and powerful player, he was appointed Scotland's captain for 1993 and then as captain of the Lions touring team to New Zealand. By profession he is a sports marketing executive.

Thorleif HAUG (Nor)

NORDIC SKIING
Thorleif Haug. b. 28 Sep 1894 Lier, d. 12 Dec 1934 Drammen.

When skiing was added to the Olympic programme at the first Winter Games at Chamonix in 1924, Haug was 29 years old but he was the star of the Games, winning three gold medals. Those were at 18km and 50km cross-country and the Nordic combination. He was also awarded the bronze medal at ski jumping, but 50 years later an error was discovered in the calculation of the scores and Haug was in fact fourth. The medal was presented to 86-

year-old Anders Haugen by Haug's daughter. Haug was second at the Nordic combined at the 1926 World Championships. He won the Holmenkollen 50km race six times. A lifesize statue of him was erected in Drammen in 1946.

Billy HAUGHTON (USA)

HARNESS RACING

William Haughton. b. 2 Nov 1923 Gloversville, New York, d. 15 Jul 1986 Valhalla, New York.

He had a record 12 years as leading money winner at harness racing in the USA, 1952-9, 1963, 1965, 1967-8, achieving a career figure of $40,160,336 and 4910 wins. A complete horseman, he became director of the US Trotting Association. He drove the winners of four Hambletonians and five Little Brown Jugs, and his son Tommy won the Hambletonian in 1982. He died ten days after receiving a severe head injury in an accident at Yonkers Raceway

João HAVELANGE (Bra)

FOOTBALL

(Dr) João Havelange. b. 8 May 1916 Rio de Janeiro.

Competed as a swimmer for Brazil in the 1936 Olympic Games and was a member of their water polo team at the 1952 Games. In 1958 he was elected president of the Sports Association of Brazil, in 1963 a member of the International Olympic Committee and in 1974 president of FIFA. A lawyer, he was president of Brazil's national bus company, with many other commercial interests in insurance and the chemicals industry. Advanced as a nominee for the 1988 Nobel Peace Prize.

John HAVLICEK (USA)

BASKETBALL

John J 'Hondo' Havlicek. b. 8 Apr 1940 Lansing, Ohio.

Havlicek is considered one of the greatest all-round athletes ever to play professional basketball. His endurance and his ability to run at full-speed for 48 minutes was legendary. After college at Ohio State, whom he helped to the 1960 NCAA title, he was drafted both by the Boston Celtics and the Cleveland Browns of the NFL, even though he did not play football in college. He played his entire NBA career with the Celtics and after Bill Russell's retirement, took over the mantle as their leader. He played on eight NBA championship teams - 1963-6, 1968-9, 1974, and 1976. He was voted to the NBA's 35th-Anniversary Team in 1980 and to the Hall of Fame in 1984. His first professional coach, Red Auerbach, called him 'the guts of the team'.

NBA career: 26,395 points av. 20.8. Play-offs: 3776 points av. 22.0.

Connie HAWKINS (USA)

BASKETBALL

Cornelius L Hawkins. b. 17 Jul 1942 Brooklyn, New York.

A star at the University of Iowa, he was approached by gamblers and asked to shave points. He was never convicted of any crime and never actually shaved points, but for being suspected he was banned from the NBA after finishing college in 1965. Thus he began his professional career with the Pittsburgh Condors and Minnesota Muskies of the ABA in 1967-9, leading the league in scoring in 1967/8 and second in 1968/9. Legal action then allowed him to enter the NBA, where he played for the Phoenix Suns 1969-76. He was quickly named to the all-NBA first team, justifying the claims of Kareem Abdul-Jabbar who once declared him the 'greatest player in the world' based on watching him play in New York city playground leagues. Because of his banishment, he was well past his prime after his first two years in the league.

Mike HAWTHORN (UK)

MOTOR RACING

John Michael Hawthorn. b. 10 Apr 1929 Mexborough, d. 27 Jan 1959 near Guildford.

In 1958 Hawthorn became the first British

world motor racing champion. In his Grand Prix career, 1952-8, he won three of his 45 races, with 127.64 points.
Trained as an engineer, Mike started racing with his father Leslie, who owned a garage, with a Riley Imp in 1951. The following year he won two Irish trophy races in a Riley Sprite, moved up to Formula Two racing, and was fourth at Spa in his first Grand Prix drive in a Cooper-Bristol. He was fourth in the World Championship both that year and in 1953 for Ferrari, when he became the first British driver to win the French Grand Prix for 30 years. He progressed to third place in 1954, but that year his father was killed in a car accident. Mike met with much press criticism in the mid 1950s, including over his involvement in the 1955 Le Mans tragedy, which deeply affected him. Both 1955 and 1956 were unsuccessful years driving a variety of cars, but in 1957 he was fourth for Ferrari, and then beat Stirling Moss by one point for the title in 1958. He then announced his retirement to concentrate on his garage business, but that was short lived, as he was killed in a road accident when his Jaguar went out of control on the Hog's Back in Surrey in 1959.

Ann HAYDON see JONES

Bob HAYES (USA)

ATHLETICS and AMERICAN FOOTBALL
Robert Lee Hayes. b. 20 Dec 1942 Jacksonville, Florida.

The Olympic 100m champion of 1964 in a world record equalling time of 10.0 (10.06 automatic timing), Hayes won with awesome power by a clear two metres margin. He won a second gold medal when he anchored the US sprint relay team to a world record.
He had run the first automatically timed sub-10 second time with 9.91 in the semi-final, but the wind, at 5.3m/s, was well over the permitted limit. In April 1963 at Walnut, California he ran the first ever sub-10 second 100 metres on hand timing with 9.9, but that too was aided by wind assistance of 5m/s.
His first world record had been an unratified 9.3 for 100 yards in 1961, and after 9.2 in 1962 he became the first to run 9.1 with a world record at St Louis on 21 Jun 1963 to take the AAU title. He was also the first to break 6 seconds for 60 yards indoors when he won the AAU title on 22 Feb 1964 in 5.9 (5.99 automatic timing) after tying the record of 6.0 six times in the preceding five weeks. He won the AAU 100y or 100m title each year 1962-4 and while at Florida A & M won the NCAA 200m in 1964.
Having played football at Florida A & M he turned professional for the Dallas Cowboys as a wide receiver and was twice chosen All-Pro. He had a sensational rookie season with 46 pass receptions for 1003 yards and an average of 21.8 yards per carry. He led the NFL in punt returns in 1968. He played with Dallas for ten years and then one year with the San Francisco 49ers. He ran into trouble with the law and served a two-year jail sentence for drugs possession and dealing.
NFL career 1965-75: Rushing: 7,414 yards av. 20.0, 71 touchdowns;

Colin HAYES (Aus)

HORSE RACING
Colin Sydney Hayes. b. 16 Feb 1924 Adelaide.

Set new records as a trainer for most winners in Australia with 241 in 1981/2 and 264 in 1984/5, passing a career total of 5000 in 1989. On 7 Feb 1987 he trained a record five Group One winners on one day, three at Morphetville, SA and two at Sandown, Victoria.
He took out his trainer's licence in 1950, and steadily built up his business, based from 1965 at his Lindsay Park Stud in South Australia. His Melbourne Cup winners have been *Beldale Ball* 1980 and *At Talaq* 1986. He has been a great pioneer of new training methods.

Elvin HAYES (USA)

BASKETBALL
Elvin Ernest Hayes. b. 17 Nov 1945 Rayville, Louisiana.

From the University of Houston, where he

was voted college player of the year in 1968 having led his team to a well-publicised upset of the UCLA Bruins, he led the NBA in scoring as a rookie, one of only three times that this has occurred. He was a power forward or small center who could play almost equally well inside or outside, playing for 16 years in the NBA and ranking second only to Kareem Abdul-Jabbar in most games played in NBA history. In 1978 he led the Washington Bullets to the NBA Championship. He spent most of his career with the Baltimore/Capitol/ Washington Bullets, although he also played for San Diego and Houston.
NBA career: 27,313 points, av. 21.0; 16.279 rebounds, av. 12.5.

Desmond HAYNES (Bar)

CRICKET

Desmond Leo Haynes. b. 15 Feb 1956 Holder's Hill, St James.

Having established himself as part of the longest lasting top-class opening partnership in Test history with Gordon Greenidge (playing together in 89 Tests and recording a record 16 century opening partnerships), Haynes has remained a mainstay of the West Indies batting. He holds the record for the most runs and the most centuries scored in one-day internationals. He has played for Barbados from 1977 and made his Test début a year later. He captained the West Indies in four Tests in 1990. Much later in his career than many West Indians he came to play in county cricket, and has been a considerable success for Middlesex from 1989.
111 Tests 1978-93: 7250 runs at 42.64, 18 100s HS 207; 65 catches.
225 One-day Ints: 8195 runs at 41.81, 16 100s HS 152; 55 catches.*
First-class 1977-92: 21,176 runs at 46.84, 50 100s HS 255; 162 catches, 1 stumping.*

Johnny HAYNES (UK)

FOOTBALL

John Norman Haynes. b. 17 Oct 1934 Kentish Town, London.

An inside-forward with an exceptionally long and accurate pass, he was one of the great stars of the 1950s, becoming the first £100 a week player in Britain. In his early days he was noted for his goalscoring abilities but later played a deeper game. He was the first player to represent England at all five international levels - Schoolboy, Youth, Under-23, 'B' and senior.
Joining the Fulham groundstaff as a schoolboy in 1950, he turned professional two years later and stayed with the club until 1970 when he went to South Africa on a free transfer. He played more than 700 games for Fulham and would almost certainly have won domestic honours had he chosen to play for a more fashionable club. He missed a whole season after being seriously injured in a car crash in August 1962. This ended his international career in which he was capped 56 times (1954-62, captain 22 times) and scored 18 goals.

Marques HAYNES (USA)

BASKETBALL

Marques Oreole Haynes. b. 3 Oct 1926 Sand Springs, Oklahoma.

Universally acclaimed as the greatest ever dribbler of a basketball. He played collegiately at Langston University, graduating in 1946. At that time no blacks played in the NBL, so he signed with the Kansas City Stars, a touring squad which was affiliated with the Harlem Globetrotters, to whom he was promoted in 1947. He starred with the Globetrotters for the next 35 years, but periodically left the team for other ventures, such as his own Fabulous Magicians (1953-72), Meadowlark Lemon's Bucketeers (1979-81), and his own Harlem Magicians (1983-90). He was approached by several NBA teams in the 1950s but rejected all offers.

Tom HAYWARD (UK)

CRICKET

Thomas Walter Hayward. b. 29 Mar 1871 Cambridge, d. 19 Jul 1939 Cambridge.

Hayward was a prolific scorer in county cricket and the second man, after W.G. Grace, to score 100 hundreds. From 1895 to 1914 he scored over 1000 runs every

year, with ten seasons over 2000 and peaks of 3170 at 54.65 in 1904 and 3518 at 66.37 in 1906. The latter figure has been exceeded only by Denis Compton and Bill Edrich in 1947. Intially batting at No.3, he opened from 1900. He also bowled quickish off-breaks and in 1897 achieved the double with 114 wickets and 1368 runs. His uncle Thomas was renowned as one of the top batsmen of the 1860s.
35 Tests 1896-1909: 1999 runs at 34.46, 3 100s HS 137; 14 wickets at 36.71, BB 4-22; 19 catches.
First-class 1893-1914: 43,551 runs at 41.79, 104 100s HS 315; 481 wickets at 22.95, BB 8-89; 492 catches.*

Spencer HAYWOOD (USA)

BASKETBALL

Spencer Haywood. b. 22 Apr 1949 Silver City, Mississippi.

The 1968 US Olympic basketball team was not expected to be one of the greatest teams ever sent to the Olympics and many people thought the 1968 team might be the first Americans ever to lose the gold medal. But the experts had not heard of Spencer Haywood, who was then an unknown freshman at the University of Detroit. Haywood was a 2.03m *6' 8"* tall player who could play either center or forward. In the Olympics he completely dominated the big men from other countries to lead the US to another gold medal. After the Olympics, Haywood returned to school for only one year. He joined the Denver Rockets of the ABA in 1969 and began an outstanding professional career. In his first year he was the Rookie of the Year, the Most Valuable Player and made first-team all-ABA. He then jumped leagues to join the NBA's Seattle Supersonics and took up where he left off by becoming one of the great forwards in the NBA. He made first-team all-NBA for three straight years, and then was named to the second-team for two years. In 1975 he was traded to the New York Knicks, where he played for four seasons before finishing his career with the Los Angeles Lakers in 1980. Haywood was briefly married to superstar model, Iman.

Vijay HAZARE (India)

CRICKET

Vijay Samuel Hazare. b. 11 Mar 1915 Sangli, Maharashtra.

Hazare was a prolific run-scorer in India. Making his début for Maharashtra in 1934/5, he scored 316* for them in 1939/40 and 309 for The Rest v Hindus out of an innings total of 387 in 1943/4. He also scored 288 in his world record partnership of 577 with Gul Mahomed for Baroda v Holkar in 1947.
He had moved to Baroda in 1941 and captained them 1950-6. Having just missed playing for India before World War II, his Test début had to wait until the Indian tour to England in 1946. In his second series, against Australia in 1947/8, he hit centuries in each innings of a Test, the first Indian to accomplish this feat. He was also a capable medium-paced bowler and captained India without much success in 14 Tests.
30 Tests 1946-53: 2192 runs at 47.65, 7 100s HS 164; 20 wickets at 61.00, BB 4-29; 11 catches.*
First-class 1934-67: 18,754 runs at 58.06, 60 100s HS 316; 595 wickets at 24.61, BB 8-90; 166 catches.*

Mike HAZELWOOD (UK)

WATER SKIING

Michael Hazelwood. b. 14 Apr 1958 Heckington, Lincolnshire.

The greatest water skier ever produced in the United Kingdom. He began skiing at age eight and made the British team when he was only 15. He reached the top in 1977 when he was the first European to win the Moomba Masters and the first Briton to become World overall champion. He won further World titles at his forté, jumping, in 1979 and 1981 and achieved the first 60m jump in 1981, improving the world record to 61.9m *203 ft* in 1986. Four times Hazelwood was the US Masters overall champion, 1978-81, and won a record nine European overall titles, 1976-83 and 1986, and seven British titles 1974, 1976-9, 1981 and 1983.

Alec HEAD (Fra)

HORSE RACING

Jacques-Alexandre Head. b. 31 Jul 1924 Mesnil le Roi.

The third son of English-born trainer Willie Head, Alec rode first on the flat and then with great success over fences before taking out a trainer's licence in 1947. He was chosen by the Aga Khan to train his horses when they were moved to France in 1951, and he was leading trainer in France each year from 1952 to 1955, in which year he moved from Maisons-Laffitte to Chantilly. He handed over to his daughter Christiane '**Criquette**' (b. 6 Nov 1948 Neuilly-sur-Seine) on his 60th birthday in 1984, by when he had trained winners of most of Europe's major races, including 4 Prix de l'Arc de Triomphe, 22 French classics and 3 English classics, including the Derby with *Lavandin* in 1956.

Freddy HEAD (Fra)

HORSE RACING

Fréderic Head. b. 19 Jun 1947 Neuilly.

French champion jockey six times, first in 1970. His grandfather Willie and father Alec were amongst the greatest of trainers. His first ride in public was in 1964, when apprenticed to his grandfather, and he rode his first winner a few days later. He shares the record with four wins in the Prix de l'Arc de Triomphe, first on *Bon Mot III* , trained by his grandfather Willie Head, in 1966, and has 23 French classic successes. He came in for some criticism in England, as some hot favourites failed to win major races, but his first English classic winner was *Zino* in the 1982 2000 Guineas, and great horses that he rode included *Relko*, the 1963 Derby winner. In the USA he won the Breeders' Cup Mile on *Miesque* in 1987 and 1988.

George HEADLEY (Jam)

CRICKET

George Alphonso Headley. b. 30 May 1909 Panama, d. 30 Nov 1983 Kingston.

The 'Black Bradman', who achieved a wonderful Test record in the 1930s and indeed played a further three Tests, although with little success, after the War. In his first Test series, against England in 1930 at the age of 20, he scored 703 runs at 87.87 with four hundreds in the four Tests. In 1948 he became the first black man to captain the West Indies. Born in Panama, he went to Jamaica when he was 10. He had insufficient opportunities to show the world his abilities, but when he did there was little doubt that he was one of the greatest of all batsmen. On his tours of England he made 2320 runs at 66.28 in 1933 and 1745 at 72.20 in 1939, when he scored a century in each innings of the Lord's Test. He later played for many years in the Lancashire leagues. Awarded the MBE. His son **Ronald** (b. 29 Jun 1939) played with much success for Worcestershire 1958-74 and in two Tests for the West Indies in 1973.

22 Tests 1930-54: 2190 runs at 60.83, 14 100s HS 270; 14 catches.

First-class 1928-54: 9921 runs at 69.86, 33 100s HS 344; 51 wickets at 36.11, BB 5-33; 76 catches.*

Jack HEARNE (UK)

CRICKET

John Thomas Hearne. b. 3 May 1867 Chalfont St Giles, Buckinghamshire, d. 17 Apr 1944 Chalfont St Giles.

For 35 years J T Hearne gave exceptional service to Middlesex as a lively medium-paced bowler and a useful batsman. He took over 100 wickets in a season 15 times, with a peak of 257 at 14.28 in 1896. In 1899 he took a Test hat-trick for England against Australia at Leeds. He became a notable coach.

He was a distant cousin of Middlesex player 'Young Jack' **J W Hearne** (b. 11 Feb 1891 Hillingdon, d. 14 Sep 1965 West Drayton), who played 24 Tests for England 1911-26, and a cousin of the Hearnes of Kent, all three of whom played in the England-South Africa Test in 1892.

12 Tests 1892-99: 126 runs at 9.00, HS 40; 49 wickets at 22.08, BB 6-41; 4 catches.

First-class 1888-1923: 7205 runs at 11.98, HS 71; 3061 wickets at 17.75, BB 9-32; 426 catches.

Thomas HEARNS (USA)

BOXING

Thomas Hearns. b. 18 Oct 1958 Memphis, Tennessee

Thomas 'The Hit Man' Hearns was exceptionally tall for a welterweight at almost 6' 3" *1.90m*. He possessed a lethal punch and, having turned professional on 25 Nov 1977, won his first world title at that weight in 1980 by stopping Pipino Cuevas. Over the next eight years, Hearns also held titles as a light-middleweight, middleweight, and light-heavyweight. His four career losses came against all-time greats Sugar Ray Leonard and Marvelous Marvin Hagler, and also against Iran Barkley who knocked out Hearns in 1988 and beat him on points in 1992 when Hearns lost the WBA light-heavyweight title. In November 1988, Hearns defeated James Kinchen to claim the super-middleweight championship of the World Boxing Organization, and claimed to be the first man to win world titles in five weight classes. The fifth title seems manufactured to most boxing historians as Kinchen was a last-minute substitute for Fulgencio Obelmejias, who at the time held the title. In all Hearns won 14 and drew 1 of 19 world title fights.
Career record: W - 50 (40), L - 4, D - 1.

Beth HEIDEN (USA)

SPEED SKATING and CYCLING

Elizabeth Lee Heiden. b. 27 Sep 1959 Madison, Wisconsin.

The sister of Eric Heiden was a great all-rounder. She became the first American to win a speed skating world title in 1979 and was second in 1980, with second place also in the World Sprints 1979-80. She was world junior champion 1978-9. An ankle injury restricted her to a 3000m bronze in the 1980 Olympics. Later that year she became the first American to win the women's world road race title at cycling, and in 1983 she won the NCAA cross-country skiing title.
Best times: 500m 41.78, 1000m 1:23.66, 1500m 2:07.87, 3000m 4:32.60, 5000m 8:06.93, all in 1980.

Eric HEIDEN (USA)

SPEED SKATING

Eric Arthur Heiden. b. 14 Jun 1958 Madison, Wisconsin.

Although all his record times have now been improved, his performances at major championships remain unsurpassed and he is still considered as the greatest speed skater of all-time. After 7th place at 1500m in the 1976 Olympics, he made his first major impact the following year, when he uniquely won the world overall, world sprints and the world junior titles. He successfully defended all three titles in 1978 and, having moved out of the junior ranks, took the world overall and the world sprints for the third straight year in 1979. In the overall championship he won all four individual events, the first time since 1912 (Oscar Mathisen) that this had been accomplished. He was in superlative form at the 1980 Winter Olympics with a unique clean sweep of all five gold medals. He set Olympic records at each distance, including 10,000m in 14:28.13, his eighth world record. After the Olympics he suffered his first defeat since 1977 at the World Championships and then retired from skating, although later in the year he came close to making the US Olympic cycling team in the 1000m time trial and he subsequently had a brief career as a professional cyclist.
Heiden attended the University of Wisconsin, the University of California at San Diego and a school in Norway before enrolling for pre-medical studies at Stanford University.
Other best times: 500m 37.63 (1980), 1000m 1:13.60 (1980), 1500m 1:54.79 (1980), 3000m 4:06.91 (1979), 5000m 6:59.15 (1980).

Harry HEILMANN (USA)

BASEBALL

Harry Edwin Heilmann. b. 3 Aug 1894 San Francisco, California, d. 9 Jul 1951 Southfield, Michigan.

Heilmann played in the major leagues for 17 years, most of them with the Detroit Tigers. He played primarily outfield and

first base but it is as a hitter that he is best remembered. He led the American League in hitting in four seasons, 1921, 1923, 1925 and 1927, each at .390 or better, with a best of .403 in 1924. He hit a lot of doubles, with 40 or more in 8 of 10 seasons between 1921 and 1930, but he was not known as a power hitter. Arthritis in his wrists ended his baseball career and he then became the radio voice of the Tigers for 17 years before he died from lung cancer at age 56.
Career 1914-32: 2660 hits Avg. .342, HR 183; RBI 1538.

Mel HEIN (USA)

AMERICAN FOOTBALL

Melvin J Hein. b. 22 Aug 1909 Redding, California, d. 31 Jan 1992 San Clemente, California.

Considered the greatest center in the early days of the NFL, when he played for 15 years with the New York Giants. In 1938, he became the first lineman to be voted NFL MVP. Playing both offense and defense, as was common in that era, Hein played linebacker on defense. He later became a collegiate coach, was a supervisor of officials for the AFL from 1966-70 and held the same position for the NFL from 1970-74. He had played collegiate football at Washington State.

Tom HEINSOHN (USA)

BASKETBALL

Thomas William Heinsohn. b. 26 Aug 1934 Jersey City, New Jersey.

Heinsohn has excelled as player, coach and broadcaster of basketball. He is the only person to have been NBA Rookie of the Year and Coach of the Year. After his college career at Holy Cross he played for nine years as a big forward with the Boston Celtics, during which time they won nine division titles and eight NBA Championships. He was famous for his hook shot which enabled him to average 18.6 points during his career. After his retirement in 1965 he began a superb coaching career in 1969 and led the Celtics to NBA crowns in 1974 and 1976, and to 68 victories in the 1973 season, still an NBA record. After his coaching career ended in 1978, he became a broadcaster for CBS Television and later for local Celtics broadcasts.

Carol HEISS (USA)

FIGURE SKATING

Carol Elizabeth Heiss. b. 20 Jan 1940 New York. Later Jenkins

America's most successful woman figure skater. The daughter of German immigrants, she showed a remarkable aptitude for the sport and at the age of seven became a pupil of Pierre and Andrée Brunet, the former Olympic and World pairs champions. Four years later she won the US Novices Championship and went on to win an abundance of senior titles. After placing fourth at her first World Championships in 1954, she improved to take the silver in 1955 and then won the World title for the next six years. She won an Olympic silver medal in 1956, a gold in 1960 and four American titles 1957-60. After winning the 1960 Olympic title she signed a movie contract and in April of that year married Hayes Jenkins (qv).

Rüdiger HELM (GDR)

CANOEING

Rüdiger Helm. b. 6 Oct 1956 Neubrandenburg.

Helm shares the record with 13 World and Olympic titles at canoeing. His first gold came at the age of 19 with the K1 1000m in 1976 and he added: K1 1000m 1978-83, K2 500m 1978, K4 500m 1983 and K4 10,000m 1978-81. Those details include the Olympic golds at K1 and K4 in 1980, and he also won three Olympic bronze medals: K1 500m and K4 1000m in 1976 and K2 500m in 1980.

David HEMERY (UK)

ATHLETICS

David Peter Hemery. b. 18 Jul 1944 Cirencester, Gloucestershire.

Olympic champion at 400m hurdles in

1968 when he won by a huge margin and smashed the world record, running a time of 48.12. Amazingly he only contested the event in four seasons. He first ran it in 1965 when he had a best of 52.8 for 440y hurdles, improving to 51.8 in 1966. After his epic 1968 season, in which he ran five British records at 440y hurdles and five more at 400m hurdles, and at the end of which he was awarded the MBE, he did not run the event again until 1972. Then he won the bronze medal at the Olympics, as well as a silver in the 4 x 400m relay.
He had started as a high hurdler and set six British records at 110m/120y hurdles with a best of 13.6 in 1969 (and 13.72 on automatic timing in 1970), winning the Commonwealth title in 1966 and 1970, the World Student Games in 1970 and taking the European silver in 1969. He won the NCAA 400mh in 1968 and the AAA 110mh 1966 and 400mh 1968 and 1972. He also competed for Britain at the decathlon (best of 6893 points).
His family had moved to Boston, USA when he was 12, returning six years later. Having started a banking career he went back to the USA, to Boston University in 1964, where he was coached by Billy Smith. With Smith's aid and that of his English coach Fred Housden he became a supreme stylist. His great strength and disciplined preparation were shown further by his success in the all-sport Superstars competitions after his retirement from athletics in 1972. Since his retirement he has worked in Britain and the USA as a coach and counsellor.

John HENCKEN (USA)

SWIMMING

John Frederick Hencken. b. 29 May 1954 Culver City, California.

Set 12 world records at individual breaststroke events, seven at 100m from 1:05.68 in 1972 to 1:03.11 in 1976, and five at 200m from 2:22.79 in 1972 to 2:18.21 in 1974. He set world records when he won all his three Olympic gold medals: 200m (2:21.55) in 1972, 100m (1:03.11 after records in both heat and semi) and medley relay in 1976, and also when he won the 1973 World 100m (1:04.02).
At the Olympics he also won the 100m bronze in 1972, and the 200m silver in 1976, when he improved his US record to 2:17.26 but was behind David Wilkie, who also beat him at 200m at the 1973 Worlds, where Hencken also won a medley relay gold.
Graduated in electrical engineering from Stanford University, for whom he won five NCAA titles. He won individual AAU titles outdoors at 100m 1972-4, 1976; 200m 1973-4, 1976; and indoors at 100y 1974-5 and 200y 1975.

Paul HENDERSON (Can)

ICE HOCKEY

Paul Garnet Henderson. b. 28 Jan 1943 Kincardine, Ontario.

Like Mike Eruzione, who scored the goal in 1980 by which the US defeated the Soviet Union in the Olympics, Paul Henderson, a superb left wing who played in both the NHL and WHA, will forever be remembered by hockey fans for one game and one goal. He started with the Detroit Red Wings, but later played for the Toronto Maple Leafs, Toronto Toros (WHA), Birmingham Bulls (WHA), and the Atlanta Flames. While playing for the Maple Leafs he was selected in 1972 to play for Team Canada against the USSR in a series of games. The Soviet Union surprised the professional NHL players and took an early lead, winning three of the first four games. In the last three games, Henderson starred, scoring tie-breaking goals in all three. In the 7th game Henderson scored on a rebound with only 34 seconds left to win that game and the series, 4-3, and preserve Canadian superiority in their national sport.
Career 1962-80 - 1067 games, 376 goals, 761 points. Best year: 1977/8: 37 goals, 66 points (WHA).

Rickey HENDERSON (USA)

BASEBALL

Rickey Henley Henderson. b. 25 Dec 1958 Chicago, Illinois.

Early in the 1991 season, Henderson stole

the 939th base of his career, beating Lou Brock's record. It confirmed him as the greatest base stealer in major league history, a fact which he proclaimed himself to the listening crowd. He passed the 1000 mark in 1992 and on 16 Jun 1993 with his 1066th passed the world record of Japanese League player Yutaka Fukumoto. Henderson has been called the greatest lead-off batter in baseball history; a good hitter who hovers around .300 for career, but who also draws a lot of walks, and his lifetime on-base percentage has been over .400 for his first 12 years in the league. Once on base, his speed has terrorised opponents. Even though he does not hit for a lot of power, he has turned many singles into doubles by stealing or simply taking the extra base. He has also been quite controversial, and has been known as a bit of a 'hot dog'. He has played outfield and designated hitter with the Oakland Athletics, except for a spell with the New York Yankees 1985-9. He has led the American League in stolen bases 11 times in his first 14 seasons, with a single season record of 130 in 1982.
Career 1979-92: 2000 hits Avg. .291, HR 199; SB 1042.

Patsy HENDREN (UK)

CRICKET

Elias Henry Hendren. b. 5 Feb 1889 Turnham Green, Middlesex, d. 4 Oct 1962 Tooting Bec, Surrey.

The third most prolific batsman ever in first-class cricket, playing for Middlesex for 30 years and most successfully for England, especially from the mid-1920s. He was also a brilliant outfielder. A short, strong man, he became a hero in the West Indies in 1930 with his devastating batting when he scored 693 runs at 115.50 in the Tests and 1765 at 135.76 in first-class games, and for his humorous banter with the crowds. He scored over 2000 runs in 12 seasons: 1920-9, 1931-4 and 1936, including over 3000 three times: 3010 at 77.17 in 1923, 3311 at 70.44 in 1928 and 3186 at 56.89 in 1933. He was also a good wing forward at soccer, playing for Brentford, Queens Park Rangers, Manchester City and Coventry, and in a 1919 'Victory' international against Wales.
51 Tests 1920-35: 3525 runs at 47.63, 7 100s HS 205; 1 wicket; 33 catches.*
First-class 1907-38: 57,611 runs at 50.80, 170 100s (22 over 200) HS 301; 47 wickets at 54.76, BB 5-43; 754 catches.*

Stephen HENDRY (UK)

SNOOKER

Stephen Gordon Hendry. b. 13 Jan 1969 Edinburgh.

He succeeded Steve Davis as the world's top snooker player in the 1990s. In 1990-1 his consistency brought him 36 successive unbeaten matches in ranking tournaments. In 1990 he became World champion, at 21 years 106 days the youngest ever, and won again in 1992 and 1993. His other major tournament wins include: UK Open 1989-90, British Open 1991, Benson & Hedges Masters 1989-93. He was awarded the MBE in 1993.
He won the British under-16 title in 1983 and a year later, at 15, became the youngest ever Scottish amateur champion. He retained that title in 1985 and then turned professional. In 1986 he won his first Scottish professional title and in 1987 became the youngest ever winner of a ranking tournament, beating Dennis Taylor 10-7 to win the Rothmans Grand Prix. When he won the Sky Sports International at Plymouth in 1993 he became the first player to score ten century breaks in one tournament.

Sonja HENIE (Nor)

FIGURE SKATING

Sonja Henie. b. 8 Apr 1912 Oslo, d. 12 Oct 1969. Later Topping, Gardiner and Onstad.

The most successful and the most popular ice skater of all-time. After winning her first Norwegian title at the age of nine, she made her Olympic début as an 11-year-old in 1924 when she finished last in a field of eight. She placed fifth in the World Championship that year and improved to take second place in 1926. This was the last defeat she ever suffered. She went on to win ten world titles, 1927-36, six European titles, 1931-36, and three Olympic gold medals, 1928, 1932 and 1936. Apart from her unparalleled competitive record, her flair and style did much to popularise the sport. She dazzled the crowds with her theatrical performances in glamourous outfits and her arrival on the scene saw the end of the days of long skirts and black boots. Her attractive appearance, engaging personality and spectacular skating talent made her a natural for Hollywood where she amassed a fortune after leaving the amateur ranks in 1936. She made ten feature films for 20th Century-Fox and her own show, *Hollywood Ice Revue*, was an unprecedented box office attraction.

She was married three times, firstly to Dan Topping from 1939 to 1946 and she became a US citizen in 1941. Her second marriage to Winthrop Gardiner, the aeroplane millionaire, lasted from 1949 to 1956 when she married Niels Onstad, with whom she built a fine art collection which was later donated to Norway as a gift to the nation. She suffered from leukaemia in later life and died while flying from Paris to Oslo with her third husband for treatment from Norwegian specialists.

Heike HENKEL (FRG/Ger)

ATHLETICS

Heike Henkel. née Redetzky. b. 5 May 1964 Kiel.

Henkel took the high jump gold medal at her third Olympics in 1992, having won the Europeans in 1990 and the Worlds in 1991 as well as the World Indoors in 1991 and European Indoors in 1990 and 1992 to complete a clean sweep of the major high jump titles of the early 1990s.

She won the first of eight national outdoor high jump titles in 1984 and steadily improved to top world-class, taking her first major medal in 1988 with silver at the European Indoors, to which she added bronze at the World Indoors in 1989. In August 1987 she cleared 2 metres for the first time. In 1990 she improved the FRG indoor high jump record, previously set in 1982 by Ulrike Meyfarth, to 2.01m. She had a brilliant season in 1991, winning the overall Grand Prix title and being clearly the world's best female high jumper, taking Meyfarth's outdoor record with 2.05. Further progress was made in 1992 with a world indoor record of 2.07. She competes for LG Bayer Leverkusen.

In May 1989 she married **Rainer Henkel** (b. 27 Feb 1964 Opladen) who was world swimming champion in 1986 at 400m and 1500m freestyle, European champion at 1500m in 1987 and silver medallist at 400m 1987 and 1500m 1985, before placing sixth at 1500m in the 1988 Olympic Games.

Best times: 400m 3:48.30 (1986) and FRG records 800m 7:57.86 (1987) and 1500m 15:02.23 (1987).

Tommy HENRICH (USA)

BASEBALL

Thomas David Henrich. b. 20 Feb 1913 Massilon, Ohio.

Henrich played outfield in the majors for 11 years with the New York Yankees, missing four years because of World War II. He was known as 'Old Reliable' for his steady defensive and hitting abilities. With Joe DiMaggio and Charlie Keller, he helped form one of baseball's great outfields. His overall hitting records were only average, but he was known for being at his best in the clutch, helping the Yankees to win six pennants and four World Series.

Career 1937-50: 1297 hits Avg. .282, HR 183; RBI 795.

Jon HENRICKS (Aus)

SWIMMING

Jon Malcolm Henricks. b. 6 Jun 1934 Sydney, New South Wales.

Olympic gold medallist in 1956 at 100m freestyle, with a second gold and a world record at the 4 x 200m relay, Henricks was one of the greatest sprint swimmers. His 100m victory in a time of 55.4, later designated the inaugural world record at long course, was his 56th in succession at that distance in three years. He had missed the 1952 Games due to an ear infection and

illness held him back in 1960 when he was favoured for another medal so that he could not qualify for the 100m final. Just before the Games he had led off the Australian team that set a world record at 4 x 220y relay.
He won three gold medals, 110y and at freestyle and medley relays at the 1954 Commonwealth Games, and was Australian champion at 110y 1953-6, 220y 1953-4.

Pete HENRY (USA)

AMERICAN FOOTBALL

Wilbur Frank Henry. b. 31 Oct 1897 Mansfield, Ohio, d. 7 Feb 1952 Washington, Pennsylvania.

An offensive and defensive tackle, considered the greatest tackle in the early days of pro football and by legendary coach John Heisman as the 'greatest punt blocker the game has ever known'. He played college football at Washington & Jefferson, graduating in 1920. He played NFL football from 1920-3 with the Canton Bulldogs, rejoined them in 1925-6, and played with the New York Giants 1927 and Pottsville Maroons 1927-8. In addition to his line play, Henry was an exceptional punter and drop-kicker. He holds the NFL record for a drop-kicked field goal with one of 52 yards for Pottsville in 1928. In 1923, he recorded a 94-yard punt which lasted as an NFL record until 1969. Henry later returned to his alma mater as football coach and athletic director.

Babe HERMAN (USA)

BASEBALL

Floyd Caves Herman. b. 26 Jun 1903 Buffalo, New York, d. 27 Nov 1987 Glendale, California.

Herman played outfield and first base for 13 major league seasons. He broke in with the Brooklyn Dodgers, but later played for the Cincinnati Reds, Chicago Cubs, Pittsburgh Pirates, and Detroit Tigers. He was a top hitter, batting over .300 in 13 seasons, with highs of .393 in 1930 and .381 in 1929, but was known as one of the worst fielding players in the National League. He led the league in errors in 1927 at first base and in 1928 in the outfield. During his career he hit for the cycle three times, a major league record he shares with Bob Meusel.
Career 1926-45: 1818 hits Avg. .324, HR 181; RBI 997.

Dick HERN (UK)

HORSE RACING

(Major) William Richard Hern. b. 20 Jan 1921 Holford, Somerset.

Leading trainer in Britain four times, 1962, 1972, 1980 and 1983. He was formerly an amateur rider at point-to-points 1938-56, and was assistant trainer to Major Michael Pope 1952-7, before taking over as private trainer to Lionel Holliday at Newmarket. In 1962 he took over Bob Colling's stables at West Ilsley. His classic successes have included six winners of the St Leger, from his first with *Hethersett* in 1962, three Oaks, one each at 1000 Guineas and 2000 Guineas, and the Derby with *Troy* in 1979 and *Henbit* in 1980. His greatest horse was *Brigadier Gerard*. Awarded the CVO in 1980.

Erika HESS (Swi)

ALPINE SKIING

Erika Hess. b. 6 Mar 1962 Aeschi.

World champion at Alpine Combination in 1980, 1982, 1985, both slalom and giant slalom in 1982 and at slalom in 1987. In the World Cup she had the first of 31 individual victories in January 1981, was second overall that year and in 1986, champion in 1982 and 1984, 3rd in 1983, and 4th in 1985 and 1987; she won the slalom title a record four times, 1981-3 and 1985, and the giant slalom in 1984. Her only Olympic medal was the bronze at slalom in 1980 as she was only fifth in the slalom and seventh in the giant slalom in 1984.
She started racing at the age of five and first came to prominence with second place in the Swiss Championships at giant slalom in 1977. Quite small at 1.63m tall, she was nonetheless a powerful skier from a notable skiing family.

Lutz HESSLICH (GDR)

CYCLING

Lutz Hesslich. b. 17 Jan 1959 Ortrand.

The Olympic sprint cycling champion in 1980 and 1988 and had the GDR not boycotted the 1984 Olympics it is probable that he would have won three consecutive gold medals, better even than the great Daniel Morelon. He was World Junior champion in 1976 and 1977 and after third place in 1977 won senior titles in 1979, 1983, 1985 and 1987, with silver medals in 1981-2 and 1986 and bronze in 1977. He was GDR champion in 1978-80, 1982-3 and 1986. He set world records for 200m with a flying start at 10.441 sec in 1984 and 10.190 in 1985.

Bob HEWITT (Aus/SAf)

TENNIS

Robert Anthony John Hewitt. b. 20 Jan 1940 Sydney, New South Wales.

One of the great doubles players of his generation with an unrivalled return of service from the right-hand court. With fellow Australian Fred Stolle he won Wimbledon in 1962 and 1964, and the Australian Championship 1963-4. He then formed an even more successful partnership with South African Frew McMillan and won Wimbledon three more times (1967, 1974, 1978) and the 1972 French and 1977 US titles. In 1967 Hewitt and McMillan were unbeaten in a run of 39 consecutive doubles matches. In the mixed doubles Hewitt won at Wimbledon 1977 and 1979, in Australia 1961 and in Paris 1970. He lacked the mobility to excel at singles, at which his best performance in a Grand Slam event was to reach the Australian semi-finals in 1960. He emigrated in 1964 and after fulfilling his three-year residential qualification he represented South Africa in the Davis Cup 1967 to 1974.

Bryan HEXTALL (Can)

ICE HOCKEY

Bryan Aldwyn Hextall. b. 31 Jul 1913 Grenfell, Saskatchewan, d. 25 Jul 1984 Poplar Point, Manitoba.

In 1940, Hextall scored an overtime goal which brought the New York Rangers the Stanley Cup for the last time. He was a right winger who was considered a vicious bodychecker. He could also score, leading the NHL in scoring with 24 goals and 56 points in 1941/2. After his career ended he went into the lumbar and hardware business and had two sons, Bryan Jr and Dennis, play in the NHL. In the 1980s, his grandson Ron played as a goalie with the Philadelphia Flyers.
NHL career 1936-48 - 447 games, 188 goals, 363 points.

Rachel HEYHOE-FLINT (UK)

CRICKET

Rachel Heyhoe. b. 11 Jun 1939. née Flint.

The leading run-scorer in women's Test cricket, with 1814 at 49.02 in 25 matches from 1960 to 1979. This included four centuries, with a highest score of 176 against Australia in 1976. In 1963 against Australia she hit the first six in a women's Test. She also scored 643 runs in one-day internationals at an average of 58.4 and captained England to victory in the first women's World Cup in 1973. Her strong, charming personality and media awareness brought the women's game to public attention. She also played for England as a goalkeeper at hockey. Awarded the MBE in 1972. Formerly a PE teacher she became a journalist and public relations consultant.

Humphrey HICKS (UK)

CROQUET

Humphrey Osmond Hicks. b. 20 May 1904 Esher, Surrey, d. 9 Jun 1986 Colyton, Devon.

The dominant figure in world croquet until the arrival of John Solomon. Although his early career was curtailed by illness, he reached the final of the 1930 Open Championship and won the title in 1932 and 1939. After the war he was the Open champion five more times between 1947 and 1952, failing to win the title only in 1951. He also won the men's championship nine times between 1930 and 1966,

the President's Cup five times (1947-8, 1951, 1954 and 1961), the men's Open doubles seven times and the mixed doubles four times. His total of 27 Championship victories remained a record until surpassed by John Solomon.
He played for the Budleigh Salterton club and is rated as one of the greatest players of all-time. Before the handicap limit was fixed at minus 5 he held the lowest ever handicap of minus 5.5.

Edward HIDE (UK)

HORSE RACING
Edward William George Hide. b. 12 Apr 1937 Ludlow.

Rode 2591 winners in his riding career in Britain, 1950-85, with his first winner in 1951 and over 100 in 1973-4, 1976-7 and 1980-1, with a peak of 137 in 1974. His father, William (1907-89), was a trainer, and Edward began his career with him, becoming champion apprentice in 1954 and 1955 (75 winners). He had six classic winners, from St Legers on *Cantelo* in 1959 to *Julio Mariner* in 1978, and he won the 1973 Derby on *Morston*. Runs a small stud farm.

Molly HIDE (UK)

CRICKET
Mary Edith Hide. b. 24 Oct 1913.

Her career was interrupted by World War II but she played in 15 Tests for England between 1934 and 1954 and was captain from 1937. She was a fluent bat, scoring 872 runs in Tests at an average of 36.33 including two 100s, and a spin bowler who took 36 wickets at 15.25. Her highest score was 141* for England v The Rest in 1952 and her best Test bowling performances were 5-5 v New Zealand in 1935 and 5-20 v Australia 1937.
Her second-wicket partnership of 235 (made in 142 minutes) v New Zealand at Christchurch in 1934 remains a Test record; Hide scored 110 and Betty Snowball 189. She played county cricket for Surrey.

Nándor HIDEGKUTI (Hun)

FOOTBALL
Nándor Hidegkuti. b. 3 Mar 1922 Budapest.

A deep-lying centre-forward who linked the inside-forwards, Puskás and Kocsis, in the team of 'Magic Magyars' in the 1950s. He made his international début in 1945 while playing for Herminamezo in Division II of the Hungarian League, but it was not until 1952, when he was a gold medallist at the Helsinki Olympics, that he won a regular place in the national side. The majority of his 68 caps and 39 international goals came after he was 30 and any doubts regarding his status as a world class player were removed when he scored three of Hungary's goals in their memorable 6-3 defeat of England at Wembley in November 1953.
After moving to MTK Budapest he won three Championship medals playing at inside-right, although he continued as centre-forward for the national team. He played in the World Cup in 1954 and retired after his second World Cup appearance in 1958. Initially, he stayed on at MTK as a coach but then spent three years coaching in Italy. Following his return to Hungary in 1963, he coached a number of teams but eventually moved to Poland in 1972.

Alex HIGGINS (UK)

SNOOKER
Alexander Higgins. b. 18 Mar 1949 Belfast.

The fiery, controversial Higgins took the snooker world by storm in 1972 when he won at his first attempt at the World Professional Championships, at 23 then the youngest ever winner of the title. He was the biggest attraction in snooker, but did not win the title again until 1982 in an emotional final against Ray Reardon. His other major tournament wins include: British Gold Cup 1980, UK Open 1983, Benson & Hedges Masters 1978 and 1981. After winning the Irish title in 1983 he went six years without a tournament win until regaining the Irish title in 1989, although he had helped Ireland to win the

World Cup in 1985-7. Also in 1989 he won the B & H Irish Masters.
His often churlish behaviour brought him increasingly into trouble and he suffered bans from the game. At his peak, though, he was a brilliant, fast player and a great entertainer.

Clement HILL (Aus)

CRICKET

Clement Hill. b. 18 Mar 1877 Adelaide, d. 5 Sep 1945 Melbourne.

A great left-handed batsman who was at his best on the hard wickets of Australia, where he scored all four of his double centuries. He was not unsuccessful, however, on his four tours to England. He declined to make two further tours in 1909 and 1912 through disagreements with the Australian Board of Control, although between those dates he captained Australia in 10 Tests. He had a crouching stance, but was quick on his feet and was both a battler and a fast scorer. He was also a magnificent outfielder. He was the first player ever to reach 2000 runs (1904) and 3000 runs (1911) in a Test career; in addition to his 100s, he had successive Test scores of 99, 98 and 97 in 1901/02.
49 Tests 1896-1912: 3412 runs at 39.21, 7 100s HS 191; 33 catches.
First-class 1892-1926: 17,213 runs at 43.57, 45 100s HS 365; 10 wickets at 32.30, BB 2-6; 168 catches, 1 stumping.*

Graham HILL (UK)

MOTOR RACING

Norman Graham Hill. b. 15 Feb 1929 Hampstead, d. 29 Nov 1975 in a plane crash at Arkley, North London.

A hugely popular driver who was world motor racing champion in 1962 and 1968, and runner-up 1963-5. He was the only driver to have also won the Indianapolis 500 (1966) and Le Mans 24-hour race (1972).
He started driving late, buying his first car at the age of 24, and began work for Lotus as a racing mechanic in 1954. He made his Grand Prix début for them in 1958 and by his retirement in 1975 had driven in a record 176 championship races of which he won 14, totalling 289 points. He drove for Lotus 1958-9 and 1966-70, BRM 1960-6 with his first win in the 1962 Dutch GP, Brabham 1971-2, Shadow and Lola 1973-5. He won that tough race, the Monaco Grand Prix, five times in seven years 1963-9.
In 1953 he had stroked London Rowing Club's eight to victory in the Grand Challenge Cup at Henley. In 1993 his son **Damon** (b. 17 Sep 1952) succeeded Nigel Mansell on the Williams Formula One team and quickly established himself as one of the top drivers.

Phil HILL (USA)

MOTOR RACING

Philip Toll Hill, Jr. b. 20 Apr 1929 Miami, Florida.

In 1961 he became the first American to win the world motor racing title, but was most noted for his success in long-distance sports car events. He won the Le Mans 24-hour race with Olivier Gendebien in 1958 and 1961-2, the Sebring 12-hours in 1958-9 and 1961, and at Monza in 1960-1.
A true motoring enthusiast and a fine engineer, he had his first race win at Carrwell Speedway, Los Angeles in 1948. In 1955 he was invited to join Ferrari as a sports car and test driver, and after a seventh place in the French Grand Prix in a Maserati made his Grand Prix début for Ferrari with third in the Italian Grand Prix in 1958. He achieved the first of his three Grand Prix wins in that race in 1960, but left Ferrari after a poor 1962 season. He retired from racing in 1967 after a win with Mike Spence in the Six Hours race at Brands Hatch. In world championship racing he scored 98 points from 48 races 1958-64.

Blanche HILLYARD, see BINGLEY

Bernard HINAULT (Fra)

CYCLING

Bernard Hinault. b. 14 Nov 1954 Yffignac, Côtes du Nord.

Hinault was one of the all-time great

cyclists on the rank behind Eddy Merckx. He was incredibly tough, earning the nickname, 'Le Blaireau', or 'The Badger'. He equalled the record of Anquetil and Merckx by winning the Tour de France five times, 1978-9, 1981-2 and 1985, and has collected the second highest totals of 77 days wearing the Maillot Jaune and 28 stage wins, with the King of the Mountains title in 1986; he was forced to retire on the 12th stage through injury in 1980 when leading the race. He is also one of the few riders to win all three major tours, adding the Giro d'Italia 1980, 1982 and 1985, and the Vuelta à España in 1978 and 1983. His only weakness was that he was not a great road sprinter. But at the end of a fast, difficult race, his sprint became quite formidable and he won many one-day races in addition to his tour victories. He was French junior champion in 1972 and turned professional in 1974, winning the French pursuit title in 1975-6.
Other major victories: 1980 World Pro Road Race; Grand Prix de Nations 1977-9, 1982, 1984; Ghent-Wevelgem 1977, Liège-Bastogne-Liège 1977, 1980; Dauphiné-Libéré 1977, 1981; Flèche-Wallonne 1979, 1983; Tour of Lombardy 1979, 1984; Paris-Roubaix and Amstel Gold Race 1981.

Jürgen HINGSEN (FRG)

ATHLETICS

Jürgen Hingsen. b. 25 Jan 1958 Duisburg.

Brilliant decathlete who set three world records, one each year 1982-4 with a best of 8798 points (8832 on current tables), and yet never won a major title. That was because he was up against Daley Thompson, to whom he was runner-up at the 1984 Olympics, the 1983 Worlds and in the 1982 and 1986 Europeans (with a 9-0 career record between the two). Even when Thompson was past his best, Hingsen could not manage it, as he did not finish at the 1987 World Championships and had three false starts in the 100m, the opening event of the 1988 Olympic decathlon.
A superbly built athlete at 2.00m and 102kg, he competed for LAV Bayer Uerdingen/Dormagen and won eight of his 28 career decathlons. His best event was the long jump, at which he had a best of 8.04m in 1982 and was FRG champion in 1983.
In 1989 he became a TV presenter with ZDF.

Clarke HINKLE (USA)

AMERICAN FOOTBALL

William Clarke Hinkle. b. 10 Apr 1912 Toronto, Ohio.

Hinkle played football from 1929-32 at Bucknell and from 1932-41 with the Green Bay Packers. He was both a running back and a superb defensive linebacker, but was also known as an excellent punter and placekicker. He was named All-Pro four times and helped the Packers win three division titles and two NFL championships.

John HIPWELL (Aus)

RUGBY UNION

John Noel Brian Hipwell. b. 24 Jan 1948 Mayfield, NSW.

During an unusually lengthy international career (1968-82) he was capped 36 times. His days as Australia's scrum-half appeared to be over after the 1978 season but he was recalled to the team in 1981 when he played in four Tests and he won his final cap against England the following season.
On his first tour to the British Isles in 1966/7 he failed to make the Test side but he went on six further tours and captained Australia in the British Isles in 1975/6.

Elroy HIRSCH (USA)

AMERICAN FOOTBALL

Elroy Leon Hirsch. b. 17 Jun 1923 Wausau, Wisconsin.

'Crazylegs' Hirsch was a whippet-like running back and wide receiver. He played collegiately at the University of Wisconsin, 1941-2, 1947, and University of Michigan, 1943-4, eventually graduating from Baldwin-Wallace University after

serving in the US Marine Corps from 1943-6. Hirsch began his pro career with the Chicago Rockets of the All-American Football Conference but joined the Los Angeles Rams in 1949 when that league folded. He played with the Rams until 1957, his greatest year coming in 1951 when he caught 66 passes for 1495 yards, and scored 102 points. That year he led the NFL in points scored, passes caught, and receiving yardage (an NFL record), tied a record with 17 receiving touchdowns, and was named Player of the Year. Hirsch later had a brief foray as an actor.
NFL career 1946-57: 7029 yards gained receiving av. 18.2, 60 touchdowns.

George HIRST (UK)

CRICKET

George Herbert Hirst. b. 7 Sep 1871 Kirkheaton, Yorkshire, d. 10 May 1954 Ludley, Huddersfield, Yorkshire.

With Wilfred Rhodes for Yorkshire he made up an unbeatable pair of all-rounders. In 1906 he achieved the unique feat of scoring 2000 runs (2385 at 45.86) and taking 200 wickets (208 at 16.50) in a first-class season. That was one of 14 doubles (1000/100) that he obtained and in two more of those he scored over 2000 runs, with a high of 2501 at 54.36 in 1904. A middle-order forcing right-handed batsman, a left-arm medium-fast inswing bowler and a magnificent fielder, he was surprisingly not very effective in Tests, but was hugely popular. He later coached at Eton College for 18 years.
24 Tests 1897-1909: 790 runs at 22.57, HS 85; 59 wickets at 30.00, BB 5-48; 18 catches.
First-class 1891-1929: 36,323 runs at 34.13, 60 100s HS 341; 2739 wickets at 18.72, BB 9-24; 604 catches.

Tommy HITCHCOCK (USA)

POLO

Thomas Hitchcock Jr. b. 11 Feb 1900 Aiken, South Carolina, d. 19 Apr 1944 Salisbury, England.

Perhaps the greatest polo player ever, he was an aggressive rather than a particularly skilful rider, but he was a long and accurate striker of the ball. He played for the US in every international match between 1920 and 1940, with only two exceptions, and was on the winning team every time except in the Cup of the Americas in 1936.
As a 17-year-old at St Paul's school he tried to enlist in the Aviation Section of the Army Signal Corps for service in World War I. Having been rejected on the grounds of his youth, he enlisted with the French forces and went overseas, later transferring to the US Air Service. He was shot down over enemy lines while flying a mission for the famous Lafayette Escadrille and spent a number of months in hospitals and prison camps. While being transferred between camps he jumped from a train as it was crossing a river and, although still wounded and walking only at nights, he covered the 100 miles to the Swiss border in just eight days.
After the war, Hitchcock was educated at Harvard and Oxford. Substantial family business interests enabled him to devote much of his time to polo and he maintained a 10-goal handicap for 18 years. At the outbreak of World War II he rejoined the Army Air Corps and served as assistant air attache to the embassy in London. His adventurous life came to an end when he was killed in an army airplane crash in England.

Kinue HITOMI (Japan)

ATHLETICS

Kinue Hitomi. b. 1 Jan 1908 Okayama, d. 2 Aug 1931 of tuberculosis.

A pioneer all-rounder, Hitomi's world records included the following bests: 100m 12.2 (1928), 200m 24.7 on a straight track (1929), 400m 59.0 (1928), long jump 5.98m (1928). She also had a wind-aided long jump of 6.075 for Japan v Germany in 1929 and took the Olympic silver medal at 800m with 2:17.6 in 1928. She set Asian records at ten standard events, from 100m to 800m and 80m hurdles on the track, high and long jumps, discus and javelin. She made her international début at the Women's World Games of 1926, when she won the long jump and standing long jump, was second at discus, third at 100m and fifth at 60m. In 1930 she retained her World Games long jump title, backed with a second and two third places.

Lew HOAD (Aus)

TENNIS

Lewis Alan Hoad. b. 23 Nov 1934 Glebe, New South Wales.

Universally recognised as one of the great players of all-time. A forceful, aggressive player with a powerful physique, he was outstanding as a junior, winning the Australian junior title in 1951, and, as a 17-year-old, reaching the fourth round at Wimbledon in 1952. In 1956 he won the Wimbledon, French and Australian singles titles but was thwarted in his bid for the Grand Slam when he lost to Ken Rosewall in the US final. The following year he defended his Wimbledon title with a 6-2, 6-1, 6-2 victory over fellow Australian Ashley Cooper, and Hoad's performance that day is still rated as one of the finest in the history of the game. This was his last match as an amateur and was a fitting climax to his brilliant but relatively brief amateur career. Between 1953 and 1957 he won six Grand Slam men's doubles titles with Ken Rosewall and two further titles with different partners. He also won the mixed doubles at the 1954 French Championships. His overall Davis Cup record was to win 11 of 13 singles and 7 of 9 doubles 1953-6, with Australia winning the Cup in three of those four years.
His professional career, which began immediately after the 1957 Wimbledon, was limited by a back injury. In 1968 he set up his own tennis ranch in Spain and after the game went Open, he came out of semi-retirement to play at Wimbledon in 1968, 1970 and 1972 but was eliminated in the early rounds each year.

Jack HOBBS (UK)

CRICKET

(Sir) John Berry Hobbs. b. 16 Dec 1882 Cambridge, d. 21 Dec 1963 Hove, Sussex.

'The Master' was the supreme English batsman, a great cover fielder and a wonderful man. He set records which may never be surpassed with 61,237 runs and 197 centuries (or 199 on a more accurate, but non-traditional assessment) in first-class cricket. But he was not especially interested in runs for the sake of runs, and it was the sheer quality that made him such a delight and so dependable for Surrey and England. He exceeded 1000 runs in 26 seasons (24 in England and 2 in South Africa), with a record 17 over 2000 and once over 3000, 3024 at 70.32 in 1925, when he set the record (passed by Denis Compton in 1947) of 16 centuries in the season. He scored an amazing 98 of his first-class centuries after the age of 40, and remained a must for England from 1907 until he was 47 in 1930. He formed notable opening partnerships with Tom Hayward and Andy Sandham for Surrey, and with these men he made 40 and 66 century partnerships respectively. Then for England he opened principally with Wilfred Rhodes and Herbert Sutcliffe (26 century partnerships, including 15 in Tests). Hobbs was the first batsman to reach 4000 runs (1926) and 5000 runs (1929) in Test cricket. He played for Cambridgeshire before making his Surrey début in 1905. He made 155 in his first Championship match and was immediately presented with his county cap. In 1953 he became the first professional to be knighted for services to cricket.
61 Tests 1907-30: 5410 runs at 56.94, 15 100s HS 211; 1 wicket; 17 catches.
First-class 1905-34: 61,237 runs at 50.65, 197 100s HS 316; 107 wickets at 25.00, BB 7-56; 339 catches.*

Gil HODGES (USA)

BASEBALL

Gilbert Raymond Hodges. b. 4 Apr 1924 Princeton, Indiana, d. 2 April 1972 West Palm Beach, Florida.

A slugging, power-hitting first baseman who played 18 years in the majors, 16 with the Brooklyn/Los Angeles Dodgers and his last two with the New York Mets. Because of injuries his career only encompassed 14 full seasons but he still hit 370 home runs

during that span. He recorded over 100 RBI for seven straight years, 1949-55, and 20 home runs for 11 consecutive seasons, 1949-59. He hit 14 grand slams, which at the time was a National League record. His greatest single game came on 31 Aug 1950 when he hit four home runs against the Braves. He was also an excellent fielder, winning three Gold Gloves. After his playing career he became a manager, first with the Washington Senators and then with the New York Mets. In 1969 he led the 'Miracle Mets' to a World Series victory, but died quite young from a heart attack after playing golf.
Career 1943-63: Avg. .273, HR 370; RBI 1274. Best season: 1954: .304, 42 HR, 130 RBI.

Gunhild HOFFMEISTER (GDR)

ATHLETICS
Gunhild Hoffmeister. b. 6 Jul 1944 Forst.

At 1500m Hoffmeister won Olympic silver medals in 1972 and 1976, European gold in 1974 and silver in 1971. At 800m she won European silver in 1974, Olympic bronze in 1972, European Indoor gold in 1972 and the World Student Games gold in 1970. She won 14 GDR titles, eight at 1500m and six at 800m between 1968 and 1976. She ran on two GDR teams that set world records at 4 x 800m, and was a member of the GDR parliament.
Best times: 800m 1:58.61 (1976), 1000m 2:35.9 (1972, world best), 1500m 4:01.4 (1976).

Ben HOGAN (USA)

GOLF
William Benjamin Hogan. b. 13 Aug 1912 Dublin, Texas.

Hogan was, with Jack Nicklaus and Bobby Jones, a contender for the title of the greatest ever golfer. He is certainly remembered as the hardest working golfer ever and 'Hogan stories' of his legendary dedication to the game are still common on the PGA Tour. His greatest year was 1953 when he became the only professional to win three legs of golf's professional grand slam, the US Open, Masters, PGA and British Open. Only the PGA eluded him in that year, but for good reason. Hogan had to qualify for the 1953 British Open as did everyone in those days. Qualifying for the British and the finals of the PGA overlapped, so he could not have played both events.
In 1948 Hogan won 10 tournaments on tour and was the leading money winner. He was the game's finest player beyond a doubt. On 13 Feb 1949, driving home from a tournament and near El Paso, Texas, his car was crushed by an oncoming bus. Hogan was also nearly crushed as he threw himself across his wife's lap to save her life. He was not expected to live, much less play tournament golf again. But he returned in 1950 to win the US Open, and had his greatest years after the accident. He later started the Ben Hogan company which manufactures golf clubs, balls, and other equipment.
Major victories: US Open 1948, 1950-51, 1953; PGA 1946, 1948; Masters 1951, 1953; British Open 1953. 63 US PGA Tour victories.

Uwe HOHN (GDR)

ATHLETICS
Uwe Hohn. b. 16 Jul 1962 Rheinsberg.

The first, and so far only, man to throw the javelin over 100 metres, with 104.80m in East Berlin on 20 Jul 1984. This, at 5.08m, was the biggest ever improvement on a world javelin record. Two months earlier he had set a European record 99.52m. Such throwing was instrumental in the javelin specification being changed from 1986 so as to reduce the distances thrown. A sports student who competed for ASK Potsdam, he won the European Junior title with a record distance of 86.56 in 1981, and went over 90 metres in 1982, when he won the European senior title. He then had a year out before his big years of 1984, when the GDR boycotted the Olympics and 1985, when he won both the European Cup and World Cup competitions.
His career was ended by back injuries which necessitated a series of operations 1986-9. These were not successful and left him 60% immobile.

Christoph HÖHNE (GDR)

WALKING

Christoph Höhne. b. 12 Feb 1941 Borsdorf.

At 50 kilometres walk he was the Olympic champion in 1968 (6th 1964, 14th 1972) and European in 1969 and 1974 (4th 1964, 2nd 1971). He also won three Lugano Trophy 50km finals, 1965, 1967 and 1970. He set two world records for 50km (with those for 30 miles en route) with 4:10:51.8 in 1965 and 4:08:05.0 in 1969, and one at 30km, 2:15:16.0 in 1971; and he had a road best for 50km of 3:52:53 in 1974. GDR champion seven times at 50km walk 1963-5, 1968-71.

Michael HOLDING (Jam)

CRICKET

Michael Anthony Holding. b. 16 Feb 1954 Half Tree Way, Kingston.

With his beautiful athletic action and smooth, light-footed accelerating run-up, Holding was a glorious fast bowler. He produced many devastating spells of bowling, none more so than on the 1976 West Indies tour of England, when he took 28 wickets in the series at 12.71; at The Oval, a wicket on which 1507 runs were scored in the match, he had the extraordinary figures of 8-92 and 6-57. He exceeded this wicket haul in the 1983/4 series against India when he captured 30 at 22.10. He played for Jamaica from 1973, captaining them shrewdly, and in England for Lancashire and Derbyshire.
60 Tests 1975-87: 910 runs at 13.78, HS 73; 249 wickets at 23.68, BB 8-92; 22 catches.
102 One-day Ints: 282 runs at 9.09, HS 64, 142 wickets at 21.36, BB 5-26; 30 catches.
First-class 1973-89: 3600 runs at 15.00, HS 80; 778 wickets at 23.43, BB 8-92; 125 catches.

Steve HOLLAND (Aus)

SWIMMING

Stephen Roy Holland. b. 31 May 1958 Brisbane.

At the age of 15 in 1973, Holland won the inaugural world title at 1500m freestyle in a world record time of 15:31.85, taking 5.95 secs off the record that he had set (for 1650y) a month earlier. Yet he swam on for another 110m, unsure of whether he had reached the finish!
He made further improvements to his 1500m world record with 15:27.79 in 1975 and 15:10.89 in 1976 and set seven world records at 800m, from 8:17.60 in 1973 to 8:02.91 in 1976. He won the Commonwealth gold at 1500m in 1974, when at 15 years 245 days he became the youngest ever male swimming gold medallist, but did not defend his world title in 1975. At the 1976 Olympics he swam 1500m in 15:04.66, two seconds inside the world record, but had to settle for the bronze medal behind the Americans Brian Goodell and Bobby Hackett; later he was fifth at 400m.
Australian champion 400m/440y 1975-6, 1500m/1650y 1974-6. He turned professional and competed successfully in surf races.

Eleanor HOLM (USA)

SWIMMING

Eleanor Holm. b. 6 Dec 1913 New York. Later married names Jarrett, Rose, Walker.

The glamorous Eleanor Holm won 29 American swimming titles and set seven world backstroke records from 1930, with short course bests of 1:16.3 for 100m in 1935 and 2:48.7 for 200m in 1936. These lasted as US records for more than 16 years. At the age of 14 she was fifth in the 100m backstroke at the 1928 Olympics and won this event at the Los Angeles Games four years later.
Having married the crooner Art Jarrett in 1933, she was selected for a third Olympic Games in 1936, but her behaviour on the boat trip to Europe incurred the disapproval of US officials and she was banned from competing. She had reportedly drunk champagne while in training, and despite a petition signed by most of the US team, Avery Brundage and his USOC officials refused to reconsider their verdict.
She sang with her husband's band, and in

1938 played Jane in the film *Tarzan's Revenge* opposite decathlete Glenn Morris. She divorced Jarrett and married Billy Rose, promoter of aquacades in which she starred.

Marshall HOLMAN (USA)

BOWLING

Marshall Holman. b. 29 Sep 1954.

With 21 career PBA Championships he stands fifth on the all-time PBA list and has the record all-time earnings of $1,592,866 to the end of the 1992 season. This fiery player has always been a big crowd favourite, wearing his emotions on his sleeve. On one occasion he punched the wall, broke his hand and had to retire from the competition. His career highlights have been his 1985 US Open and the 1976 and 1986 Tournament of Championships titles. The last put Holman over the $1 million mark in career earnings, only the third bowler to do so. In 1982, 1984, and 1987 he had the highest average on the PBA Tour and he was voted PBA Player of the Year in 1987. That was a tribute to his consistency as he did not win a championship that year. Holman has probably been bowling's most outspoken champion, often predicting victories, and his temper has earned him one suspension and the ire of some other players and fans, but he remains one of the tour's most exciting players.

Nat HOLMAN (USA)

BASKETBALL

Nathan Holman. b. 19 Oct 1896 New York.

The playmaking guard of the Original Celtics, the first nationally known basketball team. He was a superb all-round player, with a tantalising change of pace. While playing he also coached at City College of New York (CCNY), before retiring as a player in 1930. He then became well-known as a basketball coach at the New York campus and his 1950 team is the only college team to win the NIT and NCAA titles in the same year. He retired as coach in 1952 but made brief returns in 1955-6 and 1959-60.

Larry HOLMES (USA)

BOXING

Larry Holmes. b. 3 Nov 1949 Cuthbert, Georgia

Although one of the greatest ever champions, Holmes never received the plaudits of many other heavyweights. Much of this was because he succeeded such ring legends as Ali, Frazier, and Foreman. He also lacked the personality out of the ring to promote himself and suffered in the public's eye as a result. His bitterness over the lack of recognition only compounded the problem. He won the heavyweight world championship in 1978 by outpointing Ken Norton and won his first 47 bouts, including 21 world title fights. Trying to match Rocky Marciano's record of 49 victories without a loss or draw, Holmes lost the title in 1985 to Michael Spinks and also lost a return bout to Spinks. He then retired but in 1988 returned to face Mike Tyson, who knocked him out in four rounds. In 1991 Holmes began another ring comeback and continued to fight through to 1993.
Career record: W - 58 (40), L - 4, D - 0.

Márton HOMONNAI (Hun)

WATER POLO

Márton Homonnai. né Havlicsek. b. 2 Feb 1906, d. 15 Oct 1969 Rio de Janeiro, Brazil.

After a silver medal in 1928 he was captain of the Hungarian team that won the Olympic water polo tournaments of 1932 and 1936, and the European Championships of 1926-7, 1931 and 1934. He made 110 international appearances for Hungary.
He became a member of the Hungarian Nazi party and was commander of an armed party group. After the War he was declared, in his absence, a war criminal. He divorced before World War II. His daughter **Katalin Szöke** (b. 17 Aug 1935 Budapest) competed under her mother's maiden name and won gold medals at the 1952 Olympics and 1954 Europeans at 100m freestyle and relay.

Willie HOPPE (USA)

BILLIARDS

William Franklin Hoppe. b. 11 Oct 1887 Cornwall-on-Hudson, New York, d. 1 Feb 1959 Miami, Florida.

The greatest American billiards player, who won a total of 51 world titles at various different versions of the game, although he never played English billiards. He learned the games at his father's New York hotel and first played as a professional in 1901 at the age of 13. The following year he went to Europe, playing on the pro circuit in Paris. On a subsequent visit in 1906, he beat the 60-year-old Frenchman Maurice Vignaux for the World 18.1 (one shot in baulk) Championship. He won the title four more times, 1910-11 and 1913-14, before the event lost official recognition. At the 18.2 (two shots in baulk) game he held the World title in 1908, 1910-20, 1922-4 and, briefly, in 1927.

In the 1930s Hoppe concentrated on three-cushion billiards, the lone survivor among carom games, and was world champion in 1936, 1940-3 and 1947-52. In compiling this unsurpassed record of championship victories he set a host of scoring records, and his clean living image was in sharp contrast to the lifestyle of many of his pool hall contemporaries. He retired in 1952 aged 65 after spending 50 years promoting the products of the Brunswick-Balke-Collender Corporation.

Wolfgang HOPPE (GDR)

BOBSLEIGH

Wolfgang Hoppe. b. 14 Nov 1957 Apolda.

Top bobsleigh driver of the 1980s. In the two-man event he won an Olympic gold medal in 1984 and a silver in 1988, and was a three-time world champion, 1985-6 and 1989, with silver in 1987. He was equally accomplished in the four-man event, winning Olympic gold in 1984, a silver in 1988 and 1992, and taking the world title in 1991 and silver in 1987. He was also European champion at two-man 1986-7 and four-man 1987. He had been the GDR junior decathlon champion in 1976.

Rogers HORNSBY (USA)

BASEBALL

Rogers Hornsby. b. 27 Apr 1896 Winters, Texas, d. 5 Jan 1963 Chicago, Illinois.

'Rajah' Hornsby ranks with Babe Ruth, Ty Cobb and Ted Williams as one of the very greatest hitters in baseball history and is usually acclaimed as the greatest right-hander. His records are almost too numerous to list. Twice, in 1922 (.401, 250 hits, 42 HR) and 1925 (.403, 39 and 143), he won the Triple Crown, and batted over .400 a third time with .424 in 1924, which is a modern record. He led the National League in hitting seven times and in RBI four times. His career average of .358 is second lifetime only to Ty Cobb. Hornsby played multiple positions, but primarily was a second baseman. He was a difficult personality, often abrasive to the public and belligerent to the baseball executives. This led to his being traded several times, despite his great ability. He began with the St Louis Cardinals, for whom he played 12 years, but he later played with the New York Giants, Boston Braves, Chicago Cubs, and St Louis Browns. During his last 10 seasons, he spent parts of nine of them as a player-manager. It was said he was the only manager he could play for. He managed briefly again 15 years after his career ended. He never smoked or drank, even coffee, and to preserve his batting eye he refused to go to movies.
Career 1915-37: 2930 hits Avg. .358, HR 301; RBI 1584.

Paul HORNUNG (USA)

AMERICAN FOOTBALL

Paul Vernon Hornung. b. 23 Dec 1935 Louisville, Kentucky.

Hornung was known as football's 'Golden Boy' and he knew the best and worst that pro football had to offer. After winning the Heisman Memorial Trophy in his senior year (1956) at Notre Dame, he joined the Green Bay Packers. From being the worst team in the NFL they were transformed into the best by Vince Lombardi from 1958, and Hornung blossomed as a star under Lombardi's martinet-like coaching

manner. Hornung was known as a womaniser and carouser, but Lombardi forced him to concentrate on football, saying that Hornung was only an average football player in the midfield area but that he was the greatest he had ever seen when the Packers got close to scoring range. As a running back and place-kicker, Hornung helped the Packers to four NFL championships, 1961-2, 1965-6. He led the NFL in scoring 1959-61, and his total of 176 points in 1960 is a still-standing NFL record. In both 1960 and 1961 he was the NFL's MVP. He missed the 1963 season when he and Alex Karras were suspended from football for betting on games. Hornung has become a well-known television football analyst. He was elected to the College Football Hall of Fame in 1985 and the Pro Football Hall of Fame in 1986; though an obvious choice, it was felt that voters had not selected him earlier because of his gambling suspension.
NFL career 1957-66: Rushing: 3711 yards av. 4.2, 50 touchdowns. Receiving: 1480 yards av. 11.4, 12 touchdowns.

HORTENCIA (Bra)

BASKETBALL
Hortencia Maria de Fatima Marcari Oliva. b. 24 Sep 1959.

The finest women's player ever outside of the United States and the Soviet Union. At 1.74m *5'8"* she was far from the tallest player in most games, but she was a potent offensive weapon of whom it was once said by Cheryl Miller, 'She can score on anybody'. In 1983 Hortencia scored 36 and 46 points against the United States in games at the World Championships and the Pan-American Games. She spent most of her career playing professionally for Prudentinas, a club team in the small town of Presidente Prudente.

Tim HORTON (Can)

ICE HOCKEY
Myles Gilbert Horton. b. 12 Jan 1930 Cochrane, Ontario, d. 21 Feb 1974 Toronto, Ontario.

Considered by some fans as almost the equal of Doug Harvey as a defensive player. Horton was not large, but he was incredibly strong, and played tough as a result; yet he was one of the cleanest players in the game, rarely getting a penalty. Horton played his first 18 years with the Toronto Maple Leafs. He was traded several times in his last few years, finishing his career with the Buffalo Sabres. Tragically, Horton was killed in 1974, driving between Toronto and Buffalo. At the time of his death, only Gordie Howe and Alex Delvecchio had played more games in the NHL.
NHL career 1952-1974 - 1,446 games, 115 goals, 518 points.

Hazel HOTCHKISS (USA) see WIGHTMAN

Frank HOWARD (USA)

BASEBALL
Frank Oliver Howard. b. 8 Aug 1936 Columbus, Ohio.

A giant slugger, 2.01 m *6'7"*, 116 kg *255 lb*, who played outfield and first base. He began with the Los Angeles Dodgers, but is best remembered for his years with the Washington Senators. He captained the basketball team at Ohio State University, and was named All-Big Ten in 1958. In May 1968 he belted 12 home runs in 16 days, setting major league records for most home runs in six consecutive games (10), five consecutive games (8), and tying AL records for most home runs in four consecutive games (7), and most straight games with home runs (6). His season's totals of home runs 1968-70 were 44, 48, 44. Since retiring he has served mostly as a coach, although he managed for parts of 1981 and 1983.
Career 1958-73: 1774 hits Avg. .273, HR 382; RBI 1119.

Gordie HOWE (Can)

ICE HOCKEY
Gordon Howe. b. 31 Mar 1928 Floral, Saskatchewan.

The most durable player in NHL history, he amassed the pre-Gretzky NHL career records of 801 goals, 1049 assists and 1850 points in a record 1767 games over a record 26 seasons. After playing for Omaha in the AHL in 1944/5, he began playing in the NHL in 1946 with the Detroit Red Wings, and held down their right wing until 1971. In 1973 he joined his two sons on the Houston Aeros team in the fledgling World Hockey Association (WHA) and returned to the NHL for the Hartford Whalers in 1979/80 when he was 51 years old, after 34 years in the sport at the highest level.

Hall of Famer Bill Gadsby said of Howe, 'He was not only the greatest hockey player I've ever seen, but also the greatest athlete.' Hockey expert Stan Fischler listed Howe as Number One in his book, *The All-New Hockey's 100.* In his early years in the league, Howe's greatest rival was Montreal's Maurice Richard. But Richard considered Howe the best, saying 'Gordie could do *everything*'.

He led the NHL in scoring to win the Ross Trophy in 1951-4, 1957 and 1963, setting all-time records with 43 goals and 86 points in 1950/1, 47 and 86 in 1951/2, 49 and 95 in 1952/3. He won the Hart Trophy as NHL MVP six times, 1952-3, 1957-8, 1960 and 1963. He helped Detroit to four Stanley Cup victories, 1950, 1952, 1954-5 and had a record 20 seasons in the play-offs. He was selected for 12 all-star first teams, and nine second teams.

Canadian athlete of the year 1963, he has the Order of Canada and is now a cattle breeder.

Career 1946-80: 2186 games, 975 goals, 2358 points. NHL play-offs: 157 games, 68 games, 160 pts.

Lida HOWELL (USA)

ARCHERY

Lida Howell. née Scott. b. 28 Aug 1859, d. 20 Dec 1939.

Lida Scott became interested in archery in the 1870s and won her first titles, the Ohio State Championship, in 1881 and 1882. In the spring of 1883 she married Millard C. Howell and also won the first of 17 national championships of the 20 she contested between 1883 and 1907 - one of the most amazing records in any sport. Her scores in the 1895 championship set records which were not broken until 1931. She won gold medals in both events, the Double Columbia Round and the Double National Round, in 1904 when archery was contested in the St Louis Olympics by women.

Waite HOYT (USA)

BASEBALL

Waite Charles 'Schoolboy' Hoyt. b. 9 Sep 1899 Brooklyn, New York, d. 25 Aug 1984 Cincinnati, Ohio.

The New York Yankees of the 1920s are considered possibly the greatest dynasty in baseball history, and Waite Hoyt was their top pitcher during much of that era. He played for six different teams in the majors, but it was with the Yankees (1921-30) that he achieved most of his fame. He pitched in seven World Series (six with the Yankees and one with the Philadelphia Athletics in 1931), and ranks high on the World Series records lists in numerous categories.

Career pitching 1918-38: ERA 3.59; W-L 237-182, SO 1206; Best seasons: 1927: 22-7, 2.64 ERA; 1928: 23-7, 3.36 ERA.

Cal HUBBARD (USA)

AMERICAN FOOTBALL

Robert Cal Hubbard. b. 31 Oct 1900 Keytesville, Missouri, d. 19 Oct 1977 Milan, Ohio.

Hubbard played college football at both Centenary College and Geneva College. He was a tackle who later played for ten years in the NFL with the New York Giants, Green Bay Packers, and Pittsburgh Pirates. He gained most of his fame in six years with the Packers and was named All-Pro from 1928-33. During football off-seasons, Hubbard umpired minor league baseball games and after his 1936 retirement he became an American League umpire from 1936-51. From 1951 until 1969 he was supervisor of officials for major league baseball. Hubbard has been elected to the College Football Hall of Fame, the Pro Football Hall of Fame, and the National Baseball Hall of Fame, the only athlete so honoured. In 1969 he was voted the NFL's greatest tackle of the first 50 years.

DeHart HUBBARD (USA)

ATHLETICS

William DeHart Hubbard. b. 25 Nov 1903 Cincinnati, Ohio, d. 23 Jun 1976 Cleveland, Ohio.

The first black athlete to win an Olympic gold medal in an individual event, with the long jump in 1924. A year later he improved the world record from 7.76m to 7.89 to win his third consecutive NCAA title for the University of Michigan. That was just over an inch short of 26 feet, and Hubbard went over that distance by 2 $^1/_4$ inches with 7.98m at Cincinnati in 1927, but the take-off board was one inch higher than the pit and the record therefore could not count.

Hubbard won six consecutive AAU long jump titles 1922-7 as well as the triple jump in 1922-3. He was also a top class sprinter, with an indoor world best 6.2 for 60y, the NCAA 100y title in 1925 and a tie of the world record at 100y with 9.6 in 1926. Injured in 1928, he could only place 11th at the Olympics.

Carl HUBBELL (USA)

BASEBALL

Carl Owen Hubbell. b. 22 Jun 1903 Carthage, Ohio. d, 21 Nov 1988 Scottsdale, Arizona.

A left-hander, he pitched his entire 16-year major league career with the New York Giants. His best years were 1933-7 when he won over 20 games in five consecutive seasons. Famous for his screwball, he is one of only two pitchers (with Hal Newhouser) to have won two MVP awards. He is best remembered for his feats in the 1934 All-Star Game when, pitching for the National League, he consecutively struck out Babe Ruth, Lou Gehrig, Jimmy Foxx, Al Simmons, and Joe Cronin, one of the great Murderers Rows ever to grace the All-Star game. Hubbell also set a major league record which still stands when he won 24 consecutive games over the course of two seasons - 16 to end the 1936 season and 8 at the start of 1937. He underwent elbow surgery in 1938 and was never the same again.

Career pitching: 1928-43 ERA 2.98; W-L 253-154, SO 1677; Best seasons: 1936: 26-6, 2.31 ERA; 1933: 23-12, 1.66 ERA; 1935: 23-12, 3.27 ERA; 1937: 22-8, 3.19 ERA.

Peter HUDSON (Aus)

AUSTRALIAN RULES FOOTBALL

Peter Hudson. b. 19 Feb 1946 Tasmania.

The most prolific scorer in the history of Australian Rules football. In a 19-year career from 1963-81 he kicked a record 2191 goals in the VFL and Tasmania. In 1971 he equalled Bob Pratt's 1934 record of 150 goals in a season, but then missed an easy shot at goal in the Grand Final, in which his team, Hawthorn, beat St Kilda, and had no more opportunities to improve the record. He had joined Hawthorn from New Norfolk in 1967 and with 125 goals in 1968 became the first man since John Coleman in 1952 to kick more than 100. Injuries held him down to 120 in 1969, but he kicked 146 in 1970. After a brief retirement he returned with 110 goals for Hawthorn in 1977, his fourth year as VFL leading scorer. Returning to Tasmania he scored a season's record 202 goals for Glenorchy in 1981.

Sam HUFF (USA)

AMERICAN FOOTBALL

Robert Lee Huff. b. 4 Oct 1934 Edna Gas, West Virginia.

Huff established the position of middle linebacker as a glamour spot, starring on defense for the New York Giants in the late 1950s when they were the premier team in pro football. Giants defensive coach Tom Landry stated flatly that 'Sam Huff became the symbol of defensive football'. He played for the Giants 1956-63 and the Washington Redskins 1964-7 and for one more year in 1969, when Vince Lombardi was named Redskins coach. Huff was twice All-Pro and played in four

Pro Bowl Games. He played college football at West Virginia.

Merv HUGHES (Aus)

CRICKET

Mervyn Gregory Hughes. b. 23 Nov 1961 Euroa, Victoria.

When Merv Hughes started his Test career, he was taken as something of a joke by fans. With his huge moustache accentuating his glowers at batsmen, and his very primitive batting skills, the bowling proficiency of this huge man tended to be overlooked. Not only has his batting improved, but his aggressive fast-medium bowling has become more and more respected, so that by the 1993 Australian tour of England he had become one of the world's best, and on that series really established himself in the forefront of the game as he took his tally of Test wickets beyond 200. His sheer determination enabled him to triumph on unhelpful pitches. He took 22 wickets at 23.22 against India in 1991/2 and exceeded that total against England in 1993.

45 Tests 1985-93: 923 runs at 16.78, HS 72; 177 wickets at 27.88, BB 8-87; 22 catches.*

33 One-day Ints: 108 runs at 13.50, HS 20, 38 wickets at 29.34, BB 4-44; 6 catches.

First-class 1981-93: 2189 runs at 16.71, HS 72; 508 wickets at 28.49, BB 8-87; 49 catches.*

Bobby HULL (Can)

ICE HOCKEY

Robert Marvin Hull. b. 3 Jan 1939 Pointe Anne, Ontario.

Although his statistics speak for themselves, Bobby Hull was known as much for his charisma as for his hockey ability. Known as 'The Golden Jet' for his skating speed and his blond hair, which flowed behind him during one of his rink-long rushes, he was also known for the hardest shot in hockey and for his strength. But although he was built like a body builder, he refused to use it as a fighter, and was one of the cleanest hockey players of his era.

In 1965/6 Hull made hockey history when he became the first NHL player to break the 50 goal barrier with 54, also tying the points record with 97. He also scored over 50 goals in 1966/7 with 52 (80 points) and 1968/9 with 58 (107 points). In 1973, Hull switched to the nascent World Hockey Association, where he played for the appropriately named Winnipeg Jets, and scored 77 goals (142 points) in 1974/5. That family record of Hull's was broken by his youngest son, Brett Hull, who now stars in the NHL and scored more than 80 goals in both 1990 and 1991.

Career 1957-80 - 1474 games, 913 goals, 1808 points. NHL: 1063 games, 610 goals, 1,170 points. Play-offs: 119 games, 62 goals, 129 pts. Hart Trophy 1965-6; Ross Trophy 1960, 1962, 1966; Byng Trophy 1965.

Denny HULME (NZ)

MOTOR RACING

Dennis Clive Hulme. b. 18 Jun 1936 Motueka, d. 4 Oct 1992.

World motor racing champion in 1967 for Brabham when he beat his patron by just three points to take the title.

His father, Clive, who had won a wartime VC for gallantry in Crete, ran a trucking business at Pongakawa, near Te Puke, and encouraged Denny's career, which started at hill climbing in 1955. In 1960 he won a 'Driver to Europe' scholarship and this enabled him to gain valuable experience. He worked as a mechanic, joining Jack Brabham in 1962, and after success in Formula 2 in 1964 was given the opportunity of Grand Prix racing by Brabham in 1965. In Hulme's career to 1974 he won eight Grand Prix races from Monaco 1967 with a total of 248 points from 112 races. He joined his friend and compatriot Bruce McLaren in 1968 and won the Can-Am series in 1968 and 1970. He became chairman of the Grand Prix Drivers' Association.

Not a naturally gifted driver, he was a shy and modest man who made his way to the top through hard work and determination; known as 'The Bear'. He was awarded the OBE in 1992, but later that year he died of a heart attack during the Bathurst 1000 race in Australia

Geoff HUNT (Aus)

SQUASH

Geoffrey Brian Hunt. b. 11 Mar 1947 Melbourne.

World champion both as an amateur and a professional and an eight-time winner of the British Open title. In 1965, at the age of 18, he became the youngest-ever winner of the Australian Amateur and on his first visit to England, the youngest finalist in the British Amateur. Before turning professional in 1971 he won the World Amateur on the first three occasions it was held, 1967-71, the British Open in 1968, the British Amateur in 1969 and further Australian Amateur titles 1969-71. As a pro he went on to win the British Open again in 1973 and for six successive years 1976-81. At the World Open he won the first four titles 1976-80 and was almost certainly deprived of a fifth victory as the Championships were not held in 1978. He also won the Australian Open in 1980-1. By beating Jonah Barrington 13-2 in a series of exhibition matches in the 1969/70 season he clearly established himself as the world No.1, which he remained until the arrival of Jahangir Kahn. A devastating hitter and superb stroke player, he was one of the first to recognise that superb physical fitness was a vital component of a world class player's game. His exemplary court manners made him universally popular and with his retirement in April 1982 the game lost one of its favourite personalities. Awarded the MBE.

James HUNT (UK)

MOTOR RACING

James Simon Wallis Hunt. b. 29 Aug 1947 Belmont, Surrey, d. 15 Jun 1993 Wimbledon, London.

World motor racing champion in 1976, Hunt drove in Formula One for Hesketh 1973-5 and McLaren 1976-9, winning 10 Grand Prix races, six in 1976, and 179 points from 92 starts in his career. He was a natural athlete, excelling at many sports, and overcame a poor reputation as 'Hunt the Shunt' to reach the top, which ensured great popularity for this extrovert, glamorous, arrogant but intelligent driver. He raced in Formula Ford in 1968-9, then turned to Formula 3, where he teamed up with Lord Alexander Hesketh in 1972. The latter gave him his chance at Formula One in 1973 and by the time that Hesketh had to pull out of this expensive world, Hunt had made his name and he won the world title in the dramatic year of 1976. His first GP win was at Zandvoort in 1975, when he was fourth in the championship. After his retirement he became a BBC television commentator on motor racing.

Catfish HUNTER (USA)

BASEBALL

James Augustus Hunter. b. 8 Apr 1946 Hertford, North Carolina.

Catfish Hunter pitched for 15 years in the major leagues; from 1965-74 it was for the Oakland Athletics, but in 1975 he became baseball's first free agent and signed with the New York Yankees. He had been the star of the Athletics team which won three consecutive World Series 1972-4 and continued his winning ways with the Yankees, leading them to three pennants 1976-8. He then retired when relatively young because of arm problems and diabetes.
Career pitching: ERA 3.26; W-L 224-166, SO 2012; Best seasons: 1974: 25-12, 2.49 ERA; 1975: 23-14, 2.58 ERA.

Geoff HURST (UK)

FOOTBALL

Geoffrey Charles Hurst. b. 8 Dec 1941 Ashton-under-Lyne, Lancashire.

As a relative unknown, his three goals in the 1966 World Cup final brought him instant fame. This was only his eighth international and he is the only player to have scored a hat-trick in a World Cup final. He went on to win 49 caps and score 24 goals as England's centre-forward 1966-72. He signed as a professional with West Ham in 1959 and was initially a wing-half, but he only played in eight League matches in his first two seasons.

His career really took off when his manager, Ron Greenwood, moved him up front and in successive years he earned winners' medals in the FA Cup 1964, European Cup-Winners' Cup 1965 and World Cup 1966. He stayed with West Ham for 13 seasons scoring 180 goals in 410 League matches, but because of crowd abuse at Upton Park he moved to Stoke City in 1972 and then to West Bromwich Albion three years later. His final seasons were spent with Cork Celtic and Telford United as player-manager before spending 18 months as the manager of Chelsea. His days at Stamford Bridge marked the end of his active involvement with football and he pursued his various business interests. A fine club cricketer, he played once for Essex in 1962.

Don HUTSON (USA)

AMERICAN FOOTBALL

Donald Montgomery Hutson. b. 31 Jan 1913 Pine Bluff, Arkansas.

The first great wide receiver in pro football. In his pro career with the Green Bay Packers, 1935-45, he caught 488 passes for 7,991 yards and 100 touchdowns, all NFL records which lasted until the 1980s. He also set a record by leading the NFL in receiving in eight of his 11 years. In college at the University of Alabama, where his 9.8 speed for 100 yards made him very difficult to defend, Hutson had played baseball and he also signed with the Brooklyn Dodgers of the National League, but never played major league baseball. He was named a charter member of the NFL Hall of Fame in 1963.

Len HUTTON (UK)

CRICKET

(Sir) Leonard Hutton. b. 23 Jun 1916 Fulneck, Pudsey, Yorkshire, d. 6 Sep 1990 Kingston-upon-Thames.

A complete batsman on all types of wickets, his greatness all the more amazing for the fact that he made a full recovery from a wartime accident which shortened his left arm by two inches. He had made his Test début in 1937, and a year later, at the age of 22, compiled the highest ever Test score with his 364 against Australia at The Oval. Fourteen years later he became the first professional to captain England, and in all led his country in 23 Tests (with an 11-4 win-loss record), the highspots being the regaining of the Ashes in 1953 and their retention in 1954/5. From 1937 to 1953 he averaged at least 48 in every English season, with a peak in 1949 when he scored 3429 runs at 68.58 and made a record number of runs for any month, 1294 in June. He averaged over 60 in 1938-9, 1947-9 and 1952-3. His mastery was especially shown on the 1950/1 tour of Australia when he scored 533 runs in the Tests at an average of 88.83, compared to the next best Englishman at 38.77, and in the West Indies in 1953/4 when he scored 677 runs in Tests at 96.71. He was also a very fine close fielder and a useful leg spinner in his early days.

He was the first professional to be elected to membership of the MCC during a playing career and the second (in 1956) to be knighted for services to the game. His son **Richard** (b. 6 Sep 1942) played in 5 Tests for England as an all-rounder.

79 Tests 1907-30: 6971 runs at 56.67, 19 100s HS 364; 3 wickets at 77.33; 57 catches.

First-class 1934-60: 40,140 runs at 55.51, 129 100s HS 364; 173 wickets at 29.51, BB 6-76; 400 catches.

Ragnhild HVEGER (Den)

SWIMMING

Ragnhild Tove Hveger. b. 10 Dec 1920 Elsinore.

The most prolific setter of world records at swimming, with a total of 42 at individual events between 1936 and 1942, including eight at her favourite distance of 400m, from 5:14.2 (1937) to 5:00.1 (1940). Her other world record bests: freestyle - 100y 59.7, 200m 2:21.7, 220y 2:22.6, 300y 3:25.6, 300m 3:42.5, 440y 5:11.4, 500y 5:53.0, 500m 6:27.4, 800m 10:52.5, 880y 11:08.7, 1000y 12:36.0, 1000m 13:54.4, 1500m 20:57.0, 1 mile 23:11.5; backstroke - 200m 2:41.3, 400m 5:38.2.

In her very first race at the age of 13 she

won the Danish 400m title. She was silver medallist at 400m at the 1936 Olympics, but the War cost her the chance of winning an Olympic gold. She was, however, still good enough to place fifth at 400m in 1952. At the 1938 Europeans she took three gold medals, at 100m, 4 x 100m relay and by half a length at 400m.

Chuck HYATT (USA)

BASKETBALL

Charles Hyatt. b. 28 Feb 1908 Syracuse, New York, d. 8 May 1978 St Petersburg, Florida.

Hyatt was one of the stars of basketball before true professional leagues existed. He played collegiately at the University of Pittsburgh where he made first-team All-American from 1928-30. He led the nation in scoring in his sophomore and senior seasons. After graduation he played for six years for the Phillips 66 Oilers, the nation's top amateur team, and was named AAU All-American each year. Phillips were national AAU runners-up in 1937 and 1939 and champions in 1940.

Dorothy HYMAN (UK)

ATHLETICS

Dorothy Hyman. b. 9 May 1941 Cudworth, Yorkshire.

From 1957 to 1963 Hyman competed with great distinction as Britain's best ever woman sprinter. She won Commonwealth gold medals at sprint relay in 1958 and at both 100y and 220y in 1962, when she added a relay silver. After a relay silver in 1958 she was European champion at 100m and second at 200m with a relay bronze in 1962. At the Olympics she was 2nd at 100m and 3rd at 200m in 1960, but was held back by injury in 1964 and did well to make the 100m final and take a bronze medal in the relay. WAAA champion at 100m and 200m in 1959-60 and 1962-3. She retired somewhat prematurely and was prevented from resuming her career due to the then rules of amateurism, because she had received the proceeds of her biography. However, she ran again domestically in 1969, when she was WAAA champion at 200m and helped a talented squad of women sprinters from her Dorothy Hyman Track Club.

Best times: 100m 11.3 (1963), 200m 23.2 (1963).

Flo HYMAN (USA)

VOLLEYBALL

Flora Jo Hyman. b. 31 Jul 1954 Los Angeles, d. 24 Jan 1986 Matsue, Japan.

The greatest ever American volleyball player. The 1.96m *6' 5"* Hyman made the US national team in 1975 during her collegiate career at the University of Houston, where she three times made All-American. She was the top player on the US team throughout her career and was named as the outstanding player at the 1981 World Cup. At the 1984 Olympics she led the US team to the silver medals behind China. After the Olympics she began an acting career, appearing as a knife-wielding mercenary in *Order of the Black Eagle*. She also played professional volleyball in Japan, and at a tournament there collapsed and died. An autopsy revealed that her death was due to Marfan's Syndrome, a connective tissue disorder which often weakens the heart valves and aorta.

Jacky ICKX (Bel)

MOTOR RACING

Jacques Bernard Ickx. b. 1 Jan 1945 Brussels.

Set a record by winning the Le Mans 24-hour race six times, with four different co-drivers, 1969, 1975-7 and 1981-2, the first two in Fords and the next four in Porsches. He was world sports car champion 1982-3, and won the Paris-Dakar in 1983.

Ickx was three times Belgian motorcycling trials champion and European F2 champion in 1967. In his Formula One world championships career, 1966-79, he had eight wins and 181 points from 116 races. In his first full season, for Ferrari in 1968, he won the French Grand Prix, the second youngest ever GP winner, and was fourth in the championship. He was runner-up for the world title for Brabham in 1969 and

for Ferrari in 1970. He won the Can-Am series in 1979 in a Lola-Chevrolet.
His father was a famous motoring journalist.

Viktor IGUMENOV(USSR)

WRESTLING

Viktor Igumenov. b. 10 Mar 1943 Omsk.

Possibly the greatest wrestler never to have won an Olympic medal. He won five Greco-Roman world championships, at 74kg 1966-7 and 1969-71, and the European title in 1970. In 1968 he competed at the Olympics in the 78kg class but was eliminated after the third round, having lost his first round match. At the 1972 Olympics he retired after the second round with an injury.

Sándor IHAROS (Hun)

ATHLETICS

Sándor Iharos. b. 10 Mar 1930 Budapest.

Iharos had a glorious year in 1955, when he set world records at five distances: 1500m 3:40.8, 3000m 7:55.6, 2 miles 8:33.4, 3 miles 13:14.2, 5000m 13:50.8 and 13:40.6. To those he added the records for 6 miles (27:43.8) and 10,000m (28:42.8) on his début at the distance in 1956. Sadly the traumas of the Hungarian rebellion cost him the chance of Olympic glory in that year, and although he remained a fine runner for several years he was never again to recapture his peak form. After a European record 3:42.4 for 1500m in 1954 he was a disappointing 6th in the European 1500m and was also 6th at 5000m in 1958.

Raymond ILLINGWORTH (UK)

CRICKET

Raymond Illingworth. b. 8 Jun 1932 Pudsey, Yorkshire.

For long a canny and accurate off-break bowler and useful middle-order batsman, Illingworth reached the peak of his career after he had left his native county of Yorkshire and become captain of Leicestershire. After just a few matches there he took over as captain of England in 1969 when Colin Cowdrey was injured. He met with immediate success over the West Indies and produced the best batting of his life, including a century in the 2nd Test. From then until 1973 he proved to be a highly respected captain, achieving a record of 12 wins, 5 losses and 14 draws in his 31 Tests in charge. He retired as captain of Leicestershire after the 1978 season, but returned to manage and captain Yorkshire at the age of 50 in 1982-3. That was not a success, but that embattled county's members were left to reflect on what might have been if they had held on to this redoubtable player and tactician in 1969. He has become a TV commentator on the game. Awarded the CBE in 1973.
61 Tests 1958-73: 1836 runs at 23.24, 2 100s HS 113; 122 wickets at 31.20, BB 6-29; 45 catches.
First-class 1951-83: 24,134 runs at 28.06, 22 100s HS 162; 2072 wickets at 20.28, BB 9-42; 446 catches.

IMRAN KHAN (Pak)

CRICKET

Imran Ahmad Khan Niazi. b. 25 Nov 1932 Lahore.

Certainly his country's and one of the world's greatest ever all-rounders, the charismatic Imran often also seemed the one man who could hold together his national team. Personally asked by President Zia to defer his retirement as early as 1985, he captained Pakistan in 48 Tests 1982-92 (winning 14), and his career was capped when he led his team to victory in the 1992 World Cup. He has been the leading wicket-taker in the five World Cup series with 34 at 19.26. He was a hugely successful fast bowler over many years, and his batting got better and better as his career progressed.
He made his first-class début for Lahore in 1969 and came to England to go to school at Worcester Royal Grammar School prior to going to Oxford University. In England he played for Worcestershire 1971-6 and Sussex 1976-88. He also played in Kerry Packer's World Series Cricket in 1977-9. He did not play domestic cricket in

Pakistan for the last decade of his Test career, yet was always able to step straight into international cricket. His most successful Test series was against India in 1982/3 when he scored 247 runs at 61.75 and took 40 wickets at 14.00. His cousins Majid Khan (qv) and Javed Burki (b. 8 May 1938) both captained Pakistan.
88 Tests 1971-92: 3807 runs at 37.69, 6 100s HS 136; 362 wickets at 22.81, BB 8-58; 28 catches.
175 One-day Ints: 3709 runs at 33.41, 1 100 HS 102, 182 wickets at 26.62, BB 6-14; 37 catches.*
First-class 1969-92: 17,771 runs at 36.79, 30 100s HS 170; 1287 wickets at 22.32, BB 8-34; 117 catches.

Miguel INDURÁIN (Spain)

CYCLING

Miguel Induráin Larraya. b. 16 Jul 1964 Villava, near Pamplona, Navarra.

Induráin made rapid progress to become the world's leading cyclist, demonstrating his superb time-trialing ability and fine strength on the mountains to win the Tour de France for three successive years 1991-3. In 1992 he set a record average speed of 39.504 km/h. In one of his time-trialing efforts in the 1992 Tour he defeated the second best rider by over three minutes, one of the greatest single rides in Tour history. His dominance in 1993 was similar, although having won two time trials he was beaten in the third by Tony Rominger. Induráin first contested the Tour in 1985, failing to finish then or in 1986; from 1987 he placed successively 97th, 47th, 17th (including his first stage win) and 10th before his first win. In all 1989-93 he had nine stage wins. He was third in the world professional road race in 1991 and 6th in 1992.
As an amateur he was Spanish champion in 1983, competed at the 1984 Olympics and turned pro in 1985. He won the Paris-Nice race in 1989 and 1990. In 1992 he became only the sixth rider ever to win the Giro d'Italia and the Tour de France in the same year, and he won the Giro again in 1993 with consummate mastery.

Melbourne INMAN (UK)

BILLIARDS

Melbourne Inman. b. 15 Jul 1878 Brentford, London, d. 11 Aug 1951 Farnborough, Kent.

A six-time winner of the world professional billiards championship before losing the title by default. Initially a marker at a Twickenham club, he began his professional career as a 16-year-old and was declared the world champion in 1908 when the Billiards Association decided to nominate a champion in an effort to revive the championship which had been in abeyance since 1903. He went on to win the title again in 1909, 1912-14 and 1919 but during this period he lost in the final to H W Stevenson in 1910 and 1911.
After beating Stevenson for the 1919 championship he declined to defend his title in 1920 as he felt that the champion should not be required to play through the preliminary rounds. He never recaptured the title but still featured prominently in the championship until 1930.
He was a superb match player who combined a mastery of safety play with an ability to make large breaks and he once held the world record with a break of 894. He toured the world twice, was a keen racehorse owner and was one of the most popular and successful sportsmen of his generation.

Isao INOKUMA (Japan)

JUDO

Isao Inokuma. b. 4 Feb 1938 Yokosuka, Kanagawa Prefecture.

World Open champion at judo in 1965, five years after he had become, at 21, the youngest ever all-Japan champion. He lost that title in 1960 and 1961 but regained it in 1963.

Monte IRVIN (USA)

BASEBALL

Montford Merrill Irvin. b. 25 Feb 1919 Columbus, Alabama.

Irvin played eight major league seasons, seven of them with the New York Giants.

He was a solid hitter, both for average and power, and he was also outstanding defensively in the outfield and possessed good speed. But his greatest years were spent banned from major league baseball, before he became one of the first blacks to break the colour line in 1949. In the Negro Leagues he played mostly with his hometown Newark Eagles, and led the Leagues' batting in both 1940 (.422) and 1941 (.396). He was elected to the Hall of Fame in 1973.
Career batting: 1949-56 731 hits Avg. .293, HR 99; RBI 443.

Andy IRVINE (UK)

RUGBY UNION
Andrew Robertson Irvine. b. 16 Sep 1951 Edinburgh.

A brilliant attacking full-back whose elusive running was also recognised at the highest level by his selection on the wing for the British Lions. He is Scotland's most capped full-back with 47 appearances and also played four times on the wing. In his 60 matches (51 for Scotland, 9 for the Lions) he scored a then world record total of 301 points. He toured three times with the British Lions, playing twice on the wing against South Africa in 1974, at full-back in all four Tests against New Zealand in 1977, and at full-back in three Tests against South Africa in 1980.
His adventurous running added much to the game, although his dedication to attack sometimes exposed defensive weakness.

Ken IRVINE (Aus)

RUGBY LEAGUE
Kenneth John Irvine. b. 5 Mar 1940 Sydney, d. 22 Dec 1990 Brisbane, Queensland.

A high-scoring winger of exceptional speed. In 31 Tests (including 9 against Great Britain) between 1959 and 1967 he scored a record 33 tries and kicked 11 goals. He toured Great Britain three times and New Zealand twice. He played first-grade football for North Sydney 1959-70 and Manly 1971-3. A stocky, powerful man, he was Australian professional sprint champion and set a professional world record of 9.3 sec for 100 yards in 1963. He died from leukaemia.

Hale IRWIN (USA)

GOLF
Hale S Irwin. b. 3 Jun 1945 Joplin, Missouri.

One of the steadiest players in the world for over 20 years. He represented the United States in the World Cup in 1974 and in 1979, when he won with John Mahaffey and was the individual leader. In five Ryder Cup appearances, 1975, 1977, 1979, 1981 and 1991, he has 13 wins, 5 losses and 2 halves. Though he has never been the top player in the world, he has been in the US top ten money winners eight times, 1973-8, 1981 and 1990. He won the US Open in 1974, 1979 and in 1990, when he caused a major upset as he had not been a contender for several years and was only eligible via a special exemption given him by the USGA, but he became the oldest ever champion at 45 years 15 days. He won the World Matchplay in 1974 and 1975. While at the University of Colorado he was NCAA champion in 1967, and he was also an outstanding defensive back at American football.
PGA career earnings 1968-92: $4,586,940 with 19 victories.

Volmari ISO-HOLLO (Fin)

ATHLETICS
Volmari Fritjoff Iso-Hollo. b. 1 May 1907 Ylöjärvi, d. 23 Jun 1969 Heinola.

The Olympic steeplechase champion of 1932 and 1936. On the former occasion he won easily, but a judging error meant that the runners ran an extra lap; on the latter he ran a world best 9:03.8. He had run an earlier world best of 9:09.4 in 1933 and also won Olympic medals at 10,000m, 2nd in 1932 (in his best ever time of 30:12.6), and 3rd in 1936. Finnish champion at 5000m 1933 and at steeplechase 1936.
A printer by trade, he was a cheerful extrovert and a gentleman of the running tracks for 20 years.

Other bests: 1500m 3:54.3 (1936), 3000m 8:19.6 (1933), 5000m 14:18.3 (1932).

Dan ISSEL (USA)

BASKETBALL

Daniel Paul Issel. b. 25 Oct 1948 Batavia, Illinois.

A big 2.06m *6'9"* forward/small center who played for the University of Kentucky 1966-70, the Kentucky Colonels of the ABA 1970-5, and the Denver Nuggets of the ABA 1975-6 and NBA 1976-85. Although a big man, he had a soft outside shooting touch. Six times in his career he averaged over 25 points per game, topped by 30.6 in 1971/2 when he led the ABA. His awards include ABA Rookie of the Year, and he was ABA 1st or 2nd-team All-Star for six years 1971-4, 1976. He returned to the Nuggets as coach in 1988.
ABA/NBA career: 27,482 points, av. 22.6.

Maria ITKINA (USSR)

ATHLETICS

Maria L Itkina. b. 3 Feb 1932 Smolensk.

A pioneer of women's 400m running who won the first two European 400m titles, in 1958 and 1962, following her 200m victory in 1954, and who ran a world best 53.9 in 1955. After the IAAF accepted the event she ran four official records from 54.0 in 1957 to 53.4 in 1962. She had been 4th at the 1960 Olympics at both 100m and 200m, but by the time the 400m was added to the Olympics in 1964 she was no longer supreme and placed fifth, although she ran her fastest ever time of 52.9 in 1965. She won 14 Soviet titles, four each at 100m (1960-3), five at 400m (1959-60, 1963-5), six at 200m (1954, 1956-7, 1960-2). European Cup 400m winner 1965.
Other bests: 100m 11.4 (1960), 200m eight USSR records to 23.4 in 1956 and 1961.

Paula IVAN (Rom)

ATHLETICS

Paula Ivan. née Ilie. b. 20 Jul 1963 Heresti.

The world's top woman middle-distance runner of 1988 and 1989, in which years she won the IAAF overall Grand Prix and was unbeaten in 24 major races. Trained since 1983 by Ion Puica (husband of Maricica), she took the 1988 Olympic silver medal at 3000m and then ran away with the 1500m in 3:53.96, the second fastest ever run by a woman. She won the World Student Games double at both 1500m and 3000m in 1987 and 1989. In 1989 she won the European Indoor 1500m, European Cup 3000m and World Cup 1500m. She set a world 1 mile record of 4:15.61 in 1989 and a Romanian record for 3000m of 8:27.15 in 1988. Gave birth to a son in 1991.
Other bests: 800m 1:56.42 (1988), 1000m 2:34.73 (1989), 5000m 15:31.22 (1989).

Vyacheslav IVANOV (USSR)

ROWING

Vyacheslav Nikolayevich Ivanov. b. 30 Apr 1938 Moscow, Russia.

The first man to win the Olympic single sculls three times consecutively, 1956-64. The remainder of his career is likewise impressive as he won the first World Championship in single sculls in 1962 and was European champion in 1959, 1961, and 1964. Ivanov's great rival was Australian Stuart MacKenzie, whom he defeated at the 1956 Olympics. MacKenzie never again competed in the Olympics due to injuries, but Ivanov did not fare well at other meets against the Australian as MacKenzie twice defeated him in the European Championships and in Ivanov's only two attempts at the Diamond Sculls. In 1956, Ivanov lost his gold medal when, exulting during his victory celebration, he dropped the medal into Lake Wendouree, where the rowing events were held. He dived to the bottom of the Lake but could not find it. The IOC provided him with a replacement.

Bill IVY (UK)

MOTOR CYCLING

William D. Ivy. b. 27 Aug 1942 Kent, d. 12 Jul 1969 Sachsenring, GDR.

From 1959 he raced British machines, becoming a full-time professional in 1965, when he won his first British title. He shot to world recognition when he signed in 1966 for Yamaha, for whom he was world champion at 125cc in 1967. On the Isle of Man he won TT races at 125cc in 1966 and 250cc 1968, and in 1968 he became the first man to lap the TT course at over 100 mph *160.9 km/h* on a 125cc machine. A small man at 1.60m and 60kg, he was a flamboyant and hugely popular character. He had a major dispute in 1968 with his team-mate Phil Read, who beat him to the world titles at 125cc and 250cc, following which he announced his retirement, but he came back in 1969 to ride for Yawa. He was killed that year while practising for the East German Grand Prix.

Tony JACKLIN (UK)

GOLF

Anthony Jacklin. b. 7 Jul 1944 Scunthorpe.

One of the most influential British golfers. Although his time as a truly great player was fleeting, he restored the image of British golf by becoming the first European player of his era to win a US tournament, at Jacksonville in 1968, winning the British Open in 1969 (third in 1971-2) and the US Open in 1970. Prior to Jacklin, Britain had not produced a great player since Henry Cotton in the 1930s. He had 13 victories on the European Tour and three on the US PGA tour. He won the Dunlop Masters in 1967 and 1973.

Since his competitive career has been in eclipse, Jacklin was Ryder Cup captain from 1983 to 1989, inspiring winning European squads in 1985, 1987 and 1989. He played 35 matches in seven Cup appearances 1967-79, winning 13, losing 14 and halving 8. In 1969 he was part of great drama at Royal Birkdale. At that time the US had won the last five ties and 12 of the last 13, but Jacklin defeated Jack Nicklaus 4 & 3 on the last morning to keep Britain close. In the deciding match, also against Nicklaus, Jacklin holed a long birdie putt on 17 to get square. He then tied the match by halving Nicklaus on the last green.

Awarded the OBE 1970 and CBE 1990.

Alec JACKSON (UK)

FOOTBALL

Alexander Skinner Jackson. b. 12 May 1905 Renton, Dumbartonshire, d. 15 Nov 1946 Cairo, Egypt.

Although winning only 17 caps, he is acknowledged as probably the greatest Scottish right-winger. He was at his brilliant best with three goals for the 'Wembley Wizards' in Scotland's 5-1 victory over England in 1928. After playing for junior clubs in Dumbarton he emigrated to the United States while still a teenager but returned home to join Aberdeen in 1923. In his first full season he was capped three times and attracted the attention of various English clubs, and in 1925 Herbert Chapman signed him for Huddersfield Town. Within a year he had won a League Championship medal and he helped Huddersfield to the FA Cup final in 1928 and 1930 where they were the losing finalists in both years.

In September 1930, Alec Jackson went south to Chelsea, but he failed to show his earlier brilliance and the move was not a success. He lost his place in the Scottish team and stayed only two seasons at Stamford Bridge before a dispute with the management led to his joining the unknown non-League club, Ashton Nationals. The short-lived Lancashire club soon ran into financial problems and were unable to meet their commitments to Jackson who generously helped them by tearing up his contract and retiring to manage a pub. He later played very briefly for Margate and for Nice in France but his career effectively ended at the age of 27 when he played his last League game for Chelsea. He was killed in a car accident in Egypt while serving as a major in the Army.

Archie JACKSON (Aus)

CRICKET

Archibald (Alexander) Jackson. b. 5 Sep 1909 Rutherglen, Lanarkshire, Scotland. d. 16 Feb 1933 Brisbane.

A batting prodigy whose career was cruelly terminated by tuberculosis, from

which he died at the age of 23. A sublime right-handed batsman and a superb outfielder, he made his début for New South Wales at 17 and made 464 runs at 58.00 in his first season. He was promoted to opening the innings in his second season of 1927/8, and in that year he toured New Zealand with an Australian side. His feats, together with those of his team-mate Don Bradman, captivated the public. He made his Test début at the age of 19 against England at Adelaide in February 1929 and made 164 in the first innings. He made his last Test appearance in February 1931 against the West Indies, but by then his illness was already gathering momentum although he tried to keep playing cricket. He died on the day that England regained the Ashes in 1933. A huge crowd attended the funeral of this much-adored young cricketer.
8 Tests 1929-31: 474 runs at 47.40, 1 100 HS 164; 7 catches.
First-class 1926-31: 4383 runs at 45.65, 11 100s HS 182; 26 catches.

Bo JACKSON (USA)

BASEBALL and AMERICAN FOOTBALL
Vincent Edward Jackson. b. 30 Nov 1962 Bessemer, Alabama.

Bo Jackson captured public imagination by combining major league careers at both baseball and football. He had been a fine all-rounder in high school, at track and field as well as his two main sports. At Auburn University he won the Heisman Trophy as a running back in 1985, but having been the first draft selection he turned down the Tampa Bay Buccaneers of the NFL to play baseball in the AL for Kansas City Royals. A year later, however, he signed a five-year contract to play for the Los Angeles Raiders in the NFL. At baseball he had considerable success at both batting, sharing the major league record for four consecutive home runs in 1990, and at pitching, leading the league with 172 strikeouts in 1989, a year in which he also hit 32 home runs and had 105 runs batted in.
His career was threatened by a dislocated hip, but in April 1993 he hit a 400ft home run in his first game since 5 Oct 1991, having in the interim received an artifical hip.
Career batting 1986-92: 476 hits Avg. .249; HR 112; RBI 327.
NFL Football 1987-90: 2782 yards gained rushing av. 5.4, 352 yards gained receiving av. 8.8.

Don JACKSON (Can)

FIGURE SKATING
Donald George Jackson. b. 2 Apr 1940 Oshawa.

The first great Canadian male figure skater. He won the first competition he ever entered in 1950, and after winning the Canadian junior title in 1955 moved to New York to train under the great coach Pierre Brunet. From 7th in the World Championships in 1957 he made steady progress, to 4th in 1958 and 2nd in both 1959 and 1960. That year he also took the Olympic bronze medal. The 1961 Championships were cancelled following the death of the entire American team in an air crash but at the 1962 World Championships he became the first Canadian to win the title and gave an awe-inspiring display, receiving a record seven perfect marks. His landing of the first triple lutz was a particular triumph.
He won the North American title in 1959 and 1961 and was Canadian champion 1959-62, but had turned professional before the 1964 Games, so that he is possibly the greatest male skater never to win an Olympic title. His success was based on a spectacular free skating routine which was well-suited to the professional arena and he won the World Professional championship in 1965 and 1970, but after seven years of touring he tired of the itinerant life with *Ice Follies* and returned to his home town to devote his time to coaching.

Joe JACKSON (USA)

BASEBALL
Joseph Jefferson Jackson. b. 16 Jul 1889 Brandon Mills, South Carolina, d. 5 Dec 1951 Greenville, South Carolina.

'Shoeless Joe' Jackson was one of the

great hitters in baseball history, but one of its most tragic stories. His career batting average of .356 is surpassed only by Ty Cobb and Rogers Hornsby. He began his career in 1908 with the Philadelphia Athletics, was traded in 1910 to the Cleveland Indians, and played for the Chicago White Sox 1915-20. In 1919, the White Sox won the pennant but lost the World Series to the Cincinnati Reds. It later transpired that eight of the White Sox, Jackson among them, had accepted money to 'throw' the Series, which gave the team the nickname of the Black Sox. In court, however, all the players were found not guilty. Nonetheless, for his rôle in the supposed fix, Jackson was expelled from baseball by Commissioner Judge Kenesaw Mountain Landis, and this has probably prevented him from ever becoming a member of the Hall of Fame. Supposedly, as Jackson left the courthouse after the trial, a small boy ran up to him and uttered the immortal plea, 'Say it ain't so, Joe.' Jackson later denied that rumour.
Career batting: 1908-20 1774 hits Avg. .356; RBI 785. Best seasons: 1911: .408, 233 hits. 1912: .395, 226 hits. 1920: .382, 121 RBI.

Marjorie JACKSON (Aus)

ATHLETICS

Marjorie Jackson. b. 13 Sep 1931 Coffs Harbour, New South Wales. Married Olympic cyclist Peter Nelson in 1954.

Known as the 'Lithgow Flash', she was undefeated in major competition with the 100m/200m double at the 1952 Olympics and the 100y/220y double at the 1950 and 1954 Commonwealth Games, with three relay golds as well,
Her 18 world records included six at 100 yards, taking the record from 10.8 in 1950 to 10.4 in 1952 and an unratified exhibition 10.3 in 1953; three at 100m to 11.4 in 1952; four at 200m or 220y with a best of 23.4 (23.59 auto) with which she won the 1952 Olympic title; and five in relays. Australian champion at 100y and 220y 1950, 1952 and 1954. Awarded the MBE.

Peter JACKSON (UK)

RUGBY UNION

Peter Barrie Jackson. b. 22 Sep 1930 Birmingham.

An unorthodox winger who could score from the most unlikely positions. In 20 matches for England he scored six tries, none more memorable than the one against Australia in 1958 which gave England victory in the final minutes of the game.
He first played in an England Trial in 1950 when he was still with Old Edwardians, but did not win his first cap until 1956 by which time he was playing for Coventry. After winning 15 caps he lost his England place after the 1959 season and in the next three years 1960-2 he only played in one international, but in 1963, at the age of 33, he was recalled to the team and played in all four matches when England won the International Championship. On the 1959 British Lions tour he played in both Tests against Australia and in three of the four Tests against New Zealand.
His exciting and deceptive running seemed admirably suited to the style of play espoused by the Barbarians but surprisingly Peter Jackson never played for this famous touring side.

Reggie JACKSON (USA)

BASEBALL

Reginald Martinez Jackson. b. 18 May 1946 Wyncote, Pennsylvania.

Jackson's nickname was 'Mr October' because of his great success in the World Series; he played for 11 divisional champions, six pennant winners, and five World Series champions. He began his slugging career with the Oakland Athletics and led that team to three consecutive World Series victories in 1972-4. Traded to Baltimore in 1976, he was signed as a free agent in 1977 by George Steinbrenner of the New York Yankees. Many people pointed to Jackson as an abuse of the free agent system, as his season statistics were only average with the Yankees. But he led the Yankees to two more World Series victories 1977-8, and his October and World Series figures were stunning: .357 average

- almost 100 points above his regular season average; .755 slugging average, a World Series record; and 10 home runs. He was outspoken and brash, but he was a great winner. Jackson is also the only player after whom a candy bar was named, the 'Reggie' bar.
Career batting: Avg. .262, HR 563; RBI 1702. Best seasons: 1969: 47 HR, 123 Runs. 1973: 32 HR, 117 RBI.

Stanley JACKSON (UK)

CRICKET

(Rt. Hon Sir) Francis Stanley Jackson. b. 21 Nov 1870 Chapel Allerton, Yorkshire, d. 9 Mar 1947 Knightsbridge, London.

'Jacker' was a great natural cricketer, a classic batsman, great cover fielder and astute medium-pace bowler who showed supreme ability to rise to the big occasion. He did that most notably in 1905 when he captained England to a 2-0 win with three draws against Australia and personally dominated the series, scoring 492 runs at 70.28 and taking 13 wickets at 15.46. Such success came despite the fact that his business career permitted him only one full season with Yorkshire in 1898. He captained Cambridge University for two years and toured India with Lord Hawke's team in 1892/3, but thereafter did not have the time for touring.
A Conservative MP from 1915-26 and chairman of the party from 1923, he subsequently became Governor of Bengal, and was awarded the GCSI and GCIE. President of the MCC 1921.
20 Tests 1893-1905: 1415 runs at 48.79, 5 100s HS 144; 24 wickets at 33.29, BB 5-52; 10 catches.*
First-class 1890-1907: 15,901 runs at 33.83, 31 100s HS 160; 774 wickets at 20.37, BB 8-54; 195 catches.

Helen JACOBS (USA)

TENNIS

Helen Hull Jacobs. b. 6 Aug 1908 Globe, Arizona.

An often under-rated player who was overshadowed by Helen Wills-Moody for the greater part of her career. She reached the Wimbledon singles final six times but won only once, beating Fru Sperling (Ger) in 1936. She lost to Dorothy Round in the 1934 final and to Wills-Moody in 1929, 1932, 1935 and 1938. She also lost to Wills-Moody in the final of the US Championships in 1928 and the French in 1930. The only event she won when Wills-Moody was playing was the US title in 1933. The US Championships proved to be her favourite tournament, winning the singles 1932-5, the doubles 1932 and 1934-5 (all with Sarah Palfrey/Fabyan), and the mixed doubles 1934 (with George Lott). She played in 12 Wightman Cup teams (1927-37, 1939) and only Chris Evert-Lloyd has represented the US in more ties. Jacobs' main strength was her backhand drive but she was also an excellent volleyer and a fine general tactician. Her on-court rivalry with Wills-Moody was often said to extend to personal dislike but both players denied this, and it was only their contrasting personalities that precluded a closer friendship.

Hirsch JACOBS (USA)

HORSE RACING

Hirsch Jacobs. b. 8 Apr 1904 New York, d. 13 Feb 1970 Miami.

He became the leading trainer in US racing history with 3596 winners from 1924 to the 1960s, earning $15,340,354 and leading the yearly list for most races won 11 times, 1933-9 and 1941-4. His most notable success was with *Stymie*, who won 35 races and set a career record of $918,485 in 1943-7.
From the age of 8 he raised and raced pigeons, and claimed that this experience later helped him with horses. In 1923 he worked as racing secretary for three New York pigeon clubs, but a year later he quit the pigeon raising business with his partner Charlie Ferraro and started training horses, initially for Ferraro. From 1928 most of his horses raced under the colours either of his partner Isador Bieber or his wife Ethel, whom he married in 1933. Ethel was the leading owner in races won in 1936-7 and 1943.

JAHANGIR KHAN (Pak)

SQUASH

Jahangir Khan. b. 10 Dec 1963 Peshawar.

The most successful player in the history of squash, winner of a record six World Open titles, 1981-85, 1988, and ten successive British Opens, 1982-91. The son of Roshan Khan, the winner of the 1956 British Open, he began playing squash at the age of ten and at 15 won the first of his three World Amateur titles, 1979, 1983, 1985. This marked the start of an unmatched record at major championships. He is also the youngest ever winner of the World Open title at 17 years 354 days in 1981.

From April 1981, when Geoff Hunt beat him in the final of the British Open, to November 1986, when Ross Norman (NZ) beat him in the World Championship final, he was unbeaten in more than 500 matches. He also lost in the World final to Rodney Martin in 1991 and had seven wins in the Pakistan Open until Jansher Khan beat him in 1987.

In 1982 he achieved the amazing feat of winning a major international professional title without losing a point, when he defeated Maqsood Ahmed (Pak) 9-0, 9-0, 9-0 in the final of the ISPA Championship. Jahangir was totally dedicated to the game, a charming and quiet personality, yet ruthless on court with a complete game in every way.

Evelyn JAHL (GDR)

ATHLETICS

Evelyn Jahl. née Schlaak. b. 28 Mar 1956 Annaberg. Later Herberg.

Jahl was the Olympic discus champion in 1976 and 1980 and European winner in 1978. She started her international career by winning the European Juniors in 1973, and won six GDR titles as well as victories at the 1979 European Cup and 1979 and 1981 World Cups.

She succeeded Faina Melnik as world record holder with 70.72m in 1978 and 71.50m in 1980.

JAÏRZINHO (Bra)

FOOTBALL

Jaïr Ventura Filho. b. 25 Dec 1944 Caxias, Rio de Janeiro.

After signing as an amateur for Botafogo in 1961, he turned professional shortly after winning a gold medal at the 1963 Pan American Games. First capped by Brazil in 1964, he played in three matches in the 1966 World Cup but injuries, a hasty temper and some outstanding rivals prevented him establishing a regular place in the national team until the next World Cup in 1970. In Mexico he scored in each of Brazil's matches (the first player ever to do this in a World Cup Finals tournament) and his total of 7 goals was the second highest of the tournament. In 1971 a broken leg again cost him his international place but he returned to the Brazilian squad and won 87 caps, including appearances in his third World Cup in 1974, scoring in all 37 goals. Apart from a brief spell with Olympique Marseille, he remained loyal to Botafogo throughout his career. His long-striding runs, clever ball control and accurate crosses were features of his game.

Alex JAMES (UK)

FOOTBALL

Alexander Wilson James. b. 14 Sep 1901 Mossend, Lanarkshire, d. 1 Jun 1953 London.

Beginning his career in senior football with Raith Rovers in 1922, he moved to Preston North End after three years and in 1929 he was transferred to Arsenal. At Highbury, Herbert Chapman used him in a deep-lying rôle and he developed into one of the finest schemers the game has known. While he was with Arsenal they won the League four times (1931, 1933-35) and the FA Cup twice (1930, 1936). Surprisingly, he won only eight Scottish caps - 4 with Preston and 4 with Arsenal - but this was due to his disagreements with the selectors and certainly not to any lack of ability. Before Chapman changed his style of play, Alex James was an orthodox goalscoring inside-forward - while with

Raith Rovers and Preston North End he scored 80 goals in 257 appearances - but significantly he only scored 26 times in 231 matches for Arsenal. He retired in June 1937 and coached briefly in Poland. After the war he was on the coaching staff at Highbury.
With his baggy shorts he was the subject of many cartoons and caricatures and was one of the best known sportsmen in Britain between the wars.

JANSHER KHAN (Pak)

SQUASH
Jansher Khan. b. 15 Jun 1969 Peshawar.

Winner of four World titles, 1987, 1989-90, 1992, on each occasion beating the Australian Chris Dittmar in the final, as he did also in the World Pro Squash Association Championships in 1992. He was Asian junior champion in 1985, and had an amazing year in 1987 when he was 29th on the world rankings in March and 1st by December. He lost to Jahangir Khan in the final of the British Open but then succeeded him as the world's best player, beating him in the final of the Pakistan Open and in the World semi-finals. Jahangir regained his number one ranking when he beat Jansher in the finals of the World Open in 1988 and also in the British Open in 1991. Jansher won the British Open in 1992 and 1993.

Jan JANSSEN (Hol)

CYCLING
Jan Janssen. b. 19 May 1940 Nootdorp.

One of the great road sprinters of all time, an ability which helped him win a lot of races. However, he was only an average climber and this prevented him from winning more major tours. His victory in the 1968 Tour de France came by only 38 seconds over 'Joop' Zoetemelk, at the time the closest finish in Tour history. He had been points winner in the Tour in 1964-5 and 1967.
Other major victories: Vuelta à España 1967 (and points 1967-8), World professional road race 1964, Paris-Roubaix 1967, Bordeaux-Paris 1966, Zürich 1962.

Karin JANZ (GDR)

GYMNASTICS
Karin Janz. b. 17 Feb 1952 Hartmannsdorf.

While Olga Korbut was hitting the headlines at the 1972 Olympics, Janz took silver medals behind Lyudmila Turischeva in the all-around event and with the GDR team. At individual apparatus Janz added two golds, a silver and a bronze to the silver and bronze that she had won in 1968. She was the then youngest-ever European overall champion in 1969, with four of five individual titles, and won a World gold on asymmetric bars in 1970.

Douglas JARDINE (UK)

CRICKET
Douglas Robert Jardine. b. 23 Oct 1900 Bombay, India, d. 18 Jun 1958 Montreux, Switzerland.

Amid the controversy of the England tour to Australia in 1932/3, which Jardine captained, and in which he encouraged his fast bowlers to use 'Bodyline' tactics, the fact that he was a middle-order batsman of the highest class is often forgotten. After Winchester, Jardine played for Oxford University 1920-3 and Surrey 1921-33, captaining them in 1932-3. His classic batting was matched by his iron will, and he displayed that to full effect as England captain in 15 Tests between 1931 and 1933, with an unmatched 9-1 win-loss record. His best seasons were when he led the first-class averages in 1927, 1002 runs at 91.09 and 1928, 1133 at 87.15.
His father Malcolm was an Oxford blue for four years, scoring 140 in the 1892 University match, who became Advocate-General of Bombay.
22 Tests 1928-34: 1296 runs at 48.00, 1 100 HS 127; 26 catches.
First-class 1920-48: 14,848 runs at 46.84, 35 100s HS 214; 48 wickets at 31.10, BB 6-28; 188 catches.

Matti JÄRVINEN (Fin)

ATHLETICS
Matti Henrikki Järvinen. b. 18 Feb 1909 Tampere, d. 22 Jul 1985 Helsinki.

Järvinen took javelin throwing into a new era, as he set ten world records from 71.57m at Viipuri on 8 Aug 1930 to 77.23m at Helsinki on 18 Jun 1936. He threw 20 competitions over 75m from 1933 to 1940, to six for his nearest rival Yrjö Nikkanen. Järvinen won the European title in 1934 and 1938 and the Olympics in 1932, but back injury restricted him to fifth place in 1936.
He started as a gymnast and in his very first javelin competition in 1926 threw an amazing 54.26, although quickly developing javelin elbow which held him back for three years before the first of his eight Finnish titles between 1929 and 1942.
His father **Verner** (1870-1941) won Finland's first Olympic gold medal, at Greek style discus in 1906, and Matti was his fourth son. His elder brothers were **Yrjö** (1900-68), a 58.50 javelin thrower; **Kalle** (1903-41), who set two Finnish shot records to 15.92 (1932); and **Akilles** (1905-43), who was the Olympic silver medallist in 1928 and 1932 and set three world records at the decathlon.

Chet JASTREMSKI (USA)

SWIMMING

Chester Andrew Jastremski. b. 12 Jan 1941 Toledo, Ohio.

A pioneer of the modern fast-stroking sprint style for the breaststroke, he set nine world records, 17 US records and won 12 AAU titles. However, he won just one Olympic medal.
In 1956 he won his 200m heat at the US Trials, but was disqualified for using an illegal kick; then in 1960 he was second at the Trials but his coach took him off the Olympic team. Finally in 1964 he got a bronze medal at 200m, and he also swam in the heats of the medley relay in 1968. His peak form came in seven weeks from 2 July to 20 August 1961 when he improved the world record for 100m breaststroke six times, from 1:11.1 to 1:07.5, and also set records at 200m of 2:33.6 and 2:29.6. He improved the latter time in 1964 to a US record 2:28.2. He had recorded the first sub one-minute time for 100y breaststroke with 59.6 in April 1961 and was then a student at Indiana University, where he was coached by Doc Counsilman.
He won AAU titles outdoors at 100m 1960-2, 1964; 200m/220y 1961-2, 1964-5; and the Pan-American 200m breaststroke in 1963. He became a doctor and was a member of the US medical team at the 1976 Olympics.

JAVED MIANDAD (Pak)

CRICKET

Javed Miandad Khan. b. 12 Jun 1957 Karachi.

A brilliantly talented right-handed batsman who has become Pakistan's leading run-scorer in Test cricket. He made a dramatic start to his Test career, averaging 126.00 for 504 runs in his first series, three matches v New Zealand 1976, including 163 in his first match and 206 in the 3rd, when at 19 years 141 days he become the youngest double-century maker in Test history. At the age of 17 he had made a score of 311 in Pakistan first-class cricket.
A wristy, quick-footed player, he has long been an attractive batsman to watch but a difficult and provocative character. He became, at 22 years 260 days in 1980, his country's youngest ever Test captain and in five separate spells has led Pakistan in 34 Tests (winning 14 to 6 lost), but had to yield the job several times to the great Imran Khan and, after Imran had finally retired, again in 1993 to Wasim Akram.
Javed did, however, have a most successful series beating England in 1992. He has also had great success at the one-day game and is the leading run scorer in World Cup matches with 1929, av. 44.74, having played in all five series to Pakistan's triumph in 1992. He played county cricket for Sussex 1976-9 and Glamorgan 1980-5.
121 Tests 1976-93: 8689 runs at 53.30, 23 100s HS 280; 17 wickets at 40.11, BB 3-74; 93 catches, 1 stumping.*
222 One-day Ints: 7233 runs at 42.29, 8 100s HS 119; 7 wickets at 42.42, BB 2-22; 68 catches, 2 stumpings.*
First-class 1973-92: 28,248 runs at 53.90, 80 100s HS 311; 191 wickets at 33.48, BB 7-39; 337 catches, 3 stumpings.

Michel JAZY (Fra)

ATHLETICS

Michel Jazy. b. 13 Jun 1936 Oignies, Pas-de-Calais.

The hero of French athletics in the 1960s, he set nine world records from 1962, including his bests, each in 1965, at 1 mile 3:53.6, 3000m 7:49.0 and 2 miles 8:22.6, and his last, 4:56.2 for 2000m in 1966. With Ron Clarke and Kip Keino he re-wrote the record books for distance running in 1965.
He took the silver medal at 1500m, a long way behind Herb Elliott, at the 1960 Olympics, but having won the European 1500m in 1962, he determined on the 5000m for the 1964 Olympics. The favourite, he kicked away to a ten-metre lead after the bell, but tied up and finished a disappointed fourth. He ended his international career with the European 5000m gold and 1500m silver in 1966. Between 1956 and 1966 he competed in 59 internationals for France, won 11 national titles and set a record 42 French records. His final records at distances other than his world records: 800m 1:47.1 (1962), 1000m 2:19.1 (1963), 1500m 3:36.3 (1966). He also ran the 10,000m in 29:03.2 in 1965.

Dickie JEEPS (UK)

RUGBY UNION

Richard Eric Gautrey Jeeps. b. 25 Nov 1931 Willingham, Cambridgeshire.

A solid, reliable player who went on the 1955 British Lions tour of South Africa as third choice scrum-half although not yet capped by England. The quality of his service to fly-half Cliff Morgan earned him a place in all four Tests. He toured again with the Lions to Australia and New Zealand in 1959 and South Africa in 1962, playing in a total of 13 Tests which stood as a record until beaten by Willie John McBride.
On his return from his initial visit to South Africa, Jeeps won his first England cap against Wales in 1956 but was immediately dropped and did not command a regular place in the England team until the following season. He went on to win 24 caps before his retirement in 1962 and he captained England in the last 13 matches of his international career.
From school he played for Cambridge City for one season before moving to Northampton in 1949. He also appeared regularly for London Counties and Eastern Counties. After retirement he served as an England selector and was President of the RFU in 1976-7. He was awarded the CBE in 1977 and was Chairman of the Sports Council from 1978-85.

James JEFFRIES (USA)

BOXING

James Jackson Jeffries. b. 15 Apr 1875 Carroll, Ohio, d. 3 Mar 1953 Burbank, California

For his era Jeffries was a giant, standing 1.89m *6' 2 1/2"* and weighing 100 kg *220 lbs*. He had a very short career as he mainly worked as a sparring partner for other heavyweights (including heavyweight champion Jim Corbett) until he decided to turn professional in 1896. He won the world title in his 13th fight when he knocked out Bob Fitzsimmons in 11 rounds in 1899, and retired as heavyweight champion in 1905, having beaten all the worthy contenders. In 1910 he was coerced to come out of retirement as a 'great white hope' in an attempt to wrest the heavyweight championship from Jack Johnson, but Johnson knocked out Jeffries in the 15th round.
Career record: W - 18 (15), L - 1, D -2.

David JENKINS (USA)

FIGURE SKATING

David Wilkinson Jenkins. b. 29 Jun 1936 Akron, Ohio.

After placing third behind his elder brother, Hayes, at the 1956 Olympics, he kept the title in the family by winning the Olympic gold medal in 1960. Born into a skating family he was schooled in the sport from an early age but did not win his first major title until 1957 when he was the World, North American and US champion. He retained all three titles for the next two years and in 1960, after winning the North

American and US titles for a fourth successive year, he won an Olympic gold medal. Directly after his Olympic victory he announced his retirement, thus missing the chance of a fourth consecutive win at the World Championships held immediately after the Olympics. His later successes were achieved while he was a student at Case Western Reserve Medical School and after winning his Olympic gold medal he skated professionally for one year to help defray the cost of his medical studies. He is today a surgeon in Tulsa, Oklahoma.

Ferguson JENKINS (Can)

BASEBALL

Ferguson Arthur Jenkins. b. 13 Dec 1943 Chatham, Ontario.

Jenkins had one of the most unheralded careers of any great modern pitcher. He pitched with four different teams but achieved most of his fame with the Chicago Cubs 1966-73. With them he won over 20 games in six consecutive seasons 1967-72, and added a seventh 20-win season in 1974 with the Texas Rangers. Unfortunately he never played for a pennant-winning team and this probably contributed to his lack of media attention. He has had a very difficult life since his retirement from baseball. Near the end of his career, he was arrested for drug possession when returning to Canada and, although he was eventually acquitted, the notoriety hurt him a greal deal. He also lost his wife to an early death and in 1992, he had to deal with the death of his three-year-old daughter and his girlfriend.
Career pitching 1965-83: ERA 3.34; W-L 284-226, SO 3192; Best seasons: 1974: 25-12, 2.83 ERA; 1971: 24-13, 2.77 ERA; 1970: 22-16, 274 SO; 1969: 21-15, 273 SO.

Hayes JENKINS (USA)

FIGURE SKATING

Hayes Alan Jenkins. b. 29 Mar 1933 Akron, Ohio.

After spending much of his early career in the shadow of Dick Button, he finally established himself by winning the World Championship in 1953. This proved to be a major breakthrough as he went on to retain the title for the next three years and his younger brother, David, kept the title in the family for a further three years. After leading the US to a clean sweep of the medals at the 1956 Winter Olympics, Hayes turned professional and toured with an ice show for two summers to help meet the cost of his studies at Harvard Law School. In 1960 he married Carol Heiss, the five-time World champion and 1960 Olympic gold medallist, and today they live in Akron, Ohio where Hayes is a successful international attorney with the Goodyear Tire Company.

Bruce JENNER (USA)

ATHLETICS

William Bruce Jenner. b. 28 Oct 1949 Mt Kisco, New York.

The Olympic decathlon champion of 1976, when he set a world record of 8618 points (8617 on current tables), he became one of the most successful athletes at cashing in on his fame. His good looks and personality brought him many lucrative film, advertising and sponsorship contracts. The annual Bruce Jenner Classic meeting in San Jose is named in his honour.
A very gifted all-rounder rather than having any especial individual event strengths, Jenner made his decathlon début in 1970 and was tenth at the 1972 Olympics. He reached the position of world's best in 1974-6, when he won 12 and failed to finish once in 13 decathlons, with earlier world records of 8524 in 1975 and 8538 at the 1976 US Olympic Trials. AAU champion in 1974 and 1976, Sullivan Award winner 1976.

Pat JENNINGS (UK)

FOOTBALL

Patrick Anthony Jennings. b. 12 Jun 1945 Newry, Co. Down.

An outstanding goalkeeper and Northern Ireland's most capped player. Beginning his career with Newry Town in his native Ireland, he joined Watford in 1963 but

within a year moved to Tottenham where he spent 13 seasons before making a surprise move to Arsenal in 1977. While with Spurs he won an FA Cup winners medal 1967, League Cup winners medals 1971 and 1973, and a UEFA Cup winners medal 1972. In 1973 he was voted Footballer of the Year. With Arsenal he won a second FA Cup winners medal in 1979. He returned to Tottenham in 1993 as a member of the coaching staff.
A superbly efficient but unspectacular player, he was possibly the best keeper in the world at his peak and for many years had no rival for his position in Northern Ireland's team. Making his international début in 1964 he retired after the 1986 World Cup having won a then world record 119 caps. He was awarded the MBE in 1976 and later the OBE.

Sixten JERNBERG (Swe)

NORDIC SKIING

Sixten Jernberg. b. 6 Feb 1929 Lima.

Winner of a men's record nine Olympic medals for skiing: four golds, 50km 1956, 30km 1960, 50km and 4 x 10km relay 1964; three silver, 15km and 30km 1956, 15km 1960; two bronze, relay 1956 and 15km 1964. He was also 4th at 4x10 km in 1960 and 5th at 50km 1960 and 30km 1964. This magnificent record was supported with 14 World Championship medals, with golds at 50km in 1958 and 1962 and at relay in those years and 1964. He won the first of 15 individual Swedish titles at 15km and 50km in 1955. Originally a blacksmith he was a lumberman from Dalecarlia at the time of his Olympic triumphs and later became a businessman.

Gilbert JESSOP (UK)

CRICKET

Gilbert Laird Jessop. b. 19 May 1874 Cheltenham, Gloucestershire, d. 11 May 1955 Fordington, Dorset.

Throughout his career he scored at a remarkable rate, achieving many records. In his five 200s he maintained a rate of just under 100 runs an hour, while in the Hastings Festival of 1907 he made 191 in an hour and a half. 'The Croucher' was far from just a slogger, however; he was also a candidate as the greatest fielder of his era, with unerring accuracy in throwing from the covers, as well as a fast bowler. He was a fine all-round sportsman, and captained Cambridge University in his final year 1899 and Gloucestershire 1900-12. The best aggregate of his 14 seasons at over 1000 runs was 2323 at 40.75 in 1901, and he twice achieved the double, with 100 wickets in 1897 and 1900 (when he also scored 2210 runs). Typically his one Test century, against Australia at The Oval in 1902, was 104 out of 139 made off 76 balls in 77 minutes, taking England to victory.
18 Tests 1899-1912: 569 runs at 21.88, 1 100 HS 104; 24 wickets at 33.29, BB 4-68; 11 catches.
First-class 1894-1914: 26,698 runs at 32.64, 53 100s HS 286; 873 wickets at 22.80, BB 8-29; 463 catches.

JIANG Jialiang (China)

TABLE TENNIS

Jiang Jialiang.

After winning the World Cup in 1984 he took the world singles title in 1985 and 1987. He was also a member of three winning Swaythling Cup teams 1983-7.

Ben JIPCHO (Kenya)

ATHLETICS

Benjamin Wabura Jipcho. b. 1 Mar 1943.

After helping Kip Keino win the Olympic 1500m title in 1968, running the first lap in 56 seconds at the high altitude of Mexico City, Jipcho faded back to 10th place. He emerged as a top-class runner with silver medals at steeplechase at the 1970 Commonwealth Games and 1972 Olympics and in 1973 set three world records for the 3000m steeplechase, despite very rudimentary hurdling technique, from 8:20.69 at the African Games (when he also won the 5000m) to 8:13.91. Then in 1974 he had a great Commonwealth Games, winning the 5000m (in 13:14.4) and steeplechase and taking bronze at 1500m. He turned profes-

sional and was the leading money winner on the ITA circuit in 1974 and 1975.
Other bests: 1500m 3:33.16 (1974), 1 mile 3:52.17 (1973), 3000m 7:44.4 (1973), 2 miles 8:16.4 (1973).

Georges JOBÉ (Bel)

MOTO CROSS

Georges Jobé. b. 6 Jan 1961.

At the age of 18 in 1980 he won his first world title at moto cross in the 250cc category and was also in the winning Belgian team in the Trophée des Nations and Moto-Cross des Nations. He was runner-up for the 125cc world title in 1981 and 1982 and won again in 1983. Then as Suzuki, for whom he rode, pulled out of the sport, he moved up to 500cc, placing second in the championship in 1984. In 1987, on a private Honda, he won the world title, and after an unsuccessful year at 125cc in 1988, he returned to 500cc and became world champion again in 1991 and 1992 for Honda.

Egil JOHANSEN (Nor)

ORIENTEERING

Egil Ivar Johansen. b. 18 Aug 1954 Kristiansand.

One of only three men to win two world orienteering titles. He was champion in 1976 and 1978 and won the silver medal in 1979. In the relay he won a gold in 1978 and silver 1976.
He was Norwegian champion each year 1975-9 as well as winning the long distance title in 1978.

Ingemar JOHANSSON (Swe)

BOXING

Jens Ingemar Johansson. b. 22 Sep 1932 Gothenburg.

In the Olympic heavyweight final in 1952 Johansson was disqualified for not giving of his best against Edward Sanders. However, he turned professional and overcame the shame of that decision by winning 21 successive bouts to when he became world heavyweight champion by knocking out Floyd Patterson in 1959, having knocked out the number one contender, Eddie Machen, in the first round the previous year. Johansson had won the European title in 1956 and defended it successfully twice, but he lost the world title in a return with Patterson who knocked him out in the fifth round in 1960 and repeated the medicine in the sixth round a year later. Johansson came back in 1962 to regain the European title that he had been forced to relinquish on becoming world champion, but retired a year later to concentrate on his haulage business. He had been Swedish amateur champion 1950-2 and was finally awarded his Olympic medal in 1982.
Career record: W - 26 (17), L - 2, D - 0.

Ivar JOHANSSON (Swe)

WRESTLING

Ivar Johansson. b. 31 Jan 1903 Kuddby, Östergötland, d. 4 Aug 1979.

Johansson shares the record for three Olympic gold medals at wrestling with Aleksandr Medved and Carl Westergren. He is also one of the three wrestlers to have won Olympic gold medals in both classes. Two of these came in 1932 when he won the freestyle middleweight and the Greco-Roman welterweight. He added the 1936 title at Greco-Roman middleweight. At the European Championships he was nonpareil, winning nine titles between 1931 and 1939, six at Greco and three at freestyle. At Greco-Roman he was unplaced at the 1926 Europeans and 1928 Worlds, then 3rd in 1929 and 2nd in 1930 at the Europeans before beginning his unbeaten run.
A great tactical thinker, his specialist hold was the backhammer, using his exceptionally strong wrists and hands.

Karl JOHANSSON (Swe)

ORIENTEERING

b. 15 Jun 1940 Hedemora.

World orienteering champion in 1968 at the individual event and in 1966 and 1968 at relay. He also won three Swedish titles 1967-71.

Sven JOHANSSON (Swe), see TUMBA.

Barry JOHN (UK)

RUGBY UNION

Barry John. b. 6 Jan 1945 Cefneithin.

With his jink, swerve, sidestep and mastery of the drop-kick, he was the archetypal Welsh fly-half but his superlative skills were admired far beyond Welsh boundaries and even the demanding New Zealand crowds joined in calling him 'The King'.

Beginning his senior career with Llanelli he moved on to Cardiff where he teamed up with scrum-half Gareth Edwards. After being capped twice in 1966 he only established a regular place in the Welsh team after he first partnered Edwards internationally in 1967. In all but the first two of John's 25 appearances for Wales he partnered Edwards, and all five of his Tests for the British Lions were in partnership with his club-mate. He set many scoring records, which would undoubtedly have been improved on had he not decided to retire at the early age of 27.

Sabine JOHN (GDR)

ATHLETICS

Sabine John. née Möbius, then Paetz. b. 16 Oct 1957 Döbeln.

A talented all-rounder who set a world heptathlon record with 6946 points in 1984 when she won the GDR title. She also set the first of three world indoor pentathlon bests that year but was denied by the Eastern European boycott of Los Angeles of the chance to bid for Olympic glory. After a year out of competition she returned in 1988 to gain the Olympic heptathlon silver medal. She had earlier won silvers at the 1982 Europeans and 1983 Worlds behind her team-mate Ramona Neubert. A PE teacher, she competed for SC DHfK Leipzig.

Individual event bests: 100m 11.46 (1984), 200m 23.23w/23.37 (1984), 800m 2:06.14 (1988), 100m hurdles 12.54 (1984), high jump 1.83 (1982), long jump 7.12 (1984), shot 16.23 (1988), javelin 44.62 (1984).

Tommy JOHN (USA)

BASEBALL

Thomas Edward John. b. 22 May 1943 Terre Haute, Indiana.

John pitched for a record 26 years in the major leagues for six different teams, but is best known for his years with the Los Angeles Dodgers 1972-8 and New York Yankees 1979-82. In 1974 he was having an outstanding season when he ruptured the medial collateral ligament of his pitching elbow during a game. He underwent reconstructive surgery by Dr Frank Jobe, who used a revolutionary new technique. John eventually needed further surgery because of some nerve problems and sat out an entire year. But he came back to have his greatest years after the injury, winning 20 games three times between 1977 and 1980. He was primarily a sinkerball pitcher and was never an overpowering fastballer.

Career pitching: ERA 3.31; W-L 286-224, SO 2227; Best seasons: 1980: 22-9, 3.43 ERA; 1979: 21-9, 2.97 ERA.

Ben JOHNSON (Can)

ATHLETICS

Benjamin Sinclair Johnson Jr. b. 30 Dec 1961 Falmouth, Jamaica, emigrating to Canada in 1976.

Achieved worldwide infamy when he was disqualified on a positive drugs test for steroids after powering to a sensational world record time of 9.79 in the Olympic 100 metres of 1988. Subsequently he was stripped of the world titles that he had won and the records that he had set in races in 1987 both indoors at 60m (6.41) and outdoors at 100m (9.83, passing 60m in 6.38, easily a world best). That year he won all 21 finals at 100m and had also set a 50m record indoors at 5.55. Having served a two-year ban he returned in 1991 to much ballyhoo and made the World Indoor 60m final, but made little impact outdoors then or in 1992, when he went out in the semi-finals at the Olympic Games. He tested positive once again in January 1993 and this time was banned for life.

He made the Canadian Olympic team in

1980, although that team did not compete due to the boycott. Improving steadily he won silver medals at both 100m and the sprint relay at the Commonwealth Games in 1982, although he later admitted to the Dubin enquiry that his drug taking had started in those days. Only a semi-finalist at the 1983 World Championships, in 1984 he became the first Canadian sprinter to win an Olympic medal (bronze at 100m) for 20 years. He lost just once in 1986, when he won two gold medals at the Commonwealth Games and had ten sub-10.10 times, the most ever run in a season.

Dennis JOHNSON (USA)

BASKETBALL

Dennis Wayne Johnson. b. 18 Sep 1954 San Pedro, California.

One of the greatest all-round guards ever to play basketball and perhaps the finest defensive player at the guard position. He was also a great winner, improving every team he played for. Johnson played at Pepperdine University and was drafted by the Seattle Supersonics in 1976. He played for them from 1976-80, was traded to the Phoenix Suns where he played from 1980-83, and played his last six years with the Boston Celtics. Johnson played on NBA champions in 1979 (Seattle), 1984 and 1986 (Boston). He was first team All-NBA in 1981 and defensively he was a first-team on the NBA All-Defensive squad in 1979-83 and 1987. Though not a great scorer, he was at his best in pressure situations and was a clutch shooter who rarely missed when the game was on the line.

Gus JOHNSON (USA)

BASKETBALL

Gus Johnson, Jr. b. 13 Dec 1938 Akron, Ohio, d. 29 Apr 1987 Akron.

One of the strongest players ever to play professional basketball, Johnson played forward and was only 1.98m *6'6"* but at 110 kg *240 lb* he was an imposing force on the court. In the 1960s, Johnson became one of the first men to shatter an NBA backboard with a powerful dunk. Johnson played collegiate ball at Akron University and the University of Idaho. In 1963 he joined the Baltimore Bullets and played with them until 1972, when he played briefly in his last year with the Phoenix Suns before finishing his career in the ABA with the Indiana Pacers. With the Pacers Johnson finally was able to play on a championship team. He died while still in his forties from a brain tumour.

Jack JOHNSON (USA)

BOXING

Arthur John Johnson. b. 31 Mar 1878 Galveston, Texas, d. 10 Jun 1946 Raleigh, North Carolina

One of the greatest heavyweight champions ever and certainly one of the most controversial. Johnson was hated by white America because of his arrogant manner, his penchant for keeping white mistresses, and the bias of the era against blacks. He thus had to wait a long time for a title fight and did not win the heavyweight championship until he was 30 in a fight against Tommy Burns held in Sydney, Australia. This was the first of many times Johnson fought outside the United States because of bigotry and some legal problems. Johnson was convicted in 1913 of violating the Mann Act which prohibited transporting women over state lines for immoral purposes. A white prostitute certified that Johnson had done that and he fled the country. He then defended his title twice in Paris. In 1915 Johnson lost his title when he was knocked out by Jess Willard in the 26th round in Havana, Cuba. Johnson later claimed the fight was fixed, and that he had been persuaded he would be allowed to return to the US if he was no longer champion. Ring historians doubt the claims as he was 37 at the time and most feel he was squarely beaten. He was killed in a car accident.

Career record: W - 79 (46), L - 8, D -12.

Magic JOHNSON (USA)

BASKETBALL

Earvin Johnson, Jr. b. 14 Aug 1959 Lansing, Michigan.

One of the greatest all-round basketball

players ever to play the game. He first came to stardom as a freshman at Michigan State University and he led them to the NCAA title as a sophomore. He then left college and signed with the Los Angeles Lakers. During the 1980s, Johnson was the quarterback of the Laker dynasty which won five NBA championships and he was league MVP in 1987, 1989 and 1990. At 2.06m *6'9"* he is the tallest point guard ever to play basketball, but he still possessed the great ball handling skills and passing ability of much smaller men. In addition, he often played small forward and power forward because of his size. In the 1980 NBA finals against the Philadelphia 76ers he played in every position. In the concluding sixth game Kareem Abdul-Jabbar was sidelined with a sprained ankle, so Johnson played center and scored 42 points with 15 rebounds and 7 assists. In the 1990/1 NBA season, Johnson surpassed Oscar Robertson's total of 9887 to become the all-time leader in assists.

But 'Magic' Johnson is much more than his statistics. He has been the ultimate team player and leader, and his outgoing, well-nigh infectious smile earned him a multitude of fans. He became a multi-millionaire because of that popularity, which brought him many endorsement contracts. He professed a desire to come back to basketball and eventually become a team owner.

On the eve of the 1991 NBA season he announced his retirement, revealing that he had been infected with HIV, the AIDS virus. He immediately expressed a desire to help promote the fight against the deadly killer. He returned, however, to play on the Olympic gold medal winning 'Dream Team' in 1992, but hopes of an NBA return proved short-lived.

NBA career 1979-91: 17,239 points av. 19.7; 6376 rebounds, 9921 assists.

Peter JOHNSON (Aus)

RUGBY UNION

Peter George Johnson. b. 13 Sep 1937 Sydney, NSW.

At the time of his retirement he held the record as Australia's most capped player and he still holds the record as his country's most capped hooker. Between 1959 and 1972 he played 42 times for Australia, including a record 37 consecutive internationals, and he captained the Wallabies during their tour of Ireland and Scotland in 1968. He played for the Sydney club Randwick.

An economist by training, he later became a noted writer and commentator on the game. His brother, **Brian** (b. 29 Apr 1930), was also capped nine times.

Rafer JOHNSON (USA)

ATHLETICS

Rafer Lewis Johnson. b. 16 Aug 1934 Hillsboro, Texas.

A brilliant all-rounder, he set a world record for the decathlon at his fourth attempt at the event with 7985 points (7608 on current tables) in 1955 while a student at UCLA. He was second at the 1956 Olympics and after setting a new world record at 8302 points (7789) in 1959 for USA v USSR, he won the Olympic gold in another record 8683 points (7982) in 1960. In his career he won nine of eleven decathlons contested, with other titles including the 1955 Pan-Americans and the AAU of 1956, 1958 and 1960. The US flagbearer at the 1960 Games, he subsequently became a film star, and lit the Olympic flame as the last torch bearer in Los Angeles in 1984.

His outstanding individual bests included: 100m 10.3 (1957), 110mh 13.8 (1956), long jump 7.76 (1956), shot 16.75 (1958), discus 52.50 (1960), javelin 76.75 (1960).

Walter JOHNSON (USA)

BASEBALL

Walter Perry Johnson. b. 6 Nov 1887 Humboldt, Kansas, d. 10 Dec 1946 Washington, D.C.

'Big Train' Johnson is usually considered the greatest right-handed pitcher ever. He pitched his entire 21-year career with the Washington Senators who were throughout that period one of the worst teams in the American League. His 417 wins is second

only to Cy Young on the all-time list, but he did not appear in a World Series until near the end of his career in 1924. Johnson won 20 games eleven times and won over 30 games twice. He was a big (1.85m *6'1"* 91 kg *200 lb*), overpowering fastballer who also held the major league record for career strikeouts until Nolan Ryan broke it in the 1980s. Johnson led the American League in strikeouts twelve times and twice recorded over 300 in one season. He was known as a great gentleman, and later he managed for seven years but with only a modicum of success.
Career pitching 1907-27: ERA 2.17; W-L 417-279, SO 3506; Best seasons: 1913: 36-7, 1.14 ERA, 243 SO; 1912: 33-12, 303 SO, 1.39 ERA; 1914: 28-18, 1.72 ERA; 1915: 27-13, 1.55 ERA.

Bill JOHNSTON (USA)

TENNIS

William M Johnston. b. 2 Nov 1894 San Francisco, California, d. 1 May 1946 San Francisco.

Nicknamed 'Little Bill', he was, after some early successes, overshadowed by 'Big Bill' Tilden. After his first tournament win in the Bay Counties junior singles in 1910, he won the State Championships of California, Oregon and Washington in 1912 and the following year he took the first of his 10 Pacific Coast singles titles. After winning the US singles in 1915 he was again a finalist in 1916 but due to war service in the Pacific as a lieutenant in the Navy he missed the next two Nationals. In 1919 he was ranked World No.1 for the only time after beating Tilden in the US final, but he then lost to 'Big Bill' in the next six US finals. With Tilden he played on the US team which won the Davis Cup for seven consecutive years 1920-6 and which lost to France in 1927; his overall record was 14 wins in 17 singles and wins in all four doubles.
He won the singles at Wimbledon and the World Hard Court Championships in 1923, and as a doubles player he was the US champion partnering 'Peck' Griffin in 1915-16 and 1920 and he won the mixed doubles in 1921. His game was one of constant attack and was not based on any particularly outstanding stroke. He rejected all offers to turn professional and after retiring from the game became an insurance broker.

Neil JOHNSTON (USA)

BASKETBALL

Donald Neil Johnston. b. 4 Feb 1929 Chillicothe, Ohio, d. 27 Sep 1978 Bedford, Texas.

Johnston had the first legendary hook shot in pro basketball. He played for two years collegiately at Ohio State but was then ruled ineligible when he signed a professional baseball contract with the Philadelphia Phillies, for whose Class B minor league teams he played from 1949 to 1951 as a pitcher. From 1951 he played eight seasons in the NBA with the Philadelphia Warriors, leading the league in scoring three times and being elected first-team All-NBA in 1953-6. He also led the NBA in rebounding in 1955. He later coached briefly in the NBA (1959-61) and the ABL (1961-3).

Rae JOHNSTONE (Aus)

HORSE RACING

William Raphael Johnstone. b. 13 Apr 1905 New South Wales, d. 29 April 1964 Chantilly, shortly after racing at Le Tremblay.

In nine countries he rode over 2000 winners. A stylish rider, he was particularly successful in France where he was known as 'Le Crocodie', due to his late surges. He trained as an apprentice in Australia and left to ride overseas in 1931; briefly in India, and then, unable to secure a racing licence in England, settling in France in 1932. Gaining a licence at last in England he won the 1000 and 2000 Guineas in 1934, the first of 12 classic winners in England, including three in the Derby. He also rode 8 classic winners in France and 7 in Ireland.
After retiring from riding in 1957 he trained in France.

Aurel JOLIAT (Can)

ICE HOCKEY

Aurel Emile Joliat. b. 29 Aug 1901 Ottawa, Ontario.

Joliat played both professional football and professional hockey. In football, he played in the Canadian Football League as a full-back with the Ottawa Rough Riders. This was despite the fact that he weighed only about 64 kg *140 lb*. At ice hockey he played his entire career as a left winger for the Montreal Canadiens. He always played with a trademark black baseball cap on his head. He was a good scorer for his era, but his forté was stickhandling and passing. He later returned to Ottawa and became a railway passenger ticket agent before retiring. *NHL career 1922-38 - 654 games, 270 goals, 460 points. Best year: 1924/5: 29 goals, 40 points. Hart Trophy 1934.*

Andrée JOLY, see Pierre BRUNET

Alan JONES (Aus)

MOTOR RACING

Alan Jones. b. 2 Nov 1946 Geelong, Victoria.

After starting his Formula One career in a Hesketh in 1975, and driving successively for Lola, Surtees and Shadow, he joined Williams in 1978 and had three very successful years 1981-3, finishing third, first and third in the world championship. He returned to Australia to run a cattle farm, but had a few Grand Prix races in later years, although without further success. In his world championship career from 1975 to 1986 he won 12 Grands Prix from 116 races, totalling 206 points. He won the Can-Am series in 1978 in a Lola-Chevrolet. His father Stan was a racing driver, and Alan won the 1963 Australian kart championship. He first came to England in 1969.

Ann JONES (UK)

TENNIS

Adrianne Shirley Jones. née Haydon. b. 7 Oct 1938 Birmingham.

The first left-hander to win the women's singles at Wimbledon. She took the title in 1969 and also won the mixed doubles that year. She had previously been a singles finalist in 1967 and a semi-finalist on six other occasions, and had won the junior title in 1956. Her other major victories came at the French Championships where she won the singles 1961 and 1966 and the women's doubles 1963, 1968-9.

She was a member of 12 Wightman Cup teams (1957-67, 1971, 1975) winning 16 (10 singles, 6 doubles) of her 32 rubbers. In the Federation Cup she played in 18 ties, winning 21 (10 singles, 11 doubles) of her 34 rubbers.

Initially, she was an outstanding table tennis player, representing England 69 times and she reached five World finals but was runner-up on each occasion: singles 1956, women's doubles 1953 and 1956, and mixed doubles 1955-6. She was English junior champion three times in the singles 1953, 1955-6 and won the English Open doubles with Diane Rowe in 1956.

In August 1962 she married 'Pip' Jones, a Birmingham businessman, and following her retirement from the game she became a leading administrator.

Bobby JONES (USA)

GOLF

Robert Tyre Jones, Jr. b. 17 Mar 1902 Atlanta, Georgia, d. 18 Dec 1971 Atlanta, Georgia.

With Ben Hogan and Jack Nicklaus, Bobby Jones is usually considered one of the three greatest players of all time. Grantland Rice had the most moving epitaph for him when he said, 'As a young man he was able to stand up to just about the best that life can offer, which is not easy, and later he stood up, with equal grace, to just about the worst.' Jones was a child prodigy who finished 8th in his first US Open when only 18. He later won 13 major championships, capped by his unparalleled year of 1930 in which he won the US and British Open and Amateur Championships. Since termed the 'Grand Slam' of golf, Rice termed it in 1930 the 'impregnable quadrilateral'. After that stunning accomplishment, Jones retired

from competitive play at the age of 28, although in later years he would play each year in the great American tournament which he founded - the Masters. Jones suffered for the last 25 years of his life from syringomelia, a chronic, debilitating disease of the spinal cord which kept him wheelchair bound for his last decade.
Jones was one of the most popular and erudite golfers ever. He held degrees in literature and law from Harvard and Georgia Tech. Later in his life he was made an honorary member of the Royal & Ancient club and a freeman of the town of St Andrews. When he was accorded the latter honour in 1958, the entire town stood up and sang, 'Will Ye No' Come Back Again', bringing tears to the eyes of all present, including Jones.
Major victories: US Open 1923, 1926, 1929-30; British Open 1926-27, 1930; US Amateur 1924-5, 1927-8, 1930; British Amateur 1930. Won 9 and lost 1 of his 10 Walker Cup matches in the five rubbers 1922-30.

Courtney JONES (UK)

ICE DANCE

Courtney John Lyndhurst Jones. b. 30 April 1933 Poole, Dorset.

The winner of four successive world ice dance titles with two different partners, in 1957-8 with June Markham and in 1959-60 with Doreen Denny. Like other British champions of the time he received greater recognition abroad than he did at home. Denny and Jones won three British and European titles, 1959-61, and they would almost certainly have won their third (and Jones' fifth) world title in 1961 but the championships were cancelled following the loss of the entire US team in an air crash. Jones retired in 1961 when his partner turned professional, but he returned in 1963 when, with Peri Horne, a former Olympic figure skater, they introduced two new dances which soon became internationally accepted. He later served as President of the National Skating Association and was awarded first the MBE and then the OBE in 1989 for his services to the sport.

K C JONES (USA)

BASKETBALL

K C Jones. b. 25 May 1932 Tyler, Texas.

Jones is one of four basketball players to have been an Olympic, NCAA and NBA champion. His college career was at the University of San Francisco who won NCAA titles in 1955 and 1956 (although Jones missed the 1956 NCAA tourney due to an eligibility technicality). After college he played for nine years in the NBA, the first eight of which saw his Boston Celtics win the championship. He played his entire collegiate and professional career in the company of Bill Russell, and although Russell was usually given as the reason for all the championships, K C Jones was the same type of player; a defensive stalwart who always guarded the opposition's leading guard and the ultimate team player. Jones was such an outstanding athlete that he was also drafted by the Los Angeles Rams of the NFL, although he had never played college football.
After he retired as a player he became a professional coach, first as an assistant on the Celtics. His first head coaching job came for the San Diego Conquistadors in 1972 and he had a three-year stint in the mid-70s with the Washington Bullets. Jones went back to the Celtics as an assistant coach and was their head coach from 1983 to 1988, leading them to NBA Championships in 1984 and 1986. In 1990 he returned to the Seattle Supersonics as a coach and in all has won over 500 games as an NBA head coach.

Ken JONES (UK)

RUGBY UNION

Kenneth Jeffrey Jones. b. 30 Dec 1921 Blaenavon.

An Olympic sprinter who used his speed to great effect on the wing for Newport and Wales. Between 1947 and 1957 he won 44 Welsh caps - 43 of them in successive matches - and he played for the British Lions in three Tests in New Zealand in 1950. For Wales he scored 17 tries and 16 for the Lions, including two in Tests. Although speed was a vital part of his game, he also possessed a deceptive swerve and a solid defence. At the time of his retirement his total of 47 international caps (including 3 for the Lions) was a record in world rugby. In athletics he was 3rd at 220y and 6th at 100y in the 1954 Empire Games; semi-finalist at 100m and sprint relay silver medallist in the 1948 Olympics; and Welsh champion seven times at 100y and eight times at 220y between 1946 and 1954. Awarded the MBE.

Lewis JONES (UK)

RUGBY LEAGUE

Benjamin Lewis Jones. b. 11 Apr 1931 Gorseinon, Wales.

Capped 10 times by Wales and twice by the British Lions as a rugby union player, he caused a surprise by signing professional forms for Leeds in November 1952 for the then record fee of £6,000. Although a fractured arm, sustained within two months of his switching codes, delayed his impact on the League game, he went on to set many scoring records, including a season's record 496 points (194 goals, 36 tries) in 1956/7. His total of 278 points on the 1954 tour of Australia was also a record at the time. After playing 15 times for Great Britain he left for Australia in 1964 and at the age of 33 became the player-coach with Wentworthville in Sydney.

He was equally at home as a stand-off, centre, full back or winger and with his sidestep, jink, dummy and change of pace he was the archetypal Welsh three-quarter.

Michael JONES (NZ)

RUGBY UNION

Michael Niko Jones. b. 8 Apr 1965 Auckland.

A flanker with pace, anticipation and brilliant handling skills, he has been rated the best forward in world rugby in recent years. After making his international début for Western Samoa against Wales in 1986, he went on to win 31 caps for the All Blacks to 1993, scoring nine Test tries. In 1989, playing against Australia, he twisted his knee so badly that surgeons feared he would never play again. However, he came back to join New Zealand's tour of France in 1990. A devout Christian, he played in four matches when New Zealand won the World Cup in 1987, but missed the semi-final against Wales as he would not play on a Sunday. A shy, unassuming individual, he is the antithesis of the usual conception of an All Black forward.

Sam JONES (USA)

BASKETBALL

Samuel Jones. b. 24 Jun 1933 Wilmington, North Carolina.

Jones played his college basketball at North Carolina College (now North Carolina Central University) and then played for 12 years with the Boston Celtics after they drafted him first in 1957. He helped them win 10 NBA Championships. He was a shooting guard who at first had to break the Celtics guard line-up of Bob Cousy and Bill Sharman, but once in the line-up he could not be moved out. He is best known for his bank shots, usually using them on pull-up jumpers off the fast break. He was named to the NBA 25th-Anniversary All-Time Team in 1970 and to the Hall of Fame in 1983.

Lee Roy JORDAN (USA)

AMERICAN FOOTBALL

Lee Roy Jordan. b. 27 Apr 1941 Excel, Alabama.

Jordan played center and linebacker at the University of Alabama under Bear Bryant. In pro football he played defense exclusively and was a five-time All-Pro and played in six Pro Bowls. He played his entire NFL career 1963-76 with the Dallas Cowboys, helping to make them one of the NFL's premier defensive teams in the late 1960s and early 1970s. Since his retirement he has become a real estate broker.

Michael JORDAN (USA)

BASKETBALL

Michael Jeffrey Jordan. b. 17 Feb 1963 Brooklyn, New York.

For some time now Jordan has established

his position as the greatest basketball player in the world currently, and surely has consolidated his place as the greatest ever. He played collegiately at the University of North Carolina, whom he helped win the NCAA championship in 1983. In 1984 he led the United States to an Olympic gold medal and then turned to the NBA after his junior year in college. He was soon established as a scoring sensation, leading the league for seven successive years from 1986/7, when he became only the second player in NBA history to score over 3000 points in a season. He won the NBA MVP award in 1988 and 1991-2, and was MVP for three successive years in the NBA Finals as he led the Chicago Bulls to the title each year 1991-3, so completing his Triple Crown. In 1993 he averaged an all-time record 41 points per game in his team's 4-2 win in the finals over Phoenix. In 1992 he won a second Olympic gold medal as the 'Dream Team' professionals swept all before them. An immensely popular athlete, he has been marketed into a money-making machine off the court as well by his agents. Jordan plays mostly shooting guard and possesses nonpareil quickness and jumping skills, hence his nickname of 'Air Jordan', reinforced by his enormously lucrative Nike shoe contract. As at 1993 he has the highest ever scoring average in NBA history.

Jordan's NBA record

Season	*Games*	*Points*	*Average*
1984/5	82	2313	28.2
1985/6	18	408	22.7
1986/7	82	3041	37.1
1987/8	82	2868	35.0
1988/9	81	2633	32.5
1989/90	82	2753	33.6
1990/1	82	2580	31.5
1991/2	80	2404	30.1
1992/3	78	2541	32.6
Total	667	21,541	32.3

4221 rebounds, 3935 assists.
Play-offs 1984-93: 4040 points in 111 games, average 36.4.

Addie JOSS (USA)

BASEBALL

Adrian Joss. b. 12 Apr 1880 Juneau, Wisconsin, d. 14 Apr 1911 Toledo, Ohio.

Joss pitched for only nine seasons in the major leagues, all with the Cleveland Indians, and in that time he won 160 games, even though he pitched only a portion of his final season because of arm problems. He was beloved of his fellow players and fans, but his career was shortened by his untimely death from tubercular meningitis.
Career pitching 1902-10: ERA 1.89; W-L 160-97, SO 920; Best seasons: 1907: 27-11, 1.83 ERA; 1908: 24-11, 1.16 ERA.

Jackie JOYNER-KERSEE (USA)

ATHLETICS

Jacqueline Joyner-Kersee. b. 3 Mar 1962 East St Louis, Illinois.

The world's greatest all-round woman athlete, she won both long jump and heptathlon by huge margins at the 1987 World Championships and went on to do the same Olympic double in 1988. She added a second Olympic heptathlon title in 1992 with a silver at long jump, having previously taken silver at heptathlon in 1984 when she was fifth at long jump. JJK won 12 successive heptathlon competitions 1985-91, before she pulled up with a hamstring injury at the 1991 Worlds. The previous day she had retained her long jump title, but had suffered a severe ankle injury. She came back with three wins in 1992. In her career she has won 24 of 34 heptathlons to June 1993 and has set four world records, 7148 and 7158 in 1986, and 7215 and 7291 in 1988. She also set a world long jump record at 7.45m in 1987 and twice ran a world indoor best of 7.37 for 55m hurdles in 1989. She has set eleven US records outdoors, six at heptathlon, three at long jump and two at 100m hurdles, with a best of 12.61 in 1988.
The sister of **Al Joyner** (b. 19 Jan 1960) who won the 1984 Olympic triple jump title, she went to UCLA on a basketball scholarship, but there she was persuaded to try the heptathlon by the assistant track coach, Bobby Kersee. She married Kersee on 11 Jan 1986.
NCAA heptathlon champion 1982-3, and US champion at heptathlon 1982, 1987,

1991-3, and long jump 1987 and 1990-3. Sullivan Award winner 1986.
Other bests: 200m 22.30 (1987), 400m 53.64 (1990), 800m 2:08.51 (1988), 400m hurdles 55.05 (1985), high jump 1.93 (1988), triple jump 13.20 (1985), shot 16.84 (1988), javelin 50.12 (1986).

Alberto JUANTORENA (Cuba)

ATHLETICS

Alberto Juantorena Danger. b. 21 Nov 1950 Santiago de Cuba.

The double Olympic champion at 400m and 800m in 1976. His double was unique in Olympic history; he set a world record of 1:43.50 at 800m and his 44.26 for 400m was then the fastest ever at low altitude. With his huge stride (he was 1.90m tall) it was felt that he had taken middle distance running into a new era, but he made only one improvement on these times. In 1977 he ran the 800m in 1:43.44 to win the World Student Games title and he won the 400m/800m double at the inaugural World Cup. In the latter he won an epic race against Mike Boit of Kenya, who had missed the 1976 Olympics.
At 400m he won the World Student Games gold in 1973 and the Pan-American silver in 1975. A severe Achilles tendon injury prevented him from defending his Olympic 800m title in 1980 after he had placed fourth at 400m, and his career ended when he was carried off, screaming in agony and frustration after tripping over the kerb in a heat at the 1983 World Championships.
He became the president of the Cuban athletics federation and council member of the IAAF.

JUNG Kuo-tuan (China)

TABLE TENNIS

Jung Kuo-tuan. b. 1940 Hong Kong.

The first Chinese player to win the world singles title. Son of a Hong Kong seaman, he first took up the game at the age of 16 when he went to work for a fishmonger who ran a table tennis saloon for gambling purposes. Long hours of working and playing took their toll of his fragile health and he spent some time in a tuberculosis sanatorium. Early in 1958 he distinguished himself in his first appearance in a national competition by beating the Chinese champion, Wang Chu-yao. By the end of the season he was ranked as his country's No.1. His meteoric career continued the following year when, after four successive wins by Chinese players, he won the 1959 world singles, beating former champions Richard Miles (USA) and Ferenc Sidó (Hun) on the way to the title. He was also a member of the winning Chinese team in 1961. His greatest assets were the half-volley, drop-shot and forehand drive. Despite his penholder grip he also possessed an extremely effective backhand drive.

Sonny JURGENSEN (USA)

AMERICAN FOOTBALL

Christian Adolph Jurgensen III. b. 23 Aug 1934 Wilmington, North Carolina.

Jurgensen played college football at Duke University, graduating in 1957. He was a quarterback but the Blue Devils primarily ran the ball and he threw only six touchdown passes in college and had only 59 pass attempts in his senior season. He was drafted by the Philadelphia Eagles and played as back-up to Norm Van Brocklin until 1961 when he became the Eagles regular quarterback. He then played for the Washington Redskins from 1964-74. Known for his incredibly strong arm and accurate passing ability, he played for mostly mediocre teams in the NFL and never won a pro championship.
NFL career 1957-74: 32,224 yards from 2433 pass completions, 57.1%, 255TD.

Choo-Choo JUSTICE (USA)

AMERICAN FOOTBALL

Charles Justice. b. 18 May 1924 Asheville, North Carolina.

A legend as a college running back at the University of North Carolina, Justice played tailback for the Tarheels from 1946-49, forming a backfield with Olympic decathlon medallist Floyd 'Chunk' Simmons. Justice set the NCAA record for career total yardage with 5136 yards (3774 rushing, 2362 passing), was also a superb punter and scored 39 touchdowns in his college career. He was an All-American in both 1948 and 1949. He played in the NFL in 1950 and from 1952-4 with the Washington Redskins, but he never duplicated his collegiate success in the pros. The book and movie, *Everybody's All-American*, was purportedly based loosely on Justice's career and fame.

Jim KAAT (USA)

BASEBALL

James Lee Kaat. b. 7 Nov 1938 Zeeland, Michigan.

Kaat played in the major leagues in four decades from the 1950s to the 1980s. He started his career in 1959 with the Washington Senators, pitched with them and the Minnesota Twins (who had been the Senators prior to a move) until 1973 and from then with four other teams. He won 20 games in a season three times, with his best season 25-13 in 1966. A big, fireballing left-hander in his early years, he became a very crafty pitcher by the end of his career, often using a quick-pitch delivery. He is usually considered the greatest fielding pitcher of all time and won fourteen consecutive Gold Glove awards 1962-75, a record at any position surpassed only by Brooks Robinson's 16 at third base. Since retirement Kaat has become a very popular baseball announcer on television.

Career pitching: 1959-83 ERA 3.45; W-L 283-237, SO 2461.

Duke KAHANAMOKU (USA)

SWIMMING

Duke Paoa Kahinu Makoe Hulikohoa Kahanamoku. b. 24 Aug 1890 Honolulu, Hawaii, d. 22 Jan 1968 Honolulu.

In his very long swimming career he won three Olympic gold medals and swam at four Games. He bettered the world best time for 100 yards by about five seconds when swimming in the open sea off Hawaii in 1911. US swimming officials were sceptical but he soon proved his huge talent when he came to the mainland.

At his first Olympics in 1912 he won the 100m freestyle and a silver on the US 4 x 200m team. He retained his title eight years later, on his 30th birthday, in a world record time of 60.4 and recorded another world record and gold medal on the 4 x 200m team. He was beaten into second place at 100m in 1924 by Johnny Weissmuller, but was passed over for the relay team. Back again in 1928 he won no medals, but he was also an alternate, although he did not compete, on the US water polo team at the 1932 Olympics at the age of 42.

His first world record was 61.6 for 100m on a straight course in 1912. He followed this with four records for 100 yards from 54.5 in 1913 to 53.0 in 1917 and improved the 100m time to 61.4 in 1918 before that final 60.4 in 1920. US freestyle champion at 100y outdoors in 1916-7 and 1920 and indoors in 1912.

Also a superb surfer, he helped to popularise that sport with demonstrations in California and Australia, and in swimming used the 'flutter' kick that he developed as a youth to propel the surfboard. He played an island king in many movies, as befitted a man with Hawaiian royal blood. His Christian name of Duke was in honour of a visit by the Duke of Edinburgh, son of Queen Victoria, to Hawaii. He became sheriff of Honolulu.

Al KALINE (USA)

BASEBALL

Albert William Kaline. b. 19 Dec 1934 Baltimore, Maryland.

Kaline played outfield for 22 major league seasons with the Detroit Tigers. He batted over .300 nine times and only in his last two seasons did his career average drop below .300. Known as 'Mr Tiger', he played in 16 All-Star Games. Playing right field, he won 10 Gold Gloves in 11 years, 1957-9, 1961-7. Since his retirement in 1974, he has been an announcer for the Tigers television network.

Career 1953-74: 3007 hits Avg. .297, HR 399; RBI 1583. Best seasons: 1955: .340, 200 hits. 1956: .314, 128 RBI.

Irina KALININA (USSR/Rus)

DIVING

Irina Kalinina. b. 8 Feb 1959 Penza.

Olympic champion at springboard diving in 1980, having placed 4th at highboard and 7th at springboard in 1976. World champion at springboard 1975 and 1978 and highboard 1978 (after 3rd 1973 and 2nd 1975). Her first major title was the European Youth springboard in 1973 and in that year she won her first Soviet titles at both springboard and highboard diving. A year later she was a silver medallist at both events in the European Championships.

Alvin KALLICHARAN (Guy)

CRICKET

Alvin Isaac Kallicharan. b. 21 Mar 1949 Port Mourant, Berbice.

A small (1.63m *5'4"*) graceful, left-handed batsman, Kallicharan first played for Guyana in 1966 and made a sensational start in Test cricket with 100s in his first two innings against New Zealand in 1972. Throughout the 1970s he played a major part in the success of the West Indies team. He withdrew from World Series cricket in 1977 when he discovered that it would conflict with a contract he had in Queensland, and took over the captaincy of the West Indian Test team, leading them nine times but only winning one match. On the return of the Packer players, his form declined and he was then banned from Tests for playing in South Africa, as he became the first West Indian to play in the Currie Cup, for Transvaal 1981-4.
In England he played for Warwickshire from 1971 and twice exceeded 2000 runs in a season: 2120 at 66.25 in 1982 and 2301 at 52.29 in 1984. He also had occasional success with off-break bowling.
66 Tests 1972-81: 4399 runs at 44.43, 12 100s HS 187; 4 wickets at 39.50, BB 2-16; 51 catches.
31 One-day Ints: 826 runs at 34.41, HS 78; 3 wickets at 21.33, BB 2-10; 8 catches.
First-class 1966-90: 32,650 runs at 43.65, 87 100s HS 243; 84 wickets at 47.97, BB 5-45; 323 catches.*

Rohan KANHAI (Guy)

CRICKET

Rohan Bholalall Kanhai. b. 26 Dec 1935 Port Mourant, Berbice.

A batting genius, perhaps not always the most disciplined but he was nonethleless a fine captain of the West Indies who instilled some order into the team when he took over from Gary Sobers in 1972, leading them in his last 13 Tests. Kanhai made his début for the then British Guiana in 1955 and two years later came to England for the first time, initially playing as a wicket-keeper. After three Tests he concentrated on his batting, which came into full flower with his maiden Test century and his highest ever score of 256 against India in 1958/9, and some wonderful batting on the tour of Australia in 1960/1 during which he scored two centuries in the Adelaide Test. In England he played for Warwickshire 1968-77.
79 Tests 1957-74: 6227 runs at 47.53, 15 100s HS 256; 50 catches.
7 One-day Ints: 164 runs at 54.66, HS 55; 4 catches.
First-class 1955-82: 28,774 runs at 49.01, 83 100s HS 256; 18 wickets at 56.05, BB 2-5; 318 catches, 7 stumpings.

Karin KANIA (GDR)

SPEED SKATING

Karin Kania. b. 20 Jun 1961 Dresden. née Enke.

One of the very few individuals who have reached world class at both figure and speed skating. After placing ninth in the European figure skating championships in 1977 she felt that she could not improve much further and switched to speed skating. A world class time for 1500m after only 14 days specialised training confirmed her potential and in due course she became the supreme performer in her new sport. She won the first of 15 GDR titles and the World Sprint Championship in 1980, and one week later took the Olympic gold medal over 500m. Between 1980 and 1987 she won the world sprint title a record six times and at the World Championships she won the overall title a

record five times, 1982, 1984, and after taking a year off to have a baby, again in 1986-8. Her Olympic record was equally distinguished: she won a record total of eight Olympic medals (3 gold, 4 silver, 1 bronze) in the Games of 1980, 1984 and 1988.
In 1980 she married an engineer named Busch but the marriage lasted less than two years and she never competed under that name, and then in 1985 she married Rudolf Kania. She set seven world records at distances from 500m to 3000m.
Best times: 500m 39.24 (1988), 1000m 1:17.70 (1988), 1500m 1:59.30 (1986), 3000m 4:17.76 (1988), 5000m 7:39.82 (1988).

Juha KANKKUNEN (Finland)

RALLYING

Juha Kankkunen. b. 2 Apr 1959 Laukaa.

An exuberant driver, he was the first man ever to win three world rallying titles, 1986-7 and 1991. He had started rallying in 1978, driving a Ford Escort. He drove for Toyota in 1983, 1988-9; Peugeot 1986, Lancia 1987, 1990-2. After winning the 1985 Safari and the 1987 RAC he enjoyed an outstanding year in 1991 when he won four major rallies - Safari, Acropolis, 1000 Lakes and Australian. In 1992 he was runner-up for the world title although he won just once, at the Portuguese.
He switched from Lancia to Toyota for 1993 and with his usual co-driver Juha Piironen won his third Safari Rally and the Argentina Rally, to bring his number of championship race wins to 17. He also won Paris-Dakar 1988.

Jigoro KANO (Japan)

JUDO

Dr Jigoro Kano. b. 28 Oct 1860 Kobe, Hyogo Prefecture, d. 4 May 1938.

The founder of judo, he combined the principles of different forms of ju-jitsu, studying the skills while at the Imperial (now Tokyo) University. He founded the first Kodokan (judo training school) in 1882 at Shitaya, encouraging his followers to balance physical and mental discipline. The Kodokan became the centre of world judo. He was the founder president of the Japanese Amateur Sports Association in 1911 and under his guidance judo developed as a worldwide sport, although not admitted to the Olympic programme until 26 years after his death. He was an IOC member 1909-39.
He died on board ship (the *Hikawa Maru*) returning from an IOC conference in Cairo.

KAPIL DEV (India)

CRICKET

Kapil Dev Nikhanj. b. 6 Jan 1959 Chandigarh.

A splendid fast-medium bowler, who is the highest wicket-taker in one-day internationals and the second highest ever in Tests, a record that will surely be his very soon. He is also a most capable batsman, challenging Imran Khan and Ian Botham for the title of the world's leading all-rounder of the 1980s. He reached the double of 1000 runs and 100 wickets in Test cricket in 25 Tests in just 1 year 107 days from his début in 1978, and at the youngest age, 21 years 27 days. He has progressed to be the youngest to 2000/200 at 24 and 3000/300 at 28, and is the only man to achieve 4000 and 400.
In 1983 he captained India to a triumphant win in the World Cup final, and earlier in that competition the brilliance and power of his batting was shown against Zimbabwe at Tonbridge. India appeared to be heading for a sensational defeat at 17-5, but then Kapil scored 175 not out in 181 minutes in his team's 266-8 to take them to victory. Despite his World Cup success Kapil lost the Indian captaincy a year later, although he had another spell in charge in 1985-7. In all he captained India in 34 Tests, winning just 4.
He plays for Haryana in the Ranji Trophy, and played for Northants 1981-3 and Worcestershire 1984-6 with remarkably little success, obviously preferring to keep his form for the international arena.
124 Tests 1978-93: 5069 runs at 31.29, 8 100s HS 163; 420 wickets at 29.66, BB 9-83; 63 catches.

205 One-day Ints: 3642 runs at 24.77, 1 100 HS 175; 241 wickets at 26.65, BB 5-43; 63 catches.*
First-class 1975-92: 10,765 runs at 32.82, 17 100s HS 193; 798 wickets at 27.01, BB 9-83; 183 catches.

Julius KARIUKI (Kenya)

ATHLETICS

Julius Kariuki. b. 12 Jun 1961 Nyahururu.

Won the 1988 Olympic 3000m steeple-chase title in 8:05.51, the second fastest time ever, and the fastest on auto timing. A Kikuyu, he studied biochemistry at Riverside CC, California. He had been seventh in the 1984 Olympics, and won the steeplechase at the African Championships 1985, World Cups of 1985 and 1989 and Commonwealth Games in 1990. He was also World Student Games champion at 10,000m in 1989.
Other best times: 1500m 3:37.79 (1986), 1M 4:00.43 (1986), 3000m 7:47.35 (1986), 5000m 13:35.72 (1989), 10,000m 28:35.46 (1989), 2000m steeplechase 5:14.43 (1990, world best).

Béla KAROLYI (Rom/USA)

GYMNASTICS

Béla Karolyi. b. 13 Sep 1942 Cluj, Romania.

Karolyi, ably assisted by his wife Martha, was the inspirational coach of the Romanian gymnastics team for a decade, with his first star pupil being Nadia Comaneci. He defected to the USA on 30 Mar 1981 and soon became involved in the sport in his adopted country. He spent a year with Paul Ziert at the University of Oklahoma and then took charge of a gym-nastics club in Houston, Texas. By the time that Mary Lou Retton won the all-around gold medal at the 1984 Olympics, Karolyi had produced 7 Olympic and 14 World champions.
Karolyi, who graduated in PE from the University of Bucharest, had been a member of two Romanian world champion handball teams.

György KÁRPÁTI (Hun)

WATER POLO

György Kárpáti. b. 23 Jun 1935 Budapest.

Kárpáti, the best outside forward of his era, won his first Olympic gold medal in 1952 when he was only 17 years old. He was also an excellent swimmer and in the 1950s was considered the fastest water polo player in the world. He later won Olympic gold in 1956 and 1964 and a bronze in 1960. He was a member of the Hungarian team which won the European Championships in 1954 and 1962.

Rudolf KÁRPÁTI (Hun)

FENCING

Rudolf Kárpáti. b. 17 Jul 1920 Budapest.

A member of the noted Hungarian team which dominated sabre competitions for more than a decade. In team competitions he won Olympic gold medals at four suc-cessive Games 1948-1960 and was a member of the winning team at five World Championships, 1953-5, 1957-8. Individually, he was both an Olympic champion (1956, 1960) and World cham-pion (1954, 1959).
A talented musician, he was the leader of the People's Army Central Artistic Ensemble. On retirement he became President of the Hungarian Fencing Federation and a member of the world governing body where he played a major rôle in promoting the use of electronic scoring for touches.

Anatoliy KARPOV (USSR/Rus)

CHESS

Anatoliy Yevgenyevich Karpov. b. 23 May 1951 Zlatoust.

Became world chess champion in 1975 by default, having beaten Viktor Korchnoi for the right to challenge for the title, when Bobby Fischer refused to defend against him. Karpov drew with Garry Kasparov in 1984 but Kasparov defeated him to gain the title in 1985 and again in 1988. Karpov was a candidate master at age 11, European junior champion 1967-8 and World junior champion 1969, and USSR

champion 1976 and 1983. He reached international master status in 1969 and grandmaster a year later.
An economist at St Petersburg University, he is a calm, determined player, always very hard to defeat, although Nigel Short managed that in the semi-finals of the Challengers' tournament in 1992.

Pertti KARPPINEN (Fin)

ROWING

Pertti Johannes Karppinen. b. 17 Feb 1953 Vehmaa.

Olympic champion at single sculls in 1976, 1980 and 1984, and World champion in 1979 and 1985. He was also 2nd in the Worlds in 1977, 1981 and 1986, and 3rd in 1987. At double sculls he was second in the 1981 World Championships with his brother Reima (b. 27 Jan 1958).
Tall at 2.01m, his first international showing was seventh place at the 1973 European single sculls. He moved steadily up the rankings with 6th in 1974 and 4th in 1975 at the World Championships before his first Olympic gold. He was 7th in 1988 and competed in a fifth Olympics in 1992, but did not make the final.

Alex KARRAS (USA)

AMERICAN FOOTBALL

Alexander George Karras. b. 15 Jul 1935 Gary, Indiana.

A defensive tackle who played at the University of Iowa and for 13 years in the NFL with the Detroit Lions. Karras was relatively small for a tackle but was incredibly quick with great agility. He was All-Pro from 1960-2. In 1963 he and Paul Hornung were suspended from pro football because they had bet on games and during a one-year hiatus from the game he wrestled professionally. Karras retired in 1970 and has become a football analyst on television and a well-known actor. He is married to the Canadian-born actress Susan Clark and his screen roles have included parts in *Paper Lion*, *Blazing Saddles*, and *Babe*. The last was the television movie about Babe Didrikson Zaharias, in which Karras played George Zaharias, Babe's husband, while his wife portrayed the great female athlete.

Garry KASPAROV (USSR/Aze)

CHESS

Garry Kimovich Kasparov. b. 13 Apr 1963 Baku. né Harry Weinstein, he changed his name after his father was killed in a road accident.

Kasparov became the youngest ever world chess champion in 1985 when he beat Anatoliy Karpov at the age of 22 years 210 days. He successfully defended his title in 1988 and reached the highest ever ELO rating of 2800 at the end of 1989, increasing to 2805 by the end of 1992.
He won the USSR under-18 title at the age of 12 and reached international master status in 1979 and international grandmaster a year later. He was World junior champion in 1980 and joint USSR champion in 1981. Although an Azerbaijani, he played for the Russian team that won the chess Olympiad in 1992.

Sawao KATO (Japan)

GYMNASTICS

Sawao Kato. b. 11 Oct 1946 Sugadaira, Niigata Prefecture.

The 1.60m *5' 3"* Kato was the all-around Olympic gold medallist in 1968, when he held off the challenge of Mikhail Voronin, and in 1972 when he had a comfortable margin over his team-mate Eizo Kenmotsu. He added team and floor exercises gold medals with a bronze for the rings in 1968, and team and parallel bars gold medals with two silvers in 1972. In 1976 he again helped Japan to win the team title but was beaten into second place in the all-around before retaining his parallel bars title. Surprisingly he did not win an individual gold medal at World Championships.

Tatyana KAZANKINA (USSR/Rus)

ATHLETICS

Tatyana Vasilyevna Kazankina. b. 17 Dec 1951 Petrovsk. Later Kovalenko.

In 1976 she became the only woman to

achieve the Olympic double of 800m (in a world record 1:54.94) and 1500m, and she retained her 1500m title in 1980. She had started her major championships career with fourth in the 1974 European 800m and later moved up to 3000m, at which in 1983 she was third in the World Championships and won at the European Cup. She set three world records at 1500m, and one each at 2000m, 3000m and 4x800m relay. She became the first sub-4 minute women's 1500m runner when she ran 3:56.0 at Podolsk on 28 Jun 1976, improving to 3:55.0 at Moscow in July 1980 and to 3:52.47 a month later in Zürich. That time remains as the world record more than a decade later and seems untouchable, as does her 8:22.62 for 3000m in Leningrad in 1984.
A diminutive figure at 1.62m and 48kg, her range of ability was shown with her second places at 800m in the 1977 World Student Games and in the 1976 World Cross-country. In 1984 she was suspended for refusing to take a drugs test following a 5000m race in Paris (when she ran her best for that distance of 15:23.12) and although her reputation has been tarnished by that, she was a truly exceptional runner. She returned to place 5th in the 1986 Women's World 15km Road Race. She had babies in 1978 and 1982.
Other best times: 800m 1:54.94 (1980), 2000m 5:28.72 (1984), 5000m 15:23.12 (1984). USSR champion 1500m 1975-7.

Warren KEALOHA (USA)

SWIMMING

Warren Paoa Kealoha. b. 3 Mar 1904 Honolulu, Hawaii, d. 8 Sep 1972 Honolulu.

The first man to repeat an Olympic backstroke title as he won at 100m in 1920 and 1924. He set four world records at this event as he took the record from 1:14.8, which he recorded in a heat prior to his first Olympic victory in Antwerp in 1920 when he was 16, to 1:11.4 in 1926.
AAU champion six times at backstroke and twice at 50m freestyle, Kealoha was undefeated at the backstroke until 1926 when he was narrowly pipped by Johnny Weissmuller.
Warren's father was a Mr Daniels and he was adopted by a Hawaiian family. He later became a successful rancher. His brother Pua (1902-73) also swam at the 1920 Olympics, taking a gold in the 4x200m relay, silver at 100m freestyle and placing fourth at 1500m.

Moss KEANE (Ire)

RUGBY UNION

Maurice Ignatius Keane. b. 27 Jul 1948 Currow, Co. Kerry.

Although not outstanding in any particular aspect of the game, his all-round abilities as a hard-working forward won him 51 caps for Ireland 1974-84. He was only on the winning side in 17 of these matches but Ireland won the Five Nations Championship in 1974 and 1982 and shared the title in 1983. Called up for the British Lions tour of New Zealand in 1977 after Geoff Wheel failed a fitness test, he played in one Test. A former Gaelic footballer, he was the first to win international rugby union honours after the eligibility rules were changed.

Kevin KEEGAN (UK)

FOOTBALL

Joseph Kevin Keegan. b. 14 Feb 1951 Armthorpe, Nr. Doncaster, Yorkshire.

Outstanding as a forward or in midfield, he epitomised the modern player who reaped rich financial rewards from his skills. Signing as an apprentice for Scunthorpe United in 1967, he became a full professional 12 months later and in 1971 moved to Liverpool where he played on the winning team in the FA Cup 1974, the European Cup 1977, the UEFA Cup (1973, 1976) and the Football League (1973, 1976-7). In the summer of 1977 he left Liverpool for SV Hamburg and helped them to the Bundesliga title in 1979 and to the final of the European Cup in 1980. He returned to England to join Southampton in 1980 and after two years at The Dell he moved to Newcastle United where he remained until his retirement in May 1984. He returned there as manager in 1992 with immediate success as they gained promo-

tion to the Premier League as champions of Division One.
He won 63 caps for England 1973-82, and captained the team on many occasions. He was equally adept at scoring or creating goals and it is testimony to his great talent that he won five Footballer of the Year awards: European 1978-9, English 1976 and 1982, and West German 1978. He was awarded the OBE in 1982.

Willie KEELER (USA)

BASEBALL

William Henry Keeler. b. 3 Mar 1872 Brooklyn, New York, d. 1 Jan 1923 Brooklyn.

'Wee Willie' was one of the top hitters at the turn of the century even though he was only 1.64m *5'4"* tall. He batted over .300 in all but the last three years of his 19-year career, playing for the New York Giants, New York Yankees, Baltimore Orioles, and Brooklyn Dodgers. He played mostly outfield, but spent some time at third base. In his greatest season, 1897, Keeler averaged .424 from 239 hits and hit safely in 44 consecutive games, a National League record which still stands, although tied by Pete Rose. His advice was simple, 'Keep your eye on the ball and hit 'em where they ain't.'
Career 1892-1910: 2962 hits Avg. .341; RBI 810; SB 495.

Kip KEINO (Kenya)

ATHLETICS

Hezekiah Kipchoge Keino. b. 17 Jan 1940 Kipsamo.

The pioneer of the great Kenyan running tradition, and a great crowd-pleaser with his long stride and huge talent. At the 1968 Olympics he won the 1500m and was second at 5000m, and in 1972 won the 3000m steeplechase and was second at 1500m. He won Commonwealth titles at 1 mile and 3 miles in 1966 and at 1500m in 1970, when he was third at 5000m. He was also African champion at both 1500m and 5000m in 1965. He had started his international career in 1962, when he set a Kenyan mile record of 4:07.0 in the heats and was 11th at 3 miles in the Commonwealth Games. He improved to 5th at 5000m in the 1964 Olympics, and in 1965, with Ron Clarke and Michel Jazy, rewrote the record books for the distance events. That year Keino ran world records at 3000m (7:39.6) and 5000m (13:24.2) as well as claiming his 1500m/5000m double at the first African Games.
He has been coach to Kenyan teams, and for several years has run, with his wife, an orphanage in Eldoret.
Other bests: 800m 1:46.41 (1972), 1500m 3:34.91 (1968), 1 mile 3:53.1 (1967), 10,000m 28:06.4 (1968), 3000m steeplechase 8:23.64 (1972).

Ágnes KELETI (Hun)

GYMNASTICS

Ágnes Keleti. b. 9 Jun 1921 Budapest.

Hungary's most successful Olympic competitor with ten medals in all from 1948 to 1956: five gold, one in 1952 and four in 1956, three silver and two bronze. In 1956, when aged 35 years 171 days (the oldest ever female gold medallist), she won three of the four apparatus finals but a lapse in the vault in which she was 23rd meant that she had to settle for the silver behind Larisa Latynina in the all-around competition. She stayed in Australia after the Games and eventually settled in Israel, where she became national women's gymnastics coach.
She had won her first Hungarian title in 1946 and one world title, on the asymmetric bars in 1954, but again a bad lapse in the vault had cost her any chance of the all-around title. Originally a fur worker, and later a professional cellist.

George KELL (USA)

BASEBALL

George Clyde Kell. b. 23 Aug 1922 Swifton, Arkansas.

The finest major leaguer who came up during the player shortage of World War II. He joined the Philadelphia Athletics in 1944, and played in the majors until 1957. Long after the war had ended, Kell remained the top third baseman in the

American League. He later played with the Detroit Tigers, Boston Red Sox, Chicago White Sox, and Baltimore Orioles. He was the AL batting champion in 1949, and that title denied Ted Williams, who finished second, of a third Triple Crown. Kell was an outstanding fielder, leading the league in fielding seven times, and four times in assists and total chances. He later became a play-by-play announcer for the Detroit Tigers.
Career batting: 1943-57 2054 hits Avg. .306; RBI 870. Best seasons: 1949: .343. 1950: .340, 218 hits.

Carsten KELLER (FRG)

HOCKEY
Carsten Keller. b. 8 Sep 1939 Berlin.

He captained the team which won Olympic gold in 1972 and won 133 caps for Germany between 1958 and 1972 as a defender. He played for Berliner SC, as did his son **Andreas** (b. 1 Oct 1965 Berlin), who as a midfield player won 196 outdoor and 28 indoor caps for Germany from 1983 to 1992 and won an Olympic gold in 1992 after silver medals in 1984 and 1988. Andreas also won gold medals at the European Cup in 1991 and Champions Trophy 1986-8 and 1991-2.
Carsten's father **Erwin** (1905-71) won a silver medal at the 1936 Olympics.

Charlie KELLER (USA)

BASEBALL
Charles Ernest Keller. b. 12 Sep 1916 Middletown, Maryland, d. 23 May 1990 Frederick, Maryland.

'King Kong' Keller earned his nickname from his muscled body and his black, bushy eyebrows. The name aptly described his slugging abilities. He came up in 1939 with the New York Yankees and eventually played for six pennant winners with the Bronx Bombers. He played his last two full seasons with the Detroit Tigers. He later coached briefly and then retired to Maryland to run a horse farm.
Career batting 1939-52: 1085 hits Avg. .286, HR 189; RBI 760. Best season: 1941: .298, 33 HR, 122 RBI.

Thomas KELLER (Swi)

ROWING
Thomas Keller. b. 24 Dec 1924 Zürich, d. 29 Sep 1989.

Highly respected international statesman of sport and president of FISA 1958-89. He trained as a chemical engineer and became a successful businessman, president of Swiss Timing from 1972.
He joined the Grasshopper Rowing Club in Zürich in 1940, and won his first Swiss senior title at single sculls in 1950, in which year he was third in the European Championships. He won further Swiss titles at double sculls in 1955 and single sculls in 1956, when he was selected for the Olympics, but the Swiss team withdrew from the Games. He had also skied for the Swiss Universities team.

John KELLY (USA)

ROWING
John Kelly, Sr. b. 4 Oct 1889 Philadelphia, Pennsylvania, d. 26 Jun 1960 Philadelphia.

Probably the greatest sculler the United States has ever produced. Kelly began rowing in 1908 with the Chamounix and Montrose Boat Clubs, but joined the Vesper Boat Club in 1909. From then until his competitive retirement after the 1924 Olympics, he won every sculling title available to him, including both World Championship and Olympics in both singles and doubles, and many national titles in both boats.
'Available to him' is an important term; Kelly never won the Diamond Sculls at the Henley Regatta. It has often been mistakenly quoted that Kelly was denied entry for the single sculls in 1920 on the grounds that he was an artisan (a bricklayer), but this is in fact not correct. The true reason is that Kelly was a member of the Vesper Boat Club, who were barred from entry by the Henley officials due to infringements of the amateur rules back in 1905, a ban which still stood in 1920. Kelly would, however, surely have won that title had he been allowed to compete and in later years his 'bricklaying' led to a lucrative business as a contractor in Philadelphia. He fathered

two very famous children - John Kelly, Jr (b. 24 May 1927) who won Olympic bronze at single sculls in 1956, and the late Grace Kelly, the American movie star who later became Princess Grace of Monaco.

Red KELLY (Can)

ICE HOCKEY

Leonard Patrick Kelly. b. 9 Jul 1927 Simcoe, Ontario.

Kelly may have been the most well-rounded hockey player ever and perhaps the most under-rated superstar in hockey history. He began his career with the Detroit Red Wings as a defenseman and is considered by hockey cognoscenti as one of the greatest defenders ever. He pioneered the concept of a rushing defenseman years before Bobby Orr, and helped Detroit win four Stanley Cups.
In 1960, Kelly was traded to the Toronto Maple Leafs, although he resisted the trade. He actually considered retirement and challenged the NHL's prohibition against free agency by so doing. But the Leafs convinced him to join them, and switched him to center for the last seven years of his career. He was superb at that position and helped Toronto win four Stanley Cups, giving him eight championships in all, a mark surpassed by only three men in NHL history.
NHL career 1947-67 - 1316 games, 281 goals, 823 points. Best year: 1960/1: 50 assists, 70 points. Lady Byng Trophy 1951, 1953-4, 1961; Norris Trophy 1954.

Sean KELLY (Ire)

CYCLING

John James Kelly. b. 24 May 1956 Carrick-on-Suir, Tipperary.

A professional cyclist from 1977, for much of the 1980s Sean Kelly was rated the world's best in the computer rankings. This was based mainly on his many wins in the one-day classics and he became the first World Cup series winner in 1989. He was not as formidable in the major tours because he was only an average climber, and his biggest disappointment has been his inability to win the Tour de France, although he has been points winner a record four times (1982-3, 1985, 1989), his best placing being 4th in 1985. His greatest success has come in the Paris-Nice stage race, which he won for an amazing seven consecutive years 1982-8.
Other major victories: Vuelta à España 1988 (and points jersey 1980, 1985-6, 1988); Tour de Suisse 1983, Milan-San Remo 1986, 1992; Ghent-Wevelgem 1988, Paris-Roubaix 1984, 1986; Liège-Bastogne-Liège 1984, 1989; Grand Prix de Nations 1986, Paris-Tours 1984, Tour of Lombardy 1983, 1985, 1991.

Mario KEMPES (Arg)

FOOTBALL

Mario Kempes. b. 15 Jul 1954 Bellville.

South American Player of the Year 1978. He scored 20 goals in 43 internationals for Argentina, including two in the World Cup final of 1978 when Argentina beat Holland 3-1. He helped Valencia win the European Cup-Winners' Cup in 1980. He joined River Plate in 1981 and from 1985 played for several teams in Spain and Austria. He was especially noted for his goalscoring ability from free-kicks.

Eizo KENMOTSU (Japan)

GYMNASTICS

Eizo Kenmotsu. b. 13 Feb 1948 Okayama Prefecture.

Won nine Olympic medals at three Games, 1968, 1972 and 1976; three of each colour, with all three golds at the team event. At the all-around event he was 4th in 1968 and 2nd in 1972.
At World Championships he won a record 16 medals, four of each colour individually, with three gold and a silver for the team. His individual golds were the all-around and horizontal bar in 1970, and on his best exercise, the parallel bars, in 1974 and 1978. He introduced numerous original elements to his displays.
He became assistant professor at the Nippon College of Health and Physical Education and the coach to the Japanese team.

Ted KENNEDY (Can)

ICE HOCKEY

Theodore Kennedy. b. 12 Dec 1925 Humberstone, Ontario.

Kennedy spent his entire career as a center with the Toronto Maple Leafs and in 1948 replaced the revered Syl Apps as captain and acknowledged leader of the Leafs. He helped the Leafs win five Stanley Cups and was captain for two of those victories. Never flashy or dazzling, but simply a solid, productive player who always did what was necessary to help his team win. His career started when he was only 17 years old and ended when he was 30, his legs feeling the wear of 15 years in professional hockey. He later became an official of the Ontario Racing Association.
NHL career 1942-57 - 696 games, 231 goals, 560 points. Best year: 1950/1: 43 assists, 61 points. Hart Trophy 1955.

Paul KERES (USSR/Est)

CHESS

Paul Keres. b. 7 Jan 1916 Narva, Estonia. d. 5 Jun 1975 Helsinki, Finland.

Consistently amongst the world's best chess players for 30 years and winner of many major tournaments. He was Estonian champion in 1934-5, 1942-3, 1945 and 1953, Georgian champion 1946 and USSR champion 1947, 1950-1. He won the 1938 AVRO tournament beating most of the world's best, but lost chances to challenge for the world title due to the War. Thereafter he was well placed in all six candidates tournaments 1950-65, but with three second places just missed the chance to progress. He died of a heart attack while returning from the Vancouver Open.

Sean KERLY (UK)

HOCKEY

Sean Robin Kerly. b. 29 Jan 1960 Tankerton, Kent.

With 64 goals in 99 appearances he is the top goalscorer for Great Britain. He also played 79 times for England (45 goals) and won a further 20 England caps in indoor internationals. He made his international début against Poland in 1981 and after winning a bronze medal at the 1984 Olympics he won gold in 1988. At his third Games in 1992 the GB team were not among the medal winners. Other successes included a silver medal in the 1986 World Cup and in the European Cup he won silver in 1987 and bronze in 1991. A powerful striker, he played at centre-forward for Southgate, Kent, Middlesex and the South before announcing his retirement after the 1992 Olympics. He was awarded the MBE in 1992.

Cecil KERSHAW (UK)

RUGBY UNION

Cecil Ashworth Kershaw. b. 3 Feb 1895, d. 1 Nov 1972 Worthing, Sussex.

A scrum-half who formed a legendary partnership with W.J.A.Davies. In the 14 internationals they played together they were never on the losing side. Kershaw won only two caps without Davies as his partner and England lost both matches (v Wales 1920 and 1922).
Both Davies and Kershaw enjoyed distinguished Naval careers and most of their playing days were spent together with US Portsmouth. When not utilising his speedy long pass, Kershaw linked with his loose forwards and unlike current scrum-halves he seldom kicked for position. A champion fencer, he twice represented Britain at the Olympic Games, 1920-24.

Stanley KETCHEL (USA)

BOXING

Stanley Ketchel. né Stanislaus Kiecal. b. 14 Sep 1886 Grand Rapids, Michigan, d. 15 Oct 1910 Conway, Missouri.

'The Michigan Assassin' was considered the greatest middleweight ever until Sugar Ray Robinson came along. Ketchel was a great favourite of the fans because of his style which was based on aggression as he spurned attempts at defence. He won the middleweight championship in 1907 by defeating Joe Thomas in 32 rounds. In 1909, Ketchel had the temerity to challenge the feared Jack Johnson, who was 35 pounds heavier, for the heavyweight cham-

pionship. He floored Johnson in the 12th and was on the attack throughout, but Johnson recovered and knocked out Ketchel. In 1910, when only 24 and vacationing on a ranch in Missouri, Ketchel was murdered by Walter Dipley, a farmhand who was jealous of Ketchel's relationship with a female cook. Dipley unloaded both barrels of a shotgun into Ketchel's back while he was eating breakfast.
Career record: W - 55 (49), L - 4, D - 5.

Atje KEULEN-DEELSTRA (Hol)

SPEED SKATING
Atje Keulen-Deelstra. b. 31 Dec 1938 Grouw.

Winner of four overall world speed skating championships, 1970, 1972-4, a record until Karin Kania registered her fifth victory in 1987. Despite these successes, she was never an Olympic champion but won a silver and two bronze medals in 1972. She set a world record for 1500m with 2:17.2 in 1970.

Valeriy KHARLAMOV (USSR)

ICE HOCKEY
Valeriy Borisovich Kharlamov. b. 14 Jan 1948 Moscow, d. 27 Aug 1981 Moscow.

Gained international fame in 1972 when he had an excellent series for the USSR against the NHL All-Stars. His fame was cemented when the redoubtable Bobby Hull said that he was the best winger in the world. He won Olympic gold medals in 1972 and 1976 and silver in 1980, and also skated for the Soviet teams which won the world championships in 1969-71, 1973-5, and 1978-9, and the European championship from 1969-79. He played for the Central Army Sports Club team.

Anatoliy KHRAPATIY (USSR/Kaz)

WEIGHTLIFTING
Anatoliy Khrapatiy, b. 20 Oct 1963 Abatsar.

Khrapatiy was undefeated in the 90kg class from 1985, when he finished third at the European Championships, to 1990, winning the Olympic gold medal in 1988 and five consecutive World and European Championships, 1986-90. He had also been European Junior champion in 1983 and won his first two Soviet titles in 1983-4. He had missed the 1984 Olympics through the Soviet boycott, and was very disappointed that he was not selected for the 1992 Olympics, blaming the chief coach to the ex-USSR team, Vasiliy Alekseyev.

Bill KIDD (USA)

ALPINE SKIING
William Winston Kidd. b. 13 Apr 1943 Burlington, Vermont.

In 1964 he was second in the slalom at the Olympic Games, becoming the first ever Alpine skiing medallist from the USA. He achieved another such first with the first world title for the USA, when he won the Alpine Combination in 1970. He then turned pro and won the world pro titles that year at giant slalom and combined. He came to prominence with 8th at slalom and 12th at giant slalom at the 1962 World Championships. For much of the 1960s he was amongst the world's best skiers, but a broken leg in 1967 and sprained ankles prior to the Games held him back in 1968, when was fifth at the Olympic giant slalom. He has had a most successful career in the ski industry, including being ski director at Colorado Springs.

Adolph KIEFER (USA)

SWIMMING
Adolph Gustav Kiefer. b. 27 Jun 1918 Chicago, Illinois.

The Olympic gold medallist at 100m backstroke in 1936, Kiefer might well have won more medals but for the War, during which he was put in charge of swimming instruction for the US Navy. In his long career, 1935-44, he set 17 world backstroke records including four at 100m in 1935-6 from 1:07.0 to 1:04.8, three at 200m from 2:24.0 in 1935 to 2:19.3 in 1944, and other bests of 100y 56.8 (1944) and 400m 5:10.9 (1941). He was the first to swim 100 yards backstroke in less than a minute and won a total of 18 AAU titles including outdoors at 100m for nine successive years 1935-43.

Tom KIERNAN (Ire)

RUGBY UNION

Thomas Joseph Kiernan. b. 7 Jan 1939 Cork.

While playing at centre for Cork Constitution he was surprisingly chosen as full-back by Ireland, and immediately proved an outstanding success in his new position, going on to win 54 caps for Ireland (1960-73) and play in five Tests for the British Lions.

Although Ireland only won once in Kiernan's first 10 matches, he impressed sufficiently to win a place with the 1962 Lions in South Africa. He played in only one Test but he returned to South Africa as captain of the 1968 Lions. His 17 points in the first Test and 35 points in the series were then British records. Apart from Kiernan's 11 penalty goals, the only other score by the Lions in the entire Test series was a try by Willie John McBride - which Kiernan converted.

Although he retired 20 years ago, he is Ireland's most capped full-back and his record of captaining his country 24 times also remains unbeaten. After his playing days were over he became a highly successful coach for Munster and Ireland. His nephew **Michael** (b. 17 Jan 1961 Cork) became Ireland's top international points scorer with 308 from 43 matches 1982-91, playing as a centre.

Harmon KILLEBREW (USA)

BASEBALL

Harmon Clayton Killebrew. b. 29 Jun 1936 Payette, Idaho.

'The Killer' is one of the greatest sluggers in baseball history. His 573 home runs ranks him 5th all-time. At age 31 he had hit 380, ahead of Ruth's pace for career home runs, but he tailed off in the last seven years of his career. Killebrew spent his entire career with the Washington Senators/Minnesota Twins, playing outfield and first base. He led the league in home runs six times and RBI three times.

Career batting 1954-75: 2086 hits Avg. .256, HR 573; RBI 1584. Best seasons: 1962: 48 HR, 126 RBI. 1964: 49 HR, 111 RBI. 1969: 49 HR, 140 RBI.

Jean-Claude KILLY (Fra)

ALPINE SKIING

Jean-Claude Killy. b. 30 Aug 1943 Saint-Cloud, Seine-et-Oise.

Killy matched Toni Sailer's record by winning all three Alpine skiing gold medals at the 1968 Olympics in Grenoble, close to his home in Val d'Isère. Following that triumph, which made him the greatest sporting hero in France, he was made a member of the Légion d'Honneur by President De Gaulle.

A reckless youngster who left school at 15 to concentrate on skiing, he became a purposeful and brilliant expert, joining the French national team in 1961. Ill with hepatitis at the 1964 Olympics, when he was fifth at the giant slalom, he became the best of his generation; world champion at Alpine Combination 1966 and 1968 and at downhill 1966, and winner of the overall World Cup in its first two seasons 1967-8. He won all three disciplines in 1967 and the giant slalom in 1968, and in these two seasons Killy won 18 World Cup races, six downhills, five slaloms and seven giant slaloms. After the 1968 season he retired at the age of 24 to ski professionally in the USA. He became the first ski-racing millionaire. He tried motor racing in 1969 and went on to a prosperous business career. Co-president of the Organising Committee for the 1992 Winter Olympics.

Nelli KIM (USSR/Bls)

GYMNASTICS

Nelli Vladimirovna Kim. b. 29 Jul 1957 Shurab, Leninabad.

This beautiful gymnast followed Nadia Comaneci by earning perfect scores of 10.0 at the 1976 Olympics for her vault and floor exercise, winning both after she had been second to Comaneci in the all-around. She helped the Soviet team to the team gold, as she did again in 1980, when she shared first place at floor exercises

with Comaneci. Between these two Olympics she married international gymnast Vladimir Achasov.
Born of a Korean father and Russian mother, she had lived in Tajikistan from the age of seven. Her first World Championship appearance was in 1974, when she was third on the beam. She was champion at floor and vault in 1978 and second all-around, moving up to take that title in 1979, and in all she had a total of 11 World Championship medals. In the European Championships she was 2nd overall in 1975 and tied for 3rd in 1977.

KIM Soo-nyung (SKo)

ARCHERY

Kim Soo-nyung. b. 5 Apr 1971 Choong Chung Book Province.

The greatest woman archer of the modern era. In 1988 she won individual and team gold medals at the Olympics. Nicknamed 'Viper' she was women's individual and team world champion in both 1989 and 1991. By 1990, she held every women's world record at all distances, and overall as well. At the Barcelona Olympics she again helped Korea to the team gold but finished second in the individual event.

Masahiko KIMURA (Japan)

JUDO

Masahiko Kimura. b. 10 Sep 1917 Kumamoto, d. 18 Apr 1993.

The top judoka between 1938 and 1949, and unbeaten throughout his career from the age of 18 in 1935 until his retirement. Only 1.70m tall but powerful at 83kg, his throwing techniques brought him continued success against much larger opponents. He shared the All-Japan title with Ishikawa in 1949.

Ralph KINER (USA)

BASEBALL

Ralph McPherran Kiner. b. 27 Oct 1922 Santa Rita, New Mexico.

The greatest home run hitter of the post-World War II major leagues. He led the National League in home runs in his first seven seasons 1946-52, a league record, and averaged 42 homers a season. He appeared to be a threat to Babe Ruth's career marks, but because of back problems he played only three more years. He hit over 50 home runs in 1947 and 1949, the first National Leaguer to accomplish that feat. Kiner has been a long-time play-by-play announcer for the New York Mets since his retirement.
Career batting 1946-55: 1451 hits Avg. .279, HR 369; RBI 1015. Best seasons: 1949: .310, 54 HR, 127 RBI. 1947: .313, 51 HR, 127 RBI.

Betsy KING (USA)

GOLF

Elizabeth King. b. 13 Aug 1955 Reading, Pennsylvania.

The second highest money-winner in the history of women's golf. She headed the money list for the first time in 1984 and after four years in the top ten including second places in 1986 and 1987, topped the list again in 1989 when her total of $654,132 was the first over $500,000. She was second again in 1992.
She had been a semi-finalist at the 1972 USGA Junior Girls Championship and turned pro in 1977 after graduating from Furman University. Despite consistency on the tour she did not win a major until the 1987 Dinah Shore (winning that title again in 1990), but then had consecutive wins in the US Women's Open 1989 and 1990. In the 1992 LPGA at Bethesda, Maryland she swept to victory with a host of records. Her score of 267 (68, 66, 67, 66) was 17 under par, and it was the first time in a major US tournament that a woman had had four rounds in the 60s. She also won the British Women's Open in 1985.
LPGA career earnings 1977-92: $3,906,642 with 28 victories.

Billie Jean KING (USA)

TENNIS

Billie Jean King. née Moffitt. b. 22 Nov 1943, Long Beach, California.

Winner of a record 20 Wimbledon titles.

Between 1961 and 1979 she won 6 singles, 10 women's doubles and 4 mixed doubles, and in 1967 and 1973 she won all three titles in the same year. At the US, French and Australian Championships she won a total of 6 singles, 6 women's doubles and 7 mixed doubles and her total of 39 Grand Slam titles has only been exceeded by Margaret Smith-Court.

Her battles with the Australian were a feature of the game in the 1960s and the 1970 Wimbledon final when Mrs Court won 14-12, 11-9 is often rated as the greatest women's match of all-time.

In 1965 Miss Moffitt married Larry King, who later became a lawyer and sports promoter, and with his support she played a leading role in raising the status of women's tennis. She was one of the founders of the women's professional tour in 1970 and twice served as President of the Women's Tennis Association. Her contribution to the game has been immense although the significance of her much publicised victory over Bobby Riggs in the 'Battle of the Sexes' at Houston in 1973 is generally over-rated.

Her outstanding serve-volley game was supported by a devastating smash and she used these attributes to keep up a relentless attacking game.

Micki KING (USA)

DIVING

Maxine Joyce King. b. 26 Jul 1944 Pontiac, Michigan. Married Jim Hayne in 1976.

Olympic champion at springboard diving in 1972, having placed fourth in 1968 after fracturing her wrist. King was also AAU champion at springboard 1m 1967, 3m 1965, 1967, 1969-70, highboard 1969, and took the Pan-American silver at springboard 1967 and 1971.

While at the University of Michigan she was the goalkeeper for two national championship winning water polo teams. After graduating in 1966, she joined the US Air Force and was a captain at the time of her Olympic success. In 1973 she was appointed diving coach at the US Air Force Academy.

Roger KINGDOM (USA)

ATHLETICS

Roger L Kingdom. b. 26 Aug 1962 Vienna, Georgia.

The second man to win two Olympic titles at 110m hurdles. A very powerful man, he won the NCAA and Pan-American titles while at the University of Pittsburgh in 1983 and went on to win the 1984 Olympic title. After winning the TAC title in 1985 he had a quiet couple of years before becoming the second man to run 110m hurdles in sub-13.00, at high altitude in 1988, a year in which he won all 25 races at 110mh. He ran the third fastest ever time, 12.98, to take the Olympic title and improved further in 1989 with a world record 12.92 in Zürich and the fastest ever wind-aided time, 12.87, at the World Cup. That year he also won the World Student Games title. He won further TAC titles each year 1988-90.

He was World champion at 60m hurdles indoors in 1989, when he also ran a time of 7.37, corrected from the originally announced 7.36, which equalled the world record. He missed the 1991 outdoor season following two operations on his right knee, and although he came back in 1992 he was unable to make a third US Olympic team.

Nile KINNICK (USA)

AMERICAN FOOTBALL

Nile Clarke Kinnick, Jr. b. 9 Jul 1918 Adel, Iowa, d. 2 Jun 1943 Gulf of Paria, Venezuela.

Many people think Nile Kinnick could have been President of the United States. But the 1939 Heisman Memorial Trophy winner never got the chance, dying tragically in a plane crash shortly after the start of World War II. As a college footballer 1936-9 at the University of Iowa he was a classic triple threat, running, passing and kicking for the Hawkeyes. In 1939, in addition to the Heisman, Kinnick won the Maxwell Award and the Walter Camp Trophy and was chosen as America's Athlete of the Year. He also found time to graduate in four years as a Phi Beta Kappa holder. After starring in the College All-

Star Game in 1940, Kinnick, who was a first-round draft choice of the Philadelphia Eagles, turned down pro football to enrol in Iowa's Law School. He became active in Republican politics, hoping to follow his grandfather, a former Iowa Governor, into public office. He was beloved of his team-mates and opponents for his abilities, his sportsmanship, and his character. The Iowa football stadium is named in his honour.

John KINSELLA (USA)

SWIMMING

John Pitann Kinsella. b. 26 Aug 1952 Oak Park, Illinois.

The Sullivan Award winner for 1970, when he became the first man to swim 1500 metres in less than 16 minutes with 15:57.1 and also set a world record at 400m with 4:02.7. At the Olympic Games of 1968 he won a silver medal at 1500m and went on to take a gold and world record in the 4 x 200m relay in 1972.
He was AAU champion outdoors at 400m and 1500m in 1970, and indoors at 500y and 1500m each year 1970-2. While at Indiana University he was NCAA champion outdoors at 500y and 1500m each year 1971-3.
After graduating from Indiana he became a professional long-distance swimmer, crossing the English Channel in 9 hr 9 min in 1969. He is now a successful businessman.

Sachio KINUGASA (Japan)

BASEBALL

Sachio Kinugasa. b. 18 Jan 1947 Kyoto.

On 13 Jun 1987 Kinugasa, third baseman of the Hiroshima Toyo Carp, passed the record for 2130 consecutive major league baseball appearances set by Lou Gehrig and had 2215 consecutively in all. Kinugasa ended his career later that year having played 2677 games from 1965, with a lifetime batting average of .270 with 2543 hits, 1448 runs and 504 home runs. Elected the Japan League's MVP in 1984.

Karch KIRALY (USA)

VOLLEYBALL

Charles F 'Karch' Kiraly. b. 3 Nov 1960 Jackson, Michigan.

Kiraly has been considered by many to be the best volleyball player in the world, and was designated as such by the FIVB in December 1986, the first time that such a distinction had been made.
He won gold medals with the US teams at the 1984 and 1988 Olympics, 1985 World Cup when he was named the Most Valuable Player, 1986 World Championships and 1987 Pan-American Games. He played collegiately at UCLA, where he helped the Bruins to three NCAA Championships, being named NCAA MVP twice and helping them to a 124-5 record in his four years. He eschewed the chance of playing in the 1992 Olympics, as by then he had become a top exponent of professional beach volleyball. With Steve Timmons he won the first World Series in 1989 and he was the leading money winner on the beach volleyball tour from 1991 to 1993.

Ian KIRKPATRICK (NZ)

RUGBY UNION

Ian Andrew Kirkpatrick. b. 24 May 1946 Gisborne.

A high-scoring flanker whose devastating running tested the best of defences. He was first capped against France on the 1967 tour and in his second international, against Australia in 1968, he went on as a replacement for the injured Brian Lochore and scored three tries, the first All Black to do so in a Test match since 1935. From then on he played in 38 consecutive internationals, captaining New Zealand in the series against Australia in 1972, Britain and France in 1972/3 and England in 1973. He played 36 internationals as a flanker and three as a No. 8, and scored 16 international tries which at the time was an All Black record.
Awarded the MBE in 1980, he was manager of the unofficial Cavaliers tour of South Africa in 1986.

John KIRWAN (NZ)

RUGBY UNION

John James Patrick Kirwan. b. 16 Dec 1964 Auckland.

In 1983, while playing third-grade rugby, he was a surprise choice for Auckland to play against the British Lions. The following year he won his first cap and soon established himself as one of the great wingers of modern times. In 1988 he passed Stu Wilson's All Black record of 19 international tries and went on to score 34, and having played in 45 internationals he is also New Zealand's most capped winger. He would undoubtedly have improved on these records had not recurring achilles tendon and back problems and a severe injury against Pontypool in 1989 curtailed his Test appearances. He relied to a large extent on his speed and imposing physique, but he also made good use of the swerve and sidestep.

Tom KITE (USA)

GOLF

Thomas O Kite, Jr. b. 9 Dec 1949 Austin, Texas.

By 1990 Kite had earned more prize money than any golfer ever, with over $6 million on the US PGA Tour, heading the money list in 1981 and 1989, when he set a season's record with $1,395,278. In February 1993 he became the first to pass $8 million in PGA career earnings. He is one of the steadiest players ever, not a long hitter but very accurate and possessed of a superb short game. The only criticism of Kite had been his inability to win one of the four major championships, but in 1992 he ended that omission by winning the US Open at Pebble Beach. He was PGA Player of the Year in 1989, a year in which he led the US money list and won the Players Championship. He also won the Vardon Trophy in 1981 and 1982, and in 1979 was awarded the Bobby Jones Award for his meritorious contributions to the game. He has represented the USA in the 1970 World Amateur, 1971 Walker Cup, 1984 and 1985 World Cup, and six Ryder Cups 1981-9 (won 13, lost 7, halved 4). While at the University of Texas he tied with his team-mate Ben Crenshaw for the 1972 NCAA title.

PGA career earnings 1972-92: $7,612,918 with 17 victories.

Franz KLAMMER (Aut)

ALPINE SKIING

Franz Klammer. b. 3 Oct 1953 Mooswald, Carinthia.

Perhaps the greatest ever downhill racer, he was Olympic champion in 1976. Then he faced enormous pressure as the clear favourite, having won eight of nine World Cup downhill races the previous year. Last of the top seeds to race, he was down on 1972 champion Bernhard Russi en route but stormed home to take the gold medal. Klammer won his first downhill race in 1973 and won a record 25 World Cup downhill races 1974-84 (as well as one win at combined), being champion each year 1975-8 and 1983; his best overall position was third in 1975 and 1977. Surprisingly his only World title was at Alpine Combination in 1974, when he was second in the downhill. He suffered a decline in form in 1979 and 1980, when he was not even selected for the Austrian Olympic team, but after marriage came back to his best when on 6 Dec 1981 he won his first downhill race for three years. He consolidated with fifth in the World Cup downhill series in 1981/2 and then regained the title in 1982/3.

A farmer's son, he was famed for his raw courage and determination.

Chuck KLEIN (USA)

BASEBALL

Charles Herbert Klein. b. 7 Oct 1904 Indianapolis, Indiana, d. 28 Mar 1958 Indianapolis.

Playing outfield for 17 years mostly with the Philadelphia Phillies, Klein was the top National League slugger of the late 1920s and early 1930s. He had over 200 hits for five straight seasons 1929-33, and led the National League in home runs four times, doubles twice, hits twice, runs three times, slugging average three times, and batting

average once. His greatest year was 1933 when he won the Triple Crown (.368, 28 HR, 120 RBI), also leading the league in hits (223), doubles (44), and slugging. Fast for a slugger, in 1932 he led the NL in stolen bases with 20. On 10 Jul 1936, he became one of the few major leaguers to hit four home runs in one game.
Career batting 1928-44: 2076 hits Avg. .320, HR 300; RBI 1201. Other top seasons: 1929: .356, 43 HR. 1930: .386, 250 hits, 59 doubles. 1933: .368, 223 hits, 44 doubles, 28 HR, 120 RBI.

Reiner KLIMKE (FRG)

EQUESTRIAN

(Dr) Reiner Klimke. b. 14 Jan 1936 Münster.

The most successful dressage rider of all time. Although he began his career in dressage, he also helped the FRG win the European team three-day title in 1959, and in 1960 was 16th at the Olympic three-day event. At dressage Klimke has won six Olympic gold medals and eight medals overall; both Olympic records for equestrian sport. He won team gold in 1964, 1968, 1976, 1984 and 1988; and individual bronzes on *Dux* in 1968 and on *Mehmed* in 1976 as well as the individual gold in 1984 on his favourite horse, *Ahlerich*. At the world championships, Klimke has been almost as successful, winning the individual title on *Mehmed* in 1974 and on *Ahlerich* in 1982, and helping West Germany to the team title in 1966, 1974, 1982, and 1986. He was European champion on *Dux* 1967, *Mehmed* 1973 and *Ahlerich* 1985, and rode on seven winning German teams.
In 1988, *Ahlerich*, by then a 17-year-old, helped Klimke to his final team gold medal at Seoul. In all Klimke, a lawyer and notary, won ten German titles.

Bobby KNIGHT (USA)

BASKETBALL

Robert Montgomery Knight. b. 25 Oct 1940 Orrville, Ohio.

His basketball career began at Orrville High School and he then played with the great Ohio State teams which featured Jerry Lucas and John Havlicek. Soon thereafter he became an assistant coach at the US Military Academy and two years later was named head coach, at only 24 the youngest head coach in major college basketball history. There he compiled a record of 102-50 in five years and led the nation three times in team defense. He then took over as coach at Indiana University, where he has achieved legendary status in an often tempestuous career. They won the NCAA title in 1976 (with an undefeated 32-0 team), 1981, and 1987. In 1984 he was coach of the US Olympic basketball team which easily won the gold medal. In 1979, Knight coached the US Pan-American team to a gold medal in Puerto Rico, but amid great controversy, as he allegedly struck a Puerto Rican security guard at a team practice and was arrested briefly. Knight has had other very controversial moments, and his taskmaster approach to coaching has led to occasional difficulties in recruiting. But it is universally acknowledged that Knight gets more from his players than any current basketball coach.

Pete KNIGHT (USA/Can)

RODEO

Peter Charles Knight. b. 5 May 1903 Philadelphia, Pennsylvania, d. 23 May 1937 Hayward, California.

Having moved with his family to Oklahoma and then in 1914 to Canada, taking up residence in Calgary, Knight became the greatest known of all Canadian cowboys, inspired initially by the well-known Calgary Stampede. His first competition was the Crossfields Rodeo at the age of 15. His top event was saddle bronc riding, at which he first won the Calgary Stampede in 1924, was considered unofficial world champion in 1926, and won the official title in 1932-3 and 1935-6. He became famous for his many battles with *Midnight*, considered the toughest bronc ever in rodeo history. In 1926 at the Montreal Stampede, Knight drew *Midnight* and achieved a qualified ride, although he never finished a ride on the bronc that was never broken. In 1937, defending his world saddle bronc championship, he rode *Duster* to a successful ride, but the effort cost him his life, as he died only a few hours later in hospital. His legend lives on in Western Canada where he is remembered in two popular songs, 'Pete Knight, King of the Cowboys' and 'Pete Knight's Last Ride'.

Alan KNOTT (UK)

CRICKET

Alan Philip Eric Knott. b. 9 Apr 1946 Belvedere, Kent.

One of the greatest of wicket-keepers and surely the greatest wicket-keeper/batsman, with the ability to bat at his best at the highest level. Supremely fit, he made a record 65 consecutive appearances for England before going to play World Series cricket, adding another six Tests on his return in 1980-1. He followed in the great Kent wicket-keeping tradition and perhaps exceeded even the great Godfrey Evans in ability. In his 78th Test he passed Evans' record 220 dismissals (from 91 Tests). He is the only wicket-keeper to score 4000 runs and take 200 dismissals in Test cricket.
95 Tests 1967-81: 4389 runs at 32.75, 5 100s HS 135; 250 catches, 19 stumpings.
20 One-day Ints: 200 runs at 20.00, HS 50; 15 catches, 1 stumping.
First-class 1964-85: 18,105 runs at 29.63, 17 100s HS 156; 2 wickets; 1211 catches, 133 stumpings.

Finn KOBBERÖ (Den)

BADMINTON

Finn Kobberö. b. 13 Mar 1936 Copenhagen.

A brilliant stroke player who particularly excelled at doubles. He won seven men's doubles titles at the All-England Championships, six with Jørgen Hammergaard Hansen, 1955-6 and 1961-4, and one with Per Nielsen in 1960; and eight at mixed doubles, the first four with Kirsten Granlund (née Thorndahl) and then four with Ulla Strand (née Rasmussen). He also won three successive US men's doubles titles 1956-8 with Hammergaard Hansen and another with Charoen Watansin in 1960, and partnered Judy Devlin for the mixed doubles title in those four years. This debonair player later became a television commentator.

Hugo KOBLET (Swi)

CYCLING

Hugo Koblet. b. 21 Mar 1925 Zürich, d. 6 Nov 1964.

His nickname was 'The Pedaller of Charm', for the grace and ease he displayed on the bike. His greatest hour of a meteoric career came in the 1951 Tour de France which he won by 20 minutes. But it was one particular stage, on 15 July from Brive to Agen of 177 km, which established his legend. At 37 km Koblet rolled off the front in a lone breakaway. Though the peloton chased and chased, he could not be caught, winning eventually by 2:35. One of his greatest rivals, Italy's Raphael Geminiani, described his effortless ride: 'He pedalled in a state of grace. While we suffered like dogs, he rolled along like a tourist.' His brilliance was, however, short-lived; he travelled to Mexico later that winter and came down with a mysterious malady. He was never again the same sublime rider. In 1964, he took his own life by driving his car into a tree.
At the World Championships he was third in the pro pursuit in 1947 and second in 1951 and 1954. His other major victories: Giro d'Italia 1950; Tour de Suisse 1950, 1953, 1955; Zürich 1952, 1954; Grand Prix de Nations 1951.

Marita KOCH (GDR)

ATHLETICS

Marita Koch. b. 18 Feb 1957 Wismar. Later Meier.

Marita Koch had a sprinting career of unparalleled brilliance, and must rate as a prime contender for the greatest ever woman athlete. Since her retirement at the end of the 1986 season no woman has approached her final outdoor record, 47.60 in winning the 400m at theWorld Cup in Canberra in October 1985.

She succeeded another elegant runner, Irena Szewinska, as the world's best with her first world records of 22.06 for 200m and 49.19 for 400m in 1978. In all she set 16 world records: 4 at 200m (to 21.71 in 1984), 7 at 400m (1978-85), 2 at 4 x 100m relay (1979 and 1983), 1 at 4 x 200m relay (1980), 2 at 4 x 400m relay (1982 and 1984). She also set 17 world indoor bests at distances from 50m to 400m.

At 400 metres she was Olympic champion in 1980, European in 1978, 1982 and 1986 and European Indoor in 1987. She did not run the 400m at the 1983 World Championships, but still took three golds, with the 200m and both relays, and a silver at 100m. At 200 metres she won three European Indoor titles, the World Indoor Games of 1985 and the World Student Games title in 1979. In all she won 17 gold medals at major championships, with four silvers and one bronze. To that one can add 15 golds and five silvers at World and European Cup finals.

Koch, a student of paediatric medicine and a member of the Sports Club Empor Rostock, lost in the 1977 World Cup to Irena Szewinska, but after that was beaten at 400m only twice, by Jarmila Kratochvílová in 1981 and by Bärbel Wöckel in 1982. After her retirement she married her coach Wolfgang Meier; their daughter Ulrike was born in 1990.

Other best times: 50m 6.11i (1980), 60m 7.04i (1985), 100m 10.83 (1983).

Sándor KOCSIS (Hun)

FOOTBALL

Sándor Kocsis. b. 21 Sep 1929 Budapest, d. 21 Jul 1979 Barcelona, Spain.

A prolific goalscoring inside-forward for the great Hungarian team of the 1950s. After only one season in the first team with Ferencváros of Budapest, where he won his first international cap, he was directed to join the newly-formed Army team, Honvéd, who had access to the country's best players. At Honvéd he joined the great Puskás and their brilliant understanding was continued in the national team. Kocsis won five League Championship medals with Honvéd, was top scorer in the League three times and won an Olympic gold medal in 1952. He scored a total of 75 international goals, including seven hat-tricks, in 68 appearances 1949-56. He was the top scorer in the 1954 World Cup with 11 goals, including four against West Germany.

At the time of the 1956 Hungarian uprising, Kocsis was on Honvéd's South American tour and like many of the team decided not to return home. Initially, he worked as a player-coach in Switzerland but soon settled in Spain where he joined Barcelona, with whom he won two League and two Cup medals before his retirement in 1966. A modest and likeable individual, he possessed all the skills including the invaluable ability to score with either foot and with his head.

Eva KÓCZIÁN (Hungary)

TABLE TENNIS

Eva Kóczián. b. 25 May 1936 Budapest. Later Földi.

The winner of the women's singles in 1958 and 1960 at the first two European Championships to be held, she was champion for a third time in 1964 as Mrs Földi. She also won the world mixed doubles in 1955 with Kálmán Szepesi (Hun) and the European women's doubles with Erzsébet Heirits in 1966. Although she never won the world singles, she came close in 1961 when she lost 21-19 to Chui Chung-hui (Chn) in the final set.

Many of her early doubles successes were with her brother, Josef, a finalist in the 1952 World Championships, but latterly she partnered László Földi, a Hungarian international whom she married in 1960 but later divorced.

Ronald KOEMAN (Hol)

FOOTBALL

Ronald Koeman. b. 21 Mar 1963 Zaandam.

A high-class defender with a ferocious shot, he helped Holland to win the European Championship in 1988. In that year he also helped PSV Eindhoven to win the European Cup and the Dutch league championship. He moved to Barcelona, for whom he scored the winning goal when they won the 1992 European Cup as he became only the second player to win European Champions' Cup medals with two different clubs. He had also scored their only goal in the final of the European Cup-Winners Cup the previous year which they lost to Manchester United. By June 1993 he had scored 10 goals in 66 internationals and was the captain of the Dutch national team.

Thomas KÖHLER (GDR)

LUGE

Thomas Köhler. b. 25 Jun 1940 Zwickau.

Winner of six World and Olympic luge titles, a record shared with Hans Rinn (GDR). He was the first man to win three single-seater titles, the 1962 and 1967 Worlds and 1964 Olympics, and was also the two-seater champion in the 1965 and 1967 Worlds and the 1968 Olympics. Additionally, he placed second in the single-seater at the 1968 Olympics.

Ada KOK (Hol)

SWIMMING

Aagje Kok. b. 6 Jun 1947 Amsterdam. Now Van der Linden.

At 1.83m *6 ft* and 83 kg *180 lb*, this gentle giant dominated her contemporaries and was the top female butterfly swimmer of the 1960s. Her first major international successes came at the 1962 European Championships when she won gold medals at 100m and medley relay; she repeated this feat in 1966 when she also took the 400m freestyle silver medal.

Kok had disappointed Dutch hopes with second place at 100m butterfly at the 1964 Olympics and a silver in the medley relay. In 1968 she was only fourth at 100m, but made up for that by winning the 200m in an Olympic record.

Kok's butterfly world records were not beaten until 1970: three at 100m from 66.1 in 1963 to 64.5 in 1965, and four at 200m from 2:25.8 in 1965 to 2:21.0 (at the longer 220y) in 1967. She also set a world record with the Dutch medley relay team in 1964.

Claudia KOLB (USA)

SWIMMING

Claudia Ann Kolb. b. 19 Dec 1949 Hayward, California. Later Thomas.

At the age of 14 Kolb won an unexpected Olympic silver medal at 200m breaststroke. Four years later she won both 200m and 400m individual medley gold medals by huge margins, 2:24.7 to the runner-up's 2:28.8 at 200m and 5:08.5 to 5:22.2 at 400m. She set five world records at 200m medley from 2:27.8 in 1966 to 2:23.5 in 1968, and four at 400m to 5:04.7 in 1968.

Pan-American champion at both medley events in 1967; AAU champion outdoors at 100y and 220y breaststroke 1964-5, 200m IM 1966-8, 400m IM 1966-7. Coached by George Haines at Santa Clara.

Peter-Michael KOLBE (FRG)

ROWING

Peter-Michael Kolbe. b. 2 Aug 1953 Hamburg.

Surely the greatest rower never to have won an Olympic gold medal. As a single sculler, Kolbe's failure to do so was because of his great rivalry with the Finn, Pertti Karppinen, behind whom he took silver medals in 1976 and 1984. Kolbe missed the 1980 Olympics because of the boycott and in 1988 again finished second, this time to Thomas Lange. In the World Championships, however, Kolbe was nonpareil, winning the single sculls five times, 1975, 1978, 1981, 1983, and 1986. He also won the European title in 1973. He moved to Oslo in 1982 to live with his Norwegian wife, whom he met when she was a journalist at the 1975 World Championships.

Alevtina KOLCHINA (USSR)

NORDIC SKIING

Alevtina Pavlovna Kolchina. b. 11 Nov 1930 Pavlovsk, Perm region.

Although she won five Olympic medals, three of these were at the 3 x 5km cross-country relay (silver 1956, gold 1964 and bronze 1968) and she had to settle for two bronze medals at individual events, at 5km

in 1964 and 1968. It was at the World Championships that she came into her own, winning at 10km in 1958 and 1962 and at 5km in 1962 and 1966, as well as gaining gold medals on Soviet relay teams in each of these years.
Her husband **Pavel Kolchin** (b. 9 Jan 1930) won four Olympic medals: gold at relay and bronze at both 15km and 30km in 1956, and bronze at relay in 1964. Their son, Fyodor, was second in the Nordic combination at the 1977 World Juniors and 15th at the 1980 Olympics.

Hannes KOLEHMAINEN (Fin)

ATHLETICS

Johannes Pietari Kolehmainen. b. 9 Dec 1889 Kuopio, d. 11 Jan 1966 Helsinki.

The first in a long line of great Finnish distance runners and the man who 'ran Finland onto the world map'. At the 1912 Olympics he ran the first sub-15 minute time for 5000m, smashing through that barrier with 14:36.6 but only beating Jean Bouin (France) by a tenth of a second. Two days earlier he had won the 10,000m with 31:20.8, and he later added a third gold medal at cross-country with a silver in the team event, and set a world record of 8:36.9 in a heat of the 3000m team race. Kolehmainen had run his first marathon at the age of 17, and five of them at the age of 19, three on consecutive Saturdays. Apart from placing 4th in the 1917 Boston Marathon he did not run another until 1920, but that year he won the Olympic gold in an amateur world best time of 2:32:35.8.
In 1911 he won the AAA 4 miles and set a world record of 8:48.5 for 3000m. After World War I he added world records at long distances: twice at 25km to 1:25:20.0, and at 30km in 1:47:13.4, both in 1922. Two brothers also set world bests: Taavetti '**Tatu**' (1885-1967) with 1:07:40.2 at 20km (1913) and 1:26:32.6 at 25km (1915), and Wiljami '**Willie**' (1886-1967) with 2:29:39.2 for the marathon as a professional in the USA in 1912. Tatu had led for more than half of the 1912 Olympic marathon before dropping out.

Tommy KONO (USA)

WEIGHTLIFTING

Tommy Tamio Kono. b. 27 Jun 1930 Sacramento, California.

Pound for pound, Tommy Kono is probably the greatest lifter the United States has yet produced. Between 1953 and 1959 he was undefeated in world and Olympic competition, adding six successive world titles to his two Olympic gold medals in the 1952 lightweight class (67.5kg) and 1956 light-heavyweight (82.5kg). He also won gold medals in the Pan-American Games of 1955, 1959, and 1963. Kono was capable of lifting well at almost any bodyweight, as shown by his Olympic medals in three different classes (he also won a silver in the 1960 middleweight 75kg class). He is the only man ever to set world records in four different classes (26 in all: 2 at 67.5kg, 10 at 75kg, 12 at 82.5kg, 2 at 90kg), and won 11 AAU championships - at three different weights.

Ilsa KONRADS (Aus)

SWIMMING

Ilsa Konrads. b. 29 Mar 1944 Riga, Latvia.

She preceded her older brother John as a world record holder by just two days, with new bests for 800m and 880y on 9 Jan 1958 when she was aged 13. She set 12 world records in all, including 4:45.4 for 440y in 1960, four at 880y (also records for the shorter 800m) to 10:11.4 in 1959, and 19:25.7 for 1650y (also a record for 1500m and the first sub-20 minute time) in 1959. Ilsa won the Commonwealth title at 440y in 1958 to make her and John the first brother-sister individual champions in Games history, and won a silver at 440y in 1962. She suffered from nerves at major events, and at the Olympic Games in 1960 she gained a silver medal in the 4 x 100m relay but was a disappointing fourth at 400m, then the longest event for women. She also swam at the 1964 Games but did not reach a final.
Coached by John Talbot from the age of nine. Australian champion 220y 1963, 440y 1959, 1963; 880y 1958-60. She became a national magazine editor.

John KONRADS (Aus)

SWIMMING

John Konrads. b. 21 May 1942 Riga, Latvia.

In two years, 1958-60, John Konrads set 25 world records, as he and his sister Ilsa took the world of swimming by storm, John despite contracting polio as a child. At 200m he set three records to 2:02.2 (for 220y) in 1959, at 400m/440y four to 4:15.9(y) in 1960, at 800m/880y three from 9:17.7 in 1958 to 8:59.6 for 880y in 1959, and at 1500m two to 17:11.0 (for 1650y) in 1960. He improved his 220y best to 2:01.6 in 1960.

He was a triple gold medallist, 440y, 1650y and 4 x 200y, at the 1958 Commonwealth Games and won three Olympic medals in 1960: gold at 1500m, bronze at 400m and 4 x 200m. He had been a reserve for the 1956 Games and also made Australia's team in 1964, although then past his peak.

Australian champion at 110y 1959, 200m/220y and 400m/440y 1958-61, 1650y 1958-60. NCAA champion in 1963 at 1650y while at the University of Southern California.

The parents of John and Ilsa Konrads escaped from Latvia to Germany in 1944 and thence emigrated to Australia in 1949.

Raymond KOPA (Fra)

FOOTBALL

Raymond Kopaszewski. b. 13 Oct 1931 Noeux-les-Mine, Pas de Calais.

Acknowledged as the greatest French player until Platini, he was the son of a Polish miner and a French mother.

He began his career as a right-winger but later starred as a centre-forward. He started with US Noeux 1944-9 and SCO Angers 1949-51 before moving in 1951 to Reims, whom he helped to two French League titles, 1953 and 1955. A superb performance against Real Madrid in the 1956 European Cup Final prompted the Spanish club to sign him immediately. While he was with Real Madrid they won the European Cup three times 1957-9 and were twice Spanish League champions 1957-8. After his return to Reims the following season they again won the French League in 1960 and 1962.

A member of the French World Cup squad in 1954 and 1958, he won 45 caps (many as captain) between 1952 and 1962, scoring 17 goals, and was European Footballer of the Year in 1958. After his retirement in 1963 he became a successful businessman in Reims. In 1970 he became the first French footballer to be decorated with the Legion of Honour.

Lena KØPPEN (Den)

BADMINTON

Lena Køppen. b. 5 May 1973 Copenhagen.

The Danish dentist was the first women's singles world champion at badminton in 1977, also winning the mixed doubles with Steen Skovgaard. She went on to win European titles in 1978 and 1982 and was All-England singles champion in 1979 and 1980, having previously been beaten once in the final and five times in the semis in nine appearances. She won a record 25 Nordic titles, including the singles for nine successive years 1973-81, the women's doubles for 9 years in 10, and the mixed each year 1975-81.

A graceful and athletic player, and hugely popular in Denmark where she was featured on a Dkr. 2.70 stamp in 1983, she announced her retirement that year after surprise defeats in both the All-England and the World Championships.

Erland KOPS (Den)

BADMINTON

Erland Kops. né Olsen. b. 14 Jan 1937 Copenhagen.

The top badminton player of the early 1960s, winning seven men's singles titles at the All-England Championships, 1958, 1960-3, 1965 and 1967, and four at men's doubles, with Per Nielsen in 1958, and with Henning Borch 1967-9. He was US Open champion at singles in 1963, 1965 and 1967, and Nordic champion each year 1964-8.

He was a tireless retriever, with a powerful smash. He now runs restaurants in Copenhagen.

Olga KORBUT (USSR/Bls)

GYMNASTICS

Olga Valentinovna Korbut. b. 16 May 1955 Grodno.

This elfin (1.50m, 40kg) 17-year-old delighted the world with her displays of vivacity and originality at the 1972 Olympics, although she was only seventh overall after falling during a daring performance on the asymmetric bars. However, she went on to win gold medals on the beam and at floor exercises as well as on the Soviet team, although she was placed only second on the asymmetric bars to the dismay of the crowd. She had only come into the team as a reserve, but her fame was now assured.

Trained by Ronald Knysh and later by Yuriy Titov, she was the World Student Games champion in 1973 and was second overall at the 1973 Europeans and 1974 Worlds, winning the vault at the latter. She returned to the Olympics in 1976 as a member of the winning Soviet team, placing 5th overall and taking silver on the beam. She retired from competition in 1977, and then married rock singer Leonid Bortkevich; their son Richard was born in 1979. Olga taught gymnastics in the USSR, and moved with her family in 1991 to the USA where she now coaches and lives in Atlanta.

Viktor KORCHNOI (USSR)

CHESS

Viktor Lvovich Korchnoi. b. 23 Jul 1931 Leningrad.

A great defensive chess player, he achieved many major tournament victories and was beaten by Anatoliy Karpov for the world title in 1978 and 1981. He contested six further candidates tournaments 1962-85, placing second in 1968 and in 1974, when he just lost to Karpov who went on to become world champion.

He was USSR champion in 1960, 1962, 1964 and 1970, and after emigrating was Netherlands champion 1977 and Swiss 1982, 1984-5. For the USSR in six Olympiads he had 50 wins, 31 draws and just 3 losses.

Yuriy KOROLEV (USSR/Rus)

GYMNASTICS

Yuriy Korolev. b. 25 Aug 1962 Vladimir.

After winning the European Junior title in 1980 he had great success in 1981, when he was second in the Europeans, tied for the World Student Games title and won the overall World title. In all he won six individual gold medals at World Championships between 1981 and 1987, with another overall title in 1985. He was World Student Games champion in 1983 and shared the World Cup overall title with Li Ning in 1986.

Stefka KOSTADINOVA (Bul)

ATHLETICS

Stefka Georgieva Kostadinova. b. 25 Mar 1965 Plovdiv. Later Petrova.

She set world records for the high jump with 2.07 and 2.08m in 1986, and at 2.09 when she won the World title in Rome in 1987. She took the Olympic silver medal in 1988, and won the World Cup in 1985 and the European Cup in 1985 and 1987. A knee injury affected her form in 1989 and she broke a bone in her left foot when trying to return in 1990. She was 6th in the 1991 World Championships, but returned to consistent 2m-plus jumping in 1992, although she disappointed with only 1.94 for 4th in the Olympics.

Indoors she set three world bests in 1987-8 and was European Indoor champion in 1985, 1987 and 1988 and World Indoor champion in 1985, 1987, 1989 and 1993, the latter her 95th competition at two metres or higher indoors or out. A PE student, she married her coach Nikolai Petrov on 6 Nov 1989.

Rosemarie KOTHER (GDR)

SWIMMING

Rosemarie Kother. b. 27 Feb 1956 Schwerin. Later Gabriel.

A prolific world record breaker at the butterfly, stocky and powerful. She set three records in 1974 at 100m, two at the European Championships where she won triple gold, adding the 200m and the medley relay (GDR in a world record), and a further improvement to 61.88 against the USA a week later. At 200m she set six records, with her first two, 2:15.45 and 2:13.76, coming at the World Championships in 1973, when she took a second gold on the GDR medley relay team which set a world record and added a silver at 100m butterfly.

At the 1975 World Championships she swam her best time for 100m, 61.80, but was beaten by Kornelia Ender into second place. However, she again won gold medals at 200m and medley relay. On her return from these championships she married Rainer Gabriel.

In 1976 she improved her 200m record three times, with a best of 2:11.22, but at the Olympic Games she was third at 200m and only fifth at 100m, despite recording a time of 61.56. She was GDR champion at butterfly 100m 1972, 200m 1972-5.

Sandy KOUFAX (USA)

BASEBALL

Sanford Koufax. b. 30 Dec 1935 Brooklyn, New York.

Koufax had a brief, meteoric career as the top pitcher in baseball but it was enough for some experts to label him as the greatest left-hander ever. He pitched his entire 12-year career with the Brooklyn (later Los Angeles) Dodgers. Through 1960 he was known as the fastest pitcher but very wild. In 1961, however, he began to control his pitches and became almost unstoppable. In 1961-6 he won 129 games and posted an ERA of 2.20, and during his last five years his ERA was less than 2.00. This is even more impressive when one considers that in two of those six years, Koufax did not pitch a full season because of elbow problems, but he led the National League in strikeouts in all four of his full seasons, posting a major league record of 382 in 1965 (since broken). He retired after 1966 at the peak of his career (he won 27 games that year) because of an arthritic elbow condition. Cy Young Award winner 1963, 1965-6 and MVP 1963. World series MVP 1963 and 1965.

Career pitching 1955-66: ERA 2.76; W-L 165-87, SO 2396; Best seasons: 1966: 27-9, 317 SO, 1.73 SO; 1965: 26-8, 382 SO, 2.04 ERA; 1963: 25-5, 306 SO, 1.88 ERA.

Pál KOVÁCS (Hun)

FENCING

Pál Kovács. b. 17 Jul 1912 Debrecen.

Initially a hurdler of some promise, he became the Olympic individual sabre champion in 1952 after winning the bronze in 1948, and world champion in 1937 and 1953.

Noted for his calm approach, he was possibly the most highly rated of many fine sabre exponents during the years when the Hungarians were pre-eminent with this weapon. He was a member of the winning team at five successive Olympics (1936-60). In 1980 he became vice president of the international governing body, the FIE.

Alvin KRAENZLEIN (USA)

ATHLETICS

Alvin Kraenzlein. b. 12 Dec 1876 Milwaukee, Wisconsin, d. 6 Jan 1928 Wilkes Barre, Pennsylvania.

His feat of winning four gold medals at individual athletics events at the Olympic Games remains a record. In 1900 in Paris he won the 60m, 110m and 200m hurdles and long jump.

He was AAU champion at 220y hurdles 1897-9, 120yh 1898-9 and completed a treble with the long jump in 1899.

His straight-leg technique of taking a hurdle in a single stride revolutionised the event and he took the world records to 15 $^1/_5$ secs for 120y hurdles and 23 $^3/_5$ for 220y hurdles on a straight track in 1898. He also set five world records at the long jump from 7.29 to 7.43m at just two meetings, the Penn Relays and IC4A Championships in 1899.

He won eight IC4A titles in all in his three years at Pennsylvania 1898-1900. He graduated with a degree in dentistry, but did not practise and became a distinguished track coach, of German and Cuban teams as well as the University of Michigan.

Frank KRAMER (USA)

CYCLING

Frank Lewis Kramer. b. 20 Nov 1880 Evansville, Indiana, d. 8 Oct 1958 East Orange, New Jersey.

As a teenager, Frank Kramer contracted tuberculosis and his parents got him to take up cycling for his health. He became so good at it that he remains the greatest track sprinter ever produced in the United States and one of the world's greatest ever. He won only one world championship, when it was held in Newark, New Jersey in 1912, and would surely have won more but he travelled only rarely to Europe and competed in the event only one other time. Kramer did, however, win the Grand Prix de Paris in 1905 and 1906 and also won three six-day events. He was US pro sprint champion 1901-16, 1918 and 1921, having been amateur champion in 1899.

In the 1920s, when American cycling was in its heyday, Kramer was one of the best known athletes and was higher paid than any baseball player except Babe Ruth. He had a very long career, retiring on 26 Jul 1922 at age 42. The *New York Times* ran front-page stories about the event for three days. In his last race he equalled the world sprint record for one-sixth of a mile.

Ingrid KRAMER (GDR), see ENGEL

Jack KRAMER (USA)

TENNIS

John Albert Kramer. b. 1 Aug 1921 Las Vegas, Nevada.

The outstanding player in the immediate post-World War II era and a major figure in the development of professional tennis. As the 1939 Junior US doubles champion he made his Davis Cup début that year and progressed to win the US men's doubles in 1940 and 1941 with Ted Schroder, and the mixed doubles in 1941 with Sarah Palfrey Cooke. Although his career was interrupted by war service in the Navy, he won the doubles for a third time in 1943 (with Frank Parker). In 1946 he was the US singles champion and favourite to take the Wimbledon title but, playing with a badly blistered hand, he lost to Drobny in the 4th round, although he won the doubles with Tom Brown (USA). As he had announced that he would turn professional after winning the Wimbledon singles, this defeat delayed Kramer's entry into the paid ranks - but only for one year.

In 1947 he won the singles and the doubles (with Schroder) at the US Championships and at Wimbledon won both the singles, with a comprehensive 6-1, 6-3, 6-2 defeat of Tom Brown in the final, and the doubles with Bob Falkenburg. He helped the US to win the Davis Cup in 1946 and 1947 and in this competition from 1939-47 won all his six singles and 2 of 3 doubles. After turning professional in October 1947, he lost his first two matches to Bobby Riggs but then beat Pancho Gonzales 96-27 in an extended series of matches. Following his retirement in 1953 he became a tour promoter and ILTF executive. As a player his powerful serve-volley and concept of 'percentage tennis' took him to the top, and as an administrator and promoter his influence was immeasurable. He was executive director of the Association of Tennis Professionals 1972-5.

Jerry KRAMER (USA)

AMERICAN FOOTBALL

Gerald Louis Kramer. b. 23 Jan 1936 Jordan, Montana.

Considered by some as the greatest ever offensive guard in pro football history. He played collegiately at the University of Idaho and as a pro with the Green Bay Packers, whom he helped to win five NFL championships and the first two Super Bowl titles. He and Fuzzy Thurston teamed up to give the Packers a formidable guard duo who led the blocking on Green Bay's feared 'Power Sweep'. Kramer was one of the quickest offensive linemen ever. He was incredibly tough, surviving multiple operations, several of them life-threatening. He was also a place kicker for several years, played in three Pro Bowls and was a five-time All-Pro. He has authored four books about professional football and his own career.

Jarmila KRATOCHVILOVA (Cs)

ATHLETICS
Jarmila Kratochvílová. b. 26 Jan 1951 Golcuv Jenikov.

Kratochvílová was runner-up to Marita Koch at the 1980 Olympics and 1982 Europeans, but beat her in the 1981 World Cup 400m and, while Koch concentrated on the sprints, won an unprecedented double at 400m and 800m at the 1983 World Championships. There she broke Koch's world record by running 47.99 for 400m, while her 800m time of 1:54.68 was the third fastest ever. She had run a world record 1:53.28 just two weeks earlier.
The extremely powerful Czech followed that with an unusual double, 200m and 800m in the 1983 European Cup final. In 1985 she again won the European Cup 800m. In successive years from 1981 she was European Indoor champion three times at 400m and once at 200m.
She broke the national junior record for 400m in 1972, but was slowed by injuries and did not set her first national record until the age of 27 in 1978. She 'retired' in 1986, but came back to run well at 800m in 1987, when she was second in the European Cup and fifth in the World Championships.
Other bests: 100m 11.09 and 200m 21.97, both in 1981.

Barbara KRAUSE (GDR)

SWIMMING
Barbara Krause. b. 7 Jul 1959 Berlin.

Triple gold medallist at freestyle events at the 1980 Olympics, setting world records at 100m with 54.98 in her heat and 54.79 in the final, a time that was not beaten for six years, and at 4 x 100m, with an Olympic and European record 1:58.33 for 200m. She had set previous records for 100m, 55.41, and 200m, 1:59.04, in 1978 when she was world champion at 100m and silver medallist at 200m and both 4x100m relays.
She had to miss the 1976 Olympic Games through illness after winning the GDR 400m in a European record 4:11.69, which made her favourite for gold at that event.

Annichen KRINGSTAD (Nor/Swe)

ORIENTEERING
Annichen Kringstad. b. 15 Jul 1960 Oslo, Norway. Later Svensson 1983-4.

World champion in 1981, 1983 and 1985, the only woman to win the title three times, and also a member of the winning relay team in each of those years.
Norwegian born, she became a Swedish citizen, married a Swede and represented Sweden internationally. She was married briefly and competed then as Kringstad-Svensson, but after a divorce reverted to her maiden name.

Ingrid KRISTIANSEN (Nor)

ATHLETICS
Ingrid Kristiansen. née Christensen. b. 21 Mar 1956 Trondheim.

When she ran 5000m in 14:37.33 in Stockholm on 5 Aug 1986, Kristiansen became the only athlete to hold world records at 5000m, 10,000m and marathon. She is also the only athlete to have won world titles at track, road and cross-country.
She first achieved international prominence at cross-country skiing, placing 21st in the 1978 world championships, having won gold, silver and bronze medals as a member of the Norwegian team in the European Junior Championships in 1973-5. She had run in the 1971 European Championships at 15 when she was knocked down in the heats of the 1500m, but her first major successes were bronze medals in the World Championship 3000m in 1980 and European marathon in 1982. She won the Houston marathon in her fastest time just five months after giving birth to her son, Gaute, in August 1983 and went on to set a European best 2:24:26 in winning the 1984 London marathon and a world best there of 2:21:06 in 1985, although she was disappointed by her fourth place in the 1984 Olympic marathon. In 1986 she reached her peak form with superiority in distance-running unparalleled since the days of Emil Zátopek. She won her first gold medal, finishing the European 10,000m about half a

lap ahead of the runner-up, and set her third world record for 5000m, 14:37.33, and her second at 10,000m, with 30:13.74 at the Bislett Games in Oslo. All three of her world records remain unapproached seven years later.
In 1987 she won the World track 10,000m and in 1988 the World Cross-country title after third places in 1985 and 1987. She also won the World road 15km in 1987 and 1988. A bone fracture on the arch of her right foot caused her to drop out while leading the Olympic 10,000m in 1988. After her daughter Marte was born on 1 Aug 1990, she returned to place sixth in the 1991 Boston marathon. In all she has 14 major marathon wins including Stockholm 1980-2, Houston 1983-4, London 1984-5 and 1987-8; Boston 1986, 1989; Chicago 1986, New York 1989.
World road bests: 10km 30:45.7 (1986), 10 miles 50:37 (1987), 15km 47:16 (1987), half marathon 1:06:40 (1987). Other track bests: 1500m 4:05.97 (1986), 3000m 8:34.10 (1986).

Mikhail KRIVÓNOSOV (USSR/Bls)

ATHLETICS

Mikhail Petrovich Krivonosov. b. 1 May 1929 Krichev.

Krivonosov set seven world records for the hammer, including one unratified mark, from 63.34m in 1954 to win the European title to 67.32 in 1956, just prior to his Olympic silver medal behind Hal Connolly. The first of his 12 USSR records had been 59.18 in 1952. He won the European silver medal in 1958 and was the Universiade champion in 1955 and 1957 and the USSR champion in 1952 and each year 1954-8.

Rudi KROL (Hol)

FOOTBALL

Ruud Krol. b. 24 Mar 1949 Amsterdam.

An outstanding youngster, he made his début for Ajax at the age of 20 and stayed with them, playing a major rôle in their successes of the 1970s, until 1980 when after a short stay with Vancouver Whitecaps he signed for Napoli. He played 107 games for them before moving to Cannes in the French Second Division. After only ten league games for Ajax he was awarded his first international cap in November 1969. From then he played, mostly as a sweeper, in a record 83 internationals for Holland, overtaking the previous record of Puck van Heel in 1979. While coming to the end of his footballing career as captain of Ajax and Holland he was in great demand and pursued a variety of business ventures. After his retirement he became a coach, but a short stay in 1989 as manager of the Belgian club Mechelen was not successful.

Petra KRONBERGER (Aut)

ALPINE SKIING

Petra Kronberger. b. 21 Feb 1969 Pfarrwerfen, near Salzburg.

The overall World Cup winner in 1990, 1991 and 1992, she was the first woman ever to win World Cup races in all four disciplines: 6 downhill, 3 each giant slalom and slalom, 2 each super G and combined. She was world champion at downhill in 1991, but a bad fall in the Super G put her out of the rest of the championship. Having been sixth in the downhill at her first Olympic Games in 1988, she won gold medals at slalom and combined in 1992.
Quiet and shy, she won her first Europa Cup race just before her 18th birthday, followed by three Austrian junior titles. She won her first World Cup races at downhill in December 1989 and was speedily established as the world's best and a superb technician. She surprised the skiing world by declaring her retirement to return to studies in December 1992.

Roepie KRUIZE (Hol)

HOCKEY

Jan Hendrik Kruize. b. 17 Nov 1952 Heemstede, d. 14 Feb 1992 The Hague.

The leading figure in Dutch hockey in the immediate post-war years. A forward with Laren and HHIJC, The Hague, he scored 60 goals in 56 outdoor internationals 1946-54. He won an Olympic bronze medal in 1948 and a silver in 1952. His three sons each played at two Olympics, Ties (qv), Hans 1976 and 1984, and Jan Hidde 1984 and 1988.

Ties KRUIZE (Hol)

HOCKEY

Ties Kruize. b. 17 Nov 1952 The Hague.

The son of Roepie Kruize, he played in the Olympics of 1972 and 1984. Although he failed to gain an Olympic medal, he was the top scorer with 19 goals at the 1972 Games. He won gold with the Dutch team at the 1973 World Cup and 1983 European Championships. He was a penalty corner and stroke specialist with Klein Zwitserland, whom he helped to win the European Cup for Club Champions in 1979, and scored 167 goals in 202 outdoor internationals 1971-86. A serious car accident in 1975 in which he suffered a shattered upper leg surely cost him further international honours. Before the accident he played as a forward, but afterwards moved to defence. He worked as an insurance broker.

Elzbieta KRZESINSKA (Pol)

ATHLETICS

Elzbieta Krzesinska. née Dunska. b. 11 Nov 1934 Warsaw.

Twice a long jump medallist both at the Olympics (1st 1956 and 2nd 1960) and Europeans (2nd 1962 and 3rd 1954). She set four Polish long jump records, at 6.12m in 1954 and after 6.22 with two world records at 6.35 in 1956, the last when winning the Olympic title. She emerged internationally in 1952 when she was 12th in the Olympics and won the first of eight Polish long jump titles (the last in 1963). She was also Polish champion at 80m hurdles in 1957. With her husband Andrzej (pole vault) she became a notable coach.

Mike KRZYZEWSKI (USA)

BASKETBALL

Michael William Krzyszewski. b. 13 Feb 1947 Chicago, Illinois.

Krzyzewski (pronounced SHUH-shef-ski) has established himself as one of the great college basketball coaches in his tenure at Duke University. He played basketball himself at the US Military Academy (1969) under legendary coach Bob Knight. After serving five years in the Army, he resigned in 1974 as a captain and then served as an assistant coach with Knight at Indiana before his first head coaching position, 1976-80, at his alma mater. In 1980 he was appointed head coach at Duke University and he has since turned that school's basketball program into the finest in the country, with six appearances in the Final Four in seven years and five consecutively (1986, 1988-1992). This run was marked by Duke's first NCAA championships in 1991-2, the first time in 19 years that any college team had won in successive years. Krzyzewski was head coach of the US team at the 1987 World University Games and 1990 World Championships, and an assistant coach of the 1992 US Olympic basketball team.

Ferdi KUBLER (Swi)

CYCLING

Ferdinand Kubler. b. 24 Jul 1919 Adliswill.

The first Swiss rider to win the Tour de France (1950), he was also the points winner in that race in 1954. He was one of the most versatile riders ever, as he was Swiss champion in the pursuit and in cyclo-cross in addition to his road abilities. His pursuit ability manifested itself in making him a formidable road sprinter, but he was a good enough all-rounder to win four major stage races. Kubler was nicknamed 'The Swiss Cowboy' because of his penchant for wearing Stetson cowboy hats. In successive world road race championships, 1949-51, he was 2nd, 3rd and 1st.

Toni KUKOC (Cro)

BASKETBALL

Toni Kukoc. b. 18 Sep 1968 Split.

The 2.08m Croatian belies his size with point and shooting guard skills which have made him almost unrivalled in European leagues. He came to the fore with Split, with whom he won the Yugoslav title in 1988-91 and the European Champions'

Cup in 1989-91. He now plays in the Italian league with Benetton Treviso, whom he helped to win the national title in 1992 and to the final of the European Championship in 1993. He helped Yugoslavia win the European title in 1989 and 1991 and the World title in 1990. At the Olympic Games he won silver medals in 1988 for Yugoslavia and in 1992 for Croatia. In July 1993 he signed for the Chicago Bulls of the NFL.

Galina KULAKOVA (USSR)

NORDIC SKIING

Galina Alekseyevna Kulakova. b. 29 Apr 1942 Logachi, Udmurt.

The winner of a record nine world titles at cross-country skiing. Five were at individual events: 5km 1970 and 1974, 10km 1974 and the Olympic double in 1972; and four relays, 1970 and 1974 and Olympics 1972 and 1976. At the Olympics in addition to her four gold medals she won two silver and two bronze; her last in the 1980 relay was at 37 years 298 days, making her the oldest ever skiing medallist before Smetanina beat that record in 1992. In all she won 18 world or Olympic medals 1970-82 and was the winner of the first cross-country World Cup in 1979. She was a PE teacher.

Janina KURKOWSKA (Pol)

ARCHERY

Janina Kurkowska. né Spychajowa. b. 8 Feb 1901 Starosielce, d. 6 Jun 1979 in Sweden.

Kurkowska established herself as the greatest woman archer between the days of Lida Scott Howell and those of Kim Soo-nyung. She did this by winning the women's individual world championship a record seven times, 1931-4, 1936, 1939 and 1947. She was also a member of five Polish teams which won the women's team championship in 1933-4, 1936, 1938-9.

Bob KURLAND (USA)

BASKETBALL

Robert Albert Kurland. b. 23 Dec 1924 St Louis, Missouri.

Bob 'Foothills' Kurland was the first dominating seven-footer to play college basketball; so dominant, in fact, that he caused the rulemakers to outlaw goal-tending, because he could block almost every shot from going into the basket. In 1945 and 1946 he led his Oklahoma A&M team to the NCAA championship and then went on to play for six years with the Phillips 66ers, being named AAU all-America every year he played. While there he became the first man to play in two Olympic championship teams. He recalls his greatest athletic thrill as being selected to carry the US flag at the closing ceremonies of the 1952 Games, a thrill which he says still brings tears to his eyes. After the Games, Kurland joined Phillips Petroleum's marketing division and has moved up in the company to divisional manager of several offices, as well as having been sales manager of the Atlanta and Denver offices.

Aleksandr KURLOVICH (USSR/Bls)

WEIGHTLIFTING

Aleksandr Kurlovich. b. 28 Jul 1961 Grodno.

Kurlovich continued Soviet dominance of the unlimited class and claimed the title of world's strongest man by winning the super-heavyweight class at the 1988 Olympics and the 1989 Worlds. He first came to international prominence in 1983 when he was 2nd at the Europeans and Worlds to fellow Soviet, Anatoly Pisarenko. In 1984, he and Pisarenko were arrested at Mirabel Airport in Montreal when customs officials searched their luggage and found anabolic steroids. The two were convicted by Canadian authorities and fined. Soviet officials dismissed them from the national team and stripped them of their status as 'Masters of Sport', but Kurlovich returned to the team in 1987 and won the world title with a world record total of 472.5 kg.

Jari KURRI (Fin)

ICE HOCKEY

Jari Pekka Kurri. b. 18 May 1960 Helsinki.

After playing for Jokerit in Finland, Kurri

joined the Edmonton Oilers, where he played as a left wing with great effect alongside Wayne Gretzky. He was elected to the NHL All-Star team in 1985 and 1987 and played in five Stanley Cup teams. After playing for Milan in Italy 1990/1, he returned to play in the NHL for Los Angeles Kings, teaming up again with Gretzky.
NHL career - 909 games, 524 goals, 1190 points. Play-offs: 150 games, 93 goals, 205 points. Lady Byng Trophy 1985.

Janusz KUSOCINSKI (Pol)

ATHLETICS
Janusz Kusocinski. b. 15 Jan 1907 Warsaw, d. 12 Jun 1940 Palmiry, Warsaw.

In 1932 he became the first Polish male athlete to win an Olympic gold medal when he led from the start of the 10,000m and held off the challenge of Volmari Iso-Hollo (Fin) to clock the second fastest ever time of 30:11.4. Earlier that year he had set the first world record by a Polish man with 3000m in 8:18.8, and in all he set 23 Polish records from a 15:41.0 at 5000m in 1928 to 14:24.2 for 5000m in 1939. He showed his range of ability with the national title at 800m in 1:56.6 in 1932. At the 1934 Europeans he was 2nd at 5000m and 5th at 1500m (at which his best time was 3:54.0 in 1932). A great patriot, he was shot by the Gestapo for refusing to betray his colleagues in the Resistance.

Vladimir KUTS (USSR/Rus)

ATHLETICS
Vladimir Petrovich Kuts. b. 7 Feb 1927 Aleksino, Ukraine, d. 16 Aug 1975 of a heart attack.

Captured world imagination with his searing displays of distance running to capture the Olympic titles at 5000m and 10,000m in 1956.
He succeeded Emil Zátopek as world record holder at 5000m when he won the 1954 European title in 13:56.6. He lost the record to other athletes, but regained it three times with 13:51.2 in 1954, 13:46.8 in 1955 and 13:35.0 at Rome in 1957. He also set a world 10,000m record of 28:30.4 in Moscow in 1956 and recorded four world records or bests at 3 miles.
A graduate of the Leningrad Institute of Physical Culture, he participated at various sports, especially skiing, until he took part in, and won, his first cross-country race in 1948. He first entered the national championships in 1952 and emerged rapidly into world class in 1953 at the age of 26, when he won the first of four successive 5000m and 10,000m USSR doubles, with a further 5000m win in 1957.

Jackie KYLE (UK/Ire)

RUGBY UNION
John Wilson Kyle. b. 30 Jan 1926 Belfast.

First capped in 1947 while a medical student at Queen's University, Belfast he went on to play 46 times for Ireland and in six Tests for the British Lions on the 1950 tour of Australia and New Zealand. On his retirement in 1958 he was the world's most capped player and still enjoys the distinction of being Ireland's most capped fly-half. A notable feature of his international career was that in his 11 matches against Scotland, he was on the winning side each time.
A fly-half in the classic mould, he was a well-balanced, athletic player whose brilliant attacking skills were matched by his solid defence. On leaving the international rugby scene he became a doctor in Malaysia and later moved to Zimbabwe. Awarded the OBE.

Angel LABRUNA (Arg)

FOOTBALL
Angel Labruna. b. 26 Sep 1918, d. 19 Sep 1983.

After making his début for the River Plate first team in 1939 at the age of 21, he enjoyed a career of remarkable longevity and played in the 1958 World Cup Finals at the age of 40.
As a goalscoring inside-forward he was capped 36 times and scored 17 international goals. When it seemed that his international career was over, he was recalled, at the age of 37, for the 1955 South American Championships and

scored a hat-trick against Uruguay. For River Plate he scored almost 500 goals and won nine First Division Championship medals. After 20 years of First Division football with River Plate he moved to Platense when he was clearly past his best and later played briefly in Chile and Uruguay. When he finally retired he proved a successful coach with Platense and River Plate.

Michel LACHANCE (Can)

HARNESS RACING

Michel Lachance. b. 16 Dec 1950 St Augustine, Québec.

Lachance led the North American wins list at harness racing each year 1984-7. In 1986 he broke a record thought to be unbreakable, Hervé Filion's 637 winners in a year. He did not just break it, but went on to a massive total of 770 victories. Filion came back, however to improve even that mark in 1988 and 1989.
The son of a cattle farmer, Lachance was winning races at county fairs by the age of 12, and won his first major harness race at 17. Having topped the winners list he achieved his boyhood dream by driving *Goalie Jett* to win the sport's major prize, the Little Brown Jug, in 1989. A year earlier he achieved the all-time pacing record for 1 mile, driving *Matt's Scooter* to a time of 1:48 2/5.

Catherine LACOSTE (Fra)

GOLF

Catherine Lacoste. b. 27 Jun 1945 Paris. Later Mrs J. de Prado.

The daughter of René Lacoste (qv), the great French tennis player, she is easily the greatest woman golfer from continental Europe. In the 1960s only she and JoAnne Gunderson Carner among the amateurs could challenge the lady professionals. In 1967 Lacoste made history when she won the US Women's Open, but her greatest year was probably 1969 when she won the Amateur Championships of the US, Britain, France, and Spain. She was also French Open champion in 1967, 1970 and 1972, and Spanish in 1972 and 1976. She helped France to win the World Amateur Team title in 1964, and was the individual leader in 1964 and 1968. She was a strong player, known for her great length and powerful game.

René LACOSTE (Fra)

TENNIS

Jean René Lacoste. b. 2 Jul 1904, Paris.

An outstanding tactician and student of the game whose belief in the merits of the baseline game was partly forced on him by a delicate constitution which would not have withstood the rigours of an aggressive, attacking style.
One of the 'Four Musketeers', his controlled groundstrokes were equally effective on grass or hard courts and he won major titles on both surfaces. He won the singles championships of Wimbledon (1925, 1928), US (1926-7) and French (1925, 1927, 1929). With Jean Borotra he won the Wimbledon doubles in 1925 and the French title in 1925 and 1929.
Because of illness he was unable to defend his Wimbledon singles title in 1926 and although aged only 25, his poor health forced him to retire in 1929 when at his peak. The previous year he had played the last of his 26 Davis Cup ties in which he won 40 of his 51 rubbers. His greatest Davis Cup performance came in 1927 when he beat both Bill Tilden and Bill Johnston of the USA in crucial singles matches and France won the trophy for the first time.
His nickname was 'The Crocodile' and he used an embroidered crocodile on his world-renowned sports gear.

Marion LADEWIG (USA)

BOWLING

Marion Van Oosten Ladewig. b. 30 Oct 1914 Grand Rapids, Michigan.

In 1973 Ladewig was voted the greatest woman bowler of all time. She was voted bowler of the year nine times, 1950-4, 1957-9, and 1963. In 1950 she won the Women's International Bowling Congress (WIBC) all-events and team titles, and in 1955 the all-events and doubles. She was

US Open champion for the first six years of that tournament 1949-54, and won the BPAA All-Star title eight times and the World Invitational four times. She was voted the greatest female athlete in Michigan history.

Guy LAFLEUR (Can)

ICE HOCKEY

Guy Damien Lafleur. b. 20 Sep 1951 Thurso, Québec.

Lafleur starred as a right wing for 12 years (1971-83) with the Montreal Canadiens, helping them to win five Stanley Cup titles. He then retired, but could not stay away, returning in 1988 to play for the New York Rangers for three years, providing solid though less spectacular play than early in his career.
He was not large by NHL standards but was a graceful and powerful skater who was also blessed with an accurate shot. For six straight years, 1975-80, he scored 50 or more goals in each season, with a peak of 60 in 1977/8.
NHL career 1971-91 - 1126 games, 560 goals, 1353 points. Play-offs: 128 games, 58 goals, 134 assists. Hart Trophy 1977-8, Ross Trophy 1976-8, Smythe Trophy 1977, Lester Pearson Award 1976-8.

Napoleon LAJOIE (USA)

BASEBALL

Napoleon Lajoie. b. 5 Sep 1874 Woonsocket, Rhode Island, d. 7 Feb 1959 Daytona Beach, Florida.

One of the great hitters of baseball's early era, Lajoie played mostly second base with the Philadelphia Athletics 1896-1902 and then the Cleveland Indians, whom he also managed 1905-9. His .426 batting average in 1901 still stands as a National League record and is the top mark ever in the 20th century. He led the American League in hitting four times.
Career batting 1896-1916: 3251 hits Avg. .338, HR 83; SB 381. Other top seasons: 1899: .378; 1910: .384; 1904: .376; 1902: .378.

Jim LAKER (UK)

CRICKET

James Charles Laker. b. 9 Feb 1922 Frizinghall, Bradford, Yorkshire, d. 23 Apr 1986 Putney, London.

Laker's peak as a great off-spin bowler undoubtedly came in the 1956 Test series against Australia when he took 46 wickets in the series at an average of 9.60. In an astonishing display in the 4th Test at Old Trafford in July he took 9-37 and 10-53, figures all the more amazing for the fact that his Surrey spin partner Tony Lock bowled 69 overs in the match for just one wicket. This is the only instance of more than 17 wickets in a first-class match and the only instance of all ten wickets in a Test innings. Laker had also taken 10-88 for Surrey against the Australians earlier in the season. He had first played for England on the 1948 tour to the West Indies, and had taken 18 wickets in the Tests, but he played curiously little for England over the next 4 or 5 years, even though he took 8 wickets for 2 runs in a Test Trial in 1950. For Surrey he was a vital member of their matchless championship winning teams of 1952-8, and after his retirement in 1959 came back to play for Essex 1962-4. Tall and strong, he had a model action and was a master of his craft. He was also a useful lower-order batsman. Although his 1960 autobiography *Over to Me* caused ill-feeling, he became a much respected TV commentator.
46 Tests 1948-59: 676 runs at 14.08, HS 63; 193 wickets at 21.24, BB 10-53; 12 catches.
First-class 1946-65: 7304 runs at 16.60, 2 100s HS 113; 1944 wickets at 18.41, BB 10-53; 270 catches.

Allan LAMB (UK)

CRICKET

Allan Joseph Lamb. b. 20 Jun 1954 Langebaanweg, Cape Province, South Africa.

Lamb made his first-class début for Western Province in 1972/3 and came to England to play with Northamptonshire in 1978, becoming their county captain in

1989. With British parents, he qualified to play for England and made his Test début in 1982. He established himself as a determined middle-order batsman, whose pugnacious attack turned the course of many matches and was particularly effective in one-day internationals. He captained England in 3 Tests.
79 Tests 1982-92: 4656 runs at 36.09, 14 100s HS 142; 75 catches.
122 One-day Ints: 4010 runs at 39.31, 4 100s HS 118; 31 catches.
First-class 1972-92: 28,495 runs at 48.87, 79 100s HS 294; 320 catches.

Curly LAMBEAU (USA)

AMERICAN FOOTBALL
Earl Louis Lambeau. b. 9 Apr 1898 Green Bay, Wisconsin, d. 1 Jun 1965 Sturgeon Bay, Wisconsin.

Though not nearly as well-known today as the next great Green Bay Packers coach, Vince Lombardi, Curly Lambeau won more NFL championships as a coach than any man in league history, with those of 1929-31, 1936, 1939, and 1944. The three consecutive wins in 1929-31 is a feat matched only by Lombardi's Packers of 1965-7. Lambeau played one year of college football in 1918 at Notre Dame under Knute Rockne and in 1919 helped start the semi-pro Green Bay Packers football team, helped by support from the Indian Packing Company. The Packers entered the American Professional Football Association, the forerunner of the NFL, in 1921 and Lambeau coached them until 1949. The Packers home field was named after him, Lambeau Stadium. He also coached the Chicago Cardinals 1950-1 and Washington Redskins 1952-3. His career NFL record as a coach was 236-111-23.

Jack LAMBERT (USA)

AMERICAN FOOTBALL
John Harold Lambert. b. 8 Jul 1952 Mantua, Ohio.

After starring at Kent State as a middle linebacker, in 1974 he began an 11-year NFL career which was spent entirely with the Pittsburgh Steelers, who became the top team in pro football as Lambert led their legendary defense, the Steel Curtain. He was named to the Pro Bowl for nine consecutive seasons, a record at the time. He led the Steelers in tackles every year 1974-83 and played for four Super Bowl winning teams. Very small for a pro middle linebacker at only 100 kg *220 lb*, but he was incredibly tough.

Jean-François LAMOUR (Fra)

FENCING
Jean-François Lamour. b. 2 Feb 1956 Paris.

Olympic champion at the sabre in 1984 and 1988 and world champion in 1987. He prepared carefully for a third Olympics in 1992, achieving his first World Cup win since 1988 in the spring, but had to settle for bronze medals in both individual and team events in Barcelona. He also won an Olympic silver medal with the French sabre team in 1984 and was twelve times French champion, 1977-8, 1980-4, 1987-9, 1991-2. A physiotherapist by profession.

Kim LAMPARD (Aus)

WATER SKIING
Kim Lampard.

The greatest ever women's barefoot skier, world champion in 1980, 1982, 1985, and 1986 in her only four attempts at the championships. Her name has become synonymous with good sportsmanship and a dedicated approach to her sport. She grew up in a family of avid waterskiers and began barefoot skiing when only five. She retired in 1987 after winning the Masters title.

Kenesaw LANDIS (USA)

BASEBALL
Kenesaw Mountain Landis. b. 20 Nov 1866 Millville, Ohio, d. 25 Nov 1944 Chicago, Illinois.

Judge Landis was the first great commissioner in professional sports. He received a degree from Union Law School in Chicago in 1891 and in 1905 was named a federal judge by President Theodore Roosevelt. In

1919 the Chicago Black Sox scandal hit baseball, as several members of that team were accused (though never convicted) of throwing the World Series. Landis was named commissioner in 1920 and helped restore public confidence in baseball by his strict handling of the office, which he held until his death in 1944. He banned several players for life for consorting with gamblers.

Bernd LANDVOIGT (GDR)

Jörg LANDVOIGT (GDR)

ROWING

Bernd and Jörg Landvoigt. b. 23 Mar 1951 Brandenburg.

The Landvoigt twins competed in the 1972 Olympics in the eights, winning a bronze medal; they then formed a coxless pair, and were never beaten in that event. They won Olympic gold medals in 1976 and 1980, and were world champions in 1974-5 and 1978-9. Bernd is the younger of the twins by a few minutes. Jörg also rowed with the winning GDR eight at the 1973 European Championships.

John LANDY (Aus)

ATHLETICS

John Michael Landy. b. 12 Apr 1930 Hawthorn, Victoria.

Landy is best known for his second place to Roger Bannister, 3:59.6 to 3:58.8, in the 'Race of the Century' at the 1954 Empire Games, when they ran the third and fourth sub-four minute miles ever. Coached by Percy Cerutty, Landy ran at the 1952 Olympics at 1500m and 5000m but showed great improvement after that when in December he reduced his best mile from 4:10.0 to 4:02.1. There followed a series of 4:02 times, but Bannister beat him to be the first sub-four man, before Landy took the world record with 3:57.9, and a 1500m record at 3:41.9 en route, at Turku on 21 Jun 1954.

He retired from competition in 1955 but came back in 1956 to take the 1500m bronze medal at the Melbourne Olympics, where he took the oath on behalf of the athletes. Known as a gentleman on the track, he once stopped to help Ron Clarke to his feet, having accidentally tripped him in an Australian 1500m; Landy lost 50m on the leaders, but caught them and won. He was also a good Australian Rules footballer while studying agricultural sciences at Melbourne University, and he became a schoolteacher. Australian champion 880y 1953, 1 mile 1953-4 and 1956, 3 miles 1956.

Dick LANE (USA)

AMERICAN FOOTBALL

Richard 'Night Train' Lane. b. 16 Apr 1928 Austin, Texas.

Considered one of the greatest defensive backs in pro football history. He played college ball at Scottsbluff Junior College before serving four years in the US Army. He played in the NFL for Los Angeles Rams 1952-3, Chicago Cardinals 1954-9 and Detroit Lions 1960-5. Lane played in six Pro Bowls and was a five-time All-Pro, and he led the NFL in interceptions in 1952 and 1954, setting a still-standing NFL record with 14 interceptions in his rookie season of 1952. In 1970 he was named by sportswriters as the top NFL cornerback of all-time and Vince Lombardi called him the greatest he had ever seen. Lane was married to the famous blues singer Dinah Washington until her death.

Freddy LANE (Aus)

SWIMMING

Frederick Claude Vivian Lane. b. 2 Feb 1880 Sydney, d. 14 May 1969 Avalon.

The only Australian swimmer at the 1900 Olympics, he won the 200m and 200m obstacle race gold medals. He used a double over-arm stroke which was considered too strenuous for long distances, but Lane showed that to be false when he won the New South Wales 1 mile title. He took up swimming at the age of four after he was saved by his father from drowning in Sydney Harbour, and became the first man to swim 100 yards in less than a minute when he recorded 59.6 at Leicester in

October 1902, also setting a world record for 220y with 2:28.6 that year.
Australian champion at 100y 1898, 1902, and 220y 1902, he was also ASA champion in England at 100y 1902, 220y 1899, 1900 and 1902, 440y 1899.
Lane became a master printer, a partner in a printing and stationery company in Sydney.

Hermann LANG (Ger)

MOTOR RACING

Hermann Lang. b. 6 Apr 1909 Stuttgart, d. 19 Oct 1987 Stuttgart.

He was apprenticed to a motorcycle mechanic in 1923 and raced motorcycles from 1928, before joining Mercedes as a mechanic. He built a reputation as a fearless rider and was German hill-climb champion in 1931. He eventually got his chance to race cars in 1935 and was a full-time driver from 1936. He won his first Grand Prix at Tripoli in 1937 (winning this race again in 1938 and 1939), and reached his peak in 1939 when he won seven major races and was European champion. That year he was also European Mountain champion. He came back to racing after the War, with his greatest success a win in the Le Mans 24-hours with Karl Riess in 1952. He retired in 1954 and was then a service inspector for 20 years.

Thomas LANGE (GDR/Ger)

ROWING

Thomas Lange. b. 27 Feb 1964 Eisleben.

Champion single sculler who won the Olympic gold medal in 1988 and 1992, the World title in 1987, 1989 and 1991, and the World Cup in 1992. At double sculls he was World champion in 1983 and 1985 with Uwe Heppner, and was second in 1990. He first came to the fore by winning the World Junior single sculls in 1981 and 1982. GDR champion at single sculls 1987-8, German champion 1991-2, after winning GDR titles at double sculls 1983, 1985-6 and quad sculls 1984. In 1993 he won the Diamond Sculls at Henley. A medical student, he was coached at SV Halle by Lothar Trawiel.

Bernhard LANGER (Ger)

GOLF

Bernhard Langer. b. 27 Aug 1957 Anhausen, Bavaria.

The greatest German golfer ever, he is known as an extremely long hitter but one who is very accurate. His only shortcoming has been his putting, as early in his career he was unable to win because he suffered from the 'yips'. He overcame this by switching to a cross-handed style, helping him to finish second in the British Open in 1981 and 1984, and third in 1985-6, and to win the Masters in 1985. Surprisingly it was not until 1993, with a second Masters victory, that he won another major. He followed that with a fine third place in the British Open.
Langer turned professional in 1972 and has played on six Ryder Cup teams for Europe, 1981-91, with a record of won 11, lost 9, halved 5, and at seven World Cups for Germany. He has won the German Open five times. The leading money-winner in 1981 and 1984, his career European tour earnings are £2,796,004 with 27 wins 1976-92. To that he has added $1,585,247 from the US PGA tour.

Graeme LANGLANDS (Aus)

RUGBY LEAGUE

Graeme Frank Langlands. b. 2 Oct 1941.

At 1.83m *6 ft* and 78 kg *12 st 4 lb* he possessed the ideal build for either a centre or a full back and played with distinction in both positions. Learning the game in remote Wollongong, he joined the St George club in Sydney and was chosen to represent New South Wales in his first top class season, 1962. The following year he made the first of his 34 appearances for Australia 1963-75 and went on to set numerous records at international level. With 104 points he is Australia's top scorer against Great Britain and his 20 points in a match remained a record until beaten by Michael O'Connor. He is the only man to have played in six series against Great Britain and although he captained Australia in four Tests, further captaincy honours were denied him when a hand injury curtailed his appearances during the 1973 tour of Britain. After his retirement in 1976 he stayed in the game as coach to club and country.

Bob LANIER (USA)

BASKETBALL

Robert Jerry Lanier, Jr. b. 10 Sep 1948 Buffalo, New York.

After college basketball at St Bonaventure's, the 2.11m *6' 11"* center played for 14 years in the NBA, mostly with the Detroit Pistons, although he played his last four years with the Milwaukee Bucks. He played in eight All-Star Games, scored 19,248 points (av. 20.1), hauled in 9,000 rebounds and recorded 3,000 assists during his career. He was also known for having the largest feet in pro basketball, as he wore size 19 shoes.

Willie LANIER (USA)

AMERICAN FOOTBALL

Willie Edward Lanier. b. 21 Aug 1945 Clover, Virginia.

Lanier played as a middle linebacker at Morgan State and with the Kansas City Chiefs as a pro 1967-77, becoming the first black player to star at that position. He helped the Chiefs to one Super Bowl title (1970) and three AFL/AFC championships, played in five Pro Bowls and was a four-time All-Pro. Nicknamed 'Honeybear', he was quick enough to cover receivers and strong enough to be a formidable pass rusher. After his football retirement he became a mortgage banker.

Octave LAPIZE (Fra)

CYCLING

Octave Lapize. b. 20 Oct 1887, d. 14 Jul 1917.

One of the very few early greats of professional cycling also to have competed in the Olympics, he won a bronze medal in the 100 kilometre track race in 1908. He is still heralded as the only person to have won Paris-Roubaix, 'The Hell of the North', three consecutive times (1909-11). He was also the winner of the Tour de France in 1910, Paris-Brussels 1911-13 and Paris-Tours 1911. Lapize was killed in a dogfight during World War I.

Bob LaPOINT (USA)

WATER SKIING

Bob LaPoint. b. 25 May 1955 Castro Valley, California.

A slalom specialist, considered the greatest ever at his event. His first titles came in 1971-2 when he won the US Boys slalom. In 1975 he was the Masters slalom champion and he won the world championship in 1977, 1979, 1983, 1985 and 1987. He won ten US national championships (including jumping in 1980) and has set four official world slalom records.

Steve LARGENT (USA)

AMERICAN FOOTBALL

Steven M Largent. b. 28 Sep 1954 Tulsa, Oklahoma.

In his 14 years in the NFL with the Seattle Seahawks he set career records for 819 catches and 13,089 yards gained receiving. He caught a pass in 177 consecutive NFL games to set another record. As a wide receiver, he was neither fast nor big but he had exceptional hands and ran precise patterns. He was a six-time All-Pro who had played collegiately for Tulsa University.
NFL career 1976-89: 13,089 yards gained receiving av. 16.0, 100 touchdowns.

Bill LARNED (USA)

TENNIS

William Augustus Larned. b. 30 Dec 1872 Summit, New Jersey, d. 16 Dec 1926 New York.

Ranked among the top six Americans for 19 years (1892-1911), he won the US singles seven times (1901-02, 1907-11). He is the oldest-ever winner of the US title, aged 38 years 242 days at the time of his last victory.
While at Cornell University he won the 1892 Inter-Collegiate singles and from the

start of his career he showed little interest in doubles play. Although he took part in eight Davis Cup ties (1902-11) he played exclusively in the singles, winning 9 of his 14 rubbers. Very occasionally he entered for the doubles at the major tournaments, his best performances being to reach the Wimbledon semi-finals in 1905 and the final of the US Championships in 1907 with William Clothier as his partner on both occasions.

As a wealthy bachelor he had the means to indulge his passion for outdoor sports. He captained the champion ice hockey team of New York, was an accomplished golfer, an excellent rifle shot and a Master of Hounds. He was a member of the executive committee of the USLTA (1899-1916) and served in Cuba with the Rough Riders during the Spanish-American war. During World War I he was head of Air Force personnel in England. Ill health forced him to resign his seat on the New York Stock Exchange in 1922 and after enduring partial paralysis caused by spinal meningitis he took his own life while at the Knickerbocker Club, New York.

Bent LARSEN (Den)

CHESS

Jørgen Bent Larsen. b. 4 Mar 1935 Tilsted, Jutland.

An aggressive chess player, he was one of the few Western players to be able to challenge the might of the Soviet Union. He was three times a semi-finalist in the Candidates tournament and won the Danish title each time he contested it, in 1954-6, 1959, 1963-4. He reached international master status in 1955 and grandmaster a year later. He then abandoned his civil engineering studies and through to the 1980s won a large number of major tournaments.

Don LARSEN (USA)

BASEBALL

Don James Larsen. b. 7 Aug 1929 Michigan City, Indiana.

Larsen was only an average major league pitcher, and his fame rests on one game. For the New York Yankees on 8 Oct 1956 Larsen pitched the only no-hitter in World Series history and, in addition, it was a perfect game. He pitched for eight different teams, never winning more than 11 games in a single season.

Career pitching 1953-67: ERA 3.78; W-L 81-91, % .471, SO 849.

Gunnar LARSSON (Swe)

SWIMMING

Karl Gunnar Larsson. b. 12 May 1951 Malmö.

A versatile swimmer who won the Olympic gold at both 200m and 400m medley in 1972, the former in a world record 2:07.17 and the latter in 4:31.981, just 0.002 ahead of Tim McKee.

He did not make any individual finals at the 1968 Olympics, but after going to university in the USA at Long Beach, he made a great impact with three gold medals at the 1970 European Championships. Then he won both 400m freestyle and 200m medley in world records of 4:02.6 and 2:09.3, with a European record 4:36.2 at 400m medley and a silver medal at 200m freestyle. He closed his career with the 1973 world title at 200m medley. He won 32 Swedish titles, at freestyle, backstroke, medley and lifesaving, and also set Swedish records at 100m and 200m breaststroke.

Harold LARWOOD (UK)

CRICKET

Harold Larwood. b. 14 Nov 1904 Nuncargate, Nottinghamshire.

The scourge of Australia on the 'Bodyline' tour of 1932/3. His hostile fast bowling, 33 wickets at 19.51, did much to win the series for England. Ridiculously he was made the scapegoat for the controversy that the bodyline form of attack generated, and he never again played for England. His innings of 98 in 135 minutes in his last Test was at the time the highest ever by a 'night-watchman'. Although of only medium height (1.72m *5'8"*), he generated intense pace, with his superb action and long arms. In 1950 he sold his confec-

tionery shop in Blackpool and emigrated to Australia. In 1993 he was belatedly awarded the MBE, a fitting reward, no doubt influenced by a cricket-loving Prime Minister.
21 Tests 1926-33: 485 runs at 19.40, HS 98; 178 wickets at 28.41, BB 6-32; 15 catches.
First-class 1924-38: 7290 runs at 19.91, 3 100s HS 102; 1427 wickets at 17.51, BB 9-41; 234 catches.*

Yale LARY (USA)

AMERICAN FOOTBALL
Robert Yale Lary, Sr. b. 24 Nov 1930 Fort Worth, Texas.

After graduating from Texas A & M in 1952, Lary played 11 years in the NFL with the Detroit Lions, missing the 1954-5 seasons while serving in the military. He was an outstanding defensive back in the pro game but he was known as much for his punting, at which his lifetime career average of 44.3 yards ranks second only to Sammy Baugh, and he led the NFL in punting three times. He also returned punts for the Lions. While playing professional football, Lary also had a career in politics, serving two terms in the Texas State Legislature. He later opened an investment business in the Fort Worth area.

Emanuel LASKER (Ger)

CHESS
Emanuel Lasker. b. 24 Dec 1868 Berlingchen (now Barlinek), Prussia. d. 11 Jan 1941 New York, USA.

World chess champion from 1894, when he beat Steinitz, to 1921, when he lost to Capablanca. For much of that time he was a class above the rest of the world's best and he remained a major force in the game until the age of 67, an unprecedented length of top-class career.
During his long reign as champion he took time out to gain a doctorate for research into algebraic solutions in 1902. He raised the financial rewards available for chess players by demanding high fees.

Peter LATHAM (UK)

RACKETS and REAL TENNIS
Peter Walker Latham. b. 18 May 1865, Manchester, d. 27 Nov 1953 Chiswick, London.

The only man to hold the world title for rackets and real tennis simultaneously, and the leading player of court games in the latter part of the 19th century. He first challenged for the world rackets title in 1887 beating the reigning champion, Joseph Gray, and after defeating four challengers he resigned the title in 1902.
In 1895 he successfully challenged Charles Saunders for the world real tennis title and retained it against challenges from Tom Petitt (USA) in 1898 and 'Punch' Fairs in 1904. The following year, Fairs was successful in his challenge and this was the only championship match that Latham ever lost at either game. In 1907 he recaptured the title from Fairs. Beginning his career as an 11-year-old at the Manchester Racquet Club, Latham went on to become head professional at Queen's Club in 1888. In 1901 he accepted a post as the private professional to Sir Charles Rose but in 1916 returned to Queen's, where he taught many future champions.
Although Jock Soutar at rackets and Jay Gould at real tennis might be rated his equal in their individual fields, no player in history could match his skills at both games.

Grzegorz LATO (Pol)

FOOTBALL
Grzegorz Lato. b. 8 April 1950 Malborkx.

Scorer of the winning goal in the third-place match against Brazil in the 1974 World Cup, with a total of seven goals he was the leading scorer in the finals. He helped Stal Mielec to two Polish League titles (1973, 1976) and he scored 45 goals in 104 international matches 1971-84. As his career was drawing to a close he played in Belgium, Mexico and Canada. A speedy winger with great acceleration, he was one of the major contributors to the attractive football played by the Polish team in the 1970s. Now the trainer of Stal Mielec.

Larisa LATYNINA (USSR/Ukr)

GYMNASTICS

Larisa Semyonovna Latynina. née Diriy. b. 27 Dec 1934 Kherson.

The graceful Latynina won 18 Olympic medals, the record for any sport, nine gold, five silver and four bronze, and also won the greatest number of World and Olympic gymnastics gold medals with 12 individual and five team between 1956 and 1964. She took team gold with the USSR and gold at the floor exercises at each of her three Olympics and was all-around champion in 1956 and 1960 before placing second to Vera Cáslavská in 1964.

Trained as a ballet dancer from the age of 11, Latynina was national schools champion at 16 and reached her peak when she won all five individual titles at the first European Championships in 1957 and all but the floor exercises at the 1958 Worlds. She missed the 1959 Europeans through pregnancy, but won further golds at all-around and floor exercises at both the 1961 Europeans and 1962 Worlds to take her overall World medal collection to five individual and three team golds, with four silver and a bronze between 1954 amd 1966.

Later a Soviet team coach, she helped in the organisation of the 1980 Olympics and now works on the Moscow sports committee.

Niki LAUDA (Aut)

MOTOR RACING

Nikolaus Andreas Lauda. b. 22 Feb 1949 Vienna.

The most complete racing driver of his era, he was world champion in 1975, 1977 and 1984. He drove for March 1971-2, BRM 1973, Ferrari 1974-7, Brabham 1978-9, McLaren 1982-5, winning 25 Grand Prix races, earning a record 420.5 points from 171 starts. He had a horrifying accident at the Nürburgring in the 1976 German Grand Prix, but made an amazing comeback, after being on the critical list suffering from severe burns and lung damage, to race again six weeks later and place fourth at Monza. He only lost the world title that year by one point to James Hunt.

He started his racing career at hill-climbing in 1968, and his natural talent soon took him to the top, racing at Formula Vee in 1969, Formula 3 in 1970 and Formula 2 in 1971. He scored his first World Championship point in 1973 and his first win came the next year in the Spanish GP after he had joined Ferrari. During retirement in 1980-1 he created Lauda Air, now the second largest Austrian aviation company, but returned for four more years in Formula One.

Slightly built, his success at first seemed to be resented, but his smooth, meticulous, unspectacular driving soon earned respect.

Rod LAVER (Aus)

TENNIS

Rodney George Laver. b. 9 Aug 1938 Rockhampton, Queensland.

The only player to win the Grand Slam twice, first as an amateur in 1962 and again as a professional in 1969. The greatest ever left-hander, he was undefeated in singles at four successive Wimbledons. After winning the title in 1961 and 1962 he was banned as a professional for five years but returned to win the first two Open Championships in 1968-9. Apart from his four wins at Wimbledon he won the Australian (1960, 1962, 1969), French (1962, 1969) and US (1962, 1969) titles. His greatest year was 1962 when he won every major tournament he entered and took the Italian and German as well as the four Grand Slam titles. Laver also won nine major doubles titles, six men's and three mixed.

He was Australian junior champion in 1957 and a Davis Cup player from 1959 to 1962, being recalled to the team after a 10-year absence in 1973 when he won all six of his matches in the inter-zone semi-final against Czechoslovakia and in the final against the USA. In 24 Davis Cup rubbers he won all four of his doubles matches and lost only 4 of his 20 singles.

A hard-hitting, agile player, he had a delicate touch at the net and employed heavy top-spin on his attacking shots. In the opinion of many respected authorities he is the finest player of all-time.

Denis LAW (UK)

FOOTBALL

Denis Law. b. 24 Feb 1940 Aberdeen

One of the greatest inside-forwards of the post-war era. After signing amateur forms for Huddersfield in 1955, he turned professional two years later and then moved to Manchester City in 1960. After little more than a year he went to Torino but he did not settle in Italy and quickly returned to join Manchester United, with whom he won an FA Cup winners medal 1963 and Football League championship medals in 1965 and 1967. He was voted European Footballer of the Year in 1964.

He made his international début at the age of 18, when he was still with Huddersfield, and went on to win 55 caps for Scotland before retiring after the 1974 World Cup finals. A deadly shot when the ball was on the ground, he also scored many goals with soaring headers despite being only 5'9" *1.75m* tall. After his golden years at Manchester United, Denis Law returned to Manchester City for one final season after which he developed a career as a radio and TV commentator.

Bill LAWRY (Aus)

CRICKET

William Morris Lawry. b. 11 Feb 1937 Thornbury, Melbourne.

Lawry had great success on his first overseas tour to England in 1961, when he scored 2019 runs, including 429 runs at 52.50 in his first Test series. In the following year he was appointed captain of Victoria, a job he handled for ten years, and during all that time he was a stalwart of the Australian team, which he captained in his last 25 Tests from 1967 until he was sacked in favour of Ian Chappell in 1971. A tall and slender left-handed opener, he tended towards dourness but was a most dependable and patient batsman. He formed a particularly effective opening partnership with Bob Simpson and together they made nine century partnerships for Australia in Tests. He has been a regular member of the Channel 9 TV commentary team.

67 Tests 1961-71: 5234 runs at 47.15, 13 100s HS 210; 30 catches.
1 One-day Int: 27 runs; 1 catch.
First-class 1955-71: 18,734 runs at 50.90, 50 100s HS 266; 5 wickets at 37.60; 121 catches.

Aub LAWSON (Aus)

SPEEDWAY

Aubrey Lawson. b. 1916 Warialda, NSW, d. 21 Jan 1977 Western Australia.

One of the group of outstanding Australian riders who made a major contribution to the development of the sport in Britain. He began racing in Australia in 1937 and came to England two years later to join Wembley. He reached the World Championship final in 1939 but the event was abandoned due to the outbreak of war, and although he reached nine post-war finals (scoring 73 points) he never succeeded in winning the title, third in 1958 being his best placing. In 1947 he left Wembley for West Ham but moved to Norwich in 1954 when they were promoted to the First Division. He scored a record 680 points in a record 84 Test matches and was Australian champion five times, 1949-50, 1953-5. He made a comeback, aged 49, to win the 1963 NSW Championship and was a promoter at the Westland circuit in Sydney before retiring to a farm near Northam in Western Australia.

Eddie LAWSON (USA)

MOTOR CYCLING

Eddie Lawson. b. 11 Mar 1958 Upland, California.

The most successful US rider ever in World Championship motorcycling. His first major championship was the USA Western Region 750cc title in 1978 and he was the 1981 and 1982 USA Superbike champion riding Kawasaki bikes. His first Grand Prix race was on a Kawasaki at 250cc in 1981 and his first win was at 500cc on a Yamaha in 1984. From that point he was the supreme 500cc rider of the 1980s, world champion in 1984, 1986, 1988 and 1989, second in 1985 and third

in 1987, with 31 Grand Prix victories 1984-92. He rode for Yamaha 1983-8 and 1990, when he missed much of the season through injury, for Honda 1989 and Cagiva 1991-2. He achieved Cagiva's first ever GP win in Hungary 1992. He tried motor racing in 1993.
A shy man, but a cool and stylish rider and a great enthusiast for the sport.

Tommy LAWTON (UK)

FOOTBALL
Thomas Lawton. b. 6 Oct 1919 Bolton, Lancashire.

A strongly built centre-forward whose powerful shooting and strength in the air proved invaluable to the Everton and England attack. He signed as a professional for Burnley on his 17th birthday and four days later became the youngest player ever to score a hat-trick in the Football League. After only three months he moved to Everton where he took over from the legendary Dixie Dean, and in the last two pre-war seasons Lawton was the top scorer in the First Division, winning a League Championship medal in 1939.
During the war he appeared as a guest for a variety of clubs and played in 15 wartime 'Internationals'. He signed for Chelsea in 1945 for the first post-war season and moved to Notts County two years later. He won the last four of his international caps while playing for the Division III side. He had earlier won 8 caps with Everton, 11 with Chelsea and in his 23 games for England he scored 22 goals. After leaving Notts County in 1952 he played for Brentford, Arsenal and Kettering Town and held a variety of managerial posts.

Bobby LAYNE (USA)

AMERICAN FOOTBALL
Robert Lawrence Layne. b. 19 Dec 1926 Santa Ana, Texas, d. 1 Dec 1986 Lubbock, Texas.

One of the gutsiest quarterbacks ever to play football. He starred at the University of Texas and played in the NFL for the Chicago Bears 1948, New York Bulldogs 1949, Detroit Lions 1950-8, and Pittsburgh Steelers 1958-62. It was with the Lions that he had his greatest success, guiding them to four conference and three NFL titles in the 1950s. He was far from the most talented quarterback, his arm being only average, but he was a winner. Layne was also known for partying as hard as he played. After his retirement he coached quarterbacks for several NFL teams.
NFL career 1948-62: 26,768 yards from 1814 pass completions, 49.0%, 196 TD.

Tony LAZZERI (USA)

BASEBALL
Anthony Michael Lazzeri. b. 6 Dec 1903 San Francisco, California, d. 6 Aug 1948 San Francisco.

Lazzeri was a member of the 'Murderers Row' line-up on the 1927 New York Yankees. Seven times he posted over 100 RBI in a season, he hit 18 home runs in four seasons, and batted over .300 five times. He was an infielder who played all the infield positions although primarily second and shortstop. In 1925, while in the minor leagues with Salt Lake City of the Pacific Coast League, he set minor league records (since broken) with 60 home runs and 222 RBI. He was known as a great clutch hitter. On 24 May 1936, he became the first major leaguer to hit two grand slams in one game and his 11 RBI that day still stands as an American League record. Lazzeri was an epileptic who took medication throughout his career but he fortunately never had an on-field seizure.
Career batting 1926-39: 1840 hits Avg. .292, HR 178; SB 148. Best seasons: 1929: .354.

Johnny LEACH (UK)

TABLE TENNIS
John Alfred Leach. b. 20 Nov 1922 London.

World singles champion in 1949 and 1951 and the last Englishman to win the title. He learned the game while serving with the RAF, and with a technique which was built on a solid defence he developed into the most consistent British player in the imme-

diate post-war years. Although he was twice world singles champion, he never won this event at the English Open though he won the men's doubles (1951, 1953) and the mixed doubles (1950, 1952, 1954, 1956). He won 152 caps for England and was a member of the winning Swaythling Cup team in 1953.
After retirement he continued as non-playing captain of the British team and gave a great deal time to coaching, being particularly involved in the development of young players. He was awarded the MBE for services to the game.

Pavel LEDNEV (USSR/Rus)

MODERN PENTATHLON

Pavel Serafimovich Lednev. b. 25 Mar 1943 Gorkiy.

Between 1968 and 1980 Lednev won a record seven Olympic medals at the modern pentathlon. In the individual event he was successively 3rd, 3rd, 2nd and 3rd, while on the USSR team after silver in 1968 he took gold medals in 1972 and 1980, the latter making him, at 37 years 121 days, the oldest ever gold medallist at his sport. He was four times world individual champion, 1973-5 and 1978, and a member of the winning USSR team in 1973-4. A teacher, he was USSR champion in 1968 and 1973.

André LEDUCQ (Fra)

CYCLING

André 'Dédé' Leducq. b. 27 Feb 1904 Paris, d. 1990.

World amateur road race champion in 1924, although only ninth that year at the Paris Olympics. He turned professional in 1926 and set a record with 25 stage wins in the Tour de France between 1927 and 1938, wearing the yellow jersey for 35 days and winning the race in 1930 and 1932. He made an emotional farewell to the Tour in 1938 when he came in to the finish hand in hand with his great rival Antonin Magne to win the final stage. He won Paris-Roubaix in 1928 and Paris-Tours in 1931.

Dick LEE (Aus)

AUSTRALIAN RULES FOOTBALL

Walter Henry Lee. b. 19 Mar 1889 Collingwood, Melbourne, d. 11 Sep 1968 Northcote, Melbourne.

Although of only average height, his phenomenal high marks and superb goal-kicking led to his being rated one of the greatest full forwards of all-time. In a career beset by injury, he played for Collingwood for 17 consecutive seasons 1906-22, then a VFL record. In 230 games he kicked 707 goals, headed the VFL goalscoring table eight times, 1907-10, 1914, 1916-7 and 1919, and tied twice, 1910-11. He played in three premiership winning teams, 1910, 1917 and 1919; and in 1910 and 1915 was declared the Champion Player of the Colony. He was known as Dick to distinguish him from his father, also a well-known footballer.

Sammy LEE (USA)

DIVING

(Dr) Samuel Lee. b. 1 Aug 1920 Fresno, California.

The Olympic champion at springboard diving in 1948 and 1952, adding a highboard bronze in 1948. AAU champion at both events in 1942, he gave up diving to concentrate on his medical studies in 1943, but returned to win the highboard in 1948. He won Pan-American silver at highboard and bronze at highboard in 1951 and was the Sullivan Award winner in 1953.
A graduate of Occidental College before studying medicine at Southern California, Lee, who was born of Korean parentage, became a doctor specialising in diseases of the ear. He was also a distinguished coach, with his protegé Bob Webster the next man to retain an Olympic title.

Alice LEGH (UK)

ARCHERY

Alice Blanche Legh. b. 1855, d. 3 Jan 1948 Pitchcombe, Stroud, Gloucestershire.

The greatest woman archer from the British Isles, she won her first Grand National championship in 1881. For the next four years she took a back seat to her mother, who won the title four times consecutively, but Alice then took over. Between 1886 and 1922 she won 22 more championships, making 23 in all. This included runs of eight, 1902-09, and seven, 1886-92, in succession. She elected not to compete in the 1908 Olympic archery contests, held in London, which were won by fellow British archer Sybil 'Queenie' Newall, but the following week at Oxford she defeated Newall by the huge margin of 151 points.

Cecil LEITCH (UK)

GOLF

Charlotte Cecilia Pitcairn Leitch. b. 13 Apr 1891 Silloth, Cumberland, d. 16 Sep 1977 London.

A great English amateur who shares the record of four British Ladies' titles, 1914, 1920-1 and 1926, with Joyce Wethered. It is likely she would have set unmatched records had she not had to compete in the same era as Wethered. Leitch won the Canadian championship in 1921 by 17 & 15, the largest margin of victory in any final of a national championship.

She was a semi-finalist in the British Ladies Championship in 1908 at 17, and won the first of five French titles in 1912. In 1914 she won the English, French and British Ladies' and repeated that treble when they were first contested after the War with the English in 1919 and the other two in 1920. She won further French titles in 1921 and 1924.

She was an outspoken character and her strong, attacking play mirrored her personality.

Richard LEMAN (UK)

HOCKEY

Richard Alexander Leman. b. 13 Jul 1959 East Grinstead, Sussex.

Olympic gold medallist and England's most capped player at hockey. Making his England debut against Ireland in 1980 he went on to win a record 158 caps (106 outdoor, 52 indoor). He also represented Great Britain 70 times, and when he retired after the 1990 World Cup he had amassed a total of 228 international selections. He won a gold medal at the 1988 Olympics, silver at the 1986 World Cup and 1987 European Cup, and a bronze at the 1984 Olympics. A forward or midfield player, he played for East Grinstead, Sussex and the South after leaving Gresham's School.

Mario LEMIEUX (Can)

ICE HOCKEY

Mario Lemieux. b. 5 Oct 1965 Montreal, Québec.

By the early 1990s he had become generally recognised as the greatest player in ice hockey, emerging from the shadow of Wayne Gretzky. His career average of 2.03 points per game is second only to Gretzky. In 1987/8 Lemieux ousted Gretzky as league scoring champion for the first time ever, his 168 points being the highest ever for a non-playoff team member, and in 1988/9 he showed his offensive prowess by scoring 199 points, a mark only ever exceeded by Gretzky (four times). Lemieux's 85 goals in that year also placed him second to Gretzky for goals in a season. As an offensive weapon, at 1.96m and 95kg, Lemieux has no flaws; he is a brilliant and fast skater, he stickhandles well, is very strong, and has a powerful and accurate shot.

He had been a star by the age of 9 and at 13 was the top schoolboy player in Québec. He left school to play hockey at the age of 16 and joined the Pittsburgh Penguins in 1984/5, being voted rookie of the year in that first season, when he scored 100 points and was MVP in the NHL All-Star game.

His career was interrupted in 1990 by a chronic back injury from which he recovered. However, in January 1993, a more serious setback occurred when he was diagnosed with Hodgkin's Disease for which he received radiation treatment. He returned triumphantly in March, and despite those missing months was again the league's highest scorer for the season 1992/3 and won the Hart Trophy as NHL MVP.

NHL career 1984-93 - 577 games, 477 goals, 1174 points. Hart Trophy 1988, 1993; Ross Trophy 1988-9, 1992-3; Calder Trophy 1985, Lester Pearson Award 1985, 1988; Smythe Trophy 1991.

Eric LEMMING (Swe)

ATHLETICS

Eric Otto Valdemar Lemming. b. 22 Feb 1880 Gothenburg, d. 5 Jun 1930 Gothenburg.

A great pioneer of javelin throwing, who set his first world best of 49.32m at Gothenburg on 18 Jun 1899 and, with others also setting world bests during this period, made ten improvements in all and took the record up to 62.32m at Stockholm on 29 Sep 1912. This was the first mark ratified by the IAAF. He was Olympic champion in 1906 (freestyle), 1908 (both regular and freestyle) and 1912 and won 25 Swedish titles at all events, including ten at javelin. He first competed in the Olympics in 1900, when there was no javelin on the programme, but he contested six other field events, with his highest placing fourth at pole vault and hammer. In 1906 he won three Olympic bronze medals, at shot, pentathlon and tug-of-war.

Bob LEMON (USA)

BASEBALL

Robert Granville Lemon. b. 22 Sep 1920 San Bernardino, California.

Lemon, who won 20 or more games in seven seasons, and Bob Feller were the leaders of the outstanding Cleveland Indian pitching staffs of the early 1950s that also included Early Wynn, Mike Garcia and Herb Score. Lemon, who broke in as a third baseman, was an excellent hitting pitcher; a fastballer with a good sinkerball as well. After his career ended he turned to managing, leading both the Chicago White Sox and the New York Yankees in the major leagues.
Career pitching 1941-58: ERA 3.23; W-L 207-128, SO 1277; Best seasons: 1954: 23-7, 2.72 ERA; 1950: 23-11, 3.84 ERA; 1949: 22-10, 2.99 ERA; 1952: 22-11, 2.50 ERA.

Meadowlark LEMON (USA)

BASKETBALL

Meadow George Lemon, III. b. 25 Apr 1933 Lexington, South Carolina.

Meadowlark Lemon grew up in Wilmington, North Carolina. He enrolled at Florida A&M in 1952 but left after only two weeks when he was drafted. While serving in Germany he met Harlem Globetrotter coach Abe Saperstein and told him of his lifelong desire to play with the Trotters. This was based on his childhood when he saw the movie *The Harlem Globetrotters*, and also watched the team in Raleigh, North Carolina. Saperstein was impressed by Lemon and guaranteed him a job when he finished his military obligation. He joined the Globetrotters in 1954 and soon became the team's headliner, earning the nickname 'The Clown Prince of Basketball' and playing with them until 1979 when he formed his own travelling team, Meadowlark Lemon's Bucketeers.

Greg LeMOND (USA)

CYCLING

Gregory James LeMond. b. 26 Jun 1961 Lakewood, California.

The greatest road racer ever produced in the United States, he first came to prominence in 1979 when he won three gold medals at the world junior championships, the individual road race, team time trial and the individual pursuit. He turned professional in 1981 and was an immediate success, winning his first world road race title in 1983 after 2nd place in 1982. He was second again in 1985. He rode in his first Tour de France in 1984, finishing third, and it has been the scene of his greatest triumphs.
In the winter after his first Tour victory in 1986, LeMond was shot by his brother-in-law in a hunting accident. It was unclear at first if he would live, much less survive to ride again. He did, but for two years he was a shadow of his former greatness. Early in 1989, he considered retirement as he was often dropped on mountain climbs. But his form came around, and in the most dramatic Tour de France ever, he made up

58 seconds in the last stage time trial to defeat Laurent Fignon by 8 seconds, the narrowest victory margin in Tour history. A month later he won his second world road race title, and a third Tour de France victory came in 1990.
LeMond's strength is time trialing, although he is also an excellent climber. His weakness has been his inability to win the one-day classics, but he attributes this to the fact that he uses them primarily as warm-up races for the major tours.

Ivan LENDL (Cs/USA)

TENNIS
Ivan Lendl. b. 7 Mar 1960 Ostrava.

One of the greatest players never to win the Wimbledon singles, but the highest money earner in the history of tennis, with $19,172,627 to the end of 1992. In all, he won seven Grand Slam titles and was a losing finalist in eleven. He was a Wimbledon finalist in 1986 and 1987 and a semi-finalist in five other years, 1983-4, 1988-90. He won all the other majors at least twice: Australian 1989-90, US 1985-7, and French 1984, 1986-7.
He won the Wimbledon, French and Italian Junior titles in 1978 to become the first ITF World Junior champion. His finest tournament record was in the Grand Prix Masters which he won a record five times, 1981-2 and 1985-7, during a run of nine successive appearances in the final 1980-8. He rarely played tournament doubles, but despite failing to win Wimbledon he was the leading singles player of his time and was ranked No.1 in the World for a total of 270 weeks between 1983 and 1990, including 157 consecutive weeks from 9 Sep 1985 to 5 Sep 1988 and another 80 weeks 30 Jan 1989 to 5 Aug 1990. In May 1993 he won the 93rd singles title of his career. He has lived in Greenwich, Connecticut, USA since 1984.

Virginia LENG (UK)

EQUESTRIAN
Virginia Helen Antoinette Leng. née Holgate. b. 1 Feb 1955 Malta.

A highly successful three-day eventer. Riding *Priceless* she won the 1985 European and 1986 World individual titles, and had team golds in the 1981 and 1985 Europeans and 1982 and 1986 Worlds. She went on to further European individual and team golds in 1987 on *Night Cap* and in 1989 on *Master Craftsman*. She won Badminton in 1985, 1989 and 1993, and Burghley in 1983-4 and 1986. At the Olympic Games she won team silver and individual bronze in both 1984 and 1988. Born in Malta, where her father was serving in the Royal Marines, 'Ginny' was brought up in Cyprus, Canada, Singapore and the Philippines before her family settled in Devon when she was 16. She began riding at age three and her first international victory was in 1973 when she rode *Dubonnet* to the European Junior title. In 1977 she broke her left arm in 23 places, but made a gallant return. She made the 1980 British Olympic team but the equestrians did not go to Moscow.

Suzanne LENGLEN (Fra)

TENNIS
Suzanne Rachel Flore Lenglen. b. 24 May 1899 Compiègne, d. 4 Jul 1938 Paris.

An elegant player of incomparable ability, with a magnetic personality. With her balletic leaps around the court and her ultra-short skirts she drew the crowds to women's tennis as no player before had ever done. After her first win at Wimbledon in 1919, her only defeat before retiring in 1926 was to Molla Mallory in the 1921 US Championships, when she withdrew after losing the first set.
At Wimbledon she won both the singles and the doubles (with Elizabeth Ryan) every year from 1919 to 1925, with the exception of 1924 when she withdrew before her singles semi-final because of jaundice. In 1920, 1922 and 1925 she took all three Wimbledon titles. She was also the French champion in the singles and doubles from 1920 to 1926 apart from 1924 when she did not play because of illness. She also won the French mixed doubles in 1925 and 1926.
She won two Olympic gold medals in 1920 (singles and mixed doubles), and in

the World Hard Court Championships had ten victories (4 singles, 3 doubles, 3 mixed doubles) from her first singles title at the age of 15 in 1914; from 1921-3 she won all three events. Her amateur career ended at Wimbledon in 1926 when she clashed with the authorities and walked out of the Championships. She immediately turned professional and after touring for a while she opened a tennis school. At the age of 39 she died of pernicious anaemia.

Benny LEONARD (USA)

BOXING

né Benjamin Leiner. b. 7 Apr 1896 New York, d. 18 Apr 1947 New York.

Only a lightweight, Leonard was possessed of a punishing punch in both hands. It enabled him to win the world title in 1917 when he stopped Freddie Welsh in the 9th round. Leonard retained the title until retiring seven years later. His only loss in that span came in an attempt to win the welterweight title from Jack Britton in 1922. He had his first professional fight in 1911. In 1931, after losing his fortune in the stock market crash, Leonard came out of retirement and won 20 consecutive bouts. But he was knocked out by Jimmy McLarnin in six rounds on 7 Oct 1932 and retired for good. He became a professional referee in 1943, and died of a heart attack while refereeing in 1947.
Career record: W - 180 (69), L -21, D -6.

Buck LEONARD (USA)

BASEBALL

Walter Fenner Leonard. b. 8 Sep 1907 Rocky Mount, North Carolina.

Leonard is the only Negro League first baseman to be enshrined in the Hall of Fame. He teamed up with Josh Gibson to give the Homestead Grays one of the great one-two punches in baseball history. He was also an excellent fielding first baseman. His career in the Negro Leagues lasted from 1933-50. He was approached by Bill Veeck about playing in the majors in the late 1940s but Leonard felt he was past his prime and did not want to 'embarrass anyone or hurt the chances of those who might follow.' He compiled a .341 lifetime average in the Negro National League. From 1951-5 he played in the Mexican Leagues and made a brief appearance in the minor leagues in 1953 with Portsmouth of the Piedmont League.

Ray LEONARD (USA)

BOXING

Ray Charles 'Sugar Ray' Leonard. b. 17 May 1956 Wilmington, North Carolina

He was christened Ray Charles Leonard, because, he explains, 'I was supposed to be a singer'. He turned out to be quite a boxer. He was North American amateur and AAU champion 1974-5, Golden Gloves champion 1973-4, and he won gold medals at the 1975 Pan-American Games and rather easily at the 1976 Olympics in Montreal.

After the Olympics, Leonard turned professional and immediately became one of the top welterweights and a media favourite with his good looks, quick smile, and pleasant personality. In 1979 he won his first world title by defeating Wilfred Benitez for the WBC welterweight championship. In 1980 he lost that title to Roberto Duran in what remains his only loss as a professional, but regained the title in a re-match by a TKO in the eighth round. In 1981 he defeated Ayub Kalule to win the WBA junior-middleweight title and then decisioned Tommy Hearns to take the WBA version of the welterweight crown and unify the title. On that occasion he realised the largest payday ever for a professional athlete (at the time) when he took home an estimated $10 million. Leonard later won the WBC super-middleweight and light-heavyweight championship in the same fight when he knocked out Donny Lalonde in nine rounds in 1988.

Leonard retired four separate times, once because of a detached retina which threatened his eyesight; the 'final' retirement came in February 1991 after his second loss, to Terry Norris. One of the fastest boxers ever, his skills have been virtually unmatched and he deserves comparison as a fighter to his namesake Sugar Ray

Robinson. His popularity also enabled him to command ring fees that made him one of the wealthiest athletes ever.
Career record: W - 36 (25), L - 2, D -1.

LEÓNIDAS (Bra)

FOOTBALL
Leónidas da Silva. b. 6 Sep 1913 São Cristóvão.

One of the greatest and most durable Brazilian forwards who is often rated alongside the legendary Pelé. Known as the 'Black Diamond' he won 23 caps and scored 22 goals in internationals. On his international début in 1932, at the age of 18, he scored twice and so impressed his Uruguayan opponents that he was signed by Nacional, helping them win the 1933 Uruguayan Championship. The following year a knee injury led to the decision to return home where he joined Vasco da Gama and played in the 1934 World Cup. He then joined Botafogo and in 1936 moved to Flamengo where he enjoyed his best years. He opened Brazil's 1938 World Cup campaign with four goals against Poland and with a total of eight goals in four matches he was the leading scorer in the tournament. However, over-confidence meant that he was rested for the semi-final against Italy, a match that Brazil lost! In 1942 he moved to São Paulo where he won five Championship medals before retiring in 1950. He returned to take over as manager in 1953.

Gus LESNEVICH (USA)

BOXING
Gus Lesnevich. b. 22 Feb 1915 Cliffside Park, New Jersey, d. 28 Feb 1964 Cliffside Park.

Lesnevich won the world light-heavyweight title in 1941 after two earlier unsuccessful attempts against Billy Conn. With six successful defences he held the crown until 1948 when he lost a decision to Freddie Mills (UK). He attempted to win the world heavyweight title in 1949, but was knocked out by Ezzard Charles. In retirement he became a professional referee.
Career record: W - 60 (23), L - 14, D - 5.

Carl LEWIS (USA)

ATHLETICS
Frederick Carlton Lewis. b. 1 Jul 1961 Birmingham, Alabama.

A prime contender for the title of the greatest athlete of all-time and certainly the one with the greatest collection of gold medals. At full stride in sprinting and long jumping he brought a sublime combination of speed, power, grace and technique to the world of sport, maintaining his form at the top for well over a decade.
At his first Olympic Games in Los Angeles he emulated Jesse Owens by winning, as expected, four gold medals, at 100m, 200m, long jump and sprint relay. Dropping the 200m, he won the 100m and long jump in Seoul in 1988, although his gold for 100m came after Ben Johnson, who had finished a metre ahead of him, was disqualified for a positive drugs test. In 1992 Lewis suffered from a virus infection at the US Trials and did not qualify for 100m or 200m, but made it in the long jump and won a tough competition against Mike Powell to take Olympic gold, adding an eighth gold at the sprint relay.
At the World Championships of 1983 and 1987 he won gold medals at 100m, long jump and relay, and almost repeated this in 1991, when after becoming the first man to exceed the 23-year-old world record of Bob Beamon when he jumped 8.91m (with wind assistance), he was passed by Mike Powell's 8.95m. Even in defeat he produced by far the greatest ever series of jumps, with four over 8.80m, including also his best 'legal' jump of 8.87m. He won the 100 metres in 9.86, thus regaining the world record that he had set at 9.92 in Seoul, and which he had lost to Leroy Burrell at the US Trials, when he ran 9.90 to Burrell's 9.88. Lewis added another world record when he anchored the US sprint relay team to victory. Thus he has won eight World gold medals and one silver. In 1993 he concentrated on the sprints, leaving the long jump alone for a year, and made the World Championship team at both 100m and 200m.
The defeat by Powell on 31 Aug 1991 ended a run of 65 successive long jump victories by Lewis from a defeat by Larry

Myricks at the US Indoor Championships on 28 Feb 1981 Lewis consistently refused to go to high altitude to chase world records, but has set nine: five at 4 x 100m relay, two at 4 x 200m relay and the two above at 100 metres. He also set seven world low altitude bests: each year from 1981 to 1983 at both 100m and long jump, and in 1983 at 200m (19.75, his best ever). His international career had started with a Pan-American bronze medal at long jump in 1979, gold medals for 100m and 200m at the Pan-American juniors in 1980, and a win in the long jump at the World Cup in 1981. He has won five US titles at 100m, two at 200m and six at long jump. While at the University of Houston he won two NCAA titles outdoors and three indoors. Sullivan Award winner 1981. Coached from his university days by Tom Tellez, he competes for the Santa Monica Track Club, managed by Joe Douglas. His sister Carol (b. 8 Aug 1963) was the World long jump bronze medallist in 1983 and made the US Olympic teams of 1980, 1984 and 1988.

Ted 'Kid' LEWIS (UK)

BOXING

Ted 'Kid' Lewis. né Gershon Medeloff. b. 24 Oct 1894 Aldgate, London, d. 20 Oct 1970 London.

Usually considered, pound-for-pound, the greatest fighter ever produced in the UK. He began his professional career when he was only 14 and just before his 19th birthday won the British featherweight championship, adding the European title in 1914. In 1915, Lewis won the undisputed world welterweight title by outpointing Jack Britton. He held that title until 1919. Lewis was British Empire champion as a featherweight, welterweight, or middleweight from 1914-24 and had his last fight in 1929.

Career record: W - 215(71), L - 44, D - 24.

Wally LEWIS (Aus)

RUGBY LEAGUE

Walter James Lewis. b. 1 Dec 1959 Brisbane, Queensland.

An outstanding play-maker and one of Australia's greatest stand-off halves. After a rugby union tour of England with the Australian Schoolboys in 1977 he turned to rugby league and joined the Valleys club in Brisbane. In 1984 he moved to Wynnum Manly in Sydney but returned to Brisbane in 1988 when he helped form the Brisbane Broncos. During this period he played briefly for Wakefield Trinity in 1983 when he scored six tries in ten matches and was paid the record fee of £1,000 a match. He made 27 Test appearances for Australia 1984-9, captaining them against Great Britain in 1984 and 1986, and to World Cup victory in 1988. He represented Queensland 1980-9.

Maurice LEYLAND (UK)

CRICKET

Maurice Leyland. b. 20 Jul 1900 Newpark, Harrogate, Yorkshire, d. 1 Jan 1967 Scotton Banks, Harrogate.

An outstanding left-handed middle-order batsman who scored over 1000 runs in 17 successive seasons 1923-39, with over 2000 in 1930 and 1933-4. His unorthodox slow left-arm bowling was also most useful for Yorkshire. He averaged over 40 on three tours of Australia and was an invaluable member of the England team virtually throughout the 1930s. He was Yorkshire's coach 1951-63.

41 Tests 1928-38: 2764 runs at 46.06, 9 100s HS 187; 6 wickets at 97.50, BB 3-91; 13 catches.

First-class 1920-48: 33,660 runs at 40.50, 80 100s HS 263; 466 wickets at 29.31, BB 8-63; 246 catches.

LI Ning (China)

GYMNASTICS

Li Ning. b. 8 Sep 1963 Guangxi.

With wins in 1982 and 1986 (when he shared the title with Yuriy Korolev), Li is one of three men to have won two World Cup titles at gymnastics. In 1982 he also won five individual events. Li had been third overall in a very close contest at the 1984 Olympics, but had come back to take three gold medals, a silver and a bronze in the apparatus finals. He shared the world title for rings with Korolev in 1985, and was 5th overall, having been 6th in 1981 and 1983.

Eric LIDDELL (UK)

ATHLETICS and RUGBY

Eric Henry Liddell. b. 16 Jan 1902 Tientsin, China, d. 21 Feb 1945 Weihsien, China.

The film *Chariots of Fire* is based on the story of the 1924 Olympic gold medallists Eric Liddell and Harold Abrahams. Liddell's gold was at 400m, at which he set an Olympic and European record of 47.6. This time remained the British record until 1936. He had gone into the Games with a best (for 440y) of 49.6, his winning time at the 1924 AAAs, improving to 48.2 in the semi-final. He also took the Olympic bronze medal at 200m, but had concentrated on the 400m rather than the 100m due to the fact that the latter was held on a Sunday.

At Scottish championships he won the 100y and 220y for five successive years 1921-5, completing trebles with Edinburgh University's mile relay team 1921-3 and by winning the 440y in 1924 and 1925, adding a fourth success at the mile relay in 1925. He was AAA champion at 100y and 220y in 1923, running his personal best times of 9.7 (which lasted as a British record for 35 years) and 21.6.

A fine all-round sportsman, he won seven caps for Scotland on the wing at rugby football in 1922-3. In 1925 he returned to China to join his father as a missionary and died there after two years of internment in a Japanese concentration camp.

Nancy LIEBERMANN-CLINE (USA)

BASKETBALL

Nancy Lizabeth Liebermann-Cline. b. 1 Jul 1958 Brooklyn, New York.

A candidate for the greatest women's basketball player the United States has ever produced. When only 17 years old, as a high school junior, she played in the 1975 Pan-American Games gold medal team and in 1976 won an Olympic silver medal. Highly recruited, she took her talents to Old Dominion University where she was all-everything for four years. She led her team to two national championships and also won the Wade Trophy as the outstanding women's inter-collegiate player. She expected to play in the 1980 Olympics, but the boycott ended those hopes. After competing in several non-Olympic events as a member of the team, she signed the largest contract in the history of the Women's Basketball League. Unfortunately the league, never financially stable, soon folded. Since then she has made most of her headlines as the former trainer and manager of tennis superstar Martina Navratilova.

LIEM SWIE KING (Ina)

BADMINTON

Liem Swie King. b. 28 Feb 1956.

He succeeded his compatriot Rudy Hartono as the world's top badminton player, although without quite matching the latter's genius. At the All-England Championships, he won the men's singles in 1978-9 and 1981. He was beaten in the men's singles final in the World Championships of 1980 and 1983 and helped Indonesia to win the Uber Cup in 1976 and 1979, when on each occasion they swept to 9-0 victories in the final.

Tiina LILLAK (Fin)

ATHLETICS

Ilse Kristiina Lillak. b. 15 Apr 1961 Helsinki.

Her win on the final throw at the 1983 World Championships in Helsinki and the attendant roar of the crowd will long be remembered as one of the great moments in athletics history.

She set eleven Finnish javelin records from 1980 to 1983, including world records at 72.40m in 1982 and 74.76 in 1983, the first ever by a Finnish woman thrower. She went on to take the Olympic silver in 1984 even though she was held back by a broken bone in her foot. She has had further injury problems ever since and has not won another major medal, although she was fourth at the Europeans in 1986 as she had been in 1982. Finnish champion 1980-1, 1983, 1985-7, 1990.

Dennis LILLEE (Aus)

CRICKET

Dennis Keith Lillee. b. 18 Jul 1949 Subiaco, Perth.

One of the greatest fast bowlers of all-time. When he first established himself in the Australian team in the 1970s his sheer pace, along with that of his partner Jeff Thomson, demoralised many Test teams. Later he added variety and astute thinking to his bowling. In all he was a complete master of his craft, with a near-perfect action, and has become a much respected coach.

He played for Western Australia and made his Test début in 1971 against England. He took 23 wickets in four matches for Australia against the Rest of the World in 1971/2 and 31 wickets at 17.67 in England in 1972. However, in 1973 at the age of 23 it looked as if his career might be threatened due to stress fractures of the lower spine. By hard work and determination he returned to take 20 or more wickets in four successive series 1974-7, adding further such hauls four times in his career, including a peak of 39 at 22.31 in the six Tests in England in 1981 (with a record 81 in Tests in a calendar year that year) and 20 in his last series against Pakistan in 1983/4. By then he had become the leading wicket-taker in Test history, despite losing a couple of years when he played in World Series cricket, and his 167 against England is the Test record against one country. Awarded the MBE.

70 Tests 1971-84: 905 runs at 13.71, HS 73; 355 wickets at 23.92, BB 7-83; 23 catches.*

63 One-day Ints: 240 runs at 9.23, HS 42; 103 wickets at 20.82, BB 5-34; 9 catches.*

First-class 1969-88: 2377 runs at 13.90, HS 73; 882 wickets at 23.46, BB 8-29; 67 catches.*

Bob LILLY (USA)

AMERICAN FOOTBALL

Robert Lewis Lilly. b. 26 Jul 1939 Olney, Texas.

One of the great defensive tackles to have played pro football. His college career was spent at Texas Christian University (TCU) and his entire 14-year NFL career 1961-74 with the Dallas Cowboys. He played in the Pro Bowl 11 times and was a seven-time All-Pro selection. He helped Dallas win one Super Bowl and two NFC championships. After his retirement, Lilly was the first player elected to the Dallas Cowboy Ring of Honor.

LIN Hui-chang (China)

TABLE TENNIS

Lin Hui-chang.

After winning the World women's doubles in 1965, her career was inhibited when China withdrew from international competition in 1967. On her country's reappearance on the international scene in 1971 she made a spectacular return by winning all three titles at the World Championships. In 1965 she was a member of the Chinese team which won the Corbillon Cup for the first time and was the non-playing team captain when China won the Cup for a second time in 1975.

Walter LINDRUM (Aus)

BILLIARDS

Walter Albert Lindrum. b. 29 Aug 1898 Donnybrook, Kalgoorlie, d. 30 Jul 1960 Surfers Paradise, Queensland.

A complex but likeable character, the greatest of all billiards players and the only man ever to establish a clear superiority over Joe Davis. He learned the game in family-owned saloons, quickly established himself as the finest player in Australia, and took on the visiting Willie Smith in the 1928/9 season. Lindrum won the first match and Smith the second but the decider was abandoned when Lindrum's 20-year-old pregnant wife tragically died from her injuries after being struck by a bus.

The grief-stricken Lindrum immediately signed a contract with Burroughes and Watts and went to England with Smith where he made an instant impact on the game. He made the highest score of his career with a break of 4137 in January 1932 but missed the World Championship later that year as he was touring North America. However, he won the world title in 1933 and insisted that he would only defend the title in Australia. The Championship was duly held in Melbourne in 1934, the first time the event had been staged outside the UK, where Lindrum beat Clark McConachy and Joe Davis. As no further challengers were forthcoming he retained the title until he relinquished it in 1950. He did much work in charity fund raising during the war, and was awarded the MBE in 1951 and the OBE in 1958. His nephew **Horace** (1912-74) was also a gifted player and was the world snooker champion in 1952.

Ted LINDSAY (Can)

ICE HOCKEY

Robert Blake Theodore Lindsay. b. 29 Jul 1925 Renfrew, Ontario.

Lindsay was one of the roughest players, but that fact belies his skill as a left winger. Because of his toughness and proficiency with his fists, he twice led the league in penalty minutes and totalled 1808 minutes in the penalty box in his career. He received over 760 stitches from playing hockey, earning him the nickname 'Scarface' to go with his other nicknames of 'Terrible Ted' and 'Tempestuous Ted'. Lindsay played most of his career on the Production Line of the Detroit Red Wings, then with the Chicago Black Hawks in 1957-60. After retiring he returned four years later to play one last season with the Red Wings.

NHL career 1944-65 - 1068 games, 379 goals, 851 points. Best year: 1956/7: 55 assists, 85 points. Ross Trophy 1950 (55 assists, 78 points).

Ray LINDWALL (Aus)

CRICKET

Raymond Russell Lindwall. b. 3 Oct 1921 Mascot, Sydney.

From a smooth approach and powerful rhythmic action, Lindwall generated the pace and outswing that made him the most feared fast bowler in the immediate post-war decade. With Keith Miller he formed a formidable partnership and was at his peak in the 1948 Test series against England when he took 27 wickets at 19.62. Until 1954 he never averaged worse than 23 in a Test series; thereafter, although he continued to give valuable service to his country, once captaining them, he had lost some of his pace and his strike rate declined. He was nearly a genuine all-rounder, scoring two Test hundreds. He played for New South Wales 1945-54 and then for Queensland, whom he captained 1955-60. Awarded the MBE.

61 Tests 1946-60: 1502 runs at 21.16, 2 100s HS 118; 228 wickets at 23.05, BB 7-38; 26 catches.

First-class 1941-62: 5042 runs at 21.82, 5 100s HS 134; 794 wickets at 21.35, BB 7-20; 123 catches.*

Gary LINEKER (UK)

FOOTBALL

Gary Winston Lineker. b. 30 Nov 1960 Leicester, Leics.

A high-scoring marksman who played for Leicester 1978-85, Everton 1985-6, Barcelona 1986-9 and Tottenham 1989-92 before signing a lucrative contract to play in Japan for Grampus Eight of Nagoya. By then he had scored 322 goals in 631 senior games. He scored 48 goals in 80 appearances for England, just one goal short of Bobby Charlton's record for England. He also proved to be a fine captain. In 1986 with six goals he was the top scorer in the World Cup and was voted Player of the Year by both the football writers (as he was to be again in 1992) and his fellow players. In 1990 a further four goals brought his World Cup total up to 10 to make him the top British scorer in the competition. Despite his fine international record, he won few honours at home; he helped Leicester to the Division II title in 1980 and was an FA Cup finalist with Everton in 1986. With Barcelona he won the European Cup-Winners' Cup in 1989 and at last won an FA Cup winners' medal with Tottenham in 1991.

His major strengths were his superb acceleration, fine positional play and an ability to turn half-chances into goals. Above all he showed an appetite for the game that many of his contemporaries seemed to lack. Articulate and with an attractive manner, he is much in demand as a TV authority on the game. Awarded the OBE 1992.

Liselott LINSENHOFF (FRG)

EQUESTRIAN

Liselott Linsenhoff. née Schindling. b. 27 Aug 1927 Frankfurt.

The winner of five Olympic medals in dressage, including a team gold in 1968 and an individual gold in 1972. She also won two medals in 1956, a team silver and individual bronze, and two in 1972, adding a team silver to her individual gold. Both her gold medals came riding the famous Swedish stallion *Piaff*. At the World Championships she was a member of the winning team in 1974 and placed second in the individual events in 1970 and 1974. She also won individual European championships in 1969 and 1971 and was a member of the winning team in 1973.
A graduate of the University of Frankfurt, she is a successful entrepreneur. Her daughter, Ann-Kathrin, became a West German Olympic equestrian in 1988.

Natalya LISOVSKAYA (USSR)

ATHLETICS

Natalya Lisovskaya. b. 16 Jul 1962 Alegazy, Bashkir ASSR.

The top women's shot putter of the 1980s, she set three world records between 1984 and 1987, with a best of 22.63m. Apart from ninth place in the 1986 Europeans she took most of the major titles in the late 1980s, winning the World title in 1987, Olympics in 1988, World Indoors 1985 and 1987, World Student Games 1983, 1985 and 1987, European Cup 1985, 1987 and 1991, and the World Cup 1985. At the 1988 Olympics she had all six throws better than the silver medallist.
At World Championships in 1991 she was third indoors and second outdoors, and won the European Indoors in 1992, but then suffered injuries and was only ninth at the Olympics. She was USSR/CIS champion eight times between 1981 and 1992.

Sonny LISTON (USA)

BOXING

Charles Liston. b. 8 May 1932 St Francis, Arkansas, d. 30 Dec 1970 Las Vegas, Nevada.

One of the most feared heavyweight champions ever. Possessed of a dour manner and a menacing stare, he also had a long police record as an adolescent and early in his pro career was avoided by heavyweight champions for years. He finally got his chance aged 30 in 1962, and knocked out Floyd Patterson in the first round, winning the return bout a year later with a 1st-round KO as well. In 1964 he was heavily favoured in a defence against Cassius Clay, bookmakers quoting 7-1 odds on the champion. But Clay (later Ali) won when Liston could not answer the bell for round seven. Liston also lost a return match, though under very suspicious circumstances and some observers think that the fight was fixed. He continued fighting through 1969 when he was knocked out by Leotis Martin. He also died in very mysterious circumstances in 1970, his body remaining undiscovered for six days.
Career record: W - 50 (39), L - 4, D - 0.

Paul LITJENS (Hol)

HOCKEY

Paul Litjens. b. 9 Nov 1947.

One of the great penalty stroke specialists, he scored 267 goals in 177 internationals 1970-82 and made a major contribution to the Dutch victories in the 1973 World Cup and 1981 Champions Trophy. He played midfield and defence for Kampong and was, by profession, a lawyer.

Lawson LITTLE (USA)

GOLF

William Lawson Little, Jr. b. 23 Jun 1910 Newport, Rhode Island, d. 1 Feb 1968 Pebble Beach, California.

One of the greatest amateurs ever, his fame

rests on his winning of a double 'Little Slam', in which he won the US and British Amateur championships in both 1934 and 1935. In those tournaments he was unbeaten for 31 consecutive matches, and he achieved a record margin of victory in the 1934 British Amateur by defeating Jack Wallace 14 & 13. He won both his matches for the USA in the Walker Cup of 1934. He turned professional in 1936 and won the Canadian Open that year, but with just seven US PGA tour victories he never quite reached expectations, although he added another major title in winning the 1940 US Open.

Gene LITTLER (USA)

GOLF

Eugene Alec Littler. b. 21 Jul 1930 La Jolla, California.

Gene 'The Machine' Littler is considered by some experts to be possessed of the finest swing in golf history. He was US Amateur champion in 1953 and won both his matches in the Walker Cup that year. He achieved fame in 1954 when he won the San Diego Open while still an amateur. Littler was tipped, based on that win and his swing mechanics, to become the next great player but that lofty status never quite materialised. He instead became a very steady winner on the professional tours, but was able to win only one major championship, the 1961 US Open. He played for the US on seven Ryder Cup teams, 1961-75, with a record of 14 wins, 5 losses and 8 halves. Littler developed cancer in 1969 and after an operation on his left arm and shoulder region, made a tremendous comeback to return to professional golf and win several tournaments. *PGA career earnings: $1,578,626 with 29 victories. Seniors tour: $1,945,367 with 8 victories.*

Sergey LITVINOV (USSR/Rus)

ATHLETICS

Sergey Nikolayevich Litvinov. b. 23 Jan 1958 Tsukarov, Krasnodar.

Only two men have ever thrown the hammer more than 85 metres, yet Litvinov has twice thrown over this distance and lost to Yuriy Sedykh, at Cork in 1984 and at the 1986 European Championships, when he opened with 85.74. However, he beat his great rival to gain the 1988 Olympic title and he was World champion in 1983 and 1987. He was also Olympic silver medallist in 1980 and was 3rd at the Europeans in 1982 in addition to his 2nd in 1986. He set three world hammer records, 81.66m in 1980, 83.98 in 1982 and 84.14 in 1983. His best ever was 86.04 in 1986. He came to international prominence with bronze at the 1975 European Juniors and added a silver in 1977, with world junior records in 1976 and 1977. He was USSR champion in 1979 and 1983, and won the World Cup in 1979 and the European Cup in 1983 and 1987. He came back to form to take the Russian title and a third European Cup win in 1993. A teacher, he competed for Rostov-on-Don SA.

Anita LIZANA (Chile)

TENNIS

Anita Lizana. b. 1915 Santiago. Married Ronald Ellis in 1938.

The first world-class player to come from Latin America. She created a major surprise in 1937 when, in her first singles tournament in America, she won the US title without the loss of a set. She won the British Hard Court title in 1936 and was also a quarter-finalist at Wimbledon in 1936 and 1937. Her graceful strokes, particularly on the back-hand, were supplemented by a well disguised drop-shot. After her marrriage she settled in Britain. She won four Scottish titles, 1935-7 and 1946, and the British Covered Court singles in 1936.

Harry LLEWELLYN (UK)

EQUESTRIAN

(Sir) Henry Morton Llewellyn. b. 18 Jul 1911 Merthyr Tydfil, Glamorgan.

Educated at Oundle and Trinity College, Cambridge, he was a successful amateur steeplechase jockey prior to World War II, placing second on his father's horse *Ego* in the 1936 Grand National. At show jumping he won the Olympic individual bronze in 1948 and the team gold in 1952, riding his famous horse *Foxhunter* (1940-59), whom he had bought in 1947, and on whom he won 78 international events including the King George V Gold Cup in 1948, 1950 and 1953. *Foxhunter's* clear round on the last day of the 1952 Games ensured Britain of its only gold medal at Helsinki.

During the war, Llewellyn saw action in Italy and Normandy and was awarded an OBE by Field Marshal Montgomery for working as his liaison officer. Llewellyn then took up a career in the business world of Wales, which eventually led to his being knighted in 1977. In 1978, he succeeded to the Baronetcy upon the death of his older brother. He was chairman of the Sports Council for Wales 1971-81.

Clive LLOYD (Guy)

CRICKET

Clive Hubert Lloyd. b. 31 Aug 1944 Queenstown, Georgetown.

A genial man but a commander who welded the West Indies into the most professional and successful team in cricket. He was a left-handed batsman of enormous power and, before knee operations forced him into the slips, an electrifying fielder in the covers, belying the seemingly languid and shambling gait of this 1.96m *6'5"* man. He was an immediate success in Test cricket, making 82 and 78* in his first match against India and averaging over 50 in his first two series. He usually batted at number five, and after he became captain in 1974 could be relied on to produce the important innings when his side needed it most. He set a record by captaining the West Indies in 74 Tests, winning 36 of them to 12 lost. He played for Guyana and for Lancashire from 1968 (captain 1981-3 and 1986). He led the West Indies to victories in the first two World Cup finals, and his powerful batting was seen at its best when he scored 102 in the first of those at Lord's in 1975. In 1976 he equalled the record for the fastest ever double century, scoring 201* in 120 minutes for West Indies v Glamorgan at Swansea. Awarded the CBE 1992.

110 Tests 1966-85: 7515 runs at 46.67, 19 100s HS 242; 10 wickets at 62.20, BB 2-13; 90 catches.*
87 One-day Ints: 1977 runs at 39.54, 1 100 HS 102; 8 wickets at 26.25, BB 2-4; 39 catches.
First-class 1964-86: 31,232 runs at 49.26, 79 100s HS 242; 114 wickets at 36.88, BB 4-48; 377 catches.*

Pop LLOYD (USA)

BASEBALL

John Henry Lloyd. b. 25 Apr 1884 Palatka, Florida, d. 19 Mar 1965 Atlantic City, New Jersey.

With a career batting average of .342, Lloyd played for 12 different teams in a 27-year career in the Negro Leagues 1905-31. He also played for 12 seasons in Cuba. He was primarily a shortstop but played many different positions, moving to first base as he got older. He was often compared to Honus Wagner who played shortstop in the major leagues concurrently. Once, Babe Ruth was asked who was the greatest player he had ever seen. Ruth replied, 'You mean major leaguers?'. When told he could pick anyone, Ruth responded, 'In that case, I'd pick John Henry Lloyd.'

Marina LOBACH (USSR/Bls)

GYMNASTICS

Marina Lobach. b. 26 Jun 1970 Kiev, Ukraine.

In 1988, Lobach, who had never previously placed higher than 4th in a major championships overall, although she had won the 1987 world title at hoops, achieved a perfect score in each of her four routines in both preliminaries and final of the rhythmic gymnastics at the Olympic Games. She competed for Minsk Dynamo.

Yuriy LOBANOV (USSR)

CANOEING

Yuriy Lobanov. b. 29 Sep 1952 Dushanbe, Tajikistan.

Lobanov won the Olympic gold medal in

the Canadian pairs at 1000m with Vladislavs Cesiunas in 1972, and went on to win ten world titles: C2 500m 1974-5, C2 1000m 1974, 1977, 1979; C2 10,000m 1973-5, 1977, 1979. He missed the 1976 Olympics, but won a bronze medal at the 1000m pairs in 1980.

Brian LOCHORE (NZ)

RUGBY UNION

Brian James Lochore. b. 3 Sep 1940 Masterton.

A back-row forward who gave outstanding service to New Zealand rugby as a player and captain, and later as a selector and coach. He captained New Zealand in 18 of his 25 international matches and under his leadership the All Blacks won 15 Tests, which made him New Zealand's most successful captain. He made his international début against England on the 1963/4 tour and on his second visit to Britain and France in 1967 he led the team, who were unbeaten throughout the tour.

A shy, unassuming farmer, he possessed inner qualities which commanded the respect of his contemporaries. Not only was he an inspiring leader on the field, he was also an outstanding coach and guided New Zealand to victory in the first World Cup in 1987. He was awarded the OBE for his services to the game.

Tony LOCK (UK)

CRICKET

Graham Anthony Richard Lock. b. 5 Jul 1929 Limpsfield, Surrey.

A left-arm medium paced spin bowler, he was capable of very fast balls, though with a doubtful action for which he was no-balled for throwing in five matches, eventually causing him to re-model it. Having done so in 1960 he continued to enjoy much success. He formed a great spin partnership with Jim Laker for both England and Surrey, for whom he played until 1963, and enjoyed great success with their Championship winning teams 1952-8. He took 100 wickets in a season each year 1951-62, with a peak of 216 at 14.39 in 1955, the last occasion on which a bowler took over 200 wickets in a season. He played nine seasons for Western Australia from 1962/3, all but the first as their captain, and led them to the Sheffield Shield in 1967/8. He also played for Leicestershire for three seasons 1965-7, and again took 100 wickets when he captained them in both 1966 and 1967. He was a brilliant close fielder, and his career total of 830 catches is the third highest of all-time. He made the highest score of his career in his last Test innings, against the West Indies in 1968.

49 Tests 1952-68: 742 runs at 13.74, HS 89; 174 wkts at 25.58, BB 7-35; 59 ct.
First-class 1946-71: 10,342 runs at 15.88, HS 89; 2844 wickets at 19.23, BB 10-54; 830 catches.

Bobby LOCKE (SAf)

GOLF

Arthur D'Arcy Locke. b. 20 Nov 1917 Germiston, Transvaal, d. 9 Mar 1987 Johannesburg.

British Open champion four times, 1949-50, 1952 and 1957, and Open champion of South Africa nine times, 1935, 1937-40, 1946, 1950-1, 1955. His first victory was the South African boys' title at the age of 14, which he followed with SA amateur and open titles in 1935 and 1937 before turning professional in 1938. His career was interrupted by World War II in which he flew more than a hundred Liberator missions. Locke started playing the US circuit in 1947, when he was third in the US Open and won four of five successive tournaments. He was so successful that he engendered a lot of resentment among American professionals. In 1949 Locke played in the British Open and was then banned from the US tour under the pretext that he had failed to honour his American commitments by playing in Britain. The ban was lifted in 1951 but Locke never played extensively again in the United States, where in all he had 15 US PGA tour victories.

Locke's game was highly unorthodox. He was decidedly unathletic in appearance and his swing was very flat, very hands-dominated, and he played a wide, sweeping hook for all his shots. Many people consider Bobby Locke the greatest putter ever, although his style was also unorthodox, as he struck the ball a downward, inside-out blow, imparting sidespin to all his putts.

James LOFTON (USA)

AMERICAN FOOTBALL

James Lofton b. 5 Jul 1956.

A top-class long jumper when he was at Stanford University, he was ranked third in the world in 1978 when he won the NCAA and was 2nd in the AAU championships with his best ever jump of 8.23m *27' 0"*. He then joined the Green Bay Packers as a wide receiver and in his career to 1992, continuing with the Los Angeles Raiders and the Buffalo Bills, he has set the all-time record in the NFL for 13,821 yards gained receiving.

George LOHMANN (UK)

CRICKET

George Alfred Lohmann. b. 2 Jun 1865 Kensington, London, d. 1 Dec 1901 Matjiesfontein, Cape Province, South Africa.

In his ten-year Test career Lohmann has by far the best average of any bowler taking 25 or more wickets, and his strike rate, with a wicket every 34 balls, is also a record. He had a short career with Surrey which was ended by ill-health, but took over 140 wickets each year 1885-92, with 200-wicket hauls each year 1888-90. He was also an exceptional slip fielder. After two years out of action 1883-4 having contracted tuberculosis, he returned for two years 1895-6 and had extraordinary success on the matting wickets of South Africa, taking 35 wickets at 5.80 in the three Tests 1895/6: 7-38 and 8-7, 9-28 and 3-43, 7-42 and 1-45. The 9-28 was the first ever 9-wicket take in Test cricket and the 8-7 remains unparalleled. At that time he held the record for most wickets in Tests. He managed the 1901 South African team in England

18 Tests 1886-96: 213 runs at 8.87, HS 62; 112 wickets at 10.75, BB 9-28; 28 catches.*

First-class 1884-98: 7247 runs at 18.68, 3 100s HS 115; 1841 wickets at 13.74, BB 9-28; 337 catches.

Ernie LOMBARDI (USA)

BASEBALL

Ernesto Natali Lombardi. b. 6 Apr 1908 Oakland, California, d. 26 Sep 1977 Santa Cruz, California.

One of the greatest hitting catchers of all time, despite being one of the slowest runners ever to play major league baseball. He was so slow that the infield could play very deep and prevent what would have been basehits for normal runners. A good catcher but a better hitter, in a 17-year career he batted over .300 ten times, with his top averages .343 in 1935 and .342 in 1938. He was passed over for Hall of Fame during his lifetime, which greatly embittered him, but he was eventually elected in 1985 by the Veterans' Committee.

Career batting 1931-47: 1792 hits Avg. .358, HR 190.

Vince LOMBARDI (USA)

AMERICAN FOOTBALL

Vincent Thomas Lombardi. b. 11 Jun 1913 Brooklyn, New York, d. 3 Sep 1970 Washington, DC.

Undoubtedly the greatest of all professional football coaches, Lombardi has become a legendary figure. He was an excellent college football lineman at Fordham and began his coaching career at St Cecilia's High School in New Jersey. He later trained as an assistant coach under Red Blaik at the US Military Academy 1948-52. He then spent seven years as an offensive coach with the New York Giants, until in 1959 he was named head coach of the Green Bay Packers where he established his legend. He took the hapless Packers, last in the league in 1958, to second place in 1959. In 1960 they won their conference before losing in the NFL Championship Game. No Lombardi team would ever again lose a play-off game. The Packers were NFL champions in 1961 and 1962, and won three consecutive championships in 1965-7, the only time this has been accomplished in modern NFL history. The Packers won the first two Super Bowls 1966-7. Lombardi then retired only to return in 1969 as coach of the Washington Redskins, who had a good first season before he fell ill and died shortly after the start of the 1970 season. Lombardi was a dynamic personality who drove his men hard, drove himself harder, and was loved by his players. He was a forceful public speaker, often known for the statement, 'Winning isn't everything, it's the only thing.' Lombardi himself stated that what he actually meant was, 'Winning isn't everything, but making the effort to win is.'

Dallas LONG (USA)

ATHLETICS

Dallas Crutcher Long. b. 13 Jun 1940 Pine Bluff, Arkansas.

Long set seven official world records at the shot and a further three unofficial ones. At the age of 18 he became the first man to better Parry O'Brien, with 19.25m at Santa Barbara on 28 Mar 1959, and his best year was 1964 when he won the Olympic title and set his last world record of 20.68m for USA v USSR at Los Angeles on 25 July. He was the bronze medallist at the 1960 Olympics and was AAU champion in 1961 and NCAA champion while at the University of Southern California each year 1960-2. Qualified as a dentist.

Johnny LONGDEN (USA)

HORSE RACING

John Eric Longden. b. 15 Feb 1907 Wakefield, England.

Longden held the record for most wins in a career as a jockey from 1956, when he passed the total of 4870 ridden by Gordon Richards, until 1970.

He started his racing career in 1926 and when he retired in 1966 he had ridden a record 6032 winners, with total earnings of $24,665,800. He then became a trainer and in 1969, with *Majestic Prince*, became the first man to have ridden and trained a Kentucky Derby winner.

Born in England, he was raised in Canada from the age of two and became a US citizen in 1942. His first winner was in Utah in 1927 and his first jockey's championship for most wins came in 1938. He was leading money winner in the USA in 1943 and 1945, setting new records of $573,276 and $981,977 respectively, and won most races in 1947 and 1948. He rode *Count Fleet* to the Triple Crown in the USA in 1943. Nicknamed 'The Pumper' due to his vigorous riding action.

Jeanne LONGO (Fra)

CYCLING

Jeanne Longo. b. 31 Oct 1958 Annecy.

Considered by many as the greatest women's road cyclist ever, with great climbing ability coupled with her track ability as a pursuiter. She has won a record eight world titles: pursuit 1986, 1988-9; road 1985-7, 1989; and points 1989. She was French champion on the road 11 times from 1979 to 1989, pursuit 1980-9, 1992, and points 1988-9, 1992. The only omission on her record is that she has not won an Olympic title; she was sixth in the road race in 1984, but was only 21st in 1988 when she was favourite but still recovering from a hip fracture. The race was held on almost a flat course, turning it into a sprinter's race. In 1992 at Barcelona, however, she came out of retirement to earn a silver medal in the Olympic road race. She won the women's Tour de France in 1987-9.

She has set numerous world records on the track from her first in 1984, with her outdoor bests (all from 1989 at the high altitude of Mexico City): 3km 3:38.190, 5km 6:14.135, 10km 12:59.435, 20km 25:59.883, 1 hour 46.3527km; and indoors 3km 3:40.264 (1992), 5km 6:17.608 (1991), 10km 12:54.260, 20km 26:51.222 and 1 hour 45.016km (all 1989). She first set world records for the 1 hour in 1986 with 44.770km at high altitude and 43.587km at sea level.

She is married to her coach Patrice Ciprelli, a former Alpine skiing international.

Anita LONSBROUGH (UK)

SWIMMING

Anita Lonsbrough. b. 10 Aug 1941 York, Yorkshire. Later Porter.

Simultaneously Olympic, European and Commonwealth champion at breaststroke swimming. She set two world records for 200m, 2:50.3 in 1959 and 2:49.5 when winning the 1960 Olympic title, and two at 220y in 1962.

A member of the Huddersfield Borough Club, she only started at the breaststroke nine months before winning her first title at the 1958 Empire Games. There she won the 220y and a second gold on England's world record-setting medley relay team. In 1962 she won both Commonwealth 110y and 220y breaststroke titles and added a silver at the medley relay. At the Europeans she had been second at 200m breaststroke and bronze medallist at medley relay in 1958, and won silver at 400m individual medley and bronze at medley relay as well as her 200m gold in 1962. She ended her career at the 1964 Olympics, where she was 7th at 400m IM. ASA champion at 220y breaststroke 1958-62, 440y IM 1963-4, 220y freestyle 1963. Bests: 400m IM 5:30.5 and 440y IM 5:33.6 in 1964.

Voted Sportswoman of the year in two polls in Britain in both 1960 and 1962, and BBC Sports Personality of the Year 1962. Awarded the MBE 1963, the first swimmer to be so honoured. She became a swimming journalist and radio reporter. Married to cyclist Hugh Porter (qv).

Carlos LOPES (Por)

ATHLETICS

Carlos Lopes. b. 18 Feb 1947 Viseu.

Lopes sealed a distinguished career by becoming the oldest ever Olympic champion at the marathon in 1984, the oldest to set a world best with 2:07:12 to win the Rotterdam Marathon in 1985, and the oldest ever World cross-country champion in 1985. He had earlier wins in the World cross-country in 1976 and 1984, with second place in 1977 and third in 1983. He first competed in the Olympic Games in 1972, going out in the heats of 5000m and 10,000m, but he took the 10,000m silver medal in 1976. Improving with age, he ran a European 10,000m record of 27:24.39 in 1982 and was fourth in the European Championships that year, and ran 27:17.48 behind his compatriot Fernando Mamede's world record 27:13.81 in 1984.

His first marathon was a failure to finish at New York in 1982, before he ran a European best of 2:08:39 when second in Rotterdam in 1983, two seconds behind Rob de Castella. He set a total of 25 Portuguese records between 1971 and 1983 at distances from 3000m to marathon.

Other bests: 3000m 7:48.8 (1976), 5000m 13:16.38 (1984).

Nancy LOPEZ (USA)

GOLF

Nancy Marie Lopez. b. 6 Jan 1957 Torrance, California. Later Melton, then Knight.

One of the most influential, and greatest, players in the history of women's golf. She first became known when she won the New Mexico Women's Amateur championship when she was only 12 years old. She later won the US Junior Girls Championship twice and the Western Girls Championship three times. She attended Tulsa University, for whom she won the AIAW collegiate championship in 1976. She was second in her first US Women's Open in 1975.

After turning professional Lopez had immediate success. In 1978 she won nine tournaments and was the leading money winner. Her streak of five consecutive tournament victories caught the imagination of the public and focused attention on women's golf at a time when it was badly in need of a superstar; her good looks, easy smile, and pleasant personality filled that role perfectly. She has continued to be a dominant force on the women's tour, with major wins at the LPGA 1978, 1985, 1989 and the Dinah Shore 1981. After marrying former baseball star Ray Knight (New York Mets) in 1982, Lopez had two chil-

dren and now plays less frequently than before, but remains a formidable opponent.
LPGA career earnings 1977-92: $3,562,371 with 46 victories.

Greg LOUGANIS (USA)

DIVING

Gregory Efthimios Louganis. b. 29 Jan 1960 San Diego, California.

The greatest diver of all-time, with a record four Olympic and five World gold medals. His first major medal was the Olympic silver at highboard in 1976 (when he was 6th at springboard). He had to miss the 1980 Games but demonstrated his superiority to all comers with the springboard and highboard double in both 1984 and 1988. His springboard win in 1988 came despite needing stitches in between dives, after hitting his head on the board on his descent in the preliminary round.
He holds the world records for the highest marks ever achieved for 3m springboard, 755.49 in 1983, and platform, 717.41 in 1986, and set Olympic records at 754.41 and 710.91 in 1984. At the 1982 World Championships at Guayaquil in Ecuador he was the first man to achieve a score of over 700 points for the 11 dive 3m springboard test with a total of 752.67, and was awarded a perfect 10.0 score by all seven judges for his highboard inward $1^1/_2$ somersault to the pike position.
He won both world titles in 1982 and 1986 after winning the highboard in 1978. Pan-American champion at both events 1979. He has won a record 47 US titles in all, 17 each at 1m and 3m springboard and 13 at platform.
Of Samoan and Northern European ancestry, he triumphed over a difficult childhood to become a marvellously accomplished technician. His grace was augmented by many years of classical dance training. Sullivan Award winner 1984.

Tommy LOUGHRAN (USA)

BOXING

Thomas Loughran. b. 29 Nov 1902 Philadelphia, Pennsylvania, d. 7 Jul 1982 Altoona, Pennsylvania

One of the greatest ever light-heavyweight champions, although it took him eight years and almost 100 fights before he was given a title bout. In 1927 he outpointed Mike McTigue to win the world title, which he defended six times before relinquishing it to fight for the heavyweight championship. He won several fights as a heavyweight but lost a title match against the giant Primo Carnera, conceding 39 kg (86 lb). Loughran had a classic series of six fights against the renowned light-heavyweight Harry Greb. Greb won 2-1, with one draw and two no-decision bouts.
Career record: W - 123 (17), L - 30, D -12.

Joe LOUIS (USA)

BOXING

Joe Louis. né Joseph Louis Barrow. b. 13 May 1914 Lafayette, Louisiana, d. 12 Apr 1981 Las Vegas, Nevada.

Considered by many to be the greatest heavyweight champion ever, and, with Jesse Owens, the greatest black sporting hero prior to World War II. He had a good amateur record in his native Detroit and turned professional in 1934. In his 13th fight he knocked out Primo Carnera, and 'The Brown Bomber' became boxing's hottest property.
Louis was upset in 1936 by Max Schmeling (Ger) in a fight with political overtones because of Hitler's Aryan supremacy theories. But in 1937 he won the heavyweight championship by defeating James Braddock and he avenged the defeat to Schmeling with a one-round knockout in 1938. Louis remained heavyweight champion from 1937 until 1949, at 11 years 252 days the longest ever continuous reign, and made a record 25 consecutive successful title defences. He retired while still champion.
Because of financial difficulties caused by tax demands, Louis returned to the ring in 1950 and lost title bouts against Ezzard Charles and Rocky Marciano. He continued to have financial problems throughout his life and later was forced into professional wrestling and acted as a greeter at a Las Vegas casino.
Career record: W - 63 (49), L - 3, D - 0.

Spyridon LOUIS (Greece)

ATHLETICS

Spyridon Louis. b. 12 Jan 1873 Maroressi, d. 26 Mar 1940.

The first Greek Olympic champion when he won the marathon, held in Athens at 40km in 1896, in 2:58:50. He had placed fifth in the second trial race for the Games, but worked his way through the field to win the big race to the ecstatic joy of his countrymen. A modest man, he turned down numerous lucrative offers and returned to a normal village life in Amarousian, where he was a water-carrier. He never ran again.

Clyde LOVELETTE (USA)

BASKETBALL

Clyde Edward Lovelette. b. 7 Sep 1929 Terre Haute, Indiana.

A winner of championship basketball titles at every major level of competition: NCAA 1952 for the University of Kansas, Olympic 1952, and NBA with the Boston Celtics 1963-4. He was a 2.06m *6' 9"* center who was a two-time all-American in college and scoring leader at 28.4 points per game in 1952. After his Olympic success he was drafted by the Minneapolis Lakers in 1953 and he had four good years for them. He subsequently played for both Cincinnati and St Louis, playing in three NBA All-Star games and making second team all-NBA one year, before finishing his career with the Celtics as a back-up center to Bill Russell.

Lovelette was a burly fellow on the court and was known as a bit of an enforcer. He apparently took the reputation with him after his playing days as he served several years as sheriff of his hometown.

Jack LOVELOCK (NZ)

ATHLETICS

John Edward Lovelock. b. 5 Jan 1910 Cushington, d. 28 Dec 1949 New York, USA.

His Olympic 1500m victory in 1936 was one of the most complete in Olympic history, as he produced a long sustained drive for the finish and posted a world record of 3:47.8.

A Rhodes Scholar at Exeter College, Oxford, he set a world record with 3:02.2 for 3/4 mile and was 7th at 1500m in the Olympics in 1932. In 1933 he set the world record for the mile with 4:07.6 at Princeton after a great race with Bill Bonthron, and he was AAA and Empire Games champion at 1 mile in 1934. In 1935 Lovelock returned to Princeton, where he beat Bonthron and Glenn Cunningham in the first 'Mile of the Century', and won the World Student Games title at 1500m. His 3 miles best was 14:14.8 (1936).

Lovelock completed his medical studies in 1937 and practised as a doctor in London before moving to the USA in 1946. On his way home from his job as assistant director of physical medicine and director of rehabilitation at the Manhattan Hospital of Special Surgery in New York, he fell to his death beneath a subway car.

Cyril LOWE (UK)

RUGBY UNION

Cyril Nelson 'Kit' Lowe. b. 7 Oct 1891 Holbeach, Lincs, d. 6 Feb 1983 Chobham, Surrey.

Scoring 18 tries in 25 consecutive international appearances between 1913 and 1923 he was England's leading try scorer until Rory Underwood bettered his record in 1990. This remarkable record was achieved despite the fact that he failed to score in each of the five matches in his first international season of 1913.

On leaving Dulwich College he went up to Cambridge University where he won his blue in 1911-13. During the war he was an ace fighter pilot, winning the DFC and MC and rising to the rank of Group Captain. Having played for England nine times in 1913-14 he won a further 16 caps after the war and, briefly, held the record as England's most capped player.

Individually, 1914 was his best season as he scored three tries against Scotland and France and two against Wales, and that total of eight tries in one Championship season remains an England record. In his six international seasons England won the Grand Slam four times.

Douglas LOWE (UK)

ATHLETICS

Douglas Gordon Arthur Lowe. b. 7 Aug 1902 Manchester, d. 30 Mar 1981 Cranbrook, Kent.

The first athlete to retain his Olympic 800m title as he won in 1924 and 1928, on both occasions setting British records at 1:52.4 and 1:51.8 respectively. After the 1928 Games he improved that record to 1:51.2. He was also AAA champion at both 440y and 880y in 1927 and 1928. He set a world record for 600 yards with 1:10.4 in 1926.

While at Pembroke College, Cambridge he won a blue for soccer as well as for athletics. He was Hon. Secretary of the AAA from 1931 to 1938, and became a leading barrister and QC.

John LOWE (UK)

DARTS

John Lowe. b. 21 Jul 1945 Clay Cross, Derby.

Formerly a joiner, he has been one of the top players since he won his first major title, the World Masters in 1976. He won that title again in 1980 and won the World Cup singles in 1981 and 1991. He has played on seven winning England teams in the latter tournament from 1979 to 1991. He lost to Leighton Rees in the final of the first World Professional Championship in 1978, but won the title the following year and also in 1987 and 1993, being runner-up in 1981-2, 1985 and 1988.

On 13 Oct 1984 Lowe won £102,000 for achieving the first 501 scored with the minimum nine darts in a major event. This was in the quarter-finals of the first World Matchplay Championship at Slough; he went on to win the final. He won the British Open in 1977 and 1988, the British Matchplay in 1978 and 1986, the *News of the World* Championship in 1981, and with Bob Anderson the first World Pairs title in 1986.

Jerry LUCAS (USA)

BASKETBALL

Jerry Ray Lucas. b. 30 Mar 1940 Middletown, Ohio.

One of the greatest forwards ever to play basketball. In 1960, besides playing on the Olympic gold medal team, he led his Ohio State team to the NCAA championship as a sophomore center. He played mostly center in college and made all-American each year 1960-2 as well as twice being named College Player of the Year. He also led the nation in rebounding in his junior and senior years, and in field goal percentage all three of his varsity years, setting a collegiate career mark in that category. He was drafted by Cincinnati of the NBA in 1962 but instead signed with the Cleveland Pipers of the soon-to-be-defunct American Basketball League. Cleveland folded before playing a game and Lucas sat out a season before beginning his NBA career. His 11-year NBA career began with a Rookie of the Year award in 1964. He was three times named to the NBA first-team All-Stars, and three times was named second-team. In 1965 he was the MVP of the NBA All-Star game and he finished his career with the New York Knicks by helping them win an NBA title in 1973.

Since his basketball career ended, Lucas has been involved in several entrepreneurial pursuits, the best known of which are his books and schools of memory training. His own memory is phenomenal and he and partner Harry Lorayne have devised a system which they have marketed into a big business.

NBA career: 12,942 rebounds, av. 15.6.

Muriel LUCAS (UK)

BADMINTON

Muriel Lucas. Later Mrs King Adams.

The most successful player in the early days of the All-England Badminton Championships, and her total of 17 titles remains unbeaten by a woman. She was singles champion in 1902, 1905 and 1907-10, won the women's doubles 10 times in 12 years between the first championships in 1899 and 1910 with four different partners, and the mixed doubles with Norman Wood in 1908.

Sid LUCKMAN (USA)

AMERICAN FOOTBALL

Sidney Luckman. b. 21 Nov 1916 Brooklyn, New York.

After playing college football in his hometown of New York at Columbia University he played for the Chicago Bears from 1939 to 1950. During this time he rivalled Sammy Baugh as one of the two top quarterbacks in the game. Between 1940 and 1946 he helped the Bears to win four NFL championships, including the 73-0 rout of the Washington Redskins in the 1940 Championship Game. In 1943 he set an NFL record by passing for seven touchdowns in one game, a record which has yet to be broken. He coached at the US Merchant Marine Academy for 20 seasons.
NFL career 1939-50: 14,683 yards from 904 pass completions, 51.8%, 137 TD.

Christa LUDING (GDR)

SPEED SKATING and CYCLING

Christa Luding. b. 4 Dec 1959 Weisswasser. née Rothenberger.

World champion at both sprint cycling and at speed skating. She first competed at the Olympic Games at speed skating in 1980, when she was 12th at 500m and 18th at 1000m, and reached the top in 1984 when she won the Olympic gold at 500m. Four years later she won the 1000m and was second at 500m. To those three medals from the Winter Games she added silver at the Summer in 1988, when she was beaten 2-1 by Erika Salumäe in the cycling sprint. She won another medal with the 500m speed skating bronze in 1992.
Rothenberger had been persuaded by her coach Ernst Luding (whom she married in 1988) to take up cycling in the off season from skating, and quickly reached the top at that sport too, winning the world sprint gold medal in 1986. At skating she was also world sprint champion in 1985 and 1988 and won World Cup titles at 500m in 1988-9 and at 1000m 1988.

Jon LUGBILL (USA)

CANOEING

Jon Lugbill. b. 27 May 1961 Wausson, Ohio.

The top whitewater canoeist of the 1980s and winner of a record five world individual titles at canoe slalom (C1 1979, 1981, 1983, 1987, 1989) as well as seven C1 team gold medals 1979-91. With David Hearn (b. 17 Apr 1959) he was undefeated in the World Championship C1 team event 1979-91. Lugbill was also the World Cup champion each year 1988-90. When the sport returned to the Olympic programme in 1992, he came fourth.
Employed as an environmental planner for the Washington (D.C.) Council of Government.

Hank LUISETTI (USA)

BASKETBALL

Angelo Joseph Luisetti. b. 16 Jun 1916 San Francisco, California.

Luisetti is usually considered the first great player to use the now standard one-handed jump shot, rather than the two-handed set shot of his era. He starred at Stanford from 1934-8. On 1 Jan 1938, he scored 50 points against Duquesne, becoming the first collegiate player to score that many in one game. In both 1937 and 1938 he was named collegiate player of the year. In 1950 he was voted the second best basketball player of the first half-century.

D Wayne LUKAS (USA)

HORSE RACING

Darrell Wayne Lukas. b. 2 Sep 1935 Antigo, Wisconsin.

He has become the most successful trainer in the USA, leading the money lists for ten successive years 1983-92 and setting seasonal records with \$5.8m in 1984, \$11,802,701 in 1985, \$13,344,595 in 1986, \$17,842,358 in 1988 and with career earnings at \$110,948,894 from 1977-92.
He had an unconventional background, as he had coached basketball at high school for nine years and as assistant at the University of Wisconsin before starting

training in 1966. Initially he had greatest success with quarter-horses. In the 1980s he reached the top of his profession with thoroughbreds, winning the Eclipse Award as top trainer in 1985, 1986 and 1987. His first Kentucky Derby winner was *Winning Colors* in 1988 and has a record ten wins in Breeders Cup races.

Steve LUNDQUIST (USA)

SWIMMING

Stephen Kent Lundquist. b. 20 Feb 1961 Atlanta, Georgia.

His five world records at 100m breaststroke in 1982-4 culminated in 1:01.65 to take the Olympic gold medal in Los Angeles, when he added a second gold in the medley relay and was sixth at 200m individual medley. He had been on the boycotting US Olympic team of 1980. NCAA champion while at Southern Methodist University at 100m breaststroke in 1980-3, 200m breaststroke 1981-2, 200m IM 1983. World champion at 100m breaststroke and medley relay in 1982 and Pan-American champion at both breaststroke events and the medley relay in 1983, with a bronze at 200m IM. Other bests: 200m breaststroke 2:15.38 (a US record, 1983), 200m IM 2:03.24 (1983). Later an actor and model.

Janis LUSIS (USSR/Lat)

ATHLETICS

Janis Voldemarovich Lusis. b. 19 May 1939 Jelgava, Latvia.

Javelin thrower who won four European titles between 1962 and 1971 and won a complete set of Olympic medals - gold 1968, silver 1972, bronze 1964, before placing eighth in 1976. He won 12 USSR titles between 1962 and 1976, the World Student Games title in 1963, and in four European Cup Finals was first twice and second twice, for an outstandingly consistent record in a notoriously inconsistent event. A fine all-rounder, who was also a world-ranked decathlete (best of 7486 points in 1962 on the 1985 tables), he married the 1960 Olympic javelin champion, Elvira Ozolina (qv). He set his first Latvian record with 77.48m in 1961 and six USSR records from 86.04 in 1962 to world records of 91.98 in 1968 and 93.80 in 1972. He became a coach of javelin throwers in Latvia and the USSR, and with Elvira spent three years in Madagascar 1987-90.

Joe LYDON (UK)

RUGBY LEAGUE

Joseph Lydon. b. 26 Nov 1963 Wigan, Lancashire.

A deceptive and speedy runner who excelled at centre, wing or full back. As a 19-year-old he scored a try on his international début against France in 1983 and went on to win 23 caps (plus 2 appearances as a substitute). Beginning his career with Widnes he moved to Wigan in 1985 for a then world record fee of £100,000. He played in Challenge Cup winning teams for both clubs; Widnes in 1984 and Wigan each year 1988-90. During the summer of 1987 he played for Eastern Suburbs, Sydney.

Sandy LYLE (UK)

GOLF

Alexander Walter Barr Lyle. b. 9 Feb 1958 Shrewsbury, England.

Known for his prodigious length off the tee, Lyle was one of the top golfers in the world in the 1980s, and with Nick Faldo was responsible for the restoration of British golfing prestige. He was a boy international from 1972 and British Youths champion in 1977, when he played in the Walker Cup before turning professional. In 1979 he won the Scandanavian and European Opens and made his Ryder Cup début. He won the British Open in 1985, and had a great year in 1988 when he won the US Masters and World Matchplay. Thereafter he slumped somewhat and failed to make the Ryder Cup teams of 1989 and 1991. In 1992 he was back, however, to 8th on the European money list, to take his career European Tour earnings to £2,070,948 with 18 wins 1977-92, having been leading money-winner in 1979, 1982 and 1985. Awarded the MBE 1987.

Michael LYNAGH (Aus)

RUGBY UNION

Michael Patrick Lynagh. b. 25 Oct 1963 Brisbane.

The record points scorer in international rugby. In 61 matches for Australia 1984-93 he has scored a world record 762 points, achieving the remarkable feat of scoring in each of the first 59 of them. The majority of his points have come from penalties or conversions but his skills extend beyond that of place kicking. Solid in defence and enterprising in attack, his fine all-round ability played a major role in Australia's victory in the 1991 World Cup. He had to withdraw through injury from Australia's tour of Wales and Ireland in 1992.

He plays for Australia mostly at fly half, with seven games as a centre and one as replacement full back. He has played for Queensland University and Queensland.

George McAFEE (USA)

AMERICAN FOOTBALL

George Anderson McAfee. b. 13 Mar 1918 Corbin, Kentucky.

One of football's greatest running backs. His college career was spent at Duke University, whom he helped to a Rose Bowl berth in his senior year. Blessed with blinding speed, he was drafted by the Chicago Bears and played for them in 1940-1 and 1945-50, missing the interim years because of military service. His best years were probably lost because of the war. In addition to his talents as a running back, McAfee was an exceptional punt returner with a career punt return average of 12.8 yards per attempt. This remains an NFL record for those with more than 100 returns

Once, when George Halas was asked if Gale Sayers was a better runner than George McAfee, Halas replied that merely comparing any football player to McAfee was the finest compliment he could give them.

NFL career 1940-50: Rushing: 1685 yards av. 4.9, 22 touchdowns. Receiving: 1357 yards av. 16.0, 11 touchdowns.

Willie John McBRIDE (UK)

RUGBY UNION

William James McBride. b. 6 Jun 1940 Toomebridge, Co. Antrim.

During an international career which lasted from 1962 to 1975, 'Willie John' played in a record 17 Tests for the Lions and was capped 63 times (12 as captain) by Ireland. His total of 80 international caps remained a record until bettered by fellow Irishman Mike Gibson in 1979.

In an era when the robust, physical play of the All Blacks and Springboks dominated, McBride was the only forward from the Home Countries who was their match. In addition to his ability to take on the opposition, he inspired his team-mates to do the same and his outstanding leadership qualities led to his being appointed captain of the 1974 Lions in South Africa. This was his fifth Lions tour and his team stunned the Springboks by winning the Test series 3-0 with one match drawn. After retirement, he coached the Irish team and was manager of the 1983 Lions tour to New Zealand.

Stan McCABE (Aus)

CRICKET

Stanley Joseph McCabe. b. 16 Jul 1910 Grenfell, New South Wales, d. 25 Aug 1968 Mosman, Sydney.

McCabe played three of the greatest ever innings: 187* out of 360 at Sydney against England in 1932, 189* from 274-2 at Johannesburg against South Africa in 1935, and 232 out of 411 at Nottingham against England in 1938. Don Bradman himself urged his team not to miss a ball of the last, for he said they would never again see the like. A superb attacking batsman, McCabe had his most successful tour of England in 1934 with 2078 runs at 69.26. Nicknamed 'Napper', he played for New South Wales from the age of 18 and was also a useful medium-fast bowler who opened the bowling for Australia several times, and was a splendid fielder in any position.

He met his death in a fall from a cliff at the rear of his home.

39 Tests 1930-8: 2748 runs at 48.21, 6 100s HS 232; 36 wickets at 42.86, BB 4-13; 41 catches.
First-class 1928-42: 11,951 runs at 49.38, 29 100s HS 240; 159 wickets at 33.72, BB 5-36; 139 catches.

Chris McCARRON (USA)

HORSE RACING

Christopher McCarron. b. 27 Mar 1955 Dorchester, Massachusetts.

In his first season of 1974 he set a world record by riding 546 winners (from a record 2199 mounts). He again topped the most wins list in 1975 and 1980, and set prize-money records in 1981 ($8,397,604) and 1984 ($12,038,213), having also topped the money list in 1980 when he took the Eclipse Award for outstanding jockey. His great horses ridden include *John Henry* and *Alysheba*. By the end of 1992 he was third on the all-time career prize money list at $155,103,658, with 5761 winners.

Joe McCARTHY (USA)

BASEBALL

Joseph Vincent McCarthy. b. 21 Apr 1887 Philadelphia, Pennsylvania, d. 13 Jan 1978 Buffalo, New York.

One of baseball's greatest managers, but he never played major league ball, although he bounced around the minor leagues for 15 years. After retiring in 1921 he was named manager of the Louisville Colonels and managed them to an American Association pennant. In 1926 he was hired to manage the Chicago Cubs, who won the National League pennant in 1929. McCarthy became manager of the New York Yankees in 1931 and enjoyed one of the greatest managerial careers ever with the Bronx Bombers as they won eight American League pennants and seven World Series championships. He was fired by the Yankees in 1946 and managed the Boston Red Sox 1948-50 before retiring. His career record was 2125 wins and 1333 losses, with a career winning percentage of .615, a major league record.

Charlie MACARTNEY (Aus)

CRICKET

Charles George Macartney. b. 27 Jun 1886 West Maitland, New South Wales, d. 9 Sep 1958 Sydney.

Known as the 'Governor-General', he was a brilliant batsman with a wide range of strokes and, particularly when he first played for Australia, a fine slow left-arm bowler. He played throughout his career for New South Wales and reached his peak form in Tests at 40 when he scored 473 runs at an average of 94.60 in England in 1926. On the previous tour in 1921 he had scored 2317 runs at 59.42 in first-class games, and that included 345 against Nottinghamshire, still the record for scoring in one day.
35 Tests 1907-26: 2131 runs at 41.78, 7 100s HS 170; 45 wickets at 27.55, BB 7-58; 17 catches.
First-class 1905-36: 15,019 runs at 48.78, 49 100s HS 345; 419 wickets at 20.95, BB 7-58; 102 catches.

Ed MACAULEY (USA)

BASKETBALL

Charles Edward Macauley, Jr. b. 22 Mar 1928 St Louis, Missouri.

The youngest player ever elected to the Naismith Memorial Basketball Hall of Fame. 'Easy Ed' Macauley, who earned his nickname for the smooth style which characterised his play, played at St Louis University where he was a two-time All-American and collegiate Player of the Year in 1947 and 1948. Professionally he was drafted by the St Louis Hawks in 1949 as a territorial choice. He played one season with them and was traded to the Boston Celtics in 1950. Boston returned him to St Louis where he played from 1956 to 1959, helping the Hawks to the 1958 NBA title. He was a 2.03m *6'8"* forward who played in eight NBA All-Star Games. He was player-coach of the Hawks in 1958/9 and, after retiring as a player, coached them for one more year before becoming their general manager. He later entered various business ventures and has been a sports announcer in St Louis.

Liz McCOLGAN (UK)

ATHLETICS

Elizabeth McColgan. née Lynch. b. 24 May 1964 Dundee.

World champion at 10,000m in Tokyo in 1991 and at the half-marathon in 1992. A Scottish international who competed for Dundee Hawkhill, she made her first steps to world class while at the University of Alabama, USA, for whom she won the NCAA indoor mile in 1986. In that year she won Scotland's one athletics gold medal at the 1986 Commonwealth Games in Edinburgh. She retained that 10,000m title in 1990, when she was also 3rd at 3000m. In 1987 she was second in the World cross-country and smashed her bests at all events from 800m to 10,000m, at which she was 5th in the World Championships. She married international steeplechaser Peter McColgan in October 1987. In 1988, after a highly successful campaign on the roads, she took the Olympic silver medal at 10,000m. She set a 10km world road best of 30:38 at Orlando in 1989, just a week after she had taken the World indoor silver at 3000m, having led nearly all the way, and then coming back for sixth at 1500m just 13 minutes later.

She made an astonishingly fast return after her daughter Eilish was born on 25 Nov 1990 to win a series of important races and then place third in the World cross-country in March 1991. She won her first two marathon races, the fastest ever début marathon 2:27:32 at New York 1991 and 2:27:38 in Tokyo 1992, but was third in London 1993. In 1992 she ran a world indoor record of 15:03.17 for 5000m and was 5th in the Olympic 10,000m. She was BBC Sports Personality of the Year for 1991, and was awarded the MBE in the 1992 New Year Honours List.

Won UK 10,000m 1986, 5000m 1988, 3000m 1989, 1991; Scottish 3000m 1985-6.

Best times: 800m 2:05.9 (1987), 1500m 4:01.38 (1987), 1M 4:26.11 (1987), 2000m 5:40.24 (1987), 3000m 8:34.80i (1989), 8:38.23 (1991), 5000m 15:01.08 (1987). Road: 15km 47:43 (1988), Half Marathon 67:11 (1992), Marathon 2:27:32 (1991).

Mark McCORMACK (USA)

SPORTS MANAGEMENT

Mark Hume McCormack. b. 6 Nov 1930 Chicago.

Agent and impresario, founder and chief executive of International Management Group (IMG), which he started in 1962. McCormack played golf while at the College of William and Mary, and during this time met Arnold Palmer. After graduating from Yale Law School he became Palmer's business agent. He built a sporting empire with IMG so that by the beginning of the 1990s it was a company employing over 1000 people worldwide, working for top sportsmen and women and with governing bodies to promote sport, especially golf and tennis (and in television). He pioneered the use of corporate hospitality tents at major sporting events. Married tennis player Betsy Nagelsen (b. 23 Oct 1956 St Petersburg, Florida) on 1 Mar 1986.

Pat McCORMICK (USA)

DIVING

Patricia Joan McCormick. née Keller. b. 12 May 1930 Seal Beach, California.

The first diver to win both highboard and springboard diving at two Olympic Games, a feat she achieved in 1952 and 1956. The latter double came just five months after the birth of her son. Coached by her airline pilot husband Glenn, she was AAU champion at springboard both 1m and 3m 1950-1, 1953-6; highboard 1949-51, 1954 and 1956.

Pan-American champion at both events in 1955 after winning the highboard and placing second at springboard in 1951. Sullivan Award winner 1956. Her daughter Kelly McCormick dived for the USA at the 1983 Pan-American Games.

Willie McCOVEY (USA)

BASEBALL

Willie Lee McCovey. b. 10 Jan 1938 Mobile, Alabama.

McCovey became the first great hero of the new San Francisco Giants when he

joined them in 1959. Playing in only 52 games, he batted .354 and won Rookie of the Year honours. He earned the acclaim of the Bay Area fans that had strangely never been accorded Willie Mays. McCovey played most of his 22-year career with the Giants, taking only a brief foray to San Diego and Oakland before finishing his career with four seasons in San Francisco. A first baseman, he was primarily a power hitter, as he batted over .300 in only one full season (1969). He hit over 30 home runs in seven seasons and led the National League three times (44 in 1963, 36 in 1968, 45 in 1969). He also led in RBI twice, 105 in 1968 and 126 in 1969, a figure he equalled in 1970.
Career 1959-80: 2211 hits Avg. .270, HR 521; RBI 1555.

Flo McCUTCHEON (USA)

BOWLING

Floretta Doty McCutcheon. b. 22 Jul 1888 Ottumwa, Iowa, d. 2 Feb 1967 Pasadena, California.

McCutcheon was considered the finest woman bowler in the pre-tournament era. She dominated women's bowling between 1920 and the late 1930s. During that time she made several nationwide tours and gave clinics and exhibitions to over 250,000 women and children. She recorded over 8,000 matches in which she bowled over 200, bowled eleven 800 series, more than a hundred 700 series, and ten perfect 300 games. In 1938/9 she averaged 206 for the WIBC season, a record which stood until 1963/4.

Craig McDERMOTT (Aus)

CRICKET

Craig John McDermott. b. 14 Apr 1965 Ipswich, Queensland.

After making his Test début against the West Indies in 1985, McDermott made a considerable impression in England that year, when he took 30 wickets in the Test series for Australia. The Queensland fast bowler then had some indifferent years and struggled to make much impact at the highest level. However, in the 1990s he has proved to be Australia's most consistently successful bowler, with a Test series best so far of 31 wickets at 21.61 against India in 1991/2.
He was appointed to be Yorkshire's first overseas player in 1992, but had to cancel those plans through injury. He bowled well in the one-day internationals on the Australian tour to England in 1993, but then had to return home early after a stomach operation.
47 Tests 1985-93: 691 runs at 11.91, HS 42; 198 wickets at 28.34, BB 8-97; 11 catches.*
104 One-day Ints: 373 runs at 7.61, HS 37; 155 wickets at 24.91, BB 5-44; 23 catches.
First-class 1983-93: 2350 runs at 16.43, HS 74; 542 wickets at 27.12, BB 8-44; 37 catches.

Hugh McELHENNY (USA)

AMERICAN FOOTBALL

Hugh Edward McElhenny Jr. b. 31 Dec 1928 Los Angeles, California.

A running back known for his speed, his agility, and his electrifying open-field runs. In high school, McElhenny ran 100 yards in 9.7 and 120y hurdles in 14.0. He took that speed to the University of Washington, playing there 1949-51, and in the NFL from 1952-64, mostly with the San Francisco 49ers but with brief stretches at the end of his career with the Minnesota Vikings, New York Giants, and Detroit Lions. His style was often compared to George McAfee.
NFL career 1952-64: Rushing: 5261 yards av. 4.7, 38 touchdowns; Receiving: 3247 yards av. 12.3, 20 touchdowns.

John McENROE (USA)

TENNIS

John Patrick McEnroe. b. 16 Feb 1959 Wiesbaden, West Germany.

Born in Germany while his father was serving with the US Air Force, McEnroe was a brilliant tennis player with a flair, touch and passion unrivalled in the modern game. While still at Stanford University in 1977 he won the one Grand Slam mixed

doubles title of his career at the French Open (with Mary Carillo) and made a sensational Wimbledon début when, at the age of 18, he became the first qualifier and youngest player ever to reach the semi-finals. He won the NCAA singles in 1978 and went on to win Wimbledon in 1981 and 1983-4, and the US Open 1979-81 and 1984. With Peter Fleming (USA) he won the men's doubles at Wimbledon four times (1979, 1981, 1983-4) and the US Open three times (1979, 1981, 1983) and took further Grand Slam doubles titles with Mark Woodforde (Aus) at the 1989 US Open and with Michael Stich (Ger) at Wimbledon 1992.
Only Connors and Lendl have exceeded his total of 77 Grand Prix singles victories, and only Tom Okker (78) his 77 doubles titles (57 of them with Fleming). McEnroe won the Grand Prix Masters in 1979 and 1984-5. His best years were probably 1981, when he beat Borg in the final at both Wimbledon and the US Open, and 1984 when he won 13 out of 15 tournaments and again won both those titles.
He had a fine Davis Cup record and was a member of five winning US teams, 1978-9, 1981-2 and 1992, winning 9 of 10 singles and 3 of 4 doubles in finals. After variable results in 1985 he took a six-month break from the game, but on his return never quite recaptured his previous form, although he claimed some notable scalps. To the end of 1992 he was third on the all-time earnings table at $12,227,622. His abilities as an athletic, left-handed player cannot be disputed but his image was tarnished by boorish and ungracious behaviour and he drew frequent fines and suspensions for his tantrums. Marriage to Oscar-winning actress Tatum O'Neal (from whom he is now separated) in August 1986 and the birth of two sons did nothing to improve his manners, and at the 1990 Australian Open he became the first player ever to be ejected from a Grand Slam tournament. He was removed for swearing at officials during his 4th round match with Mikael Pernfors (Swe).
His brother Patrick (b. 1 Jul 1966) won the 1989 French Open and Masters doubles with Jim Grabb.

Joe McGINNITY (USA)

BASEBALL

Joseph Jerome McGinnity. b. 19 Mar 1871 Rock Island, Illinois, d. 14 Nov 1929 Brooklyn, New York.

McGinnity played only 10 years in the majors as he did not start his career until he was 28. But in those ten years he won over 20 games eight times, twice won over 30, and totalled an amazing 246 wins for 10 seasons. He was known as the 'Iron Man' because he pitched so much.
He led the league in innings pitched every year from 1899-1904 and in games pitched from 1900-7. McGinnity pitched over 300 innings every year from 1899-1907, with highs of 434 in 1903 and 408 in 1904. These were not records because of the era in which he pitched, but the 434 figure has not been surpassed since 1908. Strangely, after his major league retirement in 1908, McGinnity returned to the minor leagues and pitched for 17 more years, notching another 171 wins before he finally stopped pitching.
Career pitching 1899-1908 ERA 2.66; W-L 246-142, SO 1068; Best seasons: 1904: 35-8, 1.61 ERA; 1903: 31-20, 2.43 ERA; 1900: 28-8, 2.94 ERA; 1899: 28-16, 2.68 ERA; 1906: 27-12, 2.25 ERA.

Terry McGOVERN (USA)

BOXING

Joseph Terrance McGovern. b. 9 Mar 1880 Johnstown, Pennsylvania, d. 26 Feb 1918 Brooklyn, New York

'Terrible Terry' McGovern turned professional at 17 and had a short but meteoric career. He won the bantamweight world championship in 1899 at the age of 19 when he knocked out Pedlar Palmer in the first round. After one successful defence of that title, he annexed the featherweight crown in 1900 with a knockout of George Dixon. McGovern seemed almost invincible and won six more world title fights by knock-out until Young Corbett knocked him out in a featherweight title fight in 1901. He fought for four more years but was never the same fighter.
Career record: W - 59 (34), L - 4, D - 4.

Matt McGRATH (USA)

ATHLETICS

Matthew John McGrath. b. 18 Dec 1878 Nenagh, Co. Tipperary, Ireland, d. 29 Jan 1941 New York.

Olympic hammer champion in 1912 and silver medallist in 1908 and 1924, at the age of 45. He was also fifth in 1920 and won seven AAU titles between 1908 and 1926 as well as seven titles at 56lb weight. He set world hammer records of 52.90m in 1907 and 57.10 in 1911.

John McGRAW (USA)

BASEBALL

John Joseph McGraw. b. 7 Apr 1873 Truxton, New York, d. 25 Feb 1934 New Rochelle, New York.

Having played major league baseball 1892-99 with the Baltimore Orioles of the National League, he began his managing career with the Orioles, although he returned for one more year as a player in 1900 with the St Louis Cardinals. He then returned to managing the Orioles in 1901-2. McGraw was then hired by the New York Giants, whom he managed for 30 years from 1903, a career second only to Connie Mack's in longevity. During his tenure he managed the Giants to four National League pennants and three World Series victories. His career record was 2784 wins at a percentage of .587. He managed with an iron fist and demanded unquestioned obeisance to his authority.

Barry McGUIGAN (UK)

BOXING

Finbar Patrick McGuigan. b. 28 Feb 1961 Clones, Monaghan.

An Irish hero throughout his career. As an amateur in 1978 at bantamweight he won the Irish title and the gold medal at the Commonwealth Games. Having turned professional he won the British featherweight title in 1983 and in 1985 outpointed Eusebio Pedroza to win the world featherweight championship. He was upset in 1986 by Steve Cruz and retired briefly. He started fighting again but did not mount a serious title challenge.

Career record: W - 30 (26), L - 2, D - 0.

Willa McGUIRE (USA)

WATER SKIING

Willa McGuire. née Worthington. b. 1928 Lake Oswego, Oregon.

Willa Worthington began water skiing in 1942 at age 14 and quickly abandoned her interest in diving to become the first great female water skier. At the first four world championships she won three overall titles, 1949-50 and 1955, and five individual golds: slalom and jumping 1949 and 1955, and tricks 1950. She also won eight overall US championships, each year 1946-51 and 1954-55, with 18 individual championships, never losing at tricks, at which she was a great pioneer, and in 1949 and 1951 securing rare sweeps of all three individual events as well as the overall title. She is now known as a multi-talented artist who does primarily portraiture.

Connie MACK (USA)

BASEBALL

né Cornelius Alexander McGillicuddy. b. 22 Dec 1862 East Brookfield, Massachusetts, d. 8 Feb 1956 Germantown, Pennsylvania.

Mack had the longest career in history as a baseball manager. He first managed Milwaukee in the minors 1897-1900 and became part-owner and manager of the Philadelphia Athletics, a position he held for 50 years. In that time he managed nine American League pennant winners, five World Series champions, and holds first place among major league managers with 7878 games, 3776 wins, and 4025 losses. His lifetime winning percentage was a mediocre .484 but he is remembered more for his longevity than his brilliance.

Eugen MACK (Swi)

GYMNASTICS

Eugen Mack. b. 21 Sep 1907 Zürich, d. 29 Oct 1978.

The most successful gymnast of the 1930s

at the World Championships, at which he won five individual gold medals (the overall and three individual apparatus titles in 1934 and the vault in 1938), three silvers and a bronze. At the Olympics he won gold medals for the horse vault and team in 1928, did not compete in 1932, and took four silvers and a bronze in 1936.
He was also a trainer and a designer of gymnastic equipment.

Kitty McKANE (UK) see GODFREE

Heather McKAY (Aus)

SQUASH

Heather Pamela McKay. née Blundell. b. 31 Jul 1941, Queanbeyan, New South Wales.

Winner of a record number of major championships and unbeaten from 1962 to 1980, one of the greatest records in any sport.
The eighth of eleven children born to sporting parents, she initially took up squash to improve her fitness for hockey and two years later she was the Australian champion. On her first visit to Britain in 1962 she lost in the final of the Scottish Open to the British Open champion Fran Marshall, and this was the last competitive match she ever lost. One month after her defeat in Scotland, she won the first of her 16 consecutive British Open titles, 1962-77, and after winning 14 consecutive Australian amateur titles, 1960-73, she turned professional. She won the first two Women's World titles in 1976 and 1979 and then retired. However, after only two years she became the best racquetball player in Canada, where she had settled in 1975. She married the professional coach Brian Mackay in 1965.

Herb McKENLEY (Jam)

ATHLETICS

Herbert Henry McKenley. b. 10 Jul 1922 Clarendon.

Versatile sprinter with the unique distinction for a male athlete of making Olympic finals at 100m, 200m and 400m. He was at his best at the one-lap with world 440y bests at 46.2 in 1946 and 1947 and at 46.0 in 1948. He improved the 400m record to 45.9 (46.00 auto) at Milwaukee on 2 Jul 1948. He won Olympic silver medals at 400m in 1948 and 1952, and in the latter Games ran a 44.6 relay leg, the fastest ever at the time, for Jamaica's gold medal winning team. He was 4th at 200m in 1948 and 2nd at 100m in 1952. He also won the AAU 440y in 1945, 1947 and 1948, and the NCAA 440y for the University of Illinois in 1946 and 1947.
For many years up to 1992 'Hustling Herb' has been the head coach for the Jamaican Olympic teams.
Other bests: 100y 9.5 (1949) and 9.4w (1947), 100m 10.2 (1951), 200m 20.8 (1950), 220y straight 20.6 (1946) and 20.2w (1947).

Graham McKENZIE (Aus)

CRICKET

Graham Douglas McKenzie. b. 24 Jun 1941 Cottesloe, Perth.

A dependable fast-medium outswing bowler for Australia in the 1960s, when he became the then youngest-ever player to reach the milestones of 100, 150 and 200 wickets in Tests. Tall, and with a superb physique, he surprisingly dropped out of the Australian team before his 30th birthday but played successfully for Leicestershire 1969-75.
60 Tests 1961-71: 945 runs at 12.27; HS 76; 246 wickets at 29.78, BB 8-71; 36 catches.
1 One-day Int: 2 wickets at 11.00; 1 catch.
First-class 1959-75: 5662 runs at 15.59; HS 76; 1218 wickets at 26.98, BB 8-71; 200 catches.

Stuart MACKENZIE (Aus)

ROWING

Stuart Alexander Mackenzie. b. 5 Apr 1937 Sydney, New South Wales.

A great single sculler, the winner of a record six successive Diamond Sculls at Henley 1957-62. He began his rowing career at King's School in Sydney and contested the 1956 Australian single sculls championship because he announced that the Australian great Merv Wood, 20 years

his senior, was a bit old for Olympic selection. Mackenzie won easily to gain selection. At the Olympics he won a silver medal, although he was well beaten by Vyacheslav Ivanov. In 1959 he became the first man to win both the single and double sculls at Henley. In two of the Diamond Sculls wins, Mackenzie avenged his Olympic defeat by Ivanov. Mackenzie was also European single sculls champion in 1957-58 (both times defeating Ivanov), and won the Empire Games single sculls in 1958, with a silver medal at double sculls with Wood. He was forced to withdraw from the 1960 Olympics with anaemia and a stomach ulcer. Although a great champion, he is considered one of the most unpopular rowers ever at Henley. Among his other exuberant antics, he once stopped in mid-race to adjust his cap, allowed his opponent to catch up, and then rowed away easily to win.
He was not selected for the 1962 Commonwealth Games after refusing to return to Australia for trials, so he ended his career rowing for Britain at the 1961 and 1963 European Championships.

Chuck McKINLEY (USA)

TENNIS

Charles Robert McKinley. b. 5 Jan 1941 St Louis, Missouri, d. 11 Aug 1986 Dallas, Texas.

Although he won the Wimbledon singles in 1963, he was better known as a doubles player, winning the US title in 1961 and 1963-4 with Dennis Ralston. Due to a series of upset results he uniquely won his Wimbledon singles title without meeting a seeded player. He was also only the third player ever to win the title without losing a set in the tournament. McKinley played in 16 Davis Cup ties between 1960 and 1965, winning 17 of 22 singles and 13 of 16 doubles, and possibly the finest performance of his career came in the 1963 Challenge Round when his victory over John Newcombe in the vital fifth rubber enabled the USA to recapture the trophy from Australia. He retired in 1965 to become a stockbroker in New York, but died at the age of 45 of a brain tumour.

Rick McKINNEY (USA)

ARCHERY

Richard Lee McKinney. b. 12 Oct 1953 Decatur, Indiana.

World champion at target archery three times, 1977, 1983 and 1985. He also won five gold medals with the US team 1975-83. He competed at four Olympic Games from 1976, when he was 4th, to 1992, winning silver medals at the individual event in 1984 and team 1988. In 1980, he would probably have been a slight favourite over team-mate Darrell Pace but the Olympic boycott prevented his participation. McKinney set world records at 50m, 70m and 90m, and won nine US National Championships, 1977, 1979-83, 1985-7, and three NCAA titles, 1981-3. At all disciplines, target, indoor and field, he has won 23 national titles.
He began his archery career at the age of ten, and has been a great rival of Pace (qv), who grew up just 85 miles away from him.

Tamara McKINNEY (USA)

ALPINE SKIING

Tamara Price McKinney. b. 16 Oct 1962 Lexington, Kentucky.

Had her first World Cup race at the age of 14 and in the 13 years up to her retirement in 1990 she won 18 World Cup races, being overall champion in 1983, and taking the giant slalom title in 1981 and 1983 and the slalom in 1984. World champion at Alpine combination in 1989. Her best at the Olympic Games was 4th at giant slalom in 1984.
Her father, Rigan, was a notable steeplechase jockey and her mother was a part-time ski instructor at Mt Rose after the family moved to Nevada when Tamara was a baby. Her half-brother Steve was the first speed skier to exceed 200 km/h.

Myrtle MACLAGAN (UK)

CRICKET

Myrtle Ethel Maclagan. b. 2 Apr 1911 Ambala, India, d. 11 Mar 1993 Farnham, Surrey.

In the first women's Test played between

England and Australia at Brisbane in December 1934, Maclagan took 7-10 with her off-spinners for England in skittling Australia out for just 47. She then top-scored with 72 to ensure a 9-wicket victory for England. In the 2nd Test at Sydney in January she scored the first Test century by a woman with 119. In her 14 Tests over 17 years she became the first to reach the career figures of 1000 runs and of 50 wickets with 1007 at 41.95 and 60 at 15.60 respectively. She captained England in two Tests in 1951. She was an officer in the ATS during the War and having rejoined the Army in 1951 was awarded the MBE for her services to the WRAC in 1966. She was a fine all-rounder, also playing for the Army at hockey, lacrosse, badminton and tennis.

Archie McLAREN (UK)

CRICKET

Archibald Campbell McLaren. b. 1 Dec 1871 Whalley Range, Manchester, d. 17 Nov 1944 Warfield Park, Bracknell, Berkshire.

After making his name as a handsome batsman at Harrow, he joined Lancashire in 1890, and was their captain 1894-6 and 1899-1907. In 1895 he made 424 in 470 minutes against Somerset at Taunton; this lasted as the record score in first-class cricket for over 27 years and added 80 to WG Grace's previous record. He succeeded WG as England captain in 1899 and in all led England in 22 Tests, but was not especially successful, winning 4 to 11 losses, and he did not get the most out of his teams. At 49 he raised a team that beat the all-conquering Australians at the end of their tour in 1921. He managed the England team to South Africa in 1924/5.
35 Tests 1894-1909: 1931 runs at 33.87, 5 100s HS 140; 29 catches.
First-class 1890-1921: 22,237 runs at 34.15, 47 100s HS 424; 1 wicket; 453 catches.

Bruce McLAREN (NZ)

MOTOR RACING

Bruce Leslie McLaren. b. 30 Aug 1937, d. 1 June 1970 Goodwood.

On 22 Dec 1959 at 22 years 104 days he became the youngest ever winner of a World Championship race when he won the United States GP at Sebring. Although he never won the world title, his name became even more famous as a result of the enormous success of cars bearing his name long after his death, as McLaren won the Constructors' Championship in 1974, 1984-5, 1988-90.
His father encouraged his career initially at hill climbing, and after studying engineering at Auckland University he won the New Zealand 'Driver to Europe' scholarship in 1958, where he raced for Cooper in Formula 2. He stepped up to Formula One in 1959 and in 1960 was second to Jack Brabham in the World Championship. The Cooper cars became less competitive and at the end of 1964 he left them for his own team, which soon gained a reputation for good management. He won the Cam-Am series in 1967 and 1969, but was killed testing a prototype in 1970. In his world championship career he won four of his 101 races, with a total of 196.5 points.
He was the most popular driver of his day, with his modesty and open, friendly approach to the sport. He was left with a limp, and his left leg 4cm shorter than his right, as a legacy of a childhood illness.

Jimmy McLARNIN (USA)

BOXING

James Archibald McLarnin. b. 19 Dec 1906 Inchacore, Belfast, Northern Ireland

McLarnin was among the world's best light and welterweights for almost a dozen years. He had lost a lightweight world title fight in 1928, but won the welterweight championship in 1933 by a first-round knockout of Young Corbett III. After McLarnin moved to Vancouver as a boy he was 'adopted' by Pop Foster, a Canadian who handled him adroitly so that he made a lot of money. This was invested wisely and McLarnin retired a wealthy man after three great battles in 1934-5 with Barney Ross, who won the rubber match and claimed the world welterweight title.
Career record: W - 63 (20), L - 11, D - 3.

Hugh McLEOD (UK)

RUGBY UNION

Hugh Ferns McLeod. b. 8 Jun 1932 Hawick.

A tough prop forward from Hawick, who made his international début against France in 1954 and kept his place in the Scottish XV until his retirement in 1962 at the age of 29. Initially a tighthead prop, he later specialised in the loosehead position. His 40 caps came in consecutive matches and he toured twice with the Lions. Although he did not command a place in the Test side in South Africa in 1955, he played in all six Tests against Australia and New Zealand on his second tour in 1959. Awarded the OBE.

Maurice McLOUGHLIN (USA)

TENNIS

Maurice Evans McLoughlin. b. 18 Nov 1890 Carson City, Nevada, d. 10 Dec 1957 Hermosa Beach, California.

Although he only had a brief top-class career, he had a major influence on the development of tennis as the first notable player to rely on a serve-volley game. Because of his hard-hitting style he was known as the 'California Comet' and it was his service that first gave rise to the description 'cannonball'. Progressing from the asphalt courts of San Francisco, he won the Pacific States Championship in 1907, and when he first went East in 1909 he caused a sensation when his power game took him to the finals of the All-Comers at the National Championships. After the Challenge Round had been abolished, he took the title in 1912 and 1913. He also won three US doubles titles with Tom Bundy 1912-14. After reaching the final of the US singles in 1914-15 and the doubles 1915-16, he served in the US Navy in World War I. On his return to the game in 1919 he met with only limited success and soon retired to devote himself to his real estate business. His only appearance at Wimbledon in 1913 attracted unprecedented crowds who saw the 23-year-old American win the All-Comers title before losing to Anthony Wilding in the Challenge Round. He won 12 of 20 Davis Cup matches 1909-14. Although his style of play changed the whole pattern of the game, the fact that he was America's first champion from the public parks - rather than the wealthy élite - had a significant influence in attracting both players and spectators from a wider social background.

Johnny McNALLY (USA)

AMERICAN FOOTBALL

John Victor McNally. b. 27 Nov 1904 New Richmond, Wisconsin, d. 28 Nov 1985 Palm Springs, California.

'Johnny Blood' was one of the great running backs of the early days of pro football. He played college football only briefly at St John's of Minnesota. He was playing semi-pro football in 1924 when he saw a Rudolph Valentino movie marquee *Blood and Sand*. He re-christened himself Johnny Blood and began playing under that pseudonym, a common practice in that era to preserve amateur status. In 1925 he began a 15-year NFL career which saw him play for the Milwaukee Badgers, Duluth Eskimos, Pottsville Maroons, Green Bay Packers, Pittsburgh Pirates, and Pittsburgh Steelers. In his last year (1939), Blood was a player-coach with the Steelers. He was an undisciplined player, who was never known to pass up a drink, and he often missed practices, but he stayed in pro football because of his great athletic ability. He was, however, a terrible coach. After serving as a cryptographer in China during World War II he tried to play for the Packers again in 1945, but failed.

Dave McNAMARA (Aus)

AUSTRALIAN RULES FOOTBALL

David John McNamara. b. 22 Jan 1887 Boosey, nr. Yarrawonga, Victoria, d. 15 Aug 1967 Caulfield, Melbourne.

The greatest all-round kicker in the history of the game, who won many matches solely on his goal-kicking abilities. He began playing with St Kilda in 1905 and burst into prominence as a centre half-forward two years later, and was appointed

their captain at the age of 21 in 1908. After a dispute with the club he moved to Essendon in the VFA for three seasons, taking the side to the premiership in 1911 and 1912, when with 107 goals he became the first player to score 100 in a season. He rejoined St Kilda in 1913 and finished his career as captain of the club for the 1922/3 season; in 122 VFL matches for them he kicked 600 goals. In 1914 at St Kilda Cricket Ground he place-kicked a football 96 metres.
After retirement he became a successful racehorse trainer and served as president of the Victorian Trainers Association.

Phil MacPHERSON (UK)

RUGBY UNION

George Philip Stewart MacPherson. b. 14 Dec 1903 Newtonmore, Inverness, d. 2 Mar 1981 Thame, Oxfordshire.

One of the greatest Scottish centres who captained his country in 12 of his 26 international matches. After attending Edinburgh Academy and Fettes he went up to Oxford University and played against Cambridge in 1922-4. A fine all-round athlete, he was the Scottish long jump champion in 1929.
After serving as a Brigadier in World War II he resumed his career as a merchant banker and became a director of many major institutions. He was awarded the CBE for his work.

Helene MADISON (USA)

SWIMMING

Helene Emma Madison. b. 19 Jun 1913 Madison, Wisconsin, d. 25 Nov 1970 Seattle. Later McIver, then Kapphahu.

The treble Olympic gold medallist in 1932, at 100m in a long-course best of 66.8, 400m in a world record 5:28.5 and at 4x 100m relay in another world record, Madison broke world records at 15 distances from 100y to 1 mile in 1930-1 and was the Sullivan Award winner in 1931. Her best times included 100y 60.0, 100m 66.0, 220y 2:34.8, 440y 5:31.0, 880y 11:41.2, 1500m 23:17.2, mile 24:34.6. She won all four US titles at 100y, 440y, 880y and 1 mile in 1930 and 1931.
Retiring while still a teenager, she had a brief film career in Hollywood, but did not meet with success there or as a nightclub singer.

Freddy MAERTENS (Bel)

CYCLING

Freddy Maertens. b. 13 Feb 1952 Nieuwpoort.

Although he did not quite meet the hopes of a nation to emulate Eddy Merckx, he compiled one of the great records ever in the one-day classics. He was only an average climber, which prevented him from winning much in the major tours, but he was one of the greatest ever road sprinters.
Major victories: World Pro Road Race 1976, 1981; Vuelta à España 1977; Tour of Flanders 1982; Ghent-Wevelgem 1975-6; Amstel Gold Race 1976; Bordeaux-Paris 1985; Zürich 1976; Paris-Nice 1977; Grand Prix de Nations 1976; Points Jersey: Tour de France 1976, 1978, 1981 and Vuelta à España 1977.

Zoltán MAGYAR (Hun)

GYMNASTICS

Zoltán Magyar. b. 13 Dec 1953 Budapest.

A supreme exponent on the pommel horse at which he introduced the 'Magyar travel' and the 'spindle'. He took the Olympic gold medal in 1976 and 1980, and won three successive World titles, 1974, 1978 and 1979, and European titles, 1973, 1975 and 1977. He also won an Olympic bronze with the Hungarian team in 1980. His best all-around placing was 4th at the 1975 Europeans. He graduated from the Budapest Academy of PE and was coached at Ferencváros by László Vigh.

Larry MAHAN (USA)

RODEO

Larry 'Bull' Mahan. b. 21 Nov 1943 Salem, Oregon.

The winner of a record six Professional Rodeo Cowboy Association all-around championships, 1966-70 and 1973. He was a bit of a maverick in his early days, with flamboyant dress and behaviour which offended many older cowboys, but was a great rider. His great physical strength allowed him to ride saddle broncs, bare-backs, and bulls in the same rodeo - often consecutively. He also changed the training methods of cowboys, emphasising the need for proper diet, exercise and mental management. He retired from bull riding in 1977 and saddle bronc riding in 1979. In 1972 a movie, *The Great American Cowboy*, was made about Mahan's race for a year-end bull riding title. He retired to cattle breeding and also does a lot of promotional work.

Danny MAHER (USA/UK)

HORSE RACING

Daniel Aloysius Maher. b. 29 Oct 1881 Hartford, Connecticut, d. 9 Nov 1916 London.

Champion jockey in the USA in 1898 and in Britain in 1908 and 1913, with 1771 winners between 1895 and 1913; in nine of these years he rode over 100, with a peak of 139 winners in 1908.

He began riding at the age of 14 and three years later was champion in the USA. He went to England in 1900 and rode the first of his nine classic winners in 1901. A stylish horseman, his health declined due to excessive wasting, and by the time of the last of his 1421 winners in Britain in 1913 he was already suffering from tuberculosis. Having lost most of his money due to unwise investment in a New York hotel, he rode his last race in 1915 and died the following year.

MAHMOUD KARIM (Egypt)

SQUASH

Mahmoud Karim. b. Cairo.

Winner of four successive British Open titles, 1946-9. Starting as a ball boy at the Gezira Club in Cairo, he later became senior professional there and, with Amr Bey on diplomatic duty in London, was virtually unbeatable in Egypt. After a scheduled trip was cancelled because of the outbreak of war, he paid his first visit to England in 1946 when he beat Jim Dear to become British Open champion. Following three further victories he was again a finalist in 1950 and 1951 but lost both times to Hashim Khan. In 1953 he emigrated to Canada where he became a successful and popular coach and tournament organiser.

Frank MAHOVLICH (Can)

ICE HOCKEY

Francis William Mahovlich. b. 10 Jan 1938 Timmins, Ontario.

One of the greatest left wingers ever to play professional hockey, although the game tormented him. The Toronto Maple Leafs fans expected a lot of the talented Mahovlich. He played well but never seemed to satisfy them. The pressure mounted on him and twice he succumbed to nervous breakdowns during his career. Still, it was an outstanding one.

In 1960/1 he scored 48 goals (84 points) to approach the fabled Maurice Richard's record of 50 in a season. His personal points best for a season came in 1971/2 with 96 (43 goals). He played for six Stanley Cup champions, four in Toronto and two with the Montreal Canadiens, with whom he finished his NHL career. He played in the WHA from 1974-8 and then retired to manage his own travel agency in Toronto.

Career 1957-78 - 1418 games, 622 goals, 1335 points; NHL: 1181 games, 533 goals, 1103 points. Play-offs: 137 games, 51 goals, 118 points. Calder Trophy 1958.

Phil MAHRE (USA)

ALPINE SKIING

Phillip Ferdinand Mahre. b. 10 May 1957 Yakima, Washington.

Olympic slalom champion in 1984, having been 2nd in 1980, and World champion at Alpine Combination in 1980. A US international from 1974, he was fifth in the giant slalom at the 1976 Olympics. After 2nd place in 1978 and 3rd in 1979 and 1980, he became the first American to win a World Cup title as he was overall champion each year 1981-3, won the giant slalom in 1982-3, and the slalom in 1982. In all he won 27 World Cup events: seven giant slalom, nine slalom and eleven combined.

His twin brother **Steve** also competed at three Olympics, and won the slalom silver medal behind Phil in 1984. He was world champion at giant slalom in 1982 and won nine World Cup ski races. Their father, Dave, was an area ski manager in the White Pass area of the Cascade mountains in Washington State.

Karl MAIER (FRG)

SPEEDWAY

Karl Maier. b. 24 Aug 1957 Munich.

Maier was a motorcycle mechanic and dealer who won a record four world long-track speedway titles, 1980, 1982 and 1987-8.

Sepp MAIER (FRG)

FOOTBALL

Josef-Dieter Maier. b. 28 Feb 1944 Haar.

Winning his 40th cap in 1972 he became West Germany's most capped goalkeeper and he brought his total up to 95 before his retirement, helping his team to win the European Championship in 1972 and World Cup in 1974. He was earlier a youth and amateur international.

A qualified mechanic, he played as an amateur for Bayern Munich 1958-65 and as a professional 1965-79, making his senior début at the age of 18. With them he accumulated numerous honours, notably the European Cup-Winners' Cup 1967, European Cup 1974-6, World Club Cup 1976, the German Cup 1966-7, 1969, 1971, and the German League 1969, 1972-4, playing in 473 first division games in all. Although he was undoubtedly Germany's finest-ever goalkeeper, he suffered occasional lapses and his performance in the 1970 World Cup fell far short of the standard expected.

In 1987 he became a goalkeeper coach for Bayern Munich and for the German international team, and he now works in advertising.

Arthur MAILEY (Aus)

CRICKET

Arthur Alfred Mailey. b. 3 Jan 1886 Waterloo, Sydney, d. 31 Dec 1967 Kirrawee, New South Wales.

Mailey, who became a distinguished cartoonist and writer, entitled his autobiography *Ten for 66 and All That.* That was in recognition of his best bowling performance, for the Australians against Gloucestershire in 1921. A leg-break and googly bowler, getting prodigious turn, he had also taken 9-121 against England the previous winter, and he took over 140 wickets on both his tours to England, 1921 and 1926. His 36 wickets against England at 26.27 in his first Test series of 1920/1 remained the Australian record until 1979.

21 Tests 1920-6: 222 runs at 11.10, HS 46; 99 wickets at 33.91, BB 9-121; 14 catches*

First-class 1912-31: 1529 runs at 12.33, HS 66; 779 wickets at 24.10, BB 10-66; 157 catches.

MAJID KHAN (Pak)

CRICKET

Majid Jahangir Khan. b. 28 Sep 1946 Ludhiana, Punjab, India.

Majid became the youngest player ever to score a first-class century, at 15 years 47 days, and played his first Test at 18 years 26 days, but it was not until a decade later that he fully established himself as one of the world's best batsmen. Before then he had been a hostile fast-medium bowler, but with a suspect action, and he later bowled occasional off-spin, as his batting flourished. He impressed Glamorgan with 147 not out (including 13 sixes) in 89 minutes against them for the touring Pakistan team, so they signed him up and he had a most successful nine years with them, captaining the county 1973-6. From 1970-2 he was a student at Cambridge University, and captained them most successfully for two years. His father Dr **Jahangir Khan** (1910-88) was one of India's best fast bowlers of the 1930s, playing four Tests, and his cousins Javed Burki and Imran Khan (qv) both captained

Pakistan, as did Majid in three Tests against England in 1973.
63 Tests 1964-83: 3931 runs at 38.92, 8 100s HS 167; 27 wickets at 53.92, BB 4-45; 70 catches.
23 One-day Ints: 786 runs at 37.42, 1 100 HS 109; 13 wickets at 28.76, BB 3-27; 3 catches.
First-class 1961-85: 27,444 runs at 43.01, 73 100s HS 241; 223 wickets at 32.14, BB 6-67; 410 catches.

Timo MAKINEN (Finland)

RALLYING

Timo Makinen. b. 18 Mar 1938 Helsinki.

An ultra-fast rally driver. He joined BMC in 1963 and in Mini Coopers he had his first big win, the Tulip Rally in 1964, won the 1000 Lakes Rally 1965-7 and the Monte Carlo Rally in 1965, He was again fastest in the 1966 Monte Carlo Rally, but lost the race through disqualification for infringing a lighting regulation. After a year with Lancia he joined Ford in 1970, and in Escorts won the RAC Rally in three successive years, 1973-5, and the 1000 Lakes Rally in 1973. He also met with success at powerboat racing and won the Round Britain race in 1969. He had started rallying in 1960, while working for his father, Antero, who owned a transport fleet.

Mohamad Asad MALIK (Pak)

HOCKEY

Mohamad Asad Malik. b. 30 Oct 1941.

A forward with the Pakistan International Airlines team, he won seven medals at major tournaments. At the Olympic Games he won gold 1968 and silver 1964 and 1972, in the World Cup gold 1971, and at the Asian Games gold 1962 and 1970 and silver 1966.

Bronislaw MALINOWSKI (Pol)

ATHLETICS

Bronislaw Malinowski. b. 4 Jun 1961 Nowe, d. 26 Sep 1981 in a car crash near Grudziadz.

A determined front runner, he was European steeplechase champion in 1974 and 1978 and Olympic champion in 1980 when he gradually wore down the blazing pace that had been set by Filbert Bayi. At the Olympics he had been fourth in 1972 and second in 1976, when he ran his best time of 8:09.11 behind Anders Gärderud. His major championships career had started with the European Junior title at 2000m steeplechase in 1970.
He was a physical education graduate and concentrated on the steeplechase at which he was ranked in the world top six each year 1972-80, but he was also a fine flat race runner, with 8th at 5000m in 1971 and 4th at 10,000m in 1974 in the Europeans. He was Polish champion at 5000m three times and steeplechase four times.
Best times: 1500m 3:37.42 (1978), 1M 3:55.40 (1976), 3000m 7:42.46 (1974), 5000m 13:17.69 (1976), 10,000m 28:25.19 (1974).

Harry MALLIN (UK)

BOXING

Henry William Mallin. b. 1 Jun 1892 Shoreditch, London, d. 8 Nov 1969 Lewisham, London.

The greatest amateur boxer ever produced in the UK. He was ABA middleweight champion each year from 1919-23 and never lost a match as an amateur boxer in over 300 bouts. He won the Olympic middleweight title in both 1920 and 1924, becoming the first man to defend an Olympic boxing championship. He worked as a London policeman and in 1936 and 1952 managed the British team at the Olympics. He became a high-ranking officer in the Amateur Boxing Association. His brother **Fred**erick (1902-87) was also ABA middleweight champion five times, 1928-32.

Molla MALLORY see BJURSTEDT

Joe MALONE (Can)

ICE HOCKEY

M. Joseph Malone. b. 28 Feb 1890 Sillery, Québec, d. 15 May 1969 Montreal.

Malone was the first great scoring machine

in the NHL. In 1917/8 he scored 44 goals while playing in only 20 games - the season was much shorter in those days - and in 1918/9 his 39 goals were scored in only 24 games. He is the only player ever to average more than one goal per game for a career while playing over 100 games, and was so difficult to defend against that he was nicknamed 'Phantom Joe'.
NHL career 1917-24 - 125 games, 146 goals, 164 points. Ross Trophy 1918, 1920.

Moses MALONE (USA)

BASKETBALL
Moses Eugene Malone. b. 23 Mar 1955 Petersburg, Virginia.

Malone was a highly recruited high school player and although he signed a letter of intent to play at the University of Maryland he went directly to play professionally as a center without playing at college. He began with the Utah Jazz of the ABA in 1974, and then played in 1975-6 for the St Louis Spirits. In the NBA he started with the Buffalo Braves, but has since played for Houston, Philadelphia, Washington, Atlanta and Milwaukee, winning the NBA MVP Award in 1979, 1982 and 1983. He made first-team All-NBA in those years as well as 1985, led the NBA in rebounding six times and was chosen to play in the All-Star Game 12 times. As at January 1993 he had the all-time career record of 8395 free throws.
Career NBA/ABA 1975-93: 29,237 points, av. 21.1; 17,562 rebounds, av. 12.7. NBA: 27,066 points at 21.5; 15,940 rebounds.

Mikhail MAMIASHVILI (USSR/Rus)

WRESTLING
Mikhail Mamiashvili. b. 21 Nov 1963 Konotop, Ukraine.

Mamiashvili won the Greco-Roman middleweight Olympic gold medal in 1988 at Seoul. He probably would have been defending his title but for the 1984 Soviet Olympic boycott. He was first named to the Soviet national team in 1983, and at welterweight he won the world championship in 1983, 1985 and 1986 and the European championship in 1986. He was USSR champion in 1984, 1987-8 and the World Cup winner of 1984-5.

Graziano MANCINELLI (Italy)

EQUESTRIAN
Graziano Mancinelli. b. 18 Feb 1937 Milan.

Mancinelli succeeded the D'Inzeo brothers as a great Italian show jumper. With them he helped Italy win the Olympic team bronze in 1964, but his participation was quite controversial as he was considered a professional rider for the Milan horse dealing company of Fratelli Rivolta. He was initially banned, but was reinstated the day before the Games began. He competed in the Olympics again in 1968, 5th in the team event, and in 1972, when he won the individual gold medal on *Ambassador* . Having tied with Ann Moore (UK) and Neal Shapiro (USA), he rode a perfect round in the jump-off to win the title; he also earned another team bronze.
At the European Junior Championships he won a team gold in 1954 after silvers in 1952 and 1953. Second in the 1970 World Championships and European champion in 1963. Italian champion 1967, 1972, 1974 and 1976.

Hana MANDLIKOVÁ (Cs)

TENNIS
Hana Mandlíková. b. 19 Feb 1962 Prague. Later Sadlek.

Winner of the French Open 1981, US 1985 and Australian 1980 and 1987, but a Wimbledon singles title always eluded her although she was runner-up in 1981 and 1986. Wendy Turnbull (Aus) was her regular doubles partner but she was partnered by fellow Czech Martina Navratilova when she won her only Grand Slam doubles title at the 1989 US Open. Initially her outstanding successes as a junior (she won the French juniors and was ITF junior world champion in 1978) were repeated in the senior ranks but latterly her game was notable for its inconsistency. During the 1986 Federation Cup she married Sydney restaurant owner Jan Sedlek, but they were divorced two years later. Her career tour earnings were $3,340,959. She now coaches Jana Novotná, who reached the 1993 Wimbledon ladies singles final.

Toni MANG (FRG)

MOTOR CYCLING

Anton Mang. b. 29 Sep 1949 Inning.

In a long career, 1976-88, this aggressive rider achieved a record 33 Grand Prix wins at 250cc, with a further 8 at 350cc and one at 125cc. He started his Grand Prix career in 1974 and his first win was on a Yamaha at 350cc in 1976. For Kawasaki he was world champion at 250cc in 1980 and 1981 and at 350cc in 1982, and for Honda at 250cc in 1987. He was also 2nd at 350cc in 1980 and at 250cc in 1982 and 1985.

Edoardo MANGIAROTTI (Italy)

FENCING

Edoardo Mangiarotti. b. 7 Apr 1919 Renate Veduggio, Milan.

Winner of a record 13 Olympic medals for foil and épée from 1936 to 1960. A natural right-hander, he was forced to fence left-handed by his father Giuseppe who was 17 times professional épée champion of Italy. After making his international debut at the 1935 World Championships at the age of 16, he went on to build an unsurpassed record of successes.

In the épée team he won four Olympic gold medals (1936, 1952-60) and one silver (1948). Individually, he won one gold for épée (1952) and two bronze (1948 and 1956). As a foilist he won a team gold medal in 1956 and three silver medals (1948-52, 1960) and an individual silver in 1952. At the World Championships he won two individual épée titles (1951 and 1954). He was also a member of 13 winning teams (épée 1937, 1949-50, 1953-5 and 1957-8; foil 1937-8, 1949-50 and 1954-5). An estate agent and journalist, he became secretary-general of the Fédération Internationale d'Escrime.

His elder brother, **Dario** (b. 18 Dec 1915), won an Olympic gold in 1952 and a silver in 1948 in the team épée, and an individual silver in 1952.

Vinoo MANKAD (India)

CRICKET

Mulvantrai Himmatlal Mankad. b. 12 Apr 1917 Jamnagar, d. 21 Aug 1978 Bombay.

Having impressed against Lord Tennyson's team in India in 1937/8, Mankad had to wait until the Indian tour of England in 1946 to make his Test debút. Then, however, he met with notable success with the double of 1120 runs at 28.00 and 129 wickets at 20.76 in the season. He was a fine slow left-arm bowler and a right-handed batsman who could bat down the order or open, as he did against New Zealand in 1955/6 when he first scored 223 to equal India's highest in Tests and then 231, putting on a record 413 opening partnership with Pankaj Roy. He is one of only three cricketers to have batted in every position in the order in Tests. He performed with much distinction for India until he was into his 40s. His double of 1000 runs and 100 wickets came in 23 Tests, a record until improved by Ian Botham.

His son **Ashok** (b.12 Oct 1946) scored 991 runs at 25.41 in 22 Tests for India 1969-78.

44 Tests 1946-59: 2109 runs at 31.47, 5 100s HS 231; 162 wickets at 32.31, BB 8-52; 33 catches.

First-class 1935-64: 11,566 runs at 34.83, 26 100s HS 231; 781 wickets at 24.53, BB 8-35; 188 catches.

Madeline MANNING (USA)

ATHLETICS

Madeline Manning. b. 11 Jan 1948 Cleveland, Ohio. Later Jackson, then Mimms.

As a 20 year-old at Tennessee State University, she became Olympic champion at 800m in 1968, having won gold medals in 1967 at Pan-Ams and World Student Games. She went on to make three more US teams, but did not qualify for the 800m finals of 1972 and 1976 and could not run in 1980 due to the boycott. She did, however, add a 4 x 400m relay silver in 1972. In all she won ten TAC titles, outdoors in 1967, 1969, 1975-6 and 1980-1, and indoors in 1967-9 and 1980. She set two

world records in 1972: 2:02.0 for 880y and on the US team at 4 x 440y relay.
She set seven US records at 800m from 2:03.6 in 1967 to 1:57.90 in 1976. An accomplished gospel singer, she has made several recordings.
Other bests: 400m 52.2 (1972), 1500m 4:14.04 (1980).

Lia MANOLIU (Rom)

ATHLETICS
Lia Manoliu. b. 25 Apr 1932 Chisinau.

Manoliu competed at six Olympic Games, a unique achievement for an athlete. At the discus she started with sixth in 1952 and ninth in 1956 before taking the bronze medals in 1960 and 1964. She became the oldest ever women's athletics gold medallist at 36 years 176 days in 1968, when she set an Olympic record 58.28m on her first throw of the competition. Her Olympic career ended with ninth place in 1972, in which year, at the age of 40, she set a personal best of 62.06.
She is the only woman to have competed at five European Championships (1954-71), with a best place of 4th in 1969. An electrical engineer by profession, she won a record 12 Romanian titles between 1952 and 1970. She is now president of Romania's national Olympic committee.

Nigel MANSELL (UK)

MOTOR RACING
Nigel Ernest James Mansell. b. 8 Aug 1953 Upton-on-Severn.

Britain's most successful Grand Prix driver of the 1980s, his tenacity paid off when he became world champion in 1992, two years after declaring his retirement. He had been runner-up in the World Drivers' Championship in 1986, when he was just two points behind Alain Prost, and again in 1987 and 1991. Rash and aggressive at the outset of his career, he worked hard to achieve his eminence as a fast and determined driver.
He started at kart racing and was in the British junior team, turning to motor racing in the 1970s while also working as an aerospace engineer. He made his Grand Prix début in 1980, driving for Lotus 1980-4, Williams 1985-8, 1991-2 and Ferrari in 1989-90. His first pole position was in 1984 and his first Formula One win was in the 1985 European Grand Prix at Brands Hatch. After a short-lived retirement and much speculation he signed for Williams for 1991, reaching his peak with a brilliant year in 1992 when he won the first five Grand Prix races and took the title with 108 points to 56 by the runner-up, his team-mate Riccardo Patrese. Mansell started in pole position a record 14 times in the 16 races, and had a record nine wins. His championship year ended, however, in anger, as he left Formula One after being unable to agree terms with Frank Williams. In his career he had 30 GP wins (27 for Williams, 3 Ferrari) and 31 pole positions from 180 starts, totalling 469 points. He then joined the Newman-Haas Indy Car team in the USA in 1993, won his first race in that series and was a splendid third in his first ever drive in the Indianapolis 500. BBC Sports personality of 1986 and 1992, awarded the OBE 1991.

MANSUR ALI KHAN (India)

CRICKET
Mansur Ali Khan, Nawab of Pataudi. b. 5 Jan 1941 Bhopal.

If only! How often can that be said, and yet if only the Nawab of Pataudi had not lost most of his sight in one eye in a car accident in 1961, what batting might have been seen. He was at the time a vividly exciting batsman, who had made his Sussex début in 1957 while still at school at Winchester and who had won his blue at Oxford in 1960 and was due to captain them against Cambridge. And yet he overcame this adversity and met with considerable batting success over the ensuing years. Just a few months after his accident he made his Test début for India and became the youngest Test captain ever at 21 years 77 days against the West Indies in 1962. In all he captained India in 40 of his 46 Tests. Ajit Wadekar was controversially preferred to him for the 1971 tour to England, but Mansur Ali Khan, as he now was following the abolition of princely privileges and titles, returned to play Tests under Wadekar in 1972/3 and to captain India against the West Indies in 1974/5. In India he played first for Delhi and then Hyderabad, and he also captained Sussex in 1966.

46 Tests 1961-75: 2793 runs at 34.91, 6 100s HS 203; 1 wicket; 27 catches. First-class 1957-76: 15,425 runs at 33.67, 33 100s HS 203*; 10 wickets at 77.60; 208 catches.*

His father **Iftikhar Ali, Nawab of Pataudi** (1910-52) gained his blue at Oxford University 1929-31, setting a record for the annual match against Cambridge with 238* in 1931, and played with outstanding success in England in the early 1930s. He had three Tests for England 1932-4, scoring 144 runs at 28.80 including 102 on his début against Australia, and three for India in 1946, when he captained them on their tour of England but scored only 55 runs in the Tests. In his first-class career 1928-46 he scored 8750 runs at 48.61, with 29 100s, HS 238*.

Mickey MANTLE (USA)

BASEBALL

Mickey Charles Mantle. b. 20 Oct 1931 Spavinaw, Oklahoma.

Mantle, named by his father after the great major league catcher Mickey Cochrane, was destined to become a ball player and his father taught him the fundamentals from an early age. He took over centerfield from Joe DiMaggio and inherited his 'mantle' as the leader of the New York Yankees, roaming centerfield for them in the 1950s and 60s, and helping them to 12 pennants and seven World Series victories. He and Willie Mays were probably the first top players to combine great speed and power. Mantle hit over 500 career home runs and was considered the fastest runner in the game early in his career. Unfortunately he was hampered by injuries, which some experts consider kept him from possibly becoming the greatest player ever. His greatest year was 1956 when he won the batting Triple Crown, batting .353 with 53 home runs and 130 RBI. He was also one of only five players to hit over 50 home runs twice or more, with 54 in 1961, when he trailed his team-mate Roger Maris who broke Babe Ruth's legendary record of 60 home runs with 61 in the season. Mantle was a switch hitter and is considered the greatest power hitter ever among that category.

Career 1951-68: 2415 hits Avg. .298, HR 536; RBI 1509; SB 153.

Eero MÄNTYRANTA (Fin)

NORDIC SKIING

Eero Antero Mäntyranta. b. 20 Nov 1937 Pello, Lapland.

He competed at four Olympic Games, winning cross-country skiing medals at three of them. On the Finnish 4 x 10km relay team he won successively gold 1960, silver 1964, and bronze 1968. At his peak in 1964 he won both the 15km and 30km, and he added silver and bronze at those events in 1968 to bring his total medal haul to seven. The outgoing Mäntyranta was world champion at 30km in 1962 and 1966, with relay silver medals both years and a bronze at 50km in 1966.

He made a comeback in 1971 and competed, although unsuccessfully, at the 1972 Olympics. However, having won a big race a month later he was then found to have used amphetamines in the Finnish Olympic trials and his career was over, although he always claimed that he had been sabotaged.

Heinie MANUSH (USA)

BASEBALL

Henry Emmett Manush. b. 20 Jul 1901 Tuscumbia, Alabama, d. 12 May 1971 Sarasota, Florida.

Manush was an outfielder who played for five clubs in his career in the American League. With the Detroit Tigers for the first five years of his career, he replaced Ty Cobb in centerfield. He batted over .300 in 12 years, leading the American League in 1926 (.378), in hits twice (241 in 1928 when he again averaged .378, and 221 in 1933), in doubles twice and in triples once.

Career 1923-39: 2524 hits Avg. .330, HR 110; RBI 1183.

Deena MAPPLE (USA)

WATER SKIING

Deena Mapple. née Brush. b. 2 Mar 1960 Sacramento, California.

The top women's water skier from the mid-1980s. She was world overall champion in 1987 and 1989 and won her speciality, jumping, in 1981, 1985, 1987, and 1989. In 1988 she set a world record at 47.5m *156 ft*. She also shared the world record for slalom in 1990. She is married to **Andy Mapple** (UK, b. 3 Nov 1962), who was world slalom champion in 1981 and 1989.

Diego MARADONA (Arg)

FOOTBALL

Diego Armando Maradona. b. 30 Oct 1960 Lanus, Buenos Aires.

The first man since Pelé to be universally recognised as the world's greatest player. He played for Argentinos Júniors 1975-82, apart from a spell in 1981 with Boca Júniors, who defaulted on the transfer payment for him. Maradona was transferred for £4.8m to Barcelona in July 1982. Two years later a world record £6.9 million was paid for him by Napoli. In 1986 at the peak of his brilliance as a midfield player he led Argentina to victory in the World Cup. With Napoli he won the Italian League and Cup double in 1987, the UEFA Cup in 1989 and the Italian League for a second time in 1990. That year he again took Argentina to the World Cup final. Unable to cope with the adulation heaped on him by the Neapolitans, his private life went into sharp decline. Heavy drinking, women, drug abuse and criminal associations all contributed to his downfall and in 1991 he was arrested for the possession of cocaine and ordered by the courts in Argentina to undertake a rehabilitation programme. After a 15-month ban he signed for the Spanish club Sevilla, who despite Maradona's past record and age (32) were still willing to pay Napoli a transfer fee of £4.48 million.
Despite his unacceptable off-field behaviour, he was a player of genius and his ball control, deadly shooting and ability to beat an opponent have possibly never been matched - except by Pelé. South American Player of the Year three times (1979, 1980 and 1990), he set Argentine records with 29 goals and 82 international appearances from his début at 16 in 1977.

Rabbit MARANVILLE (USA)

BASEBALL

Walter James Vincent Maranville. b. 11 Nov 1891 Springfield, Massachusetts, d. 5 Jan 1954 New York, New York.

In his 23 seasons in the American League, Maranville was not a great hitter, as shown by his career average of .258 in an era when batting over .300 was common. But he was one of the first great fielding shortstops, known for his speed and his 'Rabbit-like' leaps, hence the nickname. He still stands first on the all-time list of putouts by a shortstop (5139), third in assists (7534), and second in chances accepted (13,124). He was also quite famous as a practical joker and clown prince of baseball. He briefly managed in the minor leagues after he retired from playing.
Career 1912-35: 2605 hits Avg. .258, HR 28; RBI 884; SB 291.

Pete MARAVICH (USA)

BASKETBALL

Peter Press Maravich. b. 22 Jun 1947 Aliquippa, Pennsylvania, d. 5 Jan 1988 Pasadena, California.

'Pistol Pete' Maravich set unmatched college scoring records while at Louisiana State University, 1138 points at an average of 43.8 per game in 1968, 1148 at 44.2 in 1969 and 1381 at 44.5 in 1970, the three highest season's averages in NCAA history, for a total 3667 in 83 games. He won all the major awards for college player of the year in 1970 and was one of the most flamboyant players ever seen on the hardcourt.
Before he went to LSU he had become a high school legend when he played basketball at Broughton in Raleigh, North Carolina where his father was coach at North Carolina State. Maravich's pro

career was also outstanding, although less spectacular. Despite his scoring ability, he was probably best known for his passing, and his spectacular ball-handling has since served as a model for many of the top stars in the 1980s. In 10 years in the NBA he scored 15,948 points at an average of 24.2 per game, with an average of 31.1 for 2273 points when he led the league in 1977. He played for the Atlanta Hawks 1970-4, New Orleans (Utah 1979) Jazz 1974-80 and Boston Celtics 1980. He was selected to play in four All-Star games and to the Basketball Hall of Fame in 1987. He died quite young while playing in a pick-up basketball game. A movie was later made of his life.

Alice MARBLE (USA)

TENNIS

Alice Marble. b. 28 Sep 1913 Beckwith, Plumas County, California, d. 13 Dec 1990 Palm Springs, California.

Although she was tall and lithe, she had a less than robust physique. Despite this she became the first woman to succeed with the serve-volley technique. In 1934 she visited Europe with the US team, but collapsed during her first match in Paris. It transpired that she was suffering from tuberculosis and she was strongly advised to give up the game. After more than two years as a semi-invalid she made a remarkable comeback.

She was a semi-finalist at Wimbledon in 1937 and 1938 before she took the title in 1939. She was also a four-time US singles champion, 1936 and 1938-40, and formed an outstanding doubles partnership with Sarah Palfrey. Together they won Wimbledon 1938-9 and took four successive US titles 1937-40. Marble had no regular partner for mixed doubles events but she won Wimbledon three times 1937-9 and the US title four times, 1936 and 1938-40, with four different partners.

Her career was interrupted by the war and in 1941 she turned professional and toured with Mary Hardwick. A glamorous personality and the first woman to play in shorts at Wimbledon, she was named one of America's ten best-dressed women and was for a time a professional singer. She was also a regular columnist for a tennis magazine and was voted the Athlete of the Year in numerous polls in both 1939 and 1940.

Gino MARCHETTI (USA)

AMERICAN FOOTBALL

Gino John Marchetti. b. 2 Jan 1927 Smithers, Wisconsin.

One of the first great defensive ends in the NFL, he was drafted in 1952 from San Francisco by the Dallas Texans, for whom he played offensive tackle. The team folded and Marchetti joined the Baltimore Colts in 1953, where he was shifted to defensive end. He played in eleven straight Pro Bowls and was named All-Pro at that position seven times. He helped the Colts win two NFL Championships in 1958-9 and retired in 1964, although he came back in 1966 for one final season. He had begun a very successful restaurant business while a player and continued managing that business after his playing retirement.

Rocky MARCIANO (USA)

BOXING

né Rocco Francis Marchegiano. b. 1 Sep 1923 Brockton, Massachusetts, d. 31 Aug 1969 Newton, Iowa.

'The Brockton Bomber' retired as the only professional fighter to have won every bout of his career. There had been a few other undefeated fighters, but all had at least one draw on their record. Some people consider Marciano the greatest heavyweight champion ever, though at 179 cm *5' 10"* and 89 kg *195 lb* he was not big for a heavyweight. He was possessed of only average skills but his stamina, punching ability and durability made him a formidable opponent.

Marciano was an excellent athlete as a schoolboy but did not shine as a boxer until he served in World War II in England. After his discharge he sought a professional career but his lack of size and skill discouraged several promoters. He finally earned a title shot in his 43rd fight, knocking out Jersey Joe Walcott in the 12th

round on 23 Sep 1952, defending the title six times to 1955. Marciano was very popular in his native Massachusetts up to his untimely death which occurred in a private plane crash.
Career record: W - 49 (43), L - 0, D - 0.

Sarunas MARCIULIONIS (Lit)

BASKETBALL

Sarunas Raimondas Marciulionis. b. 13 Jun 1963 Kaunas.

The greatest guard ever to play for the Soviet Union, prior to Lithuania gaining its independence. In Lithuania he played for Vilnius Statiba. Having earned a gold medal in the 1988 Olympics he became one of the first Soviets to turn professional, joining the Golden State Warriors, who had drafted him in the 6th round of the 1987 NBA draft. He plays shooting guard and is an excellent shooter and passer at 1.96m *6' 5"*. Marciulionis represented his 'true' nation at the 1992 Olympics in Barcelona, leading Lithuania to a bronze medal.
NBA career: 3332 points, av. 14.7.

Juan MARICHAL (Dom)

BASEBALL

Juan Antonio Marichal Sánchez. b. 20 Oct 1937 Laguna Verde.

One of the two greatest right-hand pitchers of the 1960s (with Bob Gibson). He pitched for the San Francisco Giants for 14 years 1960-73, winning over 20 games in six seasons with them, 1963-6 and 1968-9, in which period his ERA was under 3.00 every year. He was famous for his high kick and his pinpoint control of multiple pitches. His fame was tarnished in a game on 22 Aug 1965 against the Los Angeles Dodgers, when both teams were in the heat of a pennant race. While Marichal was batting, he thought Dodger catcher John Roseboro was throwing his return pitch to the mound dangerously close to his head. Marichal had already hit several Giants with pitches and Roseboro had asked the Dodger pitcher to hit Marichal, which Koufax refused. A fight broke out and Marichal used his bat to club Roseboro on the head, giving him a concussion. Marichal regretted the incident and the two later became friends. However, perhaps because the writers remembered the incident, Marichal, an obvious choice, was not elected to the Hall of Fame on his first two chances. Roseboro then campaigned for Marichal and he was elected in 1983.
Career pitching 1960-75: ERA 2.89; W-L 243-1421, SO 2303; Best seasons: 1968: 26-9, 2.43 ERA; 1963: 25-8, 2.41 ERA; 1966: 25-6, 2.23 ERA; 1969: 21-11, 2.10 ERA; 1965: 22-13, 2.14 ERA.

Humberto MARILES (Mex)

EQUESTRIAN

Humberto Mariles Cortés. b. 1913 Chihuahua, d. 6 Dec 1972 Paris, France.

The winner of three Olympic medals at the 1948 Games in London, individual and team golds at show jumping and a bronze with the Mexican three-day team. This combination of winning Olympic medals in jumping and eventing has been accomplished 13 times in all. On 14 Aug 1964 he was driving home from a party in Ciudad México when he was forced off the road. At the next traffic light, Mariles Cortés pulled out a pistol and shot the other driver. Initially imprisoned, he was released by presidential pardon. In 1972 he was arrested in Paris for drug-smuggling but died in prison before coming to trial.

Dan MARINO (USA)

AMERICAN FOOTBALL

Daniel Constantine Marino, Jr. b. 15 Sep 1961 Pittsburgh, Pennsylvania.

Marino played high school football in the steel town and college football for the University of Pittsburgh, whom he guided to 42 wins in 47 games. He was drafted in the first round of the 1983 draft by Miami Dolphins and became the first rookie quarterback ever to start in the Pro Bowl. He was NFL MVP in 1984. In his NFL career 1983-92 he has 39,502 yards gained passing from 2929 pass completions. In 1992 he completed an NFL record five successive years at more than 4000 yards.

Roger MARIS (USA)

BASEBALL

Roger Eugene Maris. né Maras. b. 10 Sep 1934 Hibbing, Minnesota, d. 14 Dec 1985 Houston, Texas.

Maris was a quiet man from Fargo, North Dakota who shunned the spotlight. But he made a terrible mistake in 1961, when as a power-hitting right fielder for the New York Yankees, he made an assault on Babe Ruth's record of 60 home runs in one season and broke it with 61. The New York press put him in the limelight all year and the pressure became a terrible burden to him. As a result, the press turned against him, and what should have been his greatest moment became terribly traumatic. He did, however, have more than one great season. He was a great fielding outfielder with a powerful arm and late in his career he helped St Louis win a World Series in 1967. But his greatest years came with the Yankees in 1960-1, when he was MVP and led the American League in RBI in both years (112 and 142). In 1960 he was just edged out of the lead in home runs, 39 to 40, by his team-mate Mickey Mantle. Maris died quite young from a brain tumour.

Career 1957-68: 1325 hits Avg. .260, HR 275; RBI 851.

Rube MARQUARD (USA)

BASEBALL

Richard William Marquard. b. 9 Oct 1889 Cleveland, Ohio, d. 1 Jun 1980 Baltimore, Maryland.

Nicknamed Rube because of his resemblance to the great pitcher, Rube Waddell, Marquard pitched in the majors from 1908-25 but was really only a top pitcher for three great years, 1911-13. In the 1912 season he won 26 games, setting a major league record of 19 consecutive wins by a pitcher in a single season, from opening day until 3 Jul 1912.

Career pitching: ERA 3.07; W-L 201-177, SO 1593; Best seasons: 1912: 26-11, 2.56 ERA; 1911: 24-7, 2.49 ERA, 237 SO; 1913: 23-10, 2.50 ERA.

Rod MARSH (Aus)

CRICKET

Rodney William Marsh. b. 4 Nov 1947 Armadale, Western Australia.

At first dubbed 'Iron gloves', Marsh improved to become one of the most skilful of wicket-keepers and holds the Australian record for most dismissals in a first-class career and the world record for dismissals in Test cricket. From his début he played in 52 successive Tests for Australia 1970-7 before moving over to World Series Cricket, and returned to play a further 44 more to 1984. He set an Australian record with 26 dismissals (all caught) in a series, in 6 Tests against the West Indies in 1975/6, and in his penultimate series took a world record 28 (again all caught) in 5 Tests against England in 1982/3. A combative personality, he played throughout his career for Western Australia and was also a forceful left-handed batsman, who scored one of his three Test centuries in the Centenary Test at Melbourne in 1977.

96 Tests 1970-84: 3633 runs at 26.51, 3 100s HS 132; 343 catches, 12 stumpings.
92 One-day Ints: 1225 runs at 20.08, HS 66; 120 catches, 4 stumpings.
First-class 1968-84: 11,067 runs at 31.17, 12 100s HS 236; 1 wicket; 804 catches, 65 stumpings.

Bryan MARSHALL (Ire)

HORSE RACING

Bryan Marshall. b. 29 Feb 1916 Cloughjordan, Tipperary, d. 9 Oct 1991 Reading, England.

Leading jumps jockey who rode 508 winners, 1932-54, including the Grand Nationals of 1953 and 1954.

His mother Binty was a fine show-jumper and he started riding from the age of three. At 11 he worked in his summer holidays with trainer Atty Persse, and at the age of 12 was apprenticed, riding his first flat race winner in 1929. His first winner over fences was in the 1932/3 season. After wartime service, being demobbed as a captain, he was second in 1946/7 and in 1947/8 won the NH jockeys title.

He was not only a natural horseman, but a marvellous judge of pace, and very strong in the finish. He married show-jumper Mary Whitehead in 1953, and trained until 1973, after which he ran a horse transport business.

Malcolm MARSHALL (Bar)

CRICKET

Malcolm Denzil Marshall. b. 18 Apr 1958 St Michael, Bridgetown.

The leader of the triumphantly successful West Indies fast bowling attack, he achieved the remarkable feat of taking 20 or more wickets in seven successive Test series from 1983 to 1986. He passed that total again with his best figures, 35 (av. 12.65) in 1988 for a West Indies-England series record. At 1.80m *5' 11"* he was no giant, but his fitness, fast approach and fast arm made him the most feared bowler in the world for many years. In 1989 he passed Lance Gibbs to become the leading wicket-taker in Tests for the West Indies. He has also often shown considerable batting skills. In the West Indies he has played for Barbados from 1977/8 and in England for Hampshire from 1979.

81 Tests 1978-91: 1810 runs at 18.85, HS 92; 376 wickets, at 20.94, BB 7-22; 25 catches.

117 One-day Ints: 955 runs at 14.92, HS 66; 157 wickets at 26.96, BB 4-18; 15 catches.

First-class 1973-92: 9863 runs at 24.53, 6 100s HS 117; 1524 wickets at 18.70, BB 8-71; 131 catches.

Billy MARTIN (USA)

BASEBALL

Alfred Manuel Martin. b. 16 May 1928 Berkeley, California, d. 25 Dec 1989 Binghamton, New York.

One of the toughest little baseball players and managers in history. He grew up in a rough area near San Francisco and he learned to use his fists well, something he never forgot. He played in the majors with seven teams, but his first seven years were spent with the New York Yankees and he always considered himself a Yankee. He played second base, was an average hitter and a good fielder, but a great winner. After retirement he became one of the best managers in baseball, albeit very controversial. He often argued with general managers and owners and was frequently fired. Still, he usually took over very poor teams and made them into winners, with what was termed 'Billy-Ball' by the press. He is most famous for managing the New York Yankees multiple times between 1975 and 1988. He argued frequently with owner George Steinbrenner, and was fired several times by him, only to be brought back every time when Steinbrenner realised the Yankees needed a winning manager. Martin also fought once on national television with superstar Reggie Jackson. Martin was killed in a car accident just before he was to begin managing the Yankees again.

Career 1950-61: 877 hits Avg. .257.

Dugie MARTIN (USA)

BASKETBALL

Slater Martin. b. 22 Oct 1925 El Mina, Texas.

A playmaking guard with the University of Texas and from 1949 in the NBA with the Minneapolis Lakers, whom he helped to five NBA championships. In 1957 he was traded to the St Louis Hawks. During his 11-year NBA career he was 2nd-team All-NBA five times and played in seven All-Star Games. He was very briefly a player-coach with the Hawks in 1957 and later coached for two years with the Houston Mavericks of the ABA in 1967-9.

Patrice MARTIN (Fra)

WATER SKIING

Patrice Martin. b. 24 May 1964 Nantes.

Martin won his first world title at tricks at the age of 15 in 1979. He won the slalom in 1985 and the tricks again in 1987 and 1991. Having determined from 1984 to become not just a tricks specialist but an overall champion, he achieved his aim with that title in both 1989 and 1991.
He was European overall champion in 1984, 1985 and again in 1992, winning at

tricks eleven times between 1978 and 1992, and at slalom in 1985.
Known as the 'Little Prince', he has been coached throughout his career by his father Joël. His temperament has made him unpopular, but there is no doubting his mastery of his sport.

Steffi MARTIN (GDR) see WALTER

Jorge MARTINEZ (Spain)

MOTOR CYCLING

Jorge Martinez. b. 29 Aug 1962 Alcira, Valencia.

The most successful rider at 80cc class in World Championship motorcycling, with 22 Grand Prix victories 1984-89. After placing fourth in 1984 and second in 1985 he was world champion each year 1986-8. He was also world champion at 125cc in 1988 and at this class had 13 Grand Prix victories to 1990.
Nicknamed 'Aspar', the cobbler, from his father's occupation, he became a national hero, riding the Spanish Derbi machines.

Josef MASOPUST (Cs)

FOOTBALL

Josef Masopust. b. 9 Feb 1931 Most, Bohemia.

In 1962 he became the only Czech player to earn the European Footballer of the Year award. After being capped at Youth level he joined the Czech Army team, Dukla Praha at the age of 20 and remained with them as an attacking midfield player for 17 years.
First capped in 1954, he went on to play 63 times for Czechoslovakia although he was dropped for more than a season in mid-career when his short-passing game no longer suited the style of play adopted by the national team. He scored his team's goal in their 3-1 defeat by Brazil in the 1962 World Cup final. In 1968 he joined Crossing Molenbeek in Belgium as a professional and on his retirement in 1971 he returned to Dukla Praha as assistant manager.

Antonio MASPES (Italy)

CYCLING

Antonio Maspes. b. 14 Jan 1932 Milan.

With Cesare Pinarello, he won a bronze medal in the tandem match sprint at the 1952 Olympics. He became one of the great professional track sprinters, winning the world title in that event seven times, 1955-6, 1959-62 and 1964.

Rie MASTENBROEK (Hol)

SWIMMING

Hendrika Mastenbroek. b. 26 Feb 1919.

The treble Olympic gold medallist in 1936, when she won the 100m and 400m freestyle with a third win on the Dutch 4x100m team. Coached by Ma Braun, she shot to fame in 1934 when she won three European golds, at 400m and 4x100m freestyle and 100m backstroke, and was second at 100m freestyle. Later that year she set the first of seven world records with bests including 440y freestyle 5:29.1 (1936), 100m back 1:15.8 (1936), 200m back 2:49.6 (1935).

Enno MATARELLI (Italy)

SHOOTING

Enno Matarelli. b. 5 Aug 1928 Bologna.

The first man to win World, Olympic and European titles for clay pigeon shooting. Twice world champion, 1961 and 1969, he was Olympic and European champion in 1964.

François MATHET (Fra)

HORSE RACING

François Mathet. b. 21 May 1908, d. 12 Jan 1983.

Mathet started with just two horses and went on to become, at Chantilly, the first trainer in Europe with more than 100 horses, and in 1965 the first trainer in the world with more than 200, reaching a peak of about 250 at six different yards. He set a French record with 111 winners in 1958. After service as a cavalry officer, winning the Croix de Guerre, he started training in

1944. His first major owner was François Dupré, for whom he trained the double Arc de Triompe winner *Tantième*. He also won the Arc with *Sassafras* in 1970 and *Akiyda* in 1982, and the Epsom Derby with *Phil Drake* in 1955 and *Relko* in 1963.

Eddie MATHEWS (USA)

BASEBALL

Edwin Lee Mathews. b. 13 Oct 1931 Texarkana, Texas.

The greatest power-hitting third baseman prior to Mike Schmidt, Mathews played for 15 years with the Braves, starting in Boston, playing all 13 years of the team's existence in Milwaukee, and during their first year in Atlanta. He was the only player to have played in all three cities for the Braves. He was a pure power hitter as he never batted for high average, passing .300 in only three seasons with a high of .306 in 1959 and 1961. He was a good fielder but made his name by hitting home runs, hitting over 40 in a season four times, and over 30 ten times.

Career 1952-68: 2315 hits Avg. .271, HR 512; RBI 1453. Best seasons: 1953: 47 HR, 135 RBI; 1959: 46 HR, 114 RBI; 1955: 41 HR, 101 RBI; 1954: 40 HR, 103 RBI.

Christy MATHEWSON (USA)

BASEBALL

Christopher Mathewson. b. 12 Aug 1880 Factoryville, Pennsylvania. d. 7 Oct 1925 Saranac Lake, New York.

Mathewson was the dominant pitcher of his era and is considered with Walter Johnson as one of the greatest right-handed pitchers ever. He was one of the original five players inducted into the Hall of Fame at its opening in 1936.

Mathewson pitched for 16 seasons with the New York Giants although he finished his career by pitching in one game for the Cincinnati Reds. He won over 20 games in a season 13 times, 12 of them consecutively 1903-14, and over 30 games four times. He had exceptional control, averaging only 1.6 walks per nine-inning game. He ranks near the top in most all-time pitching categories with 372 wins (4th), 78 shutouts (3rd), and a 2.13 ERA (5th). He enlisted in the Army shortly after his career ended in 1916 and while overseas developed tuberculosis, from the effects of which he died in 1925.

Career pitching 1900-16: ERA 2.13; W-L 373-188 SO 2502; Best seasons: 1908: 37-11, 1.43 ERA; 1904: 33-12, 2.03 ERA; 1905: 31-8, 1.27 ERA; 1909: 25-6, 1.15 ERA; 1903: 30-13, 2.26 ERA, 267 SO.

Bob MATHIAS (USA)

ATHLETICS

Robert Bruce Mathias. b. 17 Nov 1930 Tulare, California.

Mathias won the 1948 Olympic decathlon title at the age of 17, still the youngest ever male Olympic medallist at any track and field event. He was the Sullivan Award winner that year. He said 'never again' on completing his 1948 Olympic victory, but he became an all-time great, winning all 11 decathlons that he contested, from 1948 to 1956. He set three world records (with points on the current tables), 7287 in 1950, 7543 and 7592 in 1952, the latter when retaining his Olympic title. He won four AAU titles, 1948-50 and 1952, but later regretted retiring before he might have reached his peak. His bests at individual events at which he attained world top ten rankings: 110mh 13.8 (1952), discus 52.83 (1951) .

He starred in a film version of his life in 1954 and also appeared with Jayne Mansfield in a spoof of the 1896 Games, *It Happened in Athens* (1961). He was US Congressman as a Republican for California's 18th district 1966-74. In 1973 he introduced legislation to amend the US Olympic Charter, creating a 'Bill of Rights' for amateur athletes.

Oscar MATHISEN (Nor)

SPEED SKATING

Oscar Wilhelm Mathisen. b. 4 Oct 1888 Kristiana (Oslo), d. 12 Apr 1954 Oslo.

The first of only two men to win the world overall speed skating championship five times, 1908-09, 1912-4. His only defeat came in 1910 when he placed second to the Russian, Nikolay Strunnikov. In 1912 he won all four individual events, one of only four men ever to achieve this feat. He also won the European title three times in six appearances and was a prolific record breaker, setting 14 world records at distances ranging from 500m to 10,000m between 1908 and 1914. He was Norwegian champion 1907, 1909-10, 1912-13 and 1915. He turned professional in 1916 and won the 1920 World Pro title by beating the American Bobby McLean. *Best times: 500m 43.4 (1914) and 43.0 as pro (1929), 1000m 1:31.8 (1909) and 1:31.1 as pro (1929), 1500m 2:17.4 (1914), 5000m 8:36.3 (1916), 10,000m 17:22.6 (1913).*

Marjo MATIKAINEN (Fin)

NORDIC SKIING

Marjo Tuulevi Matikainen. b. 3 Feb 1965 Lohja.

The winner of a record three World Cup titles at cross-country skiing, 1986-8. In 1988 she was Olympic champion at 5km and took the bronze at 10km. In the relay she took bronze medals with the Finnish teams in both 1984 and 1988. At the World Championships she won at 5km in 1987 and 15km in 1989, and added a silver medal in 1987 and a silver and two bronze in 1989. She then retired from racing at the age of 24. She is a mining engineer and an observer for the International Ski Federation.

Ollie MATSON (USA)

AMERICAN FOOTBALL

Oliver Adrian Matson. b. 1 May 1930 Trinity, Texas.

Matson played college football at the University of San Francisco where he used his great speed to star as a running back. After graduation in 1952, he made the US Olympic team and won a bronze medal at 400m and a silver medal on the 4 x 400m relay team in Helsinki, with a best time for 400m of 46.6. He played for the Chicago Cardinals 1952-8 and then with the Los Angeles Rams, Detroit Lions and Philadelphia Eagles before he retired from football in 1966. Matson was a great all-purpose back and runner, gaining 12,844 net all-purpose yards during his pro career. He played in five Pro Bowl games and was NFL MVP in 1956.
NFL career 1952-66: Rushing: 5173 yards av. 4.4, 40 touchdowns; Receiving: 3285 yards av. 14.8, 23 touchdowns.

Randy MATSON (USA)

ATHLETICS

James Randel Matson. b. 5 Mar 1945 Kilgore, Texas.

Having set several high school records at shot and discus, Matson was the shot silver medallist as a teenager at the 1964 Olympics. He was the top shot putter of the 1960s, setting four world records and winning the Olympic title in 1968 as well as the Pan-Ams of 1967, World Student Games (and discus) 1965 and AAU six times 1964, 1966-8, 1970, 1972. His first two world records, 20.70 and 21.05 in 1965, were not ratified, but on 8 May 1965 he became the first ever 70ft putter, with 21.52m *70' 7 1/4"* at College Station Texas, his own track at Texas A & M University. At the same venue in April 1967 he set a collegiate discus record of 65.16m and later improved the shot record to 21.78. The 1967 Sullivan Award winner, he later turned professional with the ITA group. He had also been an accomplished basketball player.

Lothar MATTHÄUS (Ger)

FOOTBALL

Lothar Matthäus. b. 21 Mar 1961 Erlangen.

A midfield player who has made 98 appearances for West Germany or Germany, scoring 19 goals. In this highly successful period, Germany were runners-up in the World Cups of 1982 and 1986 and winners in 1990, and won the European Championship in 1980. He was elected as both European Footballer of the Year and by *World Soccer* as the World Footballer of the Year in 1990 for his inspirational leadership.
He started with Herzogenaurach, before

making his name playing for Borussia Mönchengladbach, scoring for them when they lost in the UEFA Cup final of 1980. From there he was signed for a German record fee by Bayern Munich, with whom he won the Bundesliga each year 1985-7 and the German Cup in 1986. In 1988 he signed for Inter Milan for £2.4 million, and with them won the Italian League 1989 and UEFA Cup 1991, in the final of which he scored from the penalty spot. Ruptured knee ligaments in April 1992 meant that he had to miss the 1992 European Championships, but he was back in the German team in 1993.

Roland MATTHES (GDR)

SWIMMING

Roland Matthes. b. 17 Nov 1950 Erfurt.

The supreme backstroke swimmer, with deceptive power from a seemingly languid stroke, he set eight world records at 100m from 58.4 in 1967 to 56.30 in 1972, and nine at 200m from 2:07.9 in 1967 to 2:01.87 in 1973. Olympic gold medallist at both 100m and 200m in 1968 and 1972, he also won two silver and bronze medals in relays. He was also European champion at both distances in 1970 and 1974, and World champion at both in 1973 and at 100m in 1975 when, tired from efforts to overcome a stomach illness, he was fourth at 200m backstroke, the first time for eight years that he had been beaten in a championships race.

A seven-year unbeaten run in any backstroke race had been ended by John Naber at Concord, California in September 1974, but Matthes continued his long career and was third behind Naber at 100m in the 1976 Olympics just six weeks after an appendectomy.

He was a fine all-round swimmer and took European silvers at 100m freestyle in 1970 and 100m butterfly in 1974, with three European records at the 100m butterfly in 1971 to 55.7, and one at 200m IM, 2:12.8 in 1970. He was GDR champion at 100m and 200m backstroke 1968-72, 1974-5; freestyle 100m 1970-2, 200m 1968; 100m butterfly 1971-2; 200m IM 1968-70. Married for a while to Kornelia Ender.

Christina MATTHEWS (Aus)

CRICKET

Christina Matthews. b. 1959.

Australia's most capped woman Test player, with 19 appearances. A wicketkeeper and right-handed bat, she holds the world Test career record of 53 dismissals (43 catches and 10 stumpings), including the most dismissals in a match, nine (8 catches and 1 stumping) against India at Adelaide in February 1991, and the most in a series, 19 (17 and 2) against India that year.

35 One-day Ints: 114 runs at 10.36; 25 catches, 12 stumpings

Stanley MATTHEWS (UK)

FOOTBALL

(Sir) Stanley Matthews. b. 1 Feb 1915 Hanley, Stoke-on-Trent.

One of the legendary names of world soccer. With his dribbling skills and swerve he destroyed the reputations of some of the game's greatest full backs and was possibly the most popular player in history.

Making his League début for Stoke City at the age of 17, he had passed his 50th birthday when he played his last League game in 1965. He remained with Stoke until 1947 when he moved to Blackpool, but in 1961 he returned to the Potteries. He twice won Football League Division II honours with Stoke, first in 1933 and, incredibly, for a second time 30 years later in 1963. With Blackpool, he played in three FA Cup finals (1948, 1951, 1953) but was on the winning side only in 1953 when his superb performance led to the match being known as the 'Matthews Final'.

Although his appearances in the England side were spasmodic during the latter part of his career, he won 54 international caps; after making his début in 1934 as a 19-year-old he played his last game for England in 1957 at the age of 41. He was the first footballer to be awarded the CBE (1957) and the first to be knighted (1965). In 1948 he was the first winner of the Football Writers' Player of the Year award and, after a 15-year interval, he again won

the award in 1963. He was also the first winner of the European Footballer of the Year award in 1956.
Following his retirement in 1965 he served as general manager of Port Vale for three years and later coached in Malta and South Africa. His son, also Stanley Matthews, played Davis Cup tennis for Britain.

Don MATTINGLY (USA)

BASEBALL

Donald Arthur Mattingly. b. 20 Apr 1961 Evansville, Indiana.

Mattingly played in six successive All-Star games for the American League 1984-9. First baseman for the New York Yankees, he led the AL in batting with an average of .343 in 1984, in RBI with 145 in 1985 when he was voted AL MVP, and in hits in 1984 (207) and 1986 (238). He shares the AL career record for the highest fielding average (.995) for a first baseman.
Career 1982-92: 1754 hits Avg. .311, HR 192; RBI 913.

Gisela MAUERMAYER (Ger)

ATHLETICS

Gisela Mauermayer. b. 24 Nov 1913 Munich.

A marvellous all-round athlete, Mauermayer set ten world records at the discus, seven in 1935 starting with 44.34m and three in 1936 culminating in 48.31, and also set three world records at the pentathlon. Other bests included a German shot record of 14.38m in 1934.
She won the discus at the 1936 Olympics and 1938 Europeans, when she also took the shot silver, won the shot and pentathlon at the 1934 Women's World Games, and won 20 German titles at all events between 1933 and 1942.

Ivan MAUGER (NZ)

SPEEDWAY

Ivan Gerald Mauger. b. 4 Oct 1939 Christchurch.

Winner of 15 world titles at speedway, including a record six individual titles, 1968-70, 1972, 1977 and 1979. He contested 14 consecutive World Championships from 1966 to 1979, gaining a total of 176 points. He won the Pairs in 1970 with Ronnie Moore after an unofficial win in 1969 with Bob Andrews, the Team title four times (three for Britain, one for New Zealand) and won the Long Track title in 1971-2 and 1976. He also holds the record for most appearances, 15, and most points, 146, in the British League Riders' Championship between 1965 and 1979.
He started riding speedway machines in New Zealand in 1956, coming to Britain a year later; then he failed to gain a regular place in the Wimbledon team and went home to New Zealand at the end of 1958. In 1963 he returned to join Newcastle in the Provincial League and had his first major success when the won the 1966 European Championship. He won League titles with Newcastle 1964, Belle Vue 1970-2 and Exeter 1974. He was awarded the MBE in 1976.

Peter MAY (UK)

CRICKET

Peter Barker Howard May. b. 31 Dec 1929 Reading, Berkshire.

A strong and elegant batsman, the finest of his generation. His talent blossomed at Charterhouse and continued in his first-class career with Cambridge University and Surrey, whom he captained from 1957 to 1962. He made a century against South Africa on his Test début at the age of 21 and batted outstandingly for England for most of the 1950s. His highest score of 285* was against the West Indies in the First Test in 1957 when, at a time when England looked in danger of an innings defeat, he put on 411 for the 4th wicket with Colin Cowdrey, still the England Test record partnership. He succeeded Len Hutton as England captain in 1955 and was highly successful in that rôle, winning 20 to 10 losses in his 41 matches in charge. However, the strain of captaincy and illness resulted in his retirement at the early age of 31. He first became one of the Test selectors in 1965, and was their chairman 1982-8. President of MCC 1980/1. He cap-

tained Cambridge at soccer, though not at cricket. Awarded the CBE 1981. An insurance broker from 1953 and an underwriting member of Lloyd's from 1962.
66 Tests 1951-61: 4537 runs at 46.76, 13 100s HS 285; 42 catches.*
First-class 1948-63: 27,592 runs at 51.00, 85 100s HS 285; 282 catches.*

Helene MAYER (Ger)

FENCING
Helene Mayer. b. 20 Dec 1910 Offenberg, d. 15 Oct 1953 Munich.

A statuesque blonde who is regarded by many as the greatest-ever woman fencer. She first became the German foil champion at the age of 13 and a gold medal at the 1928 Olympics was followed by the world title in 1929 and 1931. After only placing fifth at the 1932 Olympics, when she was handicapped by illness, she stayed in California to study international law and languages. Her decision to represent Germany at the 1936 Berlin Olympic Games was strongly criticised by the Jewish community in America. At the Olympics, she placed second to the Hungarian, Ilona Schacherer-Elek, who, to the frustration of the Nazis, was also Jewish.
The Olympic placings were reversed at the 1937 World Championships and Mayer then retired from international competition. After the Berlin Games, she returned to the United States and later became an American citizen. She competed in nine US Championships from 1934 to 1947, winning the title each time except for 1947 when she placed second. A determined competitor and a classic stylist with a superb physique, she could compete on equal terms with most of the leading male fencers of her generation. She returned to Germany shortly before she died.

Don MAYNARD (USA)

AMERICAN FOOTBALL
Donald Rogers Maynard. b. 25 Jan 1935 Crosbyton, Texas.

A wide receiver, he played college football at Texas Western (later Texas at El Paso). He joined the New York Giants in 1958 but was cut after one year and joined the Hamilton Tiger-Cats in the Canadian league until he was drafted by the fledgling AFL in 1960. He joined the New York Titans of the AFL, who soon became the New York Jets and with them Maynard became one of the top receivers in pro football. Helped by the addition of the strong-armed Joe Namath, he set many records and played through to 1973, joining the St Louis Cardinals for one season prior to his retirement.
NFL career 1958-73: 11,834 yards gained receiving av. 18.7, 88 touchdowns.

Willie MAYS (USA)

BASEBALL
Willie Howard Mays. b. 6 May 1931 Westfield, Alabama.

'The Say Hey Kid' ranks with Joe DiMaggio and his contemporary Mickey Mantle as one of the greatest centerfielders in baseball history, with his combination of speed, power, hitting for average, and great fielding ability.
He played with the New York/San Francisco Giants 1951-72, before finishing his career back in New York with the Mets. He batted over .300 ten times, seven of them consecutively in his prime, 1957-63. He hit over 40 home runs in a season six times, led the National League in home runs four times and is one of only five men to have hit 50 or more in a season more than once. Very fast, he also led the National League in stolen bases in four consecutive years early in his career, 1956-9. Strangely, Mays never led his league in RBI although he had over 100 in ten seasons, with a high of 141 in 1962.
As a fielder, his speed enabled him to get to balls few others could reach. His career total of 7095 putouts is the record for any outfielder.
Career 1951-73: 3283 hits Avg. .302, HR 660; RBI 1903; SB 338. Best seasons: 1954: .345, 41 HR, 110 RBI; 1955: .319, 51 HR, 127 RBI; 1965: .317, 52 HR, 112 RBI; 1962: .304, 49 HR, 141 RBI.

Lucien MAZAN (Fra)

CYCLING

Lucien Mazan. b. 18 Oct 1882 Plessé, d. 20 Dec 1917 Troyes.

Mazan, better known by his pseudonym of **Petit-Breton**, was the first great French rider of the 20th century. He was the first man to win two consecutive Tours de France, 1907-08, and also won the Milan-San Remo 1907 and Paris-Brussels 1908. He set a world 1 hour record with 41.110 km in 1905, passing 10km in a record 14:04.8. Petit-Breton was killed fighting in the First World War.

Bill MAZEROSKI (USA)

BASEBALL

William Stanley Mazeroski. b. 5 Sep 1936 Wheeling, West Virginia.

The top second baseman of his era and possibly the top defensive second baseman ever, 'Maz' played his entire career with the Pittsburgh Pirates. He won eight Gold Gloves but was not a great hitter, never batting over .300, although his greatest fame came while hitting. In the 1960 World Series, he won the 7th game for the Pirates by hitting a home run in the bottom of the ninth inning to defeat the Yankees. He led National League second basemen in double plays for eight consecutive seasons 1960-7, in chances accepted a record eight, and in assists a record nine. His totals of 1706 career double plays and 161 double plays in a season (1966) are major league records.
Career 1956-72: Avg. .260, HR 138; RBI: 853.

Sandro MAZZOLA (Ita)

FOOTBALL

Alessandro Mazzola. b. 8 Nov 1942 Turin.

Tall and slender, but his speed and directness made him a magnificent centre-forward and later midfield player for Inter Milan and Italy in the 1960s. He was six years old when his father **Valentino** (1919-49), the inside-left and captain of Italy and Torino, died in the Torino air disaster in 1949, and eventually emulated him as one of his country's greatest players.
He made his senior début for Inter in 1961 and for Italy in 1963. By his last international in 1974 he had won 70 caps and scored 22 goals for Italy, helping them to win the European Championship in 1968 and playing in the World Cups of 1966, 1970 and 1974. For Inter he scored 115 goals in 405 appearances to 1977.

Philip MEAD (UK)

CRICKET

Charles Philip Mead. b. 9 Mar 1887 Battersea, London, d. 26 Mar 1958 Boscombe, Hampshire.

It is curious to look back on Mead's career and see that he only won 17 Test caps for England over a 19-year span, yet he averaged nearly 50 and was for years a most prolific run scorer for Hampshire. A left-handed batsman and occasional slow left-arm bowler, his poor fielding counted against him. He went to Australia twice, yet on tours as far apart as 1911/2 and 1928/9. He played, of course, in a great era of English batsmen and while he lacked the dash and style of some, he was nonetheless a fine technician. In all he scored 1000 runs in a season 27 times, over 2000 nine times and over 3000 twice: 3179 at 69.10 in 1921 and 3027 at 75.67 in 1928.
His idiosyncratic and unchanging routine before every ball - looking round the field, pulling at his cap, and shuffling into a crouching stance - was a notable feature of his game. He played minor counties cricket for Suffolk in 1938-9, and in his youth kept goal for Southampton.
17 Tests 1911-28: 1185 runs at 49.37, 4 100s HS 182; 4 catches.*
First-class 1905-36: 55,061 runs at 47.67, 153 100s HS 280; 277 wickets at 34.70, BB 7-18; 671 catches.*

Andrea MEAD LAWRENCE (USA)

ALPINE SKIING

Andrea B Mead Lawrence. née Mead. b. 19 Apr 1932 Rutland, Vermont.

At the age of 19 she won both the slalom

and giant slalom at the 1952 Olympic Games, the first American skier to win two gold medals. In between those wins she fell twice in the downhill to finish 17th. Mead had already competed at the 1948 Games, when she was 8th at slalom. She started skiing at the age of three, and prior to her 1952 successes married US ski team member David Lawrence, who was 35th that year at the giant slalom. By 1956 she had had three children, but returned to tie for fourth place in the Olympic giant slalom.

In 1960 she was chosen to ski into the Olympic stadium at Squaw Valley, California with the Olympic torch.

She won US titles at downhill, slalom and combined in 1949, 1952 and 1955, and giant slalom in 1953. Andrea, who was divorced from David, became a TV commentator on skiing.

Richard MEADE (UK)

EQUESTRIAN

Richard John Hannay Meade. b. 4 Dec 1938 Chepstow, Monmouthshire.

With three Olympic gold medals at the three-day event, as an individual on *Laurieston* in 1972 and team in 1968 and 1972, Meade is Britain's most successful Olympic equestrian. He made his Olympic début in 1964 after his victory on *Barberry* at Burghley, and competed again in 1976, when he was fourth.

After being runner-up in the individual event at the World Championships in 1966 on *The Poacher*, he was a member of the winning British team at the 1970 and 1982 Championships and in both those years won at Badminton, on *The Poacher* and *Speculator III* respectively. He was also a member of the winning eventing team at the 1967 European Championships. Awarded the OBE in 1974.

His parents bred ponies and horses in Chepstow, so he learnt to ride at an early age. He is an engineering graduate of Cambridge University and now farms in Wiltshire; he became president of the British Equestrian Federation in 1989.

Colin MEADS (NZ)

RUGBY UNION

Colin Earl Meads. b. 3 Jun 1936 Cambridge, Auckland.

With 55 international appearances, Colin Meads is the most capped New Zealander of all-time. He made his Test début as a loose forward on the 1957 tour of Australia, but he soon settled as a lock and his international career lasted a record 15 seasons.

His uncompromising play did not always meet with the approval of referees, and against Scotland in 1967 he became only the second player to be sent off in an international. His reputation was further damaged in 1986 when, although a national selector, he accompanied the Cavaliers on their unofficial tour of South Africa. He was severely reprimanded by the New Zealand RFU and lost his place on the national selection panel at the end of the season. His brother, **Stanley** (b. 12 Jul 1938 Arapuni) played 15 Tests with Colin for the All Blacks as a forward 1961-6.

Mary T MEAGHER (USA)

SWIMMING

Mary Terstegge Meagher. b. 27 Oct 1964 Louisville, Kentucky.

In an age when world records tumble frequently, her world butterfly records of 57.93 for 100m and 2:05.96 for 200m, both set at the US Nationals in Brown Deer, Milwaukee, Wisconsin in 1981, remain well clear at the top of the world all-time lists more than a decade later. The former improved her own record of 59.26 by a staggering 1.33 secs, and the latter was her fifth world record from her first of 2:09.77 in 1979 when she scored an upset win over Tracy Caulkins at the Pan-American Games (a title she retained in 1983). Twelve years after her 200m record she still has the 12 fastest times of all-time, set between 1979 and 1986, at that event. Meagher would surely have won gold medals at the 1980 Olympics but for the US boycott; she was, however, rewarded for her patience by taking three golds in

1984, both butterfly events and the medley relay. She had won the 100m and taken silver medals at 200m and medley relay at the 1982 Worlds, and continued her career with a record-equalling six medals at the 1986 World Championships: gold at 200m butterfly, silvers at all three relays, and bronze at 200m freestyle and 100m butterfly. She ended with a bronze at 200m butterfly in the 1988 Olympics.
She won a total of 22 US national titles between 1979 and 1988. While at the University of California in Berkeley she won the NCAA title at 100y butterfly in 1985 and 1987 and the 200y in 1983 and 1985-7. Other bests: freestyle 100m 56.23 (1986), 200m 2:00.01 (1986), 400m 4:14.41.

Rick MEARS (USA)

MOTOR RACING

Rick Ravon Mears. b. 3 Dec 1951 Wichita, Kansas.

The greatest master of sustained speed on oval tracks with his uncomplicated, relaxed concentration, Mears had career record winnings of $4,299,392 from 15 starts in the Indianapolis 500, 1978-92. He had a record six pole starts and having won in 1979, 1984 and 1988, tied the record with a fourth win in 1991, having set numerous speed records during his career.
The son of former race driver Bill Mears, he started racing sprint buggies in 1970 and made his début in Indy Car racing in 1976, sharing the title of Rookie of the Year in 1978. After several accidents he retired at the end of 1992 with Indy Car career earnings of $11,050,807 and 29 victories, with the Championship in 1979 and 1981-2. An accident in practice for a race at Montreal in September 1984 required multiple surgery to his feet.

Giuseppe MEAZZA (Ita)

FOOTBALL

Giuseppe Meazza. b. 23 Aug 1910 Milan, d. 21 Aug 1979.

'Peppino' Meazza was the greatest star and captain of the Italian teams that won the World Cup in 1934 and 1938. From 1930, when he scored twice on his international début, to 1939 he played 53 times for Italy at centre or inside-forward, scoring 33 goals, a national record until surpassed by Luigi Riva. He played for Internazionale from 1927 to 1939, then occasionally for AC Milan, and he made guest appearances during the War for Juventus and Varese. He had one season for Atalanta in 1945 before becoming Inter's manager. In all he scored 269 goals in 440 Italian League First Division games. Trainer of the Italian team in 1962. The magnificent San Siro stadium in Milan is now named in his honour.

Mária MEDNYÁNSZKY (Hun)

TABLE TENNIS

Mária Mednyánszky. b. 7 Apr 1901 Budapest, d. 22 Dec 1978 Budapest. Later Klucsik.

The greatest woman player of all-time who was a match for all but the very best men of her era. She was the winner of the singles at the first five World Championships 1926-31, and was runner-up to her compatriot, Anna Sipos, in the next two. She also won the first women's doubles title in 1928 with Erika Flamm (Aut) and a further six doubles titles 1930-5 with Sipos. Her overall record total of 18 world titles between 1926 and 1935 was completed with six wins in the mixed doubles with three different partners. Her game was based on a heavy attacking spin.

Aleksandr MEDVED (USSR/Ukr)

WRESTLING

Aleksandr Vasilyevich Medved (Oleksander Medvid - Ukrainian). b. 16 Sep 1937 Belaya Tserkov, Kiev Oblast.

A giant who wrestled in the unlimited class for much of his career, he holds the record for ten world and Olympic championships won in wrestling. From his world heavyweight bronze medal in 1961 to 1972 he lost just two of 73 bouts in 15 international championships, to world champions Wilfried Dietrich (FRG) in 1961 and Ahmet Ayik (Tur) in the 1965

Worlds. He won Olympic gold as a light-heavyweight in 1964 and super-heavyweight 1968 and 1972, and world titles at light-heavyweight 1962-3 and 1966, and super-heavy 1967, 1969-71. He was European champion in 1966, 1968, and 1972. He was also Soviet champion in 1961-3 and 1966-70. As a super-heavy-weight, Medved's record is more impressive when one considers that at a maximum weight of about 110kg *242 lb* he was quite light for that class. He was by profession an engineer.

Joe MEDWICK (USA)

BASEBALL

Joseph Michael Medwick. b. 24 Nov 1911 Carteret, New Jersey, d. 21 Mar 1975 St Petersburg, Florida.

'Ducky' Medwick played in the major leagues from 1932-48, mostly with the St Louis Cardinals. An outfielder, he also played with the Brooklyn Dodgers, New York Giants, and Boston Braves. His greatest season by far was 1937 when he won the Triple Crown. Medwick was a great hitter, batting over .300 in 15 seasons, including the first 11 of his career. He led the National League in hitting only in 1937, but led in RBI from 1936-38, with a high of 154 in his Triple Crown season. *Career 1932-48: Avg. .324, HR 205; RBI 1383. Best seasons: 1937: .374, 31 HR, 154 RBI; 1936: .351, 138 RBI; 1938: .322, 122 RBI.*

Shekhar MEHTA (Kenya)

RALLYING

Shekhar Mehta. b. 20 Jun 1945 Kenya.

The winner of the Safari Rally a record five times, 1973, 1979-82. Each time he was driving a Datsun and Mike Doughty was his co-driver on the last four occasions. His career ended when he was seriously injured.

Petra MEIER (GDR)

ATHLETICS

Petra Meier. née Felke. b. 30 Jul 1959 Saalfeld.

The only woman to throw the javelin 80 metres, achieving exactly that distance at Potsdam on 9 Sep 1988. That was her fourth world record, having become the first 75m thrower in 1985. She had lost the record to Fatima Whitbread at the 1986 Europeans, when she took the silver medal, but having regained the record she took her revenge by beating Whitbread to take the 1988 Olympic title. She had a long and distinguished career from European Junior silver in 1977. In World Championships she was 2nd in 1987 and 1991 and at the Europeans was also 7th in 1982 and 3rd in 1990. Her other successes included the World Student Games title in 1989, World Cup 1991 (after 2nd in 1981 and 1985), European Cup 1986, 1987, 1989 and the GDR title each year 1984-9. Competed for SC Motor (later TuS) Jena.

Hugo MEISL (Aut)

FOOTBALL

Hugo Meisl. b. 16 Nov 1881 Vienna. d. 17 Feb 1937 Vienna.

Known as the 'Father of Austrian Football', his influence extended far beyond his own country. The son of a wealthy Jewish banker, his father was so disturbed by his enthusiasm for sport that he banished him for a time to Trieste. He played occasionally for the Cricketers and for Austria FK, but he became more interested in management and in 1912 brought the British coach Jimmy Hogan to Vienna. This was the start of the Austrian 'Wunderteam' which Meisl and Hogan played a vital part in developing. The team was the leading national side on the Continent in the early 1930s, beating Scotland 5-0, Germany 6-0 and only losing 3-4 to England at Wembley. Meisl was rightly recognised, along with England's Herbert Chapman and Italy's Vittorio Pozzo, as one of the greatest managers of the time.

As an administrator he was secretary of the Austrian FA and an influential figure in the early days of FIFA. His brother, Willy, was an international goalkeeper and an outstanding sports journalist.

Vladimir MELANIN (USSR)

BIATHLON
Vladimir Mikhailovich Melanin. b. 1 Dec 1933 Balyik Sovetskogo, Kirov region.

World biathlon champion in 1959 and 1962-3 and also a member of the winning USSR team in each of those years, he became Olympic champion in 1964.

Doina MELINTE (Rom)

ATHLETICS
Doina Melinte. née Besliu. b. 27 Dec 1956 Hudesti.

A strong middle-distance runner, she was the Olympic champion at 800m with silver at 1500m in 1984, running at each Games from 1980 to 1992. She was World Indoor champion at 1500m in 1987 and 1989, and European Indoor champion at 800m in 1982 and 1989 and at 1500m in 1985, 1988 and 1990; but in the other major outdoor championships her best was bronze at 1500m in the 1987 Worlds and 1986 Europeans.
World Student Games champion at 800m in 1981, and European Cup winner at both 800m and 1500m in 1989 and at 1500m in 1991. Later in her career she ran hard all round the Grand Prix circuit, needing to run for the money rather than being able to concentrate on championships glory. She became Member of Parliament for Bacau.
Best times: 800m 1:55.05 (1982), 1000m 2:31.85 (1990), 1500m 3:56.7 (1986), 3000m 8:37.11 (1986). World indoor bests: 1500m 4:00.27 (1990), 1 mile 4:18.86 (1988) and 4:17.14 (1990). World best 600m 1:23.5 in 1986.

Stan MELLOR (UK)

HORSE RACING
Stanley Thomas Edward Mellor. b. 10 Apr 1937 Manchester.

Broke Fred Winter's record for a jockey of 923 winners under National Hunt rules; his 1000th was on *Ouzo* at Nottingham on 18 Dec 1971, and he ended with a career total of 1049, including 14 abroad, from 1953 to 1972. He also won three flat races. He then became a trainer at Lambourn, Wiltshire.
He started as an amateur with George Owen at the age of 15, and at 16 turned professional and won on his first pro ride. He was champion jockey in 1959/60 and the following two seasons, with a peak of 118 wins in 1960/1. As a lightweight he was always able to have plenty of rides, and excelled with great timing. As a jockey he had won the Whitbread Gold Cup in 1962, and exceeded this with training successes in 1980 and 1987. Awarded the MBE in 1972.

Faina MELNIK (USSR)

ATHLETICS
Faina Grigoryevna Melnik. b. 9 Jun 1945 Bakota, Ukraine.

Set a record eleven world records for the women's discus, from 64.22m in 1971 to 70.50 in 1976. She was twice European (1971 and 1974) and once Olympic (1972) champion. She won 52 successive discus competitions between 1973 and 1976, so it was a major shock when she placed only fourth in the Olympics that year. Suddenly her all-conquering years of success were over, for she was fifth in the 1978 Europeans and failed to qualify for the 1980 Olympic final. She won nine USSR discus titles between 1970 and 1981, the World Student Games 1973, European Cup 1973, 1975 and 1977, and World Cup 1977. Her shot best was 20.03m (1976). She was married to Bulgarian discus thrower Velko Velev 1977-9.

Vera MENCHIK (UK)

CHESS
Vera Francevna Menchik. b. 16 Feb 1906 Moscow, d. 26 Jun 1944 London.

The dominant player in women's chess for many years. She was a pupil of Géza Maróczy and won the inaugural Women's World Championship in 1927, retaining the title throughout her life. World junior women's champion 1926-7.
Her family (her father was Czech and her mother English) moved to Hastings in 1921, and she became a British citizen on marrying R.H.Stevenson in 1937. She was killed in an air raid in London in 1944.

Alfredo MENDOZA (USA)

WATER SKIING

Alfredo Mendoza. b. 16 Jul 1935.

The world's premier male water skier during the early 1950s, Mendoza learned to water ski at Lake Tequesquitengo, south-west of Mexico City. His fascination with the sport convinced him to change his earlier dream of becoming a bullfighter. In both 1953 and 1955 he was world overall and jumping champion, adding the slalom in 1955. He used his tournament successes to launch a successful exhibition career at Cypress Gardens and later turned to ice skating, starring in several touring ice shows in the 1960s and 1970s.

Mal MENINGA (Aus)

RUGBY LEAGUE

Malcolm Norman Meninga. b. 8 Jul 1960 Bundaberg, Queensland.

'Big Mal', a great attacking centre, has made a record 38 international appearances for Australia at rugby league and scored a record 250 points in these games, 1982-92. A policeman from Queensland, he first came to Britain with the Kangaroos in 1982, when he was top scorer on the tour with 118 points. In 1984/5 he joined St Helens on a contract which made him the highest paid player in the game and scored 28 tries for them in 31 matches. He missed the 1988 World Cup final through injury, but returned to captain the Australian tourists in 1990.

Pietro MENNEA (Italy)

ATHLETICS

Pietro Paulo Mennea. b. 28 Jun 1952 Barletta.

The 1980 Olympic 200m champion, he competed in three further Olympic finals at this distance, 3rd 1972, 4th 1976, 7th 1984, and also ran in 1988. Also at 200m he was European champion in 1974 and 1978, World Student Games champion in 1973, 1975 and 1979, and third in the 1983 World Championships. He won ten Italian titles at 200m as well as three at 100m, at which distance he won European gold in 1978 and silver in 1974. He added two more European medals to bring his total to six, with the bronze in 1971 and silver in 1974 at 4x100m relay, was European Indoor champion at 400m in 1978, and won an Olympic bronze medal at 4x400m relay in 1980.

In his long career from 1969 to 1984 he ran 164 races at 200m in under 21 seconds, headed by his 19.72 set at high altitude in Mexico City in 1979, the longest lasting world record at the start of 1993. He also set his 100m best of 10.01 in Mexico City in 1979. He now runs his family sportswear company.

Carlos MERCENARIO (Mex)

WALKING

Carlos Mercenario. b. 3 May 1967.

With World Race Walking Cup wins at 20km in 1987 and 50km in 1991 and 1993, he became the first man to win at both distances and tied the series record with three individual wins. He was Pan-American champion at 20km in 1987 and 1991, and after placing 8th at 20km in 1988 took the Olympic silver medal at 50km in 1992. He had set a world junior best for 20km when second in the America's Cup in 1986, and a world best time of 1:19:24 in 1987. His 50km best is 3:42:03 (1991).

Joe MERCER (UK)

FOOTBALL

Joseph Mercer. b. 9 Aug 1914 Ellesmere Port, Cheshire, d. 9 Aug 1990 Hoylake.

The son of a professional footballer, he signed for Everton as a 16-year-old in 1932 and helped them to the Football League title in 1939. He played at left-half for England in all their five international matches that season but, although he played in 22 wartime internationals, he was not capped again after the war. In 1946 he lost his place in the Everton team and was transferred to Arsenal where, under the shrewd guidance of Tom Whittaker, his career was revived. With Arsenal, he won League Championship honours (1948, 1953), and an FA Cup winners medal (1950), and he was again an FA

Cup finalist in 1952. In 1950 he was voted Footballer of the Year.
Despite his frail physique he was a relentless tackler but his fragile, spindly legs always caused him problems and his playing days ended in April 1954 when he sustained a double fracture.
He went on to enjoy a highly successful career as a manager, holding appointments at Sheffield United, Aston Villa, Manchester City and Coventry. His years at Maine Road were particularly notable, as he led Manchester City to the First Division title 1968, the FA Cup 1969 and to both the League Cup and European Cup-Winners' Cup 1970. He also served as England's caretaker manager between the departure of Sir Alf Ramsey and the appointment of Don Revie. Held in high regard by his peers and universally popular with spectators, he remained closely connected with the game until he retired as a director of Coventry in 1981. He died on his 76th birthday.

Joe MERCER (UK)

HORSE RACING

Joseph Mercer. b. 25 Oct 1934 Bradford.

Rode 2810 winners in his riding career in Britain, 1950-85. His brother Manny (qv) was a brilliant jockey. Joe won his first race in 1950 and became champion apprentice in 1952 and 1953. The first of his eight English classic winners was *Ambiguity* in the 1953 Oaks, but he was perhaps the best jockey never to win the Derby. Undoubtedly the greatest horse that he rode was *Brigadier Gerard* on whom he won 17 races in 1970-2, and he rates as his greatest joy the winning of the Prix Diane on the Queen's *Highclere* in 1974. He rode over 100 winners in a season six times, first with 106 in 1964 and 1965, improving to 115 in 1978 and a peak of 164 in 1979. He was apprenticed to Major Fred Sneyd 1947-55 and then went to Bob Colling's stable at West Ilsley, which was taken over in 1962 by Dick Hern, with whom he stayed until 1976 when the racing world was amazed to hear that Mercer's services were no longer required. However, he then joined Henry Cecil and became champion jockey in 1979 at the age of 45. In 1959 he married Harry Carr's daughter Anne.
A great sportsman and enormously respected in the racing world, he was a model jockey, renowned for waiting and producing a hard, driving finish. On his retirement from the saddle he became an agent and then racing manager for Maktoum Al Maktoum.

Manny MERCER (UK)

HORSE RACING

Emmanuel Lionel Mercer. b. 15 Nov 1928 Bradford, Yorkshire, d. 26 Sep 1959 in a fall at Ascot.

Brother of Joe (qv), he was a superbly stylish jockey, apprenticed first to James Russell and then to George Colling in 1947. He surpassed 100 winners in a season first in 1953, when he rode the first of his two classic winners, *Happy Laughter* in the 1000 Guineas, and again each year 1956-9, with a peak of 125 in 1958. In all from 1947 he rode 976 winners.

Vijay MERCHANT (India)

CRICKET

Vijay Madhavji Merchant. b. 12 Oct 1911 Bombay, d. 27 Oct 1987

India's most accomplished batsman, his career average is second only to that of Don Bradman. Particularly during the War years he scored prodigiously in India, scoring four hundreds in successive innings in 1941/2, and averaging 98.75 in his career for 3639 runs in the Ranji Trophy in which he played for Bombay from 1933 to 1952. He had made his first-class début for the Hindus in the Pentangular Tournament in 1929/30. A small, compact and very sound batsman, he scored 282 and 245 runs in the 3-Test series against England in 1936 and 1946 respectively, and on the latter tour made 2385 runs at 74.53 in first-class games. He became a leading administrator of cricket in India.
10 Tests 1933-51: 859 runs at 47.72, 3 100s HS 154; 7 catches.
First-class 1937-59: 13.248 runs at 71.72, 44 100s HS 359; 65 wickets at 32.12, BB 5-73; 115 catches.*

Eddy MERCKX (Bel)

CYCLING

Eddy Merckx. b. 17 Jun 1945 Meensel-Kiezegem.

It is very rare in any sport that one is able to state that one man was undoubtedly the greatest ever. But such is the case in cycling with Eddy Merckx. He was so strong and rode hard so often that his nick-name was 'The Cannibal'. He had no weaknesses - he was the strongest time tri-alist and climber in the world, and could outsprint all but a few rivals.

His list of major victories is staggering. He has won the most titles in the following major races: 5 Tour de France (1969-72, 1974), wearing the Maillot Jaune for a record 96 days and winning a record 35 stages; 5 Giro d'Italia (1968, 1970, 1972-4); 3 world professional road race (1967, 1971, 1974), as well as the amateur title 1964; 7 Milan-San Remo (1966-7, 1969, 1971-2, 1975-6); 3 Ghent-Wevelgem, 4 Flèche-Wallonne (1967, 1970, 1972, 1975); 5 Liège-Bastogne-Liège (1969, 1971-3, 1975). He was the first man (since equalled only by Stephen Roche) to win the Tour de France, Giro d'Italia and world professional road race in the same year (1974). He is one of only four men to have ever won all three of the major tours - France, Italy and Spain (1973), but only Merckx also won the other major tour, Switzerland (1974). At the 1969 Tour de France, Merckx performed the still unequalled feat of winning the yellow jersey (overall winner), green jersey (points winner), and polka-dot jersey (King of the Mountains). He was again King of the Mountains in 1970 and points winner in 1971-2.

He set world records at Mexico City in 1972 for 10km 11:53.2, 20km 24:06.8 and 1 hour 49.431957 km. He was Belgian sportsman of the year each year 1969-74.

Other major victories: Paris-Roubaix 1968, 1970, 1973; Tour of Flanders 1969, 1975; Paris-Nice 1969-71; Het Volk 1971, 1973; Amstel Gold Race 1973, 1975; Tour of Lombardy 1971-2; Paris-Brussels 1973; Grand Prix de Nations 1973; Dauphiné-Libéré 1971; King of the Mountains - Tour de France 1969-70, Giro d'Italia 1968.

Billy MEREDITH (UK)

FOOTBALL

William Henry Meredith. b. Jul 1874 Chirk, nr. Wrexham, Wales, d. 19 Apr 1958 Manchester.

A brilliant outside-right who, like Stanley Matthews in later years, enjoyed a career of remarkable longevity. He won the first of his 48 Welsh caps in 1895 and made his final international appearance in March 1920 at the age of 45 years 229 days when Wales beat England for the first time in their history. His record of being the oldest player ever to win international honours still stands. Four years later, as he approached his 50th birthday, he was brought into the Manchester City side for the FA Cup semi-final although he had made only three League appearances in the previous two years.

After one season with Northwich Victoria he signed for Manchester City in October 1894, but after being involved in an illegal payments scandal in 1906 he was forced to leave the club. He then joined Manchester United but rejoined City in 1921. He won an FA Cup winners medal with both City, 1904, and United, 1909, and twice won League Championship honours with United, 1908 and 1911.

Billy Meredith, who always played with a toothpick in his mouth, was justifiably known as the 'Prince of Wingers' and his laconic attitude shielded the fact that he worked constantly on his dribbling skills until the end of his career. He was a founder member of the Players' Union and after retirement he returned to Manchester United in 1931 as a coach. He later ran a hotel in Manchester.

Bryn MEREDITH (UK)

RUGBY UNION

Brinley Victor Meredith. b. 21 Nov 1930 Cwmbran.

Playing in 34 internationals between 1954 and 1962, he is Wales' most capped hooker. After playing in all four Tests on the 1955 Lions tour of South Africa, he toured Australia and New Zealand in 1959 but skipper Ronnie Dawson kept him out of the Test side. In 1962, Meredith made his third Lions tour and played in all four Tests against South Africa. Apart from being an exceptionally quick striker in the scrum, his play in the loose was unusually skilful for a hooker.

Leon MEREDITH (UK)

CYCLING

Lewis Leonard Meredith. b. 2 Jul 1882 St Pancras, London, d. 27 Jan 1930 Davos, Switzerland.

The first man to win seven world championships, all in the now-defunct amateur 100 km motor-paced event, 1904-05, 1907-09, 1911 and 1913. Meredith also won seven British championships, 1902-8. At the 1908 Olympics he might well have been favourite to win the individual road race, but the event was not contested for one of the few times in Olympic history; he did win a gold medal at team pursuit. In 1912 he was 4th in the road race at the Stockholm Olympic Games. He was also British amateur roller-skating champion in 1911 and 1912. He died of a heart attack while on his annual winter holiday in Davos.

Ted MEREDITH (USA)

ATHLETICS

James Edwin Meredith. b. 14 Nov 1892 Chester Heights, Pennsylvania, d. 2 Nov 1957 Camden, New York.

As a 19-year-old he won Olympic gold medals at 800m and 4 x 400m relay in 1912, and was also 4th at 400m. Earlier that year he had set inter-scholastic records with 49.2 and 48.4 for 440y and 1:55.0 for 880y, but in the Olympic final he took a second off the 800m world record with 1:51.9, a tenth of a second ahead of Mel Sheppard, and ran to an 880y record at 1:52.5, with a third world record in the relay.
He set four more world records: at 4x440y in 1915 and in 1916 at 880y 1:52.2 and 440y (and 400m) 47.4 while at the University of Pennsylvania. He won the IC4A and AAU 440y 1914-5 and the IC4A 880y 1915. He attempted a comeback in 1920 but was eliminated in the semi-finals of the Olympic 400m. He became a real estate broker.

Carole MERLE (Fra)

ALPINE SKIING

Carole Merle. b. 24 Jan 1964 Super-Sauze, Alpes de Haute Provence.

World Cup winner at super giant slalom each year 1989-92 and at giant slalom in 1992 and 1993. By January 1993 she had achieved a French record 20 World Cup victories, including a record 11 at Super-G and 9 at giant slalom. Overall she was second in 1992 and third in 1993. Runner-up in world championships at giant slalom 1989 and super giant slalom 1991, and at her third Olympics in 1992 at super G, she became world champion at giant slalom in 1993.

Dally MESSENGER (Aus)

RUGBY LEAGUE

Herbert Henry Messenger. b. 12 Apr 1883 Balmain, Sydney, d. 24 Nov 1959 Gunnedah, New South Wales.

Nicknamed 'Dally' because of his resemblance to the Premier of New South Wales, William Dalley. He was a major influence in the successful introduction of rugby league into Australia. He came from a notable sporting family; his grandfather won the Doggett's Coat and Badge in 1862 and his father was also a champion sculler on the Thames. An outstanding centre and full back and a former rugby union star who won two caps against New Zealand, he was persuaded to play in three matches in 1907 against the visiting New Zealand professional team who were on their way to England. This resulted in his expulsion from the Union but he played so well that he was asked to join the New Zealanders on tour and proved to be their outstanding player in England. The following season he was appointed vice-captain of the first Australian team to tour England where he captained his country in two Tests. In 1910 he was captain in all three Tests when Great Britain made their first visit to Australia. Because of family and business

commitments he declined an invitation to tour Britain in 1911. A dazzling runner and a prodigious goal-kicker, he set a long-lasting record with 270 points (19 tries and 108 goals) in 1911.
After his retirement in 1913 he managed his own hotel and held a variety of jobs before finishing up as a carpenter for the Department of Public Works. Sadly, he died in relative poverty but he was the first man to win international honours in both rugby codes and he remains Australia's first great rugby league hero.

Andy MESSERSMITH (USA)

BASEBALL

John Alexander Messersmith. b. 6 Aug 1945 Toms River, New Jersey.

A good pitcher, winning 130 games in 12 seasons in the majors, but far better known for his contribution to major league ballplayers' pursuit of free agency. In 1975 he and Dave McNally tested the reserve clause by playing without a contract. At the end of the year, arbitrator Peter Seitz ruled that this freed both of them from their contracts and made them free agents, thus ushering in a new era to baseball. Messersmith was not the first free agent (Catfish Hunter was a year earlier in different circumstances) but his precedent was the most important. In 1976 he was signed by the Atlanta Braves for an estimated $1.75 million, but won only 18 games in four more major league seasons. All of today's ballplayers owe a large percentage of their astronomical salaries to Andy Messersmith and Dave McNally.
Career pitching 1968-79: ERA 2.86; W-L 130-99; SO 1625; Best seasons: 1974: 20-6, 2.59 ERA; 1971: 20-13, 2.99 ERA.

Mark MESSIER (Can)

ICE HOCKEY

Mark Douglas Messier. b. 18 Jan 1961 Edmonton, Alberta.

A rugged center who broke into pro hockey with Indianapolis of the World Hockey Association in 1978. He played only one year in the WHA before joining the Edmonton Oilers, where he formed a potent line centering for Wayne Gretzky. Together they led the Oilers to the Stanley Cup in 1984-5 and 1987-8. Messier led the Oilers to his fifth Stanley Cup win in 1990, after Gretzky had been traded. In 1991 Messier was traded to the New York Rangers, where he immediately became their leader. The Rangers won their division in 1992, but lost out early in the play-offs.
Career 1978-92: 1057 games, 453 goals, 1243 points. NHL 1979-92: 1005 games, 452 goals, 1232 points. Play-offs: 177 games, 87 goals, 229 points. Best years: 1981/2: 50 goals; 1989/90: 45 goals, 129 points. Hart Memorial Trophy 1990, 1992; Lester Pearson Award 1990, 1992; Smythe Trophy 1984.

Ralph METCALFE (USA)

ATHLETICS

Ralph Harold Metcalfe. b. 29 May 1910 Atlanta, d. 10 Oct 1978 Chicago.

A great sprinter, whose career was slightly overshadowed by that of Jesse Owens. He was a poor starter but a very powerful finisher, and at the Olympic Games he took silver at 100m and bronze at 200m in 1932 and silver at 100m and gold at 4x100m relay in 1936, when the US teams set world records in heat and final.
Metcalfe ran 220 yards on a straight course in 19.8 at Toronto on 3 Sep 1932, and although this was wind-assisted and thus ineligible for records, it was the first sub-20 seconds time. He went on to win the NCAA title in world bests of 20.5 in 1933 (20.3 at 200m) and 20.4 in 1934 before having a 200m time of 20.6 run around a quarter-turn at Budapest in 1933 ratified as a world record. He ran a world record 9.4 for 100y in 1933 and after a 10.2 to win the 1932 NCAA title for Marquette, a time that was accepted as a record by the NCAA but not ratified by the AAU or IAAF, he ran six times of 10.3 in 1933-4, the last two of which were accepted as world records. Metcalfe won the sprint double at both AAU and NCAA championships for an unparalleled three consecutive years 1932-4, and added further AAU titles at 200m in 1935 and 1936.

He was also indoor champion at 60m in 1933-4 and 1936 and was the first to run 60y indoors in 6.1 (1933).
He was for many years on the city council in Chicago, and was elected to the US Congress in 1970 for the 1st District of Illinois, serving until his death.

Murray MEXTED (NZ)

RUGBY UNION
Murray Graham Mexted. b. 5 Sep 1953 Wellington.

His Test début against Scotland in 1979 marked the start of 34 consecutive international appearances for New Zealand at No.8. Although he did not have the formidable physique of some of all his All Black colleagues, his all-round athleticism made him one of the outstanding forwards of his era.
His involvement with the 'rebel' Cavaliers tour to South Africa in 1986 effectively ended his international career, and after marrying a former Miss Universe, Lorraine Downes, he published his autobiography. His father, **Graham** (b. 3 Feb 1927), who also played at No.8, was capped by New Zealand in 1950.

Debbie MEYER (USA)

SWIMMING
Deborah Meyer. b. 14 Aug 1952 Haddonfield, New Jersey. Later Reyes.

In 1968 she won the Sullivan Award after becoming the first woman to win Olympic gold medals at three events when she won the freestyle treble of 200m, 400m and 800m, winning each by a large margin. All this despite suffering for much of the time in Mexico with an upset stomach.
In just over three years from July 1967 to August 1970, Meyer set 15 world records: 200m 2:06.7; 400m, five from 4:32.6 to 4:24.3; 800m, five 9:35.8 to 9:10.4; 1500m, four 18:11.1 to 17:19.9; thus revolutionising concepts of what women were capable of. Pan-American champion at 400m and 800m in 1967, and AAU champion at both 400m and 1500m each year 1967-70, as well as at 400m individual medley in 1969. Suffering from asthma as a child, her family moved in 1965 to the sunnier climes of California, where Meyer joined the Arden Hills club. Her coach there, Sherman Chavoor, believed that she retired before she had even scratched the surface of her ability, despite her world records.

Ann MEYERS-DRYSDALE (USA)

BASKETBALL
Ann Elizabeth Meyers. b. 26 Mar 1955 San Diego, California.

Meyers made headlines when she became the first woman to sign an NBA contract. She went to training camp with the Indiana Pacers but did not make the team cuts. She was a four-time basketball all-American 1975-8 at UCLA, where her brother, Dave, had played for the men's basketball team before playing in the NBA, and she also played two years of volleyball and track. At a school known as the greatest basketball power ever, she set all-time points scoring records and in 1978 won the Broderick Award both as the outstanding collegiate basketball player and the outstanding female athlete.
For the USA she won a silver medal at the 1976 Olympics, and played on US teams at the 1975 and 1979 Pan-American Games and World Championships and 1977 World University Games. She was also elected to carry the US flag at the 1979 Pan-Am opening ceremony. In 1979-80 Meyers played with the New Jersey Gems of the Women's Basketball League and was voted the league's co-MVP. Since the league folded, she has worked mostly as a colour commentator for women's basketball on television.

Ulrike MEYFARTH (FRG)

ATHLETICS
Ulrike Meyfarth. b. 4 May 1956 Frankfurt-am-Main. Married Dr Roland Nasse 1988.

Meyfarth captured the hearts of the crowd in Munich in 1972 when, at 16 years 123 days, she became the youngest ever individual Olympic champion, setting a world high jump record of 1.92m.
Although remaining a fine jumper, she failed to qualify for the Olympic final in

1976, and was 7th and 5th in the European Championships of 1974 and 1978. However, she returned to the top when she won the 1981 World Cup high jump and she regained the world record, 10 years and 4 days after her Munich triumph, by jumping 2.02m to win the 1982 European title. In 1983, after a silver medal in the World Championships, she set another record, with Tamara Bykova (USSR), at 2.03m in the European Cup Final. Finally, she sealed her career by regaining her Olympic title in 1984, 12 years after Munich; this was the longest ever gap between gold medals. She was 1.88m tall. She was also European Indoor champion in 1982 and 1984, and FRG champion seven times outdoors and six indoors. On retirement she became a fashion model.

Lucien MIAS (Fra)

RUGBY UNION

Lucien Mias. b. 28 Sep 1930 St Germaine de Calherbe Lozere.

One of the most influential figures in French rugby, he was the first man who was able to persuade the French players, and particularly the forwards, to blend their individual skills into a co-ordinated team effort. He was capped 29 times as a lock forward and was probably at his best on the 1958 tour of South Africa. After France had held the Springboks to a 3-3 draw in the first Test, Mias led them to a memorable 9-5 victory in the second and final Test. The following season he captained France when they won the International Championship outright for the first time, and his place in French rugby history was assured.
Played for US Carcassonne and SC Mazamet. After 17 international appearances between 1951 and 1954, he concentrated on becoming a doctor, but returned to play for France in 1958-9.

Anders MICHANEK (Swe)

SPEEDWAY

Anders Michanek. b. 30 May 1943 Stockholm.

World speedway champion in 1974 and second in 1975. In all he scored 95 points in 11 finals betweeen 1967 and 1978. A very stylish rider, he was a member of the team that won the world team title in 1970, won the pairs title each year 1973-5 and was also long track world champion in 1977.

Cary MIDDLECOFF (USA)

GOLF

(Dr) Emmett Cary Middlecoff. b. 6 Jan 1921 Halls, Tennessee.

Middlecoff won the Tennessee Amateur from 1940-43 while he was in dental school. He then served in the Army medical corps as a dentist, but still played enough to allow him to win the 1945 North and South Open while still an amateur. He was named to the 1947 Walker Cup team but withdrew to turn professional. He had an excellent professional career, winning at least one tour event every year 1947-61, with a total of 40 victories, including the US Open 1949 and 1957 and the Masters 1955. He played for the US in the Ryder Cups of 1953, 1955 and 1959. He was an excellent ball-striker whose swing had a pronounced pause at the top of the backswing, and he was very long off the tee. He was also known as the slowest player in golf. His career was ended by back problems and putting misery. He never again practised dentistry after leaving the Army. After retiring from playing golf in 1963 he became a television commentator.

Kyuzo MIFUNE (Japan)

JUDO

Kyuzo Mifune. b. 21 Apr 1883 Kuji, Iwate Prefecture, d. 27 Jan 1965.

A distinguished judoka who at the time of his death was the only 10th dan in the world, despite the fact that he was very small at 1.56m and 56kg. His *osoto-gari* throws and ankle sweeps brought him many victories and in 1923 he was appointed a teacher at the Kodokan. In 1964 he became the first living person to receive the Order of the Rising Sun (3rd class).

George MIKAN (USA)

BASKETBALL

George Lawrence Mikan, Jr. b. 18 Jul 1924 Joliet, Illinois.

The first great big man to play in the NBA. He played for DePaul in college and then the 2.08m *6'10"* center joined the Chicago Stags in the original National Basketball League. The next year he was traded to the Minneapolis Lakers, with whom he played until his retirement. He led the Lakers to five NBA championships and was first-team All-NBA in every year 1949-54. He led the NBL or NBA in scoring five times. In addition, Mikan led both Chicago and Minneapolis to NBL titles in 1947 (Chicago) and 1948 (Minneapolis). He was so dominant that the three-second rule was instituted because of him. Goaltending also became a rule during his era, presumably to counteract his dominance. He retired after the 1954 season, but came back to play for part of one more year. He coached the Lakers in 1957/8 and in 1968-9 he was commissioner of the ABA. He also attended law school in the 1960s and later practised law.

NBA career: 11,764 points, av. 22.6.

Stan MIKITA (Can)

ICE HOCKEY

Stanley Mikita. b. 20 May 1940 Sokolce, Czechoslovakia.

When he was a baby, Mikita was adopted by his aunt and uncle, who lived in St Catherine's, Ontario. There he learned to play hockey in the NHL style and became a consummate professional center, with no weaknesses. He played all 22 years of his career with the Chicago Black Hawks. Centering for Bobby Hull for many years, Mikita led the NHL in assists from 1964 until 1967 and finished his career second only to Gordie Howe for assists all-time, and third on the all-time scoring list behind Phil Esposito and Howe. Mikita accomplished all this despite a chronic back problem which forced him to wear a brace through most of his career.

NHL career 1958-80: 1,394 games, 541 goals, 1,467 points. Play-offs: 155 games, 59 goals, 150 pts. Best year 1966/7: 62 assists, 97 points. Hart Trophy 1967-8; Ross Trophy 1964-5, 1967-8; Lady Byng Trophy 1967-8.

Vern MIKKELSEN (USA)

BASKETBALL

Arild Verner Agerskov Mikkelsen. b. 21 Oct 1928 Fresno, California.

Mikkelsen played for Hamline University in St Paul, Minnesota and stayed in town to play professionally for the Minneapolis Lakers for 10 years in the NBA. A big, tough power forward, he joined with George Mikan and Slater Martin to play on four Laker championship teams. He played in six NBA All-Star games, and coached the Minnesota Muskies of the ABA for 13 games in 1968. He was disqualified on fouls more times than any player in NBA history.

Hannu MIKKOLA (Fin)

RALLYING

Hannu Olavi Mikkola. b. 24 May 1942 Joensuu.

World rallying champion in 1983, and runner-up in 1979-80 and 1984, he achieved great success in a long career, beginning in 1963. He first came to prominence in 1967 when he was third in the 1000 Lakes Rally. He has a record-equalling 19 wins in world championship races from 1973. Major wins have included the 1970 World Cup Rally, a record four in the RAC Rally with co-driver Arne Hertz (Swe), 1978-9 and 1981-2; the Safari Rally 1972 and 1987; the 1000 Lakes 1968-70, 1974-5, 1982-3. Driving in these races Ford Escorts 1968-74 and 1978-9, Toyota Corolla 1975, Audi Quattro 1981-7.

Devereux MILBURN (USA)

POLO

Devereux Milburn. b. 19 Sep 1881 Buffalo, New York, d. 15 Aug 1942 Westbury, Long Island, New York.

A fine all-round athlete who was educated

at the Hill School in Philadelphia and then Lincoln College, Oxford, graduating from there in 1903. He also earned a law degree from Harvard in 1906. While at Oxford, Milburn competed for the swimming team for four years, rowed and played for the polo team in his last two years. He was from an extremely wealthy family and used the wealth to allow him to own an unmatched stable of polo ponies. He was a member of the American polo team from 1909 to 1928, and on the winning team in the Westchester Cup against Great Britain 1909, 1911, 1913, 1921, 1924, and 1927, captaining the team in those last three years. He was rated at 10 goals from 1917 through 1928.

Rod MILBURN (USA)

ATHLETICS

Rodney Milburn, Jr. b. 18 Mar 1950 Opelousas, Louisiana.

Milburn set world records at 120y hurdles and at 110m hurdles (13.2 in 1972 and 13.1 twice in 1973). His 13.24 to win the 1972 Olympic title in Munich was later established as the first automatically-timed record. In a great season in 1971, when he won all his 28 races, he ran the first ever 13-flat times for 120y hurdles, first wind-aided on 4 June at Billings, Montana and then with a 'legal' wind of 1.95 m/s three weeks later. He ran a further 13.0 for 120y in 1973 and (unratified) in 1975 after he had turned professional with the ITA group. He was reinstated for amateur competition in 1980.

AAU high hurdles champion outdoors in 1971-2 and indoors in 1972-3, NCAA champion for Southern University in 1971 and 1973, and Pan-American champion in 1971. Indoors he set world hurdles bests at 50y (5.8 in 1973), and five times at 60y (three at 6.8 1973-4, and twice as a pro at 6.7 in 1974-5).

David MILFORD (UK)

RACKETS

David Sumner Milford. b. 7 Jun 1905 Headington, Oxfordshire, d. 24 Jun 1984 Marlborough, Wiltshire.

World rackets champion from 1937 to 1947 and the first amateur to hold the title since Sir Wiliam Hart-Dyke in 1862. While at Rugby he won the Public Schools Championship in 1923 and 1924 and at Oxford he won blues for rackets and hockey. In 1930 he won his first Amateur singles title at rackets and the first of his 25 international caps for hockey (inside-left or centre-forward). He then concentrated on hockey and did not play again in the Championships until 1935 when he won his second title. Between 1930 and 1966 he won 18 British amateur titles (7 singles, 11 doubles). After winning the British Open in 1936, he challenged Norbert Seltzer (USA) for the world title. Seltzer won the first leg in New York by a narrow margin (4-3) but Milford was an easy winner (4-0) of the second leg at Queen's and was the overall winner, 7-3. He remained world champion until he resigned the title in 1947 but, mainly because of the war, he was never called upon to make a defence.

Roger MILLA (Cam)

FOOTBALL

Albert Roger Milla. b. 20 May 1952 Yaoundé.

Milla had a long and distinguished career. He started his career with the Leopard Club, Douala and was African Footballer of the Year in 1976 when he played for Tonnere Yaoundé, whom he had helped to win the African Cup-Winners Cup the previous year. He then played for five French clubs, helping Monaco in 1980 and Bastia in 1981 to win the French Cup before retiring in 1988 after seemingly ending his career with Montpellier. In 1982 he scored six goals for the Cameroon in World Cup qualifying matches, helping them to qualify for the finals for the first time. With his country again qualifying for the finals in 1990 he came out of retirement and was a star, scoring twice when he came on as a substitute both against Romania in the first round and against Colombia in the second; he was the oldest player ever to score in a World Cup finals tournament. His feats were rewarded with a second selection as

African Footballer of the Year, 14 years after his first.

Cheryl MILLER (USA)

BASKETBALL

Cheryl Deann Miller. b. 3 Jan 1964 Riverside, California.

Considered by many to be the greatest woman basketball player of all-time. In high school she was the most coveted female hoopster ever, averaging 32.6 points for her entire high school career and leading Riverside Poly High School to a 132-4 record. She played her college ball at the University of Southern California and there became the first person, male or female, to be named first-team All-American for four consecutive years as the team won NCAA titles in 1983 and 1984. She won the Naismith Trophy, emblematic of college basketball's top player, three straight years 1982-4. She then led the US Olympic team to a gold medal in Los Angeles.

She was the first pick of the California Stars of the National Women's Basketball Association in 1986, but the league soon folded. Instead she played again for the US national team which won the Goodwill Games and the world championships in 1986. She was hoping to return to the Olympics in 1988 but extensive ligament damage to her knee caused her to miss out. She is now an announcer for televised basketball games. Her brother, Reggie Miller, plays for the Indiana Pacers of the NBA.

Johnny MILLER (USA)

GOLF

John Laurence Miller. b. 29 Apr 1947 San Francisco, California.

Miller had won the 1964 US Junior championship and signed up to caddy in the 1966 US Open. However, the 18-year-old amateur amazed the golfing world by playing and finishing 8th overall. After turning professional in 1969 he had a superb career, winning 23 tour events between 1971 and 1987. His win in the 1973 US Open was the result of a last round of 63, at the time a tournament record.

In 1974 and 1975 he was the best player in the world, leading money winner in 1974 and 2nd in 1975, although he did not play much in the last half of that year. He won 8 tournaments in 1974 and 4 in 1975. His victories in those years included several rounds in the very low 60s, and were highlighted by a 14-stroke victory at the 1975 Phoenix Open. He won the British Open in 1976 and was three times second in the US Masters. Miller no longer plays much but is a golf analyst for television broadcasts.

Keith MILLER (Aus)

CRICKET

Keith Ross Miller. b. 28 Nov 1919 Sunshine, Melbourne.

A marvellous and exciting all-rounder, a talented batsman who was both a powerful driver and a delicate late cutter, and a fiercely competitive bowler, especially fast in short spells. He was also a genius as a slip fielder. Nicknamed 'Nugget', he was a true cavalier, aggressive yet casual, uninterested in averages or aggregates

He played for Victoria 1937-47, making 181 against Tasmania on his début, then switching to New South Wales for whom he played until 1956, captaining them in some of those years. He first made his name internationally on the Australian Services tour of England in 1945, with the high spot a brilliant 185 in 165 minutes for the Dominions XI at Lord's. He made his Test début against New Zealand in 1946 and against England in 1946/7 he scored 384 runs at 76.80 and took 16 wickets at 16.87, including his best performance of 7-60 and an innings of 79 in the first Test, as he started his formidable new-ball partnership with Ray Lindwall.

He also played Australian Rules football for Victoria and New South Wales.

After his retirement he became a sports journalist. Awarded the MBE 1956.

55 Tests 1946-56: 2958 runs at 36.97, 7 100s HS 147; 170 wickets at 22.97, BB 7-60; 38 catches.

First-class 1937-59: 14,183 runs at 48.90, 41 100s HS 281; 497 wickets at 22.30, BB 7-12; 136 catches.*

Sammy MILLER (UK)

MOTOR CYCLING
Samuel Hamilton Miller. b. 11 Nov 1933 Belfast.

The greatest trials rider of his time, achieving enormous success after he had been third as a road racer in the world 250cc championship in 1957. He was British trials champion each year from 1959 to 1969 and was twice European champion. Many of his greatest successes were on the 500cc Ariel, but in 1964 he switched to Bultaco and maintained his supremacy on a 250cc two-stroke.

Tony MILLER (Aus)

RUGBY UNION
Anthony Robert Miller. b. 28 Apr 1929 Manly, New South Wales.

In an international career lasting from 1952 to 1967, he won 41 caps which was then an Australian record. He also matched Graham Cooke's record of playing for the Wallabies for 16 seasons and no Australian has had a longer international career. His final match was against New Zealand in 1967 when, at the age of 38, he became Australia's oldest-ever Test player. He won international honours at both prop and lock and was one of the most robust forwards ever to represent Australia. He would undoubtedly have been capped more often but for the fact that he was unavailable to tour for 10 years and also missed several seasons as he developed his business interests. He played a record 332 matches for the Sydney club Manly, continuing to coach them on his retirement at age 42.

MILON of Kroton (Gre)

WRESTLING
Milon of Kroton. fl. ca. 540-508 BC.

The greatest wrestler of ancient Greece. He was champion at wrestling six times at the Olympic Games (540 BC boys', and 532-516 BC), seven times at the Pythian Games, ten times at the Isthmian Games and nine times at the Nemean Games. In four Olympiads, he was *periodonikes*, meaning he won all of the four major festival titles. He was so dominant that he frequently won his championships *akoniti*, meaning that nobody would enter against him. His strength was supposedly developed when as a young boy he began carrying a wild heifer on his shoulders. As the heifer grew, Milon continued to carry him for exercise and his strength became legendary, but it eventually killed him. In a forest, he saw a tree which had been cut open with wedges in it. He decided to pull open the trunk with his massive hands. He did this but the wedges flew out and the trunk trapped his hands. He was caught in the tree and wild beasts tore him to pieces that night.

Alain MIMOUN (Fra)

ATHLETICS
Alain Mimoun O'Kacha. b. 1 Jan 1921 Le Telagh, Algeria.

A fine distance runner who achieved his greatest success at cross-country, at which he was International champion in 1949, 1952-3 and 1956. On the track he seemed the perennial runner-up to Emil Zátopek, taking silver medals at the Olympics in 1948 at 10,000m, and in 1952 at both 5000m and 10,000m and at the Europeans at both those events in 1950. He came into his own, however, with Olympic gold at the marathon in 1956 on his début at the distance, with Zátopek in sixth place.
He set French records with 32 national titles, 12 at 10,000m, eight at 5000m, six each at cross-country and marathon, and with 85 international appearances 1947-66. His 11 French records included his bests for 5000m, 14:07.4 (1952) and 10,000m, 29:13.4 (1956), and his fastest marathon was 2:21:25 in 1958. He continued to run as a veteran, setting numerous age-group records over many years.

Hiroshi MINATOYA (Japan)

JUDO
Hiroshi Minatoya. b. 1943.

World champion at 63kg in 1965 and at 70kg in 1967 and 1969. Tall (1.76m) for a welterweight, he used his long legs to hook his opponents and he possessed great stamina.

Minnie MINOSO (Cuba/USA)

BASEBALL

Saturnino Orestes Armas Minoso Arrieta. b. 29 Nov 1922 Havana, Cuba.

Minoso played major league baseball in five decades, with Nick Altlock the only player to achieve that feat. He broke in with the Cleveland Indians in 1949, and played continuously through to 1964. In 1976 his last team, the Chicago White Sox, let him play in three games near the end of the season and in 1980 he appeared in two more games with the White Sox. Minoso, by then 67 years old, attempted to play in 1990, but commissioner Fay Vincent banned the attempt as not in the best interests of baseball. Minoso led the American League in stolen bases three times, in triples twice, doubles once, and in hits once. He batted over .300 eight times. He crowded the plate a great deal, and was hit by 189 pitches in his career, an American League record.

Career 1949-80: 1963 hits Avg. .298, HR 186; RBI 1023; SB 205.

Bruce MITCHELL (SAf)

CRICKET

Bruce Mitchell. b. 8 Jan 1909 Johannesburg.

On his Test début in 1929 Mitchell scored 88 and 61* but took 575 minutes to score those 149 runs. That set the scene for his fine defensive skills as an opening batsman, although he was also a most graceful player.

Missing many opportunities due to World War II, he played in all 42 Tests for his country from then until his last match against England in 1949, when he scored 99 and 56, finishing with a career runs aggregate which remains the South African record. He toured England three times, with a peak of 2014 runs at 60.13 in 1947.

42 Tests 1929-49: 3533 runs at 46.48, 12 100s HS 206; 2 wickets; 15 catches.
First-class 1940-64: 12,614 runs at 53.67, 46 100s HS 290; 12 wickets at 49.33, BB 3-36; 73 catches.

Rosi MITTERMAIER (FRG)

ALPINE SKIING

Rosi Mittermaier. b. 5 Aug 1950 Reit-i-Winkel. Later Neurather.

She had a great year in 1976, when at her third Olympic Games she won both slalom and downhill and the silver in the giant slalom. She was also world champion at Combination and the World Cup overall champion in 1976, although she did not win any of the individual disciplines. She had previously been 4th in 1973 and 3rd in 1975 in the World Cup, and from 1969 to 1976 had ten individual victories in World Cup races.

Petite and charming, she married Christian Neurather, who was fourth in the 1973 World Cup. Her sisters both skied at the Olympics, Heidi in 1964 and Evi in 1976.

Yoshinobu MIYAKE (Japan)

WEIGHTLIFTING

Yoshinobu Miyake. b. 24 Nov 1939 Miyagi Prefecture.

Japan's greatest ever lifter and, with Waldemar Baszanowski, the most dominant lifter of the 1960s in the lighter weight classes. Just 1.55m tall, he finished second in the 1960 Olympic bantamweight (56kg) class but won gold medals at the 1964 and 1968 Olympics as a featherweight (60kg). He was also world champion at 56kg in 1962 and at 60kg in 1963, 1965-67. He set 26 world records, including ten consecutive records in the snatch from 115kg in 1961 to 125.5kg in 1969, and nine consecutive overall records in the 60kg class. He became head of the Japanese weightlifting team.

His younger brother **Yoshiyuki** (b. 30 Sep 1945) was Olympic bronze medallist at featherweight in 1968 and succeeded him as world champion in 1969 and 1971.

Johnny MIZE (USA)

BASEBALL

John Robert Mize. b. 7 Jan 1913 Demorest, Georgia, d. 2 Jun 1993 Georgia.

A power-hitting first baseman who may

have struck out less than any power hitter in history. His slugging feats are legendary and he hit three home runs in a game a record six times. Thirty times he had two home runs in a game, second only to Babe Ruth. He led the National League in home runs four times, with a high of 51 in 1947. He also batted well for average, hitting over .300 in the first nine years of his career. He played with the St Louis Cardinals 1936-41, the New York Giants 1942-9 and the New York Yankees 1949-53. *Career 1936-53: 2011 hits Avg. .312, HR 359; RBI 1337. Best seasons: 1939: .349, 28 HR, 108 RBI; 1947: .302, 51 HR, 138 RBI; 1940: .314, 43 HR, 137 RBI; 1937: .364, 25 HR, 113 RBI.*

Billie Jean MOFFITT (USA) see KING

Dietmar MÖGENBURG (FRG)

ATHLETICS

Dietmar Mögenburg. b. 15 Aug 1961 Leverkusen.

A fine high jump competitor who made a habit of winning important competitions, from his first major successes when he won the European Cup Final and European Junior high jumps at the age of 17 in 1979. He set a world and world junior record of 2.35m in 1980, a European record 2.36 in 1984 and a world indoor record 2.39 in 1985. At 2.01m he has been the tallest of the tall men who have set world high jump records.

Through his nation's boycott he lost the opportunity of competing at the 1980 Olympics, but won in 1984. He was European champion outdoors in 1982 and indoors in 1980, 1982, 1984, 1986 and 1989. Not quite so successful later in his career, he was fourth in the 1983 and 1987 Worlds and in the 1986 and 1990 Europeans, and sixth at the 1988 Olympics. He was FRG champion ten times, 1980-5 and 1987-90.

MOHIBULLAH KHAN (Pak)

SQUASH

Mohibullah Khan.

One of the five members of the phenomenal Khan family who all won the British Open. After losing three times in the final to his uncle Azam he finally won the title in 1962, after which he emigrated to America where he became the professional at the Harvard Club in Boston. He adapted well to the hardball game, winning the North American Open four times between 1963 and 1967.

Scott MOLINA (USA)

TRIATHLON

Scott Molina. b. 29 Feb 1960 Pittsburgh, California.

Known as 'The Terminator', Molina has won more triathlon championships than any other racer. He was Bud Light US Champion from 1983-6 and in 1988 finally won the Hawaii Ironman. In 1984-5 he won an amazing 40 of 47 races. His background was ideal for triathlon as he was a distance runner and age-group swimmer as a youth. He is renowned as the hardest trainer in the sport, putting in more mileage than any of the top professionals. He is married to world class triathlete Erin Baker (qv).

Silke MÖLLER (GDR)

ATHLETICS

Silke Möller. née Gladisch. b. 20 Jun 1964 Stralsund.

For long regarded as the successor to Marlies Göhr, she reached her peak in 1987 with a brilliant sprint double at the World Championships. She came to the fore when she ran for the GDR team that set a world junior record to win the European Junior title, and continued to gain maximum reward for relay running with two world records at the 4 x 100m relay, in 1983 and at the 1985 World Cup, the latter a record which still stands. She took relay golds at the 1983 Worlds and the 1986 and 1990 Europeans, and won the 100m silver at the latter. She was World Indoor champion at 60m in 1985 and won three European Indoor medals.

She missed the 1991 season through injury, but was embroiled with Katrin Krabbe and Grit Breuer in the controver-

sial drug test avoidance issue in 1992. A student teacher, she ran for SC Empor Rostock and married Dietmar Möller in October 1987.
Best times: 50m 6.12i (1988), 60m 7.04i (1988), 100m 10.86 and 10.82w (1987), 200m 21.74 (1987).

Tim MOLONY (Ire)

HORSE RACING
Tim Molony. b. 14 Sep 1919 Co. Limerick, d. 14 Dec 1989 Wymondham, near Melton Mowbray, Leicestershire.

He came to England in 1946 and was National Hunt champion jockey five times, each year from 1948/9 to 1951/2 and in 1954/5, with a peak of 95 wins in 1949/50. His first ride in public was in 1936 and he turned professional in 1940.
A bold, brave rider, known as the 'rubber man', he rode 866 winners under NH rules to April 1958, when he retired after breaking a thigh in the only bad fall of his career. Riding *Hatton's Grace* and *Sir Ken* he won four consecutive Champion Hurdles, and he rode *Knock Hard* to win the Cheltenham Gold Cup in 1953. He became a trainer in Leicestershire in 1960.
His younger brother Martin (b. 1925) showed brilliant skill, and rode the Gold Cup winner *Silver Fame* in 1951 and the winners of the 1944, 1946 and 1950 Irish Grand Nationals, but his career was cut short by a fall in September that year.

Art MONK (USA)

AMERICAN FOOTBALL
Arthur Monk. b. 5 Dec 1957 White Plains, New York.

A wide receiver, Monk achieved lasting fame in 1992 when he caught his 820th pass to surpass Steve Largent as pro football's all-time leader in receptions, taking the record to 847 by the year's end. He also caught a pass in 148 consecutive games, third on the all-time list. In 1984 he set the single season record for most receptions with 106 (since broken). He played at Syracuse and in pro football from 1980 with the Washington Redskins. A big man at 1.91m *6'3"* and 95 kg *210 lb*, he is not exceptionally fast for an NFL receiver, but he has perhaps the surest hands of any recent pro flanker. A very hard worker, he is also known for the precision with which he runs his routes.
Monk was the 1976 national inter-scholastic champion in the intermediate hurdles. He is a second cousin of the renowned jazz great Thelonius Monk.

Earl MONROE (USA)

BASKETBALL
Vernon Earl Monroe. b. 21 Nov 1944 Philadelphia, Pennsylvania.

Say the name 'The Pearl' to a basketball fan, and only one player springs to mind. Earl the Pearl Monroe was an electrifying guard who played college ball at Winston-Salem State where he averaged 41.4 points per game in his senior year. He then played 13 years in the NBA, starting with the Baltimore Bullets and being voted Rookie of the Year in 1968, but playing his last nine years with the New York Knicks, who won the NBA Championship in 1973. He was an artist on the court, head-faking and juking in a uniquely charismatic style.

Joe MONTANA (USA)

AMERICAN FOOTBALL
Joseph C Montana, Jr. b. 11 Jun 1956 Monogahela, Pennsylvania.

One of the greatest ever quarterbacks, he began his rise to greatness at Notre Dame in the 1970s, being best remembered for rallying his college from a 23-point deficit in the 1979 Cotton Bowl to defeat Houston 35-34. Montana joined the San Francisco 49ers in 1979 and moved into the starting quarterback role in 1980. He helped the 49ers win four Super Bowl titles and is also the only man to have been voted Super Bowl MVP three times, 1982, 1985 and 1990. Montana returned quickly from lumbar disc surgery in 1986, but his career stalled in 1991 due to a torn tendon in his elbow, although he returned after two years out with two touchdown passes in the final game of 1992. In April 1993 he signed a three-year contract with the Kansas City Chiefs. Montana played in eight Pro Bowls and was a six-time All-Pro. He is rated as the NFL's all-time leader for passing efficiency and holds Super Bowl career records for 11 touch-down passes, 1142 yards gained passing and 83 pass completions, including game records in the first two categories at 5 and 357 in 1990. He is married to the former Jennifer Wallace, an actress and model. *NFL career 1979-92: 35,124 yards gained passing from 3128 pass completions.*

Eugenio MONTI (Italy)

BOBSLEIGH

Eugenio Monti. b. 23 Jan 1928 Dobbiaco, Bolzano.

The greatest bobsleigh driver in the history of the sport. Including the Olympics, he won a record total of eleven world titles (8 at 2-man, 3 at 4-man) between 1957 and 1968, with a further three silver and two bronze medals. The absence of bobsled events at the 1960 Olympics almost certainly deprived him of further honours, but his total of six Olympic medals is a record for the sport. After winning two silver medals in 1956, he won two bronze in 1964 and his persistence was finally rewarded in 1968 when he won two gold medals. He then retired to become the Italian team manager.

Luis MONTI (Arg, Ita)

FOOTBALL

Luisito F. Monti. b. 15 May 1901 Argentina, d. 1983.

An attacking centre-half who uniquely played in a World Cup final for two different countries. Born of Italian parents in Argentina, he began his career with Boca Júniors and was in the Argentine side which lost to Uruguay in the finals of the 1928 Olympic Games and the 1930 World Cup. In 1931 he moved to Juventus and in 1932 won the first of his 18 caps for Italy. In 1934 he played in his second World Cup final and this time was on the winning side as Italy beat Czechoslovakia 2-1 after extra time. Renowned for his robust play, he helped Juventus to four successive league titles 1932-5.

Carlos MONZON (Arg)

BOXING

Carlos Monzon. b. 7 Aug 1942 Santa Fé.

One of the greatest middleweights of modern boxing, Monzon first won the world title in 1970 when he upset Nino Benvenuti with a 12th round knockout. He never lost again and defended his title 14 times before retiring in 1977, his three losses having come in 1963-64. In 1988 he was charged with murder after his third wife died from a fall from a balcony. *Career record: W - 89 (61), L - 3, D - 9.*

Archie MOORE (USA)

BOXING

né Archibald Lee Wright. b. 13 Dec 1916 Benoit, Mississippi.

Moore had the longest career of any modern fighter and one of the most impressive. He was world light-heavy-weight champion for ten years and would have been for longer but he was not given a title shot until he was 36 years old in 1952. He may actually have been older as his mother has claimed that he was born in 1913.

Moore was virtually unbeatable at 175 pounds, but he also challenged twice for the heavyweight championship, losing in 1955 to Rocky Marciano and in 1956 to Floyd Patterson. He was a very advanced fighter for his day, training by walking on his hands and doing 250 push-ups every day. After his retirement he served as an adviser to numerous fighters and also appeared in a few movies. Moore took his last name from an uncle, Cleveland Moore, who had helped raise him. *Career record: W - 183 (129), L - 22, D -9.*

Bobby MOORE (UK)

FOOTBALL

Robert Frederick Moore. b. 12 Apr 1941 Barking, Essex, d. 24 Feb 1992 Putney, London.

One of England's greatest defenders and captain of the team which won the 1966 World Cup. After making a record 18 appearances for England's Youth team,

whom he captained, he went on to win a then record 108 caps at senior level, 90 as captain.
Starting as an amateur with West Ham United, he signed as a professional in 1958 and made 642 League and Cup appearances for them, which was then a club record, leading them to victories in the FA Cup 1964 and the European Cup Winners' Cup 1965. He then played for Fulham 1974-7 and made a second appearance in the FA Cup final in 1975 when Fulham lost to his old club West Ham.
A master tactician and a natural leader, he was an ideal choice as captain of both club and country. He was voted Footballer of the Year in 1964 and was awarded the OBE in 1967. He served briefly as player-manager of the Danish club, Herning FC, before taking up managerial and executive appointments at Oxford City 1979-81 and Southend United 1983-6. He was then sports editor of *Sunday Sport* for three years. The exemplary off-field image which he developed later led to numerous valuable commercial contracts before his tragically early death from cancer.

Dickie MOORE (Can)

ICE HOCKEY

Richard Winston Moore. b. 6 Jan 1931 Montreal, Québec.

Moore had the unenviable task of trying to replace Maurice Richard at right wing for the Montreal Canadiens, but was such an outstanding player that he almost succeeded. In 13 years to 1964 he helped them win six Stanley Cup championships and made brief comebacks in both 1964/5 and 1967/8. He was probably as courageous a player as any to lace up skates. He often played with injuries, notably in 1959 when he played with a broken right wrist, and a left wrist which had been broken in 1957 and had never healed properly. Chronic knee problems eventually ended his career.
NHL career 1951-68 - 719 games, 261 goals, 608 points. Play-offs: 135 games, 46 goals, 110 pts. Best years: 1957/8: 36 goals, 84 points; 1958/9: 55 assists, 96 points. Ross Trophy 1958-9.

George MOORE (Aus)

HORSE RACING

George Thomas Donald Moore. b. 5 Jul 1923 Mackay, Queensland.

He started riding in Australia in 1938, with his first winner in 1940. One of his greatest feats was riding 15 winners from 29 races in the four-day Sydney Cup carnival in 1969. In 1959 and 1960 he rode for Prince Aly Khan in France, and he rode his first classic winner in England, *Taboun*, in the 2000 Guineas 1959. He returned to England in 1967, when he took over from Lester Piggott as first jockey for Noel Murless. In a marvellous season he rode 72 winners, including three classics, *Fleet* in the 1000 Guineas and *Royal Palace* in the 2000 Guineas and Derby, and the King George VI and Queen Elizabeth Stakes on *Busted*. Back in Australia from 1969, he retired in 1971, and later trained with great success in Hong Kong, with his son Gary as first jockey.
He had problems with stewards during his career, and from 1954 served two and a half years disqualification for allegedly giving false evidence at an enquiry.

Lenny MOORE (USA)

AMERICAN FOOTBALL

Leonard Edward Moore. b. 25 Nov 1933 Reading, Pennsylvania.

After starring as a flashy running back at Penn State University 1953-5, Moore joined the Baltimore Colts and was named Rookie of the Year. In the NFL he played both running back and flanker, thanks to his exceptional speed. He was nicknamed 'Spats' because of his habit of taping his shoes up over his socks in the appearance of old-style spats. He played his entire pro career with the Colts and four times led the league in rushing average, by itself a record. He scored a touchdown in 18 successive games 1963-5, still a record. At his retirement, his 113 career touchdowns trailed only Jimmy Brown and has since been surpassed only by Walter Payton.
NFL career 1956-67: Rushing: 5174 yards av. 4.8, 63 touchdowns; Receiving: 6039 yards av. 16.6, 48 touchdowns.

Ronnie MOORE (NZ)

SPEEDWAY

Ronnie Moore. b. 8 Mar 1933 Hobart, Tasmania, Australia.

Arriving in England in 1950 to ride for Wimbledon, he made a spectacular début when he reached the world final that year as a 17-year-old. He first won the title in 1954, at the age of 21, to become the youngest-ever world individual champion and he again took the title in 1959, with second places in 1955-6 and 1960. A broken leg forced his retirement in 1963 but he returned to Wimbledon six years later and won the first World Pairs title with Ivan Mauger in 1970. He finally retired from British League racing in 1972 but continued to ride in internationals and in New Zealand. In all he contested 14 World Championships between 1950 and 1971, scoring 144 points.
He had ridden as pillion in his father's 'Wall of Death' act, touring New Zealand when he was aged 11. He also tried motor racing in 1956.

Adrian MOORHOUSE (UK)

SWIMMING

Adrian David Moorhouse. b. 25 May 1964 Bradford, Yorkshire.

Winner of many major titles in a long career at breaststroke swimming, his record reads: Olympic Games: 1984 4th 100m, 1988 1st 200m, 1992 8th 100m; Worlds: 1982 4th 100m, 7th 200m; 1986 disqualified after finishing first at 100m, 4th 200m; 1991 2nd 100m; Europeans: 1981 3rd 100m, 1983 1st 200m, 2nd 100m; 1985 1st 100m; 1987 1st 100m, 3rd 200m and silver at 4x100m medley; 1989 1st 100m in world record 1:01.49; Commonwealth Games: 1982 1st 100m, 3rd 200m; 1986 1st 200m, 2nd 100m; 1990 1st 100m in world record 1:01.49, 4th 200m. He set his third 1:01.49 world record later in 1990. That was also his ninth British record from his first, 1:03.15 in 1982.
Made his international début in 1980. In 1987 he became the first man to break one minute for 100m breaststroke in a 25m pool, with 59.75. ASA long-course champion 100m 1981-3, 1985-7, 1989-91; 200m 1981-3, 1985-6. Awarded the MBE in 1987.

Pablo MORALES (USA)

SWIMMING

Pedro Pablo Morales, Jr. b. 5 Dec 1964 Chicago.

At the 1984 Olympics he won a gold medal in the 4 x 100m medley relay, and set US records in both butterfly events, taking the silver medal at 100m in 53.23 behind Michael Gross's world record and placing 4th at 200m in a US record 1:57.75; he also took a silver medal in the 200m individual medley. His disappointment at failing to win an individual gold was compounded by his failure to make the US team in 1988, with third places at both butterfly events. He retired and went to Cornell Law School (having graduated from Stanford University in 1987). However, he came back in 1992 to win the 100m butterfly and take a second gold on the US world record setting 4 x 100m medley team. This was his third world record swimming the butterfly leg on the medley relay.
He had set a world record for 100m butterfly with 53.38 at the US Olympic Trials in 1984 and regained the record from Gross with 52.84 at the US World Trials in 1986, when he also set a US record of 2:02.23 for 200m individual medley. He then went on to win gold medals at 100m butterfly and medley relay at the 1986 Worlds. Other bests: 100m backstroke 56.88 (1988), 400m IM 4:27.30 (1983). His parents had emigrated from Cuba in 1956.

Karen MORAS (Aus)

SWIMMING

Karen Lynne Moras. b. 6 Jan 1954.

At the age of 14 she won a bronze medal at 400m and was fourth at 800m at the 1968 Olympics. Two years later she won a triple at the Commonwealth Games, at 200m, 400m and 800m. In the latter event she set a second world record, improving the time of 9:09.1 that she had set when winning the Australian title to 9:02.4. In 1971 she set a world record at 400m with 4:22.6. Past her best by the 1972 Olympics she did not make the finals as she was only 11th and 13th fastest respectively at 400m and 800m. She was Australian champion 200m 1970, 400m 1968-70, 800m 1968, 1970-1. Her sister Narelle was 8th in the 1972 Olympic 800m and 5th at 400m in the 1974 Commonwealth Games.

Noureddine MORCELI (Alg)

ATHLETICS

Noureddine Morceli. b. 28 Feb 1970 Ténès.

After second place in the World Junior 1500m in 1988, Morceli became a student at Riverside Community College, USA 1989-90, and burst to the top of world middle-distance running. In 1990 he won the Grand Prix series at 1500m, and he was unbeaten in 15 races at 1500m or 1 mile in 1991, when he won World titles indoors and out. He also set a world indoor record for 1500m of 3:34.16 in 1991. In 1992, however, he lost four times and had a poor run to place only 7th at the Olympics. Nonetheless he ended the season in style with a world record of 3:28.82 at Rieti. He started his 1993 campaign in brilliant style with 3:29.20 for 1500m at the Mediterranean Games and national records at 1000m and 1 mile. Coached by his elder brother Abderahmane, who was 3rd in the World Student Games and 4th in the World Cup with a best of 3:36.26 for 1500m in 1977.
Other bests: 800m 1:44.79 (1991), 1000m 2:13.73 (1993), 1 mile 3:47.78 (1993), 3000m 7:37.34 (1991), 5000m 13:25.20 (1990).

Daniel MORELON (Fra)

CYCLING

Daniel Morelon. b. 28 Jul 1944 Bourg-en-Bresse.

After third place in 1965, Morelon won a record nine world amateur sprint titles, 1966-7, 1969-73 and 1975, and three Olympic gold medals, sprint in 1968 and 1972 and tandem sprint in 1968, with a bronze (1964) and silver (1976) in the sprint. His tandem gold medal was won with Pierre Trentin, his great countryman with whom he had many battles, and these two also won the world tandem title in 1966. He won a total of 14 French titles, and set a world record indoors for 500m with a flying start at 28.75 in 1976. Strictly a track sprinter, he saw no reason to turn professional. He became the French sprint cycling coach in 1983.

Fernando MORENA (Uru)

FOOTBALL

Fernando Morena. b. 2 Feb 1952 Montevideo.

One of the few outstanding Uruguayan internationals of the 1970s and the scorer of a record number of goals in Uruguayan football, over 650. He played for River Plate Montevideo and Peñarol, apart from two short spells abroad with Rayo Vallecano in Spain and then Flamengo in Brazil. He won a Copa Libertadores medal with Peñarol in 1982 and helped Uruguay to win the South American Championship in 1983. He won 49 international caps 1971-83, scoring 20 goals.

Howie MORENZ (Can)

ICE HOCKEY

Howarth Morenz. b. 21 Jun 1902 Mitchell, Ontario, d. 8 Mar 1937 Montreal, Québec.

Years before Eric Heiden, in the heyday of Clas Thunberg, hockey fans will swear that Howie Morenz was the fastest ice skater ever. Known as 'The Stratford Streak (or Flash)' or 'The Meteor', he was easily the fastest player in the early years of the NHL. Most of his career was spent as a center for the Montreal Canadiens, though late in his career he briefly played with the Chicago Black Hawks and New York Rangers. In his last hockey game on 28 Jan 1937 for the Canadiens against his old team-mates from Chicago, Morenz, at full speed, was checked into the boards and sustained an open, comminuted fracture of his leg. Just over a month later, he died from complications from that accident.

Career 1923-37: 550 games, 270 goals, 467 points. Best years: 1927/8: 33 goals, 51 points; 1929/30: 40 goals, 50 points; 1930/1: 28 goals, 51 points. Hart Trophy 1928, 1931-2; Ross Trophy 1928, 1931.

Lisa-Marie MOREROD (Swi)

ALPINE SKIING

Lisa-Marie Morerod. b. 16 Apr 1956 Vers-l'Eglise.

In four years, 1975-8, she won 24 World Cup races; 14 at giant slalom, at which she was champion in 1976-8, and 10 at slalom, at which she was champion in 1975-7. She took the overall title in 1977, with 2nd place in 1976 and 3rd 1978.

Cliff MORGAN (UK)

RUGBY UNION

Clifford Isaac Morgan. b. 7 April 1930 Trebanog.

One of the most talented fly-halves in the history of the game, who was at his best when partnering his Cardiff clubmate Rex Willis. He played a major role when Wales won the Grand Slam in 1952 and the following season he inspired Cardiff and then Wales to victory over the touring All Blacks. On the 1955 Lions tour of South Africa, a brilliant try in the first Test paved the way for a classic victory and he captained the Lions when they won the third Test. The series ended level at 2-2 and Morgan made an outstanding contribution to the Lions' successes.

Between 1951 and 1958 he won 29 caps for Wales and still holds the record as the most capped Welsh fly-half. On retirement, he became a successful radio and TV commentator and journalist and was later Head of Outside Broadcasts for the BBC. He was honoured with the OBE in 1977 and the CVO in 1986.

Janet MORGAN (UK)

SQUASH

Janet R.M. Morgan. b. 10 Dec 1921 Wandsworth, London, d. 29 Jun 1990. Married Joe Bisley, then Ambrose Shardlow.

Initially a top-class tennis player, she became the best squash player in the world in the 1950s. She learned both games at Surbiton Lawn Tennis Club and as a tennis player she appeared at Wimbledon 14 times and was a non-playing member of the 1946 Wightman Cup squad. She first took up squash in 1946 and within two years was a finalist in the British Open. After losing to Joan Curry in the final of the British Open in 1948 and 1949, she won the US title in 1949 and then, in 1950, won the first of ten successive British titles. Her greatest year was 1954 when she won the British, Australian and US Opens.

After giving up competitive play in 1960 due to persistent leg and back problems, she became first chairman and then president of the Women's Squash Racquets Association until 1988, and worked tirelessly to promote the sport. She especially encouraged Heather McKay, who in 1972 surpassed her record number of British Open titles. Janet also achieved a seven handicap at golf. Awarded the MBE 1961.

Joe MORGAN (USA)

BASEBALL

Joe Leonard Morgan. b. 19 Sep 1943 Bonham, Texas.

One of the cogs of 'The Big Red Machine' which dominated the National League in the early 1970s. Morgan, a second baseman, played with the Houston Colt 45s (later the Astros) from 1963-71 when he was traded to the Cincinnati Reds. He helped the Reds to four National League pennants and two World Series victories 1975-6. In both 1975 and 1976 Morgan was named National League MVP. He won five Gold Gloves at second base 1973-7. He combined power and speed more than any other second baseman, hitting 268 career home runs, including four seasons of 20 or more, and he had 689 stolen bases, with nine consecutive seasons of 40 or more 1969-77. He has since become a popular television announcer.

Career 1963-84: 2518 hits Avg. .271, HR 268; RBI 1133; SB 689. Best seasons: 1975: .327; 1976: .320.

Paul MORPHY (USA)

CHESS

Paul Charles Morphy. b. 22 Jun 1837 New Orleans, d. 10 Jul 1884 New Orleans of apoplexy.

The world's leading chess player during his two-year career at the game. A graduate of the University of Louisiana and admitted to the Louisiana bar at the age of 19, he was not permitted to practise until he reached the age of 21. So he used the opportunity to play chess and to travel. He won the unofficial US chess title in 1857, and in 1858 defeated Adolf Anderssen to take over as unofficial world champion. He beat every major player, but had his last serious match in 1859. His legal career was not a success and he became a recluse.

Arthur MORRIS (Aus)

CRICKET

Arthur Robert Morris. b. 19 Jan 1922 Dungog, New South Wales.

An elegant left-handed opening batsman for Australia in the first post-war decade. He became the first player ever to score two hundreds on his first-class début, when he made 148 and 111 for New South Wales v Queensland at Christmas 1940. He played for New South Wales until 1955, captaining them (alternating with Keith Miller) from 1947. He was at his best with the supremely powerful Australian team in England in 1948, when he headed the Test averages with 696 runs at 87.00 and made 1922 runs at 71.18 in all first-class matches. A regular vice-captain of Australia, he captained them twice in Tests. The illness and death from cancer of his first wife at the age of 33 led to his retirement in 1955. Eight years later he made a brief comeback to big cricket when he went to India with a Commonwealth team and once again demonstrated his superb stroke play. Awarded the MBE.

46 Tests 1946-55: 3533 runs at 46.48, 12 100s HS 206; 2 wickets; 15 catches.
First-class 1940-64: 12,614 runs at 53.67, 46 100s HS 290; 12 wickets at 49.33, BB 3-36; 73 catches.

Glenn MORRIS (USA)

ATHLETICS

Glenn Edward Morris. b. 18 Jun 1912 Simla, Colorado, d. 31 Jan 1974 Burlingame, California.

In 1936 he won the only three decathlons that he ever contested. In the first he broke the US record at the Kansas Relays, and then set world records to win the US Trials and the Olympic gold medal. His scores were respectively 7576, 7884 and 7900 points (7109, 7213 and 7254 points on the current tables). He won the Sullivan Award that year and went on to a brief Hollywood career, playing Tarzan in *Tarzan's Revenge* (1938). He then became a running back in the NFL. He had graduated from Colorado State in 1934.

Tom MORRIS Jr (UK)

GOLF

Tom Morris, Jr. b. 20 Apr 1851 St Andrews, Scotland, d. 25 Dec 1875 St Andrews.

'Young Tom' Morris was probably the greatest player of the featherie and early guttie period. His three consecutive wins in the British Open in 1868-70 retired the championship belt and forced the cancellation of the 1871 tournament. He won in 1872 for a fourth consecutive time. Walter Hagen in the PGA is the only other golfer to win a major championship four times consecutively and Morris remains the youngest ever British Open winner, at 17 years 249 days in 1868.

Morris was taught by his father, Old Tom Morris. They made a formidable pair and in 1875 were playing a stakes match at North Berwick when Young Tom received word that his young bride had died during childbirth. He never recovered from the anguish and his death a few months later is often attributed to 'heartbreak'.

Tom MORRIS Sr (UK)

GOLF

Tom Morris, Sr. b. 17 Jun 1821 St Andrews, Scotland, d. 24 May 1908 St Andrews.

'Old Tom' Morris was the first man to win the British Open four times, 1861-2, 1864 and 1867, the last making him still the oldest ever champion, at 46 years 99 days. He was a leading figure in Scottish golf for almost fifty years from when he was apprenticed to Allan Robertson in 1839 to learn the making of featherie balls. He was employed at Prestwick from 1851 to 1865, and then returned to St Andrews to serve as greenkeeper and professional until his death. He teamed with first Robertson and then his son, Young Tom, to make a formidable pair in stakes matches. At his death he was considered the most revered man in the game of golf.

Bobby Joe MORROW (USA)

ATHLETICS

Bobby Joe Morrow. b. 15 Oct 1935 Harlingen, Texas.

A most impressive Olympic triple gold medallist at the 100m, 200m and relay in 1956. His time at 200m was a world record 20.6 (20.75 on automatic timing). He had run 20.6 twice earlier in 1956, to win the NCAA and US Olympic Trials races, but neither was ratified. At 100m he tied the world record of 10.2 three times in 1956 and at 100 yards equalled the record with 9.3 in 1957. He also set six relay world records, two on US teams and four for Abilene Christian College, for whom he completed the NCAA sprint double in 1956 and 1957. AAU champion at 100y/100m in 1955-6 and 1958 and at 220y 1958. In 1960 he failed to make a second Olympics as he was 4th at 200m in the US Trials. He was *Sports Illustrated* Sportsman of the Year for 1956.

Angela MORTIMER (UK)

TENNIS

Florence Angela Margaret Mortimer. b. 21 Apr 1932 Plymouth, Devon. Later Barrett.

A determined player whose economic use of ground strokes enabled her to enjoy a long career despite her physical frailty. In 1955 she won the French singles and the Wimbledon doubles with Anne Shilcock, but did not win another major title until she took the Australian singles in 1958. Despite this victory she was unseeded at the 1958 Wimbledon for the first time in six years, but reached the final where she lost to Althea Gibson. Finally in 1961, at her eleventh attempt, she beat Christine Truman in three sets in the first all-British women's singles final since 1914 to become the first British winner of the title since Dorothy Round in 1937. After being eliminated in the third round of the 1962 singles she did not play at Wimbledon again, but in 1964 she played in her seventh and final Wightman Cup tie. In April 1967 she married the former British Davis Cup player, John Barrett.

Willie MOSCONI (USA)

BILLIARDS

William Joseph Mosconi. b. 27 Jun 1913 Philadelphia, Pennsylvania.

The son of a billiard hall proprietor and the winner of 15 pocket billiards titles. He won his first championship at this essentially American game in 1941 and went on to win a further 13 times in the next 16 years. After his final victory in 1957 the event was discontinued, so he is the last officially recognised pocket billiards champion.

In the 1960s he was at the forefront of the revival of pool and is now the owner of a billiards centre. He has appeared on television demonstrating trick shots and playing exhibition matches, and he was the technical adviser for the Paul Newman film, *The Hustler*.

Francesco MOSER (Italy)

CYCLING

Francesco Moser. b. 19 Jun 1951 Pal' di Giovo, Trento.

At the 1972 Olympic road race Moser came 7th, a rather inauspicious beginning for a man who would become one of the great professionals. He was supposed to be the next Italian *campionissimo* and although he won a lot of races, with his first Italian professional title in 1972 and world titles at pursuit 1976 and road 1977 (2nd 1976), he seemed to disappoint the Italian cycling cognoscenti because he

never won as much as Coppi. But Moser used his great track pursuiting ability to allow him to win many races with his sprint. In addition, his ability to mount a long, sustained attack was almost legendary. He used this to break Merckx's hour record twice with 50.808423 km and 51.15135 km at Mexico City in January 1984. Still there was some controversy surrounding this mark because Moser used a bike with many technological breakthroughs unavailable to Merckx. His final record lasted until 1993. In Mexico he also set records for 5km 5:47.163 and 10km 11:39.720. Moser also improved the low altitude 1 hour record twice with 48.54376 km and 49.80193 km at Milan in 1986. Indoors he set seven world records, with bests of 10km 11:50.36 (1988), 20km 24:12.28 (1987) and 1 hour 50.644km (1988).
Other major victories: Paris-Tours 1974, Tour of Lombardy, 1975 and 1978, Flèche-Wallonne and Zürich 1977, Paris-Roubaix 1978-80, Ghent-Wevelgem 1979, Giro d'Italia and Milan-San Remo 1984. Points Jersey Giro d'Italia 1976-8, 1982.

Annemarie MOSER-PRÖLL (Aut)

ALPINE SKIING

Annemarie Moser. née Pröll. b. 27 Mar 1953 Salzburg.

Winner of a women's record 62 races in the World Cup, at which she was overall champion each year 1971-5 and in 1979 (2nd 1977-8, 1980). She won the World Cup titles at downhill in 1971-5 and 1978-9, and giant slalom in 1971-2 and 1975. Her individual race wins comprised 36 downhill, including a record 11 consecutively from December 1972 to January 1974, 16 giant slalom, 7 combined and 3 slalom. An effervescent character, she had retired from competition and missed the 1976 Olympics following her marriage to Herbert Moser in March 1975. However, she came back to become world champion at Alpine Combination in 1978 and won her first Olympic gold medal in 1980, the downhill, having taken silvers as an 18-year-old at downhill and giant slalom in 1972.

Edwin MOSES (USA)

ATHLETICS

Edwin Corley Moses. b. 31 Aug 1955 Dayton, Ohio.

The supreme 400 metres hurdler, he dominated his event for nearly a decade, and set up the greatest ever winning streak by a track athlete, 122 successive 400mh races (107 finals) between defeats by Harald Schmid in Berlin on 26 Aug 1977 and Danny Harris in Madrid on 4 Jun 1987.
He was Olympic champion in 1976 and 1984, having to miss Moscow in 1980 due to the US boycott, World champion in 1983, won the World Cup races of 1977, 1979 and 1981, the US Olympic Trials every four years from 1976 to 1988, and was US champion in 1977, 1979, 1981, 1983 and 1987.
In the 1988 Olympic final he was third, his first ever loss in a championship race. His total career record at 400m hurdles, 1975-88, was 178 wins in 187 races. He ran 13 of the 19 times run by any athlete under 47.50 and 45 of the 89 under 48.00. He missed the 1982 and 1985 seasons through injury. He was the Sullivan Award winner for 1983 and went bobsledding with the US World Cup team 1990/1.
Moses went to Morehouse College, Atlanta, Georgia on an academic scholarship to study mechanical engineering. In his first year of 1975 he ran just one race at 440 yards hurdles, recording a time of 52.0. The next year he was sensational, running 50.1 in his first race and after improving to 49.8 and 48.8 was fourth in the US Championships in 48.94. He won the US Trials in 48.30 and then the Olympic title in his first world record of 47.63. Moses moved after graduation to Laguna Hills, California and set further world records at 47.45 in 1977, 47.11 in 1980 and 47.02 in 1983. The latter remained unbeaten until Kevin Young ran 46.79 in the 1992 Olympic final.
Moses took the Olympic oath on behalf of the competitors at the Los Angeles Olympics in 1984.
Other bests: 400m 45.60 (1977), 800m 1:48.98 (1983), 110m hurdles 13.64 and 13.5 hand-timed (1978).

Bill MOSIENKO (Can)

ICE HOCKEY

William Mosienko. b. 2 Nov 1921 Winnipeg, Manitoba.

Mosienko played his entire 14-year NHL career as a right wing with the Chicago Black Hawks. His best years came on the Pony Line with the Bentley brothers, Max and Doug. On 23 Mar 1952 he scored the fastest hat-trick in NHL history when at Madison Square Garden against the New York Rangers he scored three goals in only 21 seconds.

NHL career 1941-55 - 711 games, 259 goals, 539 points. Best Year: 1943/4: 32 goals, 70 points. Lady Byng Trophy 1945.

Stirling MOSS (UK)

MOTOR RACING

Stirling Crauford Moss. b. 17 Sep 1929 West Kensington, London.

Britain's most admired and respected motor racing driver of his era, he was unlucky never to win a world title, but won 16 of his 66 Grand Prix races 1951-61. He was runner-up to Juan Manuel Fangio in the World Drivers' Championship each year from 1955 to 1957 and by just one point to Mike Hawthorn in 1958; and in all he totalled 186.64 points. His patriotism meant that he raced uncompetitive British cars up to 1954, when he bought a Maserati and later joined their works team. He was then persuaded to sign for Mercedes in 1955, driving as number two to Fangio. That year he became the first Englishman ever to win the British Grand Prix, a success he repeated in a Vanwall in 1957, after rejoining Maserati in 1956. He also excelled in sports car racing and in 1955 he became the first Englishman to win the Italian Mille Miglia. Back in British cars he had two highly successful years with Vanwall 1957-8, and was third in the championship with Cooper in 1959 and 1960, and for Lotus in 1961. In 1962 he was severely injured in a crash at Goodwood, and after a slow recovery realised that he would never regain all his old skills. However, years later he reappeared, racing for fun, retaining all the verve and sparkle which has made him such a revered figure. Awarded the OBE in 1959.

His father Alfred had raced internationally in the 1920s and his mother Eileen had been an expert trials driver in the 1930s. His sister **Pat** (b. 27 Dec 1934), who married Erik Carlsson (qv), was a leading rally driver. Stirling started racing at 17 and in 1948 he had ten class wins in sprint and hill-climb events.

Rosa MOTA (Por)

ATHLETICS

Rosa Mota. b. 29 Jun 1958 Foz do Douro.

From her marathon début, when she won the European title in Athens in 1982 after placing 12th at 3000m, she compiled the greatest record in championship races. She improved her best time in each of her first seven marathons to the 2:23:29 that she ran behind Joan Benoit and Ingrid Kristiansen in Chicago in 1985.

She has won 14 major marathons. After 4th in the Worlds 1983 and 3rd in the Olympics 1984, she won the World title in 1987 and the Olympics in 1988 (the first ever Olympic medal by a Portuguese woman). To those she added a unique three European titles, winning again in 1986 and 1990. She has also won most of the major big city races: Rotterdam 1983, Chicago 1983-4, Tokyo 1986, Boston 1987-8, 1990; Osaka 1990, London 1991. Stomach pains caused her to drop out in the World Championships in 1991 and at London in 1992 and to miss the Olympics that year. She won the Great North Run half marathon in 1985 and 1990 (pb 1:09:33) and was second in the World Road Race Championships at 10km in 1984 and at 15km in 1986. On the track she competed for Portugal at nine European Cups 1975-87 at 1500m, 3000m or 10,000m, and in all set 19 national records from 1000m to 20 kilometres. Her sister Ana Paula Mota was Portuguese 400mh champion 1987.

Best times: 1500m 4:19.53 (1983), 3000m 8:53.84 (1984), 5000m 15:22.97 (1985), 10,000m 32:33.51 (1985), 20km 1:06:55.5 (1983, world best), 1 hour 18,027m (1983).

Marion MOTLEY (USA)

AMERICAN FOOTBALL

Marion Motley. b. 5 Jun 1920 Leesburg, Georgia.

Motley was one of the first true fullbacks, a very large, bruising running back. He was 1.88m *6'2"* and 110 kg *244 lb*, and was almost impossible to tackle one-on-one. He played college ball for the University of Nevada at Reno, and then joined the Navy after his 1944 graduation. In 1946 he joined the Cleveland Browns of the old All-American Football Conference, helping them to league and NFL championships every year of his career as they dominated pro football.

In addition to his running, Motley's size made him a punishing blocker. In 1955, he played his final NFL season with the Pittsburgh Steelers, playing mostly as a linebacker.

NFL career 1946-55: Rushing: 4720 yards av. 5.7, 31 touchdowns; Receiving: 1107 yards av. 13.0, 7 touchdowns.

Graham MOURIE (NZ)

RUGBY UNION

Graham Neil Kenneth Mourie. b. 8 Sep 1952 Opunake.

A flanker who played 21 times for New Zealand, captaining them in all but two of those games, 1977-82, including on the tour of the British Isles in 1978.

He went to Victoria University and played for Wellington, Opunake and Taranaki.

Abdollah MOVAHED (Iran)

WRESTLING

Abdollah Mohaved Arbabili. b. 10 Mar 1940.

Movahed won six consecutive world and Olympic championships between 1965 and 1970 in the lightweight freestyle class. His Olympic gold medal came about after he tied with Bulgaria's Enyu Dimov-Valchev, but he earned the championship by defeating Dimov-Valchev by decision in the final match.

Karen MUIR (SAf)

SWIMMING

Karen Yvette Muir. b. 16 Sep 1952 Kimberley.

On 10 Aug 1965, at the age of 12 years 328 days, she became the youngest competitor to break a world record at any sport, as with a time of 68.7 for 100y backstroke in a heat of the ASA junior championships she took 0.7 sec off Linda Ludgrove's mark.

The tiny South African backstroker was unable to challenge for Olympic glory due to her nation's exclusion, but she set three world records at 100m in 1968-9, with a best of 65.6, and four at 200m from 1966 to 1968 with bests of 2:23.8 and 2:24.1 for 220y.

In all she won 22 South African titles (including freestyle and medley events as well as backstroke), as well as the US titles at 100m in 1968 and 200m in 1966 and 1968.

Karl MULLEN (Ire)

RUGBY UNION

Karl Daniel Mullen. b. 26 Nov 1926 Courttown Harbour, Co. Wexford.

An outstanding hooker of the immediate post-war era who won his 25 Irish caps in consecutive matches. Noted for his brilliant tactical sense and leadership, he first captained Ireland in 1948 at the age of 21 and led them to the Grand Slam that year. In 1949 Ireland won the Triple Crown and Mullen's leadership qualities were recognised when he was chosen to lead the 1950 Lions to Australia and New Zealand. Although only managing one draw in the Test series against New Zealand, the 1950 Lions are still remembered as the most popular team ever to tour New Zealand. On his return, he led Ireland to the International Championship in 1951 and played his last international against Wales in 1952.

Egon MÜLLER (FRG)

SPEEDWAY

Egon Müller. b. 26 Nov 1948 Kiel.

The first man to win the World Long Track title four times, 1974-6 and 1978. He was also the world Individual champion in 1983 in the fifth of his seven finals, on a track that was more fitted to Long Track racing, at which he was a master, than conventional speedway. He made his international début for Germany in 1972 and rode in Britain for Coatbridge 1973 and Hull 1976.

Ellen MÜLLER (Aut) see PREIS

Gerd MÜLLER (FRG)

FOOTBALL

Gerhardt Müller. b. 3 Nov 1945 Zinsen, Bavaria.

One of the most prolific scorers in international football. With 10 goals, including two hat-tricks, he was top scorer at the 1970 World Cup finals and he succeeded Uwe Seeler as Germany's top international scorer. Seeler scored 43 goals in 73 matches but Müller surpassed this total after less than 50 games, and in all scored 68 goals in 62 matches. In 1970 he became the first German to be voted European Footballer of the Year.

His signing for Bayern Munich in 1964 marked the start of a period of unprecedented success for the club in the German Cup and League, and with Müller in the team they also won the European Cup 1974-6 and the European Cup Winners' Cup 1967. He retired from international football after scoring the winning goal in the 1974 World Cup final.

A squat, heavy-thighed figure, the strength of his game was in his close finishing and even with packed defences he was deadly in the penalty area with either foot or with his head. In all competitive games he scored 628 goals, including 365 in 427 games in the Bundesliga.

Hennie MULLER (SAf)

RUGBY UNION

Hendrik Scholtz Vosloo Muller. b. 26 Mar 1922 Witbank, Transvaal, d. 26 Apr 1977 Cape Town.

Although winning only 13 caps, he had a great influence on the development of the modern loose forward game. As a former winger he used his speed from the set pieces to catch the opposing fly-half as the ball arrived. This is now universally accepted, although current laws inhibit modern players from using the tactic with the same devastating effect.

The 1949 All Blacks were caught by surprise by the new Springbok tactics and lost all four Tests. On the 1951/2 tour of Britain and Ireland, the South Africans again won every Test and following an injury to Basil Kenyon, Muller took over as tour captain. He again captained the Springboks on the 1953 tour of Australia when they won the series 3-1 and the defeat in the second Test marked the only time he was on the losing side in a Test. He later served as the Springbok manager and coach before his early death from a heart attack.

Peter MÜLLER (Swi)

ALPINE SKIING

Peter Müller. b. 6 Oct 1957 Lambach, Austria.

At downhill he was World Cup winner in 1979, 1980 and 1982 (tied) and at last won the world title in 1987, having been 5th in 1978 and 1982 and 2nd in 1985 (and 1989). In all he won 24 World Cup races, including 19 at downhill, second only to Klammer. His best Olympic placing was 4th in 1980. He had won his first Swiss title in 1977 at giant slalom.

Known as a perfectionist and a magnificent glider. His parents were Swiss doubles champions at badminton.

Gardner MULLOY (USA)

TENNIS

Gardnar Putnam Mulloy. b. 22 Nov 1913 Washington, D.C.

A doubles specialist whose finest performance came when he had reached the veteran stage. As a singles player his best performance was as runner-up at the 1952 US Championships and he reached the semi-final stage of a Grand Slam tournament on five other occasions: Wimbledon

(1948), US (1942, 1946, 1950) and Australian (1947). In the men's doubles he had a far superior record. He won four US titles (1942, 1945-6, 1948) and was runner-up three times (1950, 1953, 1957); at the French championships he was twice runner-up (1951-2) and after being a losing finalist at Wimbledon in 1948 and 1949 he finally took the title in 1957 with Budge Patty. At the age of 43 yrs 226 days, Gardner Mulloy is the oldest player ever to win a Wimbledon Championship. Between 1946 and 1957 he played in 12 Davis Cup ties, winning 8 out of 11 doubles rubbers and, rather surprisingly, winning all three of his singles matches.

Sandro MUNARI (Italy)

RALLYING

Alessandro Munari. b. 27 Mar 1940 Milan.

The first man to win the Monte Carlo Rally four times, 1972 and 1975-7, and the first to win the event for three successive years. All his victories were in a Lancia. In 1977 he won the inaugural FIA Cup for Drivers which received official recognition as the World Championship two years later. He was Italian rally champion in 1967, when in the Corsica Rally he achieved his first major win, and in 1969, and he won the European Rally title in 1973. He ended his career after Lancia were absorbed into Ford in 1978.

Bill MUNCEY (USA)

POWERBOATING

William Muncey. b. 1929, d. 18 Oct 1981 Acapulco, Mexico.

Muncey won more powerboat races, 62, than any man in history. He won the APBA Gold Cup race three times 1977-9 with the Atlas Van Lines boat, but had won earlier versions of the Gold Cup in 1956-7, 1961-2 and 1972. He was the unlimited point winner in powerboat racing in 1960 and 1961. In 1960 he set an all-time speed record of 308.9 km/h *192.001 mph*. In 1981, while leading the world championship race, Muncey's boat went out of control and he was killed when he crashed at 282 km/h *175 mph*.

Anthony MUNOZ (USA)

AMERICAN FOOTBALL

Anthony Munoz. b. 19 Aug 1958 Ontario, California.

One of the great offensive tackles in pro football history. He played collegiately at USC, where he made All-American in both his last two years, and was the third overall pick in the 1980 NFL draft. Munoz, who played his entire career with the Cincinnati Bengals, was selected for an NFL record 11 consecutive Pro Bowls at tackle. Even late in his career, he remained one of the great pass blockers in the game. He used great techniques in blocking to complement his size (1.98 m *6'6"* and 130 kg *285 lbs*). He retired after the 1992 season.

Thurman MUNSON (USA)

BASEBALL

Thurman Lee Munson. b. 7 Jun 1947 Akron, Ohio, d. 2 Aug 1979 Canton, Ohio.

Munson played for 11 seasons as a catcher, all of them with the New York Yankees. He was their acknowledged leader in the 1970s but his career was tragically ended in a plane crash in the middle of his 11th season. He caught over 130 games in nine consecutive seasons 1970-8, and was also a top hitter, batting over .300 with more than 100 RBI in 1975-7. He was Rookie of the Year in 1970, American League MVP in 1976, and won three Gold Gloves as a catcher 1973-5.

Career 1969-79: 1558 hits Avg. .292, HR 113; RBI 701 RBI. Best seasons: 1975: .318; 1977: .308.

Billy MURDOCH (Aus/Eng)

CRICKET

William Lloyd Murdoch. b. 18 Oct 1854 Sandhurst, Victoria, d. 18 Feb 1911 Melbourne.

The first great Australian batsman and captain of Australia in 16 of his 18 Tests for them. He first toured England in 1878 and made four further tours, including that of 1880 when he captained Australia in the

first ever Test in England. In that match he scored his first ever century in first-class cricket with 153 not out. He had originally been considered as a wicket-keeper but passed that job to Jack Blackham. In 1884 at The Oval his 211 was the first double-century in Test cricket.
He played for New South Wales from 1876 to 1890, but did not play Tests as he concentrated on his legal practice from 1885 to 1890. He was then persuaded to return to lead the Australian team to England. On being dropped by Australia due to age, he came to England, for whom he played against South Africa in 1892. He captained Sussex from 1893 to 1899 and played for London County 1899-1904.
19 Tests (18 for Australia 1880-90, 1 for England 1892): 908 runs at 31.31, 2 100s HS 211; 14 catches.
First-class 1875-1904: 16,953 runs at 26.86, 19 100s HS 321; 10 wickets at 43.00, BB 2-11; 218 catches, 25 stumpings.

Noel MURLESS (UK)

HORSE RACING

(Sir) Charles Francis Noel Murless. b. 24 Mar 1910 Malpas, Cheshire, d. 9 May 1987 Newmarket.

Nine times champion trainer on the flat in England, he trained the winners of 19 classics in England between 1948 and 1973 and two in Ireland. He broke the records for highest prize money three times, being the first trainer to win more than £100,000 in a year with £116,898 from 48 winners in 1957, and the first over £200,000 with £256,899 from 60 winners in 1967.
He was a steeplechase jockey during the 1930s and after assisting the Irish brothers Frank and Hubert Hartigan, he established stables first at Hambleton Lodge, Yorkshire, taking over from Fred Darling at Beckhampton in 1947, and then moving to Warren Place, Newmarket in 1952. His Derby winners were *Crepello* 1957, *St Paddy* 1960 and *Royal Palace* 1967, and his other great horses included *Petite Etoile*.
He was knighted in the 1977 Silver Jubilee honours.

Alex MURPHY (UK)

RUGBY LEAGUE

Alexander John Murphy. b. 22 Apr 1939 St Helens, Lancashire.

A brilliant scrum half of extraordinary speed who played in four winning Challenge Cup finals for three different teams: St Helens 1961 and 1966, Leigh 1971 and Warrington 1974. On the last three occasions he was player-coach but when he devoted himself exclusively to coaching he took four teams to the final: Warrington 1975, Wigan 1984 and St Helens 1987, 1989. He won the first of his 27 Great Britain caps in Australia in 1958, when at the age of 19 he was the youngest British player ever to tour there. He played brilliantly, scoring 21 tries in 20 matches, the majority of which were attributable to his speed from the base of the scrum. He played in all three Tests and Great Britain won the series 2-1. In 1959 he equalled the GB Test match record by scoring four tries against France, a record which stood for 32 years until Martin Offiah scored five times against France in 1991.
He was also an accomplished stand-off and played some notable games at senior club level. One of the most knowledgeable men in the game, he is now a member of the TV commentary team.

Calvin MURPHY (USA)

BASKETBALL

Calvin Jerome Murphy. b. 9 May 1948 Norwalk, Connecticut.

Murphy became a legend in high school basketball in Norwalk, Connecticut where he led his team to a state title. The diminutive guard, 1.78m *5'10"*, went to Niagara University where he averaged 48.9 points/game in freshman ball. In his varsity career he averaged 33.1 for 2548 points over three seasons 1968-70. The cat-quick Murphy was a ball-handling wizard who may have been the fastest player ever to play in the NBA. Thought to be too short to play well at that level, he proved the experts wrong, surviving for 13 years as a professional, 12 of them with the Houston Rockets. He had a career free-

throw percentage of .892, second in NBA history only to Rick Barry. His season percentage of .958 in 1980/1 is an NBA record. He was also a nationally known baton twirler who frequently performed at half-times.
NBA career av. 18.8.

Isaac MURPHY (UK)

HORSE RACING

Isaac Murphy. né Isaac Burns. b. 1 Jan 1861 Fayette County, Kentucky, d. 12 Feb 1896 Kentucky.

A great black jockey of the last part of the 19th century, Murphy was the first man to ride the winners of three Kentucky Derbys, *Buchanan* in 1884, *Riley* in 1890 and *Kingman* in 1891. He rode 628 winners, which represented an extraordinary 44% of his 1412 mounts.
He changed his name from Burns to Murphy, as that was the name of his maternal grandather who brought him up following the death of his father in the Civil War. He died of pneumonia, probably brought on by the constant dieting required to maintain his riding weight.

Deryck MURRAY (Tri)

CRICKET

Deryck Lance Murray. b. 20 May 1943 Port-of-Spain.

The first-choice West Indian wicket-keeper during the 1970s, setting dismissals records that lasted until passed by Jeff Dujon. After making his first-class début for Trinidad in 1961, he first played Test cricket in 1963 when he took what was then a West Indian record 24 dismissals in the five Tests against England. In the next ten years he played only one Test series, against England in the West Indies in 1968, as he came to study at Cambridge University, whom he captained in 1966, and played county cricket for Nottinghamshire 1966-9 while he obtained a business studies degree from Nottingham University. He later played for Warwickshire 1972-5. He was a permanent member of the West Indian team from 1973, and joined the majority of his colleagues in 1977 in moving to World Series Cricket, with whom he was a prime negotiator for players' rights. He was Clive Lloyd's deputy for much of the 1970s and captained the West Indies in one Test in 1979/80. A talented batsman, he was also a part-time leg-spinner. His father Lance played for Trinidad & Tobago.
62 Tests 1963-80: 1993 runs at 22.90, HS 91; 181 catches, 8 stumping.
26 One-day Ints: 294 runs at 24.50, HS 61; 37 catches, 1 stumping.*
First-class 1961-81: 13,291 runs at 28.33, 10 100s HS 166; 5 wickets at 73.40, BB 2-50; 741 catches, 108 stumpings.*

Eddie MURRAY (USA)

BASEBALL

Eddie Clarence Murray. b. 24 Feb 1956 Los Angeles, California.

A power-hitting first baseman, Murray was the leading player on the Baltimore Orioles from his rookie year of 1977 until he was traded to the Los Angeles Dodgers in 1989, moving on to the New York Mets in 1992. He batted over .300 in six seasons and from 1977-92 he has only had three seasons (1986, 1991-2) at less than 20 home runs; five times he posted over 30. He has had over 100 RBI in a season five times. He trails only Mickey Mantle among power-hitting switch hitters. Decidedly low key on the field, Murray has often been criticised for his aloof attitude.
Career 1977-92: 2646 hits Avg. .290, HR 414; RBI 1562; SB 90. Best seasons: 1982: .316, 32 HR; 1983: .306, 33 HR; 1980: 32 HR.

John MURRAY (UK)

CRICKET

John Thomas Murray. b. 1 Apr 1935 North Kensington, London.

An immaculate wicket-keeper, Murray held the record for most dismissals in a first-class career from passing Bert Strudwick's total in 1975, until his 1527 victims was passed by Bob Taylor. In 1957 he completed the wicket-keeper's double with 1025 runs and 104 dismissals, and he exceeded 1000 runs in a season on six

occasions. His batting prowess was best demonstrated with his 112 for England against West Indies at The Oval in 1966, batting at No.9, and in a dashing century for the Rest of the World in Barbados in 1967. Awarded the MBE.
21 Tests 1961-7: 506 runs at 21.00, 1 100 HS 112; 52 catches, 3 stumping.
First-class 1952-75: 18,872 runs at 23.59, 16 100s HS 142; 6 wickets at 40.50, BB 2-10; 1268 catches, 258 stumpings.

Ty MURRAY (USA)

RODEO
Ty Murray. b. 11 Oct 1969 Phoenix, Arizona.

Murray joined the pro rodeo tour in 1988 and just a year later won the first of four successive world all-around titles. In 1990 he became the first cowboy to win over $200,000 in a year, increasing the record each year to $258,750 in 1991 from the three roughstock events. A true all-rounder, he has yet to win an individual event title.

MUSHTAQ MOHAMMAD (Pak)

CRICKET
Mushtaq Mohammad. b. 22 Nov 1943 Junagadh, Gujerat, India.

At 15 years 124 days when he made his début for Pakistan v West Indies at Lahore in 1959, Mushtaq is the youngest ever Test cricketer. He had made his first-class début at 13 years 41 days and became the youngest Test centurion at 17 years 82 days. Yet he was far from just being a prodigy, because with his exciting stroke-play and skilful leg-break bowling he had a long career at top class level. His peak Test performance came in Pakistan's innings victory over New Zealand at Dunedin in 1973, when he scored 201 and took 2-15 and 5-49. He captained Pakistan in his last 19 Tests 1976-9. He played in Pakistan for Karachi and PIA, and in England for Northants 1964-77 (captain 1975-7). His brothers Hanif (qv), **Wazir** (b. 22 Dec 1929) and **Sadiq** (b. 3 May 1945) all played for Pakistan and another brother, Raees, only narrowly missed that honour.
57 Tests 1959-79: 3642 runs at 39.17, 10 100s, HS 201; 79 wickets at 29.22, BB 5-28; 42 catches.
10 One-day Ints: 209 runs at 24.83, HS 55, 3 catches.
First-class 1956-85: 31,091 runs at 42.07, 72 100s HS 303; 936 wickets at 24.34, BB 7-18; 347 catches.*

Stan MUSIAL (USA)

BASEBALL
Stanley Frank Musial. b. 21 Nov 1920 Donora, Pennsylvania.

'Stan the Man' was one of the most consistent, classiest ballplayers, at outfield and first base for the St Louis Cardinals for his entire career. He hit for both average and power, leading the National League in batting average seven times (1943, 1946, 1948, 1950-2, 1957) and RBI twice (1948, 1956). He was elected the MVP in the league in 1943, 1946 and 1948, and he appeared in 20 All-Star Games. He also led the league in hits six times, doubles eight times, triples five times, and runs five times. He was known for his consistency and rarely suffered slumps. At his retirement in 1964, he was named director of President Johnson's National Council on Physical Fitness. A bronze statue in honour of the greatest Cardinal was later erected in front of Busch Stadium. In 1972, he was awarded the rare honour for a foreigner of being named by the Polish government as a recipient of the Merited Champions Medal.
Career 1941-63: 3630 hits Avg. .331, HR 475; RBI 1951. Best seasons: 1943: .357, 220 hits; 1946: .365, 228 hits; 1948: .376, 230 hits; 1951: .355, 205 hits.

Bogdan MUSIOL (GDR)

BOBSLEIGH
Bogdan Musiol. b. 25 Jul 1957 Swielochowice, Poland.

Won Olympic gold with the GDR 4-man bob team in 1980, when he was also third at 2-man, and went on to take silver medals in 1984 and 1988 at both 2-man and 4-man. On the latter occasion he partnered Wolfgang Hoppe and these two became world champions in 1989. Before turning to bobsledding Musiol had been a useful hammer thrower (56.50m best).

Lon MYERS (USA)

ATHLETICS

Laurence Eugene Myers. b. 16 Feb 1858 Richmond, Virginia, d. 15 Feb 1899 New York, of pneumonia.

Before world records were officially ratified he set world bests at all events from 100 yards (10.0 in 1880) to 1000 yards. He also set US records from 50 yards (5.5 in 1884) to the mile, at which his best was 4:27.6 behind Walter George in 1882. He was undefeated at 440y and 880y, at which his best times were 48 $^{4}/_{5}$ and 1:55 $^{2}/_{5}$ in 1885. In 1879, with a time of 49 $^{1}/_{5}$ in New York, he became the first amateur to run the quarter mile in less than 50 seconds.
His record 15 national titles included 100y 1880-1, 220y 1879-81 and 1884, 440y 1879-84, 880y 1879-80 and 1884. In 1880, having won four US titles in one day, he repeated the quadruple triumph a week later in the Canadian Championships. He won AAA titles at 440y in 1881 and 1885, and at 880y in 1885, and went on to further success as a professional after considerable controversy over his amateur status. Very thin but, at 1.73m tall, with long legs, his success was achieved despite being sickly for much of his life. He became a bookmaker and racehorse owner.

Larry MYRICKS (USA)

ATHLETICS

Larry Ellwyne Myricks. b. 10 Mar 1956 Clinton, Mississippi.

Although overshadowed for most of his career by Carl Lewis. Myricks was a fine long jumper. He broke his leg warming up for the 1976 Olympic long jump final, but returned to Montreal to win at the 1979 World Cup with a world low altitude best of 8.52m. He won the US Olympic Trials in 1980, but that was the year of the boycott, so he returned to the Olympics to place 4th in 1984 and 3rd in 1988. At World Championships he competed at 200m in 1983 and won long jump bronze medals in 1987 and 1991, although he had to wait nearly a year for the first before Evangelisti's alleged bronze medal distance in Rome was shown to be fraudulent. He was World Indoor champion in 1987 and 1989 and won the World Cup long jump for a second time in 1989.
US champion at long jump in 1979-80 and 1989, and at 200m in 1988; NCAA long jump champion in 1976 and 1979; Grand Prix series winner in 1987 and 1989. He tested positive for phenylpropanolamine at three meetings in Jan-Feb 1990, but an original lifetime ban imposed by TAC was shortened to one year, enabling him to compete again from April 1991.
A business graduate of Mississippi College, he became a company personnel recruiter and married Arnita Epps, who was third in the 1991 TAC 100m hurdles.
Best performances: long jump 8.74m (1988), 100m 10.26 (1987), 200m 20.03 (1983).

John NABER (USA)

SWIMMING

John Phillips Naber. b. 20 Jan 1956 Evanston, Illinois.

At the 1976 Olympic Games in Montreal, Naber won four gold medals, all in world record times, and both his backstroke records were unbeaten for seven years. At the 100m back he took 0.11 off the previous best, set by Roland Matthes, with 56.19 in his heat and improved massively to 55.49 in the final. In the 200m, at which he had set his first record with 2:00.64 a month earlier, he became the first backstroker to break two minutes with 1:59.19. He added gold medals at 4 x 100m freestyle and medley relays and took the 200m freestyle silver medal.
Naber, who had lived in Italy and England, did not start swimming until the age of 13. His first major international event was the 1973 World Championships, at which he was third at 200m backstroke. A year later he ended the seven-year win streak of Matthes by beating him at both 100m and 200m at Concord, California, and set his first US record for 200m at 2:03.55.
While at the University of Southern

California, Naber won ten individual and five relay titles ,and at the AAUs he won 18 individual and seven relay titles. He won three gold medals at his final major event, the 1977 Pan-American Games. *Freestyle bests: 200m 1:50.50 and 400m 3:53.91 in 1976.*

Nedo NADI (Italy)

FENCING

Nedo Nadi. b. 9 June 1894 Livorno, d. 29 Jan 1940 Rome.

The most versatile fencer of the 20th century. He was initially taught the foil as a child in his father's gymnasium, but by the age of 15 he had also mastered the épée and sabre and went on to win the highest honours with all three weapons. In 1912 he won the Olympic individual foil title without suffering a single defeat. After being decorated for gallantry in World War I he produced a superlative performance at the 1920 Olympics, winning five gold medals, the individual title in the foil and the sabre and leading the Italians to victory in all three team events. After this unprecedented success, he turned professional and taught in Buenos Aires for some years. On his return to Europe he was surprisingly reinstated as an amateur and from 1935 until his death he was President of the Italian Fencing Federation.

His father, Giuseppe 'Beppo', was one of the world's leading fencers at the turn of the century and his younger brother, **Aldo** (1899-1965), shared in his successes at the 1920 Olympics, winning a gold medal in all three team events and a silver in the individual sabre.

Marie-Thérèse NADIG (Swi)

ALPINE SKIING

Marie-Thérèse Nadig. b. 8 Mar 1954 Tannenboden.

Caused a major upset when she won both downhill and giant slalom gold medals aged 17 at the 1972 Olympics, soon after turning from playing soccer to ski racing. Nine years later she was the World Cup overall champion and won the downhill in 1980 and 1981. She won the bronze medal for downhill at the 1980 Olympics. From 1975 to 1981 she won 24 World Cup races: 13 downhill, 6 giant slalom, 5 combined.

Bronko NAGURSKI (Can/USA)

AMERICAN FOOTBALL

Bronislaw Nagurski. b. 3 Nov 1908 Rainy River, Ontario, Canada, d. 7 Jan 1990 International Falls, Minnesota.

One of the legendary characters in pro football history, he was born of Ukrainian parents and became a naturalised US citizen. He played collegiately at the University of Minnesota, where he was named All-American as both a fullback and a tackle, and pro football from 1930-7 and 1943 with the Chicago Bears. He played both linebacker and fullback in the NFL and helped the Bears to three Championships and five divisional title games. The barrel-chested Nagurski symbolised raw, brute power. He had a 48cm (19 inch) neck, massive thighs and arms and huge hands. His Hall of Fame ring was so big that a standard-size ring could be passed completely through it. In 1934 he also became a professional wrestler, and performed in that sport until 1960.

James NAISMITH (Can/USA)

BASKETBALL

James Naismith MD. b. 6 Nov 1861 Almonte, Ontario, Canada, d. 28 Nov 1939 Lawrence, Kansas.

Naismith graduated from McGill University, Montreal with a degree in philosophy in 1888 and then began a career as a physical education instructor. His first big job was at Springfield College, Massachusetts. In 1891 he was asked by the chairman of his department to try to develop an indoor game that the students could play for fun and to stay in shape for the spring sports seasons. Naismith shortly thereafter invented basketball, first played in December 1891. He also coached the game at the University of Kansas 1899-1909, with an indifferent record of 53-55. He earned four degrees in the disparate fields of philosophy, religion, physical education and medicine.

Koichi NAKANO (Japan)

CYCLING

Koichi Nakano. b. 14 Nov 1955 Kurume, Fukuoka Prefecture.

World professional sprint champion for ten successive years, 1977-86, a record unmatched in any cycling event. Such was his dominance that in 1985-6 only 11 and 10 riders respectively entered against him. Nakano was very strong and ideally built at 1.72m and 80kg.

His father, Mitsuyoshi, was a professional cyclist and the son followed in his path by joining the Japan Bicycle Racing school in Suzenji for ten months before making his pro début in 1970. By the time of his tenth world title win, Nakano had won 470 of his 775 races and earned 838 million yen (then $5.8 million). He was so well compensated that he would lose money by competing in the world championships. After his retirement as a match sprinter, he continued to ride in Japanese keirin races for two more years.

Akinori NAKAYAMA (Japan)

GYMNASTICS

Akinori Nakayama. b. 1 Mar 1943 Aichi Prefecture.

Nakayama was third in the Olympic all-around in both 1964 and 1968, his inconsistency depriving him of higher honours, but he won team golds on both occasions and came back to win three golds and a silver on individual apparatus in 1964 and gold and silver in 1968. At World Championships he won a total of seven golds, two silvers and three bronze, winning the floor exercises in 1966 and 1970, horizontal bar in 1966 and rings in 1970.

He was particularly innovative on the parallel bars.

Joe NAMATH (USA)

AMERICAN FOOTBALL

Joseph William Namath. b. 31 May 1943 Beaver Falls, Pennsylvania.

Namath played quarterback at the University of Alabama and in the early AFL with the New York Jets. Having spurned offers to play in the established NFL to sign with the Jets for the then unearthly figure of $400,000, he was largely responsible for the success of the AFL as a league and in 1969 pulled off one of the great upsets in football history when he led the Jets to the first win by an AFL team in the Super Bowl, beating the Baltimore Colts (he was game MVP). He played until 1977 in the now combined NFL, finishing his career riding the bench for one season with the Los Angeles Rams. By then, he had had multiple operations on both knees and was but a shadow of his former greatness. He was possessed of perhaps the strongest arm in football history. In 1967 he became the first pro quarterback to throw for over 4,000 yards in a single season. Namath has had an acting and announcing career since his football retirement. By 1992, the arthritis in his knees had progressed to the point that he underwent bilateral total knee replacements to help him walk more comfortably.

AFL/NFL career 1965-77: 27,663 yards from 1886 pass completions, 50.1%, 173 TD.

José NAPOLES (Cuba)

BOXING

José Napoles. b. 13 Apr 1940 Santiago de Cuba.

One of the great post-war welterweight champions. He won the world title in 1969 with a victory over Curtis Cokes. He lost it to Billy Backus in 1970, but only because of an eye injury and easily won the rematch, holding the title until 1975. He made one effort to claim the middleweight title but lost in 1974 to Carlos Monzon. In all he won 15 of his 18 world title fights.

Career record: W - 76 (54), L - 8, D - 0.

Laurie NASH (Aus)

AUSTRALIAN RULES FOOTBALL/CRICKET

Laurence John Nash. b. 2 May 1910 Fitzroy, Melbourne, Victoria, d. 24 Jul 1986 Heidelberg, Victoria.

Nash was a rare example of a double international for Australia at cricket and at Australian Rules football. He never played Sheffield Shield cricket, but played 17 times for Tasmania and once for Victoria. He was a tearaway fast bowler who made his Test début in the last Test against South Africa in 1932, making a dream start with 4-18 and 1-4 in Australia's innings win. He did not, however, get another chance in Tests until the last match of the 1936/7 England tour. He was again a success with 4-70 and 1-34, so that his Test record was amazingly good for one who only played twice.

He joined South Melbourne to play Australian Rules football in 1933, the year the club took the premiership. A fast, tough and versatile player, he was equally at home in attack and defence as a centre half-back or centre half-forward. His partnership with Bob Pratt was judged by many as the most brilliant combination the game has seen. In 1938 he moved to Camberwell in the Victoria FA and kicked 400 goals in his four seasons in that association. He rejoined South Melbourne in 1945 for one final season and later coached the club.

2 Tests 1932-7: 50 runs at 15.00, HS 17; 10 wickets, at 12.60, BB 4-18; 6 catches. First-class 1929-37: 407 runs at 12.33, 1 100 HS 110; 69 wickets at 28.33, BB 7-50; 19 catches.

Ilie NASTASE (Rom)

TENNIS

Ilie Nastase. b. 19 Jul 1946 Bucharest.

The first great player to come from Eastern Europe. With a repertoire of brilliant shots and a delicate touch he seemed destined to dominate his era, but he only won two Grand Slam singles titles, the US Open 1971 and the French 1972. He was also a finalist at Paris in 1971 and at Wimbledon in 1972 and 1976. He was at his best in the Masters where he was a finalist for five successive years 1971-5, losing only to Vilas in 1974. His weakness was not in his play but in his character and, regrettably, what was initially seen as a mischievous streak turned into unacceptable abuse of authority.

His game was well suited to doubles and he won the men's in Paris 1970, Wimbledon 1973 and the US Open 1975. He also won the mixed doubles at Wimbledon in 1970 and 1972 with Rosemary Casals. Possibly his greatest success was to lead Romania to the 1972 Davis Cup final in Bucharest, but his loss to Stan Smith in the opening rubber proved decisive and the USA retained the trophy. His outstanding Davis Cup record was 74 wins in 96 singles matches and 35 wins in 50 doubles. He spent 40 weeks ranked as the world number one in 1973-4 and won 57 singles and 51 doubles titles in his career.

Susan NATTRASS (Can)

SHOOTING

Susan Nattrass. b. 5 Nov 1950 Medicine Hat, Alberta.

In 1976 she became the first woman to compete in Olympic trap shooting, placing 25th. She competed at further Olympics in 1988 and 1992 and has won a record six women's world titles, 1974-5, 1977-9 and 1981. She has also achieved three world second places, 1971, 1982 and 1991, and two third places, 1983 and 1986.

She started competitive shooting in 1969 and in 1981 was awarded the Order of Canada and won the Lou Marsh Trophy as Canada's athlete of the year. Now a director of athletics and recreation.

Martina NAVRATILOVA (Cs/USA)

TENNIS

Martina Navrátilová. née Subert. b. 18 Oct 1956 Prague, Czechoslovakia.

The only woman to win the Grand Slam twice (1983-4) and undoubtedly the greatest woman player of the modern era and possibly the greatest of all-time. Only the third left-hander to have won the title, she has won the Wimbledon singles a record nine times, 1978-9, 1982-7, 1990. She also won four US (1983-4, 1986-7), three Australian (1981, 1983, 1985) and two French (1982, 1984) titles for a total of 18 Grand Slam singles victories. Starting with her Wimbledon victory in 1983 she won

six successive Grand Slam singles before losing to Helena Sukova (Cs) in the Australian Open at the end of 1984.
Her record in the women's doubles is even more impressive as she has set a record with 31 Grand Slam titles between 1976 and 1990: the Wimbledon and French seven times each, 9 US and 8 Australian Opens. Navratilova was partnered by Pam Shriver in 20 of these 31 victories and from April 1983 to July 1985 this pair won eight successive Grand Slam doubles titles and were unbeaten in 109 consecutive matches. Navratilova also won mixed doubles titles at Wimbledon 1985 and 1993, French 1974 and 1985, and the US Open 1985 and 1987. Only Margaret Court-Smith has bettered her total of 55 victories in Grand Slam events. Although she eventually lost her No.1 world ranking to Steffi Graf, victory in the 1990 Wimbledon singles, when Graf went out in the semi-finals, proved that she was still a major force at the age of 33. She maintained her challenge to the world's best as she reached the semi-finals at Wimbledon in 1992 and 1993, and with the mixed doubles in that year won her 18th Wimbledon title.
Czech born, she changed her name from Subert to that of her stepfather at the age of 10 and she became a naturalised American citizen in July 1981. She created a unique Federation Cup record when, having been on the winning Czech team in 1975, she was a member of the winning US team in 1982, 1986 and 1989. To the end of 1992 her career earnings were $18,396,526, more than $8 million ahead of any other woman, and she ranked as the world's number one for a record total of 332 weeks. By June 1993 she had won a world record 164 tournaments at singles and a further 162 at doubles.

Cottari K NAYUDU (India)

CRICKET

(Col) Cottari Kanakaiya Nayudu. b. 31 Oct 1895 Magpur, d. 14 Nov 1967 Indore.

A father figure of cricket in India, whom he captained in their first Test against England in 1932. He was then aged 36, yet his first-class career went on for another 32 years, and he is the only player to have made first-class appearances in six decades. He was a Test selector for many years and vice-president of the Indian Cricket Board of Control. He was a tall and elegant, hard-hitting batsman and an accurate slow-medium bowler. He caused a sensation in December 1926 when he hit 153 in 100 minutes for the Hindus against the MCC tourists, including 11 sixes and 13 fours.
His brother **Cottari** Subbanna **Nayudu** (b. 18 Apr 1914) played 11 Tests for India 1934-52.
7 Tests 1932-6: 350 runs at 25.00, HS 81; 9 wickets at 2.88, BB 3-40; 4 catches, First-class 1916-63: 11,825 runs at 35.94, 26 100s HS 200; 411 wickets at 23.11, BB 7-44; 170 catches, 1 stumping.

Anthony NEARY (UK)

RUGBY UNION

Anthony Neary. b. 25 Nov 1949 Manchester.

Until his record was beaten by Rory Underwood, he was England's most capped player. As a flanker with Broughton Park he played for England 43 times, but although he toured with the British Lions to South Africa 1974 and New Zealand 1977, the final match of the series against New Zealand was the only time he was called up for Test duties.
He made his international début against Wales in 1971 and, after a spell as England's captain in mid-career, he retired after England had won the Grand Slam in 1980.

Josef NECKERMANN (FRG)

EQUESTRIAN

Josef Neckermann. b. 5 Jun 1912 Würzburg, d. 13 Jan 1992 Dreieich, near Frankfurt.

Amongst the richest private citizens ever to have competed at the Olympic Games, at which he won six medals in the dressage: individual silver 1968, bronze 1960 and 1972; team gold 1964 and 1968, silver 1972. He was World champion in 1966 and European champion in 1965, 1967,

1969 and 1971. From the age of 39 his business success allowed him to pursue his ambition to be a top-class rider.
He acquired his first business in 1935 and made his fortune from mail order, becoming the owner of one of Europe's largest department stores. He also became president of Stiftung Deutsche Sporthilfe, a foundation to aid high-performance sportsmen, and was a member of the West German National Olympic Committee. His daughter **Eva-Maria Pracht** competed at the 1984 and 1988 Olympic Games for Canada, winning a team bronze in 1988, and her daughter, Neckermann's granddaughter, **Martina**, competed at the 1992 Olympic Games in dressage for Canada.

Johan NEESKENS (Hol)

FOOTBALL

Johan Neeskens. b. 15 Sep 1951 Heemstede.

A midfield player and fine all-round athlete who played a major rôle in the three successive victories of Ajax in the European Cup 1971-3. A penalty specialist, he scored Holland's only goal, and the first penalty ever in a World Cup Final, when his team lost to West Germany in 1974. After that he soon joined team-mate Johan Cruyff in Barcelona. Strong, fast and combative, he scored 17 goals in internationals for Holland. He had started his career with Haarlem.

Renaldo NEHEMIAH (USA)

ATHLETICS

Renaldo Nehemiah. b. 24 Mar 1959 Newark, New Jersey.

'Skeets' Nehemiah was the world's finest high hurdler in 1978-81, but then turned professional footballer with the San Francisco 49ers. He set three world 110m hurdles records: 13.16 and 13.00 in 1979 and 12.93 in Zürich in 1981, and he also ran a hand-timed 12.8 in 1979. A student at the University of Maryland he won AAU titles each year 1978-80, and in 1979 the NCAA, Pan-American and World Cup titles. He won the US Olympic Trials in 1980 and would have been a clear favourite for a gold medal, but was denied his chance through President Carter's boycott of the Games in Moscow. He was also AAU indoor champion at 60y hurdles in 1979.
He achieved his long-sought wish in 1986 when he was re-admitted to international competition by the IAAF. After running his fastest time (13.19) since his return, he had to withdraw through injury from the 1991 World Championships.
World junior records: 4x100m relay 1977, five at 110mh 1978. World indoor bests 1979-82 with best times: 50yh (4) 5.92 (1982), 50mh 6.36 (1979), 60yh (5) 6.82 (1982), 60mh 7.62 (1979).

Meinhard NEHMER (GDR)

BOBSLEIGH

Meinhard Nehmer. b. 13 Jan 1941 Boblin.

Nehmer was the winner of three Olympic titles as driver of the 1976 two-man and 1976 and 1980 four-man. On each occasion he was joined by his countryman Bernhard Germeshausen and they share the record for the most Olympic gold medals won by bobsledders. Additionally, he won an Olympic bronze in the two-man in 1980 and the world 4-man in 1977.
An Army sergeant and a former javelin thrower (best of 81.50m 1971), he did not take up bobsledding until he had retired from athletics and was aged 35 when he won his first Olympic medal in 1976. He became coach to the US bobsled team in 1991.

Byron NELSON (USA)

GOLF

John Byron Nelson, Jr. b. 4 Feb 1912 Fort Worth, Texas.

Byron Nelson's fame as a golfer rests principally on his amazing success in 1945, when he won 19 tournaments, 11 of them consecutively (both records). His swing is usually considered the first demonstration of the purely modern method of an upright swing with a pronounced leg drive, keeping the club along the target line for longer than any player before him. Nelson achieved his greatness despite being a

haemophiliac. He had won the US Open in 1939, the Masters in 1937 and 1942 and the US PGA in 1940 and 1945. In all he had 52 PGA tour victories. After 1945, he essentially retired to ranching in Texas, though in 1955 he won the French Open while vacationing in Europe.
Nelson was the first expert commentator on television for golf broadcasts.

Oscar NELSON (USA)

BOXING

Oscar Battling Matthew Nelson. né Oscar Nielsen. b. 5 Jun 1882 Copenhagen, Denmark, d. 7 Feb 1954 Chicago, Illinois.

The 'Durable Dane' was primarily known as one of the toughest fighters ever, able to absorb unusual amounts of punishment and take a punch well. Nelson fought three classic battles with Joe Gans. He lost to him in 1906 in 42 rounds, the longest bout ever recorded under Marquess of Queensberry rules, but in 1908 defeated Gans to win the world lightweight championship. He lost the crown in a 40th round KO by Ad Wolgast. Nelson fought for seven more years without distinction before retiring.
Career record: W -67 (39), L - 31, D - 25.

Imre NÉMETH (Hun)

ATHLETICS

Imre Németh. b. 23 Sep 1917 Kassa (later Kosice, Czechoslovakia), d. 22 Aug 1989 Budapest.

The 1948 Olympic champion at the hammer, at which he was undefeated in 73 consecutive competitions from 15 Sep 1946 to 31 Jul 1950. He was third at the 1952 Olympics and at the Europeans 4th in 1946 and 6th in 1954. He set three world records, one each year 1948-50, and in 1952 was the second man to exceed 60 metres, with his best ever throw of 60.31.
He was later the manager of the Nepstadion in Budapest.
His son Miklos (qv) emulated him as a world record holder and Olympic champion, the only such father-son combination.

János NÉMETH (Hun)

WATER POLO

János Németh. b. 12 Jun 1906, d. 1974.

A great goalscorer for the Hungarian team, which lost only once in the 110 internationals in which Németh played. These included wins in the Olympic finals of 1932 and 1936.

Miklos NÉMETH (Hun)

ATHLETICS

Miklos Németh. b. 23 Oct 1946 Budapest.

Followed his father by becoming an Olympic champion, although for Miklos it was with the javelin when in 1976 in Montreal, in the third of his four Olympic appearances, he threw a world record 94.58m in the first round to give him a record 6.66m winning margin.
In four European Championships his best placing was fifth in 1966, and he was World Student champion in 1970.
His various improvements to javelin design caused some problems in the 1990s when he pioneered the use of rough-tailed spears, which were barred by the IAAF, as was his new multi-part model thrown to what would have been a world record by Jan Zelezny in 1992.

Ondrej NEPELA (Cs)

FIGURE SKATING

Ondrej Nepala. b. 22 Jan 1951 Bratislava, d. 2 Feb 1989 Germany of cancer.

Czechoslovakia's first Olympic and World figure skating champion. In 1964 he was, at the age of 13, the youngest competitor at the Innsbruck Olympics when he finished in 22nd place. After improving to 8th in 1968, he won the Olympic gold medal in 1972. He finished his career as an amateur in 1973 after taking his third successive world title in his home town of Bratislava. He was also European champion 1969-73.

George NEPIA (NZ)

RUGBY UNION

George Nepia. b. 25 Apr 1905 Wairoa, d. 27 Aug 1986 Ruatoria.

One of the legends of New Zealand rugby who began his first-class career as a winger before becoming one of the greatest of all full-backs. As a 19-year-old he was selected for the 1924/5 'Invincibles' who started their tour in Australia before visiting Europe and Canada. Incredibly, George Nepia played in all 38 matches on the extended tour and distinguished himself with some brilliant performances. Because of his Maori blood he was not eligible for the 1928 South African tour and because of injury and illness he played in only two Tests against Australia in 1929, but the following year he played in all four Tests against the visiting British Lions. After failing to make the team for the 1935 tour of Britain he signed to play rugby league in England. Initially he played for the now defunct Streatham & Croydon club but he soon moved to Halifax and when he returned home in 1937 he won international honours. Reinstated as an amateur during the war-time amnesty, he was welcomed back to the Union code and remained in the first-class game until 1950. He later became a popular referee.

Anthony NESTY (Surinam)

SWIMMING

Anthony Nesty. b. 25 Nov 1967 Trinidad.

Became the first sportsman from his country to win an Olympic medal, when he won the gold for 100m butterfly in 1988 in the second best ever time of 53.00, beating Matt Biondi by a hundredth of a second. On his return home he was decorated as Commander of the Yellow Star, and his picture has appeared on national stamps and coins.

He competed at the 1984 Olympics at the age of 16 and the following year went to the USA, first to a private school and then to the University of Florida at Gainesville. In 1986 he set a US high school record for 100 yards butterfly, previously held by Pablo Morales. He won the Pan-American 100m butterfly title in 1987 and followed his Olympic triumph with the world title in 1991. In 1992 he took the Olympic bronze medal.

Best 200m butterfly 2:00.17 (1988).

Igor NETTO (USSR/Rus)

FOOTBALL

Igor Netto. b. 2 Sep 1930 Moscow.

Captained the USSR from the wing-half position from 1954 to 1963, winning a then record total of 57 caps. After making his Olympic début in 1952, he led his team to victory in Melbourne four years later. He also took part in the World Cup in 1958 and 1962 and played for the USSR when they won the first European Championships in 1960, despite the fact that he scored an own goal in the final.

He joined Spartak Moskva in 1948 and remained with them until his retirement in 1966; during this period he made 367 League appearances, scored 37 goals and won five League Championship medals. A stylish, unhurried player, he left the football scene after retirement and became an ice hockey trainer.

Ramona NEUBERT (GDR)

ATHLETICS

Ramona Neubert. née Göhler. b. 26 Jul 1958 Pima.

At the heptathlon Neubert set four world records, from 6670 points in 1981 to 6935 in 1983, and won the European (1982) and World (1983) titles. She also won the 1981 and 1983 European Cup finals. At the pentathlon she was fourth in the 1980 Olympics and eighth in the 1978 Europeans. GDR champion at heptathlon 1981, long jump 1982.

Best performances: 200m 23.14 (1982), 800m 2:04.73 (1984), 100mh 13.13 (1983), high jump 1.86m (1981), long jump 6.90m and 7.00w (1981), shot 15.44m (1982), javelin 49.94m (1983).

Ernie NEVERS (USA)

AMERICAN FOOTBALL

Ernest Alonzo Nevers. b. 11 Jun 1903 Willow River, Minnesota, d. 3 May 1976 San Rafael, California.

The only athlete ever to have been a professional in the three major American sports of baseball, football, and basketball, although primarily known for his football

prowess. He played all three sports at Stanford, playing a full 60 minutes of every football game in his junior and senior years. He graduated in 1925 and played with Duluth Eskimos for two years, before spending the 1929-31 seasons with the Chicago Cardinals. In 1929 he led the NFL in scoring and on 28 Nov 1929 scored all 40 points in leading the Cardinals to a 40-7 victory over the Chicago Bears. It remains an NFL record for points scored in a single game.
In the winter of 1925/6, Nevers played professional basketball for the Chicago Bruins of the American Basketball League, the first professional league, and for three seasons, 1926-8, he was a pitcher with the St Louis Browns at baseball. His career pitching record was 6-12, with a lifetime ERA of 4.63.
He later had a short coaching career before doing some public relations work in the San Francisco area.

Paula NEWBY-FRASER (Zim)

TRIATHLON

Paula Newby-Fraser. b. 2 Jun 1962 Harare.

Has a women's record five wins in the Hawaii Ironman Triathlon, 1986, 1988-9, 1991-2. In 1988 she took over 30 minutes off the fastest time by a woman with 9 hr 1 min 1 sec, which placed her an incredible 11th overall. She went even faster in 1989 with 9:00:56, and in 1992 recorded the fastest Ironman time ever by a woman with 8:55:28. She also achieved four successive wins in the Nice Triathlon 1989-92. Perhaps the finest spokesperson for her sport, she was voted in 1990 the Women's Sport Foundation Athlete of the Year.
The daughter of South African parents, she was born in Zimbabwe but grew up in Durban, South Africa, taking part in a wide variety of sports. She entered her first triathlon in January 1985 after graduating from the University of Natal, and moved to California a year later. Since then she has concentrated on her demanding sport, swimming, rowing and running practically every day.

Don NEWCOMBE (USA)

BASEBALL

Donald Newcombe. b. 14 Jun 1926 Madison, New Jersey.

The first great black pitcher in major league history, he started in the Negro Leagues, as did so many of his generation, and in 1949 was called up by the Brooklyn Dodgers, to be named the Rookie of the Year that year. His greatest year was 1956 when he won the Cy Young and MVP Awards, and by winning 27 games helped the Dodgers to a pennant. Named to the All-Star Game three times, he was a big, overpowering man with a tough fastball and was also one of the greatest hitting pitchers ever, with a lifetime .271 average, often called upon to pinch hit. He retired after the 1960 season, and later admitted to difficulty with alcohol abuse. But he overcame that and started counselling many other players with similar problems.
Career pitching 1949-60: ERA 3.56; W-L 149-90, SO 1129. Best seasons: 1956: 27-7, 3.06 ERA; 1955: 20-5, 3.19.

John NEWCOMBE (Aus)

TENNIS

John David Newcombe. b. 23 May 1944 Sydney, New South Wales.

The last amateur to win the Wimbledon singles in 1967, he won two further titles as a professional in 1970-1. His all-round power game, with its heavy serve-volley and forceful ground strokes, also earned him the US title in 1967 and 1973 and the Australian in 1973 and 1975. He might have won further Wimbledon singles honours but he was banned in 1972 when professionals under contract were banned from ILTF events, and he missed 1973 following a boycott by the Association of Tennis Professionals. He won the Australian junior title each year 1961-3. Despite his seven Grand Slam singles titles, he will be remembered as an outstanding doubles player and his partnership with countryman Tony Roche is the greatest of modern times. Together they won Wimbledon five times (1965, 1968-70, 1974), the Australian four times

(1965, 1971, 1973, 1976), French twice (1967, 1969) and US (1967). Newcombe also won five further Grand Slam men's doubles titles with different partners: Wimbledon 1966, Australian 1967, French 1973 and US 1971 and 1973. Additionally, he won the mixed doubles at the 1964 US Championships.
In 1963 he made a testing Davis Cup début when Australia faced the USA in the Challenge Round. Newcombe lost first to Dennis Ralston and then to Chuck McKinley in the deciding rubber, and many felt that, at the age of 19, too much had been asked of him. His Davis Cup career recovered and he went on to play in 26 ties to 1976, winning 16 of 24 singles and 10 of 11 doubles. His best Cup performance came in the 1973 final when Australia, calling only on Newcombe and Laver, beat the USA 5-0 indoors in Cleveland.

Tom NEWMAN (UK)

BILLIARDS

Thomas Newman. né Pratt. b. 23 Mar 1894 Barton-on-Humber, Lincolnshire, d. 5 Oct 1943 Tufnell Park, London.

Winner of a record six world billiards titles under knock-out conditions. He learned the game in the saloons owned by his father in Nottingham and later in London. In the early part of his career, he signed a three-year contract with John Roberts, Jr. with whom he toured extensively. After winning his first world title in 1921, he was the champion for four of the next five years, losing only to Willie Smith in the 1923 final. He was again a finalist each year 1928-30 but lost to Joe Davis on each occasion, although his record of playing in ten successive finals remains unsurpassed. In 1924 he made the first 1000 break in the Championship (1021).
Although he professed to have little interest in the game, he was also an accomplished snooker player and lost to Joe Davis in the 1934 World final.

John NGUGI (Kenya)

ATHLETICS

John Ngugi. b. 10 May 1962 Nyahururu.

Ngugi won a record fifth world cross-country title in 1992, after four successive wins 1986-9. He took the 1988 Olympic title at 5000m, having sprinted away from the field with a 58.2 400m lap after 1000m. He fell after 1000m in the 1990 Commonwealth Games, but got up and overtook the whole field within a lap; he led by 40m at the bell, but was pipped on the line. Later that year he set a Commonwealth 10,000m record of 27:19.15. He missed selection for the 1991 World Championships, but came into top form at the end of the year, and narrowly missed the world record for 10,000m in Brussels when he ran 27:11.62.
A Kikuyu, he has a seemingly lumbering stride, but at his best was in a class of his own over the country and highly effective on the track as well. His first important title was the East and Central African 1500m in 1985. In 1993 he refused a random drugs test and was at first suspended, but a review of the circumstances exonerated him.
Other best times: 1500m 3:37.02 (1985), 1M 3:56.75 (1990), 3000m 7:45.59 (1989), 2 miles 8:23.38 (1991), 5000m 13:11.14 (1990), Half marathon 1:01:24 (1989).

Guy NICKALLS (UK)

ROWING

Guy Nickalls. b. 12 Feb 1866 Sutton, Surrey, d. 8 Jul 1935 Leeds, Yorkshire.

The winner of a record 23 Henley medals. His son, Guy Oliver, also won 10, and had the highest number of wins (7) in the Grand Challenge Cup. Guy, the father, also won an Olympic gold medal in 1908 when he rowed with the Leander Club crew in the eights. In the Diamond Sculls, Nickalls won six times between 1888 and 1894, failing only in 1892. Between 1890 and 1897 he and his brother, Vivian, dominated the Silver Goblets pair oars, winning together in 1894-6. Guy won with Lord Ampthill in 1890-1 and with ER Balfour in 1897, while Vivian won with WAL Fletcher in 1892-3. In 1895, their father, Tom, donated the Nickalls Challenge Cup in their honour, to be given to future winners of the pair oars at Henley.

Jack NICKLAUS (USA)

GOLF

Jack William Nicklaus. b. 21 Jan 1940 Columbus, Ohio.

Jack Nicklaus' record of 20 major championship wins is unmatched in golf history, and many people consider him the greatest player ever. He was a superb amateur who won the US Amateur in 1959 and 1961, adding the NCAA Championship for Ohio in 1961. In his first year as a professional, 1962, he won the US Open, defeating Arnold Palmer in a play-off at Oakmont. Nicklaus had the misfortune to dethrone Palmer as the game's greatest player, for he was never able to match Palmer's popularity and early in his career he was not well-liked by golf fans. But his great skill won out and he eventually became universally admired and liked. Nicklaus was also one of the longest drivers ever. He continues to play both on the PGA Tour and PGA Senior Tour with some success, winning the US Senior Open in 1991 and 1993, but his primary occupation in the 1990s is as a golf course designer.
Major victories: US Open 1962, 1967, 1972, 1980; Masters 1963, 1965-66, 1972, 1975, 1986; British Open 1966, 1970, 1978; PGA 1963, 1971, 1973, 1975, 1980; World Match Play 1970.
PGA career earnings 1962-92: $5,309,130 with 70 victories.

Bill NIEDER (USA)

ATHLETICS

William Henry Nieder. b. 10 Aug 1933 Hempstead, New York.

In 1960 Nieder set three world records at the shot: 19.45, 19.99, and the first ever 20m effort, 20.06 at Walnut on 12 Aug 1960. That came in the final pre-Olympic meeting and he was advanced to the US team, having only placed fourth at the US Trials, through injury to Dave Davis. In Rome he maintained his form to beat Parry O'Brien and Dallas Long, winning clearly with an Olympic record 19.68m. Nieder had won the 1955 NCAA shot title for Kansas, and was second in the 1956 Olympics. He retired to start a pro boxing career that lasted just one round, when he was knocked out in his only fight.

Phil NIEKRO (USA)

BASEBALL

Philip Henry Niekro. b. 1 Apr 1939 Blaine, Ohio.

Niekro pitched for 24 years in the major leagues, mostly with the Milwaukee/ Atlanta Braves. He started at Milwaukee in 1964 and stayed with the Braves after their move to Atlanta from 1966 to 1983. By the time he retired at age 48, he was one of the oldest regular players in major league history. He won over 10 games in a single season 19 times. His speciality was the knuckleball, which he used to mystify National League hitters.
Career pitching 1964-87: ERA 3.35; W-L 318-274, SO 3342. Best seasons: 1969: 23-13, 2.57 ERA; 1979: 21-20; 3.39 ERA; 1974: 20-13, 2.38 ERA.

Hans NIELSEN (Den)

SPEEDWAY

Hans Hollen Nielsen. b. 26 Dec 1959 Brovst.

Winner of a record number of world titles, 19 in all between 1978 and 1991. He was a member of the winning Danish World Championship team a record nine times, he won the World Pairs title a record seven times (1979, 1986-91) and was a three-time winner of the World Individual title (1986-7, 1989). In four of his world pairs championships he was partnered by Erik Gundersen. Most of his career was spent riding for Oxford in the British League and in 1988 he totalled 563 points to set a new League record. He also won the British League Riders Championship a record three times, 1986-7 and 1990.

Gunda NIEMANN (GDR/Ger)

SPEED SKATING

Gundula Niemann. née Kleeman. b. 26 Sep 1966.

She has become the top woman distance speed-skater of the 1990s. She was world overall champion each year 1991-3, and at the Olympic Games of 1992 she won two gold medals, at 3000m and 5000m, with silver at 1500m. World Cup winner at 1500m 1991-2 and at 3000m/5000m 1990 and 1992. She had made her Olympic début in 1988, when she was 7th at both 1500m and 5000m. She set a world record for 3000m with 4:10.80 in 1990. Before turning to speed skating she had been a promising 400m hurdler.

Toni NIEMINEN (Fin)

SKI JUMPING

Toni Markus Nieminen. b. 31 May 1975.

With a team ski-jumping gold at the 1992 Games, Nieminen became, at 16 years 259 days, the youngest ever Winter Olympics gold medallist. Two days later he took the individual gold on the large hill and he also won a bronze on the normal hill. He completed a marvellous year by winning the World Cup title.

Angel NIETO (Spain)

MOTOR CYCLING

Angel Nieto Roldan. b. 15 Jan 1947 Zamora.

His 90 Grand Prix wins is second only to Giacomo Agostini's 122 wins in world championship motorcycling. This small man (1.57m), known as 'El Niño' (the infant), was hugely successful on the small bikes so popular in Spain, with 27 wins at 50cc, 1 at 80cc and 62 at 125cc between 1969 and 1985, on Derbi machines 1969-72, 1974 and 1985, Morbidelli 1973, Kreidler 1975, Bultaco 1976-7, Minarelli 1978-81 and Garelli 1982-4. In 1969 he was not only the youngest ever 50cc world champion but also the first Spaniard to win a motorcycling world title. In his career he won a record seven world titles at 125cc, 1971-2, 1979, 1981-4, and a record six titles at 50cc, 1969-70, 1972, 1975-7.
He had started racing at the age of 13 on a 50cc Derbi and a year later started work in the Bultaco racing department in Barcelona. He moved to Derbi and at 16 became a works rider for them, staying with them for his initial world successes.

Aleksey NIKANCHIKOV (USSR)

FENCING

Aleksey Nikanchikov. b. 30 Jul 1940, d. 1 Feb 1972 Minsk, Belarus.

Three-time individual world épée champion, and Olympic silver medallist in the épée team event in 1968. His three victories at the World Championships, 1966-7 and 1970, matched the record in the individual épée set by Georges Buchard (Fra) in 1933.
At the early age of 31 he was found asphyxiated in the garage of his home.

Aaron NIMZOWITSCH (Rus/Lat)

CHESS

Aaron Isaewitsch Nimzowitsch. né Niemzowitsch. b. 7 Nov 1886 Riga. d. 16 Mar 1935 Hareskov Sanatorium, Copenhagen, Denmark.

A colourful, eccentric figure, he narrowly failed to become world chess champion, but was a most influential innovator and writer on the game. His *My System* is a classic book on the game and he created a new chess vocabulary. He tied for the Russian title with Alekhine in 1914 and moved to Scandinavia in 1920, first to Sweden and then to Denmark. He called himself the 'Crown Prince of the Chess World' but did not get a chance to challenge for the world title.

Monty NOBLE (Aus)

CRICKET

Montague Alfred Noble. b. 28 Jan 1873 Sydney, d. 22 Jun 1940 Randwick, Sydney.

A master all-rounder, who was dedicated to sportsmanship and the ethics of the game, qualities he showed to good order in his 15 matches as Australian captain 1903-9. He was an accomplished medium paced off-break bowler and a fine, mostly defensive, batsman.
He worked initially in a bank, but on being denied permission to play inter-state cricket for New South Wales (whom he captained 1902-10), he trained as a dentist.
42 Tests 1898-1909: 1997 runs at 30.25,

1 100 HS 133; 121 wickets at 25.00, BB 7-17; 26 catches.
First-class 1893-1920: 13,975 runs at 41.74, 37 100s HS 284; 625 wickets at 23.11, BB 8-48; 191 catches.

Leo NOMELLINI (Italy/USA)

AMERICAN FOOTBALL

Leo Nomellini. b. 19 Jun 1924 Lucca, Italy.

Nomellini was brought to the United States by his parents when he was four years old. He grew into a giant of 1.91m *6'3"* and 120 kg *265 lb,* who became a great football lineman. After high school, he served four years in the US Marines. At the University of Minnesota he played guard and tackle and was also a shot putter and heavyweight wrestler. After graduation in 1949 he played from 1950-63 for the San Francisco 49ers as both offensive and defensive tackle, and was chosen to the All-NFL offensive team in 1951 and 1952 and the defensive team in 1953-4, 1957, and 1959. He played in ten Pro Bowl Games and was elected to the NFL Hall of Fame in 1969. Exceptionally durable, he never missed a game, playing in 266 consecutive NFL games. In the off-season, Nomellini competed as a pro wrestler under the name 'Leo the Lion'.

Gunnar NORDAHL (Swe)

FOOTBALL

N Gunnar Nordahl. b. 19 Oct 1921 Hörnefors.

The most famous of a trio of brothers who helped Sweden to the 1948 Olympic title; the others were Bertil (b. 26 Jul 1917) and Knut (1920-84). Gunnar was a robust centre-forward with a superb physique, who set many scoring records both at home and in Italy. From 1940 to 1944 he played for Degerfors before moving to IFK Norrköping, where he won four successive League Championship titles 1945-8. In his eight seasons in the major league in Sweden he topped the scoring list four times. In 1949 he became the first Swedish professional footballer to play overseas and went with his Swedish colleagues Gunnar Gren and Nils Liedholm (they were known as the Grenoli trio) to AC Milan, for whom he scored 210 goals in 257 league games, heading the Italian League scoring list in five of six consecutive seasons 1949-55. He helped Milan to win the Italian League title in 1951 and 1955. In 1956 he moved to AS Roma and returned to Sweden in 1959 where he held a variety of coaching posts.
With 43 goals in 33 internationals for Sweden he was one of the deadliest strikers in world football in the immediate post-war years.

Björn NORDQVIST (Swe)

FOOTBALL

Björn Nordqvist. b. 6 Oct 1942 Hallsberg.

A fine defender, with 115 international appearances 1963-78 he is Sweden's most capped player and was captain for many years, playing in three World Cups 1970-8. He played for Hallsberg, IFK Norrköping, PSV Eindhoven, IFK Göteborg, Minnesota Kicks and Örgyte IS.
He also played bandy in Division I of the Swedish League and ice hockey in Division II.

Wolfgang NORDWIG (GDR)

ATHLETICS

Wolfgang Nordwig. b. 27 Aug 1943 Siegmar, Chemnitz.

Nordwig won a record three European pole vault titles, 1966, 1969 and 1971, and a record four European indoor titles, 1968-9 and 1971-2. He won the Olympic bronze medal in 1968 and became champion in 1972, when he set his ninth and final GDR record of 5.50m. This came in a controversial event, as he was the only one of the leading contenders not to have to use a different pole than they were used to, following an IAAF ban on some new poles, as used by Bob Seagren and others. Nordwig had set two world records, 5.45m and 5.46 in 1970. He also won the European Cup three times and the World Student Games title in 1970, and was GDR champion for eight successive years from 1965 to 1972.

Martha NORELIUS (USA)

SWIMMING

Martha Norelius. b. 20 Jan 1908 Stockholm, Sweden, d. 23 Sep 1955. Later Wright.

She was the first woman to retain an Olympic title, winning the 400m freestyle in 1924 and 1928, when she won a third gold medal at the 4 x 100m relay. In the two and a half years from 28 Feb 1926 to 27 Aug 1928, Norelius set 17 world records, including best times of 220y 2:40.6, 400m 5:39.2, 880y 12:17.8 and 1500m 23:44.6. She was suspended by the AAU in 1929 for swimming an exhibition in the same pool as professionals and so decided to turn pro herself, winning $10,000 in a 10 mile Wrigley Marathon in Toronto. She was considered to be the first woman to swim like a man, emulating Johnny Weissmuller's action.
Her father Charles had swum on the Swedish 4 x 250m team which was fifth at the 1906 Olympics and he coached swimming for 63 years, indeed until 12 years after his daughter's death. He started coaching Martha but she switched to Louis de B Handley on emigrating to the USA. Martha married Joe Wright, a rower who won an Olympic silver medal for Canada at double sculls in 1928.

Greg NORMAN (Aus)

GOLF

Gregory John Norman. b. 10 Feb 1955 Mount Isa, Queensland.

The 'Great White Shark' has been one of the world's best golfers during the 1980s and 1990s, although his record in the majors has been marred by him losing too many titles when in strong contention, such as in play-offs for the US Open 1984, US Masters 1987 and British Open 1989. His best year was in 1986 when he led going into the final round of all four majors, although he only won one, the British Open. However, he also won the European Open and the World Matchplay and headed the money list on the US PGA tour with the then record of $653,296. He again headed the list in 1990 with $1,165,477 and was ninth on the all-time list at the end of 1992. He led the European tour in 1980, and had earlier wins in the World Matchplay in 1980 and 1983, with the Australian Masters 1980, 1983-4, Dunlop Masters 1981-2. He ranked as the world number one when the Sony Rankings were introduced in 1986, and remained at the top until passed by Nick Faldo in early 1991. In 1993 he won his second major, when he won a superb contest for the British Open at Sandwich. His total of 267 (66, 68, 69, 64) was an all-time record low aggregate, and his final round of 64, the best ever by a champion, brought him home two shots ahead of Faldo.
He had turned professional in 1976, and in that year first played for Australia in the World Cup.
PGA career earnings 1983-92: $5,247,909 with 10 victories.

Ross NORMAN (NZ)

SQUASH

Ross Norman. b. 1 Jul 1959 Whitianga.

At the World Open in 1986 Norman had a stunning victory over Jahangir Khan in the final, the latter's first loss for more than five years. This was the culmination of a determined campaign by the super-fit Norman to reach the top after a serious knee injury while parachuting in 1983. He had won the New Zealand junior title in 1977, was runner-up in the British amateur in 1979 and a quarter-finalist in the British Open in 1980 and 1984. In 1985 he was beaten by Jahangir in the final of the World Open and in 1986 won the European Open.

Dave NOURSE (SAf)

CRICKET

Arthur William Nourse. b. 26 Jan 1878 Thornton Heath, Surrey, d. 8 Jul 1948 Port Elizabeth.

South Africa's first great batsman, a very solid left-hander, and also a left-arm medium paced bowler. He had a very long career so that he became known as the 'Grand Old Man' of South African cricket.

He scored a record number of runs in South African cricket and played for Natal 1896-1925, Transvaal 1925-7 and Western Province 1927-36. His son Dudley (qv) followed in his footsteps.
45 Tests 1902-24: 2234 runs at 29.78, 1 100 HS 111; 41 wickets at 37.87, BB 4-25; 43 catches.
First-class 1896-1936: 14,216 runs at 42.81, 38 100s HS 304; 305 wickets at 23.36, BB 6-33; 171 catches.*

Dudley NOURSE (SAf)

CRICKET
Arthur Dudley Nourse. b. 12 Nov 1910 Durban, d. 14 Aug 1981 Durban.

A powerful and aggressive right-handed batsman (unlike his father Dave, qv), he had a highly successful Test career on either side of World War II. In his second Test he scored 231, then a record score for his country, in 289 minutes against Australia in December 1935. He captained South Africa in his last 15 Tests, starting with the 1948/9 series against England. In that series he made 536 runs at 76.57, having also averaged over 60 in his two previous series against England: 422 runs at 60.22 in 1938/9 and 621 at 49.00 in 1947. He was also a very safe catcher and a good baseball player.
34 Tests 1935-51: 2960 runs at 53.82; 9 100s HS 231; 12 catches.
First-class 1931-53: 12,472 runs at 51.37, 41 100s HS 260; 135 catches.*

Igor NOVIKOV (USSR)

MODERN PENTATHLON
Igor Aleksandrov Novikov. b. 19 Oct 1929 Drezna, Moscow region.

A most consistent performer at the modern pentathlon, at the four Olympic Games from 1952 to 1964 he was successively 4th, 4th, 5th and 2nd at the individual, and at the team event won two gold medals (1956 and 1964) and a silver (1960). His 5th place in 1960, when he had the misfortune to lose considerable ground on his rivals in the riding, interrupted a sequence of successive world individual titles, 1957-9 and 1961. Those wins were followed by second place in 1962 and third in 1963. Consistently strong at each discipline, he had set a record score at fencing when he won his first world title. He was also a member of the USSR team that won five successive team titles, 1957-9, 1961-2. He was the USSR individual champion in 1953, 1956, 1959 and 1964.
Novikov became a coach, chairman of the USSR Modern Pentathlon Federation, and vice president of the international governing body.

Paavo NURMI (Fin)

ATHLETICS
Paavo Johannes Nurmi. b. 13 Jun 1897 Turku, d. 2 Oct 1973 Helsinki.

Nurmi, the 'Flying Finn', won a record nine Olympic gold medals: 1500m and 5000m 1924, 10,000m 1920 and 1928; 3000m steeplechase 1924, cross-country team and individual 1920-24. He added silver at 5000m in 1920 and 1924 and at steeplechase in 1928 for a record 12 in all. He dominated the world of distance running in the 1920s, revolutionising the sport with his hard training methods.
He set 22 official and 13 unofficial world records at distances from 1500m to 20 kilometres. His best for 5000m, 14:28.2, was run just an hour after his 3:52.6 world record at 1500m. Between 1920 and 1933 he won 20 Finnish titles at distances from 800m to 10,000m and cross-country. On a barnstorming tour of the USA in the winter of 1925 he won 53 of 55 races, with 12 world indoor bests from January to March at all distances from 1500m to 5000m!
His statue stands outside the Olympic stadium in Helsinki, where he carried the Olympic flame into the stadium at the Opening Ceremony in 1952. This introverted, and even sometimes bitter man, became a wealthy businessman and building contractor.
Other bests: 1M 4:10.4 (1923), 3000m 8:20.4 (1926), 2M 8:58.2 indoors (1925), 3M 14:02.4 (1924), 6M 29:07.1 (1924), 10,000m 30:06.1 (1924), 10M 50:15.0 (1928), 20,000m 1:04:38.4 (1930), 1 Hour 19,210m (1928).

Betty NUTHALL (UK)

TENNIS

Betty May Nuthall. b. 23 May 1911 Surbiton, Surrey, d. 8 Nov 1983 New York, USA. Later Shoemaker

The daughter of tennis enthusiasts who founded the West Side Club at Ealing, she won the first of her seven British Junior titles in 1924 at the age of 13 and was unbeaten at the Championships for three years. Although it was not until 1928 that she started to serve overarm, she made her Wightman Cup début at Forest Hills the previous year at the age of 16 yr 80 days, the youngest player ever to represent Great Britain in the Cup. With a victory over the redoubtable Helen Jacobs she was the only British singles winner, and two weeks later she reached the final of the singles and women's doubles at the US Championships. She scored her greatest successes at these Championships as in 1930 she became the first overseas player to win the singles, and she also won the women's doubles in 1930-1 and 1933 (with three different partners) and the mixed doubles with George Lott (USA) in 1929 and 1931. She won the French doubles in 1931 with Eileen Whittingstall and the mixed in 1931 and 1932, the latter with Fred Perry. She surprisingly never progressed beyond the quarter-finals of the singles or the semi-finals of either doubles at Wimbledon, but won the Hard Court Championship in 1927. She played in her eighth and final Wightman Cup tie in 1939 and made her last appearance at Wimbledon in 1946 when she lost in the fourth round of the singles to Dorothy Bundy (USA) who was the daughter of the 1905 champion May Sutton. Following her marriage to American Franklin C Shoemaker, she spent her later years in America.

Tazio NUVOLARI (Italy)

MOTOR RACING

Tazio Georgio Nuvolari. b. 16 Nov 1892 Casteldario, d. 11 Aug 1953 Mantua.

With his unique style, he was the greatest driver of the 1930s. Small and wiry, he was known as *Il Campionissimo*, 'The Great Little Man'.

He raced motorcycles from 1920 to 1930, and was the Italian 500cc champion in 1924. He contested his first motor race in 1921, emerging in 1928 as a major force and going on to become a living legend with a large number of major wins up to his last race in 1950. These included, mostly in Alfa-Romeos, the major Grand Prix wins: Belgian 1933, French 1932, German 1935, Italian 1931-2, 1938, Monaco 1932.

He also excelled in sports car events, winning the Le Mans 24-hours in 1933 and the Mille Miglia in 1930 and 1933, and in sprints and hill climbs. After World War II he won the 1946 GP de Albigeois in a Maserati and in 1947 was second in the Mille Miglia before gracefully giving way to younger drivers.

Matti NYKÄNEN (Fin)

NORDIC SKIING

Matti Ensio Nykänen. b. 17 Jul 1963 Jyväskylä.

He was probably the most colourful, notorious and controversial character in the history of Finnish sports, and the ace ski jumper of the 1980s. He won a record four Olympic gold medals. In 1984 he took the silver medal at the 70m hill before winning at the 90m, and in 1988 he took all three gold medals, with the introduction of a team event. He also has a record with four World Cup jumping titles, 1983, 1985-6 and 1988, and at 18 was the youngest ever ski-jumping world champion at the 90m hill in 1982. He was World Junior champion in 1981 and also won the world title at ski-flying in 1985, in which year he set a world jumping record at 191m.

Surprisingly he did not win any more world titles, but was 2nd at normal hill in 1987, and third at large hill in 1985 and 1989.

Slightly built, he demonstrated beautiful, natural aerodynamic skill from the start of his career, allied to a daredevil temperament. Ill-tempered in his youth, he mellowed a little after his marriage. Since 1991 he has been a pop singer.

Alex OBOLENSKY (UK)

RUGBY UNION

(Prince) Alexander Obolensky. b. 17 Feb 1916 St Petersburg, Russia, d. 29 Mar 1940 Norfolk.

Educated at Trent College and Brasenose College, Oxford, he was one of the greatest wingers ever to play for Oxford but he failed to score in his two appearances in the University match (1935 and 1937). A White Russian Prince, who dropped his title in March 1936, he won all four of his England caps that year and his second try against the visiting All Blacks is still remembered as a classic and invariably referred to as 'Obolensky's try'. In the summer of 1936 he went on the RFU tour of South America and his tally of 17 tries against a Brazilian XV remains a record for representative rugby.
On leaving Oxford, he played for Rosslyn Park and the Barbarians and was the first English international to lose his life in World War II. Serving as a Pilot Officer in the RAF, he was killed in a flying training accident.

Dan O'BRIEN (USA)

ATHLETICS

Dan Dion O'Brien. b. 18 Jul 1966 Portland, Oregon.

The 1991 world champion at the decathlon, he was devastated in 1992 when he failed to clear a height in the pole vault at the US Trials for the Olympic Games. He and his colleague Dave Johnson were at the time the centre of a major Reebok advertising campaign leading up to the Olympics, but the sudden-death system meant no second chance for him to compete in Barcelona. However, in September of that year, in Talence, France, he took Daley Thompson's world record with a score of 8891 points. Born of a Finnish mother and black American father, he was adopted at the age of two by an Oregon couple. He has shown enormous natural talent, although he failed to take full advantage of this while he was at the University of Idaho. Eventually he buckled down to work, and burst into world-class in 1990 with 8483 points. He improved to a wind-aided 8844 to win the US title in 1991, just three points short of Thompson's world record, and set a US record under legal conditions at 8812 in Tokyo. In 1993 he set a world indoor record with 6476 points for the heptathlon at the World Indoor Championships, and despite injury problems took the US decathlon title at the start of his outdoor campaign.
Individual event bests: 60m 6.67i (1993), 100m 10.41/10.23w (1991), 400m 46.53 (1991), 1500m 4:33.19 (1989), 60mh 7.85i (1993), 110mh 13.94 (1991), 13.81w (1989); HJ 2.16i (1992), PV 5.25 (1991), LJ 8.08 (1992), 8.11w (1991); SP 16.69 (1992), DT 52.86 (1990), JT 62.58 (1992).

Ian O'BRIEN (Aus)

SWIMMING

Ian Lovett O'Brien. b. 3 Mar 1947 Wellington, NSW.

Olympic champion in 1964 at 200m breaststroke in a world record time of 2:27.8, with a bronze medal at the medley relay. O'Brien was a formidable competitor at breaststroke events, winning the 110y/220y double at the Commonwealth Games of 1962 and 1966. Both the latter were won in world record times of 68.2 and 2:29.3 respectively despite the fact that he was 30 lb overweight only six weeks before the Games. He also won a Commonwealth medley relay gold in 1962. He set two other world records, an earlier 68.6 for 100y and his best for 220y of 2:28.0 (worth 2:27.0 for the shorter 200m). In 1968 he was 6th at 100m in the Olympics, but then retired at the age of 21. He won 15 Australian titles including breaststroke ones at 100m/110y 1963-6, and at 200m/220y 1962-6.

Parry O'BRIEN (USA)

ATHLETICS

William Parry O'Brien. b. 28 Jan 1932 Santa Monica, California.

In a very long career as a shot putter, Parry O'Brien was Olympic champion in 1952 and 1956, won the silver medal in 1960, and was fourth in 1964. He was Pan-American champion in 1955 and 1959 and won AAU titles indoors nine times (1953-61) and outdoors eight times (1951-5, 1958-60). Sullivan Award winner 1959. The complete master of his event, and pioneer of the step-back O'Brien technique, he set the record win streak by a male athlete with 116 consecutive victories between July 1952 and June 1956. He set 15 world records with ten performances ratified by the IAAF, from 18.00m in 1953 to 19.30 in 1959. His 18.42m *60' 5 1/4"* in 1954 was the first ever 60ft put. Although he was surpassed by younger throwers, O'Brien continued to improve and recorded a best of 19.69 in 1966. While at the University of Southern California he was NCAA champion in 1952 and 1953. He also won the AAU discus title in 1955 and had a best at that event of 60.00m in 1965.

Vincent O'BRIEN (Ire)

HORSE RACING

Michael Vincent O'Brien. b. 9 Apr 1917 Churchtown, Co. Cork.

A great Irish trainer, he began his racing career as an amateur jockey and rode his first winner in 1940, before starting training in Co. Cork in 1943. In 1951 he moved to Ballydoyle House, Tipperary, where he established one of the world's great training centres, first achieving immense success as a trainer of jumpers. He won all the major National Hunt races including the Grand Nationals of 1953-5, four Cheltenham Gold Cups and the Champion Hurdle, won three times by *Hatton's Grace*. O'Brien switched to flat racing from 1959, achieving even greater success, training winners of 16 English classics, including six Epsom Derbys, and 27 Irish classics; perhaps the greatest of these was the triple crown winner *Nijinsky* in 1970. He also trained two winners of the Prix de l'Arc de Triompe: *Ballymoss* 1958 and *Alleged* 1977-8. In 1966 he began one of the greatest partnerships on the English turf, with Lester Piggott riding many great races for him. O'Brien's sons David and Charles followed him as successful trainers.

Pat O'CALLAGHAN (Ire)

ATHLETICS

(Dr) Patrick O'Callaghan. b. 15 Sep 1905 Kanturk, d. 1 Dec 1991 Clonmel.

Olympic gold medallist at the hammer in 1928 (51.39m) and 1932 (53.92). On 22 Aug 1937 he exceeded the world record with 59.56 in Fermoy, but this mark was not recognised by the IAAF as the Irish federation (NACA) was not affiliated to the world body. The IAAF had imposed the boundary rule (i.e. Northern Ireland was part of the UK) in 1935, and the NACA refused to accept the decision. In consequence no Irish team participated in the 1936 Berlin Olympic Games, and perhaps Dr Pat was thus deprived of a third gold medal. Between 1927 and 1936 he won Irish titles: six each at shot and hammer, four at 56lb weight 1928 and 1930-2, three at high jump, and one at discus 1931.

He started athletics after he had qualified as a doctor at the age of 20, too young to practise in Ireland so he served in the RAF Medical Corps from 1926 to 1928. He took up the hammer in 1927 and was Olympic champion a year later.

Luis OCANA (Spain)

CYCLING

Jesus Luis Ocana Pernia. b. 9 Jun 1945 Priego.

A great all-rounder who was primarily known as a superb climber. As he had the misfortune to race in the same era as Eddy Merckx, he was prevented from winning more major tours by the great Belgian. Ocana lacked the sprinting ability to win one-day classics so his primary efforts were directed towards the major tours. In 1971 Ocana wore the *Maillot Jaune* and led Merckx in the Tour de France until he crashed on a hairpin bend on the descent of the Col de Mente in the Pyrenées; his life was at risk but he returned to ride again. His Tour de France win in 1973 was sweet but was achieved in Merckx's absence. His best world championships placing was third in the pro road race in 1973.

Other major victories: Vuelta à España 1970 (King of the Mountains 1969), Grand Prix de Nations 1971, Dauphiné-Libéré 1972-3.

Christy O'CONNOR (Ire)

GOLF

Christy O'Connor. b. 21 Dec 1924 Dublin.

The greatest Irish golfer ever and probably, between the eras of Henry Cotton and Tony Jacklin, the best player from the British Isles. He was the dominant player in the early days of the British PGA Tour, with 24 victories and leading the Order of Merit in 1961 and 1962. He never won the British Open but finished in the top five seven times between 1958 and 1969, with a best of 2nd in 1965. He started his professional career only in his late 20s, winning his first British title in 1955 at the Swallow-Penfold Tournament. His major wins included the Dunlop Masters in 1956 and 1959, the PGA Match Play in 1957 and the World Seniors in 1976 and 1977. With Harry Bradshaw he won the World Cup for Ireland in 1958. O'Connor played in a record 10 Ryder Cup matches, consecutively from 1955 to 1973, with a record of 11 wins, 20 losses and 4 halves.
His nephew **Christy O'Connor Jr** (b.19 Aug 1948) followed him as a Ryder Cup player in 1975 and played again in 1989, when the two-iron approach shot that he hit to within tap-in distance at the 18th closed out Fred Couples and ensured victory for Europe.

Michael O'CONNOR (Aus)

RUGBY LEAGUE

Michael David O'Connor. b. 30 Nov 1960 Nowra, New South Wales.

After winning 12 international Union caps as a centre or wing, he changed codes in 1983 and signed professional forms for St George's in Sydney. After only two seasons he won international honours as a League player and on the tour of New Zealand in 1985 scored 3 tries and 13 goals in only four matches. On his first tour of Britain he broke the individual scoring record for an Anglo-Australian match. In the first Test he scored 22 points (3 tries, 5 goals) to better the previous best of 20 points which had been shared by four players.

Peter O'CONNOR (Ire)

ATHLETICS

Peter O'Connor. b. 18 Oct 1874 Ashtown, Wicklow, d. 9 Nov 1957 Upton, Newton, Waterford.

O'Connor set five world records for the long jump, the first at 7.51 in 1900 and then four more in 1901, with his last at 7.61 remaining unbeaten for 20 years. It also remained as an Irish record until 1990. In 1906 he disappointed with Olympic silver at the long jump in Athens, but came back to win gold at the triple jump. He then retired to concentrate on his solicitor's practice, but was a judge at the 1932 Olympics in Los Angeles. He was AAA champion at long jump 1901-06 and high jump 1903-04.

Ernst OCWIRK (Aut)

FOOTBALL

Ernst Ocwirk. b. 7 Mar 1926 Vienna, d. 23 Jan 1980 Vienna

The last of the great attacking half-backs, he played that rôle in the Austrian team when most other countries had abandoned this style of play. Making his international début in 1947, he played in the Olympics the following year and went on to win 62 caps. His early career was with Austria FAC and FK Austria and he moved to Italy to join Sampdoria after turning professional. He returned to FK Austria in 1961 but after only one year went back to Italy as manager of Sampdoria. In 1965 he again returned to FK Austria and after five years as manager there he spent one year in Germany as manager of Cologne and then in 1972 moved to Admira-Energie.

Mikio ODA (Japan)

ATHLETICS

Mikio Oda. b. 30 Mar 1905 Hiroshima.

When he won the triple jump in 1928 he

was the first ever Asian Olympic gold medallist at athletics. Three years later he jumped 15.58m, while on the same day Chuhei Nambu long jumped 7.98, and these were the first world records set at athletics by Asians.
Oda had placed sixth at the 1924 Olympics but was prevented by injury from being at his best for the 1932 Games and he came only 12th. In all he set a record 21 Asian records, taking the long jump from 6.90 in 1923 to 7.38 in 1928 in seven stages and setting 10 triple jump bests from 14.27 in 1923, with four at the decathlon to 6003 points in 1926. Far-Eastern champion at long jump and decathlon 1927, and triple jump 1925, 1927 and 1930. He became a distinguished leader of the sport in Japan.
Other bests: High jump 1.92m, pole vault 3.80m, long jump 7.52m (1931).

William O'DONNELL (Can)

HARNESS RACING

William A O'Donnell. b. 4 May 1948 Springhill, Nova Scotia

Canadian O'Donnell went to New England to become second trainer to Jim Doherty and having established himself there moved on to Saratoga and Meadowlands. He led the North American money winners at harness racing in 1981-2 and 1984-5. In 1985 he became the first driver to surpass $10 million in a year with $10,207,372, helped especially by *Nihilator* and *Prakas*, winners respectively of the Little Brown Jug and Hambletonian, and the greatest ever money spinners. By the end of 1992 O'Donnell was third on the all-time list at $75,555,169, having had 4705 winners.

Al OERTER (USA)

ATHLETICS

Alfred Adolph Oerter. b. 19 Sep 1936 Astoria, New York.

Oerter achieved the unique feat of winning four successive Olympic titles, with the discus at each Games from 1956 to 1968. He also won the Pan-American title in 1959, the AAU six times between 1959 and 1966, and the NCAA for the University of Kansas in 1957 and 1958. He set four world records from 61.10m in 1962 to 62.94 in 1964. The former was the first officially accepted mark over 200 ft, although Oerter himself had thrown over that mark with 61.73m at Fayetteville, Arkansas on 5 Apr 1958, but this was disallowed due to a 2.5% downhill slope.
After winning his fourth Olympic gold medal with a personal best 64.78 in 1968, he retired to concentrate on his career as a systems analyst and computer engineer in 1969. He had won each of his Olympic titles when others were favoured ahead of him and, especially in 1964, against considerable adversity, for then he had neck and rib injuries.
After a decade out of competition, however, he made an awe-inspiring comeback and improved his best to 69.46 at the age of 43 in 1980. He placed fourth that year in the US Olympic Trials, but by then the US Government had determined to boycott the Games in Moscow. If that competition had been 'for real' who can say but that his tremendous competitive spirit might not once again have returned him to the Olympic arena. Even in 1985, at the age of 49, he had a season's best of 64.38, 31 years after he had set a US high school discus record.

Martin OFFIAH (UK)

RUGBY LEAGUE

Martin Offiah. b. 29 Dec 1966 Hackney, London.

Signed by Widnes from the rugby union club Rosslyn Park, he immediately proved to be the most exciting winger to emerge in recent years. In his first four seasons as a League player he was the leading try scorer: 1987/8 (44 tries), 1988/9 (60), 1989/90 (45) and 1990/1 (49). He set a GB record by scoring five tries against France in 1991 and with 19 tries in only 21 international matches he has the best strike rate of any GB player in history. In January 1992 he signed for Wigan for a record transfer of £400,000. A fast, elusive runner, he also has the strength to break through all but the most committed tackles.

Ichiro OGIMURA (Japan)

TABLE TENNIS

Ichiro Ogimura. b. 25 Jun 1932 Shizuoka Prefecture.

A subtle player whose intelligent service variations enabled him to defeat some of the game's biggest hitters. He won the world singles in 1954 and 1956, the men's doubles in 1956 and 1959, and the mixed doubles three times in succession, 1957-61. He was a stalwart of the Japanese team which won the Swaythling Cup five times in succession, 1954-9. After retirement he became a noted coach in Japan and Europe. In 1979 he was elected deputy president of the International Table Tennis Federation and in 1987 its president.

Sadaharu OH (Japan)

BASEBALL

Sadaharu Oh. b. 10 May 1940 Tokyo.

The all-time home run king, as his 868 in Japanese leagues far surpasses both Babe Ruth and Hank Aaron. Oh hit his 756th in 1976 off Yukio Yakeshi to surpass Aaron and led the Japanese leagues in home runs 15 times, 13 of them consecutive. He won nine MVP awards and the Triple Crown in Japan in back-to-back years. He won nine Diamond Gloves, the Japanese equivalent of Gold Gloves, and led the league in RBI 13 times. He studied the Japanese martial arts of *aikido* and *kendo* to help him learn to harness his immense strength. In 1974, Aaron and Oh met in a home-run hitting contest in Japan with Aaron winning 10-9. Oh is now a sports commentator and head of the Japan Sumo Association.

Isao OKANO (Japan)

JUDO

Isao Okano. b. 20 Jan 1944 Ibaragi Prefecture.

The Olympic champion in Tokyo in 1964 and World champion in 1965 at middle-weight (80kg). A superb technician, at 85kg and 1.68m tall he was the lightest man to win the All-Japan championship, open to all weights, winning in 1967 and 1969. He was appointed national trainer in 1972.

José María OLAZÁBAL (Spain)

GOLF

José María Olazábal. b. 5 Feb 1966 Fuenterrabia.

Olazábal is establishing a formidable record as a match player at golf and his short game is one of the best in the world. In the Ryder Cup he partnered Severiano Ballesteros to three wins on his début in 1987, in 1989 was the top European player with four wins and a half, and in 1991 achieved three wins and a half with Ballesteros, although he was beaten by Paul Azinger in the singles.

The son of a San Sebastian greenkeeper, Olazábal had won the British boys, youths and amateur (the third youngest ever and first Spanish champion in 1984) titles, before winning the PGA School qualifier in 1985. In his first pro season in 1986 he was second in the Order of Merit, followed by 17th, 3rd, 2nd, 3rd, 4th and 6th places in the following years to take his 1986-92 career European Tour earnings to £2,188,097.

Bert OLDFIELD (Aus)

CRICKET

William Albert Stanley Oldfield. b. 9 Sep 1894 Alexandria, Sydney, d. 10 Aug 1976 Killara, Sydney.

Australia's finest wicket-keeper of the pre-war era, and an elegant batsman. Ever calm and unruffled, he set a world record number of dismissals in Tests (passed by Godfrey Evans in 1954). He first came to prominence for the Australian Imperial Forces team that toured England in 1919, and played for New South Wales. Awarded the MBE.

54 Tests 1920-37: 1427 runs at 22.65, HS 65; 78 catches, 52 stumpings.*

First-class 1919-38: 6135 runs at 23.77, 6 100s HS 137; 399 catches, 262 stumpings.

Brian OLDFIELD (USA)

ATHLETICS

Brian Oldfield. b. 1 Jun 1945 Elgin, Illinois.

He achieved astonishing world bests with 22.11, 22.55 and 22.86m at the shot as an

ITA professional in 1975-6. At the time the world amateur record was 21.82. He also recorded four world indoor bests in 1973-5. Before turning professional he had a best of 20.97 and was sixth at the Olympics in 1972 as well as AAU champion indoors in 1970.
As a reinstated amateur he won the US title in 1980 and set two US records, 22.02 in 1981 and 22.19 in 1984 (when he topped the world list at the age of 39), but he was ineligible for the Olympics. A graduate of Middle Tennessee State, he used the rotational technique.

Tony OLIVA (Cuba/USA)

BASEBALL

Pedro Oliva López. b. 20 Jul 1940 Pinar del Rio, Cuba.

Oliva played for 15 years in the majors with the Minnesota Twins and was one of the great hitters of the 1960s. He led the American League in hitting in 1964 and 1965, his first two full seasons; the only player to lead the American League in batting in both of his first two years. He was Rookie of the Year in 1964 and played in the All-Star Game in eight consecutive seasons, 1964-71. Unfortunately, he had injury problems with his right knee, which required surgery seven times during his career, and that limited his mobility, so his hitting suffered as a result in his last four seasons.
Career 1962-76: 1917 hits Avg. .304, HR 220; RBI 947. Best seasons: 1964: .323, 32 HR, 217 hits; 1971: .337; 1970: .325, 204 hits.

Eric OLIVER (UK)

MOTOR CYCLING

Eric S. Oliver. b. 1911 Crowborough, Sussex, d. 1981.

He was the first ever world sidecar champion in 1949, with Dennis Jenkinson as passenger, and won again in 1950-1 with Lorenzo Dobelli and in 1953 with Stanley Dibben. When sidecars were reintroduced to the Isle of Man TT in 1954, Oliver won with Les Nutt. Oliver concentrated on sidecar racing after World War II, having raced both solo machines and sidecars before then, making his TT début as a solo rider in 1937. With supreme skill and determination, in all he won 18 world championship sidecar races in his Norton/Watsonian combination and in 1954 he introduced the kneeler sidecar outfit, soon emulated by most other sidecar competitors.

Nadezhda OLIZARENKO (USSR/Rus)

ATHLETICS

Nadezhda Fyodorovna Olizarenko. née Mushta. b. 28 Nov 1953 Bryansk.

She won the 1980 Olympic title for 800m, when she improved the world record that she had set six weeks earlier of 1:54.85 to 1:53.43, and was also third at 1500m. An international class athlete for nearly two decades, she was European silver medallist at both 800m and 4 x 400m relay in 1978 and gold medallist at 800m in 1986. She also won the World Student Games 800m in 1979 and was USSR 800m champion in 1988. She added another world record at 4 x 800m in 1984. A sports instructor, she competed for Odessa SA and is married to Sergey Olizarenko (8:24.0 for 3000m steeplechase in 1978).
Other best times: 400m 50.96 (1980), 1500m 3:56.8 (1980).

Merlin OLSEN (USA)

AMERICAN FOOTBALL

Merlin Olsen. b. 15 Sep 1940 Logan, Utah.

After playing college football at Utah State he spent his entire 15-year pro career with the Los Angeles Rams as a defensive tackle, one of the very best ever to play in that position. With Deacon Jones, Rosey Grier and Lamar Lundy, Olsen made up the Fearsome Foursome for the Rams, considered perhaps the greatest defensive line ever. He played in the Pro Bowl a record 14 times and was elected to the Pro Football Hall of Fame in his first year of eligibility (1982). Olsen has stayed very visible since his retirement from football. He has been a popular football analyst on television and acted in both movies and television, including the rôle of Jonathan

Garvey, a farmer on the very popular television show 'Little House on the Prairie', that starred Michael Landon.

Ole OLSEN (Den)

SPEEDWAY

Ole Bjarne Olsen. b. 16 Nov 1946 Haderslev.

In 1971 he became the first Dane to win the world individual title. He was again the winner in 1975 and 1978 and in all scored 119 points from 12 finals. He took the Pairs title in 1979 with Hans Nielsen and was also a three-time winner of the Team championship. He became manager of the Danish national team.

Yobes ONDIEKI (Kenya)

ATHLETICS

Yobes Ondieki. b. 21 Feb 1961 Kisii.

On 10 July 1993 in Oslo he became the first man to run 10,000m in under 27 minutes, as his 26:58.38 took nearly ten seconds off the five-day-old world record set by his compatriot Richard Chelimo. Remarkably this was only the second track 10km of Ondieki's career, his previous effort being 28:25.44 in 1983.
While at Iowa State University in the USA he was second in the 1985 NCAA cross-country. He went on to study business administration in Albuquerque. He emerged into world class in 1988, when he was 12th in the Olympic 5000m, and then had a magnificent season in 1989 when he became the first man to beat Saïd Aouita at 5000m for ten years. He fell in the Commonwealth Games 5000m in 1990, but overcame his bad luck in major events with a decisive win in the 1991 World Championships 5000m, after running away from the field on the second lap. A few weeks earlier he had improved the Kenyan 5000m record that he had set at 13:04.24 in 1989 to 13:01.82. He was a little below his best in 1992, when he was 5th in the Olympic 5000m.
Other best times: 1500m 3:34.36 (1990), 1M 3:55.32 (1991), 2000m 5:01.6 (1989), 3000m 7:34.18 (1992).
Yobes married the Australian marathon runner **Lisa Martin** (née O'Dea, b. 12 May 1960 Gawler, South Australia) in February 1990. Lisa won the Commonwealth Games marathon in 1986 and 1990, and the Olympic silver in 1988. She won at Osaka in 1988, when she ran the world's fastest for a loop course, 2:23:51, and at New York in 1992, after 2nd place there in 1985-6 and 3rd in 1991. She had started as a 400m hurdler before turning to distance running. In 1992 she set her fifth Australian 10,000m record at 31:11.72.

Jonjo O'NEILL (Ire)

HORSE RACING

John Joseph O'Neill. b. 13 Apr 1952 Castletownrocke, Cork.

Champion National Hunt jockey in 1977/8, when he set a record with 149 winners, and in 1979/80; in his career 1972-86 he rode 885 winners, three times over 100 in a season.
Apprenticed for three years to Mick Connolly at The Curragh, where in 1970 he rode his first winner. He joined the stable of Gordon W Richards in 1972. He rode *Dawn Run* to her unique double of Champion Hurdle in 1983 and Gold Cup in 1986, and had previously won those races on *Sea Pigeon* in 1980 and *Alverton* in 1979 respectively.
His natural lightness meant that he had few weight problems. Highly popular, he was the first NH jockey to employ an agent. Soon after he retired he had to begin a tremendously courageous battle against cancer, but overcame that to pursue a successful training career.

Norman O'NEILL (Aus)

CRICKET

Norman Clifford O'Neill. b. 19 Feb 1937 Carlton, Sydney.

A brilliant right-handed batsman, even if he could never quite live up to the label of 'the new Bradman' that was given him when he scored 1005 runs at 83.75 in his third season in Australia. He became increasingly nervous and a most uncertain starter, but a glorious stroke-player when set. His highest Test score of 181 was made in the celebrated tie against the West Indies at Brisbane in December 1960, and in 1961, in his first tour to England, he scored 1981 runs at 60.03 in first-class matches. He played for New South Wales and was also a spectacular fielder with a brilliant, long and accurate throw. His retirement, far too early at the age of 30, was hastened by knee trouble.

His son Mark played first-class cricket for Western Australia.

42 Tests 1958-65: 2779 runs at 45.55, 6 100s HS 181; 17 wickets at 39.23, BB 4-41; 21 catches.

First-class 1955-67: 13,859 runs at 50.95, 45 100s HS 284; 99 wickets at 41.01, BB 4-40; 104 catches.

Takashi ONO (Japan)

GYMNASTICS

Takashi Ono. b. 26 Jul 1931 Noshiro, Akita Prefecture.

Ono was unfortunate to be beaten by the narrowest of margins, 0.05 points, for the Olympic all-around title in both 1956 and 1960. He was, however, the winner of Japan's first individual Olympic gold with the horizontal bar 1956, a title he won again in 1960. He also shared, with Boris Shakhlin, the horse vault gold in 1960 and won team gold in 1956 and 1964. He had won a bronze for the horse vault in 1952 and in all won five gold, four silver and four bronze medals at the Olympics.

At World Championships he won four silver medals and a bronze in 1958 and gold on the horizontal bar in 1962.

Bennie OOSTERBAAN (USA)

AMERICAN FOOTBALL

Benjamin Gaylord Oosterbaan. b. 24 Feb 1906 Muskegon, Michigan, d. 25 Oct 1990 Ann Arbor, Michigan.

He played basketball and football at Muskegon High School and was also state high school champion in the discus throw. He went to the University of Michigan where he starred as an end, making All-American three straight years 1925-7. He also played on the Wolverine basketball and baseball team, leading the conference in batting in 1927. Oosterbaan never played pro football, electing instead to become a coach. He became an assistant at Michigan, but was head basketball coach beginning in 1938. In 1948, he became head football coach and led Michigan to a national championship. He coached at Michigan until his retirement in 1958, when he moved into school administration. In 1951 he was selected to the All-Time All-American team as an end.

Bill O'REILLY (Aus)

CRICKET

William Joseph O'Reilly. b. 20 Dec 1905 White Coiffs, New South Wales, d. 6 Oct 1992 Sydney.

'Tiger' O'Reilly was an outstanding contender as the world's best-ever spin bowler. Tall (1.88m *6'2"*) and with a fast bowler's temperament, he could bowl ferociously, his leg breaks, top spinners and googlies often lifting alarmingly from hard pitches, and with great intelligence and control. In an era when the bat tended to dominate, his bowling figures were outstanding and he took 102 wickets in 19 Tests against England.

He made a slow start to his cricket career after his début for New South Wales in 1927, as he first became qualified as a teacher and spent a year or two teaching in the bush before his Test début in 1932. He took 27 wickets in his second Test series, not gaining much notice as it was the 1932/3 'Bodyline' series against England, and throughout the 1930s maintained his consistency. He lost good years due to the War and made his final Test appearance in the first post-War match against New Zealand in 1946, taking 5-14 in the first innings, his 11th 5-wicket haul in Tests. He then became a highly respected journalist for the *Sydney Morning Telegraph*. Awarded the OBE in 1971.

27 Tests 1932-46: 410 runs at 12.81, HS 56; 144 wickets at 22.59, BB 7-54; 7 catches.*

First-class 1927-46: 1665 runs at 13.13, HS 56; 774 wickets at 16.60, BB 9-38; 65 catches.*

Tony O'REILLY (Ire)

RUGBY UNION

Anthony Joseph Francis Kevin O'Reilly. b. 7 May 1936 Dublin.

A strong-running winger with great crowd appeal. After winning 28 caps for Ireland between 1955 and 1963 his international career seemed to be over, but following an injury to the first-choice winger he was recalled seven years later and made his final appearance against England in 1970. His career span of 16 seasons of international rugby has only been matched by Mike Gibson among Irish players.
Although he scored 15 tries for Ireland in the International Championship, O'Reilly really excelled on tours with the British Lions. He played in every Test in South Africa in 1955 and in Australia and New Zealand in 1959, and his six tries in the 10 Tests remains a Lions scoring record.
Well before he gave up playing, he embarked on a highly successful business career to become the 'golden boy' of Irish business, moving on to a world stage. He became president of the Heinz Corporation in the USA in 1979 and is now one of the world's highest paid executives. Additionally, he has substantial investments in a private capacity and is an influential figure in the financial world.

Bobby ORR (Can)

ICE HOCKEY

Robert Gordon Orr. b. 20 Mar 1948 Parry Sound, Ontario.

The best defenseman in the NHL, winning the Norris Trophy a record eight times 1968-75, but he was also the first one ever to be a true offensive threat. He revolutionised ice hockey and his rink-long rushes thrilled fans and resulted in many points for the Boston Bruins.
He led the NHL in scoring to win the Ross Trophy in 1970 and 1975, and in assists five times, setting season's records of 87 in 1969/70 and 102 in 1970/1 (when he achieved his own points best with 139). He assisted the Bruins to Stanley Cup victories in 1970 and 1972, winning the Smythe Trophy as the play-offs MVP in both years. He also won the Hart Trophy as NHL MVP three times, 1970-2.
A tough and vigorous player, he started playing at the age of 4 and began his pro career with the Bruins at 18, the earliest permitted age. His prowess was immediately recognised with the Rookie of the Year trophy for 1966/7. He was Canadian male athlete of the year 1970.
Orr was not huge, but was very strong and was one of the two or three fastest skaters in the league in his early years. However, he had multiple operations for ligament damage to both knees and late in his career he was but a shadow of his early greatness. He was traded to the Chicago Black Hawks for one last attempt at a comeback in 1976/7, but his knees allowed him to play only a few games before retiring. If he had had two good legs, it is likely no player ever would have compared to him.
His nickname among his team-mates was 'Bobby God' and when team-mate Phil Esposito was the game's most prolific scoring machine and to most observers the second best player in the NHL, he commented in a *Sports Illustrated* article that 'I'm not good enough to lace up Bobby Orr's skates.'
NHL career 1966-79: 657 games, 270 goals, 915 points. Lester Pearson Award 1975.

Phil ORR (Ire)

RUGBY UNION

Philip Andrew Orr. b. 14 Dec 1950 Dublin.

The world's most capped prop forward. The first of his 49 consecutive matches for Ireland was against France in 1976 and after this sequence was interrupted in 1986 he won nine further caps to bring his total to a record 58 international appearances. He toured with the British Lions to New Zealand in 1977, when he played in the first Test. He also toured with the 1980 Lions to South Africa but failed to command a place in the Test team. He retired after the 1987 World Cup.
A clothing manufacturer, he went to Trinity College, Dublin and played his club rugby for Old Wesley.

Hans-Henrik ØRSTED (Den)

CYCLING

Hans-Henrik Ørsted. b. 13 Dec 1954 Grenå.

One of the greatest professional pursuiters in history. He turned professional in 1980 and in the next seven years won 3 gold (1984-6), 2 silver, and 2 bronze at the world individual pursuit championships. He set amateur world records outdoors at 4000m 4:40.23, 5000m 5:50.68, 10km 11:54.906, 20km 24:35.63 and 1 hour 48.200 km at high altitude in Mexico City in 1979. Then as a professional in 1985 he improved the 5km time to 5:45.646, which he followed with his greatest ride, shortly after the World Championships, when he broke the low-altitude world hour record, which had stood since 1967, as he recorded 48.144 kilometres. He also set indoor world records at 4km, 5km and 10km as an amateur and twice at 5km as a pro.

Ørsted was also a strong six-day rider, but his size and lack of climbing ability hampered his efforts to turn successfully to the road.

Carlos ORTIZ (PR)

BOXING

Carlos Juan Ortiz. b. 9 Sep 1936 Ponce.

Not possessed of great knock-out power, Ortiz was an excellent boxer who reigned as a world champion for nine years. His first world title came in 1959 when he claimed the NBA light-welterweight championship by stopping Kenny Lane in two. He lost that title in 1960 to Duilio Loi and also lost a re-match to Loi in 1961.

In 1962 Ortiz moved down to the lightweights and won that title, which he held until 1968, continuously except for 1965 when he lost the title and then regained it against Ismael Laguna. Ortiz was stopped only once in his career, that coming in his last fight in 1972 when Ken Buchanan finished him in six.

Career record: W - 61 (30), L - 7, D - 1.

Manuel ORTIZ (USA)

BOXING

Manuel Ortiz. b. 2 Jul 1916 Corona, California, d. 31 May 1970 San Diego, California

Ortiz was born of Mexican parents and began professional boxing in 1938. He won the world bantamweight title in 1942 and held it for eight years with only a short pause in 1947 when he lost it and then regained it from Harold Dade. He lost the title in 1950 to Vic Toweel and then boxed for five more years before retiring in 1955. Ortiz won 21 of his 23 world title fights.

Career record: W - 95 (49), L - 29, D - 3.

Harold OSBORN (USA)

ATHLETICS

(Dr) Harold Marion Osborn. b. 13 Apr 1899 Butler, Illinois, d. 5 Apr 1975 Champaign, Illinois.

The only man to win Olympic titles at both decathlon and an individual event (high jump), with both titles in 1924. In that year he also set world records at high jump, 2.02m and 2.03m, and decathlon, 7710 points (6476 on the current tables). His best high jump was 2.04 (and 2.056 in an exhibition) in 1924.

He tied for the NCAA high jump title while at Illinois in 1922 and in all won 18 AAU titles in six different events, including high jump 1922 and 1925-6, and decathlon 1923, 1925-6; as well as indoors at high jump 1923-6 and at standing long jump 1925-7. He competed well into the 1930s and made his career as an osteopath.

Carl OSBURN (USA)

SHOOTING

Carl Townsend Osburn. b. 5 May 1884 Jacksontown, Ohio, d. 28 Dec 1966 Helena, California.

Winning five gold, four silver and two bronze medals, he is the most successful Olympic marksman of all-time. His record total of 11 medals was accumulated at the Games of 1912, 1920 and 1924, with three of his five gold medals coming in 1920. Essentially a military rifle specialist, he was also an excellent shot with the small bore rifle and in the running deer event. After graduating from the US Naval Academy in 1906 he pursued a naval career and rose to the rank of Commander.

Bennie OSLER (SAf)

RUGBY UNION

Benjamin Louwrens Osler. b. 23 Nov 1901 Aliwal North, d. 23 Apr 1961 Belville.

A tactical fly-half who relied extensively on shrewd kicking. With long kicks to touch or to the corners, he played to the forward strength of the South African team. As long as the Springboks were successful, criticism of his style was restrained but when South Africa decided to run the ball for the Australian visit in 1933, Osler, who was playing under orders, opened up the game at every opportunity - Australia won the series and Osler never played for the Springboks again.
His 17 caps came in consecutive matches 1924-33, during which he scored 2 tries, 6 conversions, 4 penalties and a tally of 4 dropped goals in Test matches which stood as a record until 1951. He was captain of the Springbok team to the British Isles in 1931/2. His brother, Stanley, also won a Springbok cap in 1928.

Micheline OSTERMEYER (Fra)

ATHLETICS

Micheline Ostermeyer. b. 23 Dec 1922 Berck-sur-Mer, Pas-de-Calais.

At the 1948 Olympics she took gold medals for shot and discus and bronze at the high jump. Up against stiffer competition in the European Championships, with the USSR athletes also competing, she was 2nd in the shot in 1946, and third at 80m hurdles and shot in 1950. She would obviously have benefited from multi-event competition, but the pentathlon was not added to the Olympic programme until years later.
She won 12 French titles, six at the shot (1945-8 and 1950-1), two at pentathlon and one each at 60m, 80m hurdles, high jump and discus. Her 18 French records included her bests for high jump 1.61 (1946), shot 13.79 (1948), and discus 44.40 (1950).
She started her athletics career with Orientale Tunis, competing for them 1942-5 and 1947-9, moving to Stade Français 1950-2. She became a distinguished concert pianist.

Nina OTKALENKO (USSR)

ATHLETICS

Nina Otkalenko. née Pletnyova. b. 23 May 1928 Kursk.

She ran seven world records for 800 metres, of which five were ratified, from 2:12.0 in 1951 to 2:05.0 in 1955, but that distance did not return to the Olympics until 1960. She was European champion in 1954 and won four Soviet titles, 1951-4, followed by four second places and a third up to 1960.
She also ran world bests for 400m of 55.5 in 1954 (improving to a pb 55.0 in 1955) and for 1500m of 4:37.0 in 1955, and ran on five world record teams at 4 x 800m relay.

Mel OTT (USA)

BASEBALL

Melvin Thomas Ott. b. 2 Mar 1909 Gretna, Louisiana, d. 21 Nov 1958 New Orleans, Louisiana.

Playing for the New York Giants, mostly in the outfield, Ott was one of the great power hitters in National League history. He did it with a singular style in which he lifted his right leg fully off the ground at least a foot in the air while the pitch was on the way. Ott possessed the requisite perfect timing and very quick wrists. This enabled him to hit 511 home runs in his career, and to lead the National League in hitting six times. He was player-manager of the Giants for his last six seasons and later became a broadcaster.
Career 1926-47: 2876 hits Avg. .304, HR 511; RBI 1860. Best seasons: 1929: .328, 42 HR, 151 RBI; 1930: .349, 25 HR, 119 RBI; 1934: .326, 35 HR, 135 RBI.

Merlene OTTEY (Jam)

ATHLETICS

Merlene Joyce Ottey. b. 10 May 1960 Jamaica.

Consistently in the medals in major championships and ranked in the world's top ten women sprinters each year from 1980 to 1992. She reached her peak when she won 73 successive sprint finals (and 15 heats) from 21 May 1989 to 8 Mar 1991, when beaten by Irina Privalova in the World Indoor 60m. Her unbeaten runs at 100m, 57 consecutive finals from her third place in the 1987 World Championships, and 36 finals at 200m from 6 May 1989, were ended in disappointment at Tokyo in 1991 when she failed to win the expected gold medals at individual events. Third at both, she has a record five bronze medals at World Championships, but returned to her best to anchor the Jamaican team to sprint relay gold. In 1992 she similarly disappointed at the Olympics, where she was fifth at 100m and 3rd at 200m. She had also won Olympic bronze medals at 200m in 1980 and at both 100m and 200m in 1984. She was 4th at 200m when below par through injury in 1988. In the World Championships she won more bronze at both 100m and 200m in 1987, and at the sprint relay in 1983, when she had been 4th at 100m, 2nd at 200m.

At the Commonwealth Games, however, she won three gold medals: 200m 1982, 100m and 200m 1990, with silver at 100m 1982 and bronze at sprint relay in both years. She was also World Indoor champion at 200m in 1989 and 1991 (3rd and 2nd respectively at 60m).

She has set seven Commonwealth records at 200m and five at 100m, 1980-91, with bests of 21.64 and 10.78. In 1990 she set a one year record of seven sub-22.00 200m times and has a record 37 legal times sub-11.00 for 100m to the end of 1992. Indoors she set many world bests at 300 yards (best 32.63 in 1982) and 300m (best 35.83 in 1981), three times at 200m to her 21.87 in 1993, and with 6.96 for 60m in 1992. While at Nebraska University she won NCAA titles outdoors at 100m 1982-3 and 200m 1983. She was TAC champion at 100m 1984-5 and 200m 1982 and 1984-5, and the overall Grand Prix winner in 1987 and 1990. Formerly married to hurdler/high jumper Nat Page (USA), she now competes for Larios of Spain, and lives in Italy with boyfriend Stefano Tilli, the European Indoor champion at 60m in 1983 and 200m in 1985.

Jim OTTO (USA)

AMERICAN FOOTBALL

James Edwin Otto. b. 5 Jan 1938 Wausau, Wisconsin.

Jim Otto was big 'Double Zero', wearing the uniform number '00' for the bulk of his pro career as a center, for the Oakland Raiders 1960-74, having played collegiately at the University of Miami. He was All-Pro in the AFL for all ten years of that league's existence and started every regular season game (210) of his career with the Raiders, despite numerous injuries. He retired after six operations on his right knee when he decided he could not play because of his most recent operation, which involved a total knee replacement. Otto actually wore number 50 for his first pro season and did not switch to the famed Double Zero until 1961.

Kristin OTTO (GDR)

SWIMMING

Kristin Otto. b. 7 Feb 1966 Leipzig.

Otto won six gold medals at the 1988 Olympics, a women's record at one Games for any sport. She demonstrated unique versatility by winning 100m titles at three strokes: freestyle, backstroke and butterfly as well as golds at the 50m freestyle and 4 x 100m freestyle and medley relays. She had won the same events, except the 50m, at the 1987 Europeans, having placed second at 100m freestyle and won golds on both freestyle relay teams in 1983.

At the World Championships she won three gold medals in 1982, 100m backstroke and both freestyle and medley relays; and four gold medals, 100m freestyle, 200m individual medley and both 4 x 100m relays, in 1986, when she also took silver at 50m freestyle. On the first leg of the 4 x 100m freestyle she was

timed in 54.73, a time which beat the six year-old world record of Barbara Krause, and which itself was unbeaten for nearly six years. She also set a world record at 200m freestyle with 1:57.75 in 1984.
Other bests, in 1988 except where shown: 50m freestyle 25.49; backstroke: 50m 29.12 (European record), 100m 60.89, 200m 2:11.82 (1982); 100m butterfly 59.00 (European record), 200m IM 2:15.56 (1986). In a short-course 25m pool she became the first woman to break the minute barrier for 100m backstroke, with 59.97 in 1983.
After her multiple medal efforts the powerful Otto, 1.85m tall and weighing 70 kg, had a quiet time at the 1989 Europeans, restricting herself to just two events - and two gold medals - at 100m backstroke and medley relay.
She started swimming at the age of six and, as customary for top East German hopes, started sports school at 11. Her first GDR senior title was at 100m backstroke in 1982. Now coaches in Hanover and commentates on German TV.

Francis OUIMET (USA)

GOLF

Francis Desales Ouimet. b. 8 May 1893 Brookline, Massachusetts, d. 3 Sep 1967 Wellesley, Massachusetts.

Ouimet's fame rests primarily on his victory in the 1913 US Open, when he was an amateur well-known only in Massachusetts. He was persuaded to enter the Open, which was scheduled at The Country Club in Brookline, near his home, only at the last moment, but he went on to tie for the championship with Britain's favoured Harry Vardon and Ted Ray. In the play-off, Ouimet won quite easily and his victory is often credited with starting the golf boom in the United States.
He won the US Amateur title in 1914 and 1931 and was a member of every Walker Cup team from 1922 to 1934, with a playing record of 8 wins, 5 losses and 2 halves, before being non-playing captain from then until 1949. In 1951 he was the first non-British national to be elected captain of the Royal and Ancient Golf Club.

Steve OVETT (UK)

ATHLETICS

Steven Michael James Ovett. b. 9 Oct 1955 Brighton.

Brilliant middle-distance runner, who led the way for the British domination of these events in the 1970s and 1980s. He competed at three Olympic Games, winning the gold medal at 800m in 1980, when he was also third at 1500m.
He started his championship success at 400m with the English Schools Junior title in 1970 and AAA Youth titles in 1971 and 1972, and emerged internationally in 1973 when he won the European Junior 800m. In 1974 he set a European junior record and took silver against his seniors in the European Championships. He was fifth in the 1976 Olympic 1500m and took a second European 800m silver in 1978 before winning the 1500m title and thereafter concentrating on longer distances, winning 45 successive races at 1500m or 1 mile 1977-80. Indeed he seemed unbeatable at that time, with a devastating win in the 1977 World Cup 1500m in Düsseldorf. However, it was at his original distance of 800m that he took Olympic gold, only to lose to Coe at 1500m.
Ovett had professed himself uninterested in records, which went regularly to Coe, but in 1980-1 he gave chase and set three world records at 1500m and two at 1 mile. He lost the 1982 season due to a training accident when he impaled his thigh on some church railings, but came back in 1983 to take fourth place in the World 1500m. He was very disappointed with that and determined to do better at the 1984 Olympics, but there he suffered severe bronchial problems and had to trail in last at 800m and pull out of the 1500m final. He won the UK 1500m 1977 and 1981 and AAA 800m 1974-6, 1500m 1979-80. Awarded MBE in the New Year Honours 1982.
He was able to compete outstandingly at a wide range, but the longer distances did not hold the same attraction for him, although at 5000m he won the 1986 Commonwealth title. His final major championship appearance was 10th in the 1987 World 5000m. Now settled in

Scotland, he is a regular commentator on athletics for ITV.
Best times: 800m 1:44.09 (1978), 1000m 2:15.91 (1979), 1500m 3:31.36 (1980), 1 mile 3:48.40 (1981), 2000m 4:57.71 (1982), 3000m 7:41.3 (1977), 2 miles 8:13.51 (1978, world best), 5000m 13:20.06 (1986).

Dicky OWEN (UK)

RUGBY UNION
Richard Morgan Owen. b. 17 Nov 1876 Llandore, Swansea, d. 27 Feb 1932 Swansea. Although always known as Owen, his birth was actually registered as Owens.

A scrum-half with Swansea whose 35 international appearances for Wales between 1901-12 remained a record until beaten by Ken Jones in 1955. He was first choice for Wales during their first 'Golden Era' and was in the team which won the Triple Crown four times and the Championship on two other occasions. Always an innovative player, it was his unorthodox pass which led to the Welsh try when they beat the 1905 All Blacks 3-0. A steelworker and later a licensee, he took his own life.

Steve OWEN (USA)

AMERICAN FOOTBALL
Stephen Joseph Owen. b. 21 Apr 1898 Cleo Springs, Oklahoma, d. 17 May 1964 New York.

Having grown up in Indian Territory in Oklahoma, Owen attended Phillips University in 1917-8, where he was the football team's star tackle and captain both years. He then worked in the Oklahoma oil fields, but joined the NFL in 1924 with the Kansas City Cowboys. He played for parts of the next ten seasons with various teams and became a star tackle. From 1931 to 1953 he coached the New York Giants (serving as player-coach in 1931 and 1933). In this time the Giants won eight conference titles and two NFL Championships. He was known as a great innovator and in 1950 he introduced the umbrella defense, a forerunner of the 4-3-4 defense which was standard by the late 1950s. Owen was released by the Giants in 1953, but later coached in college at Baylor, in the Canadian League and briefly as an assistant with the Philadelphia Eagles.

Jesse OWENS (USA)

ATHLETICS
James Cleveland Owens. b. 12 Sep 1913 Decatur, Alabama, d. 31 Mar 1980 Tucson, Arizona.

Three unsurpassed achievements top the list of honours in the brilliant career of Jesse Owens: he won four gold medals at the 1936 Olympic Games, 100 and 200m, long jump and sprint relay; he set six world records in one day; and his world long jump record lasted for 25 years 79 days.
Owens won his first national title with the AAU long jump in 1933, and repeated that win in 1934 and 1936, adding the 100m in 1936 and indoor long jump in 1934 and 1935. While at Ohio State University he won the NCAA titles at each of 100y/m, 200m/220y, 220y hurdles and long jump in both 1935 and 1936. Indoors Owens equalled the world bests for 60 yards at 6.1 (twice) and 60m with 6.6 in 1935 and made three improvements on the long jump best in 1934-5.
His day of world records was at Ann Arbor on 25 May 1935 in the Big Ten Championships, when within one hour he contested four events and set six records. He had started the day worried about a sore back, but the pain left him when the gun went for the first event. His programme was: 3.15pm - 100 yards in 9.4, 3.25pm - long jump of 8.13m *26' 8 1/4"*, 3.45pm - 220y in 20.3 (also a record for 200m), 4.00pm - 220 yards hurdles in 22.6 (also record for 200m). This is also the only occasion on which an athlete has set a track and a field record on the same day. The 100 yards time of 9.4 was the fourth of six times that Owens equalled this world record, but the first to be ratified as a record. The long jump was the first ever 8 metre jump, and was not bettered until Ralph Boston did 8.21m in 1960. Owens

twice more exceeded 8m, including 8.06 at the 1936 Olympic Games and jumped 26 ft *7.92m* or more 15 times in 1935-6, yet it was 12 years before any other athlete exceeded that distance more than once. Owens also set world records in 1936 for 100m at 10.2 and three at the Olympic Games in Berlin: 20.7 for 200m (round a turn) and twice at 4 x 100m relay for the USA.
After running in some post-Olympic meetings in Europe, Owens ended his amateur career at the age of 23. He travelled extensively as a popular speaker and was a great gentleman and example to all.

Elvira OZOLINA (USSR/Lat)

ATHLETICS

Elvira Anatolijevna Ozolina. b. 8 Oct 1939 Leningrad (St Petersburg). Later Lusis, then Baslina.

Olympic javelin champion in 1960 and European in 1962, she set four world records from 57.92m in 1960 to 61.38m in 1964, although the latter was not ratified by the IAAF.
After such a brilliant start to her career she faded somewhat in relative standings and was fifth in the 1964 Olympics and 1966 Europeans, but added a fifth Soviet title in 1973 to those won in 1961-2, 1964 and 1966. Her best throw was a Latvian record 63.96m in 1973, nine years after her final world record.
Her family had moved in the days of Tsarist Russia from Isikula in Latvia to St Petersburg. After marrying the great javelin thrower Janis Lusis she came to live in Riga.

Darrell PACE (USA)

ARCHERY

Darrell Owen Pace. b. 23 Oct 1956 Cincinnati, Ohio.

The world's top archer in the 1970s and early 1980s. He was US Champion seven times, 1972-6, 1978 and 1984, and first competed internationally in 1973, finishing 23rd at the World Championships. By 1975 he held every world record and he won the world title in 1975 and 1979, when he set a FITA single round record of 1341 which lasted for ten years. He also won five team gold medals with the US team 1975-83. In 1976 he set new best ever figures for FITA double rounds with his 2570 at the US Olympic Trials and 2571 when he won the Olympic gold. He went on to further Olympic triumphs, although he had to miss the 1980 Games when he would have battled team-mate Rick McKinney for the title. In 1984 McKinney was more highly rated, but Pace won the gold medal at Los Angeles. He broke all five Olympic records in 1976 and 1984. In 1988, Pace was 9th individually but helped the United States win a silver medal in the team round at Seoul. He was also world indoor record holder with a score of 588 at 18m and won gold medals at team and individual at the 1991 Pan-American Games, having won the individual silver in 1979.
From 1976 to 1981 he was a systems specialist on electronics and computers for the US Air Force, and is now a radio technical supervisor for the Ohio Department of National Resources.

Ann PACKER (UK)

ATHLETICS

Ann Elizabeth Packer. b. 2 Mar 1942 Moulsford, Berkshire. Later Brightwell.

In 1964 at the Tokyo Olympics she sealed her athletics career with a storybook win at 800 metres in a world record time of 2:01.1 in her first year at the event. She had been favoured to win the 400m, but although she ran a European record time of 52.20 she had to settle for the silver behind Betty Cuthbert, while her fiancé **Robbie Brightwell** (b. 27 Oct 1939) had been disappointed with his fourth place in the men's 400m. After her success Robbie went on to gain a silver medal at 4x400m. They were married after the Games and Ann retired at the age of 22. Both were awarded the MBE in 1969.
Their son Gary was a useful 400m runner, and his two younger brothers Ian and David became professional footballers with Manchester City, Ian playing for England Schools, Youths and Under-21.

Ann's athletic success had started with the English Schools 100y title in 1959 and she won WAAA titles at long jump 1960 and 440y 1964. In 1962 she surprised by reaching the final of the European 200m and later that year she was 6th at 80m hurdles and took a silver medal in the sprint relay at the Commonwealth Games. She reached world class when she moved up to 400m in 1963.
Other bests: 100m 11.7w/12.0 (1960), 200m 23.7 (1964), 80mh 11.4 (1960), LJ 5.92m (1960).

Charles PADDOCK (USA)

ATHLETICS

Charles William Paddock. b. 11 Aug 1900 Gainesville, Texas, d. 21 Jul 1943 Sitka, Alaska.

Famed for his leap across the finish line of sprint races, which caught the eye of the judges even if it did not gain him territorial advantage, Paddock was the Olympic champion at 100m and sprint relay in 1920, and also took the silver medal at 200m in both 1920 and 1924. At a third Olympics in 1928 he did not qualify for the 200m final. He was AAU champion at 220y in 1920 and at both 100y and 220y in 1921 and 1924.
He came to prominence in winning the Inter-Allied 100m in 1919 and went on to attend the University of Southern California. In all he set 19 world records, of which 11 were officially ratified. He ran the 100y seven times in 9.6, but his most startling achievement was when he ran the 110 yards in 10 $^{1}/_{5}$ at Pasadena on 18 Jun 1921. Officials did not put the time forward for ratification as the 100m record because the distance at 100.58m was too long! His other record bests: 220y straight 20.8 (1921 and 1924), 300y 30.2 (1921), 300m 33.2 (1921). He also set a world record with the 1920 US 4 x 100m team in 1920.
He died in a plane crash when serving as a captain in the Marines in World War II.

Sabine PAETZ (GDR), see JOHN.

Alan PAGE (USA)

AMERICAN FOOTBALL

Alan C. Page. b. 7 Aug 1945 Canton, Ohio.

One of the great defensive ends in football history. He was quite small for a defensive lineman in the 1970s, but made up for his lack of size with tremendous quickness. He played college ball at Notre Dame and played for the Minnesota Vikings from 1967-77, helping make up the famed Purple People Eater defense. He made All-Pro every year 1970-7. Page became a long-distance runner during his career and completed a marathon in the mid-70s, dropping his weight from 110 kg *244 lb* to as low as 95 kg *210 lb*. This caused the Vikings to trade him to the Bears as they thought he was too small to be effective. While playing pro football, Page also went to law school in the off-season and earned his degree from the University of Minnesota in 1978. After he retired from football in 1981 he began a law practice. In 1992, Page ran for and was elected to a seat on the Minnesota Supreme Court, making him the first black man to earn such a position in the state.

Satchel PAIGE (USA)

BASEBALL

Leroy Robert Paige. b. 7 Jul 1906 Mobile, Alabama.

Satchel Paige is considered by many experts as the greatest pitcher in baseball history, but the archaic prohibition against blacks in the major leagues prevented him from having the stage he needed to show off his skills. He began pitching in the Negro Leagues in 1926 and had a 22-year career with various teams. He did not reach the major leagues until he was 42 years old and by then he was well past his prime. His greatest legacy was the many exhibition games he pitched against major league all-star teams, prompting Joe DiMaggio to label him as 'The best I've faced and the fastest.' In exhibition games, he was famous for calling in his outfield and striking out the side. Unfortunately records from the Negro Leagues are very sketchy, leaving only the legend to be most of what we know about Satchel Paige, probably baseball's greatest victim of racial discrimination.

Lyudmila PAKHOMOVA (USSR)

ICE DANCE

Lyudmila Alekseyevna Pakhomova. b. 31 Dec 1946 Moscow, d. 17 May 1986 Moscow. Later Gorshkov.

With her husband Aleksandr Gorshkov she won the first Olympic gold medal for ice dancing in 1976 and a record six world titles, 1970-4 and 1976. They also won the European title six times. After the 1976 Olympics she retired and took over direction of the ballet trainers' section of the Institute of Theatrical Arts of which she was herself a graduate. She died at the early age of 39 after a long illness.

Sarah PALFREY (USA)

TENNIS

Sarah Hammond Palfrey. b. 18 Sep 1912 Sharon, Massachusetts. Later Fabyan, then Cooke, then Danzig.

An outstanding doubles player who won nine US women's doubles titles (1930, 1932, 1934-5, 1937-41) and was the Wimbledon champion with Alice Marble in 1938 and 1939. Apart from her successes in the women's doubles she won the US singles in 1941 and 1945 and was runner-up to Helen Jacobs in 1934 and 1935, and won the US mixed doubles four times (1932, 1935, 1937, 1941) as well as the French mixed doubles in 1939.
Coming from a large tennis-playing family with their own court, all five Palfrey sisters won at least one national junior championship but only Sarah distinguished herself in the senior ranks. Throughout her career she was coached by Hazel Hotchkiss. The strength of her doubles play was her excellent volleying but she also had a fine backhand and this combination kept her in the top flight for many years. She was ranked No.4 in the US as early as 1929 and in 1945 she was No.1 before she relinquished her amateur status the following year. She married three times, firstly in 1934 to Marshall Fabyan Jr, then in 1940 to T Elwood Cooke, and finally in 1951 to Jerry Danzig, a radio and television executive and a special assistant to Governor Rockefeller.

Arnold PALMER (USA)

GOLF

Arnold Daniel Palmer. b. 10 Sep 1929 Latrobe, Pennsylvania.

Undoubtedly the most popular golfer of all time. Now in his sixties, he still plays on the PGA Senior Tour and usually is accompanied by the largest galleries, the remainder of 'Arnie's Army' of his youth. Palmer was popular for his style and charisma, which showed his expressions, whether happy or sad, to their fullest. His style was one of all-out attack, as he was a muscular, attractive young man who drove the ball a long way. He always went for the pin and for birdies, and early in his career he managed several spectacular come-from-behind victories, which earned the sobriquet of 'Palmer's Charges'. He was a gracious loser as well, and he had to suffer the disappointment of never winning the PGA Championship and being runner-up four times in the US Open.
Palmer was the first player to win over $1 million on the PGA tour and made a fortune off the course as well because his manner and popularity made him so attractive to advertisers. Even in 1990, Palmer was still considered by US business magazines to make the most money among athletes from commercial endorsements. Despite his popularity, fortune, and skill, he was very popular among his fellow professionals; this was certainly due to the fact that Palmer always treated them with respect and as friends, and also because much of the great increase in golf purses in the 1960s and 1970s was due to Palmer's charismatic television personality.
Major victories: US Open 1960; British Open 1961-2; Masters 1958, 1960, 1962, 1964; World Match Play 1964, 1967; US Amateur 1954.
PGA career earnings 1955-92: $1,902,698 with 60 victories.

Jim PALMER (USA)

BASEBALL

James Alvin Palmer. b. 15 Oct 1945 New York.

Palmer pitched for 19 years in the major leagues, all with the Baltimore Orioles. He retired after the 1984 season but attempted an ill-fated comeback in 1991, after his election to the Hall of Fame. He was the top American League pitcher of the 1970s, winning 20 games eight times. In his last few years he had difficulty with arm problems. He won the Cy Young award in 1973, 1975-6 and led the league in wins 1975-7 and in ERA 1973 and 1975. Since his retirement he has become a television announcer and a model, using his lithe body in underwear advertisements.
Career pitching: ERA 2.86; W-L 268-152, SO 2212. Best seasons: 1970: 20-10, 2.71 ERA; 1971: 20-9; 2.68 ERA; 1972: 21-10, 2.07 ERA; 1973: 22-9, 2.40 ERA; 1975: 23-11, 2.09 ERA; 1976: 22-13, 2.51 ERA; 1977: 20-11, 2.91 ERA; 1978: 21-12, 2.46 ERA.

Kristjan PALUSALU (Est)

WRESTLING

Kristjan Palusalu. b. 10 Mar 1908, d. 17 Jul 1987.

Palusalu can claim, more than any other wrestler, that for one year he was the ultimate wrestling champion. In that year, 1936, he won Olympic gold in the unlimited class at both Greco-Roman and freestyle. Ivar Johansson and Källe Anttila also won Olympic gold in both styles of wrestling, but only Johansson in the same year. Palusalu won only one other major title, the 1937 European championship in Greco-Roman. He was voted Estonia's greatest sportsman of all-time in 1991.

Abdon PAMICH (Italy)

WALKING

Abdon Pamich. b. 3 Oct 1933 Fiume.

Excelled at the 50km walk at which he was Olympic champion in 1964 and European champion in 1962 and 1966 (2nd 1958). He competed at five Olympic Games in all, 1956-72, with 3rd in 1960 and 4th in 1956 at 50km, and amassed 40 Italian titles at various distances. He set a world track record at 4:14:02.4 in 1961 and a road 50km best of 4:03:02 in 1960.

Robert PAPAREMBORDE (Fra)

RUGBY UNION

Robert Paparemborde. b. 5 Jul 1948 Luruns.

An immensely powerful prop who was the strength in the French front row for nine seasons. Between 1975 and 1983 he played in 55 internationals, which remains the record for a French prop, and with eight international tries he holds the world scoring record for a prop forward.

Jean-Pierre PAPIN (Fra)

FOOTBALL

Jean-Pierre Papin. b. 5 Nov 1963 Boulogne-sur-Mer.

European Footballer of the Year in 1991 and the inspiration of the Marseille team which won four consecutive French league titles in 1989-92. Papin was the leading goalscorer in France in each of those years and scored 102 goals 1988-92. He started his career with INF Vichy, then had spells with Valenciennes and the Belgian club FC Brugge before joining Marseille in 1986. He was transferred to AC Milan for £10 million in the summer of 1992 and helped them to win the Italian league in 1992/3. He made his international début for France in 1986 and played in the team that was third in the World Cup that year. To November 1992 he scored 21 goals in 37 appearances for the national team.

László PAPP (Hun)

BOXING

László Papp. b. 25 Mar 1926 Budapest.

Papp is, with Téofilo Stevenson, one of the two Olympic boxers to win three consecutive gold medals. He was so renowned in Hungary that, having won three Olympic titles (middleweight 1948 and light-middleweight 1952 and 1956), he was allowed

to turn professional, the only professional from a Communist country until the era of *glasnost* in the late 1980s. The southpaw quickly established the same dominance among professionals, winning the European middleweight title in 1962. By 1965, Papp was in line for a world title fight, but the Hungarian authorities recanted and stopped him from fighting any more as a pro. He was forced to relinquish his European crown and retire from professional boxing. He had won European amateur titles in 1949 and 1951. For two decades, 1971-92, he was a successful chief coach of the Hungarian national team.
Career record: W - 26 (15), L - 0, D - 3.

Bernie PARENT (Can)

ICE HOCKEY
Bernard Marcel Parent. b. 3 Apr 1945 Montreal, Québec.

Began his NHL career with the Boston Bruins and later played with the Toronto Maple Leafs and then the Philadelphia Blazers of the WHA, but Parent is best remembered as the goalie for the Philadelphia Flyers in the late 1960s and early 70s, winning the Stanley Cup in both 1974 and 1975. Parent was beloved of Philadelphia fans who were often seen with a bumper sticker on their cars which said, 'Only the Lord Saves More than Bernie Parent!'
Career 1965-79 - 671 games, 2.55 GAA, 57 shutouts. NHL 608 games, 2.55 GAA, 55 shutouts. Vezina Trophy and Smythe Trophy 1974-5.

Vladimir PARFENOVICH (USSR/Bls)

CANOEING
Vladimir Parfenovich. b. 2 Dec 1958 Minsk.

Set a record by winning three Olympic gold medals for canoeing at one Games in 1980, when he won the kayak singles at 500m and the pairs with Sergey Chukray at both 500m and 1000m. Including these events he won world titles at K1 500m 1979-83, K2 500m 1979-82 and K2 1000m 1980-2. He won his first Soviet title at K1 in 1977.

Brad PARK (Can)

ICE HOCKEY
Douglas Bradford Park. b. 6 Jul 1948 Toronto, Ontario.

One of the greatest defensemen ever to play in the NHL. Unfortunately, he never won a Norris Trophy (symbolising the top defenseman in the league) because his career clashed with that of Bobby Orr. Park played for the New York Rangers 1968-75, Boston Bruins 1975-83, and the Detroit Red Wings 1983-5. He was the consummate defensive player, possibly even superior to Orr, but Orr was also skilled on the attack. Park was first-team All-NHL in 1970, 1972, 1974, and 1976, but he never had the good fortune to skate for a Stanley Cup winner in his 17-year career.
NHL career 1968-85 - 1113 games, 213 goals, 896 points. Play-offs: 161 games, 90 assists, 125 points. Best year: 1973/4: 25 goals, 82 points.

PARK Joo-bong (SKo)

BADMINTON
Park Joo-bong. b. 5 Dec 1964.

The winner of a record number of world titles at badminton, with the men's doubles in 1985 and 1991 and the mixed doubles with Yoo Sang-hee in 1985 and with Chung Myung-hee in 1989 and 1991. His doubles expertise was further shown by four All-England titles at men's doubles and four at mixed doubles, all with Chung Myung-hee, 1986, 1989-91. In 1992 he won the Olympic doubles title with Kim Moon-soo. Tall and speedy, with a whiplash smash, he made his Thomas Cup début in 1982.

Ace PARKER (USA)

AMERICAN FOOTBALL
Clarence McKay Parker. b. 17 May 1913 Portsmouth, Virginia.

He helped to establish the legend of the Iron Dukes when he was a single-wing quarterback at Duke University 1934-6. A tremendous all-round athlete, Parker lettered in basketball one year for Duke and also starred for the baseball team in left field for three years. After college, Parker played in the NFL 1937-46 (missing a few years in the middle for military service), for the Brooklyn Dodgers, Boston Yanks, and New York Yankees (All-American Football Conference). Although probably a better college player, he was eventually elected to both the College and Professional Football Halls of Fame. He also played infield for two years 1938-9 with the Philadelphia Athletics at baseball. After his playing career ended he became an assistant football coach at Duke and later served as their head baseball coach.

Charlie PARKER (UK)

CRICKET

Charles Warrington Leonard Parker. b. 14 Oct 1882 Prestbury, Gloucestershire, d. 11 Jul 1959 Cranleigh, Surrey.

The total of 3278 wickets taken by this slow-medium left-arm bowler, who spun the ball fiercely, is the third highest of all-time in first-class cricket, yet he played only one Test Match. His chances were perhaps not helped by the fact that he was strongly opinionated. He made his début for Gloucestershire in 1903, but it was not until 1920, when he was 37, that he first took 100 wickets in a season; however, he did so every year from then until 1935, with more than 200 in 1922, 1924-6 and 1931. On retiring at the age of 52, he turned to golf, at which he was a fine player.
1 Test 1921: 3 runs, HS 3; 2 wickets at 16.00, BB 2-32.*
First-class 1903-35: 7951 runs at 10.48, HS 82; 3278 wickets at 19.46, BB 10-79; 248 catches.

Frank PARKER (USA)

TENNIS

Frank Andrew Parker. b. 31 Jan 1916 Milwaukee, Wisconsin. né Franciszek Andrzej Paikowski.

Although possessing a fine backhand he lacked power on the forehand and his game was particularly well suited to the slower clay courts. Ranked in the top ten in America for 17 consecutive years 1933-49, he won the US doubles in 1943 and the singles in 1944 and 1945. He also won the French singles in 1948-9 but never won the singles at Wimbledon where his best performance was to reach the semi-finals in 1937. He was, however, the Wimbledon men's doubles champion with Pancho Gonzales in 1949, and they also won the French title that year before both turning professional. Parker had a fine Davis Cup record, losing only two of the 14 singles matches he played between 1937 and 1948. Although he did not have an armoury of powerful shots, his game was noted for his command of length and control.

Jack PARKER (UK)

SPEEDWAY

Jack Parker. b. 9 Oct 1908 Aston Manor, Warwickshire.

A great speedway rider whose career stretched from 1928 to the 1950s. He was runner-up in the British final of the first Star Championship in 1929 and won this title in 1934. In the World Championships he was fourth in 1939, but had to wait until the competition started again in 1949 for his next chance. Then he came second to Tommy Price, after being slowly away in the crucial heat against his great rival. He had a record seven British Match Race wins between 1932 and 1951 and was British Riders Champion in 1947. He rode in the first England v Australia Test match in 1930 and by the early post-war years had amassed more points in Tests than any other English rider.
Parker joined BSA in 1927, working in their experimental department, later designing and producing their speedway machines. His brother **Norman** (b. 14 Jan 1910) was also a speedway international.

Jim PARKER (USA)

AMERICAN FOOTBALL

James Thomas Parker. b. 3 Apr 1934 Macon, Georgia.

The first modern prototype of an offensive lineman, combining size with great speed and quickness. He played college football at Ohio State, graduating in 1957, and spent his entire 11-year NFL career with the Baltimore Colts. He started at offensive tackle but moved to guard in his last four seasons. He played in eight Pro Bowl games and helped the Colts to win five conference championships and two NFL titles.

Jonty PARKIN (UK)

RUGBY LEAGUE

Jonathan Parkin. b. 5 Nov 1897 Sharlston, Yorkshire, d. 9 Apr 1972 Wakefield, Yorkshire.

During a 10-year international career he won 17 Great Britain caps and was the first man to make three tours of Australasia (1920, 1924 and 1928, the last two as captain). Although injured for much of the 1928 tour, his qualities of leadership played a major part in Britain's entirely unexpected victory in the Test series against both Australia and New Zealand. After joining Wakefield Trinity as a boy of 15, he remained with the club for 17 years before asking for a transfer in 1930. As Wakefield were anxious to retain his services they demanded what they thought was an unacceptably high transfer fee for a player nearing the end of his career. Parkin paid the fee out of his own pocket, declared himself a free agent and signed for Hull Kingston Rovers. Wakefield and the League authorities were outraged by this early example of 'player power' and the rules were changed to prohibit players paying their own transfer fees.
An astute and resilient scrum half, he had a fine tactical brain, but his brilliant leadership was perhaps his finest quality.

Nawab of Pataudi (Ind) see MANSUR ALI KHAN

Riccardo PATRESE (Italy)

MOTOR RACING

Riccardo Patrese. b. 17 Apr 1954 Padua.

With 250 starts from 1977 to the end of 1993 he has contested more Formula One Grand Prix races than any other driver. He has totalled 272 points, with six wins: just Monaco 1982 and South Africa 1983 before 1991, when he had his best season with three wins and third place in the World Drivers' Championship, matching his 1989 place, and 1992 when he was runner-up to his Williams team-mate Nigel Mansell in the Championship and won the Japanese GP.
At karting he raced from the age of 12 and was world champion in 1973-4. He was the FIA European F3 champion in a Chevron-Toyota in 1976 and in 1982 was second in the World Endurance Championship for Lancia. He made his Grand Prix début for Shadow in 1977, and drove for Arrows 1978-81, Brabham 1982-3 and 1986-7, Alfa 1984-5, Williams 1987-92, Benetton 1993.
Aggressive in his early days, he became one of the steadiest drivers on the circuit.

Floyd PATTERSON (USA)

BOXING

Floyd Patterson. b. 4 Jan 1935 Waco, North Carolina

Patterson won the middleweight gold medal at the 1952 Olympics. Trained by Cus D'Amato, he had established an excellent amateur record, as in 1951-2 he had won six major amateur titles, including the National AAU and New York Golden Gloves championships. Less than a month after the Games, Patterson fought his first professional fight against Eddie Godbold and knocked him out in four rounds. He grew out of the middleweight class, and although light for a heavyweight, on 30 Nov 1956 he defeated light-heavyweight champion Archie Moore for the vacant world title, then, at 21 years 10 months, the youngest ever heavyweight champion. In 1959 he lost his title to Ingemar Johansson, who knocked him out in three rounds, but on 20 Jun 1960 he became the first man to regain the heavyweight crown when he knocked out Johansson in the fifth round. Patterson defended the title twice before losing by KO in the first to Sonny Liston. He fought twice more for the unified title, against Liston and then Muhammad Ali, but he was knocked out both times. He also lost a WBA heavyweight title bout

in 1968 against Jimmy Ellis. He then retired before returning in 1970 to win nine fights, before being stopped by Ali in seven rounds on 20 Sep 1972.
Career record: W - 55 (40), L - 8, D - 1.

Gerald PATTERSON (Aus)

TENNIS

Gerald Leighton Patterson. b. 17 Dec 1895 Preston, Melbourne, Victoria, d. 13 Jun 1967 Melbourne.

The leading player in the post-World War I era, he won the Wimbledon singles at his first attempt in 1919. The following year he lost to Bill Tilden in the 1920 Challenge Round but had the consolation of winning the mixed doubles. Patterson did not come to Europe in 1921 but he recaptured his title in 1922 after the abolition of the Challenge Round to become the first Wimbledon champion to 'play through'. At home he was runner-up in the Australian singles in 1914, 1922 and 1925 and won the title for the only time in 1927. He had a better record in the doubles, being the Australian champion five times, 1914, 1922, 1925-7 and winning the US doubles in 1919.
Between 1919 and 1928 he played in 16 Davis Cup ties, winning 21 of 31 singles and 11 of 15 doubles, and was the non-playing captain of the Australian team in 1946. With his big serve and forceful net play he was the first Australian power player. After winning an MC in World War I, he was appointed a representative for the sporting equipment firm, A.G.Spalding, in 1920 and by 1935 had risen to become managing director of their Australian subsidiary. He inherited a considerable fortune from his parents and from his mother's sister, opera singer Dame Nellie Melba, and he became one of Australia's most successful businessmen, serving on the Board of many Public Companies.

Rodney PATTISSON (UK)

YACHTING

Rodney Stuart Pattisson. b. 15 Aug 1943 Campbeltown, Argyleshire.

Britain's most successful Olympic yachtsman who won medals in the Flying Dutchman class with different partners on each of his three Olympic appearances. He won Olympic gold in 1968 (with Iain MacDonald-Smith) and 1972 (with Chris Davies), and took the silver in 1976 (with Julian Brooke-Houghton). During this period, he was unrivalled in the Flying Dutchman class and was World and European champion from 1968 to 1972. He was awarded the MBE for his Olympic successes. After his victory in 1968 he resigned his commission in the Navy and joined a boat building firm which allowed him more time for training than his naval duties had permitted. In 1983 he was co-skipper of *Victory*, Peter de Savary's entry in the America's Cup.

Mel PATTON (USA)

ATHLETICS

Melvin Emery Patton. b. 16 Nov 1924 Los Angeles.

After two world record-equalling times of 9.4 for 100 yards, Patton became the first man to run the distance in 9.3 at the West Coast Relays on 15 May 1948. Later that year he won the US Olympic Trials for 200m in a world best around a turn of 20.7. The clear Olympic favourite, he disappointed with 5th place at 100m but won gold at 200m and 4x100m relay. A nervous runner, he never entered the AAU Championships but won each NCAA title he contested for the University of Southern California, the 100y or 100m 1947-9 and 200m/220y 1948-9. In 1949 in the USC-UCLA dual meet he ran the 100y in a wind-assisted 9.1 and then, with the wind below the allowable limit, set a world record for 220 yards straight with 20.2. He also twice ran on USC world record-setting 4 x 220 yards relay teams in 1949 and only lost three races in his years of sprinting dominance 1947-9.

Budge PATTY (USA)

TENNIS

John Edward Patty. b. 11 Feb 1924 Fort Smith, Arkansas.

After winning the US Junior title, Patty

served with the Army in Europe and won the Allied Forces tournament in Marseilles in 1945. He decided to settle in Paris and never returned to America to live, although he returned occasionally to play in selected tournaments. He was a quarter-finalist in the singles at the US championships in 1951, 1953 and 1957 and his best performance in the doubles was to reach the final in 1957. He made his only Davis Cup appearance in 1951 when he won both his singles and the doubles against Canada in Montreal.

He was at his best in Europe, winning both the French singles and Wimbledon in 1950, the German title in 1953-4 and the Italian in 1954. His duels with Jaroslav Drobny captured the public imagination and produced some of the classic matches of the era. The most notable came in the third round at Wimbledon in 1953 when Drobny won in five sets in a match which lasted a then record total of 93 games. In the doubles Patty won the French mixed in 1946, and at Wimbledon in 1957 the 33-year-old Patty and his 43-year-old partner, Gardnar Mulloy, claimed a stunning victory in the men's doubles when they beat the great Australians Neale Fraser and Lew Hoad in the final.

Patty had one of the most effective forehand volleys in the history of the game, and his fluent all-round game and good looks made him a great favourite of the crowd. During his years in Paris he was a prominent member of the social set and was the escort of many international beauties. He later moved to Switzerland where he developed a successful business.

Ivan PATZAICHIN (Rom)

CANOEING

Ivan Patzaichin. b. 26 Nov 1949 Tulcea.

Shares the men's record for World and Olympic titles at Canadian canoeing, with 13 in all. At the Olympics he won seven medals: gold at 1000m in 1968, 1980 and 1984 at C2 and in 1972 at C1, with silvers at 1000m C2 in 1972 and at 500m C2 in 1980 and 1984. He was partnered by Serghei Covaliov in 1968 and 1972, by Petre Capusta at 500m in 1980 and by Toma Simionov at 1000m in 1980 and in 1984. His world titles were at C2 500m 1979, C2 1000m 1970, 1973, 1981; C1 1000m 1977, C1 10,000m 1978. He competed for Dinamo Bucharest.

Axel PAULSEN (Nor)

FIGURE and SPEED SKATING

Axel Rudolf Paulsen. b. 18 Jul 1855 Aker, d. 9 Feb 1938 Oslo.

One of the innovative pioneers of figure skating whose name is perpetuated by the jumps they evolved. It is doubtful, however, if the early 'Axel' was anything more than a crude version of a one and a half turn jump, bearing little resemblance to the smooth and complicated modern variations which have evolved. As a pioneer of international competition, he also made a great contribution to the development of speed skating. Official championships were not held until after he had retired but he travelled extensively in search of competition. In 1883 he visited England and North America but a proposed match at Southport against the British professional champion, George Smart, did not materialise and in Canada he was unable to master the sharp turns of the indoor rinks. The following year he enjoyed a successful tour of America where he competed over longer distances on outdoor rinks. Although official world records were not then recognised, his winning time of 1hr 33min 28sec for a 25 mile race in New York has seldom been bettered. He was the winner of the first ever international speed skating competition at Hamburg in 1885 and he set an interesting record at Amsterdam in 1888 when he skated one mile backwards in 3min 31.6 sec.

Jerzy PAWLOWSKI (Pol)

FENCING

Jerzy Pawlowski. b. 25 Oct 1932 Warsaw.

Winner of three individual sabre titles at the World Championships (1957, 1965-6) and runner-up four times. He also had an outstanding record at the Olympics, winning individual gold in 1968 and silver in 1956 and three team medals (silver 1956-

60, bronze 1964). An Army major with a master's degree in law, he was highly thought of by the Polish Government and was asked to become a spy on their behalf. When he refused, he was framed as being a spy himself and was sentenced to 25 years imprisonment and his name was removed from all Polish sporting records.

Walter PAYTON (USA)

AMERICAN FOOTBALL

Walter Jerry Payton. b. 25 Jul 1954 Columbia, Mississippi.

Statistically the greatest runner in pro football history; his fluid, quick running style earned him the nickname 'Sweetness'. Payton played college football at Jackson State University and spent his entire NFL career with the Chicago Bears from 1975-87. He led the NFC in rushing yardage four times but led the NFL only once (1977). Because of his durability, however, in 1984 he broke Jim Brown's record of 12,312 yards for career yards gained rushing and finished with a career record 16,726 yards (av. 4.4). He also had 492 catches for 4538 yards receiving and 15 touchdowns. He rushed for 1000 yards in 10 of his 13 seasons and topped 100 yards in 77 games, with an NFL record 275 yards against Minnesota on 20 Nov 1977. During his career he appeared in nine Pro Bowls. He was known for his tremendous strength, bench-pressing over 175 kg (385 lb) and leg-pressing over 275 kg (600 lb).

Eulace PEACOCK (USA)

ATHLETICS

Eulace Peacock. b. 27 Aug 1914 Dothan, Alabama.

A great rival of Jesse Owens, he lost his chance to challenge him for the 1936 Olympic titles through leg injuries. He matched the world record for 100m at 10.3 in both 1934 and 1935. In 1935 in the AAU Indoor Championships Peacock set a world best for long jump with 7.71m, but Owens beat him, improving that record twice. After Owens had achieved his six world records in one day, Peacock was runner-up to him at 100y and long jump in the NCAAs. However, he then beat Owens to win both events at the AAUs. There he became the second 8m long jumper with exactly that distance. Twice more the following week Peacock beat Owens at 100m. Although his best long jump days were behind him, Peacock was a fine all-rounder, and won the AAU pentathlon title in 1937 and 1943-5 to add to his wins in 1933 and 1934.

Bobby PEARCE (Aus/Can)

ROWING

Henry Robert Pearce. b. 30 Sep 1905 Sydney, New South Wales, d. 20 May 1976 Toronto, Canada.

Son of the Australian professional sculling champion Harry Pearce, Bobby was the first man to defend the Olympic single sculls title, winning the gold in that event in both 1928 and 1932. He grew up in Australia, but later emigrated and became a Canadian citizen in the mid-1930s. He was denied entry to the Henley Diamond Sculls in 1928 because of his profession as a carpenter, but in 1930 he became a whisky salesman in Toronto and this allowed him to enter the Diamond Sculls, which he won in 1931. He turned pro in 1933 and won the world professional sculling championship, holding that title until his retirement just before World War II.

Eric PEARCE (Aus)

HOCKEY

Eric Robert Pearce. b. 29 Oct 1931 Jubbalpore, India.

One of five brothers who played international hockey. The eldest brother, Cec, retired before Australia made their Olympic hockey debut in 1956 but Mel (1956), Gordon (1956-60 and 1968) and Julien (1960-64 and 1968) were all Olympic players. Eric's feat of playing in four Olympics (1956-68) has only been matched by Rik Charlesworth among Australian hockey players.

Eric Pearce, who learned the game as a child in India, won Olympic bronze in 1964 and silver in 1968 and was for many years a stalwart of the Western Australian team which won numerous Australian titles.

Roger PECKINPAUGH (USA)

BASEBALL

Roger Thorpe Peckinpaugh. b. 5 Feb 1891 Wooster, Ohio. d. 17 Nov 1977 Cleveland, Ohio.

The premier shortstop of his era, spending his entire career in the American League, mostly with the New York Yankees, although he also played with the Washington Senators, Cleveland Indians, and Chicago White Sox. He was voted MVP in 1925. In 1914 he was a player-manager with the Yankees and later again became the Yankee manager until 1933, with one more year at their helm in 1941.
Career 1910-27: 1876 hits Avg. .259; SB 207.

Eusebio PEDROZA (Pan)

BOXING

Eusebio Pedroza. b. 2 Mar 1953 Panama City.

For a featherweight Pedroza packed a tremendous punch. He turned professional when he was 20 and won the world title in 1978 by knocking out Cecilio Lastra. Pedroza remained the champion for seven years and made 19 successful title defences, five of which were against past or future world champions. He lost his crown to Barry McGuigan in 1985.
Career record: W - 39 (24), L - 5, D -1.

Robert PEEL (UK)

CRICKET

Robert Peel. b. 12 Feb 1857 Churwell, Yorkshire, d. 12 Aug 1941 Morley, Yorkshire.

A top-class slow left-arm bowler, who was also a formidable batsman and an excellent cover point fielder. Three times he took 20 wickets or more in a Test series against Australia. His partnership of 292 with Lord Hawke for Yorkshire v Warwickshire in 1896 is still the English record for the 8th wicket; Peel scored 210* in that match. He took 100 wickets in a season eight times with a high of 180 at 14.97 in 1895 and he did the double in 1896. Sadly his county career came to an abrupt end due to an incident when he took the field drunk.
22 Tests 1884-96: 427 runs at 14.72, HS 83; 102 wickets at 16.81, BB 7-31; 17 catches.
First-class 1882-99: 12,191 runs at 19.44, 7 100s HS 210; 1776 wickets at 16.19, BB 9-22; 214 catches.*

PELÉ (Bra)

FOOTBALL

Edson Arantes do Nascimento. b. 23 Oct 1940 Tres Coracoes, Minas Gerais.

The best known of all footballers and arguably the world's most famous sportsman. A complete master of all the skills, he fully justified his legendary status and he was admired throughout the world.
A first-team regular for Santos in 1956 at the age of 16, he scored on his début for Brazil the following year and his international reputation was established in the 1958 World Cup, when he scored a hat-trick in the semi-final and twice in the 5-2 defeat of Sweden in the final. Because of injury, his contribution to the next two World Cup campaigns (1962, 1966) was minimal but he came back in 1970 and took his second winners' medal. For Santos he won a host of domestic League and Cup honours and helped them to the World Club Championship in 1962 and 1963. He won his 111th and final cap in 1971 and scored 97 international goals (77 goals from 92 games on a stricter international match definition). He retired at the end of the 1974 season but a lucrative contract with the New York Cosmos brought him out of retirement the following year. When he finally retired in 1977 he had scored 1281 goals in 1363 first-class games, later adding two in special appearances.
His many business interests have brought him immense wealth, but despite his material success he remains a modest and likeable individual, characteristics which served him well in his political aspirations.

Henri PÉLISSIER (Fra)

CYCLING

Henri Pélissier. b. 22 Jan 1889 Paris, d. 1 May 1935 Dampièrre.

A great all-round cyclist who struggled for many years before finally winning the Tour de France in 1923. At the 1919 Tour he was cautioned for dangerous riding. That night he quit the race, declaring that he would not tolerate being treated like a convict. In his statement, he coined the term which is now a favoured description of the members of the peloton, '*forçats de la route*' or 'convicts of the road'. His first major win, the 1911 Tour of Lombardy, was hardly planned at all. At a Paris railway station he met Lucien Petit-Breton, who talked him into going for a week's racing in Italy. Pélissier ran home and packed his bags, winning the Tour of Lombardy ten days later. He won the race again in 1913 and 1920.

Other major victories: Milan-San Remo 1912, Paris-Roubaix 1919, 1921; Bordeaux-Paris 1919, 1922, 1924; Paris-Brussels 1920, Paris-Tours 1922.

John PENNEL (USA)

ATHLETICS

John Thomas Pennel. b. 25 Jul 1940 Memphis, Tennessee.

Pennel set nine world records at the pole vault from 4.95m at Memphis on 23 Mar 1963 via the first 17ft clearance (17ft 0 3/4 in *5.20m*) at Coral Gables, Florida on 24 Aug 1963, to 5.44m at Sacramento on 21 Jun 1969, although only four of these were officially accepted. Such was the rate of progress of the world standard in the early days of the fibreglass pole, especially in 1963 when the record was broken or equalled ten times in all, that recognition of several of his efforts was not applied for. He also set two world indoor bests in 1966.

Sullivan Award winner 1963 and winner of both AAU and World Student Games titles in 1965. He disappointed at the Olympics, placing 11th in 1964 and 5th in 1968.

Willie PEP (USA)

BOXING

Willie Pep. né Guiglermo Papaleo. b. 19 Sep 1922 Middletown, Connecticut.

Pep was so difficult to hit that he was nicknamed 'Will o' the Wisp'. He was one of the busiest boxers ever, contesting 242 bouts in his career after turning professional at age 17. He won the world featherweight title in 1942, aged only 20, and held the title for six years until knocked out by Sandy Saddler in four rounds in 1948. But Pep pulled off a major upset four months later when he outpointed Saddler. In 1950, however, he lost the rubber match to Saddler after three successful title defences. Pep continued to fight continuously until he retired in 1958, but in 1965 at age 43 he made a brief comeback and won 9 of 10 fights. He then became a referee.

Career record: W - 230 (65), L - 11, D - 1.

Pascual PEREZ (Arg)

BOXING

Pascual Pérez. b. 4 Mar 1926 Tupungati, Mendoza, d. 22 Jan 1977 Mendoza.

Pérez had won the Olympic flyweight gold medal in 1948 but did not turn professional until he was 26. Only 1.50m tall he was nonetheless a hard puncher and in 1954 he became the first Argentinian to win a world boxing title, beating Yoshio Shirai in Tokyo. He had eight successful defences but, after a run of 59 consecutive wins was ended in a non-title fight by Sadao Yaoita in 1959, he lost the title to Pone Kingpetch in 1960. Kingpetch also won the re-match.

Career record: W - 83 (56), L -6, D - 2.

Guy PÉRILLAT (Fra)

ALPINE SKIING

Guy Périllat. b. 24 Feb 1940 La Clusaz, Haute-Savoie.

World combined champion in 1960, when he showed his all-round ability by finishing in the first six at all three Alpine events at the Olympic Games: 3rd downhill, 6th slalom and giant slalom. At subsequent Olympics, in 1964 he was 6th at downhill,

10th at giant and 12th slalom, and he ended his career in 1968 when he took the silver at downhill and was 4th at giant slalom. He turned professional, joining Bob Beattie's team in the USA, in 1969. In 1961 he achieved the unique feat of winning all the classic downhill races of the season. After military service in Algeria, Périllat was below his best at the 1962 World Championships, but took the slalom silver medal. He gained his second world title in 1966, when he won the giant slalom and was second at slalom.

Kieren PERKINS (Aus)

SWIMMING

Kieren John Perkins. b. 14 Aug 1973 Brisbane, Queensland.

Perkins set world records at 400m (3:46.47), 800m (7:46.60) and 1500m (14:48.40) in early 1992, and improved the 1500m time to 14:43.48 when he won the Olympic title. He also improved at 400m to 3:45.16 but was beaten into second place by the Russian Yevgeniy Sadovyi. He has also set world short course records for 1500m of 14:32.40 in 1992 and 14:26.52 in 1993, and for 800m of 7:34.90, the latter improving a record set by Michael Gross in 1985.
He won silver medals at 1500m in the 1990 Commonwealth Games and the 1991 World Championships, when, with 14:50.58, he was just 0.22 sec behind Jörg Hoffman (Ger). Later in 1991 he won the Pan-Pacific 400m and 1500m, recording a world record for 800m en route to the 1500m win.
Best 200m 1:48.92 (1992).

Fred PERRY (UK)

TENNIS

Frederick John Perry. b. 18 May 1909 Stockport, Cheshire.

The outstanding British player of modern times and one the world's greatest players of all-time. Since he turned professional in 1936, no British male has won a Grand Slam singles title whereas Perry won eight: three at Wimbledon 1934-6, three US at Forest Hills 1933-4 and 1936, and the 1935 French and 1934 Australian Championships. He was the first player to win all four major singles but as he did not hold the titles concurrently he missed the distinction of being the first winner of the Grand Slam.
Perry also won the Australian and French doubles with Pat Hughes in 1933 and took four Grand Slam mixed doubles titles with three different partners. His claim to greatness was enhanced by his superb Davis Cup record. In 20 ties between 1931 and 1936 he lost only 7 of his 52 matches and just one of his ten singles in the Challenge Rounds, as he helped the British team to win the Cup for four consecutive years 1933-6. In both the 1933 and 1936 finals Perry won the vital fifth rubber to clinch the match 3-2 for Great Britain.
After winning the 1936 US singles he turned professional and played a series of classic matches with Ellsworth Vines and Don Budge. His great strength was his running forehand drive and he had a confident, aggressive attitude to the game.
In the days of the 'gentleman amateur' Perry was unique in that he did not come from a wealthy background and his father was a Labour Member of Parliament. Initially, his main sport was table tennis, at which in 1929 he was the world singles champion. He became an American citizen and served with the US Forces during World War II but in his later years he spent more time in England.

Gaylord PERRY (USA)

BASEBALL

Gaylord Jackson Perry. b. 15 Sep 1938 Williamston, North Carolina.

Perry pitched for 22 years in the major leagues with eight different teams. He was renowned because of the rumours that persisted that he was able to win mostly because he threw spitballs. He entitled his autobiography *Me and the Spitter*. He was an excellent pitcher, whether or not the allegations are true. He is the only man to have won the Cy Young Award in both leagues (1972 AL, 1978 NL), was named to the All-Star team five times, and five times led his league in wins.

Career pitching 1962-83: ERA 3.10; W-L 314-265, SO 3534. Best seasons: 1966: 21-8, 2.99 ERA; 1970: 23-13, 3.20 ERA; 1972: 24-16, 1.92 ERA; 1974: 21-13, 2.52 ERA; 1978: 21-6, 2.72 ERA.

Joe PERRY (USA)

AMERICAN FOOTBALL

Fletcher Joseph Perry. b. 27 Jan 1927 Stevens, Arkansas.

A running back known for his speed and quickness. He played college football at Compton Junior College before entering the US Navy in 1945. He joined the San Francisco 49ers in 1948 and played for them in both the All-American Football Conference 1948-50 and the NFL 1951-60, then spent two seasons with the Baltimore Colts before returning to finish his career in 1963 with the 49ers. Perry led the AAFC in rushing once and the NFL twice. He was named All-Pro three times. At his retirement, Perry's career rushing yardage gained was an NFL career record, later broken by Jim Brown.
AAFC/NFL career 1948-63: Rushing: 9723 yards av. 5.0, 71 touchdowns. Receiving: 2021 yards av. 7.8, 12 touchdowns.

Atty PERSSE (Ire/UK)

HORSE RACING

Henry Seymour Persse. b. Jun 1869 Galway, Ireland d. 4 Sep 1960 Windsor, Berkshire.

Great trainer, first of jumpers and later on the flat. He trained the winners of four classics, but his greatest horse was *The Tetrarch*, and he was particularly renowned for his fast two-year-olds. His first Classic winner was in 1912, *Sweeper II* in the 2000 Guineas. He was champion trainer in 1930. Persse was a boxer while at Oxford University and an amateur steeplechase jockey before starting training in Ireland in 1902, moving to England in 1906. From 1909 he trained at Stockbridge, Hampshire and then at Kingsdown, Upper Lambourn, Berkshire until his retirement in 1953.

Michael PETER (FRG)

HOCKEY

Michael Peter. b. 7 May 1949 Heidelberg.

One of the most skilful defenders in the world, he was seen at his brilliant best when he helped the FRG team win the Olympic gold in 1972. An insurance agent who played his club hockey for Stuttgart Kickers and HC Heidelberg, he made his international début in 1969 and also played at the Olympics in 1976 and in 1984, when he won a silver medal. In all, to 1985, he won 217 outdoor and 45 indoor caps, a German record, and captained the team in the latter stages of his international career. He played in five World Championships, won four European Indoor titles and one outdoor.

Martin PETERS (UK)

FOOTBALL

Martin Stanford Peters. b. 8 Nov 1943 Plaistow, London.

A tireless and gifted player whose roving style of play did much to change the pattern of the game. A former schoolboy international, he started his professional career with West Ham in 1960 where he won 33 caps and scored England's second goal in the 1966 World Cup final. After his move to Tottenham in 1970 he played for England a further 34 times and captained the team on several occasions. The circumstances of his departure from West Ham have never been fully revealed but there is no doubt that his free-flowing style was better appreciated at Tottenham where he fully justified his record transfer fee. Although he never won an FA Cup or League winners medal, he won a European Cup-Winners' Cup medal 1965 with West Ham and with Spurs he was in the winning team in the League Cup final (1971, 1973) and the UEFA Cup (1972). In 1975 he moved to Norwich City where he enjoyed five successful seasons, after which he spent a short time as manager of Sheffield United. This ended his involvement with the game and he joined his former World Cup colleague, Geoff Hurst, in the insurance broking business.

Mary PETERS (UK)

ATHLETICS

Mary Elizabeth Peters. b. 6 Jul 1939 Halewood, Lancashire.

Peters won the Olympic pentathlon title with a world record 4801 points (4841 on the 1984 tables) on her third attempt in 1972, after placing fourth in 1964 and ninth in 1968. She needed to run a personal best in the last event, the 200m, to win, and did just that, although she had an agonising wait to see if the gap between her and Heide Rosendahl who had won that race in 22.96 to the 24.08 by Peters was sufficiently small. It was, and Peters won by 10 points.
She was Commonwealth pentathlon champion for Northern Ireland in 1970 and 1974 and also won the shot in 1970. She won eight pentathlon and two shot WAAA titles and set British records at 100m hurdles 13.29 (1972), two at shot with bests of 16.31m (1966) and 16.40m indoors (1970), and six at pentathlon. Awarded the MBE 1973 and the CBE 1990, and a most successful team manager of UK squads.
Other bests: 200m 24.08 (1972), high jump 1.82m (1972), long jump 6.04m (1972).

Ronnie PETERSON (Swe)

MOTOR RACING

Bengt Ronald Peterson. b. 14 Feb 1944 Örebro, d. 11 Sep 1978 Monza, Italy.

One of the finest drivers never to win the world title, very fast with exceptional reflexes. He had been runner-up in the championship in 1971 with four second places, but did not win a Grand Prix race until the French GP of 1973. However, that year he won three of the last four races to take third place in the championship and he won three more races in 1974 when fifth, all for Lotus. The Lotus cars became less competitive and he earned only six points in 1975. He returned to March and won the 1976 Italian GP. He had an unsuccessful year with Tyrrell in 1977 but in 1978 was again second in the championship for Lotus as number two to Mario Andretti. In his career, 1970-8, he won 10 of his 123 Grand Prix races, scoring 206 points. He died of injuries following an accident at Monza.
His father, Bengt, had been a notable amateur racing driver in Sweden. Ronnie started at motorcycle, moto-cross and speedway racing in his teens, turning to kart racing at 17. By the age of 19 he had won the first of three successive Swedish national kart titles. He had his first Formula 1 drive for March in 1970, and in 1971 was European Formula 2 champion.

Lucien PETIT-BRETON (Fra), see Lucien MAZAN

Tigran PETROSYAN (USSR)

CHESS

Tigran Vartanovich Petrosyan. b. 17 Jun 1929 Tbilisi, Georgia (of Armenian parents who died in World War II), d. 13 Aug 1984 Moscow.

Petrosyan became world chess champion by defeating Mikhail Botvinnik in 1963, and after a successful defence against Boris Spassky in 1966, he lost to Spassky in 1969. Armenian champion 1946, USSR champion in 1959, 1961, 1969 (joint) and 1975, he achieved both international master and grandmaster status in 1952. A very careful, persistent player.

Aleksandr PETROV (USSR)

BASKETBALL

Aleksandr Pavlovich Petrov. b. 14 May 1939 Baku, Azerbaijan.

One of the early stars of Soviet basketball. He won silver medals in the 1960 and 1964 Olympics and also helped the national team to win European championships in 1959, 1961, 1963, 1965 and 1967, and a world championship in 1967.

Drazen PETROVIC (Cro/Yug)

BASKETBALL

Drazen Petrovic. b. 22 Oct 1964 Sibenik, Croatia, d. 8 Jun 1993 Germany.

Petrovic was considered the greatest player ever produced in Yugoslavia, for whom he began playing in 1981 when only 17. A 1.97m guard, he helped Yugoslavia to a bronze medal at the 1984 Olympics, a silver medal at the 1988 Olympics, and a European championship in 1989. With Zagreb he won the European Champions Cup in 1985 and 1986 and the Cup of Cups in 1987. He was the youngest Yugoslav player to play professionally in another country when he signed a four-year contract with Real Madrid which began shortly after the 1988 Olympics. For them he scored 56 points in the final of the Cup of Cups in 1989. That year he joined the Portland Trail Blazers in the NBA but had a slow start with them and was later traded to the New Jersey Nets. By the time of his death he was establishing a formidable record with them, averaging 20.6 points in the NBA in 1991/2 and 22.3 in 1992/3. He led Croatia in 1992 at Barcelona when they won a silver medal, losing only to the 'Dream Team'. At the peak of his career he died in a car accident.

Natalya PETRUSEVA (USSR)

SPEED SKATING

Natalya Petruseva. née Pertileva. b. 2 Sep 1955 Pavlovsky Posad, Moscow.

A fine all-round speed skater who made her international début in 1978 and won women's overall world titles in 1981-2 and the world sprint title in 1982. At the 1980 Olympics she won the 1000m and placed 3rd in the 500m, and in 1984 won bronze medals at 1000m and 1500m with 6th place at 500m. Coached by her husband.
Best times: 500m 40.51 (1984), 1000m 1:19.31 (1983), 1500m 2:04.04 (1983), 3000m 4:29.31 (1984), 5000m 7:51.8.

Bob PETTIT (USA)

BASKETBALL

Robert Lee Pettit, Jr. b. 12 Dec 1932 Baton Rouge, Louisiana.

The top forward in basketball in the 1950s and one of the very greatest players in NBA history. After playing for Louisiana State (LSU) in college he was drafted by the Milwaukee Hawks in 1954 and played his entire 11-year NBA career with them, although the last 10 years were spent in St Louis after the Hawks moved there in 1955. Pettit was 2.06m *6'9"* and possessed the rebounding skills of a Bill Russell, the shooting touch of a Rick Barry, and was also a great leader. He played in the All-Star Game every year he was in the league and was named to the All-NBA First Team every year except his last. He twice led the league in scoring, and once in rebounding. In 1958 he led the Hawks to an upset NBA Championship over the Boston Celtics, one of only two times in Bill Russell's career that the Celtics failed to win the title. Pettit has been chosen on both the 25- and 35-year NBA All-Time teams. No forward in history has ever been so dominant in both scoring and rebounding.
NBA career: 20,880 points, av. 26.4; 12,849 rebounds, av. 16.2.

Richard PETTY (USA)

MOTOR RACING

Richard Lee Petty. b. 2 Jul 1937 Level Cross, North Carolina.

The king of US stock car racing, he holds the record for race victories at 200, nearly double the second highest (David Pearson 105), from 1185 starts from 1958 to his retirement at the end of 1992. His last win was in 1984, and he had career earnings of $7,763,174. He had a record 27 wins (from 48 races) in a season in 1967, which included a record ten in successive races, and was NASCAR champion a record seven times, 1964, 1967, 1971-2, 1974-5 and 1979. He also won the Daytona 500 a record seven times, 1964, 1966, 1971, 1973-4, 1979 and 1981.
His father **Lee** (b. 4 Mar 1914), winner of the first Daytona 500 in 1959, held the previous NASCAR records, with three championships 1954 and 1958-9, and 54 Grand National wins, a total passed by Richard in 1967 when he set a season's record with 20 wins (27 in all races), improving to 21 in 1971. In that year Richard became the first NASCAR driver to exceed $1 million in career earnings. Richard's brother Maurice (b. 27 Mar 1939) was the top engine-builder and his son Kyle also became a leading driver.

Brian PHELPS (UK)

DIVING

Brian Eric Phelps. b. 21 Apr 1944 Chelmsford, Essex.

Britain's finest diver, he won an Olympic bronze medal at springboard in 1960, gold medals for both events at the Commonwealth Games of 1962 and 1966, and golds for highboard at the European Championships of 1958 and 1962. At 14, in 1958, he was the youngest ever European champion after taking the high-board silver at the Commonwealth Games. He was sixth at highboard at the 1964 Olympics. Unbeaten by a British competitor from 1958 to 1966, he won 14 ASA titles from his first at 13 in 1957 to 1966. Married to gymnast Monica.

Andre PHILLIPS (USA)

ATHLETICS

Andre Lamar Phillips. b. 5 Sep 1959 Milwaukee.

For many years the closest American challenger to Ed Moses, he succeeded him as Olympic champion at 400m hurdles in 1988. Phillips was fifth in the 1983 World Championships and won at both 400m hurdles and 4 x 400m relay at the 1985 World Cup. He also developed into a world-class high hurdler in 1985. NCAA champion when at UCLA in 1981, and TAC champion 1985.

Best times: 200m 20.55 (1986), 400m 44.71 (1986), 110mh 13.25 (1985), 400mh 47.19 (1988).

Mark PHILLIPS (UK)

EQUESTRIAN

Mark Anthony Peter Phillips. b. 22 Sep 1948 Cirencester, Gloucestershire.

He achieved a record four Badminton victories: 1971-2 on *Great Ovation*, 1974 on *Columbus* and 1981 on *Lincoln* before Lucinda Green surpassed his feat. A reserve for the 1968 Olympics, he won a team gold in 1972, although *Great Ovation* fell twice in the cross-country and theirs was the discard score. With the British team he won team golds in the 1970 Worlds and 1971 Europeans. In 1988, Phillips again competed at the Olympics in the three-day event. He was forced to withdraw before the cross-country stage because his horse *Cartier* had pulled a muscle, but he earned a silver medal as the fourth member of Britain's second-placed team.

In 1973, Captain Phillips married **HRH The Princess Anne** (b. 15 Aug 1950), who had won the 1971 European three-day event title on *Doublet* and competed for Britain at the 1976 Olympics, but the marriage was dissolved in 1992. In 1974 he was appointed a Commander of the Victorian Order. He was educated at Marlborough and RMA Sandhurst and now farms at Gatcombe, Gloucestershire.

Cory PICKOS (USA)

WATER SKIING

Cory Pickos. b. 17 Apr 1964 Kenosha, Wisconsin.

Considered as the greatest trick skier of all time. He set 22 world records and 25 US records in tricks to a peak score of 10,990 points on 15 Jul 1989. He was a six-time tricks champion at the Masters Meet as well as winning the world title in 1981 and 1983.

Nicola PIETRANGELI (Italy)

TENNIS

Nicola Pietrangeli. b. 11 Sep 1933 Tunis, Tunisia.

The most prolific Davis Cup player in history. Although born in Tunis of a French father and Russian mother, he established an Italian qualification and between 1954 and 1972 played a record 164 rubbers in 66 ties for Italy, winning 78 of his 110 singles and 42 of his 54 doubles.

At singles he won the French title in 1959 and 1960, the Italian in 1957 and 1961 and the German in 1960. As a superb touch player his game was also well-suited to doubles and with Davis Cup team-mate Orlando Sirola he won the French doubles in 1959, the Italian in 1960 and was a Wimbledon finalist in 1956.

Lester PIGGOTT (UK)

HORSE RACING

Lester Keith Piggott. b. 5 Nov 1935 Wantage.

The greatest jockey of the modern age on the English turf. From his first winner, *The Chase* at Haydock Park on 18 Aug 1948 at the age of 13, to May 1993 he rode over 5300 winners worldwide, including 4450 in Britain. There were a record 30 classic winners between 1954 and 1992: 5 in the 2000 Guineas, 2 the 1000 Guineas, 6 The Oaks, 8 the St Leger, and a record 9 in the Derby, a race with which he is most especially connected in the minds of his admiring public, from *Never Say Die* in 1954 to *Teenoso* in 1983. In 1970 he rode *Nijinsky,* whom he considered the best of many brilliant horses that he had ridden, to the Triple Crown.

A child wonder, and twice champion apprentice, he surpassed 100 winners in a season 25 times between 1955 and 1984 and was champion jockey eleven times between 1960 and 1982, with a peak total of 191 winners in 1966, but he sought to find the best rides rather than to maximise the number of his wins, particularly after he had startled the racing world by turning freelance. He became undoubtedly the richest British sportsman. He had been first jockey to Sir Noel Murless 1954-66, in the 1970s rode many major race winners for Vincent O'Brien, and in the early 1980s teamed up with Henry Cecil.

His grandfather Ernest had ridden three Grand National winners, his father Keith trained at Newmarket and his mother Iris was the sister of the famous jockeys Bill and Fred Rickaby. A solitary and withdrawn character, due to his partial deafness and speech impediment, Lester brought great strength to bear, driving his horses to many a perfectly-judged finish, and he was both a brilliant horseman and a marvellous judge of a horse. In his early days his ruthless will to win cost him a series of suspensions from the Turf for dangerous riding. He had marvellous balance and needed it as he rode exceptionally short. He retired on 29 Oct 1985 to train at Newmarket with his wife Susan (daughter of the famous trainer Sam Armstrong), and his first winner was sent out from his Eve Lodge stables within weeks. In October 1987 he was sentenced to three years imprisonment for a £2.8 million tax fraud, and was released a year later. This cost him the OBE awarded earlier. He obviously missed riding and made a comeback on 15 Oct 1990 at the age of 54, starting to add to his winners the following day and soon showing that he had lost little of his supreme ability, riding the winner of the Breeders' Cup mile in the USA. A record 30th classic winner came in 1992 with *Rodrigo de Triano* in the 2000 Guineas.

Kustaa PIHLAJAMÄKI (Fin)

WRESTLING

Kustaa Pihlajamäki. 7 Apr 1902 Nurmo, Österbotten, d. 10 Feb 1944 Helsinki.

Finland's greatest ever wrestler; the winner of three Olympic freestyle medals, gold in 1924 at bantamweight and 1936 at featherweight, and silver in 1928 at feather. He and Carl Westergren are the only two wrestlers to have won gold medals 12 years apart. Pihlajamäki won nine European championships - seven in Greco-Roman (1930-1, 1933-4, and 1937-8) and two in freestyle (1931, 1937). He never competed in the world championships but won a record 29 Finnish titles. A policeman, he was renowned for his speed. A statue in his honour was erected in Helsinki. He came from a family of great wrestlers. His brothers, Arvi and Paavo, won multiple Finnish championships, and his cousin **Hermanni** (1903-82) won two Olympic medals, including a gold in featherweight freestyle in 1932, when Kustaa unsuccessfully tried a heavier category, the lightweight, in order to allow Hermanni his chance. He died at the age of 41 of a ruptured appendix

Lyudmila PINAYEVA (USSR)

CANOEING

Lyudmila Pinayeva. née Khvedosyuk. b. 14 Jan 1936 Krasnove, Leningrad region.

The most successful woman kayak canoeist of her era, she won the Olympic kayak singles in 1964 and 1968 and added world titles at this event in 1966 and 1970-1. In the pairs she took the Olympic bronze in 1968 before winning with Yekaterina Kuryshko in 1972.

Laffit PINCAY (Pan/USA)

HORSE RACING

Laffit Pincay, Jr. b. 29 Dec 1946 Panama City, Panama.

At $170,325,931, in his career 1964-92 he has the all-time record for jockey's earnings, in 1985 passing Bill Shoemaker, to whom he is second for career wins with 7888. He headed the jockeys' money-winning table in the USA in 1970-4, 1979 and 1985 and won the Eclipse Award for outstanding jockey in 1971, 1973-4, 1979 and 1985.

His first winner was in Panama City on 19 May 1964. Two years later he won on his first mount in the USA, at Arlington Park on 1 Jul 1966. He won the Belmont Stakes in three successive years 1982-4, and in the last also rode *Swale* to win the Kentucky Derby.

Martin PIPE (UK)

HORSE RACING

Martin Charles Pipe. b. 29 May 1945 Taunton, Somerset.

In the years from 1988 to 1992 he smashed all records for training horses to win National Hunt races in Britain. Previously an amateur point-to-point rider, he began training for the 1974/5 season, with his first winner *Hit Parade* at Taunton on 29 May 1975, and obtained a full licence in 1977. His first five years brought only 19 winners, but his number of winners increased each year from 1978/9 to 1989/90; he first trained 50 winners in a season in 1984/5, 106 in 1986/7 and broke Michael Dickinson's season's record of 120 with 129 in 1987/8. He left these figures far behind as in 1988/9 he was responsible for 208 winners. In 1989/90 he again bettered the record, reaching 200 winners on 7 May 1990, 12 days ahead of the previous year, and ending with 224 wins from 639 runs. A high proportion of his winners were ridden by Peter Scudamore, as he too set brilliant new records. In 1990/91 Pipe added to his records, becoming the first NH trainer to win over £1 million in a season with £1,203,014, and with 230 winners. He was again champion with 224 winners in 1991/2 and 194 in 1992/3.

Nelson PIQUET (Bra)

MOTOR RACING

Nelson Piquet Soutomaior. b. 17 Aug 1952 Rio de Janeiro.

Three times world champion at Formula One in 1981, 1983 and 1987. His first F1 Grand Prix race was in an Ensign in 1978, and since then he has driven for McLaren 1978, Brabham 1979-85, Williams 1986-7, Lotus 1988-9, Benetton 1990-1. A gifted driver, with fine mechanical acumen, he won 23 Grand Prix races from his first, the US GP West in 1980, amassing a career total of 485.5 points, third behind Alain Prost and Ayrton Senna, from 204 races, and he achieved 24 pole positions.

His first successes were in his home country where he started at kart racing, and in Volkswagens he won the Brazilian 2-litre sports car championship in 1972, the Brazilian Sports 2000 title in 1973 and the Brazilian Formula Super Vee title in 1976. In his first season in Europe in 1977 he was third in the F3 championship.

His career was ended by a serious accident at Indianapolis on 25 May 1992, when he suffered multiple leg injuries.

Gordon PIRIE (UK)

ATHLETICS

Douglas Alastair Gordon Pirie. b. 10 Feb 1931 Leeds, d. 7 Dec 1991 Lymington, Hampshire from cancer.

Great distance athlete who helped revolutionise attitudes to hard training. He set five world records: in 1953 at 6 miles and at 4x1500m relay, and three in 1956. The first of these was in Bergen on 19 June when he ran 5000m in 13:36.8 (25 secs off his best), beating Vladimir Kuts in 13:39.6 as both beat the old mark of 13:40.6. Three days later at Trondheim he ran 3000m in 7:55.6, a time which he improved to 7:52.7

in Malmö in September when he beat the great Hungarian trio of Rozsávölgyi, Iharos and Tábori. Later that year at the Olympics he ran an epic race at 10,000m against Kuts, but had to yield and ended eighth; he came back to gain the 5000m silver behind Kuts. At the 1952 Olympics he was 7th at 10,000m and 4th at 5000m, and in 1960 he went out in the heats of the 5000m. In 1958 he was third in the European 5000m and fourth in the Empire Games at both 1 mile and 3 miles. He was AAA champion at 3 miles 1953 and 1961 and at 6 miles 1951-3 and 1960.
He set 24 British records at distances from 2000m to 10,000m, and excelled at cross-country, at which he was English National champion each year 1953-5.

Anatoliy PISARENKO (USSR)

WEIGHTLIFTING
Anatoliy Pisarenko. b. 10 Jan 1958 Kiev.

Pisarenko was another in the long line of Soviet super-heavyweight champions who could claim to be the world's strongest man. In 1978 he was second in the European Juniors and third in the World Juniors, and he won three successive World heavyweight titles in 1981-3, succeeding Sultan Rakhmanov, who had taken the crown at the end of Vasiliy Alekseyev's career. In 1984, Pisarenko and Aleksandr Kurlovich were arrested at Mirabel Airport in Montreal when customs officials searched their luggage and found anabolic steroids. The two were convicted by Canadian authorities and fined. Soviet officials dismissed them from the national team and stripped them of their status as 'Masters of Sport'. Pisarenko was allowed back in the national team at the end of 1986 and competed at the European Championships in 1987, but failed to total. That effectively ended his career.

Frantisek PLÁNICKA (Cs)

FOOTBALL
Frantisek Plánicka. b. 2 Jul 1904 Prague.

A top Contintental goalkeeper of the 1930s who ranked with Zamora (Spa) and Hiden (Aut) as one of the world's best. After signing as a professional for Slavia Praha in 1925, he remained with the club throughout his career and played more than 1,000 matches. His 73 caps stood as a Czech record until 1966 and he captained the national team on many occasions, including the 1934 World Cup when Czechoslovakia only lost to hosts Italy in the final after extra-time. He retired from the first-class game in 1939 but continued to play in veterans matches for another 30 years.

Eddie PLANK (USA)

BASEBALL
Edward Stewart Plank. b. 31 Aug 1875 Gettysburg, Pennsylvania, d. 24 Feb 1926 Gettysburg.

One of the top pitchers of the first few years of the 20th century, playing mostly with the Philadelphia Athletics. In 1915 he jumped to the St Louis Terriers of the new Federal League, but returned to the majors to finish his career with two years at the St Louis Browns of the American League. He won 20 games in a season eight times and was a finesse pitcher who was very serious and, for his era, very slow and deliberate on the mound.
Career pitching 1901-17: ERA 2.35; W-L 326-193, SO 2246. Best seasons: 1904: 26-16, 2.14 ERA; 1905: 24-12, 2.26 ERA; 1907: 24-16, 2.20 ERA; 1912: 26-6, 2.22 ERA; 1915: 21-11, 2.08 ERA.

Herma PLANK-SZABÓ (Aut)

FIGURE SKATING
née Herma Szabó. b. 22 Feb 1902 Vienna, d. 7 May 1985 Admont. Later Plank-Szabó, then Jaross-Szabó, then Stark-Szabó.

The greatest female skater of the immediate post-World War I era and the only person to win a world title for both singles and pairs. Of Hungarian origin, she won the first of her six Austrian singles titles in 1922 and that year she captured the first of her five successive world singles titles. In 1925 she also won the world pairs with her fellow-Austrian Ludwig Wrede, and this 'double' remains unique in the history of the Championships. After placing third with Wrede in 1926, they won the pairs for a second time in 1927 but Plank-Szabó lost her singles title that year to Sonja Henie after a disputed decision. She had previously beaten the Norwegian at the 1924 and 1926 World Championships and the 1924 Olympic Games, where she took the gold medal. On her return to Vienna after her Olympic victory, the whole city came to a halt as thousands turned out to greet her. She was also an excellent skier and swimmer and her free skating routine of jumps and spins inspired many skaters who followed her, including Henie. She won her first three World titles under the name Plank-Szabó, Plank being the name of her first husband, and her titles of 1925-6 after she had married for a second time, as Jaross-Szabó. After she retired she married for a third time.

Jacques PLANTE (Can)

ICE HOCKEY

Joseph Jacques Omer Plante. b. 17 Jan 1929 Mont Carmel, Québec.

Plante had one of the longest careers of any goaltender and won the Vezina Trophy as the top goalie a record seven times, 1956-60, 1962, 1969. He played with several teams but his peak fame came with the Montreal Canadiens in the late 1950s and early 60s. In addition to leading Montreal to six Stanley Cups, Plante pioneered the use of a mask as a goalie, being the first top goalie to use one regularly in games, beginning in the 1959/60 season. 'Jake the Snake' was cocky and used that trait to allow him to roam widely from the net, often helping out his defensemen in clearing the puck.

Career 1952-75 - 868 games, 2.38 GAA, 83 shutouts. NHL: 837 games, 2.38 GAA, 82 shutouts. Hart Trophy 1962.

Michel PLATINI (Fra)

FOOTBALL

Michel Platini. b. 21 Jun 1955 Joeuf.

The only man to win the European Footballer of the Year award for three successive years, 1983-5. From AS Joeuf he joined Nancy in 1972, moving to AS St Etienne in 1979 and then to Juventus in 1982. He scored 41 goals for France in 72 international appearances (50 as captain) 1976-87, which included the final stages of three World Cups, and in 1984 he captained France to victory in the European Championship.

He won French Cup winners' medals with Nancy in 1978 and St Etienne in 1979 and 1982, and the League Championship with St Étienne in 1981. While he was with Juventus they won the Italian Cup in 1983, the European Cup-Winners' Cup and Italian League in 1984, and the European Cup in 1985. In this tragic Heysel final Platini scored the only goal from a penalty. He retired in 1987 having scored 348 goals in 648 professional games, and took over as manager of the French national team on 1 Nov 1988.

His long, precise passes, his use of the dead ball and his exceptional scoring ability for a midfield player contributed substantially to the success of the French team in the early 1980s.

Gary PLAYER (SAf)

GOLF

Gary Jim Player. b. 1 Nov 1936 Johannesburg.

His dedication to become a great player was probably matched only by Ben Hogan's. Early in his career, Player, small at 1.70m *5'7"*, was a very short hitter. Realising he needed to drive the ball farther to become a champion, he started lifting weights and exercising fanatically. He gained the length he needed and became one of four men to win all four of the major championships, the US Open 1965; Masters 1961, 1974, 1978; British Open 1959, 1968, 1974; and PGA Championship 1962, 1972. In addition, Player's record in the US tournaments would surely have been greater had he confined himself to that tour. But more than any golfer, he travelled the world, playing on all continents and winning multiple tournaments in Africa, Australia, Europe and South America as well.

Other victories included World Match Play 1965-6, 1968, 1971, 1973; South African

Open 1956, 1960, 1965-9, 1972, 1975-7, 1979, 1981; Australian Open 1958, 1962-3, 1965, 1969-70, 1974.
PGA career earnings: $1,811,251 with 21 victories. Seniors tour: 1985-92 $2,795,978 with 16 victories.

Michael PLUMB (USA)

EQUESTRIAN
John Michael Plumb. b. 28 Mar 1940 Islip, New York.

After being a member of the three-day event team which won the silver medals at three successive Olympics (1964, 1968, and 1972), Plumb won a team gold and an individual silver at the 1976 Games. He won a second team gold in 1984 and his total of six Olympic medals is a record for a US equestrian. He has competed in seven Olympic Games (1960-76, 1984, 1992), and actually made eight Olympic teams, but his participation in 1980 was prevented by the boycott. He may yet achieve that record eighth participation in 1996.
Double gold medallist at the Pan-American Games of 1967, having taken team golds in 1959 and 1963. At the World Championships he won the silver medal and took team gold in 1974. A graduate of the University of Delaware, he farmed in Maryland.

Simon POIDEVIN (Aus)

RUGBY UNION
Simon Paul Poidevin. b. 31 Oct 1958 Goulburn, New South Wales.

A tough, hard-working loose forward who made his début against Fiji in 1980 and announced his retirement in 1988 after becoming the first Australian to win 50 caps. He soon made a comeback and went on to win a total of 59 caps to 1992, which stands as a record for an Australian flanker.
Poidevin, who was of French descent, played a vital role in the Australian successes of the 1980s and was in the winning team in five Test series. A graduate of New South Wales University, he played for Randwick.

Roger POINCELET (Fra)

HORSE RACING
Roger Poincelet. b. 3 Mar 1921 Paris, d. 1 Nov 1977.

In his career he rode over 2500 winners, from the Aly Khan's *Manchuria* in 1937 to his retirement, and was French champion jockey nine times. He rode for Marcel Boussac from soon after World War II, and the latter set Poincelet up as a trainer in 1970 at his Villa Djebel stable.
He had three wins in both the Prix de l'Arc de Triomphe and the Grand Prix de Paris. His first English classic winner was *Thunderhead* in the 2000 Guineas 1952 and he also won the Oaks with *Never Too Late* in 1960 and the Derby with *Psidium* in 1961.

Judit POLGAR (Hun)

CHESS
Judit Polgar. b. 23 Jul 1976.

A chess prodigy, on 20 Dec 1991 she became the youngest ever grandmaster at 15 years 150 days, an honour previously held by Bobby Fischer. She was also only the second ever woman grandmaster, the first being her sister **Zsusza** (b. 19 Apr 1969) earlier in 1991. By the end of 1992 Judit had the highest ever Elo rating for a woman at 2595; Zsusza was rated second at 2560 and a third sister Sofia (b. 2 Nov 1974) was the world's sixth-rated woman player. Their father László, a psychologist, had encouraged his daughters to play chess from the age of four.

Fritz POLLARD (USA)

AMERICAN FOOTBALL
Frederick Douglas Pollard. b. 27 Jan 1894 Chicago, Illinois, d. 11 May 1986 Silver Spring, Maryland.

Pollard was probably the first great black footballer. As a halfback at Brown he was named All-American in 1915, only the second black player so chosen (center William Lewis of Harvard was first in 1892-3). Pollard also ran track at Brown as a hurdler; although fairly good, he never won a national championship as has been rumoured. After graduation he enrolled at Penn Dental School, but left to play pro football from 1919-26 with various teams (Akron Pros, Milwaukee Badgers, Hammond Pros, and Providence Steamrollers). He was a player-coach with both Akron and Hammond, making him the first black to coach a pro football team. After his playing retirement, Pollard coached for several years and then became a film producer. His son **Fritz Pollard, Jr**. (b. 18 Feb 1915) won a bronze medal in the 110m hurdles at the 1936 Olympics and was also an All-American halfback at the University of North Dakota.

Jim POLLARD (USA)

BASKETBALL

James Clifford Pollard. b. 9 Jul 1922 Oakland, California, d. 22 Jan 1993 Stanford, California.

Pollard helped Stanford to an NCAA title in 1942, but did not finish college because he served in the military 1942-5. He then played two years of AAU basketball with the San Diego Dons and the Oakland Bittners, before joining the Minneapolis Lakers of the old National Basketball League, helping them win one NBL title. He later played on five NBA championship teams with the Lakers until he retired in 1955. He was a tough forward who was a top jump-shooter and rebounder. He later coached in college at LaSalle and also briefly in both the ABA and NBA.

Marjorie POLLARD (UK)

HOCKEY and CRICKET

Marjorie B Pollard. b. 3 Aug 1899 Rugby, d. 21 Mar 1982 Bampton, Oxfordshire.

A high-scoring international hockey player, who also captained England at cricket, and played tennis and golf to county standard. Her international hockey career was divided into two parts, 1921-8 and 1931-7, and she won a total of 41 caps. Details of the scorers in some of the earlier matches have not been reliably recorded, but it is known that she scored more than 115 goals in international matches. Amongst her scoring feats were 13 of England's 20 goals against Wales in 1926, and the following season, seven out of eight against Ireland, all five against Scotland and all eight against Germany. After some outstanding performances as a Peterborough schoolgirl, she joined the town club and later founded the North Northants HC. As a journalist she wrote for several national newspapers, and edited the magazines *Hockey Field* 1946-70 and *Women's Cricket* for 20 years. She was also the first woman radio commentator on cricket. She served as acting president of the All-England Women's Hockey Association and was a founder member of the Women's Cricket Association. In 1965 she was awarded the OBE for services to sport.

Graeme POLLOCK (SAf)

CRICKET

Robert Graeme Pollock. b. 27 Feb 1944 Durban.

One of the world's greatest ever batsmen, who had only a limited time to show the power and beauty of his glorious left-handed batting before South Africa was isolated from international cricket. In each of his last two Test series, against Australia in 1966/7 and 1969/70, he scored over 500 runs at averages of 76.71 and 73.85, with his highest ever score of 274, a record for South Africa in Tests, in that final series. He played for Eastern Province, for whom he made his first Currie Cup hundred at the age of 16, moving to Transvaal in 1978. 1.89m *6'2 $^1/_2$"* tall, he holds the record for most runs in the Currie Cup competition. Now a marketing consultant for insurance brokers.

23 Tests 1963-70: 2256 runs at 60.97, 7 100s HS 274; 4 wickets at 57.00, BB 2-50; 17 catches.

First-class 1961-87: 20,940 runs at 54.67, 64 100s HS 274; 43 wickets at 47.95, BB 3-46; 248 catches.

His father had kept wicket for Orange Free State, and his elder brother **Peter** Maclean **Pollock** (b. 30 Jun 1941) played in 28 Tests for South Africa 1961-70 as a fast bowler, capturing 116 wickets at 24.18, with 485 at 21.89 in his first-class career.

Igor POLYANSKIY (USSR)

SWIMMING
Igor Polyanskiy. b. 20 Mar 1967 Novosibirsk.

Polyanskiy's best for 200m backstroke of 1:58.14, set in 1985, lasted as a world record for six years. At that distance he lost just one race in 1985-8, when he was pipped by team-mate Sergey Zabolotnov by a hundredth of a second in the 1987 European Championships (where he won a gold medal at medley relay), and he was the double backstroke champion at the 1985 Europeans and 1986 Worlds (with bronze at medley relay in the latter). In 1988 he set three world records for the 100m, with 55.17, 55.16 and 55.00, so he was a solid favourite for the Olympic Games. However, just before the Games the American David Berkoff improved Polyanskiy's 100m record twice. Polyanskiy duly won the 200m but at 100m he took the bronze, a place behind Berkoff as both were surprisingly beaten by Daichi Suzuki of Japan. For the first 30 metres or so all three men used the underwater backstroke style that had been pioneered by Berkoff; this style was banned after the Games, with the backstrokers allowed to swim only the first 10m (later 15m) underwater.

Natalya PONOMARYEVA (USSR), see RUMYANTSEVA

Nina PONOMARYEVA (USSR)

ATHLETICS
Nina Apollonovna Ponomaryeva. née Romashkova. b. 27 Apr 1929 Sverdlovsk.

The Olympic discus champion of 1952 and 1960 and bronze medallist in 1956. She was European champion in 1954 and won eight Soviet titles between 1951 and 1959. She set a world record at 53.61m in 1952 and her best ever was 56.62m in 1955, but she achieved notoriety for allegedly shoplifting some hats from C & A Modes in Oxford Street, London, as a result of which the UK v USSR match in 1956 was cancelled. She was 6th in the 1962 Europeans and was 11th at her fourth Olympics in 1964.

Bill PONSFORD (Aus)

CRICKET
William Harold Ponsford. b. 19 Oct 1900 North Fitzroy, Melbourne, d. 6 Apr 1991 Kyneton, Victoria.

The only man to make two scores of over 400 in first-class cricket, Ponsford has the third highest average of all batsmen to have scored more than 10,000 runs in their career and was also a superb outfielder. He took a while to get a place in the Victoria team, but made 162 in his second first-class game and in just his fourth innings produced a world record score of 429 against Tasmania in 1923. He made 1043 runs at 86.92 in his first eight first-class innings. Such scoring made him an obvious selection for Australia and he made 110 on his début against England in December 1924, and 128 in the second Test. He had little success in England in 1926, but was sensational in the next two Australian seasons, scoring 1229 runs at 122.90 in 1926/7 and 1217 at 152.12 in 1927/8, including a new world record 437 against Queensland. Thereafter Bradman stole his thunder for run-scoring and he was affected by illness and injuries, though he had a glorious tour to England in 1934, scoring 1784 runs at 77.56, including topping the Test averages with 569 runs at 94.83. At The Oval he scored 266 and 22 in his last Test, retiring all too early at the age of 33. In his Sheffield Shield career he scored 5413 runs at 84.57.
29 Tests 1924-34: 2122 runs at 48.22, 7 100s HS 266; 21 catches.
First-class 1920-35: 13,819 runs at 65.18, 47 100s HS 437; 71 catches.

Dick POPE (USA)

WATER SKIING
Richard Downing Pope, Jr. b. 12 Dec 1930.

The first great water skier. He won his first of four consecutive US overall titles in 1947 and that year also became the first man known to ski barefooted. He competed in the first World Championships in 1949, but lost the title when he went all-out and made some crucial mistakes. In 1950 at his home water of Cypress

Gardens, Pope won the overall title and the slalom. He pioneered the use of a single ski for slalom and in his last tournament in early 1952 he also perfected a 540° turn on the jumping ramp. He then entered the Marine Corps and his competitive career was essentially over. After his return in 1955, Pope became manager of the US water ski team and President of the World Water Ski Union 1956-8. He succeeded his father (who with his brother Malcom had been a pioneer of boat stunts from the 1920s) as president of Cypress Gardens in 1962.

Hugo PORTA (Arg)

RUGBY UNION

Hugo Porta. b. 11 Sep 1951 Buenos Aires.

The greatest Argentinian player in history who was possibly the best fly-half in the world during his peak years. Deceptively quick off the mark, he was able to fall back on his superlative kicking skills when he lost some of his speed during the latter part of his career.

First capped in 1971, he played for his country 49 times (mostly as captain) before retiring in 1990 and he also played eight times for South America during a series of matches in 1980-84. His club rugby was played for Banco Nacion.

Porta's kicking was the major single factor in the emergence of Argentina as a power in world rugby. Against France in 1977 he kicked all 18 points in a drawn match and against the All Blacks in 1985 he again kicked all 21 points in another drawn game. He twice scored 23 points in a Test match and his total of 564 international points (514 for Argentina; 50 for South America) was the world record until passed by Michael Lynagh, although some of Porta's points came in matches against 'minor' countries. He twice dropped three goals in an international in Buenos Aires, against Australia in 1979 and against New Zealand in 1985.

A graduate of Buenos Aires University and an architect by profession, he was appointed Argentinian ambassador to South Africa in September 1991.

Hugh PORTER (UK)

CYCLING

Hugh William Porter. b. 27 Jan 1940 Wolverhampton, Staffordshire.

The finest ever British pursuit cyclist; in addition to his four world professional titles, 1968, 1970, 1972-3, he was second in 1967 and 1969, and third in 1971. As an amateur he won a bronze medal at the 1963 world championships in the pursuit, but had difficulty at the 1964 Olympics, losing in the quarter-finals at Tokyo, before winning the 1966 Commonwealth gold. He competed on the road as well, including the 1968 Tour de France (he did not finish), but with less success. Porter married British swimming gold medallist Anita Lonsbrough (qv) on 1 Jun 1965. Awarded the MBE.

John PORTER (UK)

HORSE RACING

John Porter. b. 2 Mar 1838 Rugeley, d. 21 Feb 1922 Newbury.

Betweeen 1868 and 1900 he trained the winners of over 1000 races, including 23 English classics, with a record-equalling seven Derbys. In all, in 43 seasons he trained the winners of 1063 races. He was apprenticed to John Barham Day in 1852, and rode occasionally. He became a trainer in 1863 for Sir Joseph Hawley, first at Cannons Heath and then at Kingsclere, Berkshire, which he bought on his patron's death in 1875. His best horses included the triple crown winners *Ormonde, La Flèche, Common* and *Flying Fox*. After his retirement from training in 1905 he managed Newbury racecourse.

Gert POTGIETER (SAf)

ATHLETICS

Gerhardus Cornelius Potgieter. b. 16 Apr 1937 Pietermaritzburg.

Potgieter set three world records for 440y hurdles, starting with 50.7 in 1957, improving to 49.72 when he won the 1958 Commonwealth title in Cardiff (adding a second gold at the 4 x 440y relay), and then to 49.3 to win his fifth consecutive

South African 440y hurdles title in April 1960. He was also SA champion at 220y hurdles in 1959-60.
His clash with Glenn Davis was keenly anticipated at the 1960 Olympics, but Potgieter had a road accident in Europe on his way to Rome. He sustained serious injuries, including the loss of his left eye. Although he returned to athletics and won the SA decathlon title in 1966 he was never able to recapture his hurdling form. As a 19-year-old in 1956 he was on the way to a possible medal in the Olympic 400m hurdles final, but fell at the tenth hurdle and came in sixth and last.
Other bests: 440y 46.3 (1959), 110m hurdles 14.5 (1960), 220y hurdles 23.1 (1957).

Jonathan POTTER (UK)

HOCKEY

Jonathan Nicholas Mark Potter. b. 19 Nov 1963 Paddington, London.

Great Britain's most capped player. A talented half-back, he made his début for Britain against Pakistan in 1983 and went on to win a record 128 caps, also playing 82 times for England. After winning a bronze medal at the 1984 Olympics, he won silver at the 1986 World Cup and 1987 European Cup and an Olympic gold medal in 1988. Before making his third Olympic appearance at Barcelona, he won a bronze medal in the 1991 European Cup. After graduating from Southampton University he played for Hounslow.

Denis POTVIN (Can)

ICE HOCKEY

Denis Charles Potvin. b. 29 Oct 1953 Ottawa, Ontario.

As a player in Junior A hockey in Canada, Potvin heralded was what to come when he broke Bobby Orr's scoring record. He eventually succeeded Orr as the top defenseman in the NHL and no less an authority than Stan Fischler actually rates Potvin ahead of Orr in the all-time list of defensemen. Potvin played his entire career with the New York Islanders and guided them to four straight Stanley Cup victories in 1980-3.
NHL career 1973-88 - 1060 games, 310 goals, 742 assists, 1052 points. Play-offs: 185 games, 56 goals, 164 points. Best year: 1978/9: 31 goals, 101 points. Norris Trophy 1976, 1978-9; Calder Trophy 1974.

Annet PÖTZSCH (GDR)

FIGURE SKATING

Annet Pötzsch b. 3 Sep 1960 Karl-Marx-Stadt. Married Axel Witt, older brother of Katarina (qv).

Twice a world champion and East Germany's first Olympic figure skating gold medallist. After winning the first of her four East German titles as a 16-year-old in 1976, she went on to become a three-time European champion and engaged in a series of classic contests with Linda Fratianne (USA). The American beat her at the 1977 and 1979 World Championships but Pötzsch was the winner at the 1978 and 1980 World Championships and at the 1980 Olympic Games.

Raymond POULIDOR (Fra)

CYCLING

Raymond Poulidor. b. 15 Apr 1936 Masbaraud-Merignat.

The most popular rider of his time and one of the best-loved French cyclists ever. His acclaim was mostly for his grace in defeat for he rarely won the major victories often expected of him. It was his bad fortune to ride in the same era as Anquetil and then Merckx. In the Tour de France, Poulidor started 14 times between 1962 and 1976, and placed 2nd three times (1964-5, 1974) and 3rd five times (1962, 1966, 1969, 1972, 1976). He won seven stages in his 14 Tours, but despite this he never wore the yellow jersey for even a day.
In the world professional road race he was second in 1974 and third in 1961, 1964 and 1966.
Major victories: Milan-San Remo 1961, Flèche-Wallonne and Grand Prix de Nations 1963, Paris-Nice 1972-3, Vuelta à España 1964, Dauphiné-Libéré 1966.

Ronald POULTON (UK)

RUGBY UNION

Ronald William Poulton. b. 12 Sep 1889 Oxford, d. 5 May 1915 Belgium. Later Poulton-Palmer.

The outstanding player in English rugby immediately prior to World War I. An elusive runner on the wing or in the centre and a deadly finisher, he scored a record five tries in the 1909 Oxford v Cambridge match and four tries for England against France in 1914 which was then a record for an international. In all, he scored eight tries for England in 17 internationals and 24 points for Oxford in three University matches 1909-11. He also won a hockey blue in these three years.
On inheriting a fortune from his uncle, he changed his name to Poulton-Palmer in 1913 and on leaving Oxford he joined the family biscuit firm of Huntley and Palmer. A handsome, popular officer, he was killed by a sniper's bullet while serving with the Berkshire Regiment.

Mike POWELL (USA)

ATHLETICS

Michael Anthony Powell. b. 10 Nov 1963 Philadelphia.

He won an epic long jump contest at the World Championships in Tokyo in 1991 to end the winning streak of Carl Lewis and to take, with a jump of 8.95m, the world record that Bob Beamon had set back in 1968. He won silver medals behind Lewis at the Olympic Games of 1988 and 1992, and won the World Student Games long jump in 1987 and the US title in 1990 and 1992-3. He has a sociology degree from UCLA, and was formerly at UC/Irvine. An effervescent character, he is proving a great crowd pleaser at meetings all round the world.

Jean PRAT (Fra)

RUGBY UNION

Jean Prat. b. 1 Aug 1923 Lourdes.

With 51 caps (one at centre, the rest as a flanker), including 12 as captain, between 1945 and 1955 he was the dominant figure in the revival of French rugby after the war. Unusually for a forward, he dropped five goals in internationals and his total of 145 international points is a record for a forward. He was also an inspirational captain, leading France to their first away wins against Wales 1948 and England 1951. In 1954 he captained France and scored the winning try in their first-ever win over New Zealand, and that year France took a share in the Five Nations Championship for the first time in their history. His brother, **Maurice** (b. 17 Sep 1928 Lourdes), also won 31 caps as a centre. Nicknamed 'Monsieur Rugby', throughout his career Jean played for Lourdes and helped them to six French championships between 1948 and 1958, with another as their coach in 1960. His book *Mêlée Ouverte* was published in 1968.

Steve PREFONTAINE (USA)

ATHLETICS

Steven Roland Prefontaine. b. 25 Jan 1951 Coos Bay, Oregon, d. 1 Jun 1975 Eugene, Oregon.

Although he did not win an Olympic medal or set a world record, 'Pre' was a legend even before his untimely death at the age of 24 when his sports car went out of control as he was returning home, having dropped off Frank Shorter at Kenny Moore's house following a post-meeting party.
He was the leader of the resurgence in US distance running and his flamboyant style made him a national hero, with a growing industry in 'Go Pre' T-shirts. At the University of Oregon he won a record four successive titles at 3 miles/5000m in 1970-3. He was the 1971 Pan-American champion at 5000m, placed fourth at the 1972 Olympics and was AAU champion at 3 miles in 1971 and 1973. He set US records at each distance from 2000m to 10,000m in 1974: 2000m 5:01.4, 3000m 7:42.6, 2M 8:18.29, 3M 12:51.4, 5000m 13:21.87, 6M 26:51.8, 10,000m 27:43.6.
Other bests: 1500m 3:38.1 and 1M 3:54.6, both in 1973.
The Prefontaine Classic meeting has been held annually in his memory at Eugene from 1976.

Ellen PREIS (Aut)

FENCING

Ellen Preis. b. 6 May 1912 Berlin. Married name Müller.

The first woman fencer to compete in five Olympic Games (1932-56); winner of the Olympic foil title in 1932 and a bronze medallist in 1936 and 1948. She was world champion in 1947, 1949 and in 1951, when she shared the title with Renée Garilhe (Fra).

Paddy PRENDERGAST (Ire)

HORSE RACING

Patrick J Prendergast. b. 5 Aug 1909 Co. Kildare, d. 20 Jun 1980 Kildare.

A great Irish trainer, whose Meadow Court stables were at Maddenstown near the Curragh. After an unsuccessful career as a jumps jockey, he worked in Australia and for the Epsom trainer Harry Hedges before being granted his trainer's licence in Ireland in 1941. He trained 17 Irish classic winners and four in England, where he was leading trainer 1963-5. His sons Kevin (b. 5 Jul 1932) and Paddy Jnr (b. 19 Mar 1935) both became trainers.

Alan PRESCOTT (UK)

RUGBY LEAGUE

George Alan Prescott. b. 17 Jun 1927.

After starting his career as a winger he later moved into the pack and in 1956 became the first forward ever to captain Great Britain. He signed for Halifax in 1946 as a winger but moved to loose forward when his weight increased and after he transferred to St Helens in 1948/9 he developed into an outstanding prop forward. In an international career which started in 1951 he won 28 caps and led the British team to victory in the 1958 Test series in Australia. As was to be expected from a former winger, he showed unusual speed for a forward and scored an exceptional try when St Helens won the 1956 Challenge Cup final. After he retired, he stayed on as a coach at St Helens.

Irina PRESS (USSR)

ATHLETICS

Irina Natanovna Press. b. 10 Mar 1939 Kharkov.

Hugely powerful all-rounder who won Olympic titles at 80m hurdles in 1960 and at pentathlon in 1964. She also ran on the USSR's fourth-placed sprint relay team in 1960 and was third at 80m hurdles and sixth at shot in 1964.
The younger of the Press sisters, she set six world records at 80m hurdles from 10.6 in 1960 to 10.3 in 1965 and eight at pentathlon to the 5246 points that she recorded to win the Olympic title in Tokyo 1964.
Other bests: 60m 7.2 (1961), 100m 11.4 (1960), 200m 24.2, high jump 1.67m, long jump 6.24m, shot 17.21m (1964).

Tamara PRESS (USSR)

ATHLETICS

Tamara Natanovna Press. b. 10 May 1937 Kharkov.

Bestrode the world of women's shot and discus throwing in the 1960s. Tamara was Olympic champion at shot in 1960 and 1964 and at discus in 1964 (silver in 1960). She won the European double in 1962 after winning the shot and placing third at discus in 1958. In the Soviet Championships she won nine shot (1958-66) and seven discus (1960-6) titles.
She set six world records at the shot from 17.25m in 1959 to 18.59m in 1965 and six at the discus from 57.15m in 1960 to 59.70m in 1965. Her 77cm improvement to 18.55m at Leipzig on 10 Jun 1962 was the biggest ever for a world shot record. Both Tamara and her younger sister Irina retired from the sport in 1966; perhaps coincidentally with the advent of sex testing.

Jozef PRIBILINEC (Cs)

WALKING

Jozef Pribilinec. b. 6 Jul 1960 Kremnica.

Compiled a most successful record at the 20 kilometres walk in the 1980s, winning the European title in 1986 and the Olympic title in 1988. Earlier he had gained silver

medals at the 1982 Europeans and both the 1983 and 1987 World Championships. He also won the World Cup in 1983, and his only disqualification in a major race was after finishing first in the 1985 World Cup race. He first came to prominence by winning the 1979 World Junior title at 10,000m walk, and indoors at the 5000m walk he was European champion in 1987-8 and 2nd in the Worlds in 1987. A sports instructor, he competed for Dukla Banská Bystrica. After a four-year retirement he returned to competition in 1993, immediately regaining his place among the world's élite.
World track walk bests: 3000m 11:00.2 (1985), 5000m 18:42.0 (1985), 10,000m 38:02.60 (1985), 15,000m 58:22.4 (1986), 1 hour 15447m (1986). World road best: 20km 1:19:30 (1983).

Ryan PRICE (UK)

HORSE RACING

(Captain) Henry Ryan Price. b. 16 Aug 1912 Hindhead, d. 16 Aug 1986 Finton, W Sussex.

Leading NH trainer in 1954/5, 1958/9, 1961/2, 1965/6 and 1966/7. He took out a trainer's licence in 1937, and, after war service as a commando, saddled his first winner at Plumpton in 1946. He trained in Sussex at Wisborough Green and Lavant before moving to Findon in 1951. His horses won the Champion Hurdle three times, the Grand National (*Kilmore* 1962), and Cheltenham Gold Cup (*What A Myth* 1969). In the 1960s he began to train more horses for the flat, and in 1970 handed over his jumpers to Josh Gifford so as to concentrate on the flat, winning the Oaks in 1972 and St Leger in 1975 before retiring in 1982.

Tommy PRICE (UK)

SPEEDWAY

Thomas Price. b. 11 Jun 1911 Cambridge.

In 1949 he became the first Englishman to be world speedway champion, on the resumption of that event for the first time since 1938. He had won the British Championship in 1946. He captained Wembley and later emigrated to Australia, where he lives in Perth.

Joe PRIMEAU (Can)

ICE HOCKEY

Joe Primeau. b. 24 Jan 1906 Lindsay, Ontario.

Primeau played center for the Toronto Maple Leafs for all nine years of his NHL career and is best known for centering the famed Kid Line with Busher Jackson and Charlie Conacher. He was an unselfish player who passed up individual fame to make his team and his team-mates better. Surprisingly, he retired when he was only 30 years old. He attempted a career as a businessman, but was lured back into coaching. He eventually became the only man to coach winners of the Memorial Cup (winners of the Canadian Junior A championship), the Allan Cup (the Canadian amateur team trophy), and the Stanley Cup.
NHL career 1927-36 - 310 games, 66 goals, 243 points. Best year: 1931/2: 37 assists, 50 points. Lady Byng Trophy 1932.

John PRINCE (NZ)

CROQUET

John G. Prince. b. 23 Jul 1945 Lower Hutt, Wellington.

In 1963 when he made his Test début for New Zealand at the age of 17 years 190 days, he became the youngest player ever to appear in the MacRobertson Shield. He has gone on to make a record seven appearances in this series to 1990. On 30 Mar 1970 he became the first to achieve a sextuple peel in competition and in 1983 the first to achieve two sextuple peels in a day. His first of more than 30 NZ titles was in 1969, and when in 1974 he beat Nigel Aspinall in all three matches for NZ v England he was recognised as the world's best player.

Meyer PRINSTEIN (USA)

ATHLETICS

Meyer Prinstein. b. Dec 1880 Poland, d. 10 Mar 1925 New York.

The winner of five Olympic titles. He started with 2nd at long jump and 1st at triple jump in 1900, before winning both

events in 1904 and the long jump in 1906. AAU long jump champion 1898, 1902, 1904 and 1906.
First came to prominence with a US record 7.19m at the 1898 IC4As and two weeks later a world record 7.23. After five improvements on this by Alvin Kraenzlein, Prinstein came back with 7.50 to beat his great rival easily at the 1900 Penn Relays. Best triple jump 14.47m (1900).
A graduate of Syracuse University, he practised as a lawyer before his early death.

Mike PROCTER (SAf)

CRICKET

Michael John Procter. b. 15 Sep 1946 Durban.

Procter played just two Test series as well as playing in all five Rest of the World v England games in 1970; then he was lost to international cricket through South Africa's isolation. His Test bowling record shows just how much of an impact he would have made, with 26 wickets at 13.57 against Australia in 1969/70.
He was a magnificent all-rounder, an inspiration to the teams for whom he played, Natal 1965-9 and 1976-89, Western Province 1969/70, Rhodesia 1970-6, and Gloucestershire 1965-81. He was immensely popular in his adopted county, whom he captained from 1977-81, giving himself wholeheartedly to their cause. A recurring knee injury brought his retirement although he did make a later comeback with Natal.
He was capable of fearsome pace as a fast bowler, amazingly off the wrong foot, also bowled off-breaks successfully from time to time, and was a classical and hard-hitting batsman. In England he took 100 wickets in a season twice and scored 1000 runs nine times. For Rhodesia in 1970/1 he equalled the world record with six successive centuries.
7 Tests 1966-70: 226 runs at 25.11, HS 48; 41 wickets at 15.02, BB 6-73; 4 catches. First-class 1965-89: 21,936 runs at 36.01, 48 100s HS 254; 1417 wickets at 19.53, BB 9-71; 325 catches.

Marcel PRONOVOST (Can)

ICE HOCKEY

Joseph René Marcel Pronovost. b. 15 Jun 1930 Lac la Tortue, Québec.

Pronovost was a tough defenseman during his 15 years with the Detroit Red Wings and 5 years with the Toronto Maple Leafs. He played with reckless abandon and was oft-injured, but it never seemed to slow his intensity. In the 1961 Stanley Cup finals, he played with a broken ankle. Before each game he would remove the cast stabilising the ankle, lace up his skates and play the game, and then replace the cast after the game.
NHL career 1950-70 - 1206 games, 88 goals, 345 points.

Alain PROST (Fra)

MOTOR RACING

Alain Prost. b. 24 Feb 1955 St Chamond.

The most successful and most complete motor racing driver of all-time. He has set records with 51 Formula One Grand Prix wins and 776.5 points from his 194 starts from 1981 to the end of July 1993. He was world champion in 1985-6 and 1989, and was runner-up in 1983-4, 1988 and 1990, and had a peak of seven wins in two of those years, 1984 and 1988.
After making his Karting and Formula Renault début in 1976, he was the 1979 European Formula Three champion and had his first Formula One start in the 1980 Argentine GP for McLaren. Switching to Renault, he had his first win in the 1981 French GP. He was 5th, 4th and 2nd in the championship 1982-4, losing by just half a point to Niki Lauda in the final year. He then returned to McLaren and his yearly championship placings in 1985-90 were 2, 1, 1, 4, 2, 1, 2. He drove for Ferrari in 1991, but had a year off in 1992 before returning in 1993 to drive for Williams, winning his first race back and continuing in his accustomed dominant fashion, taking pole position in nine of the first ten races of the season and winning seven of these up to and including the German Grand Prix, which was his 51st Formula One success compared to 39 by the next

best of Ayrton Senna. A master of tactics, cool, rational and economical, he also has a fine mechanical understanding of his cars.

Ludmila PROTOPOPOV (USSR) see BELOUSOVA

Oleg PROTOPOPOV (USSR)

FIGURE SKATING

Oleg Alekseyevich Protopopov. b. 16 Jul 1932 Leningrad.

Partnering his wife, Ludmila (née Belousova), he won the Olympic pairs title in 1964 and 1968 and they also won the world title for four successive years, 1965-8. After taking up the sport in 1948 at the relatively late age of 16, he joined the navy in 1951 and two years later placed third in the USSR pairs championship. Having been given time off from his naval duties, he began training in earnest in 1954 at a Moscow rink where he first met Ludmila Belousova and they were married the following year.

Maricica PUICA (Rom)

ATHLETICS

née Maricica Luca. b. 29 Jul 1950 Bucharest. Married to her trainer Ion Puica.

A consistently top-class distance runner throughout the 1980s, Puica won the 1984 Olympic title at 3000m, in that epic race when Mary Decker tripped over Zola Budd. She was world cross-country champion in 1982 and 1984, and had the added distinction of being the first woman ever to beat Grete Waitz in a road race.
Surprisingly her only other final placing at four Olympics, 1976-88, was 7th at 1500m in 1980, while she was silver medallist at 3000m in the 1987 Worlds and the Europeans of both 1982 and 1986, after placing 4th in 1978.
She set two world records, for 1 mile in 1982 and for 2000m in 1986.
Best times: 800m 1:57.8 (1979), 1000m 2:31.5 (1986), 1500m: 3:57.22 (1984), 1 mile 4:17.33 (1985), 2000m 5:28.69 (1986), 3000m 8:27.83 (1985), 5000m 15:06.04 (1985).

Aubert PUIG (Fra)

RUGBY LEAGUE

Aubert Puig. b. 24 Mar 1925 Andernach, Germany. aka Puig-Aubert

An automatic choice as full back for his country from 1946 to 1956, during which period he won 46 international caps and scored a record 361 points. He was at his best on the 1951 tour of Australia when the unfancied French team surprisingly took the series with a 35-14 win in the third Test. His record of 236 points on the tour bettered Jim Sullivan's record and although that record has now been beaten, no one has bettered Puig's feat of kicking 18 goals from 18 attempts in the three 1951 Test matches. Stocky and powerful at 1.67m tall and weighing 100kg by the end of his career, he played on six French championship winning teams and five cup winners, five and four respectively with Carcassone between 1945 and 1953 and once each with the XIII Catalan in 1957-9. He took charge of the French national team from 1969.

John PULMAN (UK)

SNOOKER

John Pulman. b. 12 Dec 1923 Teignmouth, Devon.

Pulman turned professional after winning the English Amateur snooker title in 1946 and steadily progressed until he reached the World Matchplay championship semi-final in 1954. He was beaten by Fred Davis in the final in 1955 and 1956 but won in 1957, when the event was held for the last time. When the World Championship was revived in 1964 Pulman was challenged by Fred Davis for the title and won 19-16. He retained the title against six successive challenges in 1964-8, but was beaten by John Spencer in the first round in 1969 when the Championship was contested for the first time since 1951 as a knock-out tournament. In 1970 he was beaten by Ray Reardon in the final. His standard declined thereafter, but he reached the world semi-final in 1978. From the 1970s he has commentated regularly on the game for television.

Ferenc PUSKÁS (Hun, Spa)

FOOTBALL
Ferenc Puskás. née Purczeld. b. 2 Apr 1927 Budapest.

One of the greatest inside-forwards of the post-war era. He won his first international cap aged 18 in 1945 and went on to play for Hungary 84 times, including one sequence of 36 consecutive appearances, scoring a record total of 83 goals. He was later capped four times by Spain, three of them in the 1962 World Cup.
Starting his career with Kispest in 1943 he remained with the club after it was strengthened with Army players to become Honvéd and while with them won five Hungarian League titles and an Olympic gold medal in 1952.
At the time of the 1956 Hungarian uprising Puskás was on a South American tour with Honvéd and like his team-mates, Kocsis and Czibor, decided not to return home. He spent a year in Vienna and then joined Real Madrid where he became one of the stars of a superlative team, scoring 35 goals in 39 European Cup matches for them including four in the 1960 final against Eintracht Frankfurt and another hat-trick in 1962 against Benfica. With Real, Puskas won the European Cup and World Club Championship 1960, the Spanish League each year 1961-5 and the Spanish Cup 1961.
He retired in 1966 and coached all over the world, with spells in Canada, the USA, Saudi Arabia, Egypt, Paraguay and Chile, and notably as manager of the Greek champions Panathinaikos, where he achieved the remarkable feat of taking them to the 1971 European Cup final. Director of international relations for the Hungarian Soccer Federation, in 1993 he returned temporarily to manage the Hungarian national team.
Renowned for his goal-scoring abilities, Puskás was known as the 'Galloping Major' due to his Army rank; in 1992 he was promoted to lieutenant-colonel.
He topped the Hungarian League scoring list four times between 1947 and 1954 and was the leading scorer in the Spanish League in four of the five seasons between 1960 and 1964.

Emiel PUTTEMANS (Bel)

ATHLETICS
Emiel Puttemans. b. 8 Oct 1947 Leuwen.

A brilliant distance runner, who set world records for 3000m 7:37.6 (1972), 2 miles 8:17.8 (1971) and 5000m 13:13.0 (1972). His pattering strides were well suited to tight indoor tracks and he set long-lasting standards indoors in 1973: 2000m 5:00.0, 3000m 7:39.2 and 2 miles 8:13.2, and in 1976 for 5000m 13:20.8. His championship record did not do justice to his abilities. He competed at four Olympic Games but only once met with any success, in 1972 when he was 2nd at 10,000m and 5th at 5000m. He did, however, win the European Indoor 3000m in 1973 and 1974.

Janusz PYCIAK-PECIAK (Pol)

MODERN PENTATHLON
Janusz Pyciak-Peciak. b. 9 Feb 1949 Warsaw.

Olympic champion at modern pentathlon in 1976 and 6th in 1980, and World champion in 1977 and 1981. With the Polish team he won World Championship gold medals in 1977-8 and 1981.

QAMAR ZAMAN (Pak)

SQUASH
Qamar Zaman. b. 11 Apr 1951 Quetta, Baluchistan.

One of the most adventurous squash players, his game was built on a superb natural ability and a wide range of attacking shots. At times these talents made him virtually unbeatable, but his reluctance to play the orthodox game when holding commanding leads prevented him from winning more major titles. Coached by his father, Mohammed Ayub, his first important titles were the Pakistan Under-16 in 1967 and Under-18 in 1968-9. He first came to England in 1972 and the following year reached the final of the British Amateur and the semi-finals of the Open. In 1974 he again lost in the final of the Amateur but in 1975 he scored his greatest success when he won the British Open after beating the holder, Geoff Hunt, in the quarter-finals. Although he again beat Hunt soon afterwards, the Australian remodelled his game and Zaman never repeated his victories. He won the World Masters in 1979, the International Squash Players Championship in 1977 and 1979 and was runner-up in the World Open four times, 1977, 1979-80 and 1984, and the British Open four times.

Don QUARRIE (Jam)

ATHLETICS

Donald O'Reilly Quarrie. b. 25 Feb 1951 Kingston.

Quarrie won a complete set of Olympic medals: gold at 200m and silver at 100m in 1976, with bronze at 200m in 1980. He added a sprint relay silver medal in 1984. He had been selected for the 1968 Olympics at the age of 17 but was injured in training and unable to compete, so he first came to worldwide attention with sprint trebles, 100m, 200m and relay, at the 1970 Commonwealth and 1971 Pan-American Games. He had three more Commonwealth successes, at 100m and 200m in 1974 and at 100m in 1978, and set four world records: at 100m, a 9.9 at Modesto in 1976, and at 200m, three times of 19.8. The first, also auto-timed at 19.86, was when he won the Pan-American title at the high altitude of Cali, Colombia in 1971. Then he twice ran 19.8 at Eugene in June 1975. The second was when he won the third of his AAU 200m titles (he also won two at 100m), and in both those 1975 races he beat Steve Williams, whom he considered his greatest sprint rival.

Ana QUIROT (Cuba)

ATHLETICS

Ana Fidelia Quirot Moret. b. 23 Mar 1963 Palma Soriano, Santiago de Cuba.

A fine middle distance runner who won 39 successive 800m finals from the Grand Prix final in 1987 to her third place in Zürich 1990. She was unable to take part in the 1988 Olympics, but won a bronze medal at 800m in 1992. In the World 800m she was 4th in 1987 and 2nd in 1991. Perhaps her peak achievement came with a triple win at 400m, 800m (in her personal best time of 1:54.44) and 4x400m relay at the 1989 World Cup. She also achieved this triple at the Central American Games of 1986 and 1990, and the 400m and 800m at the 1989 World Student Games and 1990 Goodwill Games. At the quadrennial Pan-American Games she has won eight medals between 1979 and 1991, including the 400m and 800m double in 1987 and 1991. She was five times a Grand Prix series winner: 800m 1987, 1989, 1991; 400m 1988 and 1990.

Formerly married to Raúl Cascaret, world freestyle wrestling champion at 74kg 1985-6, she was a graduate of the Havana Institute of PE. Her career was threatened when she suffered severe burns in a household accident in January 1993, after which she give birth prematurely to a daughter, who died a few days later.

Other bests: 200m 23.07 (1988), 400m: 49.61 (1991) and hand-timed 49.2 (1989), 1000m 2:33.12 (1989).

Adrian QUIST (Aus)

TENNIS

Adrian Karl Quist. b. 23 Jan 1913 Medindie, South Australia.

An outstanding doubles player and one of the finest ever left court players. Remarkably, his two Wimbledon doubles titles were separated by an interval of 15 years: he won first in 1935 with John Crawford and again in 1950 with John Bromwich. Quist also had the unusual record of holding the Australian doubles title from 1936 to 1950 and although the Championships were not held during the war years 1941-5 he still won 10 consecutive titles, the first two with Don Turnbull and the next eight with Bromwich. Additionally, he won the French doubles in 1935 with Crawford and the US doubles in 1939 with Bromwich.

In the singles he was at his best at the Australian Championships where he was a three-time winner (1936, 1940, 1948) but away from home he never progressed beyond the quarter-finals of a Grand Slam event, reaching this stage at Wimbledon

1936 and Forest Hills 1933. Between 1933 and 1948 he played in 23 Davis Cup ties, winning 42 of his 55 rubbers, but it was his doubles partnerships with John Bromwich which secured his place among the all-time greats.

Charles RADBOURN (USA)

BASEBALL

Charles Gardner Radbourn. b. 11 Dec 1854 Rochester, New York, d. 5 Feb 1897 Bloomington, Illinois.

'Old Hoss' was one of the great pitchers of the 19th century, with incredible durability. In 1883 he started 68 games and finished 66 of them, winning 48. In 1884 he completed all 73 games which he started and he won 60 games, still a major league record, though it should be considered in the light of the era. He pitched in a submarine, underhand-type style, which possibly explains his ability to pitch so often. Radbourn won his 310 games in only 11 seasons, averaging over 28 wins per season. He played mostly in the National League with Providence and Boston, but spent 1890 in the new Players' League with their Boston affiliate.

Career pitching 1880-91: ERA 2.68; W-L 310-195, SO 1830. Best seasons: 1884: 60-12, 1.38 ERA, 441 SO; 1883: 48-25, 2.05 ERA.

Paul RADMILOVIC (UK)

SWIMMING and WATER POLO

Paulo Radmilovic. b. 5 Mar 1886 Cardiff, Glamorgan, Wales, d. 29 Sep 1968 Weston-super-Mare, Somerset.

Won Olympic gold medals for water polo with the British team at successive Games, 1908, 1912 and 1920, and also for 4 x 200m freestyle swimming in 1908. He also competed at the Games of 1924 and 1928. He had a Yugoslav father and an Irish mother, and eventually competed in international swimming and water polo for almost 30 years. In swimming, he won a fourth gold medal in 1908 as a member of Britain's 4 x 200 metre relay team. He won nine ASA championships at an amazing range of distances and time span: 100 yards in 61.0 in 1909, 440y 1925, 880y 1926, 1 mile each year 1925-7 and the long-distance swim of five miles in the River Thames in 1907, 1925 and 1926. His first Welsh title was at 100y in 1901 and his last the 440y in 1929 at the age of 41 in a championship record that stood for nine years. In 1967 he was the first Briton inducted into the International Swimming Hall of Fame.

Helmut RAHN (Ger)

FOOTBALL

Helmut Rahn. b. 16 Aug 1929 Essen.

A brilliant right-winger whose two goals in the 1954 World Cup final gave West Germany a 3-2 victory over Hungary. In the 1958 World Cup finals he scored six goals in six games. His immoderate lifestyle almost certainly precluded him from winning more than 40 caps. He played for five different German clubs, with his only domestic honours coming in 1955 when Rot-Weiss Essen won the Championship, and ended his career with Enschede in Holland.

A mercurial player whose greatest asset was his ability to unleash a superb shot after dribbling past a host of defenders.

Wayne RAINEY (USA)

MOTOR CYCLING

Wayne Wesley Rainey. b. 23 Oct 1960 Los Angeles, California.

Winner of the 500cc world motorcycling championship for Yamaha for three successive years 1990-2. He was USA Superbike champion riding for Kawasaki in 1983 and for Honda in 1987, but had only one year of Grand Prix racing, at 250cc for Yamaha in 1984, behind him when he replaced Randy Mamola on the 500cc Yamaha team for 1988. His smooth style brought him immediate success and with consistent performances he came third in the championship series, winning the British GP. He moved up to second in 1989 before his winning years, when he won 14 races in his three seasons as champion. He added three more wins in the first eight races of 1993.

Sonny RAMADHIN (Tri)

CRICKET

Sonny Ramadhin. b. 1 May 1929 Esperance Village.

With just two trial games his only first-class experience, Ramadhin was selected for the 1950 West Indies tour of England. There, with the left-armer **Alf Valentine** (b. 29 Apr 1930), also an unknown, he mesmerised the England batsmen and took West Indies to a remarkable series success. He took 26 wickets at 26.23 and Valentine 33 at 20.42 in the series, and in all first-class matches they took 135 wickets at 14.88 and 123 at 17.94 respectively. Ramadhin's variety of bowling was remarkably hard to pick, mixing leg breaks in with his off breaks, and he reaped much devastation in Tests, although he was savaged by the Australian batsmen in 1951/2. His best Test analysis was his 7-49 in 31 overs at Edgbaston in the first innings of the First Test of the 1957 series against England, but that was followed by 98 overs, the most ever in first-class cricket, taking 2-179 in the second innings, when Peter May and Colin Cowdrey with resolute batting and much pad-play overcame his challenge.

He never quite recovered from such over-bowling, although he took 119 wickets on tour that summer, and had little further success in Tests. He did, however, take huge quantities of wickets in league cricket in England and played for Lancashire in 1964-5.

43 Tests 1950-61: 361 runs at 8.20, HS 44; 158 wickets at 28.96, BB 7-49; 9 catches. First-class 1950-65: 1092 runs at 8.66, HS 44; 758 wickets at 20.24, BB 8-15; 38 catches.

Alf RAMSEY (UK)

FOOTBALL

(Sir) Alfred Ernest Ramsey. b. 22 Jan 1920 Dagenham, Essex.

Although he was England's regular choice at right-back for four seasons, he is best remembered for his shrewd managerial skills. Beginning his professional career with Southampton, he made his first-team début in 1946 and won his first England cap shortly before moving to Tottenham in May 1949, helping them to win the Football League Division II in 1950 and the First Division in 1951. He went on to win 32 caps - including a run of 29 consecutive appearances - before retiring in 1955. That year he was appointed manager of Ipswich Town and repeated the rare feat he had accomplished at Tottenham as a player by taking them to the Division II and I titles in successive years, 1961-2. In May 1963 he was appointed England's manager, the most successful ever, winning the World Cup in 1966 and losing only 17 out of 113 matches to May 1974. He was knighted in January 1967 for his rôle in England's World Cup success. In 1977 he had a brief spell as manager of Birmingham City.

Mary RAND (UK)

ATHLETICS

Mary Denise Rand. née Bignal. b. 10 Feb 1940 Wells, Somerset. Later Toomey.

A brilliantly talented all-rounder, who made up for the disappointment of placing ninth in the long jump at the 1960 Olympics when favourite for the title by winning in great style in 1964, when she set three British and Olympic records culminating in a world record 6.76m. That year she also won the silver medal at pentathlon with a British record 5035 points and bronze in the sprint relay; she was 4th at 80m hurdles in 1960.

She set the first of her six British records at pentathlon at the age of 18 when 7th in the European Championships in 1958, and that year she won the Commonwealth long jump silver medal. She set 11 British records at the long jump from 6.19 in 1959, and also set British records at 100y 10.6 (1964) and 80m hurdles 10.8 (1963). Four months Mafter the birth of her daughter she won European long jump and sprint relay bronze medals in 1962, and she won the Commonwealth long jump in 1966. WAAA champion at 80m hurdles 1959, 100m hurdles 1966, high jump 1958, long jump 1959, 1961, 1963-5; pentathlon 1959-60. She married in 1960 rower Sidney Rand

and in 1969 Bill Toomey (qv), from whom she is now divorced.
Other bests: 100m 11.7 (1963), 200m 23.9 and 23.6w (1967), high jump 1.72m (1964).

Kumar Shri RANJITSINHJI (India)

CRICKET
HH the Maharajah Jam Sahib of Nawangar, Kumar Shri Ranjitsinhji. b. 10 Sep 1872 Sarodar, d. 2 Apr 1933 Jamnagar.

A batting genius, who exhilarated cricket fans at the turn of the century and opened up new techniques with his scintillating play and exquisite timing. From a small princely state in India he came to Cambridge University, although he did not gain his blue until 1893. He burst into prominence, however, when he started playing for Sussex in 1895, and he made his England début in 1896 with 62 and 154* in his first match against Australia. That year he scored 2780 runs in first-class cricket at 57.92, beating the record seasonal aggregate set by W.G. Grace. He missed the 1898 season but then dominated with successive seasons (1899-1901) scoring 3159 runs at 63.18, 3065 at 87.57 and 2468 at 70.51. He captained Sussex from 1899 to 1903, but ended his full-time cricket after 1904, except for part seasons on his return to England in 1908 and 1912. He became the Maharajah of Nawangar in 1907 and thereafter became involved in state affairs and was a delegate at the League of Nations after World War I. The Ranji Trophy was instituted in his memory in India a year after his death.
15 Tests 1896-1902: 985 runs at 44.95, 2 100s HS 175; 1 wicket; 13 catches.
First-class 1893-1920: 24,692 runs at 56.37, 72 100s HS 285; 133 wickets at 34.59, BB 6-53; 233 catches.*

Johnny RAPER (Aus)

RUGBY LEAGUE
John William Raper. b. 12 Apr 1939 Sydney.

A footballer of unusual versatility who played at the top level at stand-off, centre or second row but made his reputation as a loose forward. After touring Britain in 1959 and 1963, he was vice-captain on the 1967 tour. He took over the captaincy after Reg Gasnier was injured, and after losing the first Test led Australia to victory in the series. His nine-year international career ended in 1968 when he was captain of the winning Australian team in the World Cup. His club career started with Newtown in 1956, moving on to St George 1959-69, West Newcastle 1970-2 and Kurri Kurri 1973, after which he became a coach.

Abdul RASHID (Pak)

HOCKEY
Abdul Rashid, Jr. b. 3 Mar 1947.

Pakistan's most prolific goalscorer, he won gold medals at all the major tournaments: Olympic Games 1968 (with silver 1972 and bronze 1976), World Cup 1971, Asian Games 1970 and 1974. He played for the Pakistan International Airways team.

Seppo RÄTY (Fin)

ATHLETICS
Seppo Henrik Räty. b. 27 Apr 1962 Helsinki.

Räty was one of the most surprising World athletics champions of 1987, when he twice improved his national record in Rome to win the javelin with 83.54m. Since then he has proved to be a most consistent competitor at major meetings, 3rd at 1988 Olympics, 2nd at 1991 Worlds and 1992 Olympics. Finnish champion in 1985-6, 1989-91. In 1991 he sensationally twice improved his best by five metres with world records with the roughened-tail javelin at 91.98 and 96.96. With that spear ruled illegal he took the Finnish record to 90.60 in 1992.
Very powerfully built at 1.89m tall and weighing 110kg. A former factory worker, he competed for Tohmajärven Urheilijat.

Betsy RAWLS (USA)

GOLF
Elizabeth Earle Rawls. b. 4 May 1928 Spartanburg, South Carolina.

One of the greatest golfers in the early

years of the LPGA Tour. As an amateur at the University of Texas in 1950 she finished second in the US Open. After graduating the following year in physics, she turned professional and immediately won her first of four US Women's Opens, winning again in 1953, 1957 and 1960. Her other major wins were the LPGA in 1959 and 1969 and the Western Open in 1952 and 1959. She was leading money-winner on the LPGA Tour in 1952 and 1959, and her 55 victories is the third highest ever. Her career in the late 1950s would surely have been more impressive had she not had the redoubtable Mickey Wright as a fellow competitor. After her competitive retirement, she served as LPGA Tournament Director from 1975-81. She was not a long hitter but was known as having the best short game in women's golf.

Phil READ (UK)

MOTOR CYCLING

Philip William Read. b. 1 Jan 1939 Luton, Bedfordshire.

Eight times world motorcycling champion, at 250cc in 1964-5, 1968 and 1971, at 125cc in 1968, all riding for Yamaha; at 500cc for MV in 1973-4 and at Formula One for Honda in 1977. In his career between 1961 and 1975 he achieved 52 Grand Prix victories: 10 at 125cc, 27 at 250cc, 4 at 350cc and 11 at 500cc, 39 for Yamaha, 11 MV Augusta and 2 Norton. He won eight Isle of Man TT races 1961-77.

He bought his first bike, a 250cc side-valve Matchless, at the age of 13, started racing in 1956 when he was an apprentice engineer, and had his first win at Castle Combe in 1957. His first major wins were on Nortons before being selected by Geoff Duke to ride for Gilera in 1963; after that unsuccessful year he started his hugely successful Yamaha era. A most determined competitor, his feud with Bill Ivy brought him some notoriety in 1968, and he enjoyed fierce rivalry with Giacomo Agostini when they were team-mates in 1973. Awarded the MBE in 1979.

Ray REARDON (UK)

SNOOKER

Raymond Reardon. b. 8 Oct 1932 Tredegar, Monmouthshire.

Reardon was the top snooker player of the 1970s, winning the world title at his second attempt in 1970, each year 1973-6 and in 1978, the latter making him, at 45 years 6 months, the oldest ever champion. He was ranked as world number one from the introduction of rankings in 1976 until 1980 and again in 1982. Other major wins: Benson & Hedges Masters 1976, British Open 1982. He was also the BBC TV Pot Black champion in 1969 and 1979. He helped Wales to win the World Cup in 1979 and 1980.

His first important success was at 17 when he won the first of six successive Welsh Amateur titles, 1950-5. He left his colliery job in Wales to become a policeman when his family moved to Stoke-on-Trent. It was not until 1964 that he won the English Amateur title and he turned pro in 1967. Awarded the MBE in 1985.

Steve REDGRAVE (UK)

ROWING

Steven Geoffrey Redgrave. b. 23 Mar 1962 Amersham, Buckinghamshire.

Olympic gold medallist in 1984 at the coxed fours and in 1988 at the coxless pairs with **Andrew Holmes** (b. 15 Oct 1959), with whom he also took the bronze at coxed pairs. He equalled the all-time record with a third Olympic gold in 1992, at the coxed pairs with **Matthew Pinsent** (b. 10 Oct 1970) and cox **Garry Herbert** (b. 3 Oct 1969).

He was world champion at coxless pairs with Holmes in 1987 and with Pinsent in 1991, and at coxed pairs in 1986. In that year he became the first rower ever to win three gold medals at the Commonwealth Games, at single sculls and with Holmes at coxless and coxed pairs.

He was runner-up in the World Junior double sculls in 1980 and made his World senior début with 8th and 6th at Quad sculls in 1981-2. He won the Diamond Sculls at Henley in 1983 and 1985 and had five consecutive successes at the Wingfield Sculls from 1985-1989. In 1989 he took up bobsledding and was a member of the crew which won the British 4-man championship that year.

Jim REDMAN (Rho)

MOTOR CYCLING

James A Redman. b. 8 Nov 1931 Hampstead, London.

Winner of six world motorcycling titles in four years. Born in Britain, he emigrated to Rhodesia at the age of 18, racing there before returning to Europe. His first year, 1958, was unsuccessful but in 1960 he started racing for Honda, and for them won the world title at 250cc 1962-3 and 350cc 1962-5. In all, between 1962 and 1965 he won 18 Grands Prix at 250cc, 21 at 350cc and 4 at 125cc, as well as 2 at 500cc in 1966. On the Isle of Man he won the Junior TT and 250cc races each year 1963-5. When Honda moved out of racing in 1966, Redman retired and returned to South Africa.
A stylish and cool professional rider, he was awarded the MBE in 1964.

Tom REECE (UK)

BILLIARDS

Thomas Reece. b. 12 Aug 1873 Oldham, Lancashire, d. 16 Oct 1953 Lancing, Sussex.

Although he failed in his lifetime ambition to win the world billiards title, his break of 499,135 assures him of a place in the history of the game. This phenomenal score was made in London in the summer of 1907 and took almost five weeks to compile. Even then it was 'unfinished' but it was not officially recognised as the press and public were not continually present. The break was based on 249,552 'cradle' or 'anchor' cannons, involving repeated use of the same shot. After a rule restricting the number of ball-to-ball cannons to 25 was introduced, Reece devised the 'pendulum' cannon which led to further inflated scores. It soon became apparent that the game would suffer if unlimited scoring, entirely by specialist means, was permitted and in 1932 the important Baulk line rule was introduced.
He reached the final of the World Championship six times, 1912-14, 1921 and 1924-5, but lost to Melbourne Inman in his first three finals and to Tom Newman in the next three.

Robin REED (USA)

WRESTLING

Robin Lawrence Reed. b. 20 Oct 1899 Pettigrew, Arkansas, d. 20 Dec 1978 Salem, Oregon.

America's greatest wrestler in the pre-war era, and possibly the greatest ever. In a career that began in high school, and then continued at Oregon State, he was never defeated, winning three AAU titles in 1921-2 and 1924. He was not tremendously strong, but worked endlessly on improving his moves to better himself.
He was also a bit of a character. While hitchhiking his way across the country to join the 1924 US Olympic team in New York, he stopped at Iowa State and asked the coach if he could work out when the team came to practice. When the coach refused, Reed asked if he could do so if he pinned every man on the team. He then stood in the doorway and grabbed each team member as he came to practice, pinning all of them in quick succession.
Reed weighed only 135 lb, but at the Paris Olympics he won a bet when he pinned Harry Steel, the American heavyweight gold medallist, five times within 15 minutes. In his own event, the featherweight class, Reed was not challenged as he won the gold medal by pinning all his opponents.

Willis REED (USA)

BASKETBALL

Willis Reed, Jr. b. 25 Jun 1942 Hico, Louisiana.

A huge center who played college basketball at Grambling and for 10 years in the NBA with the New York Knicks. Until his retirement in 1974 he was one of the two or three top centers in the league and one most feared by opponents as he was a massive 2.08 m *6'10"*, 115 kg *255 lb*. He led the Knicks to two NBA championships in 1970 and 1973. In the first in 1970, against the Lakers led by Wilt Chamberlain at center, Reed was injured in the sixth game, and it was thought the Knicks could not win without their big man at center. He did not warm up before Game 7, but hobbled out shortly before tip-off to a huge ovation, and his mere presence inspired the Knicks who went on to win after he had scored the first basket of the game with a turn-out jumper.

Reed was known for his soft shooting touch around the basket, which belied his size. He played on the great Knicks teams which epitomised team basketball, but he was the clear leader.

He later became a coach, first in the NBA with the Knicks, then with Creighton College, and more recently with the New Jersey Nets.

Dai REES (UK)

GOLF

David James Rees. b. 31 Mar 1913 Barry, Wales, d. 15 Nov 1983.

Surpassed only by Ian Woosnam as the greatest ever Welsh golfer. In his 35-year career Rees had 20 British PGA tour victories, but never the one he most wanted, the British Open, in which he was runner-up three times and third once.

He won the Dunlop Masters in 1950 and 1962 and the *News of the World* Match Play in 1936, 1938 and 1949-50. Rees made nine Ryder Cup appearances as a player between 1937 and 1961, winning 7, losing 10 and halving 1 of his 18 matches, and captained the British PGA team that won the Cup for the first time for 24 years in 1957. He was also selected for the match in 1939 which was cancelled due to the outbreak of War, and was non-playing captain in 1967. He was a smallish man, but was known as a long hitter, especially for his size.

His father was the professional at Aberdare GC and Rees was assistant there 1929-34, before taking up appointments at Surbiton and Hindhead. Awarded the CBE.

Dick REES (UK)

HORSE RACING

Frederick Brychan Rees. b. 30 Nov 1894 Tenby. d. 14 Aug 1951 Lewes, Sussex.

The son of a Pembrokeshire vet, he was a complete horseman. Employing tactical mastery and with the ability to produce his mounts with driving finishes, he was the first great jumping jockey in Britain. After riding as an amateur for two years, he turned professional in 1921 and won the Grand National that year on *Shaun Spadah*. His elder brother **Billy** won the following year on *Music Hall*, and his nephew **Bill** rode *Pas Seul* to win the 1960 Cheltenham Gold Cup. Dick was five times champion NH jockey, in 1920-1, 1923-4, 1927.

As with so many jockeys, weight troubles curtailed his career.

Pee Wee REESE (USA)

BASEBALL

Harold Henry Reese. b. 23 Jul 1918 Ekron, Kentucky.

Reese was the premier fielding shortstop of his era, playing from 1940-58 with the Brooklyn/Los Angeles Dodgers. He was named to the All-Star team nine times during that 16-year career (he missed three years to military service). Reese also proved his greatness as a man when he befriended Jackie Robinson and helped ease his acceptance by other players when Robinson broke the major league colour line. Never a great hitter for average, Reese was valuable for his clutch hitting, his fielding, and his leadership. He was one of the best-liked Dodgers on that very popular team.

Career 1940-58: Avg. .269, HR 126; RBI 885; SB 232.

John REID (NZ)

CRICKET

John Richard Reid. b. 3 Jun 1928 Auckland.

Reid's hitting ability was shown when he hit a world record 15 sixes in an innings of 296 for Wellington v Northern Districts in 1963. He made his Test début in 1949

against England and from then played in 58 successive Tests for New Zealand until his retirement 16 years later, having established himself as one of the world's best all-rounders, adding fast-medium or off-break bowling, fine close fielding and occasional wicket-keeping to his powerful batting. He captained New Zealand for a decade, in 34 Tests from 1956. He scored a record 1915 runs (at 68.39) in a South African season when New Zealand toured there in 1961/2, with 546 runs and 11 wickets in the Test series. Awarded the OBE. He coached in New Zealand and South Africa.
58 Tests 1949-65: 3428 runs at 33.28, 6 100s HS 142; 85 wickets at 33.35, BB 6-60; 43 catches, 1 stumping.
First-class 1947-65: 16,128 runs at 41.35, 39 100s HS 296; 466 wickets at 22.60, BB 7-20; 240 catches, 7 stumpings.

William RENSHAW (UK)

TENNIS
William Charles Renshaw. b. 3 Jan 1861 Leamington, Warwickshire, d. 12 Aug 1904 Swanage, Dorset.

Winner of a record seven singles titles at Wimbledon (1881-6, 1889) and five doubles with his twin **Ernest** (1884-6, 1888-9). In 1880 and 1881 they also won the Oxford doubles which was recognised as the premier event prior to the introduction of the official All-England doubles championship at Wimbledon in 1884.
In ten singles appearances at Wimbledon, William Renshaw lost only three matches. His defeat by O.E.Woodhouse in the 3rd round on his début in 1880 was followed by six successive Championships and in 1887 he did not defend his title. In 1888 he lost to Irishman Willoby Hamilton in the quarter-final although family honour was restored as Ernest Renshaw won the title that year. William was again champion in 1889 and on his last appearance in 1890 he lost again to Hamilton. The Renshaws are generally recognised as the founders of modern tennis and credited with turning a game into a sport. The twins, who came from a wealthy family and were both educated at Cheltenham, had tremendous crowd appeal and after their retirement, attendances at Wimbledon dropped significantly. Although not the inventor of the overhead serve and smash, William developed their technique and was the first to employ them consistently and effectively. Marginally the older of the twins, William had the better championship record but both were well ahead of their contemporaries.

Jim RENWICK (UK)

RUGBY UNION
James Menzies Renwick. b. 12 Feb 1952 Hawick.

Starting with a a try on his international début against France in 1972, he went on to win 52 Scottish caps, scoring 67 points, including 8 tries. He shares the record of being Scotland's most capped player and when he retired in 1983 he was the world's most capped centre. He toured South Africa with the British Lions in 1980 and played in one Test.

Anfissa RESTSOVA (USSR/Rus)

SKIING/BIATHLON
Anfissa Restsova. b. 1964. née Romanova.

At the 1988 Olympics she won a silver medal at 20km cross-country skiing and a gold on the Soviet 4 x 5 km relay team, Four years later she became the first woman individual Olympic champion at the biathlon, to which she added a bronze medal in the biathlon relay. At cross-country skiing she had earlier won the silver medal at the 1985 and 1987 World Championships at 20km, and was second in the World Cup in 1987.

Mary Lou RETTON (USA)

GYMNASTICS
Mary Lou Retton. b. 24 Jan 1968 Fairmont, West Virginia.

The darling of the crowds at the Los Angeles Olympic Games in 1984, the year of the Eastern European boycott. Small at 1.44m *4' 8 3/4"*, but powerful, she had missed the 1983 Worlds through a wrist injury although at the end of that year she defeated many of the world's best at the Chunichi Cup. The Olympics were her major championships début at the age of 16. She fulfilled the dreams of her supporters and coach Béla Karolyi by gaining a perfect ten score on her floor exercises, the final event of the all-around competition, to tie for the gold with Ecaterina Szabo. She added a silver and two bronze medals at individual apparatus and a team silver. She married Shannon Kelley, former University of Texas quarterback, on 29 Dec 1990.

Carlos REUTEMANN (Arg)

MOTOR RACING

Carlos Alberto 'Lole' Reutemann. b. 12 Apr 1942 Santa Fé.

Runner-up for the world championship in 1981, when he was just one point behind Nelson Piquet. He started racing in 1965, and in his Formula One career he drove for Brabham 1972-6, Ferrari 1976-8, Lotus 1979, Williams 1980-2, and won five of his 146 Grand Prix races, scoring 310 points. His first win was the 1974 South African GP.

He is now state governor of Santa Fé and is running for the Presidency of Argentina in 1995.

Yvonne REYNDERS (Bel)

CYCLING

Yvonne Reynders. b. 4 Aug 1937 Schaarbeek-Brussels.

With Beryl Burton of Britain, Reynders was one of the two great women road riders of the 1960s. She won 12 medals at the women's world championships: road race - 4 gold (1959, 1961, 1963, 1966), 2 silver; pursuit - 3 gold (1961, 1964-5), 3 silver.

Butch REYNOLDS (USA)

ATHLETICS

Harry Lee Reynolds, Jr. b. 8 Jun 1964 Akron, Ohio.

In 1988 Reynolds smashed Lee Evans' 20-year-old world record of 43.86 by running 43.29 in Zürich, but he was surprisingly defeated at the Olympics when he was second to Steve Lewis, although he took a gold medal in the relay. In 1987 Reynolds, a student at Ohio State University, had run the three fastest ever low-altitude times, 44.10, 44.13 and 44.15, and won NCAA and TAC titles, but was beaten into third place (with a relay gold) at the World Championships. He set a further low-altitude record of 43.93 to win the US Trials in 1988.

He received a two-year ban after a positive drugs test in 1990 for Nandrolene at Monaco, but was reinstated by TAC in 1991 due to alleged irregularities in testing procedure. However, the IAAF ban was retained and there was considerable confusion when he was allowed by court rulings to run in the 1992 Olympic Trials. He placed fifth, and that qualified him for the US Olympic relay squad, but he was not permitted to run in Barcelona. Throughout the controversy Reynolds vociferously protested his innocence. The IAAF extended his ban to the end of 1992 for bringing the sport into disrepute. On 14 Dec 1992 the US District Court in Columbus, Ohio awarded for him against the IAAF: $6,839,902 for loss of earnings during his two-year suspension, and $20,356,008 punitive damages. The IAAF did not accept the jurisdiction of the court, but Reynolds returned to competition, won the 1993 World Indoor 400m title and later qualified for the US team at the outdoor World Championships. His brother Jeff had a 400m best of 44.98 in 1988.

Valeriy REZANTSEV (USSR/Kaz)

WRESTLING

Valeriy Grigoryevich Rezantsev. b. 8 Oct 1946 Novomoskovsk, Tula Oblast.

Rezantsev won seven consecutive Greco-Roman championships at the Olympics and World Championships at light-heavyweight (90kg): Olympic gold in 1972 and 1976, and World gold in 1970-1 and 1973-5. He was also European champion in 1970 and 1973-4 and Soviet champion 1970-5.

George RHODEN (Jam)

ATHLETICS

Vincent George Rhoden. b. 13 Dec 1926 Kingston.

After being overshadowed for some years by his compatriots Herb McKenley and Arthur Wint, Rhoden came through to beat McKenley for the first time in the 1949 AAU 400m and to win the Olympic title in 45.9 (46.09 on auto timing) in 1952 before anchoring the gold medal-winning Jamaican relay team. He had been an Olympic semi-finalist in 1948 and won a record ten medals at the Central American and Caribbean Games between 1946 and 1954.
Other bests: 100m 10.3 (1950), 200m 21.0 (1950), 220y straight track 20.5 (1952).

Wilfred RHODES (UK)

CRICKET

Wilfred Rhodes. b. 29 Oct 1876 Kirkheaton, Yorkshire, d. 8 Jul 1973 Branksome Park, near Poole, Dorset.

The greatest wicket-taker of all-time in first-class cricket, and an all-rounder whose runs total is exceeded by only 15 batsmen. Throughout his exceptionally long career he was a masterly slow left-arm bowler, and his sound batting progressed so that from an England No.10 or 11 in his first series in 1899 he developed to be able to open the innings in the period 1909-21, mostly with Jack Hobbs, with whom he made 8 century opening partnerships. He is one of only three cricketers to have batted in every position in the order in Tests. His 16 doubles of 1000 runs and 100 wickets in a season is the all-time record, as is his 23 seasons of 100 or more wickets. He captured 154 wickets at 14.60 in his first season of 1898, and went on to his peak seasons with 261 wickets at 13.81 in 1900 and 251 at 15.12 in 1901. He averaged under 20 runs per wicket in each season from then until 1930, apart from 1904 and 1911-13, when for a while he concentrated on his batting. He scored over 1000 runs in each of the 20 seasons in England between 1903 and 1926, with a peak of 2261 runs in 1911. At Kingston, Jamaica in 1930 he became, at 52 years 165 days, the oldest ever Test player and his span as a Test cricketer of 31 years 315 days is easily the record. He made a record number of 1107 first-class appearances. He later coached at Harrow School.
58 Tests 1899-1930: 2325 runs at 30.19, 2 100s HS 179; 127 wickets at 26.96, BB 8-68; 60 catches.
First-class 1898-1930: 39,802 runs at 30.83, 58 100s HS 267; 4187 wickets at 16.71, BB 9-24; 764 catches.*

Eugène RIBÈRE (Fra)

RUGBY UNION

Eugène Ribère. b. 14 Jun 1902 Thuir.

His total of 34 caps (1924-33) stood as a French record until surpassed by Jean Prat in 1954. He was on the losing side in his first 11 internationals, but the first-ever French victory over England in 1925 ended the string of defeats. A mobile loose forward, he captained France 12 times including the game against England in 1931 which was the last match France played in the Five Nations Championship before being banned from the competition for 16 years for infringing the amateur regulations.
He played for USA Perpignan and then Quillan and Narbonne. He took charge of French team selection in 1960.

Jerry RICE (USA)

AMERICAN FOOTBALL

Jerry Lee Rice. b. 13 Oct 1962 Starkville, Mississippi.

Rice was a good college footballer at Mississippi Valley State, graduating in 1985, but never really hinted that he would someday become possibly the greatest professional wide receiver of all time. He was drafted by the San Francisco 49ers and immediately made an impact on the league as he formed in the late 1980s, with quarterback Joe Montana, one of the great passing/receiving duos in league history. Rice was big (1.88m *6'2"*, 97 kg *215 lb*) and exceptionally fast, making him a great deep threat. In 1987, when he was the NFL MVP despite playing only 12 games, he caught 22 touchdown passes to beat the previous NFL record of 18 in a season, and during 1992 in only his 8th NFL season he caught his 101st touchdown pass, breaking Steve Largent's career NFL record, taking his total to 103 by the end of the season. By the end of his career, he could possibly put that record out of reach of future receivers. He has also equalled the record for seven consecutive NFL seasons at over 1000 yards receiving and has caught 610 passes, 9th all-time, in only eight years, including catching a pass in 111 consecutive games to the end of 1992. He helped San Francisco to Super Bowl victories in 1989 and 1990 and was the MVP in 1989, when he set a record for 215 yards gained receiving and tied the record with 11 pass receptions in the game.

Jim RICE (USA)

BASEBALL

James Edward Rice. b. 8 Mar 1953 Anderson, South Carolina.

Rice played outfield and designated hitter for the Boston Red Sox. He was an immensely powerful man, who early in his career gave indications that many power-hitting records were in jeopardy. Despite tailing off in his last few seasons, his career average was .300. From 1977-9 he had slugging averages of .593, .600, and .596, which were figures so good that they were almost anachronistic for the era. Strangely he had a troubled career, as Boston fans, often rumoured to be racist, never accepted the quiet, handsome, black man. He grew ill at ease with the media and the fans, and was often surly in his last years. It was sad, for his first ten years in the league warranted better treatment for him.

Career 1974-88: Avg. .300, HR 379; RBI 1423. Best seasons: 1977: .320, 39 HR, 114 RBI; 1978: .315, 46 HR, 139 RBI; 1979: .325, 39 HR, 130 RBI; 1983: .305, 39 HR, 126 RBI.

Sam RICE (USA)

BASEBALL

Edgar Charles Rice. b. 20 Feb 1890 Morocco, Indiana, d. 13 Oct 1974 Rossmor, Maryland.

An outfielder who played his entire 20-year career with the Washington Senators, he was a speedster who hit for good average, but with little power. He hit a lot of singles (2272 of his career 2987 hits) and also used his speed to garner a lot of triples. Between 1921 and 1930 he had 10 or more triples in every season. Six times he posted over 200 hits in one season.

Career 1915-34: 2987 hits Avg. .322; RBI 1078; SB 351. Best seasons: 1924: .334, 216 hits; 1925: .350, 227 hits; 1926: .337, 216 hits.

Henri RICHARD (Can)

ICE HOCKEY

Joseph Henri Richard. b. 29 Feb 1936 Montreal, Québec.

Henri Richard played his entire 20-year career with the Montreal Canadiens. As a center, he skated alongside his brother, Maurice, for the first five years of his career. Dubbed 'The Pocket Rocket' because he was only 170 cm *5' 7"* and 73 kg *160 lb*, he was able to perform well while playing in the shadow of his older brother and his career after he was out of that shadow became even more brilliant. While Maurice was intense and exciting, Henri was smooth and calculating. His record of skating on 11 Stanley Cup winners is the best in NHL history and may well stand forever.

NHL career 1955-75 - 1256 games, 358 goals, 1046 points. Playoffs: 180 games, 49 goals, 129 points. Best year: 1957/8: 52 assists, 80 points.

Maurice RICHARD (Can)

ICE HOCKEY

Joseph Henri Maurice Richard. b. 4 Aug 1921 Montreal, Québec.

'The Rocket' was possibly the most beloved player ever to don *le rouge, blanc et bleu* of the Montreal Canadiens. He played right wing and was idolised for his skill and for his intensity. In 1944/5, he set the modern standard for goalscoring when he totalled 50 in a 50-game NHL season. That goals-per-game average would remain a modern NHL record until 1982

when Wayne Gretzky scored 92 in 80 games. Richard helped Montreal win the Stanley Cup eight times. He was once described as 'the epitome of recklessness, of untrammelled fire and fury and abandon on the ice.' He used that intensity to become one of the greatest players ever, rivalled during his playing days only by Gordie Howe. He was probably not the all-round player that Howe was, but no hockey player was ever more exciting.
NHL career 1942-60 - 978 games, 544 goals, 965 points. Play-offs: 132 games, 82 goals, 126 points. Hart Trophy 1947.

Barry RICHARDS (SAf)

CRICKET

Barry Anderson Richards. b. 21 Jul 1945 Durban.

Richards played just one Test series, a gloriously successful one against Australia, and also played all five matches for the Rest of the World against England in 1970, but the South African ban cost him the chance of further Test honours. In the early 1970s he was probably the best batsman in the world, forming a formidable opening partnership for Hampshire, for whom he played from 1968-78, with Gordon Greenidge.

He played in South Africa for Natal (captain 1973-6). He was the first man to score 1000 runs in a Currie Cup season, 1971/2 and 1972/3. He also had a highly successful season in Australia in 1970/1, scoring 1538 runs at 109.86, including one of the greatest innings ever seen there, 356 for South Australia v Western Australia at Perth. That included 325* on the first day of the match.

He was very successful with World Series cricket, but the lack of an international challenge meant that he eventually tired of county cricket, a stage not big enough for him to display the full majesty of his talents. A right-handed batsman and also a useful off-break bowler and a brilliant slip fielder.
4 Tests 1970: 508 runs at 72.57, 2 100s HS 140; 1 wicket at 26.00; 3 catches.
First-class 1964-83: 28,358 runs at 54.74, 80 100s HS 356; 77 wickets at 37.48, BB 7-63; 367 catches.

Bob RICHARDS (USA)

ATHLETICS

Robert E Richards. b. 20 Feb 1926 Champaign, Illinois. Ordained in 1948.

Known as 'The Vaulting Vicar', Richards was the best pole vaulter of the early 1950s, winning the Olympic title in 1952 and 1956, the Pan-American title in 1951 and 1955, and the AAU nine times outdoors, each year 1948-57 except 1953, and eight indoors 1948, 1950-3, 1955-7. Having won the bronze medal in 1948, he is the only man to win pole vault medals at three Olympics. At the University of Illinois he tied for the NCAA vault title in 1947. A great all-rounder, he was also AAU decathlon champion in 1951, 1953-6, and took silver at the 1955 Pan-Ams. Although Richards never bettered the world records set by Cornelius Warmerdam, he followed him by becoming the second 15 ft *4.57m* vaulter, and cleared 15ft or higher in 126 competitions between 1951 and 1957. His best was 4.72m indoors in 1957, with 4.70 outdoors in 1956. He won 50 successive pole vault competitions 1950-2 and was unbeaten outdoors 1953-5.

The Sullivan Award winner of 1951, he founded the Bob Richards Motivational Institute. His son Bob, with the benefit of a fibre glass pole, exceeded his father's best with 5.33 in 1973.

Gordon RICHARDS (UK)

HORSE RACING

Sir Gordon Richards. b. 5 May 1904 Oakengates, d. 10 Nov 1986 Kintbury, Berkshire.

Richards bestrode the Turf in Britain, where he rode a record 4870 winners (over 2000 more than the previous record) and was champion jockey a record 26 times. In that final year he rode his one Epsom Derby winner, *Pinza*, just a few days after it had been announced that he was to be the first professional jockey to be knighted. The first of his 14 classic winners had been *Singapore* in the 1930 St Leger, and his greatest success came in winning the fillies Triple Crown on *Sun Chariot* in 1942.

At the age of 15 he answered an advertisement for stable-lads and joined the trainer Martin Hartigan. He had his first ride in public in October 1920 and his first winner was *Gay Lord* at Leicester on 31 Mar 1921. Champion with 118 winners in 1925, he contracted tuberculosis in 1926 but returned as champion with 164 winners the following year, and from then until 1953 he was champion every year except 1930, when Freddie Fox beat him by one, and 1941 when he broke a leg. He surpassed Fred Archer's season's record with 259 winners in 1933, when on 3-5 October he rode a world record 12 successive winners. He improved the season's record to 269 in 1947, with 12 years in all at 200 or more. After an accident in 1954 he retired from riding, and trained from 1955 to 1970, when he became a racing manager. He was first jockey to Tommy Hogg 1925-31, Fred Darling 1932-47, and then for Noel Murless.

A strong and determined, if unorthodox jockey, riding on a long rein, he displayed perfect balance and said that his success came from his will to win. Unlike some of his rivals he had little difficulty in making his riding weight of less than 8 stone.

He was a model sportsman, adored by the racing public and respected by his colleagues.

Vivian RICHARDS (Ant)

CRICKET

Isaac Vivian Alexander Richards. b. 7 Mar 1952 St John's, Antigua.

An imperiously powerful batsman, the best in the world for many years in the 1970s and 1980s, and a useful medium pace and off-break bowler. He made a brilliant start in Test cricket with 192* in his second Test, against India in December 1974, and in 1976 he made a world record of 1710 runs (av. 90.00) in a calendar year, including 829 runs, average 118.42, in 4 Tests against England. He captained the immensely powerful West Indies team to 27 wins in 50 Tests between 1980 and 1991 and made many marvellous attacking innings, often keeping his very best for the biggest occasions, particularly the Tests and Cup finals at Lord's. He played a match-winning innings of 138* in the 1979 World Cup final.

At Old Trafford in 1984 he made what remains the highest ever score in a one-day international, with 189 not out, all the more remarkable as the West Indies were in severe trouble at 102-7 at one stage. In 1986 at St John's, Antigua he made a sensational 110* against England, reaching his 100 off just 56 balls, the fastest ever in Test cricket. He scored a record number of runs for the West Indies in Test cricket and was at one time the leading run-scorer in one-day internationals.

He made his first-class début for the Leeward Islands. In England he played county cricket for Somerset 1974-86, helping them to win their first major trophies, the Gillette Cup and John Player League in 1979, and Glamorgan 1990-3. He also played for Antigua at football, including a World Cup qualifying match.

121 Tests 1974-91: 8540 runs at 50.23, 24 100s HS 291; 32 wickets, at 61.37, BB 2-17; 122 catches.

187 One-day Ints: 6721 runs at 47.00, 11 100s HS 189; 118 wickets at 35.83, BB 6-41; 101 catches.*

First-class 1972-92: 34,977 runs at 49.40, 112 100s HS 322; 219 wickets at 44.90, BB 5-88; 447 catches, 1 stumping.

Ernest RICHARDSON (Can)

CURLING

Ernest Richardson. b. 4 Aug 1931 Regina, Sakatchewan.

The skip of four Canadian curling world championship teams, 1959-60 and 1962-3. These remarkable teams were made up of the Richardson family, Ernie as skip, Arnold third player, Garnet 'Sam' second and Wes the lead. They were pioneers of the long-sliding delivery and wide-open take-out method to the sport.

Richie RICHARDSON (Ant)

CRICKET

Richard Benjamin Richardson. b. 7 Mar 1952 Five Islands, Antigua.

A highly talented right-handed batsman,

who succeeded his fellow-Antiguan Vivian Richards as captain of the West Indies. As characters they are very different, with Richardson seemingly much more diffident than the rumbustious Richards. He is, however, a determined cricketer, and has started his spell as captain of the West Indian nations auspiciously.

He made his début for the Leeward Islands in 1982, but was one of the few top West Indian cricketers not to play county cricket in England until he joined Yorkshire in 1993. He is the only Test batsman nowadays not to use a batting helmet, and his distinctive floppy hat has become world famous.

71 Tests 1983-93: 5231 runs at 46.70, 15 100s HS 194; 77 catches.

185 One-day Ints: 5307 runs at 34.23, 5 100s HS 122; 65 catches.

First-class 1982-92: 9863 runs at 43.25, 29 100s HS 194; 5 wickets at 40.80, BB 5-40; 144 catches.

Tom RICHARDSON (UK)

CRICKET

Thomas Richardson. b. 11 Aug 1870 Byfleet, Surrey, d. 2 Jul 1912 St Jean d'Arvey, France.

A splendidly-built fast bowler, at his prime in the 1890s he was the world's finest bowler. He made his début in 1892 and the following year took 174 wickets at 15.40, figures that he improved in 1894 to 196 at 10.33, and in 1895 to 290 at 14.38. That total was the season's record until Tich Freeman took 304 wickets in 1928. Richardson again took over 200 wickets with 246 in 1886 and 273 in 1897, but thereafter although he exceeded 100 wickets in five more seasons, his form began to decline, and eventually increasing weight cost him his county place. He reached 1000 wickets in first-class cricket in just 174 matches, easily the all-time record.

14 Tests 1893-8: 177 runs at 11.06, HS 25; 88 wickets at 25.22, BB 8-94; 5 catches.*

First-class 1892-1905: 3424 runs at 9.65, HS 69; 2104 wickets at 18.43, BB 10-45; 125 catches.

Annegret RICHTER (FRG)

ATHLETICS

Annegret Richter. née Irrgang. b. 13 Oct 1950 Dortmund.

Olympic champion at 100m in 1976, having set a world record on auto timing at 11.01 in the semi-finals. She also won silver medals at 200m, in an FRG record of 22.39 just 0.02 behind Bärbel Wöckel, and at sprint relay. In 1972 she had won Olympic gold at the relay, running the third leg on the FRG team that set a world record time of 42.81, and was fifth at 100m.

In the European Championships at the sprint relay she had won gold in 1971 and silver in 1974, when she was fifth at 100m. She was also European Indoor champion at 60m in 1973 and won a total of 15 German titles outdoors and 12 indoors.

Ulrike RICHTER (GDR)

SWIMMING

Ulrike Richter. b. 17 Jun 1952 Goerlitz.

In the four years 1973-6 Richter set nine world records at the 100m backstroke, taking the record from 65.39 to 61.51, and two at 200m, 2:18.41 and 2:17.35 in 1974. Three swimmers improved that 200m record before the 1976 Olympic Games, but there Richter beat them all and won the 100m and 200m double in Olympic records of 61.83 and 2:13.43. She added a third gold medal as she led off the GDR team to a world record in the medley relay. At the World Championships in 1973 she beat the double Olympic champion Melissa Belote (USA) to win the 100m, and led off the GDR medley relay team with her second world record (64.99) setting her team on its way to a world record and upset victory over the USA. She helped the GDR improve that record at the 1974 Europeans, where she made it three golds with the backstroke double. In 1975 she retained her world titles at 100m and on the medley relay, but was third at 200m backstroke. Her best 200m time was 2:13.27 in the GDR trials 1976, and she was GDR backstroke champion 100m 1973-6, and 200m 1974, 1976.

David RIGERT (USSR/Rus)

WEIGHTLIFTING

David Adamovich Rigert. b. 12 Mar 1947 Nagrnoe, Kokchetav Oblast, Kazakhstan.

Rigert was one of the greatest weightlifters ever, but at the highest level of the sport, the Olympic Games, he suffered abject failure twice. He was World champion at 90 kg five times, 1971 and 1973-76, and also won at 100 kg in 1978, and was European champion at 90kg 1971-76, 1978 and 1980, and at 100kg 1979. In 1972, 1976 and 1980 he was the clear favourite in his class at the Olympics. In 1976 he came through as expected and won the gold medal. But in both 1972 and 1980 he failed to lift a weight in three snatch attempts and was eliminated from the competition. Rigert set 63 world records at 82.5, 90 or 100kg during the 1970s.

John RIGGINS (USA)

AMERICAN FOOTBALL

John Riggins. b. 4 Aug 1949 Centralia, Kansas.

A durable fullback who played college ball at the University of Kansas, where he broke Jayhawk records for rushing which had been set by Gale Sayers. Riggins played professionally for the New York Jets and Washington Redskins. He was not a back who was expected to make big gains, but he was a punishing, bruising runner who could be counted on in third and short yardage situations.
NFL career 1971-85: Rushing: 11,352 yards av. 3.9, 104 touchdowns. Receiving: 2090 yards av. 8.4, 12 touchdowns.

Bobby RIGGS (USA)

TENNIS

Robert Larimore Riggs. b. 25 Feb 1918 Los Angeles, California.

A precocious teenager who beat the US No.2, Frank Shields, in 1934 when he was only 16. He won the US Clay Court singles and doubles two years later and successfully defended both titles in 1937 and 1938. After uniquely winning all three titles on his only appearance at Wimbledon in 1939, he also won the US singles that year but lost in the French final to Donald McNeil (USA). He lost again to McNeil in the final of the 1940 US singles but won the mixed doubles that year and took the singles for a second time in 1941 before turning professional. As a pro he beat Don Budge on both the 1946 and 1947 tours and surprised Jack Kramer in the early matches of his first tour, but Kramer recovered to take the series by a wide margin. A brilliant touch player and a shrewd tactician, Riggs' career was interrupted by World War II and because of the missed opportunities he is often under-rated. He returned to the public eye in 1973 when he beat the great Margaret Court in a much publicised 'battle of the sexes', though later in the year he lost to Billie Jean King in straight sets before a record TV audience of 50 million.

Frank RIJKAARD (Hol)

FOOTBALL

Franklin Rijkaard. b. 30 Sep 1962 Amsterdam.

A classy and adaptable midfield player, he helped Holland to win the European Championship in 1988, AC Milan the European Cup in 1989 and 1990, when he scored the winning goal in the final against Benfica, and Ajax the European Cup-Winners' Cup in 1987. He also played for Sporting Lisbon before being transferred for £2.5 million in 1988 to Milan, whom he helped to win the Italian league in 1992-3. By June 1993 he had scored 6 goals in 63 internationals.

Ronald RILEY (Aus)

HOCKEY

Ronald William Riley. b. 14 Sep 1947.

Australia's greatest centre-forward who was rated the best in the world in that position during his peak years. He won Olympic silver medals in 1968 and 1976, and although Australia only placed fifth in 1972, Riley was the top scorer in the Olympic tournament with ten goals. He won a total of 70 caps before retiring from international hockey after the Montreal Olympics, but his impressive form for the Sydney club St George and for New South Wales led to his being selected for the 1980 Olympic squad. The withdrawal of the Australian team from the Moscow Games deprived him of a fourth Olympic appearance.

Fred RIMELL (UK)

HORSE RACING

Thomas Frederick Rimell. b. 24 Jun 1913 Newmarket, d. 12 Jul 1981 Upton upon Severn, Worcestershire.

Leading National Hunt trainer in 1950/1, 1960/1, 1968/9, 1969/70, 1975/6, and the first to win over £1 million in prize money. First apprenticed to his father, Tom, at Kinnersley, Worcestershire, he switched from flat racing, at which he rode his first winner at the age of 12, to the jumps in 1932 and was champion NH jockey four times between 1938/9 and 1945/6. A natural horseman, he brought both power and balance to his steeplechase riding. He took a trainer's licence in 1945 and, after injury, retired from riding in 1947. His horses won the Grand National four times, the Cheltenham Gold Cup twice and Champion Hurdle twice. After his death, his wife Mercy (née Cockburn) carried on training at Kinnersley.

Jochen RINDT (FRG)

MOTOR RACING

Karl Jochen Rindt. b. 18 Aug 1942 Mainz, d. 5 Sep 1970 Monza.

Posthumous winner of the world motor racing title in 1970. Orphaned when 15 months old in the War, he was brought up by his grandparents in Graz, Austria. He was a naturally brilliant, brave driver, who made a reputation with daring driving in 1962-4 on the European circuit, so that he was given his Formula One chance by Rob Walker in 1964 at Zeltweg. He dominated Formula Two racing with nine wins for Brabham in 1967, but did not have competitive Formula One cars with Cooper 1965-7 and Brabham in 1968, until 1969 when he joined Lotus. He won the United States GP that year and five races in 1970, when he crashed going flat out in practice at the Italian Grand Prix and died on the way to hospital.

In his World Championship career he had six wins and earned 109 points from 60 starts.

Jim RINGO (USA)

AMERICAN FOOTBALL

James Stephen Ringo. b. 2 Nov 1932 Orange, New Jersey.

Ringo is considered by many people the greatest center in pro football history. He played collegiately at Syracuse and was drafted in 1953 by the Green Bay Packers. He played 15 years in the NFL, eleven with Green Bay and his final four with the Philadelphia Eagles. He was named All-Pro eight times and played in 10 Pro Bowls. His strength and endurance helped him play in 182 consecutive games, at the time an NFL record. After his playing retirement he became an NFL coach, mostly as an offensive co-ordinator though he was head coach of the Buffalo Bills for 1976-7.

Hans RINN (GDR)

LUGE

Hans Rinn. b. 19 Mar 1953 Langewiesen.

Winner of six World and Olympic titles, a record shared with Thomas Köhler (GDR). He was Olympic two-seater champion in 1976 and 1980, world champion at single-seater in 1973 and 1977 and two-seater in 1977 and 1980. Additionally, he won an Olympic bronze in the single-seater in 1976.

Cal RIPKEN (USA)

BASEBALL

Calvin Edwin Ripken, Jr. b. 24 Aug 1960 Havre de Grace, Maryland.

Ripken has become one of the great shortstops in baseball history, playing with the Baltimore Orioles. Huge for a shortstop at 1.93 m *6'4"* and 100 kg *220 lb*, and also possessed of unusual power for that posi-

tion, he has great range and a strong arm and is a solid, though unspectacular, fielder. He was voted Rookie of the Year in 1982 and MVP in 1983 and hit over 20 home runs in each of the first ten years of his career. To the end of 1992 he had played in 1735 consecutive games, which is second in baseball history, trailing only Lou Gehrig's legendary record of 2130. Only 32 years old and quite healthy, barring an injury Ripken may threaten Gehrig's heralded mark during the 1995 season.
Career 1981-92: 1922 hits Avg. .277, HR 273; RBI 1014. Best seasons: 1991: .323, 210 hits, 34 HR, 114 RBI; 1983: .318, 211 hits, 47 doubles, 102 RBI.

Gus RISMAN (UK)

RUGBY LEAGUE

Augustus John Risman. b. 21 Mar 1911 Barry, Wales.

Equally talented as a centre or full back, his career spanned 27 seasons and included tours of Australia in 1932, 1936 and, as captain, in 1946. Between 1932 and 1946 he won 17 caps and has the longest international career of any Great Britain rugby league player.
He signed for Salford shortly before his 18th birthday in 1929 and led them to victory in the 1938 Challenge Cup. He remained with the club until 1946 when he moved to Workington as player-manager. After winning the Championship in 1951, Workington won the 1952 Challenge Cup and after a 14-year interval the 41-year-old Risman won his second Cup winner's medal and achieved the distinction of being the oldest player ever to appear in a Cup Final. His son **Bev** (b. 23 Nov 1937) won rugby union international honours for England and the Lions at fly-half before turning professional. Like his father, he captained his country and led Great Britain from full back in the 1968 World Cup.

Ville RITOLA (Fin)

ATHLETICS

Viljo Eino Ritola. b. 18 Jan 1896 Peräseinäjoki, d. 24 Apr 1982 Helsinki.

Second only to Paavo Nurmi as an Olympic medal winner in the 1920s. In 1924 he had eight races in eight days; he won the steeplechase (in his first ever race at the event!) and the 10,000m, improving his six weeks old world record from 30:35.4 to 30:23.2, and took his gold medal haul to four with the team 3000m and cross-country. The two great Finns met on the track for the first time at these Games, but Nurmi won the 5000m in 14:31.2 to Ritola's 14:31.4 and the order was the same in the individual cross-country, although Ritola was nearly a minute and a half behind. Four years later Ritola traded wins with Nurmi, winning the 5000m and taking silver at 10,000m (in his best time of 30:19.4).
The 14th of 20 children, he left home to go to the USA at the age of 17, and there won 14 AAU titles. He trained exceptionally hard and first made his mark with second in the 1922 Boston Marathon. Indoors he ran world bests at 2 miles, 9:03 3/4 (1925) and four at 3 miles to 13:56.2, the first sub-14 minute time indoors or out, en route to 14:23.2 for 5000m in 1925. That time was five seconds faster than Nurmi's outdoor world record. He returned to Finland only in 1924 and 1928, and never competed at the national championships.

Luigi RIVA (Italy)

FOOTBALL

Luigi Riva. b. 7 Nov 1944 Leggiuno.

A former left-winger whose devastating shooting led to a brilliant career as a striker. He joined the unfashionable Sardinian club, Cagliari, in 1963 and helped take them into the Italian First Division in his first season. He won his first cap in June 1965, when he came on as a substitute against Hungary, but he failed to command a regular place in the national team until 1967. He scored an Italian record 35 goals from his 42 international appearances, including the opening goal in the replayed European Championship final in 1968, which Italy won. In 1969/70 he played a major rôle in taking Cagliari to their first-ever championship and that season he scored 7 of Italy's 10 goals in their World Cup qualifying matches.

Possibly too much was expected of him in the Mexico finals where, although scoring twice against Mexico in the quarter-final and once against Germany in the semi-final, he did not feature prominently in the final.
At his peak he was Italy's highest paid player and he refused even greater rewards to join Juventus. He suffered a succession of injuries during his career and twice broke his leg, and eventually he was forced to retire through injury in 1977.

Roberto RIVELINO (Bra)

FOOTBALL
Roberto Rivelino. b. 19 Jan 1946 São Paulo.

Initially a midfield player, he later played on the left-wing where his powerful left foot proved a highly effective weapon. His ability to curve free-kicks around a wall and his fierce shooting on the run made him a valued member of Brazil's winning team at the 1970 World Cup when he scored three goals. He again scored three times in the 1974 finals but his performance in the 1978 finals was a disappointment and he soon left Brazil to play for Al-Ahly in Saudi Arabia.
After joining Corinthians as a junior he progressed through the ranks to their first team - a rare feat in the free-spending club who normally filled the team with expensive acquisitions. He remained with them until 1975 when he moved to Fluminense. With 120 appearances (1968-79) he is Brazil's most capped player although this total includes matches against club sides and representative selections and on a stricter definition he played in 94 internationals in which he scored 26 goals.

Gianni RIVERA (Ita)

FOOTBALL
Gianni Rivera. b. 18 Aug 1943 Valle S Bartolomeo, Alessandria.

A talented inside-forward who, despite his apparently frail physique, possessed a powerful shot. Starting with his hometown club, Alessandria, in 1958 he moved to AC Milan in 1960 and gave them exceptional service, being elected vice president of the club while still playing. He was team captain when they won the double of World Club Championship and European Cup in 1969. They also won the European Cup in 1963 and the Cup-Winners' Cup in 1968 and 1973 and other honours included Italian League championships 1962 and 1968, and Italian Cup in 1967 and 1972-3.
A classic stylist with phenomenal ball control, he was voted European Footballer of the Year in 1969. He won 60 international caps and was a member of the Italian team which finished as runners-up in the 1970 World Cup.

Jean-Pierre RIVES (Fra)

RUGBY UNION
Jean-Pierre Rives. b. 31 Dec 1952 Toulouse.

A brilliant open-side flanker who won 59 caps between 1975 and 1984 and captained France in a record 34 matches. Renowned for his dashing style and flowing locks, he led France to many triumphs, notably a victory over the All Blacks in Auckland in 1979 and the Grand Slam in 1981.
Because of injury he missed the 1975 tour of South Africa and the home series against New Zealand in 1977. After retirement he appeared in several films, his sculptures were widely exhibited and he was a prominent figure in French society. His autobiography, *A Modern Corinthian*, published in 1986, was a chronicle of his life both on and off the field.

Roger RIVIÈRE (Fra)

CYCLING
Roger Rivière. b. 23 Feb 1936 Saint-Etienne.

Rivière was world professional pursuit champion 1957-9 and when he turned to the road in 1959, French cycling fans turned to him, looking for a hero they could embrace. Though they had Jacques Anquetil, he was never loved by them. After Rivière had broken Anquetil's world hour record with 46.92342km in 1957 and

47.3469km in 1958, setting records en route at 10km and 20km on both occasions, great things were expected of him. In the Tour de France he finished 3rd in 1959 behind Anquetil, who in 2nd lost his only Tour, and Rivière was favoured in 1960 as Anquetil opted to race the Giro instead. Rivière was on course to win, with several of his favourite time trials remaining, when he crashed off the side of the Col de Perjuret in the Tarn Gorges. The broken back he sustained ended his promising career and he never raced again.

Phil RIZZUTO (USA)

BASEBALL

Philip Francis Rizzuto. b. 25 Sep 1917 Brooklyn, New York.

'Scooter' Rizzuto played shortstop for 13 seasons with the New York Yankees, missing three years in military service. He was a solid but unspectacular hitter for a shortstop. In the field, he was quick with sure hands and helped the Yankees to nine pennants and eight World Series victories. On his retirement he immediately became a Yankee announcer, famous for his expression 'Holy Cow', and continued into the 1980s.

Career 1941-56: 1588 hits Avg. .273; SB 163.

Joél ROBERT (Bel)

MOTO-CROSS

Joél Robert. b. 24 (11?) Nov 1943 Chatelet.

At 20 Robert was the youngest ever moto-cross world champion and in all gained a record six 250cc world titles, 1964, 1968-72, and won a record 50 Grand Prix races. He started racing in 1959 and won the Belgian junior title in 1960. He rode the Czechoslovakian bikes CZ in his Grand Prix successes from 1964 to 1968 but switched to Suzuki for 1970.

An exceptionally talented rider, his flamboyant style and extrovert personality made him a popular celebrity.

Andy ROBERTS (Ant)

CRICKET

Anderson Montgomery Everton Roberts. b. 29 Jan 1951 Urlings Village.

One of the fastest and most dangerous of bowlers, he was the first Antiguan to play for the West Indies and became the third West Indian to take 200 wickets in Test cricket. He made his Test début with one match in 1974 and in his next series took 32 wickets at 18.28 against India in 1974/5. His next most successful series was against England in 1976 with 28 wickets at 19.17, including his 100th Test wicket after just 2 years 144 days. When needed he also showed himself able to bat very well. He played for the Leeward Islands and for Hampshire. In 1974 he was the most successful bowler in England with 119 wickets at 13.62. Awarded the CBE.

47 Tests 1974-83: 762 runs at 14.94, HS 68; 202 wickets at 25.61, BB 7-54; 9 catches.

56 One-day Ints: 231 runs at 10.04, HS 37; 87 wickets at 20.35, BB 5-22; 6 catches.*

First-class 1970-84: 3516 runs at 15.69, HS 89; 889 wickets at 21.01, BB 8-47; 52 catches.

John ROBERTS (UK)

BILLIARDS

W. John Roberts Jr. b. Aug 1847 Ardwick, Manchester, d. Dec 1919.

The first great billiards player, who made a record seven successful defences of the world title he first won in 1870. Initially raised in Lancashire, he moved to London in 1866 when his father took a saloon at Leicester Square. At the first World Billiards Championship in February 1870, William Cook beat John Roberts, Sr. but within weeks John Roberts, Jr. avenged his father's defeat by taking the title from Cook, an odds-on favourite. In the early days, the championship was decided by challenge matches and Roberts played in 11 challenges, winning eight and losing three. After beating Joseph Bennett in June 1885 he declined to make any further

defences, mainly owing to a dispute over the rules, but he remained supreme for at least another decade.
During his peak years, the title sometimes passed to lesser players, as Roberts preferred to tour the world rather than play in the Championships. He visited Australia three times and went twice to New Zealand and America and once to South Africa, but 11 times to India for supervision of the billiard-table factory he owned in Calcutta, and due to his appointment as court billiards player to the Maharajah of Jaipur. This involved an annual visit of one month to the Palace and carried a salary of £500 a year.
An arrogant, self-assured and wealthy man, he finally retired from competitive play in 1906 when problems with his eyesight worsened, but he was one of the greatest sporting heroes of his time and a great entertainer.

Kenny ROBERTS (USA)

MOTOR CYCLING

Kenny Roberts. b. 31 Dec 1951 Modesto.

The first American to win a motorcycling world title at 500cc in 1978. Riding for Yamaha, he retained the title in 1979 and 1980 and won a total of 22 Grand Prix 500cc races between 1978 and 1983 and two 350cc races in 1978.
The Californian started motorcycling at the age of 15 and rapidly achieved success, winning his first national junior title in 1971. After sweeping all before him in the USA he first raced in Europe in 1974. In the USA he set overall speed records to win the Daytona 200 in both 1983 and 1984, having earlier won in 1975 and 1978. He managed the successful Yamaha team in the 1980s.

Robin ROBERTS (USA)

BASEBALL

Robin Evan Roberts. b. 30 Sep 1926 Springfield, Illinois.

Roberts pitched for 19 years in the major leagues, most of them with the Philadelphia Phillies. He was a tough competitor but his problem was giving up home runs. He won 20 or more games in six straight seasons 1950-5, but then developed shoulder problems and was never again so dominant. He later coached collegiate baseball at the University of South Florida.
Career pitching 1948-66: ERA 3.40; W-L 286-245, SO 2357. Best seasons: 1950: 20-11, 3.02 ERA; 1951: 21-15, 3.03 ERA; 1952: 28-7, 2.59 ERA; 1953: 23-16, 2.75 ERA; 1954: 23-15, 2.96 ERA; 1955: 23-14, 3.28 ERA.

Alan ROBERTSON (UK)

GOLF

Alan Robertson. b. 1815 St Andrews, Scotland, d. Sep 1858.

The greatest player of the pre-tournament and featherie era, who died two years before the first real championship, the British Open, was started. The tournament was actually begun to settle the argument of who was the best player in the world, an argument which had a pat answer while Robertson was alive - it was Robertson. It was said he never lost an individual stakes match. He never faced the other great player of that era, Old Tom Morris, in an individual match, though it is recorded that they were unbeaten as a team. They later had a parting of the ways when Morris began making gutta percha balls, which Robertson saw as a threat to his trade of making featheries. Robertson's fame is also based on his great feat of once going round St Andrews in 147 strokes for 36 holes.

Bruce ROBERTSON (NZ)

RUGBY UNION

Bruce John Robertson. b. 9 Apr 1952 Hastings.

Playing in 34 internationals between 1972 and 1981, he was at the time of his retirement New Zealand's most capped centre. He had an unusually lengthy international career for a back and it would have been even longer had he not refused to play against South Africa in 1981. A powerful, thrusting runner, he is rated as one of New Zealand's greatest centre-threequarters.

Oscar ROBERTSON (USA)

BASKETBALL

Oscar Palmer Robertson. b. 24 Nov 1938 Charlotte, Tennessee.

'The Big O' is rated by many as the greatest guard ever to play basketball. He started at Crispus Attucks High School in Indianapolis and then at the University of Cincinnati, where for three consecutive years (1958-60) he led the NCAA in scoring, made first-team all-America, and was named collegiate Player of the Year. In his junior year, he broke the NCAA career scoring mark which had been set in a four-year career, totalling 2973 points at an average of 33.8 per game.

Robertson was 1.96m *6' 5"* tall and was a natural guard, though he was probably the biggest man ever to play that position at the time. At the 1960 Olympics, where he won a gold medal, he often played forward because of his size and jumping ability. In the NBA he played for the Cincinnati Royals 1960-70 and then with the Milwaukee Bucks, for whom, in 1971, he finally played on an NBA championship winning team.

In his 14-year pro career, Robertson rewrote the record book. He was 10 times named to first team all-NBA and twice, in the twilight of his career, was named to the second team. He was Rookie of the Year in 1961 and MVP in 1964, rare feats for a guard. His greatest honour probably came in 1980 when he was named to the NBA's 35th anniversary All-Time team.

Perhaps the best measure of his dominance is the triple-double, a new term coined to describe the exploits of Magic Johnson, and which refers to a game in which a player scores double figures in points, rebounds, and assists. It was not until the seventh year of his career that Robertson's career averages fell below a triple-double standard.

He set the NBA career record for assists that lasted until surpassed by Magic Johnson.

NBA career: 26,710 points av. 25.7; 9887 assists, av. 9.5.

Paul ROBESON (USA)

AMERICAN FOOTBALL

Paul Bustill Robeson. b. 9 Apr 1898 Princeton, New Jersey, d. 23 Jan 1976 Philadelphia, Pennsylvania.

Paul Robeson was a legendary character quite apart from being a tremendous athlete. He was a black man who in high school excelled in academics, sports, debating and sang in the choir. He achieved the highest score on a statewide examination for entrance to Rutgers College. He later recalled that, 'Equality might be denied, but I knew I was not inferior.' At Rutgers, Robeson was the only black student and was not accepted at first by his team-mates. Eventually they allowed him to join them but several teams refused to play Rutgers because of Robeson, who continued his excellence in multiple fields. He made Phi Beta Kappa, was valedictorian of his class, and was the top debater in the school. He earned 12 varsity letters in football, basketball, baseball, and track & field. Best known as a football end, he made All-American in his junior and senior years and Walter Camp termed him the greatest defensive end of his era. He competed in the discus, javelin, and pentathlon for the track team.

Robeson played professional football with the Hammond Pros, Akron Pros, and Milwaukee Badgers 1920-2, using the sport to finance his law school studies at Columbia. He briefly practised law although he was denied membership of the bar because of his race, but gave that up to start a lucrative singing and acting career that saw him star on the Broadway stage. In the 1930s he became politically active, and was an outspoken opponent of fascism and racism. He spent a lot of time in Europe criticising American racial policies and this led to his investigation and censure by the House Un-American Activities Committee, led by the notorious Senator Joseph McCarthy. The State Department took away his passport and his career went into oblivion. Perhaps one of the most obvious victims ever of racial injustice, he has never been elected to the College or Pro Football Halls of Fame.

Brooks ROBINSON (USA)

BASEBALL

Brooks Calbert Robinson. b. 18 May 1937 Little Rock, Arkansas.

Universally acclaimed as the greatest fielding third baseman ever. He won a Gold Glove at third base for sixteen consecutive seasons 1960-75; the record for the most won at any position, and for the most won consecutively. He played for the Baltimore Orioles and was a good batter, though not spectacular. He was at his best in the World Series, highlighted by his performance in the 1970 Series when he was MVP, after robbing the Cincinnati Reds multiple times defensively and batting .429 for seven games. When he retired, this Baltimore legend stepped right into a position as the Orioles announcer on television.
Career 1955-77: 2848 hits Avg. .267, HR 268; RBI 1357. Best seasons: 1964: .317, 28 HR, 118 RBI; 1962: .303, 23 HR.

Frank ROBINSON (USA)

BASEBALL

Frank Robinson. b. 31 Aug 1935 Beaumont, Texas.

One of baseball's all-time great power hitters, though never given the acclaim of Mays, Aaron, or Mantle. He played for the Cincinnati Reds 1956-65 and then joined the Baltimore Orioles. Though he finished his career with a few other teams, he is best associated with those two. He was voted MVP in both leagues (1961-NL, 1966-AL), and the latter was his greatest year as he won the Triple Crown and led the Orioles to a World Series championship. He played mostly outfield with some time at first base late in his career. His 586 home runs is the 4th highest all-time. In 1975 he became a playing manager with the Cleveland Indians. This made him the first black man to manage in the major leagues. He has since managed several teams, notably the Orioles in the 1980s.
Career 1956-76: 2943 hits Avg. .294, HR 586; RBI 1812; SB 204. Best seasons: M1966: .316, 49 HR, 122 RBI; 1962: .342, 39 HR, 136 RBI; 1961: .323, 37 HR, 124 RBI; 1959: .311, 36 HR, 125 RBI.

Jackie ROBINSON (USA)

BASEBALL

Jack Roosevelt Robinson. b. 31 Jan 1919 Cairo, Georgia, d. 24 Oct 1972 Stamford, Connecticut.

A tremendous all-round athlete who broke the colour line by becoming the first black player in the major leagues in the 20th century. He became a great hero to blacks, and late in his career became an outspoken supporter of black causes. His eulogy was delivered by the Rev. Jesse Jackson. In 1987 major league baseball renamed the Rookie of the Year Award in his honour. Robinson attended UCLA where he lettered in football, baseball, basketball, and track. At long jump he topped the world rankings in 1938 with 7.78m and won the NCAA title in 1940. He reached the semi-finals of the National Negro Tennis Tournament, and also briefly played semi-pro football with the Honolulu Bears. After spending a minor league season in Montreal, he joined the Brooklyn Dodgers, who had signed him in 1946, and was an immediate sensation. A second baseman, he was voted Rookie of the Year in 1947, and in 1949 won the MVP Award. He was a fiery competitor who used his great speed to torment opposing defenses. He played only 10 years in the major leagues, although because of his late start, he was by then 37 years old.
Career 1947-56: 1518 hits Avg. .311, HR 137; RBI 734; SB 197. Best seasons: 1949: .342, 16 HR, 124 RBI, 37 SB. 1951: .338, 19 HR, 88 RBI, 25 SB.

Jem ROBINSON (UK)

HORSE RACING

James Robinson. b. 1793 Newmarket, d. 1865.

His total of 24 classic winners, between 1817 and 1848, is still the third highest ever for a jockey, including a record 9 in the 2000 Guineas and the former record of 6 Derbys. He was apprenticed to Robert Robson, and learnt much from champion jockey Frank Buckle. A ruthless rider, his career ended with a bad fall in 1852, which left him with a permanent limp.

Sugar Ray ROBINSON (USA)

BOXING

Sugar Ray Robinson. né Walker Smith. b. 3 May 1921 Detroit, Michigan, d. 12 Apr 1989 Culver City, California.

Many boxing experts consider Sugar Ray Robinson, pound-for-pound, the greatest boxer of all time. He can boast of the following feats: between 1943 and 1951 he won 91 consecutive fights; he won the middleweight championship five times; he fought 22 world championship bouts; he lost only 19 of 202 professional fights and he was never knocked out.

Walker Smith began professional boxing in Detroit in 1940. He acquired the name Ray Robinson when he substituted for a boxer by that name. He later became Sugar Ray Robinson when his trainer George Gainsford was told that his boxer was 'sweet as sugar'. He first won the world welterweight title in 1946 and held it for four years before relinquishing it to campaign as a middleweight. He became world middleweight champion for the first time in 1951 and between 1946 and 1960 he held some version of a world championship in all years. Robinson also fought for the light-heavyweight title in 1952 but lost to Joey Maxim.

Career record: W - 175 (110), L - 19, D -6.

Bobby ROBSON (UK)

FOOTBALL

Robert William Robson. b. 18 Feb 1933 Langley Park, Co. Durham.

Having played 20 times for England as an inside-forward 1957-62, later becoming a right-half, he managed the England football team 1982-90. In his Football League career he scored 133 goals in 584 games for Fulham 1950-6 and 1962-7, and West Bromwich Albion 1956-62. In 1968 he played for the Vancouver Whitecaps, before managing Fulham, November 1968 to January 1969, and Ipswich Town 1969-82. After his career as England manager, which culminated in incessant hounding by the tabloid press, he managed the Dutch team PSV Eindhoven and then Sporting Lisbon in Portugal. Awarded CBE 1990.

Bryan ROBSON (UK)

FOOTBALL

Bryan Robson. b. 11 Jan 1957 Chester-le-Street, Co. Durham.

After being on the books of West Bromwich Albion as a schoolboy and an apprentice, he signed professional forms in 1974. In 1981 he moved to Manchester United for the then record British fee of £1.5 million and while with United he became the first captain to lead a team to three victories in the FA Cup (1983, 1985, 1990). Although he missed many games, he helped United to their first League title in 26 years in 1992/3.

After a fine performance in the 1982 World Cup he was forced out of the next two competitions (1986, 1990) because of injury. He was troubled by injuries throughout his career but he still won 90 caps (with 26 goals) and took over the captaincy of England and Manchester United from Ray Wilkins in 1982. He is recognised as one of the most complete midfield players ever to represent England.

Robert ROBSON (UK)

HORSE RACING

Robert Robson b. 1765, d. 2 Apr 1838 Newmarket.

He set a record, later surpassed by John Scott, by training the winners of 34 English classics between 1793 and 1827, including records for the Oaks (12), 1000 Guineas (9), Derby (7), many for the 3rd and 4th Dukes of Grafton. He was known as 'The Emperor of Trainers'. He started as private trainer at Lewes, Sussex to Sir Ferdinand Poole in 1793, when he achieved his first classic success, the Derby with *Waxy*, and then moved to Newmarket.

Andy ROBUSTELLI (USA)

AMERICAN FOOTBALL

Andrew Robustelli. b. 6 Dec 1926 Stamford, Connecticut.

Robustelli was an unexpected star in pro football. He played college ball at little-known Arnold College, making Little

All-American three consecutive years. He was only a 19th-round pick in the NFL draft, but played with the LA Rams 1951-5 as a defensive end, twice making All-Pro. In 1956 he was traded to the New York Giants and made All-Pro five more times with them. He made seven Pro Bowl appearances and was the 1962 NFL MVP.

Pedro ROCHA (Uru)

FOOTBALL

Pedro Rocha. b. 3 Dec 1942 Salto.

A constructive, tactical player who was well-suited to the introduction of the 4-2-4 formation. Starting with his local provincial club, he moved to Peñarol in Montevideo at the age of 17 and featured in their team which won the League Championship in seven of the eight years between 1960 and 1968. During this golden era Peñarol also won the World Club Championship in 1966.

Rocha played in the 1962 and 1966 World Cups and captained Uruguay on his third World Cup appearance in 1970, although he missed most of the tournament after being injured early in the first match. Due to the depressed economy, many Uruguayan clubs were forced to sell their top players and Rocha was one of the first stars to go abroad when he moved to São Paulo in Brazil shortly after the 1970 World Cup. At the time he had won 75 international caps and with his talent and experience he soon became a valuable asset to his new club.

Stephen ROCHE (Ire)

CYCLING

Stephen Roche. b. 20 Nov 1959 Dublin.

Roche had a year in 1987 that has been matched by only one rider ever - the great Eddy Merckx. He won both the Tour de France and Giro d'Italia and also won the rainbow jersey as world road champion. His Tour de France win was the stuff of high drama. In second place entering the Alps, with Pedro Delgado close in 3rd, Roche fell off the pace as Delgado attacked up the Villard de Lans. Delgado took over the race, and was the leader on the road, as he opened up a huge margin. But Roche countered and closed to within four seconds at the finish. It was an almost superhuman effort which earned him the yellow jersey but also put him in hospital overnight. However, he recovered enough to race the next day and keep the yellow jersey into Paris. Roche's career was hampered by knee problems both before 1987 and in the ensuing years.

He was 45th in the Olympic road race in 1980 and turned pro in 1981, winning the Paris-Nice and the Tour of Corsica in his first season. He was third in the world pro road race in 1983 and in the Tour de France in 1985.

Tony ROCHE (Aus)

TENNIS

Anthony Dalton Roche. b. 17 May 1945 Wagga Wagga, New South Wales.

One of the great doubles players, whose partnership with fellow-Australian John Newcombe was particularly successful. Together they won Wimbledon five times (1965, 1968-70, 1974), the Australian title four times (1965, 1971, 1973, 1976) and the French (1967, 1969) and US (1967) titles. Having been Australian junior champion in 1964 the left-handed Roche failed to achieve the success some felt he deserved in the major singles. Although he won the French and Italian titles in 1966 and was runner-up at Wimbledon in 1968 and Forest Hills in 1969 and 1970, he surprisingly never reached an Australian final. In 11 Davis Cup ties 1964-7 and 1974-8 Roche won 7 of 11 singles and 7 of 9 doubles. His career was hampered by an injury to his left elbow which was apparently cured after much publicised treatment by a Philippine faith healer.

Knut(e) ROCKNE (Nor/USA)

AMERICAN FOOTBALL

Knute Kenneth Rockne. b. 4 Mar 1888 Voss, Norway, d. 31 Mar 1931 near Bazaar, Kansas, USA.

Often considered the greatest college football coach ever. He compiled a career record of 105-12-5 while coaching Notre

Dame from 1918 to 1930 before his untimely death in a plane crash. His .881 winning percentage is the highest of all-time among college football coaches, and his teams were considered unofficial national champions three times. He played football at Notre Dame 1910-14 and is considered the pioneer of the forward pass as a true offensive weapon. Rockne also competed in track at Notre Dame and once held the school pole vault record. After college he played semi-pro football for the Massillon Tigers.

Bill RODGERS (USA)

ATHLETICS

William Henry Rodgers. b. 23 Dec 1947 Hartford, Connecticut.

Rodgers sprung to prominence at the age of 27 with third place at the 1975 International cross-country championships. A month later he entered the Boston Marathon for his sixth race at the distance and improved his best from the 2:19:34 that he had run there in 14th place in 1974 to 2:09:55, the fourth sub-2:10 time. He went on to lead the US marathon running boom, winning again at Boston each year 1978-80, including his fastest ever time of 2:09:27 in 1979, and four times in New York, each year from 1976 to 1979. Sadly Rodgers did not gain success at the major international championships, finishing 40th in the 1976 Olympic marathon when suffering from a foot injury.
Track bests: 5000m 13:42.0 (1978), 10,000m 28:04.42 (1976) and world records for 15,000m 1:14:11.8 and 15 miles 1:11:43.1 en route (1979).

Guy RODGERS (USA)

BASKETBALL

Guy William Rodgers, Jr. b. 1 Sep 1935 Philadelphia, Pennsylvania.

Rodgers played college ball at Temple and for 12 years in the NBA mostly for the Warriors, first in Philadelphia and later in San Francisco, before his last three years with various teams. He was a short play-making guard who was best known for his passing ability and twice led the NBA in assists with six years at second. He played in four NBA All-Star Games. He once handed out 28 assists in a single game, a long-standing NBA record. He ranks fifth in all-time NBA assists.

Irina RODNINA (USSR)

FIGURE SKATING

Irina Konstantinova Rodnina. b. 12 Sep 1949 Moscow. Later Zaitsev.

As the winner of three Olympic gold medals and ten times world champion, both records, she is the greatest pairs skater in history. Her ten World Championship victories came in successive years, 1969-78, the first four with **Aleksey Ulanov** (b. 4 Nov 1947) and the next six with her husband, Aleksandr Zaitsev. During this decade of complete domination she also won the Olympic title in 1972 partnering Ulanov and again in 1976 and 1980 with Zaitsev. She also won a record eleven European titles, 1969-78 and 1980, the last seven with Zaitsev, and it was at the 1973 Europeans that this superlative pairing received an unprecedented maximum six marks from all twelve judges. Her initial partnership with Ulanov broke up when he became emotionally involved with Lyudmila Smirnova at the 1972 Olympics. Rodnina began training with Zaitsev on 15 Apr 1972 and Ulanov formalised his relationship with Smirnova both on and off the ice. In 1973 the re-arranged foursome met at the World Championships when victory went to Rodnina and Zaitsev, who were married three years later.

Gaston ROELANTS (Bel)

ATHLETICS

Gaston Roelants. b. 5 Feb 1937 Opvelp.

The world's best steeplechaser in the early 1960s and a great cross-country runner. At the steeplechase he won the 1962 European and 1964 Olympic titles as well as setting two world records, 8:29.6 in 1963 and 8:26.4 in 1965. He had been 4th in the steeplechase at the 1960 Olympics, and after a bronze at the 1966 Europeans he turned with great success to longer dis-

tances, setting world records at 20km (58:06.2) and 1 hour (20,664m) that year and later improving those records to 57:44.4 and 20,878m in 1972. He won a silver (1969) and a bronze (1974) in European marathon races.
He equalled the record by winning four International cross-country titles, 1962, 1967, 1969 and 1972, with three second places and in all nine top ten placings between 1960 and 1975. His long career continued into his 40s, and he won five world titles in his first year in veterans' ranks.

Budge ROGERS (UK)

RUGBY UNION
Derek Prior Rogers. b. 20 Jun 1939 Bedford.

One-time holder of the record as England's most capped player. He played in 34 internationals between 1961 and 1969, captaining the team seven times, and in two Tests for the British Lions in South Africa in 1962. His foraging, fast-breaking play from the open side of the scrum is said to have been one of the influences that led to a change in the laws which restricted the activities of roving wing-forwards. He remained loyal to the Bedford club throughout his career and, after retiring, served England as a coach and a selector. He was awarded the OBE for his services to the game.

Walter RÖHRL (FRG)

RALLYING
Walter Röhrl. b. 7 Mar 1947 Regensburg.

One of only two men to have won the Monte Carlo Rally four times and also to have had three successive victories in the event: 1980 in a Fiat, 1982-3 Opel, 1984 Audi Quattro. He shares both records with Sandro Munari. Röhrl was world champion in 1980 and 1982 and the first man to win the title twice, with 14 world championship race wins. His regular co-driver has been **Christian Geistdorfer** (FRG, b. 1 Feb 1953).
His first big win was at Wiesbaden in 1971. Joining Opel in 1973, he was European champion in 1974. He retired after helping Audi to win the 1990 German touring car championship.

Aleksandr ROMANKOV (USSR)

FENCING
Aleksandr Romankov. b. 7 Nov 1953 Korsakov, Sakhalin.

Winner of a record five world foil titles, 1974, 1977, 1979, 1982-3. Despite these successes he was never an Olympic champion but won an individual silver in 1976 and a team silver and individual bronze in 1980. He won his first Soviet title in 1976. A teacher, he competed for Dynamo Minsk.

Aleksandr ROMANOV (USSR)

CYCLING
Aleksandr Romanov. b. 11 May 1953 Moscow.

A superb track rider who was best known as a motor-paced time trialist. Oddly, he never competed in the amateur motor-paced event at the world championships. He did compete in the individual pursuit, however, and was third in the world juniors in 1983. Romanov set the following world records behind a motorbike, with all his best times coming in 1987: Outdoors three over 50 km, his best being 35:21.108; three at 100 km to 1 hr 10:50.940; and three at one hour to 84.710km. Indoors he set eight world records over 50 km (best 32:56.746); six at 100 km to 1 hr 05:58.031; and six at one hour to 91.131km.

Nina ROMASHKOVA (USSR), see PONOMARYOVA

Henry RONO (Kenya)

ATHLETICS
Henry Kipwambok Rono. b. 12 Feb 1952 Kaprirsang, Nandi Hills.

His brilliant talent was shown by an outstanding series of world records. He was kept away from Olympic competition in 1976 and 1980 by Kenyan boycotts, so

that left 1978 as his great year, with doubles at 5000m and 3000m steeplechase at the Commonwealth Games and at 10,000m and steeplechase at the African Games. That year he also set three world records: 13:08.4 for 5000m in Berkeley on 8 April, 8:05.4 for 3000m steeplechase in Seattle on 13 May, and 27:22.4 for 10,000m in Vienna on 11 June. In 1981 he returned to improve his 5000m record to 13:06.20 at Knarvik, Norway.
His rise to world prominence had come while at Washington State University. Sadly, although he made some tentative running comebacks over the next decade, including a 2:19:12 marathon in 1986, he ran into difficulties with drink and the law.

ROOP SINGH (India)

HOCKEY

Roop Singh. b. 8 Sep 1910, d. 16 Dec 1977.

Winner of Olympic gold medals in 1932 and 1936 and a prolific scorer from the inside-left position. At the 1932 Olympics he scored 10 goals in India's 24-1 victory over USA and his elder brother, Dyan Chand, contributed eight.

Keke ROSBERG (Fin)

MOTOR RACING

Keijo E. Rosberg. b. 6 Dec 1948 Solna, Sweden.

Won the driver's world title in a closely contested championship in 1982. After winning Scandinavian and Finnish karting titles and the 1973 European title, he worked up through the formulas to his Formula One début for the Theodore team in 1978. Apart from third place in the 1980 Argentine GP he had little success until joining Williams in 1982, when after a consistent year he won the Swiss GP and the world title. Remaining with Williams he was 5th, 8th and 3rd in the championship 1983-5, and sixth for McLaren in 1986, when he retired with career figures of five victories in 114 races and 159.5 points. From 1990 he took up racing sports cars for Peugeot, and achieved his first win in 1991.

Lionel ROSE (Aus)

BOXING

Lionel Rose. b. 21 Jun 1948 Warragul, Victoria

The only Aboriginal to win a world title at any sport, Rose began fighting professionally in 1964, became Australian champion in 1966, and won the world bantamweight title by outpointing Japan's Fighting Harada in 1968. He defended his title three times before losing the championship in 1969 to Ruben Olivares. Shortly after that loss, Rose was awarded an MBE for his contributions to Australian boxing. He later campaigned with less success as a lightweight and at junior-lightweight, at which he lost a controversial world title fight in 1971, and retired in 1976. He had been Australian amateur bantamweight champion in 1963.
Career record: W - 42 (12), L - 11, D - 0.

Mauri ROSE (USA)

MOTOR RACING

Mauri Rose, b. 26 May 1906 Columbus, Ohio, d. 1 Jan 1981 Detroit, Michigan.

Won the Indianapolis 500 three times, 1941, 1947-8, and, qualifying for 15 consecutive races, was also second in 1934 and third in 1940 and 1950. A development engineer with several manufacturers, including Hupmobile, Chevrolet and General Motors, he compiled an outstanding record despite being a part-time driver for most of his career.
Began his racing career on dirt tracks in Indiana and Ohio. US (AAA) National driving champion in 1936 and second in 1934.

Murray ROSE (Aus)

SWIMMING

Iain Murray Rose. b. 6 Jan 1939 Birmingham, England.

The hero of the swimming events at the Olympic Games in Melbourne in 1956, when he became the youngest triple gold medallist in Olympic history, winning the 400m and 1500m and taking the third leg on the world record-setting Australian team at 4 x 200m relay. After becoming a

student at the University of Southern California, he retained his 400m title in 1960 with his colleague at USC, Tsuyoshi Yamanaka of Japan, taking the silver medal, just as in 1956. Also in 1960 Rose took the silver behind John Konrads at 1500m and won a bronze medal in the relay. A vegetarian, he was known as the 'Seaweed Streak'.
He set the last short course record at 400m freestyle with 4:25.9 in 1957, and his 4:27.0 in the 1956 Olympics was recognised as the inaugural long course record. Other world records included 800m, 8:51.5 in 1962, and 1500m, 17:59.5 in 1956 and 17:01.8 in 1964. Despite world records at 800y and 1500m in 1964, Rose was denied a place on that year's Australian Olympic team as he refused to return from the USA for the Australian Championships. He was Commonwealth champion in 1962 at 440y and 1650y, with two more golds in the relays. Australian champion 220y 1955, 440y 1955-6; US 400m and 1500m 1958 and 1962; NCAA 1650y 1961-2.
His Scottish parents had emigrated to Australia when he was a baby. Rose later briefly pursued a film career in Hollywood.

Pete ROSE (USA)

BASEBALL
Peter Edward Rose. b. 14 Apr 1941 Cincinnati, Ohio.

Rose, known as 'Charlie Hustle', played for 24 years in the major leagues and was known throughout his career as one of the greatest competitors in baseball history. Best known for his years with the Cincinnati Reds, 1963-78, he later played for six seasons with the Philadelphia Phillies, and half of one year with the Montreal Expos, before returning to Cincinnati to finish his career in 1985-6. On 11 Sep 1985, he surpassed the long standing record of 4190 hits in a career by Ty Cobb; a tribute to his greatness and his durability. Earlier in his career he had been known as one of the leaders of the 'Big Red Machine' which dominated the National League in the early 1970s. In 1978 with the Phillies, Rose mounted a serious threat to Joe DiMaggio's record 56-game hitting streak when he hit safely in a National League record 44 consecutive games. On his retirement, Rose became the Reds manager. In 1989, major league baseball mounted an investigation against him for purportedly betting on baseball games. He was banned from baseball for this and the rules were also changed to keep him out of the Hall of Fame. He also served time in prison in 1991 for income tax problems.
Career 1963-86: 4256 hits Avg. .303; HR 160; RBI 1314; Runs: 2165; SB 198. Best seasons: 1969: .348, 218 hits; 1968: .335, 210 hits; 1973: .338, 230 hits; 1976: .323, 215 hits; 1975: .317, 210 hits.

Ralph ROSE (USA)

ATHLETICS
Ralph Waldo Rose. b. 17 Mar 1885 Louisville, d. 16 Oct 1913 San Francisco of typhoid fever.

Olympic shot champion in 1904 and 1908 and second in 1912. He won a third gold medal at the two-handed shot in 1912 and won silver and bronze medals at discus and hammer (1904). He won four AAU shot titles, 1907-10, as well as the discus 1905 and 1909 and javelin 1909.
A huge man at 1.98m and 130kg, Rose set eight pre-IAAF shot records, from 14.81m in 1904 to 15.54 in 1909. The latter stood for a record duration of 18 years 241 days. His most remarkable achievement, however, came in an unsanctioned meet at Healdsburg, California on 26 Jun 1909, when he put the shot an unconfirmed 16.56, a mark unsurpassed by anyone until Jack Torrance in 1934, and also exceeded the world hammer best with 54.38m. In 1912 he achieved a world two-handed shot record at 28.00 (15.39 right, 12.61 left). He attended the University of Michigan and later studied law at Chicago.

Bernd ROSEMEYER (Ger)

MOTOR RACING
Bernd Rosemeyer. b. 14 Oct 1909 Lingen. d. 28 Jan 1938 on the Frankfurt - Darmstadt autobahn.

A former motorcycle racer, especially for

DKW, a member of the Auto Union group, he raced their cars from 1934, joining their works team in 1935. In 1936 he had a brilliant season, almost single-handledly matching the all-powerful Mercedes, as he took the difficult-to-handle Auto Unions to victories in the Italian, Swiss and German Grands Prix.
Having exceeded 250 mph for the first time on a road, with 252.46 mph *406.28km/h* in October 1937, he was killed three months later when attempting speed records, as his car turned over at a speed of over 250 mph in a savage cross-wind.

Heide ROSENDAHL (FRG)

ATHLETICS

Heidemarie Rosendahl. b. 14 Feb 1947 Hückeswagen. Later Ecker.

A highly talented all-rounder, she won Olympic gold medals at long jump and sprint relay in 1972, and in between these events had an epic battle against Mary Peters in the pentathlon. During the competition Rosendahl long jumped 6.83m, just one centimetre short of the world record that she had set two years earlier, and in the final event ran a brilliant 22.96 200m, but she would have needed to run 0.1 sec faster to beat Peters and finished ten points behind the latter's world record of 4801 points for a silver medal.
In the European Championships she missed the events of 1969 due to the West German boycott, but was second at pentathlon in 1966 and won that event in 1971, when she took the bronze at long jump. She was European Indoor long jump champion in 1971, and won a total of 27 FRG titles between 1966 and 1972, including outdoors five each at pentathlon and long jump and one at 100mh, and 12 indoors. Her father Heinz Rosendahl was FRG discus champion in 1951 and 1953.
She set four world records at pentathlon 1969-72 and one at long jump in 1970.
German records: two at 200m to 22.96, six at 100m hurdles, best 13.1 (1970); five at long jump to 6.84 (1970), six at pentathlon.
Other bests: 100m 11.3 (1971) and 11.2w (1968), high jump 1.70m (1970), shot 14.28m (1968), javelin 48.18m (1966).

Albert ROSENFELD (Aus)

RUGBY LEAGUE

Albert Aaron Rosenfeld. b. 28 Jul 1885, d. Oct 1970 England.

A member of the first Australian team to tour England in 1908/9, he left his Sydney team, Eastern Suburbs, to sign for Huddersfield at the end of the tour and although his career was curtailed by World War I, he set a host of scoring records, a number of which remain unbeaten. A small man at 1.65m *5'5"* but with dazzling skills, he was the leading try scorer in the country for five consecutive seasons and his feat of scoring 80 tries for Huddersfield in 42 matches in 1913/4 has never been surpassed. This bettered his own record of 78 tries set two seasons earlier. As part of an outstanding Huddersfield three-quarter line he benefited from his close understanding with centre Harold Wagstaff.
Prior to his retirement in 1924 he played briefly for Wakefield Trinity and Bradford Northern, but he will be remembered essentially as a Huddersfield player and as the most prolific try scorer the game has known. In 1964 he made a return visit to Australia for the first time since leaving in 1909.

Ken ROSEWALL (Aus)

TENNIS

Kenneth Robert Rosewall. b. 2 Nov 1934 Sydney, New South Wales.

An elegant stylist, whose classic ground strokes, particularly on the backhand, made him one of the most admired players of all-time. With his abundant talent he won every major honour except the Wimbledon singles, although he was a losing finalist four times, 1954, 1956, 1970 and 1974. He reached his peak as a professional before the Open era readmitted the pros to Wimbledon in 1968.
His career was remarkable for its longevity: he was Australian junior champion in 1950 and 1952, and won his first Grand Slam title in 1953 and his last in 1972. During this 19-year period he won 8 Grand Slam singles (4 Australian, 2 US, 2 French), 9 men's doubles (2 Wimbledon, 3

Australian, 2 US, 2 French) and the mixed doubles at the 1956 US championships. He reached the final of the US singles for a fourth time in 1974 at the age of 39 and did not finally retire from Grand Prix tennis until 1979. He played in 11 Davis Cup ties 1953-6, 1973 and 1975, and his record was 17 wins in 19 singles and 2 of 3 doubles.

ROSHAN KHAN (Pak)

SQUASH

Roshan Khan.

The 1956 British Open champion at squash. Born in poor circumstances, he worked as assistant professional to his father at the Rawalpindi Club before joining his elder brother, Nasrullah, in Karachi in 1951. After winning his third Pakistan Professional Championship he overcame inter-clan rivalry and made the journey to England. Azam and Hashim Khan, his relatives by marriage, had been visiting England for some years and usually proved more than a match for him. In 1953 he lost in the semi-final of the British Open to Azam, the following year he was eliminated by Hashim, again at the semi-final stage, and although he made the final in 1955 he again lost to Hashim. He finally got the better of Hashim in the 1956 final but because of knee injuries he was forced to miss the next two Championships. He was a finalist for a third time in 1960 but only managed to take one point from Azam, who beat him in the semi-finals in the next three years. His last major victory was the Canadian Open in 1961.
He declined many attractive offers from overseas, preferring to remain in Pakistan where he coached his two sons. His eldest son, Torsam, was ranked in the world's top ten before he died of a heart attack during a tournament in Australia in 1979, and his youngest son, Jahangir, became the greatest player in the world.

Barney ROSS (USA)

BOXING

né Barnet David Rosofsky. b. 23 Dec 1909 New York, d. 17 Jan 1967 Chicago, Illinois.

Ross's grocer father was murdered by gunmen in Chicago when he was only 14. After working as a messenger for mobsters he turned professional to help support the family. He became known for his speed and in 1933 he won the world lightweight and junior-welterweight championships from Tony Canzoneri. He added the welterweight title in 1934, when he outpointed Jimmy McLarnin, and held these three world titles simultaneously for a few months. He had three classic fights with McLarnin, exciting their Irish and Jewish ethnic supporters in New York, with Ross winning the rubber bout.
Ross retired in 1938 after losing to Henry Armstrong. In World War II he served as a Marine on Guadalcanal where he was wounded. For his valour, however, he was awarded the Congressional Medal of Honor. Ross later fought drug addiction which grew out of the wounds he suffered. He eventually died of cancer after a long illness.
Career record: W - 73 (22), L - 4, D - 3.

Paolo ROSSI (Ita)

FOOTBALL

Paolo Rossi. b. 23 Sep 1956 Prato.

Initially a winger, who was converted into a centre-forward, he began his career with Juventus, making his First Division début in 1977, and then moved to Como, Lanerossi Vicenza and Perugia before returning to Juventus in 1981. There his honours included the European Cup-Winners' Cup 1984 and the European Cup 1985.
At the height of his career he was suspended for three years for allegedly 'fixing' a match between Perugia and Avellino. His sentence was later reduced to two years and he was immediately recalled to the national team for the 1982 World Cup where, with a dazzling display of his goalscoring abilities, he helped Italy win the trophy. He was elected European Footballer of the Year that year. He later played for Milan 1985-6 and Verona 1986-7. He scored 20 goals in 48 international appearances 1977-86.

Mark ROTH (USA)

BOWLING

Mark Stephen Roth. b. 10 Apr 1951 Brooklyn, New York.

Roth won 33 titles on the PBA Tour, trailing only Earl Anthony's 41. He was also the second player (after Anthony) to earn $1 million in tournament winnings and to the end of 1992 his career earnings totalled $1,410,141. He was voted PBA Player of the Year four times, 1977-9 and 1984. He did not, however, win a major championship until he won the US Open in 1984. In 1978 Roth won eight titles, still a PBA record for a single year, and he also won the PBA High Average Award a record six times (1976-9, 1981, 1988).
His career might have been even greater had he not duelled against Anthony for much of it. He is considered by some to be the father of the modern game, epitomised by his hard-throwing, hard-cranking style.

Christa ROTHENBURGER, see LUDING.

Frank-Peter RÖTSCH (GDR)

BIATHLON

Frank-Peter Rötsch. b. 19 Apr 1964 Güstrow.

In 1988 Rötsch won Olympic biathlon gold medals at both 10km and 20km. He came to international prominence as a member of the winning GDR team at the 1981 and 1982 World Junior Championships, taking the individual silver medal at 10km in the second year. In 1983 he was runner-up at 20km in the World Championships with a second silver medal on the GDR relay team, and a year later made his Olympic début with the 20km silver.
He was World champion at 10km in 1985 (and 2nd again at 20km) and won both 10km and 20km in 1987, with relay golds both years. He was also the World Cup winner in 1984-5 and 1987.

Dorothy ROUND (UK)

TENNIS

Dorothy Edith Round. b. 13 Jul 1909 Dudley, Worcestershire, d. 12 Nov 1982 Kidderminster, Worcestershire. Later Little.

The outstanding British player of the 1930s. After being runner-up to Helen Wills Moody at Wimbledon in 1933 she beat Helen Jacobs in the final the following year, when with Fred Perry winning the men's title this was the first British 'double' in the Wimbledon singles since 1909. Although the top seed, she was eliminated at the quarter-final stage at Wimbledon in both 1935 and 1936, but in 1935 she had become the first overseas player to win the Australian women's title. She regained her Wimbledon title in 1937 and married Dr Douglas Little later that year. She did not defend her title in 1938 and as Mrs Little made her last Wimbledon appearance in 1939 when she was eliminated in the fourth round.
She won the mixed doubles at Wimbledon with the Japanese Davis Cup captain, Ryuki Miki, in 1934 and with Fred Perry in 1935 and 1936. In view of her Championship successes, she had a surprisingly poor Wightman Cup record, winning only 4 of her 11 singles and losing both doubles. An unspectacular player, her strength was her forehand drive which she supplemented with a shrewd drop-shot. A dedicated Sunday School teacher, she refused to play on Sundays which on one occasion posed difficulties for the authorities at the French Championships.

Stanley ROUS (UK)

FOOTBALL

(Sir) Stanley Ford Rous. b. 25 Apr 1895 Mutford, Lowestoft, Suffolk, d. 18 Jul 1986.

One of the most influential figures in the history of football. He trained as a teacher at St Luke's College, Exeter, where he was captain of soccer and tennis. After war service he accepted his rather modest playing abilities and took up refereeing. He took charge of 34 international matches throughout Europe from 1920 to 1934,

when he left his teaching job to become secretary of the Football Association. He remained in that job until 1961 when he was appointed president of FIFA, a position he held until his retirement in 1974. He was one of the founders of the Central Council for Physical Recreation (CCPR) and a member of many sporting bodies, all of whom benefited immensely from his forward thinking and planning talents.
He was awarded the CBE in 1943 and knighted in 1949.

Edd ROUSH (USA)

BASEBALL
Edd J Roush. b. 8 May 1893 Oakland City, Indiana, d. 21 Mar 1888 Bradenton, Florida.

Roush was major league baseball's top hitter in the dead-ball era in which he played. He was an outfielder who played with five major league teams, but is best known for the 12 years he spent with the Cincinnati Reds. He twice led the league in batting (1917, 1919) and batted over .300 in thirteen different seasons. He was known for using the heaviest bat in baseball to slap hits to all fields.
Career 1913-31: 2376 hits Avg. .323; RBI 981. Best seasons: 1921: .352; 1922: .352; 1917: .341; 1924: .348.

Diana ROWE (UK)

TABLE TENNIS
Diana Rowe. b. 14 Apr 1933 Marylebone, London. Later Schöler.

An identical twin who played left-handed and formed a brilliant partnership with her right-handed sister, Rosalind. Together they won the world doubles in 1951 and 1954 and were runners-up in 1952-3 and 1955. They also won six consecutive English Open doubles 1950-5, after which the partnership broke up following Rosalind's marriage.
Diana continued tournament play and won six more English doubles titles with three different partners and she also won the singles for the first time in 1962. She won European team titles in 1958 and 1964 and women's doubles titles in 1962 and 1964, and was again a finalist in 1970. She married the West German champion Eberhard Schöler in 1966 and reached the quarterfinals of the world mixed doubles with him in 1971.

Rosalind ROWE (UK)

TABLE TENNIS
Rosalind Rowe. b. 14 Apr 1933 Marylebone, London. Later Cornett.

An orthodox player who shared in the early successes of her left-handed twin sister, Diana. She retired from Championship play following her marriage in October 1955 to Jack Cornett, a ship's doctor whom she had met two years earlier when the twins travelled by sea to play in New Zealand. Prior to her marriage, she and her sister had reached the final of the world women's doubles for five successive years 1951-5, and were the winners in 1951 and 1954. They also won six consecutive English women's doubles 1950-5, and Rosalind was the English singles champion in 1953 and 1955.

Angelica ROZEANU (Rom)

TABLE TENNIS
Angelica Rozeanu. née Adelstein. b. 15 Oct 1921 Bucharest.

Succeeded Gizi Farkas as the world No.1 woman player in the years immediately following World War II. She first won the Romanian singles title as a 15-year-old in 1936 and held it every year until her retirement, except for the period of the German occupation. She made her World Championships début in 1936 and reached the third round of the singles. Two years later she scored her first major international success with a victory in the Hungarian Championships, but she was denied a passport for the World Championships in London by the strongly anti-semitic Romanian Government. She returned to international competition in 1950 when she won the first of her record six successive world singles titles and led the Romanian women to the first of five victories in the team event. She also won three women's doubles and three mixed

doubles at the World Championships between 1951 and 1956. Her greatest year came in 1953 when she won the singles, both doubles and was a member of the winning Corbillon Cup team. She won European women's doubles titles in 1958 and 1960.
At home, she was either showered with honours or was the victim of political and racial purges, and finding these inconsistencies unacceptable, she emigrated to Israel in 1960 and closed her international career with a victory at the 1961 Maccabiah Games. Initially, her game was built on defence but after the war she developed into an attacking player and could hit with authority on either wing.

Pete ROZELLE (USA)

AMERICAN FOOTBALL

Alvin Ray Rozelle. b. 1 Mar 1926 South Gate, California.

In 1960 he succeeded Bert Bell as commissioner of the NFL. The decision came as a big surprise and Rozelle, then general manager of the Los Angeles Rams, was felt to be a compromise choice. But in the next 29 years he became universally acclaimed as the finest commissioner in the history of US professional sport. He controlled football in an ironclad fashion and made the professional game highly popular. He was able to negotiate several lucrative television contracts and helped make the game highly visible on television. In 1963 he was named Sportsman of the Year by *Sports Illustrated*. He retired rather unexpectedly at the end of the 1989 season.

Wilma RUDOLPH (USA)

ATHLETICS

Wilma Glodean Rudolph. b. 23 Jun 1940 St Bethlehem, Tennessee. Later Ward.

A heroine of the 1960 Olympics when she was triple sprint gold medallist with 100m, 200m and relay. In 1956 she had won Olympic bronze on the US sprint relay team, but did not qualify from the heats of the 200m. She missed the 1958 season through the birth of her first child, but reached world class in 1959, when she was second at 100m and took relay gold at the Pan-American Games, and won the first of four successive US titles at 100m/100y. She was AAU indoor champion at 50y 1959-60 and 220y 1960 and set her first world record when she won the 1960 outdoor title with 22.9 for 200m.
She added the world record for the 100m with 11.3 (11.41 on automatic timing) in the Olympic semi-final, running a wind-aided 11.0 (11.18) in the final. She improved the 100m record to 11.2 in 1961 and also ran on US relay teams that set world records in 1960 at the Olympics and in 1961 against the USSR. She was the 1961 Sullivan Award winner.
The 20th of 22 children, she lost the use of her left leg for a while after suffering from double pneumonia and scarlet fever at the age of four and had to wear a leg brace until she was 8. She has formed the Wilma Rudolph Foundation, and works with underprivileged children.

Red RUFFING (USA)

BASEBALL

Charles Herbert Ruffing. b. 3 May 1904 Granville, Illinois, d. 17 Feb 1986 Mayfield Heights, Ohio.

Ruffing began his career with the Boston Red Sox in 1924. Though he had previously been at best a mediocre pitcher, he was traded to the New York Yankees in 1930 and became one of the top pitchers in baseball and the leader of the staff that helped the Yankees win multiple pennants in the 1930s. He won 20 games in a season each year 1936-9 and his World Series record was a redoubtable 7-2.
He was also an excellent hitter, and his season's average of .364 in 1930 is the second best ever posted by a pitcher. He accomplished his feats despite having lost four toes in a mine accident as a young boy.
Career pitching 1924-47: ERA 3.80; W-L 273-225, SO 1987. Best seasons: 1936: 20-12, 3.85 ERA; 1937: 20-7, 2.99 ERA; 1938: 21-7, 3.32 ERA; 1939: 21-7, 2.94 ERA. Batting: 512 hits Avg. .269.

Frank RÜHLE (GDR)

ROWING
b. 5 Mar 1944 Dehna.

Rühle was a member of the renowned Einheit Dresden four (with Frank Forberger, Dieter Grahn and Dieter Schubert), who competed for 11 years and were never beaten in international competition. See Frank Forberger for details.

Karl-Heinz RUMMENIGGE (FRG)

FOOTBALL
Karl-Heinz Rummenigge. b. 25 Sep 1955 Lippstadt, Westphalia.

After winning a European Cup winners medal and the World Club Cup with Bayern Munich in 1976, he helped Germany win the European Championship in 1980 and was voted European Footballer of the Year in 1980 and 1981. A winger, he scored 45 goals in 95 international appearances 1976-88, and after a poor showing by Germany in the 1978 World Cup, Rummenigge skippered them to the final in 1982 and 1986, but they lost on both occasions. He had played for Borussia Lippstadt before joining Bayern Munich in 1974. Moved to Inter Milan in 1983, then to Servette Geneva 1987-9. Now a TV commentator with ARD.
His younger brother **Michael** (b. 3 Feb 1964) played twice for Germany.

Natalya RUMYANTSEVA (USSR)

WATER SKIING
Natalya Rumyantseva. b. 18 Mar 1963 Dubna. Later Ponomaryeva.

World water skiing champion at tricks in 1979, 1983, and 1987, with six world records for the event. She was European overall champion a record five times, 1982, 1984, 1987, 1989 and 1992, and in tricks she has won 14 European medals. In 1985 she was awarded the Soviet Badge of honour for Sports and received a degree in sports instruction from the Institute of Physical Culture in Moscow. In 1990 after *glasnost* she started competing professionally in the United States. Natalya attended music school as a child and is an excellent pianist.

Adolph RUPP (USA)

BASKETBALL
Adolph Rupp. b. 2 Sep 1901 Halstead, Kansas, d. 10 Dec 1977 Lexington, Kentucky.

Rupp learned basketball as a player at the University of Kansas under the legendary coach Forrest 'Phog' Allen. After graduating in 1923, Rupp coached at several high schools, and also earned a master's degree in education administration from Columbia. From 1930 to 1972 he was head coach at the University of Kentucky, winning 874 games with a winning percentage of .825. He coached Kentucky to four NCAA titles (1948, 1949, 1951, and 1958). His last years as a coach were marked by his refusal to recruit black players and his opposition to blacks playing major college basketball.

Roman RURUA (USSR/Geo)

WRESTLING
Roman Vladimirovich Rurua. b. 25 Nov 1942 a Georgian village.

He was Soviet champion each year 1963-70 at 63 or 69 kg Greco-Roman, and at the Olympic Games won a featherweight (63kg) silver medal in 1964 and gold in 1968. From 1966 Rurua was undefeated in international competition for five years. He won world championships at featherweight in 1966-7 and 1969, and at lightweight in 1970.

Ian RUSH (UK)

FOOTBALL
Ian James Rush. b. 20 Oct 1961 St Asaph, Flintshire.

One of the most dangerous strikers of recent years. After winning Welsh international honours at Schoolboy, Youth and Under-21 level, he made his début in a full international in 1980. In June 1993 he scored his 25th goal in his 60th international match. Joining Liverpool from Chester City as a teenager in 1980, he soon became a vital member of the superb team which won the European Cup 1984, FA Cup 1986, 1989 and 1992, Football

League Cup 1981-4 and the League Championship 1982-4, 1986 and 1990. Rush missed Liverpool's League Championship success of 1988 as he spent that season with Juventus in Italy.

Wim RUSKA (Hol)

JUDO

Wilhelm Ruska. b. 29 Aug 1940 Amsterdam.

Ruska, hugely powerful and fast despite his size at 1.90m and 118kg, was the first man to win four judo world titles, succeeding at the over-93kg class in 1967 and 1971, and adding the Olympic golds in 1972 at both over-93kg and Open. He was European Open champion in 1969 and 1972 and at over-93kg in 1967, 1969 and 1971-2. He became coach to the Dutch judo team.

Bill RUSSELL (USA)

BASKETBALL

William Fenton Russell. b. 12 Feb 1934 Monroe, Louisiana.

Perhaps he was the greatest basketball player ever, perhaps only its greatest champion, but it matters little, for Bill Russell forever changed the shape of professional basketball. He turned it into the consummate team game, where defensive ability, rebounding and hustle were as important as great offensive skills.
Russell played for the University of San Francisco, the 1956 US Olympic gold medal team, and the Boston Celtics. Although most of the records were being set by his arch-rival, Wilt Chamberlain, Russell was the ace winner. His character refused to allow his team to lose, as his teams won 13 of the 16 championships open to them, and one loss occurred when he was injured in the NBA championship finals. He played on two NCAA championship teams, and won 10 NBA championships with the Celtics, eight of those in succession.
Russell was five times the NBA's Most Valuable Player, and was virtually always first or second-team all-NBA, often alternating the honour with Chamberlain. He was named *The Sporting News* Athlete of the Decade in 1970, and was also named Sportsman of the Year in 1968 by *Sports Illustrated.* After his retirement he was named to the NBA's 25th and 35th Anniversary All-Time Teams and was named the NBA's greatest player ever in a poll of basketball writers.
Russell also coached in the NBA, but with mixed success. He twice led the Celtics to NBA titles as a player-coach, but later could do little to help the Seattle Supersonics. He now works as a basketball commentator for CBS Sports, as well as serving as a spokesman for several companies in television commercials.
NBA career: 14,522 points, av. 15.1; 21,620 rebounds, av. 22.5.

Bernhard RUSSI (Swi)

ALPINE SKIING

Bernhard Russi. b. 20 Aug 1948 Andermatt.

Olympic downhill champion in 1972 and silver medallist in 1976. In World Cup races he had nine downhill wins and one at giant slalom, 1970-7, winning the downhill series in 1971-2.

Babe RUTH (USA)

BASEBALL

George Herman Ruth. b. 6 Feb 1895 Baltimore, Maryland, d. 16 Aug 1948 New York.

Considered by many to be the greatest player in baseball history. Ruth began his career as a pitcher with the Boston Red Sox, winning 80 games 1915-19. In 1920 he was traded to the New York Yankees and there he was shifted to playing right field full-time. Already known as a powerful hitter, his abilities blossomed and he became the game's greatest power hitter. His records are almost too numerous to mention. They are topped by his records of 60 home runs in 1927 and 714 career home runs. He hit over 50 home runs in a season four times, the only player to accomplish that feat more than twice, and had eleven seasons of over 40 home runs. He had a career batting average of .342, and six sea-

sonal marks over .370. His career slugging average of .690 has never been approached - only four other players have a career mark over .600. He is the all-time leader in walks, equal second in runs, second in home runs and runs batted in (both to Hank Aaron), and is fifth in total bases. Ruth is also widely considered to have 'saved' baseball, regenerating interest in the sport after the Black Sox scandal of 1919. Shortly after he joined the Yankees, they built Yankee Stadium, always known since as 'The House that Ruth Built'. He was mourned by millions of Americans when he died from throat cancer in 1948, three weeks after the première of the movie *The Babe Ruth Story*.
Career 1914-35: 2873 hits Avg. .342, HR 714; RBI 2209; SB 123. Best seasons: 1927: .356, 60 HR, 164 RBI; 1921: .378, 59 HR, 171 RBI; 1920: .376, 54 HR, 137 RBI; 1928: .323, 54 HR, 142 RBI; 1923: .391, 41 HR, 130 RBI; 1931: .373, 46 HR, 163 RBI. Career pitching: ERA 2.28; W-L 94-46.

John RUTHERFORD (UK)

RUGBY UNION
John Young Rutherford. b. 4 Oct 1955 Selkirk.

Retiring in 1987 after 42 international appearances, he was Scotland's most capped fly half. In 35 of these matches he partnered scrum half **Roy Laidlaw** (b. 5 Oct 1953 Jedburgh) which was a world record for an international half-back pairing. Once he had made his début against Wales in 1979, Rutherford was never dropped by Scotland though he missed several matches due to injury. On the British Lions tour of New Zealand in 1983 he was second choice to Ollie Campbell (Ire) for the fly half position but he played at centre in the third Test and scored one of the Lions' two tries. He scored 12 drop-goals in internationals.

Birger RUUD (Nor)

SKIING
Birger Johannes Ruud. b. 23 Aug 1911 Kongsberg.

The only skier to win Olympic events at both Alpine and Nordic disciplines, as in 1936 he won the Alpine downhill race as well as taking gold medals for ski jumping in 1932 and 1936. The downhill was not a separate event in 1936, but part of the Alpine combined, so that although Ruud won that event he fared less well at slalom and finished just out of the medals in fourth place. In 1948 Ruud travelled to the Olympic Games in St Moritz as coach to the Norwegian team, but in view of the poor weather he decided to compete instead of a less experienced competitor and took the silver medal; at 36 he remains the oldest Olympic ski-jumping medallist. In addition to his Olympic titles, Ruud was world champion at ski jumping in 1931, 1935 and 1937, and second in 1939. His older brother **Sigmund** (b. 30 Dec 1907 Kongsberg) won the Olympic silver medal for ski jumping in 1928 and the world title in 1929, and another brother, **Asbjörn** (b. 6 Oct 1919, d. 1989), became the then youngest ski-jumping world champion at 18 in 1938, and was 7th at the Olympics in 1948.

Bunny RYAN (USA)

TENNIS
Elizabeth Montague Ryan. b. 5 Feb 1892 Anaheim, Los Angeles, California, d. 6 Jul 1979 Wimbledon, London, England.

Winner of a record 19 Wimbledon doubles titles (12 women's, 7 mixed) between 1914 and 1934. It was not until 1979 that this figure was exceeded by Billie Jean King. Ryan's supremacy as a doubles player was underlined by numerous victories at other major championships: French (4 women's), US (1 women's, 2 mixed), Italian (1 women's, 1 mixed) and World Hard Court (2 women's, 2 mixed). In eight of her 20 major women's doubles victories she was partnered by Suzanne Lenglen (6 Wimbledon, 2 World Hard Court). Her singles victories were limited to the British Hard Court title in 1924 and 1925 and the Italian title in 1933 but she came close to winning a major singles on more than one occasion. She was the losing finalist at Wimbledon in 1921 and 1930 and at the

US Championships in 1926.
Bunny Ryan made her home in England after her first visit in 1912 and spent most of her life in her adopted country, becoming probably the most assiduous tournament player in history. Reputedly, she won 659 tournaments - including the last championship of Imperial Russia in 1914 - and finished as runner-up in more than 800 others! Her record shows her to have been the greatest of all doubles players and her strengths were a chop stroke and chop volley at the net. Appropriately, she died at Wimbledon the day before Billie Jean King broke her record for the number of titles won.

Nolan RYAN (USA)

BASEBALL

Lynn Nolan Ryan. b. 31 Jan 1947 Refugio, Texas.

The greatest strikeout artist in baseball history as a result of his blazing fastball and his great durability, due in great part to his assiduous physical conditioning. From his début in 1966 with the New York Mets, through his career with the California Angels 1972-9, Houston Astros 1980-8 and the Texas Rangers 1989-92, he has achieved 5668 strikeouts, by far the all-time record. He was the first pitcher to achieve 4000 in July 1985 and 5000 on 23 Aug 1989, and became the first to strike out 300 or more batters in three consecutive seasons in 1972-4 and the oldest to do so in a season in 1989; his 383 in 1973 is a modern major league record. He led the American League for strikeouts nine times (1972-4, 1976-9, 1989-90) and the National League twice, 1987-8. While with Houston he also led the NL for earned run average in 1981 and 1987.
Ryan's early wildness, and the poor teams with which he has played, are reflected in his being the all-time major league leader in career walks, and being 3rd (through 1992) on the list of career losses by a pitcher. Still, he managed to win his 300th game in 1990 and he also pitched his 7th no-hitter in that season, when he was 43 years old; the next best figure being Sandy Koufax's four.
His fast pitch, the 'Ryan Express', was measured at 100.9 mph *162.3 km/h* in 1974, and he maintained express speed throughout his career.
Career pitching 1966-92: ERA 3.17; W-L 319-287, SO 5668. Best seasons: 1973: 21-16, 383 SO; 1974: 22-16, 367 SO; 1972: 329 SO; 1976: 327 SO; 1977: 341 SO; 1989: 301 SO.

Nolan Ryan - Strikeouts

1966	6	1980	200
1967	-	1981	140
1968	133	1982	245
1969	92	1983	183
1970	125	1984	197
1971	137	1985	209
1972	329	1986	194
1973	383	1987	270
1974	367	1988	228
1975	186	1989	301
1976	327	1990	232
1977	341	1991	203
1978	260	1992	157
1979	223		

Pam RYAN (Aus)

ATHLETICS

Pamela Ryan. née Kilborn. b. 12 Aug 1939 Melbourne.

Her first major titles were the Commonwealth 80m hurdles and long jump in 1962. She retained her hurdles title in 1966 and 1970 and took her gold collection to six with the sprint relay in 1966 and 1970. At the Olympics she was 3rd in 1964 (in 10.56 to 10.54 for winner Karin Balzer) and 2nd in 1968 at 80m hurdles, and at the lengthened distance of 100m hurdles she was 4th in 1972. On the flat she tied the world record for 60m with an unratified 7.2 in 1968. Over hurdles she set world records for 80m at 10.5 in 1964 and 10.4 in 1965, with an auto-timed best of 10.41 in the heats of the 1968 Olympics (before 10.46 in the final behind team-mate Maureen Caird's 10.39); at 100m with 12.5 (12.93 auto timing) in 1972; and at 200m five records to 25.7 in 1971.
Between 1963 and 1972 she won a women's record 17 Australian titles: 7 at 80mh, 3 each long jump and pentathlon, 2 at 100mh and one each at 100y and 200mh.
Other bests: 100m 11.5 (1967) and 11.2w

(1969), 200m 23.6 (1968), long jump 6.24 (1966) and 6.26w (1962).

Yakov RYLSKY (USSR)

FENCING

Yakov Rylsky. b. 25 Oct 1928 East Kazakhstan Oblast.

A soldier, he is one of only three men to have won the world individual sabre title three times (1958, 1961, 1963). Fourth place in 1964 represented his best individual Olympic placing but he won a team bronze in 1956 and a gold in 1964.

Jim RYUN (USA)

ATHLETICS

James Ronald Ryun. b. 29 Apr 1947 Wichita, Kansas.

A prodigy, he became by far the youngest four-minute miler at 17 in 1964. Before he left his teenage years he was the world's supreme middle-distance runner, with his first world records, 1:44.9 for 880 yards and 3:51.3 for the mile, at 19 in 1966. Later that season he set a US record for 2 miles at 8:25.2 and at the end of the year won the Sullivan Award.

Coached by Bob Timmons at Kansas State University, for whom he won the 1967 NCAA mile title, he won his third successive AAU mile title in 1967 in 3:51.1 having led from the gun, finishing with a devastating last lap in 52.5. Two weeks later he took an amazing 2.5 seconds off the world record for 1500m that Herb Elliott had set at the 1960 Olympics, as with 3:33.1 Ryun left Kip Keino well beaten on 3:37.2.

At just over 20 years of age Ryun had the world at his feet, but set no more world records and won no more titles. He was second to Kip Keino in the 1968 Olympic 1500m, beaten mentally by the high altitude in Mexico City and the way that Keino blazed away despite that apparent handicap. Ryun had the desperate misfortune to fall in the heats of the 1972 Olympic 1500m. He ran for a while with the ITA pro group and later as a veteran but never again approached the brilliant style of his glory days.

Jaano SAARINEN (Fin)

MOTOR CYCLING

Jaano Saarinen. b. 11 Dec 1945 Turku, d. 1973 Monza.

He was the new star of motorcycling, and leading the World Championship at both 250 and 500cc when he was killed in a 50-machine pile-up on the first lap in the Italian 250cc Grand Prix at Monza in 1973.

The Finnish ice racing champion of 1965, he developed in motorcycle racing until he won the 1971 Czechoslovakian GP. This led to works rides in 1972, and he immediately became World 250cc champion. He had staggered critics by beating Giacomo Agostini on the MV-3. He started 1973 by winning the Daytona 200 in the USA, and the dashing rider swept to a series of wins before tragedy struck.

Arvidas SABONIS (Lit)

BASKETBALL

Arvidas Romas Sabonis. b. 19 Dec 1964 Kaunas.

At 2.21m *7'3"* and 127 kg *280 lbs* Sabonis is considered the greatest big basketball player ever produced outside of the United States. He began playing with the Soviet national team in 1981 and Indiana coach Bobby Knight immediately labelled him 'The best young player in the world'.

He helped the USSR to win the World title in 1982, European title 1981 and 1985, and World Cup 1986. He was drafted to play in the NBA by the Atlanta Hawks in 1985 and by the Portland Trail Blazers in 1986, but never played in the NBA as two Achilles tendon ruptures threatened his career so that he played only one major event in the late 1980s, helping the USSR to the 1988 Olympic gold.

He later rejoined European professional leagues and played for Lithuania at the Barcelona Olympics. For his size, Sabonis possessed incredible basketball skills, being able to handle the ball well and even shoot the three-point basket well.

Sandy SADDLER (USA)

BOXING

Joseph Saddler. b. 23 Jun 1926 Boston, Massachusetts

Saddler was the son of a West Indian but was raised in Harlem. He turned professional at 17 but had over 100 fights before he earned a title shot in 1948, when he defeated Willie Pep to claim the world featherweight championship. Saddler lost a return match but then defeated Pep in their third and fourth bouts. He remained featherweight champion until 1956, when a car accident caused an eye injury which forced his retirement.
Career record: W - 144 (103), L - 16, D -2.

Toni SAILER (Aut)

ALPINE SKIING

Anton Sailer. b. 17 Nov 1935 Kitzbühel.

The first man to win the treble at the Alpine skiing events at the Olympics, with giant slalom, slalom and the downhill in 1956, when he won each event by substantial margins and also became, at 20 years 73 days, skiing's youngest ever male champion. He was World champion at Alpine combination in 1956, and retained that title as well as winning the downhill and giant slalom in 1958, at which point he retired to become a hotelier. He was also an actor and singer, making 15 films and 18 records, but retained his winter sports links, becoming technical director of the Austrian Ski Association from 1972.
A brilliant and daring skier, he pioneered the hip-swinging style in the giant slalom.

Henri SAINT CYR (Swe)

EQUESTRIAN

Julius Henri Révérony Saint Cyr. b. 15 Mar 1902 Stockholm, d. 27 Jul 1979.

The first rider to win two individual Olympic gold medals in dressage, in 1952 and 1956. He also helped Sweden win team dressage gold medals at both Games. He began his Olympic career in 1936 with the Swedish three-day event team and in 1960 completed five Olympic appearances with five different horses. In 1956 he took the oath on behalf of the competitors at the equestrian events, held in Stockholm.

Yves SAINT-MARTIN (Fra)

HORSE RACING

Yves Saint-Martin. b. 8 Sep 1941 Agen, Lot et Garonne.

French champion jockey 15 times between 1959 and 1983, with wins in most of the major races throughout Europe, including nine in the Prix du Jockey Club and 29 French classics in all, and wins in all five English classics. His first winner was in 1958 when he was apprenticed to François Mathet, whom he had joined in 1955 and with whom he stayed at Chantilly until 1970, the year that he had the first of his four wins in the Prix de l'Arc de Triomphe on *Sassafras*. His first English classic winner was *Monade* in the 1962 Oaks, and great horses that he rode included *Relko*, the 1963 Derby winner, and *Allez France*, winner of the Prix de l'Arc in 1974. From 1971 to 1977 he rode for Daniel Wildenstein. He retired in 1988 having ridden 3314 winners.
Typically riding very short, yet with fine balance, he proved a cool judge of a race. His son Eric is a jockey.

Carlos SAINZ (Spain)

RALLYING

Carlos Sainz. b. 12 Apr 1962 Madrid.

World rallying champion in 1990 and 1992, and second in 1991. With his co-driver Luis Moya his 13 championship race wins include the Monte Carlo Rally 1991 and RAC 1990 and 1992, driving a Toyota Celica GT4. Spanish champion in 1987 and 1988. He started rallying in 1980 with Renault and later drove for Ford and Toyota before switching to Lancia for 1993.

Hitoshi SAITO (Japan)

JUDO

Hitoshi Saito. b. 2 Jan 1961 Aomori.

One of only three men to have won two Olympic gold medals at judo, as he won the over-95kg category in both 1984 and 1988. He was also World open champion in 1983. A huge, squat figure, he weighed 140kg at a height of 1.80m. A graduate of Kokushikan University, and now a lecturer.

Ulrich SALCHOW (Swe)

FIGURE SKATING

Karl Emil Julius Ulrich Salchow. b. 7 Aug 1877 Copenhagen, Denmark, d. 18 Apr 1949 Stockholm.

Winner of a record ten world singles figure skating titles, the first Olympic gold medallist and a nine-time European champion between 1898 and 1913. After finishing second at the World Championships in 1897, 1899 and 1900. Salchow won every world title from 1901 to 1911, except for 1906 when he did not compete. Although he had retired by the time the Championships were revived after the war in 1922, he had earlier placed fourth in the 1920 Olympics in an unsuccessful defence of the title he had won in 1908. Apart from his outstanding championship record he will also be remembered as the originator of the Salchow jump which is now an integral part of most free skating routines. After retirement he continued to be a major influence in the sport when he served as a forceful, but not universally popular, president of the International Skating Union from 1925 to 1937.

Ilmari SALMINEN (Fin)

ATHLETICS

Ilmari Salminen. b. 21 Sep 1902 Elimäki, d. 5 Jan 1986 Kouvola.

A late starter at athletics, he won three major 10,000m titles in his 30s when he was a sergeant in the Finnish army. He was Olympic champion in 1936 (and from then was the 'Golden Sergeant') and European champion in 1934 and 1938, while at 5000m he was European 3rd in 1934 and Olympic 6th in 1936, when he fell with just two laps to go. He broke Nurmi's 13-year-old world record for 10,000m with 30:05.5 in 1937 and won four Finnish titles at this event, 1934-5, 1937 and 1942, as well as the 5000m in 1942. He raced regularly until his late 40s.

Other bests: 3000m 8:22.8 (1935), 5000m 14:22.0 (1939).

Tatyana SAMOLENKO (USSR), see DOROVSKIKH.

Vladimir SALNIKOV (USSR)

SWIMMING

Vladimir Valeryevich Salnikov. b. 21 May 1960 Leningrad.

The greatest long-distance swimmer of all time, he set 13 world records: six at 400m from 3:51.41 in 1979 to 3:48.32 in 1983; four at 800m from the first sub 8-minute time, 7:56.43 in 1979 to 7:50.64 in 1986; three at 1500m from the first sub-15 minute time, 14:58.27 at the 1980 Olympics, to 14:54.76 in 1983. His first European records had been 3:53.32 (1978), 8:13.35 (1976) and 15:29.45 (1976).

His first major title was the European 1500m in 1977, and he retained that title in 1981 and 1983, adding the 400m in 1983 with silver at 400m in 1981. He was World champion at both 400m and 1500m in 1978 (with silver at 4x200m) and 1982, and won three Olympic gold medals, 400m, 1500m and 4x 200m in 1980; but he missed the 1984 Games through the Soviet boycott.

After winning 61 consecutive finals at 1500m from 1977, Salnikov finished only fourth in the World Championships in 1986. The following year he failed to qualify for the final of the Europeans, and it seemed that his brilliant career was drawing to an end. However, this most popular man and dedicated sportsman, trained by his wife Marina, determined to have one last shot at Olympic glory, and succeeded by winning the 1500m in 1988, when at 28 he became the oldest champion for 56 years.

Erika SALUMAË (USSR/Est)

CYCLING

Erika Salumaë. b. 11 Jun 1962 Pärnu.

While competing for the USSR she

became the first Estonian woman to win an Olympic gold medal, with the sprint title in 1988. She won again in 1992, this time in the colours of her own nation, competing at the Games in its own right for the first time since 1936. She was also world sprint champion in 1987 and 1989 and runner-up in 1984 and 1986. In USSR Championships she won 10 gold, 3 silver and 3 bronze medals.

She came to sports late, taking up cycling in 1981 and making the Soviet national team in 1984. She has set 17 world records with her outdoor flying start 1km time of 1:10.463 lasting from 1984 and her indoor records for unpaced flying start of 29.655 (for 500m) and 1:05.232 lasting from 1987. Her 1km standing start bests: 1:14.249 outdoors 1984 and 1:13.377 indoors 1983.

Juan Antonio SAMARANCH (Spain)

ADMINISTRATOR

Juan Antonio Samaranch Torello. b. 17 Jul 1920 Barcelona.

An IOC member in Spain from 1966, he was appointed 1st vice-president 1974-8 and then president of the International Olympic Committee in 1980. He was Spanish ambassador to the USSR and Mongolia from 1977 to 1980, so that he was in Moscow at the time of the 1980 Olympic Games. He had been president of the Spanish Skating Federation, a member of the Spanish Olympic Committee from 1954 (president 1963-70), and was Chef de Mission to Spanish Olympic teams in 1956, 1960 and 1964. Appointed Marques de Samaranch in 1991.

Pete SAMPRAS (USA)

TENNIS

Pete Sampras. b. 12 Aug 1971 Washington, D.C.

In 1990, at 19 years 28 days, he became the youngest ever winner of the men's singles title at the US Open. He had won his first title on the ATP tour in February that year and leapt up the world rankings from 81 at the end of 1989 to 5th at the end of 1990. He ended that year by winning the inaugural Grand Slam Cup in Munich for the greatest ever prize in tennis, $2 million. A gifted strokemaker, it surprisingly took him nearly three years before he won another Grand Slam title, but that came in 1993 at Wimbledon. He had reached the World No.1 ranking in April 1993 and fully justified his top seeding at Wimbledon with impressive wins over Andre Agassi, Boris Becker and Jim Courier in his last three matches. In 1991-2 he suffered at times from shin splints, but won the ATP World Championships at Frankfurt in 1991. In 1992, after comfortably beating defending champion Michael Stich in the quarter-finals at Wimbledon, he then lost to Goran Ivanisevic in the semis; and he was beaten by Stefan Edberg in the final of the US Open.

Sampras has a strong all-round game, hitting his ground strokes with great power and is a fine serve and volley exponent. At the end of 1992 he had career tour earnings of $4,557,225. In the Davis Cup his record 1991-2 is won 5, lost 3. In 1992 he played in the doubles with John McEnroe, helping the US to win the trophy.

Joan SAMUELSON (USA)

ATHLETICS

Joan Samuelson. b. 16 May 1957 Cape Elizabeth, Maine. née Benoit, married Scott Samuelson on 29 Sep 1984.

Benoit ran the first sub-2:25 marathon with a stunning 2:22:43 at Boston in 1983, and the following year the waif-like figure ran away from the field in the first Olympic marathon at Los Angeles to win in 2:24:52. That victory was all the more remarkable for the fact that she qualified by winning the US Trials race only seventeen days after undergoing arthroscopic surgery on her right knee. She won eight of her thirteen marathons from 1979 to 1985, when she improved further to win at Chicago in 2:21:21. That was her fifth US record and the world best for the distance. She was the Sullivan Award winner 1985. She did not run another marathon until her third place in New York in 1988, having given birth to daughter Abigail on 24 Oct 1987. Her son Anders was born on 24 Jan

1990. She returned to top form after many injuries with a great run for fourth in the 1991 Boston marathon, and later was sixth in New York, but was unable to regain an Olympic place in 1992, although she won the Columbus marathon that year in 2:32:18. She began as a cross-country skier and had been a useful track runner, winning the Pan-American 3000m in 1983, but undoubtedly her forté was on the roads, where she also set US bests for 10 miles 53:18 in 1986 and at half marathon 1:08:34 in 1984.
Best track times: 1500m 4:24.0i (1983), 1M 4:36.48i (1983), 3000m 8:53.49 (1983), 5000m 15:40.42 (1982), 10,000m 32:07.41 (1984).

Salvador SÁNCHEZ (Mex)

BOXING

Salvador Sánchez. b. 3 Feb 1958 Santiago Tainguistenco, d. 12 Aug 1982 Queretaro.

In the late 1970s and early 1980s Sánchez was considered the world's finest boxer. He was killed in a motor vehicle accident while in the prime of his career. He first won the world featherweight championship in 1980 by knocking out Danny López. For a featherweight he possessed a tremendous knockout punch and he used it to successfully defend his title nine times through 1982 before his untimely death.
Career record: W - 44 (32), L - 1, D - 1.

Earl SANDE (USA)

HORSE RACING

Earl Sande. b. 13 Nov 1898 Groton, South Dakota, d. 20 Aug 1968 Jacksonville, Oregon.

Leading money-winner in the USA in 1921, 1923 and 1927, Earl Sande rode the winners of 196 stakes races, 18 of them in his first full year of riding thoroughbreds, 1918. In 1923 he won 39 such races, including the Kentucky Derby, Belmont Stakes and a match with the Epsom Derby winner *Papyrus* on *Zev*. *Man O'War* was the greatest horse that he rode.
He began as a rodeo broncobuster before racing for Joe Goodman in 1917 and came to fame when riding for Commander J K L Ross of Canada; he then rode for Harry Sinclair and finally for William Woodward. The latter persuaded him to return from a two-year retirement, during which he trained unsuccessfully, to ride *Gallant Fox* on whom he won the Triple Crown in 1930. He recommenced his training career in 1932, and in 1953 returned unsuccessfully as a jockey with one win from ten rides. In all he won 968 of 3673 races, including three Kentucky Derbys and five Belmont Stakes. He was nicknamed 'The Dutchman' or 'Handy Guy'.

Anne SANDER (USA)

GOLF

Anne Sander. b. 31 Aug 1937 Everett, Washington. Later Quast, then Decker, then Welts.

Anne Sander won the US Women's Amateur championship under three different names: in 1958 as Anne Quast, 1961 as Anne Decker and 1963 as Anne Welts. She later added a British Women's Amateur title as Anne Sander in 1980 and is one of only 10 women to have won both championships. Sander was also twice low amateur in the US Women's Open and finished 4th in that tournament as late as 1973. She played on six Curtis Cup teams between 1958 and 1980, a record for American women. She might well have won more championships in the 1960s had her great rival JoAnne Gunderson Carner turned professional earlier. She also won the Western Women's Amateur in 1956 and 1961, and the US Senior Women's Amateur in 1987, 1989-90.

Tessa SANDERSON (UK)

ATHLETICS

Theresa Ione Sanderson. b. 14 Mar 1956 St Elizabeth, Jamaica.

The Olympic javelin champion in 1984, she is the only British athlete to compete at five Olympic Games from her 10th place in 1976 to 4th in 1992. Other highlights of a 20-year international career include three Commonwealth titles, 1978, 1986 and 1990, and after five top-three placings a

win in her sixth European Cup in 1991, with a win in the 1992 World Cup in her last competition. She was fourth in the World Championships in 1983 and 1987 and won the European silver in 1978. She won the UK title in 1977 and 1978 and nine WAAA titles, 1975-7, 1979-80, 1985, 1989-90, 1992.
She started her senior international career at the Commonwealth Games (5th) and Europeans (13th) in 1974, and set the first of her ten UK records at the javelin with 56.14 in 1976, taking the record to 73.58 in 1983. The last five were also Commonwealth records, as were her heptathlon scores of 5857 and 6125 points in 1981. In all she made 57 international appearances for Britain 1974-92. She had a great rivalry with Fatima Whitbread, and although Whitbread was superior in the period 1984-7, overall Sanderson had a 27-18 advantage in clashes between them 1977-88. She has become a TV presenter, first with Sky and now with the BBC. Awarded MBE in New Year Honours 1985.

Andrew SANDHAM (UK)

CRICKET

Andrew Sandham. b. 6 Jul 1890 Streatham, Surrey, d. 20 Apr 1982 Westminster, London.

Sandham was a top-class opening batsman, forging a great partnership with Jack Hobbs, with whom he shared 66 century partnerships, mostly for Surrey. But with Herbert Sutcliffe partnering Hobbs for England, Sandham did not get many Test opportunities. However he scored the first Test treble century, 325 v West Indies at Kingston in 1930. A small man, he was a fine hooker and cutter, and was also a splendid outfielder. He scored over 1000 runs in a season 18 times, with eight years over 2000 and bests of 2565 at 51.30 in 1929 and 2532 at 58.88 in 1928. He coached at The Oval 1946-58 and then scored for Surrey for a further 12 years.
14 Tests 1921-30: 878 runs at 38.17, 2 100s HS 325; 4 catches.
First-class 1911-37: 41,284 runs at 44.83, 107 100s HS 325; 18 wickets at 31.11, BB 3-27; 158 catches.

Viktor SANEYEV (USSR/Geo)

ATHLETICS

Viktor Danilovich Saneyev. b. 3 Oct 1945 Sukhumi.

At the triple jump Saneyev won three successive Olympic titles, 1968, 1972 and 1976, and added a silver medal in 1980. He was European champion in 1969 and 1974, and won the silver medal in 1971 and 1978. He also won six European Indoor titles (and one silver medal), the World Student Games title of 1970 (second 1973) and eight USSR championships for the greatest ever record at the event. At the 1964 European Junior Championships he won silver medals at both long and triple jumps, and he won the European Cup Final TJ in 1967, 1973 and 1975. He set three world records, two at the 1968 Olympics (17.23m and 17.39 in a final when the record went four times) and his best of 17.44 in his home-town of Sukhumi on 17 Oct 1972.
Long jump best 7.90m (1967).

Manuel SANTANA (Spain)

TENNIS

Manuel Martinez Santana. b. 10 May 1938 Madrid.

The greatest ever Spanish tennis player and the first Spaniard to win a Grand Slam singles title. Starting as a ball boy, he went out in the first round on his Wimbledon début in 1958 but progressed to take the French title in 1961 and 1964, beating Nicola Pietrangeli in the final on both occasions. In 1965 he won the US championship and then took the 1966 Wimbledon title. In 1967 he set a Wimbledon record when he became the only holder of the men's singles to be eliminated in the first round the following year, losing to Charles Pasarell (USA) in four sets. His only major doubles title came at the 1963 French Championships when he partnered Roy Emerson. He is easily his country's most prolific and successful Davis Cup player, winning 69 out of 86 singles and 23 of his 34 doubles in 46 ties 1958-73; although lacking the support of truly world class players, he took Spain to the Challenge

Round in 1965 and 1967. In the latter year he played both singles and the doubles in all seven ties.
A universally popular champion, he is rated with Cochet and Nastase as one of the great touch players of all-time.

Djalma SANTOS (Bra)

FOOTBALL

Djalma dos Santos. b. 27 Feb 1929 São Paulo.

The greatest-ever South American right-back. In an international career which lasted from 1952 to 1968 he played in four World Cup final tournaments (1954-66) and helped Brazil take the trophy in 1958 and 1962. Starting his professional career in 1948 with Portuguesa de Desportos, he moved to Palmeiras in 1958 and 10 years later he joined Atlético Paranaense where he ended his playing days. He won 100 caps (1952-68), a South American record, and played in his last international at the age of 39. A scrupulously fair player, he also distinguished himself as Brazil's penalty-taker.

José SANTOS (USA)

HORSE RACING

José Adeon Santos. b. 26 Apr 1961 Concepción, Chile.

The leading money-winning jockey in the USA each year from 1986 to 1989, he set a new season's record with $14,877,298 in 1988, when he won the Eclipse award as the nation's leading rider. Started riding in Chile.

Nilton SANTOS (Bra)

FOOTBALL

Nilton dos Santos. b. 16 May 1925 Ilha do Governador.

Initially a high-scoring striker, then a centre-half and finally an attacking left back, he developed a fine partnership with his unrelated namesake, Djalma dos Santos, in the Brazilian national team. They played together in Brazil's World Cup triumphs in 1958 and 1962. Nilton came to the fore in the 1949 South American Championships but was a reserve for the 1950 World Cup. He played in 1954 but was sent off in the quarter-final. He won 74 international caps - occasionally captaining the team - and after joining Botafogo from Flecheiras in 1948 remained with the Rio de Janeiro club until his retirement in 1963.

Gene SARAZEN (USA)

GOLF

Gene Sarazen, né Eugenio Saraceni. b. 27 Feb 1902 Harrison, New York.

The first man to win the four tournaments now considered the major championships - US Open 1922 and 1932, British Open 1932, PGA 1922 and 1933, and Masters 1935. He won the Masters in a play-off with Craig Wood, although late in the fourth round he trailed Wood by three strokes with four holes to play. On the 15th hole at Augusta National, a par five of 520 yards over water, Sarazen holed his second shot with a three-wood to record a doub' eagle. He then parred the last three holes and defeated Wood by five strokes in a play-off the next day. Sarazen also gained fame as the inventor of the sand wedge, which he designed to help his own play out of bunkers. In all he had 38 US PGA tour victories and played for the US in six Ryder Cups with a match record of 7 wins, 2 losses, 3 halves. He won the PGA Seniors title in 1954 and 1958, scored a hole-in-one at the age of 71 in the 1973 British Open and, now in his 90s, still takes the first stroke at the Masters each year.

SARFRAZ NAWAZ (Pak)

CRICKET

Sarfraz Nawaz Malik. b. 1 Dec 1948 Lahore.

An underrated fast-medium bowler, this aggressive and powerful man was his nation's best bowler during the 1970s. At 1.90m *6'3"*, he was able to seam and swing the ball both ways. A hard-hitting tail-ender, he was the third Pakistani to reach the double of 1000 runs and 100

wickets in Tests. A graduate of Government College, Lahore, in Pakistan he played mainly for Lahore and in England for Northamptonshire 1969-82.
55 Tests 1969-84: 1045 runs at 17.71, HS 90; 177 wickets at 32.75, BB 9-86; 26 catches.
45 One-day Ints: 221 runs at 9.60, HS 34, 63 wickets at 23.22, BB 4-27; 8 catches.*
First-class 1967-85: 5709 runs at 19.35, HS 90; 1005 wickets at 24.62, BB 9-86; 162 catches.

György SÁROSI (Hun)

FOOTBALL

György Sárosi. b. 16 Sep 1912 Budapest. né Stefancsis.

A highly talented all-round footballer who scored 42 goals in his 61 international appearances for Hungary from 1931 to 1943, including seven against Czechoslovakia in 1937. He was the star player and captain when Hungary were runners-up in the 1938 World Cup. He played for Ferencváros, and was signed by Juventus, although he never played for them. After some time in the USA, he coached in Italy for Bologna, Roma and Juventus. As well as success at a variety of other sports, he obtained a post-graduate law degree.

Ilmari SAVOLAINEN (Fin)

GYMNASTICS

(Dr) Heikki Ilmari Savolainen. b. 28 Sep 1907 Joensuu.

Savolainen won nine Olympic medals at gymnastics over a record 24-year span. He started in 1928, when he was a medical student, with a bronze at the pommel horse, and 20 years later was involved in a three-way tie for the gold at this event. In 1948 he also won a team gold, and he won three team bronze medals, 1932, 1936 and 1952, when at 44 years 297 days he became and remains the oldest ever gymnastics medallist. In that year he gave the Olympic oath on behalf of the competitors at the opening ceremony. In 1932 he achieved his highest overall position with third, adding a silver on horizontal bar and bronze on parallel bars. He was also World champion in 1931.

Terry SAWCHUK (Can)

ICE HOCKEY

Terrance Gordon Sawchuk. b. 28 Dec 1929 Winnipeg, Manitoba, d. 31 May 1970 New York, USA.

Sawchuk played for five teams in his 21-year goaltending career, but he was best known for his years with the Detroit Red Wings, whom he helped to win three Stanley Cups in the early 1950s. His 103 career shutouts is an NHL record, and he recorded 12 in one season three times (1952, 1954-5). Sawchuk, who pioneered the 'crouch' style of netminding, is considered by some hockey experts as the greatest goalie ever. He was certainly one of the toughest as he played despite numerous injuries and required multiple operations in the off-season to recuperate from those injuries.
NHL career 1949-70 - 971 games, 2.52 GAA, 103 shutouts. Vezina Trophy 1952-3, 1955, 1965; Calder Trophy 1951.

Gale SAYERS (USA)

AMERICAN FOOTBALL

Gale Eugene Sayers. b. 30 May 1943 Wichita, Kansas.

If greatness in pro football was based on only three-year careers, Gale Sayers would be considered the greatest running back ever. He played college ball at the University of Kansas and in 1965 was the first-round draft choice of the Chicago Bears. Sayers was stunning in his rookie season, breaking or tying eight NFL records, including one for most touchdowns in a season as he scored 22 that year. He also tied an NFL record by scoring six touchdowns in one game. He led the NFL in rushing in 1966 and 1969 and led the league in kick-off returns in 1966. He was fast, quick, and electrifying, with moves that had to be seen to be believed. But in 1968 he sustained a serious knee injury and was never again the same runner. He played through the 1971 season before retiring, as he also sustained further

knee injuries. He was nonetheless named All-Pro every year from 1965 to 1969. His career kick-off return average of 30.6 is an NFL record.
Sayers was ranked third on the world junior long jump list at 7.58m and his brother Roger was one of only two men ever to beat Bob Hayes at 100y.
NFL career 1965-71: Rushing: 4956 yards av. 5.0, 39 touchdowns; Receiving: 1307 yards av. 11.7, 9 touchdowns.

Ilona SCHACHERER-ELEK (Hun) see ELEK

Karl SCHÄFER(Aut)

FIGURE SKATING
Karl Schäfer. b. 17 May 1909 Vienna, d. 23 Apr 1976 Vienna.

His record of seven world figure skating titles has only been surpassed by Ulrich Salchow. Beginning his international career in 1927, he placed third in both the European and World Championships when Austria took all three medals in both events. The following year he improved to place second at both championships and was fourth at the Olympics. In 1929 he won the first of his eight successive European titles but lost to Gillis Grafström, who had been absent from the European meet, at the Worlds. From 1930 to 1936 he was World champion each year and he was also the Olympic champion in 1932 and 1936, when he retired.
For many years he was one of Europe's leading breaststroke swimmers, setting Austrian records with 1:15.4 for 100m and 2:48.2 for 200m, and was a member of one of the most distinguished families in the history of figure skating, who between them won no less than 32 gold medals at major championships. Schäfer won 17 major gold medals (2 Olympic, 7 World and 8 European); his cousin, Herma Plank-Jaross-Szabó, eight (1 Olympic and 7 World); his sister-in-law, Helene Engleman, four (1 Olympic and 3 World) and his father-in-law, Edouard Engleman, three (3 European).

Erich SCHÄRER (Swi)

BOBSLEIGH
Erich Schärer. b. 1 Sep 1946 Zürich.

Winner of the world two-man bob title in 1978-9 and 1982 and the Olympic champion in 1980. In all these events he was the driver with Josef Benz as brake man. In the four-man bob, he won the world title in 1971, 1973 and 1975, and drove the Swiss team into second or third places for the next seven years. His total of seven bobsled victories at the World Championships and Olympic Games has only been exceeded by Eugenio Monti. Schärer also won Olympic silver in the four-man event in 1976 and 1980 and bronze in the 1976 two-man, and at the World Championships five silver and five bronze medals. He had been a useful decathlete, scoring 6441 points in 1973.

Dolph SCHAYES (USA)

BASKETBALL
Adolph Schayes. b. 19 May 1928 New York.

One of the greatest, and most durable, NBA players ever. After starring at New York University (NYU) he played for 16 years with the Syracuse Nationals, who in Schayes' last season moved to Philadephia and became the 76ers. From 1952 to 1961 he played in 764 consecutive games. He was a big 2.03m *6'8"*, 100 kg *220 lb* forward who excelled as both a scorer and rebounder, averaging over 10 rebounds a game in his career. Six times he was named to the All-NBA first team, 1952-5 and 1957-8, and six other times he was on the second team. He finished as a player-coach at Philadelphia and later coached in the NBA for six years. He was coach of the year in 1966 with the 76ers. His son Danny has also played for over 10 years in the league.
NBA career 19,249 points, av. 18.2.

Jody SCHECKTER (SAf)

MOTOR RACING
Jody Scheckter. b. 29 Jan 1950 East London.

Scheckter was world drivers' champion in 1979 in his first year with Ferrari. His father had a Renault dealership, and Jody started racing karts, then motorbikes, progressing to be the leading driver in South Africa before coming to Europe at the age of 21. He started his Formula One career in 1974 with Tyrrell and placed third in the championship, winning the Swedish and British Grands Prix. He was third again in 1976 and second in 1977 when he joined Wolf. After an unsuccessful year in 1980 he retired with career figures of ten victories in 112 races and 255 points. As head of the drivers' association he worked hard for circuit safety.

Norbert SCHEMANSKY (USA)

WEIGHTLIFTING

Norbert Schemansky. b. 30 May 1924 Detroit, Michigan.

The only man to win four medals in Olympic weightlifting (gold at 90kg 1952, with silver 1948 and bronze 1952 and 1964 at heavyweight). He first became prominent internationally when he finished second in the 1947 World Championships behind John Davis. He won three World titles, at 90kg in 1951 and 1953 and at heavyweight in 1954, with three silver medals. He won nine AAU titles between 1949 and 1965 and also won the heavyweight gold medal at the 1955 Pan-American Games.

Ard SCHENK (Hol)

SPEED SKATING

Adrianus Schenk. b. 16 Sep 1944.

After tying for the silver medal at 1500m in 1968 he won three gold medals at the 1972 Olympics in Sapporo, Japan, setting Olympic records at 1500m, 2:02.96 and at 10,000m, 15:01.35, and also winning at 5000m, 7:23.61. He took all three titles by clear margins. Two weeks later in Norway, he became the only the fourth speed skater to win all four events at the World Championships. He has also won the world all-round title in 1970 and 1971 and the European title in 1966, 1970 and 1972. Turning professional he won the pro World and European titles in 1973. From 1966 to 1972 he set 18 world records at distances from 1000m to 10,000m.

Best times: 500m 38.9, 1000m 1:18.8 (1971), 1500m 1:58.7 (1972), 3000m 4:08.3 (1972), 5000m 7:09.8 (1972), 10,000m, 14:55.96 (1971).

Vitaliy SCHERBO (Bls)

GYMNASTICS

Vitaliy Scherbo. b. 13 Jan 1972 Minsk.

The most successful sportsman at the 1992 Olympic Games, when he won six gold medals, adding four individual apparatus titles to the all-around and the team gold that he won with the Unified team from the CIS. He became a member of the Soviet national team at 15 and became the USSR overall champion in 1990. That year he was second in the World Cup and won three individual events at the European Championships. He was runner-up to his compatriot Grigoriy Misyutin at the 1991 World Championships with a team gold and two silvers and a bronze at individual events, and went on to win the 1993 World title, with additional golds on vault and parallel bars and one silver. At the first World Championships for individual apparatus in 1992 he won at rings and tied for first place at the pommel horse. He was also European champion all-around in 1992.

Jef SCHERENS (Bel)

CYCLING

Jozef Scherens. b. 7 Feb 1909 Wercher, d. 1988.

Known as having the greatest acceleration ever in track sprinting, 'The Cat' was the first cyclist to win six consecutive world championships (1932-7) in the same event before placing second to Arie van Vliet (Hol) in 1938. He had also been third in 1931. He had a very long career, winning his last world title in 1947, 15 years after his first, and but for World War II he might have won several more titles.

Juan SCHIAFFINO (Uru, Ita)

FOOTBALL

Juan Alberto Schiaffino. b. 28 Jul 1925 Montevideo.

An outstanding forward who played a major rôle in Uruguay's 1950 World Cup victory. Against Bolivia he scored a World Cup single-match record of 5 goals. He joined Peñarol as an 18-year-old and after graduating through their lower teams went on to win 22 caps for Uruguay.
Immediately after the 1954 World Cup he was transferred for a world record fee of £72,000 to AC Milan where he was an instant success, winning with them three Italian league titles. He was capped four times by Italy, his eligibility coming through his parents. In 1960 he moved to Roma and remained with them until his retirement two years later.
After an absence of 12 years he returned to Uruguay where he concentrated on his substantial business interests, but he retained an interest in the game as a coach and scout. His generalship, allied with his exceptional scoring ability despite his slight build, led to his being rated as one of the greatest Uruguayan players of all-time.

Harald SCHMID (FRG)

ATHLETICS

Harald Schmid. b. 29 Sep 1957 Hanau.

He was the last man to beat Edwin Moses at 400m hurdles (at the 1977 ISTAF meeting) before the latter's long winning streak, and was consistently in the world's top three 1977-87, when he never failed to gain a medal at a major championships: Olympics 3rd 1984; Worlds 2nd 1983, 3rd 1987; Europeans 1st 1978, 1982 and 1986. His first Olympic medal had been a bronze at 4 x 400m relay in 1976, when he was a hurdles semi-finalist. In that year he also set a world junior record.
He has a men's record of five European Cup wins (400mh 1979, 1983, 1985, 1987; 400m 1979) with second places at 400mh in 1981 and 1989. At Turin in 1979 he had a unique triple, helping the West German team to win the 4x400m relay as well, and at 400m hurdles he set his first European record with a time of 47.85. He improved that record to 47.48 at the 1982 Europeans, and equalled it when he was but 0.02 secs behind the winner, Moses, in the 1987 World Championships. He won the FRG 400m hurdles title 12 times, a record for any event, 1977-8, 1980-9. FRG sportsman of the year 1979 and 1987.
In his career he ran 128 sub-50.00 400mh times, including 65 sub-49.00, 8 sub-48.00. He married Elzbieta Rabsztyn (7th European 100mh 1978 for Poland).
Other bests: 400m 44.92 (1979), 800m 1:44.83 (1987).

Birgit SCHMIDT (GDR/Ger)

CANOEING

Birgit Schmidt. née Fischer. b. 25 Feb 1962 Brandenburg.

The most successful woman in the history of canoeing. In GDR colours she won the K1 Olympic title in 1980 and added gold medals at K2 and K4 in 1988. After a three-year break, during which time she gave birth to her second child, she returned for the united German team in 1992, when she again won the K1 for a women's record four gold medals. She has won a further 19 gold medals at world championships: K1 1981-3, 1985, 1987; K2 1977-8, 1981-3, 1985, 1987; K4 1978-9, 1981-3, 1985, 1987.
By profession a PE teacher, she competed for ASK Vorwärts (later OSC) Potsdam. Her husband Jörg was world champion at C1 1000m in 1982 and took the Olympic silver medal at C1 500m in 1988.

Joe SCHMIDT (USA)

AMERICAN FOOTBALL

Joseph Paul Schmidt. b. 18 Jan 1932 Mt Oliver, Pennsylvania.

One of the great middle linebackers in pro football history, playing for 13 years with the Detroit Lions. He was only a 7th-round draft choice of the Lions from Pittsburgh, but played in the Pro Bowl for nine years. He was not huge, but was very quick and was able to cover receivers well as a linebacker. He helped the Lions to two NFL championships.
After his retirement, Schmidt coached the Lions from 1967 to 1973. He later became a very successful businessman in the Detroit area.

Jozef SCHMIDT (Pol)

ATHLETICS

Jozef Schmidt. b. 28 Mar 1935 Michalkówice, Katowice province.

Speedy and a superb technician, Schmidt was the world's best triple jumper of the early 1960s, although his career went on to 1972. He was Olympic champion in 1960 and 1964 and European champion in 1958 and 1962 (5th 1966, 11th 1971). He also won ten Polish championships between 1958 and 1971, and when winning that title at Olsztyn on 5 Aug 1960 he became the first 17-metre triple jumper with 17.03m. That lasted as a world record until 1968 and was his seventh Polish record, starting with 16.06 in 1958. He set Olympic records when he won at 16.81 in 1960 and 16.85 in 1964, yet jumped even further with 16.89 when he was only 7th in the amazing competition in 1968 at high altitude in Mexico City, where his world record was improved five times by three different men.

Other bests: 100m 10.4 (1961), long jump 7.84 and 7.96w (1963).

Mike SCHMIDT (USA)

BASEBALL

Michael Jack Schmidt. b. 27 Sep 1949 Dayton, Ohio.

Now considered by many experts as the top third baseman in baseball history, and certainly the greatest as a power hitter. Though probably surpassed in the field by Brooks Robinson, Schmidt was still accomplished enough to win 10 Gold Gloves at the hot corner. Thirteen times in 17 seasons (all with the Philadelphia Phillies) he hit over 30 home runs in a season, which trails only Hank Aaron (15 times); and 11 times he hit over 35 home runs (trailing only Babe Ruth with 12). Schmidt led the National League in homers a record eight times, and the major leagues seven times, a mark bettered only by Ruth's nine. He also led the senior circuit in RBI four times, 1980-1, 1984 and 1986, and was named to the All-Star team 12 times in 17 seasons. Late in his career, he was shifted to first base occasionally.

Career 1972-89: Avg. .267, HR 548; RBI 1595. Best seasons: 1980: 48 HR, 121 RBI; 1979: 45 HR, 114 RBI; 1983: 40 HR, 109 RBI.

Milt SCHMIDT (Can)

ICE HOCKEY

Milton Conrad Schmidt. b. 5 Mar 1918 Kitchener, Ontario.

Schmidt played his entire career of 16 years for the Boston Bruins, although he missed four years in the prime of his career while serving in World War II. Despite that, he is still acclaimed as one of the greatest centers ever. He made his fame centering the Kraut Line, alongside Woody Dumart and Bobby Bauer, and was renowned for his toughness and his ability to play his best in the biggest games. He played for two Stanley Cup champions and four regular season first-place teams. After he retired, he coached the Bruins for seven years and then became their general manager.

NHL career 1936-55 - 778 games, 229 goals, 575 points. Hart Trophy 1951, Ross Trophy 1940 (30 assists, 52 points).

Oscar SCHMIDT (Bra)

BASKETBALL

Oscar Daniel Schmidt Bezzera. b. 16 Feb 1958 Natal.

Schmidt, who is known only by his first name in his native Brazil, began playing basketball at age 14 in his hometown of Natal. He has since become Brazil's greatest ever player and one of the most potent offensive threats ever, leading Brazil to an upset of the USA in the final of the 1987 Pan-American Games, when he scored 46 points. He was voted best player at the 1986 World Championships.

At 2.03m *6'8"* tall but relying primarily on his superb outside shot, he plays professionally for Caserta in the Italian league. He was drafted in the 6th round of the 1984 NBA draft by the New Jersey Nets but never played in the United States. Oscar has been the leading scorer in every league in which he has played.

Wolfgang SCHMIDT (GDR/FRG)

ATHLETICS

Wolfgang Schmidt. b. 16 Jan 1954 Berlin.

A great discus thrower in the late 1970s and early 1980s, he fell from favour for contacts with the West and was imprisoned in the GDR. He was eventually allowed to leave the country, and made a fine return to top-class competition for the FRG in 1988 after missing five seasons. In 1989 he was second in the world rankings, and was top in 1990, as he had been in 1975 and 1977-9. In 1991 he was fourth at the World Championships, but sadly was not selected for the 1992 Olympics.

He came to prominence with gold at discus and silver at shot in the 1973 European Juniors, improving steadily to set a world record of 71.16m in 1978, in which year he was European champion at discus and took a bronze medal in the shot. At the Olympics he was second in 1976 and fourth in 1980. He won the World Student Games gold in 1979 and the European Cup Final in 1975, 1977 and 1979, as well as the inaugural World Cup competitions in 1977 and 1979. He was GDR champion each year 1975-80 and later FRG champion in 1990 and 1991, when the Germanys were unified.

His father, Ernst Schmidt, who became a national coach, won the 1942 German decathlon title and ten GDR titles (5 shot, 4 discus, 1 decathlon) 1950-4, and he set 12 GDR shot records to 15.85m in 1952, 8 discus to 46.24m in 1954 and two decathlon.

Best at shot: 20.76 (1978).

Petra SCHNEIDER (GDR)

SWIMMING

Petra Schneider. b. 18 Feb 1963 Teutschenthal.

Her fourth world record for 400m individual medley, 4:36.10 to win the 1982 world title, still stood 11 years later; only Mary Meagher's butterfly world records have lasted as long.

At the 400m Schneider was unbeaten in 25 consecutive finals from 1978 to 22 Aug 1983, when Kathleen Nord beat her for the European title. In that period she had won the 1980 Olympic, 1981 European and 1982 World titles at that event, adding Olympic silver at 400m freestyle in 1980, European silver at 200m medley in 1981 and World gold at 200m medley and silver at 400m freestyle in 1982. She had also taken the World bronze at 400m medley in 1978.

Schneider's first world record had been 4:39.36 for 400m medley in 1980, a time that she improved to 4:38.44 and to 4:36.29 in winning the Olympic title in 1980. That year she also set a 200m medley record of 2:13.00.

Vreni SCHNEIDER (Swi)

ALPINE SKIING

Vreni Schneider. b. 26 Nov 1964 Elm.

Double Olympic gold medallist at slalom and giant slalom in 1988, after falling in the combined. World champion at giant slalom in 1989 and 1991, and slalom in 1991. At the World Cup she was overall champion in 1989, and has won a record four giant slalom titles, 1986-7, 1989 and 1991, as well as the slalom in 1989-90 and 1992-3. She won a record 14 World Cup races in a season, including all seven slalom, in 1988/9, with a career 41 wins to January 1993, the fourth highest ever total. Her brother Andreas was world champion at Alpine combination in 1978 and the overall World Cup winner in 1980.

Karl-Heinz SCHNELLINGER (FRG)

FOOTBALL

Karl-Heinz Schnellinger. b. 31 Mar 1939 Duren.

His record of playing in four World Cups (1958-70) has only been matched by Uwe Seeler among German players. When only 19 he made his World Cup début in 1958 as a right-half but later developed into one of Europe's most respected left-backs. On his return from the 1958 World Cup he left his local club, Duren, and signed for FC Cologne and in 1963 he moved to Italy where he played for AS Roma, Mantua and AC Milan. His best years were with Milan and he helped them win the Italian

Cup in 1967, the Italian Championship and European Cup-Winners' Cup in 1968 and the European Cup and World Club Championship in 1969. He was capped 48 times and although not noted for his mobility, his tackling was awesome.

Alwin SCHOCKEMÖHLE (FRG)

EQUESTRIAN

Alwin Schockemöhle. b. 29 May 1937 Osterbeck/Emsland.

The Olympic show jumping champion of 1976 on *Warwick Rex*, when as a 39-year-old factory owner he became the first rider since 1928 to complete the competition without a fault. He won a complete set of team medals: gold in 1960, silver 1976 and bronze 1968.

Until he won the European title in 1975 he was known as the 'champion without a championship'. At the Europeans he was 2nd in 1963, 1969 and 1973; 3rd in 1965 and 1967. He won a team silver at the European Juniors in 1954. He had begun as a three-day eventer before, angry at not being selected for the 1956 Olympic team, he concentrated on show jumping. German champion 1961, 1963 and 1967, and winner of the King George V Gold Cup in 1975. He became a coach and is now a horse breeder and dealer.

Paul SCHOCKEMÖHLE (FRG)

EQUESTRIAN

Paul Schockemöhle. b. 22 Mar 1945 Vechta.

Followed his brother Alwin into the world show jumping élite and became the largest private breeder of horses in Germany.

After second place in 1979, Paul won three successive European titles on his great horse *Deister* in 1981, 1983 and 1985, with team gold in 1981. He also won the King George V Gold Cup on *Deister* in 1983. At the Olympics he was 7th equal in 1984, when he won a team bronze to add to the silver that he had won with Alwin in 1976. German champion 1974, 1980, 1982-3, 1986-7. In the World Cup he was 3rd in 1980 and 2nd in 1982.

Garry SCHOFIELD (UK)

RUGBY LEAGUE

Garry Edward Schofield. b. 1 Jul 1965 Leeds

An outstanding junior with Hunslet Parkside, he captained the Great Britain amateur youth team to New Zealand in 1983 and signed for Hull that year. In his first season as a professional he topped the League scoring list with 38 tries, and at the age of 18 years 10 months he was selected for the tour of Australia to become the youngest-ever member of a Great Britain touring party. His brilliant play in the centre brought him a host of scoring records and his four tries against the formidable New Zealanders in 1985 remains one of his finest performances.

Financial difficulties at Hull caused the club to sell many of their leading players in 1987/8 and Schofield commanded the then record transfer fee of £155,000 when he moved to Leeds. He has won 33 caps for Great Britain and only Mick Sullivan has bettered his total of 26 international tries. In his more recent games he has proved an inspiring captain of the Great Britain team.

Don SCHOLLANDER (USA)

SWIMMING

Donald Arthur Schollander. b. 30 Apr 1946 Charlotte, North Carolina.

The first swimmer to win four gold medals at one Olympic Games, with the 100m and 400m individual titles and both freestyle relays in 1964, all but the 100m in world record times. In the 4 x 200m relay he contributed a 1:55.6 split, two seconds faster than any other competitor, as with 7:52.1 the USA became the first team to break the 8 minute barrier. He was awarded numerous sportsman of the year trophies, including the Sullivan Award. Schollander added a fifth Olympic gold at 4 x 200m relay in 1968, when he was also silver medallist at 200m, having failed to make the US team to defend his 100m and 400m titles.

The 200m, which was not on the Olympic programme in 1964, was Schollander's

best distance and at this he set nine world records, from becoming the first man to break two minutes with 1:58.8 in 1963 to 1:54.3 in 1968. He also set three world records at 400m with a best of 4:11.6 in 1966 and shared eight freestyle relay records; and set US records for 100m 54.0 (1964) and 800m 9:04.0 (1963).
At the Pan-American Games he was second at 400m in 1963 and champion at 200m in 1967, when he added golds on both freestyle relay teams. He won AAU titles outdoors at 100y 1964, 1966-7; 200m/220y 1962-4, 1966-7; 440y 1963-4, 1966; and indoors at 220y 1963-7 and 500y 1964.
Coached by George Haines at the Santa Clara club, Schollander graduated from Yale University, for whom he was NCAA champion at 200y in 1968.
Schollander, whose mother Martha had performed swimming stunts in *Tarzan* films, used an immaculate, seemingly effortless stroke.

Briek SCHOTTE (Bel)

CYCLING

Albéric Schotte. b. 7 Sep 1919 Canegem.

Schotte was primarily known for his great sprinting ability, which enabled him to win a number of one-day classics, but his lack of ability in time trials and the mountains prevented him from being a factor in the major tours. Most of his victories came in his native Belgium, although he did win the world road championship two years out of three on foreign ground (1948 and 1950).
Major victories: Tour of Flanders 1942, 1948; Ghent-Wevelgem 1950, 1955; Paris-Brussels 1946, 1952; Paris-Tours 1946-7

Beate SCHRAMM (GDR/Ger)

ROWING

Beate Schramm. b. 21 Jun 1966 Leisnig.

Schramm was World champion at double sculls with Sylvia Schurabe in 1986, with Jana Sorgers in 1989, and with Kathrin Boron in 1990 and 1991. At the Olympics she won a gold medal in the GDR quad sculls in 1988. She won the World Cup for single sculls in 1992, but failed to finish in her Olympic semi-final.
She first came to the fore by winning the World Junior single sculls in 1983 and 1984. A member of Potsdamer RG she is 1.86m tall and 79kg, and is coached by Lothar Trawiel.

Karl SCHRANZ (Aut)

ALPINE SKIING

Karl Schranz. b. 18 Oct 1938 St Anton, Arlberg.

Schranz was a world-class skier from 1956, but in a long and distinguished career never won an Olympic gold. He was world champion at Alpine Combination and downhill in 1962 and at giant slalom in 1970, and the World Cup overall champion in 1969 and 1970, winning both downhill and giant slalom in 1969 and tying for the downhill in 1970. From 1969 to 1972 he won 12 World Cup races, 8 at downhill and 4 at giant slalom. At the Olympics, he was silver medallist at giant slalom in 1964, and at downhill 7th in 1960 and 5th in 1968. He was at one time declared the winner of the slalom in 1968. After a mysterious figure was alleged to have crossed his path, he stopped and was allowed a re-run, when he recorded a time faster than Jean-Claude Killy. However, after much debate he was controversially disqualified for missing earlier gates on his first run. He delayed his retirement to have a final try for Olympic glory in 1972. However, IOC President Avery Brundage, in his last tilt at commercialism, attacked what he saw as blatant abuse by Alpine skiers by concentrating his campaign on Schranz, who had been outspoken in his criticism of Brundage. Schranz was reputed to be earning some $50,000 a year as a tester and designer for ski manufacturers and just three days before the opening of the Games in Sapporo the IOC voted 28-14 to bar him from the Games. Schranz returned to Austria to a hero's reception and a ticker-tape parade. He announced his retirement, but in 1988 the IOC awarded him a symbolic medal as a participant in 1972.

Dieter SCHUBERT (GDR)

ROWING

Dieter Schubert. b. 11 Sep 1943 Pirna

Schubert was a member of the renowned Einheit Dresden four (with Frank Rühle, Dieter Grahn and Frank Forberger), who competed for 11 years and were never beaten in international competition. See Frank Forberger for details.

Jürgen SCHULT (GDR)

ATHLETICS

Jürgen Schult. b. 11 May 1960 Neuhaus, Kr. Hagenow.

In 1986 he added over two metres to the world record for the discus with 74.08m. Since then, although he has not got near that distance, he has been most consistent, winning 1987 World, 1988 Olympic and 1990 European titles, and being undefeated in 1988 and 1989. He also won the 1989 European and World Cup events and was 2nd in the 1992 Olympics. He won the European Junior title in 1979 and came to top world-class in 1983, when he won the European Cup and the first of eight successive GDR titles at the discus. A trainee journalist, he competes for the Schwerin club.

Margit SCHUMANN (GDR)

LUGE

Margit Schumann. b. 14 Sep 1952 Wallershaugen

Olympic champion in 1976 and a four-time winner at the World Championships. After taking third place at the 1972 Olympics, she maintained an unbeaten record for the next five years. She was world champion from 1973-7, a winning sequence which included the Olympic title in 1976. On her third and final Olympic appearance, she placed sixth in 1980.

Barbara Ann SCOTT (Can)

FIGURE SKATING

Barbara Ann Scott. b. 9 May 1928 Ottawa, Ontario. Later King.

The first Canadian to win an Olympic or World figure skating title. Although denied the opportunity to meet the top Europeans during the war, she built a fine championship record at home. After winning her first Canadian title in 1944 she took the North American Championship in 1945 and 1946 and the following year won the World Championship in Stockholm and then the European title in Davos on her first visit to Europe. She returned in 1948 to defend both titles successfully. The highlight of 1948 was, however, her Olympic gold medal when, although not accustomed to outdoor rinks, she again beat Eva Pawlik (Aut), who also finished as runner-up at the World and European Championships. Scott then turned professional and in 1955 married Tommy King, a former pro basketball player with the Detroit Falcons, whom she had met when he was working as publicist for the professional ice shows. The married couple settled in Chicago where Barbara Ann Scott-King became one of the leading equestriennes in the United States.

Dave SCOTT (USA)

TRIATHLON

Dave Scott. b. 4 Jan 1954 Woodland, California.

A legend in triathlon circles because of his performance in the biggest race of all, the Hawaii Ironman, which he won six times - 1980, 1982-4, and 1986-7. He has raced less frequently in the shorter races. Scott attended the University of California at Davis where he was a swimmer and water polo player. He was the first athlete to make training and racing in triathlons his full-time occupation.

Elisha SCOTT (UK)

FOOTBALL

Elisha Scott. b. 24 Aug 1894 Belfast, d. 16 May 1959 Belfast.

Possibly the greatest goalkeeper of his era. After making his début for Liverpool in 1913 he went on to make 430 appearances for the club, which stood as a record for almost a quarter of a century. His reflex saves were a significant factor in Liverpool winning the League Championship in 1921 and 1922. At a time when Ireland only played the other Home Countries he won 31 caps between 1920 and 1936 and on his last international appearance he was approaching his 42nd birthday. In 1934 he left Liverpool to become player-manger of Belfast Celtic. He retired as a player in 1936 but remained as manager until 1949, even though the club had by then dropped out of League football. Exceptionally lithe and agile, he had superb judgement and many of his contemporaries, including the great 'Dixie' Dean, rated him the finest goalkeeper they ever played against.

John SCOTT (UK)

HORSE RACING

John Scott. b. 1794 Chippenham, near Newmarket, d. 4 Oct 1871 Malton, Yorkshire.

Trained the winners of a record 40 English classics between 1827 and 1863 at his Whitewall stable in Malton. His total was made up of 16 winners of the St Leger, eight of the Oaks, seven 2000 Guineas, five Derby and four 1000 Guineas. His most notable horses were *Touchstone* and *West Australian*, who in 1853 became the first Triple Crown winner. His brother **Bill** (1797-1848), his stable jockey for his first 18 years at Whitewall, rode 19 classic winners, including a record nine of the St Leger, but died prematurely due to heavy drinking.

Peter SCUDAMORE (UK)

HORSE RACING

Peter Michael Scudamore. b. 13 Jun 1958 Hoaruntby, Herefordshire.

Scudamore has been the most successful jockey in National Hunt history having ridden a total of 1678 winners from 7521 mounts, from his first in 1979 at Devon and Exeter to his retirement after winning on his last ride, at Ascot on 7 Apr 1993. In the 1988/9 season he rode 221 winners (from 663 rides) compared to the previous record of 149. Having shared the jockey's championship title in 1981/2 with his first century (120 winners), he was champion for seven successive seasons from 1985/6 to 1991/2. On 18 Nov 1989 he passed John Francome's career record 1138 winners. His most important winners have been in the Champion Hurdle: *Celtic Shot* in 1988 and *Granville Again* in 1993. He rode for David Nicholson and for Fred Winter before beginning his record-breaking partnership with Martin Pipe. Awarded the MBE in 1990.

His father **Michael** (b. 17 Jul 1932) rode a total of 496 winners under NH rules 1952-69, including *Oxo* to win the 1959 Grand National.

Bob SEAGREN (USA)

ATHLETICS

Robert Lloyd Seagren. b. 17 Oct 1946 Pomona, California.

The 1968 Olympic pole vault champion, and silver medallist in 1972, he set five world records outdoors from 5.32m at Fresno on 14 May 1966 to 5.63 at Eugene on 2 Jul 1972 and eight indoors with successive improvements from 5.18, the first indoor 17ft clearance, at Albuquerque on 5 Mar 1966 to 5.33m *17' 6"* at Los Angeles on 8 Feb 1969. NCAA champion while at the University of Southern California in 1967 and 1969, he was AAU champion outdoors in 1966 and 1969-70, and indoors in 1966-7 and 1970.

He achieved great success on the televised Superstars competition, winning the inaugural US event in 1973 and the first World event in 1977, and he appeared in numerous television rôles.

Tom SEAVER (USA)

BASEBALL

George Thomas Seaver. b. 17 Nov 1944 Fresno, California.

'Tom Terrific' was indeed a terrific pitcher throughout his 20 years in the major leagues. Seaver is best known for the first 11 years he spent with the New York Mets 1967-77. He then played with the Cincinnati Reds 1977-82, the Mets again 1983, then the Chicago White Sox and Boston Red Sox. He was a power pitcher

who was possessed of almost perfect technique. He won over 20 games in a season five times and struck out more than 200 batters in a season 10 times. He was a very hard-working player who was known as a true gentleman. Seaver's father, Charles, was a top amateur golfer who played for the United States in the 1932 Walker Cup match against Great Britain.
Career pitching 1967-86: ERA 2.86; W-L 311-205 SO 3640. Best seasons: 1969: 25-7, 2.21 ERA; 1971: 20-10, 1.76 ERA; 1972: 21-12, 2.92 ERA; 1975: 22-9, 2.38 ERA; 1977: 21-6, 2.59 ERA.

Frank SEDGEMAN (Aus)

TENNIS

Frank Allan Sedgeman. b. 29 Oct 1927 Mount Albert, Victoria.

After five successive victories by American players, he won Wimbledon in 1952 to become the first Australian singles champion since Jack Crawford in 1933. He also won the men's and mixed doubles in his last year at Wimbledon in 1952 and is the last man to win all three titles in one year. The Australian junior champion in 1946, he won the Australian title in 1949 and 1950 and became the first Australian to win the US singles in 1951 and 1952.
He won the Wimbledon men's doubles on his first appearance in 1948 with John Bromwich, with whom he also won the US doubles in 1950. He then joined Ken McGregor to form the most formidable partnership of the era. They won all four Grand Slam titles in 1951 and only a five-set loss to Mervyn Rose (Aus) and Vic Seixas in the US Championships prevented them from repeating the feat in 1952.
Sedgeman's partnership with Doris Hart in the mixed doubles was only marginally less successful than his pairing with McGregor in the men's event. Together they won the Australian title in 1949 and 1950 and were the Wimbledon, US and French champions in both 1951 and 1952.
To this roll of tournament victories, Sedgeman could add a superb Davis Cup record: he won 16 of his 19 singles, was unbeaten in his nine double matches and was a member of the team which won the trophy for three successive years 1950-2.
He turned professional in January 1953 and enjoyed continuing success in the paid ranks. A lithe, agile player, he was particularly strong on the forehand and the volley and set a fine example both in his play and his behaviour.

Yuriy SEDYKH (USSR/Rus)

ATHLETICS

Yuriy Georgiyevich Sedykh. b. 11 Jun 1955 Novocherkassk.

The greatest hammer thrower of all-time. His first Olympic title came at the age of 21 in 1976, with the defending champion, his coach Anatoliy Bondarchuk, third. While others have threatened his position, he consistently came through to win the major titles, the European in 1978, 1982 and 1986 and the Olympics again in 1980. At the 1986 European Championships he responded to Sergey Litvinov's opening 85.74 with five throws averaging 86.16, following the world record of 86.74 with 86.68 and 86.62!
Sedykh set world junior records in 1973 and 1974, and won the European Junior title in 1973. In 1980 he started with two world records at 80.38 and 80.64, but the latter was passed by Litvinov a week later with 81.66. Sedykh, as always, rose to the occasion and with the very first throw of the Olympic final sent his hammer out to a new record of 81.80 to secure the title.
After missing the 1984 Games through the Soviet boycott he took the silver medal in 1988, but was not selected in 1992, although still throwing regularly over 80 metres, as he was 4th in the CIS trials.
He was second in the 1983 World Championships and often treated odd years as low-key, but after non-selection for the Europeans in 1990, he triumphed in Tokyo in 1991 to garner the one major title that had eluded him, World champion, the oldest ever at 36.
In all he set eight Soviet records, including six world records: the three in 1980, 86.34 in 1984, 86.66 and 86.74 in 1986. He also set three world bests at the 35lb weight to 23.46 in 1979.
Sedykh has been a great innovator in

hammer throwing. His hallmark has been a finely grooved technique accentuated with great speed in the circle. His post-graduate dissertation for the Kiev Institute of Physical Culture was on 'The effectiveness of power building means in hammer throw training', and he certainly seemed to find the secret.

Uwe SEELER (FRG)

FOOTBALL

Uwe Seeler. b. 5 Nov 1936 Hamburg.

First capped when only 17, he was one of West Germany's most popular sportsmen. Included in his record total of 72 caps, 1954-70, were 21 appearances in matches at four World Cup finals (1958-70); only Wladyslaw Zmuda has matched this total. Despite his lack of height, he could rise above most opponents in the air and his acrobatic shooting led to him topping the German League scoring list five times between 1955 and 1964.
Throughout his playing career, 1953-71, he remained loyal to SV Hamburg and helped them to the West German League title 1960 and Cup 1963. One of the great centre-forwards, he coupled his skills with unremitting effort and his 43 goals in international matches were a major contribution to West Germany's successes in the 1960s. He captained Germany in the World Cup in 1966 and 1970 (to 2nd and 3rd places respectively), and in 1968 he took Hamburg to the final of the European Cup Winners Cup. He became a successful business executive, owning a clothing company.

Henry SEGRAVE (UK)

MOTOR RACING

(Sir) Henry O'Neal Dehane Segrave. b. 22 Sep 1896 Baltimore, USA of Irish father and American mother, d. 13 Jun 1930 Lake Windermere.

The first man to hold the world land and water speed records simultaneously. He set the world land speed record at Daytona, USA, with 327.96 km/h (203.79 mph) in a Sunbeam in 1927 and 372.47 km/h (231.445 mph) in the 23-litre Irving Napier *Golden Arrow* in 1929. In that year he also won the International Championships for racing boats. He was killed attempting to improve the world water speed record, which he had set at 98.76 mph, when his *Miss England II* hit an underwater obstruction.
A wartime pilot and aviation attaché in the USA, he had a successful motor racing career from 1917 until retiring in 1927 to concentrate on speed records, with a record of 31 wins in 49 races which included the 1923 French and 1924 San Sebastian Grands Prix in Sunbeams. He had joined the Sunbeam Talbot-Darracq works team in 1921. Knighted in 1929 for services to British prestige.

Pancho SEGURA (Ecu)

TENNIS

Francisco Segura. b. 20 Jun 1921 Guayaquil.

Although enjoying only limited success as an amateur, he became one of the most popular and entertaining players on the pro circuit. While at the University of Miami (Florida) he won the NCAA singles 1943-5 and remains the only player to have won the title for three consecutive years. He won the 1944 US Clay Court title and the 1946 US Indoor, but never won a Grand Slam tournament. His best performance as an amateur was to finish as runner-up in the French doubles in 1946. In the singles he was a quarter-finalist at the US Championships in 1946 and 1947. On turning professional in 1947, his exceptional double-fisted forehand, penetrating lob and speed around the court led to some outstanding victories, although with Gonzales, Kramer and Rosewall as his contemporaries on the circuit he did not win a large number of titles.

Peter SEISENBACHER (Aut)

JUDO

Peter Seisenbacher. b. 25 Mar 1960.

In 1984 he was the first Austrian to win a major judo title when he won the Olympic gold medal at middleweight (86kg). In 1988 he became the first judoka to retain an Olympic title. He first came to international prominence when 3rd in the European Juniors in 1979 and 2nd in the Europeans in 1980. He was World champion in 1985 and European champion 1986.

Vic SEIXAS (USA)

TENNIS

Elias Victor Seixas Jr. b. 30 Aug 1923 Philadelphia, Pennsylvania.

Winner of the Wimbledon singles in 1953 and the French and US titles in 1954, but more successful as a doubles player winning 13 Grand Slam titles. He set a Wimbledon record by winning the mixed doubles for four successive years, partnering Doris Hart 1953-5 and Shirley Fry in 1956. He also won three US Championships, 1953-5, and the French in 1953 with Hart. In the men's doubles he won the US Championship in 1952 with Mervyn Rose (Aus) and four further Grand Slam titles with Tony Trabert: French 1954-5, US 1954 and Australian 1955. Notwithstanding these successes possibly his finest performance was in the Challenge Round of the Davis Cup in 1954 when he defeated Rosewall in the singles and won his doubles with Trabert, as the USA recaptured the trophy from Australia after losing in the previous four finals. He played in 19 Davis Cup ties 1951-7, winning 38 of his 55 rubbers.

An unorthodox player and always in excellent physical condition, he was noted for his gentlemanly conduct both on and off the court. Unlike most of his contemporaries, he never became a professional and was one of the top players in the last days of amateur tennis.

Toshihiko SEKO (Japan)

ATHLETICS

Toshihiko Seko. b. 15 Jul 1956 Kuwana, Mie Prefecture.

He disappointed in the 1984 Olympics, finishing only 14th, after single-minded preparation and five successive marathon wins since 1979. He failed again with ninth in 1988. In all, of his 16 marathons, 1977-88, he won 10: the prestigious annual race at Fukuoka in 1978-80, 1983; Boston 1981 and 1987; Tokyo 1983, London and Chicago (his best time of 2:08:27) 1986, Otsu 1988. At 10,000m he was the Asian Games bronze medallist in 1986 and set two Asian records, with a best of 27:42.17 in 1985. He set world records for 25,000m 1:13:55.8 and 30,000m 1:29:18.8 in 1981. A graduate of Waseda University, he was coached by Kiyoshi Nakamura, who had run at 1500m in the 1936 Olympics.

Monica SELES (Yug)

TENNIS

Monica Seles. b. 2 Dec 1973 Novi Sad.

As a 15-year-old she was an unseeded semi-finalist at the French Open in 1989 and she became the youngest-ever winner of the title at 16yr 169d the following year. Only Lottie Dod, who won Wimbledon as a 15-year-old in 1887, has won a women's Grand Slam singles at a younger age. In 1991 Seles won three more Grand Slam singles as a 17-year-old when she was the youngest winner of the Australian Open and took the French and US titles, with a season's record earnings of $2,457,758. She improved that record to $2,622,352 in 1992, by when she was firmly established as the world's number one and had taken her career earnings to $6,971,393, the fourth highest all-time. She again won the Australian title in 1992 and 1993 and won the French in 1992 but, as in 1991, defeat at Wimbledon spoiled her chances of completing the Grand Slam.

A stab wound in the left shoulder blade at the German Open in May 1993 put her out of action, for how long remains to be seen.

Philippe SELLA (Fra)

RUGBY UNION

Philippe Sella. b. 14 Feb 1962 Clairac.

The world's most capped centre. In addition to winning 84 caps in his specialist position, he was capped six times as winger and once at full-back. His total of 91 international appearances has only been exceeded by his team-mate, Serge Blanco; and these two share the French record with 42 International Championship appearances. His exceptional attacking skills were matched by his solid defensive play. A great opportunist, he scored a try in each of the Five Nations matches in 1986 and 26 in all internationals.

Lee Roy SELMON (USA)

AMERICAN FOOTBALL

Lee Roy Selmon. b. 20 Oct 1954 Eufaula, Oklahoma.

Selmon played college football at the University of Oklahoma as a defensive end. In his senior years he won both the Outland and Lombardi Trophies as the top college lineman. In 1976 he was made the first choice of the entire NFL draft by the Tampa Bay Buccaneers, for whom he played defensive end for 10 years. He made All-Pro from 1979-84 and from 1979-81 was considered the top defensive lineman in football.

Frank SELVY (USA)

BASKETBALL

Franklin Delano Selvy. b. 9 Nov 1932 Corbin, Kentucky.

Selvy played nine years in the NBA but he is best known for his feats as a college star at Furman University. There, in 1954 as a senior, he led the nation in scoring with an unheard-of average of 41.5 points per game. Included in that magic season were nine games in which he scored over 50 points. In one of those, Selvy scored 100 points against Newberry College of South Carolina; that remains an NCAA record in a single game.

Uljana SEMJONOVA (Lat)

BASKETBALL

Uljana Larionovna Semjonova. b. 9 Mar 1952 Daugavpils.

At 2.16m *7'1"* and 129 kg *285 lb*, Semjonova played at centre for Daugawa Riga, the dominant team in the European Champions' Cup for many years, and won Olympic gold medals with the USSR team in 1976 and 1980, and world championships in 1971, 1975, and 1983. She also helped the Soviets to ten European championships from 1970. She was finally dropped from the team when, despite her great size, she was no longer able to run the guard adequately to keep up with the whippet-quick American players.

Ayrton SENNA (Bra)

MOTOR RACING

Ayrton Senna da Silva. b. 21 Mar 1960 São Paulo.

The dominant driver on the Grand Prix circuit in 1988-91, who first became world champion at Formula One in 1988 when he won eight races, an all-time record for one season.

Sponsored by his millionaire father he finished second twice and fourth once in the world karting championships in 1979-81. In 1981 he abandoned his university studies and won 13 of 18 Formula Ford races in Britain. He progressed rapidly, dominating Formula Ford 2000 racing in 1982 and the British Formula Three championship in 1983, when he won 12 rounds, before making his début in Formula One the following year, driving for Toleman. He made an immediate impression with second at Monaco and third in the Portuguese Grand Prix, achieving his first win in the latter race for Lotus in 1985. In the World Championship for Lotus he was fourth in 1985 and 1986 and third in 1987 before switching to McLaren in 1988. With McLaren he was second in 1989, won again in 1990 and 1991 and was 4th in 1992. He started 1993 without a team contract but he continued to drive for McLaren on a race by race basis and displayed consummate skill to win two of the first three races of the year. By the end of 1993 he had won 39 Grands Prix, many by leading from start to finish, from 152 races, in 61 of which (easily an all-time record) he started in pole position, including a season's record 13 in both 1988 and 1989. His score of 584 points is second only to Alain Prost.

A totally dedicated and intelligent driver, his unyielding attitude brought him into conflict with other drivers, especially with his leading rival Alain Prost.

Patrick SERCU (Bel)

CYCLING

Patrick Sercu. b. 27 Jun 1944 Roeselare

Began his career as a great track sprinter, winning the world amateur title in 1963, the Olympic gold for the kilometre time trial in 1964 and the world pro sprint in 1967 and 1969, with second places in 1965 and 1968. He set indoor world records for 1 kilometre with a flying start of 1:01.23 in 1967 and with a standing start of 1:07.35 in 1972, and an outdoor kilometre record of 1:02.46 in 1973. Later in his career he finished the Tour de France twice and was points winner in 1974, but he will be remembered as one of the greatest six-day racers ever, as from 1964 to 1983 he won a record 88 of 233 such races contested with several different partners. He coached the Belgian Olympic team in 1984.

His father Albert won the Het Volk and was second in the world pro road race in 1947.

Joe SEWELL (USA)

BASEBALL

Joseph Wheeler Sewell. b. 9 Oct 1898 Titus, Alabama.

Sewell, a shortstop, played 14 seasons in the American League, mostly with the Cleveland Indians. He was primarily famous for the fact that in over 7000 at bats, he struck out only 114 times in his career, a mark never threatened. In five seasons (1925, 1929-30, 1932-3) he struck out only three or four times for the entire season. He was also a solid hitter for average, with a career mark of .312 and ten seasonal averages over .300, topped by his .353 in 1923. His career average of one strikeout per 62.6 at bats is nonpareil in baseball history, second place on the all-time list being Lloyd Waner with one strikeout per 44.9 at bats.

Career 1920-33: 2226 hits Avg. .312; RBI 1053.

Boris SHAKHLIN (USSR/Ukr)

GYMNASTICS

Boris Anfiyanovich Shakhlin. b. 27 Jan 1932 Ishim, Tyumen region.

Shakhlin won six individual event Olympic gold medals at gymnastics, one in 1956, four (two shared) in 1960 and one in 1964, to which he added the team gold in 1956, with four silver and two bronze for 13 medals in all. Prior to his 1960 Olympic domination he had won the World title at pommel horse in 1954, and was World combined exercises champion in 1958, when he also won three other individual gold medals and the team gold. He won a further World team gold, with three silvers and two bronze, in 1962 and in all won 14 World Championship medals. He was European overall champion in 1955. At 1.71m and 70kg he was larger than usual for a gymnast. His height and reach made him particularly successful on the horizontal bar, but he was weak at the floor exercises.

Bill SHANKLY (UK)

FOOTBALL

William Shankly. b. 2 Sep 1913 Glenbuck, Ayrshire, d. 28 Sep 1981 Liverpool.

The driving force behind the emergence of Liverpool Football Club as a great team. A fine player himself, he played for Carlisle United before transferring to Preston North End in 1933. With them he won an FA Cup winners medal in 1938, and played five times for Scotland 1938-9. In 1949 he returned to Carlisle as manager, moving on to Grimsby 1951, Workington 1953 and Huddersfield 1955, before joining Liverpool in December 1959. There he developed a strong youth policy and teams that would become the powerhouse of English football. They won Division 2 in 1962 and began their drive to the top with the Division 1 title in 1964. Under Shankly Liverpool won the Football League again in 1966 and 1973, the UEFA Cup in 1973, and the FA Cup in 1965 and 1974, after which he retired. Under his chosen successor Bob Paisley, Liverpool went on to even more titles and honours. Awarded the OBE in 1974.

Shankly was one of five brothers who played professional football; one of them, Bob, managed Dundee when they won the Scottish Championship in 1962.

Jack SHARKEY (USA)

BOXING

né Joseph Paul Zukauskas. b. 26 Oct 1902 Binghamton, New York.

Sharkey was small for a heavyweight but was a skilful boxer known for his attack on the body. He first fought for the heavyweight title in 1930 but lost to Max Schmeling when he was disqualified for a low blow. Sharkey won the rematch in 1932 to claim the heavyweight championship but lost it one year later to Primo Carnera. In 1936 Sharkey made another attempt to win the title against Joe Louis but was knocked out in the third round and retired. In October 1990 he became the longest-lived world heavyweight champion.
Career record: W - 38 (14), L - 13, D - 3.

Bill SHARMAN (USA)

BASKETBALL

William Walton Sharman. b. 25 May 1926 Abilene, Texas.

One of the great shooting guards in NBA history. He played at the University of Southern California and then spent almost all his 11-year NBA caréer with the Boston Celtics, winning four championships. There he teamed with Bob Cousy to form one of the great guard tandems in NBA history. He was the best free-throw shooter in the NBA, leading the league in percentage seven times, and ending with a career percentage of .883 from the line, later surpassed only by Rick Barry and Calvin Murphy. Sharman played in eight All-Star Games and in 1970 was named to the NBA 25-year Anniversary All-Time Team. He was also a top baseball player in the Dodgers organisation and in the minor leagues 1950-5. After his playing career ended he became a coach, first in the ABL, later in college and the ABA, and eventually in the NBA with the Los Angeles Lakers.

Henry SHARPE (UK)

FIGURE SKATING

Henry Graham Sharpe. b. 19 Dec 1917 London.

The first of only two Britons to win the men's world figure skating singles title. He took up skating in 1930 at his father's ice rink in Bournemouth and made his British Championship début there in 1933 when he placed second to Jack Page's 11th and final British title. Sharpe was never beaten again in a British singles event, winning in 1934-8 (twice in 1937) and 1947. He was 5th in the 1936 Olympics; at the World Championship he was 6th in 1934, 2nd each year 1936-8 and won in 1939, and at the Europeans he was 4th in 1934, 2nd 1937-8 and winner in 1939. In that year his team-mate Freddie Tomlins was second at both Europeans and Worlds. The outbreak of war denied him the chance of Olympic honours when at his peak but after serving in the Army he came back to win his eighth and final British title in 1947. Internationally, his comeback was short-lived; he placed 7th at the 1948 Olympics and 6th at the World Championships.

Alfred SHAW (UK)

CRICKET

Alfred Shaw. b. 29 Aug 1842 Burton Joyce, Nottinghamshire, d. 16 Jan 1907 Gedling, Nottinghamshire.

The bowler of the first ball in Test cricket, he was England's finest bowler of his era, and a useful batsman as well. At medium or slow-medium pace he employed flight and artistry and was relentlessly accurate. His fluent, easy action enabled him to bowl for long spells. He was involved in six tours to Australia, captaining the England team that toured there in 1881/2, and later acting as manager. He played for Nottinghamshire for over 30 years, captaining them in 1883-6, when they were the unofficial county champions each year. A strong personality, he fought hard to improve conditions for professional cricketers. He was a first-class umpire from 1898 to 1905.
7 Tests 1876-82 (captain in 4): 111 runs at 10.09, HS 40; 12 wickets, at 23.75, BB 5-38; 4 catches.
First-class 1864-97: 6585 runs at 12.83, HS 88; 2027 wickets at 20.12, BB 10-73; 368 catches.

Tim SHAW (USA)

SWIMMING

Timothy Andrew Shaw. b. 11 Nov 1957 Long Beach, California.

In August 1974, at the age of 16, he matched the feat of Jon Konrads by simultaneously holding world records at 200m, 400m and 1500m freestyle. His times, set in four days at the AAU Championships, were 1:51.66, 3:56.96 (heat) and 3:54.69, and 15:31.75. In 1975 he was world champion at each of those distances and added two more records at 400m, 3:53.95 and 3:53.31, two at 800m, 8:13.68 and 8:09.60, and 15:20.91 at 1500m; he was also AAU 400m champion. For those endeavours he won the Sullivan Award, but in 1976 his 3:52.54 for 400m left him silver medallist behind Brian Goodell at the Olympics.
Best 200m backstroke 2:03.75 (1978).
Eight years later Shaw won a second Olympic silver medal - for the USA at water polo.

Wilbur SHAW (USA)

MOTOR RACING

Warren Wilbur Shaw. b. 13 Oct 1902 Shelbyville, Indiana, d. 30 Oct 1954 Fort Wayne, Indiana in a plane crash.

The winner of the Indianapolis 500 three times, in 1937, 1939 and 1940, and second three times, 1933, 1935 and 1938; he persuaded Anton Hulman Jr. to save the track from becoming an industrial site in 1945, and was from then its general manager until his death.
Noted for his daring and aggressive driving, he built his own car at 18, competing in the early 1920s on board tracks and in midget racing, and having made his début at Indianapolis in 1927 he reached the top of auto racing in the 1930s.

Tatyana SHCHELKANOVA (USSR)

ATHLETICS

Tatyana Shchelkanova. b. 18 Apr 1937 Yeysk, near Rostov.

She set four world records for the women's long jump from 6.48m in 1962 to 6.70m in 1964. Her absolute best was a wind-assisted 6.96m in the 1966 Soviet Championships, and she also set nine world indoor bests to the 6.73 with which she won the first European Indoor title in 1966. She was European champion in 1962 and third in the 1964 Olympics; World Student Games champion at long jump in 1963 and 1965 and at pentathlon in 1965, when she was also second at 80m hurdles.
Other bests: 100m 11.7 (1961), 80m hurdles 10.8 (1963), pentathlon 4863 points (1963).

Patty SHEEHAN (USA)

GOLF

Patricia Leslie Sheehan. b. 27 Oct 1956 Middlebury, Vermont.

In 1992 Sheehan became the first woman to win the US and British Opens in the same year. An ebullient player, she had previously been runner-up in the US Open three times. By the end of the year she was fourth on the all-time LPGA money list at $3,591,290, having completed eleven successive years ranked in the top eight. In June 1993 she won her 31st tournament on the circuit when she won her third LPGA Championship. Her first major successes came with consecutive LPGA Championship wins in 1983-4, achieving the then record low aggregate of 272 and the record lowest round of 63 in 1984.
She was formerly a top junior skier, whose father Bobo coached the US Olympic team in 1956, and before turning pro she won all four of her matches in the 1980 Curtis Cup.
LPGA career earnings 1980-92: $3,591,290 with 29 victories.

Barry SHEENE (UK)

MOTOR CYCLING

Barry Sheene. b. 12 Sep 1950 Holborn, London.

A charismatic motorcycling champion, he overcame serious injuries to attain success and great popular esteem. He was world champion at 500cc for Suzuki in 1976 and 1977, and still holds the record for the fastest ever average speed for a world championship race, 217.37 km/h (135.07

mph) with a lap record at 220.721 km/h (137.150 mph) at Spa-Francorchamps, Belgium in 1977. His first Grand Prix wins were for Suzuki in 1971, one at 50cc and three at 125cc. Then he won 19 at 500cc between 1975 and 1981, the last for Yamaha, all the others for Suzuki.
His father Frank Sheene was a notable rider and his brother-in-law Paul Smart raced in Britain and the USA in the 1960s and 1970s. Barry made his racing début in 1968, won the British 125cc title in 1970 and was just beaten by Angel Nieto to the world 125cc title in 1971. He was awarded the MBE in 1978 and retired in 1984.
From 1987 he has lived in Queensland, Australia where he is a TV commentator.

Martin SHERIDAN (USA)

ATHLETICS
Martin Joseph Sheridan. b. 28 Mar 1881 Bohola, Co. Mayo, Ireland, d. 27 Mar 1918 New York.

The Olympic discus champion in 1904, 1908 and at the Intercalated Games of 1906, with further gold medals at the Greek-style discus in 1908 and the shot in 1906. He also won three silver medals at the standing high and long jumps and the stone throw in 1906, and bronze at standing long jump in 1908. Between 1904 and 1911 he won four AAU titles at discus, one each at shot and Greek-style discus, two at pole vault for distance and three all-around championships. Before the standardisation of the discus circle he made eight improvements on the best from a 2.50m circle, including the first ever throw in excess of 40 metres in 1902. His best performance was 43.69m in New York in 1905, about which some doubts have been expressed, or 43.54m in 1909.
Sheridan came to the USA at the age of 16 and later became a policeman in New York, but died prematurely of pneumonia.

Albert SHESTERNYEV (USSR)

FOOTBALL
Albert Shesternyev. b. 20 Jun 1941 Moscow.

Shesternyev made 89 international appearances for the USSR, captaining them at the World Cups of 1966 and 1970, having earlier played in 1962, and when they were runners-up in the European Championships of 1964. He played for the FIFA team which beat Brazil 2-1 in 1968. He was a speedy full-back, capable of running 100 metres in 11.0 seconds.

Peter SHILTON (UK)

FOOTBALL
Peter Leslie Shilton. b. 18 Sep 1949 Leicester.

As goalkeeper for England 125 times between 1970 and 1990 he is the most capped player in the world. After making his début for Leicester City as a 16-year-old he later played for Stoke City 1974-7, Nottingham Forest 1977-82, Southampton 1982-7, Derby County 1987-92 and Plymouth Argyle as player-manager 1992-3. His major honours came when he was with Forest, helping them win the European Cup 1979 and 1980, the League title 1978 and the League Cup 1979.
A complete master of all the goalkeeping skills, he has made a total of 1374 senior UK appearances, including a record 991 League appearances with his six clubs 1966-93. For his contribution to the game he was awarded the MBE in 1986 and OBE 1990.

SHIN Geum-dan (NKo)

ATHLETICS
Shin Geum-dan. b. 3 Jul 1938 Pyongyang.

A rather mysterious athlete, as her nation did not compete at the Olympics. At the 1963 Games of the New Emerging Forces in Djakarta, which were not recognised by the IAAF, on successive days she ran an Asian record 23.5 for 200m, the first sub-2 minute time by a woman at 800m with 1:59.1, and 400m in 51.4, compared to the official world record of 53.4 and her own earlier mark of 53.0. The following year in Pyongyang she improved her times to 51.2 and 1:58.0.
She had emerged in world class in 1959 and in 1961 had run an unofficial world record for 800m with 2:01.2.

Bill SHOEMAKER (USA)

HORSE RACING

Billie Lee Shoemaker. b. 19 Aug 1931 Fabens, Texas.

'The Shoe' passed the record career wins of 6032 by Johnny Longden in 1970 and went on to a total of 8833 winners from 40,350 mounts to his retirement on 3 Feb 1990, with $123,375,524 in purses, having been, in 1985, the first to reach $100 million. He headed the money-winning list in the US ten times, 1951, 1953-4 and 1958-64 and rode a record 1009 stakes winners. He started to ride in Winters, Texas, where his grandfather was a ranch foreman. In 1949 he had his first ride in public on 19 March, his first winner on 20 April, and ended the year with 219 winners for second place nationwide. The following year he tied for first with 388 victories and led in race wins five times, in 1951, 1953, when he set a single year record of 485 winners, 1954, 1958 and 1959.
He won the Kentucky Derby four times from *Swaps* in 1955 to *Ferdinand* in 1986, when he became, at 54, the oldest ever winning jockey of the race. He also rode the winners of two Preakness Stakes and five Belmont Stakes, and was the Eclipse outstanding jockey as well as winning the Merit award in 1981, having been given a Special award in 1976.
Shoemaker stood 4ft 11in and weighed 95lb. Although paralysed from the neck down in a car accident on 8 Apr 1991, he continues to work as a trainer.

Eddie SHORE (Can)

ICE HOCKEY

Edward William Shore. b. 25 Nov 1902 Fort Qu'Appelle, Saskatchewan.

Considered by many hockey experts to be the greatest defenseman ever to play in the NHL. Except for ten games at the end of his last season with the New York Americans, Shore played his entire career with the Boston Bruins. His ability was based on three skills: he was an extraordinary skater, he was an excellent stick-handler, and he was probably the toughest player ever seen in the NHL. Tales of his fearlessness abound among old-time hockey players and during his career, his face became criss-crossed by hundreds of stitches but he rarely came out of a game. The Norris Trophy signifying the league's best defenseman was not awarded until 1953, but Shore would probably have won it seven or eight times. From 1931 to 1939 he was a first-team All-Star seven times.
NHL career 1926-40 - 553 games, 105 goals, 284 points. Hart Trophy 1933, 1935-6, 1938.

Frank SHORTER (USA)

ATHLETICS

Frank Charles Shorter. b. 31 Oct 1947 Munich, Germany.

While at Yale University, Frank Shorter was a useful distance runner winning the NCAA 6 miles title in 1969, but he did not emerge into world class until after graduation. On the track he won five AAU titles at 6M/10,000m between 1970 and 1977 and the 5000m in 1970, and the Pan-Am 10,000m title in 1971 as well as third place in 1979. He twice set US records for 10,000m with a best of 27:51.4 for 5th place at the 1972 Olympics.
It was, however, as a marathon runner that he secured his place in the history books. He made his début in 1971, placing second to Kenny Moore in the AAUs and going on to win the Pan-American title and the first of four victories in the international race at Fukuoka, Japan. In 1972 he won the Olympic title in Munich and in 1976 took the silver medal. His best time was 2:10:30 at Fukuoka in 1972 and that year he won the Sullivan Award.
Shorter, who earned a law degree in 1974, became a very successful businessman with his own chain of sports goods stores, as well as a TV commentator.

Jim SHOULDERS (USA)

RODEO

James Arthur Shoulders. b. 13 May 1928 Henryetta, Oklahoma.

Thirty years after he last competed, Shoulders is still a legend among rodeo cowboys. His record of 16 world titles is still a PRCA record. That included five all-around titles, 1949, 1956-9; four for bareback bronc riding, 1950, 1956-8; and seven for bull riding, 1951, 1954-9. He set money-winning records which enabled him to start his own rodeo stock ranch. He was considered rodeo's greatest competitor and competed almost endlessly during his ten-year career despite numerous injuries. He then became well-known through a series of television commercials in the United States.

Stanley SHOVELLER (UK)

HOCKEY

Stanley Howard Shoveller. b. 2 Sep 1881 Kingston Hill, Surrey, d. 24 Feb 1959 Broadstone, Dorset.

The first man in Olympic history to win two gold medals for hockey and England's highest scoring player. After Kingston Grammar School, he joined Hampstead and represented Surrey and the South before making his international debut in 1902. He went on to win 35 caps for England at centre-forward and accumulated a record total of 79 goals, scoring in all but ten of his international matches. He captained England from 1909 until his retirement in 1921 when he became a leading administrator. During World War I he won an MC serving as a captain in the Rifle Brigade.

Arthur SHREWSBURY (UK)

CRICKET

Arthur Shrewsbury. b. 11 Apr 1856 New Lenton, Nottinghamshire, d. 19 May 1903 Gedling, Nottinghamshire.

W G Grace's famous tribute was 'Give me Arthur', when asked which of his contemporaries he rated the highest. For much of his career Shrewsbury was the finest professional batsman in the country, a master of the turning ball, and he was the first player to reach 1000 runs in Test cricket (1893). With James Lillywhite and Alfred Shaw he helped to organise four tours to Australia in the 1880s, and he captained two of them, winning five of the seven Tests played on those. In an age of much lower scoring than at any time since, he consistently scored at a higher rate than anybody but Grace, and made 10 double hundreds. He shot himself less than a year after his final first-class match, unable to cope with life after cricket.

23 Tests 1881-93: 1277 runs at 35.47, 3 100s HS 164; 29 catches.
First-class 1875-1902: 26,505 runs at 36.65, 59 100s HS 267; 376 catches.

Pam SHRIVER (USA)

TENNIS

Pamela Howard Shriver. b. 4 Jul 1962 Baltimore, Maryland.

In 1978, at the age of 16, she set a record as the youngest-ever finalist at the US Open, but despite this brilliant start to her career she has not reached the final of a Grand Slam singles since. She did, however, become an outstanding doubles player and between 1981 and 1989 won 20 Grand Slam titles with Martina Navratilova (7 Australian, 5 Wimbledon, 4 French, 4 USA). Together they won a record eight consecutive Grand Slam women's doubles titles and from April 1983 to July 1985 they won 109 successive matches in all tournaments. They also won a record 79 doubles titles together in their careers. Shriver also won a gold medal with Zina Garrison when tennis was reintroduced into the Olympic programme in 1988, the US women's doubles in 1991 with Natalya Zvereva (USSR) and the French mixed doubles in 1987 with Emilio Sánchez (Spa). At the end of 1992 her career earnings were $4,870,516. Her exceptional height (5'11" *1.80m*) has enabled her to develop a superb service.

Alf SHRUBB (UK)

ATHLETICS

Alfred Shrubb. b. 12 Dec 1879 Slinfold, Sussex, d. 23 Apr 1964 Boumanville, Ontario, Canada.

The world's greatest distance runner at the turn of the century, he set world records from 2 miles to 1 hour, many of which lasted for a very long time. His greatest

run was at Glasgow on 5 Nov 1904, when his world records included those for 6 miles 29:59.4, 10,000m 31:02.4, 10 miles 50:40.6 and 1 hour 18,742m. That last time remained a British record for 48 years 296 days. Earlier in 1904 he had set records at 2, 3, 4 and 5 miles.
He won the first two International cross-country races 1903-4, but did not compete at the 1904 Olympics as Britain did not send a team. At the end of that year the AAA declared him to be a professional.
He won the English National cross-country each year 1901-4 and was AAA champion at 1 mile 1903-4 and 4 miles 1901-4.

Yelena SHUSHUNOVA (USSR/Rus)

GYMNASTICS

Yelena Shushunova. b. 23 May 1969 Leningrad.

The all-around champion at the 1988 Olympics, when she added a silver and bronze at individual apparatus and a team gold. She had won her first Soviet title in 1982, and was the European overall champion in 1985, when she also won three of the four individual events. She went on to be the World Cup winner in 1986 and won a record six gold medals at the 1987 World Student Games. At the World Championships she won the vault in 1985 and 1987 and shared the floor exercises gold in 1987, when she was second overall. Only 1.48m tall but courageous and powerful, she competed for the Army Sports Club, Leningrad.

Janusz SIDLO (Pol)

ATHLETICS

Janusz Sidlo. b. 19 Jun 1933 Szopienice, d. 2 Aug 1993 Warsaw.

Sidlo had a long career, ranked in the world's top ten javelin throwers each year from 1953 to 1970, and competed in five Olympic Games, but only once gained a medal, silver in 1956. He fared better in European Championships, winning in 1954 and 1958 and taking the bronze in 1969 as well as 7th places in 1962 and 1966. He won 15 Polish titles between 1951 and 1970 and appeared in a record 61 internationals for Poland. He made a sensational improvement in 1953 when he added 6.88m to the Polish javelin record, throwing 80.15m, which was also a European record. He improved that with a world record 83.66 in 1956, although he set three more national records with a best 14 years later at 86.22 in 1970. He also set a record with five wins between 1951 and 1959 at the World Student Games.

Jon SIEBEN (Aus)

SWIMMING

Jonathon Scott Sieben. b. 24 Aug 1966 Coorparoo, Brisbane.

The surprise Olympic champion of 1984 at 200m butterfly, when he improved his pre-Games best from 2:01.17 to a world record 1:57.04 in the final to beat the clear favourite Michael Gross. Four years later in Seoul he was fourth at 100m butterfly in an Australian record 53.33.

Paul SILAS (USA)

BASKETBALL

Paul Theron Silas. b. 12 Jul 1943 Prescott, Arizona.

A bruising power forward who played for 16 years in the NBA, including three Championship teams: Boston Celtics 1974 and 1976, and the Seattle Supersonics 1979. In college at Creighton he was known as a rebounder, still holding the all-time career rebound record among college players, and is one of only seven players to average over 20 points and 20 rebounds for a college career. He coached for three season with the San Diego Clippers from 1980-3.

Daniela SILIVAS (Rom)

GYMNASTICS

Daniela Silivas. b. 9 May 1971.

In 1990 Silivas revealed that she had been born a year later than previously claimed. That meant that she had won the gold medal for balance beam at the 1985 World Championships at the age of 14 years 185 days, making her the youngest ever world champion. She was European champion in 1987, when she also took gold medals at three of the four individual apparatus events, and won further world titles with the Romanian team in 1987, sharing the gold for floor exercises in 1987 and 1989 and on the beam in 1989. At the 1988 Olympics she took the all-around silver medal, being passed by Yelena Shushunova in the last event, but came back to win three of the four apparatus finals.

Sara SIMEONI (Italy)

ATHLETICS

Sara Simeoni. b. 19 Apr 53 Rivoli, Verona. Later Azzaro.

A charming high jumper whose rivalry with Rosi Ackermann made her event a highlight for many years. She first competed at the Olympic Games in 1972, when she was 6th, and went on to win three Olympic medals, gold in 1980 and silver in 1976 and 1984. She was European champion in 1978, bronze medallist in 1974 and 1982 and placed 9th in 1971. She won four European Indoor and two World Student Games titles, and was Italian champion 13 times. She twice cleared a world record 2.01m in August 1978, first at Brescia and then at Prague to win the European Championship. These brought her tally of Italian records to 21 from 1.71m in 1970 when she made her international début.
A physical education instructor, she became the presenter of a TV sports programme in 1986.

Al SIMMONS (USA)

BASEBALL

Aloysius Harry Simmons. né Aloys Szymanski. b. 22 May 1902 Milwaukee, Wisconsin, d. 26 May 1956 Milwaukee.

An outfielder, best remembered for the 12 years he spent with the Philadelphia Athletics. In his career, he batted over .300 15 times, leading the American League in 1930 (.381) and 1931 (.390). His best average was 1927 at .392. Six times he had over 200 hits in a season, topped by his stunning 253 in 1925 (4th all-time); he also led the league with 216 in 1932. One of Simmons' goals was to reach 3,000 hits for his career, but missing a year to military service in 1942 and most of his last three years to injuries prevented this. The legendary manager Connie Mack considered Simmons the greatest player he had ever managed.
Career 1924-44: 2927 hits Avg. .334, HR 307; RBI 1827,

Nikita SIMONIAN (USSR/Arm)

FOOTBALL

Nikita Simonian. b. 12 Oct 1926 Armavir.

Unusually small for a centre-forward but exceptionally fast, he was one of the most prolific scorers in Russian football. Starting his career in Georgia, he moved to Moscow in 1946 to join Krilia Sovietov before transferring to Spartak Moskva three years later. With the country's premier club he won four League and two Cup medals. He scored 12 goals in his 23 internationals, won a gold medal at the 1956 Olympics and retired soon after playing in the 1958 World Cup. Initially he was a trainer with the Soviet Football Federation and in 1960 became manager of Spartak. One of the few Armenian players to reach the top flight, he made an immeasurable contribution to the emergence of the USSR as a world soccer power.

Allan SIMONSEN (Den)

FOOTBALL

Allan Rodenkam Simonsen. b. 15 December 1952 Vejle.

An attacking midfield player, he was European Footballer of the Year in 1977 when he played for Borussia Mönchengladbach, with whom he won UEFA Cup winners medals in 1975 and 1979. With Barcelona he won the European Cup-Winners' Cup in 1982, before returning to Denmark to play for Vejle BK. He scored 21 goals in 55 internationals to the 1986 World Cup for Denmark. He had a short spell in England with Charlton Athletic.

Bobby SIMPSON (Aus)

CRICKET

Robert Baddeley Simpson. b. 3 Feb 1936 Marrickville, New South Wales.

A reliable opening batsman, useful leg-break bowler and one of the greatest ever slip fielders. He made his mark early, playing for New South Wales from the age of 16 and making his Test début at 21, yet most surprisingly it took him over 6 years and 30 Tests before he scored his maiden century in Test cricket. On that occasion, however, at Old Trafford in 1964 against England, he went on to score 311, and he added another nine centuries in Tests. On that tour he had taken over as Australian captain from Richie Benaud, and he led his country in 39 matches altogether. These included 10 matches in 1977-8, when he returned to Tests after a ten-year absence to take over the side which had been severely affected by the defection of most of the best players to World Series Cricket. His original retirement at the age of 32 had seemed premature, and he showed great dedication to score 539 runs (av. 53.90) with two centuries in a 5-Test series against India, which was won 3-2. He was, however, less successful in the following series against the mighty West Indians. He played for Western Australia 1956-61. A strong disciplinarian, he later managed Leicestershire and Australia.

62 Tests 1957-78: 4869 runs at 46.81, 10 100s HS 311; 71 wickets at 42.26, BB 5-57; 110 catches.

2 One-day Ints: 36 runs at 18.00; HS 23; 2 wickets at 47.50; 4 catches.

First-class 1952-78: 21,029 runs at 56.22, 60 100s HS 359; 349 wickets at 38.07, BB 5-33; 383 catches.

O J SIMPSON (USA)

AMERICAN FOOTBALL

Orenthal James Simpson. b. 7 Jul 1947 San Francisco, California.

One of the greatest running backs in football history. 'The legend' began with 'the run' that O J Simpson made for USC in the final game against UCLA in 1967. Late in the game, Simpson made an electrifying run with USC behind, scoring a game-winning touchdown from 64 yards out, considered one of the single great runs in football history. It was only a prelude to a great career.

In Simpson's senior year he won the Heisman Memorial Trophy. In his college days he was also a fine sprinter, helping USC set a world record in the 4 x 110 yard relay and with a 100y best time of 9.4. In 1969 he was drafted by the Buffalo Bills in the first round. He languished with the Bills for two season before new head coach Lou Saban established Simpson as the key to the Bills offense. In 1973 Simpson smashed the NFL rushing record with 2003 yards and in his career for the Bills to 1977 and then two seasons with the San Francisco 49ers he gained 11,236 yards and scored 61 touchdowns. Since his retirement as a player he has become a very well known sports announcer on television.

NFL career 1969-79: Rushing: 11,236 yards av. 4.7, 61 touchdowns. Receiving: 2140 yards av. 10.5, 14 touchdowns.

Tommy SIMPSON (UK)

CYCLING

Thomas Simpson. b. 30 Nov 1937 Co. Durham, d. 13 Jul 1967 Mont Ventoux, France.

Tommy Simpson was the first truly great British road professional, and he remains the greatest yet produced by the British Isles. He turned professional in 1960 after an amateur career which included an Olympic bronze medal in the 1956 team pursuit and a silver in the individual pursuit at the 1958 Commonwealth Games. He lacked only the ability to climb strongly, which made him more of a factor in one-day classics than in the major tours. In 1962 he became the first Briton to wear the *maillot jaune* at the Tour de France, though he held it only for a day. His greatest year was 1965 when he won the Tour of Lombardy and the world professional road race. Those wins occurred after a disastrous fall in the Tour de France when doctors feared they might need to amputate his arm.

In 1967, Simpson was ascending Mont

Ventoux in the Tour de France when he collapsed and fell from his bike. He could not be revived and died that day. He was later found to have been quite heavily drugged with stimulants and his death was directly responsible for many of the anti-drug regulations put in place by international sporting organisations.
Other major victories: Tour of Flanders 1961, Bordeaux-Paris 1963, Milan-San Remo 1964, Paris-Nice 1967.

Matthias SINDELAR (Aut)

FOOTBALL
Matthias Sindelar. b. 11 Feb 1903 Kozlor-next-Iglau, Czechoslovakia, d. 23 Jan 1939 Vienna.

The star centre-forward of the brilliant Austrian 'Wunderteam' of the 1930s. Tall and extremely thin, his dribbling skills played havoc with opposing defences and he created many opportunities for his team-mates in addition to scoring valuable goals himself. In 1928 he scored three times in Austria's 5-1 defeat of Hungary and in 1932 he scored both goals when Austria beat Italy 2-1. Later in the season he claimed a hat-trick in Austria's 8-2 victory over Hungary. In 44 internationals he scored 27 times. Virtually all his playing career was spent with FK Austria where he won three Cup winners' medals and twice helped them win the League. In 1934 he was a member of the team which reached the semi-finals of the World Cup.
Although Czech-born, he spent most of his life in Austria where, as a Jew, he suffered from the rise of Hitler. After being betrayed by a colleague in the 'Wunderteam' who was a dedicated Nazi, Sindelar gassed himself.

Mike SINGLETARY (USA)

AMERICAN FOOTBALL
Michael Singletary. b. 9 Oct 1958 Houston, Texas.

Now considered to be the last of the great middle linebackers in pro football. He played college ball at Baylor and pro football from 1981-92 with the Chicago Bears. He played in all nine Pro Bowls 1983-91 and was named NFL Defensive Player of the Year in 1985, when he led the Bears defense as they won the Super Bowl with what is considered one of the great defensive teams in NFL history, and in 1988, when he had a season's high 170 tackles from a career total of 1488. Modern pro football usually employs four linebackers, two inside and two outside, and true middle linebackers, such as Singletary, are now quite rare.

Anna SIPOS (Hun)

TABLE TENNIS
Anna Sipos. b. 1908 Szeged.

Winner of 11 world titles between 1929 and 1935, including all three in 1932. She had a great rivalry with her team-mate Maria Mednyánsky, losing to her in the singles final in 1930 but beating her to win the title in 1932 and 1933. Together they won six successive women's doubles titles, 1930-5. Sipos also won the world mixed doubles in 1929 with István Kelen and in 1932 and 1935 with Viktor Barna.

Cornelia SIRCH (GDR)

SWIMMING
Cornelia Sirch. b. 23 Oct 1966 Jena.

She was only 15 when she won her first world title in 1982, finishing five seconds ahead of the runner-up at 200m backstroke in a world record 2:09.91. She never managed to better that time but retained her title in 1986 and was European champion at that event in 1983, 1985 and 1987. At the Europeans she also won gold at 4 x 200m freestyle and silver at 100m backstroke in 1983, silver at 400m medley in 1985, and gold at 200m medley in 1987. At the 400m medley she was 4th at the 1986 Worlds. She ended her career at the 1988 Olympics with silver at 100m and bronze at 200m.
Coached by Wolfgang Fricke at SC Turbine Erfurt, she was GDR backstroke champion 100m 1986, 200m 1982-3, 1985, 1987-8; 200m IM 1987.
Other bests: 100m backstroke 61.48 (1983), 200m IM 2:15.04 (1987), 400m IM 4:45.65 (1986).

George SISLER (USA)

BASEBALL

George Harold Sisler. b. 24 Mar 1893 Manchester, Ohio, d. 26 Mar 1973 Richmond Heights, Ohio.

Sisler played primarily first base during his major league career, spent mostly with the St Louis Browns. He is considered the greatest ever Browns player. He was a superb hitter for average and a great base stealer for his era. He batted over .300 every year of his career except his rookie year (1915) and twice he batted over .400. In 1920 he led the league with a .407 average and his 257 hits that year remains a major league record for a single season. He also recorded 246 hits in 1922 when he batted .420. Sisler led the American League in stolen bases four times, topped by 51 in his great season of 1922 when he was the league's MVP. He originally began his career as a left-handed pitcher, but his hitting was too valuable for him not to play every day. He did pitch in 24 games in seven different seasons between 1915-28, with a career mark of 5 wins, 6 losses. *Career 1915-30: 2812 hits Avg. .340, HR 101; RBI 1175; SB 375.*

Omar SIVORI (Arg, Ita)

FOOTBALL

Enrique Omar Sivori. b. 2 Oct 1935 San Nicolás.

A goalscoring inside-forward with superb ball skills who was capped both by his native Argentina and by Italy. Beginning his career with River Plate, he was a member of the team which brought the 1957 South American Cup to Argentina, and immediately afterwards moved to Italy together with the two other members of Argentina's brilliant inside trio.

Sivori went to Juventus whom he helped to three Italian First Division titles (1958, 1960-61). With 27 goals he was top scorer in the League in 1959, and in 1961 he was voted European Footballer of the Year. Because of his Italian father, he was capped 9 times by Italy including two games in the 1962 World Cup, and he had earlier won 12 caps for Argentina.

In 1965, following differences with the Juventus coach, he moved to Napoli but, mainly because of injury, he played only 12 games in four seasons. In 1969 he returned to Argentina where he took up various coaching appointments.

Patrik SJÖBERG (Swe)

ATHLETICS

Jan Niklas Patrik Sjöberg. b. 5 Jan 1965 Göteborg.

Sjöberg set a world record for the high jump with 2.42m in 1987, shortly before winning the World title, and has compiled a record of outstandingly consistent success for more than a decade. That was his 12th Swedish record from his first in 1982. As a teenager he took the Olympic silver medal in 1984, and added bronze in 1988 and silver in 1992. Indoors he set world bests at 2.38 in 1985 and 2.41 in 1987, and won four European Indoor titles, 1985, 1987-8 and 1992, and the World Indoor Games 1985. He was the World Cup winner in 1985 and 1989 and has an extraordinary record for the Swedish team, having never lost in 22 appearances from his début in 1981, at the age of 16, to 1993. He was Swedish champion each year 1981 to 1987 and in 1989. He competes for Örgryte IS, Göteborg and lives in Brussels; renowned for his extrovert lifestyle.

Ragnar SKANÅKER (Swe)

SHOOTING

Ragnar Skanåker. b. 8 Jun 1934 Stora Skedvi.

A gunmaker, he has a twenty-year span as an Olympic medallist; at free pistol he won the gold medal in 1972, silver in 1984 and 1988, and bronze in 1992. Adding to a remarkable Olympic record he was also 5th in 1976 and 7th in 1980.

He was world champion at standard pistol in 1978, free pistol in 1982 and air pistol in 1983, 2nd at free pistol in 1978, and third at air pistol in 1979 and 1981, with a further gold, two silver and two bronze medals in team events. In the European Championships he won the free pistol in

1989 and also has three individual silver medals.

Lidiya SKOBLIKOVA (USSR)

SPEED SKATING

Lidiya Pavlovna Skoblikova. b. 8 Mar 1939 Zlatoust, Chelyabinsk.

The winner of six Olympic gold medals, a record for skating until 1988 when Karin Enke-Kania won her eighth medal, and twice world champion. She was nearing her best when speed skating events for women were introduced into the Olympic programme in 1960 and she won gold medals in the 1500m and 3000m, setting a world record 2:25.2 in the former. Four years later she became the first woman to win all four events at one Olympics, winning a gold medal on four consecutive days, with new Olympic records at 500m, 1000m and 1500m, although slushy ice conditions precluded a fourth record in the 3000m. A teacher from Siberia, she made a third Olympic appearance in 1968 when she was 11th in the 1500m. She also set world records at 1000m, 1:31.8 in 1963, and 3000m, 5:05.9 in 1967.

After three successive bronze medals, 1959-61, in the overall competition at the World Championships, she improved to take second place in 1962 and was then overall champion in 1963 and 1964, winning all four individual events in both years.

Arkadiusz SKRZYPASZEK (Pol)

MODERN PENTATHLON

Arkadiusz Skrzypaszek. b. 20 Apr 1968.

He became the world's best modern pentathlete with the world title in 1991 and the Olympic gold in 1992. He had been runner-up in the World Juniors in 1987 before making his Olympic début in 1988.

Andrew SLACK (Aus)

RUGBY UNION

Andrew Gerard Slack. b. 24 Sep 1955.

He led Australia a record 19 times during a career in which he won 39 caps between 1978 and 1987. A steady but unspectacular centre, he was dropped from the team on more than one occasion. He captained the Wallabies for the 1987 World Cup but after defeats by France and Wales, Australia finished a disappointing fourth and Slack retired.

Mary SLANEY (USA)

ATHLETICS

Mary Thereza Slaney. né Decker. b. 4 Aug 1958 Flemington, New Jersey.

A great distance runner who won the World Championships double of 1500m and 3000m in 1983. She became the youngest ever US international at 14 years 224 days when she ran 1 mile indoors against the USSR in 1973. Later that year she won at 800m v USSR, and she set a world indoor best for 880y in 1974. For the next four years she rarely competed due to a series of injuries; throughout her career she was troubled by leg injuries and in all has had some dozen operations, yet she consistently overcame them to dominate US distance running, setting 22 US records at all distances from 800m to 10,000m. She set world records at 1 mile in 1980, at 1 mile, 5000m and 10,000m in 1982, and again at the mile in 1985, when she was in invincible form and won the women's overall Grand Prix title. She was often seen at her best indoors, with her long flowing stride, and she set 16 world indoor bests between 1974 and 1985.

She won the US Olympic Trials at 1500m in 1980, 3000m in 1984, 1500m and 3000m in 1988, but her Olympic career was blighted. She missed the 1980 Games due to the US boycott, then she fell in the 3000m at Los Angeles in 1984. In 1988 she was 8th at 1500m and 10th at 3000m and she narrowly failed to make the US team in 1992 when she was 4th in the Trials at 1500m. She was Pan-American champion at 1500m in 1979 and won US titles at 800m 1974, 1500m 1982-3, 3000m 1983.

She was at the University of Colorado. Formerly married to 2:09:32 marathon runner Ron Tabb, she married British discus thrower Richard Slaney (best of

65.16m in 1985) on 1 Jan 1985. She gave birth to a daughter, Ashley Lynn, on 30 May 1986.
Best times: 800m 1:56.90 (1985), 1000m 2:34.65 (1988), 1500m 3:57.24 (1985), 1 mile 4:16.71 (1985), 2000m 5:32.7 (1984), 3000m 8:25.83 (1985), 5000m 15:06.53 (1985), 10,000m 31:35.3 (1982), marathon 3:09:27 at age 12!

Fergus SLATTERY (Ire)

RUGBY UNION

John Fergus Slattery. b. 12 Feb 1949 Dun Laoghaire.

With 61 international appearances between 1970 and 1984 he was Ireland's most capped flanker. On the Lions tour of New Zealand in 1971 he was unable to command a place in the Test side but on his second Lions tour in 1974 he played in all four Tests against South Africa. He made his international début against the touring Springboks in 1970 and played in 28 consecutive matches before he lost his place through injury. After returning to the side he made a further 33 consecutive appearances for Ireland.

Enos SLAUGHTER (USA)

BASEBALL

Enos Bradsher Slaughter. b. 27 Apr 1916 Roxboro, North Carolina.

'Country' Slaughter, Roxboro's finest, was one of the hardest working, toughest ballplayers ever to play in the major leagues. He played mostly with the St Louis Cardinals, although he played for three other teams at the end of his career. He was an outfielder with only average speed, best remembered for his play in the last inning of the 7th game of the 1946 World Series, when he went from 1st base to home on a single to win the game and Series for the Cardinals. At the end of his career he became a baseball coach at Duke University, before retiring to his tobacco farm in Roxboro.
Career 1938-59: 2383 hits Avg. .300, HR 169; RBI 1304. Best seasons: 1949: .336; 1918: .318; 1948: .321.

Tod SLOAN (USA)

HORSE RACING

James Forman Sloan. b. 10 Aug 1873 Bunker Hill, nr. Kokomo, Indiana, d. 21 Dec 1933 Los Angeles.

He started his career in the USA, and after winning 132 races in 1896, 137 in 1897, and an amazing 186 of 362 races in 1898, he went to England, where he rode with great success, winning 254 races from 801 mounts. He popularised the forward seat, low crouch position, known as the 'monkey crouch', from the expression 'monkey up a stick', and this was soon adopted universally.
Orphaned at the age of 5, in 1890 he went to St Louis to join his elder brother, Cassius, who was established as a jockey. He was soon recognised as a brilliant jockey himself. His childhood nickname was 'Toad', but he shortened that to 'Tod'. An excellent shooter, he competed at the 1900 Olympics in that sport.
A stocky man with short legs, he was a heavy gambler, regarded as greedy, arrogant and dishonest, but a genius on a horse. His licence to ride was revoked in 1900, and although he stayed in England for 15 years in the hope that he could return to the saddle, that never happened and he was eventually deported for breaking the gambling laws. He died of cirrhosis of the liver.

Ilona SLUPIANEK (GDR)

ATHLETICS

Ilona Slupianek. née Schoknecht. b. 24 Sep 1956 Demmin. Later Briesenick.

She started her career with the European Junior shot title in 1973 (and was second at discus). She was fifth in the 1976 Olympics, but was disqualified for drug abuse after winning the shot at the 1977 European Cup Final. Just one year and 16 days later she returned to win the 1978 European title, and went on to further wins: Olympics 1980, European 1982, European Indoor 1979 and 1981. Seven times GDR champion, she also won the World Cup shot three times, the European Cup twice and took the 1983 World bronze

medal. She set world records at 22.36m and 22.45m in 1980 after eleven world junior records in 1973-4.
Although throwing lesser distances, she continued her career into the late 1980s, and was 2nd in the 1987 World Indoors. She competed for SC Dynamo Berlin and was at one time a deputy in the GDR national assembly. She married **Hartmut Briesenick** (b. 17 Mar 1949), European shot champion in 1971 and 1974.

Raisa SMETANINA (USSR)

NORDIC SKIING

Raisa Petrovna Smetanina. b. 29 Feb 1952 Mokhcha, Komi ASSR.

The winner of a record ten medals at Olympic skiing. These were four gold: 10km and relay 1976, 5km 1980 and relay 1992; five silver: 5km 1976, relay 1980, 10km 1984 and 1988, 20km 1984; and the bronze at 20km 1988. World champion at 20km in 1982, in all she has won the record number of 23 World and Olympic medals 1974-92. She was the World Cup winner in 1981, and was second in 1979 and 1984.
Her Olympic relay gold in 1992 came 20 years after her international début and just 13 days before her 40th birthday to make her the oldest ever Olympic skiing medallist.

Charlie SMIRKE (UK)

HORSE RACING

Charles James William Smirke. b. 23 Sep 1906 Lambeth.

Winner of 11 classics in England from Derby winners *Windsor Lad* in 1934 to *Hard Ridden* in 1958. Six of these, including *Mahmoud* in 1936 and *Tulyar* in 1952, were owned by the Aga Khan for whom he rode for 30 years. He was apprenticed to Stanley Wootton from 1920 and rode his first winner in 1922. His most wins in a year was 78 in 1924. A cocky, cheerful Cockney, he lost his licence to ride in 1928 due to a miscarriage of justice by the Stewards of the Jockey Club and did not regain it until 1933.

Arthur SMITH (UK)

RUGBY UNION

Arthur Robert Smith. b. 23 Jan 1933 Castle Douglas, d. 3 Feb 1975 Edinburgh.

After playing in only three matches for Scotland he was chosen for the 1955 Lions tour of South Africa but he broke his hand in the first match and did not play again until the end of the tour. In 1962 he again toured South Africa with the Lions, this time as captain, and in the three Tests he played the Lions won twice and drew once. Between 1955 and 1962 he was capped 33 times on the wing and scored 12 tries with his fast elusive running. A brilliant scholar, he also was the Scottish long jump champion but after his early death at the age of 42 he will be best remembered for his outstanding qualities as a captain.

Cecil SMITH (USA)

POLO

Cecil Smith. b. 14 Feb 1904 Llano County, Texas.

A contender for the title of greatest polo player of all time, he was rated at 10 goals longer than any player in history - 25 years 1938-62 (also in 1934). He was a bit of an anomaly in the early years of polo, as he was not wealthy . He grew up on a ranch and worked stock as a young boy, learning many aspects of a rodeo cowboy's life. In 1924 he was hired by a local horse-buyer to level out a polo field and train his ponies. There he discovered his abilities and within ten years he had achieved his 10-goal rating. He once played on the first 40-goal team in polo history, with Tommy Hitchcock, Stewart Iglehart and Mike Phipps. Despite living most of his life in San Antonio, Texas, Smith played most his career with the Oak Brook club of Illinois and the Old Westbury Club of Long Island. He has spent most of his life in the career he first learned, as a rancher, breeding and raising horses. For many years he battled for ratings, handicaps, and team match-ups with the Eastern, aristocratic polo establishment because he was not 'one of them'. In the end, he simply outplayed them all.

Dean SMITH (USA)

BASKETBALL

Dean Edwards Smith. b. 28 Feb 1931 Emporia, Kansas.

Smith played basketball at the University of Kansas 1949-53 under the legendary coach Forrest 'Phog' Allen. Having been a reserve on the 1952 NCAA Championship team, he served in the US Air Force and was an assistant coach at the US Air Force Academy in 1957-8. In 1959 he moved to the University of North Carolina as an assistant to Frank McGuire, whom he succeeded as head coach in 1962 when McGuire moved to the NBA. In the last 30 years at the University of North Carolina, Smith has established a collegiate basketball programme second to none. Through 1993 he is second among college coaches (to Adolph Rupp) in career victories, and first in NCAA victories, having qualified for the NCAA tournament for 19 consecutive years, made the final six for 13 consecutive years and won in 1982 and 1993. He coached the US Olympic team to a gold medal in 1976 at Montreal. His programme is noted for the excellent graduation rate (c. 97%) among his players.

Doug SMITH (UK)

HORSE RACING

Douglas Smith. b. 21 Nov 1917 Shottesbrooke, Nr Maidenhead, d. 11 Apr 1989 (when he committed suicide at his home in Suffolk).

Champion jockey in Britain in 1954-6, 1958-9, in all he rode 3111 winners, 1931-67, with a highest season's total of 173 in 1947, when runner-up to Gordon Richards. The son of a Berkshire farmer, he won prizes in the show ring before starting his career as an apprentice jockey, with his brother Eph, to Major Fred Sneyd. His first ride was at Salisbury in 1931, and his first winner in the same race a year later. His first classic success was on the King's *Hypericum* in the 1946 1000 Guineas, when retained by Cecil Boyd-Rochfort. He won the 2000 Guineas on *Pall Mall* in 1958 and the 1000 Guineas on *Petite Etoile* in 1959. He excelled on stayers, notably the great *Alycidon*, and won the Cesarewitch five times. He trained in Newmarket 1968-79, winning the Oaks with *Sleeping Partner* 1969, and then became a bloodstock agent. His brother **Eph** (1915-72) rode 2313 winners 1930-65, including three classics, the 2000 Guineas and Derby on *Blue Peter* in 1939, and the St Leger on *Premonition* 1953.

G O SMITH (UK)

FOOTBALL

Gilbert Oswald Smith. b. 25 Nov 1872 Croydon, d. 6 Dec 1943 Lymington, Hampshire.

The greatest centre-forward of his day. Educated at Charterhouse and Oxford University he was the quintessential amateur in the Corinthian mould. He won the first of his 20 England caps (1893-1901) while still at Oxford and was a member of the Old Carthusian team which won the FA Amateur Cup in 1897. He was also a fine cricketer, winning his blue at Oxford and scoring a century against Cambridge in 1896. He also played cricket for Hertfordshire and Surrey. For many years he was joint Headmaster of Ludgrove Preparatory School with another England soccer international, William Oakley. Although lacking speed and a robust physique, he possessed a lethal shot and was a consummate tactician.

Harvey SMITH (UK)

EQUESTRIAN

Robert Harvey Smith. b. 29 Dec 1938 Bingley, Yorkshire.

A Yorkshire farmer, he recorded his first major show jumping win in 1958 with *Farmer's Boy*. He went on to win the King George V Gold Cup in 1970 and set records for seven wins in the John Player Trophy and four in the British Jumping Derby. Smith took part in both the 1968 and 1972 Olympics but failed to win a medal. He earned a World bronze medal in 1970, European silver in 1967 and 1971, and bronze in 1963.

His worldwide fame is due as much to his

fighting spirit and his no-holds-barred approach to his sport as to his prowess as a rider. He also wrote several popular books about equestrian sport and now trains National Hunt horses. His son **Robert** (b. 12 Jun 1961) became the youngest ever winner of the King George V Gold Cup in 1979.

Ian SMITH (UK)

RUGBY UNION

Ian Scott Smith. b. 31 Oct 1903 Melbourne, Australia, d. 18 Sep 1972 Edinburgh.

Although educated at a soccer school (Winchester), he became the leading international try scorer after he concentrated on rugby at Oxford. After winning his blue in 1923 he went on to win 32 caps on the wing for Scotland between 1924 and 1933 and set a host of scoring records. On his international début against Wales in 1924 he scored three tries and the following season he scored four tries against both Wales and France. In all, he scored a record 24 tries for Scotland but on the Lions tour of South Africa in 1924 he failed to cross the line in the two Tests he played. He captained Scotland in his last season (1933) when they won all three matches, their first Triple Crown for eight years.

Jeff SMITH (UK)

MOTO-CROSS

Jeffrey Vincent Smith. b. 14 Oct 1934 Colne.

World 500cc moto-cross champion in 1964-5. A qualified engineer, he had started scrambling at 20 and won the first of his nine ACU Stars scrambling titles at 500cc in 1955, having won the trials titles in 1953 and 1954, riding for BSA virtually throughout his career. He was awarded the MBE in 1970 and later moved to Canada to pursue his engineering career.

Jimmy SMITH (USA)

BOWLING

Jimmy Smith. né James Mellilo. b. 19 Sep 1882 Brooklyn, New York, d. 21 Apr 1946.

The top bowler of the early part of the 20th century. He combined an effortless style with great ability to teach bowling. Between 1915 and 1925 he was considered the match game king of the sport. From 1910 to 1915 and again from 1916 to 1925, he made nationwide exhibition tours, bowling several thousand matches during the tour.

John SMITH (USA)

WRESTLING

John William Smith. b. 9 Aug 1965 Del City, Oklahoma.

America's most successful international freestyle wrestler, with Olympic titles in 1988 and 1992 and world titles in 1987, 1989-91, all at featherweight (62kg). He began wrestling at the age of six, and won two NCAA championships while at Oklahoma State. His first major international victory was at the Goodwill Games in 1986. He defended that title in 1990 and was also Pan-American champion in 1987 and 1991. From 1986 to 1990, Smith's international record was 150-3. In 1990 he became the first and only wrestler to win the Sullivan Award.
He is the younger brother of Lee Roy Smith, who helped coach John and who was also an NCAA champion and finished 2nd in the world championships in 1983.

Margaret SMITH (Aus)

TENNIS

Margaret Jean Smith. b. 16 Jul 1942 Albury, New South Wales. Later Court.

The winner of a record 62 championships in Grand Slam tournaments. She won 24 singles (11 Australian, 5 USA, 5 French, 3 Wimbledon), 19 women's doubles (8 Australian, 5 USA, 4 French, 2 Wimbledon), 19 mixed doubles (8 USA, 5 Wimbledon, 4 French, 2 Australian).
She also won a further 26 major titles at the Italian, German and South African Championships (9 singles, 8 women's doubles, 9 mixed doubles).
Her phenomenal record of successes exceeds anything achieved by any other player, either man or woman, and several

judges rate her as the finest woman player of all-time. Her first major victory was in the 1960 Australian singles and in 1963 she uniquely won a mixed doubles Grand Slam with Ken Fletcher. In 1970 she became only the second woman in history to take a singles Grand Slam.
Superbly athletic, she had a powerful serve and the strength of her volleying brought a new dimension to the women's game. Her incredible record might have been even greater but she did not play in 1967 because of staleness. In October of that year she married Australian Barry Court. She also missed the 1972 and 1974 seasons when she was having children and when she became pregnant for a third time in 1977 she retired. She was awarded the MBE in recognition of her achievements.

Mike SMITH (UK)

CRICKET

Michael John Knight Smith. b. 30 Jun 1933 Westcotes, Leicestershire.

A free-scoring batsman in county cricket for Leicestershire 1951-55 and then for Warwickshire, whom he captained from 1957-67. He had won a blue at Oxford University 1954-6, scoring a century in the University match each year, including 201* in 1954. He scored 1000 runs in a season 19 times, with six over 2000 and a peak of 3245 at 57.94 in 1959. At Test level he did not quite establish himself as a batsman, although he was a highly respected captain of England for 25 matches 1963-6, especially successful as a tourist.
He was also a brilliant short-leg fielder and was the last man to double as an international for England at cricket and rugby, at which he won one cap as a fly-half in 1956. He played for Leicester and formed a notable half-back combination at Oxford with the Welsh scrum-half Onllwyn Brace. Awarded the OBE.
50 Tests 1958-72: 2278 runs at 31.63, 3 100s HS 121; 1 wicket; 53 catches.
First-class 1951-76: 39,832 runs at 41.84, 69 100s HS 204; 5 wickets; 593 catches.

Robin SMITH (UK)

CRICKET

Robin Arnold Smith. b. 13 Sep 1963 Durban, South Africa.

Smith was marked out as a potentially great batsman from an early age, and is fulfilling that promise. A brilliant all-round athlete, rugby player and cricketer at school, he followed his elder brother **Chris** (b.15 Oct 1958) in leaving South Africa to play for Hampshire and qualify for England. Chris played in 8 Tests 1983-6, but Robin has established himself as one of the world's best batsmen and an England regular from his début in 1987. Two years later against Australia, while the side was disintegrating around him, he scored 553 runs at 61.44. He hits a cricket ball with a ferocious power, particularly strong in square driving and cutting. That power was shown to best effect in his marvellous 167* in a one-day international against Australia in 1993. He played for Natal 1980-5 and for Hampshire from 1982.
40 Tests 1987-93: 2954 runs at 49.23, 8 100s HS 148; 29 catches.*
58 One-day Ints: 2068 runs at 42.20; 4 100s HS 167; 18 catches.*
First-class 1980-93: 14,806 runs at 44.59, 35 100s HS 209; 12 wickets at 57.58, BB 2-11; 156 catches.*

Stan SMITH (USA)

TENNIS

Stanley Roger Smith. b. 14 Dec 1946 Pasadena, California.

Although winning only two Grand Slam singles titles he formed a brilliant doubles partnership with Bob Lutz. They first teamed up at the University of Southern California and while still students enjoyed an outstanding year in 1968 when they won the US Inter-Collegiate, US Clay Court and both the US National and Open Championships. They won the US Open three more times (1974, 1978, 1980) and lost only one of the 12 Davis Cup doubles they played together between 1968 and 1979. They also won the Australian title in 1970 and are the only pair to have won a

US National title on all four surfaces - clay, grass, hard and indoor.
After winning the first Masters title in 1970, Smith won the US title and was a finalist at Wimbledon in 1971, and won the 1972 Wimbledon singles when he beat Nastase in a classic final. Possibly his greatest singles performance came later in 1972 when he met Nastase again in the Davis Cup final in Bucharest. Faced with a hostile crowd, biased officials and some appalling behaviour by his opponent, he claimed a second win against the Romanian in the opening rubber and put the US on their way to an unexpected victory. His overall Davis Cup record was to win 15 of 19 singles and 19 of 22 doubles 1968-79. As a founder member of the Association of Tennis Professionals he was obliged to support the Wimbledon boycott in 1973 and was unable to defend his title, but he returned in 1974 and made his 19th and final appearance in 1983. Standing 1.93m *6'4"* he had the ideal physique for the serve-volley game and his strength in this department more than compensated for the lack of penetration of his ground strokes. In his career he won 39 singles and 61 doubles tournaments.

Tommie SMITH (USA)

ATHLETICS

Tommie C Smith. b. 12 Jun 1944 Acworth, Texas.

A claimant to the title of the world's greatest ever 200m runner, and just as good at 400m on his rare attempts at that distance. He ran the fastest time ever recorded for 220 yards, with 19.5 on a straight course at San Jose in 1966, improving his own world record of 20.0 run there in 1965. Around a full turn he set further world records with 20.0 for 220y in 1966 and 19.8 (19.83 on auto timing) when he won the Olympic title at 200m in 1968. He beat Lee Evans by five yards to set world records at 400m 44.5 and 440y 44.8 at San Jose in 1967, and also contributed a 43.8 leg for the first ever sub 3-minute 4 x 400m relay time, run by the USA against the Commonwealth in 1966.
Smith had a phenomenal ability to change pace at high speed - his 'Tommie-Jet gear' - and many observers believe that he never reached his peak, particularly at the one lap. His career was blighted by his principled black power protest on the victory rostrum at the 1968 Olympics, following which he was expelled from the Olympic village. At 200m/220y he was AAU champion in 1967-8 and both NCAA and World Student Games champion in 1967, also winning a silver medal in the latter at 100m.
After graduation from San Jose State University in 1969, Smith played three seasons of pro football with the Cincinnati Bengals and also ran some pro track. He became professor and athletic director at Oberlin College and later in Los Angeles.
Other bests, all in 1966: 100y 9.3, 100m 10.1, long jump 7.90m.

Willie SMITH (UK)

BILLIARDS

William Smith. b. 25 Jan 1886 Darlington, Co. Durham, d. 2 Jun 1982 Leeds, Yorkshire.

The winner of the world billiards title in 1920 and 1923, on the only two occasions he played in the championships. Although the latter was his last major win, he remained a force in the game during the dominant years of Inman, Davis and Lindrum. The son of a sporting journalist, he was declared a professional at the age of 15 for accepting a modest amount of travel expenses after playing in a Middlesbrough club. He made a sensational London début in 1912 with a break of 736 to beat the renowned Tom Newman and his score of 2743 against Newman in 1928 is often considered to be the finest break ever made as it did not include any repetitive cannons and was compiled solely by all-round play. He toured Australia in 1929 for a series of matches against Walter Lindrum and was instrumental in persuading the Australian to come to England after the death of his young wife.
Smith was also an outstanding snooker player, losing to Joe Davis in the final of the World Championship in 1934 and

1936. Never a relaxed character, he became increasingly morose and awkward as the years passed and was constantly at loggerheads with the governing bodies, retaining a cynical view of their capabilities until his death at the age of 96.

Vasiliy SMYSLOV (USSR)

CHESS

Vasiliy Vasiliyevich Smyslov. b. 24 Mar 1921 Moscow.

He beat Mikhail Botvinnik to win the world chess title in 1957, but lost it in the re-match a year later. Joint USSR champion 1949, he achieved grandmaster status in 1950. In 1982 at the age of 61 he became the oldest ever to qualify for the Candidates tournament, but lost in the final to Anatoliy Karpov.

Sam SNEAD (USA)

GOLF

Samuel Jackson Snead. b. 27 May 1912 Hot Springs, Virginia.

One of the greatest ever golf champions, but perhaps best known for the tournament he never won, the US Open, although he finished second three times. He won every other major title and a record 81 PGA Tour events from 1936 to 1965. A tremendous natural athlete, he possessed a fluid, almost lyrical, natural swing, which he used to become a very long hitter and one of the best strikers in the history of the game.
It is estimated that Snead won between 135-160 titles worldwide, a total surpassed only by Roberto de Vicenzo. Snead won the Vardon Trophy in 1938, 1949-50, and 1955 on the US Tour. He was US leading money-winner in 1938, and 1949-50. He played on 8 Ryder Cup teams between 1937 and 1959 (won 10 matches, lost 2, halved 1). In 1979 he played in the Quad Cities Open on the regular tour and shot his age twice, posting scores of 67 and 66 in that event. He continued to have success into the mid-80s on the senior tour. Major victories: Masters 1949, 1952, 1954; British Open 1946; PGA 1942, 1949, 1951. His nephew J C Snead played on the US Ryder Cup teams of 1971, 1973 and 1975.

Peter SNELL (NZ)

ATHLETICS

Peter George Snell. b. 17 Dec 1938 Opunake.

The surprise winner of the Olympic 800m in 1960, he not only retained his title in 1964 but also won gold at 1500m, winning both events confidently and easily. He won the Commonwealth 880 yards and 1 mile double in 1962 and set the following world records: 800m 1:44.3 and 880y 1:45.1 in 1962, 1000m 2:16.6 (1964), 1 mile 3:54.4 in 1962 and 3:54.03 in 1964, as well as at 4 x 1 mile with the NZ team in 1961.
Snell's 800m record took an amazing 1.4 seconds off the six and a half year-old record of Roger Moens, although he had given notice of his potential with a 1:44.8 relay leg in 1960. His first mile record, which took 0.1 off Herb Elliott's mark, was his first ever sub-four and was run on a grass track at Wanganui. A very strong runner, at his best he seemed invincible. NZ champion at 880y 1959-60, 1962 and 1964, 1 mile 1959, cross-country 1962.
A good tennis player, he did not take up running seriously until he was 18, from when he was coached by Arthur Lydiard. He is now a noted exercise physiologist, living in Dallas, Texas.
Best 1500m 3:37.6 (1964).

Duke SNIDER (USA)

BASEBALL

Edwin Donald Snider. b. 19 Sep 1926 Los Angeles.

Snider was a centerfielder and top power-hitter for the Brooklyn Dodgers. He was one of the New York triumvirate of great centerfielders in the 1950s, sharing the honour with Mickey Mantle and Willie Mays. He hit over 40 home runs in five consecutive seasons 1953-7 and batted over .300 in seven seasons. In both the 1952 and 1955 World Series, he hit four home runs, the only man to accomplish that feat twice.
Career 1947-64: 2116 hits Avg. .295, HR 407; RBI 1333. Best seasons HR/RBI: 1953: 42/126, 1954: 40/130, 1955: 42/136, 1956: 43/101, 1957: 40/92.

John SNOW (UK)

CRICKET

John Augustine Snow. b. 13 Oct 1941 Peopleton, Worcestershire.

England's best fast bowler in a period when he was often the only top-class fast bowler in the team. He played for Sussex from 1961 to 1977, and took over 100 wickets in a season in 1965, in which year he made his England début, and in 1966, but in later years tended to reserve his best for the big occasions. He had a smooth, high action, generating genuine pace despite his relatively slim build. He could be a useful tail-end batsman, notably when he made 59* and put on 128 for the last wicket with Ken Higgs against West Indies at The Oval in 1966. He made his highest score of 73 against India at Lord's in 1971, but was excluded from the next Test for colliding with Sunil Gavaskar. His autobiography was appropriately titled *Cricket Rebel.*

49 Tests 1965-76: 772 runs at 13.54, HS 73; 202 wickets at 26.66, BB 7-40; 16 catches.

9 One-day Ints: 9 runs at 4.50, HS 9; 14 wickets at 16.57, BB 4-11; 1 catch.*

First-class 1961-77: 4832 runs at 14.17, HS 73; 1174 wickets at 22.72, BB 8-87; 125 catches.*

Betty SNOWBALL (UK)

CRICKET

Elizabeth Alexandra Snowball. b. 1906, d. 1988.

As a wicket-keeper Betty Snowball was likened to Bert Oldfield by the Australian press. She claimed 21 victims (13 catches, 8 stumpings) in her ten Tests, including four stumpings in an innings for England against Australia at Sydney in 1935. She was also a prolific opening bat, making the highest score by an England Test player of 189 in 222 minutes, including 22 boundaries, against New Zealand at Christchurch in 1935. In that match she contributed heavily to a record 2nd-wicket partnership of 235 with Molly Hide. Snowball was the England vice-captain from 1934 to 1948 and also represented her native Scotland at both lacrosse and squash.

Gary SOBERS (Bar)

CRICKET

(Sir) Garfield St Aubrun Sobers. b. 28 Jul 1936 Bay Land, Bridgetown.

The world's greatest ever all-round cricketer. A year after making his first-class début for Barbados, Sobers first played for the West Indies as an orthodox slow left-arm bowler at the age of 17, batting at No.9. Very soon his batting blossomed, so that just four years later against Pakistan at Kingston he scored 365 not out, exceeding the world Test record score that Len Hutton had set nearly 20 years earlier. In this series against Pakistan Sobers scored 824 runs in the 5 Tests at 137.33. He displayed his glorious batting all round the world through the 1960s and into the 1970s, twice averaging more than 100 in a Test series against England: 709 runs at 101.28 in the West Indies in 1960, and 722 at 103.14 in England in 1966. He played for South Australia for three seasons 1961-4, and at that time added fast-medium left-arm bowling to his repertoire, so successfully that it was with this style that he gained many of his wickets, three times obtaining 20 or more in Test series in the 1960s. His all-round brilliance extended also to his fielding, initially anywhere in the field, and later as a close-in catcher. An obvious choice to succeed Frank Worrell as captain of the West Indies, he led them for 39 successive Tests 1965-72. He set a wondrous example but was not as effective a captain as he perhaps might have been, veering between over-generosity, as when he declared and allowed England to win at Port-of-Spain in 1968, and over-defensiveness. In 1968 he came to play for Nottinghamshire and there he was an inspiration until 1974, captaining them in four of these seasons. This delightful man was knighted for services to cricket in 1975.

93 Tests 1954-74: 8032 runs at 57.78, 26 100s HS 365; 235 wickets at 34.03, BB 6-73; 110 catches.*

1 One-day Int: 1 wicket; 1 catch.

First-class 1953-74: 28,315 runs at 54.87, 86 100s HS 365; 1043 wickets at 27.74, BB 9-49; 407 catches.*

SÓCRATES (Bra)

FOOTBALL

Sócrates Brasileiro Sampaio de Sousa Vieira de Oliveira. b. 19 Feb 1954 Belem.

He scored 22 goals in 60 international appearances for Brazil and played in the 1982 and 1986 World Cup competitions. He played for Flamengo and was South American Player of the Year in 1983, but made little impact when he came to Europe to play for Fiorentina in Italy.

Magnar SOLBERG (Nor)

BIATHLON

Magnar Solberg. b. 4 Feb 1937 Soknedal.

The first man to win two individual Olympic gold medals at the biathlon, winning at 20km in 1968 and 1972. His first win came when as a 31-year-old policeman he was a virtual unknown. He added a silver medal on the Norwegian relay team in 1968. In the World Championships he took bronze at 20km in 1969 and 1971, and relay silver each year 1969-71.

David SOLE (UK)

RUGBY UNION

David Michael Barclay Sole. b. 8 May 1962 Aylesbury, Bucks.

By leading Scotland in 1990 to only the third Grand Slam in their history, David Sole joined the immortals of Scottish rugby. A regular in the front row since 1986, he took over the captaincy from Finlay Calder in 1990 and led Scotland to their Grand Slam success in his first season as captain. He announced his retirement after the 1992 game against Wales but was persuaded to lead Scotland on their 1992 tour of Australia, where Sole had earlier played in all three Tests for the 1989 Lions. Having won 44 caps and captained Scotland a record 25 times he finally retired after the Australian tour.

John SOLOMON (UK)

CROQUET

John William Solomon. b. 22 Nov 1931 Wandsworth, London.

The most successful and possibly the greatest croquet player of all-time. He made his tournament debut in 1948 while still a schoolboy at Charterhouse and went on to win 31 major British events. Between 1951 and 1972 he won the Open championship, the men's championship and the men's doubles ten times each and the mixed doubles once. He also won the President's Cup on nine occasions, 1955, 1957-9, 1962-4, 1968 and 1971, and was a four-time winner of the Champion of Champions tournament. After first representing England in New Zealand in 1950, at the age of 19, he went on to play in a record 25 Test matches over five tours and captained England in Australia in 1969. Some traditionalists held the view that his play was rather too adventurous but his unsurpassed record provides undeniable proof of his abilities.

Javier SOTOMAYOR (Cuba)

ATHLETICS

Javier Sotomayor Sanabria. b. 13 Oct 1967 Limonar, Matanzas.

A high jump prodigy, he set world age bests each year from 2.17m at 15 in 1983 and an amazing 2.33 in 1984 at 16 through to a world junior record 2.36 in 1986, and world records at the age of 20, 2.43 in 1988, and 21, 2.44 in 1989. The latter was the first ever 8-foot jump. He advanced that to 2.45 in 1993. He also set a world indoor record 2.43 in 1989.
At 1.95m tall he is ideally built for a high jumper, but has suffered from injuries which restricted him to 9th in 1987 and 2nd in 1991 at World Championships, but after Cuba had boycotted previous Games he earned his due reward with Olympic gold in 1992. He was World Junior champion in 1986, won the Pan-American title in 1987 and 1991, the World Student Games in 1989, and World Indoors in 1989 and 1993. He cleared 2.30m or better in 130 meetings (44 at 2.35 or more) from 1984 to the end of July 1993.
A graduate of Havana Institute of PE, he is a master technician, with a very fast, head-on approach. Married high jumper Maria del Carmen Garcia (1.90m 1990) in 1989.

Graeme SOUNESS (UK)

FOOTBALL

Graeme James Souness. b. 6 May 1953 Edinburgh.

A masterly midfield player whose precision passing was a feature of his game, although he was thought by many to adopt an unnecessarily aggressive attitude. Initally an apprentice with Tottenham Hotspur, he was transferred to Middlesbrough in 1972 for £30,000 without ever playing a League game for Spurs, and helped them win promotion to the First Division in 1974. In 1978 he moved to Liverpool and became a key player in the brilliant team which won the European Cup (1978, 1981, 1984), the Football League (1979-80, 1982-84) and the Football League Cup (1981-84). In June 1984 he signed for Sampdoria in Italy, but returned home in 1986 to become player-manager of Rangers, whom he took to the Scottish League Championship in 1987, 1989 and 1990. In 1991 he took over as manager of Liverpool and won the FA Cup in 1992 after undergoing heart surgery, but by their own high standards the club have not fared well under his stewardship.
After winning Scottish International honours at Schoolboy, Youth and Under-23 level, he went on to win 54 senior caps between 1975 and 1986.

Warren SPAHN (USA)

BASEBALL

Warren Edward Spahn. b. 23 Apr 1921 Buffalo, New York.

Spahn is possibly the greatest left-handed pitcher ever. He pitched mostly for the Boston/Milwaukee Braves, missing 1943-5 due to the war. In 13 of his 21 full seasons, he won over 20 games, a major league record for one league. He was a high-kicking pitcher with a good fastball, but he had control of multiple pitches.
In the early 1950s, he and Johnny Sain were the mainstays of an otherwise mediocre Braves pitching staff, which became immortalised by the jingle, 'Spahn and Sain/And pray for rain'. Spahn pitched two no-hitters in his career. He loved pitching and after he was unable to make it in the majors, he pitched in Mexico and the minor leagues until 1967.
Career pitching 1942-65: ERA 3.08; W-L 363-245, SO 2583. Best seasons: 1947: 21-10; 1949: 21-14; 1950: 21-17; 1951: 22-14; 1953: 23-7; 1954: 21-12; 1956: 20-11; 1957: 21-11; 1958: 22-11; 1959: 21-15; 1960: 21-10; 1961: 21-13; 1963: 23-7.

Walter SPANGHERO (Fra)

RUGBY UNION

Walter Spanghero. b. 21 Dec 1943 Parra-sur-l'Hers, Aude.

Playing in three different forward positions, he won 51 caps between 1964 and 1973 and in seven of these matches he played alongside his brother, **Claude** (b. 5 Jun 1948, 22 caps in all). After publishing a book *Rugby au Coeur* in 1970 which was critical of the selectors, he was out of favour for a while but was recalled to the team in 1971. After France had gone 10 matches without a win Spanghero was appointed captain for the 1972 match against England and led his country to a stunning 37-12 victory in the last international played at Colombes Stadium. He retained the captaincy until his retirement in 1973. He toured South Africa in 1964 and 1967, and captained the French team in Australia in 1972.
Despite his huge physique he was exceptionally fast and is rated as one of the greatest-ever French forwards. He played for R.C.N.

Boris SPASSKY (USSR)

CHESS

Boris Vasiliyevich Spassky. b. 30 Jan 1937 Leningrad.

He was a boy prodigy at chess and achieved international master status in 1953 and grandmaster in 1955, when he was World Junior champion. He studied journalism at Leningrad University. He beat Mikhail Tal to win the Candidates tournament in 1965, but narrowly lost to Tigran Petrosyan for the world title in 1966. After a Candidates win in 1968 he

became world champion, defeating Petrosyan in 1969.
After losing his title to Fischer in 1972 he drifted into comparative obscurity, becoming a French citizen and falling in the world rankings to 99th place by the time that Fischer made his dramatic comeback in a series of games against him for what the promoters billed as 'The World Championship of Chess'. He was USSR champion in 1961 and 1973.

Tris SPEAKER (USA)

BASEBALL

Tristram E Speaker. b. 4 Apr 1888 Hubbard, Texas, d. 8 Dec 1958 Lake Whitney, Texas.

One of the first players inducted into the Hall of Fame, where his plaque reads, 'The greatest centerfielder of his day'. He played mostly with the Boston Red Sox 1907-15 and the Cleveland Indians 1916-26, including being player-manager there 1919-26. Other than his first two years and 1919, he batted over .300 in every season, and his career average ranks him 6th equal all-time. He interrupted Ty Cobb's 12 years leading the American League in hitting 1907-19 by taking top place at .386 in 1916.
Early in his career he was also a top base stealer, stealing over 20 bases every year from 1909-18. He was also known for his prowess as an outfielder and led Boston's legendary outfield of Speaker, Duffy Lewis, and Harry Hooper.
Career 1907-28: 3515 hits Avg. .345 HR: 117; RBI 1528; SB 433. Best seasons: 1925: .389; 1012: .383, 222 hits, 53 doubles; 1916: .386, 211 hits; 1920: .388, 50 doubles; 1923: .380, 59 doubles; 1926: 52 doubles.

Freddie SPENCER (USA)

MOTOR CYCLING

Freddie Burdette Spencer. b. 20 Dec 1961 Shreveport, Louisiana.

In 1985, riding for Honda, he became the first man ever to win the 250cc and 500c world motorcycling titles in the same year. Also 500cc world champion in 1983, between 1982 and 1985 he had 27 Grand Prix wins, 20 at 500cc and 7 at 250cc. Surprisingly he did not win another Grand Prix race after his double triumph.
He started dirt track racing at the age of six and as a teenager established himself in the USA before making his Grand Prix début in 1980.

John SPENCER (UK)

SNOOKER

John Spencer. b. 18 Sep 1935 Radcliffe, Lancashire.

Having played snooker as a boy, he did not play from the age of 18 to 28. Then he succeeded in winning a series of money matches, and was persuaded to enter the 1964 English Amateur Championship. He lost in the final, as he did in 1965, but he won in 1966, when he was also runner-up in the World Amateur. In 1969 he entered the World Professional Championship, played that year for the first time since 1951 on a knock-out basis, and he won. A period of great success followed, with Pot Black wins in 1970-1 and 1976, and the World title again in 1971 and 1977. It was, however, a major shock when he was beaten in the 1972 final by Alex Higgins. His last major success was when he was a member of the England World Cup winning team in 1981.

Michael SPINKS (USA)

BOXING

Michael Spinks. b. 13 Jul 1956 St Louis, Missouri.

In 1976 the brothers **Leon** (b. 11 Jul 1953 St Louis) and Michael Spinks both won gold medals at the Montreal Olympics, Leon at light-heavyweight and Michael at middleweight. At the time Leon was much the better known, although Michael had won the 1976 Golden Gloves Association of America title.
After turning professional Leon won the world heavyweight title when he defeated Muhammad Ali in 1978, but he lost the rematch and two other world title fights. Michael Spinks went on to enjoy the superior career. Early on he won all his bouts

but some said he didn't fight enough to make real progress. However, he won the WBA light-heavyweight championship in 1981 by defeating Eddie Mustafa Muhammad and in early 1983 he won a much ballyhooed unification title fight with WBC champion, Dwight Muhammad Qawi (né Braxton). In 1985 Spinks outpointed Larry Holmes to win the IBF world heavyweight championship, becoming the first reigning light-heavyweight champion to win that title. In 1988 Spinks fought a bout with Mike Tyson in a heavyweight unification fight, but was knocked out in 91 seconds and promptly retired. It was the only loss of his career.
Career record: W - 31 (21), L - 1, D - 0.

Mark SPITZ (USA)

SWIMMING

Mark Andrew Spitz. b. 10 Feb 1950 Modesto, California.

Spitz set a record for any sport when, in Munich in 1972, he won seven gold medals at one Olympic Games. Three of these were in relays, and all were in new world records. In all he set 26 world records at individual events 1967-72 (number and bests at each event): freestyle 100m (3) 51.22, 200m (4) 1:52.78, 400m (3) 4:07.7; butterfly 100m (7) 54.27, 200m (9) 2:00.70; all of these bests except for the 400m freestyle were set in Munich. He also set six world records on relay teams and a US record for 100m backstroke with 57.70 in 1972.
His triumph in Munich was partially inspired by his determination to make up for his disappointment of four years earlier when he had been strongly fancied to take six gold medals, but ended with two relay golds, a silver at 100m butterfly and a bronze at 100m freestyle. In his final race, the 200m butterfly, he was the current world record holder and fastest in qualifying, but, his confidence shattered and tired from an exhaustive programme, he finished last. It was fitting that this event was the first of his 'golden surge' in 1972.
Coached by George Harris at the Santa Clara Swimming Club from 1964 and at Indiana University by Doc Councilman, Spitz won eight NCAA titles in 1969-72 and in all he won 24 AAU titles. His first international titles were the four gold medals that he won at the Maccabiah Games in 1965. He also won five golds, 100 and 200m butterfly and three relays, at the 1967 Pan-American Games. Sullivan Award winner 1971.
He capitalised successfully on his Olympic fame following his graduation in 1972, and in 1991 made a return to competition with the stated aim of making the 1992 Olympic team, but despite his best endeavours found that he could not match swimmers half his age.

Frederick SPOFFORTH (Aus)

CRICKET

Frederick Robert Spofforth. b. 9 Sep 1853 Balmain, Sydney, d. 4 Jun 1926 Long Ditton, Surrey, England.

'The Demon' was so named for his bowling feats in the early Test matches, when at various times he was the leading wicket taker. He started his career as an out-and-out fast bowler, adding variations of pace and break. In his second Test at Melbourne in January 1879, he had innings analyses of 6-48 and 7-62, and the former included the first hat-trick in Tests. He did even better at The Oval in 1882 when he became the first bowler to take 14 wickets in a Test match, with 7-31 and 7-40. His record on tours to England in first-class matches was exceptional, including 97 wickets at 11.00 in 1878, 157 at 13.24 in 1882, and 207 at 12.82 in 1884. He took 764 wickets at 6.04 and 763 at 5.49 in all matches of the Australians' long international tours in 1878 in five countries and in 1880.
He played for New South Wales 1874-88 and after his fifth tour in 1886 settled in England, playing occasionally for Derbyshire as well as club cricket for Hampstead, and becoming a very successful businessman.
18 Tests 1877-87: 217 runs at 9.43, HS 50; 94 wickets at 18.41, BB 7-44; 11 catches.
First-class 1874-97: 1928 runs at 9.88, HS 56; 853 wickets at 14.95, BB 9-18; 83 catches.

Ken STABLER (USA)

AMERICAN FOOTBALL
Kenneth Michael Stabler. b. 25 Dec 1945 Foley, Alabama.

The greatest left-handed quarterback in NFL history, Stabler played collegiately at the University of Alabama and in the NFL achieved most of his fame as quarterback of the Oakland Raiders from 1970-9, but he finished his career with a few years at the Houston Oilers and New Orleans Saints. Stabler directed the Raiders to AFC Championships in 1974-6 and a Super Bowl Championship in 1976. He was nicknamed 'The Snake' because of his lizard-quick pass release and swiftness of foot. He was also known for his fast lifestyle.
NFL career 1970-84: 27,938 yards from 2270 pass completions, 59.8%, 194 TD.

Jean STABLINSKI (Fra)

CYCLING
Jean Stablinski. b. 21 May 1932 Thun-Saint-Ammand.

A superb all-round cyclist whose record would have been better had Jacques Anquetil not been riding at the same time. He was world professional road champion in 1962 after his close friend Seamus Elliott had broken away. When Jos Hoevenaars chased Elliott, Stablinski went with him and eventually dropped the other two. Shortly before the finish Stablinski punctured, but he was allowed to borrow a spectator's bike and rode that across the line to win his only world title. Other major victories: Vuelta à España 1958, Paris-Brussels 1963, Tour of Henninger Tower 1965, Amstel Gold Race 1966.

Amos STAGG (USA)

AMERICAN FOOTBALL
Amos Alonzo Stagg. b. 16 Aug 1862 West Orange, New Jersey, d. 17 Mar 1965 Stockton, California.

Stagg played football at Yale while he was studying for the ministry and in 1889 was named to the first All-American football team. He eventually gave up the study of divinity to become a physical educator. In 1893 Stagg came to the University of Chicago and coached there until the mandatory retirement age of 70 in 1932. He coached four undefeated football teams, won seven Western Conference championships and won 255 games, and also coached basketball. In 1933 he was named head coach at the College of the Pacific and in 1943, at age 81, he was selected Coach of the Year. In 1946, Stagg retired as a head coach and served as an assistant coach to one of his sons at Susquehanna College for the next six years. Amazingly he then returned to the West Coast, serving as punting and kicking coach at Stockton Junior College until he retired at age 98 in 1961 after 71 years of college coaching. His career head coaching record of 314-181-35 was unmatched for years until Bear Bryant surpassed his total number of career victories.

Anisoara STANCIU (Rom)

ATHLETICS
Anisoara Stanciu. née Cusmir. b. 28 Jun 1962 Bralia.

She set the first of her four world long jump records at 7.15m in 1982. In 1983 she improved to 7.21, 7.27 and 7.43, the last two in the same competition on 4 June at Bucharest. The next year she became Olympic long jump champion, having already gained silver medals in the 1982 European and 1983 World Championships. She was also World Student Games champion in 1983 after placing second in 1981.

Andy STANFIELD (USA)

ATHLETICS
Andrew William Stanfield. b. 29 Dec 1927 Washington, D.C, d. 15 Jun 1985 Livingston, New Jersey.

He won the Olympic gold medals at 200m and sprint relay in 1952 and the 200m silver medal in 1956, and was AAU champion at 220y in 1949 (also at 100y), 1952 and 1953. He set two world records at 20.6, the first at 220y in 1951 and the second at 200m in 1952. He was AAU indoor champion at 60y in 1950 and long

jump in 1951. While at Seton Hall he was IC4A champion outdoors at 100y 1949-51 and 220y 1951, and indoors at 60y 1949-51 and long jump 1951.
Other bests: 100y 9.5 (1950), 100m 10.3 (1949), 220y hurdles 22.9 (1951), long jump 7.85m (1951).

Willie STARGELL (USA)

BASEBALL
Wilver Dornel Stargell. b. 6 Mar 1940 Earlsboro, Oklahoma.

Stargell played for 21 years with the Pittsburgh Pirates, mostly in the outfield and at first base, and was a great leader of their team in the 1970s after Roberto Clemente's death. He was primarily a power hitter, who twice hit balls out of Dodger Stadium, the only player to accomplish that feat. His greatest season was 1979 when he was voted the MVP and led the Pirates to a World Series victory. He was voted Series MVP as he set Series records of 25 total bases and seven extra base hits. That year he was voted Sportsman of the Year by *The Sporting News* and co-Sportsman of the Year (with Terry Bradshaw) by *Sports Illustrated*. He was elected to the Hall of Fame in his first year of eligibility.
Career 1962-82: 2232 hits Avg. .282, HR 475; RBI 1540. Best seasons: 1971: 48 HR, 125 RBI; 1973: 44 HR, 119 RBI.

Greville STARKEY (UK)

HORSE RACING
Greville Michael William Starkey. b. 21 Dec 1939 Lichfield, Staffordshire.

Winner of five English classics including the Derby on *Shirley Heights* in 1978. He rode his first winner at Pontefract in 1956, when he was apprenticed to H.Thomson Jones, and retired in 1989. He was first jockey to John Oxley 1961-9 and Henry Cecil 1970-4, before a spell as a freelance and then teaming up with Guy Harwood. His highest number of winners in a season was 107 in 1978, and he also reached exactly 100 in 1978 and 103 in 1982-3. He now owns a stud farm in Newmarket.

Bart STARR (USA)

AMERICAN FOOTBALL
Bryan Bartlett Starr. b. 9 Jan 1934 Montgomery, Alabama.

His coach, Vince Lombardi, said he considered Starr the greatest quarterback in football history because he led his team to more championships than any other and that was all that mattered. It is a plausible argument, though many experts consider Johnny Unitas, Joe Montana, Roger Staubach and Otto Graham to have been superior at the position. Starr played in college at the University of Alabama but was only a 17th-round draft choice of the Packers. He struggled for three years until Lombardi became coach in 1959 and handed Starr the starting position. Under Starr, the Packers won six conference championships, five NFL championships and the first two Super Bowls, in both of which Starr was voted the MVP. He played in the Pro Bowl four times and still holds NFL records for most consecutive passes without an interception (294), fewest interceptions in a season (3), and lowest percentage of interceptions in a season (1.2%). In eight NFL Championship and Super Bowl games, he had only two passes intercepted out of 192 attempts. In those games, he completed 59% of his passes, and threw for 14 touchdowns. Starr retired after the 1973 season and later became a head coach in the NFL, coaching the Packers for several years.
NFL career 1956-71: 24,718 yards from 1808 pass completions, 57.4%, 152 TD.

Peter STASTNY (Cs)

ICE HOCKEY
Peter Stastny. b. 18 Sep 1956 Bratislava.

He joined the Czech national team in 1976, starring on a line with his brothers, Marian and Anton. A few months after the 1980 Olympics, Peter and Anton were vacationing in Austria when they contacted representatives of the Québec Nordiques, with whom they had been in contact for over a year. They were prepared to defect, although Marian wished to stay behind. Once in North America,

Stastny established himself as one of the stars of the NHL, and in the 1980s became one of the most consistent scorers in the league. He was traded in 1990 to the New Jersey Devils with whom he played through 1993.
NHL career 1980-93: 954 games, 444 goals, 1221 points. Play-offs: 84 games, 33 goals, 103 points. Best years: 1981/2: 46 goals, 139 points; 1982/3: 47 goals, 124 points. Calder Trophy 1981.

Brian STATHAM (UK)

CRICKET
John Brian Statham. b. 17 Jun 1930 Gorton, Manchester.

A wonderfully accurate fast bowler for England in the 1950s, forming famous partnerships with Frank Tyson and with Fred Trueman. His effectiveness was marked not just by his own fine figures, but by the enormous help that his relentless accuracy gave to his partners. After just one part-season in which he had taken 37 wickets for Lancashire, he was a replacement on the England tour of Australasia in 1950/1, making his Test début against New Zealand. His best Test series figures were 27 wickets at 18.18 against South Africa in 1960 and he exceeded 100 wickets in 13 English seasons, all at an average of 21.63 or better, with a low of 12.29 for his 134 wickets in 1958. In 1963 he held the record for most wickets in Tests for two months, before Trueman overtook him. Nicknamed 'George', he captained Lancashire in 1965-7. Awarded the CBE in 1966.
70 Tests 1951-65: 675 runs at 11.44, HS 38; 252 wickets at 24.84, BB 7-39; 28 catches.
First-class 1950-68: 5424 runs at 10.80, HS 62; 2260 wickets at 16.36, BB 8-34; 230 catches.

Roger STAUBACH (USA)

AMERICAN FOOTBALL
Roger Thomas Staubach. b. 5 Feb 1942 Silverton, Ohio.

'The Dodger' was one of the great quarterbacks in football history. He played collegiately at the US Naval Academy and there as a junior won the Heisman Memorial Trophy, quarterbacking the Midshipmen to second in the national polls and a spot in the Cotton Bowl against number one Texas, who defeated the Navy 28-6. Staubach's senior year saw him hampered by injuries and he failed to win the Heisman again. Because of the five-year service commitment, it was not expected that Staubach would play pro football. But the Dallas Cowboys drafted him and after five years in the Navy, Staubach joined the Cowboys in 1969. Staubach was a back-up for two seasons, but from 1971-9 he was the starting quarterback at Dallas. He led the Cowboys to four Super Bowl appearances, winning in 1972, when he was MVP, and 1978. He was a very accurate passer with a strong arm but was also known for his scrambling abilities. It is possible, had Staubach not missed five years of his prime, that he would have become the greatest quarterback ever.
NFL career 1969-79 : 22,700 yards from 1685 pass completions, 57.0%, 153 TD.

Ernie STAUTNER (USA/Ger)

AMERICAN FOOTBALL
Ernest Stautner. b. 20 Apr 1925 Cham, Germany.

The son of Bavarian immigrants and brought up on a New York farm. After graduating from high school he served in the Marines from 1943-6, before enrolling at Boston College. He earned All-American recognition in his last two years and in 1950 was drafted by the Pittsburgh Steelers, with whom he played his entire NFL career to 1963 as a defensive tackle. He played in nine Pro Bowls. He has became an offensive line coach in the NFL with both the Dallas Cowboys and the Steelers.

Renate STECHER (GDR)

ATHLETICS
Renate Stecher. née Meissner. b. 12 May 1950 Süptitz.

A very powerful sprinter, who achieved a great championships record in the 1970s.

Olympics: 1972 1st 100m and 200m, 2nd 4x100m; 1976 1st 200m and 4x100m, 2nd 100m; Europeans: 1969 1st 4x100m, 2nd 200m; 1971 1st 100m and 200m, 2nd 4x100m; 1974 1st 4x100m, 2nd 100m and 200m. She was European Indoor champion at 60m 1970-2 and 1974, and won the 100m/200m double at the World Student Games in 1970 and European Cup in 1973 and 1975. GDR champion at 100m and 200m 1970-2 and 1974 and at 100m 1975. Her first international success was a gold medal in the sprint relay at the European Juniors in 1966, and at those Championships in 1968 she won silver medals at both sprints and the relay.
At 100m she equalled or bettered the hand-timed record eight times from 11.0 in 1970 to 10.8 in 1973 and set an auto-timed best of 11.07 when she won the 1972 Olympic title by 0.16 sec. She also set three world records at 200m to 22.1 (22.38 auto) in 1973 and seven in relays. Indoors her world records included three at 6.0 (and 6.19 auto) for 50m, and two at 7.1 (7.16 auto) for 60m.
She was coached throughout her career by Horst-Dieter Hille and ran for SC Motor Jena.

Dorothy STEEL (UK)

CROQUET

Dorothy Dyne Steel. b. 1884, Woodsetts, Yorkshire, d. 22 Jan 1965, Biddenham, Bedfordshire.

The greatest woman croquet player of all-time who was the equal of any of her male contemporaries. The daughter of a Yorkshire clergyman, she learned the game on the vicarage lawn, and with her effective but unexciting style she won 4 Open Championships (1923, 1933, 1935-6), 15 women's Championships (8 of them in succession), 5 women's doubles and 7 mixed doubles for a total of 31 titles. She also won the President's Cup six times and she rated her last victory in 1937 as the best of her many fine performances.
She played for England in 1925, 1928 and 1939 but refused to go on the 1927 tour of Australia following a dispute over expenses. After the War, when her hands were crippled by arthritis, she was forced to give up playing but continued to make her presence felt in the game as a notable team manager. DD, as she was always known, spent much of her life at Biddenham, Bedford where she played croquet for the local club and was a keen rider to hounds.

Mavis STEELE (UK)

BOWLS

Mavis M Steele. b. 9 Sep 1928 Kenton, Middlesex.

A world champion bowler and leading administrator of the game. At the World Championships she won six medals: gold in the fours and team event in 1981, three silver (singles and pairs 1973, triples 1981) and one bronze at fours 1985. She won the Commonwealth games bronze medal at triples in 1982 and was runner-up in the World indoor singles in 1989.
She won a total of 11 English titles, including the singles in 1961-2 and 1969, and represented England internationally for 33 successive years. During the latter part of her career she became involved in the administration of the game and served as assistant secretary of the English Women's Bowling Association and as President of the English Women's Indoor Bowling Association in 1989-90. In 1983 she was awarded the MBE for her services to the game.

Les STEERS (USA)

ATHLETICS

Lester LeRoy Steers. b. 16 Jun 1917 Eureka, California.

Steers, who was 1.87m tall and weighed 87kg, set three world records for high jump in 1941, 2.10m, 2.105 and 2.11. He perfected the recently formulated straddle technique and was reported to have cleared half an inch over 7 feet (the first man to do so) in an exhibition in Eugene in February 1941. He was AAU champion in 1939 and 1940 and NCAA winner for the University of Oregon in 1941.

William STEINITZ (Aut)

CHESS
William Steinitz. b. 17 May 1836 Prague, d. 12 Aug 1900 New York.

World chess champion 1866-94, the longest ever reign. He became a full-time player soon after going to study in Vienna in 1858 and represented Austria in the first international match in 1862 in London, to where he moved later that year. His win over Adolf Anderssen in 1866 is recognised as the beginning of his career as world champion, although he did not use that title until 1886, four years after he had moved to New York. A profound thinker, he pioneered a new outlook on strategy. Following his defeat by Emanuel Lasker in 1894 he suffered a nervous breakdown and died as a pauper.

Bill STEINKRAUS (USA)

EQUESTRIAN
William Clark Steinkraus. b. 12 Oct 1925 Cleveland, Ohio.

One of the first members of the American Pony Club before he took up show jumping in 1938. He first joined the US Equestrian Team (USET) in 1951. He was appointed captain of the USET in 1955, holding the post until his retirement in 1972, and later became its president.
His greatest achievement came in 1968 when he became the first US competitor to win an individual gold medal in an Olympic equestrian event, riding *Snowbound* to the show jumping title. He also won team bronze in 1952 and silver in 1960 and 1972, and in all competed at five Olympic Games, being prevented from making a sixth appearance when his horse went lame at the last minute in Tokyo in 1964, and twice won team gold medals at the Pan-American Games. Steinkraus is an accomplished amateur musician and worked as a book editor.

Casey STENGEL (USA)

BASEBALL
Charles Dillon Stengel. b. 30 Jul 1890 Kansas City, Missouri, d. 29 Sep 1975 Glendale, California.

Stengel studied dentistry for three years at Western Dental College but left in 1910 to play minor league baseball. Thus began one of the most colourful baseball careers ever seen. He played fourteen years as a major league outfielder in the National League with five different clubs, and developed a reputation as a prankster, exemplified by the time he caught a bird in the outfield and put it under his hat, only to let it escape when he doffed his cap to the fans. He starred for the New York Giants in the 1922 and 1923 World Series. He began coaching and managing in the minor leagues in 1924 and his first job in the major leagues was in 1934 with the Brooklyn Dodgers, whom he managed until 1943, when he was relegated to the minors again. From 1949 to 1960 he achieved the most dominant tenure of any major league manager ever, taking the New York Yankees to ten American League pennants and seven World Series championships, five of them consecutively 1949-53. He then was named to manage the hapless expansion club, the New York Mets, but could not get them out of the National League cellar. He was the first manager to effectively use platooning and followed his intuition and gambled on the percentages a great deal. He was known for many malapropisms, several of which were uttered during a hysterical testimony recorded during a Senate investigation of major league baseball.
Career 1912-25: 1219 hits Avg .284 HR 60.

Ingemar STENMARK (Swe)

ALPINE SKIING
Ingemar Stenmark. b. 18 Mar 1956 Tärnaby.

With 86 wins (46 giant slalom and 40 slalom) from 287 races, he has easily the greatest record for the World Cup at Alpine skiing. This included a men's record 13 wins in one season in 1978/9, of which ten were part of a record 14 successive giant slalom wins. He was the overall winner each year 1976-8, but, refusing to contest the downhill, was second in 1975 and 1980-4. He won the slalom title eight

times 1975-81 and 1983, and the giant slalom seven times, 1975-6, 1978-81 and 1984.
He had taken the bronze at giant slalom at the 1976 Olympics, and won both his speciality events at the 1978 Worlds and 1980 Olympics, and the slalom at the 1982 World Championships.
A shy man, he was an idol in his native Sweden, regularly beating Björn Borg as his nation's most popular sportsman. Like Borg, he went to live in Monte Carlo.

Galina STEPANOVA (USSR)

SWIMMING

Galina Nikolayevna Stepanova. née Prozumenshchikova. b. 26 Nov 1948 Sevastopol.

A fine breaststroker, who was the first Russian Olympic swimming champion with the 200m in 1964 at the age of 15, adding silver at 200m and bronze at 100m in both 1968 and 1972. Her usual style was to blaze ahead from the gun, but after establishing a clear lead she faded badly in both the 1968 and 1972 Olympics.
She set four world records at the longer distance, from 2:47.7 for 220y in 1964 to 2:40.8 in 1966, and also one at 100m, 1:15.7 in 1966. In that year she won her first European title at 200m, and in 1970 she not only retained that title in a European record 2:40.70, but added a gold for the 100m, included on the European programme for the first time. She won silver medals on the USSR medley relay team in both years. She improved her best time for 100m with a European record 1:14.70 in 1971. USSR champion 100m 1966-8, 200m 1963, 1965-8.

Marina STEPANOVA (USSR/Rus)

ATHLETICS

Marina Stepanova. née Makeyeva. b. 1 May 1950 Meglevo.

In 1986 she won the European 400m hurdles title in 53.32, becoming the oldest woman ever to set a world record. She improved further to 52.94 at Tashkent on 17 September at the age of 36 years 139 days. After sixth place in the 1978 Europeans, she had also set a world record with 54.78 in 1979, in which year she won the European Cup and was second in the World Cup at this event, a new one on the women's programme. A sports instructress, she competed for Leningrad Dynamo. Gave birth to daughter Marina in December 1981.
Other bests: 200m 22.5 (1986), 400m 51.25 (1980), 800m 1:59.8 (1980).

Helen STEPHENS (USA)

ATHLETICS

Helen Herring Stephens. b. 3 Feb 1918 Fulton, Missouri.

Stephens had a phenomenal two and a half year career as a teenager, setting many world records, although none were officially ratified. In her first race, just a few days after her 17th birthday in 1935, she equalled the world indoor best of 6.6 for 50m and beat the great Stella Walsh. She improved to 6.4 twice in 1936.
Outdoors in 1935 she set world marks at 100 yards, running 10.8 three times. At 100m she started with two 11.9s, then an 11.8 and twice 11.6, the second to win the AAU title, and at 200m recorded a 24.4 with 23.9 for 220 yards on a straight track. Finally at Toronto in September she ran times that could scarcely be believed, 10.4 for 100y and 23.2 for 220y. Still only 18, in 1936 she improved at 100m, running 11.5 twice, and won Olympic gold medals at 100m and sprint relay. In the three years 1935-7 she won 14 AAU titles: outdoors at 100m 1935-6, 200m 1935 and at shot and discus in 1936; and indoors at 50m and shot 1935-7, 200m 1937 and standing long jump 1935-6.
With an impressive 1.83m *6 ft*, 75kg *165 lb* physique, she dwarfed her rivals and also set US records with 13.61m and 13.70 indoors at the 8lb shot, and had a discus best of 40.70m. She turned professional as a runner and basketball player, and after a career at the Defense Mapping Agency Aerospace centre in St Louis, coached at her old school in Missouri. Her physical abilities remained strong and she took seven gold medals at the 1981 Senior Olympics.

Arthur STEPHENSON (UK)

HORSE RACING

William Arthur Stephenson. b. 7 Apr 1920.

Although he came from a notable training family, he made a late start to his career as a trainer, farming at Bishop Auckland until he took a licence in 1959. Then he speedily became established. In 1969/70 he became the first man to train more than 100 winners in a National Hunt season in Britain. While he did not exceed that season's total of 114, he went on to top the 100 mark seven times in all, each year to 1974 and again in 1975/6 and 1976/7 and was champion trainer ten times. His cousin **Willie** (b. 9 Oct 1911) trained the three-time Champion Hurdle winner *Sir Ken*, the 1951 Derby winner *Arctic Prince*, and the 1959 Grand National winner *Oxo*.

Peter STERLING(Aus)

RUGBY LEAGUE

Peter Sterling. b. 16 Jun 1960 Toowoomba, Queensland.

A great halfback, after making his representative début with Sydney Seconds in 1981 he was one of the sensations of the undefeated Australian tour of Britain and France the following year, touring again in 1986. He played for Parramatta 1978-89, helping them to Sydney premierships in 1981-3 and 1986, and in 1984/5 in England for Hull, helping them to the Challenge Cup final.

Charlotte STERRY (UK) see COOPER

H W STEVENSON (UK)

BILLIARDS

Henry William Stevenson. b. 15 Jul 1874 Hull, Yorkshire, d. 11 Jun 1964 Isleworth, Middlesex.

Universally known by his initials 'H W', he was the dominant figure in world billiards after the retirement of John Roberts,Jr. Beginning as a marker in his native Hull, he made a name for himself in South Africa where he lived for a number of years before playing his first pro game in England. After finishing as runner-up to Charles Dawson in the 1900 World Championship, he beat Dawson for the title in 1901. Over the next decade the title changed hands frequently and Stevenson claimed the Championship four more times. He was still a contender in 1919 and 1920 when well past the age of 50.

Many professionals of the time went on tour to boost their earnings but Stevenson travelled more than most. In 1921, accompanied by Claude Faulkiner, he embarked on a tour which lasted almost two years and took him to South and East Africa, India, Burma, China, Japan, New Zealand and Australia.

Téofilo STEVENSON (Cuba)

BOXING

Téofilo Stevenson Lawrence. b. 29 Mar 1952 Dcilias.

The greatest heavyweight boxer that never became the world's professional champion, as he was not allowed by the Cuban authorities to turn pro. His first international appearance was at the 1971 Pan-American Games in Cali, Colombia, where he lost a decision in the semi-finals to Duane Bobick (USA). In 1972, at Munich, Stevenson won a re-match with Bobick en route to winning his first Olympic gold medal.

Stevenson also won the Olympic heavyweight gold medal in 1976 and 1980, making him one of only two men to win three Olympic boxing gold medals (Hungary's László Papp is the other). In addition, Stevenson won golds at the 1975 and 1979 Pan-American Games, and was world amateur champion in 1974, 1978, and 1986. It is likely that Stevenson would have won a fourth Olympic gold medal at Los Angeles, had the Cubans not boycotted the 1984 Olympics. He was not beaten in a major competition until a loss to Francesco Damiani (Ita) in 1982.

American professional boxing promoters coveted Stevenson's talent, his good looks, and bodybuilder's physique. But he refused all entreaties to turn professional and remained an amateur to continue boxing for the honour of his country.

Ian STEWART (Aus)

AUSTRALIAN RULES FOOTBALL
Ian Harlow Stewart. b. 1943 Queenstown, Tasmania.

One of only four players to have won the Brownlow Medal three times. He was honoured with St Kilda in 1965 and 1966 and with Richmond in 1971. A talented centre, he played a total of 205 VFL games for the two clubs, 128 for St Kilda and 77 for Richmond. Only 1.79m tall and 79kg, his brilliant reading of the game more than compensated for his modest physique. After a brief spell with Carlton in 1978 he coached South Melbourne 1976-81.

Ian STEWART (UK)

ATHLETICS
b. 15 Jan 1949 Handsworth, Birmingham.

A determined competitor who compiled a fine racing record, taking gold medals at 5000m in the 1969 Europeans and 1970 Commonwealth Games (in a European record of 13:22.8), at 3000m in the 1969 and 1975 European Indoors, and the World cross-country title in 1975. At the Olympic Games 5000m he was 3rd in 1972 and 7th in 1976.
Coached by Geoff Warr from the age of 15, he worked very hard and in 1968 set five European Junior records from 3000 to 5000 metres. He won the AAA 5000m in 1969 and indoor 3000m in 1972-3 and 1975, and the UK 10,000m in 1977.
He took up cycling and now coaches and works to promote distance running.
Other British records: 1500m 3:39.12 (1969), 2000m 5:02.97 (1975), 2 miles 8:22.0 (1972). Other bests: 1 mile 3:57.3 (1969), 3000m 7:46.83 (1976), 10,000m 27:43.03 (1977).
His brother and sister also won European Indoor titles, **Peter** (b. 8 Aug 1947) the 3000m in 1971, and **Mary** (b. 25 Feb 1956) the 1500m in 1977. Peter set British records at 1500m 3:38.22 and 1 mile 3:55.3 in 1972, and Mary set British records for 1000m 2:39.42 (1974) and 1 mile 4:36.1 (1977) and won the 1978 Commonwealth 1500m, at which her best time was 4:06.0 (1978).

Jackie STEWART (UK)

MOTOR RACING
John Young Stewart. b. 11 Jun 1939 Dumbarton.

Britain's most successful driver, world champion in 1969, 1971 and 1973, and runner-up in 1968 and 1972. In his Formula One career from 1965 to 1973 he set a record, since surpassed by Alain Prost, with 27 Grand Prix wins and 360 points (from 99 races), driving for BRM 1965-7, Matra 1968-9, March 1970 and Tyrrell 1971-3.
His father was a Jaguar dealer and his elder brother Jimmy had raced in the 1950s. At trap shooting Jackie won a series of major events, including the British Championships in 1959-60, but was bitterly disappointed to fail at the trials for the 1960 Olympic Games. He first raced in 1960 and his ability was soon apparent, as he was the most successful British driver in club races in 1963 and won 11 Formula Three races for Cooper-BMC in 1964. Signed by BRM for Formula One in 1965 he was an immediate success, with a point in his first race, a win in the Italian GP at Monza and third place overall. He campaigned hard to sell the sport, pushing it into a modern big business enterprise, and he became by far the sport's biggest money-earner. After he retired at the top of his profession, he continued his jet-set life, promoting the sport and campaigning vigorously for improved driver safety standards. BBC Sports Personality of the Year 1973 and *Daily Express* Sportsman of the Year 1971 and 1973. Awarded the OBE in 1972.

Nels STEWART (Can)

ICE HOCKEY
Nels Stewart. b. 29 Dec 1902 Montreal, Québec, d. 21 Aug 1957 Wasaga Beach, Ontario.

Stewart began his NHL career in 1926 with the Montreal Maroons, although he later played for both the Boston Bruins and New York Americans. He was primarily a center and a top goalscorer, but he skated many shifts as a defenseman. In his rookie

season of 1925/6 he scored 34 goals, leading the league, and until Maurice Richard came along, Stewart would reign as the all-time career goalscorer in the NHL. He was not much of a skater, but he had a laser shot, and simply camped out in front of the opponent's net, waiting to launch his deadly weapon on the opposing goaltender. He was nicknamed 'Ole Poison' for his work around the enemy net.
Career 1925-40 - 654 games, 324 goals, 515 points. Hart Trophy 1926, 1930; Ross Trophy 1926.

Payne STEWART (USA)

GOLF

William Payne Stewart. b. 30 Jan 1957 Springfield, Missouri.

Noted as the most colourful dresser on the PGA tour, in his distinctive plus-fours and wearing the colours of NFL teams, Stewart is also compiling a fine career record and is now well established in the all-time top ten money-winners. He first broke into the top ten on the tour in 1986 when he ranked 3rd, was 2nd in 1989 and 3rd in 1990. His majors have been the 1989 PGA and 1991 US Open, belying his previous reputation of fading under pressure. He then had a couple of poor years until he came back to form in 1993, when he was 2nd in the US Open and shot a tournament record-equalling 63 in the final round of the British Open.
He turned professional after completing his golf scholarship at Southern Methodist University. Member of the US Ryder Cup team in 1987, 1989 and 1991.
PGA career earnings 1981-92: $5,394,697 with 8 victories.

Andrew STODDART (UK)

CRICKET and RUGBY

Andrew Ernest Stoddart. b. 11 Mar 1863 South Shields, d. 4 Apr 1915 London by suicide.

The only player to captain England at both rugby and cricket. He made his first-class cricket début for Middlesex and the first of his ten appearances for England at rugby (four as captain, including uniquely on his first appearance) in 1885. He took England cricket teams to Australia in 1894/5 and 1897/8.
A stockbroker, he made 221 in his last first-class innings in cricket and scored prolifically for Hampstead in club cricket, including the then record score of 485 in 1886. He was a right-handed opening batsman and medium paced bowler.
16 Tests 1988-98: 996 runs at 35.57, 2 100s HS 173; 2 wickets at 47.00, BB 1-10; 6 catches.
First-class 1885-1900: 16,738 runs at 32.12, 26 100s HS 221; 278 wickets at 23.63, BB 7-67; 257 catches.

Fred STOLLE (Aus)

TENNIS

Frederick Sydney Stolle. b. 8 Oct 1938 Hornsby, New South Wales.

An outstanding doubles player who was also noted for his 'near misses' in major singles events. He shares with Von Cramm the record of finishing as runner-up in the Wimbledon singles for three successive years 1963-5. He was also the losing finalist at the US, Australian and Italian Championships in 1964 and was again runner-up at the Australian Championships in 1965. He won his first Grand Slam singles in 1965 when he took the French title and in 1966 was the US and German singles champion.
His men's doubles record of eight Grand Slam victories give a truer indication of his abilities. With Bob Hewitt he won the 1963-4 Australian and 1962 and 1964 Wimbledon titles, and with Roy Emerson he won the 1965-6 US, 1966 Australian and 1965 French Championships. He also won six Grand Slam mixed doubles titles: Wimbledon 1961, 1964, 1969; US 1962 and 1965 and Australian 1962. In view of his record it is surprising that he only played in four doubles rubbers in the Davis Cup. He won three of these but he also had an impressive singles record, winning 10 out of 12 rubbers. A former Sydney bank clerk, he turned professional early in 1967. He had a powerful serve-volley game but his greatest strength was his return of service on the backhand.

Dwight STONES (USA)

ATHLETICS

Dwight Edwin Stones. b. 6 Dec 1953 Irvine, California.

Stones won an Olympic bronze medal for the high jump as a teenager in 1972, and maintained his position amongst the world's best jumpers for the ensuing decade. He set three world high jump records: 2.30 in 1973, 2.31 and 2.32 in 1976, and a fourth US record 2.34 in 1984; and seven world indoor bests from 2.26 to 2.30 in 1975-6. He cleared 7ft *2.13m* or more in some 500 competitions in his career from 1971 to 1986.
He was US champion six times, 1973-4, 1976-8, 1983, won a second Olympic bronze medal in 1976 and was fourth in 1984. Sixth place in the 1983 Worlds and second in the 1977 World Cup completed a good record, but one without a major international win for this flamboyant character, who stood 1.96m *6'5"* tall.
A graduate of Cal State-Long Beach, for whom he won the 1976 NCAA title, he became a highly respected TV commentator on track and field athletics.

Michael STOUTE (UK)

HORSE RACING

Michael Ronald Stoute. b. 22 Oct 1945 Barbados.

Son of the Chief of Police in Barbados, he came to Britain and worked for Pat Rohan at Malton 1965-8, Douglas Smith 1968-70 and H.Thomson Jones 1970-2, before gaining his trainer's licence in 1972.
He first trained over 100 winners in a year in 1980 and was champion trainer in 1981 and again in 1986 and 1989. His progressive record has been: 101 winners in 1980, 103 in 1982, 120 in 1985. In 1986 he set a record for worldwide earnings by a British trainer of £2,778,405 and in 1989 he set a record in Britain of £2,000,330.
His first classic winner was *Fair Salinia* in the 1978 Oaks and his first English and Irish Derby winner the ill-fated *Shergar* in 1981.

Curtis STRANGE (USA)

GOLF

Curtis Northrup Strange. b. 30 Jan 1955 Norfolk, Virginia.

Strange first gained fame in the United States as a collegian at Wake Forest University when he won the NCAA championship as a freshman in 1974. After he turned professional he did not initially have the success predicted of him, but he gradually improved and in the late 1980s was considered the top American player and one of the two or three best in the world. In 1988-9 he became the first man since Hogan in 1951 to win two successive US Opens. He is an intense player who has been often criticised for his demeanour on the course, but to his colleagues and friends he is well-liked and considered a warm friend.
He had his first PGA tour victory in 1979 and led the tour in earnings in 1985 and 1987-8, becoming the first to win over $1 million in a season with $1,147,644 in 1988. At the end of 1992 he was third on the all-time earnings list.
PGA career earnings 1976-92: $5,779,864 with 17 victories.

Astrid STRAUSS (GDR)

SWIMMING

Astrid Strauss. b. 24 Dec 1968 Berlin.

Strauss won European gold medals at 400m, 800m and 4x200m in both 1983 and 1985, with silver at 200m in 1983. In 1986 she became World champion at 800m, with silver at 400m. Both then and at the 1987 Europeans she was a member of the GDR 4x200m team that took the title in world record times, but at the latter took the silver medals at 400m and 800m.
She did not achieve any world records at individual events, but set three European records at both 400m, to 4:07.66 in 1984, and 800m, to 8:26.52 in 1986, and one at 1500m, 16:13.55 in 1984.
She improved her 800m best to 8:22.09 when second to Janet Evans at the 1988 Olympics. She won a treble of 200m (in her best ever time of 1:59.80), 400m and 800m at the GDR Championships in 1983,

retaining the latter two titles each year 1984-6.
A commanding figure at 1.87m and 82kg, she was prevented from attempting further Olympic success by a drugs ban in 1992.

Shirley STRICKLAND (Aus)

ATHLETICS

Shirley Barbara Strickland. b. 18 Jul 1925 Guildford, Western Australia. Later De la Hunty.

The first Australian woman athlete to win a medal at the Olympics, she went on to set an all-time record with seven. Her glittering collection would have been one more if there had been an examination of the photo-finish for the 200m in 1948, when she was actually 3rd rather than the official 4th place. In 1948 she won bronze medals at 100m and 80m hurdles with a sprint relay silver. She then won the 80m hurdles in both 1952 (with world records of 11.0 in a heat and 10.9 in the final) and 1956, adding a bronze at 100m in 1952 and a third gold and another world record at 4x100m in 1956. She also set a world record for 100m with 11.3 in 1955 and her time of 10.89 in the Olympic semi in 1956 was then the fastest ever on auto timing. At the Empire Games she secured three golds, in the hurdles and two relays, and two silvers, 100y and 220y, in 1950, but missed the 1954 Games after the birth of her son. Australian champion at 440y in 1950, 1952, 1956. Her father had been a champion professional runner. A graduate of the University of Western Australia, she became a teacher of mathematics and physics, and later an athletics coach.
Other bests: 100y 10.6 (1955), 200m 24.1 (1955).

Herbert STRUDWICK (UK)

CRICKET

Herbert Strudwick. b. 28 Jan 1880 Mitcham, Surrey, d. 14 Feb 1970 Shoreham, Sussex.

England's best wicket-keeper of his era, he set a record number of first-class career dismissals from his Surrey début in 1902. His 91 dismissals in his first full season was at the time a record. Better batsmen were often preferred to him in the Test team and he was aged 41 before he kept in a Test in England. He was quiet and unobtrusive but very quick on his feet. He became Surrey's scorer for many years.
28 Tests 1910-26: 230 runs at 7.93, HS 24; 60 catches, 12 stumpings.
First-class 1902-27: 6445 runs at 10.89, HS 93; 1 wicket; 1242 catches, 255 stumpings.

Christine STÜCKELBERGER (Swi)

EQUESTRIAN

Christine Stückelberger. b. 22 May 1947.

The most successful woman ever in international dressage events, with five Olympic medals: an individual gold and team silver in 1976, team silver in 1984, and team silver and individual bronze in 1988. She was equally successful at the World Championships, winning the individual title in 1978 and silvers in 1982 and 1986, with team medals in 1974, 1978, 1982, and 1986. At the European Championships, Stückelberger claimed six team medals between 1973 and 1987, and five individual medals, including golds in 1975 and 1977. In 1980 she also won the Dressage Festival held one week after the Olympics for riders who had boycotted the Moscow Games, at which most of the world's top dressage riders competed. Each year from 1970-9 she was Swiss champion.

Eric STURGESS (SAf)

TENNIS

Eric William Sturgess. b. 10 May 1920 Johannesburg.

South Africa's greatest tennis player. He won his first SA singles titles in 1939 and 1940 and then joined the South African Air Force, in which he was a pilot instructor and flew Spitfires in the War. Shot down in 1944, he was a prisoner-of-war in Germany until 1945. He completed a total of 11 SA singles titles with wins in 1946, 1948-54 and 1957. He was 27 before he embarked on the international circuit, having lost his best years during the War, but he still met with considerable success. His quick reflexes and thinking, and control of the lob, made him an especially good doubles player. In 1949 he had his best Wimbledon Championships, as he was beaten by Ted Schroeder (USA) in five sets in the semi-finals of the singles, lost to Pancho Gonzales and Frank Parker when he played with Budge Patty in the men's doubles semi, and won the mixed doubles with Sheila Summers (SAf), beating John Bromwich and Louise Brough in the final. He had a further Wimbledon mixed doubles success in 1950 with Louise Brough, and was runner-up in the men's doubles with Jaroslav Drobny in 1951 and with Vic Seixas in 1952, losing to Sedgeman and McGregor both years. In the French Open he was twice runner-up in the men's singles but he won the men's doubles with Eustace Fannin in 1947 and the mixed doubles with Sheila Summers in 1947 and 1948. He was beaten in the final of the US singles in 1948 by Pancho Gonzales. The Americans said of him that he had the most perfect court manners in the world.

Luis SUÁREZ (Spa)

FOOTBALL

Luis Suárez Miramonte. b. 2 May 1935 La Coruña.

One of the greatest of all Spanish forwards, playing usually as an inside-left. He joined FC Barcelona from the junior leagues in 1953. After winning the European Footballer of the Year award in 1960 he moved to Inter Milan in 1961 where he enjoyed his greatest successes. He helped the Italian club to three League titles and the European Cup and World Club Championship in 1964 and 1965. His career with Inter ended in 1970 when he was suddenly transferred to Sampdoria. He played in the 1962 and 1966 World Cups. This appeared to be the end of his international career but six years later he was recalled to the national side and won his 32nd cap against Greece at the age of 37. He scored 14 goals in international matches. He became manager of Genoa in 1973, and after working with Cagliari and Como he returned to Spain and joined the technical staff of the Spanish federation. Appointed manager of the Spanish national team in 1988.

Louise SUGGS (USA)

GOLF

Louise Suggs. b. 7 Sep 1923 Atlanta, Georgia.

She helped establish the LPGA Tour with her great rivals, Patty Berg and Babe Zaharias, although she did not become as well known as those two. Suggs won both the US (1947) and British (1948) Amateur titles and won 11 major professional championships, with 50 LPGA victories for fourth on the all-time list. She was the leading money winner on the tour in 1953 and 1960. Major victories: US Women's Open 1949, 1952; LPGA 1957; Titleholders 1946, 1954, 1956, 1959; Western Open 1946-7, 1949 53.

Naim SULEYMANOGLÜ (Bul/Tur)

WEIGHTLIFTING

Naim Suleymanoglü. né Naim Suleimanov. b. 23 Jan 1967 Ptichar, Bulgaria. aka Naum Shalamanov.

Pound-for-pound possibly the strongest man who has ever lived, and certainly the greatest weightlifter of the 1980s. Trained by Ivan Abadjiev, at the age of 14 he won the gold medal at 52kg at the World Juniors in 1982, when his total of 250kg ranked him second in the world at senior level. In 1983 he moved up to 56kg and became the youngest ever world record holder with snatch and total records at the age of 15, but he was beaten into second place in the World Championships. At the 1984 Europeans he became the second man (after Stefan Topurov) to lift three times bodyweight overhead and he was the first man to snatch 2.5 times his own bodyweight (27 Apr 1988). In all he set 33 world records at 56kg or 60kg weight categories, culminating in his world records for snatch, jerk and total at the 1988 Olympics.
A member of the Turkish minority in Bulgaria, he had earlier been forced to take

a Bulgarian version of his name, Naum Shalamanov, and sought political asylum in Turkey after the 1986 World Cup in Melbourne. As Shalamanov for Bulgaria he was world champion at 60kg in 1985 and 1986. As Naim Suleymanoglü for Turkey, after the Turkish government had made a large payment to Bulgaria to clear his status, he won the 1988 Olympic and 1989 world titles. He also won the World Cup in 1984-6 and was European champion at 56kg 1984 and 60kg 1985-8.
After a pause he returned to win the world title in 1991 and his second Olympic title in 1992.

Jim SULLIVAN (UK)

RUGBY LEAGUE

James Sullivan, b. 2 Dec 1903 Cardiff, Wales, d. 14 Sep 1977 Wigan.

The most prodigious goal kicker of all-time. Between 1921 and 1946 he kicked 2867 goals and scored 6192 points in club, representative and international matches. When he was signed by Wigan from the Cardiff rugby union club he had the distinction of being, at the age of 17, the youngest player ever to represent the Barbarians. He toured Australia in 1924, 1928 and as captain in 1932. In 1936 he became the only player ever to be selected for a fourth tour but declined the invitation. He made a record 60 international appearances, 25 of which were for Great Britain and the remainder for Wales and Other Nationalities. His 160 goals and 329 points is a record at international level.
He played in five successive Test match victories during his three visits to Australia and kicked 246 goals on the tours. It was the consistency of his goal kicking that made him unique among full backs, and he kicked more than 100 goals in every season except 1946. His best year was 1934 with the then record total of 204 goals.
He played 921 games for Wigan, setting a record for the most appearances by a player for one club. On his retirement he stayed on at Wigan as coach and later coached briefly at St Helens.

John L SULLIVAN (USA)

BOXING

John Lawrence Sullivan. b. 15 Oct 1858 Boston, Massachusetts, d. 2 Feb 1918 Abingdon, Massachusetts

The great John L Sullivan was a massive fighter for his time who boasted that he could lick 'any sonofabitch in the house'. He first claimed the world championship in 1882 when he defeated Paddy Ryan and although he did not fight Britain's best at the time, there was little doubt that he was the best heavyweight in the world. He was as renowned for his love of liquor as he was for his boxing and was one of the best-loved American boxers ever. Sullivan lost his title as world champion in 1892 when he was knocked out by James J Corbett. It was his first, and only, fight under the Queensberry Rules. After his retirement, Sullivan swore off liquor, married his childhood sweetheart and toured the nation lecturing against the evils of drink.
Career record: W - 38 (33), L - 1, D - 3.

Mick SULLIVAN (UK)

RUGBY LEAGUE

Michael Sullivan. b. 12 Jan 1934.

Britain's most capped player with 46 caps for Great Britain 1954-63 and a further 5 for England; he also scored a record 45 international tries. On the 1958 tour of Australia he scored a record 38 tries and he set a further record by making 36 consecutive international appearances, thereby emphasising his clear superiority over his contemporaries.
Mick Sullivan, who was not related to the legendary Jim Sullivan, won three amateur caps for England and turned professional in 1952, from when he played for Huddersfield, Wigan and St Helens during his peak years and later for York, Dewsbury and the Australian club Junee.
At international level his speed, swerve, sidestep and devastating tackling made him the most formidable winger of his era. Although his speed gradually diminished, his other talents remained and served him well when he played at loose forward after his international career ended.

John SURTEES (UK)

MOTOR CYCLING and MOTOR RACING
John Surtees. b. 11 Feb 1934 Tatsfield, Kent.

The only man to have become world champion on both two wheels and four. In his motorcycling career for MV Agusta 1956-60 he won 38 Grand Prix races, 22 at 500cc and 15 at 350cc, including the unprecedented feat of winning all of the 25 world championship events he contested in 1958 and 1959, being world champion at 350cc and 500cc in both those years and in 1960.
His father Jack had a motorcycle business in Croydon and John acted as his passenger, racing sidecars on grass tracks before becoming an engineering apprentice with Vincent, on whose machines he achieved his earliest successes. He made his solo début in 1951 and in 1955, racing for Norton, beat the great Geoff Duke in 68 out of 76 races, He began his brilliant career with MV in 1956 when he won the Senior TT and the world championship at 500cc. On the Isle of Man he won further Senior TT races in 1958-60 and Junior in 1958-9.
Surtees, awarded the MBE in 1961 for his services to motorcycle racing, started motor racing in 1960, when he made his Formula One début in a Lotus and was second in the British Grand Prix. Driving for Ferrari, he was world champion in 1964 and runner-up in 1966, but halfway through that season left Ferrari for Cooper. In 1967-8 he ran the Honda team and placed fourth in the 1967 world championship. In 1969 he moved to BRM and in 1970 he built his own Formula One car, but ended his own racing career in 1972, with a record of six wins and 180 points from 111 Grand Prix races. He also won the first Can-Am Challenge in 1966.
Introspective, but determined and with plenty of skill, based on mechanical ability.

William SURTEES (UK/USA)

RACKETS
William James Conyers Surtees. b. 29 June 1947 Windsor, Berks.

World rackets champion 1972-3 and again from 1975-81, and an eight-time winner of the US Amateur singles, 1971-72, 1974-79. After winning the Public Schools rackets championship for Rugby in 1965 he attended Balliol College, Oxford before settling in America where he now works in real estate in Florida.
When winning his second US Amateur title in 1972 he beat Howard Angus for the world title which had fallen vacant following the retirement of Geoffrey Atkins. Angus reversed the decision when he challenged in 1973 but Surtees reclaimed the title in 1975 and remained the champion until 1981.

Bert SUTCLIFFE (NZ)

CRICKET
Bert Sutcliffe. b. 17 Nov 1923 Ponsonby, Auckland.

The most prolific run-scorer in New Zealand cricket, where he played for Otago 1946-62 and Northern Districts 1962-6. An attractive left-handed batsman, he often had to carry the NZ batting. His most successful Test series were in 1949 against England with 423 runs at 60.42 (and 2627 runs at 59.70 on tour) and in 1955/6 against India with 611 runs at 87.28. His 385 for Otago v Canterbury in 1952/3 is the highest ever in first-class cricket by a New Zealander. He was also a useful slow left-arm bowler.
42 Tests 1988-98: 2727 runs at 40.10, 5 100s HS 230; 4 wickets at 86.50, BB 2-38; 20 catches.*
First-class 1942-66: 17,283 runs at 47.22, 44 100s HS 385; 86 wickets at 37.95, BB 5-19; 158 catches, 1 stumping.

Herbert SUTCLIFFE (UK)

CRICKET
Herbert Sutcliffe. b. 24 Nov 1894 Summer Bridge, Harrogate, Yorkshire, d. 22 Jan 1978 Crosshills, near Keighley, Yorkshire.

Immaculate of appearance, Sutcliffe was a hugely reliable and prolific opening batsman, who formed memorable opening partnerships with Jack Hobbs for England and with Percy Holmes for Yorkshire. He played for Yorkshire 2nd XI in 1914 and

his first-team career fitted exactly into the period between the Wars, the First, in which he had been commissioned as a 2nd Lieutenant, delaying his début in first-class cricket until he was 24. He was then an immediate success, scoring over 1000 runs each season, over 2000 runs each year 1922-35 and 1937, with three years over 3000: 3002 at 76.97 in 1928, 3006 at 96.96 in 1931 and 3336 at 74.13 in 1932. In that last year he made his highest score, 313, for Yorkshire v Essex at Leyton, putting on a world record 555 runs for the first wicket with Holmes. He has the best record of any England batsman against Australia, his 2751 runs being made at an average of 66.85. He became a successful businessman and was a Test selector 1959-61. His son Billy captained Yorkshire 1956-7.
54 Tests 1924-35: 4555 runs at 60.73, 16 100s HS 194; 23 catches.
First-class 1919-45: 50,138 runs at 51.95, 149 100s HS 313; 14 wickets at 40.21, BB 3-15; 466 catches.

May SUTTON (USA)

TENNIS

May Godfray Sutton. b. 25 Sep 1886 Plymouth, Devon, England. d 4 Oct 1975 Santa Monica, California. Later Bundy.

The English-born daughter of a naval captain, she went to California as a young child when the family emigrated. She learned all her tennis in America and with her masculine-type serve and speed around the court she won her first Southern California championship at the age of 13. In 1904, when still only 17, she won both the singles and the women's doubles at the US Championships. She was the top-ranked player in the US that year, and although playing infrequently, maintained that ranking for several years. In 1905 she became the first overseas player - man or woman - to win a Wimbledon title on her début there, beating former champion Dorothea Douglass in the final. She lost to Douglass in the 1906 Challenge Round, but won the title for a second time in 1907 when she again met Douglass (now Mrs Chambers) in the final.
In 1912 she married Thomas Bundy, an American Davis Cup player and US doubles champion of 1912 and 1914, and although she gave birth to three children she continued to play top-class tennis for many years. She played in the Wightman Cup in 1925 and in 1929 she made her fourth and last appearance at Wimbledon when she reached the quarter-finals at the age of 42. She later became a tennis instructor and although she retired from coaching in the 1950s, she continued playing until three years before her death. One of her star pupils was her daughter, **Dorothy** 'Dodo' Bundy Cheney (b. 1 May 1916), who was also a Wightman Cup player and in 1938 became the first American to capture the Australian women's singles title.

Mike SUYDERHOUD (USA)

WATER SKIING

Michael Albert Suyderhoud. b. 16 Mar 1950 Surabaja, Indonesia.

A legendary figure in American water skiing, partly for his overall ability, but especially for his jumping, at which some people consider he was the greatest ever. He won seven overall US national championships and in 1967 and 1969 won the world overall title. In 1971 he failed to defend his crown but that year won both the slalom and jumping world championships. In 1977 he came back to again win the world jumping championship. In his career he set four world jumping records and was the first man to exceed 160 feet (48.8m). Suyderhoud was also one of the first skiers to practise the freestyle event and helped promote the early freestyle tournaments of the 1970s. He now runs his own water ski school in California.

Gunde SVAN (Swe)

NORDIC SKIING

Gunde Anders Svan. b. 12 Jan 1962 Skamhed, Vansbro.

With eleven titles he has won the greatest number of world and Olympic gold medals at cross-country skiing; seven individual: world 15km 1989, 30km 1985 and 1991,

50km 1985 and 1989, with the Olympic 15km 1984 and 50km 1988; and four relays: world 4 x 10km 1987 and 1989 and Olympics 1984 and 1988. His four gold medals ties the record for Olympic skiing, and in 1984 in addition to his two gold medals he took a silver at 50km and a bronze at 30km. At 22 he was the youngest ever Olympic cross-country skiing champion. He also won a world bronze at relay in 1985 and three silver medals in 1991. Svan also has a record five World Cup titles at cross-country skiing, winning in 1984-6 and 1988-9, with 2nd in 1983 and 1990 and 3rd in 1987 making eight successive years in the top three.
After competing at the World Junior Championships each year from 1980 to 1982, winning a gold and two silvers at the relay and an individual 15km bronze in 1981, he first competed at the World Championships in 1982, when he was 13th at 15km. In 1984 he won all four Swedish titles, three individual and the relay, a feat he emulated in 1989. He excelled at freestyle, realising less success at the classic style at which, at the 1988 Olympics, he was 13th at 15km and 10th at 30km. His final world title in 1991 over 30km was, however, at the classic style. From 1965 to 1991 he won 372 of his 615 races including 30 individual World Cup races 1983-91 and 16 national titles (including 7 in relays).

Oscar SWAHN (Swe)

SHOOTING

Oscar Gomer Swahn. b. 20 Oct 1847 Tanum, d. 1 May 1927 Stockholm.

A legend in Olympic shooting. He was aged 64yr 258 days when he won a gold medal in the single-shot running deer team event in 1912 and is the oldest-ever Olympic champion. He is also the oldest-ever Olympic medallist and Olympic competitor, being 72yr 280 days when he won a silver medal in the double-shot running deer team event in 1920.
At the Games of 1908, 1912 and 1920 he won a total of three gold, one silver and two bronze medals, all in running deer. In 1924, at the age of 76, he qualified for his fourth Olympics but was unable to compete because of ill health. He first started shooting in 1863 and in his 65-year career he won more than 500 prizes, all of which he donated to the Army Museum in Stockholm. His son **Alfred** (1879-1931) was also an outstanding marksman, at the Olympics winning three gold, joining his father on the winning team in both 1908 and 1912 and winning the individual single-shot running deer title in 1912, three silver and three bronze medals. His nine medals is a Swedish record for summer Olympians.

Lynn SWANN (USA)

AMERICAN FOOTBALL

Lynn Curtis Swann. b. 7 Mar 1952 Alcoa, Tennessee.

At high school near Los Angeles, Swann played football and was also a good long jumper, at which he had an all-time best of 7.67m. He went to college at Southern California, where he became an All-American wide receiver in 1973. Drafted by the Pittsburgh Steelers in 1974, he played for nine years for them in the NFL, helping them to four Super Bowl titles in the 1970s, being the MVP in Super Bowl X in 1976. He played in three Pro Bowls and was a four-time All-Conference selection.
NFL career 1974-82: 5462 yards gained receiving av. 16.3, 51 touchdowns.

Frank SWIFT (UK)

FOOTBALL

Frank Victor Swift. b. 24 Dec 1913 Blackpool, d. 6 Feb 1958 Munich, Germany.

After signing professional forms for Manchester City in 1932, he made his first-team début in 1933 and proved so successful that he did not miss a match for the next five years, making 192 consecutive League appearances.
He was goalkeeper in the City team which won the FA Cup in 1934 and the Football League in 1937. After that Cup final the 20-year-old Swift collapsed from nervous exhaustion. Despite these pre-war suc-

cesses, he did not win the first of his 19 full England caps until 1947. In 1948 he became the first goalkeeper to captain England. After his retirement he became a licensee and soccer journalist and lost his life in the Munich air disaster while working for the *Sunday Empire News*. A spectacular goalkeeper who was immensely popular with the crowd, he would undoubtedly have won further international honours had his career not been interrupted by World War II.

Walter SWINBURN (Ire/UK)

HORSE RACING

Walter Robert John Swinburn. b. 7 Aug 1961 Oxford.

Hailed as a boy wonder when he won his first Derby on *Shergar* in 1981, by 1993 he had ridden seven English and nine Irish classic winners. His father Wally was a top Irish jockey when Walter began his apprenticeship with 'Frenchie' Nicholson in 1977 and had his first winner at Kempton Park the following year. In 1983 he was retained as first jockey by Michael Stoute and in that year rode *All Along* to victory in the Prix de l'Arc de Triomphe as well as three major races in North America, culminating in the Washington International. In 1984 he rode 99 winners in Britain and achieved his first century with 111 in 1990.

Madge SYERS (UK)

FIGURE SKATING

Florence Madeline Syers. née Cave. b. 1882, d. 9 Sep 1917 Weybridge, Surrey.

The most influential figure in the development of women's skating. As there was, at the time, no specific rule prohibiting women, she entered the 1902 World Championships and caused a sensation by finishing second to the great Ulrich Salchow. The authorities immediately barred women from the Championships and in 1906 introduced a separate World Championship for Ladies. Cave easily won the title in 1906 and 1907 and the gold medal at the 1908 Olympics by a huge margin. She also won the British title in 1903 and 1904, beating the leading male skaters on both occasions. She owed much to her husband, Edgar Syers, who encouraged her to give up the restrictive 'English' and adopt the free-flowing 'International' style. Together they won the bronze medal in the pairs at the 1908 Olympics.

Miklós SZABADOS (Hungary)

TABLE TENNIS

Miklós Szabados. b. 18 Mar 1912 Budapest, d. 2 Dec 1962 Sydney, Australia.

One of the greatest of the early Hungarian players whose total of 10 men's world titles has only been bettered by his countryman, Viktor Barna. Together they won the world men's doubles six times between 1929 and 1935 and Szabados won the mixed doubles three times with Maria Mednyánsky. In this time he also played on five winning Swaythling Cup teams. His only victory in the singles came in 1931, when he completed the treble, but he was a singles finalist on three other occasions, losing in 1929 to Fred Perry, the future Wimbledon tennis champion, and in 1932 and 1935 to Barna.

While on a tour of Australia in 1937 he found the country so attractive that he immediately settled in Sydney and never once returned to Europe. He became an Australian citizen and was for many years the country's No.1 player. He will be remembered for his superb footwork and his gentlemanly behaviour.

Ecaterina SZABO (Rom)

GYMNASTICS

Ecaterina Szabo. b. 22 Jan 1967 Zágon.

Szabo was the most successful female gymnast at the Los Angeles Olympic Games in 1984, although overshadowed by the publicity surrounding Mary Lou Retton, with whom she tied for the all-around title, as she won three of the four apparatus finals and also won a team gold. This petite (1.43m, 35kg) and elegant gymnast was European Junior champion in 1980 and 1982, and had won the gold medal for floor exercises and placed 4th overall at the 1983 World Championships.

Jerzy SZCZAKIEL (Pol)

SPEEDWAY

Jerzy Szcakiel. b. 28 Jan 1949 Grudziadz.

After winning the World Pairs title in 1971, he became the first East European to win the World Individual Championship when he took the 1973 title in his native Poland. He is the biggest outsider ever to win the championship and his success was a remarkable contrast to his first appearance in the World finals in Sweden two years earlier when he failed to score a single point.

Irena SZEWINSKA (Pol)

ATHLETICS

Irena Szewinska. b. 24 May 1946 Leningrad. née Kirszenstein.

One of the greatest woman athletes of all time and a very gracious lady. Starting as a sprinter and long jumper, her long smooth strides were ideally suited to the 400m to which she progressed later in her career. Her collection of 41 medals from major championships is unrivalled and she set 13 world records from 1965 to 1976: 100m 11.1 in 1965 and 11.19 in 1968; 200m: four from 22.7 in 1965 to 22.0 (22.21 auto) in 1974; 400m: three from the first sub-50 second time, 49.9 in 1974 (in just her second race at the distance) to 49.29 in 1976; two at 440y and two at 4x100m relay. Two of those world records were set while winning Olympic titles, 200m in 1968 and 400m in 1976. In all she won seven Olympic medals: in 1964 at 18 she took silver at 200m and long jump with gold on the Polish sprint relay team; in 1968 she also took bronze at 100m; and in 1972 a bronze at 200m. She was supreme at 400m in the mid-1970s, winning 34 consecutive finals in that period, including the 1976 Olympics when she won by some ten metres. Her Olympic career ended in anticlimax as she pulled a muscle in the semi-finals of the 400m in 1980.

At European Championships she collected a record five gold medals: 200m, LJ and 4x100m in 1966, 100m and 200m 1974, with a silver and four bronze in her four championships to 1978.

At the first World Cup in 1977 Szewinska received the trophy on behalf of the winning European team; she had won an individual double with the 200m and 400m, in which she had run a marvellous race to beat Marita Koch in a world record 49.52 to 49.76, Koch's last defeat at 400m for four years. Szewinska contested the biennial European Cup competition from 1965 to 1979 amassing a record total of points, including four 1sts, two 2nds and three 3rds in individual events. Her other honours included two golds, a silver and two bronze at European Indoors, gold and silver at European Juniors, and two golds at the World Student Games. Szewinska also set a world indoor record with 7.1 for 60m in 1974.

In all she set 38 Polish records and won 19 Polish titles at four individual events. She married her coach Janusz Szewinski on 25 Dec 1967.

Other bests: 100m 10.9 and 11.13 (1974), 400m hurdles 56.62 (1977), long jump 6.67m (1968).

Pat TAAFFE (Ire)

HORSE RACING

Patrick Taaffe. b. 12 Mar 1930 Rathcoole, Dublin d. 7 Jul 1992 Dublin.

A superb horseman who rode the winner of the Grand National twice (*Quare Times* 1955 and *Gay Trip* 1970), the Irish Grand National a record six times and the Cheltenham Gold Cup four times, including thrice on the supreme champion *Arkle*. He was the second son of jumping trainer Tom Taaffe. After riding as an amateur from 1945 (with his first winner in 1947) he turned professional in 1950, when he became first jockey to Tom Dreaper. Turning to training after his retirement in 1970, he trained *Captain Christy* to the Cheltenham double, Champion Hurdle in 1972 and Gold Cup in 1974.

Koki TAIHO (Japan)

SUMO WRESTLING

Koki Taiho. né Koki Naya. b. 29 May 1940 Sakhalin, Russia.

Taiho, Japanese for 'Great Bird', is considered the greatest and most revered sumo wrestler ever. He began his career in 1960 as a *sumotori*, but was acclaimed a *yokozuna*, or grand champion, in late 1961, the fastest anyone had ever risen to that level in the sport. During his career he won 32 Emperor's Cup victories, 20 more than any other grand champion, and eight with perfect 15-0 match scores. He won 872 bouts, 45 of them consecutively, and won his final Emperor's Cup victory at the 1971 New Year's tournament and then retired. He was then permitted to open the 106th sumo school as a rare honour, as that put the Sumo Association over the limit of 105 licensed *sumotori* .

Naoto TAJIMA (Japan)

ATHLETICS

Naoto Tajima. b. 15 Aug 1912 Iwakuni, Yamaguchi Prefecture, d. 4 Dec 1990.

The Olympic champion of 1936 when he became the first man to triple jump 16 metres, his 16.00 lasted as a world record for 14 years. He had a pre-Games best of 15.40, jumped 15.76 in the first round, just 2cm down on the world record, and then achieved the record in the fourth round. Two days earlier he had won the bronze medal in the long jump with 7.74w, to equal his 1935 best. A graduate of Kyoto University, in 1932 he had been sixth in the Olympic long jump and in 1934 he won the long jump and was third at triple jump at the Far Eastern Games. Japanese champion at triple jump in 1932 and 1935. He became director of the Japan Amateur Sports Association and chairman of the Japan University Sports Board.

Mikhail TAL (USSR/Lat)

CHESS

Mikhail Nelchemyevich Tal. b. 9 Nov 1936 Riga. d. 28 Jun 1992 Moscow.

In 1957, when he graduated from Riga University, he became the youngest ever Soviet chess champion at 20 and an international grandmaster, despite never having been awarded master status (contrary to FIDE rules). An attacking genius, he won the candidates tournament in 1959 and went on to beat Mikhail Botvinnik and become world chess champion in 1960. He lost the rematch a year later when he was ill. Health problems affected him for some years, but while not fully recapturing his youthful heights he achieved much international success and was USSR champion again in 1958, 1967 (joint), 1972, 1974 (joint) and 1978 (joint) to equal the record of six titles set by Botvinnik. In seven Olympiads for the USSR, 1958-80, he achieved 59 wins, 31 draws and had two losses.

Satoko TANAKA (Japan)

SWIMMING

Satoko Tanaka. b. 3 Feb 1942 Sasebo, Nagasaki Prefecture. Now Takeuji.

Between 1959 and 1963 Tanaka set 10 world records for the 200m backstroke, taking the record from 2:37.1 to 2:28.2. That event was not then on the Olympic programme, however, and she was restricted to bronze at 100m in 1960.

Toshiaki TANAKA (Japan)

TABLE TENNIS

Toshiaki Tanaka. b. 24 Feb 1935 Otaru, Hokkaido Prefecture.

During a brief but brilliant career he was twice the world singles champion. After taking the title in 1955, he lost to his teammate, Ichiro Ogimura, in the 1956 final, but reversed that result the following year. During those three years he was also a member of the winning Swaythling Cup team. A small man at 1.60m and 52kg. Graduate of the Nippon University.

Elaine TANNER (Can)

SWIMMING

Elaine Tanner. b. 22 Feb 1951 Vancouver.

At the age of 15 the 5ft 2in Tanner, known as 'Mighty Mouse', won four gold (110y and 220y butterfly, 440y individual medley and freestyle relay) and three silver medals (110y and 220y backstroke and medley relay) at the 1966 Commonwealth Games. Her best stroke was the backstroke and at the 1967 Pan-American Games she set world records for both the 100m in 67.3 (improving to 67.1 on the first leg of the medley relay in which Canada came second) and the 200m in 2:24.4. There she added a silver at 100m butterfly and the 4x100m freestyle relay and had two fourth places. Although she improved her 100m best to 66.7 at the 1968 Olympics, she had to settle for the silver medal behind the 66.2 world record by Kaye Hall (USA). Tanner had earlier won a silver at the 200m backstroke, and added a bronze in the freestyle relay. Between 1965 and 1968 she won 17 Canadian titles, including the 100m/110y butterfly and 200m/220y backstroke each year. Other best times: freestyle 100m 61.5, 200m 2:14.8, 400m 4:43.8; butterfly 100m 65.4, 200m 2:29.9; medley 200m 2:31.8, 400m 5:26.3.

Hadyn TANNER (UK)

RUGBY UNION

Hadyn Tanner. b. 9 Jan 1917 Gowerton, Glamorgan.

As an 18-year-old schoolboy he played scrum half in the Swansea team which defeated the 1935 All Blacks 11-3. As a result of his impressive display he was immediately brought into the Welsh XV and again played a significant part in a second defeat (13-12) of the touring New Zealanders. He won 13 caps with Swansea before the war and a further 12 after the war when he played for Cardiff.
His international career lasted 14 seasons (1935-49) and matches the longest of any Welsh international. In addition to his 25 Welsh caps he played in one Test on the Lions tour of South Africa in 1938. A penetrating runner in attack and solid in defence his greatest attribute was his ability to serve his fly-half in the most adverse playing conditions.

Leonid TARANENKO (USSR/Bls)

WEIGHTLIFTING

Leonid Arkadyevich Taranenko. b. 13 Jun 1956 Malorita.

Taranenko was dominant at the 110kg class from 1980 until 1985. In 1980 he won the World, European and Olympic titles. He would almost certainly have defended his Olympic title successfully in 1984 had the Soviets not boycotted the Games, as he won the Friendship Games in Varna, Bulgaria with lifts which would have won the Olympic gold by 52.5 kg. In 1988 he won the European title, but missed the Olympics through injury. He then went on to win the super-heavyweight World title in 1990, having set world records in Canberra in 1988 for jerk at 266kg and total 475kg that remain unsurpassed five years later. USSR champion 1979, 1983, 1986-7.

Fran TARKENTON (USA)

AMERICAN FOOTBALL

Francis Asbury Tarkenton. b. 3 Feb 1940 Richmond, Virginia.

Fran Tarkenton holds most of the NFL career passing records. He was a quarterback in college at the University of Georgia, making All-American in 1960. He was drafted by Minnesota and played most of his NFL career with the Vikings until 1978, except for five seasons 1967-71 with the New York Giants. Tarkenton was an amazingly durable player, not missing a start until his 16th season. He was a good passer, but was actually known better for his superb scrambling ability, which frustrated many defensive linemen. Tarkenton holds NFL records for most passes attempted (6467), most passes completed (3686), touchdown passes (342), and yards gained passing (47,003). The only negative in Tarkenton's career was that, although he led the Vikings to four Super Bowls, he never managed to play on a winning Super Bowl team.

Jordi TARRÈS (Spain)

MOTOR CYCLING

Jordi Tarrès. b. 10 Sep 1966 Barcelona.

With four world titles, 1987, 1989-91, Tarrès has become the most successful Trials rider ever. He was also second in the 1988 championship.

Maurice TATE (UK)

CRICKET

Maurice William Tate. b. 30 May 1895 Brighton, Sussex, d. 18 May 1956 Wadhurst, Sussex.

Originally a slow-medium bowler, like his father **Fred** (1867-1943) who played once for England in 1902, Tate became the best medium-fast bowler of his era for Sussex and England. A powerful man, he swung the ball late and generated considerable pace off the pitch from a short run. He was a genuine all-rounder, achieving 1000 runs and 200 wickets in a season each year 1923-5; three of six times that this feat has ever been achieved. He had eight doubles of 1000/100 in England and one in India and Ceylon in 1926/7. He took a wicket with his first ball in Test cricket, and his most successful series was in Australia in 1924/5 when he took 38 wickets at 23.18.
39 Tests 1924-35: 1198 runs at 25.48, 1 100 HS 100, 155 wickets at 26.16, BB 6-42; 11 catches.*
First-class 1912-37: 21,717 runs at 25.04, 23 100s HS 203; 2784 wickets at 18.16; BB 9-71; 284 catches.

Ulrike TAUBER (GDR)

SWIMMING

Ulrike Tauber. b. 16 Jun 1958 Karl-Marx-Stadt (Chemnitz). Later Wanja.

One of the all-powerful GDR women team of world record breakers in the mid-1970s. Her world marks came at individual medley events, with six improvements at 200m and four at 400m. Her first records came at the 1974 Europeans when in the medley events she was timed at 2:18.97 and 4:52.42, winning by the huge margins of 5.00 and 6.36 seconds. In 1975 she won the World title at 400m but was second to Kathy Heddy (USA) at 200m.
Her final record for 400m was when she won the 1976 Olympic title in 4:42.77, and after retaining her European medley titles in 1977 she set her last mark for 200m with 2:15.85. In 1978 she took the 400m IM World silver, but was 6.69 seconds behind Tracy Caulkins. She also set a European record for 200m backstroke with 2:21.13 in 1974 and had a best at 200m butterfly of 2:12.50 when she won the Olympic silver in 1976. She won eight GDR medley titles from 1974 to 1979.

Luigi TAVERI (Swi)

MOTOR CYCLING

Luigi Taveri. b. 19 Sep 1929 near Zürich.

World motorcycling champion at 125cc in 1962, 1964 and 1966, he won a total of 30 Grand Prix races, 22 at 125cc, 6 at 50cc and 2 at 250cc. He started racing as a passenger for his elder brother Hans in 1947, and went solo a year later. After riding various machines his first wins came for MV Agusta, and he rode for them 1955-7 and 1960, for Ducati in 1958 and for Honda from 1961 to 1966.
A small man, he allied an extrovert personality off the track to stylish riding on the circuit. Now runs a car repair business.

Hugh TAYFIELD (SAf)

CRICKET

Hugh Joseph Tayfield. b. 30 Jan 1929 Durban.

'Toey' Tayfield was easily South Africa's leading wicket-taker in Test cricket, and one of the world's best off-break bowlers. He earned his nickname from his habit of stubbing his toe into the ground before bowling each ball. Meticulously accurate, he took at least 10 wickets in each of his eight Test series, with best returns of 37 at 17.18 in 1956/7 against England and 30 at 28.10 against Australia in 1952/3. He played mostly for Transvaal, having started with Natal, then Rhodesia.
37 Tests 1949-60: 862 runs at 16.90, HS 75; 170 wickets at 25.91, BB 9-113; 27 catches
First-class 1945-63: 3668 runs at 17.30, HS 77; 864 wickets at 21.86, BB 9-113; 149 catches

Alec TAYLOR (UK)

HORSE RACING

Alexander Taylor. b. 15 Mar 1862 Fyfield, Wiltshire, d. 28 Jan 1943 Thorpe, near Chertsey, Surrey.

Champion trainer in Britain 13 times, 1907, 1909-10, 1914, 1917-23, 1925-6. He was the first to pass £50,000 in a season in 1910, when his total was £52,929 from 47 races. Known as 'The Wizard of Manton', he trained over 1100 winners. His 21 English classic successes between 1905 and 1927 included eight of the Oaks, and the colts' Triple Crown winners *Gay Crusader* 1917 and *Gainsborough* 1918. He took over the Manton stables from his father, Alec senior, whose horses had won 12 classics, from 1902. He retired after the 1927 season and died a very wealthy man. His brother Tom was also a leading trainer.

Bob TAYLOR (UK)

CRICKET

Robert William Taylor. b. 17 Jul 1941 Stoke-on-Trent, Staffordshire.

Apart from one Test in 1971, Taylor had to wait a long time for his chance at international level, for while his excellence as a wicket-keeper was well known, he had to act as reserve for the great Allan Knott, who was five years younger than him. Knott, however, went to play in World Series cricket, and at the age of 36 Taylor was at last in the England team. For the next six years he showed himself the best 'keeper in the world. Against India at Bombay in February 1980 he equalled the world Test record with seven dismissals in the first innings and with three more in the second set a world Test record of ten dismissals (all caught).

He ended his career with a record number of dismissals in first-class cricket. He was also a most useful batsman, who sadly just missed a Test hundred when he made his then highest-ever score of 97 for England v Australia at Adelaide in 1979. He captained Derbyshire in 1975-6.

Awarded the MBE.

57 Tests 1971-84: 1156 runs at 16.28, HS 97; 167 catches, 7 stumpings.

27 One-day Ints: 130 runs at 13.00, HS 26; 26 catches, 6 stumpings.*

First-class 1960-88: 12,065 runs at 16.92, 1 100 HS 100; 1 wicket; 1473 catches, 176 stumpings.

Dennis TAYLOR (UK)

SNOOKER

Dennis Taylor. b. 19 Jan 1949 Coalisland, Co. Tyrone.

The hugely popular Taylor won one of snooker's greatest ever matches when he defeated Steve Davis in the final of the World Professional Championship in 1985. His 18-17 victory came on the black in the last frame in the early hours of the morning, watched by 18.5 million people, by some definitions the largest viewership ever for a sporting event on UK television. Taylor had won the British junior billiards title in 1968 and after representing England on a residential qualification in 1971 he turned professional. He reached the World Championship semi-final in 1975 and 1977 and lost in the final to Terry Griffiths in 1979. He won the Irish Professional championship in 1982 and 1985-7, the Rothmans Grand Prix in 1984 and the Benson & Hedges Masters in 1987. He was a member of the Irish team that won the World Cup three times 1985-7.

Herbie TAYLOR (SAf)

CRICKET

Herbert Wilfred Taylor. b. 5 May 1889 Durban, d. 8 Feb 1973 Newlands, Cape Town.

Taylor was especially successful batting on the matting wickets of South Africa, although he first made his name in England in the Triangular Tournament of 1912. In 1913/4, when Sydney Barnes took 49 wickets at 10.93, Taylor was outstanding with 508 runs at 50.80 in the series for South Africa. He captained his country in 18 consecutive Tests 1913-24, and by the time of his retirement after a 20-year Test career he had scored a record number of runs for South Africa. He also played rugby football for Natal. He was awarded the Military Cross during World War I.

42 Tests 1912-32: 2936 runs at 40.77, 7 100s HS 176; 5 wickets at 31.20, BB 3-15; 19 catches.

First-class 1909-36: 13,105 runs at 41.86, 30 100s HS 250; 22 wickets at 25.45, BB 4-36; 75 catches.*

J H TAYLOR (UK)

GOLF
John Henry Taylor. b. 19 Mar 1871 Northam, Devon, d. 10 Feb 1963 Northam.

Taylor, with Harry Vardon and James Braid, comprised the 'Great Triumvirate' of golf at the turn of the century. He won the British Open five times, 1894-5, 1900, 1909 and 1913, and was also second five times. He also won the PGA in 1904 and 1908, the French Open in 1908-9 and the German Open in 1912, and was second in the 1900 US Open. He represented England nine times against Scotland and frequently partnered Vardon or Braid in stakes matches.

He had started as a caddy on the Westward Ho golf course, and soon became a professional, first at Burnham, then successively at Winchester, Wimbledon and Royal Mid-Surrey.

Lawrence TAYLOR (USA)

AMERICAN FOOTBALL
Lawrence Taylor. b. 4 Feb 1959 Williamsburg, Virginia.

Some experts consider Lawrence Taylor the greatest linebacker in football history. He played in college at the University of North Carolina and was the second player chosen in the 1981 NFL draft.

An outside linebacker who combined size (1.91m *6'3"*, 111 kg *245 lb*) with great quickness and speed, he played his entire NFL career with the New York Giants. He was named Rookie of the Year and NFL Defensive Player of the Year and played in nine Pro Bowls. In 1986 he was named the NFL MVP, a rare honour for a defensive player. Taylor had a brief problem with substance abuse during his career but recovered well from that to dominate the line of scrimmage in the late 1980s for the Giants. He was expected to retire at the end of 1992, but although that season ended early with a torn Achilles tendon, he agreed in 1993 a $5 million two-year deal to stay with the Giants.

Major TAYLOR (USA)

CYCLING
Marshall Walter Taylor. b. 26 Nov 1878 Indianapolis, Indiana, d. 6 Jul 1932 Chicago, Illinois.

Major Taylor was the first great black athlete and the first to achieve national acclaim in the United States. Beginning in 1893, he raced initially in Worcester, Massachusetts and won consistently in the northeast, later travelling widely to display his talents. In 1899 he won the world amateur sprint title and in 1900 the US national professional championship, after two previous titles were taken from him by conspiracy because of his colour. He raced in Europe from 1901 to 1904, winning many championships and the acclaim of the Europeans. He lived strictly for his era, neither smoking nor drinking, and in his spare time he became a published poet.

Levan TEDIASHVILI (USSR/Geo)

WRESTLING
Levan Kitoyevich Tediashvili. b. 15 Mar 1948 Gegmoubani, Sagaredzhojskiy region, Georgia.

Considered the greatest technical wrestler in Soviet history. He won Olympic freestyle gold medals at middleweight (82kg) in 1972 and light-heavyweight (90kg) in 1976. He also won World championships at 82kg in 1971 and 90kg in 1973-5, and Europeans in 1974, 1976 and 1978. In the Olympics, he relegated the United States' Peterson brothers, John in 1972 and Ben in 1976, to silver medals. Tediashvili studied law, and was known as a brash performer who often played to the crowd. He did not lose a match between 1971 and 1976. He was also a Soviet and World champion at sombo, the Russian self-defence sport.

Sachin TENDULKAR (India)

CRICKET
Sachin Ramesh Tendulkar. b. 24 Apr 1973 Bombay.

A batting genius, who by his 20th birthday was well established as a Test batsman. In

a school match in 1988, with Vinod Kambli who later joined him in the Indian Test team, he set a world record partnership at any level of cricket with 664 runs unbeaten; Tendulkar scored 326* and Kambli 349*. Tendulkar made his Test début at 16 years 205 days in 1989, India's youngest ever player, and in 1990 became, at 17 years 112 days, the second youngest century-maker in Test history. He became Yorkshire's first ever overseas player in 1992. His impressive range of strokes is allied to a calm, mature approach which quite belies his youthful looks. He is also a useful medium pace bowler.
25 Tests 1989-93: 1522 runs at 44.76, 4 100s HS 165; 4 wickets at 40.25; BB 2-10; 18 catches.
56 One-day Ints: 1520 runs at 31.66, HS 84; 13 wickets at 56.00, BB 4-34; 13 catches.*
First-class 1988-92: 4708 runs at 54.74, 10 100s HS 159; 16 wickets at 73.25, BB 3-60; 28 catches.

Igor TER-OVANESYAN (USSR)

ATHLETICS
Igor Aramovich Ter-Ovanesyan. b. 19 May 1938 Kiev, Ukraine.

He achieved greatest success in the European Championships, with three gold and two silver medals at long jump between 1958 and 1971. He also won European Indoor titles in 1966 and 1968 and a silver medal in 1971; the European indoor best of 8.23m that he set to win the first of those titles was not equalled until 1985. Outdoors he set six European records from 8.01 in 1959 to 8.31 in 1962 and 8.35 in 1967, the latter two also world records.
He competed at five Olympic Games from 1956 to 1972, and won bronze medals in 1960 and 1964, with fourth place in 1968. He also won five World Student Games and a record 12 Soviet titles between 1957 and 1961. Amazingly he was second in the long jump in all nine USSR v USA matches from 1958 to 1971.
He became coach to USSR teams and vice-president of the Soviet (now Russian) track and field association. His father Aram set two USSR discus records in 1933.
Other bests: 100m 10.4 (1961), decathlon 7196 (on current tables) (1958).

Bill TERRY (USA)

BASEBALL
William Harold Terry. b. 30 Oct 1898 Atlanta, Georgia, d. 9 Jan 1989 Jacksonville, Florida.

The last National League player to bat over .400, with his .401 average (254 hits) in 1930. He had only fair power, but was the best defensive first baseman of his era and batted over .300 every year of his career with the New York Giants. He went .350 or over four times (also 1929 - .372, 226 hits; 1932 - .350, 1934 - .354). His career average ranks him 12th equal all-time. He was a player-manager from 1932-6 and continued managing the Giants to 1941, leading them to three National League pennants and a World Series victory in 1933.
Career 1923-36: 2193 hits Avg. .341, HR 154; RBI 1078.

Federico TESIO (Italy)

HORSE RACING
Federico Tesio. b. 17 Jan 1869 Turin, d. 1 May 1954 Milan.

The success of the racing industry in Italy is almost entirely due to his genius. After serving as a cavalry officer and becoming champion amateur jockey in Italy, he founded his Dormello stud on the shores of Lake Maggiore in 1898. He won the first of his 22 Italian Derbys with *Guio Reni* in 1911, and steadily developed great blood lines of thoroughbreds from relatively modest mares, including the finest Italian racehorses, *Donatello*, *Nearco* and *Ribot*, although he died just two months before the latter's first race. In the early 1930s he went into partnership with Marchese Mario Incisa della Rochetta to create the Dormello-Olgiata stud near Rome. Known as 'The Wizard of Dormello', his other big race totals are unmatched anywhere in the world: 23 winners of the Gran Premio di Milano and 21 of the Criterium Nazionale.

THEAGENES of Thasos (Greece)

WRESTLING

Theagenes of Thasos. fl. ca. 480-460 BC.

Theagenes is credited with over 1400 victories in various sporting festivals in ancient Greece, but he named his son Dysolympios (twice-Olympian) in celebration of the Olympic titles he won in 480 BC in boxing and in 476 BC in the pankration. He and Kleitomachos of Thebes were the only two men to win these two events at Olympia. The Thasians erected a statue to him after his death. A former athlete, who hated him, attacked the statue one night and it fell on him and killed him. The Thasians followed Draconian law and threw the statue into the sea. A great drought fell upon the island of Thasos and crops suffered, with many animals dying as a result. The oracle at Delphi told them this could be corrected by bringing all their exiles back to their country. They did this but the drought and famine continued. They then consulted the wise Pythia at Delphi, who told them, 'You have forgotten your great Theagenes, whom you threw in the sand, where he now lies, though before he won a thousand prizes.' Several Thasian fishermen hauled the statue back in their nets, it was re-erected in its former position, and the drought ended. After this the Thasians sacrificed to Theagenes as a god of healing.

David THEILE (Aus)

SWIMMING

David Egmont Theile. b. 17 Jan 1938 Maryborough, Queensland.

The Olympic 100m backstroke champion of 1956, when he set a world record time of 62.2, and 1960, in 61.9. He also won a medley relay silver medal in 1960.
A quiet, unassuming personality, Theile was Australian junior champion in 1954 and won his first senior title at 100y the following year in a national record. He won the 100y backstroke title again in 1956 and 1959-60, missing the years 1957-8 while he concentrated on his medical studies. He graduated from the University of Queensland and became a Fellow of the Royal Australian College of Surgeons.

Philippe THIJS (Bel)

CYCLING

Philippe Thijs. b. 8 Oct 1890 Anderlecht-Brussels, d. 16 Jan 1972 Brussels.

The first man to win the Tour de France three times, 1913-14 and 1920. He rode almost exclusively in France and had no major wins outside of his homeland. He was helped by the rules in 1913 which required all riders to make their own repairs. Going over the Pyrenées, Eugene Christophe was leading the race when he broke his front fork. He carried his bike to the nearest town, found a blacksmith's shop and fixed the bike himself. The three-hour delay handed the lead to Thijs, who held on to win the race.

Gustavo THOENI (Italy)

ALPINE SKIING

Gustavo Thoeni. b. 28 Feb 1951 Trafoi.

Olympic champion at giant slalom in 1972 and silver medallist at slalom in 1972 and 1976. He was world champion at Alpine Combination in 1972 and 1976 and both slalom and giant slalom in 1974. In the World Cup he was overall champion each year 1971-3 and 1975 (2nd 1974, 3rd 1970, 1976), won titles at giant slalom 1970-2 and slalom 1973-4 and had 24 individual race wins.
His cousin Roland (b. 17 Jan 1951) won the bronze medal at the 1972 Olympics, one place behind Gustavo in the slalom.

Sven THOFELT (Swe)

MODERN PENTATHLON

Sven Alfred Thofelt. b. 19 May 1904 Stockholm, d. 1 Feb 1993 Stockholm.

Over a 20-year period he won Olympic medals of all colours before helping to found the International Modern Pentathlon Union in 1948, and being its secretary-general 1948-60 and then president 1960-88. He had a distinguished military career as an artilleryman, retiring from the Swedish army as a Brigadier General, having commanded his country's northern defence forces.
He first contested a modern pentathlon

competition at the age of 19, and five years later took the Olympic gold medal in Amsterdam. He had the misfortune to draw poor horses at the Olympic Games of 1932 and 1936 and was placed fourth on each occasion. At the three Olympics from 1928 to 1936 he was successively 2nd, 1st and 3rd at swimming in the modern pentathlon competition and he developed into a fine fencer, winning four Swedish titles at épée. It was at that sport that he won his other Olympic medals, taking the team silver in 1936 and bronze in 1948. He was Swedish modern pentathlon champion 1927-31 and 1934. He was team manager of Sweden's modern pentathlon team from 1936 to 1948 and a member of the IOC 1970-6, being elected an honorary member in 1976.

His son **Björn** (b. 19 Jun 1955) was world champion at modern pentathlon in 1954, but did not finish at the 1956 Olympics.

George THOMAS (UK)

BADMINTON

(Sir) George Alan Thomas Bt. b. 14 Jun 1881 Constantinople (now Istanbul), Turkey, d. 23 Jul 1972 London.

Between 1903 and 1928 Thomas won 21 All-England badminton titles, still the record. He was singles champion each year 1920 to 1923, won the men's doubles nine times with three different partners and the mixed doubles eight times with five partners. A magnificent stylist, he played in every England international match from 1903 to 1929.

In 1934 he was elected president of the newly formed International Badminton Federation, and remained in that office for 21 years. In 1940 he donated the Thomas Cup for the men's world team championship, although it was not until 1949 that it was first contested.

He was British champion at chess in 1923 and 1934 and represented England at lawn tennis, at which he reached the Wimbledon doubles semi-finals in 1907 and 1912. He also played hockey for Hampshire.

Isiah THOMAS (USA)

BASKETBALL

Isiah Lord Thomas, III. b. 30 Apr 1961 Chicago, Illinois.

One of the quintessential point guards in basketball history. He played collegiately for Bob Knight at Indiana University, winning the NCAA Championship in 1981. He was selected for the 1980 US Olympic team which did not play because of the boycott. He has played in the NBA since 1981 with the Detroit Pistons, where his playmaking and scoring has been brilliant. Twice he has led the Pistons to NBA Championships, 1989-90, being named the finals MVP in 1990. In 1984/5 he averaged an NBA record 13.9 assists for the season. He has been a controversial player who has not always been well-liked by opponents. This led to the decision in 1992 not to include him on the US Olympic basketball team - the 'Dream Team' - although he was surely deserving.

NBA career: 17,966 points, av. 19.5; 8662 assists (third all-time).

John THOMAS (USA)

ATHLETICS

John Curtis Thomas. b. 3 Mar 1941 Boston, Massachusetts.

In 1959 the teenage Thomas shot to the top with six world indoor high jump bests from 2.11m to 2.16, including the first 7ft *2.13m* jump under cover. He caught his left (take-off) foot in an elevator shaft, and the injury was so serious that he missed the outdoor season. However, in 1960 he added another four indoor bests, this time in excess of the outdoor world record of 2.16, taking the record up from 2.17 to 2.20, and then outdoors set five world records from 2.17 to 2.22. Then, however, he disappointed his fans with third place at the Olympics and for the rest of his career he remained one of the world's best but was overshadowed by Valeriy Brumel, behind whom he won the Olympic silver in 1964. AAU champion outdoors in 1960 and 1962 and indoors seven times 1959-64 and 1966, and NCAA winner for Boston University in 1960-1.

Kurt THOMAS (USA)

GYMNASTICS

Kurt BiHeraux Thomas. b. 29 Mar 1956 Miami, Florida.

He was America's first world champion at gymnastics, at floor exercises in 1978, with two more gold medals and three silvers, including the all-around, in 1979. The US boycott cost him a strong chance of gold medals at the Olympics in 1980 and he then retired from competition. He had been 21st in the 1976 Olympics, NCAA champion while at Indiana University in 1977, and the winner at the America Cup in 1977 and 1979. An innovative gymnast, he developed the 'Thomas Flair', a whirling leg movement on the pommel horse and floor exercises.

Daley THOMPSON (UK)

ATHLETICS

Francis Morgan Thompson. b. 30 Jul 1958 Notting Hill, London.

Th. world's greatest decathlete, so often displaying unparalleled competitive ability. Olympic champion in 1980 and 1984, World in 1983, European in 1982 and 1986 and Commonwealth in 1978, 1982 and 1986. He set four world records (8648 in 1980, 8730 and 8774 in 1982, 8847 in his Olympic triumph at Los Angeles 1984). He contested his first decathlon in 1975 and a year later took part in the Olympics, learning much while placing 18th. He progressed fast, with three world junior records 1976-7 and the first of ten UK and Commonwealth records in 1976. He won 19 decathlons in all, including twelve in succession from his European silver in 1978 to his 9th in the World Championships in 1987, when he had his preparations marred by a groin injury. He came back to place 4th at the 1988 Olympics, but after an operation to remove a bone growth in his left knee in September 1989 and further injuries, he was unable to achieve his goal of a fifth Olympics in 1992 and announced his retirement. Curiously he never contested a decathlon in England!
He was a top class performer at a wide range of events, winning sprint relay medals in 1986 with Commonwealth silver and European bronze, and taking national titles at the long jump, AAA in 1977 and UK in 1979. Awarded the MBE 1982.
Individual event bests: 100m 10.26 (1986), 200m 20.88 (1979), 400m 46.86 (1982), 1500m 4:20.3 (1976), 110mh 14.04 (1986), 400mh 52.14 (1986), high jump 2.14i (1982), 2.11 (1980); pole vault 5.25 (1986), long jump 8.01 (1984), 8.11w (1978), shot 16.10 (1984), discus 49.10 (1986), javelin 65.38 (1980).

David THOMPSON (USA)

BASKETBALL

David O'Neil Thompson. b. 13 Jul 1954 Shelby, North Carolina.

It is said that the saddest of possible words are 'What might have been?', words that echo in the memory when thinking of David Thompson. He led North Carolina State to a 27-0 record during his sophomore year, but the team could not contest the NCAAs because it was on probation. They won that title, however, in 1974, defeating perennial champions UCLA in the semi-finals. Thompson's NBA career was spent with the Denver Nuggets, for whom he was a high-flying guard, known for his acrobatic drives and leaps, in the manner of Julius Erving and later Michael Jordan. As an offensive threat he seemed unstoppable. After six seasons in which he averaged over 25 points per game, and 73 points in the final game of 1978 when he was attempting to wrest the NBA scoring title from George Gervin, his game fell away. He had begun using drugs, especially cocaine, and it eventually ended a career that probably never reached its potential. He later found a front-office position with the Charlotte Hornets.
NBA career 11,264 points, av. 22.1.

Tiny THOMPSON (Can)

ICE HOCKEY

Cecil Thompson. b. 31 May 1905 Sandon, British Columbia, d. 9 Feb 1981 Calgary, Alberta.

Thompson won the Vezina Trophy four

times, 1930, 1933, 1936, 1938, in only a 12-year NHL career. He played mainly for the Boston Bruins, helping them win the regular season championship six times in ten years. His best year may have been his rookie season when he recorded a goals-against average of 1.18 and had 12 shutouts. He finished his career with the Detroit Red Wings after the Bruins signed the phenomenal Frankie Brimsek. After his playing days he became the chief scout in Western Canada for the Chicago Black Hawks.
NHL career 1928-40: 553 games, 2.08 GAA, 81 shutouts.

Lothar THOMS (GDR)

CYCLING
Lothar Thoms. b. 18 May 1956 Guben.

Usually considered to be the greatest track kilometre time trialist ever. In addition to his four world titles, 1977-9 and 1981 (and 2nd 1982), his Olympic victory in 1980 was achieved in a time of 1:02.955, which stood as a world record until 1989. His victory margin in that stunning performance was almost two seconds - the most dominant ever in the Olympics.

Jeff THOMSON (Aus)

CRICKET
Jeffrey Robert Thomson. b. 16 Aug 1950 Greenacre, Sydney.

The speed of 160.45 km/h *99.7 mph* recorded for Thomson when bowling for Australia against West Indies in 1975 is the highest ever for a fast bowler. That came at his peak of fame in an era when he and Dennis Lillee terrorised opposing batsmen. Thomson's exceptional pace came from a slingy action with a long range of movement and very powerful arm, shoulder and back muscles.
He did not impress in his first match against Pakistan in December 1972, but when next tried he was devastating, taking 33 wickets at 17.93 against England in 1974/5. He had four more hauls of 20 wickets or more in Test series in the 1970s, but then seemed to lose some of his fire. He played for Middlesex in 1981, but only for part of the year due to injury. On his return to Australia, however, he made a fine comeback and took 22 wickets at 18.68 in the series against England in 1982/3. He then lost his place but returned again, this time without much success, in two Tests in England in 1985, although that allowed him to reach 200 wickets in Tests. He played for New South Wales 1972-4 and for Queensland 1974-86.
51 Tests 1972-85: 679 runs at 12.81, HS 49; 200 wickets at 28.00, BB 6-46; 20 catches.
50 One-day Ints: 181 runs at 7.54, HS 21; 55 wickets at 35.30, BB 4-67; 9 catches.
First-class 1972-86: 2065 runs at 13.58, HS 61; 675 wickets at 26.46, BB 7-27; 63 catches.

Peter THOMSON (Aus)

GOLF
Peter William Thomson. b. 23 Aug 1929 Melbourne, Victoria.

The first great golfer from Australia. He has since been overshadowed in some people's minds by Greg Norman, Bruce Crampton and Bruce Devlin, but his five British Open wins, 1954-6, 1958 and 1965, makes him the leading winner of majors amongst Australian players. He played a low, running shot which was not well-suited to American courses and, preferring the small ball, he rarely played in the USA, although he won the 1956 Texas Open and finished 5th in the 1957 Masters. He turned pro in 1950 and that year won the first of nine New Zealand Opens, his last being in 1971. He won the Australian Open in 1951, 1967 and 1972 and had 20 PGA victories in Britain. He had a great record in the Canada Cup, which with Kel Nagle he won for Australia in 1954 and 1959. These two were second in 1955 and 1961 and 3rd in 1960 and 1962, and Thomson had been third with Ossie Pickworth in 1953.
Thomson later helped develop the Asian golf circuit. Since his playing days, he has served as a golf architect, golf journalist and as President of the Australian PGA. Awarded the CBE.

Øyvin THON (Nor)

ORIENTEERING

Øyvin Thon. b. 25 Mar 1958 Drammen.

One of only three men to have won two world orienteering titles. He was champion in 1979 and 1981 and took the silver medal in 1983. A excellent relay runner, he won five gold medals, at each of the biennial championships 1981-9. He also won the World Cup in 1988. He won 15 Norwegian titles, including the standard distance in 1980 and the long distance in 1981, 1983 and 1986.

Cliff THORBURN (Can)

SNOOKER

Cliff Thorburn. b. 16 Jan 1948 Victoria, British Columbia.

The World Professional champion at snooker in 1980 when he beat Alex Higgins 18-16 in a great final. He had been a beaten finalist in 1977, having turned pro in 1973. In 1983 he was beaten 18-6 by Steve Davis in the final, but had scored the first maximum 147 break in World Championship history against Terry Griffiths in the second round.
He had started playing at the age of 16, scoring his first century break at 19. He won the first Canadian Open in 1974, with further wins each year 1978-80, and won the Benson & Hedges Masters in 1983 and 1985-6. A tough match player, he would wear down his opponents by his determined, steady play.

John THORNETT (Aus)

RUGBY UNION

John Edward Thornett. b. 30 Mar 1935.

One of three remarkably talented brothers who all won international honours. John himself won 37 caps for Australia (1955-67), brother **Dick** (b. 23 Sep 1940) won 11 caps at rugby union and 10 in rugby league, and a third brother, Ken, was also a rugby league international. Initially a flanker and a lock, John later switched to prop and he toured eight times for Australia, four of them as captain.
Educated at Sydney Boys' High School, he graduated in engineering from Sydney University. Awarded the MBE in 1966.

Jim THORPE (USA)

ATHLETICS and AMERICAN FOOTBALL

James Francis Thorpe. b. 28 May 1888 Bellemont, Oklahoma, né Wa-tho-huck (Sac and Fox Indian name meaning 'Bright Path'), d. 28 Mar 1953 Lomita, California.

Voted America's greatest athlete of the first half of the 20th century in 1950, Thorpe was a great American footballer and was the Olympic champion at decathlon and pentathlon in 1912, setting world records at both events. The gold medals that he won for those events in Stockholm were lost a year later, when he had to forfeit them for having earned some $15 per week playing baseball. The IOC decided in 1982 to restore the medals to Thorpe posthumously and replicas were presented to one of his daughters.
He had won the Olympic titles by huge margins, scoring 8412 points in the decathlon to 7724 by Hugo Wieslander (6564 to 5965 on the current tables) and was also fourth at high jump. His individual event bests included 15.0 for 120y hurdles, 1.95m high jump, 7.08m long jump and 14.84m shot put, all top world-class marks in 1912.
Thorpe's father was part Irish and part a Sac and Fox Indian, and his mother was part Indian and part French. He attended the Carlisle Indian School where he established a reputation as a phenomenal athlete and was acknowledged as one of the greatest ever college footballers as a running back. As an All-American in 1911 and 1912 he scored 25 touchdowns and 198 points from 14 games. He played professionally for the Canton Bulldogs and was their player-coach when that team joined the new American Professional Football Association in 1920. Thorpe was named as the president of that association, the league owners hoping to capitalise on Thorpe's name. His team became the Cleveland Indians in 1921, but a year later Thorpe formed his own team and after playing for various teams ended his football career with the Chicago Cardinals in 1928.

He also played major league baseball in 1913-9 with the New York Giants, Boston Braves, and Cincinnati Reds, and was known for his great speed as a base runner. After his sports career ended he became a bit player in movies, but problems with alcohol prevented him from holding jobs for long and he died penniless. A story of his life, *Jim Thorpe - All-American*, starring Burt Lancaster, was released in 1951; Thorpe had sold the film rights for $1500 in 1931 and was not paid anything further for them.

Petra THÜMER (GDR)

SWIMMING

Petra Thümer. b. 29 Jan 1961 Karl-Marx-Stadt.

Olympic champion at 400m and 800m at the 1976 Olympic Games in world record times of 4:09.89 and 8:37.14 respectively. She seized her chance, having placed second to Barbara Krause in the GDR 400m, with Krause's withdrawal through illness. At the longer distance she had set her first world record with 8:40.68 in June, only to lose the mark to Shirley Babashoff three weeks later. At the Games at the end of July both smashed the new mark, with Thümer proving the stronger.
In 1977 Thümer won a treble at 200m (2:00.29), 400m in a world record 4:08.91, and 800m (8:38.32) at the European Championships.

Clas THUNBERG (Fin)

SPEED SKATING

Clas Arnold Robert Thunberg. b. 5 Apr 1893 Helsinki, d. 28 Apr 1973 Helsinki.

The first of the great modern speed skaters, whose severe training schedule provided the basis for an unusually long world-class career. A colourful and temperamental athlete, he won his first Finnish title at the age of 26 and his first world title two months before his 30th birthday, but went on to win 31 individual events at World and European Championships. His World Championship début was in 1922 when he placed third overall and his final appearance was in 1935, aged 42. During this 14-year span he did not compete at the Championships in 1926, 1930 or 1932 but still won the overall title five times, which equalled the record number of wins. He was individual champion seven times at 1500m, six at 500m and once at 5000m . His best year was in 1925 when he took the overall title after winning three individual events and placing second in the 10,000m. His record at the Olympic Games was equally impressive, winning five gold medals, one silver and one bronze, in 1924 and 1928. He would almost certainly have added to his tally of medals had he not, like many other Europeans, declined to compete in 1932 as he objected to the mass-start style of racing used by the Americans at Lake Placid. He set five world records, from the age of 35 to his last, 500m in 42.6 at the age of 38 in 1931. By profession a building contractor, he was a national hero and was elected a Member of the Finnish Parliament.
Other best times: 1000m 1:27.4 (unofficial, his 1:28.4 of 1930 lasted for 25 years), 1500m 2:18.1, 3000m 5:00.6, 5000m 8:32.6, 10,000m 17:34.8.

Albert THURGOOD (Aus)

AUSTRALIAN RULES FOOTBALL

Albert John Thurgood. b. 11 Jan 1874 North Melbourne. d. 8 May 1927 Prahran, Melbourne, Victoria.

A brilliant all-round player who was a major influence on the development of the game. He began with Essendon in 1892 and then, after he had gone to Western Australia seeking work, played for Fremantle 1895-7 before returning to Essendon. He did not play in 1903-5 but played his last games for them in 1906. Injury and difficulty in obtaining a permit to play in the VFL effectively restricted his playing career to eight seasons. Although he played mainly at ruck and half-forward, he was the first outstanding goal-kicker in the game and in a low-scoring era set the record with 64 goals in a season (1893). After retirement he owned a number of successful race horses. He died as a result of injuries sustained in a motor accident.

Nate THURMOND (USA)

BASKETBALL

Nathaniel Thurmond. b. 25 Jul 1941 Akron, Ohio.

A great center, although overshadowed by Wilt Chamberlain and Bill Russell and later by Kareem Abdul-Jabbar. Thurmond, though not a spectacular scorer, was almost unstoppable as a rebounder and excelled at defense. He played for 14 seasons in the NBA, all of them with the San Francisco/Golden State Warriors. He played in seven All-Star Games and in 1983 was elected to the Hall of Fame.
NBA career: 14.464 rebounds, av. 15.0.

Luis TIANT (Cuba/USA)

BASEBALL

Luis Clemente Tiant Vega. b. 23 Nov 1940 Marianao, Cuba.

One of the craftiest pitchers ever. Not possessed of great speed, he threw multiple pitches from a variety of deliveries, baffling batters who had no idea what pitch was coming or where it was coming from. He had his greatest statistical year in 1968 with the Cleveland Indians, but he is best known for the eight years (1971-8) he spent with the Boston Red Sox. He remains one of the best loved Red Sox players.
Career pitching 1964-82: ERA 3.30; W-L 229-172, SO 2416. Best seasons: 1968: 21-9, 1.60 ERA; 1972: 15-6, 1.91 ERA; 1973: 20-13, 3.34 ERA; 1974: 22-13, 2.92 ERA; 1976: 21-12, 3.06 ERA.

Casey TIBBS (USA)

RODEO

Casey Tibbs. b. 5 Mar 1929 near Fort Pierre, South Dakota, d. 28 Jan 1990 Ramona, Colorado.

Considered by many as the greatest bronc rider ever, Tibbs started rodeoing at the age of 14 in Fort Pierre. In 1948 he won his first Rodeo Cowboys' Association (RCA) saddle bronc world championship, the youngest rider ever to do so, and between 1949 and 1959 won nine world championships and became known as the 'Babe Ruth' of rodeo, thanks as much to his colourful personality as his riding ability. He won the all-around cowboy world championship in 1951 and 1955, despite competing in the same era as the redoubtable Jim Shoulders, and won the saddle bronc title six times, 1949, 1951-4, and 1959, as well as the bareback bronc title in 1951. He also won more Madison Square Garden championships than any other cowboy. He retired in 1964 but returned for one last great year in 1967, when he won titles at nine of the first ten rodeos he entered. A documentary movie *Born to Buck* was made with Tibbs as the model.

Dick TIGER (Nig)

BOXING

né Dick Ihetu. b. 14 Aug 1929 Amaigo, Orlu, d. 14 Dec 1971 Nigeria.

Tiger turned professional at 23 and began boxing in Liverpool, England before moving to America after defeating future middleweight champion Terry Downes. In 1962 Tiger won the world middleweight title by defeating Gene Fullmer. He eventually lost that title in 1966 to Emile Griffith, moved up a division and defeated José Torres to claim the world light-heavyweight championship. He defended that title twice before being knocked out by Bob Foster in 1968, the only time he was stopped in his career. It was Tiger's last fight and he died of cancer only three years later.
Career record: W - 61 (3), L - 17; D - 3.

Aleksandr TIKHONOV (USSR)

BIATHLON

Aleksandr Ivanovich Tikhonov. b. 2 Jan 1947 Chelyabinsk region.

The winner of a record four Olympic gold medals at the biathlon, with relay gold medals on the USSR team at each Games from 1968 to 1980. He also won the individual silver medal at 20km in 1968, and at that distance was 4th in 1972 and 5th in 1976. Adding his World titles at 20km in 1969-70 and 1973 and at 10km in 1977 with a further six relay titles, he has a world record total of 14 biathlon gold medals. In the World Championships at 20km he was also 2nd in 1971 and 1979 and 3rd in 1977.

Bill TILDEN (USA)

TENNIS

William Tatem Tilden. b. 10 Feb 1893 Germantown, Pennsylvania, d. 5 Jun 1953 Los Angeles, California.

Universally recognised as one of the greatest players of all-time. A tall, imposing figure, he brought a sense of theatre to the courts and his devastating service and brilliant all-round attacking strokes revitalised the game after World War I. After losing in the final of the US Championship in 1918 and 1919 he went on to win the title seven times, 1920-5 and 1929. In 1920, at the age of 27, he became the first American to win the men's singles at Wimbledon, but after successfully defending his title in 1921 he did not return for the next five years. After losing in the semi-finals to Cochet in 1927 and 1929 and to Lacoste in 1928, 'Big Bill' Tilden won his third Wimbledon singles title in 1930. He was aged 37 and this victory, which came 10 years after his first success, was his last major singles title.

For six successive years 1920-5 he was ranked as the World No.1 and during this period of near-invincibility also won the World Hard Court title and was unbeaten in his 12 singles matches in Davis Cup Challenge Rounds. His overall Davis Cup record 1920-30 comprised wins in 25 of 30 singles and 9 of 11 doubles. He had some notable successes as a doubles player, winning the US men's, 1918, 1921-3 and 1927, and Wimbledon men's 1927, and the mixed at the US 1913-14, 1922-3, and French 1930. After a dispute with the US authorities over the question of 'shamateurism', he turned professional in December 1930 and continued his winning ways in the paid ranks, as late as 1945 winning the US Pro doubles with Vince Richards.

The son of a wealthy Philadelphia wool merchant, he attended the University of Pennsylvania and throughout his life he had aspirations as an actor and playwright but his ambitions were never fulfilled. His homosexuality led to two jail sentences in the less tolerant age in which he lived.

Ulf TIMMERMANN (GDR)

ATHLETICS

Ulf-Béla Timmermann. b. 1 Nov 1962 Berlin.

Top shot putter who won the Olympic title in 1988, when he made four improvements to the Olympic record. He also won the Europeans 1990, World Indoors 1987 and 1989, European Indoors 1987 and 1989, and had two wins in the World Cup and three in the European Cup 1987-91. He set world shot records with 22.62m in 1985 and 23.06 in 1988. Earlier he had taken silver medals at the 1983 Worlds and 1986 Europeans. GDR champion 1988-90 and German 1992.

Both his parents had been talented athletes, and Ulf speedily reached world class after taking the silver medal at the 1981 European Juniors.

Steve TIMMONS (USA)

VOLLEYBALL

Stephen Dennis Timmons. b. 29 Nov 1958 Newport Beach, California.

With three medals, two of them gold, Timmons has won more Olympic medals at volleyball than any other man. At the University of Southern California he was twice named All-American and he joined the national team in 1981. He led the US to Olympic gold medals in 1984 and 1988, when he was the best blocker, and to wins in the 1985 World Cup and 1986 World Championships. In 1989 the 1.96m *6' 5"* Timmons left the US to play professional volleyball for Il Messaggero in Rome, and, with fellow-US star Karch Kiraly led this team to win the 1991 World Club Championship. He then returned to the US team and won a bronze medal at the 1992 Olympics. He owns a beach sportsware company and is married to the former Jeanne Buss, the daughter of the owner of the Los Angeles Lakers.

Guillermo TIMONER (Spain)

CYCLING

Guillermo Timoner Obrador. b. 24 Mar 1926 Felanitx.

Timoner has the best record ever in the professional motor-paced cycling event. In addition to his six world championships, 1955, 1959-60, 1962, 1964-5, he twice finished second, 1956 and 1958. He was a masterful competitor, as he never set a world motor-paced record against the clock but was almost unbeatable head-to-head.

Scott TINLEY (USA)

TRIATHLON

Scott Tinley. b. 25 Oct 1956 San Diego, California.

Tinley was one of the pioneers of triathlon racing in the United States. He began competing in triathlons in 1976 and has won numerous races. These include two victories at the Hawaii Ironman (1982 and 1985) and one runner-up finish in 1990. He was triathlete of the year in 1985 and has won eight Bud Light series races in his career.

Having previously worked as a PE teacher, a fireman and as a paramedic, he later became a full-time triathlete. At first primarily a runner, he became equally proficient at swimming and cycling.

Janou TISSOT (Fra)

EQUESTRIAN

née Janou Lefèbvre. b. 14 May 1945 Saigon, Vietnam.

Lefèbvre won Olympic silver medals in team jumping in both 1964 and 1968, with 14th and 32nd places individually. In 1970 she won the inaugural world ladies' show jumping championships. She then married and as Janou Tissot defended that title in 1974 at La Baule, France. The championship has since been discontinued as the women now compete alongside the men in a single, combined world championship. She was also European women's champion in 1966 and French champion in 1961, 1963 and 1965.

Yuriy TITOV (USSR)

GYMNASTICS

Yuriy Yevlampiyevich Titov. b. 27 Nov 1935 Omsk.

Titov was a member of the Soviet team that won Olympic gold in 1956 and silver in 1960 and 1964, and he placed third overall at the first two Games. At individual apparatus he won a silver and a bronze in 1956 and 1960, with a silver in 1964. He had a total of four gold, three silver and three bronze medals at World Championships, including winning the vault in 1958, and the overall and rings in 1962.

A graduate of the Kiev Physical Culture Institute, he was also European champion in 1959, with a record four individual event golds, and second overall in 1957 and 1961. He became head coach to the Soviet team, and after four years on the executive committee was elected president of the International Gymnastics Federation in 1976.

Y A TITTLE (USA)

AMERICAN FOOTBALL

Yelberton Abraham Tittle. b. 24 Oct 1926 Marshall, Texas.

At Louisiana State University (LSU), Tittle played defensive back as well as quarterback and helped LSU to the Cotton Bowl in 1946.

He played with the Baltimore Colts of the All-American Football Conference (AAFC) in 1948-9, earning Rookie of the Year honours in 1948. He joined the NFL in 1950, but then played for the San Francisco 49ers 1951-60 and for the New York Giants 1961-4. He enjoyed his greatest success in New York as he led them to two NFL championship games. In 1962 he threw 33 touchdown passes and had a career best 3224 yards. In 1963 he set a league record with 36 touchdowns for the season, and in one game that year he threw for seven touchdowns in one game. He was the NFL's Most Valuable Player in 1961 and 1963.

NFL career 1948-64: 38,339 yards from 2118 pass completions, 55.2%, 242 TD.

Nadezhda TKACHENKO (USSR)

ATHLETICS

Nadezhda Vladimirovna Tkachenko. b. 19 Sep 1947 Kremenchug, Ukraine. Later Sapronova.

The Olympic champion at pentathlon in 1980, having placed 9th in 1972 and 5th in 1976. She was also World Student Games champion in 1973, European in 1974, and four times Soviet champion. She 'won' the 1978 European title but was disqualified for failing a doping test. At the 1980 Olympics she became the first woman to exceed 5000 points on the 1971 scoring tables.

Best performances: 200m 24.1/24.20, 800m 2:05.2, 100m hurdles 13.0/13.24, high jump 1.86m, long jump 6.72m, shot 16.86m.

Cindy TODD (USA)

WATER SKIING

Cindy Hutcherson Todd. b. 27 Apr 1956 Akron, Ohio.

Todd followed the redoubtable Liz Allan-Shetter as the world's best women's water skier. She won the world overall title in 1977 and 1979, the slalom in 1977, 1981, and 1983, and jumping in 1979 and 1983. Her best discipline was probably slalom at which she held the world record between 1975 and 1984. She retired at the end of 1989 and now devotes her time to church work and the Fellowship of Christian Athletes.

Mark TODD (NZ)

EQUESTRIAN

Mark James Todd. b. 1 Mar 1956 Cambridge, New Zealand.

A show jumper before he switched to the three-day event, Todd first rode in the World Championships in 1978, and in 1980 on *Southern Comfort* he became the first New Zealander to win at Badminton. Hardly a wealthy horseman, as he made his living as a dairy farmer, in 1984 he was forced to sell most of his herd to finance his trip to Los Angeles. There he became the first Kiwi to win an equestrian medal at the Olympic Games when he won the individual three-day event. In 1988, riding *Charisma* as he had in 1984, he successfully defended his Olympic title and he won a further Olympic medal with the team silver in 1992, although his chances in the individual event went when his horse was injured in the cross-country. He was the winner at Burghley in 1987, 1990 and 1991, and in 1990 helped New Zealand to win the team eventing title at the World Championships.

Alberto TOMBA (Italy)

ALPINE SKIING

Alberto Tomba. b. 19 Dec 1966 San Lazzaro di Savena, Bologna.

The extrovert 'La Bomba', with his powerful and dashing style, has become the Italian sporting superstar of the late 1980s and early 1990s. Double Olympic gold medallist with slalom and giant slalom in 1988, he was also the World Cup winner at both events in 1988 and 1992, and at giant slalom in 1991. He stormed back to form in 1991/2 when he retained his Olympic giant slalom title and had nine World Cup wins. At World Championships, however, he has won just one bronze medal (in 1987). He has a career total of 28 World Cup wins pre-1993. His concentration solely on slalom and giant slalom makes it very hard for him to win the overall title against men who also contest the downhill and super giant slalom, but he was second in 1988 and 1991-2, and third in 1989. Coached by the previous Italian skiing superstar Gustavo Thoeni.

Bill TOOMEY (USA)

ATHLETICS

William Anthony Toomey. b. 10 Jan 1939 Philadelphia

At the decathlon he won the Olympic title in 1968 and set world records with 8234 points (8096 on current tables) in 1966 and 8417 (8309) in 1969. A week after that second record, Toomey married Olympic long jump champion and world record holder Mary Rand (qv), from whom he is now divorced. He also won decathlon titles

at the 1965 World Student Games and 1967 Pan-American Games and was AAU champion each year 1965-9 following pentathlon wins in 1960-1 and 1963-4. Sullivan Award winner 1969.
A graduate of the University of Colorado, with a master's degree in education from Stanford, Toomey had a successful career in television and marketing before coaching at the University of California, Irvine.
Individual event bests included: 100m 10.3 and 10.41 auto, 400m 45.68, 110m hurdles 14.2, 400m hurdles 51.7, long jump 7.87m (and 7.93 wind-aided), discus 47.00m and javelin 68.78m.

Stefan TOPUROV (Bul)

WEIGHTLIFTING

Stefan Petrov Topurov. b. 11 Aug 1964 Asenovgrad.

Topurov was the first man to lift three times his own bodyweight overhead, performing the feat in the clean and jerk at the 1983 World Championships, when he was second overall at featherweight (60kg). He probably would have won the gold at the 1984 Olympics were it not for the boycott. That year he won the European title and at the Friendship Games achieved a total 40 kg more than the winning total in Los Angeles. He was World Junior champion in 1982 and World champion in 1987. In 1988 he won the Olympic silver, losing to Bulgarian defector Naim Suleymanoglü, who represented Turkey. Topurov had to lose 8kg to compete against Suleymanoglü, but he did so because the Bulgarians were eager to have one of their weightlifters defeat the expatriate.

Jayne TORVILL (UK)

ICE DANCE

Jayne Torvill. b. 7 Oct 1957 Nottingham, Notts. Later Christensen.

Partnering Christopher Dean she won four world titles and the 1984 Olympic gold medal with their interpretation of Ravel's *Bolero*, which was one of the most memorable and dramatic performances in the history of any sport. Having won a British junior and senior title with Michael Hutchison, she joined Dean and they won the first of a record six successive British Championships in 1978. *See Dean's entry for details.*
In September 1990 Torvill married Phil Christensen, a technician with the Phil Collins show. Along with other professionals, Olympic eligibility was returned to Torvill and Dean in 1993.

TOSTÃO (Bra)

FOOTBALL

Eduardo Gonçalves de Andrade. b. 25 Jan 1947 Belo Horizonte.

A high scoring centre-forward often known as the 'White Pele'. After playing for a variety of junior teams he joined Cruzeiro in 1963 where he was an immediate success. In 1966 he made his international début and was a member of Brazil's World Cup squad. A serious eye injury in 1969 put his World Cup place in doubt but he recovered sufficiently to turn in some brilliant performances at the 1970 World Cup finals in Mexico, playing in every match for Brazil. Two years later he moved to Vasco da Gama for a record fee but a further eye injury curtailed his career. He scored 32 goals in 55 international matches for Brazil. South American Player of the Year 1971.

Diane TOWLER (UK)

ICE DANCE

Gay Diane Margaret Towler. b. 16 Dec 1946 London.

Four-time World, European and British ice dance champion with Bernard Ford (qv for details).

Forrest TOWNS (USA)

ATHLETICS

Forrest Grady 'Spec' Towns. b. 6 Feb 1914 Fitzgerald, Georgia, d. 9 Apr 1991 Athens, Georgia.

His 13.7 for 110mh, the first sub-14 sec run, at Bislett Stadium, Oslo on 27 Aug 1936 was his third world record at 110m hurdles that year, when he also won the

Olympic, AAU and NCAA titles and the US Trials. In 1937 he won his second NCAA 120y hurdles title. Indoors in 1938 he won the AAU title at 65m hurdles and twice equalled the world record (five flights) at 60y hurdles with 7.4 at the Millrose Games.
Towns was 6ft 3in *1.905m* tall. He had not run in high school as his family were too poor to buy him track shoes. At the University of Georgia, Athens he was an assistant coach from 1938 and head coach 1942-75. The university's track was named in his honour in 1990.

Tony TRABERT (USA)

TENNIS
Marion Anthony Trabert. b. 16 Aug 1930 Cincinnati, Ohio.

The world's leading amateur for only a brief period, winning the US championship in 1953 and 1955, the French 1954-5 and Wimbledon 1955. Remarkably he won his Wimbledon and both US titles without the loss of a single set throughout the tournament. The only other man to have won the Wimbledon and US titles in the same year without conceding a set was Laurie Doherty in 1903 when he only had to contend with a Challenge Round at Wimbledon.
Trabert also won the French men's doubles with Bill Talbert in 1950 and then, with Vic Seixas, won the 1954-5 French and 1954 US titles. Trabert had an impressive Davis Cup record, winning 27 (16 singles, 11 doubles) of his 35 rubbers, and with Seixas was responsible for bringing the Davis Cup back to America in 1954 by beating Australia in the Challenge Round in Sydney.
Although particularly strong on the backhand, Trabert was generally an unspectacular player which may account for his often being underrated. At the end of the 1955 season, he turned professional and lost heavily to Pancho Gonzales on tour. He later became a successful Davis Cup captain and in recent years has been the tennis commentator for CBS television.

Jerry TRAVERS (USA)

GOLF
Jerome Dunstan Travers. b. 19 May 1887 New York, d. 30 Mar 1951 East Hartford, Connecticut.

Second only to Bobby Jones with four US Amateur titles (1907-8, 1912-3) and one of only five amateurs to win the US Open (1915). The son of a wealthy man, Travers devoted all his time to learning golf. It was said that he possessed the ideal golf temperament, but he was most famed for his ability as a putter. He was known for his wildness off the tee and frequently drove with an iron. Late in his life he had financial difficulties and turned professional, though he did little in that career. He spent the last years of his life as an aircraft engineer.

Walter TRAVIS (USA)

GOLF
Walter John Travis. b. 10 Jan 1862 Malden, Victoria, Australia, d. 31 Jul 1927 Denver, Colorado.

Travis took up the game of golf only in his mid-thirties but quickly became a top player. He was still good enough to win the Metropolitan Amateur in his mid-50s. After his third US Amateur (1900-1, 1903) he travelled to Britain hoping to annex that title. He did so in 1904, but made few friends in the process. In addition to his brusque, taciturn manner, the British were upset with his putter, the so-called 'Schenectady Putter'. That model was a centre-shafted mallet which was unheard of in Britain and rare in the US in that era. The British responded by banning centre-shafted models. Travis later worked as a golf architect and editor of *The American Golfer* magazine.

Harold TRAYNOR (USA)

BASEBALL
Harold Joseph 'Pie' Traynor. b. 11 Nov 1899 Framingham, Massachusetts, d. 16 Mar 1972 Pittsburgh, Pennsylvania.

The first great third baseman in baseball history. He played 15 full seasons for the

Pittsburgh Pirates. He was an excellent hitter for average, batting over .300 in 10 seasons. He had very little power, but was a superb fielder with a strong arm and excellent range at third. He became a player-manager in 1934 and managed through 1939, winning 457 games. He then became a scout for the Pirates until his death.
Career 1920-37: 2416 hits Avg. .320; RBI 1273; SB 158. Best seasons: 1930: .366; 1929: .356; 1927: .342; 1923: .338.

Kel TREMAIN (NZ)

RUGBY UNION

Kelvin Robin Tremain. b. 21 Feb 1938 Auckland.

An outstanding loose-forward who was noted for his try-scoring abilities. In 38 internationals (1959-68) he scored nine tries which was then a record for a New Zealand forward. He won 36 of his caps as a flanker and played once at No.8 and once as prop. Immensely strong and with sharp reflexes, he was difficult to contain when close to the opposition line.

Vladislav TRETYAK (USSR)

ICE HOCKEY

Vladislav Aleksandrovich Tretyak. b. 25 Apr 1952 Moscow Oblast.

Possibly the greatest goalie ever to play ice hockey. He joined the Central Army sports team in 1969 and made his international début in 1970 for the USSR, leading them to Olympic gold in 1972, 1976 and 1984. In 1980, Tretyak was replaced in goal after the first period of their Olympic match with the United States, and the US went on to defeat the Soviets in that game, so that Tretyak took a silver medal. His team also won nine world titles, 1970, 1973-5, 1978-89 and 1981-3, and he starred for the USSR during the 1972 series against the NHL All-Stars. He was coveted by NHL teams and was drafted by the Montreal Canadiens but he was never allowed to play, although he became close friends with Canadien goalie Ken Dryden. After *glasnost* and *perestroika*, Tretyak was hired by the Chicago Black Hawks as a goalie coach. He is the only Soviet who is in the Hockey Hall of Fame. In 1978 he was awarded the Order of Lenin.

Lee TREVINO (USA)

GOLF

Lee Buck Trevino. b. 1 Dec 1939 Dallas, Texas.

Trevino was a driving-range pro in El Paso in 1966 when he entered and qualified for the US Open. The following year he was 5th and was named Rookie of the Year. In 1968 and 1971 he won the US Open, in 1971 and 1972 the British Open and in 1974 and 1984 the PGA. He won the Vardon Trophy in 1970-2, 1974 and 1980. Trevino had an unusual swing, but students of the game thought it highly efficient. He played the ball very low, usually with a slight fade, and was considered one of the straightest drivers in the game.
As great a player as he became, Trevino was almost better known for ability as a raconteur. He loved to laugh and often joked with the galleries as he played. This made him the most popular golfer since Arnold Palmer. Trevino now plays on the PGA Senior Tour, at which he is having huge success, heading the money list with over $1 million in 1990 and 1992, and has spent time as a golf analyst on television broadcasts.
PGA career earnings 1967-92: $3,478,450 with 27 victories. Seniors tour 1989-92: $2,949,942 with 15 victories.

Charles TRIPPI (USA)

AMERICAN FOOTBALL

Charles Louis Trippi. b. 14 Dec 1922 Pittston, Pennsylvania.

An elusive running back who enjoyed his greatest fame in college playing for the University of Georgia. In 1946 he won the Maxwell Award as the nation's top football player but finished second in the Heisman voting to Glenn Davis. His college records included 32 touchdowns rushing and he also threw for 11 touchdowns. He also played baseball, making All-American as a shortstop and batting .464 in his senior year, and played one year of minor league baseball before signing with the Chicago Cardinals of the NFL in 1947. He played with the Cardinals until 1955. He later became a coach, coaching both his alma mater and the Cardinals in the NFL.

Bryan TROTTIER (Can)

ICE HOCKEY

Bryan John Trottier. b. 18 Jul 1956 Val Marie, Saskatchewan.

The center of the New York Islanders during their reign as Stanley Cup champions from 1980-3. It is hard to single out one outstanding facet of Trottier's game, but that was probably what made him so great. He did everything well - face-offs, scoring, penalty-killing, leading the power play. Though not quite the scorer that Gretzky is, Trottier plays a much more physical, intimidating game. He was traded to the Pittsburgh Penguins and was a big reason that the Penguins won the Stanley Cup in 1991 and 1992. He is considered by hockey expert Stan Fischler as one of the four or five best centers ever to play in the NHL.
NHL career 1975-92 - 1238 games, 520 goals, 1410 points. Play-offs: 219 games, 71 goals, 184 pts. Best years: 1978/9: 77 assists, 123 points; 1979/80: 87 assists, 134 points. Hart Trophy and Ross Trophy 1979, Calder Trophy 1986, Smythe Trophy 1980.

Mike TROY (USA)

SWIMMING

Michael Francis Troy. b. 3 Oct 1940 Indianapolis.

Troy set six world records at the 200m butterfly from 2:19.0 in 1959 to the 2:12.8 that he recorded to win the Olympic title in 1960. He added another Olympic gold on the 4 x 200m freestyle team. A student at Indiana University, he was second in the 200m butterfly and gold medallist in the 4x200m relay at the Pan-American Games of 1959, and butterfly champion in the AAU 100m 1958 and 200m 1959-60, NCAA 100y and 200y 1960.
Decorated for valour while serving with the US Navy in the Vietnam war, he works in estate brokerage in California.

Fred TRUEMAN (UK)

CRICKET

Frederick Sewards Trueman. b. 6 Feb 1931 Scotch Springs, Stainton, Yorkshire.

A great fast bowler, who devastated the Indians on his Test début in 1952 and went on to become the first man to take over 300 wickets in Test cricket. He was all that a fast bowler needed to be, aggressive and strong with a perfect action. As his career progressed and he lost a little of his extreme pace, his skill, late outswinger and control of line and length meant that he retained his wicket-taking ability. He was a hard-hitting and effective tail-end batsman and a brilliant fielder, either at short-leg or in the deep, where he was a fine thrower. Early in his career 'Fiery' Fred's forthright views and behaviour brought him some trouble with selectors but he matured into a most astute cricketer and a fine captain when he deputised for Yorkshire. After playing for his native county from 1949 to 1968 he played in Sunday League games for Derbyshire in 1972. A great personality, he has become a regular radio and TV commentator on cricket and a notable speaker. Awarded the OBE 1989.
67 Tests 1952-65: 981 runs at 13.81, HS 39; 307 wickets at 21.57, BB 8-31; 64 catches.*
First-class 1949-68: 9231 runs at 15.56, 3 100s HS 104; 2304 wickets at 18.29, BB 8-28; 439 catches.

Hugh TRUMBLE (Aus)

CRICKET

Hugh Trumble. b. 12 May 1867 Abbotsford, Melbourne, d. 14 Aug 1938 Hawthorn, Melbourne.

A most effective medium-fast or off-break bowler and a fine slip fielder. He was a very astute tactician, employing an impeccable length from his high action. He played for Victoria, captaining them in the last five seasons, and made five tours to England, taking more than 120 wickets on four of them. He took two hat-tricks in Tests against England at Melbourne, the

second during an analysis of 7-28 in his last first-class match - going out at the top! He then held the record for most wickets in Tests for ten years. He deputised for Joe Darling as Australian captain twice in 1901/2. He was secretary of Melbourne CC 1911-38.
32 Tests 1890-1904: 851 runs at 19.79, HS 70; 141 wickets at 21.78, BB 8-65; 45 catches.
First-class 1887-1904: 5395 runs at 19.47, 3 100s HS 107; 929 wickets at 18.44, BB 9-39; 328 catches.

Victor TRUMPER (Aus)

CRICKET

Victor Thomas Trumper. b. 2 Nov 1877 Darlinghurst, Sydney, d. 28 Jun 1915 Darlinghurst.

A brilliant batsman, he set the standards for style and elegance against which others were judged. Not the most prolific of scorers, but the one that spectators of his generation remembered. He played in 48 consecutive Test matches, never being dropped for nearly 13 years from his début in 1899 until 1912 when he did not come to England after a dispute with the Australian Board of Control. His peak came perhaps in 1902 when, in a wet summer, he made 2570 first-class runs at 48.49 with 11 hundreds. Those included the first ever century before lunch in a Test match, at Old Trafford. He was a fine all-round athlete, and shortly before his premature death from Bright's disease he instigated the meetings that resulted in the formation of the New South Wales Rugby League, breaking away from the rugby union body.
48 Tests 1899-1912: 3163 runs at 39.04, 8 100s HS 214; 8 wickets at 39.62, BB 3-60; 31 catches*
First-class 1894-1914: 16,939 runs at 44.57, 42 100s HS 300; 64 wickets at 31.73, BB 5-19; 172 catches.*

Galina TSAREVA (USSR)

CYCLING

Galina Tsareva. b. 19 Apr 1950 Velikiye-Luki.

Tsareva first made the Soviet national team in 1969 and was still considered for the 1988 Olympic team, an amazingly long career. She was world sprint champion six times, 1969-71 and 1977-9, and Soviet national champion in 1969-71, 1973 and 1975-7. Competed for Leningrad Trade Union sports society. She set a world record outdoors for 500m with a flying start at 31.70 in 1978, and indoors recorded a series of records: with a standing start 5km 6:42.237 (1982), 10km 13:41.519 (1983) and 20km 27:46.73 (1983); with a flying start, four at 200m from 12.163 in 1980 to 11.361 in 1987, 500m 32.302 (1980) and 1km 1:09.077 (1980).

Mitsuo TSUKAHARA (Japan)

GYMNASTICS

Mitsuo Tsukahara. b. 22 Dec 1947 Tokyo.

The winner of nine Olympic medals between 1968 and 1976, his final 9.9 on the horizontal bar ensuring his team of victory over the USSR in 1976. An innovator with such moves as his somersault descent from the high bar and the spectacular cartwheel on a 1 $^1/_2$ back somersault vault that is now known as the 'Tsukahara'. From 1983 he was a coach to the Japanese team. He won three successive Olympic gold medals with the Japanese team and the individual golds on the horizontal bar in 1972 and 1976. World champion at vault in 1970, he helped Japan to win three World team titles.

Yoshiyuki TSURUTA (Japan)

SWIMMING

Yoshiyuki Tsuruta. b. 1 Oct 1903 Kogoshima Prefecture, d. 24 Jul 1986.

The only man to retain an Olympic 200m breaststroke title, as he won in 1928 and 1932. His first victory was Japan's first at Olympic swimming, ushering in a supremely successful era for his national team. He set a world record for 200m breaststroke of 2:45.0 in 1929.

Sven TUMBA (Swe)

ICE HOCKEY and GOLF

né Sven Johansson. b. 27 Aug 1931 Stockholm.

Sven Johansson was known as the greatest Swedish ice hockey player in the days before Sweden sent its best players to the NHL. He became so famous that he became known by the name of Tumba, the Stockholm suburb where he grew up. He had the unusual distinction of winning Olympic ice hockey medals 12 years apart, bronze in 1952 and silver in 1964. He also played five internationals at football for Sweden, and after his hockey and football career ended took up golf and became a top player in that sport. He won the International Scandinavian match-play championship in 1970 and represented Sweden in the World Cup in 1974.

Emlen TUNNELL (USA)

AMERICAN FOOTBALL

Emlen Tunnell. b. 29 Mar 1925 Bryn Mawr, Pennsylvania, d. 22 Jul 1975 Pleasantville, New York.

Tunnell was considered perhaps the best defensive back of his era. He began his college career at the University of Toledo, starring there more as a basketball player, playing on the team which went to the finals of the NIT Tournament. He dropped out of Toledo to enrol in the Coast Guard, but returned to college at the University of Iowa, although he did not play in his senior season because of an eye injury. Tunnell signed with the New York Giants as a free agent and played 14 years in the NFL - 11 with the Giants and his last three with the Green Bay Packers before retiring in 1961. In 1952 and 1953, Tunnell's interception return yardage would have placed him in the top three among NFL running backs, had he gained the yardage on offense. At his retirement, he held the NFL record for most interceptions with 79, interception yardage (1282), punt returns (258), and punt return yardage (2209). His interception total remains second on the all-time NFL list.

Gene TUNNEY (USA)

BOXING

James Joseph Tunney. b. 25 May 1897 Greenwich Village, New York, d. 7 Nov 1978 Greenwich, Connecticut.

From a wealthy Connecticut family, Tunney became a professional boxer against their wishes. After serving as a marine in World War I and winning the American Expeditionary Force championship as a light-heavyweight, he turned professional.

In 1922 he won the US light-heavyweight championship but a few months later was beaten for that title by Harry Greb. It would remain the only defeat of Tunney's career and he avenged the defeat with four victories over Greb. Tunney then moved up to the heavyweight ranks and eventually gained a title shot against Jack Dempsey, whom he beat by a decision to win the title in 1926.

Tunney also won the re-match, the famed 'Battle of the Long Count', when he was knocked down in the seventh round and was down at least 14 seconds. Dempsey failed to go to a neutral corner and the count was delayed until he did so. That gave Tunney the time he needed to recover and he eventually won on points.

After one more fight, against Tom Heeney, Tunney retired - undefeated as a heavyweight.

He became a successful businessman, married an heiress, was a friend of George Bernard Shaw and had a son who became a US congressman.

Career record: W - 77 (45), L - 1, D - 3.

Zinaida TURCHINA (USSR)

HANDBALL

Zinaida Turchina. b. 17 May 1946 Kiev, Ukraine.

Turchina won gold medals with the USSR handball teams at the Olympic Games of 1976 and 1980 and at the 1975 World Championships, and was a star player for Spartak Kiev, whom she helped to ten of their European Cup wins.

Lyudmila TURISHCHEVA (USSR)

GYMNASTICS

Lyudmila Ivanovna Turishcheva. b. 7 Oct 1952 Grozny, Checheno-Ingushskaya ASSR.

The queen of Soviet and world gymnastics when she won all-around titles at the 1972 Olympics, at the World Championships of 1970 and 1974, at the 1971 and 1973 Europeans, and at the first World Cup in 1975, when she won all five individual events. In all she won five individual World gold medals, two silver and two bronze and two team golds. Her run of success was ended at the 1975 Worlds, although an injured back was a contributory factor. She won team gold medals at the Olympic Games of 1968, 1972 and 1976, and took silver on the floor and bronze at vault in both 1972 and 1976. A bronze at all-around in 1976 took her total Olympic medal tally to nine.

While she was never beaten by Olga Korbut in a major competition, her grace and beauty was overshadowed by the excitement generated by the new generation of tiny girls. She married sprinter Valeriy Borzov on 10 Dec 1977 and became coach of the Soviet team.

Charles TURNER (Aus)

CRICKET

Charles Thomas Biass Turner. b. 16 Nov 1862 Bathurst, New South Wales, d. 1 Jan 1944 Manly, Sydney.

A prolific wicket-taker, this medium-fast bowler smashed the record for the most wickets taken in a first-class season, with 283 at 11.68 in 1888 on the first of his three tours to England. He made a formidable partnership with J J Ferris in both 1888 and 1890, when Turner took 179 wickets at 14.21 in first-class matches in England. He made the ball nip sharply off the wicket, usually bowling quick off-breaks. On his Test début in January 1887 he took 6-15, bowling unchanged with Ferris (4-27) as they bowled England out for 45. In the following season he became the only man ever to take over 100 wickets in an Australian season, 106 at 13.59.

17 Tests 1887-95: 323 runs at 11.53, HS 29; 101 wickets at 16.53, BB 7-43; 8 catches.
First-class 1882-1910: 3836 runs at 15.54, 2 100s HS 103; 992 wickets at 14.24, BB 9-15; 85 catches.

Glenn TURNER (NZ)

CRICKET

Glenn Maitland Turner. b. 26 May 1947 Dunedin.

Having made his début for Otago in 1964/5, Turner came to England to play for Worcestershire in 1967. At first, while possessed of a very sound defence, he seemed to lack the ability to score at any speed. His professional approach, however, steadily transformed him into a very free-scoring batsman. From 1970 when he scored 2379 runs at 61.00, he averaged over 50 in 11 of his 13 years in England, going out at the top with 1171 runs at 90.07 in his last season in 1982, which included a stunning innings of 311* against Warwickshire; that was also his 100th hundred. In his only 5-Test series he scored 672 runs at an average of 96.00, with a top score of 259 against the West Indies in 1972. Regrettably he fell out with the New Zealand authorities and did not play Test cricket from 1977 after ten matches as captain, apart from two matches in 1983. He left both Test and first-class cricket at the peak of his powers and could surely have added substantially to his run-gathering at both.

41 Tests 1969-83: 2991 runs at 44.64, 7 100s HS 259; 42 catches.
41 One-day Ints: 1598 runs at 47.00, 3 100s HS 171; 14 catches.*
First-class 1964-83: 34,346 runs at 49.70, 103 100s HS 311; 5 wickets at 37.80, BB 3-18; 410 catches.*

Rebecca TWIGG (USA)

CYCLING

Rebecca L Twigg. b. 26 Mar 1963 Honolulu, Hawaii.

Probably the best-known woman rider produced by America during the cycling explosion of the 1980s. She was at her best as a track pursuiter, world champion in 1982, 1984-5 and 1987, but was forced to turn to the road race when only that event was chosen for women's cycling at the 1984 Olympics. There she only narrowly missed winning a gold medal when Connie Carpenter-Phinney outsprinted her. After the Games in 1984 she smashed the 10-year-old 3km standing start world record of 3:52.5 with a time of 3:49.78 in Barcelona. She was also popular for her good looks and her brilliant mind - she skipped high school completely, matriculating at the University of Washington when only 14. Twigg retired in 1987 but returned in late 1991 and won a bronze medal in the individual pursuit at the 1992 Olympics in Barcelona.

Jack TWYMAN (USA)

BASKETBALL

John Kennedy Twyman. b. 21 May 1934 Pittsburgh, Pennsylvania.

A star forward with the Cincinnati Royals for 11 years, after playing college basketball at the University of Cincinnati. He was a scoring machine in his early years, averaging over 31 points per game for the 1959/60 season. He was a very accurate shooter and teamed with Oscar Robertson to give the Royals a potent one-two offensive punch in the early 1960s. He was also responsible for much of the care of Maurice Stokes, who had been Twyman's teammate from 1955-7. Stokes' promising career was struck down by encephalitis, which crippled him and left him wheelchair-bound until his untimely death at age 36.

Johnny TYLDESLEY (UK)

CRICKET

John Thomas Tyldesley. b. 22 Nov 1873 Roe Green, Worsley, Lancashire, d. 27 Nov 1930 Monton, Manchester.

A stylish and quick-footed right-hand batsman and brilliant fielder for Lancashire and England. He exceeded 1000 runs in a season each year 1897-1914 and in 1919, over 2000 five times and had a peak of 3041 at 55.29 in 1901. After his retirement he became the Lancashire coach.

His younger brother **Ernest** (1889-1962) scored 38,874 runs at 45.46 with 102 100s in first-class cricket 1909-36, including 990 at 55.00 in 14 Tests 1921-9.
31 Tests 1899-1909: 1661 runs at 30.75, 4 100s HS 138; 16 catches.
First-class 1895-1923: 37,897 runs at 40.66, 86 100s HS 295; 3 wickets; 355 catches.*

Frank TYSON (UK)

CRICKET

Frank Holmes Tyson. b. 6 Jun 1930 Farnworth, Lancashire.

Tyson had a short but dramatic career. Selected for the 1954/5 England tour of Australia after just one full season in county cricket for Northamptonshire, his very fast bowling, in combination with Brian Statham, did much to win the series for England as he took 28 wickets at 20.82. Now known as 'Typhoon', he added 11 wickets at 8.18 against New Zealand and 14 at 18.42 in 1955 against South Africa, but thereafter injuries, perhaps exacerbated by his ungainly action, limited his appearances and effectiveness, A graduate of Durham University, he emigrated to Australia where he has been a teacher, coach, journalist and TV commentator.
17 Tests 1954-9: 230 runs at 10.95, HS 37; 76 wickets at 18.56, BB 7-27; 4 catches.*
First-class 1952-60: 4103 runs at 17.09, HS 82; 767 wickets at 20.89, BB 8-60; 85 catches.

Mike TYSON (USA)

BOXING

Michael George Tyson. b. 30 Jun 1966 Brooklyn, New York

Tyson turned professional in March 1985 shortly after narrowly failing to make the 1984 US Olympic team. He quickly became known among heavyweights for his lethal punching power. In 18 months he won 27 bouts, 25 by knockout. This earned him a title shot against Trevor Berbick who lasted less than two rounds as Tyson claimed the WBC version of the heavyweight championship. Aged just 20 years

144 days, he was the youngest ever heavyweight champion. He added the WBA title with a victory over James 'Bonecrusher' Smith at 20 years 249 days and unified the championship when he defeated Tony Tucker in 1987. At that time 'Iron Mike' Tyson was thought to be unbeatable, but after ten successful world heavyweight title fights he was knocked out by James 'Buster' Douglas, who had been given no chance, on 11 Feb 1990. This came shortly after Tyson had a few brushes with the law, several well-publicised romantic squabbles including the break-up of his marriage to actress Robin Givens, and also had legal difficulty with several of his former managers.

From reform school at the age of 13 he was taken by the great trainer Cus D'Amato into his home in the Catskills; after D'Amato's death in 1984, Jim Jacobs took over as his manager. In 1991 Tyson was arrested and charged with rape. He was convicted of that crime in March 1992 and began serving a six-year prison sentence.
Career record: W - 36 (31), L - 1, D - 0.

Wyomia TYUS (USA)

ATHLETICS

Wyomia Tyus. b. 29 Aug 1945 Griffin, Georgia. Later Simburg.

The first sprinter to retain an Olympic title, Tyus set eight world records, four of them at the Olympic Games. She won the 100m in 1964 with 11.2 (11.23 auto) and in 1968 with 11.0 (11.08), and at the 4 x 100m relay she ran on the US squad's world record in the heats before taking the silver medal in the final in 1964, and on the winning team in 1968. She was 6th at 200m in 1968. She also equalled the world records with 10.3 for 100y and 11.1 for 100m in both 1965 and 1968. At 200m she was the 1967 Pan-American champion and had a best of 23.08 in 1968.

Tyus first came to notice at the AAU Girls' Championship when she was 2nd at 75y and 3rd at 100y in 1961; a year later she won a triple with the 50y, 75y and 100y, and progressed to an international début in 1963. She went to Tennessee State University and was AAU champion at 100y/100m in 1964-6 and 200m/220y in 1966 and 1968, with the indoor 60y/60m title in 1965-7. Indoors she set world bests in 1966 at 50y with 5.6, and three times at 60y with 6.7, 6.6 and 6.5. She equalled the final time as a professional with the ITA group in 1974.

Carlo UBBIALI (Italy)

MOTOR CYCLING

Carlo Ubbiali. b. 24 Apr 1929 Bergamo.

Winner of nine world motorcycling titles, a record until surpassed by Mike Hailwood; six at 125cc, 1951, 1955-6 and 1958-60; and three at 250cc, 1956 and 1959-60. He won a total of 39 Grand Prix races, 26 at 125cc and 13 at 250cc, riding for Mondial 1950-2 and for MV Agusta 1953-60. On the Isle of Man he won TT races at lightweight 125cc in 1955-6, 1958 and 1960, and at 250cc in 1956, and had seven second places. He retired after the 1960 season.

A small man, ideally built for the light machines, he was a great tactician with a calm temperament.

Betty UBER (UK)

BADMINTON

Elizabeth Uber. née Corbin. b. 1907, d. 30 Apr 1983. Poole, Dorset.

One of the finest badminton players, especially at doubles, in her very long career she set an English record with 37 international appearances from 1926 to 1951, winning every match until 1948. In 1956 she donated the Uber Cup to the International Badminton Federation, and that has since been regularly contested as the women's world team championship.

She was the British junior champion at lawn tennis. At the All-England Badminton Championships she won 8 mixed doubles titles in 9 years, first from 1930 to 1932 with her husband **Bertie**, then 1933-6 with Donald Hume and in 1938 with Bill White. She was women's singles champion in 1935 and won the women's doubles with Marianne Horsley in 1931, Diane Doveton 1937-8 and Queenie Allen 1949.

UDAM SINGH (India)

HOCKEY

Udam Kullar Singh. b. 4 Aug 1928.

With gold medals in 1952, 1956 and 1964 and a silver in 1960 he matched the record of team-mate Leslie Claudius as the most successful Olympic hockey player of all-time.

Peter UEBERROTH (USA)

OFFICIAL

Peter Victor Ueberroth. b. 2 Sep 1937 Evanston, Illinois.

Born on the day that Pierre de Coubertin died, Ueberroth is unique among sports administrators as having served at the top of two of the largest sporting organisations. He was president of the Los Angeles Olympic Organizing Committee from 1979 to its triumphant conclusion in 1984. Shortly thereafter he was chosen as commissioner of major league baseball, an office which he held until 1989. Ueberroth attended San Jose State where he played water polo. His business career began to bloom in 1961 when he started a travel consultant firm, which became the largest travel enterprise in North America after American Express. As LAOOC president he angered many Europeans by bringing pure capitalism to the Games, but they made a huge profit - a bit too huge for some people's tastes. He was also not well-liked by the press and ran the committee with an iron hand. He had similar problems as a baseball commissioner and did not stand for re-election after one term. Now a very wealthy man, Ueberroth was recently rumoured to be considering a political run for the Senate and he also made approaches to buy several major airlines.

Frank ULLRICH (GDR)

BIATHLON

Frank Ullrich. b. 24 Jan 1958 Trusetal.

The winner of a record six individual world biathlon titles, four at 10km 1978-81 including the 1980 Olympics and two at 20km 1982-3, and four gold medals with the GDR relay team 1978-9 and 1981-2.
He won a further three Olympic medals, a relay bronze in 1976 and silver medals at 20km and relay in 1980. At his third Olympics he was 5th at 20km and 4th in the relay in 1984. At the World Championships he was 2nd at 20km in 1981 and at 10km in 1982.
He was World Junior champion at 15km in 1977 and also has a record four wins in the World Cup, 1978 and 1980-2, with second place in 1979 and third in 1983.

Svetlana ULMASOVA (USSR)

ATHLETICS

Svetlana Ulmasova. née Glukharyeva. b. 4 Feb 1953 Novo-Balakly, Bashkir ASSR.

European champion at 3000m in 1978 and 1982, she also won the 1979 World Cup 3000m and was fourth in the 1983 World Championships. She had set a Soviet record of 8:48.4 in 1976 and a world record of 8:26.78 in 1982, when she won her third USSR title (she had also won in 1978-9).
A teacher, after two years out she returned briefly to top-class competition in 1986, when she won the USSR 5000m.
Other bests: 800m 2:00.8 (1979), 1000m 2:33.6 (1979), 1500m 3:58.76 (1982), 1 mile 4:23.8 (1981), 5000m 15:05.50 (1986), 10,000m 32:14.83 (1986).

Vegard ULVANG (Nor)

NORDIC SKIING

Vegard Ulvang. b. 10 Oct 1963 Kirkenes.

A star of the 1992 Winter Olympics, when he won three cross-country skiing gold medals, at 10km and 30km classical and with the Norwegian relay team. He was also the silver medallist at the 25km combined. In 1988 he had won a bronze medal at 30km and was 4th at 50km. He won the cross-country World Cup in 1990, 2nd in 1989 and 1992, 3rd equal 1991 and 3rd 1993. In the summer of 1991 he skied across the Greenland ice pack. At the World Championships at the classical style events at 10km he was 3rd in 1989 and 1993, and at 30km 2nd in 1989 and 1993, 3rd in 1991.

Gintautas UMARAS (USSR/Lit)

CYCLING

Gintautas Umaras. b. 20 May 1963 Klaipeda.

One of the greatest ever pursuit cyclists. He first made the Soviet national team in 1981 and would have been a favourite at the 1984 Olympics, had the USSR not boycotted. He was USSR champion from 1984-7 and world individual (and team) pursuit champion in 1987, after second places in 1985 and 1986. After the 1988 Olympics, when he won gold medals at both individual and team pursuit, Umaras was one of several prominent Soviet riders allowed to turn professional. He set amateur world records at unpaced standing start 4km twice outdoors in 1985 and 1987 (4:31.160) and once indoors.

Polly UMRIGAR (India)

CRICKET

Pahlan Ratanji Umrigar. b. 28 Mar 1926 Sholapur, Maharashtra.

India's top scorer in Test cricket until Sunil Gavaskar, he was a powerful right-handed batsman. He also showed himself to be a shrewd captain, leading Bombay to five successive Ranji Trophies from 1958/9 and captaining India 8 times, including when he scored India's first double century in Tests, 232 against New Zealand in 1955. He scored 4102 runs at an average of 70.72 in his Ranji Trophy career. He was also a fine fielder and a medium paced off-break bowler, and later became a Test selector and manager of Indian teams.

59 Tests 1948-62: 3631 runs at 42.22, 12 100s HS 223; 35 wickets at 42.08, BB 6-74; 33 catches.

First-class 1944-68: 16,155 runs at 52.28, 49 100s HS 252; 325 wickets at 25.69, BB 7-32; 216 catches.*

Derek UNDERWOOD (UK)

CRICKET

Derek Leslie Underwood. b. 8 Jun 1945 Bromley, Kent.

With his medium pace left-arm spin bowling Underwood fully lived up to his nickname of 'Deadly', for so he was on any sort of wicket that gave him some assistance. In an age when pace bowling dominated, he could and should have played more often for England, for he was from time to time left out of the team. Despite that, he took nearly 300 wickets in Tests. He also lost the chance to play Test cricket when he played World Series Cricket in the late 1970s and when he went on a rebel tour to South Africa in 1981. He first played for Kent at 17 and in that first season showed impressive maturity to take 101 wickets at 21.12. That was the first of ten 100-wicket hauls, despite the fact that most of his career was played at a time when the number of first-class games was reduced and that target very rarely achieved. At his peak from 1966 to 1984 he averaged less than 20 runs per wicket in 12 seasons in England. Awarded the MBE 1981.

86 Tests 1966-82: 937 runs at 11.56, HS 45; 297 wickets at 25.83, BB 8-51; 44 catches.*

26 One-day Ints: 53 runs at 5.88, HS 17; 32 wickets at 22.93, BB 4-44; 6 catches.

First-class 1963-87: 5165 runs at 10.19, 1 100 HS 111; 2465 wickets at 20.28, BB 9-28; 261 catches.

Rory UNDERWOOD (UK)

RUGBY UNION

Rory Underwood. b. 19 Jun 1963 Middlesbrough, Yorkshire.

A measure of his brilliance and consistency is that he is both England's most capped player and their leading try scorer. He was the first English player to win 50 caps, and in 60 matches to April 1993 has scored 36 tries, including a record five against Fiji in 1989. First capped in 1984, he played in the World Cup in New Zealand in 1987. He also toured with the British Lions to Australia in 1989 and to New Zealand 1993 (three Tests on each tour, with a try on the second), but his duties as an RAF officer (fighter pilot) prevented him from joining a number of other touring teams. Primarily a left-winger, he could play with equal facility on the opposite wing. He announced his retirement after helping England to their second successive Grand Slam in 1992 but reversed the decision early the following season and again made himself available for international selection. His brother **Tony** (b. 17 Feb 1969 Ipoh, Malaysia) played with him for England in 1992-3 and also went on the Lions tour to New Zealand 1993.

Johnny UNITAS (USA)

AMERICAN FOOTBALL

John Constantine Unitas. b. 7 May 1933 Pittsburgh, Pennsylvania.

Considered by many as the greatest quarterback ever to play professional football. He was born to a poor coal-mining family of Lithuanian descent but he used his athletic abilities to earn a football scholarship to the University of Louisville after several schools rejected him as being too small. In the NFL, he was also spurned. He was signed as a 9th-round draft choice in 1955 by his hometown Pittsburgh Steelers, but they quickly released him and he caught on with the semi-pro Bloomfield (NJ) Rams where he played for $6 a game. In 1956 he signed with the Baltimore Colts and his legendary NFL career began. He quarterbacked the Colts until 1972, helping them win NFL titles in 1958-9, and he led them to a Super Bowl in 1971. He was the NFL MVP in 1957, 1964, and 1967, made All-Pro five times and was chosen as Player of the Decade for the 1960s. He finished his career with two desultory seasons 1973-4 with the San Diego Chargers.
Unitas' records are almost endless. He threw a touchdown pass in 47 consecutive games from Dec 1956 through Dec 1960; this is considered pro football's most unbreakable record. At his retirement, Unitas had set quarterback records for passes thrown (5186), completions, touchdowns, and yards gained. But records alone could not measure Unitas. His coolness under pressure, his radar-like accuracy in the last two minutes with the game on the line, and his toughness in holding the ball until the last possible moment despite intense defensive pressure, all contributed to his legend.
NFL career 1956-73: 40,239 yards from 2830 pass completions, 54.6%, 290 TD.

Wes UNSELD (USA)

BASKETBALL

Westley Sissel Unseld. b. 14 Mar 1946 Louisville, Kentucky.

Named in 1969 as the NBA's Rookie of the Year and MVP; a double honour he shares only with Wilt Chamberlain. From the University of Louisville, he played at center for 13 years in the NBA, all with the Baltimore/Capitol/Washington Bullets. Although he was very short at 2.01m *6'7"* for that position, he overcame that with his size, 111 kg *245 lb*, his intensity, and his desire. During his career, he averaged 14.0 rebounds per game (total 13,769) despite that relatively diminutive height. He played on an NBA Championship team in 1978 and led the league in rebounding in 1975. Since his retirement he has become a top coach with his old team.

Al UNSER (USA)

MOTOR RACING

Alfred Unser. b. 29 May 1939 Albuquerque.

Unser matched A J Foyt's record by winning the Indianapolis 500 four times, 1970-1, 1978 and 1987. On the last occasion he was, at 47 years 11 months, the oldest ever winner. He was third when his son Al Unser Jr won the race in 1992, and is third on the all-time money list for the Indy 500 with $3,378,018 from 27 races to 1993. He won the USAC National Championship in 1970 and the Indy Car World Series in 1983 and 1985. To the end of 1992 he had Indy Car series career earnings of $6,545,973 with 30 victories.
He began driving modified stock cars like his brother and made his Indy 500 début in 1965 to finish ninth. He was second there in 1968, in which year he was also voted NASCAR 'Rookie of the Year'. A smooth and controlled driver.
Three sons of Swiss immigrants who settled in Colorado before the first World War, Jerry, Josef and Louis Unser were the first to reach the summit of Pike's Peak on motorbikes. Louis, in 1934, was the first of the Unser family to win the annual race up the mountain, and he won for the ninth

time in 1953. Al joined six other Unsers in winning at Pike's Peak, ending brother Bobby's winning streak in 1964.
Al was the fourth and Bobby (qv) the third son of Jerry Unser. The elder son Louis Jr twice won the Pike's Peak climb and second brother **Jerry** (1932-59) was the 1957 USAC Stock champion.
Al's son **Al Unser Jr** (b. 19 Apr 1962 Albuquerque) was Indy Car champion in 1990 and 1992, with career earnings in the Indy Car series of $10,771,590 and 18 race wins to the end of 1992. In the Indianapolis 500 itself he is fourth on the all-time money list with $2,888,877 from 11 races to 1993. He also won the Can-Am series in 1982.

Bobby UNSER (USA)

MOTOR RACING

Robert William Unser. b. 20 Feb 1934 Colorado Springs.

Winner of the Indianapolis 500 in 1968, 1975, and 1981 (then the oldest ever winner), and winner of the USAC National Championship in 1968 and 1974.
He began driving modified stock cars at 15 in New Mexico. Following the family tradition he won the Pike's Peak championship car class in 1956 and in all set records with 13 wins in 18 runs at the mountain. He made his Indy début in 1963, and in 1972 he became the first driver in USAC history to qualify at over 200 mph average for four laps. Retired from driving after the 1981 season. He had career Indy Car series earnings of $2,674,516 and 35 victories. He is a commentator for ABC Television.

Nicole UPHOFF (Ger)

EQUESTRIAN

Nicole Uphoff. b. 25 Jan 1967 Duisburg.

Riding *Rembrandt,* who had joined her father's stable at the age of three in 1980, Uphoff won her first major event in 1987 and then took individual and team Olympic gold medals for dressage in 1988 and 1992. German champion in 1988 and 1989, she won team and individual gold medals at the 1989 Europeans and 1990 Worlds and was the runner-up with a team gold at the 1991 Europeans.
She first rode a horse in 1976. Now employed as a haulage agency clerk, she married 1992 Olympic show jumper Otto Becker (b. 3 Dec 1958) after her Olympic success in 1992.

Gene UPSHAW (USA)

AMERICAN FOOTBALL

Eugene Upshaw Jr. b. 15 Aug 1945 Robstown, Texas.

One of the greatest offensive guards in football history. He played in college at Texas A & I, where he was named to the NAIA All-American teams. In the pros he played for the Oakland Raiders 1967-82. He was very tough, playing in 209 consecutive games during his 16-year career. He was named All-Pro four times and helped the Raiders to two Super Bowl victories. In 1980, he was elected the president of the NFL Players' Association for his leadership abilities. He remained in that rôle through 1992, helping the players in their legal battles with the owners in an attempt to be granted the right to free agency.

Jean URRUTY (Fra)

PELOTA

Jean Urruty. b. 19 Oct 1913 Saint-Palais, Pyrénées-Atlantiques.

A small, unspectacular player whose economy of movement and classic style enabled him to enjoy a career of remarkable longevity. He took over as the world's No.1 from the legendary Chiquito de Cambo in 1938 and it was thought that he would be past his best when competition was resumed after World War II. Surprisingly, these proved to be his greatest years and he carried on playing until 1970, when he retired at the age of 57 after 40 years as a top-class player.

Frank URSO (USA)

LACROSSE

Frank Urso. b. 15 Apr 1954 Long Island, New York.

Urso played collegiate lacrosse at the University of Maryland and was a four-time All-American 1973-6, becoming the first freshman in 25 years to be so named. He was voted the Nation's Outstanding Lacrosse Player as both a junior and senior. Even as a freshman, Urso, who led Maryland to two national championships, was being compared to the greatest lacrosse players ever. He was a midfielder but still scored over 200 points in his collegiate career, with 127 goals.

Yelena VÄLBE (USSR/Rus)

NORDIC SKIING

Yelena Välbe. née Trubizina. b. 24 Feb 1968 Magadan, Siberia.

World Cup winner at cross-country skiing 1989 and 1991-2, second in 1990 and 1993. A beautifully smooth skier. World champion at 10km 1989 and 1991, 15km 1991 and 1993, and 30km 1989 (2nd in 1991), she was expected to dominate at the 1992 Olympics, but she had to settle for bronze medals at all four individual events before taking a gold with the CIS relay team. Her husband Urmas Välbe (Est) (b. 8 Nov 1966) was the world junior champion at 15km in 1987 and competed at the 1992 Olympics. Their daughter was born in 1987.

Fernando VALENZUELA (Mex/USA)

BASEBALL

Fernando Valenzuela Anguamea. b. 1 Nov 1960 Sonora, Mexico.

Valenzuela began his major league career in 1980 with the Los Angeles Dodgers and only pitched a few times that year, but he had a tremendous season in 1981 when he earned Rookie of the Year honours. Spurred on by the large Hispanic population in Los Angeles, he was responsible for 'Fernandomania' which accompanied his frequent starts. In a strike-shortened season he won ten consecutive decisions and tied a rookie record with eight shutouts. His main pitch was 'Fernando's Fadeaway' or a screwball, felt to be the best since Carl Hubbell's. In his best season, 1986, Valenzuela also emulated Hubbell by recording five consecutive strikeouts in the All-Star Game. After two years out he returned to play in 1993. *Career pitching 1980-90: ERA 3.31; W-L 141-116, SO 1759. Best season: 1986: 21-11.*

Bohumil VANA (Cs)

TABLE TENNIS

Bohumil Vana. b. 17 Jan 1920 Prague.

An all-out attacking player whose matches with the defensive Richard Bergmann were a feature of the international scene in the years immediately before and after World War II. Vana first played in the World Championships as a 15-year-old in 1935, won the singles in 1938 and 1947 and was runner-up in 1948 and 1949. He also won the men's doubles, 1947-8 and 1951, and the mixed doubles, 1937, 1939 and 1951. The greatest of all Czech players, he was a member of five winning Swaythling Cup teams.

Marco VAN BASTEN (Hol)

FOOTBALL

Marco van Basten. b. 31 Oct 1964 Utrecht.

An accomplished striker who began his career with Ajax and was three times top scorer in the Dutch League. He scored the winning goal for Ajax in the 1987 final of the European Cup-Winners' Cup and between 1982 and 1987 he helped Ajax to win the Dutch League and Cup three times each. After moving to AC Milan he was voted European Footballer of the Year in 1988 and 1989 and again in 1992, to equal the record for most wins. He helped the Italian club win the European Cup in 1989 (scoring twice in the final) and 1990 and the Italian championship in 1988 and 1992-3. Top scorer in Italy in 1989/90 and 1991/2.

He scored a spectacular winning goal when the Dutch team won the 1988 European Championship and in 58 international appearances to May 1993 he has scored 24 goals. He was held back in 1993 by surgery to his right ankle early in the year.

Jack VAN BERG (USA)

HORSE RACING

John Charles Van Berg. b. 7 Jun 1936 Columbus, Nebraska.

He set the record for most wins in a year by a trainer in the USA with 496 in 1976, and led the list for most winners eight times between 1968 and 1984. His world record career total for winners, 5389 from 1965 to 1989, was passed by Dale Baird in 1990.

In 1971 he took over the stables of his father, Marion, who set a previous record of 4691 winners trained. Won the Eclipse Award as Trainer of the Year in 1984. His best horse has been *Alysheba*.

Norm VAN BROCKLIN (USA)

AMERICAN FOOTBALL

Norman Van Brocklin. b. 15 Mar 1926 Eagle Butte, South Dakota, d. 2 May 1983 Social Circle, Georgia.

Known as 'The Dutchman' he was one of football's top quarterbacks and toughest competitors. He played for the University of Oregon, graduating in 1949. He was drafted by the Los Angeles Rams that year and played with them to 1957, leading them to their only NFL championship in 1951. Van Brocklin was forced to share quarterback duties with Bob Waterfield, forming a great 1-2 passing duo, but he did not like the situation and asked to be traded. So he joined the Philadelphia Eagles in 1958 and led them to the NFL championship in 1960. He was voted the NFL Player of the Year and promptly retired. During his career, he played in ten Pro Bowls, five NFL championship games, and led the NFL in passing three times. He coached the Minnesota Vikings 1961-67 and the Atlanta Falcons 1968-74.

NFL career 1970-84: 23,611 yards from 1553 pass completions, 53.6%, 173 TD.

Steve VAN BUREN (USA)

AMERICAN FOOTBALL

Steve Van Buren. b. 28 Dec 1920 La Ceiba, Honduras.

Van Buren played running back for Louisiana State (LSU) and in the NFL for the Philadelphia Eagles. He graduated from LSU in 1944 and was the first-round draft choice of the Eagles, with whom he played through the 1951 season. In college, Van Buren was actually used mostly as a blocking back for Alvin Dark, who later became a well-known major league baseball player. With the Eagles, Van Buren became the top runner in the NFL. He led the league in rushing four times and helped the Eagles win two championships. He was the second runner to gain 1,000 yards in a single season, and the first to surpass that mark twice (1947 and 1949). At his retirement, Van Buren held NFL records for career rushing attempts (1320), and most career rushing yards gained (5860).

Arthur VANCE (USA)

BASEBALL

Clarence Arthur Vance. b. 4 Mar 1891 Orient, Iowa, d. 16 Feb 1961 Homosassa Springs, Florida.

A fireballing right-handed pitcher, 'Dazzy' Vance was a colourful personality who, it has been said, 'led his Dodger team-mates everywhere but to a pennant'. He began his major league career in 1915 with the Pittsburgh Pirates but spent most of his 16-year career with the Brooklyn Dodgers. He led the National League in strikeouts for seven consecutive seasons 1922-8. He also led the league in ERA three times and in shutouts four times. In 1924 he was voted MVP for his 28-6 record. He had an excellent career strikeout/walk ratio with 2045 strikeouts and only 840 walks.

Career pitching 1915-35: ERA 3.24; W-L 197-140, SO 2045. Best seasons: 1924: 28-6, 2.16 ERA, 262 SO; 1925: 22-9, 3.53 ERA, 221 SO; 1928: 22-10, 2.09 ERA.

Harold VANDERBILT (USA)

YACHTING and BRIDGE

Harold Stirling Vanderbilt. b. 6 Jul 1884 Oakdale, Long Island, New York, d. 4 Jul 1970 Newport, Rhode Island.

Defender of the America's Cup for the USA in 1930, 1934 and 1937, and the only man to skipper and steer in three successive defences in three different yachts. After beating Ernest Heard (GB) in four straight races in 1930 aboard *Enterprise*, he sailed *Rainbow* in 1934 and after losing the first two races to the British challenger Tommy Sopwith, he won the next four despite strong protests from the British. In 1937 he retained the Cup with *Ranger*, winning in four straight races against Sopwith who was making his second unsuccessful challenge. These three Cup races were the only ones contested by J Class yachts and they soon disappeared, proving too expensive to maintain and race - even for the Vanderbilt millions.

Harold Vanderbilt was a member of the family which amassed a huge fortune in the pioneering years of the railways. He was the Commodore of the New York Yacht Club and the greatest yachtsman of his time, but will probably be better remembered as the inventor of Contract Bridge. He devised the game while on a cruise in 1925 and it soon swept the world, replacing the prevailing Auction version of the game.

Flory VAN DONCK (Bel)

GOLF

Flory van Donck. b. 23 Jun 1912 Tervueren.

Until the advent of Severiano Ballesteros and Bernhard Langer in the late 1970s, van Donck was considered the greatest player ever produced by continental Europe. Van Donck's fame rested on his great putting ability, though his style was unorthodox as he kept the toe of his putter in the air, similar to Isao Aoki. Van Donck won his own national title 16 times between 1935 and 1968, and held most of the national titles in Europe at one time or another, including the Dutch Open 1936-37, 1951, 1953; French Open 1954, 1957-8; German Open 1953, 1956; Swiss Open 1953, 1955. He was second in the British Open in 1956 and 1959.

Yvonne VAN GENNIP (Hol)

SPEED SKATING

Yvonne Marie Therese van Gennip. b. 1 May 1964 Haarlem.

Only the second woman to win three Olympic gold medals for speed skating at one Games. In 1964, Lidiya Skoblikova (USSR) won all four events but in 1988 Yvonne van Gennip came close to this record with victories in the 1500m, 3000m and the 5000m which was included in the Olympic programme for the first time. In the two longer events she set world records, 4:11.94 and 7:14.13 respectively, and the following month she set an unofficial record for 10,000m at 15:25.25. She also had a fine season in 1987 when she was the winner of the World Cup at 1500m and 3000m. At the World Championships she was 2nd in the all-round in 1988 and 3rd in 1987 and 1989.

Other bests: 500m 41.54 (1987), 1000m 2:00.68 (1988).

Paul van HIMST (Bel)

FOOTBALL

Paul van Himst. b. 2 Oct 1943 Leeuw-Saint Pierre.

A high scoring centre-forward who later switched to inside-forward with a midfield rôle. Signing for Anderlecht when only 9, he progressed through their junior teams to make his League début at the age of 16 and to win his first international cap in 1960. At the age of 17 he was voted Belgium's Footballer of the Year. He again won the award in 1962 and 1965. He topped the Belgian League scorers in 1964, 1966 and 1968, and while he was with Anderlecht they won the Belgian League eight times, with the League and Cup double in 1972. Together with his Anderlecht colleagues he declined to play for Belgium in 1967-8 and after being blamed in many quarters for Belgium's poor showing in the 1970 World Cup he announced that he would never play for his country again. A change of heart brought him back into the national team for the 1972 European Championships where he won his 69th cap to beat the long-standing Belgian record of Vic Mees. Had he not declared himself unavailable for a number of matches he would, undoubtedly, have won many more than the 82 caps he recorded, scoring 30 goals. He stayed with

Anderlecht to 1975 and ended his career with RWD Molenbeek 1975-6 and Alost 1976-7. He was trainer with Anderlecht 1982-5 and technical director at RWDM 1987-9.

Rik VAN LOOY (Bel)

CYCLING

Rik van Looy. b. 20 Dec 1932 Grobbendonk.

Prior to Eddy Merckx, van Looy won more classics than any professional cyclist ever. This was mainly due to his tremendous ability as a road sprinter, unmatched in the peloton at the time. Only the Grand Prix de Nations (a time trial) and the Bordeaux-Paris are missing from his list of major classic victories. Having been third in the 1953 world road race championship as an amateur, he won the professional title twice, 1960-1, and was second in 1956 and 1963. His lack of strength as a time trialist was his greatest weakness, as he had 38 stage wins in the three big tours but did not win any of them. He was not a great climber, though he was better than average and won the King of the Mountains title in the Giro d'Italia 1960. Van Looy also won 11 six-day races, nine of them with Peter Post.

Other major victories: Ghent-Wevelgem 1955-7, 1962; Paris-Brussels 1956, 1958; Milan-San Remo 1958; Paris-Tours 1959, 1967; Tour of Lombardy 1959; Tour of Flanders 1959, 1962; Liège-Bastogne-Liège 1961; Paris-Roubaix 1961-2, 1965; Flèche-Wallonne 1968; Points Jersey - Tour de France 1963; Vuelta à España 1959, 1965.

Keetie VAN OOSTEN-HAGE (Hol)

Keetie Hage. b. 1949 Maartensdijk. Now van Oosten.

One of the strongest woman cyclists in the world. In her brilliant career she collected six world and 22 national titles. At pursuit she was world champion in 1975-6 and 1978-9, second in 1971-3, and third in 1968-9 and 1974, and she was world road race champion in 1968 and 1976, as well as second in 1966, 1973 and 1978, and third in 1971 and 1974-5. In the Munich Olympic stadium in 1978 she added nearly 2 kilometres to the women's 1 hour record with a distance of 43.08292km, setting records en route at 5km 6:44.75, 10km 13:34.39 and 20km 27:26.66.

She was Dutch pursuit champion each year 1966-77 and road champion 1969-76 and 1978.

Lionel VAN PRAAG (Aus)

SPEEDWAY

Lionel Maurice Van Praag. b. 17 Dec 1908 Sydney, New South Wales, d. 19 May 1987 Sydney.

He secured a place in speedway history at Wembley in September 1936 when he won the first World Championship. At the end of the scheduled programme he was tied with Eric Langton at 26 points, but Van Praag won the decider after what is still recognised as being one of the most exciting races ever. He started racing at 16 and came to England in 1931 to join Wembley, becoming captain of the team in 1934. His career was interrupted by four years' war service as a transport pilot in the RAAF, during which he was awarded the George Medal in 1941, but he continued to ride in England until 1954 when he returned to his native Australia to become managing director of the International Speedway Club in Sydney.

Rik VAN STEENBERGEN (Bel)

CYCLING

Henrik van Steenbergen. b. 9 Sep 1924 Oud-Turnhout, Arendonck.

Van Steenbergen had a 24-year career as a top cyclist, retiring at age 42 in 1966. He equalled the record of three victories in the world professional road race (1949, 1956-7) and was also third in 1946. He rode almost continually, taking only a short mid-summer break. On the track he won 1314 events, and his record of 40 victories in six-day races stood for almost 20 years. His track ability allowed him to win many one-day classics because of his ability as a road sprinter. Although he won the 1956 Vuelta à España, his difficulty climbing

usually prevented him from being a factor in the major stage races.
Other major victories: Tour of Flanders 1944, 1946; Paris-Roubaix 1948, 1952; Flèche-Wallonne 1949, 1958; Paris-Brussels 1950; Milan-San Remo 1954.

Tom VAN VOLLENHOVEN (SAf)

RUGBY LEAGUE

Karel Thomas van Vollenhoven. b. 19 Apr 1935 Bethlehem, Orange Free State.

Although he was not the first South African rugby union international to switch to rugby league in England, he was undoubtedly the one who made the greatest impact. After winning seven Springbok caps he signed for St Helens in 1957. As an outstanding sprinter he had unrivalled speed and his impressive physique and natural rugby skills made him the greatest winger of his era. In his ten-year career with St Helens, he scored 397 tries; his 62 tries in the 1958/9 season remains a club record and he twice scored six tries in one match. One of his finest scoring efforts came when St Helens beat Hunslet in the 1959 Championship final and he scored another superb try in the 1961 Challenge Cup final to clinch victory for St Helens over Wigan.

Yurik VARDANYAN (USSR/Arm)

WEIGHTLIFTING

Yurik Norayrovich Vardanyan. b. 13 Jun 1956 Leninakan.

Though he won only one Olympic medal, a gold in 1980, Yurik Vardanyan was the dominant weightlifter in the world in the late 1970s and early 1980s. He won his first world title in 1977 in the 75kg class. Moving up to 82.5kg, he won again in 1978, 1979, and 1981, along with his 1980 Olympic win with a total of 400 kg, which still stands as an Olympic record. He was again world champion at 82.5kg in 1983 and 1985 and almost certainly would have won another gold in 1984 but for the Soviet boycott. USSR champion 1976-82. A PE teacher at the Armenian State Institute.

Harry VARDON (UK)

GOLF

Harry Vardon. b. 9 May 1870 Grouville, Jersey, d. 20 Mar 1937 Totteridge, London.

The greatest player of the guttie era and considered the greatest ever until the advent of Bobby Jones. Vardon won six British Opens, 1896, 1898-9, 1903, 1911 and 1913, still a record, and was second four times and in the top five six other times. He also won the US Open in 1900 and lost the play-off in 1913. He had a serious illness in 1901, after which it was said he never completely recovered his old dominance, but he won the 1911 German Open and 1912 British PGA. The overlapping grip, which he popularised, is still often termed the 'Vardon grip'. A calm and likeable man, he was known primarily for his upright, graceful swing and his tremendous talent as a fairway wood player.

Obdulio VARELA (Uru)

FOOTBALL

Obdulio Jacinto Varela. b. 1917.

A legend in Uruguayan soccer after leading his team to victory in the 1950 World Cup. A roving centre-half and an inspiring leader, he rallied his team to a 2-1 victory over the seemingly invincible Brazilians after Uruguay had been a goal down. He made a second World Cup appearance in 1954 at the age of 37 but an injury in the quarter-finals led to his retirement from the game. He had the distinction of never being on the losing side in a World Cup match.
He made his First Division début with Wanderers in 1938 and had already won the first of his 52 caps when he moved to Peñarol in 1942. After retirement he stayed on at Peñarol as coach for two seasons but then distanced himself from the game.

Margaret VARNER (USA)

BADMINTON

Margaret Varner. b. 4 Oct 1927 El Paso, Texas. Later Bloss.

But for being a contemporary of Judy

Devlin/Hashman, Varner would have compiled an even more formidable record in women's badminton. Known as the 'Texan Bronze', she beat her great rival to become All-England singles champion in 1955-6 and was a finalist on three other occasions. She won the women's doubles with Heather Ward (Eng) in 1958.
She interrupted Devlin's run of success to win the US women's singles in 1955 and captained the US team which won the Uber Cup when it was first contested in 1957 and 1960. She achieved the unique distinction of representing the USA not only at badminton but also at tennis and squash - all within two years and all on the winning side. At tennis she won her doubles match in the Wightman Cup in both 1961 and 1962, and with Margaret du Pont was a women's doubles finalist at Wimbledon in 1958. At squash she was US singles champion each year 1960-3.

Ari VATANEN (Fin)

RALLYING

Ari Pieti Uolevi Vatanen. b. 27 Apr 1952 Tuupovaara.

World champion in 1981 and winner of 10 Championship series races including the Safari (1983), RAC (1984), 1000 Lakes (1981 and 1984), and Monte Carlo (1985). He was at his best in the Paris-Dakar Rally, winning for a fourth time in 1991 driving a Citroen; his first three victories having been in Peugeots in 1987 and 1989-90.
An out-and-out speedster, his first major win was in 1979 for Ford. He switched to Opel in 1983 and to Peugeot 1984-88. He had a near-fatal accident in 1985, but recovered to return to top form, driving in the Championship races for Mitsubishi 1989-90 and after that for Subaru. He also set a record time for the Pike's Peak race when he won in 1988.

VAVÁ (Bra)

FOOTBALL

Edvaldo Izidio Neto. b. 12 Nov 1934 Recife, Pernambuco.

A bustling centre-forward whose style of play was more European than South American. During his career as an amateur with Vasco da Gama he played in the 1952 Olympics, and after turning professional he starred as the leader of the Brazilian attack when they won the World Cup in 1958 and 1962. After the 1958 World Cup, Vavá joined Atlético Madrid in Spain but returned to Brazil in 1960 where he joined Corinthians before moving to Palmeiras.
In his second World Cup campaign he scored four goals to add to the five he had scored in 1958 and, in all, he scored 15 times for Brazil in 20 international appearances. He ended his playing career in Mexico and later became a manager in Spain.

Jorge VELASQUEZ (Pan/USA)

HORSE RACING

Jorge Luis Velasquez. b. 28 Dec 1946 Chepo, Panama.

The top US rider with 438 winners in 1967, he headed the money list in 1969 and in 1988 became the fourth rider to earn over $50 million in prize money. By the end of 1992 his money winnings had reached $120,028,481 with 6570 winners from 1965.
After breaking records set by Braulio Baeza as an apprentice in Panama, Velasquez went to the USA in 1965. He won the Kentucky Derby and Preakness Stakes with *Pleasant Colony* in 1981.

Dilip VENGSARKAR (India)

CRICKET

Dilip Balwant Vengsarkar. b. 6 Apr 1956 Bombay.

A century at Lord's is the dream of all top batsmen. Vengsarkar achieved this on each of his first three tours, 1979, 1982 and 1986, to become the first visitor to score three centuries at cricket's headquarters.
An orthodox right-handed batsman, he had brilliant success for India from his Test début in 1976. He took over as captain in 1987/8, but after an outstanding first series in the job when he averaged 101.66 for 303 runs in 3 Tests against the West Indies, his batting fell away, and even after he had

lost the captaincy he could not regain his previous Test form.
116 Tests 1976-92: 6868 runs at 42.13, 17 100s HS 166; 78 catches.
128 One-day Ints: 3508 runs at 34.73, 1 100 HS 105; 37 catches.
First-class 1975-92: 17,868 runs at 52.86, 55 100s HS 258; 1 wicket; 179 catches.*

Ken VENTURI (USA)

GOLF
Ken Venturi. b. 15 May 1931 San Francisco, California.

In the late 1950s Venturi was hailed as the next great player in golf - the next Hogan. He had near misses in the Masters tournament in 1956 and 1958 and then his game went into eclipse. He was almost ready to quit the tour in late 1963, but attempted a comeback. His play in early 1964 was sporadic, but in June he won the US Open title in searing heat at the Congressional Country Club near Washington. On the last day of 36 holes, Venturi was near collapse at the end of 18 holes. He was attended to between rounds by a doctor and a priest and advised to withdraw. But he refused, playing the final round almost in a stupor, and held on to win in what is considered the most dramatic victory ever in the US Open. Venturi later suffered problems with his hands which ended his career, having won 14 PGA Tour events. He has since become a television announcer covering golf tournaments.

Hedley VERITY (UK)

CRICKET
Hedley Verity. b. 18 May 1905 Headingley, Leeds, Yorkshire, d. 31 Jul 1943 Caserta, Italy.

The world's best slow medium left-arm spinner of the 1930s and the most famous cricketing casualty of World War II, when he died of his wounds in an Italian prisoner-of-war camp as a captain in the Green Howards. With Wilfred Rhodes in the Yorkshire team, he had to wait until he was 25 for his début, but then followed in his county's great tradition of bowlers of his type and was an immediate success, as in his first season of 1930 his 64 wickets averaged just 12.42. His impressive record continued as he took at least 150 wickets in each season for the rest of the decade - his worst seasonal average was 17.63 - to have the best career average figures for any major bowler of the 20th century. He took over 200 wickets each year 1935-7. In 1932 for Yorkshire v Notttinghamshire he took 10-10, the most economical ten-wicket haul ever and the only one to include a hat-trick. In 1934 for England against Australia at Lord's he took 7-61 and 8-43, these 15 wickets being the most to fall to a bowler on one day of Test cricket.
He was a useful batsman, who was pressed into service to open the innings for England in one Test against South Africa in 1937.
40 Tests 1931-9: 669 runs at 20.90, HS 66; 144 wickets at 24.37, BB 8-43; 30 catches.*
First-class 1930-9: 5605 runs at 18.08, 1 100 HS 101; 1956 wickets at 14.90, BB 10-10; 269 catches.

Yrjö VESTERINEN (Fin)

MOTOR CYCLING
Yrjö Vesterinen.

He was Finnish junior champion at trials in 1969, joining Bultaco in 1974, and on their machines was 2nd in 1975 and then won a record three world trials motorcycling titles, 1976-8. Ever composed, he had the ideal sense of balance and concentration for a trials rider.

Georges VEZINA (Can)

ICE HOCKEY
Georges Vezina. b. 7 Jan 1888 Chicoutimi, Québec, d. 26 Mar 1926 Chicoutimi.

The first truly great goaltender in the NHL, minding the nets for the Montreal Canadiens throughout his ten-year professional career. It was once written of him, 'He has a calmness not of this world.' His career would probably have been greater had illness not claimed him so early. In a game in late 1925, he collapsed in the goal crease, suffering from tuberculosis and

with a temperature of 40.6°C (105°F) at game time. He died only a few months later. The Vezina Trophy, emblematic of the NHL's top goaltender each year, was named in his honour.
NHL career 1917-26:191 games, 3.28 GAA, 13 shutouts.

Guillermo VILAS (Arg)

TENNIS

Guillermo Vilas. b. 17 Aug 1952 Buenos Aires.

One of the greatest South American players. In 1981 he played a major role in taking Argentina to the final of the Davis Cup where they lost to the USA indoors in Cincinnati. His first major victory was in the 1974 Masters, and he won the French title in 1977 and was the losing finalist on three other occasions (1975, 1978, 1982). He also won the US and South African titles in 1977, the Australian in 1978 and 1979, and the Italian in 1980. In 1977-8 he had a professional tour record of 46 consecutive match wins, and in 1977 tied the record with 15 singles titles. He had career earnings of $4,923,132.
He was one of the most reclusive players on the circuit and spent much of his time off-court writing poetry, several volumes of which were published. A left-hander, he was at his best as a hard court player.

Pierre VILLEPREUX (Fra)

RUGBY UNION

Pierre Villepreux. b. 5 Jul 1943 Pompadour.

A brilliant attacking full-back and a superb long-range place kicker. During the early part of his international career he shared the position of full back in the French team with Claude Lacaze but soon established himself as first choice for the position. In 34 internationals 1967-72 he kicked 32 penalties and 29 conversions, including a record five in one match against England in 1972. After retirement he was an innovative and highly successful coach at his club Toulouse, but expectations that his talents would be used at a national level were never fulfilled.

Ellsworth VINES (USA)

TENNIS

Henry Ellsworth Vines. b. 28 Sep 1911 Los Angeles, California.

Regarded in the 1930s as the hardest ever hitter of a tennis ball. The power of his serve and forehand was devastating, and when only 19 he won the 1931 US singles. The following year he successfully defended his US title and won Wimbledon at his first attempt. In 1933 he again reached the Wimbledon final but lost to Jack Crawford in five sets, and that year he also lost to both Austin and Perry of Great Britain in the Davis Cup and to Bitsy Grant at the US Nationals. In the men's doubles he won the 1932 US and 1933 Australian titles, and the US mixed doubles followed in 1933. In the Davis Cup he won 13 of 16 singles in 1932-3. His brilliant, brief and meteoric amateur career ended when he turned professional in October 1933. Although Vines lost to the 41-year-old Tilden on his pro début, he soon adjusted his game to suit the indoor surfaces and reigned as the top professional for five years. After winning the US Pro singles title in 1939 he gave up tennis for golf and won several amateur tournaments. In 1942 he became a professional golfer and won five Open tournaments in 1944-5. He ranked high among the money winners for the next few years and in 1951 reached the semi-finals of the PGA Championship. After he gave up tournament golf he became the professional at La Quinta Country Club in Palm Springs.

Lasse VIREN (Fin)

ATHLETICS

Lasse Artturi Viren. b. 22 Jul 1949 Myrskylä.

Viren won the Olympic double of 5000m and 10,000m in both 1972 and 1976. This great runner showed above all the ability to peak when it really mattered, with devastating sustained pace over the later stages of a race. After his Olympic triumphs his form in lesser events was often indifferent; in European Championships he was 7th and 3rd at 5000m, and 17th and

7th at 10,000m in 1971 and 1974 respectively. He was also fifth in the Olympic marathon (2:13:11) in 1976 and at 10,000m in 1980. His tenacity and quick thinking was shown when he fell in his first Olympic final, at 10,000m in 1972, yet got up to win in a world record 27:38.35. In that year he also set world records for 2 miles at 8:14.0 and 5000m 13:16.4, and a Finnish record for 3000m of 7:43.2.
He came to prominence with brilliant wins in the Finnish junior and senior 5000m races in 1969, and won further senior titles at 1500m (1972 and 1974) and 5000m (1976).

Gundappa VISWANATH (India)

CRICKET

Gundappa Ranganath Viswanath. b. 12 Feb 1949 Bhadravati, Mysore.

A most popular and attractive batsman. He hit 230 on his first-class début for Karnataka in 1967 and at the age of 20 made his Test début against Australia, when after a duck in the first innings he made 137 in the second. For the next 13 years, he led the Indian batting with his brother-in-law Sunil Gavaskar. A kind and gentle man, he was only 1.63m *5'4"* tall, but his immaculate technique and stylish, wristy play brought him continuing success. His 222 against England at Madras in 1982 was then India's highest ever Test score. He captained India twice.
91 Tests 1969-83: 6080 runs at 41.93, 14 100s HS 222; 1 wicket; 63 catches.
25 One-day Ints: 439 runs at 19.95, HS 75; 3 catches.
First-class 1967-88: 17,970 runs at 40.93, 44 100s HS 247; 15 wickets at 48.60; 226 catches.

Yuriy VLASOV (USSR/Ukr)

WEIGHTLIFTING

Yuriy Petrovich Vlasov. b. 5 Dec 1935 Makeyevka, Dontsk Oblast.

Vlasov succeeded American Paul Anderson as the claimant to the title of 'The World's Strongest Man'. In the process he began the long line of Soviet champions in super-heavyweight lifting. He first achieved international prominence in 1959 when he won the European and World titles, adding three more World titles 1961-3 and five more Europeans 1960-4. At the Olympics he easily won the gold medal in 1960 and was heavily favoured to repeat the feat in 1964, but was upset by a fellow Soviet, Leonid Zhabotinsky. Vlasov, a graduate of Zhukovsky Air Force Academy, was USSR champion each year 1959-63 and also set 32 world records in the super-heavyweight class: 7 press, 8 snatch, 9 jerk (197.5kg 1959 to 215.5kg 1964) and 8 total. After his retirement from weightlifting, Vlasov turned to his first love and became a renowned poet.

Berti VOGTS (FRG)

FOOTBALL

Hans-Hubert Vogts. b. 30 Dec 1946 Büttgen, Lower Rhine.

A compact, strong-tackling, attacking full-back, he was a stalwart of the German team in the 1970s, making 96 international appearances, including 18 in World Cup Finals tournaments 1970-8, winning in 1974. He was appointed German captain in 1977. From VIR Büttgen he played for Borussia Mönchengladbach from 1966 to 1979, helping them to win the UEFA Cup in 1975 and 1979, German league 1970-1 and 1975-7 and Cup 1973. He became a coach in 1979 and in 1990 took over as manager of the German national team.

Rudi VÖLLER (FRG)

FOOTBALL

Rudolf Völler. b. 13 Apr 1960 Hanau.

A striker who scored 43 goals in 85 international appearances for Germany 1982-92. He helped his team to win the World Cup in 1990 and scored in the 1986 final which Germany lost 2-3 to Argentina. Appointed German captain for the 1992 European Championships, he broke his arm in the first game. Before his senior international début in 1982 he played 19 times for the German junior team.
He started his career with Kickers

Offenbach 1977-80, moving to TSV 1860 Munich 1980-2, Werder Bremen 1982-7 and then to AS Roma, whom he helped to win the Italian Cup in 1991. In 1992 he was transferred to Marseille, and with them won the European Cup and the French league in 1993.

Gottfried VON CRAMM (Ger)

TENNIS

Baron Gottfried Alexander Maximilian Walter Kurt Von Cramm. b. 7 Jul 1909 Nettlingen, nr. Hanover, d. 9 Nov 1976 Alexandria, Egypt.

Germany's greatest player until the arrival of Boris Becker. He was a finalist in seven Grand Slam singles but only won two, the French in 1934 and 1936, as he was runner-up in the French in 1935, the US in 1937 and at Wimbledon for three successive years 1935-7, a distinction he shares with Fred Stolle. In the doubles he won the mixed at Wimbledon in 1933 and the men's at the US and French Championships in 1937. He won 11 German titles (6 singles, 2 doubles, 3 mixed doubles) between 1932 and 1949, and as a member of the Davis Cup team won 82 out of 102 rubbers in 37 ties 1932-53.

A classic stylist, noted for his exemplary sportsmanship, he initially received the support of the Nazis but he refused to embrace their cause and in 1938 was imprisoned for six months on politically motivated charges of homosexuality. On his release he accepted an invitation from the King of Sweden to live in that country, but he returned to Germany when war broke out and served on the Eastern front. After the war he continued to play in tournaments and won the German championship in 1948-9. He was married briefly, 1955-60, to the Woolworth heiress Barbara Hutton, and was killed in a car crash in Egypt where he lived.

Chris VON SALTZA (USA)

SWIMMING

Susan Christina von Saltza. b. 3 Jan 1944 San Francisco. Married Robert Olmstead 1969.

Her three golds (400m freestyle and two relays) and a silver medal (behind Dawn Fraser at 100m) at the 1960 Olympics heralded a resurgence in US swimming. Coached by George Haines, she had won her first US title at 220y backstroke at the age of 13 in 1957. She won again at 200m backstroke in a world record 2:37.4 in 1958 and won freestyle titles at 100m/110y 1958-60, 200m/220y and 400m/440y 1959-60, years in which she was limited to three events. She won five gold medals, 100m, 200m and 400m freestyle with two relays, at the 1959 Pan-American Games, and by the time she retired at 16 she had set about 75 US records and a further world record with 4:44.5 for 400m freestyle in 1960. A year later she went to Stanford University, from which she graduated in history.

Arkadiy VOROBYEV (USSR/Rus)

WEIGHTLIFTING

Arkadiy Nikitich Vorobyev. b. 3 Oct 1924 Mordovo, Tambov Oblast.

Vorobyev has had a very varied career in multiple fields. He won three Olympic medals, gold in the 90kg class in 1956 and 1960 following bronze at 82.5kg in 1952. He was also World champion at 82.5kg 1953 and 90kg 1954-5 and 1957-8; and European champion at 82.5kg 1950 and 1953, 90kg 1954-5 and 1958. He set 18 world records 1950-60, 7 at 82.5kg and 11 at 90kg. After his lifting career ended he became a doctor, and wrote several textbooks on weightlifting. He then took over as Soviet national weightlifting coach. Prior to starting his career in lifting, he had been a deep-sea diver.

Mikhail VORONIN (USSR)

GYMNASTICS

Mikhail Yakovlevich Voronin. b. 26 Mar 1945 Moscow.

The overall World champion of 1966 and European champion of 1967 and 1969, Voronin won nine Olympic medals: two gold, three silver and a bronze in 1968 and two silver in 1972. In 1968 he was, however, pipped for the all-around gold by

Sawao Kato (Japan). A specialist on the high bar, where he pioneered the 'Voronin hop', he started as a footballer, being persuaded to take up gymnastics by Moscow Dynamo coach Vitaliy Belyayev.
His wife **Zinaida Voronina** (née Druginina, b. 10 Dec 1947) won a team gold and was second overall at the 1968 Olympics, where she also won two bronze medals. She was third in the 1970 World Championships.

Inga VORONINA (USSR) see ARTAMONOVA

Rube WADDELL (USA)

BASEBALL

George Edward Waddell. b. 13 Oct 1876 Bradford, Pennsylvania, d. 1 Apr 1914 San Antonio, Texas.

One of baseball's first great strikeout artists, leading his league seven times, six of them consecutively 1902-07. In 1903 (302) and 1904 he became the first modern pitcher to record 300 strikeouts in two consecutive seasons, a feat not matched until Sandy Koufax in 1965-6 and not broken until Nolan Ryan 1972-4. His 349 strikeouts in 1904 was an American League record which lasted until Ryan broke it in 1974. Waddell also won 20 games in four straight years, 1902-05. He was known as a wildman off the field; he wrestled alligators in Florida, hung around firehouses, married two women who left him, and frequented saloons. His erratic behaviour and lack of training eventually caused his arm to go out and he had a rather short, but meteoric career.
Career pitching 1897-1910: ERA 2.16; W-L 193-143, SO 2316. Best seasons: 1902: 24-7, 2.05 ERA; 1903: 21-16, 2.44 ERA; 1904: 25-19, 1.62 ERA; 1905: 27-10 1.48, ERA, 287 SO.

Virginia WADE (UK)

TENNIS

Sarah Virginia Wade. b. 10 Jul 1945 Bournemouth, Hampshire.

Wade's victory in the 1977 Wimbledon singles was received with acclaim by the spectators: this was Wimbledon's Centenary year and success by a home player was particularly welcome. Approaching her 32nd birthday this was Wade's 16th challenge for the title and although she had been a world class player for many years, previous Grand Slam singles honours had been restricted to the 1968 US and 1972 Australian titles. She gained her only major clay-court success in 1971 when she took the Italian title.
At women's doubles she won the US, French and Australian Championships in 1973 and the US title again in 1975; all with Margaret Court, but they did not play together at the 1973 Wimbledon and missed the opportunity of a Grand Slam of doubles titles that year.
Although born in Hampshire, Wade was raised in South Africa where her father was Archdeacon of Durban. She returned to England when she was 15 and then took a science degree at Sussex University. Although she later settled in New York, Wade remained a loyal member of British teams and played in more Federation Cup rubbers (100) and more ties (57) than any player of any country, winning 36 of 56 singles and 30 of 44 doubles. She also played in a record 20 Wightman Cup ties. Apart from her prowess as a player she did much for the game and in 1983 became the first woman to be elected to the Wimbledon Championships Committee. No woman has exceeded the 25 Wimbledon Championships at which she played.

Lanny WADKINS (USA)

GOLF

Lanny Wadkins. b. 5 Dec 1949 Richmond, Virginia.

Fourth on the all-time career earnings list for the US tour, he has shown his most redoubtable form in the Ryder Cup competition, where his record is 18 wins, 10 losses and 2 halves over his seven Cups 1977-91. He was US Amateur champion in 1970, when he also helped the US win the World Amateur team title. As a pro his most important wins have been the US PGA and World Series of Golf in 1977 and

the Tournament Players Championship in 1979. He has never headed the PGA money list, but was 2nd in 1985 and 3rd in 1977 and 1983.
A fast player, he is an accurate driver and a fine putter and bunker player. His younger brother Bobby has won $2,034,175 on the PGA tour 1973-92, despite not winning a tournament.
PGA career earnings 1971-92: $5,632,713 with 21 victories.

Honus WAGNER (USA)

BASEBALL

John Peter Wagner. b. 24 Feb 1874 Mansfield, Pennsylvania, d. 6 Dec 1955 Carnegie, Pennsylvania.

'The Flying Dutchman' is usually acknowledged as the greatest shortstop in baseball history, with tremendous speed and range. He broke in with the Louisville Colonels of the National League but spent most of his career, his last 18 years, with the Pittsburgh Pirates. He led the National League in hitting eight times with a high average of .381 in 1900. He also led the league in RBI five times and in doubles eight times. He was big and barrel-chested but was also possessed of great speed, stealing over 20 bases every year from 1898-1915 and leading the league five times. He had one of the shortest managing careers in baseball history, just five games as player-manager in his last year before he decided against it. He played semi-pro baseball for seven more years and was a Pirate coach from 1933-51. His fame continues to this day as one of his early baseball cards is considered the most valuable by collectors, with the very few available copies selling for more than $200,000. The card was manufactured by a cigarette company, but Wagner despised smoking and demanded the card be withdrawn after only a few copies had been made.
Career 1897-1917: 3430 hits Avg. .327; RBI 1732; SB 722. Best seasons: 1900: .381, 22 Triples; 1905: .363; 1903: .355, 19 Triples; 1908: .354, 201 hits, 19 Triples, 109 RBI; 1901: .353, 126 RBI.

Harold WAGSTAFF (UK)

RUGBY LEAGUE

Harold Wagstaff. b. 19 May 1891 Huddersfield, Yorkshire, d. 19 Jul 1939 Huddersfield.

A teenage prodigy who is universally recognised as the 'Prince of Centres', he first played for Huddersfield at the age of 15y 175 days, represented Yorkshire aged 17y 141 days and was only 17y 228 days of age when he became the youngest-ever international for England. In order to convince sceptics among the Huddersfield supporters who doubted his age, a facsimile of his birth certificate was printed in the official match programme.
He led Great Britain to Australia in 1914 and 1920 and established himself in the legends of the game as captain of the winning team in the famous 'Rorke's Drift Test' in 1914 when Great Britain won 14-6 despite being reduced to 10 men after 50 minutes play.
He won every honour in the game, but World War I curtailed his international career and he played in only 12 matches for Great Britain. After retirement he coached at Halifax and Broughton Rangers, and at the time of his death was the licensee of a hotel in Huddersfield and a committee member of his former club.

John WAITE (SAf)

CRICKET

John Henry Bickford Waite. b. 19 Jan 1930 Johannesburg.

A most successful wicket-keeper and a sound right-handed batsman, he played in a record 50 Tests for South Africa. His 26 dismissals (23 catches and 3 stumpings) against New Zealand in 1961/2 was at the time a record for a Test series.
He played for Eastern Province 1948-52 and Transvaal 1953-66, and became the director of the Transvaal Cricket Council.
50 Tests 1951-65: 2405 runs at 30.44, 4 100s HS 134; 124 catches, 17 stumpings. First-class 1948-65: 9812 runs at 35.04, 23 100s HS 219; 426 catches, 86 stumpings.

Grete WAITZ (Nor)

ATHLETICS

Grete Waitz. née Andersen. b. 1 Oct 1953 Oslo. She married Jack Waitz (né Nilsen) in 1975.

She was the first world champion at the women's marathon in 1983, fitting recognition of her ability and her pioneering rôle in women's distance running. She ran world bests in her first three marathons annually at New York from 1978 to 1980, her times 2:32:29.8, 2:27:32.6 and 2:25:41. She set a fourth world best with 2:25:29 in London on 17 Apr 1983 and went on to complete nine wins in the New York Marathon, winning each year 1982-6 and in 1988.

In all she won 13 of her 19 marathons from 1978 to 1990, including London again in 1986 in her best ever time of 2:24:54. She was also runner-up to Joan Benoit in the first women's Olympic marathon in 1984.

She first competed in the European Championships in 1971 at 800m and 1500m, and in the Olympics at 1500m in 1972. On the track she set a European junior 1500m record in 1971 and two world records at 3000m: 8:46.6 in 1975 and 8:45.4 in 1976, with a European 5000m record of 15:08.80 in 1982; yet apart from her World Cup win at 3000m in 1977 she did not win any major titles, taking European bronze medals at 1500m in 1974 and at 3000m in 1978.

Before her marathon success she was at her best in road races, where her first ever loss was to Maricica Puica in 1981, and at cross-country, where she was unbeaten for twelve years and achieved a record five wins (1978-81 and 1983) in the World Championships (also third in 1982 and 1984).

She won 33 Norwegian senior titles from 1971 to 1983 and set 23 Norwegian records at track events from 800m to 5000m. A statue of her was erected outside the Bislett Stadium in Oslo in 1984.

Other bests: 800m 2:03.1 (1975), 1500m 4:00.55 (1978), 1 mile 4:26.90 (1979), 3000m 8:31.75 (1979).

Wavell WAKEFIELD (UK)

RUGBY UNION

William Wavell Wakefield. b. 10 Mar 1898 Beckenham, Kent, d. 12 Aug 1983 Kendal, Cumbria.

Both as a player and an administrator he made an immeasurable contribution to the sport. A wing forward for Leicester, Harlequins, RAF, Cambridge University and England, he pointed the way to the advantages of mobile forward play and he introduced the concept of the back row working together as a team. His 31 caps (1920-7) remained an England record until beaten by 'Budge' Rogers in 1969, he captained England 13 times and led them to three Grand Slams. He entered Parliament as a Conservative in 1935, served as President of the RFU in 1950-1 and was a member of the International Board from 1954-61. In 1963 he became the first Baron Wakefield of Kendal.

Douglas WAKIIHURI (Kenya)

ATHLETICS

Douglas Wakiihuri Maina. b. 26 Sep 1963 Mombasa.

Wakiihuri was a surprise winner of the 1987 World marathon title, but went on to compile a brilliant record over the next three years, taking the Olympic silver medal in 1988 and the Commonwealth gold in 1990.

A Kikuyu, the son of a prison officer, he went to Japan in 1983 to train under the late Kiyoshi Nakamura. He ran 2:16:26 in his marathon début in 1986, improving to 2:13:34 for sixth in Beppu 1987 and then won the world title in 2:11:48. Seventh in the Tokyo marathon in 1988 before placing second in Seoul in 2:10:48. He seemed not to bother much about fast times, looking to run well within his ability; his fastest time, 2:09:03, came when he won the London marathon in 1989. In 1990 he also won the New York marathon. His career faltered thereafter, and he was only 36th at the 1992 Olympics.

Best track times: 3000m 7:56.69 (1989), 5000m 13:24.01 (1988), 10,000m 27:59.60 (1988).

Stanislawa WALASIEWICZ (Pol)

ATHLETICS

Stanislawa (née Stefania) Walasiewicz. b. 11 Apr 1911 Wierzchownia, d. 4 Dec 1980 Cleveland, Ohio, USA. Known in the USA as Stella Walsh (later Olson).

The most successful competitor in women's athletics in the 1930s, although a cloud was put over her career by the fact that her femininity was questioned, not least when a post-mortem after she had been shot in a parking lot at a Chicago department store revealed that 'she' had male sex organs but no female ones.
A total of 37 marks were posted by Walasiewicz as outdoor world records, although just 14 were ratified as many were never submitted for approval. Her best performances included: 100y 10.5u (1944), 100m 11.6 (1937) and 11.2u (1945), 200m 23.6 (1935), long jump 6.12 (1939).
Her parents emigrated to the USA when she was two, but she was unable to gain US citizenship so she competed for Poland at the Olympic Games, where she won the 100m in 1932 and was second at 200m in 1936. She was Women's World Games champion at 60m, 100m and 200m in 1930 and 60m in 1934; and European champion at 100m and 200m in 1938 with second at long jump and 4x100m. She was also the winner of 18 Polish titles at just five championships contested between 1933 and 1946, and of 40 AAU titles in the USA between 1930 and 1951 at a wide variety of events. These included a record 11 at 220m/220y 1930-1, 1939-40, 1942-8 and long jump 1930, 1939-46, 1948, 1951. She became a naturalised American in 1947 and eventually became a US citizen by marrying Harry Olson in 1956, but, by now 45, could not make the US team that year.
In her native Poland she held all the recognised running event records as well as those for long jump and pentathlon from the late 1930s to the early 1950s, with other bests including 60m 7.3, 800m 2:18.4, 1000m 3:02.5, 80m hurdles 12.2.

Clyde WALCOTT (Bar)

CRICKET

Clyde Leopold Walcott. b. 17 Jan 1926 Bridgetown.

A commanding batsman, the biggest and most powerful of the celebrated three Ws. He combined wicket-keeping with batting for the first part of his Test career, but achieved his peak success when he concentrated on his batting, and averaged over 75 in each of three Test series 1953-5, including 827 runs at 82.70 against Australia in 5 Tests in 1955. He went even higher in 4 Tests against Pakistan in 1958, with 385 runs at 96.25. He also bowled at fast-medium pace. His highest score was early in his career with 314* when he set a then world record partnership of 574 runs with Frank Worrell for Barbados v Trinidad in 1946. Awarded the OBE.
44 Tests 1948-60: 3798 runs at 56.68, 15 100s HS 220; 11 wickets at 37.09, BB 3-50; 53 catches, 11 stumpings.
First-class 1942-64: 11,820 runs at 56.55, 40 100s HS 314; 35 wickets at 36.25, BB 5-41; 174 catches, 33 stumpings.*

Jersey Joe WALCOTT (USA)

BOXING

né Arnold Raymond Cream. b. 31 Jan 1914 Merchantville, New Jersey.

Having turned professional when he was only 16, he took the name of Joe Walcott after the former welterweight champion. He boxed without notice until 1944 when he retired at age 30. He worked odd jobs for the next few years until he agreed to box some exhibitions for a local promoter. This led to an exhibition, which eventually received title recognition, against Joe Louis. Walcott fought well, though he lost the decision, and continued to fight. In 1951 he defeated Ezzard Charles to claim the heavyweight championship; at 37, this made him the oldest heavyweight champion ever. A year later he was knocked out by Rocky Marciano in 13 rounds. In 1953, Walcott was again knocked out by Marciano, this time in one round, and he then retired for good.
He became a referee, twice overseeing

world heavyweight contests, and was briefly mayor of Camden, New Jersey.
Career record: W - 50 (30), L - 18, D - 1

Björn WALDEGÅRD (Swe)

RALLYING

Björn L-O Waldegård. b. 12 Nov 1943 Rö.

One of the most successful rally drivers of all-time, he was world champion in 1979 and won the Monte Carlo Rally in 1969 and 1970 and the RAC in 1977. He shares the record of 19 world championship race wins. His first major win was in 1968, the first of three successive Swedish Rally wins for Porsche. He won that race again in 1975 for Lancia and 1978 for Ford. He has four wins in the Safari Rally, in 1977 in a Ford Escort and in Toyotas in 1984, 1986 and 1990.

Jan-Ove WALDNER (Swe)

TABLE TENNIS

Jan-Ove Waldner. b. 3 Oct 1965 Stockholm.

World men's singles champion in 1989 and runner-up in 1987 and 1991, and Olympic champion in 1992. He was also on the Swedish team that won the Swaythling Cup in 1989, 1991 and 1993. In European Championships he has won 11 medals from 1982, doubles champion in 1986 and 1988, and with four team wins, 1986, 1988, 1990 and 1992. His singles best was runner-up in 1982.
Other major titles won include the Masters 1989, World Cup 1990, and the European Top-12 tournament 1983-4, 1986, 1988-9. He was a brilliant junior, winning the European title at doubles each year 1980-2 and at singles each year 1981-3.

Chet WALKER (USA)

BASKETBALL

Chester Walker. b. 22 Feb 1940 Benton Harbor, Michigan.

Once considered the most unstoppable one-on-one player in the NBA. He played his college basketball at Bradley, and then for 13 years as a forward in the NBA with various teams. He was most renowned for his years with the Philadelphia 76ers with whom he earned an NBA Championship in 1967. He later became a television movie producer.
NBA career: 18.831 points av. 18.2.

Doak WALKER (USA)

AMERICAN FOOTBALL

Ewell Doak Walker, Jr. b. 1 Jan 1927, Dallas, Texas.

Walker starred as a running back for Southern Methodist University (SMU) in 1944 and from 1946-9, with one year out for Army duty. He was the quintessential 'triple threat', running well, passing sharply, and kicking long and with accuracy. He was named All-Southwest Conference all four full years at SMU, and was a three-time All-American. He won the Maxwell Award in 1947 and the Heisman Memorial Trophy in 1948 as a junior. Injury in his senior season prevented him from repeating as Heisman winner. Walker played in the NFL from 1950-4 with the Detroit Lions and was named All-Pro for four of his five years, but he is far better remembered for his heroics at SMU.
NFL career 1950-5: Rushing: 1520 yards av. 4.9, 12 touchdowns; Receiving: 2539 yards av. 16.7, 21 touchdowns.

John WALKER (NZ)

ATHLETICS

John George Walker. b. 12 Jan 1952 Papakura.

Walker became the world's first sub-3:50 miler when he ran 3:49.4 at Gothenburg on 12 Aug 1975. He also set a world record for 2000m with 4:51.4 at Oslo in 1976 prior to winning the Olympic gold medal at 1500m in Montreal. He leapt to international prominence at the 1974 Commonwealth Games when he took the silver medal at 1500m, behind Filbert Bayi's world record, and the bronze at 800m. He had, however, run on the New Zealand team that ran a world record for 4 x 1500m in Oslo in 1973 on the first of his annual tours of Europe, when he main-

tained an amazing level of consistency and success over nearly two decades. He ran his 100th sub four-minute mile on 17 Feb 1985, the first to achieve such a feat. Sadly, boycotts and injuries prevented him from competing at the Olympics of 1980 and 1988, and he was eighth at 5000m in 1984. At Commonwealth Games he was second at 1500m and fourth at 800m in 1982 and fifth at 5000m in 1986, but any chance of a dream finish to his great career was denied when he was brought down in the 1500m final in his home town of Auckland in 1990. He won 15 New Zealand titles, eight at 800m and seven at 1500m. He now breeds horses near Auckland.
Best times: 800m 1:44.94 (1974), 1000m 2:16.57 (1980), 1500m 3:32.4 (1975), 1 mile 3:49.08 (1982), 2000m 4:51.52 (1976), 3000m 7:37.49 (1982), 2 miles 8:20.57 (1975), 5000m 13:19.28 (1986).

Mickey WALKER (USA)

BOXING
Edward Patrick Walker. b. 13 Jul 1901 Elizabeth, New Jersey, d. 28 Apr 1981 Freehold, New Jersey

Many people consider Walker the toughest and hardest-hitting non-heavyweight of all time. He turned professional in 1919 and in his 46th fight, in 1922, won the world welterweight championship by defeating Jack Britton. He lost the title four years later and moved up to the middleweights, winning the world title in November 1926 by decisioning Tiger Flowers. Walker also made two unsuccessful attempts to win the light-heavyweight title in 1929 and 1933, and he fought for a time as a heavyweight. After he retired, he had several jobs, six wives, and took up painting, at which he was very successful.
Career record: W - 94 (61), L - 19, D - 4.

Maria WALLISER (Swi)

ALPINE SKIING
Maria Walliser. b. 27 May 1963 Mosnang.

World champion at downhill racing in 1987 and 1989 and at the super G in 1987. She was the World Cup overall winner in 1986 and 1987, as well winning the downhill 1984 and 1986, super G 1987 and tying for the giant slalom in 1987. In all she won 25 World Cup races, 1983-90, including 14 at downhill.

Courtney WALSH (Jam)

CRICKET
Courtney Andrew Walsh. b. 30 Oct 1962 Kingston.

A most valuable member of the West Indian pace attack from the mid-1980s, and captain of Jamaica from 1991. His most successful Test series was against India in 1987/8 when he took 26 wickets at 16.80 in 4 Tests. He has also played in England for Gloucestershire from 1984, and has twice taken most wickets in an English season, 118 at 18.17 in 1986 and 92 at 15.96 in 1992.
59 Tests 1984-93: 518 runs at 9.25, HS 30; 202 wickets at 25.61, BB 6-62; 8 catches.*
111 One-day Ints: 203 runs at 8.45, HS 29; 124 wickets at 31.04, BB 5-1; 13 catches.*
First-class 1981-92: 2969 run at 12.68, HS 63; 989 wickets at 22.49, BB 9-72; 68 catches.*

Ed WALSH (USA)

BASEBALL
Edward Augustine Walsh. b. 14 May 1881 Plains, Pennsylvania, d. 26 May 1959 Pompano Beach, Florida.

The last major league pitcher to win 40 games in a season, when in 1908 he pitched 464 innings, still a record for the 20th century. 'Big Ed' pitched mostly with the Chicago White Sox, although he finished his career with one season for the Boston Braves. His primary pitch was a spitball. Walsh later became a major league umpire for one season (1922) and then returned to the White Sox as a coach.
Career pitching 1904-17: ERA 1.82; W-L 195-126, SO 1736. Best seasons: 1908: 40-15, 1.42 ERA, 269 SO; 1911: 27-18, 2.22 ERA; 1912: 27-17, 2.15 ERA.

Stella WALSH, see WALASIEWICZ.

Fritz WALTER (FRG)

FOOTBALL
Fritz Walter. b. 31 Oct 1920, Kaiserslautern.

After making his international début against Romania in 1940, when he scored a hat-trick in a 9-3 win, he won two more caps before joining a parachute regiment. Resuming his career immediately after the war, he went on to win a total of 61 caps until his retirement in 1958 after a German record 18-year international span, scoring 33 goals. The highlight of his career came in 1954 when, as captain and midfield tactician, he led Germany to victory in the World Cup. He was again a major force in the 1958 World Cup when Germany reached the semi-finals.
Throughout his career he remained loyal to the Kaiserslautern club with whom he won League Championship honours in 1951 and 1953, playing for them until he was 40. A shrewd and imaginative tactician, he had a fine understanding with the West German manager, Sepp Herberger, and together they did much to influence the revival of German football after the war. His brother **Otmar** shared his honours with Kaiserslautern and also played with Fritz in the national team on numerous occasions, including the 1954 World Cup final.

Steffi WALTER (GDR)

LUGE
Steffi Walter. née Martin. b. 17 Sep 1962 Schlema.

Olympic champion in 1984 and 1988 and the only woman to win two Olympic luge titles. She was European junior champion in 1981 and World champion in 1983 and 1985. In 1984 she shared the World Cup with her East German team-mate, Bettina Schmidt.

Doug WALTERS (Aus)

CRICKET
Kevin Douglas Walters. b. 21 Dec 1945 Dungog, New South Wales.

A brilliant batsman, especially on hard wickets, but one who generally disappointed on his tours of England, perhaps because his technique, depending much on his eye and reflexes, was found to be suspect on slower pitches. He was also a handy medium-paced bowler, useful for stand-breaking, and a splendid fielder at cover point. He first played for New South Wales in 1962/3 and captained them in four seasons. He burst onto the international scene with 410 runs at 68.33 against England in 1965/6, including 155 on his début a few days before his 20th birthday. He went on to average over 100 in two of his next three series to 1969, but had some disappointing results in the early years of the 1970s, before possibly his best batting from 1973 to 1977. Awarded the MBE.
74 Tests 1965-81: 5357 runs at 48.26, 15 100s HS 250; 49 wickets at 29.08, BB 5-66; 43 catches.
28 One-day Ints: 513 runs at 28.50, HS 59; 4 wickets at 68.25; BB 2-24; 10 catches.
First-class 1962-81: 16,180 runs at 43.84, 45 100s HS 253; 190 wickets at 25.69, BB 7-63; 149 catches.

Bill WALTON (USA)

BASKETBALL
William Theodore Walton, Jr. b. 5 Nov 1952 LaMesa, California.

College player of the year for three consecutive years 1972-4 at UCLA, whom he led to two NCAA championships. Drafted by the Portland Trail Blazers, great things were expected of the red-headed center. He seemed to combine everything needed in a big man - intensity, size, rebounding, defense - but he added great moves and an offensive presence rarely seen at that position. In addition he seemed the ideal team man who made everyone around him play better. He quickly made an impact, leading Portland to the NBA Championship in 1977 and for a brief period, he was the dominant center in the game. Some experts predicted he could become the best center ever, but he then developed foot problems and underwent multiple operations. He played until 1987, earning one more NBA Championship ring in 1986 with the

Boston Celtics, but after his injuries he was never the same player. He briefly attended law school during one injury-induced sabbatical from basketball and has since become a television basketball commentator.

Fulke WALWYN (UK)

HORSE RACING

Fulke Thomas Tyndall Walwyn. b. 8 Nov 1910 Wrexham, d. 18 Feb 1991 Upper Lambourn.

A fine trainer under National Hunt Rules, he saddled a total of 2188 winners in a 50-year career, 1939-90. His horses won all the major races, one Grand National (*Team Spirit* in 1964), four Cheltenham Gold Cups, two Champion Hurdles and seven times the Whitbread and Hennessy Gold Cups. Perhaps the best horses he trained were *Mandarin* and *Mill House*. He was a master of getting his horses right for the big occasion.
The son of an army officer, a career he followed after school until 1935, he started riding as a youngster. The peak of his amateur career, 1929-36, was his win on *Reynoldstown* in the 1936 Grand National. He then turned professional, but switched to training at Lambourn in 1939, after serious injuries from falls. He was leading trainer in 1946/7, in which year he started training for Dorothy Paget, and again in 1947/8, 1948/9, 1957/8 and 1963/4. In 1973 he took over from Peter Cazalet as trainer of the Queen Mother's horses. Awarded the CVO.

Lloyd WANER (USA)

BASEBALL

Lloyd James Waner. b. 16 Mar 1906 Harrah, Oklahoma, d. 22 Jul 1982 Oklahoma City, Oklahoma.

Waner was the younger half of one of baseball's most famous brother combinations. Known as 'Little Poison', he was an outfielder who spent most of his career with the Pittsburgh Pirates. He was a top hitter for average, batting over .300 eleven times in his career, and was also an excellent centerfielder, leading the league in putouts four times because of his great speed.
Career 1927-45: 2459 hits Avg. .316; RBI 598. Best seasons: 1927: .355, 223 hits; 1929: .353, 234 hits; 1928: .335, 221 hits

Paul WANER (USA)

BASEBALL

Paul Glee Waner. b. 16 Apr 1903 Harrah, Oklahoma, d. 29 Aug 1965 Sarasota, Florida.

'Big Poison' Waner played together with his younger brother for the Pittsburgh Pirates 1927-40. He led the National League in hitting in 1927, 1934 and 1936 and batted over .300 14 times, notably for his first 12 seasons in the majors. He was known for his hard-drinking ways after games and this prevented him from ever being considered as a manager. He spent much of his playing retirement as a hitting coach.
Career 1926-45: 3152 hits Avg. .333, HR 113; RBI 1309; SB 104. Best seasons: 1927: .380, 237 hits, 131 RBI; 1936: .373, 218 hits; 1928: .370, 223 hits, 142 runs; 1932: .341, 62 doubles, 215 hits; 1930: .368, 217 hits.

WAQAR YOUNIS (Pak)

CRICKET

Waqar Younis. b. 16 Nov 1971 Burewala, Vehari.

In early 1993 Waqar took his 100th wicket in 20 Test matches after three years of devastating fast bowling. He was raised in Sharjah, but was spotted on his return to Pakistan so that at 17 he was brought into the one-day team and then to Tests. He took ten wickets in his first ten Tests, but then came 29 at 10.86 in 3 matches against New Zealand in 1990, and he has been consistently successful ever since. His pace, late swing and penetrating yorker have made him a scourge of opponents of Pakistan and of Surrey, who he joined that year. Although only 21, he was appointed vice-captain of Pakistan to his fast bowling colleague Wasim Akram in 1993. In February 1993 he became the youngest (21 years 77 days) and quickest (59 matches)

to take 100 wickets in one-day internationals.
23 Tests 1989-93: 194 runs at 8.81, HS 29; 121 wickets at 19.62, BB 7-76; 2 catches.
71 One-day Ints: 211 runs at 11.72, HS 37; 127 wickets at 19.89, BB 6-26.
First-class 1984-92: 2981 runs at 22.24, 3 100s HS 123; 455 wickets at 22.34, BB 7-42; 39 catches.

Monte WARD (USA)

BASEBALL

John Montgomery Ward. b. 3 Mar 1860 Bellefonte, Pennsylvania, d. 4 Mar 1925 Augusta, Georgia.

Ward played only seven seasons of major league ball, topped by his 1879 season in which he won 47 games, but is known mostly for his administrative skills. He campaigned for players' rights and in 1890 helped to form the Players' League which folded after one season. He managed for various teams in 1880, 1884, and from 1890-4. He then left baseball to begin a law career and continued to champion players' rights as their advocate, frequently representing players in contract disputes.
Career pitching 1878-84: ERA 2.10; W-L 164-102, SO 920. Best seasons: 1879: 47-19, 2.15 ERA, 239 SO; 1880: 39-24, 1.74 ERA, 230 SO.

Paul WARFIELD (USA)

AMERICAN FOOTBALL

Paul Dryden Warfield. b. 28 Nov 1942 Warren, Ohio.

Warfield played wide receiver in college at Ohio State and in the NFL with both the Cleveland Browns 1964-9 and Miami Dolphins 1970-4. In college he was also a world-class long jumper, 2nd at the NCAAs in 1962 and 3rd in 1963, and second to Ralph Boston at the 1962 AAU, with a best of 7.92m (7.98w). He and quarterback Bob Griese formed a potent passing duo for the Dolphins and Warfield was instrumental in helping the team finish the 1972 season 17-0 and win the Super Bowl. In 1975 he jumped to the Memphis Southmen of the World Football League along with Dolphin team-mates Larry Csonka and Jim Kiick, but returned to the NFL to play one last season in 1976 with the Cleveland Browns. During his career he played in seven Pro Bowls and was named All-Pro five times. His career average of 20.1 yards per catch is an NFL record for receivers with over 300 career catches.
NFL career 1964-77: 8565 yards gained receiving av. 20.1, 85 touchdowns.

Dutch WARMERDAM (USA)

ATHLETICS

Cornelius Anthony Warmerdam. b. 22 Jun 1915 Long Beach, California.

The first 15ft pole vaulter dominated his contemporaries more than any other man in history. His career best of 4.78m indoors, with a bamboo pole, was not bettered until Robert Gutowski (USA) cleared 4.82m at Austin on 15 Jun 1957, 14 years 87 days later. Warmerdam first cleared 15ft *4.57m* at Berkeley on 13 Apr 1940, adding three centimetres to the world record, and he cleared 15ft or higher in 43 competitions between 1940 and 1944. No other vaulter cleared 15ft until Bob Richards succeeded at 15ft 1in *4.59m* indoors in New York on 27 Jan 1951.
Warmerdam made seven improvements to the world record outdoors to 4.77m in 1942 and six indoors from 4.42m in 1939 to 4.79m at Chicago in 1943. AAU champion outdoors 1938 and 1940-4, and indoors in 1939 and 1943. He won the Sullivan Award for 1942.
He was the third son of a Dutch immigrant to the USA and went to Fresno State University, after he had been recommended to them by a travelling salesman who had seen him practising in a spinach patch!

Pelham WARNER (UK)

CRICKET

(Sir) Pelham Francis Warner. b. 2 Oct 1873 Port-of-Spain, Trinidad, d. 30 Jan 1963 West Lavington, Sussex.

A stylish batsman, he dedicated much of his life to cricket. He was a Test selector on various occasions between 1905 and 1938 and managed the England team to

Australia in 1932/3. His services to the game were recognised by a knighthood in 1937. He was for 60 years on the MCC committee and president in 1950/1. He played for Oxford University 1894-6 and for Middlesex, whom he captained from 1908 to 1920. He captained England 10 times, leading them on several overseas tours. He founded the *Cricketer* magazine in 1921.
15 Tests 1899-1912: 622 runs at 23.92, 1 100 HS 132; 3 catches.*
First-class 1894-1929: 29,028 runs at 36.28, 60 100s HS 244; 15 wickets at 42.40, BB 2-26; 183 catches.

Pop WARNER (USA)

AMERICAN FOOTBALL

Glenn Scobey Warner. b. 5 Apr 1871 Springville, New York, d. 7 Sep 1954 Palo Alto, California.

Warner played football at Cornell from 1892-5, graduating with a degree in law, which he practised only briefly before becoming a great football coach. His many appointments were with: Georgia 1896, Cornell 1897-8 and 1904-06, Carlisle Indian School 1899-1903, 1907-14; Pittsburgh 1915-23, Stanford 1924-32, Temple 1933-8, San Jose State (adviser) 1939-40. In his 44 years as a coach he compiled a career record of 312-104-32. His greatest player was Jim Thorpe whom he coached at Carlisle in 1908-10. Warner, voted Coach of All the Years in 1951, was an innovator who made multiple contributions to coaching theory. The football equivalent of little league baseball carries the name Pop Warner League Football.

Cyril WASHBROOK (UK)

CRICKET

Cyril Washbrook. b. 6 Dec 1914 Barrow, Clitheroe, Lancashire.

After playing one Test against New Zealand in 1937, Washbrook lost a major part of his career to World War II, but for the first five post-war years he was Len Hutton's regular opening partner for England. His best seasons were those of 1946 and 1947 when he scored 2400 runs at 68.57 and 2662 at 68.25 respectively in first-class cricket. After more than five years out of Test cricket, Washbrook, by then a selector, was recalled against Australia in 1956 at the age of 41, and proved any doubters wrong with an innings of 98, coming in at No.5 with his side then 17-3. He captained Lancashire from 1954 to 1959. His benefit of £14,000 in 1948 remained the record until 1971. Awarded the CBE 1991.
37 Tests 1937-56: 2569 runs at 42.81, 6 100s HS 195; 1 wicket; 12 catches.
First-class 1933-64: 34,101 runs at 42.67, 76 100s HS 251; 7 wickets at 44.14, BB 2-8; 212 catches.*

WASIM AKRAM (Pak)

CRICKET

Wasim Akram. b. 3 Jun 1966 Lahore.

By the 1992 Test series against England, when with Waqar Younis he swept aside the opposition's batsmen, Wasim had become one of the world's great match-winning cricketers, a fast left-arm bowler with a devastating yorker, and a dashing batsman. In January 1993 he took over as captain of Pakistan, but his start was not auspicious, with overwhelming defeat in a series against the West Indies. In February 1993 he became the second player ever to take 200 wickets in one-day internationals. On being spotted by Javed Miandad he took 7-50 on his first-class cricket début, in the first innings for a Patron's XI against the visiting New Zealand tourists. He then made his international one-day début and within two months was selected to tour New Zealand, taking ten wickets in the match in his 2nd Test at the age of 18. The start was amazing, but although he has had a few injury setbacks he has fully lived up to the impression he made. He has played for Lancashire from 1988.
48 Tests 1985-93: 1057 runs at 19.57, 1 100 HS 123; 186 wickets, at 24.56, BB 6-62; 16 catches.
153 One-day Ints: 1267 runs at 13.47, HS 86; 215 wickets at 23.27, BB 5-16; 29 catches.
First-class 1984-92: 2981 runs at 22.24, 3 100s HS 123; 455 wickets at 22.34, BB 7-42; 39 catches.

WASIM BARI (Pak)

CRICKET
Wasim Bari. b. 23 Mar 1948 Karachi.

The regular wicket-keeper for Pakistan for 15 years, he has the fourth highest career total of dismissals in Test history. A safe and agile 'keeper and a useful batsman, he also captained Pakistan capably in six Tests in 1977-8. In 1979 against New Zealand at Auckland he set a Test record with seven catches in an innings. In Pakistan he played mostly for Karachi and PIA.
81 Tests 1967-84: 1366 runs at 15.85, HS 85; 201 catches, 27 stumpings.
51 One-day Ints: 221 runs at 17.00, HS 34; 52 catches, 10 stumpings.
First-class 1964-84: 5749 runs at 21.69; 2 100s, HS 177; 1 wicket; 676 catches, 146 stumpings.

Thomas WASSBERG (Swe)

NORDIC SKIING
Thomas Lars Wassberg. b. 27 Mar 1956 Lennartsfors.

Olympic cross-country skiing champion at 15km in 1980, when he was timed in 41:57.63 to beat Juha Mieto (Fin) by the minute margin of 0.01 second, and at 50km in 1984 with the smallest ever margin in an Olympic 50km skiing race of 4.9 seconds. He also won relay gold medals in 1984 and 1988 and competed in the 1976 Games. He was World champion at 50km in 1982 and at 30km and relay in 1987, with three silvers (15km 1985, 15km and 50km 1987) and one bronze (relay 1985). He won the World Cup in 1977, was 2nd in 1980, 1982, 1984 and 1987, and 3rd in 1985.

Osamu WATANABE (Japan)

WRESTLING
Osamu Watanabe. b. 21 Oct 1940 Hokkaido.

Possibly the greatest wrestler ever, pound-for-pound. He had a very short career but was never beaten or scored upon during it. It is known that he won at least 187 consecutive matches until his victory in the 1964 Olympics at Tokyo when he won the featherweight freestyle gold medal. In that tournament he won all his matches without sacrificing a single point. This followed victories in the 1962 and 1963 world championships. He was not immensely strong, but was very quick and his technical skills were unmatched in his era.

Bob WATERFIELD (USA)

AMERICAN FOOTBALL
Robert Waterfield. b. 26 Jul 1920 Elmira, New York, d. 25 Mar 1983 Burbank, California.

Known as 'The Rifle' for his strong arm, Waterfield was a quarterback at UCLA where he also competed on the gymnastics team. He missed one year in 1944 while in the army, when he competed for the 176th Infantry at Fort Benning, Georgia. He graduated in 1945 and was drafted by the Cleveland Rams, quarterbacking them to the NFL Championship, the first rookie to achieve that feat. When the Rams moved to Los Angeles in 1946, Waterfield became a media favourite and eventually married his former high school classmate, glamorous movie actress Jane Russell. He was NFL MVP in 1945 and 1950 and led the Rams to another NFL Championship in 1951, when he split quarterback duties with Norm Van Brocklin.
NFL career 1945-52: 11,849 yards from 813 pass completions, 50.3%, 98 TD.

David WATKINS (UK)

RUGBY UNION/LEAGUE
David Watkins. b. 5 Mar 1942 Blaina, Wales.

After winning 21 rugby union caps for Wales 1963-7, he signed professional forms for Salford in 1967. An entertaining stand-off and superlative goal-kicker, his 221 goals in 47 matches in 1972/3 remains the record for the most goals kicked in one season; this was in the midst of his record sequence of scoring for Salford in 92 consecutive matches. Despite these talents, he only won two caps for Great Britain. He left Salford in 1979 and spent two seasons with Swinton before becoming managing director of the Cardiff Blue Dragons, but the attempt to revive rugby league in Wales was short lived. In 1986 he was awarded the MBE for his services to the sport.

Ken WATSON (Can)

CURLING

Kenneth Watson. b. 12 Aug 1904 Minnedosa, Manitoba.

Generally considered the greatest curler ever. He first led the Manitoba bonspiel in 1923 and later won 7 Manitoba Curling Association grand aggregate titles, including an unprecedented six in succession 1942-7. He won 32 major championships in a career which lasted until 1971. These included four Manitoba Consols titles, and Brier Championships in 1936, 1942 and 1949. Watson later became an author on curling, writing four well-read instructional books.

Tom WATSON (USA)

GOLF

Thomas Sturges Watson. b. 4 Sep 1949 Kansas City, Missouri.

Watson dominated golf worldwide in the late 1970s and early 1980s. He was leading money-winner on the US Tour from 1977-80 and won the most tournaments yearly from 1977-81. He was at one time the leading career money-winner, but is now second all-time.
Watson's fame also rested on his performance in major tournaments with his eight victories, including five at the British Open, 1975, 1977, 1980, 1982-3, the Masters 1977 and 1981, and US Open 1982. He had also won the Vardon Trophy and was named US PGA Player of the Year each year 1977-9. Watson's game slumped somewhat in the mid-1980s as he had putting problems. He has always been known as a long hitter and a great putter. Selected as captain of the 1993 US Ryder Cup team.
PGA career earnings 1971-92: $6,028,927 with 32 victories.

Matthew WEBB (UK)

SWIMMING

(Captain) Matthew Webb. b. 19 Jan 1848 Dawley, Shropshire, d. 24 Jul 1883 Niagara Falls, Canada.

Webb earned his place in history by being the first person to swim the English Channel. On 24-25 Aug 1875 he took 21 hr 45 min to cross from Dover to Calais, swimming an estimated 61 km *38 miles* to make the 33 km *21 mile* crossing. No other swimmer matched this feat until 1911 and his time was not beaten until 1934.
He had learnt to swim at the age of eight and at the time of his crossing was a captain in the Merchant Navy, standing 1.73m *5ft 8in* and weighing 92 kg *14 1/2 stone.* The previous year he had been awarded the Stanhope Gold Medal for the bravest deed of 1874, having jumped overboard in heavy seas in a vain attempt to save one of his crew. He drowned in 1883 in attempting to swim the rapids above the Niagara Falls.

Dick WEBER (USA)

BOWLING

Richard Anthony Weber. b. 23 Dec 1929 Indianapolis, Indiana.

One of the two or three greatest bowlers in history and regarded as the ambassador of the game. He has made many trips around the world to promote it.
He got his start in bowling in Indianapolis when he bowled recreationally while he was working as a mailman. He began bowling professionally in the mid-1950s and was a charter member of the PBA in 1958, winning three of its first four Tournaments. He eventually won 26 PBA Tour titles, and four BPAA US Open championships, 1962, 1963, 1965-6. He was voted Bowler of the Year in 1961, 1963 and 1965, and PBA Player of the Year in 1965.
His son **Pete** has also become one of the top bowlers on the PBA Tour and by the end of 1992 was in second place on all-time earnings with $1,427,012 and 19 titles.

Robert WEBSTER (USA)

DIVING

Robert David Webster. b. 25 Oct 1938 Berkeley, California.

Olympic champion at highboard diving in 1960 and 1964, on both occasions coming from behind with his last three dives. He was Pan-American champion at highboard 1963, and won the bronze medal at highboard 1959; and he won AAU titles at highboard 1964 and indoor 1m springboard 1962.

From Santa Clara Junior College he transferred to the University of Michigan, where he was coached by 1948 Olympic champion Bruce Harlan and by Dick Kimball, and he was later coached by Dr Sammy Lee.

Webster became a diving coach at various universities and of US teams.

Everton WEEKES (Bar)

CRICKET

Everton de Courcy Weekes. b. 26 Feb 1925 Bridgetown.

A dazzling stroke-player who annihilated the bowling attacks of many teams. He twice averaged over 100 for a Test series against India: 779 runs at 111.28 in 1948/9 and 716 at 102.28 in 1953. With a century against England in 1948 and four in that series against India in 1948/9 he completed five centuries in successive innings in Tests, a unique achievement. He added 90 and 56 in his next two innings.

In England in 1950 he scored 338 runs at 56.33 in the 4 Tests and led the tour averages with 2310 runs at 79.65, including five double centuries. He played for Barbados, captaining them for several years, and was a highly popular and successful player in league cricket in England. He was a brilliant fielder and bowled legbreaks. Awarded the OBE. He later became an international bridge player.

48 Tests 1948-58: 4455 runs at 58.61, 15 100s HS 207; 1 wicket; 49 catches.

First-class 1945-64: 12,010 runs at 55.34, 36 100s HS 304; 17 wickets at 43.00, BB 4-38; 125 catches, 1 stumping.*

Ullrich WEHLING (GDR)

NORDIC SKIING

Ullrich Wehling. b. 8 Jul 1952 Halle.

The winner of a unique three Olympic gold medals at the Nordic Combination of cross-country skiing and ski-jumping, in 1972, 1976 and 1980. He was also World champion in 1974 and took a bronze medal in 1978, having started his championship career with gold at the European Juniors in 1971. He became a leading sports official in the GDR and with the International Ski Federation.

Jens WEISSFLOG (GDR)

NORDIC SKIING

Jens Weissflog. b. 21 Jul 1964 Erlabrunn.

Top ski jumper who had his greatest year in 1984, when he won the World Cup series and Olympic gold on the normal hill (70m) and silver on the large hill. He was also second in the World Cup in 1989. He was World champion at normal hill in 1985 and 1989, and at the large hill was second in 1989 and third in 1991. At ski-flying World Championships he was second in 1985 and 3rd in 1990.

Johnny WEISSMULLER(USA)

SWIMMING

Peter John Weissmuller. né Petr Jánös Weiszmüller. b. 2 Jun 1904 Freidorf, then Hungary, d. 20 Jan 1984 Acapulco, Mexico.

The best known swimmer of all time, not only because of his speed in the pool which brought him five Olympic gold medals and 24 world records, but also because he became the most famous of all the screen Tarzans, playing him in 19 movies from 1934 to 1948.

His revolutionary freestyle stroke enabled him to smash concepts of swimming times, from his first world records for 300y and 300m at the age of 17 in 1922 to perhaps his greatest, 51.0 for 100 yards in 1927, a record which lasted for 17 years. On that same day he was timed in 2:08.0 for 200m, a time that improved his own five-year-old record by 7.6 sec, and this record stood for seven years. Having turned professional, however, Weissmuller recorded an amazing 48.5 for 100y at the age of 36 in Billy Rose's World Fair Aquacade. He was also the first man to better the minute barrier for 100m when he recorded 58.6 in 1922, improving to 57.4 in 1924, and the first to break five minutes for 400m with 4:57.0 in 1923, a 9.6 sec improvement on his own world record.

At his first Olympics in 1924 he won both 100m and 400m freestyle with a third gold at 4 x 200m relay and a bronze medal for water polo. In 1928 he added two more golds, retaining his 100m title and ending his Olympic career with another relay win. He won a men's record 36 US titles including: outdoors 100y/m and 440y 1922-3, 1925-8; 220y 1921-2, 880y 1925; indoors 100y 1922-5, 1927-8; 220y 1922-4, 1927-8; and 150y backstroke 1923.

Allan WELLS (UK)

ATHLETICS

Allan Wipper Wells. b. 3 May 1952 Edinburgh.

Olympic champion at 100 metres in 1980, when at the age of 28 he was then the oldest ever champion at the event. Due to the US boycott he was denied the opportunity of showing that he could have beaten the top Americans in Moscow, but he did so after the Games and when he won the IAAF Golden Sprints and the World Cup 100m (2nd at 200m) in 1981.

Although in his first season of athletics in 1970 he won the Scottish junior triple jump title, he only took up sprinting seriously six years later at the age of 24. He won a record six medals at the Commonwealth Games, gold at 200m and sprint relay in 1978, and gold at both 100m and 200m (when he tied with Mike McFarlane) in 1982; he was second at 100m in 1978 and earned a bronze medal on Scotland's relay team in 1982. He was 4th at both 100m and 200m at the 1983 Worlds. He would have loved to have sealed his career with success in his home town at the Commonwealth Games of 1986, but was unable to get fit enough in time, although he returned to place fifth at both 100m and 200m in the European Championships a month later. Qualified as a marine engineer.

Best times: UK records at 100m 10.11 and 200m 20.21 in 1980. Long jump best 7.32m (1972).

Mike WENDEN (Aus)

SWIMMING

Michael Vincent Wenden. b. 17 Nov 1949 Liverpool, NSW.

The winner of both 100m and 200m freestyle titles at the 1968 Olympics by six-tenths margins, this 'swimming machine' also took a silver and a bronze on the Australian relay teams. At the shorter distance he set a world record time of 52.2, and his 200m race was a classic, with his quick, rough-stroking, whirling action in vivid contrast to the smooth Don Schollander.

He won 13 medals at the Commonwealth Games, to equal the record for any sport set by fencer Ivan Lund, with nine gold, including the 100m freestyle at each Games he contested 1966, 1970 and 1974, the 200m in 1970 and five relay wins. At the first World Championships in 1973 he took the 100m bronze medal in 52.22 and a 4x200m relay silver. He was Australian champion at 100m 1966, 1968, 1970-3; 200m 1966-8, 1970, 1972.

A super-fit athlete, Wenden put in some 12 to 15 kilometres a day in the pool at his peak, hitherto unheard-of distance for a swimmer. With his coach Vic Arneil he developed the use of isometric exercises for swimmers as a supplement to pool sessions. Awarded the OBE.

Hanni WENZEL (Lie)

ALPINE SKIING

Hanni Wenzel. b. 14 Dec 1956 Staubirnen, Germany.

The first Alpine skier to win four Olympic medals. She moved to Liechtenstein at the age of one, and was granted citizenship after winning the slalom at the 1974 World Championships. She won the first ever Olympic gold medals for her adopted country with the bronze at slalom in 1976 and gold medals at both slalom and giant slalom in 1980, as well as the downhill silver that year. Also in that year she was world champion at Alpine combination. At the World Cup she was overall champion in 1978 and 1980 (2nd 1975 and 1979, 3rd 1974 and 1981), and won the giant slalom in 1974 and 1980 and the slalom in 1974, winning 33 races in all 1974-84.

Her brother **Andreas** (b. 18 Mar 1958 Planken) was world champion at Alpine combination in 1978 and the overall World Cup winner in 1980 with 14 race wins in all 1978-85, as well as winning Olympic silver at giant slalom in 1980. Their sister Petra (b. 20 Nov 1961) competed at the 1980 Olympics and their father was the World Student Games champion at Alpine combination in 1954.

Ed WERENICH (Can)

CURLING

Edrick Werenich. b. 23 Jun 1947 Benito, Manitoba.

The Scarborough, Ontario fireman has skipped eight Ontario and four National Firefighters title rinks. His titles are numerous and include: four Ontario Consuls titles, skip of the 1983-4 Ontario Tankard winners, skip of the 1983 Silver Broom winner, two-time winner of the Royal Canadian Classic and the Thunder Bay Grand Prix.

Jerry WEST (USA)

BASKETBALL

Jerry Alan West. b. 28 May 1938 Cheylan, West Virginia.

In the 1960 Olympics, West teamed with Oscar Robertson to form the greatest guard tandem ever to play on a basketball team. Robertson has the edge from basketball experts as the greatest ever guard, but some go for West. After West Virginia University, where he was the NCAA Tournament MVP when his team were runners-up, West performed his magic with the Los Angeles Lakers for 14 years. He became known as 'Mr Clutch'. In the last few seconds, if the game was close, the Lakers' main play was 'Give the ball to Jerry!'. He was 11 times NBA All-Star first-team, and twice second-team. He held NBA play-off records for field goals made, field goals attempted, free throws made, assists, and scoring average with 29.1 from 4457 points (now surpassed by Michael Jordan). In 1965 he set the single season play-off record by averaging 40.6 points for 11 games. After retiring as a player he was the head coach of the Lakers for three seasons, later filled in briefly as an interim coach during a coaching shake-up, and has since settled into an executive position with them.

NBA career: 25,192 points av. 27.0.

Carl WESTERGREN (Swe)

WRESTLING

Carl Oscar 'Calle' Westergren. b. 13 Oct 1895 Malmö, d. 5 Aug 1958.

Westergren competed at four Olympic Games (1920-32), winning three gold medals in Greco-Roman, a record: middleweight 1920, light-heavyweight 1924, and unlimited 1932. In 1928 he withdrew after losing in the first round and failed to medal. He won the 1922 middleweight Greco-Roman world championship and at the European Championships he also won three titles in three different weight classes: 1925 middleweight, 1930 light-heavyweight, and 1931 in the unlimited class. He was a cab proprietor in Malmö.

Mike WESTON (UK)

RUGBY UNION

Michael Philip Weston. b. 21 Aug 1938 Durham.

Playing in 29 internationals between 1960 and 1968, he once held the record as England's most capped three-quarter and was a brilliant tactical player at either fly-half or centre. He toured with the Lions to South Africa in 1962 when he played in all four Tests, and to Australasia in 1966 when after playing in both Tests against Australia he suffered from injury and loss of form and failed to make the team for the matches against New Zealand. Between these two Lions tours, he captained England on a short tour of Australia and New Zealand in 1963.

Born and educated in Durham, he remained loyal to the local club throughout his career. After retirement, he served as an England selector for many years and was chairman of the selection panel in 1985-6.

Joyce WETHERED (UK)

GOLF

Joyce Wethered (Lady Heathcoat-Amory). b. 17 Nov 1901 Maldon, Surrey.

Usually considered, with Mickey Wright and Babe Zaharias, as one of the greatest female golfers ever. Bobby Jones once commented that he had never seen a better player - male or female. She played in the British Ladies' Amateur only six times, winning four (1922, 1924-5, 1929), losing once in the final to Cecilia Leitch, and being a semi-finalist on the other occasion. She retired from individual competition after 1925 but came back in 1929 to play this championship at St Andrew's, where in the final she defeated the great American champion, Glenn Collett. She was English Ladies' Amateur champion each year 1920-4, but after 1925 she limited her competitive play to such events as the Worplesdon Mixed Foursomes, which she won eight times with various partners. She did, however, play in the Curtis Cup in 1932 and toured the USA as a professional in 1935.
Her brother **Roger** (1899-1983) was British Amateur champion in 1923 and tied for the British Open in 1921, before losing the play-off to Jock Hutchison.

Zach WHEAT (USA)

BASEBALL

Zachary Davis Wheat. b. 23 May 1888 Hamilton, Missouri, d. 11 Mar 1972 Sedalia, Missouri.

Zach Wheat played the first 18 of his 19 major league seasons with the Brooklyn Dodgers, finishing his outfielding career with the Philadelphia Athletics. He played almost exclusively left field and usually batted clean-up for the Dodgers. For his era he was a power hitter, though he was eclipsed in the 1920s by Ruth and the cross-town rival Yankees. He is the all-time leader in games played as a left fielder.
Career 1909-27: 2884 hits Avg. .317, HR 132; RBI 1248; SB 205. Best seasons: 1923: .375; 1924: .375, 212 hits; 1925: .359, 221 hits; 1918: .335.

Gary WHETTON (NZ)

RUGBY UNION

Gary William Whetton. b. 15 Dec 1959 Auckland.

New Zealand's most capped player. His 58 international appearances included a run of 40 consecutive games which stands as the All Black record. A formidable lock and line-out jumper, he succeeded Wayne Shelford as the New Zealand captain in 1990. In many of his internationals his twin brother, **Alan**, who won 35 caps, was also in the team and they are the only twins to have played for the All Blacks. Both twins played for Auckland, and in 1993 Gary led Castres to the French title.

Wilson WHINERAY (NZ)

RUGBY UNION

Wilson James Whineray. b. 10 Jul 1935 Auckland.

New Zealand's greatest captain who led the All Blacks a record 30 times (winning 22 of those games). Between 1957 and 1965 he played a total of 32 Test matches, captaining the team on tours of South Africa, Australia, Britain and France and in the home series against Australia (twice), the British Lions, France, and South Africa. All his international appearances were as a prop forward, but at club and representative level he produced some fine performances as a No. 8.
He was the NZ Universities heavyweight boxing champion in 1956. He set a fine standard by his exemplary behaviour both on and off the field and was awarded the OBE in 1961. On retirement he continued in the game as a coach and administrator and also became one of New Zealand's most successful businessmen.

John WHITAKER (UK)

SHOW JUMPING
John Whitaker. b. 5 Aug 1955 Huddersfield.

Riding *Milton* he has achieved one of the most successful partnerships in show jumping history, taking European team gold and individual silver in 1987, team and individual gold in 1989, and winning the World Cup in 1990 and 1991, with second place in 1993.
On *Ryan's Son* he won his first national title in 1976, and was most unlucky to miss selection for the Olympic Games that year. They also missed the 1980 Games due to the team's boycott, taking team and individual silver at the alternative Games, but won team silver at the 1984 Olympics. He has won the King George V Gold Cup twice - on *Ryan's Son* in 1986 and on *Milton* in 1990. On *Hopscotch* he won European team gold and individual bronze in 1987 and World team silver in 1986. Awarded the MBE 1991. Married to Claire Barr, whose father owned *Ryan's Son*. His brother **Michael** (b. 17 Mar 1960) has shared his three European team gold medals and Olympic silver, and was the individual silver medallist at the 1989 European Championships on *Monsanta*. The brothers learned to ride at their family's farm in West Yorkshire. John is a very controlled and steady rider, Michael more pushing.

Pernell WHITAKER (USA)

BOXING
Pernell Whitaker. b. 2 Jan 1964 Norfolk, Virginia.

The 1984 Olympic lightweight champion has gone on to become one of the most highly regarded world champions in modern boxing, with dazzling speed. As an amateur he won 201 of 215 fights and since turning professional in November 1984 he has lost just once. That defeat came in his first world title fight in March 1988 when despite the fact that he had seemed to outclass the WBC lightweight champion, José Luis Rámirez (Mex) was given the verdict. Whitaker did not have long to wait for a world title, however, as he beat Greg Haugen to take the IBF lightweight title in February 1989 and then beat Ramirez to add the WBC version in August. He continued to dominate the lightweights and added the WBA crown to unify the three leading organisations in 1990. After nine successful world title fights, he relinquished his lightweight titles to move up and win the IBF junior welterweight title in 1992 and then the WBC welterweight in 1993.
Career record: W - 32, L - 1, D - 0

Fatima WHITBREAD (UK)

ATHLETICS
Fatima Whitbread. b. 3 Mar 1961 Stoke Newington, London. Born of Cypriot parents, former name Vedad, and adopted by Margaret Whitbread, UK javelin coach and ex-international.

Fatima set a world javelin record of 77.44m at 9.18 am in qualifying for the 1986 European Championships and went on to win that event and the 1987 World title. At Commonwealth Games she placed successively 6th in 1978, 3rd in 1982 and 2nd in 1986, and at the Olympics, after failing to qualify for the final in 1980, took bronze in 1984 and silver in 1988. She won the European Junior title in 1979 and was WAAA champion five times (1981-4, 1986-7) and UK champion seven times (1981-5, 1987-8). Her career was ended by a series of injuries to her back and shoulder. Awarded MBE in Queen's Birthday Honours List 1987.

Jimmy WHITE (UK)

SNOOKER
Jimmy White. b. 2 May 1962 Tooting, London.

Surely the finest snooker player never to win the World title, although he has been a top-ranked player for a decade, since winning the English Amateur title at 16 and in 1979 becoming, at 18 years 191 days, the youngest ever amateur world champion. In the World Professional Championship he was beaten in the final in 1984 and for four consecutive years 1990-3. In 1992 he scored a maximum 147 break in the first round. He made his first century break at 13 and won the British boys (under-16) title in 1977. Since then his outstanding natural talent has brought the left-hander rich reward. His major titles include: British Open 1987 and 1992; UK Open 1992, Benson & Hedges Masters 1984, and European Open 1992.

JoJo WHITE (USA)

BASKETBALL

Joseph Henry White. b. 16 Nov 1946 St Louis, Missouri.

Pan-American gold medallist in 1967, Olympic gold medallist in 1968, and an NBA champion in 1974 and 1976, 'JoJo' White missed only an NCAA title to add to his trophies. But he tried, as he was the top player at Kansas in the late 1960s, twice being named All-American and MVP of the Big Eight Conference. In 1969 he was drafted first by the Boston Celtics with whom he played for 10 seasons. He had an excellent career as a pro, quarter-backing the Celtics to two NBA titles. He was named to the All-Rookie team in 1970, and was twice named NBA All-Star second team. He was named to play in seven consecutive NBA All-Star games, from 1971 through 1977. JoJo finished his career with two seasons with Golden State and Kansas City before retiring in 1981. He has since gone into college coaching, starting out with his alma mater, the Kansas Jayhawks.

Randy WHITE (USA)

AMERICAN FOOTBALL

Randy Lee White. b. 15 Jan 1953 Pittsburgh, Pennsylvania.

Nicknamed 'The Manster', because he was such a dominating defensive tackle that he was felt to be a man-monster, White played collegiately at the University of Maryland and in his senior year won the Outland Trophy and the Lombardi Award as college football's top lineman. He was drafted by the Dallas Cowboys and played for them from 1975-88. He played in every Pro Bowl from 1977-85 and helped the Cowboys to a Super Bowl title in 1978. With team-mate Harvey Martin, White was co-MVP of Super Bowl XII in 1978.

Reggie WHITE (USA)

AMERICAN FOOTBALL

Reginald Howard White. b. 19 Dec 1961 Chattanooga, Tennessee.

A great defensive end. While at the University of Tennessee he twice made All-American, and then began his pro career in the now defunct United States Football League. After one season he began his outstanding NFL career with the Philadelphia Eagles. At the end of the 1992 season, by when he was a perennial All-Pro and all-time leader in sacks, he declared himself a free agent. He signed a multi-million dollar contract to play for the Green Bay Packers in 1993. Highly religious, he is an ordained minister.

Whizzer WHITE (USA)

AMERICAN FOOTBALL

Byron Raymond White. b. 8 Jun 1917 Fort Collins, Colorado.

A great running back, whose other abilities were overshadowed by his football skills at the University of Colorado. He also played on the Colorado baseball and basketball teams and was valedictorian of his class in 1938, graduating Phi Beta Kappa and earning a Rhodes Scholarship. In his senior year of 1937 he led the nation in rushing, scoring and total offense. White played in the NFL in 1938 with the Pittsburgh Steelers before he left for Oxford to study. He returned in 1940 and played two more NFL seasons with the Detroit Lions. He twice led the league in rushing (1938, 1940) in his three seasons. Between 1942 and 1946, White served in the Navy as an intelligence officer and won two Bronze Stars and a Presidential Unit Citation. He graduated from Yale University Law School in 1946 and then returned to Denver to practise law. In 1962, President John F. Kennedy selected White to fill a position on the United States Supreme Court, and White has served in that position through 1992.

NFL career 1938-41: Rushing: 1319 yards av. 3.4, 11 touchdowns. Receiving: 301 yards av. 18.8, 1 touchdown.

Mal WHITFIELD (USA)

ATHLETICS

Malvin Groston Whitfield. b. 11 Oct 1924 Bay City, Texas.

The world's best two-lap runner, when from June 1948 to the end of the 1954 season he lost only three of 69 races at 800m or 880y. He was Olympic champion at both 800m and 4 x 400m relay in 1948 and at 800m in 1952, with bronze at 400m in 1948 and silver at the relay in 1952, when he was sixth at 400m. He won the Pan-American treble at 400m, 800m and relay in 1951 and won eight AAU titles: 400m 1952, 800m/880y 1949-51, 1953-4; and indoor 600y 1953 and 1000y 1954. Although he never approached the world record for 800m that Rudolf Harbig had set at 1:46.6 in 1939, Whitfield set two world records at 880y, 1:49.2 in 1950 and 1:48.6 in 1953, and one at 1000m, 2:20.8 in 1953, as well as further records at 4 x 440y and at 4 x 880y. He also set world bests for 500m 1:01.0 (1948) and at 660y 1:17.3 (1952,) and his 400m best was 45.9 in 1953. Indoors, Whitfield ran two world bests at both 500m and 600y.

He was NCAA two-lap champion in 1947 and 1948 for Ohio State University, and was in the US Air Force when he won his first Olympic gold medal. He was the Sullivan Award winner in 1954 and retired after placing fifth at 800m in the US Olympic Trials in 1956. He worked for the US Intelligence Service.

Charlie WHITTINGHAM (USA)

HORSE RACING

Charles Whittingham. b. 13 Apr 1913 San Diego.

In 1982 he became the first trainer to exceed $4 million in prize money in a season. Despite being the top stakes winner of all time, and heading the list for money won seven times between 1970 and 1982, he did not win the Kentucky Derby until he was 73, when *Ferdinand* won in 1986. He won the Eclipse Award as outstanding trainer in 1971, 1982 and 1989. He earned a trainer's licence in 1931, and became assistant trainer to Horatio Luro in 1939. Nicknamed 'Bald Eagle' after losing his hair due to a tropical disease contracted in World War II.

Kathy WHITWORTH (USA)

GOLF

Kathrynne Ann Whitworth. b. 27 Sep 1939 Monahans, Texas.

Whitworth has won the most tournaments of any female golfer, passing Mickey Wright's record of 82 wins in 1982 and taking the record to 88 with her last win in 1985. She was the leading money winner on the LPGA tour eight times, 1965-8, 1970-3, and became the first to pass $1 million in her career. Like Sam Snead among the men, her very long career lacked only a victory in the US Open, but she has rarely enjoyed a lot of publicity as a great player. Early on she was overshadowed by Wright and later by Nancy Lopez and some of the glamour girls of the LPGA such as Laura Baugh and Jan Stephenson. Whitworth was possessed of an unorthodox swing but had a tremendous short game. Her major wins: LPGA 1967, 1971 and 1975; Titleholders 1965-6, Western Open 1967.

LPGA career earnings 1959-92: $1,722,440 with 88 victories.

Tracey WICKHAM (Aus)

SWIMMING

Tracey Lee Wickham. b. 24 Nov 1962.

The Commonwealth Games champion at 400m and 800m and second at 200m in both 1978 and 1982. In 1978 her time for 800m of 8:24.62 bettered her own world record of 8:30.53 set earlier in the year. Less than a month later she won the World titles at 400m in a world record 4:06.28 and 800m by 4.41 secs in 8:24.94. Both these world records remained unbroken for nine years until Janet Evans broke them in 1987. At 1500m Wickham set world records with 16:14.93 in 1978 and 16:06.63 in 1979. Her best ever time for

200m was 2:00.60 in 1982. Her marvellous year in 1978, when she won further Commonwealth medals (silver at medley relay and bronze at freestyle relay), was rounded off by the award of an MBE in the New Year Honours. She won her first Australian title at 400m in 1976.

Lones WIGGER (USA)

SHOOTING

Lones Wesley Wigger, Jr. b. 15 Aug 1937 Great Falls, Montana.

The greatest competitive rifle shooter from the USA, he won Olympic gold medals in 1964 at small bore rifle 3 positions (and silver at prone), and in 1972 at free rifle. He also made the US Olympic team in 1968 and 1980. In all he won 24 world titles and set 29 world records as well as winning 85 US national championships in his illustrious career from 1963. He was a member of six Pan-American teams and six World Championship teams.

From 1987 he has been director of the US Shooting Team. His daughter **Deena** (b. 27 Aug 1966) was silver medallist at 3-position and a member of the US gold medal winning small-bore rifle team at the 1990 World Championships, and set a world record for the air rifle in 1990, having finished tenth at air rifle in the 1988 Olympics.

Hazel WIGHTMAN (USA)

TENNIS

Hazel Virginia Wightman. née Hotchkiss. b. 20 Dec 1886 Healdburg, California, d. 5 Dec 1974 Chestnut Hill, Massachusetts.

The winner of 16 US Championships (4 singles, 6 doubles, 6 mixed doubles) between 1909 and 1928, and the donor of the Wightman Cup. She herself played in five doubles matches, winning three, between the first Wightman Cup match in 1923 and 1931, and was captain of the US team on each occasion, continuing as non-playing captain until 1948. At the Jubilee Wightman Cup match at Boston in 1973 she was awarded an Honorary CBE.

Other success included victories in the women's doubles with Helen Wills in 1924 at Wimbledon and the Olympic Games, and she won a second Olympic gold medal that year with Dick Williams in the mixed doubles.

Her career spanned World War I although following her marriage to George Wightman in 1912 it was often interrupted by the birth of their five children. Her husband, a wealthy lawyer, served as president of the USLTA in 1924 and the marriage ended in divorce in 1940. In addition to her 16 victories at the main US Championships she also won 17 indoor US titles (2 singles, 10 doubles, 5 mixed doubles), one clay court mixed doubles and 11 veterans' doubles. She was a fine player of all racket games and was the US squash champion in 1930.

Mats WILANDER (Swe)

TENNIS

Mats Arne Olof Wilander. b. 22 Aug 1964 Växjö.

A teenage prodigy who at 17 yrs 288 days, when he won the 1982 French Open, was at the time the youngest-ever men's singles Grand Slam winner. He was also the first unseeded player to win a Grand Slam event in the era of Open tennis. He won the French title again in 1985 and in 1988 when, adding the Australian and US Open titles, he was the first man to win three Grand Slam titles in one year since Jimmy Connors in 1974. He had also won the Australian Open in 1983 and 1984. Surprisingly, he never progressed beyond the quarter-final stage of the singles at Wimbledon, but he won his only Grand Slam doubles title there with his countryman Joakim Nyström in 1986. Wilander played in six Davis Cup finals, winning three (1984-5, 1987) and losing three (1983, 1988-9).

After his triple singles success of 1988, his form deteriorated alarmingly in 1989 and he announced that he was tired of tennis and lacked motivation. He lost his No.1 world ranking to Lendl after the Australian Open. His best performance in 1990 was to reach the semi-finals at the Australian Open. His career earnings were $7,377,193.

Jimmy WILDE (UK)

BOXING

Jimmy Wilde. b. 15 May 1892 Tylorstown, Wales, d. 10 Mar 1969 Cardiff

Considered the first flyweight champion of the world and one of the greatest ever, Wilde was a very unorthodox boxer with tremendous hitting power for his size. This earned him several nicknames, such as 'The Mighty Atom', 'The Tylorstown Terror', and 'The Ghost With a Hammer in His Hand'. Wilde won the British fly-weight title in 1916 by stopping Joe Symonds, and a few months later he defeated Johnny Rosner and claimed the world title, confirming that with a win over Young Zulu Kid later in the year. He retired after he was defeated in 1921, when he attempted to wrest the bantamweight championship from Pete Herman. He came out of retirement in 1923 but was knocked out in a title bout against Pancho Villa. He later became a boxing journalist.
Career record: W - 132 (101), L - 6, D - 2.

Anthony WILDING (NZ)

TENNIS

Anthony Frederick Wilding. b. 31 Oct 1883 Christchurch, d. 9 May 1915 Neuve Chapelle, France.

One of the most popular tennis players ever. After some modest successes in his native New Zealand, he went up to Trinity College, Cambridge and played against Oxford in 1904 and 1905. He first played at Wimbledon in 1904 and won the Australian singles and doubles in 1906. While in Sydney on Davis Cup duty, he again took the singles in 1909.
On leaving University, he based himself in England and was a regular competitor at Wimbledon. He won the singles for four successive years 1910-13, and was denied a fifth win when he lost in the 1914 Challenge Round to Norman Brookes. He was at his best in the 1910 All Comers' final when he beat Beals Wright (USA) after losing the first two sets. Wilding also won the Wimbledon doubles with Brookes in 1907 and 1914, and with Ritchie in 1908 and 1910. His Davis Cup record 1905-09 and 1914 was 15 wins from 21 singles and 6 from 9 doubles.
Handsome, athletic and with impeccable manners, he had all the qualities that appealed to Edwardian society: a Cambridge blue, barrister, qualified pilot and the owner of fast cars and motor cycles; he was idolised by the public. It was not only the teenagers who grieved when he was killed by shell fire on the Western Front while serving as a captain in the Royal Marines.

Hoyt WILHELM (USA)

BASEBALL

James Hoyt Wilhelm. b. 26 Jul 1923 Huntersville, North Carolina.

One of the first great knuckleball pitchers. He also became one of baseball's first great relief pitchers, the career leader in appearances in relief and in relief wins (143). He played for eight different teams in his 21-year major league career and started only 52 games in his 1070 major league appearances, mostly due to his 27 starts for the Baltimore Orioles in 1959. Wilhelm hit his only major league home run in his first at-bat in the majors, and his only major league triple in his second at-bat. He also pitched a no-hitter, for Baltimore against the powerful New York Yankees in 1958 in only his ninth starting assignment.
Career pitching 1952-72: ERA 2.52; W-L 143-122, SO 1610. Best season: 1952: 15-3, 2.43 ERA.

Lenny WILKENS (USA)

BASKETBALL

Leonard Randolph Wilkens. b. 28 Oct 1937 Brooklyn, New York.

A smooth, playmaking guard who played for 15 years in the NBA after his college career at Providence. He broke in with the St Louis Hawks in 1960 but later played for Seattle, Cleveland, and Portland. He was a good scorer, but made his living passing the ball and still ranks third in all-time assists (7211) for an NBA player, trailing Magic Johnson and Oscar Robertson. He was a player-coach in the league for three years with the Seattle Supersonics 1969-72 and in his last season with Portland. He has coached continuously in the league since 1974, both with Seattle and recently with the Cleveland Cavaliers, and has won over 800 games as a coach in the NBA.

David WILKIE (UK)

SWIMMING

David Andrew Wilkie. b. 8 Mar 1954 Colombo, Sri Lanka.

In 1976 he became the first British male swimmer for 68 years to win an Olympic title, when he set a world record of 2:15.11 in the 200m breaststroke. At this event he had been a silver medallist in 1972, after which he went on a scholarship to the University of Miami in Florida, and he also took the 100m silver in 1976.

Born in Sri Lanka, his family returned to Scotland in 1965. Tall and broad-shouldered, he won three world titles, 100m in 1975 and 200m in both 1973 (in his first world record, 2:19.28) and 1975, setting European records at both events (1:04.26 and 2:18.23) in 1975. He also won world bronze medals at 200m medley in 1973 and at medley relay in 1975.

Wilkie's first major championships medal was a Commonwealth bronze at 200m breaststroke (also 5th at 100m) in 1970. Four years later he won gold medals at both 200m breaststroke and at 200m IM, with a silver at 100m breaststroke.

In all he set 17 British individual event records, five at 100m breaststroke from 1:06.20 in 1972 to 1:03.43 in 1976; seven at 200m breaststroke from 2:32.50 in 1970 to 2:15.11 in 1976; and five at 200m IM to 2:06.25 in 1976. ASA champion at breaststroke 100m 1973-4, 200m 1972-4; 200m IM 1974. NCAA breaststroke champion 100y 1974, 200y 1973 and 1976. Awarded the MBE in 1974.

Dominique WILKINS (USA)

BASKETBALL

Jacques Dominique Wilkins. b. 12 Jan 1960 Sorbonne, Paris, France.

A strong forward, he was All-American at the University of Georgia before being drafted by the Utah Jazz, who sold his rights to the Atlanta Hawks, with whom he has played his entire NBA career from 1982. He ruptured his Achilles tendon in January 1992 but returned to play in 1992/3, when he averaged 29.9 points per game and passed 20,000 career points. At 2.03m *6'8"* Wilkins is known for his slashing drives and spectacular dunks, which earned him the nickname 'The Human Highlight Film'. With 2366 points av. 30.3, he led the NBA in scoring in 1986, the last man to do so before Michael Jordan's seven consecutive seasons' monopoly. His brother Gerald also plays in the NBA.

NBA career: 22,096 points, av. 26.5; 5814 rebounds.

Mac WILKINS (USA)

ATHLETICS

Maurice Mac Wilkins. b. 15 Nov 1950 Eugene, Oregon.

'Multiple Mac' was a highly proficient performer at all four throwing events, but specialised at the discus. He set four world discus records in 1976, first with 69.18m at Walnut; then a week later, at San Jose on 1 May, he set the most world records in one competition. On his first three throws he set records at 69.80, 70.24 and 70.86, for the first 70m throws in official competition. He sealed a great year with Olympic victory. He went on to make the next three US Olympic teams, winning the Trials in 1980 and 1988. Unable to compete through the boycott in 1980, he won a silver medal in 1984 and was fifth in 1988. A graduate of the University of Oregon, for whom he won the NCAA title in 1973, he was US champion seven times, 1973, 1976-80 and, after three years in semi-retirement, in 1988. He was also Pan-American champion in 1979 and second in the World Cups of 1977 and 1979. His discus best was a US record 70.98 in 1980,

Other bests: shot 21.06 indoors (1977), hammer 63.66 (1977), javelin 78.44 (1970).

Bluey WILKINSON (Aus)

SPEEDWAY

Arthur George Wilkinson. b. 27 Aug 1911 Millthorpe, New South Wales, d. 27 Jul 1940 Roes Bay, NSW.

Having won the unofficial New South Wales speedway championship, a fund was raised to send him to race in England in 1927. There Wilkinson was initially rated a 'no hoper', but the tenacious red-haired Australian persevered to become the very best. He raced with West Ham from 1931 and was unlucky not to win the first official World Championship in 1936, as he won all five races in the final but, as a result of a system which credited riders with bonus points from the qualifying rounds, he failed to place in the first three. However, he did take the world title in 1938, beating the defending champion, Jackie Milne of America. His Test match record was superb, with 181 points from 23 matches against England, and in the five matches for Australia v England at Sydney in 1937/8 he became the only rider to have scored maximum points in every match of a Test series. Australian champion 1934-5 and 1938, he retired at the end of the 1938 season and became the promoter at Sheffield, but before he became established, he returned to Australia in 1940 and lost his life in a road accident.

Billy WILLIAMS (USA)

BASEBALL

Billy Leo Williams. b. 15 Jun 1938 Whistler, Alabama.

Williams quietly established himself as one of baseball's great players during the 1960s. He played mostly with the Chicago Cubs although he spent his last two years with the Oakland Athletics. He batted over .300 five times, but was always hovering around that figure in other years. From 22 Sep 1963 to 2 Sep 1970 he played in a National League record 1117 consecutive games (since broken by Steve Garvey). He was the NL Rookie of the Year in 1961, played in six All-Star Games, and led the league in hitting in 1972. He later became a hitting coach for the Cubs.

Career 1959-76: 2711 hits Avg. .290, HR 426; RBI 1475. Best seasons: 1972: .333, 37 HR, 122 RBI; 1970: .322, 42 HR, 129 RBI, 205 hits, 137 Runs.

Bleddyn WILLIAMS (UK)

RUGBY UNION

Bleddyn Llewellyn Williams. b. 22 Feb 1923 Taff's Well.

After playing in three Services and seven Victory internationals, he made his full international début for Wales as a fly-half against England in 1947. In all of his further 21 internationals he played in the centre. To his powerful midfield play he added perfectly-timed passes to his wing, and these attributes made him a valuable member of the 1950 Lions party in Australasia, when he played in five Tests and only injury prevented him from appearing in the sixth. He captained the Lions in three Tests and although he only captained Wales five times they won each match. He was a master of all the skills of the game and in the 1947/8 season scored 41 tries in 31 matches for Cardiff. In 1953 he led Cardiff to a memorable victory over the touring All Blacks. One of the legends of Welsh rugby, he later became a respected writer on the game.

Bryan WILLIAMS (NZ)

RUGBY UNION

Bryan George Williams. b. 3 Oct 1950 Auckland.

His international career began in 1970 and when he retired in 1978 he was New Zealand's most capped winger. A formidable attacking player, he played on the wing in 36 internationals, won two further caps as a centre and scored 10 tries in Test matches. Including matches other than internationals, he played 113 times for the All Blacks scoring a record 66 tries. He was also a useful place-kicker, converting two tries and kicking nine penalties in Tests. On retirement he continued his association with Auckland as a coach and, being of Samoan descent, he helped Western Samoa with their preparations for their successful 1991 World Cup campaign.

Dick WILLIAMS (USA)

TENNIS

Richard Norris Williams II. b. 29 Jan 1891 Geneva, Switzerland, d. 2 Jun 1968 Bryn Mawr, Pennsylvania.

Born in Switzerland where his father, a Philadelphia lawyer, lived for health reasons, Williams won the Swiss Championship before leaving to enrol at Harvard in 1912. With his father he set out for America aboard the ill-fated *Titanic*, and although Dick survived the disaster, his father perished. He made his Davis Cup début in 1913 when the USA recaptured the trophy and he was again on the winning team in 1921, 1923 and 1925-6, winning 6 of his 9 singles and all four doubles 1913-26. He won the US singles in 1914 and 1916, the men's doubles in 1926 and the mixed doubles in 1912. He also won the men's doubles at Wimbledon in 1920 and a gold medal in the mixed doubles at the 1924 Olympic Games. After leaving Harvard in 1916, he enrolled in the Field Artillery the following year and his knowledge of European languages led to his appointment as a staff officer in France. He was discharged with the rank of captain in 1919 and resumed his tennis career. His game was one of constant attack but had he introduced an element of prudence into his play he would certainly have won more major titles.

Freddie WILLIAMS (UK)

SPEEDWAY

Freddie Williams. b. 12 Mar 1926 Port Talbot.

A Welshman who, with victories in 1950 and 1953, became the first British rider to win two world championships. At the time of his 1950 win he was still using a provisional licence on the road, later passing his motorcycle test.

Ike WILLIAMS (USA)

BOXING

Isiah Williams. b. 2 Aug 1923 Brunswick, Georgia.

Williams turned professional in 1940 and earned his first title shot in 1945, when he won the NBA lightweight championship by knocking out Juan Zurita. Known as a crafty boxer with great defensive skill, he defended the lightweight crown seven times before he lost it to Jimmy Carter in 1951. He continued to box until 1955 but never again fought for a title.
Career record: W - 162 (40), L - 23, D -11.

J P R WILLIAMS (UK)

RUGBY UNION

John Peter Rhys Williams. b. 2 Mar 1949 Cardiff.

The most capped Welsh player. Always known as 'J P R' he was initially an outstanding tennis player and won the Wimbledon Junior singles in 1966. After deciding to concentrate on rugby, he was first chosen for Wales in 1969 and went on to play 55 times for his country and 8 times for the Lions at full back. Unusually, he also played in one international as a flanker on the 1978 Welsh tour of Australia.

The ferocity of his tackling commanded immense respect from his opponents and apart from his resolute defence he was a brilliant counter-attacking runner. During the years he spent in London as a medical student he played for London Welsh, but after he had qualified as an orthopaedic surgeon he was welcomed back to Bridgend where he finished his playing career.

'J P R' had been a member of the team which won the Triple Crown six times and captained Wales in the 1978/9 season after which he retired from international rugby, although he returned to play one last game against Scotland in 1981. One of the greatest full backs of all-time, he was certainly rated as the best in the world in that position on his two Lions tours of South Africa (1971 and 1974). He was awarded the MBE in 1977 for his outstanding contribution to the game.

Percy WILLIAMS (Can)

ATHLETICS

Percy Williams. b. 19 May 1908 Vancouver, BC, d. 29 Nov 1982 Vancouver, by suicide.

Williams was the surprise winner of the Olympic titles at both 100m and 200m in 1928. The frail-looking 20-year-old impressed throughout in Amsterdam, from when he tied the Olympic record at 10.6 in the second round of the 100m. Two years later he improved the world record for 100m to 10.3 in winning the Canadian title and that year won gold medals at 100y and sprint relay at the first Empire Games. He was, however, past his best when he failed to make the finals of the 100m and 200m at the 1932 Olympics.

Rex WILLIAMS (UK)

BILLIARDS

Rex Williams. b. 20 July 1933 Stourbridge, Worcestershire.

British junior (under-16) champion at snooker and billiards in 1948-9; he excelled at both games in the senior ranks. After winning the English Amateur snooker title in 1951, he was largely responsible for the revival of the World Professional Championships in 1964 and twice challenged John Pulman for the title, but lost on both occasions, 1964-5. He then concentrated on billiards and won the 1968 World Championship when the event was revived after an interval of 17 years. After four successful defences he lost to Fred Davis in 1980 but was again the world champion in 1982 and 1983. He decided not to defend his title in 1984 and reverted to snooker and the development of his business interests. He was a regular member of the early TV commentary teams and his involvement in the leisure industry included the ownership of a successful pool and snooker table manufacturing business.

Ted WILLIAMS (USA)

BASEBALL

Theodore Samuel Williams. b. 30 Aug 1918 San Diego, California.

He had many nicknames, 'The Splendid Splinter', 'The Kid', and 'Teddy Ballgame', but Ted Williams had only one stated ambition. 'Someday, when I walk down the street, I want people to say "There goes the greatest hitter who ever lived".' It is likely that he achieved his ambition. His lifetime batting average of .344 was surpassed by several others, but in the era in which he played, it was non-pareil. And none of the players with higher averages approached the power which Williams possessed. He won the Triple Crown (average, home runs and runs batted in) twice, in 1942 and 1947, one of only two hitters to do so. He hit 521 career home runs, despite playing in a park where right field was very deep and prevented many of his best hits from being home runs, and he might still have approached Babe Ruth's lifetime record of 714 home runs but for his missing 5 years serving in the Air Force in both World War II and the Korean War. In the latter he became a war hero when his plane was shot down. He remains the last major leaguer to hit over .400, having batted .406 in 1941.
Career 1939-60: 2654 hits Avg. .344, HR 521; RBI 1839. Best seasons: 1941: .406, 37 HR, 120 RBI; 1957: .388, 38 HR, 87 RBI; 1948: .369, 126 RBI; 1942: .356, 36 HR, 137 RBI; 1947: .343, 32 HR, 114 RBI; 1954: .345, 29 HR, 136 RBI.

Yvette WILLIAMS (NZ)

ATHLETICS

Yvette Winifred Williams. b. 25 Apr 1929 Caversham, Dunedin. Later Corlett.

A multi-talented athlete who won the Olympic gold medal for long jump in 1952 and Commonwealth gold medals for long jump in 1950 and 1954 and for shot and discus as well in 1954. Those two throwing events were not on the Empire Games (as it then was) programme at Auckland in 1950 but she won a silver medal at the javelin. Unfortunately for her, there was no pentathlon at the championships in those days. At the 1952 Olympics, where she was also sixth at the shot, she flirted with disaster in the long jump final, for she only qualified for the final six in the third round after two no-jumps. In the fourth round, however, her 6.24m was just 1cm short of the world record set nine years earlier by Fanny Blankers-Koen. Williams thus became the first NZ woman to win

Olympic gold, and she got that world record with a jump of 6.28 in 1954. Awarded the MBE.
For a decade she dominated the New Zealand athletics championships, winning the shot each year 1947-54 and long jump 1948-54 as well as the discus 1951-4, javelin 1950 and 80m hurdles 1954. Her younger brother Roy won the Commonwealth decathlon in 1966.
Other bests (all in 1954): 80m hurdles 11.3w, shot 13.95m, discus 47.84m.

Bob WILLIS (UK)

CRICKET

Robert George Dylan Willis. b. 30 May 1949 Sunderland, Co. Durham. He added his third name as a teenager in honour of Bob Dylan.

Bob Willis peaked for Test matches, leading the England attack with his often devastating fast bowling. His best return, 8-43 at Headingley in 1981, gave England an unlikely victory over Australia by 18 runs. He played for Surrey 1969-71, making his Test début in Australia in 1970/1 while still an uncapped county player. He then moved to Warwickshire, whom he captained for his last five years in the game 1980-4, also captaining England in 18 matches 1982-4. Very tall at 1.98m *6'6"*, he was an awkward-looking but most effective bowler, who established himself as a Test regular from the mid-1970s, and he passed Fred Trueman's record of most wickets for England in his 84th Test (Trueman had played fewer at 67) against New Zealand in January 1984. Since his retirement he has worked with the England management and as a TV commentator. Awarded the MBE.
90 Tests 1970-84: 840 runs at 11.50, HS 28; 325 wickets at 25.20, BB 8-43; 39 catches.*
64 One-day Ints: 83 runs at 10.37, HS 24; 80 wickets at 24.60, BB 4-45; 22 catches.
First-class 1969-84: 2690 runs at 14.30, HS 72; 899 wickets at 24.99, BB 8-32; 134 catches.

Helen WILLS (USA)

TENNIS

Helen Newington Wills. b. 6 Oct 1905 Berkeley, California. Later Moody, then Roark.

Successor to the great Suzanne Lenglen as queen of women's tennis. She was unbeaten from the autumn of 1926 until the final of the US Championships in August 1933 and did not lose even one set in a singles match between June 1927 and the Wimbledon final of 1933. This run included 12 Wightman Cup singles, her only defeats in this competition having come in 1924 when she lost to both Kitty McKane and Phyliss Covell. She also won gold medals in the singles and women's doubles at the 1924 Olympic Games.
She won 31 major championships. In the singles she won Wimbledon 8 times (1927-30, 1932-3, 1935, 1938), a record surpassed only by Martina Navratilova; the US Championships a record-equalling 7 times (1923-5, 1927-9, 1931) and the French 4 times (1928-30, 1932). In the women's doubles she won Wimbledon 3 times (1924, 1927, 1930), the US 4 times (1922, 1924-5, 1928) and the French twice (1930, 1932) and in the mixed doubles she won Wimbledon in 1929 and the US in 1924 and 1928.
She dominated the game to an extent which few others - men or women - have even approached, but all her successes were accepted without any display of emotion and she was dubbed 'Little Miss Poker Face'. She graduated from the University of California in 1928 with a degree in fine arts and later became a noted artist and illustrator. In December 1929 she married stockbroker Frederick Moody, whom she had met at her only match with Lenglen at Cannes three years earlier. They were divorced in 1937 and in October 1939 she married the polo-playing writer Adrian Roark in Las Vegas.

Maury WILLS (USA)

BASEBALL

Maurice Morning Wills. b. 2 Oct 1932 Washington, D.C.

Wills was the top base-stealer of the 1960s, leading the National League in stolen bases from 1960-5, topped by 104 in 1962 to break Ty Cobb's long-standing mark of 96 for a single season. Wills also threatened triple-figures in 1965 with 94 steals. His marks dropped off a bit after that year. He was also a good fielding shortstop who won Gold Gloves in 1961-2 and played mostly with the Los Angeles Dodgers.
Career 1959-72: 2134 hits Avg. .281; RBI 458; SB 586.

Betty WILSON (Aus)

CRICKET

Elizabeth Rebecca Wilson. b. 21 Nov 1921 Melbourne.

Wilson achieved the best bowling analysis in women's Test cricket with 11-16 in the match for Australia v England at St Kilda's, Melbourne in February 1958. During the first innings she took a hat-trick, the first by a woman in Tests, and she also scored a century to become the first man or woman to score a century and take ten wickets in a Test match. She achieved the best all-round performances in a Test for Australia and three times took five wickets in an innings and scored a century, adding 111 and 29 and 6-23 against England at Adelaide in 1949, and 127 and 6-71 against England at Adelaide in March 1958. She set Australian Test career records with 862 runs at 57.46 and 68 wickets at 11.80.
Joan Hawes said of Betty Wilson in her book *The Golden Triangle*: 'Undoubtedly Australia's greatest all-rounder and probably the finest cricketer of any era.'

Gerry WILSON (UK)

HORSE RACING

Gerald Wilson. b. 12 Oct 1903 Wing, Buckinghamshire, d. 29 Dec 1968 Wantage, Berkshire.

Champion National Hunt jockey a record seven times, each year 1932/3 to 1937/8 and in 1940/1. He rode *Golden Miller* to win both Cheltenham Gold Cup and Grand National in 1934. In 1935 he completed the Cheltenham double, on *Golden Miller* again and in the Champion Hurdle on *Lion Courage*. As a trainer he won the latter race with *Brains Trust* in 1945, and later was the landlord of a pub near Newbury. His brother Anthony was also a leading jumps jockey.

Hack WILSON (USA)

BASEBALL

Lewis Robert Wilson. b. 26 Apr 1900 Ellwood City, Pennsylvania, d. 23 Nov 1948 Baltimore, Maryland.

Wilson was a barrel-chested, power-hitting outfielder who played for 12 years in the National League with four different teams. Short and stocky at 1.68m *5'6"* and 89 kg *195 lb*, his 1930 season is one of baseball's greatest ever. He hit 56 home runs, still the National League record, and batted in 190 runs, still a major league record, averaging .356.
In later years he slumped badly, probably due to problems with alcohol. He was kept out of the Hall of Fame for many years but finally, in 1979, he was elected by the Veterans' Committee.
Career 1923-34: 1461 hits Avg. .307, HR 244; RBI 1062.

Jocky WILSON (UK)

DARTS

John Thomas Wilson. b. 22 Mar 1950 Kirkclady, Fifeshire.

At 1.62m and 102kg he is probably one of the least athletic people in this book, but a fine and popular darts player who was World champion in 1982 and 1989. He did not start playing darts until he was in his 20s, but progressed to become one of Scotland's best players and to win his first major event with the British Matchplay in 1980. He retained that title in 1981, when he won the first of a record four British Professional Championships (winning again in 1983, 1986, 1988), and a year later he had his finest year, winning the British Open as well as the World title. He also won the World Pairs with Ritchie Gardner in 1988.

Stu WILSON (NZ)

RUGBY UNION

Stuart Sinclair Wilson. b. 22 Jul 1955 Gore.

In his 34 Tests he scored 19 tries which stood as a New Zealand record until the arrival of John Kirwan. These included a hat-trick in the final Test against the British Lions at Auckland in 1983. Usually a winger but occasionally a centre, he had established himself on the right wing for the All Blacks when, due to the unavailability of Andy Dalton, he was called upon to captain the 1983 tour of England and Scotland. The appointment was not a success as Wilson did not enjoy the responsibilities which went with the position, and being on the wing was certainly not the best position to lead a side of the calibre of the All Blacks. The Test against Scotland was drawn and after losing to England, Wilson retired from international rugby. He played his club rugby for Wellington.

Jean-Pierre WIMILLE (Fra)

MOTOR RACING

Jean-Pierre Wimille. b. 26 Jun 1908 Paris, d. Jan 1949 Buenos Aires, Argentina.

Was at his peak in 1947-8, when he drove for Alfa Romeo, winning the Belgian and Swiss Grands Prix in 1947 and the French and Italian GP in 1948. He made his Grand Prix racing début in a Bugatti in 1930, and in 1931 was second in the Monte Carlo Rally. Won the French GP in a Bugatti in 1936 and at Le Mans in 1937 and 1939. He died after hitting a tree when practising for the Buenos Aires Grand Prix.

Brett WING (Aus)

WATER SKIING

Brett Wing.

The greatest ever barefoot skier, he was never defeated at national or international level. He won the world overall barefoot championship in 1978, 1980 and 1982. In 1980 he scored a grand slam by sweeping all the events -wake slalom, tricks, start methods, and jumps - in addition to the overall title. From 1982 he turned his attention to exhibition and show skiing.

Hans Günter WINKLER (FRG)

EQUESTRIAN

Hans Günter Winkler. b. 24 Jul 1926 Wuppertal-Barmen.

Showed great all-round horsemanship from his competitive début in 1948 and first international in 1952 to his retirement in 1986. In all he made 108 appearances for the German national team, 37 of them winning ones. Winkler won six Olympic medals (five gold and one silver) at show jumping at six Olympics 1956-76, but only one in the individual event. That was his win in 1956 on *Halla (1945-79)*, whom he had started riding in 1951 and on whom he was World champion in 1954 and 1955. With the German team he won Olympic golds in 1956, 1960, 1964, and 1972 and silver in 1976. At European Championships he won gold in 1957, silver in 1962 and three bronzes. German champion 1952-6 and 1959. Also a successful businessman.

His father was a riding instructor, who was killed at the end of the war

Arthur WINT (Jam)

ATHLETICS

Arthur Stanley Wint. b. 25 May 1920 Manchester, Jamaica, d. 20 Oct 1992 Kingston.

A hugely popular figure with his enormous stride (he was 1.95m tall), he represented Britain in five international matches 1946-51. However, he competed for his native Jamaica at the Olympic Games, winning gold medals at 400m in 1948, in his personal best 46.2, and at 4 x 400m in 1952, when Jamaica set a world record of 3:03.9 with Wint running the first leg. That made up for the fact that he had collapsed with cramp on the third leg in 1948 when exactly the same team was in medal contention. He also won silver medals behind Mal Whitfield at 800m in 1948 and in 1952.

At his second Olympics he had run 46.3 in a semi-final of the 400m, but went out too fast in the final (200m in 21.7) and faded to 5th in 47.0.

Wint's international career had begun at the age of 17 when he won the 800m and was third at 400mh in the 1938 Central American Games. He retained his CAG 800m title in 1946, when he also won gold medals at 400m and 4x400m relay. He was AAA champion at 440y 1946 and 1952, and at 880y 1946, 1950-1. His best ever two-lap time was 1:49.6 for 880 yards (equal to 1:48.9 for 800m) in 1951.

He came to Britain in 1944 to serve as a pilot in the RAF in World War II and then qualified as a surgeon (FRCS 1963) from St Bartholomew's Hospital. Awarded the MBE in 1954 and made a Member of the Order of Jamaica in 1989. From 1974 to 1978 he was Jamaican High Commissioner to Britain.

Fred WINTER (UK)

HORSE RACING

Frederick Thomas Winter. b. 20 Sep 1926 Andover, Hampshire.

Acclaimed by his contemporaries as the greatest ever rider under National Hunt Rules, he set a new record with a total of 923 winners (929 from 4298 races including overseas) until his retirement in 1964, when he became a highly successful trainer.

The son of a jockey/trainer, also Fred (1894-1965) who rode the winner of the Oaks in 1911, he rode at show jumping and then on the flat, with his first winner in 1939 at the age of 13 at Salisbury. After war service as a lieutenant in the Parachute regiment, he had his first jumps success in 1947. His partnership with Ryan Price began in 1949, and in 1951/2 he rode 81 winners for second place. The following year he became champion jockey with a new record of 121 wins, and the first century since 1924. He was champion jockey again in the three years from 1955/6. He twice rode the winner of the Grand National, *Sundew* in 1957 and *Kilmore* in 1962, and trained the winner in his first two years: *Jay Trump* in 1965 and *Anglo* in 1966. His Gold Cup winners were two as a jockey, *Saffron Tartan* in 1961 and *Mandarin* in 1962, and *Midnight Court* in 1978 as a trainer; and in the Champion Hurdle he had three wins as a jockey and four as a trainer. Leading trainer eight times, 1970/1 to 1974/5, 1976/7, 1977/8 and 1984/5. Awarded the CBE in 1963.

Peter WINTERBOTTOM (UK)

RUGBY UNION

Peter James Winterbottom. b. 31 May 1960 Horsforth, Leeds, Yorkshire.

England's most capped forward. A hard-driving flanker who won 58 caps for England from making his international début against Australia in 1982 to the declared end of his International Championships career in 1993. Among English players, only Rory Underwood has won more caps.

He played club rugby in South Africa and New Zealand (for Hawkes Bay in 1982/3) and returned to New Zealand with the 1983 and 1993 Lions, playing in all seven Tests on these two tours. Initially with Headingley, he moved to Harlequins at the start of the 1989/90 season.

John WISDEN (UK)

CRICKET

John Wisden. b. 5 Sep 1826 Brighton, Sussex, d. 5 Apr 1884 Westminster, London.

The founder of *Wisden Cricketers' Almanack*, first issued in 1864. A tiny man, he was an outstanding bowler for Sussex with fast off-breaks, and in the pre-Test match era played for the All-England and United England XIs. At Lord's on 15 Jul 1850 for the North v South he became the first and only bowler to take all ten wickets, all bowled, in a first-class innings.
First-class 1845-63: 4140 runs at 14.12, 2 100s HS 148; 1109 wickets; 169 catches, 1 stumping.

Katarina WITT (GDR)

FIGURE SKATING

Katarina Witt. b. 3 Dec 1965 Karl-Marx-Stadt.

Olympic gold medallist in 1984 and 1988, the first woman figure skater since Sonja Henie to retain an Olympic title, and four-time world champion, 1984-5 and 1987-8. She won the first of her eight GDR titles as a 15-year-old in 1981 and at the European Championships was successively 14th, 13th and 5th each year from 1979 before taking the silver medal in 1982 and winning the first of six successive titles in 1983. Her World Championships progression was 10th, 5th and 2nd 1980-2, before slipping to 4th in 1983. She ended her amateur career with a beautiful interpretation of the opera heroine Carmen. A lucrative professional career beckoned, but initially she only made guest appearances in professional ice shows until in 1991 she topped the bill in a new series of contests put together by French and American interests. Along with other professionals, Olympic eligibility was returned to Witt in 1993.

Bärbel WÖCKEL (GDR)

ATHLETICS

Bärbel Wöckel. née Eckert. b. 21 Mar 1955 Leipzig.

She set an Olympic record for a woman athlete by taking four gold medals, with the 200m and sprint relay in both 1976 and 1980. She first made her mark with European Junior titles and records at 200m and 100m hurdles in 1973. In 1974 she was 7th in the European 100m and won a gold medal on the GDR relay team. She shared three GDR world records at 4 x 100m and one at 4 x 200m relay in 1980, and at her second European Championships in 1982, she won the 200m, was second at 100m and added a relay gold.

She showed her one-lap capabilities by running on both GDR winning 4 x 400m relay teams at the 1981 World Cup. A student of education, she ran for SC Motor Jena.

Best times: 100m 10.95 (1982) and 10.92w (1980), 200m 21.85 (1984), 400m 49.56 (1982), 100m hurdles 13.17 and 13.14w (1973).

Alex WOJCIECHOWICZ (USA)

AMERICAN FOOTBALL

Alexander Francis Wojciechowicz. b. 12 Aug 1915 South River, New Jersey.

Wojciechowicz was the center who was the top player on Fordham's fabled Seven Blocks of Granite line. He made All-American in both 1936 and 1937 and led Fordham to three great seasons in which they lost only two games. One of his linemates at Fordham was Vince Lombardi. Wojciechowicz played for 13 years in the NFL, from 1938-50. He started out with the Detroit Lions, playing center for them through 1946, and played his last four years with the Philadelphia Eagles. In the pros, 'Wojo' also played linebacker. He earned All-Pro honours four times. In 1968 he was instrumental in helping form the NFL Alumni Association.

Mamo WOLDE (Eth)

ATHLETICS

Mamo Wolde. b. 12 Jun 1932.

He competed at four Olympic Games, starting unnoticed when he was eliminated in the heats of the 800m, 1500m and 4 x 400m relay in 1956. In 1964, however, he came to prominence with fourth at 10,000m and he went on to win three medals: in 1968 he was 2nd at 10,000m and then won the marathon, and in 1972 he was third in the marathon. At 36 and 40 respectively he became the oldest Olympic gold medallist and the oldest medallist at any running event. He was also African marathon champion in 1973.

Best times: 5000m 13:38.8 (1967), 10,000m 28:31.8 (1964), marathon 2:15:09 (1972).

WONG Peng-soon (Sin/Mal)

BADMINTON

Wong Peng-soon. b. 1918.

Renowned for his sparkling footwork, he was the inspiration of the Malayan team that dominated the Thomas Cup, winning it the first three times it was contested, in 1949, 1952 and 1955. He won his first All-Malayan Open singles title in 1940, winning again in 1941, in 1947 when the event was resumed after the war, and each year 1949-53. He was the All-England singles champion in 1950-2 and 1955, the last at the age of 37 when he beat defending champion Eddy Choong in a 67-minute marathon match. He became a professional coach in Singapore. Awarded an MBE.

Gar WOOD (USA)

POWERBOATING

Garfield Arthur Wood. b. 4 Dec 1880 Mapleton, Iowa, d. 19 Jun 1971 Miami, Florida.

'The Gray Fox' was the first legendary figure in powerboat racing and the first man to crack the 100mph *161 km/h* barrier on water. He dominated the international Harmsworth Trophy competition, winning on eight successive occasions between 1920 and 1933, driving a series of boats which he named Miss America (I through X). He won five consecutive APBA Gold Cups 1917-21, a record which stood until 1987 when broken by Chip Hanauer. Wood's last water-speed record was 200.9 km/h *124.9 mph*, set on the St Clair River near Algonac, Michigan. Named after the US President and Vice-President in office on the day he was born - James Garfield and Chester Arthur - Wood graduated from the Armour Institute of Technology in Chicago and became a millionaire as a designer and builder of boats. He made numerous boats for the US Navy and one of his designs became the P.T. boat. He also financed the well-known Chris Craft corporation.

Howard WOOD (Can)

CURLING

Howard 'Pappy' Wood. b. 29 Aug 1888 Winnipeg, Manitoba, d. 28 Dec 1978 Winnipeg.

Wood had the longest career of any great curler. He competed in the Manitoba bonspiel for 65 consecutive years, 1908-72, winning eight Manitoba Curling Association bonspiel grand aggregate titles. He skipped MacDonald Brier winners in 1925, 1930, and 1940.

Mervyn WOOD (Aus)

ROWING

Mervyn Thomas Wood. b. 30 Apr 1917.

Wood began his Olympic rowing career in 1936 when he was in seat five of the Australian Police eight that represented Australia. He would certainly have competed in the Olympics in both 1940 and 1944 but for the war. Still he competed in four Olympics to 1956, one of the longest careers ever. In 1948, Wood won both the Olympic single sculls and the Diamond Sculls at Henley. In 1952 he lost the Olympic sculls title to Yuriy Tyukalov, but he again won the Diamond Sculls. Although Wood still rowed singles, he was unable to overcome Australia's new great, Stuart Mackenzie, and the remainder of his international appearances were in doubles. In 1956 he won an Olympic bronze with Murray Riley at the doubles. At the Empire Games he won four gold medals: single sculls 1950, double sculls with Riley in 1950 and 1954, and coxed fours 1954, adding a silver medal at double sculls with Mackenzie in 1958. He was Australian single sculls champion 1946-52 and 1958. Amazingly he rowed with a partially withered hand throughout his career. New South Wales Police Commissioner 1977-9. Awarded the MVO and MBE.

Lynette WOODARD (USA)

BASKETBALL

Lynette Woodard. b. 12 Aug 1959 Wichita, Kansas.

She took over the mantle from Cheryl Miller as the top player in women's basketball. She played collegiately at the University of Kansas 1978-81, setting the women's career NCAA record with 3,649 points. She made the 1980 US Olympic team which did not compete and then worked as a volunteer assistant coach at Kansas, while studying for a Master's degree. In 1984 she earned a gold medal with the US Olympic team. Her other international medals include gold from the 1979 World University Games, 1983 Pan-American Games, the 1986 Goodwill Games, and the 1986 World

Championships; and silver from the 1983 World University Games and 1983 World Championships. In 1985 she became the first female member of the Harlem Globetrotters. Woodard is an attractive, poised, sophisticated woman who has been a delight with the media.

John WOODEN (USA)

BASKETBALL

John Robert Wooden. b. 14 Oct 1910 Hall, Indiana.

Wooden was one of the greatest guards ever to play basketball, but has made his name as perhaps the greatest coach ever. At Purdue he was a three-time All-American 1930-2, and college basketball's Player of the Year in 1932. He began college coaching at Indiana State 1946-8, and then moved to UCLA where he coached to 1975. With the UCLA Bruins, Wooden established a never to be equalled record as he won ten NCAA championships, including seven consecutively 1967-73; no other coach has won more than three. He finished with a record of 885 wins, 203 losses, and a winning percentage of .813. He was named collegiate coach of the year six times, 1964, 1967, 1969-70, and 1972-3. In 1970 he was named *Sports Illustrated*'s Sportsman of the Year. Wooden is the only person who has been inducted to the Naismith Memorial Basketball Hall of Fame both as a player (1960) and a coach (1972).

Sydney WOODERSON (UK)

ATHLETICS

Sydney Charles Wooderson. b. 30 Aug 1914 Camberwell, London.

Denied by World War II of some of his best years, he won European titles before and after, the 1500m in 1938 and 5000m in 1946. In the latter he posted the second fastest ever time with 14:08.6. Two years later he sealed his career with the 1948 English National cross-country title.
The small (1.68m), bespectacled Wooderson looked anything but a world-beater but he had both speed and strength, with world records at 800m/880y 1:48.4/1:49.2 in 1938 and 1 mile 4:06.4 in 1937. He was AAA champion at the mile each year from 1935 to 1939 and at 3 miles in 1946, when he set a British record of 13:53.2.
An untimely cracked ankle cost him the chance of Olympic success in 1936, although he beat Jack Lovelock in four of six mile races in 1934-6. Lovelock, however, had beaten him to win the 1934 Empire Games title. In 1939 Wooderson ran a world best 2:59.5 for 3/4 mile and after the War set his third British mile record with 4:04.2 (with his best 1500m of 3:48.4 en route) behind Arne Andersson in 1945.

Bill WOODFULL (Aus)

CRICKET

William Maldon Woodfull. b. 22 Aug 1897 Maldon, Victoria, d. 11 Aug 1965 near Tweed Heads, New South Wales.

A most effective opening batsman, and a determined defender of his stumps for Victoria and Australia, captaining his state from 1926 to 1934 and Australia in 25 of his 35 Tests from 1930-4. He was much respected by his team, and led them during the controversial 'Bodyline' series with quiet dignity. He became headmaster of Melbourne High School and was awarded the OBE for his services to education.
35 Tests 1926-34: 2300 runs at 46.00, 7 100s HS 161; 7 catches.
First-class 1921-35: 13,388 runs at 64.99, 49 100s HS 284; 1 wicket; 78 catches.

Sammy WOODS (Aus)

CRICKET and RUGBY UNION

Samuel Moses James Woods. b. 14 Apr 1867 Ashfield, Sydney, d. 30 Apr 1931 Taunton, Somerset.

A great natural games player, the effervescent Woods played cricket for both Australia (1888) and England (1895/6), three Tests apiece, and rugby football 13 times for England. A double blue at Cambridge University, he was a very strong wing-forward for England 1890-5. In 1886 he made his début as a fast bowler for Somerset, whom he captained from

1894 to 1906. He was their secretary for 30 years, and was a much loved character there. His bowling declined with age, but at the same time his hard-hitting batting improved

6 Tests 1888-96: 154 runs at 15.40, HS 53; 10 wickets at 25.00, BB 3-28; 5 catches.

First-class 1886-1910: 15,345 runs at 23.42, 19 100s HS 215; 1040 wickets at 20.82, BB 10-69; 279 catches.

Stanley WOODS (Ire)

MOTOR CYCLING

Stanley Woods. b. 1903 Dublin.

The outstanding motorcycling champion of the 1920s and 1930s, the great hero of an era regarded by many as a golden age of the sport in Britain. He set a record with ten TT victories on the Isle of Man, a record eventually surpassed by Mike Hailwood. His first win was the Junior TT on a Cotton in 1923; on Nortons he won the Junior TT in 1932-3 and Senior 1926, 1932-3; both Lightweight 250cc and Senior on a Moto Guzzi in 1935; and the Junior on a Velocette in 1938-9. During these years he set numerous lap speed records.

He started his racing career as a Cotton works rider, having simply written to them asking for a ride. He was a successful businessman as a toffee manufacturer in his native Dublin.

Frank WOOLLEY (UK)

CRICKET

Frank Edward Woolley. b. 27 May 1887 Tonbridge, Kent, d. 18 Oct 1978 Halifax, Nova Scotia, Canada.

A peerless left-hander, whose beautiful batting has long been cited as the model for all aspiring cricketers. A big man, he was also a great all-rounder, a graceful slow left-arm bowler and a brilliant slip fielder, with a career total of catches well clear of any other player in the history of the game. From his Test début in 1909 he played in 52 successive Tests for England until 1926. His total of 28 seasons with 1000 runs matches the record held by WG Grace, and he had 13 years over 2000 and a peak of 3352 at 60.94 in 1928. Despite that, he was not selected for the England tour of Australia in 1928/9. In eight of these years he also took 100 wickets, and had a record four years at over 2000 runs and 100 wickets.

64 Tests 1909-34: 3283 runs at 36.07, 5 100s HS 154; 83 wickets at 33.91, BB 7-76; 64 catches.

First-class 1906-38: 58,969 runs at 40.75, 145 100s HS 305; 2068 wickets at 19.85, BB 8-22; 1018 catches.*

Ian WOOSNAM (UK)

GOLF

Ian Harold Woosnam. b. 2 Mar 1958 Oswestry, Shropshire.

The greatest Welsh golfer ever, reaching the status of world number one in 1991 shortly before winning his first major - the US Masters. Just 1.64m *5' 4 1/2"* tall, Woosnam is a powerful hitter who turned pro in 1976, although he did not qualify for the European tour until 1978. In 1982 he had his first tour victory in the Swiss Open and leapt from 104th in the European Order of Merit in 1981 to 8th. Since then he has been in the top ten each year, being ranked first in a marvellous year in 1987, when he had five wins including the World Matchplay and set a money record of £439,075. Adding overseas earnings, with three more wins including the first Sun City challenge, he set a world record with £1,062,662, and also in that year partnered David Llewellyn to Wales' first World Cup win. After being runner-up in 1989 he again won the World Matchplay in 1990, when top ranked on the European tour with a new record of £574,166. His total European tour earnings 1978-92 are £3,031,164 with 21 wins.

He first played for Wales in the World Cup in 1980 and was the top individual in both 1987 and 1991. He played in each Ryder Cup 1983-91, and had great success playing with Paul Way in 1985 and Nick Faldo in 1987, but in 1991 he disappointed, and his overall playing record is 8 wins, 10 losses and 3 halves in 21 matches.

Frank WOOTTON (Aus)

HORSE RACING

b. Dec 1893 Sydney, Australia, d. 4 Apr 1940 Sydney.

A boy prodigy as a jockey, he was riding winners in South Africa in 1903 at the age of nine. Son of Australian trainer Dick Wootton (1866-1946), his family then moved to England, where he became the youngest ever champion jockey at 15 in 1909, with further titles each year from 1910 to 1912 and a peak of 187 winners in 1911. After returning from war service he was too heavy to ride on the flat, having ridden 882 winners from 3886 mounts 1906-13 before his 21st birthday. He then fared well as a jump jockey, being runner-up to Dick Rees in 1921, and later became a trainer at Epsom before returning to Australia in 1933.

Frank WORRELL (Bar)

CRICKET

(Sir) Frank Mortimore Maglinne Worrell. b. 1 Aug 1924 Bank Hall, Bridgetown, d. 13 Mar 1967 Mona, Kingston, Jamaica.

A very great batsman, and an inspirational captain. It took a long time for him to take his rightful place as captain of the West Indies with the long-time prejudice against black players for the job, but he eventually led them with distinction in his last three series 1960-3; his first match was that magical tie against Australia in 1960 and in all, 9 of his 15 Tests in charge were won. He made his first-class début for Barbados as a slow left-arm bowler, but soon established himself as a right-handed batsman, and two years later made 318* in an unbroken partnership of 502 with John Goddard against Trinidad. Three years later he had an even higher partnership against Trinidad as he scored 255* while adding 577 unbeaten with Clyde Walcott. In the first Test series West Indies played after the War he scored 294 runs at an average of 147.00 against England in 1947/8. Due to his studies at Manchester University and playing league cricket in England he missed a few series in the ensuing years, but his second Test series was also very successful as he scored 599 runs at 89.83 against England in 1950. He developed his left arm medium-fast paced bowling and took 17 wickets in the 1951/2 Test series in Australia. He later played for Jamaica, where he became a senator in their parliament, and was knighted for services to cricket in 1964, three years before his tragically early death from leukaemia.
51 Tests 1948-63: 3860 runs at 49.48, 9 100s HS 261; 69 wickets at 38.73, BB 7-70; 43 catches.
First-class 1942-64: 15,025 runs at 54.24, 39 100s 308; 349 wickets at 28.98, BB 7-70; 139 catches.*

Lorne WORSLEY (Can)

ICE HOCKEY

Lorne John Worlsey. b. 14 May 1929 Montreal, Québec.

'Gump' Worsley is one of the great characters in the history of professional hockey. He played for ten different clubs in his 24-year professional career, leaving a hilarious trail of Worsley anecdotes wherever he played. In the NHL he played primarily with the New York Rangers and the Montreal Canadiens. He was considered too short, too fat, and, for much of his career, too old, to be an effective NHL goaltender, yet he had lightning quick reflexes and nerves of steel. His face was round, with large jowls and hound-dog eyes, giving the impression of nonchalance as he carefully minded the nets for his teams.
NHL career 1952-74: 862 games, 2.90 GAA, 43 shutouts. Vezina Trophy 1966, 1968; Calder Trophy 1953.

Harry WRAGG (UK)

HORSE RACING

Harry Wragg. b. 10 Jun 1902 Hallam, Yorkshire, d. 20 Oct 1985 Newmarket.

A fine tactician, nicknamed the 'Head Waiter', he was champion jockey in England in 1941 when Gordon Richards was injured, having been runner-up to that great man five times between 1928 and 1940. In all he rode 1762 winners in Britain and Ireland, with five years over

100 and a season's peak of 110 in 1931. He rode 13 classic winners, his first being *Felstead* in the 1928 Derby. Apprenticed to Bob Colling, he rode from 1921 to 1946. He trained at Abington Place, Newmarket, sending out winners of six English and nine Irish classics before handing over to his son Geoffrey in 1983. Perhaps the best horse he trained was *Darius*, winner of the 1954 2000 Guineas.

Billy WRIGHT (UK)

FOOTBALL

William Ambrose Wright. b. 6 Feb 1924 Ironbridge, Shropshire.

The first British player to win 100 caps. A versatile player in any of the half-back positions, he won a total of 105 England caps: 51 at right-half, 46 at centre-half in consecutive matches and 8 at left-half. He captained England in 90 games.
Joining the ground staff of Wolverhampton Wanderers as a boy, he remained with the club throughout his career, making 490 League appearances in 13 seasons, helping them win the FA Cup in 1949 and the Football League in 1954, 1958 and 1959. Following his retirement in 1959, he held a number of coaching and football-related posts before taking over as manager of Arsenal in 1962. He was, however, unable to repeat his successes on the field as a manager and his contract was terminated in June 1966. He was never even cautioned on the field, and was elected an Honorary Life Member of the FA. Voted Footballer of the Year in 1952, and in 1959 awarded the CBE for his services to sport.

George WRIGHT (USA)

BASEBALL

George Wright. b. 28 Jan 1847 Yonkers, New York, d. 21 Aug 1937 Boston, Massachusetts.

Wright was considered the first 'franchise' player in baseball history. He was recruited by his older brother Harry, who formed the first true professional baseball team, the Cincinnati Red Stockings. Wright was a shortstop who dominated baseball through the 1870s, playing from 1871-82, mostly with the Boston Red Stockings. He retired to start up a sporting goods business. His son, **Beals** Wright, became a tennis champion, winning two Olympic gold medals in that sport in 1904. Beals never won a US tennis championship but was the first American to advance to the final of the All-Comers' round at Wimbledon in 1910.
Career batting: Avg. .256.

Mickey WRIGHT (USA)

GOLF

Mary Kathryn Wright. b. 14 Feb 1935 San Diego, California.

Probably the greatest women's player ever. Even the most doubting will at least accord her equal status with Joyce Wethered and Babe Zaharias. Her career was quite short, as she played the LPGA Tour seriously only for a decade. Overall she won 82 tournaments between 1956 and 1973, a record surpassed by Kathy Whitworth after almost 30 years on the tour. Wright was leading money winner each year 1961-64, and won 10 or more tournaments in all four of those years, with a record 13 in 1963. Her low round of 62 on tour remains the lowest score ever in women's professional competition (since equalled).
She began playing aged 8 and won the US Girls Junior in 1952, and the World Amateur in 1954.
Major victories: US Women's Open 1958-9, 1961, 1964; LPGA 1958, 1960-1, 1963; Titleholders 1961-2; Western Open 1962-3, 1966; Dinah Shore 1973.

Roy WRIGHT (Aus)

AUSTRALIAN RULES FOOTBALL

G Roy Wright. b. 1929.

The only ruckman to win two Brownlow Medals, 1952 and 1954. A giant, but remarkably agile, he played 194 games for Richmond 1946-59 and also represented Victoria seven times. He overcame severe childhood illness and suffered from rheumatic fever, so it was amazing that he achieved so much in football, despite many injuries.

Gus WYNN (USA)

BASEBALL

Early Wynn. b. 6 Jan 1920 Hartford, Alabama.

Wynn pitched for 23 seasons in the major leagues with the Washington Senators, Cleveland Indians, and Chicago White Sox. He struggled in his first few years in the league but hit his stride in the early 1950s as a member of the Indians' great pitching staff. He won 20 games in five separate seasons. He hung on to pitch past his prime in an attempt to win 300 games, and hit the number right on the button. He was a tough competitor, who worked with a grim, fierce appearance.
Career pitching 1939-63: ERA 3.54; W-L 300-244, SO 2334. Best seasons: 1951: 20-13, 3.02 ERA; 1952: 23-12, .2.90 ERA; 1954: 23-11, 2.72 ERA; 1956: 20-9, 2.72 ERA; 1959: 22-10, 3.16 ERA.

Aleksandr YAKUSHEV (USSR)

ICE HOCKEY

Aleksandr Sergeyevich Yakushev. b. 2 Jan 1947 Balashikh, Moscow Oblast.

Olympic gold medallist with the winning USSR team in 1972 and 1976. In the 1972 series between the USSR and the NHL, Yakushev became known to the many North Americans who had not seen this wonder play hockey before. He was lightning fast, considered by many as the fastest skater in the world. He also skated for the Soviets on their world championship teams in 1967, 1969-70, 1973-5 and 1979, and played for the Spartak Club in the Soviet leagues. On his retirement he was 4th on the all-time goalscoring list among Soviet players.

Yasuhiro YAMASHITA (Japan)

JUDO

Yasuhiro Yamashita. b. 1 Jun 1957 Yabe, Kumamoto Prefecture.

The greatest judo player of his generation, he retired in 1985 after winning 203 successive contests from 1977, nearly all by *ippon*. In that time he won nine successive All-Japan Championships, four world titles (over 95kg 1979, 1981 and 1983 and the Open in 1981) and the Olympic Open gold medal in 1984.
He learnt his skills under the *sensei* Reisuki Shirashi, going on to Tokai University, and was 19 when he won his first Japanese title, making him the youngest ever champion. Four years later he became the first to win two gold medals at one World Championship. Missed the 1980 Olympics through the boycott but was supreme in Los Angeles, when at 1.80m tall he weighed 127 kg.

YANG Chuang-kwang (Tai)

ATHLETICS

Yang Chuang-kwang. b. 10 Jul 1933 Taitung.

Yang made his decathlon début by winning the Asian Games title in 1954 and was encouraged to persist at this discipline by Bob Mathias on a visit to Taiwan. In his next competition at the multi-event, Yang added over 1000 points to his score for 8th place at the 1956 Olympics. He reached the world top three in 1958 when he was second at the AAU Championships to Rafer Johnson, whom he joined as a student at UCLA. These training companions had a titanic duel at the 1960 Olympics, with Johnson winning narrowly.
Following Johnson's retirement Yang became the world's best all-rounder and the first man to exceed 9000 points on any scoring tables with his world record 9121 (8009 on the current tables) in 1963. Taking advantage of the benefits of the newly introduced fibre-glass pole he vaulted 4.84m in this competition, higher than the tables had a score for! He was ranked sixth in the world that year at the vault, with a best of 5.00. The change in the scoring tables in 1964 adversely affected him, bringing down his pole vault scores, and he was disappointing in finishing fifth in the Olympic decathlon.

YANG Yang (China)

BADMINTON

Yang Yang. b. 8 Dec 1963 Sichuan Province.

A small and wiry left-hander, with wins in 1987 and 1989 he was the first man to win two singles titles at the World Badminton Championships. In 1989 he also won the All-England title and at the time was unbeatable in major events. He had made his Thomas Cup début in 1984, when he beat the world champion Icuk Sugiarto even though China lost to Indonesia in the final, but was in the winning team in 1986 and 1988. In 1992 he coached the Malaysian team that won the Thomas Cup.

Cale YARBOROUGH (USA)

MOTOR RACING

William Caleb Yarborough. b. 23 Mar 1939 Timmonsville, South Carolina.

Winner of the NASCAR Winston Cup series each year 1976-8 and of the Daytona 500 four times, 1968, 1977, 1983-4.
He started soap-box racing at the age of ten, and after working in the family tobacco fields, gained his NASCAR licence in 1957. In 1968 he topped the Grand National circuit for big-bore stock cars with a record $126,066, and in 1977, when he was driver of the year for the first time, set a money record with $431,576. Once second in the all-time list for money earnings, he has been outstripped by some of the younger drivers but has a career total of $5,003,716 and is fifth in the NASCAR all-time list of race wins at 83.

George YARDLEY (USA)

BASKETBALL

George Harry Yardley. b. 23 Nov 1928 Hollywood, California.

The first great professional scorer at basketball. He played collegiately at Stanford and joined the NBA in 1953 with the Fort Wayne Pistons. In 1957 the Pistons moved to Detroit and Yardley thrilled the Detroit fans when he became the first NBA player to score 2,000 points in one season. Twice during that year he scored over 50 points in one game. In a seven-year career he played in six All-Star Games and finished his career with one season at Los Angeles in the soon defunct American Basketball League.

Lev YASHIN (USSR/Rus)

FOOTBALL

Lev Yashin. né Ivanovich. b. 22 Oct 1929 Moscow, d. 21 Mar 1990 Moscow.

One of the great stars of Soviet soccer and the only goalkeeper to be voted European Footballer of the Year (1963). Beginning as an ice hockey player with Moscow Dynamo, he began to take soccer seriously in 1951 and won 78 caps for the USSR from 1954-67. After winning a gold medal at the 1956 Olympics he played in three World Cups from 1958 to 1966 and helped the USSR to win the European Championship in 1960.
Known as the 'Black Panther', he helped Dynamo win the Russian League five times and the Cup twice, and with his striking personality and acrobatic performances he was Russia's most popular sportsman and was honoured by the State with many Orders and Decorations.
His retirement was marked by a testimonial game at the Lenin Stadium in 1971 when he captained Dynamo against a Rest of the World selection. He was appointed manager of Dynamo the following day.
His popularity extended far beyond his native Russia and his death from stomach cancer was mourned throughout the world of soccer.

Carl YASTRZEMSKI (USA)

BASEBALL

Carl Michael Yastrzemski. b. 22 Aug 1939 Southampton, New York.

'Yaz' took over left field for the Boston Red Sox from Ted Williams and became almost as much of a Hub legend to baseball fans. He never became quite the hitter that Williams was, but he led the American League in hitting three times, 1963 and 1967-8, led by his Triple Crown season of 1967 in which he batted .326, hit 44 home runs and had 121 RBI. In that year he led the Red Sox to their 'Impossible Dream' as they won the pennant after finishing 9th in 1966. In 1967 as the Sox leader he batted .523 in the last 12 games, going 7-for-8 in the last two games, as the Sox needed to win frequently in the last two

weeks to take the pennant over the Detroit Tigers and Minnesota Twins. He competed in another World Series in 1975, again leading the Red Sox. In addition to his hitting, he was a superb fielder in left field with a very strong arm. He won seven Gold Gloves and led the American League in outfield assists seven times.
Career 1961-83: 3419 hits Avg. .285, HR 452; RBI 1844; SB 168.

Vyacheslav YEKIMOV (USSR)

CYCLING
Vyacheslav Yekimov. b. 4 Feb 1966 Vyborg.

Yekimov first took up cycling in 1980 and immediately made his name as a great pursuiter, with a record-equalling three world titles an an amateur, 1985-6 and 1989 (2nd 1987), to which he has added another as a professional, 1990. He was world junior champion at points and team pursuit and runner-up in the individual pursuit in 1984. In 1988 in Seoul he won an Olympic gold medal at team pursuit, but was not chosen for the individual event with the availability of team-mate Gintautas Umaras. In late 1989, Yekimov made history when he was allowed to turn professional. Riding for Panasonic from 1990, he immediately became known as one of the fastest road sprinters and he added a further world title with the Points event in 1991.
Yekimov has set many world records on the track, including indoor records for the 1 hour 49.672 km in 1986, 4km 4:28.900 (1986), 5km 5:43.514 (1987) and 5:40.872 pro (1990); 10km 11:31.968 (1989), 20km 23:14.553 (1989).

Galina YERMOLAYEVA (USSR)

CYCLING
Galina Yermolayeva. b. 4 Feb 1937 Tula.

The most successful woman sprint cyclist at the World Championships, where between 1958 and 1973 she won 14 medals: 6 gold (1958-61, 1963, 1972), 5 silver, and 3 bronze. She failed to medal only in 1962 and 1966. She set a 1 kilometre standing start record with 1:16.2 in 1965.

Miruts YIFTER (Eth)

ATHLETICS
Miruts Yifter. b. 15 May 1944. Name in his native language of Beja - Yefter Mururuse.

His age was always shrouded in mystery, but there is no doubt that 'Yifter the Shifter' was pretty old when he won a wonderful 5000m and 10,000m double at the 1980 Olympics, even if he was not quite as old as he looked.
Yifter's first international success had been a third place at 10,000m in the Eastern and Central African Championships in 1970. A year later, running 5000m for Africa v USA, he miscounted the laps and hared off with two to go but stopped just as the gun went for the last lap! He came back the next day to win the 10,000m, however. He won the Olympic bronze at 10,000m in 1972 in a time of 27:40.96, which remained his best ever, but was left weeping as the 5000m final got underway, for he could not find the entrance to the track. He would very likely have starred in 1976, but was denied the chance of Olympic competition at the very last minute due to the African boycott. Misfortune came again at the end of his career when he was one of the Ethiopian team that misjudged the laps at the 1981 World Cross-country, and put in their burst a lap early.
He won gold at 10km and silver at 5km at the 1973 African Games and in both 1977 and 1979 the tiny (1.62m) man won the 5000m and 10,000m double at the World Cup, winning each race with his distinctive and devastating finishing kick. That kick came even off the fast pace at which the 5000m was run in 1977, when with 13:13.82 he missed the world record by just 0.9 sec.

Cy YOUNG (USA)

BASEBALL
Denton True Young. b. 29 Mar 1867 Gilmore, Ohio, d. 4 Nov 1955 Newcomerstown, Ohio.

His 511 wins stands as the all-time record for pitching in baseball history . He pitched for 22 seasons, averaging 23.2 wins per season. In his honour, the Cy

Young Award is given annually to the top pitcher in each league. He won over 20 games in 15 seasons, and over 30 games in five seasons. Having started 817 games, the most in history, he also lost a record 316 games. He was not a strikeout pitcher but had superb control, averaging only 1.5 walks per game throughout his career, which began with the Cleveland Spiders in the National League 1890-8, then the St Louis Cardinals 1899-1900, Boston Red Sox 1901-08, and Cleveland Indians 1909-11, with a brief foray with the Boston Braves to end his career.
Career pitching 1890-1911: ERA 2.63; W-L 511-316, SO 2803. Best seasons: 1892: 36-12, 1.93 ERA; 1893: 34-16, 3.36 ERA; 1895: 35-10, 3.24 ERA; 1901: 33-10, 1.63 ERA; 1902: 32-11, 2.15 ERA.

George YOUNG (UK)

FOOTBALL
George Lewis Young. b. 27 Oct 1922 Grangemouth, Stirlingshire.

At centre-half or right-back he dominated the defence for club and country in the seasons immediately following World War II. Only 18 months after joining Rangers in 1941 he played for Scotland in a wartime international. After the war he won a record 53 caps in full internationals, captained Scotland a record 48 times and set a record for the number of consecutive matches played for Scotland. Although these records have now been surpassed, he had the finest record of any Scottish international up to his time.
George Young remained loyal to Rangers throughout his playing career and helped them to win six Scottish League Championships, the Scottish Cup four times and the Scottish League Cup twice. In 1949 they won the treble for the first time in their history. Following his retirement in May 1957 he concentrated on his business interests which included a newspaper column and hotel management, but from 1959 to 1962 he was manager of Third Lanark. A man of imposing physique with a devastating tackle and an immensely powerful kick, he is sometimes only remembered for physical aspects of his game but he was also a fine tactician with excellent ball skills.

Jack YOUNG (Aus)

SPEEDWAY
Jack Young. b. 16 Apr 1924 Adelaide, d. Nov 1987 Adelaide.

In the early 1950s, a great period for speedway, Young was the greatest rider. In 1951, while riding for Edinburgh, he became the first Second Division rider to win the World Championship. The following year he moved to West Ham and again won the title to become the first man to win the World Championship twice. An immaculate and fearless rider, in all he rode in seven world finals, scoring 70 points in 35 races.

Kevin YOUNG (USA)

ATHLETICS
Kevin Curtis Young. b. 16 Sep 1966 Los Angeles.

Young smashed the 9-year-old world record of Ed Moses when he won the 1992 Olympic title for 400m hurdles in 46.78. A sociology graduate of UCLA, competing for Santa Monica Track Club, he had placed fourth at the 1988 Olympics and the 1991 World Championships, but had reached world number one status in 1990 before an unbeaten triumphant season in 1992. In 1993 he stretched his unbeaten run to 25 before being narrowly beaten by the 1991 World champion Samuel Matete (Zambia) in London in July. From 1989 he has usually run 13 strides all the way, as opposed to his previous practice of 12 strides between the first 4-5 hurdles of the event. He was NCAA champion 1987-8 and US champion 1992-3.
Other best times: 400m 45.11 (1992), 110mh 13.65 (1992), 200mh 22.74 (1992).

Sheila YOUNG (USA)

SPEED SKATING and CYCLING
Sheila Grace Young. b. 14 Oct 1950 Birmingham, Michigan. Later Ochowicz.

World sprint champion at two sports,

speed skating and cycling, in both 1973 and 1976, winning also at speed skating in 1975 and at cycling in 1981. At speed skating she narrowly missed the 1968 Olympic team, was 4th at 500m in 1972 and won three Olympic medals in 1976: gold at 500m, silver at 1500m, and bronze at 1000m. That year she set her third world record for 500m at 40.68. She won her first US speed skating title in 1970. After marriage to US Olympic cyclist Jim Ochowicz in 1976, she raced for a while under this name, but reverted to her maiden name out of courtesy to announcers.

Robin YOUNT (USA)

BASEBALL

Robin R Yount. b. 16 Sep 1955 Danville, Illinois.

One of the great shortstops of the late 20th century, with exceptional power. He has been a great team man, playing for the Milwaukee Brewers since he was their number one draft pick in 1973, excelling as a base runner and clutch hitter. On 9 Sep 1992 he became the 17th major league player to record 3000 hits, and only Ty Cobb and Hank Aaron have done so at a younger age. He has averaged over .300 in six seasons with a peak of .331 in 1982, when he had 210 hits, 29 HR and 114 RBI. He was named American League MVP in both 1982 and 1989. Yount underwent shoulder surgery in 1984, and his weakened arm forced him to move to the outfield for the Brewers. He is a fine all-round sportsman, with particular interest in motorcycling.
Career 1973-92: 3025 hits Avg. .287, HR 243; RBI 1355; SB 262.

Mario ZAGALO (Bra)

FOOTBALL

Mario Jorge Lobo Zagalo. b. 10 Mar 1928 Maceio.

After playing at outside-left in Brazil's World Cup winning team in 1958 and 1962, he was manager of the team which won the Cup in 1970. He began his professional career with Flamengo but moved to Botafogo in 1959 and helped them to the League title 1961-2. After winning 35 caps he retired in 1964 but stayed with Botafogo as a coach. He was appointed coach of the national side in March 1970 and only three months later masterminded their World Cup victory. Surprisingly, Botafogo did not retain his services at the end of the season and he moved to Fluminense who won the Rio Cup and the League Championship in 1971. The following season he was with Flamengo but after a poor showing by Brazil in the 1974 World Cup he took up a coaching appointment in Kuwait. Efficient rather than spectacular, but these qualities served him well both as a player and as a manager.

ZAHEER ABBAS (Pak)

CRICKET

Zaheer Abbas Syed. b. 24 Jul 1947 Sialkot.

The first Pakistan batsman to score 5000 runs in Test cricket and the first to score 100 centuries in first-class cricket, he excelled in going on to big scores when well set. Most notably he scored double centuries in Tests on his first two tours to England, 274 at Edgbaston in his second Test in 1971 (when he averaged 96.50 in the series), and 240 at The Oval in 1974. His highest run aggregates in Test series came against India, 583 at 194.33 in 1978/9 and 650 at 130.00 in 1982/3.
A most attractive stroke-player, he made his début for Karachi Whites in 1965, and played for Gloucestershire 1972-85. His most successful year in England was in 1976, when he scored 2554 runs at 75.11. He holds the record for eight times scoring a century in both innings of a first-class match, and for four of those being a double hundred with a hundred. Rather too diffident for a captain, he nonetheless led Pakistan in 14 Tests 1983-5.
78 Tests 1969-85: 5062 runs at 44.79, 12 100s HS 274; 3 wickets at 44.00, BB 2-21; 34 catches.
62 One-day Ints: 2572 runs at 47.62, 7 100s HS 123; 7 wickets at 31.85, BB 2-23; 16 catches.
First-class 1965-87: 24,843 runs at 51.54; 108 100s HS 274; 28 wickets at 37.82, BB 5-15; 262 catches.

Aleksandr ZAITSEV (USSR)

FIGURE SKATING
Aleksandr Gennadiyevich Zaitsev. b. 16 Jun 1952 Leningrad.

The most successful male pairs skater in history. Before he joined his future wife, Irina Rodnina, his best placing in the USSR Championships had been 16th, but they immediately became a brilliantly successful pair, winning their first USSR title in January 1973 and going on to six World (1973-78) and seven European (1973-8 and 1980) titles. Together, they also won the Olympic gold medals in 1976 and 1980.

Irina ZAITSEV (USSR) see RODNINA

Yuriy ZAKHAREVICH (USSR)

WEIGHTLIFTING
Yuriy Zakharevich. b. 18 Jan 1963 Mochshina, Ukraine.

By the late 1980s he was so dominant at 110kg that the super-heavyweights feared he might attempt to move up to their weight class. After second place in 1980, he was World Junior champion in 1981 and second to Blagoev in the senior championships at 90kg. Moving up to 110kg, he won the World Juniors but just lost at the seniors. He was undefeated from 1984, when Leonid Taranenko beat him at the Friendship Games, to 1988, when he smashed the world records for snatch with 210kg and total 455kg to win the Olympic title. Those records, plus his 1988 jerk record of 250.5kg and his 440kg total record at 100kg, remain unsurpassed five years later.
He was world champion each year 1985-7 and in both the 1986 Worlds and 1988 Olympics his total would have been enough to earn him the silver in the super-heavyweight class. Starting as a light-heavyweight, he set over 40 world records in all. In 1983, Zakharevich dislocated his elbow and was told he would never lift again, but he had surgery in which a synthetic tendon was used to rebuild the elbow and he returned better than before.

Tony ZALE (USA)

BOXING
né Anthony Florian Zaleski. b. 29 May 1913 Gary, Indiana.

Zale won 87 of 95 amateur fights, with 50 inside the distance. He turned professional in 1934 at age 21 and fought 28 times in his first year. After that he retired and did not return to boxing for two years. In 1940 he earned a middleweight title shot against Al Hostak and won by a knockout in 13. He unified the title a year later by defeating Georgie Abrams. Earlier in 1941 his fight against Billy Pryor attracted the highest non-paying audience to a fight, with 135,132 at Juneau Park, Milwaukee. Zale then joined the US Navy and did not box until the end of 1945. He fought six early bouts after his return before beginning three savage, memorable bouts with Rocky Graziano. Zale won the first and third fights. Three months later he defended his middleweight championship against Marcel Cerdan. Cerdan won in 12 and Zale promptly retired.
Career record: W - 67 (45), L - 18, D - 4.

Ricardo ZAMORA (Spa)

FOOTBALL
Ricardo Zamora Martinez. b. 21 Jan 1901 Barcelona, d. 18 Sep 1978 Barcelona.

Rated as the best goalkeeper in the world in the 1930s, his reputation was ruined in English eyes when he conceded seven goals against England at Highbury in 1931. At home he was idolised. He played for Español 1916-19 and 1922-30, Barcelona 1919-22, and FC (later Real) Madrid 1930-36. With Madrid he won two League and two Cup winners medals, having earlier won two Cup medals with Barcelona and one with Español.
Internationally, he won 46 caps for Spain in full internationals and an Olympic silver medal in 1920. In 1939 he became manager of Atlético Madrid and continued as a manager after World War II with a number of clubs, including his former club Español.
He made up for his lack of height with his brilliant anticipation and athleticism, and

his flamboyant style was typical of Continental goalkeepers of the era. His son Ricardo Zamora Jr played for Atlético Madrid and Valencia as a goalkeeper.

Carlos ZARATE (Mex)

BOXING

Carlos Zarate. b. 23 May 1951 Tepito.

Zarate may be the hardest puncher ever in the lighter weight classes. He won his first 23 bouts by KO, won one decision and then followed up with 28 consecutive knockouts. In 1976 he won the world bantamweight championship by knocking-out Rodolfo Martinez, and held that title until 1979 when he was decisioned by Lupe Pintor and then retired. His only other loss came in 1978 when he attempted to wrest the super-bantamweight title from Wilfredo Gomez, a bout matching two of the hardest punchers ever for small men. Zarate was stopped (round five) for the only time in his career. He eventually came back to twice challenge for the WBC super-bantamweight title in 1987 and 1988, but he was defeated by Jeff Fenech and Daniel Zaragosa respectively.

Career record: W -57 (54), L - 4, D - 0.

Emil ZÁTOPEK (Cs)

ATHLETICS

Emil Zátopek. b. 19 Sep 1922 Koprivnice, Moravia.

A running genius, whose dedicated hard work brought him unprecedented success. His seemingly agonised, head-rolling gait belied his control and indeed his charming personality. In 1948 he won the Olympic gold medal at 10,000m and silver at 5000m, when he left his sprint finish far too late, and in 1952 he completed a unique triple with wins at both these events and the marathon in his first attempt at the distance. In his last Olympic appearance he was 6th in the 1956 marathon. His first Czech records were set in 1944 and he was national champion eight times at 5000m and twice at 10,000m. He won his first 38 races at 10,000m from 1948 to 1954, including the European titles of 1950 and 1954, and in his whole career won 261 of 334 races at all distances. At 5000m he was 5th in the Europeans of 1946, 1st in 1950 and 3rd in 1954. At his peak supremacy, the three years 1949-51, he won all 69 races at various distances and was far superior to anyone else in the world. In all he set 18 world records: five at 10,000 from 29:28.2 in 1949 to 28:54.2 in 1954, the latter just one day after he had run a world record 13:57.2 for 5000m; two each at 6 miles, 20km, 1 hour, 15 miles, and 25km; and one each at 10 miles and 30km. At Stara Boleslav in 1951 he became the first to run more than 20km in an hour, 59:51.6 at 20km and 20,052m in all, passing 10 miles in a record 48:12.0. Zátopek was a national hero, but his support for the 'Prague Spring' cost him his Communist Party membership and his rank as a colonel in the army. After some hardship, however, he returned to public life, his indomitable spirit triumphing as always. The new freedom in his country has meant that once again he can accept invitations to travel around the world. A wonderfully warm-hearted man, he has been a hero to generations of runners.

Dana ZÁTOPKOVÁ (Cs)

ATHLETICS

Dana Zátopková. b. 19 Sep 1922 Tryskat. née Ingrova.

Wife of the great Emil Zátopek, and born on the same day, she was a major star in her own right as a javelin thrower. She competed in four Olympics, winning in 1952, just after Emil had been awarded the gold medal for the 5000m. She was second in the 1960 Olympics, and won the European titles of 1954 and 1958. She also won thirteen national titles between 1946 and 1960. Her personal best was 56.67m in 1958, having achieved a world record of 55.73 earlier that year at the age of 35 years 255 days, making her at the time the oldest ever women's world record holder.

Jan ZELEZNY (Cze)

ATHLETICS

Jan Zelezny. b. 16 Jun 1966 Mlada Boleslav.

Zelezny set his first world record at 87.66

in 1987, and later that year was third in the World Championships. In 1988 he took the Olympic silver but then failed to qualify for the finals of the 1990 Europeans and 1991 World Championships. In 1990 he had regained the world record, for just six days, with 89.66, and in 1991 he won at the European Cup, but in those years he was overshadowed by Steve Backley. In 1992, however, he was brilliant and won the Olympic gold medal in splendid style. The only drawback was that his 94.74 throw in Oslo in July was not allowed as a world record as it was made with a new 'Németh' javelin ruled to be illegal by the IAAF. However, in April 1993 in Pietersburg, South Africa he smashed Backley's 91.46 record with a tremendous 95.54 effort.

Leonid ZHABOTINSKY (USSR/Ukr)

WEIGHTLIFTING

Leonid Ivanovich Zhabotinsky. né Leonid Zhabotynsky. b. 28 Jan 1938 Uspenka, Sumskaia Oblast.

Zhabotinsky took over from Yuriy Vlasov as claimant to the title 'The World's Strongest Man'. Vlasov was heavily favoured to defend his Olympic title in 1964 at Tokyo, but Zhabotinsky, who had been 2nd in the Europeans and 3rd in the Worlds in 1963 behind Vlasov, defeated him by breaking the world record with 217.5kg in the clean and jerk. Zhabotinsky followed this with World titles in 1965 and 1966 and the 1968 Olympic title. He also won European Championships in 1966 and 1968. Zhabotinsky set 17 world records: 201.5kg press 1967, eight in the snatch from 165kg in 1963 to 183.5 in 1973, six in the jerk from 213kg in 1964 to 20 in 1968, and two for total, 560kg in 1964 and 590 in 1967.

Igor ZHELEZOVSKIY (USSR/Bls)

SPEED SKATING

Igor Zhelezovskiy. b. 1 Jul 1963 Orsha, Belarus.

With six titles, in 1985-6, 1989 and 1991-3, he holds the record for overall world sprint championships at ice skating. He also won the World Cup at 1000m in 1991-2 and at this distance set a world record of 1:12.58 in 1989. He had earlier set a 1500m world record of 1:52.50 in 1987. He disappointed at the Olympic Games as at his speciality of 1000m he was 3rd in 1988 and 6th in 1992. He was also 6th and 8th at 500m and 4th and 10th at 1500m at these Games.
Other best times: 500m 36.49 (1985).

ZHU Jianhua (China)

ATHLETICS

Zhu Jianhua. b. 29 May 1963 Shanghai.

Became the first Chinese male athlete to set an officially ratified world record when he high jumped 2.37m in 1983. He improved the record to 2.38 that year and to 2.39 in 1984, but he disappointed slightly at the major events as he took the bronze medals at both the World Championships in 1983 and the Olympics in 1984. He had set the first of seven Asian records at the age of 18 in 1981, when he won the first of four Asian titles with 2.30. His form declined with injuries in the later 1980s.
The ideal height at 1.96m tall, and very fast, he was, however, perhaps not strong enough for long competitions. He was a physical education student, continuing his studies at Cal State LA University, USA in 1991.

ZICO (Bra)

FOOTBALL

Artur Antunes Coimbra. b. 3 Mar 1953 Rio de Janeiro.

An impressive striker and midfield player who scored 66 goals in 88 internationals from 1975 (54 from 78 on a stricter definition). He was voted South American Footballer of the Year three times (1977, 1981-2) but the outcome of his three World Cup campaigns was disappointing. In 1978 and 1986 his appearances were restricted by injury, and in 1982 the Brazilian defence failed to match the abilities shown by their brilliant attacking players.
Apart from a spell in Italy with Udinese

1982-5, all his playing career from 1971 was with Flamengo where he was a member of the team which won the South American and World Club Championship in 1981. He retired in 1990 and was appointed Brazil's Minister for Sport. In 1993 he returned to play in Japan with Antlers of Kashima.

Nikolay ZIMYATOV (USSR)

NORDIC SKIING

Nikolay Zimyatov. b. 28 Jun 1955 Rumyantsevo, Moscow.

The winner of four Olympic gold medals at cross-country skiing, a treble in 1980 with 30km, 50km and relay, and the 50km in 1984, when this Soviet army captain added a relay silver; at 15km he was 4th in 1980 and 6th in 1984. He also won a World Championship relay title in 1982 with the USSR team.

ZITO (Bra)

FOOTBALL

Jose Eli de Miranda. b. 8 Aug 1932 Roseira.

An outstanding player whose brilliant midfield understanding with Didi made a major contribution to Brazil's World Cup victories in 1958 and 1962.
Beginning his career with Taubate, he was signed by Santos in 1952 and played in a variety of positions from striker to full-back before settling as a wing-half. Starting the 1958 World Cup as a reserve, he was brought into the team against Russia and retained his place for the remainder of the tournament and for the next World Cup in 1962. He only missed playing in his third World Cup in 1966 because of injury. When he retired in 1967 he had won 53 international caps, four Brazil Cup medals and two South American Cup and World Club Championship winners medals.

Wladyslaw ZMUDA (Poland)

FOOTBALL

Wladyslaw Zmuda. b. 8 Jun 1954 Lublin.

Played in 21 matches in the final stages of four World Cup tournaments (1974-86); only Uwe Seeler (Ger) has matched this total (1958-70).
Zmuda made 92 international appearances in all as a defender. He won championship medals with Slask Wroclaw and Widzew Lodz before leaving Poland in 1982 to play for Verona and later Cremonese in Italy.

Joop ZOETEMELK (Hol)

CYCLING

Gerardus Jozef Zoetemelk. b. 3 Dec 1946 The Hague.

Zoetemelk is the only winner of the Tour de France also to have won an Olympic gold medal, which came in the 100 kilometre team time-trial in 1968. He had a very long career, retiring after the 1987 season. He was a great all-rounder with few weaknesses but was unable to prevail over Merckx and Hinault for most of his career. In the Tour de France, which he contested until 1986, he had 10 stage wins and set a record by finishing the race 16 times and placing 11 times in the first five, wearing the Maillot Jaune for 22 days between 1971 and his triumph in 1980, when Hinault was forced to retire with knee problems. In 1985 he capped his career by outsprinting Greg LeMond to win the rainbow jersey of world professional road champion.
Major victories: Vuelta à España 1979 (and King of the Mountains 1971), Paris-Nice 1974, 1975, 1979; Flèche-Wallonne 1976; Paris-Tours 1977, 1979; Amstel Gold Race 1987.

Dino ZOFF (Ita)

FOOTBALL

Dino Zoff. b. 22 Feb 1942 Mariano del Friuli, Gorizia.

After an uncertain start to his career, he developed into one of the world's great goalkeepers. After playing for Udinese and Mantova he went to Napoli in 1967 and won the first of his record 112 caps (1968-83) for Italy the next season. In his first international season he was in the team

which won the European Championship, but it was only after moving to Juventus in 1972, at the age of 30, that he achieved star status. He won five League championships, two Italian Cups, the UEFA Cup, and captained Italy to victory in the 1982 World Cup. In all he made 570 First Division and 74 Second Division appearances in the Italian League to 1983. In 1988 he was appointed coach to Juventus, later moving to Lazio, and also coached the Italian Olympic team.
His record in defending his line was phenomenal and between September 1972 and June 1974 he played in 12 consecutive international matches (1143 minutes of play) without conceding a goal.

Gyula ZSIVÓTZKY (Hun)

ATHLETICS
Gyula Zsivótzky. b. 25 Feb 1937 Budapest.

A highly consistent hammer thrower throughout the 1960s. His championships record: Olympics: 1960 2nd, 1964 2nd, 1968 1st, 1972 5th; European: 1958 3rd, 1962 1st, 1966 2nd, 1969 4th, 1971 11th; World Student Games: 1963 2nd, 1965 1st. He was Hungarian champion each year from 1958 to 1970 and AAA champion in 1965 and 1966. He set two world records, in 1965 and 1968, the latter his best mark of 73.76m. He made a great recovery from a serious and life-threatening intestinal complaint at the end of 1963.

Pirmin ZURBRIGGEN (Swi)

ALPINE SKIING
Pirmin Zurbriggen. b. 4 Feb 1963 Saas-Almagell, Valais.

An outstanding, naturally talented, all-round skier, he was Olympic champion at downhill in 1988, when some thought that he might win at least three events. World champion at Alpine Combination and downhill 1985, giant slalom and super giant slalom 1987; he won the overall World Cup in 1984, 1987, 1988 and 1990, winning downhill 1987-8, giant slalom 1987 and super giant slalom each year 1987-90, making him one of only three men to have won at each of these disciplines. He made his World Cup début in 1980, when he was the European junior champion at downhill, and retired having won 40 World Cup races from 1982 to 1990, then the third highest ever total.
His sister Bernadette was a top-class downhill racer.

Galina ZYBINA (USSR)

ATHLETICS
Galina Ivanovna Zybina. b. 22 Jan 1931 Leningrad. Later Fyodorova.

Zybina set 14 world records in succession at the shot, from 15.19m in 1952 to 16.76m in 1956. Of these improvements eight were ratified by the IAAF. Her all-time best was 17.50m in 1964, by which time the record had been raised to 18.55m by Tamara Press. Zybina also set three world indoor bests between 1953 and 1958. Other bests: discus 48.62 (1955), javelin 54.98 (1958).
Her outstanding championships career record at the shot read: Olympics: 1st 1952, 2nd 1956, 7th 1960, 3rd 1964; Europeans: 4th 1950, 1st 1954, 3rd 1962, 4th 1966. She won European bronze medals at javelin in 1950 and discus in 1954, and was USSR champion at shot 1952-6 ,with nine second places and two thirds between 1951 and 1968, and at javelin 1952 and 1957.

w = whelped.

BALLYREGAN BOB

w. May 1983. Brindled dog *Ballyheigue Moon - Evening Daisy.*

He won a world record 32 successive races from 9 May 1985 to 9 Dec 1986. Bred by Robert Cunningham of Ballagh, Ireland, he won his one race in Ireland before coming to England where he was owned by Cliff Kevern and trained by George Curtis. In all he won 42 of his 48 races in Britain, 1984-6, setting 15 track records, and retired to stud with his run unbroken.

BRILLIANT BOB

w. 1931. *Other Ways - Birchfield Bessie.*

He was the first greyhound ever to win three classics in one year, when in 1934 he won the Laurels, Scurry Gold Cup and Cesarewitch, although only fourth in the Greyhound Derby. Bred in Co. Tipperary by Billy Quinn. As a puppy in 1933 he won the Tipperary Cup for coursing and, turning to track racing, won the Easter Cup and Irish St Leger. He was sold in 1934 for £2000 to the trainer Sidney Orton and retired to stud after his outstanding year.

FUTURE CUTLET

w. April 1929. Brindled dog *Mutton Cutlet - Wary Guide.*

He won four classics over a four year period, the Laurels in 1931, Cesarewitch 1931-2, and after second place in 1932, the Greyhound Derby in 1933, at four the oldest ever winner. Born and bred in Ireland, he was bought for £600 by W A Evershed and sent to Sidney Probert at Wembley. A beautifully proportioned dog and an exceptionally fast starter.

MICK THE MILLER

w. June 1926 Ireland, d. 5 May 1939. Brindled dog *Lei Glorious Event - Na Boc.*

The most famous of all racing greyhounds. Originally owned by Father Martin Brophy, he was a weakly pup and made a late start to racing, but won his first race at Shelbourne Park on 18 Apr 1928. He won 15 of 20 races in Ireland, where he was trained by Mick Horan, before going to England in 1929, where after a sensational trial he was sold for a record 800 guineas at auction to London bookmaker Albert Williams. In his first races he won the preliminary three rounds and then the Greyhound Derby itself; he was then sold for 2000 guineas to Mrs Arundel Kempton, who sent him for training to Sidney Orton of Aylsham, Norfolk.

In 1930 he become the first dog to win the Derby twice, and only two days later won the Cesarewitch. He was again first past the post in the 1931 Derby, but that was declared 'no race' after other dogs became involved in fighting, and he was only fourth on the re-run. In all he won 46 of his 61 races in Britain, including 19 in succession in 1929-30. In his last race he won the St Leger over 700 yards, the longest distance he ever raced, at Wembley on 3 Oct 1931. He set numerous national and world records and was at his best at distances from 525 to 700 yards. A calm dog, he was content to sit in behind the fast starters, cutting into the rails and winning on his stamina. He starred in the film of his life *Wild Boy* in 1935, and after his death his body was embalmed and sent for display to the Natural History Museum in London.

MILE BUSH PRIDE

w. 1956. *Grand Champion - Witching Dancer.*

This brindled dog became, in 1959, the second greyhound ever to win the triple crown of English, Welsh and Scottish Derbys. Later in that year he added the Cesarewitch. He was bred by Nora Johnston in Co. Wexford, Ireland, bought by Noel Purvis and sent to Jack Harvey at Wembley. He retired after placing third in the 1960 Greyhound Derby.

PATRICIA'S HOPE

w. July 1970 Ireland. *Silver Hope - Patricia.*

This speedy white and fawn dog was only the second to win two Greyhound Derbys. He came to England in 1972 for that race, winning as a rank outsider by four lengths. Trained by Adam Jackson at Clapton, within a month he won £14,000 by becoming the third greyhound ever to win the triple crown of English, Welsh and Scottish Derbys. He then retired to John O'Connor's stud in Ireland. Initially owned by Basil Marks and Brian Stanley, John O'Connor later purchased Mr Stanley's share and it was mainly through his influence that *Patricia's Hope* returned to racing in 1973 to win his second Derby.

PIGALLE WONDER

w. March 1956, d. January 1969. Brindled dog *Champion Prince - Prairie Peg.*

The winner of the 1958 Greyhound Derby, where he set a record time of 28.44 (for 525y) in his semi-final. Later that year he dead-heated for the Cesarewitch with *Ryland Pleasure*. He was bred and reared in Ireland by Tom Murphy, and originally named *Prairie Champion* when he won his first race at Kilkenny on 10 Oct 1957 by ten lengths. Bought by Al Burnett and trained by Jim Syder Jr at Wembley, he went on to spectacular success, winning almost £8000 in prize money and starting at odds-on in 52 of his 60 races in Britain. After his last race at Shelbourne Park on 13 Aug 1960 he had a most successful stud career. He was sold in 1963 for £3500, a record for a greyhound after its racing career, to Mr A H Lucas of Bray, Wicklow.

SCURLOGUE CHAMP

w. July 1982. Black dog *Sand Man - Old Rip.*

In his spectacular greyhound racing career, he won 51 of his 63 races in Britain, including the Cesarewitch in 1985 and the BBC Television Trophy in 1985-6. These were races of between 815 and 853m, and he excelled at such distances, for he set 20 track records at between 663 and 888m. His usual racing tactic was to seemingly show no interest for the first 500m, often being trailed off by up to 20 lengths, but then to storm through the field. He was bought for £1700 by Ken Peckham at Shelbourne Park and made his début with a win at the White City on 7 Jul 1984. He was unsuccessful at stud.

SHERRY'S PRINCE

w. Apr 1967. d. 1978.

His record of being undefeated in the Grand National for three successive years is one of the greatest feats in the history of greyhound racing. After giving up flat racing in April 1969 he developed into the greatest hurdler in history. Between April 1970 and May 1972 he won 70 races and was second 15 times in 105 starts. *Sherry's Prince* won his first Grand National in 1970 and the following year equalled the record of *Juvenile Classic* by winning the event for a second time. In 1972 he won for an unprecedented third time and, as in the two previous years, he also won his heat and semi-final. Throughout his life he was owned by Mrs Joyce Mathews of Sanderstead, Surrey.

TREV'S PERFECTION

w. 1944. Brindled dog *Trev's Dispatch - Friar Tuck.*

In 1947 he became the first greyhound to win the triple crown of English, Welsh and Scottish Derbys. He had been bought by Fred Trevillion for £900 despite going 18 months without a win, and given this, his third name, achieving immediate success with a first win at the White City, followed by success in the Gold Collar and his grand slam. He was bred and reared by H G Hunn in Cumbria as *Highland Perfection*. In 1946 he was bought by Nora Rose and raced as *Matt's Regret*. Noted for his speed from the trap, courage and track-craft, he went to the USA in 1948 but met with no success in five races.

On the first line for each horse, is shown: colour (b - bay, br - brown, ch - chestnut, gr - grey); c for colt, f for filly, g for gelding; date of foaling (and death); sire - dam.

ABERNANT

gr c. 1946, d. 1970. *Owen Tudor - Rustam Mahal.*

Brilliant sprinter, who was Britain's top-rated colt at 2, 3 and 4. In all he won 14 races worth £26,394. At two he won four times, including the Middle Park Stakes. In 1949 he was beaten a short head by *Nimbus* in the 2000 Guineas, before reverting to sprinting. He won the July Cup and Nunthorpe Stakes in both 1949 and 1950, and the King's Stand Stakes in 1949. He was bred by Lady Macdonald-Buchanan, and trained by Noel Murless. During his long stud career he sired the winners of over 1000 races.

AFFIRMED

ch c. 1975 near Ocala, Florida. *Exclusive Native - Won't Tell You (Chenille?).*

In 1978 he won the US Triple Crown, although later beaten twice by the 1977 Triple Crown winner *Seattle Slew*. As a four-year-old he lost two races but ended with seven successive wins and was voted Horse of the Year for the second year in succession. In his career he was the first horse to exceed $2 million, $2,393,818 from 22 wins (including 14 Grade One races) in 29 starts in 1977-9. Bred and raced by Louis Wolfson's Harbor View Farm and trained by Lazaro Barrera.

ALCIDE

b c. 1955, d. 1973. *Alycidon - Chenille.*

A difficult horse to train, yet lazy on the racecourse. He was favourite for the Derby in 1958, but was unable to contest the race due to an accident at the stables, thought by some to his being 'got at'. He was nonetheless rated the top horse in Europe that year, after he had returned to win the Great Voltigeur Stakes and St Leger in spectacular fashion At four he was second in the Ascot Gold Cup after rapping a joint just two weeks earlier, and then won his last race, the King George VI and Queen Elizabeth Stakes. In all he won eight races, worth £56,042. Owned by Sir Humphrey de Trafford and trained by Cecil Boyd-Rochfort. *Alcide* stood as a sire at the National Stud, West Grinstead.

ALLEGED

b c. 1974 Kentucky. *Hoist The Flag - Princess Pout.*

He won nine of his ten races 1976-8, earning £338,614, then a record for a horse trained in the British Isles. His successes were headed by the Prix de l'Arc de Triomphe at 3 and 4, only the sixth horse to win this great race twice. Bred in America by June McKnight, he was bought as a yearling for just $40,000 by Monty Roberts, who sold him six months later for $175,000 to Robert Sangster. As he was considered unsuitable for racing on dirt in the USA, he was sent to Vincent O'Brien in Ireland. Rather backward, he raced only once at two, but won then by eight lengths. At three his preparations were aimed at an autumn campaign. The only defeat of his career was at odds-on in the 1977 St Leger to *Dunfermline*. After his two triumphs in the Arc he was syndicated as a stallion for around $7 million, and has proved a success at Walmac Farm in Kentucky.

ALLEZ FRANCE

b f. 1970, d. Dec 1989 Kentucky. *Sea Bird II - Priceless Gem.*

A filly rated the best horse in Europe at four in 1974, when she won all her five races including the Prix Ganay and Prix de l'Arc de Triomphe. As a two-year-old she won both her races, and at three she won 3 from 7, the Poule d'Essai des Pouliches, Prix de Diane and Prix Vermeille, and was second in the Arc to *Rheingold*. Owned by Daniel Wildenstein and trained at Chantilly, first by Albert Klimscha and then by Angel Penna. Magnificent looking and impeccably bred, with 13 wins in 21 races from 1972 to 1975, she won £493,100, a total exceeded at that time among European-based horses only by *Dahlia*, yet she beat *Dahlia* on all six occasions that they met. Retired to the USA, but failed as a brood-mare.

ALYCIDON

ch c. 1945, d. 1963. *Donatello II - Aurora.*

One of the greatest stayers of all time, in 1949 he was the first since 1879 to win the triple of Ascot, Goodwood and Doncaster Cups. He then retired having won 11 races worth £37,201. Bred by the 17th Earl of Derby and trained by Walter Earl. Very powerful, but tending to laziness, he was equipped with blinkers and provided with pacemakers both in training and for his big races. Twice unplaced at two, at three he won six times. He was second in the St Leger that year, 1948, the last defeat of his career. Standing at the Woodpark Stud, he was consistently high in the leading sires list, and champion in England in 1955. His progeny included *Alcide* and *Meld.*

ALYDAR

f. 1975 Calumet Farm, Lexington, Kentucky, d. 15 Nov 1990 Lexington. *Raise A Native - Sweet Tooth.*

In 1978 he was runner-up to *Affirmed* in all three races of the US Triple Crown, a unique achievement, losing by margins of 1.5 lengths, a neck and a head. That final race, the Belmont Stakes, in which they raced head-to-head for 1 $^{1}/_{2}$ miles, is considered the greatest American horse race of all time. In his career he won three of his ten clashes with *Affirmed*, and in all, 14 of his 26 races: 5/10 at two, 7/10 at three (including four Group One races) and 2/6 at four, earning a total of $957,195.
Possessed of brilliant acceleration, he went on to be a major stallion at Calumet Farm, sire of 45 stakes winners during his lifetime, including such noted horses as *Alysheba*, *Easy Goer* and *Turkoman*.
He had to be put down after breaking a leg in a stall accident (later questioned).

ALYSHEBA

f. 3 Mar 1984. *Alydar - .*

Passed *John Henry's* record by winning $6,679,242 in his career 1986-88, with 11 wins from 26 races. At two he won just one of his seven races. In 1987 he won three of ten races, including the Kentucky Derby and Preakness Stakes, but was beaten by a nose by *Ferdinand* in the Breeders' Cup Classic. In 1988 he won that, his last, race and was US Horse of the Year, having won seven of his nine races. Retired to stand at stud at Land's End Farm, Kentucky.
A tough and consistent horse, he was bred by Preston Madden, who sold him for $500,000 at the Keeneland Sales to the Scharbauer family. Trained by Jack Van Berg.

ARKLE

f. 19 Apr 1957, d. 31 May 1970 Bryanstown, Co. Kildare. *Archive - Bright Cherry.*

The greatest steeplechaser of all-time. He won the Cheltenham Gold Cup in 1964, 1965 and 1966. By the last year, when he won by 30 lengths, he was 3 stone superior to any other steeplechaser. His other wins included the Irish Grand National 1964, Whitbread Gold Cup and King George VI Chase 1965; Hennessy Gold Cup 1964-5, Leopardstown Chase 1964-6. He lost the first of five races against *Mill House* when he slipped on landing at the final ditch in the 1963 Hennessy, but won the next, an epic clash in the 1964 Cheltenham Gold Cup, and was totally dominant in all subsequent encounters.
Bred by Mary Baker in Co. Dublin, his dam had won six chases and a hurdle race. *Arkle* was bought by Anne, Duchess of Westminster for 1150 guineas as a 3-year-old, and trained by Tom Dreaper. His career ended prematurely when he broke a pedal bone in the King George VI Chase on 26 Dec 1966. In all he raced 35 times, won 1/3 on the flat, 4/6 at hurdles and of his 26 steeplechases won 22 and was second twice and third twice, winning the then record prize money of £78,824. He

was a noble, kind and intelligent animal, a brilliant chaser, who never fell on the racecourse, and hugely popular.

BAHRAM

b c. 1932, d. 24 Jan 1956 Argentina. *Blandford - Friar's Daughter.*

The winner of all his nine races, he was the best of his generation at two, when he won five races, and at three, when he won the Triple Crown in England in 1934. Owned and bred by the Aga Khan, and trained by Frank Butters at Newmarket. At stud he had some success in England and was sold to an American syndicate for $160,000 in 1940, but was not successful in the USA or later in Argentina.

BALLYMOSS

ch c. 1954. *Mossborough - Indian Call.*

With eight wins in 17 races 1956-8, he became the first horse from the British Isles to win over £100,000 with a total of £114,150. After placing second to *Crepello* in the Epsom Derby, he won two classics, the Irish Derby and St Leger, but reached his peak at four when he won the Coronation Cup, Eclipse Stakes, King George VI and Queen Elizabeth Stakes and Prix de l'Arc de Triomphe, to be rated the champion of Europe. At two he had won only one of his four races.
Owned by American John McShain, who paid 4,500 guineas for him as a yearling, and trained by Vincent O'Brien in Ireland. He was champion sire in England in 1967, in which year his son *Royal Palace* won the Derby.

BEACH TOWEL

f. 1987. *French Chef - Sunburn.*

As a 3-year-old in 1990 this powerful pacer became the first harness horse to win over $2 million in a year, with $2,091,860 from 18 wins in 23 races, ending with the Breeders' Crown which he won in a race record 1:51 2/5. Trained and driven by Ray Remmen (Can), he had been bought for a bargain $22,000 at Lexington by Seth Rosenfeld as a yearling. As a 2-year-old he had won $478,479 with 11 wins in 13 races, and after his brilliant year in 1990 retired to stand at stud at Walnridge Farm, Cream Ridge, New Jersey. His great grandsire was *Nevele Pride.*

BOLD RULER

br c. 6 Apr 1954, d. July 1971. *Nasrullah - Miss Disco.*

US Horse of the Year in 1957, when he won 11 of 16 races, including the Preakness Stakes. He became a noted sire of fast, early maturing horses at Claiborne Farms, Kentucky, and headed the American list eight times, 1963-9 and 1973, when his son *Secretariat* won the Triple Crown. At two he had won seven of his ten races, placing second in the Free Handicap, and at four won four races before injuring an ankle in his last race. Bred by Ogden Phipps and trained by Jim Fitzsimmons.

BRET HANOVER

b c. 19 May 1962 Pennsylvania. d. Nov 1992. *Adios - Brenna Hanover.*

The first two-year-old to be named Harness Horse of the Year, in 1964 when unbeaten in 24 races. He then became the first harness horse to achieve this honour three times, as he repeated in 1965 and 1966. In these three years he won 62 races from 68 starts, with five seconds and a third, and earned a total of $922,616, then an all-time record.
In 1965 he won pacing's Triple Crown of the Little Brown Jug, Messenger and Cane Futurity, and became the first horse to achieve prize money of over $300,000 in a season with $341,784. That figure was increased to $407,534 in 1966. He ran mile records in 1965 of 1:55 at Indianapolis on a mile track and 1:57 at Delaware, Ohio on a half-mile track, and in 1966 ran a time trial in 1:53.3 at Lexington.
Bought for $50,000 as a yearling by Richard Downing, he was trained and driven by Frank Ervin. Purchased for $2 million and retired to stud after the 1966 season.

BRIGADIER GERARD

b c. 1968, d. 29 Oct 1989 Newmarket. *Queen's Hussar - La Paiva.*

Bred by John Hislop, this handsome 16.2 hands horse won 17 of his 18 races, four at two, including the Middle Park Stakes, and a European record 13 pattern races in 1971-2; six Group 1, six Group 2 and one Group 3, starting with a win over two great horses, *Mill Reef* and *My Swallow,* in the 2000 Guineas. There were four other wins at 1 mile in 1971, and he ended that year with a win at 1m 2f in the Champion Stakes. In 1972, when he was a unanimous choice for British Racehorse of the Year, he won seven races from 1m to 1m 4f, the latter the King George VI and Queen Elizabeth Stakes. His one loss, after 15 successive wins, was to *Roberto* in the Benson & Hedges Gold Cup at York. That year he achieved a *Timeform* rating of 144, the second equal highest ever, having also been joint top-rated at 141 the previous year. He was trained by Dick Hern and ridden in all his races by Joe Mercer.
A most powerful and handsome horse, his prowess over a mile has been matched in England only by *Tudor Minstrel*. He retired to stand at the Egerton Stud in Newmarket.

BROWN JACK

br g. 1924, d. 1948. *Jackdaw - Querquidella.*

A great stayer, and one of the most popular horses of the century. Gelded as a yearling, he raced until the age of ten, winning the Queen Alexandra Stakes, ridden by Steve Donoghue, six times 1929-34, a record for any major race this century. In all from 1926 to 1934 he had 65 races, winning 25. Most unusually he was a hurdler, winning seven of ten races in 1928 including the Champion Hurdle, before his flat racing success. He was bred in Ireland by George Webb, and bought for 750 guineas by the Hon. Aubrey Hastings for Sir Harold Wernher.

BUCKPASSER

b c. 1963 Lexington, Kentucky, d. 6 Mar 1978 Paris, Kentucky. *Tom Fool - Busanda.*

US Horse of the Year in 1966, despite missing the classic races because of a cracked bone in his ankle, when he won 13 of 14 races, setting a world record for the mile of 1:32 $^{3}/_{5}$ in the Arlington Classic. He had won nine of 11 starts at two and went on to a further three wins in six races at four for a career record of 25 wins from 31 races. Bred and owned by Ogden Phipps. He retired to Claiborne Farms where he was syndicated for $4,800,000.

The BYERLEY TURK

c. 1680.

The first of the three stallions from whom all modern thoroughbreds descend in the male line, particularly from his great great grandson *Herod* (f. 1758). He was taken by Captain (later Colonel) Robert Byerley when Buda was captured from the Turks in 1687. The Turk was ridden by his owner at the Battle of the Boyne in 1689, and was sent to stud, first at Middridge Grange in County Durham and then at Goldsborough Hall, near York.

CAPTAIN CHRISTY

b g. 1967, d. 1977. *Mon Capitaine - Christy's Bow.*

A tearaway and a difficult horse to handle, but at his best a top-class steeplechaser. He won the King George VI Chase in 1974 and 1975 and the Cheltenham Gold Cup in 1974.
Bred by George Williams in West Cork, he was sold as a yearling for 290 guineas. After several owners, he was bought for Mrs Jane Samuel in 1972 and trained by Pat Taaffe. In his career 1971-75, he won 2/7 on the flat, 6/15 over hurdles, including the 1973 Irish Sweeps Hurdle, and 12/24 chases. His career ended prematurely due to tendon problems after a devasting 30 lengths win over *Bula* in his last race, the 1975 King George VI Chase.

CARBINE

b c. 1885 Sylvia Park, Auckland, NZ, d. 1914. *Musket - Mersey.*

Racing mainly in Australia, he had 33 wins in 43 races, and the only time he went unplaced was due to lameness. He won the 1890 Melbourne Cup in record time, 3:28 $^1/_4$, with 10st 5lb, still the heaviest winning weight. His career total of £59,252 was an Australian record for 25 years. His sire and dam were both English horses exported to New Zealand. Owned by Dan O'Brien, he was unbeaten as a two-year-old in New Zealand. Sent to Australia, he went from strength to strength, with his Melbourne Cup win at five the climax of his career. He started his stud career in Australia, but was bought for 13,000 guineas by the Duke of Portland, who brought him to England in 1895 to stand at the Welbeck Stud. He sired the 1906 Derby winner *Spearmint*. After his death his remains were shipped back to Australia.

CITATION

b c. Apr 1945 Lexington, Kentucky, d. 8 Aug 1970 Lexington. *Bull Lea - Hydroplane II.*

The first horse to win over $1 million. In 1948 he became the second US Triple Crown winner for his owner Warren Wright. Ridden by Eddie Arcaro, he won each race by clear margins, 3$^1/_2$, 4$^1/_2$ and 18 lengths. Trained by Benjamin Allyn 'Jimmy' Jones at Calumet Farm, he won 8 of 9 races as a 2-year-old and 14 of 20 at three, when he was voted Horse of the Year, at all distances from 4$^1/_2$ furlongs to 2 miles. He then suffered a fetlock injury and was out of racing for over a year, but was kept in training and in 1951 became the first equine dollar millionaire when winning the Hollywood Gold Cup. He was then retired to stud, but there disappointed. His career total, with 32 wins in 45 races, was $1,085,760, including a season's record $709,470 in 1948. There is a life-sized statue of *Citation* at Hialeah Park.

COLIN

br c. 1905 Lexington, Kentucky d. 1932 Middleburg, Virginia. *Commando - Pastorella.*

Unbeaten in his 15 races 1904-5, all in the state of New York; 12 at two and 3 at three before a leg injury ended his career. Owned by James R Keene and trained by James Rowe before being sent to Sam Darling in England in an unavailing attempt to get him racing again.

COTTAGE RAKE

br g. 1939, d. Fermoy, Co. Cork. *Cottage - Hartingo.*

A quick, brilliant jumper, he was the first great horse trained by Vincent O'Brien. He was the second horse to win three successive Cheltenham Gold Cups, 1948-50, in each of which he was ridden by Aubrey Brabazon. He was bred by Dr TJ Vaughan, and had his first race, on the flat, at the age of 6 in 1945. He won his next two races, including a hurdle race, and was sold in 1946 for £1000 to Frank Vickerman, who was the first owner for O'Brien. *Cottage Rake* won his first steeplechase, at Leopardstown on 26 Dec 1946, by 20 lengths and on the flat won the Irish Cesarewitch in 1947. The 1950 Gold Cup was his last win, although he continued to race occasionally for the next three years. He won 16 of his 39 races, 1945-53.

COUNT FLEET

br c. Mar 1940 Paris, Kentucky. d. 3 Dec 1973 Paris. *Reigh Count - Quickly.*

The US Triple Crown winner in 1943, ridden by Johnny Longden. Bred by Mrs Francis Hertz and trained by Dan Cameron, he was temperamental and slightly built, but soon showed his class by winning ten of 15 races as a 2-year-old. At three he was unbeaten in his six races, winning the Kentucky Derby by three lengths, when at 1-2 he was the shortest price favourite ever for that race. He was at even more prohibitive odds of 3-20 for the Preakness, which he won by eight lengths, and at 1-20 when he won the Belmont in a record time of 2:28 $^1/_5$ by 25 lengths, a record distance until bettered by *Secretariat*. He carried the distinctive black and yellow colours of his owner John D Hertz, the rental car magnate. Unfortunately a bowed tendon injury sustained in that race caused the termination of his racing career. He became a leading sire.

CREPELLO

ch c. 1954, d. 1974. *Donatello II - Crepescule.*

A strong and handsome colt standing 16.2 $^{1}/_{2}$ hands, but with weak legs, he was brilliantly trained by Noel Murless. Lester Piggott considered him at the time the best horse he had ever ridden when he steered him to victory in the 2000 Guineas and Derby in 1957. Bred and owned by Sir Victor Sassoon, he was retired to stand at Eve Stud, Newmarket without being able to show the full extent of his ability due to tendon strain after racing just five times with three wins. He was leading sire in 1969.

DAHLIA

ch f. 1970. *Vaguely Noble - Charming Alibi.*

In her racing career 1972-6, *Dahlia* won 15 of her 35 races and £1,535,443, a world earnings record for fillies or mares that nearly doubled the previous best, yet she lost on all six encounters with *Allez France*. She won races in Canada, England, France, Ireland and the USA. Voted Horse of the Year in Britain 1973, when her six wins included the Irish Oaks, King George VI and Queen Elizabeth Stakes (by six lengths from a talented field) and the Washington DC International, and in 1974, when her five wins were the Grand Prix de Saint-Cloud, King George again, the only horse ever to win this race twice, Benson & Hedges Gold Cup, Man O'War Stakes and Canadian International Championship. In 1975 she won the Benson & Hedges for the second time. Bred and owned by Nelson Bunker Hunt and trained by Maurice Zilber.

DANCING BRAVE

b c. 11 May 1983 Glen Oak Farm, Kentucky. *Lyphard - Navajo Princess.*

One of the greatest of racehorses, yet beaten in the 1986 Derby by *Shahrastani*, for which many blamed his jockey's tactics. He won both his races at two, before his 3-year-old season when he was the Horse of the Year in Britain and France, and of his eight races won six, including the 2000 Guineas, Eclipse Stakes, King George VI and Queen Elizabeth Stakes and Prix de l'Arc de Triomphe, the latter in record time, and earned £980,310. His *Timeform* rating of 141 was the highest of the decade.

He was bought as a yearling for $200,000 for Prince Khalid bin Abdullah, and trained in England by Guy Harwood. He had a brilliant finish, but it was not quite enough to make up ground lost in the Derby at Epsom. At the end of his great season he was sent to California for the Breeders' Cup Turf, but trailed in fourth. He was then syndicated for £14 million to stand at Sheikh Mohammed's Dalham Hall Stud.

Through illness he made a slow start as a stallion and was sold at the end of 1991 to Japan, where, standing at the Shizunai Stallion Stud, Hokkaido, he is becoming most successful.

DAN PATCH

b c. 1896 Oxford, Indiana, d. 11 Jul 1916 Minneapolis. *Joe Patchen - Zelica.*

Hugely popular pacer, who reduced the mile record of 1: 59 $^{1}/_{4}$ each year from 1902 to a time of 1: 55 $^{1}/_{4}$ at the Red Mile in Lexington in October 1905. That time stood as a record for 33 years. Bred by Hoosier Dan Messner Jr, he was sold in 1901 for $20,000 to M E Sturgis of Buffalo and then in 1902 to M W Savage of Minneapolis for $60,000. By then he had exhausted legitimate competition on his tours around the USA, and entered a series of exhibition races against records. Savage's promotion made *Dan Patch* a national celebrity who thrilled crowds all over the country until he retired undefeated in 1909, the holder of nine world records. His heartbroken owner died the day after his great horse.

The DARLEY ARABIAN

b c. 1700 Aleppo, Syria, d. 1730 Aldby, Yorkshire.

The second of the three stallions from whom all modern thoroughbreds descend in the male line, to be brought to England. His male line has become much the most important of the modern era. An Arabian horse of the Manicha race, a bay with three white feet, he was exported by the British Consul in Aleppo, Thomas Darley, to his brother's stud in Yorkshire at the age of four.

DAWN RUN

b m. 1978 Ireland, d. 27 Jun 1986 Auteuil. *Deep Run - Twilight Slave.*

The first horse to complete the Champion Hurdle/Gold Cup double at Cheltenham, the former in 1984, the latter in 1986; she was killed in a fall in the Grande Course de Haies at Auteuil just three months later. She was bought as a yearling for 5800 guineas by Charmian Hill, who rode *Dawn Run* to her first victory in a 'bumper' race on the flat, at the age of 62, and trained by Paddy Mullins at Goresbridge, Co. Kilkenny. After a brilliant hurdling campaign in 1983/4 with eight wins in nine races, she won her first race over fences in November 1984, but was then absent from the racecourse for 13 months before winning the Gold Cup in just her fifth race over fences. In her career *Dawn Run* won 18 of her 28 races under National Hunt rules (13/21 hurdles, 5/7 chases), setting a record with £278,837. She also won three of seven flat races.

DESERT ORCHID

gr g. 11 Apr 1979 Ab Kettleby, Leicestershire. *Grey Mirage - Flower Child.*

The most popular steeplechaser in the British Isles since *Arkle*. The striking, near-white horse was the subject during his racing career of books and TV documentaries, fully justified by brilliant steeplechasing campaigns. Although not suited by left-handed tracks, he won the Cheltenham Gold Cup in 1989 and was third in 1990 and 1991. He showed his best form in the King George VI Chase at Kempton, which he won a record four times 1986, 1988-90, but retired after falling in that race on 26 Dec 1991. He also won the 1988 Whitbread Gold Cup, and in all a record £654,413 in prize money with 34 wins from his 72 races, 1983-91.
Bred by James Burridge, whose son Richard retained a half-share in *Desert Orchid* and sent him for training to David Elsworth. After indifferent running in his first season, he won 6/8 hurdle races in 1983/4, although unplaced in the Champion Hurdle. A poor season with just one win from 9 races in 1984/5 was followed by his chasing début on 1 Nov 1985 at Devon & Exeter, the first of four successive wins in novice chases. He showed his greatness in his first race at 3 miles, when he won the 1986 King George by 15 lengths. National Hunt Horse of the Year each year from 1986/7 to 1989/90.

DIOMED

ch c. 1777, d. 1808. *Florizel* - a *Spectator* mare.

Winner of the first Derby in 1780, and much later a great sire in the USA. He was bred by Richard Vernon of Newmarket and sold to Sir Charles Bunbury. After winning his seven races as a 3-year-old he had a fairly unsuccessful racing career. His stud career was disappointing until at the age of 21 he was sold for 50 guineas to John Hoomes of Virginia, who shipped him across the Atlantic and sold him for £1000 to Colonel Miles Selden. Despite a poor reputation, he proved an immediate success, creating the dominant line in America in the 19th century.

DR FAGER

b c. 1964 Ocala, Florida *Lyphard - Navajo Princess.*

In his racing career, 1964-6, he won 18 of 22 starts, including the fastest ever mile, 1:32.2 when carrying 134 lbs in the 1968 Washington Park Handicap, and amassed total career earnings of $1,002,642. He was Horse of the Year in the US in 1968, when he was also voted champion sprinter, best grass horse and champion handicapper. Bred by W L McKnight and trained by John Nerud, he was an immediate sensation at two, when he won his first four races by an average of seven lengths. He was champion sire in the USA in 1977.

EASTER HERO

ch g. 1920 near Greenogue, Co. Dublin, Ireland, d. 1948. *My Prince - Easter Week.*

A brilliant jumper, this handsome horse was thought of as the first of the 'new' chasers, and achieved unrivalled popularity. He won the Cheltenham Gold Cup in 1929 and 1930, both by 20 lengths, but failed in his bids at the Grand National. In 1928 he misjudged the Canal Turn and caused a pile-up, and in 1929 he ran a gallant second with 12st 7lb despite a twisted plate.

Bred by Larry King who sold him to Mr Bartholomew, for whom he ran eight times, winning once in 1924-5. Then sold to Frank Barbour, who improved his jumping so that he won five of nine races in 1926/7, before being sold on the eve of the Gold Cup (and thus ineligible to run) for the huge sum of £7000 (and an additional £3000 if he won the National) to Captain Alfred Lowenstein (Bel). The latter was mysteriously lost in an aircraft over the North Sea in July 1928, and then *Easter Hero* was bought for £11,000 by 'Jock' Whitney, who sent him for training to Jack Anthony at Letcombe, Berkshire. In his career, 1925-31, he won 20 of his 40 races, before being retired to his owner's farm in Virginia.

EASY GOER

ch c. 21 Mar 1986. *Alydar - Relaxing.*

Retired at the age of four in 1990 having won a total of $4,873,770, then the fourth highest total ever, with 14 wins from 20 races. As a two-year-old he won two Group One races and the Eclipse Award. In 1989 he had four Group One wins, contesting the US Triple Crown with *Sunday Silence*. The latter surprised him to win the Kentucky Derby by 2 1/2 lengths, and won again in the Preakness Stakes, but by a nose only. *Easy Goer* finally came into his own with a win in the Belmont Stakes, beating his rival by eight lengths in the second fastest ever time, 2:24.9.

He was owned and bred by Ogden Phipps, and trained by Claude McGaughrey. His retirement came after a bone chip was found in his right ankle.

ECLIPSE

ch c. 1764, d. 27 Feb 1789. *Marske - Spiletta.*

The greatest racehorse of the 18th century. A great, great-grandson of *The Darley Arabian*, he was bought for 75 guineas by Smithfield meat salesman William Wildman at the dispersal sale of the Duke of Cumberland in 1765. *Eclipse* won all his 18 races, nine as a 5-year-old and nine at six, with eight of them walk-overs as the opposition were frightened away. Eleven of his victories were in King's Plates, races at 4 miles in which he had to carry 12 stone. After his first two races Wildman sold a half-share in *Eclipse* for 650 guineas to Dennis O'Kelly and a year later the second half for 1100 guineas. His progeny won 862 races and £158,000, and almost all the great horses of the 20th century trace back to him.

A big horse for his era, at 15.3 hands, he was a dark chestnut with a white blaze. The annual Eclipse Awards in the USA are named after him, as is the oldest Group 1 flat race over a mile and a quarter in England. His skeleton was re-assembled and stands in the National Horse Racing Museum in Newmarket.

FLYING CHILDERS

b c. 1714 d. 1741 Chatsworth, Derbyshire. The *Darley Arabian - Betty Leedes.*

Perhaps the first great racehorse in England, he was a pure-bred Arab with four white feet bred by Leonard Childers of Doncaster. Owned by the Duke of Devonshire, to whose stud at Chatsworth he retired, he was described contemporaneously as the fastest horse that ever ran at Newmarket and apparently won all his races easily.

GALLANT FOX

b c. 23 Mar 1927 Maryland, d. 13 Nov 1954 Paris, Kentucky. *Sir Galahad III - Marguerite.*

The second horse to win the US Triple Crown, which he achieved in 1930 when he won nine of his ten races and was ridden by Earl Sande. His sole defeat, by *Jim Dandy*, a 100-1 chance in the Travers Stakes at Saratoga on a muddy track, is regarded as one of the shock results of the century. Owned by William Woodward Sr and trained by Jim Fitzsimmons, he had been nothing special at two, with two wins in seven races, but at three he became the first thoroughbred to win over $300,000 in a year, and after winning the Jockey Club Gold Cup retired to stud with career earnings totalling a record $328,165.
He was outstandingly successful at stud and his first crop of foals included the next Triple Crown winner, *Omaha* (1935).

GALLORETTE

ch f. 1942. *Challenger II - Gallette.*

In her career from 1944 to 1947 she won 21 of 72 races, with earnings totalling $445,535. In 1956 the American Trainers' Association named her the best female horse in US turf history.
She was bred by Preston Burch and trained by E A Christmas. She stood 16 hands and was beautifully proportioned.

GAY CRUSADER

b c. 1914, d. 14 Sep 1932. *Bayardo - Gay Laura.*

Triple Crown winner in 1917, and described by Steve Donoghue as the greatest horse he ever rode. He was bred and owned by Alfred Cox and trained by Alec Taylor at Manton. He was injured before he could race at four and retired to a disappointing stud career. Won one of his two races at two, and six of seven at three.

GLADIATEUR

b c. 1862, d. 1876 Essex. *Monarque - Miss Gladiator.*

In 1865 he achieved the unique feat of winning the English Triple Crown and the Grand Prix de Paris. He was the first foreign-bred Derby winner, and earned the nickname 'Avenger of Waterloo'. He was bred and owned by Comte Frédéric de Lagrange, who sent him for training to Tom Jennings at Newmarket. A large, backward colt, he won two of his four races at two, and perhaps even greater than his 3-year-old successes was his win by 40 lengths in the Ascot Gold Cup, one of six wins in six races in 1866 despite problems with his off-fore fetlock joint. He proved a disappointment at stud in France and England. His statue now stands at the entrance to Longchamp racecourse.

The GODOLPHIN ARAB

br c. 1724, d. 1753 Gogmagog, Cambridgeshire.

The last of the three stallions, from whom all modern thoroughbreds descend in the male line, to be brought to England. There are varying accounts of his origin, but he may have originated from the Yemen, and was one of four Arabian horses sent from the stud of the Bey of Tunis to Louis XIV, King of France.
He was later sold to Edward Coke of Derbyshire and then acquired by Lord Godolphin, at whose country seat he died at the age of 29. His line was particularly strong through his grandson *Matchem* (1748-81).

GOLDEN MILLER

b g. 1927 d. 1957 Stanstead, Essex. *Goldcourt - Miller's Pride.*

Winner of the Cheltenham Gold Cup a record five times 1932-6, completing a unique double when ridden by Gerry Wilson to victory in the Grand National in 1934 when he set a record time of 9 min 20.4 sec, carrying 12st 2lb. Favourite for the National in 1935, he had a gallant battle with *Thomond II*, whom he had just

beaten at Cheltenham, before refusing at Valentine's. A great stayer, with a long, raking stride, he was an intelligent and even lazy horse. Also second to *Morse Code* in the 1938 Gold Cup, after the race was not run in 1937.
He was bred in Ireland by Laurence Geraghty, and first sold for 100 guineas at Goffs Sales to Paddy Quinn. He was then bought for 500 guineas by Dick Farmer for Philip Carr, who sold him in 1931, after two wins as a 3-year-old, to Dorothy Paget. Trained by Basil Briscoe 1930-5, then Owen Anthony. He never fell, although losing his partner in his first Grand National in 1933, and in all he won 29 and was placed in a further 13 of his 55 races from 1930 to 1939. A statue to him was unveiled at Cheltenham in 1989.

GRUNDY

ch c. 1972 Tewkesbury, d. May 1992 Japan. *Great Nephew - Word From Lundy.*

In 1975, after winning the Irish 2000 Guineas, the Derby and Irish Derby, he won the 'race of the century' from *Bustino*, with *Dahlia* third, in the King George VI and Queen Elizabeth Stakes at Ascot. His time was 2:26.98 for the 1.5 miles, a race record by 2.36 seconds. This race took its toll and he was fourth to *Dahlia* in his final race, the Benson & Hedges Gold Cup, three weeks later and retired to stand at the National Stud with a career record of 8 wins from 11 races, including all four at two to top the Free Handicap, and British record earnings of £326,421; he was unbeaten at a mile and a half. He was bought in 1983 by the Japan Racing Association and spent the rest of his life at stud in Japan.
A bright chestnut with three white feet, he was bought for 11,000 guineas as a yearling for Dr Carlo Vittadini, and trained by Peter Walwyn.

HAMBLETONIAN

b c. 5 May 1849 Sugar Loaf, New York, d. 27 Mar 1876 Sugar Loaf. *Abdallah - Charles Kent.*

The foundation sire of harness racing did little racing, but won prizes as a show horse. His sire was a thoroughbred, but his dam was a crippled mare owned by New York farmer Jonas Seely, who sold both mare and colt to William Rysdyk for $125. *Hambletonian* commanded stud fees which started at $10 but which rose to $500 by 1866 to make his owner's fortune. A high proportion of the 1300 foals that he sired became good racers. Nearly all Standardbreds can trace their lineage to him and the leading annual trotting race is named in his honour.

HIGHFLYER

c. 1774, d. 1793. *(King) Herod* - a mare by *Blank.*

He won all his 12 races from 1776 to 1779, before retiring to stud at Ely where he was a great success, his progeny winning 1108 races, including eight classics, and £170,000. Bred by Sir Charles Bunbury, and later owned by Lord Bolingbroke and Richard Tattersall. The latter built Highflyer Hall from the fortune he earned from stud fees and founded the famous auctioneers.

HYPERION

ch c. 1930, d. 1960. *Gainsborough - Selene.*

The Derby and St Leger winner of 1933, when ridden by Tommy Weston, became one the greatest of sires. The smallest Derby winner for 93 years at 15.1 hands, he was owned and bred by the 17th Earl of Derby, trained by the Hon. George Lambton 1932-3 and by Colledge Leader in 1934. He was a lazy horse at home, yet his Derby was won in record time and in all he won nine of his 13 races 1932-4. He was leading sire six times, 1940-2, 1945-6, 1954, and his offspring won 752 races, including 11 classics, and also had enormous influence on breeding lines.

ISINGLASS

f. 1890, d. 5 Dec 1901 Cheveley Park Stud. *Isonomy - Deadlock.*

After winning all three races at two, he

won the Triple Crown in 1893 and lost only one of his 12 races 1892-5, to *Raeburn* in the Lancaster Plate at Manchester, earning a total of £58,655, which remained the record in Britain until *Tulyar* broke it in 1952. At four *Isinglass* won the Eclipse Stakes and in his one race at five the Ascot Gold Cup. Bred and owned by Col. Harry McCalmont and trained by Jimmy Jewitt at Newmarket, he went on to a successful stud career, champion in 1905.

JAPPELOUP

c. 12 Mar 1975. *Tyrol II - Vénérable.*

Awarded the trophy as best French show jumper six times 1982-7, he was ridden by Pierre Durand for the European title in 1987 and Olympic gold in 1988. In the World Cup final he was third in 1986 and second in 1988 and 1990. Retired after the 1990 season in which he was part of the winning French team at the World Championships.

JOHN HENRY

g. Mar 1975 Paris, Kentucky.

Winner of a record $6,597,947, winning 39 of his 83 races 1977-84, including a record 25 Graded stakes wins in North America: 16 Grade I, 3 Grade II and 6 Grade III. In 1981 he was ridden by Bill Shoemaker to win the first Arlington Million, then a non-graded race, and won this race again when ridden by Chris McCarron in 1984; in both those years he was voted America's Horse of the Year. He won on dirt tracks but was best on grass, voted the US top horse on that surface four times, 1980-1 and 1983-4. He also won the Santa Anita Handicap twice and the Jockey Club Gold Cup.
Sold for just $1100 as a yearling and for $25,000 when bought by Sam Rubin as a three-year-old, he blossomed into a top-class horse late in his career.

KELSO

br g. 4 Apr 1957 Paris, Kentucky, d. 17 Oct 1983 Chesapeake, Michigan. *Your Host - Maid of Flight.*

American horse of the year for five consecutive years 1960-4; winning the 2 mile Jockey Club Gold Cup each year. He won 39 of his 63 races from 1959 to 1965, with record earnings of $1,977,896. He was gelded as a yearling because of his small size and lack of promise as a stallion, but he grew to over 16 hands by the age of five. He won just once with two seconds at two, but at three won eight of nine races despite not starting racing until the end of June, running spectacular times including a US record for 2 miles (3:19.4) in the Jockey Club Gold Cup. At four he won 7/8 and at five 6/12, not peaking until the autumn due to minor problems. In 1963 he won 9/12 for a total of $569,762 and in 1964 he ended the year with his first win in the Washington DC International in 2:23.8, the fastest time ever recorded in the USA for 1 $^1/_2$ miles. He was forced to retire in March 1966 when he fractured an off-fore sesamoid bone, but he was hunted by his owner and took part in jumping and dressage events.
A great-grandson of *Man O'War*, he was bred and owned by Mrs Allaire Du Pont, and trained from three by Carl Hanford.

KILBARRY

b g. 1946 Ireland, d. 13 Apr 1957. *Malbrouck -.*

He was bought as a five-year-old for racing by Major Frank Weldon from a Nottinghamshire farmer but his racing career was ruined by a bout of coughing, although he won a point-to-point in 1953. A big horse at 16.3 hands, he then went eventing and was ridden to second place by Weldon in the inaugural European Championships in 1953. Two years later they won this title, and in 1956 won Badminton and took Olympic team gold and individual silver. He was killed in 1957 when he broke his neck in a fall.

KINCSEM

ch f. 1874. *Cambuscan - Water Nymph.*

One of the best mares ever to race in Europe, and surely the best horse from Hungary, where she was bred at the

Imperial Stud at Kisber. She set a record for an undefeated career of 54 wins, 10 at two, 17 at three, 15 at four and 12 at five, winning in five countries at distances from 5 furlongs to 2.5 miles. Her one race in England was an easy win in the Goodwood Cup in 1878. This was followed by a triumph in the Grand Prix de Deauville and then a win in the Grosser Preis von Baden at Baden-Baden, a race she won for the third time the following year. A big mare at 16.1 hands, she was owned and bred by Erno de Blascovitz and trained by Robert Hesp.

KSAR

c. 1918. *Brûleur - Kizil Kourgan.*

Winner of the Prix de l'Arc de Triomphe in 1921 and 1922. He was bred by M E de Saint-Alary in Normandy and bought by Edmond Blanc for the then record price of 151,000 francs at the Deauville Sales. Although beaten, through poor jockeyship, in the Grand Prix de Paris in 1921, he had a series of major race victories at three and four. He went on to prove a most influential stallion.

LA FLECHE

b f. 1889, d.22 Apr 1919 Sledmere Stud, Yorkshire. *St Simon - Quiver.*

Winner of the fillies' Triple Crown in 1892. Bred by Queen Victoria at the Royal Stud at Hampton Court, as a yearling *La Flèche* was bought for a record price of 5500 guineas by Baron Maurice de Hirsch. Trained by John Porter, she was unbeaten in four races as a two-year-old and won eight of nine at three, when her only loss was due to poor riding in the Derby. She went to Richard Marsh at Newmarket at four, and, although never as dominant, won the Ascot Gold Cup and Champion Stakes in 1894. In her career this wiry filly won 16 of 24 races, setting a world record with earnings of £39,583. On the Baron's death in 1896 she was sold for 12,600 guineas to the Sledmere Stud of Sir Tatton Sykes.

L'ESCARGOT

ch g. 1963 Mullingar, Co. Westmeath, Ireland, d. 1984 Powhatan, Virginia, USA. *Escart III - What A Daisy.*

The only steeplechaser since *Golden Miller* to win the Cheltenham Gold Cup (1970 and 1971) and the Grand National (on his fourth attempt in 1975 when he beat the favourite *Red Rum*, after second in 1974). He was also fourth at Cheltenham in 1972 and 1973.

Bred by Barbara O'Neill in Mullingar, he was bought in 1966 for 3000 guineas for Raymond Guest (USA) and trained by Dan Moore on the Curragh. Won his first race, 2 miles on the flat at Navan in 1967, and in all won three of eleven hurdles races and nine of 41 chases, as well as two of eight flat races, 1967-75.

LEXINGTON

b c. 1850 Woofford County, Kentucky, d. 1 Jul 1876 Medway, Kentucky. *Boston - Alice Carneal.*

America's greatest sire of the 19th century, and champion a record 16 times. A great great-grandson of *Diomed*, he began his career named *Darley*, and after winning his first two races was sold by his breeder Dr Warfield to Richard Ten Broeck, who changed the horse's name to the Kentucky town. After a successful racing career, including two wins in three races against his great rival *Lecomte*, *Lexington* was sold by Ten Broeck for a US record price of $15,000 and stood as a sire at Woodburn Farm, Kentucky. About 40 per cent of his *c*.600 foals were winners, with earnings of $1,159,321 in North America.

MAN O'WAR

ch c. 29 Mar 1917 Lexington, Kentucky, d. 1 Nov 1947 Lexington. *Fair Play - Mahubah.*

Generally considered as the greatest ever American racehorse. In his two-year career he lost just one of his 21 races, to *Upset* in the Sanford Memorial Stakes at Saratoga on 12 Aug 1919, and that when he nearly caught the field despite being left at the start. He retired to stud with record earnings of $249,465. He started odds-on every time that he raced (three times at 1-100!) Bred by Major August Belmont II, he was bought by Samuel D Riddle for $5000 in 1918 and sent to Louis Feustel to train. As a 3-year-old he was the first horse to win the three most prestigious races, the Withers Stakes, Belmont Stakes (by 20 lengths) and Lawrence Realization Stakes. Retired to stud in Lexington, where he set a new stud fee record of $5000 and, although restricted to 25 mares a year, he sired 379 foals that won a total of 1300 races. His son *War Admiral* won the Triple Crown in 1937.

A strong, fiery chestnut of 16.2 hands, nicknamed 'Big Red', he was notable for his huge stride and muscular build, and set numerous speed records between 1 mile and 1 mile 5 furlongs.

MANDARIN

b g. 1951. *Deuz Pour Cent - Manada.*

Ridden by Fred Winter, he became a legend through his gallant victory in the Grand Steeplechase de Paris at Auteuil on 17 Jun 1962 when his rubber bit snapped at the third fence, leaving his jockey to steer him with his knees. That concluded his greatest season in which he had won all his five races, including the Hennessy Gold Cup for the second time and the Cheltenham Gold Cup, and he was then retired.

Bred in France by his owner Peggy Hennessy, he was trained by Fulke Walwyn, emerging from an erratic jumper to wins in the Hennessy Gold Cup and King George VI Chase in 1957. He was second three times in the Whitbread Gold Cup, including its first running in 1957, and won the King George again in 1959. In his career, 1954-62, this tough little horse won a record £51,496 from 19 wins in 52 races.

MANIFESTO

b g. 1888 near Navan, Ireland. *Man O'War - Vae Victis.*

Until *Red Rum* this big, bay horse was perhaps the best Grand National horse, with two wins, in 1897 (11st 3) and 1899 (12st 7). He had been fourth in 1895 and fell in 1896. In 1900 at 12, he had to carry 12st 13lb but still contended hard and was only beaten into third place in the last 100 yards. He was third again in 1902 and 1903, before running last of six at the age of 16 in 1904.

He was bred in Ireland by Harry Dyas, who sold him after his first National win for £4000 to Joseph Bulteel. He fell in his first race, in 1892, but won his next - a 2 mile hurdle. In his fifth race that year he won the Irish Champion Chase. Needing time to develop, he was lightly raced over the following years, and his National win in 1897 was only his 15th race, soon after he had been sent for training to Willie Macauliffe at Eversleigh. In his career, 1892 to 1905, he won nine of his 35 races, including one walk-over.

MARCROIX

c. 1919. d. c. 1943. *Marsan - Coquet.*

The only horse to be ridden to two Olympic three-day event gold medals, by Charles F. Pahud de Mortanges who had bought him in 1928, for the Netherlands in 1928 and 1932. Bred in France at Corbary, near Charolles by the Marquis de Croy, his sire was an English thoroughbred *Marsan* and his dam a half-bred mare. He was used as a draft horse under the German occupation in World War II, when he died.

MELD

b f. 1952, d. 14 Sep 1983 Ireland. *Alycidon - Daily Double.*

Winner of the fillies' Triple Crown and the Coronation Stakes in 1955, she raced sparingly, just six times, winning all but her first race. She was owned and bred by Lady Zia Wernher and trained at Newmarket by Cecil Boyd-Rochfort. She was possessed of dazzling acceleration and won the St Leger despite having started to cough on the eve of the race. She became the only Triple Crown filly to be the dam of a classic winner - *Charlottown*, the Derby winner in 1966 - and the longest lived, to the age of 31.

MILL HOUSE

br g. 1957, d 31 May 1970 Bryanstown, Co. Kildare. *King Hal - Nas Na Riogh.*

A big horse at 17.2 hands, he was a powerful and fluent jumper and but for his contemporary *Arkle,* might have become one of the greatest steeplechasers of all-time. From 1961-8 he won 17 of his 36 races.
He was bred near Naas by the Lawlors of County Kildare, and bought by Bill Gollings, who sent him for training to Syd Dale for a season and then to Fulke Walwyn. After winning two of six hurdles races, he fell badly in his first steeplechase, but in only his sixth won the 1963 Cheltenham Gold Cup by twelve lengths. From December 1962 to February 1964 he was supreme, winning six successive chases including his first clash with *Arkle* in the 1963 Hennessy Gold Cup and the King George VI Chase. *Arkle* had slipped in the Hennessy (when *Mill House*, who gave him 5 lb, was the only horse ever to beat him at anything worse than 21 lb better terms!) and the great horse beat *Mill House* in the 1964 and 1965 Gold Cups, and won their two other clashes in devastating fashion.
Mill House had one more moment of glory, when he won the Whitbread Gold Cup in 1967. At Cheltenham he fell in 1967 and 1968.

MILL REEF

b c. 1968, d. 2 Feb 1986. *Never Bend - Milan Mill.*

A brilliantly successful racehorse and a huge influence as a sire when he stood at the National Stud in Newmarket. In his 14 races, 1970-2, he won 12 and was second twice, to *My Swallow* in 1970 and to *Brigadier Gerard* in 1971, earning a British record £314,212. British Racehorse of the Year in 1971, when he won five races, the Greenham Stakes, Derby, Eclipse Stakes, King George VI and Queen Elizabeth Stakes (by six lengths) and the Prix de l'Arc de Triomphe in record time. His career ended after he had won both his races, the Prix Ganay and Coronation Cup, as a four-year-old when he sustained a fracture of the off-foreleg. An operation to repair the injury was, however, successful.
He was bred in Virginia by his owner Paul Mellon, and trained by Ian Balding at Kingsclere, England. Beautifully made, but quite small at 15.2 hands. He was champion sire in 1978 and 1987.

MILTON

gr c. Apr 1977. *Marius - Epaulette.*

In September 1992 he became the first show jumper to win over £1 million. Bred by John Harding-Rolls and owned by Tom and Doreen Bradley, he was nurtured by their daughter Caroline until her tragically early death in 1983. From then he was ridden by John Whitaker and from 1986 achieved a host of successes, including the European Championship of 1989, the King George V Gold Cup 1990 and the World Cups of 1990 and 1991 with second place in 1989. His name was prefixed at various times by sponsors *Next*, *Henderson* and *Everest*.

MONKSFIELD

c. 1972, d. Feb 1989 Redthorn Stud, Co. Kildare. *Gala Performance - Regina.*

Winner of the Champion Hurdle in 1978 and 1979, in each year rated the top National Hunt horse in Britain. Unusually for a top-class hurdler, he raced until the age of eight as an entire horse.
A small and exceptionally brave horse, he was bred by Peter Ryan in Ireland and bought as a two-year-old for 740 guineas (Irish) by Des McDonagh, who trained him for Dr Michael Mangan. He won his first race over the flat at two and his first two hurdles races. Second to *Night Nurse* in his first Champion Hurdle in 1977, he beat *Sea Pigeon* the next two years but lost to his great rival in 1980, after which he was retired to the Amgrove Stud in Co. Laois. In his career he won five flat races and over hurdles won 49, placing 2nd 11, 3rd 10 and 4th 4 times.

NASHUA

c. 14 Apr 1952 Paris, Kentucky. *Nasrullah - Segula.*

Winner of 22 of his 30 races 1954-6, setting an earnings record of $1,288,565. He was voted American champion 2-year-old in 1954 and Horse of the Year in 1955, when he won 10 of 12 races, including the Preakness and Belmont Stakes.
Trained by Jim Fitzsimmons and owned by the Belair Stud, where he became an influential stallion.

NASRULLAH

b c. 1940, d. 1959. *Nearco - Mumtaz Begum.*

Bred by the Aga Khan in County Kildare, although not a great racehorse he had a great influence on American breeding after his export to stand at stud in Kentucky.
He proved temperamental and, trained by Frank Butters, raced only at Newmarket during the war years, with two good wins: the Coventry Stakes at two and the Champion Stakes at three.
He was bought by Joe McGrath for 19,000 guineas and stood at stud in Ireland. He was champion sire in 1951, a year after he was sold for £130,000 to a syndicate of American breeders. He was five times champion sire in the USA and at his death had sired the winners of 292 races in the British Isles and 615 races worth $5,886,468 in America.

NASHWAN

ch c. 1 Mar 1986. *Blushing Groom - Height of Fashion.*

In 1989 he became the first horse to win the 2000 Guineas, Derby, King George VI and Queen Elizabeth Stakes and the Eclipse Stakes in the same year, but then lost a minor race in France and retired to his owner Hamdan Al Maktoum's stud. Powerfully built with an enormous stride and a beautifully fluent action. Won both his races as a two-year-old.

NATIVE DANCER

gr c. 27 Mar 1950 Lexington, Kentucky. d, 16 Nov 1967 Philadelphia. *Polynesian - Geisha.*

American Horse of the Year in 1952, when he won all nine races, and as a four-year-old in 1954, when he won all three. His one loss in his career of 22 races was his second to *Dark Star* in the 1953 Kentucky Derby, when he was impeded, but he won the Belmont and Preakness Stakes and was also voted as the three-year-old colt of the year. He started at odds-on in every race but his first. A large (16.3 hands) and powerful colt, he was a nasty animal, but a very great racehorse.
Bred and owned by Alfred G Vanderbilt, he was trained by Bill Winfrey, and he went on to be a hugely successful sire.

NEARCO

b c. 1935, d. 1957. *Pharos - Nogara.*

This great racehorse won all his 14 races in Italy and France, seven each in 1937 and 1938. Bred, owned and trained by Federico Tesio. He was sold to Martin Benson for the then record price of £60,000 in 1938 and stood at Beech House Stud in Newmarket, where he became one of the most influential sires of the century, being leading sire in 1947 and 1949 and in the top three places each year from 1952 to 1959.
He possessed brilliant speed, yet won at distances from five furlongs up to the mile and seven furlongs of the Grand Prix de Paris in 1938, his only race outside Italy.

NEVELE PRIDE

b c. 1962. *Star's Pride - Thankful.*

Emulated *Bret Hanover* by being named Harness Horse of the Year three times, in 1967-9. In those three years he won 57 races from 67 starts, including 28 of 29 as a two-year-old, 21 of 24 at three including the trotting Triple Crown of Hambletonian, Kentucky Futurity and Yonkers Trot, and 8 of 14 at four. A difficult horse to manage, he was supremely fast and set world

records each year to his 1:54.8 mile at Indianapolis in 1969.
Bred by Mr and Mrs E C Quin in Pennsylvania and originally named *Thankful's Major*, he was bought by Charles Slutsky for Nevele Acres, who renamed him. He was trained and driven by Stanley Dancer and became a stallion standing at Stoner Creek Stud in Kentucky, when he was syndicated for $3 million in 1969.

NIATROSS

c. 30 Mar 1977 Hanover, Pennsylvania. *Albatross - Niagara Dream.*

Voted Harness Horse of the Year in 1979 and 1980, and Horse of the 1980s, even though he raced for only the first year of the decade. In 1980, driven by Clint Galbraith, he took three seconds off the world record for the 1 mile by a pacer, with 1:49.2 at Lexington and a world race record of 1:52.2 at Inglewood, and won the Little Brown Jug. He ran a record 24 sub 2-minute miles that year, including 18 in succession, and set a career earnings record of $2,019,213, including a single season record, the first over $1 million, $1,414,313 in 1980.

NIGHT NURSE

b g. 1971. *Falcon - Florence Nightingale.*

Winner of the Champion Hurdle in 1976 and 1977, before being beaten by *Monksfield* in 1978. In 1976/7 he achieved the highest ever *Timeform* rating for a hurdler of 182.
Bought as a yearling for 1300 guineas, he showed little ability on the flat although he won once at three, but as a hurdler he was immediately successful, winning five of seven races in his first year and all eight in his second, 1975/6, including the Champion Hurdles of England, Scotland and Wales, and the Irish Sweeps Hurdle. In his first race after his second Champion Hurdle he had a gruelling race when beaten by *Monksfield* at Liverpool, to end with five wins in seven races that year, and was never as good again. However, he did turn successfully to steeplechasing, placing second in the 1981 Cheltenham Gold Cup and securing his last major win in the Mandarin Handicap Chase in 1982. In all he had 32 wins from 64 races under NH rules, earning a record £181,770. Trained by Paddy Broderick.

NIHILATOR

c. 1982, d. 1991.

Set an earnings record for a pacer, with $3,225,653. That included an individual race record $1,080,500 for the Woodrow Wilson two-year-old race at Meadowlands, New Jersey in 1984. He was Harness Horse of the Year in 1985, when he won 23/25 to take his career record to 35 wins in 38 races, 1984-5. Driven by William O'Donnell, at East Rutherford in 1985 he set the race record for a mile by a pacer, 1:49.6.
He was put down after he contracted laminitis, a hoof disease

NIJINSKY

b c. 1967 Windfields Farm, Canada, d. 15 Apr 1992 Paris, Kentucky. *Northern Dancer - Flaming Page.*

In 1970 this brilliant colt became the first horse for 35 years to win the British Triple Crown of 2000 Guineas, Derby and St Leger. He also won the Irish Derby and the King George VI and Queen Elizabeth Stakes (easily, yet by six lengths), but after a virulent attack of ringworm was surprisingly beaten in the Prix de l'Arc de Triomphe by *Sassafras*, and in the Champion Stakes by *Lorenzaccio*. He had won all six races at two in 1969, and in his career won £282,223 from 11 wins in 13 races.
Bred by Eddie Taylor, he was bought for a Canadian record $84,000 by Charles Engelhard, and trained by Vincent O'Brien in Ireland. He was ridden to his English classic victories by Lester Piggott, and possessed that priceless ability to quicken. A big horse at 16.3 hands, after his racing career he was a brilliant success as a stallion at Bill Hancock's Claiborne Farm stud in Kentucky.

NORTHERN DANCER

b c. 1961 Canada, d. 16 Nov 1990. *Neartic - Natalma.*

The most influential sire of modern times, he was responsible for 634 foals, of which 143 were stakes winners, the record for any stallion, and 44 were champions in various countries. A grandson of *Native Dancer*, he was small (less than 15.3 hands) and failed to reach his $25,000 reserve at the sales as a yearling, so his breeder Eddie Taylor kept him. Like his grandsire he was a difficult horse. At two he won five of seven races in Canada, before moving to the USA where he was trained by Horatio Luro, winning twice at two and seven of nine races as a three-year-old, including the Kentucky Derby (in record time of 2 minutes) and Preakness Stakes. His total racing earnings were $580,806.

As a stallion he stood at Taylor's Windfields Farm in Chesapeake City, Maryland. Within his lifetime three of his sons - *Nijinsky, The Minstrel* and *Secreto* - and three of his grandsons, all won the Derby, and he was leading sire in Britain in 1970, 1977 and 1984.

When he first stood at stud his covering fee was $10,000, but twenty years later such was his success that breeders were allegedly paying $1m for his services. In all, 295 of his progeny were sold at public auction for a total of $183,758,632, an average of $622,910, yet when he went to stud the world record price paid for a yearling was $170,000; one of his sons, *Snaafi Dancer*, fetched $10.2 million and even this was exceeded by the $13.1 million paid by Robert Sangster and partners for *Seattle Dancer* at Keeneland, Kentucky on 23 Jul 1985. Many of his sons also became champion sires.

OH SO SHARP

ch f. 1983. *Kris - Oh So Fair.*

Winner of the fillies' Triple Crown in 1986 when she raced sparingly. Owned and bred by Sheikh Mohammed al Maktoum and trained by Henry Cecil at Newmarket. She won all three races at two and four of six at three, placing second to *Petoski* in the King George VI and Queen Elizabeth Stakes and to *Commanche Run* in the Benson & Hedges Gold Cup. She then retired to stud.

ORMONDE

b c. 1883, d. 21 May 1904 California. *Bend Or - Lily Agnes.*

The greatest racehorse of the 19th century, he was unbeaten in 16 races, including the Triple Crown in 1886. Owned and bred by the 1st Duke of Westminster, he was trained by John Porter. Big and backward, he did not race at two until October, but won three races that year, and at three he swept all before him until at the end of the year he developed a wind infirmity. Nonetheless he remained the champion at four. He stood unsuccessfully at stud in England for two years and then was sold to Argentina for £12,000. In 1894 he was sold again and went to California.

PERSIAN WAR

b g. 1963, d. 1984. *Persian Gulf - Warning.*

The third horse to win the Champion Hurdle three times, 1968-70, each time ridden by Jimmy Uttley; he was also second in 1971. Bred by Sir John 'Jakie' Astor and trained on the flat by Dick Hern, he was bought by Henry Alper for £10,000 in January 1967, and by the end of that season he had won the Victor Ludorum and Daily Express Triumph Hurdles. His last victory was in June 1972. His owner placed him with five different trainers.

PETITE ETOILE

gr f. 1956. *Petition - Star of Iran.*

She won a British female record of £72,624 which lasted to 1969, winning 14 of 19 races, with many brilliant rides from Lester Piggott. She was Horse of the Year in Britain and the top 3-year-old filly in Europe in 1959, when her six victories included the 1000 Guineas and the Oaks. She retained her form in 1960, when she won the Coronation Cup, a race she won again in 1961. Owned by Prince Aly Khan (and after his death in 1961 by his son the Aga Khan) and trained by Noel Murless. Temperamental, but possessed of brilliant speed.

PHAR LAP

ch g. 26 Oct 1926 Seadown Stud, near Timaru, New Zealand. d. 5 Apr 1932 Menlo Park, California, USA. *Night Raid-Entreaty.*

The greatest ever Australasian racehorse, who won 37 of his 51 races, including 32 of the last 35. Bred by Alick Roberts, his sire had been exported from England to Australia. A fiery chestnut, known as the 'Red Terror', he was bought as a yearling for a mere 160 guineas by David Davis and trained by Harry Telford. Big and backward, he was gelded and took time to mature, as he won only once and was unplaced eight times in his first ten races in Australia. At three he came into his own and won the AJC and Victoria Derbys, both in record time, and both St Legers. At four he won 14 successive races, including the Melbourne Cup when he conceded at least a stone all round, carrying 9st 12lb *62.5 kg*. At five he won his first eight races, but could only place eighth in the Melbourne Cup when set to carry 10-10, before being sent to race in America. He won the Agua Caliente Handicap over 2000m in record time, but he died soon afterwards in mysterious circumstances. The cause was not satisfactorily determined, but it may have been from eating grass contaminated by pesticide.
A huge horse, standing 17.0 $^1/_2$ hands, his mounted hide and skeleton are on display in the National Museums in Melbourne and Auckland respectively.

PRETTY POLLY

ch f. 1901, d. August 1931 Ireland. *Gallinule - Admiration.*

Winner of the fillies' Triple Crown of the 1000 Guineas, Oaks and St Leger in 1904, all by three-length margins. Owned and bred by Major Eustace Loder and trained by Peter Purcell Gilpin. She won her first race, at Sandown Park in 1903, by a huge margin, and soon gathered a large public following. After 15 consecutive wins, 9 at two and 6 at three, she was sensationally beaten by *Presto* in heavy going, to which she was unsuited, at Longchamp. She retained her form in 1905, when she won the Coronation Cup at Epsom in a course record for 1.5 miles that was not beaten until by *Mahmoud* in the 1936 Derby. She retired after the 1906 Ascot Gold Cup, when she was beaten for only the second time in 24 races.

PRINCE REGENT

b g. 1935 *My Prince - Nemaea.*

The idol of Irish racing, he was deprived by the war years of racing in England, yet, although past his best, he was still good enough to win the 1946 Cheltenham Gold Cup by five lengths.
Bought for £350 by Harry Bonner for James V Rank, he was trained by Tom Dreaper, who considered him his greatest horse until *Arkle* had won his second Go' Cup. He reached true greatness in 1942, when he had to carry very heavy weights yet won four of his seven races including the Irish Grand National at 12-7. At that same weight he was second in that race in 1943 and 1944. Nearly 17 hands, in his career 1940-9 he won 20 of his 49 races.

RED RUM

b g. May 1965. *Quorum - Mared.*

The only horse to win the Grand National three times; he became a legend in his lifetime and had an enormous public following. In his first win in 1973 he carried 10-5 giving 21 lbs to *Crisp*, whose valiant effort he overcame in the finish, but the following year he carried 12 stone to victory and after second places in 1975 and 1976, won again with 11-8 in 1977. A 'National' horse par excellence, in his career 1967-78 he won 24 of his 100 races under National Hunt rules (3/24 hurdles, 21/76 chases) for a money record of £145,234, and three of ten flat races.
He was bought as a yearling for 400 guineas for Maurice Kingsley and he dead-

heated in his first flat race at two. He started jumping with Bobby Renton, but did not win for him in 14 races in 1969-70. He showed promise in 1970/1, when he won three novice chases as he was trained by first Tommy Stack, then Anthony Gillam. He was then sold by Mrs Lurline Brotherton to Noel le Mare for 6000 guineas in 1972 and trained by his taxi-driver Donald 'Ginger' McCain on the sands at Southport. In late 1972 he had five successive wins, before building up to his first National. A life-size statue of him was unveiled at Aintree in 1988.

RIBOT

b c. 1952, d. Apr 1972. *Tenerani - Romanella.*

This great racehorse won all his 16 races, three as a 2-year-old, five at three, including the Gran Premio del Jockey Club and the Prix de l'Arc de Triomphe, and seven at four when he won the King George VI and Queen Elizabeth Stakes and his second Arc by a record margin of six lengths. He was bred by Federico Tesio at the Dormello Stud near Lake Maggiore in Italy, owned by Tesio's partner the Marchesa Incisa della Rochetta, trained by Ugo Penco, and ridden in all his races by Enrico Camici.

He stood at Lord Derby's Woodland Stud for two years, at his owner's Olgiata Stud in Italy 1959-60, and then at the Darby Dan Stud in the USA, where, proving increasingly difficult to handle, he stayed until his death. His progeny made him leading sire in Britain in 1963 and 1968, but he was even more influential in the USA.

RUFFIAN

bl f. 1972 Paris, Kentucky. d. 1975 Belmont, New York. *Reviewer - Shenanigans.*

A big, powerful filly, *Ruffian* is rated the best ever in the USA, where she won the fillies' Triple Crown of Acorn Stakes, Mother Goose Stakes and Coaching Cub of America Oaks in 1975. Bred at Claiborne Farm, in her first race at two she won by 15 lengths and equalled the track record at Belmont Park. She completed her two-year-old career undefeated but then suffered a hairline fracture of her right hind leg which kept her out of racing for six months. After ten wins in ten races she took on the Kentucky Derby winner *Foolish Pleasure* in a match at Belmont Park but pulled up lame three furlongs into the race. After emergency surgery she lashed out, broke the cast and had to be put down.

ST SIMON

b c. 1881, d. 1908 Welbeck. *Galopin - St Angela.*

The greatest sire of the 19th century, he won all his nine races with ease, five at two and four at three, at distances from six furlongs to 2 $^1/_2$ miles. His sire won the 1875 Derby, but he was entered in only one classic, the 2000 Guineas. However, that entry was cancelled on the death of his breeder Prince Batthyany (Hun). Bought for 1600 guineas for the Duke of Portland, *St Simon* won the Ascot Gold Cup at three in his first year of racing, when he beat the previous year's winner by 20 lengths. Trained by Mat Dawson and ridden in most of his races by Fred Archer; both considered him the greatest racehorse they had known. He possessed the electric change of pace that marks the true champion. He was leading sire nine times, 1890-6, 1900-1, and ten of his offspring won 17 classics, a record he shares with *Stockwell*. His skeleton was presented to the Natural History Museum in London.

SCEPTRE

b f. 1899, d. 5 Feb 1926 Exning Stud, Newmarket. *Persimmon - Ornament.*

Uniquely the winner of four classics, all bar the Derby in 1902. Standing 16.0 $^1/_2$ hands, she was a magnificent filly, who set a world record for winnings with £39,583 for 13 wins from 25 races 1901-03.

Bred by the 1st Duke of Westminster, her sire was the son of *St Simon* and her dam was the sister of *Ormond*. On the Duke's death she was bought as a yearling for the record sum of 10,000 guineas by American gambler Bob Sievier, who sent her for training to Charles Morton at Wantage. She won two of her three races at two, and at three Sievier trained her himself. Mistrained perhaps, for he set her a demanding schedule, but after a narrow defeat in the Lincolnshire Handicap she contested all five classics. Poorly ridden, she was fourth in the Derby, but won all the others. At four she was sold for 25,000 guineas to Sir William Bass and trained by Alec Taylor at Manton. She won her last four races at four, but was below her best in three races at five.

SEA-BIRD II

ch c. 1962, d. 1973 (of an intestinal blockage). *Dan Cupid - Sicalade.*

Perhaps the greatest ever French racehorse. In 1965 as a three-year-old he won all his five races in brilliant style, Prix Greffulhe, Prix Lupin, Epsom Derby, Grand Prix de Saint-Cloud, Prix de l'Arc de Triomphe, the latter by six lengths, achieving the highest rating, 145, ever awarded by *Timeform*. Bred and owned by Jean Ternynck, trained by Etienne Pollet and ridden by Pat Glennon, he stood just over 16 hands, had a white blaze and two stockings behind. An unprepossessing two-year-old, he did not race until September and won two of his three races, his only loss being to his stable companion *Grey Dawn*. *Sea-Bird* came into his glory at three. At stud he stood for five years in the USA, before returning to France in 1972.

SEABISCUIT

f. 1933 Paris, Kentucky, d. 18 May 1947 Paris. *Hard Tack - Swing On.*

Bred by the Wheatly Stable, he was initially trained by James Fitzsimmons. He made a very slow start, as it took him 18 races at two to win even a minor event. After three wins in eleven starts at three, he was bought by Charles S Howard for $8000 in 1936, and sent for training to 'Silent Tom' Smith. This tough little horse progressed to greatness, becoming the top money-winning horse in the USA in 1937, and Horse of the Year in 1938. His finest triumph was his three-length win over 1937 Triple Crown winner *War Admiral* in a match over 9.5 furlongs at Pimlico in 1938. In all, he won 33 of his 89 races, 1935-40, setting an earnings record of $437,730.

He was injured in 1939 but came back in 1940 to win the San Antonio and Santa Anita Handicaps, setting a record time in the latter, his last race.

SEA PIGEON

br g. 1970. *Sea Bird II - Around The Roses.*

He was bred to be a classic winner, and indeed he was a top-class flat racer, but achieved his pre-eminence as a speedy hurdler, winning the Champion Hurdle in 1980 and 1981 (oldest ever at 11) after the race distance was shortened by 200 yards to 2 miles. He had struggled for the longer distance in his three previous attempts.

He was seventh in the 1973 Derby, when trained by Jeremy Tree. Gelded in 1974, he was bought by Pat Muldoon and sent for training to Gordon W Richards and then to Peter Easterby. Apart from considerable hurdling success, he won the Chester Cup on the flat in 1977 and 1978, the former in his first flat race for two years. In all he won 16 of 45 races on the flat and 21 of 40 under NH Rules, winning £277,045.

SEATTLE SLEW

br c. 1974 Lexington, Kentucky. *Bold Reasoning - My Charmer.*

Despite being bought for a mere $17,500 as a yearling by Mickey and Karen Taylor, he won the US Triple Crown in 1977, the first horse bought at public auction so to do. He had been left at the gate in the Kentucky Derby but worked his way through the field to win by two lengths. Bred by Ben Castleman, he was trained by Billy Turner to 1977 and then by Doug Peterson, and was US champion at two, three and four, and Horse of the Year at three. In his career he won 14 of his 17 races, with earnings of $1,208,726. His first loss was to *J.O.Tobin* in the Swaps Stakes after his Triple Crown triumph.

In retirement, after being syndicated for $12 million, he became champion sire in the USA, standing at the Spendthrift Farm in Kentucky, and by 1985 his stud fee reached a peak of $750,000.

SECRETARIAT

ch c. 30 Mar 1970 Doswell, Virginia, d. 4 Oct 1989 Paris, Kentucky. *Bold Ruler - Somethingroyal.*

The greatest American racehorse since *Man O'War*. He won eight of his nine races as a 2-year-old and eight of twelve at 3 in 1973, when, trained by Lucien Laurin and ridden by Ron Turcotte, he became the first horse for 25 years to win the US Triple Crown. He set track records in the Kentucky Derby and Belmont Stakes, winning the latter by the astonishing margin of 31 lengths in the world record time of 2:24.0 for 1.5 miles.

He was syndicated by Seth Hancock for an unprecedented $6.08 million after his 2-year-old season, on the death of owner Christopher Chenery. Horse of the Year in both 1972 and 1973, he retired having won a total of $1,316,608 and stood as a stallion at Claiborne Farms. Known as 'Big Red' he was a big (16.2 hands), bright chestnut with three socks and a diamond-shaped star between his eyes; majestic looking and hugely powerful with an enormous stride, he was the perfect racing machine.

SHERGAR

b c. 1978, d. Feb 1983. *Great Nephew - Sharmeen.*

Shergar was a great racehorse, winner of the 1981 Derby by a record ten lengths, but he achieved even greater fame when he was kidnapped. The kidnappers, Irish republican terrorists, demanded a ransom, but this was not to be met by the syndicate who owned him.

He was bred by the Aga Khan and trained by Michael Stoute. At two, after a win in his first race in September he was second in the William Hill Futurity. At three, he swept to wins by huge margins in two preparatory races and then in the Epsom and Irish Derbys and the King George VI and Queen Elizabeth Stakes, but he lost his sparkle in his last race, placing fourth in the St Leger, before retiring to the Aga Khan's Ballymany Stud in Co. Kildare. From there he was taken on 9 Feb 1983 and presumably slaughtered soon afterwards.

SIR IVOR

b c. 1965 Mill Ridge Farm, Lexington, Kentucky, USA. *Sir Gaylord - Attica.*

Considered by Lester Piggott as the best horse he had ridden to that time when he won the 2000 Guineas and Derby in 1968. Very powerful at 16.2 hands, he only just lasted the mile and a half distance, winning at Epsom when his devastating speed was conserved, but he was beaten by *Ribero* in the Irish Derby and by *Vaguely Noble* in the Prix de l'Arc de Triomphe, two of four losses before he came back to win the Champion Stakes and Washington International. At two he had won 3/4, so his career record was eight wins in 13 races at two and three, setting a British record £227,100.

Bred by Alice Chandler in Kentucky, he was bought for $42,000 as a yearling by Raymond Guest (USA), who sent him for training to Vincent O'Brien in Ireland. After his racing career he stood at stud for one year in Ireland and then at Claiborne Farms in Kentucky.

SIR KEN

b g. 1947. *Laeken - Carte Grise II.*

The second horse to win the Champion Hurdle in three successive years, 1952-4. He was bred in France, where he was trained by Maurice Adele before being bought by the trainer Willie Stephenson, who passed him to Maurice Kingsley after he won his first race at four. He won all 16 hurdles races contested in his first three years in England, but lost three times in 1953/4 before his third Cheltenham triumph. He was fourth there in 1955, and in 1955/6 won four of six races over fences, but was unsuccessful a year later. He was then hunted by Rodney Ward.

SPECTACULAR BID

gr c. 1976 Paris, Kentucky. *Bold Bidder - Spectacular.*

He won $2,781,607, to set a new world record, with 26 wins in 30 races, 1978-80. In 1979 he won the Kentucky Derby and Preakness Stakes and was third in the Belmont Stakes after treading on a pin and injuring a hoof before the race. He was US Horse of the Year at four in 1980, when he won all nine races. Bought for the bargain price of $37,000 as a yearling at the Keeneland Sales by Harry Meyerhoff. Trained by Grover C 'Bud' Delp. Stood at Claiborne Farms Stud, Lexington until 1991 when he moved to the Milfer Farm, Unadilla, New York.

SUN CHARIOT

br f. 1939, d. June 1963. *Hyperion - Clarence.*

Bred at the National Stud in Ireland, trained by Fred Darling and racing in the colours of King George VI, to whom she was leased, she was ridden by Gordon Richards to victory in four classics, all bar the Derby, in the war year of 1942. She was highly temperamental, but won all four races at two and four of five at three. She bred seven winners at the National Stud.

SUNDAY SILENCE

c. 25 Mar 1986. *Halo - Wishing Well.*

He won the record figure of $4,578,454 in the USA in 1989, when he won two legs of the Triple Crown, the Kentucky Derby and the Preakness Stakes, the latter in the third fastest ever time, before losing to arch-rival *Easy Goer* in the Belmont Stakes. He then beat *Easy Goer* in the Breeders' Cup Classic and his success took him to the Eclipse Award as the Horse of the Year. In his career he won $4,968,554, then the third highest ever figure, with nine wins in 14 races before his retirement after tearing a ligament in 1990 to stand first at Arthur Hancock's Stone Farm Stud in Paris, Kentucky and now in Japan.
He was bred in Kentucky and sold for $17,000 at the Keeneland Yearling Sales. Eventually he had a trio of owners, Arthur Hancock, trainer Charles Whittingham and Dr Ernest Gaillard.

SWAPS

ch c. 1 Mar 1952 Chino, California, d. 1972 Lexington, Kentucky. *Khaled - Iron Reward.*

The first great thoroughbred raised in California, he beat the favourite *Nashua* to win the Kentucky Derby in 1955 and was Horse of the Year in the USA in 1956. Owned and bred by Rex C Ellsworth and trained by Meshack Tenney, he won three of seven races at two and eight of nine at both three and four with career earnings of $848,900. Very fast, he set five world records during his career.
After fracturing a bone in his left hind leg in October 1956 he went to stud at John Galbraith's farm in Lexington. He was later syndicated for $2 million and moved to Spendthrift Farm, Lexington.

SYSONBY

b c. 1902. *Melton - Optime*, d. 17 Jun 1906 Sheepshead Bay, New York.

Trained by James Rowe, he won 14 of his 15 races in 1904-5 at all distances up to 2 $^1/_4$ miles, with earnings of $184,438, and is rated as a contender for the fastest horse on American tracks. He won five times at two and nine at three. His one loss was third to *Artful* and *Tradition* in the Futurity in 1904. He died at the age of four due to an attack of septic poisoning. Ater being buried in the stable yard his skeleton was exhumed and displayed in the American Museum of Natural History in New York.

THE MINSTREL

ch c. 1974, d. 3 Sep 1990 Lexington, Kentucky, USA. *Northern Dancer - Fleur.*

Bred in Canada by E P Taylor, he was bought by Robert Sangster for $200,000 as a yearling and won all three races at two, including the Dewhurst Stakes. After third place in the 2000 Guineas and second in the Irish 2000 Guineas, he won the Derby

(Lester Piggott's eighth winner), the Irish Sweeps Derby and the King George VI and Queen Elizabeth Stakes. His earnings in 1976-7 set a British record of £333,197, with seven wins in nine races. He retired to stud in the USA, when a half-share in him was sold for $4,100,000 to his breeder's Windfields Stud. Small (15.2 hands), with four white feet.

THE TETRARCH

gr c. 1911, d. 1935. *Roi Hérode - Vahren.*

Unbeaten in his seven races as a two-year-old when he was rated 10lb superior to the best of his rivals; he is a candidate for racing's fastest ever horse. He was unable to run thereafter due to leg trouble, but he became a most influential sire. Although only getting 130 foals, 80 of them won races and six won classics.
He was of bizarre colouring, elephant grey with white and lime patches, nicknamed 'the Spotted Wonder' or 'the Rocking Horse'. He had blistering speed, but his trainer, Atty Persse, who bought him for 1300 guineas as a yearling for Major Dermot McCalmont, believed that he would have won the Derby and that he would not have been beaten at any distance. Bred by Edward Kennedy in Co. Kildare, Ireland.

TROY

b c. 1976, d. May 1983. *Petingo - La Milo.*

He was the best three-year-old colt in Europe in 1979 when he won six consecutive races including the 200th Derby by seven lengths, the biggest margin for 54 years, the Irish Sweeps Derby, the King George VI and Queen Elizabeth Stakes and the Benson & Hedges Gold Cup, in all of which he was ridden by Willie Carson. His earnings that year set a British record of £450,428. Owned by Sir Michael Sobell and Sir Arnold Weinstock, and trained by Dick Hern. With a syndication value of £7.2 million he started well at stud, but died at seven from a perforated intestine.

TUDOR MINSTREL

br c. 1944. *Owen Tudor - Sansonnet.*

One of the best ever racehorses at 1 mile. Bred by John Dewar and trained by Fred Darling, he was unbeaten in four races at two, and at three won the 2000 Guineas by eight lengths, but was unable to handle the left-handed turn in the Epsom Derby, despite the best endeavours of Gordon Richards, and finished fourth. In all he won eight races worth £24,629. He was a success at stud and was exported to the USA in 1959.

VAGUELY NOBLE

b c. 1965, d. 19 Apr 1989 Gainesway Farm, Lexington, Kentucky, USA. *Vienna - Noble Lassie.*

Winner of the Prix de l'Arc de Triomphe and three other races in France in 1968, when he was rated the top 3-year-old colt in Europe despite the fact that he had not been entered for any of the classics. In the Arc he beat *Sir Ivor* by three lengths. Bred by Major Lionel Holliday, he was bought on the latter's death by Dr Robert Franklyn for 136,000 guineas, having won the Observer Gold Cup when trained by Walter Wharton as a 2-year-old. Trained at three by Etiénne Pollet at Chantilly. A commanding, strong horse, he won two of four races at 2 and 4/5 races at 3. He became leading sire in Britain in 1973 and 1974 and sired 29 Group One winners in Europe; especially successful as a sire of fillies, notably *Dahlia* from his first crop.

WEST AUSTRALIAN

b c. 1850, d. 2 May 1870. *Melbourne - Mowerina.*

The first horse to win the Triple Crown in England, in 1853. Bred and owned by John Bowes, and trained by John Scott. He was beaten just once, at two, and went on to win the Ascot Gold Cup in 1854. He was sold for £4750 as a stallion to Lord Londesborough and was later owned by the Emperor Napoleon in France.

WHIRLAWAY

c. 2 Apr 1938 Lexington, Kentucky, d. 6 Apr 1953 Falaise, France. *Blenheim - Oustwhirl.*

Son of the 1930 Epsom Derby winner, bred and raced by Warren Wright and trained by Benjamin Allyn Jones. He won the US Triple Crown in 1941 when, ridden by Eddie Arcaro, he totally dominated the three races. He was voted Horse of the Year at three (nine wins) and at four (11 wins) in 1941-2. In his career he had 32 wins from 60 races, losing often through his habit of veering to the right when under pressure.

His career earnings, 1940-2, were $561,161, then a record, but he was unsuccessful as a sire in the USA and France.

Aleksandra Chudina
Babe Didrikson
Ray Ewry
Jürgen Hingsen
Kinue Hitomi
Bruce Jenner
Sabine John
Rafer Johnson
Jackie Joyner-Kersee
Alvin Kraenzlein
Carl Lewis
Bob Mathias
Glenn Morris
Ramona Neubert
Dan O'Brien
Yobes Ondieki
Harold Osborn
Micheline Ostermeyer
Jesse Owens
Eulace Peacock
Mary Peters
Irina Press
Mary Rand
Heide Rosendahl
Daley Thompson
Jim Thorpe
Nadezhda Tkachenko
Bill Toomey
Yvette Williams
Yang Chuang-kwang

Australian Rules football
Haydn Bunton
Jack Clarke
John Coleman
Gordon Coventry
Jack Dyer
Ken Farmer
Peter Hudson
Dick Lee
Dave McNamara
Laurie Nash
Ian Stewart
Albert Thurgood
Roy Wright

Badminton
Tonni Ahm
Eddy Choong
Flemming Delfs
Frank Devlin
David Freeman
Morten Frost
Gillian Gilks
Han Aiping
Rudi Hartono
Judy Hashman
Finn Kobberö
Lena Køppen
Erland Kops
Liem Swie King
Muriel Lucas
Park Joo-bong
George Thomas
Betty Uber
Margaret Varner
Wong Peng-soon
Yang Yang

Baseball
Hank Aaron
Pete Alexander
Sparky Anderson
Cap Anson
Luis Aparicio
Richie Ashburn
Earl Averill
Frank Baker
Ernie Banks
James Bell
Johnny Bench
Chief Bender
Yogi Berra
Wade Boggs
Barry Bonds
Bobby Bonds
Jim Bottomley
Lou Boudreau
Harry Breechen
Roger Bresnahan
George Brett
Lou Brock
Mordecai Brown
Jim Bunning
Roy Campanella
Rod Carew
Max Carey
Steve Carlton
Orlando Cepeda
Frank Chance
Jack Chesbro
Roger Clemens
Roberto Clemente
Ty Cobb
Mickey Cochrane
Rocky Colavito
Eddie Collins
Earle Combs
Sam Crawford
Joe Cronin
Candy Cummings
Ray Dandridge
Dizzy Dean
Ed Delahunty
Bill Dickey
Dom DiMaggio
Joe DiMaggio
Larry Doby
Bobby Doerr
Don Drysdale
Dennis Eckersley
John Evers
Red Faber
Roy Face
Bob Feller
Rollie Fingers
Carlton Fisk
Curt Flood
Whitey Ford
Nellie Fox
Jimmy Foxx
Frank Frisch
Steve Garvey
Lou Gehrig
Charlie Gehringer
Bob Gibson
Josh Gibson
Lefty Gomez
Goose Goslin
Hank Greenberg
Burliegh Grimes
Lefty Grove
Gabby Hartnett
Harry Heilmann
Rickey Henderson
Tommy Henrich
Babe Herman
Gil Hodges
Rogers Hornsby
Frank Howard
Waite Hoyt
Carl Hubbell
Catfish Hunter
Monte Irvin
Bo Jackson
Joe Jackson
Reggie Jackson
Ferguson Jenkins
Tommy John
Walter Johnson
Addie Joss
Jim Kaat
Al Kaline
Willie Keeler
George Kell
Charlie Keller
Harmon Killebrew
Ralph Kiner
Sachin Kinugasa
Chuck Klein
Sandy Koufax
Nap Lajoie
Kanesaw Landis
Don Larsen
Tony Lazzeri
Bob Lemon
Buck Leonard
Pop Lloyd
Ernie Lombardi
Joe McCarthy

Willie McCovey
Joe McGinnity
John McGraw
Connie Mack
Mickey Mantle
Heinie Manush
Rabbit Maranville
Juan Marichal
Roger Maris
Rube Marquard
Billy Martin
Eddie Mathews
Christy Mathewson
Don Mattingly
Willie Mays
Bill Mazeroski
Joe Medwick
Andy Messersmith
Minnie Minoso
Johnny Mize
Joe Morgan
Thurman Munson
Eddie Murray
Stan Musial
Don Newcombe
Phil Niekro
Sadaharu Oh
Tony Oliva
Mel Ott
Satchel Paige
Jim Palmer
Roger Peckinpaugh
Gaylord Perry
Eddie Plank
Charles Radbourn
Pee Wee Reese
Jim Rice
Sam Rice
Cal Ripken
Phil Rizzuto
Robin Roberts
Brooks Robinson
Frank Robinson
Jackie Robinson
Pete Rose
Edd Roush
Red Ruffing
Babe Ruth
Nolan Ryan
Mike Schmidt
Tommy Seaver
Joe Sewell
Al Simmons
George Sisler
Enos Slaughter
Duke Snider
Warren Spahn
Tris Speaker
Willie Stargell
Casey Stengel
Bill Terry
Luis Tiant
Harold Traynor
Fernando Valenzuela
Arthur Vance
Rube Waddell
Honus Wagner
Ed Walsh
Lloyd Waner
Paul Waner
Monte Ward
Zach Wheat
Hoyt Wilhelm
Billy Williams
Ted Williams
Maury Wills
Hack Wilson
George Wright
Gus Wynn
Carl Yastrzemski
Cy Young
Robin Yount

Basketball

Kareem Abdul-Jabbar
Phog Allen
Nate Archibald
Paul Arizin
Red Auerbach
Charles Barkley
Rick Barry
Elgin Baylor
Walt Bellamy
Sergey Belov
David Bing
Larry Bird
Carol Blazejowski
Bill Bradley
Larry Brown
Wilt Chamberlain
Kresimir Cosic
Bob Cousy
David Cowens
Adrian Dantley
Bob Davies
David DeBusschere
Theresa Edwards
Julius Erving
Patrick Ewing
Walt Frazier
Joe Fulks
Artis Gilmore
Gail Goodrich
Hal Greer
Dick Groat
Alex Groza
Cliff Hagan
John Havlicik
Connie Hawkins
Elvin Hayes
Marques Haynes
Spencer Haywood
Tom Heinsohn
Nat Holman
Hortencia
Chuck Hyatt
Dan Issel
Dennis Johnson
Gus Johnson
Magic Johnson
Neil Johnston
K C Jones
Sam Jones
Michael Jordan
Bobby Knight
Mike Krzyzewski
Toni Kukoc
Bob Kurland
Bob Lanier
Meadowlark Lemon
Nancy Liebermann
Clyde Lovelette
Jerry Lucas
Hank Luisetti
Ed Macauley
Moses Malone
Pete Maravich
Sarunas Marciulionis
Dugie Martin
Ann Meyers
George Mikan
Vern Mikkelsen
Cheryl Miller
Earl Monroe
Calvin Murphy
James Naismith
Aleksandr Petrov
Drazen Petrovic
Bob Pettit
Jim Pollard
Willis Reed
Oscar Robertson
Guy Rodgers
Adolph Rupp
Bill Russell
Arvidas Sabonis
Adolph Schayes
Oscar Schmidt
Frank Selvy
Uljana Semjonova
Bill Sharman
Paul Silas
Dean Smith
Isiah Thomas
David Thompson
Nate Thurmond
Jack Twyman
Wes Unseld
Chet Walker
Bill Walton

Jerry West
JoJo White
Lenny Wilkens
Dominique Wilkins
Lynette Woodard
John Wooden
George Yardley

Biathlon
Vladimir Melanin
Anfissa Restsova
Frank-Peter Rötsch
Magnar Solberg
Aleksandr Tikhonov
Frank Ullrich

Billiards
See also Snooker
Raymond Ceulemans
Joe Davis
William Hoppe
Melbourne Inman
Walter Lindrum
Willie Mosconi
Tom Newman
Tom Reece
John Roberts
Willie Smith
H W Stevenson
Rex Williams

Bobsleigh and luge
Nino Bibbia
Eddie Eagan
Billy Fiske
Bernhard Germeshausen
Wolfgang Hoppe
Thomas Köhler
Eugenio Monti
Bogdan Musiol
Meinhard Nehmer
Hans Rinn
Erich Schärer
Margit Schumann
Steffi Walter

Bowling
Earl Anthony
Mike Aulby
Don Carter
Ned Day
Marshall Holman
Marion Ladewig
Flo McCutcheon
Mark Roth
Jimmy Smith
Dick Weber

Bowls
Janet Ackland
Tony Allcock
Percy Baker
Peter Belliss
David Bryant
David Cutler
Mavis Steele

Boxing
Muhammad Ali
Henry Armstrong
Max Baer
Reg Baker
Carmen Basilio
Wilfred Benitez
Nino Benvenuti
James Braddock
Al Brown
Joe Brown
Tony Canzoneri
Primo Carnera
Georges Carpentier
Jimmy Carruthers
Marcel Cerdan
Ezzard Charles
Julio César Chavez
Billy Conn
Henry Cooper
James J. Corbett
Jack Dempsey
George Dixon
Roberto Duran
Jackie Fields
James Figg
Bob Fitzsimmons
George Foreman
Bob Foster
Joe Frazier
Kaosai Galaxy
Joe Gans
Wilfredo Gomez
Rocky Graziano
Harry Greb
Emile Griffith
Marvin Hagler
Thomas Hearns
Larry Holmes
James Jeffries
Ingemar Johansson
Jack Johnson
Stanley Ketchel
Benny Leonard
Ray Leonard
Gus Lesnevich
Ted 'Kid' Lewis
Sonny Liston
Tommy Loughran
Joe Louis
Terry McGovern
Barry McGuigan
Jimmy McLarnin
Harry Mallin
Rocky Marciano
Carlos Monzon
Archie Moore
José Napoles
Oscar Nelson
Carlos Ortiz
Manuel Ortiz
László Papp
Floyd Patterson
Eusebio Pedroza
Willie Pep
Pascual Pérez
Sugar Ray Robinson
Lionel Rose
Barney Ross
Sandy Saddler
Salvador Sánchez
Jack Sharkey
Michael Spinks
Téofilo Stevenson
John L. Sullivan
Dick Tiger
Gene Tunney
Mike Tyson
Jersey Joe Walcott
Mickey Walker
Jimmy Wilde
Ike Williams
Tony Zale
Carlos Zarate

Canoeing
Greg Barton
Ian Ferguson
Richard Fox
Gert Fredriksson
Rüdiger Helm
Yuriy Lobanov
Jon Lugbill
Vladimir Parfenovich
Ivan Patzaichin
Lyudmila Pinayeva
Birgit Schmidt

Chess
Alexandre Alekhine
Adolf Anderssen
Mikhail Botvinnik
José Capablanca
Machgielis Euwe
Bobby Fischer
Nona Gaprandashvili
Anatoliy Karpov
Garry Kasparov
Paul Keres
Viktor Korchnoi
Bent Larsen
Emanuel Lasker
Vera Menchik

Paul Morphy
Aron Nimzowitsch
Tigran Petrosyan
Judit Polgar
Valeriy Smyslov
Boris Spassky
Wilhelm Steinitz
Mikhail Tal

Cricket
Abdul Qadir
Bobby Abel
Terry Alderman
Gubby Allen
Curtly Ambrose
Leslie Ames
Dennis Amiss
Denise Annetts
Warwick Armstrong
Asif Iqbal
Mohammad Azharuddin
Trevor Bailey
Enid Bakewell
Warren Bardsley
Sidney Barnes
Ken Barrington
Bishen Bedi
Alec Bedser
Richie Benaud
John Blackham
Colin Blythe
David Boon
Allan Border
Ian Botham
Geoffrey Boycott
Don Bradman
Mike Brearley
Janette Brittin
Bhagwant Chandrasekhar
Greg Chappell
Ian Chappell
Brian Close
Denis Compton
Learie Constantine
Colin Cowdrey
Martin Crowe
Alan Davidson
Stewart Dempster
Ted Dexter
Basil D'Oliveira
Martin Donnelly
John Douglas
Mary Duggan
Jeff Dujon
Bill Edrich
John Edrich
Godfrey Evans
Aubrey Faulkner
Fazal Mahmoud
Tich Freeman
Charles Fry
Joel Garner
Mike Gatting
Sunil Gavaskar
Lance Gibbs
George Giffen
Graham Gooch
David Gower
W G Grace
Tom Graveney
Gordon Greenidge
Jack Gregory
Syd Gregory
Tony Greig
Clarence Grimmett
Wallace Grout
George Gunn
Richard Hadlee
Wes Hall
Walter Hammond
Hanif Mohammad
Neil Harvey
Lindsay Hassett
Desmond Haynes
Tom Hayward
Vijay Hazare
George Headley
Jack Hearne
Patsy Hendren
Rachel Heyhoe-Flint
Molly Hide
Clement Hill
George Hirst
Jack Hobbs
Michael Holding
Merv Hughes
Len Hutton
Raymond Illingworth
Imran Khan
Archie Jackson
Stanley Jackson
Douglas Jardine
Javed Miandad
Gilbert Jessop
Alvin Kallicharan
Rohan Kanhai
Kapil Dev
Alan Knott
Jim Laker
Allan Lamb
Harold Larwood
Bill Lawry
Maurice Leyland
Dennis Lillee
Ray Lindwall
Clive Lloyd
Tony Lock
George Lohmann
Stan McCabe
Charlie Macartney
Craig McDermott
Graham McKenzie
Myrtle Maclagan
Archie McLaren
Arthur Mailey
Majid Khan
Vinoo Mankad
Mansur Ali Khan
Rodney Marsh
Malcolm Marshall
Christina Matthews
Peter May
Philip Mead
Vijay Merchant
Keith Miller
Bruce Mitchell
Arthur Morris
Billy Murdoch
Deryck Murray
John Murray
Mushtaq Mohammad
Cottari K. Nayudu
Montague Noble
Dave Nourse
Dudley Nourse
Bert Oldfield
Norman O'Neill
Bill O'Reilly
Charlie Parker
Robert Peel
Graeme Pollock
Bill Ponsford
Mike Procter
Sonny Ramadhin
K S Ranjitsinhji
John Reid
Wilfred Rhodes
Barry Richards
Vivian Richards
Richie Richardson
Tom Richardson
Andy Roberts
Andrew Sandham
Sarfraz Nawaz
Alfred Shaw
Arthur Shrewsbury
Bobby Simpson
Mike Smith
Robin Smith
John Snow
Betty Snowball
Gary Sobers
Frederick Spofforth
Brian Statham
Andrew Stoddart
Herbert Strudwick
Bert Sutcliffe
Herbert Sutcliffe
Maurice Tate
Hugh Tayfield

Bob Taylor
Herbert Taylor
Sachin Tendulkar
Jeff Thomson
Fred Trueman
Hugh Trumble
Victor Trumper
Charles Turner
Glenn Turner
Johnny Tyldesley
Frank Tyson
Polly Umrigar
Derek Underwood
Dilip Vengsarkar
Hedley Verity
Gundappa Viswanath
John Waite
Clyde Walcott
Courtney Walsh
Doug Walters
Waqar Younis
Pelham Warner
Cyril Washbrook
Wasim Akram
Wasim Bari
Everton Weekes
Bob Willis
Betty Wilson
John Wisden
Bill Woodful
Sammy Woods
Frank Woolley
Frank Worrell
Zaheer Abbas

Croquet
Nigel Aspinall
Cyril Corbally
Edmond Cotter
Lily Gower
Humphrey Hicks
John Prince
John Solomon
Dorothy Steel

Curling
Ernest Richardson
Ken Watson
Ed Werenich
Howard Wood

Cycling
Jean Aerts
Rudi Altig
Jacques Anquetil
Maurice Archambaud
Federico Bahamontes
Ercole Baldini
Gino Bartali
Alfredo Binda
Chris Boardman
Louis Bobet
Gianni Bugno
Beryl Burton
Connie Carpenter
Claudio Chiapucci
Fausto Coppi
André Darrigade
Pedro Delgado
Eric de Vlaeminck
Roger de Vlaeminck
Oscar Egg
François Faber
Leandro Faggin
Laurent Fignon
Urs Freuler
Tamara Garkushina
Charly Gaul
Felice Gimondi
Costante Girardengo
Andy Hampsten
Reg Harris
Beth Heiden
Lutz Hesslich
Bernard Hinault
Miguel Induráin
Jan Janssen
Sean Kelly
Hugo Koblet
Frank Kramer
Ferdi Kubler
Octave Lapize
André Leducq
Greg LeMond
Jeannie Longo
Christa Luding
Freddy Maertens
Antonio Maspes
Eddie Merckx
Leon Meredith
Daniel Morelon
Francesco Moser
Koichi Nakano
Luis Ocana
Hans-Henrik Ørsted
Henri Pélissier
Lucien Petit-Breton
Hugh Porter
Raymond Poulidor
Yvonne Reynders
Roger Rivière
Stephen Roche
Aleksandr Romanov
Erika Salumaë
Jeff Scherens
Briek Schotte
Patrick Sercu
Tommy Simpson
Jean Stablinski
Major Taylor
Philippe Thijs
Lothar Thoms
Guillomer Timoner
Galina Tsareva
Rebecca Twigg
Gintautas Umaras
Rik van Looy
Keetie van Oosten-Hage
Rik van Steenbergen
Vyacheslav Yekimov
Galina Yermoleyeva
Sheila Young
Joop Zoetemelk

Darts
Bob Anderson
Eric Bristow
John Lowe
Jocky Wilson

Discus
Adolfo Consolini
Ludvik Danek
Luís Delis
Nina Dumbadze
Fortune Gordien
Evelyn Jahl
Lia Manoliu
Faina Melnik
Al Oerter
Nina Ponomaryeva
Mike Powell
Wolfgang Schmidt
Jürgen Schult
Martin Sheridan
Mac Wilkins

Diving
Phil Boggs
Joaquin Capilla
Pete Desjardins
Klaus Dibiasi
Ingrid Engel
Gao Min
Irina Kalinina
Micki King
Sammy Lee
Greg Louganis
Patricia McCormick
Brian Phelps
Robert Webster

Equestrian events
David Broome
Frank Chapot
Bruce Davidson
Charles Pahud De Mortanges
Piero D'Inzeo
Raimondo D'Inzeo
Pierre Jonquères d'Oriola

Lucinda Green
Reiner Klimke
Virginia Leng
Liselott Linsenhoff
Harry Llewellyn
Graziano Mancinelli
Humberto Mariles
Richard Meade
Josef Neckermann
Mark Phillips
Michael Plumb
Henri Saint Cyr
Alwin Schockemöhle
Paul Schockemöhle
Harvey Smith
William Steinkraus
Christine Stückelberger
Janou Tissot (Lefèbvre)
Mark Todd
Nicole Uphoff
John Whitaker
Hans-Günter Winkler

Fencing
Georges Buchard
Christian d'Oriola
Ilona Elek
Anja Fichtel
Lucien Gaudin
Aladár Gerevich
Cornelia Hanisch
Rudolf Kárpáti
Pal Kovács
Jean-François Lamour
Eduardo Mangiarotti
Hélène Mayer
Nedo Nadi
Aleksey Nikanchikov
Jerzy Pawlowski
Ellen Preis
Aleksandr Romankov
Yakov Rylsky

Football
See also American football, Australian Rules football, Rugby League, Rugby Union
Marques Ademir
Florian Albert
Carlos Alberto
José Altafini
Manuel Amoros
José Andrade
Ossie Ardiles
Jimmy Armfield
Alan Ball
Gordon Banks
Franco Baresi
Billy Bassett
Cliff Bastin
Jim Baxter
Franz Beckenbauer
Igor Belanov
George Best
Danny Blanchflower
Oleg Blokhin
Steve Bloomer
Vsevolod Bobrov
Giampiero Boniperti
Jozsef Bozsik
Liam Brady
Andreas Brehme
Paul Breitner
Charles Buchan
Matt Busby
Emilio Butragueño
Antonio Carbajal
Johnny Carey
Raich Carter
Herbert Chapman
John Charles
Bobby Charlton
Jack Charlton
Hector Chumpitaz
Brian Clough
Mario Coluña
Bob Crompton
Johan Cruyff
Teofilo Cubillas
Kenny Dalglish
Dixie Dean
Kazimierz Deyna
Jimmy Dickinson
Didi
Alfredo Di Stefano
Duncan Edwards
Eusebio
Giacinto Facchetti
Falcão
Elias Figueroa
Tom Finney
Just Fontaine
Karl-Heinz Forster
Artur Friedenreich
Hughie Gallacher
Garrincha
Paul Gascoigne
Francisco Gento
Germano
Gerson
Gilmar
Alain Giresse
Jimmy Greaves
Ruud Gullit
Kurt Hamrin
Gerhard Hanappi
João Havelange
Johnny Haynes
Nándor Hidegkuti
Geoff Hurst
Alec Jackson
Jairzinho
Alex James
Pat Jennings
Kevin Keegan
Mario Kempes
Sandor Kocsis
Ronald Koeman
Raymond Kopa
Rudi Krol
Angel Labruna
Grzegorz Lato
Denis Law
Tommy Lawton
Leonidas
Gary Lineker
Sepp Maier
Diego Maradona
Josef Masopust
Lothar Matthäus
Stanley Matthews
Sandro Mazzola
Giuseppe Meazza
Hugo Meisl
Joe Mercer
Billy Meredith
Roger Milla
Luis Monti
Bobby Moore
Fernando Morena
Gerd Müller
Johan Neeskens
Igor Netto
Gunnar Nordahl
Björn Nordqvist
Ernst Ocwirk
Jean-Pierre Papin
Pelé
Martin Peters
Frantisek Plánicka
Michel Platini
Ferenc Puskas
Helmut Rahn
Alfred Ramsey
Frank Rijkaard
Luigi Riva
Roberto Rivelino
Gianni Rivera
Bobby Robson
Bryan Robson
Pedro Rocha
Paolo Rossi
Stanley Rous
Karl-Heinz Rummenigge
Ian Rush
Djalma Santos
Nilton Santos
Györgi Sárosi
Juan Alberto Schiaffino
Karl-Heinz Schnellinger

Elisha Scott
Uwe Seeler
Bill Shankly
Albert Shesternyev
Peter Shilton
Nikita Simonian
Allan Simonsen
Matthias Sindelar
Omar Sivori
G O Smith
Sócrates
Graeme Souness
Luis Suárez
Frank Swift
Tostão
Marco van Basten
Paul van Himst
Obdulio Varela
Vavá
Berti Vogts
Rudi Völler
Fritz Walter
Billy Wright
Lev Yashin
George Young
Mario Zagalo
Ricardo Zamora
Zico
Zito
Wladyslaw Zmuda
Dino Zoff

Golf
Amy Alcott
Willie Anderson
Isao Aoki
Tommy Armour
John Ball Jr
Severiano Ballesteros
Patty Berg
Michael Bonallack
Julius Boros
Pat Bradley
James Braid
JoAnne Carner
Billy Casper
Bob Charles
Glenna Collett Vare
Henry Cotton
Fred Couples
Ben Crenshaw
Beth Daniel
Jimmy Demaret
Roberto de Vicenzo
Chick Evans
Nick Faldo
Ray Floyd
Walter Hagen
Ben Hogan
Hale Irwin
Tony Jacklin
Bobby Jones
Betsy King
Tom Kite
Catherina Lacoste
Bernhard Langer
Cecilia Leitch
Lawson Little
Gene Littler
Bobby Locke
Nancy Lopez
Sandy Lyle
Cary Middlecoff
Johnny Miller
Tom Morris Jr
Tom Morris Sr
Byron Nelson
Jack Nicklaus
Greg Norman
Christy O'Connor
José Maria Olazábal
Francis Ouimet
Arnold Palmer
Gary Player
Betsy Rawls
Dai Rees
Alan Robertson
Anne Sander
Gene Sarazen
Patty Sheehan
Sam Snead
Payne Stewart
Curtis Strange
Louise Suggs
J H Taylor
Peter Thomson
Jerry Travers
Walter Travis
Lee Trevino
Flory Van Donck
Harry Vardon
Ken Venturi
Lanny Wadkins
Tom Watson
Joyce Wethered
Kathy Whitworth
Ian Woosnam
Mickey Wright
Babe Zaharias

Gymnastics
Nikolay Andrianov
Vladimir Artemov
Polina Astakhova
Dmitriy Bilozerchev
Svetlan Boginskaya
Alberto Braglia
Vera Cáslavská
Miroslav Cerar
Viktor Chukarin
Nadia Comaneci
Aleksandr Dityatin
Aurelia Dobre
Yukio Endo
Maxi Gnauck
Koji Gushiken
Karin Janz
Béla Karolyi
Sawao Kato
Ágnes Keleti
Eizo Kenmotsu
Nelli Kim
Olga Korbut
Yuriy Korolev
Larisa Latynina
Li Ning
Marina Lobach
Eugen Mack
Zoltán Magyar
Akinori Nakayama
Takashi Ono
Mary Lou Retton
Heiki Savolainen
Vitaliy Scherbo
Boris Shakhlin
Yelena Shushunova
Daniela Silivas
Ecaterina Szabo
Kurt Thomas
Yuriy Titov
Mitsuo Tsukahara
Lyudmila Turishcheva
Mikhail Voronin

Hammer
Harold Connolly
John Flanagan
Mikhail Krivonosov
Sergey Litvinov
Matthew McGrath
Imre Németh
Pat O'Callaghan
Yuriy Sedykh
Gyula Zsivotzky

Handball
Gheorghe Gruia
Zinaida Turchina

Harness racing
John Campbell
Stanley Dancer
Hervé Filion
Billy Haughton
Michel Lachance
William O'Donnell

High jump
Rosemarie Ackermann
Iolanda Balas

Debbie Brill
Valeriy Brumel
Tamara Bykova
Charles Dumas
Dick Fosbury
Heike Henkel
Stefka Kostadinova
Ulrike Meyfarth
Dietmar Mögenburg
Sara Simeoni
Patrik Sjöberg
Javier Sotomayor
Lester Steers
Dwight Stones
John Thomas
Zhu Jianhua

Hockey
Richard Allen
Balbir Singh
David Bell
Stefan Blöcher
Rik Charlesworth
Leslie Claudius
Dhyan Chand
Carsten Fischer
Carsten Keller
Sean Kerly
Roepie Kruize
Ties Kruize
Richard Leman
Paul Litjens
Mohamad Asad Malik
Eric Pearce
Michael Peter
Marjorie Pollard
Jonathan Potter
Abdul Rashid
Ronald Riley
Roop Singh
Stanley Shoveller
Udam Singh

Horse racing
Eddie Arcaro
Fred Archer
Cash Asmussen
Braulio Baeza
Ron Barry
Terry Biddlecombe
Cecil Boyd-Rochfort
Scobie Breasley
Frank Buckle
Frank Butters
Enrico Camici
Morny Cannon
Willie Carson
Steve Cauthen
Henry Cecil
Sam Chifney
Angel Cordero Jr
Fred Darling
Mat Dawson
Pat Day
Kent Desormeaux
Michael Dickinson
Steve Donoghue
Richard Dunwoody
Pat Eddery
Charlie Elliott
James Fitzsimmons
Nat Flatman
George Fordham
John Francome
Edward Garrison
Josh Gifford
Bill Hartack
Colin Hayes
Alec Head
Freddy Head
Dick Hern
Edward Hide
Hirsch Jacobs
Rae Johnstone
Johnny Longden
D Wayne Lukas
Chris McCarron
Danny Maher
Bryan Marshall
François Mathet
Stan Mellor
Joe Mercer
Manny Mercer
Tim Molony
George Moore
Noel Murless
Isaac Murphy
Vincent O'Brien
Jonjo O'Neill
Atty Persse
Lester Piggott
Laffit Pincay
Martin Pipe
Roger Poincelet
John Porter
Paddy Prendergast
Ryan Price
Dick Rees
Gordon Richards
Fred Rimell
Jem Robinson
Robert Robson
Yves Saint-Martin
Earl Sande
Jose Santos
John Scott
Peter Scudamore
Bill Shoemaker
Tod Sloan
Charlie Smirke
Doug Smith
Greville Starkey
Arthur Stephenson
Michael Stoute
Walter Swinburn
Pat Taaffe
Alec Taylor
Federico Tesio
Jack Van Berg
Jorge Velasquez
Fulke Walwyn
Charlie Whittingham
Gerry Wilson
Fred Winter
Frank Wootton
Harry Wragg
Maurice Zilber

Hurdling
John Akii-Bua
Karin Balzer
David Burghley
Lee Calhoun
Willie Davenport
Glenn Davis
Harrison Dillard
Yordanka Donkova
Guy Drut
Annelie Ehrhardt
Greg Foster
Glenn Hardin
David Hemery
Roger Kingdom
Rod Milburn
Edwin Moses
Renaldo Nehemiah
Andre Phillips
Gert Potgieter
Pam Ryan
Harald Schmid
Shirley Strickland
Forrest Towns
Kevin Young

Ice hockey
Sid Abel
Syl Apps
Jean Beliveau
Doug Bentley
Max Bentley
Hector Blake
Mike Bossy
Frank Boucher
Johnny Bower
Frankie Brimsek
Punch Broadbent
Walter Broda
Dit Clapper
Bobby Clarke
Paul Coffey

Charles Conacher
Lionel Conacher
Bill Cook
Yvan Cournoyer
Alex Delvecchio
Marcel Dionne
Ken Dryden
Bill Durnam
Phil Esposito
Tony Esposito
Vyacheslov Fetisov
Frank Frederickson
Bernie Geoffrion
Wayne Gretzky
George Hainsworth
Glenn Hall
Douglas Harvey
Paul Henderson
Bryan Hextall
Tim Horton
Gordie Howe
Bobby Hull
Aurel Joliat
Red Kelly
Ted Kennedy
Valeriy Kharlamov
Jari Kurri
Guy Lafleur
Mario Lemieux
Ted Lindsay
Frank Mahovlich
Joe Malone
Mark Messier
Stan Mikita
Dickie Moore
Howie Morenz
Bill Mosienko
Bobby Orr
Bernie Parent
Brad Park
Jacques Plante
Denis Potvin
Joe Primeau
Marcel Pronovost
Henri Richard
Maurice Richard
Terry Sawchuk
Milt Schmidt
Eddie Shore
Peter Stastny
Nels Stewart
Tiny Thompson
Vladislav Tretyak
Bryan Trottier
Sven Tumba (Johansson)
Georges Vezina
Lorne Worsley
Aleksandr Yakushev

Javelin
Steve Backley
Ruth Fuchs
Uwe Hohn
Matti Järvinen
Erik Lemming
Tiina Lillak
Janis Lusis
Petra Meier (Felke)
Miklos Németh
Elvira Ozolina
Seppo Räty
Tessa Sanderson
Janusz Sidlo
Fatima Whitbread
Dana Zátopková
Jan Zelezny

Judo
Cathy Arnaud
Ingrid Berghmans
Karen Briggs
Brigitte Deydier
Shozo Fujii
Anton Geesink
Isao Inokuma
Jigoro Kano
Masahiko Kimura
Kyuzo Mifune
Hiroshi Minatoya
Isao Okano
Wilhelm Ruska
Hitoshi Saito
Peter Seisenbacher
Yasuhiro Yamashita
Guus van Mourik

Lacrosse
Billy Fitzgerald
Gary Gait
Paul Gait
Frank Urso

Long jump
Bob Beamon
Ralph Boston
Galina Chistyakova
Lynn Davies
Heike Drechsler
DeHart Hubbard
Elzbieta Krzesinska
Larry Myricks
Peter O'Connor
Myer Prinstein
Tatyana Shchelkanova
Anisoara Stanciu
Igor Ter-Ovanesyan

Luge - see Bobsleigh

Marathon
See also Running
Abebe Bikila
Rob De Castella
Spyridon Louis
Rosa Mota
Bill Rodgers
Toshihiko Seko
Douglas Wakiihuri

Modern pentathlon
András Balczó
Willie Grut
Lars Hall
Pavel Lednev
Igor Novikov
Janusz Pyciak-Peciak
Arkadiusz Skrypuszek
Sven Thofelt

Moto cross
Georges Jobé
Joël Robert
Jeff Smith

Motor cycling
Giacomo Agostini
Kork Ballington
Rolf Biland
Johnny Cecotto
Geoff Duke
Joey Dunlop
Klaus Enders
Wayne Gardner
Mike Hailwood
Bill Ivy
Eddie Lawson
Toni Mang
Jorge Martinez
Sammy Miller
Angel Nieto
Eric Oliver
Wayne Rainey
Phil Read
Jim Redman
Kenny Roberts
Jaarno Saarinen
Barry Sheene
Freddie Spencer
John Surtees
Jordi Tarrès
Luigi Taveri
Carlo Ubbiali
Yrjo Vesterinen
Stanley Woods

Motor racing
See also Motor sports, Rallying
Bobby Allison

Mario Andretti
Michael Andretti
René Arnoux
Alberto Ascari
Gerhard Berger
Jack Brabham
Rudolf Caracciola
Louis Chiron
Jim Clark
Ralph De Palma
Dale Earnhardt
Bill Elliott
Luigi Fagioli
Juan Manuel Fangio
Nino Farina
Enzo Ferrari
Emerson Fittipaldi
A J Foyt
Don Garlits
Dan Gurney
Mike Hawthorn
Graham Hill
Phil Hill
Denny Hulme
James Hunt
Jacky Ickx
Alan Jones
Hermann Lang
Niki Lauda
Bruce McLaren
Nigel Mansell
Rick Mears
Stirling Moss
Tazio Nuvolari
Riccardo Patrese
Ronnie Peterson
Lee Petty
Richard Petty
Nelson Piquet
Alain Prost
Carlos Reutemann
Jochen Rindt
Keke Rosberg
Mauri Rose
Bernd Rosemeyer
Jody Scheckter
Ayrton Senna
Wilbur Shaw
Jackie Stewart
Al Unser
Bobby Unser
Jean-Pierre Wimille
Cale Yarborough

Motor sports
Donald Campbell
Malcolm Campbell
John Cobb
George Eyston
Henry Segrave

Orienteering
Åge Hadler
Egil Johansson
Karl Johansson
Annichen Kringstad
Øyvin Thon

Pelota
Chiquito de Cambo
Jean Urruty

Pole vault
Sergey Bubka
Wolfgang Nordwig
John Pennel
Bob Richards
Robert Seagren
Cornelius Warmerdam

Polo
Thomas Hitchcock
Dev Milburn
Cecil Smith

Powerboating
Renato della Valle
Chip Hanauer
Bill Muncey
Gar Wood

Rackets and Real tennis
Howard Angus
Geoffrey Atkins
Edgar Baerlein
Willie Boone
Wayne Davies
James Dear
Pierre Etchebaster
Jay Gould
Peter Latham
David Milford
William Surtees

Rallying
Markku Alén
Didier Auriol
Miki Biasion
Stig Blomqvist
Erik Carlsson
Juha Kankkunen
Timo Makinen
Shekhar Mehta
Hannu Mikkola
Sandro Munari
Walter Röhrl
Carlos Sainz
Ari Vatanen
Björn Waldegård

Real tennis *see Rackets*

Rodeo
Bob Askin
Everett Bowman
Roy Cooper
Lewis Feild
Tom Ferguson
Don Gay
Pete Knight
Larry Mahan
Ty Murray
Jim Shoulders
Casey Tibbs

Rowing
Giuseppe Abbagnale
Carmine Abbagnale
Rodica Arba
Ernest Barry
Jutta Behrendt
Jack Beresford Jr
Siegfried Brietzke
Olga Bularda
Paul Costello
Frank Forberger
Dieter Grahn
Christine Hahn
Ned Hanlan
Alf Hansen
Frank Hansen
Vyacheslav Ivanov
Pertti Karppinen
Thomas Keller
John Kelly
Peter-Michael Kolbe
Bernd/Jörg Landvoigt
Thomas Lange
Stuart Mackenzie
Guy Nickalls
Angelika Noack
Bobby Pearce
Steve Redgrave
Frank Rühle
Beate Schramm
Dieter Schubert
Mervyn Wood

Rugby League
Georges Ailleres
Eric Ashton
William Batten
Gilbert Benausse
Brian Bevan
Billy Boston
David Brown
Frank Burge
Clive Churchill
Douglas Clark
Lionel Cooper
Mick Cronin
Shaun Edwards

Joseph Egan
Keith Elwell
Neil Fox
Bob Fulton
Jean Galia
Reg Gasnier
Kenneth Gee
Andy Goodway
Andy Gregory
Ellery Hanley
Ken Irvine
Lewis Jones
Graeme Langlands
Wally Lewis
Joe Lydon
Mal Meninga
Dally Messenger
Alex Murphy
Michael O'Connor
Martin Offiah
Jonty Parkin
Alan Prescott
Aubert Puig
Johnny Raper
Gus Risman
Albert Rosenfeld
Garry Schofield
Peter Sterling
Jim Sullivan
Mick Sullivan
Tom Van Vollenhoven
Harold Wagstaff
David Watkins

Rugby Union
Pierre Albaladejo
Georges André
Rob Andrew
Billy Bancroft
Johnny Bannerman
Grant Batty
Bill Beaumont
Phil Bennett
Pierre Berbizier
Roland Bertranne
Serge Blanco
André Boniface
Naas Botha
Gerhardt Brand
Jeff Butterfield
Guy Cambérabéro
Ollie Campbell
David Campese
Will Carling
Ken Catchpole
Michel Celaya
Johan Claasen
Don Clarke
Jean Condom
Fran Cotton
Ronnie Cove-Smith
Michel Crauste
Danie Craven
Andrew Dalton
Benoît Dauga
Gerald Davies
W J A Davies
Greg Davis
John Dawes
Ronnie Dawson
Dawie De Villiers
Philippe Dintrans
Amédée Domenech
David Duckham
Fritz Du Preez
Jean Dupuy
Gareth Edwards
Mark Ella
Jan Ellis
Jannie Engelbrecht
Eric Evans
Grant Fox
Jean Gachassin
Mike Gibson
Sid Going
Arthur Gould
Ken Gray
Andy Haden
Dusty Hare
Gavin Hastings
John Hipwell
Andy Irvine
Peter Jackson
Dickie Jeeps
Barry John
Peter Johnson
Ken Jones
Michael Jones
Moss Keane
Cecil Kershaw
Tom Kiernan
Ian Kirkpatrick
John Kirwan
Jackie Kyle
Brian Lochore
Cyril Lowe
Michael Lynagh
Willie John McBride
Hugh McLeod
Phil MacPherson
Colin Meads
Bryn Meredith
Murray Mexted
Lucien Mias
Tony Miller
Cliff Morgan
Graham Mourie
Karl Mullen
Hennie Muller
Tony Neary
George Nepia
Alex Obolensky
Tony O'Reilly
Phil Orr
Bennie Osler
Dicky Owen
Robert Paparemborde
Simon Poidevin
Hugo Porta
Robert Poulton-Palmer
Jean Prat
Jim Renwick
Eugène Ribère
Jean-Pierre Rives
Bruce Robertson
Budge Rogers
John Rutherford
Philippe Sella
Andrew Slack
Fergus Slattery
Arthur Smith
Ian Smith
David Sole
Walter Spanghero
Andrew Stoddart
Haydn Tanner
John Thornett
Kelvin Tremain
Rory Underwood
Pierre Villepreux
Wavell Wakefield
Mike Weston
Gary Whetton
Wilson Whineray
Bleddyn Williams
Bryan Williams
J.P.R. Williams
Stu Wilson
Peter Winterbottom
Sammy Woods

Running
See also Athletics, Marathon
Harold Abrahams
Arne Andersson
Saïd Aouita
Evelyn Ashford
Roger Bannister
Filbert Bayi
David Bedford
Livio Berruti
Abdi Bile
Olga Bondarenko
Valeriy Borzov
Raelene Boyle
Lyudmila Bragina
Valerie Brisco
Doris Brown
Olga Bryzgina
Zola Budd

Sabine Busch
Henry Carr
Chris Chataway
Waldemar Cierpinski
Ron Clarke
Sebastian Coe
Alberto Cova
Steve Cram
Joaquim Cruz
Glenn Cunningham
Betty Cuthbert
Hal Davis
Gail Devers
Tatyana Dorovskikh
Arthur Duffey
Herb Elliott
Lee Evans
Malcolm Ford
Brendan Foster
Anders Gärderud
Walter George
Marlies Göhr
Florence Griffith-Joyner
Gunder Hägg
Murray Halberg
Rudolf Harbig
Armin Hary
Bob Hayes
Gunhild Hoffmeister
Dorothy Hyman
Sandor Iharos
Volmari Iso-Hollo
Maria Itkina
Paula Ivan
Marjorie Jackson
Michel Jazy
Ben Jipcho
Ben Johnson
Alberto Juantorena
Julius Kariuki
Tatyana Kazankina
Kipchoge Keino
Marita Koch
Hannes Kolehmainen
Jarmila Kratochvílová
Ingrid Kristiansen
Janusz Kusocinski
Vladimir Kuts
John Landy
Eric Liddell
Carlos Lopes
Jack Lovelock
Douglas Lowe
Liz McColgan
Herb McKenley
Bronislaw Malinowski
Madeline Manning
Gisela Mauermayer
Doina Melinte
Pietro Mennea
Ted Meredith
Ralph Metcalfe
Alain Mimoun
Silke Möller
Noureddine Morceli
Bobby Joe Morrow
Laurence Myers
John Ngugi
Paavo Nurmi
Nadezhda Olizarenko
Nina Otkalenko
Merlene Ottey
Steve Ovett
Ann Packer
Charlie Paddock
Mel Patton
Gordon Pirie
Steve Prefontaine
Maricica Puica
Emiel Puttemans
Don Quarrie
Ana Quirot
Butch Reynolds
George Rhoden
Annegret Richter
Ville Ritola
Gaston Roelants
Henry Rono
Wilma Rudolph
Jim Ryun
Ilmari Salminen
Joan Samuelson
Shin Keum-dan
Frank Shorter
Alfred Shrubb
Mary Slaney
Tommie Smith
Peter Snell
Andrew Stanfield
Renate Stecher
Marina Stepanova
Helen Stephens
Ian Stewart
Irena Szewinska
Wyomia Tyus
Svetlana Ulmasova
Lasse Viren
Grete Waitz
Stanislawa Walasiewicz
John Walker
Allan Wells
Mal Whitfield
Percy Williams
Arthur Wint
Bärbel Wöckel
Mamo Wolde
Sydney Wooderson
Miruts Yifter
Emil Zátopek

Shooting
Gary Anderson
Anatoliy Bogdanov
Malcolm Cooper
Luciano Giovanetti
Enno Matarelli
Susan Nattrass
Carl Osburn
Ragnar Skanåkar
Oscar Swahn
Lones Wigger

Shot
Udo Beyer
Nadezhda Chizhova
Helena Fibingerová
Natalya Lisovskaya
Dallas Long
Randy Matson
Bill Nieder
Parry O'Brien
Brian Oldfield
Ralph Rose
Ilona Slupianek
Ulf Timmermann
Galina Zybina
Tamara Press

Show jumping - *see Equestrian events*

Figure skating
Tenley Albright
Jeanette Altwegg
Ludmila Belousova
Natalya Bestemyanova
Brian Boitano
Pierre Brunet
Dick Button
Cecilia Colledge
Robin Cousins
John Curry
Christopher Dean
Sjoukje Dijsktra
Peggy Fleming
Bernard Ford
Gillis Grafström
Dorothy Hamill
Scott Hamilton
Carol Heiss
Sonja Henie
Don Jackson
David Jenkins
Hayes Jenkins
Courtney Jones
Ondrej Nepela
Lyudmila Pakhomova
Axel Paulsen
Herma Plank-Szabó
Anett Pötzsch

Oleg Protopopov
Irina Rodnina
Ulrich Salchow
Karl Schäfer
Barbara Ann Scott
Henry Sharpe
Madge Syers (Cave)
Jayne Torvill
Diane Towler
Katarina Witt
Aleksandr Zaitsev

Speed skating
Hjalmar Andersen
Inga Artamonova
Ivar Ballangrud
Bonnie Blair
Jaap Eden
Andrea Ehrig
Aleksandr Gorshkov
Yevgeniy Grischin
Tomas Gustafsson
Beth Heiden
Eric Heiden
Karin Kania
Atje Keulen-Deelstra
Christa Luding
Oscar Mathisen
Gunda Niemann
Natalya Petruseva
Ard Schenk
Lidiya Skoblikova
Clas Thunberg
Yvonne van Gennip
Sheila Young
Igor Zhelezovskiy

Skiing
Berit Aunli
Hallgeir Brenden
Christl Cranz
Bjørn Dæhlie
Irene Epple
Michela Figini
Marc Girardelli
Marielle Goitschel
Nancy Greene
Johan Grøttumsbråten
Cristl Haas
Veikko Hakulinen
Marja-Liisa Hämäläinen
Thorleif Haug
Erika Hess
Sixten Jernberg
Bill Kidd
Jean-Claude Killy
Franz Klammer
Alevtina Kolchina
Petra Kronberger
Galina Kulakova
Tamara McKinney
Phil Mahre
Eero Mäntyranta
Marjo Matikainen
Andrea Mead Lawrence
Carole Merle
Rosi Mittermaier
Lisa-Marie Morerod
Annemarie Moser-Pröll
Peter Müller
Marie-Thérèse Nadig
Matti Nykänen
Guy Périllat
Anfissa Restsova
Bernhard Russi
Birger Ruud
Toni Sailer
Vreni Schneider
Karl Schranz
Raisa Smetanina
Ingemar Stenmark
Gunde Svan
Gustavo Thoeni
Alberto Tomba
Vegard Ulvang
Yelena Välbe
Maria Walliser
Thomas Wassberg
Ullrich Wehling
Jens Weissflog
Andreas Wenzel
Hanni Wenzel
Nikolay Zimyatov
Pirmin Zurbriggen

Snooker
See also Billiards
Eddie Charlton
Fred Davis
Joe Davis
Steve Davis
Walter Donaldson
Allison Fisher
Terry Griffiths
Stephen Hendry
Alex Higgins
John Pulman
Ray Reardon
John Spencer
Dennis Taylor
Cliff Thorburn
Jimmy White

Soccer - *see Football*

Speedway
Barry Briggs
Peter Collins
Peter Craven
Vic Duggan
Ove Fundin
Erik Gundersen
Aub Lawson
Karl Maier
Ivan Mauger
Anders Michanek
Ronnie Moore
Egon Müller
Hans Nielsen
Ole Olsen
Jack Parker
Tommy Price
Jerzy Szczakiel
Lionel Van Praag
Bluey Wilkinson
Freddie Williams
Jack Young

Squash
Abdelfattah Amr Bey
Azam Khan
Jonah Barrington
Vicki Cardwell
Susan Devoy
Hashim Khan
Geoff Hunt
Jahangir Khan
Jansher Khan
Heather McKay
Mahmoud Karim
Mohibullah Khan
Janet Morgan
Ross Norman
Qamar Zaman
Roshan Khan

Sumo wrestling
Koki Taiho

Surfing
Tom Carroll

Swimming
see also Diving
Shirley Babashoff
Mike Barrowman
Alex Baumann
Matt Biondi
Ian Black
Jean Boiteaux
Arne Borg
Mike Burton
Rick Carey
Kiki Caron
Tracey Caulkins
Buster Crabbe
Lorraine Crapp
Ann Curtis
Charles Daniels
Tamás Darnyi

Victor Davis
Willy den Ouden
Donna de Varona
John Devitt
Trudy Ederle
Krisztina Egerszegi
Kornelia Ender
Janet Evans
Dawn Fraser
Heike Friedrich
Rowdy Gaines
Ute Geweniger
Brian Goodell
Shane Gould
Judy Grinham
Michael Gross
Gary Hall
John Hencken
John Henricks
Steve Holland
Eleanor Holm
Ragnhild Hveger
Chet Jastremski
Duke Kahanamoku
Warren Kealoha
Adolph Kiefer
John Kinsella
Ada Kok
Claudia Kolb
Ilse Konrads
John Konrads
Rosemarie Kother
Barbara Krause
Freddy Lane
Gunnar Larsson
Anita Lonsbrough
Steve Lundquist
Helene Madison
Rie Mastenbroek
Roland Matthes
Mary T. Meagher
Debbie Meyer
Adrian Moorhouse
Pablo Morales
Karen Moras
Karen Muir
John Naber
Anthony Nesty
Martha Norelius
Ian O'Brien
Kristin Otto
Kieren Perkins
Igor Polyanskiy
Ulrike Richter
Murray Rose
Vladimir Salnikov
Petra Schneider
Don Schollander
Tim Shaw
Jon Sieben
Cornelia Sirch
Mark Spitz
Galina Stepanova
Astrid Strauss
Satoko Tanaka
Elaine Tanner
Ulrike Tauber
David Theile
Petra Thümer
Mike Troy
Yoshiyuki Tsuruta
Chris von Saltza
Matthew Webb
Johnny Weissmuller
Mike Wenden
Tracey Wickham
David Wilkie

Synchronised swimming
Sylvie Fréchette

Table tennis
Mikael Appelgren
Viktor Barna
Stellan Bengtsson
Richard Bergmann
Chuang Tse-tung
Gizi Farkas
Jiang Jialing
Jung Kuo-tuan
Eva Kóczián/Földi
Johnny Leach
Lin Hui-chang
Maria Mednyanszky
Ichiro Ogimura
Diane Rowe
Rosalind Rowe
Angelica Rozeanu
Anna Sipos
Miklós Szabados
Toshiaki Tanaka
Bohumil Vana
Jan-Ove Waldner

Tennis
Andre Agassi
Arthur Ashe
Bunny Austin
Tracy Austin
Boris Becker
Pauline Betz
Blanche Bingley/Hillyard
Molla Bjurstedt
Björn Borg
Jean Borotra
John Bromwich
Norman Brookes
Louise Brough
Mary Browne
Jacques Brugnon
Don Budge
Maria Bueno
Rosemary Casals
Pat Cash
Henri Cochet
Maureen Connolly
Jimmy Connors
Ashley Cooper
Charlotte Cooper
Jim Courier
Jack Crawford
Max Decugis
Charlotte Dod
Lawrence Doherty
Reginald Doherty
Dorothea Douglass
Jaroslav Drobny
Margaret Du Pont
Stefan Edberg
Roy Emerson
Chris Evert
Neale Fraser
Shirley Fry
Althea Gibson
Kitty Godfree
Pancho Gonzales
Evonne Goolagong
Wentworth Gore
Steffi Graf
Darlene Hard
Doris Hart
Bob Hewitt
Lew Hoad
Helen Jacobs
Bill Johnston
Ann Jones
Billie Jean King
Jack Kramer
René Lacoste
William Larned
Rod Laver
Ivan Lendl
Suzanne Lenglen
Anita Lizana
John McEnroe
Chuck McKinley
Maurice McLoughlin
Hana Mandlikova
Alice Marble
Angela Mortimer
Gardnar Mulloy
Ilie Nastase
Martina Navratilova
John Newcombe
Betty Nuthall
Sarah Palfrey
Frank Parker
Gerald Patterson
Budge Patty
Fred Perry

Nicola Pietrangeli
Adrian Quist
William Renshaw
Bobby Riggs
Tony Roche
Ken Rosewall
Dorothy Round
Bunny Ryan
Pete Sampras
Manuel Santana
Frank Sedgeman
Pancho Segura
Vic Seixas
Monica Seles
Pam Shriver
Margaret Smith/Court
Stan Smith
Fred Stolle
Eric Sturgess
May Sutton
Bill Tilden
Tony Trabert
Guillermo Vilas
Ellsworth Vines
Gottfried Von Cramm
Virginia Wade
Hazel Wightman
Mats Wilander
Anthony Wilding
Dick Williams
Helen Wills (Moody)

Tobogganing - *see Bobsleigh*

Triathlon
Mark Allen
Erin Baker
Scott Molina
Paula Newby-Fraser
Dave Scott
Scott Tinley

Triple jump
Willie Banks
Galina Chistyakova
Mike Conley
João Carlos de Oliveira
Adhemar Ferreira da Silva
Mikio Oda
Viktor Saneyev
Jozef Schmidt
Naoto Tajima

Volleyball
Flo Hyman
Karch Kiraly
Steve Timmons

Walking
Daniel Bautista
Ernesto Canto
Maurizio Damilano
Hartwig Gauder
Vladmir Golubnichiy
Raúl Gonzalez
Christoph Höhne
Carlos Mercenario
Abdon Pamich
Jozef Pribilinec

Water polo
Deszö Gyarmati
Olivér Halassy
Márton Homonnai
György Kárpáti
János Németh
Paul Radmilovic

Water skiing
Liz Allan-Shetter
Guy de Clercq
Sammy Duvall
Mike Hazelwood
Kim Lampard
Bob LaPoint
Willa McGuire
Deena Mapple
Patrice Martin
Alfredo Mendoza
Cory Pickos
Dick Pope Jr
Natalya Rumyantseva
Mike Suyderhoud
Cindy Todd
Brett Wing

Weightlifting
Vasiliy Alekseyev
Paul Anderson
Waldemar Baszanowski
Blagoi Blagoyev
Louis Cyr
John Davis
Imre Földi
Peter George
Anatoliy Khrapatiy
Tommy Kono
Aleksandr Kurlovich
Yoshinobu Miyake
Anatoliy Pisarenko
David Rigert
Norbert Schemansky
Naim Suleymanoglü
Leonid Taranenko
Stefan Topurov
Yurik Vardanyan
Yuriy Vlasov
Arkadiy Vorobyev
Yuriy Zakharevich
Leonid Zhabotinskiy

Wrestling
Kalle Anttila
Nikolay Balboshin
Sergey Beloglazov
Wilfried Dietrich
Arsen Fadzeyev
Dan Gable
Dick Garrard
Frank Gotch
George Hackenschmidt
Viktor Igumenov
Ivar Johansson
Mikhail Mamiashvili
Aleksandr Medved
Milon of Kroton
Abdollah Movahed
Kristjan Palusalu
Kustaa Pihljamäki
Robin Reed
Valeriy Rezantsev
Roman Rurua
John Smith
Levan Tediashvili
Theagenes of Thasos
Osamu Watanabe
Carl Westergren

Yachting
Dennis Conner
Paul Elvstrøm
Rodney Pattisson
Harold Vanderbilt

Index of additional names

Many sports men and women, who do not have separate entries, have brief details shown under a distinguished family member. So for Davey Allison, for instance, see under Bobby Allison.

The following notable sports men and women do not have their own entries, but some details can be found under the names shown of colleagues, husbands, wives, coaches etc.: